IN THE BEGINNING

IN THE BEGINNING

Development in the
First Two Years of Life

JUDY F. ROSENBLITH
WHEATON COLLEGE

JUDITH E. SIMS-KNIGHT
SOUTHEASTERN MASSACHUSETTS UNIVERSITY

BROOKS/COLE PUBLISHING COMPANY
Monterey, California

Brooks/Cole Publishing Company
A Division of Wadsworth, Inc.

Printed in the United States of America.

10 9 8 7 6 5 4 3 2 1

Library of Congress Cataloging in Publication Data
Rosenblith, Judy F.
  In the beginning

  Bibliography: p.
  Includes index.
  1. Child development.   2. Infant psychology.   3. Fetus.
I. Sims-Knight, Judith E.   II. Title.
RJ131.R647 1985   612'.65   85-4105
ISBN 0-534-02846-2

Cover Illustration: *Maternal Caress*, by Mary Cassatt (drypoint and
aquatint). Courtesy of The Metropolitan Museum of Art. Gift of Paul J.
Sachs. Used by permission.

Sponsoring Editor: C. Deborah Laughton. *Editorial Assistant:* Mary Tudor.
Production: Unicorn Production Services, Inc. *Interior Design:* Jerry Wilke.
Cover Design: Sharon L. Kinghan. *Interior Illustration:* Cyndie
Clark-Huegel, Wayne S. Clark, and Parry Clark. *Photo Researcher:* Erika
Petersson. *Typesetting:* Achorn Graphic Services, Inc. *Printing and Binding:*
R.R. Donnelley & Sons, Inc.

Photograph Acknowledgments: Page ii, Susan Edmonds. Page x, Courtesy of Dr. Jerome Kagan, Harvard
University. Page 18 and Figure 6–7c, page 231, Peter Vandermark/Stock Boston. Page 20, from *Living
Images* by G. Shih and R. Kessel; © 1982 by Jones and Bartlett Publishers, Inc. Page 65, Courtesy of Cy-
togenetics Laboratory, Brigham and Women's Hospital, Harvard Medical School, Boston, MA. Page 102,
Jim Anderson/Stock Boston. Page 155, Phaneuf/Gurdziel/The Picture Cube. Figure 5–2, page 164, James
Holland/Stock Boston. Following page 203 and Figure 6–5, page 222, M. Konner/Anthro-Photo File. Fig-
ure 6–6, page 224, Heath Paley/The Picture Cube. Figure 6–7b, page 231, Alan Oransky/Stock Boston.
Page 258, Courtesy of Dr. Lewis P. Lipsitt; photograph by Jason Lauré. Page 341, George Bellerose/Stock
Boston. Page 399, Judith Sedwick/The Picture Cube. Figures 10–2, page 407, and 10–6, page 415, from *Pri-
mate Bio-Social Development*, S. Chevalier-Skolnikoff and F.E. Poirier, Eds.; © 1977 by Garland Publish-
ing Co. Figure 10–8, page 421, Elizabeth Crews/Stock Boston. Page 449, Richard Wood/The Picture
Cube. Figures 11–5 (bottom), page 468, and 12–5 (bottom), page 504, from the collections of the Library
of Congress. Page 478, Andrew Brilliant/The Picture Cube. Figure 12–1, page 484, (left) Polly Brown/The
Picture Cube; (right) David A. Krathwohl/Stock Boston. Page 520, Martha Stewart/The Picture Cube.
Figures 6–1, page 208, 6–7a, page 231, 8–8, page 311, and 8–9, page 314, courtesy of J.F. Rosenblith. All
other photographs courtesy of the authors.

P R E F A C E

The study of infants was one of the first areas in which scientific observations of humans were gathered. It has enjoyed several spurts of popularity, most recently from the 1960s to the present, but very few infancy texts are currently available. Because of this paucity, and because we had enjoyed teaching an infancy course together, we decided to write this book. The finished product represents our equal and joint contributions.

The text is designed for a broad range of students, including undergraduates with little exposure to psychology. Students in our classes have ranged from sophomores to seniors and from psychology or biopsychology majors to art, history, or literature majors. We tested preliminary versions in several classes, and students demonstrated in their classroom and examination performance that they learned from it. We have tried to make the book interesting and relevant to other disciplines, particularly nursing and human development, and have included references that would be informative to this broad spectrum of students. In addition, the comprehensive coverage in the text and its orientation toward evaluation of empirical research make this an appropriate introductory text for graduate students.

This book has two major aims not often seen in textbooks. One is to embed the presentation of current data on, and ideas about the functioning of infants in, an historical context. For example, we do not just describe some history of the field in Chapter 1, we also consider historical studies in the context of specific topics.

The second major aim is to present the material in a way that will maximize learning about the process of studying infants as well as the content derived from that study. To do this we use several techniques.

1. Research issues. One goal of this book is to help students acquire a reading understanding of research methodology. Infancy research continues to grow at a rapid rate, and it is inevitable that facts learned today may be replaced by different or new facts tomorrow. The most valuable tool students can have is a way to evaluate new research. Then in later years when they are faced with new outcomes that suggest particular actions, they can themselves evaluate the quality of the research and determine whether the new conclusions are reasonable or applicable. Many curricula leave such learning to methods courses, but we feel that students in those courses often learn the rules but not the ability to apply them. We try to help students develop that ability by using techniques that are consistent with the understanding of learning that has been developing in the field of cognition. Recent research has demonstrated clearly that people remember material better when it is learned in a meaningful context. Thus, we present research issues in the context of the research

in which they appear. Memory research also demonstrates, however, that material learned in a specific context is often tied to that context. To solve this problem, we take a skills theory approach (see Chapter 10). We assume that learning a concept is a skill that develops by combining, differentiating from, and intercoordinating with other skills, and that each of these represents a separable step or task. Therefore, we present the same methodological point in several contexts and relate those different instances in sections at the ends of chapters. Instructors who wish to do so may easily eliminate the research issues sections.

2. Major issues of infancy. We follow a similar strategy in elucidating general themes that permeate the study of infancy. Topics such as the influences of heredity and environment and their interactions are presented in each of their several contexts. Discussion sections at the ends of chapters extract major issues from their context and interrelate them. A given issue is discussed only in the chapters in which research pertinent to it has been discussed.

3. Practical implications of infancy research. Each chapter also has a section on the implications of the research presented there for parenting or other practical applications. These sections summarize conclusions applicable to parenting and draw out implications of other research findings. Again, an instructor may choose not to assign these sections.

4. Theoretical perspectives. We present major theories in the context of the general or specific issues to which they are relevant. For example, we describe Freudian theory when we consider nonnutritive sucking (Chapter 6) and attachment (Chapter 12). We do not devote a chapter to theories as such because we want theories to be understood in the context of the research designed to test the hypotheses derived from them.

5. Vocabulary. Many words that students think are merely vocabulary are considered by instructors to be major concepts. Other words, although not of major importance, are important because they are necessary to understand a point central to the study of infancy. We assume that many students are likely to be unfamiliar with or to forget the meaning of many terms and we have tried

always to define them parenthetically or in footnotes. Major concept words are printed in boldface when we define them (as are page numbers in the Index that indicate the page on which a word is defined). Students need to know these words to understand infant research. Our choices are necessarily somewhat idiosyncratic; the backgrounds of students and choices of instructors will also affect which words students need to have emphasized.

It is difficult to acknowledge the numerous contributions to this text. Feedback from students over the years has informed both structure and content. To colleagues we owe many more debts than we can acknowledge. Some colleagues have been especially helpful in reading chapters where our own expertise was more limited. Dr. Elizabeth Lloyd White's careful reading of the embryology section is especially noteworthy. The chapter on genetics was read by Dr. Sidney Beck and Prof. Maurice S. Fox. The chapter on sensation and perception profited from the suggestions of Rachel K. Clifton, Eleanor J. Gibson, and Holly Ruff. Any errors that remain are the responsibility solely of the authors.

An earlier version of the first five chapters profited from the editorial suggestions of Wesley Allinsmith. We are also indebted to the following reviewers of various parts of the manuscript: Richard N. Aslin of the University of Rochester; Alyce Blackmon of California State University, Northridge; Carol Bruner; Dianne Draper of Iowa State University; Alice Honig of Syracuse University; Jerome Kagan of Harvard University; Kathleen McCluskey of West Virginia University; Douglas B. Sawin of The University of Texas at Austin; Ned W. Schultz of California Polytechnic State University; and Albert Yonas of the University of Minnesota.

In a completely different category, we want to thank Paula Menyuk for writing the chapter on language development. Her expertise in this area far outdoes that of both authors. In addition, we appreciate Allyssa McCabe's comments on that chapter. Finally, a special debt is owed Raymond Knight, who consulted with us on issues both scientific and pedagogical throughout the writing of this book.

JUDY F. ROSENBLITH
JUDITH E. SIMS-KNIGHT

CONTENTS

PART ONE
CONCEPTION THROUGH BIRTH

PART TWO
BIRTH TO TWO YEARS

HISTORICAL AND METHODOLOGICAL INTRODUCTION

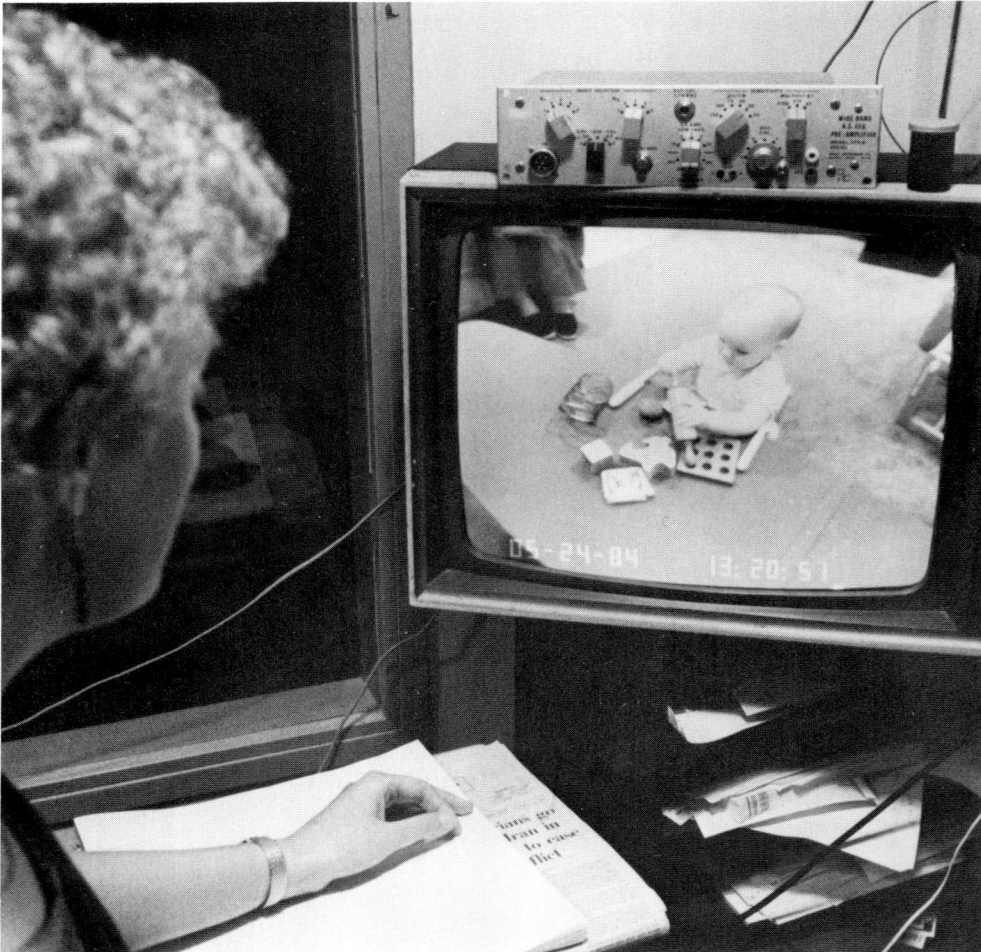

CHAPTER 1

Studying infants has become an extremely popular enterprise in psychology today. Research journals are filled with reports of studies of infants and one journal is devoted entirely to infancy. Many colleges and universities have added courses on infancy to their curricula. Similar excitement over the study of infancy has recurred several times in the history of psychology. The general reason for such intense interest in infancy is obvious: To fully understand any psychological process, one must understand its origins.

In this chapter we have two goals. The first is to introduce the reader to the history of the study of infancy, a study that predates the experimental study of humankind. The second is to show how various scientific methods developed in the course of this research. We begin by discussing reasons for studying infants, as described in the 19th century and today. We then proceed to describe, in the sequence in which they developed, the various ways in which researchers study infants and the strengths and weaknesses of each approach. We conclude with a discussion of the major methodological points.

REASONS FOR STUDYING INFANTS

Infancy is unique in all the ages of humankind in that it marks the beginning of life outside the womb. Through the study of infancy, researchers can explore (1) the roles of heredity and the environment in development, (2) the impact of experiences, particularly the possibly critical early influence of parents on infants' development, and (3) the impact on parenting of educating parents about the normal course of development.

Early Interests

These issues also motivated early researchers. The Department of Education of The American Social Science Association sponsored a group of papers on infant development at their 1881 meeting in Saratoga, New York, and published the papers in the *Journal of Social Science*, November, 1882. Mrs. Emily Talbot, Secretary of the Department, discussed what is perhaps the all-time favorite issue in infant research, the question of the roles heredity and the environment play in development.

... *That a child does most of his actions by inherited instincts seems to me most plausible. I think, as comparing children with dogs, that, aside from the physical condition, the inherited taste is first shown. Little puppies of a retriever breed will begin to take things hither and thither in their mouths long before puppies of an uneducated ancestry, though there will be a difference in talent and exceptions. In children, besides the natural self-assertion of a young child, there will continually crop out a hint of an inherited facility, which he uses without being taught. Then there is association. Having always seen a dog about, he has no fear of a dog, wants to pull him and roll about with him, does not fear the bark of a dog, though a little startled, if sharp; but of horses he has fear, and a certain fascinated interest,— wants to know them, and yet is afraid.* (Talbot, 1882, p. 15)

Charles Darwin focused on some specific issues concerning environmental influences, particularly the role parental influence plays in the development of intelligence and individual differences.

This knowledge [of infants] would probably give a foundation for some improvement in our education of young children, and would show us whether the same system ought to be followed in all cases.

I will venture to specify a few points of enquiry which, as it seems to me, possess some scientific interest. For instance, does the education of the parents influence the mental powers of their children at any age, either at a very early or somewhat more advanced stage? ...

As observation is one of the earliest faculties developed in young children, and as this power would probably be exercised in an equal degree by the children of educated and uneducated persons, it seems not impossible that any transmitted effect from education could be displayed only at a somewhat advanced age.

It is well known that children some-
times exhibit at a very early age strong spe-
cial tastes, for which no cause can be as-
signed although occasionally they may be
accounted for by reversion to the taste or oc-
cupation of some progenitor; and it would be
interesting to learn how far such early tastes
are persistent and influence the future career
of the individuals. In some instances such
tastes die away without apparently leaving
any after effect; but it would be desirable to
know how far this is commonly the case, as
we should then know whether it were impor-
tant to direct, as far as this is possible, the
early tastes of our children. It may be more
beneficial that a child should follow ener-
getically some pursuit, of however trifling a
nature, and thus acquire perseverence, than
that he should be turned from it, because of
no future advantage to him. (Darwin, 1882,
pp. 6–7)

Harris was interested in the role that
learning about their infants can play in
mothers' abilities to rear them. He believed
that through observing their babies,

the mother shall learn to study the growth of
her child, and learn what constitutes a stage
of progress, and how to discover and remove
obstacles to this growth, as well as to afford
judicious aid to the child's efforts at master-
ing the use of his faculties. One intelligent
woman who is interested in this subject will
kindle an interest which will spread through-
out an entire town. The wisdom gained
through these observations will extend
gradually to all families, and will elevate the
character of infant education incalculably.
When the mother becomes observant of
the actions of the child as a matter of educa-
tion, and when there comes to be a stock of
generalized experiences on this subject, how
much will be done toward correcting evil
tendencies upon their first manifestations! It
is a trite remark, that the shaping of a tree is
an easy affair if undertaken while it is a
sapling, but impossible after the tree has at-
tained its growth. The education that goes
on within the family is the object which now
calls with most importunity on us for our at-
tention as students of social science. (Harris,
1882, p. 5)

Current Interests

These crucial questions still motivate infancy
researchers, although a century of research has
both narrowed the range of acceptable hypotheses and dramatically increased the precision
with which they can be stated. For example,
researchers have identified the genetic mechanisms underlying certain specific disorders and
can now examine the ways in which the environment interacts with that genetic potential.
Even when specific mechanisms are not
known, techniques now exist that enable assessment of whether there is an inherited component to certain behavioral characteristics.
Such research has led to the understanding that
inheritance always acts through the environment. Thus the important question is how
does heredity interact with environment, not
what are the relative contributions of each.

Research has also demonstrated that **innate** characteristics (those present at birth) are
not purely inherited; that is, the environment
influences individuals long before they are
born. For example, it is no longer assumed that
an hour-old baby who is very active has inherited a tendency to high activity. Researchers
now try to distinguish between characteristics
that are stable within individuals because they
are inherited and those that are stable because
the environment has permanently affected the
individual or because the environment has remained stable.

A related issue is that of innate ideas. Interest in whether infants are born with some
understanding of how the world is organized
derives from the philosophical study of **epistemology** (the study of knowledge), although
the psychological exploration is quite distinct.
Because newborn babies have not experienced
the world outside the womb, particularly the
visual world, they are perfect subjects for this
endeavor. If, for example, researchers could
show that newborns act as if they know what
an object is—that it is three dimensional, has
tactual attributes, and exists independent of
the infant—they would have to conclude that
humans have innate ideas (*a priori* synthetic
ideas, according to Kant).

Just as research in the last 100 years has
led to more complex questions about the influence of heredity, it has led to differentiation
among different kinds of environmental in-

fluences. Foremost in this domain has been the study of **critical periods.** During a critical period a baby is particularly sensitive to certain kinds of environmental influence. Learning takes place rapidly and easily during that time, but at other times the same environmental events will not have the same effects. The effects of environmental stimulation during critical periods are permanent. The timing of a critical period is determined by an individual's biological timetable; thus critical periods actually represent an interaction between heredity and environment. The mechanism of critical periods was discovered in **embryology** (the science that deals with the origin and development of the individual organism), but it has been applied to many aspects of psychological development. For example, Sigmund Freud hypothesized that infancy was a critical period for the baby to establish the basic ability to love.

Other kinds of environmental influences also are crucial to development. When and how babies learn by making associations and by imitating have interested some researchers in both the 19th and 20th centuries. Other researchers have focused on learning via cognitive structures. Explicit or implicit in all this research has been the question of when and how infants' early experiences affect their development.

All of the conceptualizations of the roles of heredity and environment considered together form the basis from which parents' roles in their infants' development can be examined. Researchers no longer ask simply whether a characteristic or behavior of parents has an effect or not. Rather they must ask to which of their parents' behaviors do infants respond, and how such parental influences interact with other influences. They have learned that it is especially important to differentiate between immediate effects and long-term effects. It is no longer an unassailable truth that parental influences in infancy determine their offspring's entire life.

Finally, the role that educating parents may have in improving the quality of their parenting is still of vital concern, but researchers no longer assume that it is sufficient simply to expose parents to knowledge of how infants develop. Rather they most frequently focus on parents' skills at interacting with their infants.

Thus in infancy research, as in other areas, the more things change the more they remain the same. Although the research has become much more sophisticated, the basic questions remain the same. Likewise, although the answers to these questions are undoubtedly more accurate today than they were a century ago, they still remain tentative. As Herbert Feigl, a well-known philosopher of science, was fond of saying, answers in science are always only true until further notice (personal communication, 1968).

THE BEGINNINGS OF BEHAVIORAL STUDY OF INFANTS

The history of the psychological study of infants begins with a series of baby biographies in the 19th century. The rise of such detailed descriptions of babies was part of a general burst of interest in naturalistic observations. Indeed, Charles Darwin, a naturalist and one of the originators of the theory of evolution, was also an early baby biographer. The first baby biography, however, had been published in the year 1787 by a German philosopher, Dietrich Tiedemann, and several more appeared in published form before the "evolutionary" era of the next century. The most famous study of infancy was that by Wilhelm Preyer in the 1860s. He was a German physiologist whose account of his son's first year of life was somewhat more scientific than earlier accounts (Preyer, 1881/1893). It is probably for this reason that Preyer, not Tiedemann, is often credited with being the father of child psychology.

Of the dozens of early naturalistic observations, all but one were of infant development. The exception was the Swiss educator Pestalozzi's diary of his attempts to educate his 4-year-old son. Most of the subjects of these biographies were boys and the authors were their fathers. A notable exception was A. Bronson Alcott's observations of his daughters, especially Anna and Louisa May.

Baby biographies became so popular during the 19th century that the Department of Education of The American Social Science Association in the 1880s sponsored a systematic register of baby biographies for the purpose of unlocking "some portion of the secrets of the mental and physical development of infants" (Talbot, 1882, p. 6).

Strengths and Weaknesses of Baby Biographies

Examination of the early baby biographies can show both the strengths and the weaknesses of this approach. Do not think that baby biographies are only of historical interest. One of the major contributors to current understanding of infants, Jean Piaget, based his theories on naturalistic observations of his own three children—that is, on baby biographies. Like Preyer, Piaget was highly systematic in making observations and presented his children with numerous informal experimental situations. The baby biography is still a way of achieving scientific insight, and we hope that the following discussion will both help readers evaluate existing baby biographies and will guide those who wish to write their own.

Let us first consider the strengths of such naturalistic observations. Descriptions of behaviors in naturalistic situations provide the starting point of science. There is much to learn about babies from simply watching them without interfering in their functioning. The following example from Tiedemann is a description of behaviors that today would be identified as **reflexes** (innate, automatic responses to specific stimuli).

. . . *He had no idea as yet of purposely grasping anything; grasping occurred only by instinctive reflex, by which the fingers, like the leaves of flowers of certain sensitive plants, contract when their inner surfaces are touched by a foreign object (Tiedemann, 1787/1927, pp. 207–208).*

. . . *If he was held in arms and then suddenly lowered from a considerable height, he strove to hold himself with his hands, to save himself from falling; and he did not like to be lifted very high.[1] Since he could not*

possibly have had any conception of falling, his fear was unquestionably a purely mechanical sensation, such as older persons feel at a steep and unaccustomed height, something akin to dizziness. (Tiedemann, 1787/ 1927, p. 216)

Observers can also record newborns' responses to visual, auditory, and tactual stimuli, and thus answer the question of whether newborn babies can see and hear. The first of the following extracts is from Tiedemann's baby biography. The second is from Alcott's letter to the Department of Education of The American Social Science Association for its 1881 meeting. The last three are from the register of baby biographies sponsored by that organization and reported at that meeting.

. . . *It was observed that the boy, when hearing sound, always turned his face in the direction whence it came; so he had already learned to tell what he heard through the right ear, and what through the left, had also accustomed himself to think of spaces in some sort of relation to his body. (Tiedemann, 1787/1927, p. 217)*

. . . *During the first days after birth she slept most of the time. As she gradually awoke and was exposed to the light, she opened her eyes as if intent on adjusting these for the purpose of seeing. Luminous objects particularly attracted her notice. While viewing these her hands moved instinctively, her arms were extended and drawn toward the mouth, which also appeared to be sensitive to the stimulus by frequent movements of the lips and tongue. (Alcott, 1882, p. 8)*

. . . *Medical works give six to ten hours as the earliest time at which hearing is possible, but my boy, born at 1:30, certainly heard, and nervously started at the sound of the cock crowing at 4:30. (Talbot, 1882, p. 12)*

. . . *He recognized [responded to] the light of a window [evidently] at the age of 20 hours, as he was looking at it he was turned round so as to bring the other side towards the window, and at once turned his head towards it. He recognized sounds in a day or*

---

[1] This excerpt also shows the early baby biographers' carelessness in interpretation. This reflex represents an innate automatic response to loss of support and thereby does not require that the infant know that loss of support might be followed by falling.

two. The younger (twin) recognized light and sound in the same way a day or two later. . .

. . . (Ten days old) Both evidently noticed a piano played in another room, stopped their incessant baby motions to listen, and put on the same listening look as adults do. This was repeated for a day or two, at times when the piano played; but afterwards as the sound grew familiar they ceased to notice it. (Talbot, 1882, p. 16)

A second achievement permitted by longitudinal observations of one infant or of a group of infants is the plotting of developmental changes over age such as the disappearance of reflexes and the development of other observable behaviors such as grasping and language.

The intensive observations of baby biographers can have an advantage over other kinds of studies, cross-sectional or normative. The changes in development can be charted against the background of the infant's own past, and the behaviors can be placed in the context of the environment and the other behaviors of that infant. Thus, the baby biography provides the potential for a rich and full understanding of the meaning of infants' behaviors in a fashion unique to the method. Unfortunately, those same characteristics make baby biographies more vulnerable to error and misinterpretation than are more controlled techniques, as we will explain later.

A good example of the richness of knowledge to be gleaned from baby biographies can be seen in the following excerpt from Tiedemann's description of his son's language development.

. . . On November 29th one could observe a signification of [the] sort that indicated a certain amount of complexity in his ideas, and spoke of some amount of original composition on his part. He had been taught to reply to the question, "How big are you?" ["Wie gross bist du?" in German] by lifting up his hands; now he was required to say the word "grandmama" ["grossmama"] and as the "big" ["gross"] was too difficult for him to pronounce, he lifted up his hands and at the same time said "mama." (Tiedemann, 1787/1927, p. 221)

Tiedemann was able to describe language development accurately when he was dealing with explicit behaviors that he could clearly observe. Such observations of behaviors and developmental sequences of behaviors are just the first step in the study of infants. The ultimate goal of such studies, for both early baby biographers and modern researchers, is to discover the meaning of the behaviors they describe. They want to know, for example, what infants understand when they say "mama" for the first time. They also want to know how the infant came to be able to say "mama." Was it because his parents had rewarded him for making similar sounds; was it simply because his vocal apparatus or his brain had matured sufficiently; or were both factors involved?

It is neither straightforward nor easy to assess the meaning of behaviors. Infant investigators, including both some early baby biographers and modern experimentalists, undertake their studies to find out whether their ideas about some aspect of development are correct or not. Their expectations are quite likely to influence their findings unless the investigation is carefully controlled. A good example of the power of such expectations is found in a study by Rubin, Provenzano, and Luria (1974). They showed pictures of newborn babies to adults. Half the subjects were told that a particular picture was of a boy baby and the other subjects were told the same picture was of a girl. Even though they saw the same picture, the subjects' descriptions were that the "girl" babies were cuter, smaller, and quieter, and that the "boy" babies were larger, stronger, and more vigorous.

Expectations may affect observations in several ways. They may encourage people to see behaviors that don't exist. Rubin and colleagues' subjects not only saw behavioral differences that didn't exist, but also physical differences that didn't exist. Expectations may also cause people to fail to notice behaviors that are there. The best example of this is that psychologists, physicians, nurses, and parents during most of this century believed that newborn babies could not see or hear, because such early-developing abilities did not fit into the theoretical framework of the times. They overlooked behaviors that suggested these abilities and ignored the baby biographers' accounts which had documented such behaviors, as shown in the excerpts quoted earlier.

What can be done to control expectations?

Much of the scientific methodology developed in the last century has been a response to this problem. Two major strategies can be used in infant biographies or observational studies. The first is for the observer to separate interpretations from descriptions of behaviors observed and to insist that the actual behaviors of the infant provide the basic data. The second strategy is to develop techniques to ferret out alternative interpretations and to test the validity of each alternative interpretation.

The first strategy can and should always be used, even by parents making baby biographies of their own children. The following example from Tiedemann demonstrates an observation that does not clearly separate behavior from interpretation:

Are, then, all the movements of children at this age unintentional? Or could there already be some purpose and acquired knowledge? One circumstance, I think, indicates that even at such an early stage some learning process may occur. The mother was yet unable to offer the child the food which nature intended for him [therefore, baby is under one week of age]; artificial feeding was so far avoided for the reason mentioned above, so he had to suffer some want, and, as he was healthy, some hunger. For the relief he sought to put his own and, if possible, other people's fingers into his mouth in order to suck them, though indeed he did not find his mouth save after many vain attempts. Herein, methinks we can discern something learned, something intentional. (Tiedemann, 1787/1927, pp. 207–208)

We are hard pressed to determine the validity of Tiedemann's statements in this example. We don't know whether his father assumed the baby was suffering or whether the child did something (such as fuss and cry) that was interpretable as suffering. We don't know what the infant did to make his father think he was intending to put fingers in his mouth for relief, or even why Tiedemann thought they provided relief. Subsequent, more behaviorally based observations do not support the notion that babies intend to relieve hunger by sucking fingers in the first week of life.

Now consider this example from Taine's baby biography:

. . . From about ten months, when asked, "Where is grandfather?" she turns to this portrait and laughs. Before the portrait of her grandmother, not so good a likeness, she makes no such gesture, and gives no sign of intelligence. From eleven months when asked "Where is mamma?" she turns toward her mother, and she does the same for her father. I should not venture to say that these actions surpass the intelligence of animals. A little dog, here, understands as well when it hears the word, sugar; *it comes from the other end of the garden to get a bit. There is nothing more in this than an association, for the dog, between a sound and some sensation of taste, for the child between a sound and the form of an individual face perceived; the object denoted by the sound has not as yet a general character. . . . For if we supplied the word, we did not supply the meaning; the general character which we wished to make the child catch, is not that which she has chosen. She caught another, suited to her mental state. . . . (Taine, 1877, p. 26)*

Here is a clear differentiation between behaviors, described in the first three sentences, and the interpretation, everything from "I should not venture . . ." to the end of the excerpt. Notice the difference between the excerpt from Taine and this one from Tiedemann on the same point:

Now he learned also to comprehend a few sentences; on the 14th he knew already what was meant by: "Make a bow," "Swat the fly," which he always accompanied by the appropriate motions. (Tiedemann, 1787/1927, p. 220)

Tiedemann concluded that his son understood certain phrases because he always accompanied them by the appropriate motions. The behaviors observed are parallel, but the interpretations differ.

Observations of infants that clearly differentiate behaviors from interpretations provide two advantages over other observations. First, readers know that the infant did something to warrant an interpretation. Second, they can evaluate the reasonableness of the interpretation for themselves.

Once behaviors and interpretations are separated, the observer's interpretation can be evaluated critically. An effective way of doing this within an observational framework is to compare it to alternative interpretations. Once an alternative interpretation is generated, one can see that the original interpretation may be wrong. We have just provided such an example for the development of word meaning by comparing Tiedemann's conclusions to those of Taine.

Although the early baby biographers rarely did so, it is possible to consider alternative interpretations while doing systematic observations. Piaget's observations are replete with examples, such as the following one.

OBS. 1. On the very night after his birth, T. was wakened by the babies in the nearby cots and began to cry in chorus with them. At 0;0 (3)[2] he was drowsy, but not actually asleep, when one of the other babies began to wail; he himself thereupon began to cry. At 0;0 (4) and 0;0 (6) he again began to whimper, and started to cry in earnest when I tried to imitate his interrupted whimpering. A mere whistle and other cries failed to produce any reaction.

There are two possible interpretations of these commonplace observations, but neither of them seems to justify the use of the word imitation. On the one hand it may be that the baby was merely unpleasantly affected by being wakened by the cries of his neighbors, yet without establishing any relation between the sounds he heard and his own crying, whereas the whistle or other sound left him indifferent. On the other hand, it is possible that the crying occurred as a result of its repetition, owing to a kind of reflex analogous to that we saw in the case of suction . . . , but in this case with intensification of the sound through the help of the ear. In this second case, the crying of the other babies would increase the vocal reflex through confusion with his own crying.

Thus in neither case is there imitation, but merely the starting off of a reflex by an external stimulus. . . . (Piaget, 1945/1962, p. 7)

Piaget considered three alternative interpretations, one that claimed the newborn im-

itates and two that claimed other processes were involved. This alone helps us to become aware that any one interpretation may be wrong. Notice also that Piaget considers imitation to be an inappropriate interpretation here. Arguing that imitation requires the assumption that infants are more advanced (more cognitively complex) than do the other two alternatives, Piaget has, in good scientific tradition, accepted the simpler explanation or the one that demands fewest assumptions: that infants respond reflexively to crying. In scientific terminology, he has applied the principle of **parsimony,** known historically as "Occam's razor."

In our earlier comparative example, Taine applied the principle of parsimony, but Tiedemann did not. Taine concluded that infants can respond appropriately to certain words or phrases without necessarily understanding them. The process of associating a motoric response to a verbal stimulus is simpler than the process of understanding.

Accepting the more parsimonious explanation is often a good strategy, but it is not necessarily correct. Sometimes the more complex interpretation will be supported by later research. Indeed, investigators are still trying to ascertain whether imitative-like responses in newborns are truly imitation or not, as we shall see in Chapter 7.

Piaget employed two other techniques in his baby biographies to try to decide among alternative hypotheses. One was to collect a number of different instances of behavior that were consistent with his favored interpretation. The second was to introduce informal experiments into the observations. In the example that follows, Piaget used both of these techniques to support his interpretation that babies progress (from the earlier crying example) to a stage in which they truly imitate, but imitate only those actions that are already familiar to them.

OBS. 9. At 0;6 (25) J. invented a new sound by putting her tongue between her teeth. It was something like pfs. *Her mother then made the same sound. J. was delighted and laughed as she repeated it in her turn. Then came a long period of mutual imitation. J. said* pfs, *her mother imitated her, and J. watched her without moving her lips. Then*

---

[2] These numbers refer to years of age; months of age (days of age).

when her mother stopped, J. began again and so it went on. Later on, after remaining silent for some time, I myself said pfs. *J. laughed and at once imitated me. There was the same reaction the next day, beginning in the morning (before she had herself spontaneously made the sound in question) and lasting throughout the day.*

At 0;7 (11) and on the following days, I only had to say pfs *for her to imitate me correctly at once.*

At 0;7 (13) she imitated this sound without seeing me or realizing where it was coming from. (Piaget, 1945/1962, pp. 19–20)

In this excerpt Piaget was trying to establish that J.'s vocalization was truly imitation. To do so he varied the situation to eliminate alternative interpretations. He ascertained that J. would imitate both Mommy and Daddy; this demonstration eliminated the hypothesis that the behavior was simply an interactive game with Mommy. He then found that J. would imitate even in situations in which she had not just made the response herself; this eliminated the alternative hypothesis that J. could reproduce actions only if she was in the midst of repeating them anyway. Finally, he demonstrated that it was not a learned response to Mommy's and Daddy's faces and bodies by demonstrating that J. imitated the sound even when she could not see Daddy.

In this same section Piaget goes on to demonstrate that this is not merely a vocal response to one specific vocal stimulus by presenting examples of the imitation of other sounds.

OBS. 11. At 0;7 (17) J. at once imitated the sounds pfs, bva, mam, abou, hla, *and a new phoneme* pff *which she had been trying out for several days, differentiating between them, and without having made them herself immediately before. She was enjoying the imitation, and no longer producing one sound instead of another. (Piaget, 1945/1962, pp. 20–21)*

Piaget next provided examples of his infants at the same stage imitating motoric actions, such as sticking out their tongues, opening and closing their hands, and "waving." He always gathered as many examples as he could to support his interpretation and did informal experiments to differentiate between alternative hypotheses. Following is a particularly clear example of his use of informal experiments:

At 0;4 (23) without any previous practice, I showed L. my hand which I was slowly opening and closing. She seemed to be imitating me. All the time my suggestion lasted she kept up a similar movement and either stopped or did something else as soon as I stopped.

There was the same reaction when I repeated the experiment at 0;4 (26). But was this response of L. merely due to an attempt at prehension? To test this, I then showed her some other object. She again opened and closed her hand, but only twice, then immediately tried to seize the object and suck it. I resumed the experiment with my hand, and she clearly imitated it, her gesture being quite different from the one she made on seeing the toy. (Piaget, 1945/1962, p. 23)

Although Piaget's techniques provided a decided improvement over the more limited ones used by earlier baby biographers, they still have their limitations. The observer-experimenter's biases may still play a large role. For example, we have to take Piaget's word that L.'s gestures were different in the two instances described in the last excerpt. We have to assume that Piaget was not ignoring many behaviors that were nonimitative. For example, J. may have responded *pfs* only 35% of the times she heard *pfs*. Piaget, who believed that she could imitate, may have tended to focus on the instances in which she did imitate and may have missed the instances in which she did not. If *you* believed that 7-month-old infants could not imitate, would *you* consider that imitation in 35% of the instances was sufficient to be called imitation and not chance responding?

Another problem looms large in baby biographies. Piaget, for example, derived his entire theory of infancy (and three books) from observations on his three children. No three children are an adequate basis from which to **generalize** (to apply the result) to all children, and three children of a brilliant father who are interacted with intensively throughout their infancies provide an even less adequate sample. For these reasons, American psychologists are unwilling to accept research based solely on baby biographies. Rather they insist that findings such as those reported by Tiedemann and Piaget be replicated by well-controlled systematic studies of relatively large groups of infants, who ideally represent a clearly defined group.

Normative/Descriptive Studies

The problem of generalization, characteristic of baby biographies, is solved by **normative/ descriptive** studies, which first developed about 50 years after the first baby biography. In such a study infants in a group are observed with respect to selected behaviors. The primary goals of such research are to establish that a particular sequence of development occurs and to determine the average age at which each step in the sequence occurs. The former goal describes development and the latter establishes **norms;** hence the name. These studies have an advantage over the infant biographies in that their samples provide a better representation of infants in general than did the beloved offspring of the erudite baby biographers.

The earliest known normative study was a thesis, *Observations on the Normal Functioning of the Human Body*, written by Heinrich Feldman, a physician, and published in 1833. The first 6 pages of his 35-page paper were devoted to walking and speaking in 35 healthy infants. Examples of the kind of data he gathered are the average ages at which the babies walked unaided and uttered their first words.

Feldman's infant study was **longitudinal** as well as normative/descriptive; that is, the same children were studied at several ages. Studies that are not longitudinal are **cross-sectional;** that is, the children studied at one age are different from those studied at each of the other ages. Baby biographies are by definition longitudinal, but normative/ descriptive studies may be either cross-sectional or longitudinal. Early researchers seem to have been more patient than modern investigators, because they favored longitudinal studies, but most present day research is of the more rapidly completed cross-sectional type.

The next landmark normative study, by Kussmaul, another physican, was published in 1859. Although his first pages are devoted to the development of the soul in the first postnatal days, the last two thirds of his treatise is a sophisticated scientific report on his own and other people's findings on the functioning of various senses in the newborn period, including taste, smell, touch, pain, sight, and hearing. He also included a section on the intelligence of newborns and on the responses of premature newborns (babies who were born before they were due).

Many similar studies were done later in the 19th century, some of which were intensive studies of a single response, such as the force of sucking. There is also a doctoral dissertation from this period (Genzmer, 1873) that repeated many of Kussmaul's earlier experiments, often with large numbers of infants. This is an early example of a **replication** study, a study designed to test whether previous findings can be obtained again. Replicability is a crucial test of the validity of scientific findings. (By the way, Kussmaul's findings generally did replicate.)

Normative/descriptive studies continue to be an important area of research. We will describe modern normative/descriptive studies of infant physical, motor, and intellectual milestones and discuss the meaning and legitimate uses of such norms in Chapter 8. Other normative/descriptive studies focus on the typical sequence of changes of behaviors rather than the ages at which each kind of behavior is typical. For example, in a descriptive study designed to study Piaget's notions of imitation, the reactions of a number of babies to adult actions were observed to see whether the sequence Piaget described held for children other than his own. Many such studies will be described in Chapter 10, which focuses on Piaget's theory and related research.

Normative/descriptive studies serve very important practical purposes, such as enabling doctors and psychologists to decide whether a given child is severely delayed in achieving developmental milestones. They also can serve as the basis for theoretical interpretations of behaviors. They do not, however, permit researchers to decide among alternative explanations for behaviors (or developmental sequences of behaviors). Experiments and correlational studies are necessary for that.

MODERN RESEARCH TECHNIQUES

Since the establishment of the first psychological laboratories in the 1880s and 1890s, much of the history of psychology has consisted of the development of research methods that permit more probing analyses into questions of age-old interest. This has also been true for studies of infant development. As techniques have improved, researchers have been better able to test causal hypotheses with respect to developmental sequences.

Experiments

Experiments provide the most convincing evidence upon which to judge alternatives. The nature of experiments is perhaps most easily understood in a situation in which the interpretation being tested is whether one event causes another. For example, Tiedemann noticed that his newborn son did not use his hands to grasp and did not understand distances, because he struck his own face with his hands. Later, he noticed, his child reached for things accurately. Tiedemann concluded that touching things must ''aid sight in forming a conception of external and removed bodies'' (distances). The best way to test whether his hypothesis is true is by an experiment in which babies in one group are prevented from using their hands (as by swaddling) and in another group are allowed to use their hands. If Tiedemann is correct, babies who used their hands would understand distances (reach more accurately, not strike their faces) at an earlier age than the babies who had not used their hands. If no differences were obtained between the two groups, the alternative hypothesis (interpretation), that touching is not necessary to form a conception of depth, would be supported.

Because experiments are so important, let us consider their characteristics carefully. The experimenter manipulates the hypothesized cause, the **independent variable**, and measures the consequences on the hypothesized effect, the **dependent variable.** In the example above, experience with the hands is the independent variable and accurate reaching is the dependent variable. Experiments are the one sure way to test causal relations (Does experience with their hands influence babies to learn about distance?) because they are the only studies in which the researcher has adequate control over the relevant variables.

The experimenter sets up the study so that the only difference between the two groups is the hypothesized cause (in this case, use of the hands). This is accomplished by two means. First, the experimenter makes sure that all other conditions are constant: the ages at which the children are tested, the kind of test of reaching they are given, and so forth. Second, the experimenter assigns subjects to groups randomly; that is, subjects are put in a particular group on the basis of pure chance. In the above example, flipping a coin could be used to assign subjects to the groups. If the coin came up heads, the infant would be in the experimental group (prevented from using hands); if the coin came up tails, the infant would be in the control group (allowed to use hands). **Random assignment of subjects** to these groups controls for variations among subjects that might result from other methods of assignment. For example, if the mothers of the infants were allowed to choose whether to swaddle their babies and if differences in the accuracy of their reaching were found, the differences might have more to do with the mothers' other actions than with the experimental restrictions of the babies' hands. The mothers who asked that their babies' hands be free might be more concerned with the babies' motoric development and might spend more time explicitly training their infants to reach, grasp, and so on. If that were the case and the nonswaddled group developed motor coordination of their hands more rapidly, the experimenter would not be able to tell whether the more rapid development was due to the lack of swaddling or to the mothers' training. The mothers' actions are called **extraneous variables** and can be said to have **confounded** the experiment; that is, confounded our ability to find out whether the infants' experience with their hands produced accurate reaching. The confounding occurs because *either* the independent variable *or* the extraneous variable may produce any observed effects.

If infancy researchers could experimentally assess all the issues in which they were interested, they would have much less difficulty in establishing and expanding knowledge of babies and their development. Unfortunately many interesting phenomena cannot be studied by the experimental method, especially not with humans. The swaddling study would actually not be done with humans for both ethical and practical reasons. Ethically, the problem is that some parents would be asked to behave toward their babies in ways that make them uncomfortable and to make changes in their infant care techniques that might have long-term negative effects on their babies. Practically, it would be very difficult for parents who were assigned to a condition that did not match their natural inclinations to comply with the experimenter's instructions. Thus, the experimental manipulation itself would fail. Failure to find a difference between the two groups would then falsely suggest the treatment had no effect when there had been no "treatment." In these and other circumstances, different techniques must be used.

Correlational Studies

Correlational studies, the major alternative to experiments, are studies that measure a relation between two variables. If the swaddling study were a correlational one, the investigator would assess the degree of arm movements babies experience in their everyday lives. The result might be two categories (babies with free arm movements versus babies with restricted arm movements) or a range of scores (most to least arm movements). The development of the babies' understanding of distance would be assessed in the same way as in the experiment. The relation between these two variables then would be assessed by statistical means, most often by a statistic called the correlation coefficient. A significant correlation between the variables indicates there is a relation between the amount of swaddling and the development of understanding of distance. No relation between the variables indicates that swaddling did not make a difference in the development of understanding of distance.

The limitations of correlational research become apparent when attempts are made to interpret the findings. The causal hypothesis is that the amount of arm movement (the independent variable) influences the development of perception of distance (the dependent variable). In a correlational study, however, this interpretation or conclusion is not warranted. It may be that the babies' developing depth perception determined how much they moved their arms; that is, that babies move their arms to reach for something when they know it is at an appropriate distance.

Furthermore, these two exactly opposite conclusions are not the only possibilities. Because subjects were not randomly assigned to groups, extraneous subject variables were not controlled. Thus, an extraneous variable may produce both the amount of arm movements and the perception of distance. For example, mothers who are concerned that their babies receive sensory stimulation are likely both to allow babies free arm movements and to provide whatever experiences are crucial for development of perception of distance. Thus, the mothers' actions to stimulate their babies may cause the variation in both measures and make it look—wrongly—as if the two variables were themselves causally related.

Although causality cannot be tested directly in a correlational study, there are indirect methods. Some are similar to those used by Piaget to check on interpretations of behavior. They are all less convincing than having the results of true experiments but they do provide valuable ways of assessing the merits of alternative hypotheses. Correlational studies sometimes try to approximate the equivalence of groups that should result from random assignment of subjects by establishing that the 2 (or more) groups under study do not differ on various extraneous variables that the researcher thinks might be relevant to the outcome of the study (age of babies, marital status of mothers, education of mothers, birth weights of babies, and so on). This helps improve our confidence in the outcomes, but does not replace random assignment of subjects. The latter should result in the random distribution of extraneous variables that are not thought of in advance. Furthermore, random assignment should result in random distributions of combinations of variables (for example, second-born children of mothers under 25) in the treatment groups. Testing for comparability on a list of single variables can never be exhaustive and will never account for such combinations. Several varieties of the indirect method will be discussed throughout this book.

Correlational studies are also used in contexts other than those in which the question of causality (or what leads to what) is of prime importance. One such use is in exploring the stability of individual differences. For example, researchers wish to know whether height and weight of newborns (or 2-year-olds) relate to these same qualities in adulthood. They also are interested in whether complex traits such as intelligence are stable from infancy to later childhood. To find out, they determine the correlations between the given characteristics at the two ages. If the relations are strong (correlations high), then the adult characteristic can be predicted from the infant characteristic. The issues of stability of traits will be raised in numerous places in this book.

RESEARCH ISSUES

We discuss methodological issues in the context of specific studies throughout this book. We do this to demonstrate how methodological issues determine the conclusions that can reasonably be drawn from studies, not to subject readers to a study of methodology for its own sake. This approach has the advantage of making what might otherwise seem to be dry, abstract, and often difficult material become more concrete, meaningful, and alive. For example, it may be much easier to understand what a longitudinal study is if the term is introduced as part of the description of a particular longitudinal study. This strategy has the disadvantage that learning about a term or concept only in a particular context may make it more difficult to understand in its more general sense, and may actually distort the general meaning because of peculiarities of that specific context. Therefore, at the end of each chapter we will discuss the major methodological points in more general form and will relate them to other contexts.

In this chapter we have followed this general plan with respect to the methodological issues of baby biographies, but we have also described alternative research designs as topics in themselves. Thus our discussion of research issues follows our general model but is somewhat more extensive and includes more new information than comparable sections in other chapters.

Sampling

One major problem in infancy research is avoiding biased samples. Subjects used in one particular study may or may not be representative of all the subjects in the world. What baby biographies found about the behaviors of children of highly intelligent, well-educated adults might not be true for children from other life circumstances. This is called the problem of **biased samples.** The word *sample* refers to the subjects selected for a study, and the sample is called *biased* when it is not representative of a large group (called a **population**), which in many cases in this book is all babies (or all babies in a society). Modern studies include a broader range of babies than did the baby biographies, but their samples are usually still rather restricted. Many studies rely on volunteers obtained from notices put up around university areas or from newspaper advertisements. Such volunteers are likely to be highly educated, middle class, nonworking mothers who have time to bring their babies in for study. Other studies may draw their samples from the clinic populations in urban hospitals. Such samples are likely to be primarily composed of minorities from lower socialeconomic classes who are relatively uneducated.

Studies with such biased samples are not useless, because their findings can be applied to the groups that the sample represents. For example, if a study used subjects from a clinic population of a center city hospital, conclusions could be generalized from that sample to other poor, urban babies. By the same token, remember that those conclusions might not hold for rural, middle class infants.

The number of subjects in a sample also influences its bias. No matter how carefully a sample of babies is chosen, if there are only a few of them, they may be an unusual sample. Simply by bad luck the babies in a sample of 3 or 5 subjects may be all small, or all sleepy, or all advanced in development. As more and more subjects are added, a sample is more and more likely to include individuals who differ on any relevant dimension. A sample with more than 30 subjects is less likely to be biased by chance (it may still be biased by the way the subjects were selected, as described above). The Department of Education of The American Social Science Association, whose work in the 1880s we have referred to, was aware of the biasing likely to occur with small samples. They sponsored the collection of a large number of baby biographies to provide a more representative sample from which to draw conclusions about development.

Research Design

The design of a study depends on what researchers want to know and how much control they have over the conditions of the study. We introduced two major kinds of design distinctions in this chapter. The first is whether the study is normative/descriptive, correlational, or experimental. The second is whether the study is cross-sectional or longitudinal.

Normative/descriptive studies chart developmental sequences and are designed to answer the questions of when something develops and how it develops in the sense of what aspects develop early and what aspects develop late. Correlational and experimental studies most often try to find out what causes something to develop. Both of these latter kinds of studies investigate at least two variables and typically identify one as the cause, or independent variable, and the other as the effect, or dependent variable.

Because the ultimate goal for many psychologists is to determine what causes behavior, or what in the environment determines the course and speed of development, they must always keep in mind the strengths and limitations of each of these kind of studies. Normative/descriptive studies cannot in themselves determine what causes behaviors, although the early baby biographers did not always realize this. Making such causal inferences from descriptive studies is inappropriate because the investigators do not have control over extraneous variables.

To determine that one environmental event or condition causes babies to behave or to develop in a particular way, researchers must set up a controlled study. They specify one or more causal factors, called independent variables, and choose one or more behavioral effects, called dependent variables. The research goal is to establish that the independent variable causes the behavior of interest, the dependent variable. To do this, all other possible causes, called extraneous variables, must be eliminated. This is achieved by two kinds of experimental controls. The first attempts to eliminate all extraneous variables in the procedures of the study. For example, all subjects must be treated in as much the same way as possible. The second results from the random assignment of subjects to experimental conditions; that is, subjects are put into one condition or another by chance and only by chance. That means that subjects in each condition are essentially not different from subjects in another condition with respect to extraneous variables such as physical and intellectual level, family background, or influences of mother. If differences are found between groups then, it can be assumed that they are due to the purported independent variable (so long as there are enough subjects, preferably over 30 in each group). Because only in experiments are subjects randomly assigned to groups, it is only in experimental results that we can be confident that a causal relation exists between the independent and dependent variables. Correlational studies can eliminate extraneous variables in the procedure, but not those that are intrinsic to subjects. This is the reason for the very common statement, "Correlations cannot prove causality."

The second major variation in designs of studies concerns the number of samples and the times at which they are run. Researchers may (1) study one sample at one time, (2) compare two samples at one time, or (3) study one sample at two or more times. In developmentally oriented research, comparisons of behavior at two or more ages is often the focus of attention. Such studies may be either cross-sectional (type 2) or longitudinal (type 3). The number of ages studied is determined by the goals and resources of the particular project and is not a function of the type of study. All of the baby biographies and most of the early normative studies were longitudinal. They studied the same children at more than one age. Cross-sectional studies use a different group of children for each age. Such studies can be completed more rapidly. In a matter of weeks a very large age span (say newborns, 8-month-olds, and 2-year-olds) can be studied. Longitudinal investigators must wait for the children in their studies to grow up. If, however, the study is of a rare or hard-to-find group, such as Black identical twins, then the longitudinal design provides the advantage that fewer subjects are needed.

Cross-sectional studies are often a short-cut approach to longitudinal studies. They assume that two groups of infants at different ages are no different from one group of infants at two ages. Therefore, researchers reason, it is not necessary to wait for the younger group to grow older to find out how they will behave when they are older. A group of similar babies who have already reached that older age can be substituted. This assumption is valid only if the samples at each age are comparable on all variables other than age (for example, on sex, race, social class, or any other potentially relevant variable). Some research questions do not permit this short cut. For example, if researchers want to explore the effects of early experience on later development, they have to follow the same infants from early infancy to later infancy and hence must do a longitudinal study.

Replicability

Another important criterion for judging any research is its replicability. Replication means that a study is repeated and the same results or relations are found. Regardless of the nature of the study (cross-sectional or longitudinal; normative/descriptive, experimental, or correlational), replicability is the test of its value in predicting or understanding behavior and its development. It may sound like a waste of time to redo a study, but it is by no means a foregone conclusion that the same results or relations will be obtained. Science provides only an approximate method of discovering truth, and the results of research are always subject to revision when the next study comes along. Because humankind has found no foolproof way of finding truth, scientists and consumers of science have to be satisfied with this approximate method and must be alert to its problems and guard against its errors. One of the best

ways to do this is to repeat studies to see if they replicate. If they do, there is a measure of confidence that methodological flaws are not responsible for the results.

Some of the methodological flaws that may make a study nonreplicable have been discussed in this chapter. If the sample is biased or different, the findings may not replicate with a new sample. If extraneous variables have not been controlled, they may differ in the replication study from what they were in the original study and thus lead to nonreplication. Common examples are: the social class of the second study may differ from that in the original study, or the first study may have included only first-borns but the second included many second- and third-born children.

Another type of extraneous variable that may be important resides in the researcher rather than only in those studied. One researcher may expect that a study will support a particular hypothesis and a second investigator replicating the study may not share that bias or may have the opposite one. Good research methods minimize the role of experimenter expectations. Nevertheless, some evidence, although controversial, suggests that even in the best-controlled situations, experimenter expectations may subtly influence the results. Parents' expectations may play a similar role.

Replication studies often add new variations that are designed to test additional hypotheses such as the influence of particular extraneous variables. For example, a researcher who believes that certain research results were obtained because the sample was largely middle class might repeat the study with separate middle class and lower class samples and would predict that the results would replicate only for the middle class sample. A less careful experimenter might replicate the study using only a lower class sample to compare with the results from the previous study. This strategy is much less acceptable because a number of extraneous variables are likely to be controlled for in the first strategy that are not controlled for in the second. Time itself is often associated with changes that may be relevant to the outcome measures of a study (for example, feeding practices or use of anesthesia in childbirth may have changed). Locales may differ and may be associated with potentially relevant extraneous variables. What seems lower class in one community might seem middle class in another; hence a researcher working in the latter community and replicating an original study done in the former type of community might replicate the original finding for the middle class group with the "lower class" group, even though the hypothesis that the result is class linked was correct.

Many studies fail to replicate because of methodological flaws or unanticipated confounding variables. Note, however, that a single study, no matter how well done, may in some instances be incorrect. The best way to ferret out those incorrect conclusions is to replicate the research. Note also that research needs to be replicated over time because the extraneous variables may change over time.

SUMMARY

The summaries in this book relate specifically to the substantive concepts described in each chapter. When these concepts relate to one of the overriding themes presented at the ends of chapters (research issues, parenting, heredity and the environment) they will be summarized as part of those sections.

The study of infants has fascinated researchers for 200 years because it provides the mechanism for studying basic questions of (1) the roles of heredity and the environment in development, (2) the impact of early experience on development, and (3) the impact of teaching parents about their infants. The sophistication with which these questions are asked has increased greatly but the basic interests are the same. The scientific study of infants began in the 18th century with the first published baby biography, by Dietrich Tiedemann. By the end of the 19th century, making detailed observational histories of sons had become a popular pastime among sophisticated naturalistic-minded fathers. Such baby biographies can provide useful descriptions of developmental sequences of behaviors when the observers take care both to make clear distinctions between behaviors and interpretations and to look for alternative interpretations. Observers cannot, however, conclusively distinguish among alternative interpretations, although they can make progress in that direction by (1) applying the law of parsimony, (2) gathering multiple examples that fit only one of the alternative interpretations, and (3) introducing informal experiments.

The next kind of studies to appear were normative/descriptive studies. They are an improvement over baby biographies in that they are based on larger and more representative samples, which in turn allows production of norms. They share with baby biographies the limitation that they do not permit decisions among alternative interpretations.

Since the first psychological laboratories were established at the end of the 19th century, research techniques using experiments and correlational studies have dominated the field. In experiments researchers manipulate the independent variable (the hypothesized cause) and measure its effect on the dependent variable (the effect). Experimental conditions are controlled by isolating the independent variable and subject variables by random assignment of subjects to groups. Thus experiments are less likely than any other research design to suffer from confounding variables.

Correlational studies can in principle control procedural conditions, but cannot eliminate extraneous variables due to subject variations because they cannot randomly assign subjects to groups. Thus, results from such studies are less convincing and it is difficult to determine the existence or nature of the causal relation.

REFERENCES

Alcott, A.B. (1882). Letter to Mrs. Talbot with notes from his diary. *Journal of Social Science, 15,* 8–10.

Darwin, C. (1882). Letter to Mrs. Talbot. *Journal of Social Science, 15,* 6–8.

Feldman, H. (1833). *Observations on the normal functioning of the human body.* Bonn: C. Georgie.

Genzmer, A. (1873). *Investigations on sensory perception in newborn humans.* (National Institute of Health Library (NIH-74-230c), Trans.). Unpublished doctoral dissertation, University of Halle-Wittenberg.

Harris, W.T. (1882). Speech to 1881 meeting of Social Science Association. *Journal of Social Science, 15,* 1–5.

Kussmaul, A. (1859). *Untersuchungen über das Seelenleben des neugenborenen Menschen.* Heidelberg and Leipzig: C.F. Winter.

Piaget, J. (1962). *Play, dreams and imitation in childhood* (C. Gattegno & F.M. Hodgson, Trans.). New York: Norton. (Original work published 1945.)

Preyer, W. (1893). *The mind of the child, Part I: The senses and the will* (N.W. Brown, Trans.). New York: Appleton. (Original work published in 1881).

Rubin, J.L., Provenzano, F.J., & Luria, Z. (1974). The eye of the beholder: Parents on sex of newborns. *American Journal of Orthopsychiatry, 44,* 512–519.

Taine, M.H. (1877). Paper on infant development. *Mind, 1,* 252–259. (Original work published in *Revue Philosophique* 1876).

Talbot, E. (1882). Papers on infant development. *Journal of Social Science, 15,* 5–6.

Tiedemann, D. (1927). Tiedemann's observations on the development of the mental faculties of children (S. Langer, Trans.). *Pedagogical Seminary and Journal of Genetic Psychology, 34,* 205–230.

CONCEPTION THROUGH BIRTH

DEVELOPMENT FROM CONCEPTION TO BIRTH

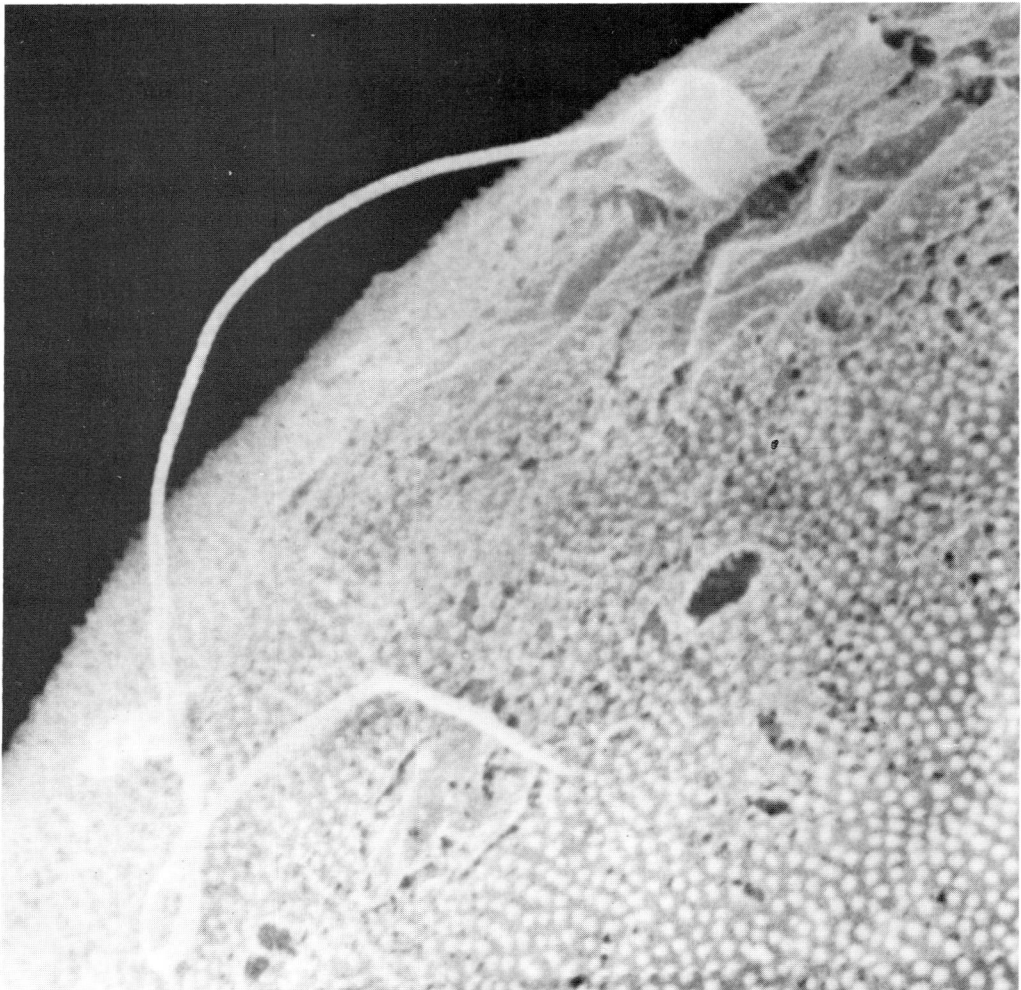

CHAPTER 2

In western cultures, birth is celebrated as the beginning of life, but the study of infancy must begin much earlier. Infants at birth are already products of their genetic makeup and the interactions of that genetic makeup with the **prenatal** environment (environment before birth). This chapter describes the normal course of prenatal growth and development. It provides the basic information necessary to understand the following three chapters, which describe things that can go wrong genetically, prenatally, and during the birth process.

In addition to acquiring this necessary background knowledge, the reader should also learn two things about normal development. The first is to appreciate the many complex and interrelated processes that work together to produce a human infant. The second is to see that despite its amazing complexity, these processes all work sufficiently well in the vast majority of pregnancies to produce normal, healthy babies.

Although students who use this book are not expected to become experts on embryology, we do want them to learn something of the basic processes and to have an overview of the development of a few systems. The heart (or circulatory system) and the respiratory system are singled out for more attention than the liver or kidneys because they are systems whose functioning undergoes particularly dramatic changes at birth. These changes are crucial to the proper development of the infant and are relevant to our later discussion of problems associated with labor and delivery. The sexual system is also described in somewhat more detail than others, both because we assume that it may be of particular interest to students and because it provides such excellent examples of the interaction of genetics and environment. In addition, certain aspects of the development of the organ most crucial to human functioning—the brain—are described.

OVERVIEW OF PRENATAL DEVELOPMENT

It is difficult to know exactly where to begin. We could consider the processes that lead to the formation of the **spermatozoa** (sperm, in the male) and the development of an **ovum** (egg, in the female) that is ready for fertilization. Some of what can go wrong with development occurs during these processes. Between the development of the millions of sperm and of the ovum and fertilization, much happens that helps determine whether the ovum will be fertilized and which particular sperm cell will fertilize it. Another set of changes occurs between penetration of the ovum by the sperm and the point of the first cleavage division. Such discussions, however, are more appropriate for biology texts.

Fertilization and Earliest Development (Zygote Stage)

We will start at the point at which an ovum and a sperm cell unite. Each of these cells has 23 **chromosomes** (barlike structures in cells that carry all the genetic information; see Figure 3–1). The two cells approach, join, and reform into a fertilized egg with 46 chromosomes (see Figure 2–1), a process that takes about 24 hours. Thus this new cell, or **zygote**, has the same number of chromosomes as all other cells in the body. It could be said that the potential for a new human being has then been created. Whether or not this potential is realized depends on many hereditary and environmental influences, as we shall see. Table 2–1 and the figures showing developing embryos will be helpful for the next sections.

Fertilization usually occurs in the **Fallopian tubes**, through which an ovum normally passes every month on its trip from the ovaries, where it has ripened, to the **uterus** or womb. It takes 2 to 3 days for the zygote to reach the uterus. The unfertilized egg is the largest cell in the body, and during its first few days as a zygote it stays the same size although it subdivides several times; that is, after each cell division, the cells inside the zygote become smaller (see Figure 2–2). Even at this stage of the first cell divisions environment is important in determining what happens to the genetic message of the **DNA** (deoxyribonucleic acid, the carrier of genetic information in cells). The DNA located in the cell **nucleus** (the part of a cell that governs growth, metabolism, and reproduction) depends upon the **cytoplasm** (protoplasm outside the nucleus) in the

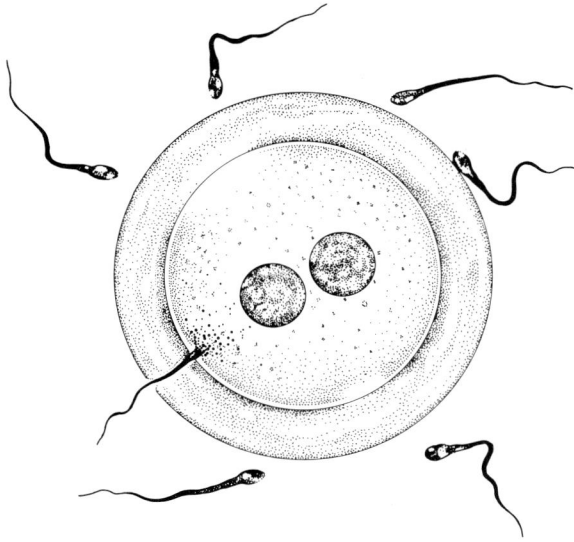

FIGURE 2–1. The process of fertilization of an ovum by a sperm. One sperm has penetrated the jelly-like coating around the egg cell. Its head has detached and swelled as it approached the nucleus of the egg cell (the two circles in the center of the cell are the head of the sperm and the nucleus of the egg). The head of the sperm cell (containing 23 chromosomes from the father) and the nucleus of the egg cell (containing 23 chromosomes from the mother) are now in the position from which they will each release their chromosomes to combine into a new cell with 46 chromosomes. The moment of combination is called fertilization. (Adapted with permission from S. Parker & J. Bavosi, Life Before Birth: The Story of the First Nine Months. *Cambridge, England: British Museum (Natural History) & Cambridge University Press, 1979.)*

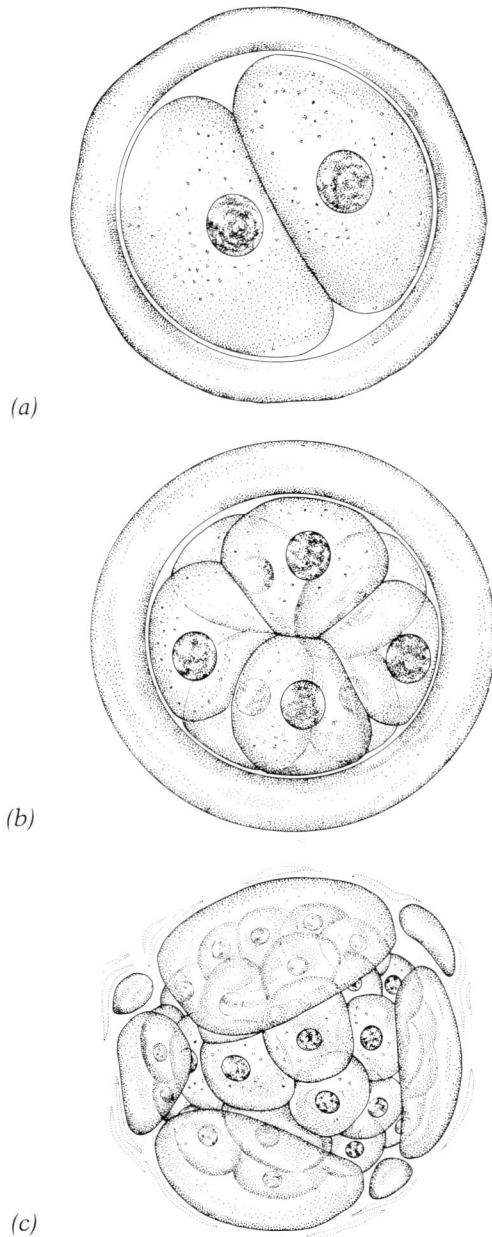

FIGURE 2–2. Initial cell division of fertilized egg. (a) After first cell division. (b) At eight-cell stage. (c) At blastocyst stage. There are about 40 cells and the outer cells are reproducing more rapidly and flattening. (Adapted with permission from S. Parker & J. Bavosi, Life Before Birth: The Story of the First Nine Months. *Cambridge, England: British Museum (Natural History) & Cambridge University Press, 1979.)*

rest of the cell body and the nutrients contained in it to be able to replicate itself properly.

During the process of so-called **cleavage** divisions, all of the cells are identical. The original cells had to rely almost entirely on their own reserves for nutrients, but by the time there are 8 cells (Figure 2–2b) they can utilize a number of external nutrients. By the time the zygote has reached the uterus, a journey of 3 or 4 days, cleavage has proceeded to the point where the zygote has 12 to 16 cells. It now has a new technical name, morula, although more generally it is still called a zygote.

By 4 days of age (the number of days

TABLE 2–1
Timetable for Prenatal Development

	Time After Fertilization	Events
Zygote[a]	0–40 hours	Cleavage divisions.
Morula	40 hours to 4 days	Reaches uterus; embryonic cell masses develop.
Blastocyst	4–8 days	Development of two-layered (bilaminar) disc. Implantation begins; embryonic membranes start to develop.
Embryo	12–13 days	Implantation complete.
	14 days	Mature placenta begins to develop.
	3 weeks (15–20 days)	Development of three-layered (trilaminar) disc. Neural tube begins to form. Disc becomes attached to wall by short, thick umbilical cord. Placenta develops rapidly.
	4 weeks (21–28 days)	Eyes begin to form. Heart starts beating. Crown–rump length 5 mm (less than $\frac{1}{4}$ in.); growth rate about 1 mm per day. Neural tube closes (otherwise spina bifida). Vascular system develops (blood vessels). Placenta maternal–infant circulation begins to function.
	5 weeks	Arm and leg buds form.
	7 weeks	Facial structures fuse (otherwise facial defects).
	8 weeks	Crown–rump length 3 cm (slightly more than 1 in.); weight 1 g (about 1/30 oz). Major development of organs completed. Most external features recognizable at birth are present.
Fetus	8–12 weeks	Movement of arms and legs. Startle and sucking reflexes first appear. Facial expressions appear. External sex organs appear. Fingerprints develop. Respiratory and excretory systems develop but are not functional. Lanugo develops.
	End of first trimester	Length 7.6 cm (about 3 in.); weight 14 g (about $\frac{1}{2}$ oz). Simple abortion by curettage no longer possible.
	13–16 weeks	Skin and true hair develop. Skeleton becomes bony.

Table 2–1 (continued)

Time After Fertilization	Events
17–20 weeks	Length 20 cm (about 8 in.); weight 450 g (less than 1 lb). Movements become obvious to mother ("quickening"). Heartbeat can be heard through a stethoscope. Old cells discarded, replaced by new ones.
25–28 weeks	Begins to acquire subcutaneous fat. Terminals of lung and associated blood vessels develop.
End of second trimester	Good chance of survival if born prematurely.
By 38 weeks	Fetus becomes plump. Lanugo usually shed. Testes of male descended.

[a]The organism is called a zygote until the time of implantation.

counted from conception, commonly called *conceptional age*) the egg mass contains 16 to 64 cells, each about the size of normal cells. They are beginning to change shape and position for the first time and thus are given a new technical name, the blastocyst, although it is also still called a zygote (Figure 2–2c). The dividing cells pull away from the center of the mass and a cavity forms. Then the cells separate into two layers, a small inner layer of cells that will form the infant, and a large mass of flattened cells on the outside of the cell mass that will form the related structures that will provide for the developing organism (Figure 2–3). The outside layer will eventually become the placenta, (the structure through which exchange of food, oxygen, and wastes between the mother and the offspring takes place, and which functions as an endocrine gland), the amnion or amniotic sac (which surrounds the infant), and other related structures. At this early time the blastocyst starts to absorb fluids from the uterine lining where it is floating.

Implantation and the Development of the Placenta and Related Structures

Once the two-layered disc has developed sufficiently, about 7 or 8 days after conception, the egg mass begins to implant in the wall of the uterus as a result of many complex interactions between the zygote and the uterine lining. Implantation normally takes place in the upper posterior (back) portion of the uterus. The location on the uterine wall where the implantation occurs is one of the determinants of the outcome of the pregnancy. The blood supply varies in different parts of the uterus and in some places may be inadequate to allow com-

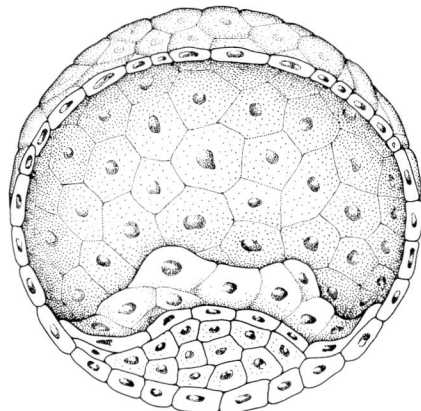

FIGURE 2–3. *Differentiation of cells into organism and support structures. (Adapted with permission from S. Parker & J. Bavosi,* Life Before Birth: The Story of the First Nine Months. *Cambridge, England: British Museum (Natural History) & Cambridge University Press, 1979.)*

pletion of the pregnancy or may result in an undernourished newborn. If the zygote attaches to the bottom of the uterus, the placenta may detach too early or may block delivery, and some placements of the placenta may make it more difficult to shed after delivery. Inappropriate placements are likely to result in hemorrhage during labor and delivery, endangering the lives of both mother and child.

The situations described above refer to implantation within the uterus. Sometimes, however, the zygote implants in one of the Fallopian tubes or somewhere else in the pelvic cavity (a small gap between the ovaries and Fallopian tubes in humans makes such misses possible). Such ectopic (outside the uterus) pregnancies usually terminate in the first 2 to 3 months, either by severe bleeding when the placenta becomes detached, or by rupture of the tube, or both. The most common symptoms are abdominal pain and vomiting. This condition requires immediate medical attention because death can result from loss of blood in as little as 6 hours after the symptoms start. According to recent newspaper reports (*Boston Globe*, 1983), ectopic pregnancies have increased in frequency in the last decade, but fewer deaths have resulted. There is no known explanation for this.

THE PROCESS OF IMPLANTATION
The outer layer of cells of the two-layered egg mass (those that will eventually form the placenta and membranes surrounding the developing organism) are responsible for implantation and for providing nutritional support for the developing organism. These cells thicken and develop amoeba-like projections that invade the uterine lining and transport nutrients from the maternal blood and other fluids in the uterine lining[1] to the zygote (Figure 2–4). The zygote takes in these nutrients by means of osmosis (gradual diffusion) because no circulatory system has yet developed. Human eggs, unlike those of chickens, have no yolk, so the supply of nutrients provided by the ovum is extremely limited. Direct contact between tis-

---

[1] The uterine lining, or endometrium, is made up of tissue, blood, and other fluids. The surface portion of the endometrium is sloughed off during menstruation when pregnancy has not occurred.

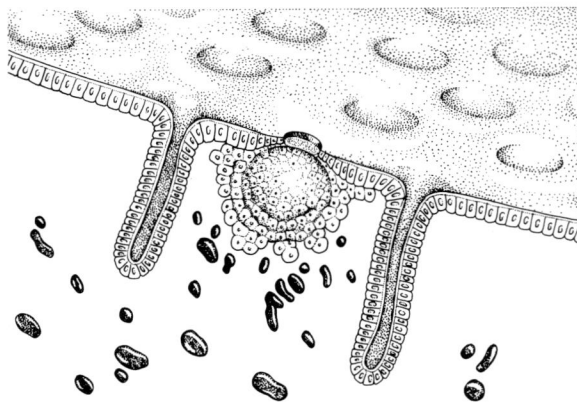

FIGURE 2–4. Implantation of zygote into uterine wall. The cells on the outside of the ball are absorbing nutrients from the mother's cells; the nutrients are, in turn, absorbed by the internal cells. (Adapted with permission from S. Parker & J. Bavosi, Life Before Birth: The Story of the First Nine Months. *Cambridge, England: British Museum (Natural History) & Cambridge University Press, 1979.*)

sue from the zygotic system and the uterine lining provides a supply system to tide the zygote over until the placental system develops.

DEVELOPMENT OF SUPPORT STRUCTURES
During this phase of direct contact all parts of the embryonic system develop. In the second week after conception the embryonic membranes begin to develop. The **amnion** is the "bag" in the phrase "bag of waters." It contains a clear fluid in which the developing organism floats and which protects it from blows, bounces, and shakes. The other three membranes (allantois, chorion, and yolk sac, which develops in humans even though human eggs have no yolk) play roles in the development of the placenta and the umbilical cord. The **placenta** is a disk-shaped mass of tissues in which small blood vessels from both mother and potential infant intertwine without joining; the **umbilical cord**, which contains two arteries and one vein, connects the baby to the placenta (see Figure 2–5). Small molecules can pass from maternal to infant vessels and back, but large ones cannot. Among the substances that can pass the placental barrier are food, oxygen, water, and salts from maternal blood,

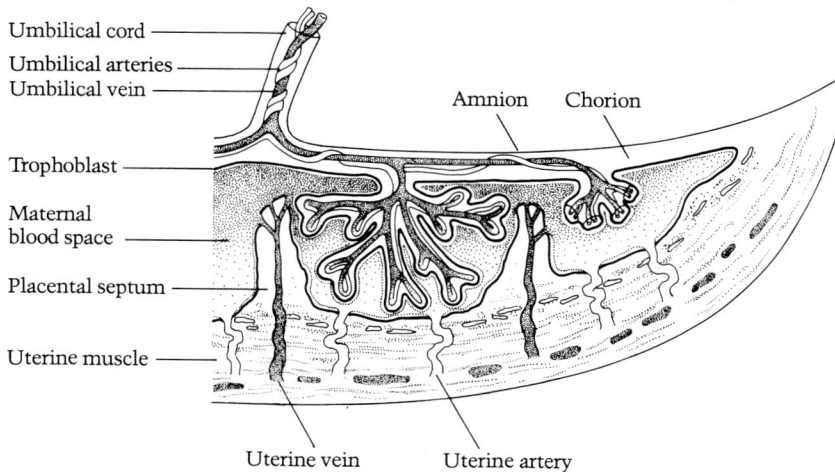

FIGURE 2–5. Diagram of the placenta attached to the uterine wall. The umbilical cord, at the top of the diagram, takes depleted blood from the developing organism to the placenta, where it disperses through small blood vessels that extend into the maternal blood supply. The placental barrier, which keeps the blood supply of the developing offspring separate from the maternal blood supply, is indicated in this diagram by the dark line labeled the trophoblast. (Adapted with permission from L.B. Arey, Developmental Anatomy: A Textbook and Laboratory Manual of Embryology *(7th Ed.). Philadelphia: Saunders, 1965.)*

and carbon dioxide and digestive wastes from infant blood. Among the large molecules that cannot pass the placental barrier are red blood cells and many harmful substances, such as most bacteria and a variety of maternal wastes, toxins, and hormones that could damage the potential child.[2]

The mature placenta starts to develop around the fourteenth day and by the end of the third week after conception it covers 20% of the uterus. Thus it soon takes over the digestive, respiratory, and excretory functions of the embryonic system. The placenta also functions as a gland and produces hormones that are crucial to the proper maintenance of pregnancy. Its role as a source of hormones becomes increasingly important as pregnancy progresses. Both estrogen and progesterone-like hormones are produced and are important not only in the growth of certain systems but in the maintenance of pregnancy.[3] Changes in the secretions of hormones probably play an important role in delivery also, but the mechanisms that normally lead to delivery are very little understood.[4]

It is important to remember that some of the placenta and all the fetal membrane systems are derived from the fertilized egg cell and are not structures grown by the mother to help her potential offspring develop. There are, of course, changes in her uterine lining that help these processes and that are the direct contribution of the maternal organism.

---

[2] The whole question of the many mechanisms that govern and control exchange (technically, transport or transfer) across the placental barrier is a highly complex field of study in itself.

[3] Note that the very name of one of the placental hormones (progestogen) implies the function of maintaining pregnancy. Pregnancy is also called **gestation**; hence this hormone is pro (or in favor of) gestation.

[4] Hormones also play an important role in conception, successful implantation, and lactation. Many of these roles are fairly well known and understood, but many are not. Any student particularly interested in these questions is referred to the book *Biology of Reproduction* (Hogarth, 1978).

Embryonic Stage of Development

INITIAL DIFFERENTIATION OF EMBRYO INTO THREE LAYERS

While the egg mass is becoming implanted in the uterine wall, the embryonic cells are differentiating into two layers of cells, called **germ** (or basic cell) **layers**. At this time the name of the organism changes from zygote to **embryo.** The inner layer of germ cells is the precursor of the **endodermal** cells (from *endon*, within, and *derma*, skin) that eventually form the linings of the internal organs, such as the digestive tract, respiratory system, bladder, vagina, and urethra. The outer germ layer gives rise to two kinds of cells: (1) the precursors of the **ectodermal** (outer covering) cells in the second week after conception, and (2) the precursors of the **mesodermal** (middle layer) cells in the third week. Ectodermal cells form the skin, sense receptors (for seeing, hearing, tasting, feeling), nerve cells, mammary and pituitary glands, and the mucus membranes of the mouth and anus. The mesodermal cells eventually form all of the muscles (including heart muscle), connective tissue (such as bone and cartilage), circulatory system (blood vessels and heart), and most of the excretory and reproductive systems.

Every part of the body develops from these three kinds of cells: endoderm, mesoderm, and ectoderm. In general, the endoderm develops into the most internal structures of the body, the mesoderm into the structures surrounding the internal organs, and the ectoderm into the surface structures, as shown in Table 2–2. This characterization is useful yet oversimplified.

We will use the ear as an example of the complexity of embryonic differentiation. Figure 2–6 is a diagram of the ear that shows the major structures and their origins. The ectoderm, as the forerunner of external structures, is the origin of most of the structures: the external ear, the outer tympanic membrane (outer part of eardrum), the sense receptors themselves (collectively known as the Organ of Corti, they transform sound into nerve impulses), and the semicircular canals (structures that have to do with the vestibular system, or balance). The other two types of cells also produce vital structures of the ear. The endoderm forms the inner tympanic membranes (inner part of eardrum) and the Eustachian tube (that goes from ear to throat), and the mesoderm differentiates into the middle tympanic membrane (the middle part of the eardrum); the hammer, anvil, and stirrup (three small bones in the middle ear that transmit sound); and the mastoid bone (the bone behind the ear). Even though the functions of these various structures may be unfamiliar, it is possible to appreciate the integrated way in which the various parts of the ear differentiate from the three basic cell types into a coordinated, functioning whole.

The first phase of embryonic differentiation results in a number of spontaneous abortions. These abortions are often of embryos

TABLE 2–2
Systems that Develop from Three Layers of the Blastocyst

Ectoderm	Central nervous system: brain and spinal cord
	Peripheral nervous system
	Sensory receivers of ear, nose, eye
	Outer skin layers and associated structures: nails, hair, tooth enamel
	Mammary and pituitary glands
Mesoderm	Circulatory system: heart, blood, lymph
	Skeleton: bone, cartilage
	Muscles and connecting tissues
	Excretory system: kidneys
	Reproductive system
	Inner layer of skin (dermis)
	Outer layers of digestive tube
Endoderm	Respiratory system: lungs
	Digestive system: pharynx, stomach, and intestines

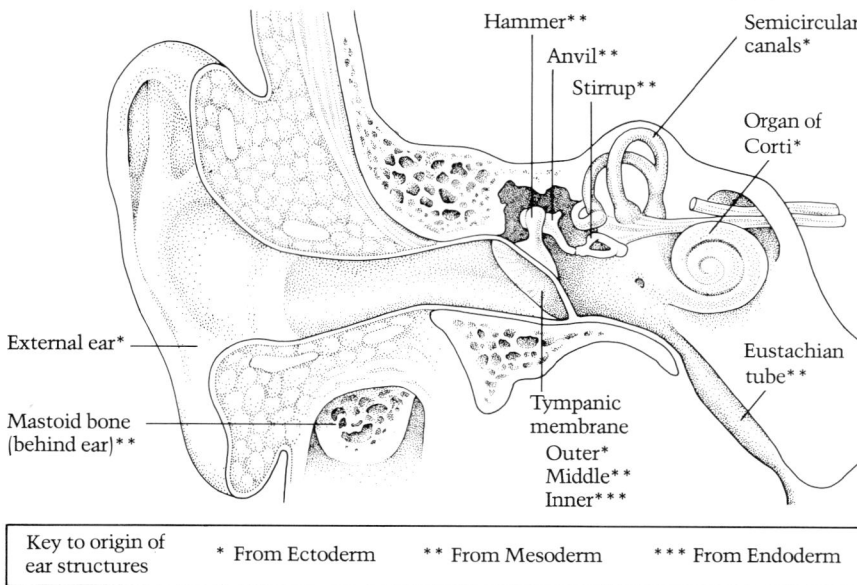

FIGURE 2–6. *Ear structures showing their derivation from the three-layered disc.*

with major chromosomal defects. They are aborted at this time and not earlier because this is the first stage of development that is governed by the embryonic cell nucleus (its DNA, to be exact). Earlier cleavage divisions are governed by the ribonucleic acid (RNA) that still survives from the original (or unfertilized) ovum.

The whole process of early differentiation is much more complex than we describe here. Not only do the cells differentiate, but many of them move from one place in the embryo to another along very specific pathways. Some differentiations are apparently self-determined and would happen even if the relevant cells were isolated from the embryo. Other differentiations depend on the chemical actions of their new neighbors and therefore depend on cell migration. Students who are interested in learning more about the details of the process of initial differentiation (called *gastrulation*) should consult a good biology text.

EMBRYONIC DEVELOPMENT 3 TO 4 WEEKS AFTER CONCEPTION

The differentiation of the mesodermal layer is not all that is happening during the third week after conception. The most critical period of physical development commences then, before most women even know they are pregnant.

During the third week the neural tube, destined to become the spinal cord, is developing (Figure 2–7a). At about 21 days the eyes begin to form. By 24 days the heart, although still just a tube, begins to flutter and then to beat. Also during the fourth week, the embryo gradually develops a head fold and a tail fold. The prominent part of the head fold is the brain and the tail bud closes off the spinal cord (Figure 2–7b). These foldings result in an organism with a distinguishable head (crown) and rump, with tail. Yes, embryonic humans have a tail (called the coccyx but with no more than 4 coccygeal vertebrae), which is more cartilaginous than bony. From this point on the embryo's length is measured from crown to rump with callipers. It is approximately 5 mm long in the fourth week. A severe defect called **spina bifida** may occur during this week if the neural tube does not close properly. Victims of this disorder suffer paralysis, deformity, and sometimes brain damage (Figure 2–8).

Also during the fourth week the first rudiments of the urogenital system are established.

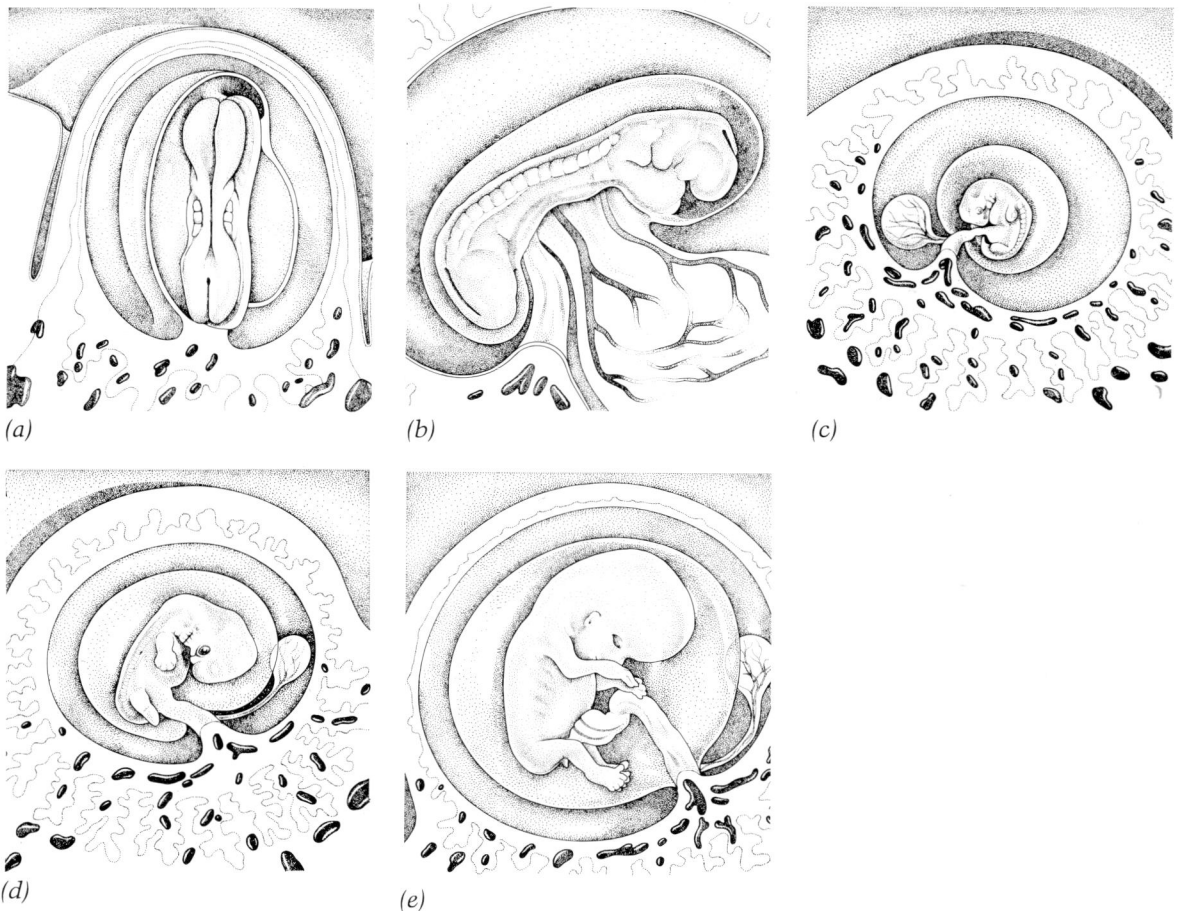

(a)   *(b)*   *(c)*

(d)   *(e)*

FIGURE 2–7. The developing embryo (not drawn to scale). In (a) the embryo is less than 5 mm long and in (e) it is 30 mm long. (a) The third week after conception. The two bulges at the top are the brain. The long groove that runs most of the way from the brain to the rump at the bottom is the start of the spinal tube. (b) The embryo a few days later, after the spinal tube has closed. The developing brain with its three bulges and spinal cord make up most of the embryo. The gut and the heart have also been enclosed by the folding together of the head and tail ends. (c) About 5 weeks after fertilization. The arm and leg buds and the tail extending below the leg buds, which developed in the fourth week, are clearly visible. (d) About 6 weeks after fertilization. The opening that looks like a mouth is the developing ear. (e) Two months after fertilization. Organogenesis is complete and the offspring is now called a fetus. (Adapted with permission from S. Parker & J. Bavosi, Life Before Birth: The Story of the First Nine Months. Cambridge, England: British Museum (Natural History) & Cambridge University Press, 1979.)

Arm and leg buds appear. The heart develops into a four-chambered structure. Primitive blood cells are manufactured and blood vessels first start to form. These developments of the vascular system of the embryo and simultaneous developments of the placental system permit the onset of mature placental functioning. From this point on there is a closed circuit in which embryonic circulation is completely separate from maternal circulation.

EMBRYONIC DEVELOPMENT 5 TO 8 WEEKS AFTER CONCEPTION

In the fifth week after conception (Figure 2–7c), the cells inside the arm and leg buds are differentiating into those that will ultimately become muscle cells, cartilage cells, and bone cells. In the sixth week (Figure 2–7d) arms and legs are more differentiated and the face has started to form but is still unrecognizable. During this time the liver, gallbladder, pancreas, and the major divisions of the intestinal tract develop. In the seventh week the facial structures fuse. Errors in this process produce hare lip, cleft nose, cleft chin, and cleft palate. Such errors are very common in the United States, affecting 1 in every 500 births (Pratt, 1982). They occur most often when 3 factors are all operative: (1) The embryo has a genetic predisposition; (2) the mother has a genetic predisposition; and (3) environmental factors such as exposure to drugs, hormones, or chemicals are present. By the end of 8 weeks the organism weighs about 1 g (about 1/30 oz) and is about 3 cm (slightly over 1 in.) long. It looks rather like a human, although its head is very large due to the rapid development of its brain (Figure 2–7e). By this time, the major steps in the development of the organs are completed, and the organism is no longer called an embryo.

These first two months are called the period of **organogenesis.** When systems are forming, they are particularly vulnerable to changes in the environment. Thus many defects of heart, lungs, ears, and other organs are produced by exposure to adverse environmental events during this period. These will be discussed in Chapter 4.

Fetal Stage of Development (2 to 9 Months)

During the next 32 weeks of development, the potential baby is known as the **fetus.** The already distinct organs are further differentiated and move to their final positions as well as grow to the size and proportions they will have at birth. Growth of crown–rump length, although not steady, averages about 1.5 mm per day.

In the third lunar month (weeks 8–12) the fetus first moves its arms and legs, although the mother may not yet be aware of these movements. The first reflexes appear during this month—startle first and then, by the end of the month, sucking. Facial expressions such as squinting, frowning, and looking surprised appear. External sex organs develop sufficiently in this month to identify the sex of the fetus. The finger, palm, and toe prints are developed enough to enable the fetus to be identified by them. Respiratory and excretory systems develop greatly in this month but are not yet functional. Part of the fetus is covered by fine hair called lanugo; some of this hair may still be present at birth. By the end of this month the fetus is 7.6 cm (3 in.) long and weighs 14 g (0.5 oz).

This marks the end of the first trimester. All major organ systems have been developed, but those necessary for survival are not yet functional. During the second trimester (weeks 13–26) much of the remaining development of these systems occurs.

In the fourth lunar month (weeks 13–16) the first layer of skin and true hair develops. The skeleton becomes bony enough (rather than cartilaginous) to be detected by X rays. In the fifth lunar month (weeks 17–20) the fetal movements become obvious to the mother, and the fetal heartbeat can be heard through a stethoscope. The fetus is now sloughing off skin and respiratory cells and replacing them with new ones. The sloughed off cells remain in the amniotic fluid and provide the basis for a method of detecting chromosomal abnormalities by a procedure called **amniocentesis.** In this procedure a needle is inserted through the mother's abdominal wall into the amniotic fluid, taking care to avoid the fetus and placenta, whose position can be determined by ultrasound (a technique using inaudible high-frequency sound waves that bounce back from various tissues at different speeds and thereby outline the shape and position of the fetus). A small sample of fluid is extracted. The sloughed-off cells of the fetus can be cultured and processed to detect chromosomal abnormalities; the fluid can be processed biochemically to detect products of many genetic defects; and the presence of excess spinal fluid (or alpha-fetoprotein), can be detected, which indicates that the neural tube has not closed and

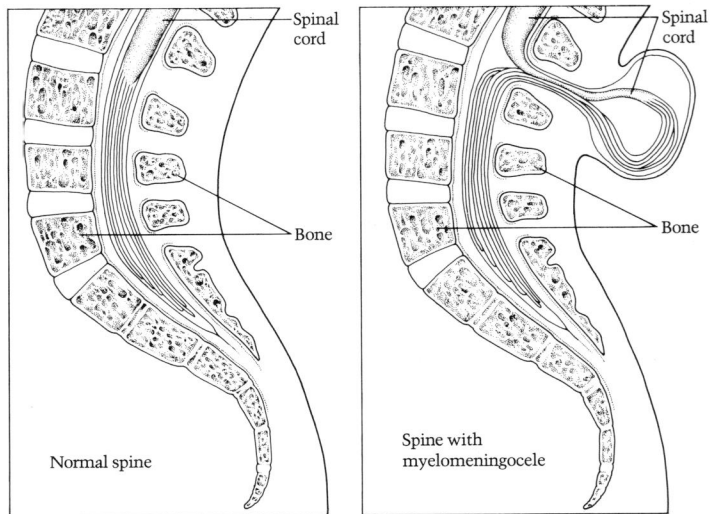

FIGURE 2–8. Spina bifida. This child has spina bifida. The drawings show a normal spine and a spine with myelomeningocele, the most severe form of spina bifida. (Photograph courtesy of the March of Dimes Birth Defects Foundation.)

the fetus thus suffers from spina bifida or other neural tube defects. Chromosomal abnormalities, genetic defects, and issues concerning amniocentesis will be discussed more thoroughly in Chapter 3.

Much of the potential infant's structural development takes place during its first five lunar months, but it reaches only 10% of its birth weight during this time. At 18 weeks it is still only 203 mm (8 in.) long and weighs less than 450 g (less than 1 lb). Its life support systems are still nonfunctional, so it could not live outside its mother's uterus. Much of the fetus's subsequent development is in physical growth and in the final development of the structures necessary for survival on its own.

In the seventh month (24–28 weeks) subcutaneous fat begins to develop, allowing increased weight gain. The infant needs this subcutaneous fat to use immediately after birth because breast milk does not start flowing for several days after birth. The terminal portions of the air passages of the lungs and the blood vessel network around them also develop in the seventh month.

By the 28th week the fetus is 28–40 cm (11–16 in.) long and weighs about 1,000 g (about 2¼ lb). The lungs are developed enough that it has a good chance of surviving on its own.

In the last trimester (27–38 weeks) the baby continues to grow rapidly. The number and size of brain cells also expand rapidly. Some recent research indicates that the protein intake of the mother is particularly important at this time to ensure optimal brain development.

By birth the fetus has acquired the plump appearance of the normal newborn, its lanugo is usually shed, and the testes (if male) are descended. We will describe the birth process in Chapter 5.

Transitions at Birth

Birth brings about profound changes in the way many organ systems function. Great demands are thus placed on the newborn. As examples we will describe the basic changes in the circulatory and respiratory systems.

In the prenatal circulatory system the umbilical arteries and veins carry blood to and from the placenta where the fetal blood is oxygenated. There are also three by-passes or shunts in the prenatal system that must not continue after birth. Furthermore, there is no complete separation of arterial blood (which is full of oxygen) and venous blood (which has yielded its oxygen to the body) until birth. However, the separations that do exist send the most highly oxygenated blood to the upper half of the body, including the brain, and the lower half receives blood with a much lower oxygen content. In fact, the prenatal circulatory system could be called a "make do" situation for the lower half of the body, especially the extremities. Indeed, this poorly oxygenated blood may be a factor in the relatively slow development of the lower body during prenatal growth. This differential development in favor of the upper half of the body is an example of a general principle of development both before and after birth, the principle of **cephalocaudal** development. This means that development proceeds from head (cephal) to tail (cauda) or from top to bottom.

The other system intimately linked to circulation is the respiratory system, primarily the lungs. This system does not function to deliver oxygen to the fetus prior to birth; the fetus gets its oxygen from that in the mother's blood by means of the placental and umbilical systems.

At birth the walls of the umbilical vessels contract and the umbilical arteries no longer pulsate. How this comes about is not fully known. When the lungs start to operate, the bypasses or shunts close rapidly, resulting in full separation of deoxygenated (venous) and aerated (arterial) blood. At first these closings are not anatomical or physical closures. They are what are called physiological or functional closures. Their action depends on a number of factors including the degree of oxygenation of the fetus. The closures may not always work perfectly in the first hours or even days or weeks of the infant's life. Nevertheless, they normally become structurally closed relatively quickly. Although failures can occur in these processes, as happens in so-called blue babies, it is extraordinary how many complex interactions take place in embryological development and usually do so without producing major problems. From this time on, the lungs become responsible for the oxygenation of the blood in the circulatory system.

Before birth the lungs are solid but contain fluid. Normally pressure on the chest during birth expels most of the fluid. Doctors and nurses often assist this process by dangling the baby by the feet, by slapping on the back, and by applying gentle suction to draw out more fluid. At birth the respiratory center of the brain is stimulated by impulses from the cold receptors of the skin and by chemoreceptors sensitive to the blood gasses, so that the baby starts to make breathing movements. (Actually, the baby may have made some sporadic breathing movements *in utero* which may account for some of the fluid in the lungs.) If the baby is slow to respond to these forces, further stimulation may be used in the form of more slapping of the back, snapping the soles of the feet, or providing oxygen. These measures usually suffice. When breathing starts, the terminal air sacs of the lungs (alveoli) expand and the other vessels (including the lymphatics) open up. However, the majority of the terminal air sacs have not developed by the time of birth. Even among those that are developed, not all suddenly open after the first cry (which brings air and thus oxygen into the lungs). After birth, then, the lungs continue to grow in complexity as well as in size.

We will indicate the complexity of the relations of the respiratory and circulatory systems by describing the interaction between them in closing one of the by-passes mentioned earlier. The expansion of the lungs greatly increases the volume of blood in the lungs, and the pressure from this increased volume of blood distends the left auricle of the heart. Receptors in the wall of the auricle trigger a reflex that leads to closure of a duct that has been important in fetal circulation (the *ductus arteriosus*). If it remained open, it would prevent proper circulation of the blood once the infant is separated from the placental circulatory system. In the normal course of events this biological reflex will function once and once only. If the reflex does not function, the infant will have serious problems because there will be insufficient oxygen for the cells. This is particularly important because the brain cells are among those most affected because the brain is still in a period of rapid growth after birth. Today this defect can usually be corrected surgically.

It has often been said that the lungs provide the real limits to viability outside of the

TABLE 2–3
The Course of Sexual Development

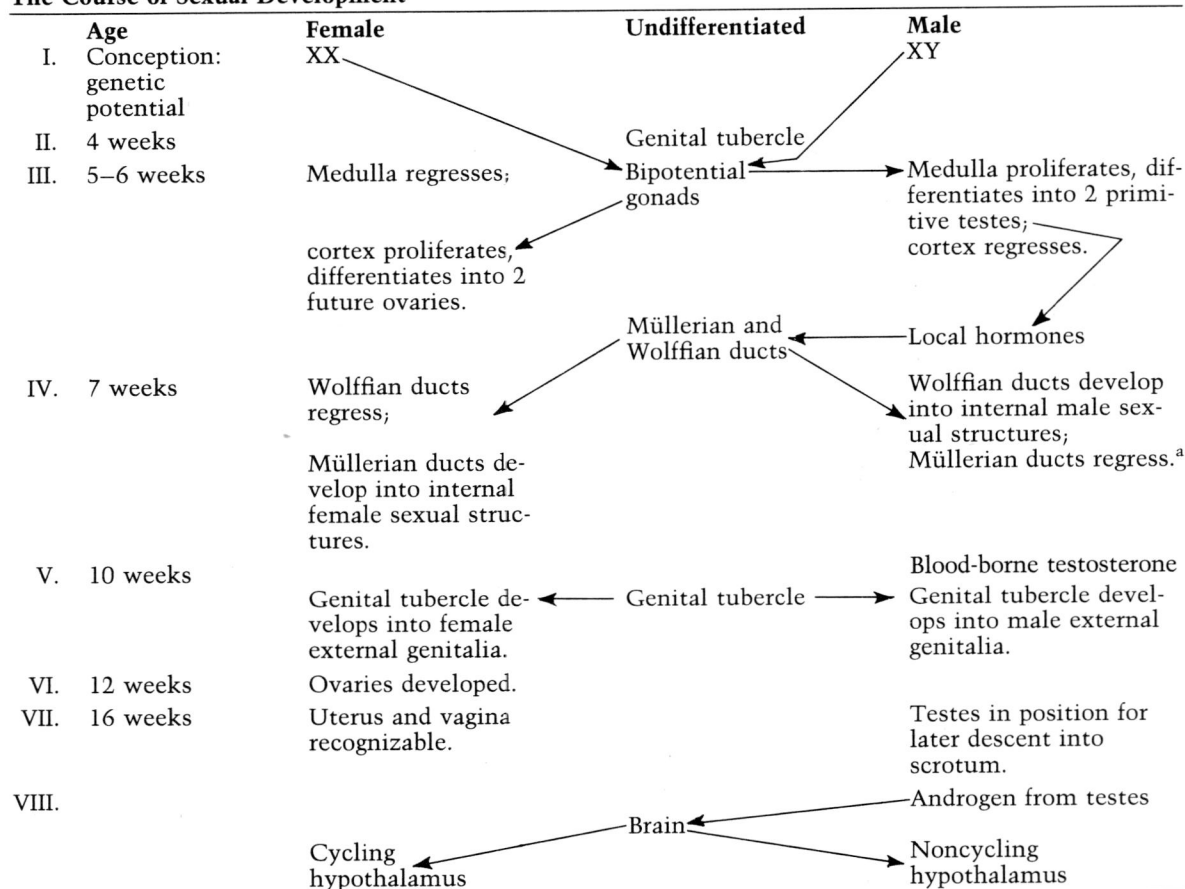

	Age	Female	Undifferentiated	Male
I.	Conception: genetic potential	XX		XY
II.	4 weeks		Genital tubercle	
III.	5–6 weeks	Medulla regresses;	Bipotential gonads	Medulla proliferates, differentiates into 2 primitive testes; cortex regresses.
		cortex proliferates, differentiates into 2 future ovaries.		
			Müllerian and Wolffian ducts	Local hormones
IV.	7 weeks	Wolffian ducts regress;		Wolffian ducts develop into internal male sexual structures; Müllerian ducts regress.[a]
		Müllerian ducts develop into internal female sexual structures.		
V.	10 weeks	Genital tubercle develops into female external genitalia.	Genital tubercle	Blood-borne testosterone Genital tubercle develops into male external genitalia.
VI.	12 weeks	Ovaries developed.		
VII.	16 weeks	Uterus and vagina recognizable.		Testes in position for later descent into scrotum.
VIII.		Cycling hypothalamus	Brain	Androgen from testes Noncycling hypothalamus

[a]But remnant forms prostatic pouch.

uterus. One important problem of premature infants is their tendency to develop respiratory distress syndrome (RDS) or hyaline membrane disease. Although much progress has been made in understanding and controlling this disorder in recent years, it is still a major problem of prematurity.

DEVELOPMENT OF ORGAN SYSTEMS OF SPECIAL INTEREST
Sexual Differentiation (Urogenital System)

We have chosen to discuss this aspect of embryological development in some detail for three reasons. (1) Prospective parents are usu-

ally intensely interested in the sex of their expected child, and most people are interested in topics related to sex and gender identity. (2) The interactions of heredity and the environment are particularly clear cut in this development. (3) There are a number of viable genetic anomalies involving the sex chromosomes (see Chapter 3). For all these reasons, development of the urogenital system is of particular interest.

The course of sexual development is outlined in Table 2–3 and illustrated in Figure 2–9. Development proceeds from top to bottom, both in the table and in the figure. In the text we will refer to the various sections or developmental periods in the table by the roman numerals in the left margin.

The process of sexual differentiation is

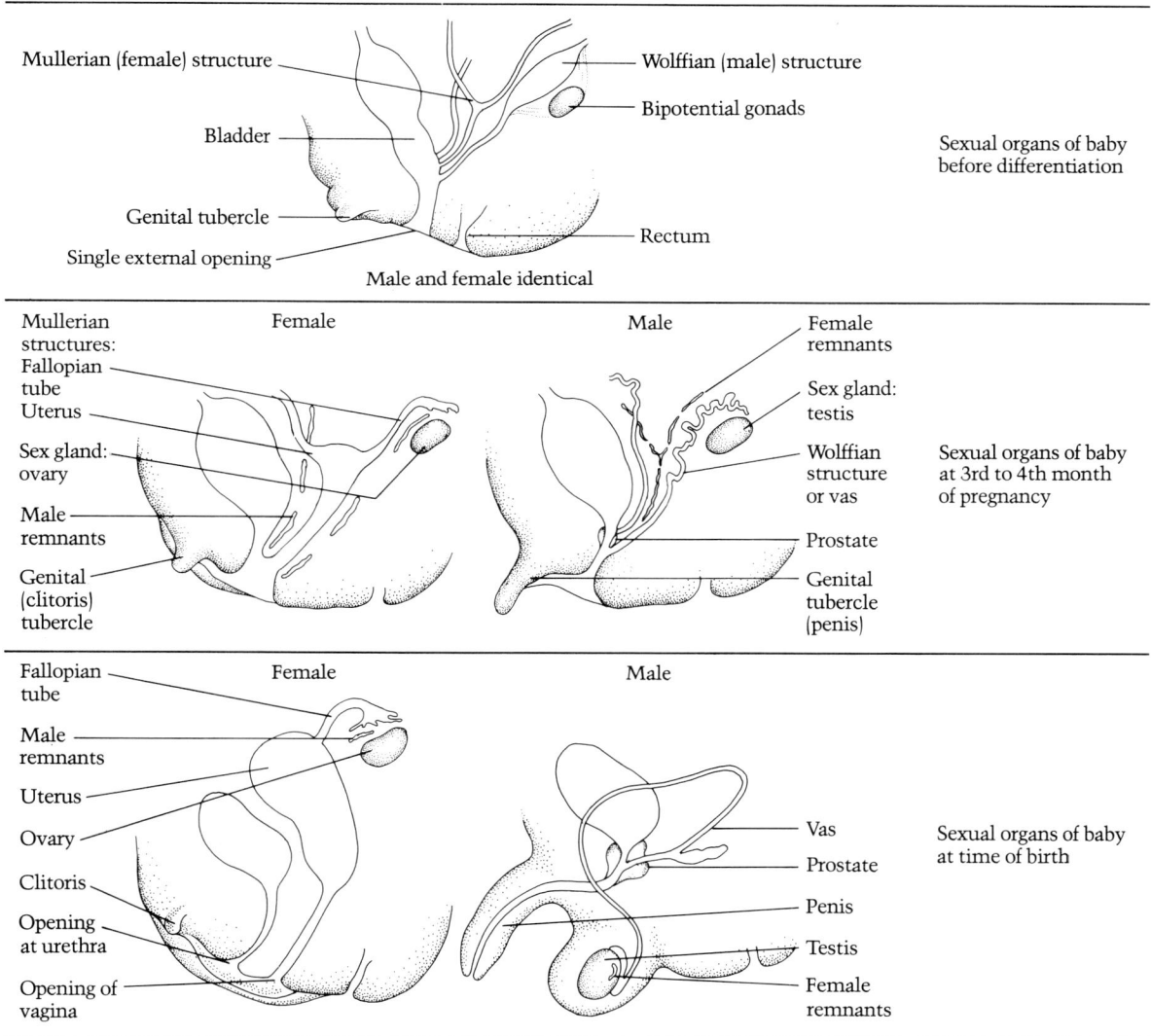

Mullerian (female) structure

Wolffian (male) structure

Bipotential gonads

Bladder

Sexual organs of baby before differentiation

Genital tubercle

Single external opening

Rectum

Male and female identical

Mullerian structures:
Fallopian tube
Uterus

Female

Male

Female remnants

Sex gland: testis

Sex gland: ovary

Wolffian structure or vas

Male remnants

Prostate

Sexual organs of baby at 3rd to 4th month of pregnancy

Genital (clitoris) tubercle

Genital tubercle (penis)

Fallopian tube

Female

Male

Male remnants

Uterus

Ovary

Vas

Prostate

Clitoris

Penis

Opening at urethra

Testis

Opening of vagina

Female remnants

Sexual organs of baby at time of birth

FIGURE 2–9. Differentiation of reproductive organs, Part 1: Internal sexual differentiation. Notice the progression from undifferentiated to differentiated states. Most of sexual development is completed in the first trimester. (Part 2 overleaf.)

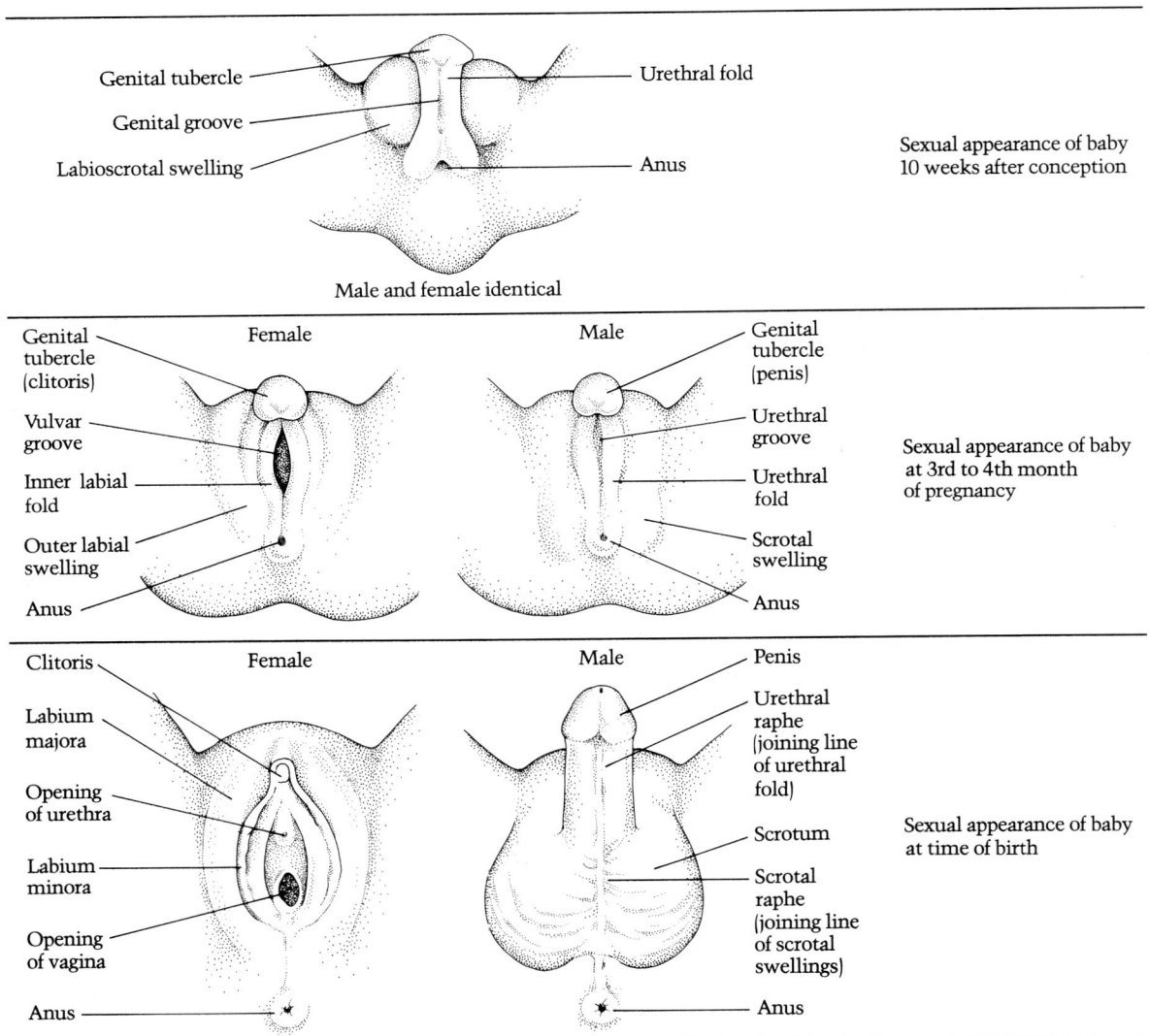

Genital tubercle

Genital groove

Labioscrotal swelling

Urethral fold

Anus

Sexual appearance of baby 10 weeks after conception

Male and female identical

Genital tubercle (clitoris) — Female

Vulvar groove

Inner labial fold

Outer labial swelling

Anus

Male — Genital tubercle (penis)

Urethral groove

Urethral fold

Scrotal swelling

Anus

Sexual appearance of baby at 3rd to 4th month of pregnancy

Clitoris — Female

Labium majora

Opening of urethra

Labium minora

Opening of vagina

Anus

Male — Penis

Urethral raphe (joining line of urethral fold)

Scrotum

Scrotal raphe (joining line of scrotal swellings)

Anus

Sexual appearance of baby at time of birth

FIGURE 2–9. Differentiation of reproductive organs, Part 2: External genital differentiation. Again, notice the progression from undifferentiated to differentiated states.

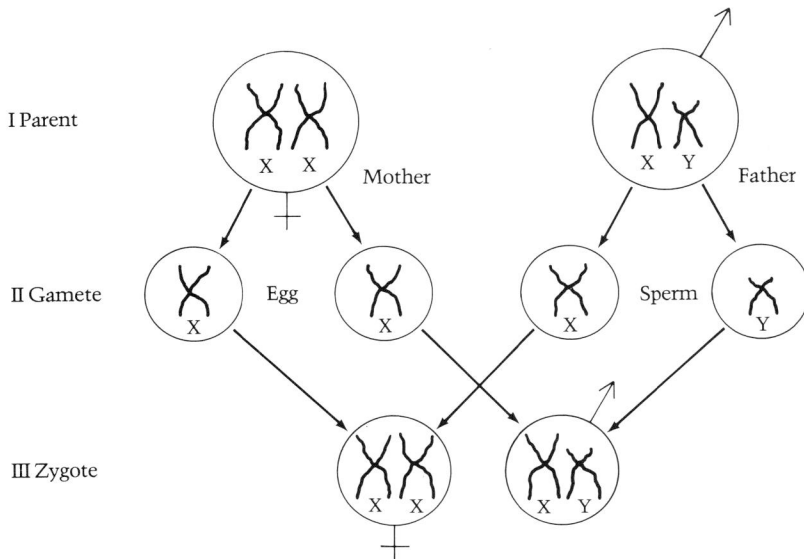

FIGURE 2–10. Meiosis. During this type of cell division, a maternal cell produces two eggs, both of which have the X chromosome, and a paternal cell produces two sperm cells (or spermatozoa), one with an X chromosome and one with a Y. If an X sperm fertilizes an egg, the zygote has the female sex chromosome combination (XX); if a Y sperm fertilizes an egg, the zygote is male (XY).

triggered by the genes on the sex chromosomes (see Figure 3–1 for a picture of human chromosomes). Female humans have two similar sex chromosomes (symbolized XX) and males have two dissimilar sex chromosomes (symbolized XY). A **gamete**, also called a **germ cell** (either an egg or a sperm cell), has 23 chromosomes, one from each of the 23 pairs of chromosomes of the parent. Thus, each gamete has one sex chromosome. Because women have two X chromosomes, it does not matter which of their chromosomes is reproduced in the egg; the egg will always have an X chromosome. Males, in contrast, contribute an X chromosome to half their sperm and a Y to the other half. If a Y sperm fertilizes the egg, the offspring is genetically male; if an X sperm fertilizes the egg, the offspring is genetically female. Therefore fathers are the sole genetic determiners of their children's sex. This process is diagrammed in Figure 2–10.

Sexual determination begins with the genetic potential of the fertilized ovum, but is only a potential at that time (see section I, Table 2–3). In the time that elapses between the fertilization of the ovum and its implanta-

tion in the uterine wall (the period of the zygote), no physical differences can be detected as a result of this genetic difference. Early in embryological development three undifferentiated sexual structures develop. They are called undifferentiated because, in this first primitive form, no differences between male or female forms can be detected. They are (1) the genital tubercle, which eventually develops into the external genitalia (it develops at section II and differentiates at section V of Table 2–3); (2) the bipotential gonad, which develops into ovaries or testes (see section III of Table 2–3); and (3) the Müllerian and Wolffian ducts, which differentiate into the internal sexual structures (sections III and IV of Table 2–3). All of these undifferentiated structures are bipotential because they can develop into either male or female structures.

The differentiation of each of the primordial (precursor) sexual structures occurs at different times during organogenesis. Thus there is a repeated pattern of going from an undifferentiated form to sexually differentiated forms. This pattern is emphasized in Table 2–3 by the arrows that radiate from the center column (the undifferentiated states) to the two side columns (the differentiated male and female forms).

The first primordial structure to differentiate sexually is the bipotential gonad, which starts differentiating at 5 to 6 weeks after conception (section III of Table 2–3). Because the female can be considered the basic sex in humans (as will become clear as we proceed), we will describe female development first. The surface (cortex) of the bipotential gonad or genital gland begins to proliferate and the internal part (medulla) begins to regress. The single structure differentiates into two parts, each of which will become an ovary. At 7 weeks after conception the internal sexual structures begin to differentiate. In females the Müllerian ducts develop into internal female structures and the Wolffian ducts start to regress (see section IV of Table 2–3).

This course of development is governed by the X chromosomes. If the embryo has a Y chromosome, then an additional step takes place that changes the development radically. At 5 to 6 weeks the central part of the genital gland (medulla) starts to proliferate and the surface portion (cortex) regresses (see section III of Table 2–3). When the genital gland differentiates into two primitive testes, these testes secrete fetal androgen (a male hormone similar to the testosterone produced by adult male testes) and another hormone that has not yet been identified. The androgen acts to stimulate the development of the Wolffian ducts and the unidentified hormone acts to suppress the development of the Müllerian ducts, that is, to change the course of development (see section IV of Table 2–3). This initial action of the hormones is local (that is, limited to the region that is adjacent to the testes) because there is as yet no circulatory system. This is known because in a mammalian species such as the rat, if the testis on one side is removed but that on the other is not, the ducts will undergo the changes that make them masculine on the side where the testis remains, but they will become like those of the female on the castrated side. This also shows why we said that female is the basic sex. The presence of male hormones produces male development: Remove the androgen (by removing the testis) from an embryo with male genes and it will develop female

structures. We will return to this point after we complete the description of the developmental sequence.

A similar pattern of development produces the external genitalia (clitoris, labia, and so forth in females and penis, scrotum, and so forth in males). At 10 weeks after conception the single genital tubercle, which appeared at 4 weeks, has developed a vertical groove (which separates it into two urethral folds), a urogenital slit, and two labioscrotal swellings. All of these structures are still bipotential (see Figure 2–9). In the female, who does not receive stimulation from male hormones, the tubercle itself will regress in size and become the clitoris. In the male, in whom male hormones are produced, it will grow to become the penis. In the female the two urethral folds will remain two separate structures and develop into the labia minora (the minor or inner lips surrounding the vagina). In the male the two folds will fuse to form the urethra (urinary opening) and scrotal pouch. In the female the two labioscrotal swellings will develop into the two labia majora (the major or outer lips) and the single mons. In the male they will fuse to form the scrotum. The single urogenital slit will deepen in the female to form the vestibule and opening portion of the vagina.

In females the ovaries are developed by 12 weeks (section VI of Table 2–3), and in the male the urethra, prepuce (foreskin), and the penile (or urethral) meatus (opening) are forming. By 16 weeks the differentiation of the sexual structures of the human male is complete (section VII of Table 2–3).

We would like to return now to the statement that female is the basic sex. What was true for early gonadal development is true throughout sexual differentiation. If genetic male mammals (rats and guinea pigs are common choices in this research) are denied their androgen by castration during sexual differentiation, they will not develop male organs appropriately and will show signs of those aspects of female physiology that develop after that time. In adulthood, if given hormone therapy, they will even develop some of the appropriate female sexual behaviors (although they will be sterile). Researchers know that the absence of male hormones produces this potential for female sexual behavior because male rats castrated after adulthood has been reached will not develop female sexual behaviors even if given female hormones.

The reverse can also happen. If genetic females are injected with male hormones at the time of sexual differentiation, they will develop dwarfed ovaries and some masculine physiology. When they reach adulthood they will not exhibit normal female sexual behaviors, even if given large doses of female hormones. There is an unfortunate human analog to this research on the masculinizing of genetic females by hormones. For a short time androgens were given to pregnant women as part of a medical treatment. Their girl babies were often born with partially developed male organs and inadequately developed female organs. Genetically female infants developing in mothers with certain conditions that cause the adrenals to secrete large quantities of male hormones may also be physically masculinized.

Let us summarize the major points from this research. Sexual differentiation occurs at particular points in development. If no male hormones are present in the first of these, the organism develops female internal sexual characteristics. If male hormones are present, the organism develops male internal sexual characteristics.[5] This happens even when the hormonal situation does not match the genetic sex. The same thing happens slightly later with respect to external sexual characteristics. The hormones are known to be the cause of the differentiation, and not the testes themselves, because injecting androgen into developing females is as effective as transplanting testes into them. The resulting sexual differentiation (whether or not it matches genetic sex) produces permanent changes that cannot be undone by hormone treatment after birth.

Sexual differentiation does not end with the development of the physical sexual structures. Appropriate sexual behavior also becomes encoded physiologically in the brain (section VIII of Table 2–3). One of the major

differences between male and female rat sexual behavior is that females are cyclical; males are not. The female cycle is produced by regular changes in levels of several different hormones (both gonadal and pituitary), and the regulation of these hormones is governed by the hypothalamus, a center in the brain close to the pituitary gland. The cyclical pattern of the hormones in females produces an ovulatory period followed by a nonovulatory period. Female mammals are typically most receptive sexually around the time they ovulate and they are then said to be "in heat." In many mammalian species, nonovulatory females will reject sexual advances.

Other sexual behaviors, such as lordosis in the female (the sexual crouch in which the female arches her back and exposes her genitalia) and male approach, mounting, and intromission behaviors, also appear to be at least partially set in the brain. For example, injecting the female hormone estrogen into male rats results in *male* sexual behaviors, not in female sexual behaviors (Fisher, 1967).

The brain includes many other structures and is involved in many behaviors other than those directly related to sexual activities. The degree to which other brain structures and behaviors related to them become permanently differentiated is currently a highly controversial area of research. Three areas of behavior are most discussed in this context: (1) aggression, including rough-and-tumble play, (2) spatial reasoning, and (3) other behaviors that are somewhat gender specific (including those thought to be related more to the functioning of the left or right sides of the brain). Roughly speaking, the above order of these topics represents the amount of evidence supportive of them (from most to least), although in none of these areas does sufficient evidence exist to demonstrate convincingly to the majority of experts in the field that these are biologically-based sex differences. Furthermore, all of these aspects of behavior are multiply determined. Thus any one individual can show both "masculine" and "feminine" behaviors, and many people are more like the other sex than their own. For example, many males are less aggressive than many females and many females are better spatial reasoners than many males. For these reasons we shall refrain from further con-

---

[5] The male hormones may not be the only hormones active in this process. It has been hypothesized that the higher levels of progesterone found in female as compared to male fetuses may act as an antiandrogen during the developmental periods when the fetus is particularly sensitive to the masculinizing action of gonadal or adrenal androgens.

sideration of sexual differences in relation to brain differentiation.

The Central Nervous System (Brain and Spinal Cord)

We have chosen to discuss the development of the central nervous system here because the brain is crucial for that intelligent behavior that marks humans. That is only part of its importance. The **central nervous system (CNS)** as a whole (the brain and spinal cord) governs all bodily functions. The brain structures get their start shortly after conception when the neural tube develops from specialized ectodermal cells. Before the neural tube closes in the fourth week of conceptional age (sixth week postmenstrual age),[6] the neural cells have proliferated into many layers. At first these cells appear to be all alike, but soon some of them, the future motor neurons, send fibers beyond the neural tube to surrounding tissues. After the neural tube closes, three bulges appear at the head end of the tube (see Figure 2–7b). They are the precursors of the three main divisions of the brain: the forebrain, midbrain, and hindbrain. At this time the extraordinary proliferation of cells in the CNS has already started. From the time the bulge at the head of the neural tube appears, the head of the embryo and fetus is very large in proportion to the rest of the body.

CELL GROWTH

Neurons, also called nerve cells, are the basic unit by which messages are sent throughout the brain, spinal cord, and peripheral nerves. The adult brain contains one million million neurons (1,000,000,000,000). Neurons are not the only cells in the brain, however. About half the cellular volume of the brain is made up of **neuroglia** or **glial cells**, which serve

a supportive role for the neurons. They transmit food (glucose and amino acids) from the blood supply to the neurons, some probably serve as scaffolding, and others manufacture **myelin** (the fatty insulating sheath that is deposited around the neurons and is necessary for the proper conduction of nerve impulses in many nerves). The development of each kind of cell has an initial phase during which there is rapid proliferation of the number of cells, followed by a period in which the previously formed cells increase in size and new ones continue to develop, followed by a final phase in which cells continue to increase in size and in myelination, but no new cells develop.

The neurons develop first, primarily between 8 and 16 weeks after conception. They originally consist only of their nuclei and a bare minimum of cytoplasm (the part of the cell surrounding the nucleus) and hence continue to grow in size for some time. The process of cell division to produce new cells probably stops earlier for neurons in the cortex than for most other cell types (by 28 weeks postconception). The glia develop later than the neurons. They start to form at about 13 weeks postconception, reach their peak of cell division from 18 weeks after conception to 4 months after birth, and cease to form new cells by 15 to 24 months postnatally. In summary, then, most cells in the brain are formed during the fetal and early postnatal period and no new cells are formed after a person reaches 2 years of age.

This should not, however, be construed to mean that no further development occurs after this age. First, the development of axons and dendrites, those processes that connect one neuron to another, is extremely rapid during the first 3 years of life, then gradually slows down to reach its adult rate by puberty, and never stops. Second, the **myelin sheath** also develops after neuron cell division has stopped. The development of the myelin sheath is necessary for normal functioning of the CNS. Much of the helplessness of newborns stems from the lack of myelination of their nervous systems. The efficiency and degree of control with which they can suck and swallow (an important fact for many studies done with infants) stems from the fact that the nerves involved in these processes are completely

---

[6]We have consistently labeled prenatal age as time from conception. It is common in some areas (such as research in neural development) to measure prenatal age from the mother's last menstrual cycle (approximately 2 weeks before conception), a date that is more reliably obtained in humans than the actual date of conception. We have converted the postmenstrual dates commonly used in the literature on this topic to postconception dates or conceptional age.

myelinated at birth. The importance of myelin is dramatically illustrated by victims of multiple sclerosis (MS), a disease in which a virus attacks the myelin sheath. As a result, MS victims gradually lose functioning of various parts of the CNS, resulting in paralysis, numbness, blindness, deafness, unsteady gait, impairment of speech, and mental changes.

Myelination develops in different brain areas at different times. Functional rather than geographical units determine the timetable for myelination. The nerve fibers carrying impulses from the senses to specific cortical areas myelinate at the same time as those carrying motor impulses from those areas to the periphery. For example, the neurons to and from the auditory system begin to myelinate in the sixth prenatal month and myelination continues until the fourth year of age. In the visual system the sensory and motor neurons start to myelinate just before birth but complete the process rapidly. The neurons that connect the cerebellum (the center of coordination and balance) to the **cortex** or forebrain (the part of the brain that governs higher processing) begin to myelinate only after birth and the process continues until 4 years of age. The efficiency of these connections, which myelination brings about, are necessary for the precise control of voluntary movement. Other structures continue to myelinate until puberty or beyond. These examples demonstrate that each neural system has its own specific myelination timetable, which may differ in nature, in time of onset, and in its course from other timetables.

One way to gain an overall view of the phenomenal early growth of the brain is to chart brain weight. From early fetal life the brain is closer to its adult weight than is any other organ (except perhaps the eye, which is partly an outgrowth from the brain, as we shall see shortly). By birth the brain weighs one fourth as much as it will in adulthood. Its rate of growth during infancy continues to be phenomenal, even though neurons cease to increase in number. By 6 months it weighs half as much as an adult brain, and at 2 years, when it has tripled its weight since birth, it achieves three quarters of its adult weight. This is by far the most rapid growth in the body, which explains why the heads of embryos, fetuses, and young babies always look so large in relation to

the rest of their bodies. Compare this rapid growth to the much slower growth of total body weight. At birth, a baby's weight is about 5% that of an adult's, and a child does not reach half an adult's weight until about 10 years of age.

DEVELOPMENT OF THE CORTEX

The cortex or forebrain is of particular interest because it is the seat of higher intellectual processes. Its growth has been painstakingly mapped by Conel (1939–1967) at 6, 7, and 8 months (postmenstrual age), at birth, and at increasing intervals throughout infancy (five ages from 1 to 24 months). It is first identifiable 6 weeks after conception, and by 24 weeks after conception it has the beginnings of the six-layered structure typical of the adult organ. In the first 2 years after birth the most advanced parts are the primary motor area whose cells govern most movements. Within the primary motor areas, those controlling the upper limbs and trunk develop first and appear quite mature and functional by 1 month after birth. This is another example of the cephalocaudal (or head to tail) course of development. By 3 months after birth all of the primary motor areas are relatively mature.

Next to develop are the primary sensory areas. The area for touch is first, followed by the visual area and then the auditory area. Cells in the visual area show the most rapid rate of maturation a few weeks before birth. All of the association areas with their integrative functions lag behind these primary areas, but they develop in relation to them and in the same order. Note that maturation of structure is closely linked to function.

DEVELOPMENT OF THE EYES

The development of the eyes illustrates the complex interaction between the CNS and other bodily structures (in this case, ectoderm) that occurs during development. The beginnings of eye development occur at $3\frac{1}{2}$ weeks post conception, right after the first bulges of the top of the neural tube develop (see Figure 2–7a). Two spherical bulges, called the optic vesicles, appear on each side of the forebrain. They enlarge until they reach the surface, or ectodermal layer. This contact causes the latter to thicken and change into a circular depression that ultimately separates from the surface and becomes the lens vesicle (see Figure 2–11). The latter will in turn develop into the lens of the eye, whereas each optic vesicle will form the optic nerve cell and pigmental layers of the retina.

The interaction between the optic vesicle and the lens vesicle provides another classic example of the importance of local environments in determining normal differentiation of organs. Our earlier example was the local action of testicular hormones in producing appropriate internal male organs. As in that case, local chemical effects act to induce change: in this case the optic vesicle induces the lens to form. That the optic vesicle is crucial is shown by the fact that if it is removed, no lens will form. If it is transplanted at the appropriate developmental stage, a lens will be formed from the ectoderm at the site of the transplant; for example, if the optic vesicle is transplanted to a leg, the chemicals produced by the optic vesicle will induce the leg ectoderm to form a lens vesicle.

HOW WE KNOW ABOUT PRENATAL DEVELOPMENT

How have researchers learned all this about the development of organisms who are shielded from view by women's bodies, and who cannot be extracted from their mothers' bodies or probed and manipulated in any way without running the risk of maiming or killing them? Much of the existing knowledge comes from studies of other mammals, particularly rats, guinea pigs, and pigs, because most involved Americans believe that the gains in knowledge and practical help to humans offset the unpleasant realities of sacrificing the animals to study embryological and fetal development. Animal experimentation, although necessary and invaluable, is not enough by itself. Differences between any two species are enormous. Even in the species closest to humans—chimpanzees and gorillas—physical and psychological systems may differ markedly. In technical terms, it is dangerous to generalize from one species to another. Therefore researchers always need to **corroborate** animal observations (to verify or make sure of the ade-

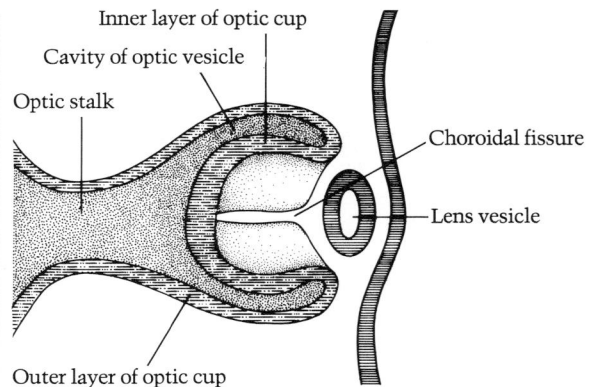

FIGURE 2–11. Embryological development of the eye. The optic vesicle has migrated to the surface, which has caused the ectodermal tissue to thicken into the lens vesicle. (Adapted with permission from F. Beck, D.B. Moffat, and J.B. Lloyd, Human Embryology and Genetics. Oxford: Blackwell Scientific Publications, 1973.)

quacy of the generalization) with studies of humans.

In studies of embryological development, the products of spontaneous abortions have been used to corroborate animal studies. This does not give a very good view of normal development because many of these abortions are of abnormal embryos or fetuses (as will be further discussed in Chapter 3). It would be better to study the products of legal abortions because a large proportion of them will be normal. The United States has contributed relatively little in this area of research because of the controversy over abortion and over study of the products of abortion.

Before the Supreme Court ruled in 1973 (Rowe v. Wade) that women might legally have abortions even if not in severe physical or emotional danger, legal abortions were rare and often occurred for cases where the fetus might not be normal. Many medical and psychological researchers and practitioners hoped that the change in abortion laws would allow the useful side effect of promoting research in prenatal development. This has not happened, however. All research in this area was stopped for a period while representative groups of concerned persons debated the ethics of such research. It is not yet clear what the long-term outcome of this debate will be, although some types of research are now permitted.

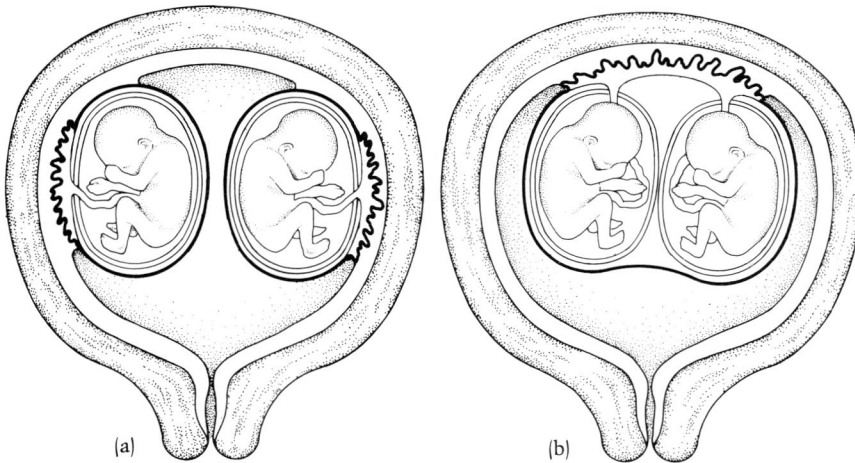

FIGURE 2–12. Twins in utero. (a) These twins could be fraternal or identical; they have individual placentas, amniotic sacs, and chorions. (b) These identical twins have a single placenta and chorion, but individual amniotic sacs. The amnions are the thin white lines, the chorions are the black lines, and the endometrium is the thick white line surrounding the chorion. (Adapted with permission from L.B. Arey, Developmental Anatomy: A Textbook and Laboratory Manual of Embryology (2nd Ed.). Philadelphia: Saunders, 1965.)

VARIANTS OF PRENATAL DEVELOPMENT

We have described the typical course of prenatal development, but the development of many babies varies from this normative description in various ways. Two relatively common variations, twinning and prematurity, are discussed here because of the importance of contrasting them with typical prenatal development.

Twinning

Twinning is a common variant of prenatal development; it occurs in 1 in every 80 pregnancies. There are two types of twins: **identical** or **monozygotic** twins, who share the same genetic blueprint, and **fraternal** or **dizygotic** twins, who do not. Identical twins come from a single ovum fertilized by a single sperm, hence the name monozygotic. In the early stages of cell division (the zygote stage), the cells split off into two separate organisms. Most monozygotic twins result from division of the inner mass at the blastocyst stage when the organ-

ism is implanting in the uterine wall and the embryonic membranes are starting to develop. These twins have only one placenta and chorion (the outermost membrane surrounding the developing organism) but usually have two umbilical cords and amniotic sacs (see Figure 2–12a). Sometimes the split occurs earlier, during cleavage divisions, and hence the two organisms implant separately and have two chorions and two placentas. About one fourth of all twins with two chorions are monozygotic.

The separation of an embryo into two babies sometimes takes place still later and does not result in complete separation. Such twins are called "Siamese" twins, because a pair of them who were widely exhibited in side shows early in this century happened to be from Siam. Such twins may be joined at various parts of their bodies and may share various organ structures. Whether they can be surgically separated to enable one or both to survive and whether they can lead normal lives depends on the degree of sharing and the particular structures shared.

Fraternal twins result from the fertilization of two different ova by two different sperm, hence the name dizygotic, or two-egged. Each zygote implants separately and develops a separate placenta, chorion, and so forth (see Figure 2–12b). Fraternal twins are actually siblings, and share the genetic characteristics of their parents to the extent that any nontwin brothers and sisters do. In fact, there has been at least one documented case in which fraternal twins were half brothers rather than full brothers. This fact was obvious because the two fathers were of different races. Fraternal twins develop from both different ova and different sperm. The latter means that fraternal twins may be of different sexes, but identical twins, who develop from the same fertilized ovum, are always the same sex.

The mechanisms that produce twins also produce multiple births with still more offspring. The base rate for these has been 1 in 6400 for triplets and 1 in 512,000 for quadruplets. Such multiples may be either fraternal or identical. In recent history the number of fraternal multiple births has increased markedly, primarily as a result of the use of hormones to treat infertility. These hormones stimulate ovulation, and sometimes they work too well. The woman releases many mature eggs and a number of them may be fertilized and develop. Because a uterus is of finite size, the more developing babies there are, the more likely they are to die in utero, or to be born early or have very low birth weights, or both.

The intrauterine environments for sets of twins, whether identical or fraternal, are not identical. For those with separate placentas, one may implant at a more favorable spot than the other. Those who share a placenta are competing for limited resources and one may get less nourishment than the other. Growth appears not to be retarded prior to 30 weeks gestational age (Naeye, Benirschke, Hagstrom, & Marcus, 1966). The different health or nutritional status of members of twin pairs appears to also be related to their birth order. Second-born twins are more likely to be stillborn or to have a lower Apgar score (an assessment of their functional status; see Chapter 5). The risk to the second born appears to be greater for homozygous or identical pairs than for fraternal pairs (Yazbak & Holden, 1966).

Because monozygotic twins have the same genetic makeup, they are of interest to those who wish to study the roles of heredity and environment in development and behavior. Fraternal twins provide a nice control group because they have no more in common genetically than any other siblings. Nontwin siblings provide another important control group for assessing the effects of greater similarity of environments for twins. These comparisons then provide an experiment of nature, albeit one with flaws.[7]

Babies Born Too Soon or Too Small

Babies are born at different weights, and not all have been gestating for 40 weeks, which is normally taken as the end of fetal development. Those born too early in fetal development or born very small have difficulty surviving. The systems we described earlier that must radically change their function at birth are not yet sufficiently developed. Although remarkable strides have been made in providing care that enables survival, survival is still highly dependent on the degree of development as well as on the sophistication of the medical care available (see Figure 2–13).[8] Prematurity may affect future development both directly and indirectly because the very aspects of prenatal care that help insure survival may themselves have good or bad effects on later development.

The prevention of low birth weight (LBW) and premature births is widely considered to be the most important factor in improving neonatal health. Progress in this direction has been made (the rate declined from 7.8% to 7.1% between 1971 and 1977), but a large number of such births still occur each year. Almost 250,000 LBW babies were born in the United states in 1979 (Institute of Medicine, 1982).

It is possible to distinguish between babies born less than 40 weeks after conception (premature or preterm) and babies who are small

---

[7] For an overview of the potential role of twin studies and descriptions of some of the important twin studies in North America, see the April, 1983, issue of *Child Development*. The first 16 articles in this issue are devoted to developmental behavioral genetics and cover adoption studies as well as twin studies.

[8] An excellent review of the effects of LBW prior to current intensive care practices can be found in Caputo and Mandell (1970) and Harper and Wiener (1965), and of psychological effects in Wiener, Rider, Oppel, and Harper (1965, 1968).

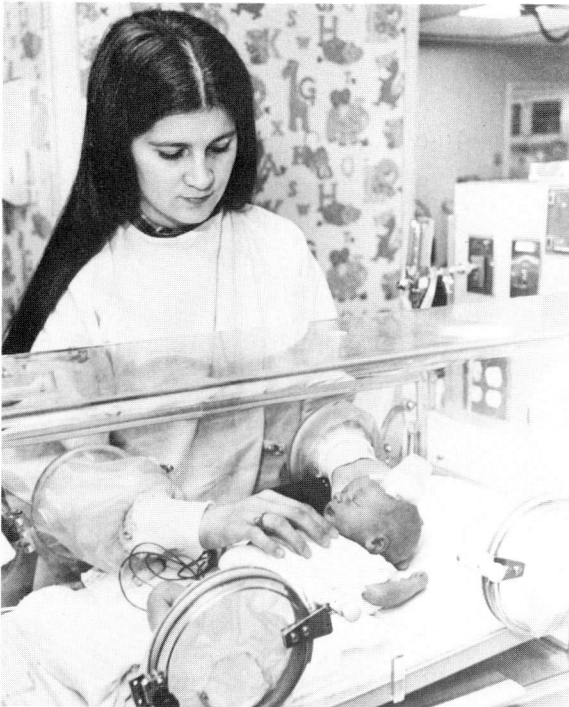

FIGURE 2–13. A premature baby in an isolette, wired to a variety of monitors that keep track of physiological functions. Although this baby is relatively large or close to term, it is still fairly small in relation to the hand of the caregiver. (Photo courtesy of the Office of Research Reporting, National Institute of Child Health and Human Development, Washington, D.C.)

for their gestational age (SGA, sometimes called small for dates, SFD), and there seem to be differences between these two groups in the degree to which they are at risk and in the kinds of problems they face. Unfortunately, most older studies assessed neither prematurity nor size in relation to gestational age. Instead, a birth weight of just under 2500 g (under $5\frac{1}{2}$ lb) was used as the **operational definition** (the definition that operates) of prematurity. This was largely because doctors did not trust mothers' reports of the time of conception or even of the time of onset of the last menstrual period. Today a number of schemes have been developed to determine the gestational age of babies. The best known are those of Dubowitz, Dubowitz, and Goldberg (1970) and of Lubchenco and colleagues (Lubchenco, 1970; Lub-

chenco, Hansman & Boyd, 1966; Lubchenco, Hansman, Dressler, & Boyd, 1963). Many recent studies use these schemes or reliable maternal reports, or both, to separate premature from SGA babies. (For an up-to-date review of these distinctions see Rosen in Institute of Medicine, 1982.) Because there are so many studies that have not made such distinctions, we will sometimes use the term "premature" when all we really know is that the baby was small.

CAUSES OF PREMATURITY OR LOW BIRTH WEIGHT

Babies may be born early or at a lower weight than normal for a variety of reasons. Infants with chromosomal or genetic defects are often spontaneously aborted very early. In addition, conditions associated with the fetus such as infections and Rh problems may cause low birth weight or prematurity or both, but some survive long enough to be born.

A second category of problems stems from the functioning of the placenta. The placenta may have implanted in an inappropriate part of the uterus so that it cannot properly provide adequate nourishment. The placenta may not have attained an adequate size and structure, or it may later develop problems due to such causes as infection or exposure to damaging agents. All of these can lead to prematurity or growth retardation or both. Twins and other multiple births are likely to be born prematurely or be SGA because they must compete for limited resources. The larger the number, the smaller and the more premature they are apt to be.

Finally, many maternal problems are related to early birth or low birth weight: Some examples are chronic disease, viral infections, drugs (including alcohol), smoking, and conditions of pregnancy such as toxemia. Many of these will be discussed in Chapter 4. In addition, a number of maternal factors that may not be directly causal are nevertheless correlated with the likelihood of prematurity and low birth weight. Examples are socio-economic status (SES), race, and lack of prenatal care.

Part of the difficulty in studying the effects of prematurity stems from this multiplicity of established and possible causes. Some causes may be more dangerous or harmful to later development than others.

FACTORS ASSOCIATED WITH PREMATURITY OR LOW BIRTH WEIGHT

Much of the research on prematures has focused on trying to assess the later outcomes for babies who had nothing wrong with them other than the fact that they were premature. Although this is an interesting research question, in real life prematures often do have something else wrong with them. Whatever caused their prematurity or low birth weight may have affected them in other ways, particularly neurologically. These babies are also more prone to be damaged in the birth process and in the postbirth period, and these associated problems have their own effects. They are more likely to suffer from anoxia (insufficient oxygen) and hyperbilirubinemia (too much of a substance called bilirubin that leads to jaundice and, in the extreme, to kernicterus, which damages the brain). Anoxia and hyperbilirubinemia have been shown (in a sample of low SES Blacks) to be related to the degree of impairment in prematures where prematurity itself was not (Braine, Heimer, Wortis, & Friedman, 1966). These findings have been corroborated by subsequent research (Goldstein, Caputo, & Taub, 1976). In the past prematures have been more likely to suffer from retrolental fibroplasia (RLF) as a result of too much oxygen in the neonatal period. This condition, which may lead to blindness, is also associated with lower IQ than that normally found for infants of equivalent birth weight but with no RLF (Genn & Silverman, 1964). Now that the cause of RLF is known, hospital personnel no longer expose premature babies to such high oxygen levels.

Another condition associated with low birth weight is spastic diplegia (a severe form of cerebral palsy), which was found in 10% of infants weighing less than 1500 g born in a London hospital in 1961–1964 (McDonald, 1964b). It too has decreased greatly in frequency; there were no low birth weight babies with spastic diplegia in that same hospital from 1965 to 1970 (Davies & Tizard, 1975).

Most of the research we will review has either ignored the problem of factors associated with low birth weight and prematurity or has isolated the various factors involved. Another strategy, currently becoming popular, is to consider the probability of deficits as a function of the number of negative factors present. The knowledge gained from all of these strategies will prove helpful when doctors face the practical issues of counseling parents about expectations for their prematures.

EFFECTS OF PREMATURITY OR LOW BIRTH WEIGHT

The problems of measuring the effects of prematurity are as difficult as those of determining its cause. Three related problems are of particular concern. First, the presence of short-term effects does not mean there will necessarily be long-term effects. This problem will reappear in other contexts in later chapters (as, for example, in the discussion of the effects of drugs used during childbirth). Prematures and SGA babies are initially retarded in many areas of development, but by middle or late childhood most will have caught up.

Second, because premature infants are younger in terms of conceptional age than full-term infants born on the same day, a lag would be expected in most behaviors that depend largely on physiological maturity. Thus to say that developmental retardation has occurred, researchers would have to determine that premature babies were farther behind than their conceptional age would indicate. A baby who is 4 weeks premature and is 4 weeks behind developmentally is not retarded. To indicate that a handicap is caused by prematurity, researchers must show a developmental lag that is greater than the amount of prematurity (for example, 6 weeks behind developmentally but only 4 weeks premature). Developmental lags are difficult to detect in very young infants because only a limited number of developing behavior systems can be measured. Furthermore, such developmental lags as are measured may be only temporary. Slowly developing babies often catch up to more rapidly developing babies. Prematures would be expected to catch up from their developmental lags unless they also suffer from specific damage of some sort, such as inadequate brain cell development or mild brain damage.

This brings us to the third problem: how to detect long-term deficits. Many researchers use as their dependent measure average performance on some measure such as IQ (measured by any one of several standardized intelligence tests). They then examine the average or mean differences in IQ between premature and term

TABLE 2–4
Survival and Degree of Impairment of Low Birth Weight Infants as a Function of Birth Weight and Year Born[a]

	Low Birth Weight			Very Low Birth Weight		
	1960	1971–1975	1976	1960	1971–1975	1976
Died (%)	72	54	33	92	80.5	50
Severely Abnormal (%)	6.7	4.5	7.6	2.3	2.8	5.7
Moderately Abnormal (%)	14	23.5	10.5	4.0	3.2	7.3
Normal (%)	7.2	17.8	48.6	1.7	13.5	36.5

[a]Adapted from a report (Budetti, McManus, Barrand, & Heinen, 1981) for the Congressional Office of Technology Assessment, Washington, D.C.

children. The average difference between the two groups may be very small. More important, such a measure masks the potentially most important effect of prematurity: that such babies are at greater risk for serious defects than are full-term babies. If the researchers had measured frequency of occurrence of IQs at various levels, they might have found a disproportionate number of low IQs in the premature group. The study by Wiener and colleagues (1968), which found just that, will serve as a good example. They found an average (or mean) difference of only about 5 points at 8 to 10 years of age between the IQs of a group of prematures and those of term infants (all infants with IQs below 50 had been eliminated). Despite the similar averages, there were twice as many prematures with IQs between 50 and 80 (the two least retarded categories of retardation). There are several problem areas both in infancy studies and in other aspects of psychology and medicine where the number of persons seriously handicapped by a given condition may be more relevant than the average difference between those with the condition and the controls or normals who do not have the condition.

Immediate Effects. It is clear that low birth weight babies are more likely to die in their first hours, days, or weeks of life than are normal weight babies. The smaller the neonate, the greater the risk. Babies born too soon as well as too small often lack the necessary physiological development to enable their circulatory and respiratory systems to function adequately. They may be unable to make the rapid and extensive changes at birth that allow adequate breathing and circulation.

Great strides have been made in the care of

very small babies, and their mortality rate has been decreasing (see Table 2–4; see also Bowes, Halgrimson, & Simmons, 1979; Paneth, Kiely, Wallenstein, Marcus, Pakter, & Susser, 1982). For example, adequate means of tube feeding and more adequate ideas of their nutritional requirements make it less likely that they will be further undernourished or that they will develop pneumonia as a result of inhaling formula because of their immaturity. Special care nurseries are now kept very warm because prematures have poor temperature regulation. Better methods of monitoring physiological functioning have been developed, enabling problems to be caught more rapidly and actions taken that may prevent not only death, but also permanent damage. Since 1965, for example, bilirubin (a factor that can lead to brain damage) has been kept at a much lower level; and since 1970 hypoglycemia (low blood sugar level), another factor that can cause brain damage, has been much less frequent.

Despite all these advances, premature and very small newborns are still at risk for their lives. Those that survive have problems that the term, normal weight baby rarely has (Jones, Cummins, & Davies, 1979). Finding the optimal level of oxygen to administer that will avoid causing retrolental fibroplasia and still provide enough for normal brain growth may be difficult. Oxygenation of the brain may be particularly important around the time of normal birth, because the brain undergoes a growth spurt then (Gluck, 1977).[9]

---

[9]Lack of oxygen in very premature babies seems to lead to less brain damage than it does in full-term babies. For example, visual placing is retarded in full-term babies deprived of oxygen at birth, but not in prematures so deprived (Rosensheim, Davidson, Reuter, Walters, & Walk, 1978).

Short-term Behavioral Effects. General developmental retardation is clear. Premature babies are likely to lack sleep–wake cycles, to be unable to maintain attention to visual stimuli (while still preterm), to lack normal neonatal reflexes (see Chapter 8), and generally to be retarded in sensory–motor development. They start to catch up in many of these areas, such as sleep–wake cycles and basic visual attention, by the time they reach the age at which they should have been born (Kopp & Parmelee, 1979; Parmelee & Sigman, 1976). One group observed in detail (Blacks) were awake more, changed state more often, and fussed and cried more than full-term controls when both were normal term age and neither was stimulated. When stimulated by auditory and tactile stimuli, the preterms responded in the same ways as healthy term neonates, but, when aroused to a crying state, they were more difficult to soothe (Friedman, Jacobs, & Werthmann, 1982; Jacobs, Friedman, & Werthmann, 1979).

Long-term Effects. One correlate of low birth weight that is permanent is physical size. One study of 10-year-olds who had been very small at birth (under 1500 g or 3½ lb) found that 41% of them weighed less and 47% were shorter than 90% of other children their age (Lubchenco, Horner, et al., 1963; see also Drillien, 1964). Even here not everyone is equally affected and newer nutritional practices with prematures may affect these outcomes. More recent studies have corroborated these long-term physical effects using SGA rather than birth weight as a basis (Kopp & Parmelee, 1979). Furthermore, very low birth weight girls have been found to give birth to low birth weight babies themselves (Thomson, 1959; Thomson & Billewicz, 1963).

Findings with respect to long-term effects on intelligence are probably the most controversial because the conclusions vary with the time period in which the study was made, the sample studied (including type of nursery care, race, SES, and whether it excluded severely damaged infants), and with how prematurity and LBW were defined. If the measure of long-term effects used is the rate of moderate to severe intellectual impairment or neurological problems, then prematurity (or LBW, or both) is a serious problem. Some 5 to 40% of such

children, depending on the study, are later moderately or severely impaired.

Recently more attention has been paid to outcome measures other than IQ and obvious neurological impairment. School performance, language development, and visual processing or visual–motor behaviors have received special scrutiny. Outcomes on a wide variety of school-related measures made when study participants were in grades 1 to 5 were poor for LBW children, but not for prematures as such (Rubin, Rosenblatt, & Balow, 1973). An index that included problems in school also distinguished LBW infants (less than 2000 g, born between 1966 and 1977) when they were 6 to 7 years of age (Drillien, Thomson, & Burgoyne, 1980). Rubin and colleagues' study (1973) also points to some of the hazards in understanding research in this area. Although there were no sex differences in the objective test performances of their children, there were sex differences in the outcomes. LBW preterm males were most at risk. SFD infants were next most at risk regardless of their gestational age at birth. Two thirds of the LBW males and over half of all SFD children had problems that led to special educational placement or the need for special services in school. The figures were not as high in children born a few years later studied by Drillien (Drillien et al., 1980).

A number of studies indicate that language development may be especially affected in LBW children. A relatively short-term study (Crawford, 1982) found decreased vocalization to be the only difference between a sample of prematures and well-matched controls that lasted beyond 14 months of age. Richman (1980) found normal intelligence and relatively normal achievement of developmental milestones (see Chapter 8) in a sample of prematures. Nevertheless, they were delayed in verbal expression and in vocabulary skills. These problems persisted through their follow ups at 6½ years when 48% of the LBW children had speech problems compared to 6% of normal birthweight controls.[10] Language abilities at 22 months were found to be even more retarded than would be expected on the basis of concep-

---

[10] This may well be a function of the fact that 42% of the LBW children had hearing deficits compared to 9% of the normals, a figure that seems high in view of other data (Abramovich, Gregory, Slemick, & Stewart, 1979).

tional age (Ungerer & Sigman, 1983). This was no longer the case at 3 years of age. Siegel (1982), looking at risk factors in relation to outcomes for both LBW (less than 1500 g) and term infants, also showed that birth weight was related to language comprehension at 3 years of age. Unfortunately, hearing was not assessed in that study.

Poorer visual information processing has been found at 1 year of age (Rose, 1983) and at 3 years (Ungerer & Sigman, 1983). Poorer performance on a task requiring visual–motor integration (the Beery VMI test) as assessed by copying forms has been found at 5 years (Siegel, 1983).

Play and personal–social interactions might be expected to be more affected by postnatal experience and less by biological maturity. It is therefore interesting to note that clear effects of conceptional age on these behaviors are present at $13\frac{1}{2}$ months and some at 22 months (Ungerer & Sigman, 1983).

From all of these data it is possible to conclude that LBW children are more likely to have language and school problems than they are to have lowered IQs.

CAUSES OF THE EFFECTS OF PREMATURITY OR LOW BIRTH WEIGHT

What is it about prematurity or LBW that produces long-term effects? This question is crucial to the effort to understand why some babies seem much more at risk than others. This could be related to what had caused their premature birth (biological), to factors associated with their birth (again biological), or to their immediate post-birth environment (the neonatal intensive care unit), which could cause biological changes or social ones. First let us summarize the biological causes to highlight their complexity.

Biological. Prematurity and low birth weight or low birth weight for gestational age may be caused by many different fetal, placental, and maternal conditions. Some, if not all of these, surely can have a direct effect on the offspring independent of the prematurity they may cause. To give just one example, a fetal infection transmitted from the mother may lead to small size and to neurological damage in the fetus, which may lead to its early birth and to most, if not all, of any subsequent defi-

cit or damage. Other conditions that may lead to retarded prenatal growth and to premature birth (or both) may retard brain growth and lead to permanent deficit. Conditions in the baby such as a genetic defect (see Chapter 3) may also lead to small size or prematurity, or both, and to later defects.

At the time of birth the shock to the baby's biological systems of being born too early may be greater than those systems can fully recover from, especially in view of their greater fragility. (We will discuss the special problems of prematures connected with childbirth in Chapter 5.) In addition, the stresses of extrauterine life on the immature systems of the premature may cause lasting effects.

Whether prematurity or retarded intrauterine growth can themselves cause permanent damage, especially if not accompanied by neurological damage, is a very controversial question. For the heavier LBW babies the evidence suggests that prematurity or retarded growth, or both, do not themselves give rise to permanent intellectual deficits. The long-term effects found for very small or very premature babies may be caused by these conditions or by associated neurological damage or other correlated factors, or by later events in the infants' lives.

Immediate Postnatal Environment. In addition to all the ways described above that premature or LBW infants may have been biologically damaged, there is another factor to consider. What are the possible effects of life in a neonatal intensive care unit? On theoretical grounds the damaging effects of such an environment have been suggested both with respect to biology and with respect to handicaps to the mother–infant relationship. The latter will be discussed in Chapter 5, but we want to consider the former briefly here.

Constant light and sound tend to deprive the newborn of patterned stimulation, and this has been pointed to as possibly affecting their physiological organization. The smaller or more premature the infants, the longer they would be in this environment and the more likely it would be that it could have a lasting biological effect upon them. For example, such effects could be responsible for the fact that although in some respects the sleep patterns of prematures look more mature than those of their term counterparts (which might be expected on the basis of the premature's longer independence from the maternal system), in other respects they look less mature (Booth, Leonard, & Thoman, 1980; Parmelee, Wenner, Akiyama, Schultz, & Stern, 1967). The lesser maturity could be ascribed to the infants not experiencing normal light–dark cycles or patterned stimuli generally. This view has received recent support from a study of prematures exposed to patterned kinesthetic and auditory stimulation. Not only were their immediate behaviors improved, but better sleep organization was one of the specific findings. They also showed fewer abnormal reflexes, another sign of greater neurological organization. In order to separate the effects of prematurity from those of intensive care, prematures have been compared with sick term babies in intensive care. Both were also compared with healthy term babies kept in the hospital (but not in intensive care) because of the illness of their mothers (Holmes, Nagy, Slaymaker, Sosnowski, Prinz, & Pasternak, 1982). The preterm infants were less mature motorically and had more deviant reflexes and less varied states than either group of term infants. They were more like the sick term infants than like the healthy term infants. Their behavior was not related to their gestational age, but to their illness, sex, obstetric complication, and to the length of time they had been hospitalized. The longer they had been in the hospital, the more their physiological organization was affected. In contrast, the babies who had been ill had their interactive processes more affected.

Post-hospital Environment. It has long been known that the effects of prematurity depend in part on the kind of postnatal environment in which the infant was reared. Most of the research on the social causes of poor outcomes of prematurity has focused on crude measures of environment such as SES, race, or maternal education. In some cases the environment has been assessed more directly, as for example by the HOME scales.[11] In others mother–infant interactions have been assessed according to the protocols of the specific study. In all cases there is concern with specifying particular aspects of maternal and home stimulation that can help children avoid deficits resulting from prematurity.

Studies have rather consistently found that although conditions around the time of birth (perinatal factors) are important predictors of short-term problems, social factors that operate during postnatal development become the best predictors of outcome in long-term studies (see Kopp & Parmelee, 1979, for a review of this literature). Premature children of high SES appear able to overcome their early developmental retardation, but those from lower SES homes frequently appear to suffer long-term deficits. In order to confirm this hypothesis statistically researchers would need to find that 2 conditions hold: (1) There is no difference between premature and full-term children from middle class homes, and (2) there is a difference between prematures and full-term children from lower class homes. When this occurs, it is called an **interaction effect**. This means that 2 independent variables (class and prematurity in this case) influence each other as to how they influence the outcome (or dependent variable). Such interactions have been found in numerous studies (including Bakeman & Brown, 1980; Douglas, 1956; Drillien, 1961, 1964; Drillien et al., 1980; Werner, Simonian, Bierman, & French, 1967). However, at least one well-done study (Wiener et al., 1965) found no such interaction. Inconsistencies in the outcomes of methodologically sound research usually occur because not all of the important factors have been identified. For example, even within lower SES groups, mothers' IQs and educations consistently predict their infants' later IQs. This suggests that lower SES mothers with higher IQs and educations may be able to compensate for the potential cognitive risks of their premature babies. Thus Wiener and colleagues (1965) may have failed to find SES differences because their lower SES population may have been relatively less disadvantaged on IQ, education, or other variables

---

[11] HOME, an Inventory of Home Stimulation (Bradley & Caldwell, 1977), examines maternal–infant interactions and home environment using both direct observation and questioning of the mother. It has six subscales: Emotional and verbal responsivity of the mother, avoidance of restriction and punishment, organization of physical and temporal environment, provision of appropriate play materials, maternal involvement with child, and opportunities for variety in daily stimulation.

that influence the stimulation they provide for the development of their children's IQs. In short, social class or SES is too crude an index and includes no specific behaviors, hence it would be wise to look for more exact aspects of the environment that protect the vulnerable child.

When actual characteristics of the home environment are examined there is the possibility of determining differential importance of specific variables, and determining whether they are the same for two groups such as prematures and term infants. This question has been examined by Siegel (1982). All six subscales of HOME administered at 12 months were significantly related to IQ at 3 years of age for preterms, but only two scales were for term infants. Five of the subscales were related to language comprehension (and three to language expression) for preterms, compared to one and none for full-term infants. The total HOME scale score was highly correlated with IQ and language comprehension for preterm infants ($r = .66$ and $r = .55$) but was not significantly correlated with either for full-term infants. This was true regardless of SES or developmental level for the prematures. Relations between outcomes and the HOME scales only occurred for those full-term infants who were developmentally delayed. One could conclude from these data that all aspects of the home environment are important for the development of infants at risk because of prematurity or other factors, but that they are not extremely relevant to the outcomes of "normal" children. Such a conclusion would find further support in data showing that mean IQs of prematures from responsive environments did not differ as a function of the number of neonatal complications they had, but they did differ as a function of complications if they were reared in less responsive environments (Cohen, Parmelee, Sigman, & Beckwith, 1982).

Other studies have measured specific mother–infant interactions at different ages. Several of them agree in finding that mothers of preterm babies were much more responsive than mothers of term babies during their early infancy (for example, Bakeman & Brown, 1980; Beckwith & Cohen, 1978; Beckwith, Cohen, Kopp, Parmelee, & Marcy, 1976). The Bakeman and Brown study, however, did not find that infant outcomes at 3 years were predicted by

these early social interactions. Neither social ability (in a day camp) nor IQ was. Mothers' responsiveness to their infants when they were 20 months old did relate to both the infants' IQs and their social abilities at age 3. Preterm babies in this study were not very handicapped. They differed by only 10 IQ points at age 3 and did not differ at all from term babies in social variables. For this group of only moderately premature infants from a socially disadvantaged Black sample, the influence of maternal interactions on intellectual development was only moderate and not operative in early infancy.

PREDICTION OF OUTCOMES

It is clear that both parents and doctors would like to be able to predict which premature infants are likely to have long-term problems and which are not. Much of what we have already discussed is relevant to this question, but we now want to address it specifically.

First, it is commonly accepted that the smaller the premature, or the more premature, or the smaller for gestational age, the more likely it is that there will be problems for those that survive. Even this conclusion is challenged by some data (Cohen & Parmelee, 1983; Cohen, Parmelee, Sigman, & Beckwith, 1982).

Second, in the effort to determine what the deleterious effects of prematurity itself (that is, without other complications) are, researchers have established that the presence or absence of neurological damage is an important determiner of outcome. Drillien and colleagues (Drillien et al., 1980) found that for LBW infants (at or below 2000 g) born between 1966 and 1970, those who were neurologically normal during the first year of life did not differ from controls at 6 to 7 years of age. Two other studies, each using different techniques of assessing neurological damage, similarly found birth weight to be unrelated to later IQ when those with neurological damage were eliminated from the sample (McDonald, 1964a; Wiener et al., 1965). Neurological factors also appear to mediate deficits in school functioning (Rubin et al., 1973). Furthermore, head circumference, a crude measure of brain growth (see Chapter 8), appears to be a good indicator of the degree of later neurobehavioral problems (Lipper, Lee, Gartner, & Grellong, 1981). Abnormal outcomes are more than twice as likely in those with a head circumference below the 10th percentile for gestational age.

A third factor, already discussed, that helps to predict outcome is the general nature of the home in which the child will be raised. We will not discuss this further but will turn to studies that have tried to look at a variety of factors in relation to the long-term outcomes.

An opportunity to examine multifactorial determinants of outcome is provided by the UCLA prospective study of cognitive development in prematures. (For a similar view of interaction in a longitudinal study, see Meyer-Probst, Rosler, & Teichmann, 1983). It started in 1972 when neonatal care units were already quite sophisticated (see Parmelee, Sigman, Kopp, & Haber, 1976, for a description). The sample studied was diverse in ethnic and SES makeup, in the degree of prematurity (25 to 37 weeks), and in birth weight (800–2495 g). Two short-term problems identified by this group (and others) were visual attention (at term date) and sleep patterns (at term date and 3 months later). The caregiving environment was assessed at 1, 8, and 24 months. When visual fixation at term was examined together with an overall index of the responsiveness of caregiving in the first 2 years, both were seen to affect the outcome. The effects of the caregiving environment were greater than those of the neurological organization of visual attention at term age (40 weeks). (Incidentally, prematures fixate a visual stimulus longer than term babies, as if their attention is captured by it.) The average IQs of 5-year-olds who had short fixation times at term and relatively responsive caregiving were 19 points higher than those who had had long fixation times and less responsive caregiving in the first 2 years (Beckwith, 1976; Beckwith & Parmelee, 1983). Nevertheless, the amount of variation in the outcomes means that individual prediction would still be hazardous.

The maturity of the quiet sleep pattern appeared to be a more potent biological indicator of trouble (Beckwith & Parmelee, 1983, 1984). Taken by itself it made a 10-point difference in IQ at age 5. Together with responsive caregiving there was a 23-point difference. When the maturity of active sleep at 3 months was examined it made as big a difference as the responsiveness of caregiving (13 and 14 points). The best combination was 19 points better than the

poorest. It thus appears that this biological indicator of neurological organization is a powerful factor in relation to later IQ. Nevertheless, the power of the influence of the environment is shown by the fact that no infant from the responsive group had an IQ below 100, whereas those from the more mature sleep group ranged from 80 to 134 and those from the less mature group from 40 to 138.

Two things are striking in these data. First, they do seem to offer real hope that someday researchers will be able to find a group of indicators that will be reasonably good predictors of the chances for normal development. Second, the IQs found in the study group were on the average rather high—mostly in the normal range or above. It cannot be assumed that this is typical for all prematures, despite the good characteristics of the sample studied, because these families had more than the usual amounts of support for dealing with their premature infants. This point takes us to the next matter we wish to discuss. Are there steps that can be taken to reduce any adverse effects of prematurity?

INTERVENTION STUDIES

We shall examine two types of interventions: short-term (during the hospital stay) and long-term interventions focused on the mother. All the interventions we will discuss are behavioral, not medical.

Hospital Interventions. Hospital interventions began because premature infants are likely to have received care that is different from the care mature newborns receive, and to have received that different care for relatively long periods. This may affect the parent–child interaction and hence the later development of the child.

Traditionally the premature infant has been placed in an incubator or isolette immediately after birth (see Figure 2–13). In these devices, temperature, oxygen levels, and humidity can be controlled. The infant is not taken to the mother for feeding, and the mother may not be encouraged to visit the baby in the special-care nursery. The nursery nurses often handle premature infants less than other babies. The premature is exposed to constant light and noise (the nursery is kept light so that observation is easy, and the incubator or isolette machinery makes a considerable amount of noise). As we noted earlier, constant light and noise may deprive the infant of normally patterned sensory experience; such deprivation has been shown to have a negative effect on sensory and perceptual development in animals (see Chapter 9).

Extra stimulation in hospitals has often been provided by giving extra handling, stroking, and rocking. Handling and stroking might be expected to be an important missing ingredient in the lives of newborns in special nurseries, because studies of handling in newborn rats suggest that such treatment allows the subjects to deal with later stress more effectively. Knudtson (1978) found just that. She gave sick and well prematures a total of 30 minutes of stroking spread throughout the day and both before and after feedings during their hospital stay. She measured their physiological reaction to stress (by measuring variations in cortisol, a chemical that is involved in stress reactions) and their behavioral organization (assessed by the Brazelton neonatal scale). She found that the stroked infants had consistently better adaptation to stress and had better behavioral organization than nonstroked infants. Three months after they left the hospital she gave them the Bayley and the Gesell infant development tests (described in Chapter 8). The stroked infants were significantly higher than the nonstroked ones on the mental part of the Bayley tests. They were also superior on sensory responsiveness and fine motor development (as measured by two of the Lodge subscales of the Bayley tests). These findings corroborate those of a smaller study that also found effects at 7 to 8 months of age (Solkoff, Yaffe, & Weintraub, 1967).

Rocking motion is another form of stimulation to which the normally gestating in utero baby is exposed and which the premature lacks. Several studies have shown that rocking in the isolette or handling leads to better weight gain and organization of behavior in the immediate newborn period (Korner, 1979; Korner, Kraemer, Haffner, & Cosper, 1975; Neal, 1968). We do not know the long-term effects of such experiences because the relevant follow-up studies of these infants have not been done. Nevertheless, many people have become concerned about the kind of neonatal care prematures receive. They feel that if such minor

interventions can produce such strong short-term effects, more drastic interventions could lead to even more important changes.

A group of investigators from Albert Einstein College of Medicine (Rose, 1980; Rose, Schmidt, Riese, & Bridger, 1980; Schmidt, Rose, & Bridger, 1980) have combined tactual stimulation (massage) with rocking. They were interested in whether such stimulation improved preterm infants' responsivity to stimulation. For the intervention group, both behavioral and heart rate responses to tactual stimuli were between those of term infants and comparable prematures who had not received the extra stimulation (Rose et al., 1980). The effects of the same stimulation was studied using cardiac and motor responses to the sound of a heartbeat and to tactual stimulation during sleep (Schmidt et al., 1980). The results were extremely complex, suggesting no straightforward positive effects except that the full-term and the intervention group of preterms exhibited cardiac response to the tactual stimulation, but the control preterm infants did not (Schmidt et al., 1980). A study that provided patterned kinesthetic and auditory stimuli (Barnard & Bee, 1983) showed improved organization during the hospital period. It also found effects on the Bayley Mental Development Index at 2 years of age, although there had been no differences at 8 months. The effects were considerable, with experimentals differing from controls by 16 to 33 points.

It is clear from these studies that preterm babies can profit from receiving some of the experiences that they would naturally have if they were in a home environment. This has led to a reform movement oriented toward providing handling, rocking, and enriched sensory stimulation (patterned).[12] The reform movement oriented toward mother–infant interactions in the hospital will be discussed in Chapter 5.

Social Interventions During Infancy. The basis for early social intervention was dis-

---

[12] Another reform in the making is the provision of sucking experience for prematures. This will be discussed in Chapter 6. Doctors are, however, beginning to warn about the dangers of overstimulating small prematures. This is especially true for tactile stimulation, because the skin is not well enough developed to protect the baby.

cussed as early as 1971 (Wright, 1971). The pioneering study in this area looked at intervention primarily directed toward mothers or families (a description is in Bromwich and Parmelee, 1979). A later study (Field, Widmayer, Stringer, & Ignatoff, 1980) looked at intervention with a population triply at risk: premature infants of lower SES Black teenage mothers. Half of the 60 mothers who volunteered for the intervention program were randomly assigned to it and the other half were assigned to a control group. In addition, 30 full-term infants of teenage mothers and 30 preterm and 30 term-infants of adult mothers were assessed as control groups. The intervention consisted of half-hour visits (twice a week for 4 months and monthly thereafter) designed to (1) educate the mothers about normal development and child rearing practices, (2) teach them age-appropriate exercises and stimulation methods, and (3) facilitate mother–infant interactions in the hope of promoting both communication skills and harmonious mother–infant relations. The infants were assessed at birth and at 4 and 8 months.

When adult preterm and teen preterm control mothers were compared, the teen mothers had less realistic expectations and less desirable child-rearing attitudes at 4 months and they rated their infants' temperaments as more difficult at both 4 and 8 months. At 8 months their infants had lower Bayley mental scores. These data suggest that the target group needed the kind of intervention the experimental group was receiving.

Compared to all preterm controls, preterm infants who received intervention did better at 4 months. They had higher scores on a developmental screening test (the Denver), weighed more, and were taller. Their mothers also differed. They had more realistic expectations, more desirable child-rearing attitudes, and rated their babies' temperaments as less difficult. Although feeding interactions in general did not differ for the two groups, both mothers and infants in the intervention group received more optimal face-to-face interaction ratings. The same pattern continued at 8 months: The intervention group babies had higher Bayley mental scores (110 versus 101), the mothers received higher ratings on the HOME scales, and the mothers rated their infants as having easier temperaments (on the Carey scales). On the HOME scales the mothers in the intervention program showed higher emotional and verbal responsivity and involvement with their infants than the mothers in the control groups. They saw their babies as more adaptable, more persistent, and having more optimal thresholds on the Carey temperament scales.

Although research on how the environment compensates for problems associated with prematurity has only begun to unravel the mysteries of the subject, practical applications are easy to make. Parents are well advised to optimize the environment of their prematures, because such factors as mother's education, class status, and positive attitudes and caregiving behaviors are related to higher IQ. Enrichment day care can also compensate for general SES disadvantages in other settings (see Chapter 13). Such care may not be sufficient to counteract all risks associated with prematurity, but it is likely to help and unlikely to hurt.

Although preventing bad outcomes resulting from prematurity is important, preventing prematurity would be an even greater achievement. Good health care, including nutrition, prior to and during pregnancy could prevent a large proportion of premature births. Studies have indicated that the vast majority of premature births occur in women with fewer than 3 prenatal visits to a doctor (Avery & Taeusch, 1984). This fact probably reflects many aspects of the mother's life, not just the effect of medical visits. Hence, education on the importance of prenatal care in all its aspects and the availability of care for all would seem the most important changes to seek.

DISCUSSION ISSUES
Critical Periods

The notion of critical periods is central in developmental psychology. Students who have had a previous course in psychology may have learned about critical periods in the course of studying either animal behavior or human development. Nowhere is this concept needed more nor studied better than in a course on infant development; hence it will be encountered frequently in this book.

The origins of the concept of critical periods are in embryology. The term originally referred to the periods in embryonic development in which a particular system is sensitive to an environmental event. We discussed two examples of critical periods, sexual differentiation and development of the lens of the eye. Consider the development of Müllerian and Wolffian ducts in sexual differentiation (see Figure 2–9). During the critical period (6 to 7 weeks after conception), whether the ducts develop into male or female sexual structures depends on whether male hormones are present in their immediate vicinity. The presence of the male hormones and of a not yet well-understood hormone secreted by the testes results in development of the Wolffian ducts into male sexual structures and regression of Müllerian ducts. The absence of such hormones means that the Müllerian ducts will develop into female sexual structures and the Wolffian ducts will regress. If male hormones are injected later in development, they cannot reverse the changes that have already taken place; that is, there is a critical period for their action. There is also a critical period for the development of external genitalia and presumably for sexual brain differentiation. In the development of the eye lens, the optic vesicle plays the same role that the male hormones do in sexual differentiation. The ectodermal tissue will develop into the eye lens only if the optic vesicle migrates to it and only if this happens before differentiation has proceeded beyond a certain point.

Several characteristics of critical periods are important to note. First, the structure that is developing during a critical period has the potential to develop in several ways. This is called **plasticity.** The course of development can be such that the Müllerian or Wolffian ducts develop into either female or male structures. Although the lens of the eye typically develops from the ectodermal tissue of the eye, there is nothing special about the ectodermal tissue. If its environment (the lens vesicle) is removed, the ectodermal tissue will not form a lens. If the lens vesicle is moved to a leg, the ectodermal tissue there will form a lens. Thus the ectodermal tissue is plastic; it may develop into a lens or into leg skin, depending upon its environment.

Second, the outcome of the critical period is determined by an environmental event ex-

ternal to the developing tissue. The environmental factor in the case of the Müllerian and Wolffian ducts is the male hormones secreted by the testes. The factor in the case of the lens of the eye is the influence of the chemicals associated with the lens vesicle.

Third, the period of plasticity is of limited duration. The same environmental event will not have the same effect later. For example, if a male embryo failed to develop a testis on one side, the Müllerian ducts on that side would develop into female internal sex organs. Even if fetal androgen is subsequently carried to that side from the other testis, when the circulatory system develops, it would arrive too late. The critical period would be past for the influence of androgen on these structures and they would remain female.

Thus the critical period is a time in which the environment influences the outcome of development. In the examples we have given so far, the environments were internal or internally produced. In Chapter 4 we will look at examples in which environmental agents external to the embryo, such as those coming from the mother, affect the potential baby. In exactly the sense we have been discussing, harmful external agents such as drugs and viruses are most harmful during certain periods. These periods turn out to be those in which particular structures are differentiating (during organogenesis).

Many psychologists interested in the development of behavior patterns after birth have been attracted to the notion of critical periods. It has been hypothesized, for example, that there is a critical period for the development of the concept of mother, for the development of the concept of one's own sex, for the development of intellectual prowess, and for the development of language. All these instances of hypothesized critical periods for psychological development share some characteristics with critical periods as described for embryological developments. At a particular time a particular system is developing. While it is developing it is receptive (or vulnerable) to certain environmental events. Once the critical period has passed, the same events have lesser effects or no effect. Although embryological critical periods clearly exist, whether critical periods in psychological development exist in a completely analogous fashion is very unclear.

This leads to a very important implication of the critical periods hypothesis. Because the organism is neither particularly receptive nor vulnerable to the crucial environmental events after the critical period, it is easy to view development as remaining fixed forever after. Similar thinking led Sigmund Freud to his famous theory that everything crucial to a child's personality occurs by 5 years of age. Although irreversibility occurs in embryological or structural development, whether it occurs in psychological development is much more in doubt.

Research Issues

In this chapter, three central research issues were discussed: (1) the limitations on generalizability when humans cannot be used as subjects for a study, (2) the limitations on interpretation imposed by operational definitions, and (3) the nature of joint causation and ways of dealing with such situations (controlling extraneous variables and analyzing multiple variables).

GENERALIZABILITY

The study of prenatal development raises two major issues about generalizability: the problem of generalizing from one species to another, and the problem of generalizing from possibly abnormal embryos and fetuses to normal ones. Researchers are more or less forced to accept such generalizations when they are unable to study the organisms in which they are directly interested. Researchers certainly cannot select a random sample of pregnant women and ask them to have abortions at different stages of their pregnancies so that the development of their embryo or fetus can be studied. There is occasionally an opportunity for such study when a pregnant woman has died from accidental causes, and some induced abortions allow the possibility for doing this in a relatively unbiased population. Physical study of the dead embryo or fetus is possible in both of these cases. In an earlier period, study of a fetus until it died after an induced abortion was considered to add so much potential knowledge that it was justified. Today the rights of the fetus are being redefined and the future of such research is currently in doubt.

Both of these issues of generalization tend to occur when ethical or practical problems (or both) prevent the study of normal humans. This occurs for many basic problems at all stages of development; hence researchers encounter these problems constantly and are forced to make assumptions about the similarities of the organisms they are studying to those in which they are directly interested. Such assumptions often turn out to be inappropriate, which may be shown if it becomes possible to test them, or if they are accidentally tested. When making assumptions about one species based on findings from another, researchers need to check on the similarities in as many ways as possible and choose a species with the greatest number of similarities in the domain of their interest. In the case of embryological development, it has been possible to specify species whose physical development is most like that of humans, and sometimes to verify knowledge gained in one species by examining the products of induced abortions of presumably normal human embryos or fetuses. We shall see in subsequent chapters that satisfactory solutions to questions of generalization across species are at least as difficult in other studies, for example those on the effects of drugs on prenatal development (see Chapter 4).

The question of generalizing from abnormal (or possibly abnormal) embryos and fetuses to those that are normal is perhaps somewhat more limited to the concerns of this chapter, at least as far as the psychology of infancy is concerned. Nevertheless, the same basic problem exists if an environmental manipulation is found to raise IQs by 15 points for an "at risk" population: The assumption cannot be made that it would do so for a normal population (and vice versa). The problems of generalization are a central issue in the understanding and use of psychological research.

OPERATIONAL DEFINITIONS

The second major issue of interpretation of research is that of operational definitions. An operational definition is the definition of a variable in terms of the procedure by which it is measured in a study. It is often contrasted with the notion of a conceptual definition, which is equivalent to a dictionary definition and is not limited by the criterion that it can be measured in a scientific fashion. The conceptual definition of prematurity is being born before the end of the normal period of gestation. The operational definition—the one used in research—is often weighing less than 2500 g (5½ lb). Thus the way something is measured may give it a meaning quite different from the ordinary definition.

Operational definitions may also vary in different studies. This can be extremely important because the conclusions reached using one operational definition may be quite different from those reached using another. For example, studies that use birth weight below 2500 g as the operational definition of prematurity may produce different conclusions than studies that use birth weight below 1300 g (about 3 lb). The former could conclude that prematurity does not lead to long-term IQ deficits but the latter studies would conclude that it does. Both might differ from a study that used less than 35 weeks gestational age to define prematurity. This is another problem of generalization. In considering how and to whom to apply research findings, it is important to consider not only the size and nature of the sample used but also the operational definitions of the concepts studied.

Although we did not label it as such, we discussed another problem of operational definitions in the section on the effects of prematurity. We noted that the results of studies may be very different depending on whether average differences between prematures and term infants or proportions of moderately or severely damaged children are measured. Each of these is a different operational definition of intellectual deficit in a group, and research using the two differing definitions often leads to different conclusions. Thus operational definitions refer to both independent and dependent variables.

MULTIPLE CAUSATION

The third research issue discussed in this chapter was joint causation. Prematurity presented a typically complex research situation. Researchers in this area have usually been interested in studying prematurity in its conceptual definition of short gestation and have not wanted results that are influenced by associated variables such as neurological problems, prenatal growth retardation, anoxia, social class, and race. Hence these have all been con-

sidered to be extraneous variables. In other words, researchers wished to make certain that these extraneous variables, rather than prematurity, were not actually responsible for the results. One technique for doing this is to separate various "subtypes of prematurity": SGA babies were separated from those who suffered short gestations, and in both groups subjects who had detectable neurological or other medical problems were separated (and often eliminated from consideration). To control for variables related to the mothers, such as social class and race, several techniques are used. One is to study only one class or race. Another is to match samples on both variables. A third, and the most elegant, is to use mothers as their own controls (the normal weight baby of a mother is compared to the premature baby of that same mother). These are all examples of controlling for extraneous variables by keeping them constant. These strategies allow researchers to discover whether prematurity in and of itself causes various outcomes. This is a good strategy to follow when the independent variable produces powerful effects and the extraneous variables are **nuisance variables**; that is, they get in the way, but do not provide much information about the issues at hand. In the case of prematurity, however, researchers discovered that research outcomes were often changed by such control procedures. For example, anoxia, an associated variable, was related to impairment but prematurity itself was not. This indicates that the extraneous variables were not merely nuisance variables, but were important variables in their own right. Such a sequence of events is typical of the history of research in many areas, and subsequent research must then consider these additional variables in conjunction with the original independent variable.

When several independent variables are considered at the same time, researchers often find that they influence each other in terms of their effects on the outcome variable. In the interaction of prematurity and social class, for example, predicted lower IQs were found for lower class children but not for middle class children. It is extremely important to identify interactions when they exist. To see why, consider this example again. Reliance on the outcome of a study that included only middle class children (a common state of affairs in psychology), would lead to the conclusion that prematurity has no long-term consequences for IQ. This would be wrong, because prematures who grow up in lower class environments have been found in several studies to have lower average IQs. Also, the failure to identify an interaction when it exists often produces a group of studies that will be inconsistent in their findings.

This example also demonstrates that interactions are often more complex than they first appear. Our simple two-variable interaction of prematurity and social class is likely to involve additional variables. Social class itself is comprised of many component parts. Some of these may help preterm babies compensate for their potential deficits (such as language stimulation) and others may not. Thus the same measure of social class may by chance yield samples that vary in the crucial component (language stimulation) in one study and samples that do not in another study. The interaction between prematurity and social class would be found only in the first study.

Parenting

Yes, pregnancy is part of parenting. From the point of view of a naive observer, a pregnant woman and her developing offspring have a mismatch in development. The most radical changes occur in the offspring during the first 8 weeks, before the woman looks pregnant and, in many cases, before she even suspects she is pregnant. Indeed, the major signs that a woman may be pregnant are missed periods and nausea. Some women who have irregular periods may not see the first missed period as a sign of pregnancy, and some women have enough flow after pregnancy that they do not know they have missed a period. Some women do not become nauseous and others who are nauseous but do not expect to be pregnant may assume they have a flu. Hence many women who do not expect to become pregnant may be unaware of their pregnancy during most, if not all, of organogenesis. This is a decided problem because organogenesis is the time of many critical periods in which certain environmental events, particularly certain diseases and drugs, can startlingly alter the course of embryonic development. Many birth defects result from

such events, as we shall see in Chapter 4. Thus good health care prior to any possibility of pregnancy, as well as during early pregnancy, is important for optimal development of the next generation. (See Guyer, Wallach, & Rosen, 1982, and Hemmink & Stanfield, 1978, for some convincing data.)

Later in pregnancy the mother's form changes radically because the fetus is growing rapidly in size and weight. Drugs and diseases generally are much less dangerous at this point (with some notable exceptions, as we shall see in Chapter 4). The mother's diet, however, is very important. Recent evidence suggests that the protein intake of the mother particularly affects brain development during the later part of pregnancy.

Parents of twins (who are often preterm) and of other preterm infants in some respects face similar problems of how to treat infants who are potentially at risk. In both cases it is important to keep in mind that having an infant at risk does not mean that the infant is necessarily doomed to a lower potential. Most twins and preterm infants do not suffer significant long-term deficits, especially if they are raised in good caregiving environments. One long-term effect that has been found (and it has been found for both twins and very low birth weight babies) is a slightly lower IQ. The average decrement in IQ, however, is typically on the order of only 5–7 points, a difference so small that it is difficult to attribute any practical significance to it. Thus most preterm and twin babies will be within the normal range of IQ, and any deficit within that range is probably not crucial. It appears that school performance may be affected more than IQ.

The little evidence that exists on social development among prematures also suggests that they do not differ from normals. In spite of these reassuring findings, twins and prematures are at risk. However, the methodological cautions we have raised make a conclusion arrived at by Kopp and Krakow (1983) with respect to all kinds of risk research appropriate here: ". . . although a considerable amount of information has been obtained about developmental phenomena subsequent to biological risk, our research literature is fragmented and difficult to synthesize" (p. 1086).

The limited evidence suggests that enrichment experiences are probably successful, so it makes sense for parents to take pains to provide intellectual and emotional support for an at risk infant. It is important that they do so in a relaxed and supportive environment that does not suggest to the child that he or she does not measure up.

SUMMARY

In nine months a single cell grows and differentiates into an amazing complex being who can survive on its own as well as into a number of structures that help support this development. The egg is fertilized while it is still in the Fallopian tubes and it has already reproduced itself several times by the time it reaches the uterus. By the fourth day the cell mass has 16 to 64 cells and has begun to differentiate into two layers, one of which will eventually be the baby and the other the placenta and other support structures. By 7 or 8 days after conception the zygote begins to implant itself in the uterine lining. By 14 days, which is approximately when the mother misses her first period, implantation is complete and the embryonic cells are differentiating into endoderm, ectoderm, and, a few days later, mesoderm. In the third week the neural tube and the placenta begin to develop. During the next 6 weeks, the period of organogenesis, all the organs of the body take form and some of them, such as the heart and circulatory system, actually function, although not in the same fashion they will after birth. By this time (8 weeks after conception) such external features as eyes, ears, and hands, are recognizable. In the third month the fetus first moves its arms and legs and first exhibits reflexes. The external sex organs are developed enough to identify sex, and identifiable fingerprints develop. This marks the end of the first trimester. The fetus is still so small that its mother does not yet look pregnant and she does not feel its movements, nor can it survive if removed from her body.

In the fifth lunar month (weeks 17–20) the fetus's movements become obvious to the mother. This time historically has been called the time of quickening. The fetal heartbeat is strong enough to be heard through a stethoscope placed on the mother's abdomen. The fetus sloughs off skin and respiratory cells into the amniotic fluid. Doctors can gather these cells by amniocentesis and process them to detect many chromosomal, genetic, and developmental abnormalities.

In the last half of its time in the womb, the fetus develops greatly in size and weight. The organ systems undergo the development necessary to allow them to function and hence to allow the fetus to have a chance to survive if born prematurely. The number and size of brain cells expands rapidly during this period. Embryos start to develop structures characteristic of their genetic sex at 5 weeks after conception. For each stage of sexual differentiation (that is, of the gonads or sex glands, the internal sexual structures, the external genitalia, and the brain) development proceeds from undifferentiated primordia. These structures have the potential to develop into either distinct male or female forms. In each case the female form develops unless hormones produced by male gonads intervene and change the course of development.

Before birth the fetal blood receives its oxygen from the maternal blood via the placenta rather than from the fetal lungs. At birth, when the lungs first draw air and the respiratory system begins to function, the circulatory system changes reflexively so that venous and arterial blood are separated. The lungs then function to provide oxygen. Immature respiratory development and malfunctions in the transition from fetal to infant respiratory and circulatory systems create many of the problems faced by newborns, particularly premature ones.

The neural tube, the primordium of the central nervous system, is one of the first structures visible in the embryo. It continues to develop earlier and more rapidly than most other organ systems. The first brain cells (neurons) develop at 8 weeks after conception. Brain cells increase in number until about 24 months after birth when glial cells stop reproducing. Although this is the most important period for the formation of the brain, the development of the myelin sheath and of neuron processes and connections (that is, of axons, dendrites, and synapses) continues long after cell division has ceased.

The areas of the cortex develop in a regular and integrated sequence. The primary motor areas develop before the sensory and association areas, and their order of development follows the cephalocaudal sequence. Next to develop are the primary sensory areas of the cortex in the order of touch, vision, and audition. The association areas develop last.

Twins are an interesting variant on normal prenatal development. Because they can be either genetically identical or merely siblings conceived simultaneously (or nearly so), they offer a testing ground for looking at genetic and environmental contributions to development. There are, however, many methodological and even statistical problems in such studies.

Prematurity, or being born too soon or too small, is one of the most common variants of development and is often considered to be a major neonatal health problem. The effects of this variant are widely studied, but usually as defined in terms of low birth weight, not gestational age. Thus, babies who have suffered prenatal growth retardation (SGA babies) have often been included in studies with prematures whose weight is normal for their gestational age.

Low birth weight (prematurity) can be caused by problems of the fetus, of the placenta, or of maternal health or nutrition. It is more often associated with birth complications than are term births. What research finds to be the outcomes for LBW babies often depends on the research strategy adopted and on the hospital care available at the time and place of the study. Clearly, the risk of death is greater, especially among very small prematures, as is the risk of short-term developmental lags in physiological, sensory, and motor development. Long-term physical growth is compromised. Questions about the degree of neurological and intellectual handicap (and intellectual handicap in the absence of neurological problems) have less certain answers. Some evidence suggests that language development and school performance may be more affected than IQ.

Are the long-term effects of being born too soon or too small, or both, a result of biological insults or of social and environmental handicaps? Or do they depend on a combination or interaction of both? There is evidence to suggest that the environment of the neonatal intensive care unit can retard neurological organization. Environmental effects are very important for long-term development. Even

relatively subtle biological or neurological damage also plays a role. Crude measures of environment such as SES or maternal IQ, as well as those using instruments designed for direct assessment of mother–infant interaction and stimulation available in the home, are related to outcomes. These factors appear more important in determining the outcomes for children at risk because of their prematurity than for normal term infants. Prediction of the long-term outcomes for too soon–too small babies appears to be more accurate when both biological and environmental factors are taken into account.

The factors identified as affecting outcomes can be manipulated in intervention programs to try to improve outcomes. Intervention during the hospital stay to provide more patterned sensory stimulation has been found to improve sensory–motor and neurological organization with fairly long-lasting effects. Interventions focused on various kinds of education for and support of mothers of prematures have shown effects over varying periods of time.

Overall, it appears that the outlook is favorable for prematures who are not neurologically damaged, and that some interventions may allay the effects even of neurological damage. It still may be that the proportions who have some handicap will be higher, but further evidence is needed.

REFERENCES
Embryology Source Books

Some understanding of embryology is necessary to understand the complexities of the constitution of the newborn, but it is clearly beyond the scope of this book. Consequently, the section of Chapter 2 that deals with embryology is not referenced in the conventional way. The books we have made most use of in writing this portion of the chapter are listed below. In addition, numerous other sources have influenced the ways we have used these materials as well as our feeling for the importance of this period.

Arey, L.B. (1965). **Developmental Anatomy: A Textbook and Laboratory Manual of Em-**

bryology (7th ed.). Philadelphia & London: Saunders.

Beck, F., Moffat, D.B., & Lloyd, J.B. (1973). **Human Embryology.** Oxford: Blackwell.

Ehrhardt, A.A., & Baker, S.W. (1974). Fetal androgens, human animal nervous system differentiation and behavioral sex differences. In R.C. Friedman, R.M. Richart, & R.L. Vande Wiele (Eds.), **Sex Differences in Behavior.** New York: Wiley.

Haines, R.W., & Mohiuddin, A. (1968). **Human Embryology** (4th ed.). Edinburgh & London: E. & S. Livingston, Ltd.

Hogarth, P. (1978). **Biology of Reproduction.** New York: Wiley.

Money, J., & Ehrhardt, A. (1972). **Man and Woman, Boy and Girl**. Baltimore: Johns Hopkins University Press.

Springer, S.P., & Deutsch, G. (1981). **Left Brain Right Brain.** San Francisco: Freeman.

Tanner, J.M. (1978). **Fetus into Man.** Cambridge, MA: Harvard University Press.

Other References

Abramovich, S.J., Gregory, S., Slemick, M., & Stewart, A. (1979). Hearing loss in very low birthweight infants treated with neonatal intensive care. *Archives of Diseases of Children, 54,* 421–426.

Avery, M.E., & Taeusch, H.W. (1984). *Schaffer's diseases of the newborn* (5th Ed.). Philadelphia: Saunders.

Bakeman, R., & Brown, J.V. (1980). Early interaction: consequences for social and mental development at 3 years. *Child Development, 41,* 437–447.

Barnard, K.E., & Bee, H.L. (1983). The impact of temporally patterned stimulation on the development of preterm infants. *Child Development, 54,* 1156–1167.

Beckwith, L. (1976). Caregiver–infant interactions and the development of the high-risk infant. In Tjossem, T. (Ed.), *Intervention strategies for high-risk infants and young children.* Baltimore: University Park Press.

Beckwith, L., & Cohen, S.E. (1978). Preterm birth: Hazardous obstetrical and postnatal events as related to caregiver–infant behavior. *Infant Behavior and Development, 1,* 403–411.

Beckwith, L., Cohen, S.E., Kopp, C.B., Parmelee, A.H., & Marcy, T.G. (1976). Caregiver–infant interaction and cognitive development in preterm infants. *Child Development, 47,* 579–587.

Beckwith, L., & Parmelee, A.H. (1983, July). *Preterm infants from birth to five years: Social factors and cognitive development.* Presented in a symposium on follow-up studies of children born at risk, at the International Society for the Study of Behavioral Development, Munich.

Beckwith, L., & Parmelee, A.H. (1984, April). *Infant sleep states, EEG patterns, caregiving and 5 year IQs of preterm children.* Presented in a symposium on sleep at the International Conference on Infant Studies, New York.

Booth C.L., Leonard, H.L., & Thoman, E.B. (1980). Sleep state and behavior patterns in preterm and full term infants. *Neuropediatrics,* (formerly *Neuropediatrie), 11,* 354–364.

Bowes, W.A., Halgrimson, M., & Simmons, M.A. (1979). Results of the intensive perinatal management of very-low-birth-weight infants (501 to 1,500 grams). *The Journal of Reproductive Medicine, 23,* 245–250.

Bradley, R.H., & Caldwell, B.M. (1977). Home observation for measurement of the environment: A validation study of screening efficiency. *American Journal of Mental Deficiency, 81,* 417–420.

Braine, M.D.S., Heimer, B., Wortis, H., & Friedman, A.M. (1966). Factors associated with impairment of the early development of prematures. *Monographs of the Society for Research in Child Development, 31* (4, Serial No. 106).

Bromwich, R.M., & Parmelee, A.H., Jr. (1979). An intervention program for pre-term high-risk infants and their parents. In T.M. Field, A.M. Sostek, S. Goldberg, & H. H. Shuman (Eds.), *Infants born at risk.* New York: Spectrum.

Budetti, P., McManus, P., Barrand, N., & Heinen, L.U. (1981, August). *The implications of cost-effectiveness analysis of medical technology. Case study No. 10: The costs and effectiveness of neonatal intensive care.* Congress of the United States, Office of Technology Assessment. Washington, DC: U.S. Government Printing Office (341-844/1016).

Caputo, D.V., & Mandell, W. (1970). Consequences of low birth weight. *Developmental Psychology, 3,* 363–383.

Cohen, S.E., Parmelee, A.H., Sigman, M., & Beckwith, L. (1982). Neonatal risk factors in preterm infants. *Applied Research in Mental Retardation, 3,* 265–276.

Cohen, S.E., & Parmelee, A.H. (1983). Prediction of

five-year Stanford-Binet scores in preterm infants. *Child Development, 54,* 1242–1253.

Conel, J. (1939–1967). *The posnatal development of the human cerebral cortex* (Vols. I–VIII). Cambridge, MA: Harvard University Press.

Crawford, J.W. (1982). Mother–infant interaction in premature and full-term infants. *Child Development, 53,* 957–962.

Davies, P.A., & Tizard, J.P.M. (1975). Very low birth weight and subsequent neurological defect (With special reference to spastic diplegia). *Developmental Medicine and Child Neurology, 17,* 3–17.

Douglas, J.W.B. (1956). Mental ability and school achievement of premature children at eight years of age. *British Medical Journal, 1,* 1210.

Drillien, C.M. (1961). The incidence of mental and physical handicaps in school-age children of very low birth weight. *Pediatrics, 27,* 452–464.

Drillien, C.M. (1964). *The growth and development of the prematurely born infant.* Edinburgh: Livingstone.

Drillien, C., Thomson, A., & Burgoyne, K. (1980). Low birthweight children at early school age. *Developmental Medicine and Child Neurology, 22,* 26–47.

Dubowitz, L.M.S., Dubowitz, V., & Goldberg, C. (1970). Clinical assessment of gestational age in the newborn infant. *Journal of Pediatrics, 77,* 1–10.

Field, T.M., Widmayer, S.M., Stringer, S., & Ignatoff, E. (1980). Teenage, lower-class, black mothers and their preterm infants: An intervention and developmental follow-up. *Child Development, 51,* 426–436.

Fisher, A.E. (1967). Chemical stimulation of the brain. In *Psychobiology: The biological basis of behavior.* San Francisco: Freeman.

Friedman, S.L., Jacobs, B.S., & Werthmann, M.W., Jr. (1982). Preterms of low medical risk: Spontaneous behavior and soothability at expected date of birth. *Infant Behavior and Development, 5,* 3–10.

Genn, M.M., & Silverman, W.A. (1964). The mental development of ex-premature children with retrolental fibroplasia. *The Journal of Nervous and Mental Disease, 138,* 79–86.

Gluck, L. (Ed.) (1977). *Intrauterine asphyxia and the developing fetal brain.* Chicago: Year Book Medical Publishers.

Goldstein, K.M., Caputo, M.M., & Taub, H.B. (1976). The effects of prenatal and perinatal complications on development at one year of age. *Child Development, 47,* 613–621.

Guyer, B., Wallach, L.A., & Rosen, S.L. (1982). Birth-weight-standardized neonatal mortality rates and the prevention of low birth weight: How does Massachusetts compare with Sweden? *The New England Journal of Medicine, 306,* 1230–1233.

Harper, P.A., & Wiener, G. (1965). Sequelae of low birth weight. In A.C. DeGraff (Ed.), *Annual Review of Medicine, 16,* 405–420.

Hemmink, F., & Stanfield, B. (1978). Prevention of low birth weight and preterm birth: Literature review and suggestions for research policy. *Milbank Memorial Fund Quarterly, 56,* 339–361.

Holmes, D.L., Nagy, J.N., Slaymaker, F., Sosnowski, R.J., Prinz, S.M., & Pasternak, J.F. (1982). Early influences of prematurity, illness, and prolonged hospitalization on infant behavior. *Developmental Psychology, 18,* 744–750.

Institute of Medicine. (1982). Summary of workshop on low birth weight infants. In Institute of Medicine, *Infants at risk for developmental dysfunction.* Washington, DC: National Academy Press.

Jacobs, B.S. Friedman, S.C., & Werthmann, M.W., Jr. (1979, April). *A comparison of temperament in pre-term, full-term and post-term infants.* Paper presented at the meeting of the Eastern Psychological Association, Philadelphia.

Jones, R.A.K., Cummins, M., & Davies, P.A. (1979). Infants of very low birth weight: A 15-year analysis. *Lancet, i,* 1332–1335.

Knudtson, F.W. (1978). *Effects of tactile stimulation on responsivity to stress in high-risk premature infants.* Paper presented at the Invited Symposium: Effects of Early Experience on Infant Development, Western Psychological Association, San Francisco.

Kopp, C.B., & Krakow, J.B. (1983). The developmentalist and the study of biological risk: A view of the past with an eye to the future. *Child Development, 54,* 1086–1108.

Kopp, C.B., & Parmelee, A.H. (1979). Prenatal and perinatal influences on infant behavior. In J.D. Osofsky (Ed.), *Handbook of infant development.* New York: Wiley.

Korner, A.F. (1979). Maternal rhythms and waterbeds: A form of intervention with premature infants. In E.B. Thoman (Ed.), *Origins of the infant's social responsiveness.* Hillside, NJ: Erlbaum.

Korner, A.F., Kraemer, H.C., Haffner, M.E., & Cosper, L.M. (1975). Effects of waterbed floatation on premature infants: A pilot study. *Pediatrics, 56,* 361–367.

Lipper, E., Lee, K., Gartner, L.M., & Grellong, B. (1981). Determinants of neurobehavioral outcome in low-birth-weight infants. *Pediatrics, 67,* 502–505.

Lubchenco, L.O. (1970). Assessment of gestational age and development at birth. *Pediatric Clinics of North America, 17,* 125–145.

Lubchenco, L.O., Hansman, C., & Boyd, E. (1966). Intrauterine growth in length and head circumference as estimated from live births at gestational ages from 26 to 42 weeks. *Pediatrics, 37,* 403–408.

Lubchenco, L.O., Hansman, C., Dressler, M., & Boyd, E. (1963). Intrauterine growth as estimated from liveborn birth-weight data at 24 to 42 weeks of gestation. *Pediatrics, 32,* 793.

Lubchenco, L.O., Horner, F.A., Reed, L.H., Hix, I.E., Jr., Metcalf, D., Colig, R., Elliott, H.C., & Bourg, M. (1963). Sequalae of premature birth. *American Journal of Diseases of Children, 106,* 101–115.

McDonald, A.D. (1964a). Intelligence in children of very low birth weight. *British Journal of Preventive and Social Medicine, 18,* 59–74.

McDonald, A.L. (1964b). The aetiology of spastic diplegia. *Developmental Medicine and Child Neurology, 6,* 277–284.

Meyer-Probst, B., Rosler, H.-D., & Teichmann, H. (1983). Biological and psychosocial risk factors and development during childhood. In D. Magnusson & V.L. Allen (Eds.), *Human development: An interactional perspective.* New York: Academic.

Naeye, R.L., Benirschke, K., Hagstrom, J.W.C., & Marcus, C.C. (1966). Intrauterine growth of twins as estimated from live birth weight data. *Pediatrics, 37,* 409–416.

Neal, M.V. (1968). Vestibular stimulation and developmental behavior of the small premature infant. *Nursing Research Report, 3,* 1, 3–5.

Paneth, N., Kiely, M.A., Wallenstein, S., Marcus, M., Pakter, J., & Susser, M. (1982). Newborn intensive care and neonatal mortality in low-birth-weight infants. *The New England Journal of Medicine, 307,* 149–155.

Parmelee, A.H., Jr., & Sigman, M. (1976). Development of visual behavior and neurological organization in pre-term and full-term infants. In *Minnesota Symposium on Child Development* (Vol. 10). Minneapolis: University of Minnesota Press.

Parmelee, A.H., Sigman, M., Kopp, C.B., & Haber, A. (1976). Diagnosis of the infant at high risk for mental, motor, and sensory handicaps. In T. Tjossem (ed.), *Intervention strategies for high risk infants and young children.* Baltimore: University Park Press.

Parmelee, A.H., Wenner, W.H., Akiyama, Y., Schultz, M.S., & Stern, E. (1967). Sleep states in premature infants. *Developmental Medicine and Child Neurology, 9,* 70–77.

Pratt, R.M. as cited in the *NIH Record,* Sept. 28, 1982, p. 6.

Richman, L.C. (1980, August). *General intellectual and specific language development of low birth weight children.* Paper presented at the meeting of the American Psychological Association, Montreal.

Rose, S.A. (1980). Enhancing visual recognition memory in preterm infants. *Developmental Psychology, 16,* 85–92.

Rose, S.A. (1983). Differential rates of visual information processing in full-term and preterm infants. *Child Development, 54,* 1189–1198.

Rose, S.A., Schmidt, K., Riese, M.L., & Bridger, W.H. (1980). Effects of prematurity and early intervention on responsibility to tactual stimuli: A comparison of preterm and full-term infants. *Child Development, 51,* 416–425.

Rosensheim, J.J., Davidson, P.W., Reuter, S.H., Walters, C.P., & Walk, R.D. (1978). *The visual placing response in oxygen deprived infants.* Paper delivered at the meeting of the American Psychological Association.

Rowe v. Wade, 410 U.S. 113 (1973).

Rubin, R.A., Rosenblatt, C., & Balow, B. (1973). Psychological and educational sequelae of prematurity. *Pediatrics, 52,* 352–363.

Schmidt, K., Rose, S.A., & Bridger, W.H. (1980). The effect of heartbeat sound on the cardiac and behavioral responses to tactual stimulation in sleeping, premature infants. *Developmental Psychology, 16,* 175–184.

Siegel, L.S. (1982). Reproductive, perinatal, and environmental factors as predictors of the cognitive and language development of preterm and full-term infants. *Child Development, 53,* 963–973.

Siegel, L.S. (1983). Correction for prematurity and its consequences for the assessment of the very low birthweight infant. *Child Development, 54,* 1176–1188.

Solkoff, N., Yaffe, S., & Weintraub, D. (1967). *Effects of handling on the development of premature infants.* Paper presented at the meeting of the Eastern Psychological Association, Boston.

Thoman, E.B. (1982). A biological perspective and a behavioral model for assessment of premature infants. In Bond, L.A. & Joffe, J.M. (Eds.), *Primary prevention of psychopathology, Vol. 6: Facilitating infant and early childhood development*. Hanover, NH: University Press of New England.

Thomson, A.M. (1959). Maternal stature and reproductive efficiency. *Eugenics Review, 51,* 157–162.

Thomson, A.M., & Billewicz, W.Z. (1963). Nutritional status, maternal physique and reproductive efficiency. *Proceedings of the Nutrition Society, 22,* 55.

Ungerer, J.A., & Sigman, M. (1983). Developmental lags in preterm infants from one to three years of age. *Child Development, 54,* 1217–1228.

Werner, E., Simonian, K., Bierman, J.M., & French, F.E. (1967). Cumulative effect of perinatal complications and deprived environment on physical, intellectual, and social development of preschool children. *Pediatrics, 39,* 480–505.

Wiener, G., Rider, R.V., Oppel, W.C., & Harper, P.A. (1965). Correlates of low birth weight: Psychological status at 6–7 years of age. *Pediatrics, 35,* 434–444.

Wiener, G., Rider, R.V., Oppel, W.C., & Harper, P.A. (1968). Correlates of low birth weight: Psychological status at 8–10 years of age. *Pediatric Research, 2,* 110–118.

Wright, L. (1971). The theoretical and research base for a program of early stimulation care and training of premature infants. In J. Hellmuth (Ed.), *The exceptional infant: Studies in abnormalities* (Vol. II). New York: Brunner/Mazel.

Yazbak, F.E., & Holden, R.H. (1966). Birth order of twins, Apgar score, and perinatal mortality. *Rhode Island Medical Journal, 49,* 595–597.

GENETIC ABNORMALITIES AND GENETIC COUNSELING

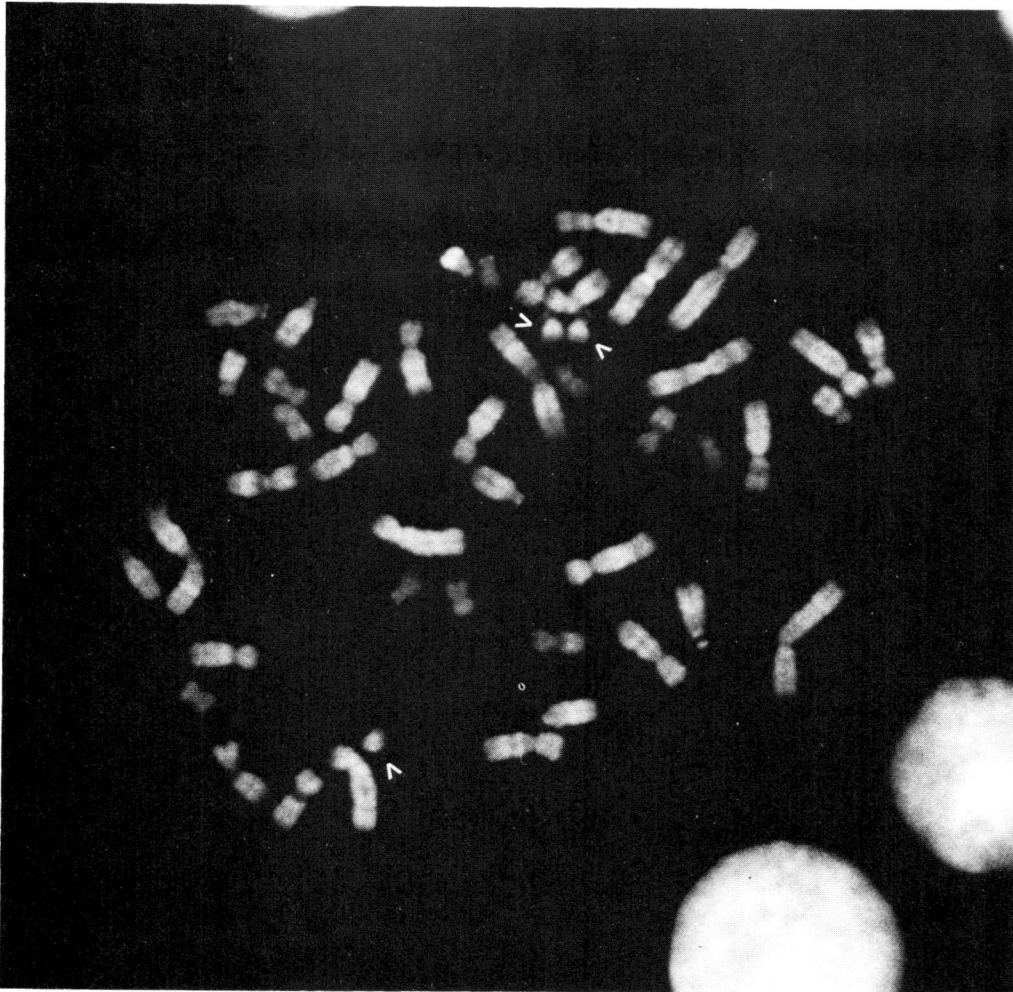

CHAPTER 3

We have examined the history of infancy studies and the ways in which we can study infants. We have also studied the prenatal growth and development of normal infants. In this chapter we shall look at a number of genetic factors that affect development before and after birth.

HEREDITY, ENVIRONMENT, AND CONSTITUTION

The set of biological and behavioral characteristics babies have at birth is called their **constitution.** Many aspects of this constitution are inherited; that is, they are transmitted from parents to offspring through the genes. Some characteristics may be genetic in a different sense: They result from an error in the genetic material (mostly in the chromosomes, occasionally in specific genes) that is not inherited. The environment during the prenatal period may also affect the constitution. Thus, every baby is born with a constitution that is the product of both heredity and environment. Developmental problems arising from inherited and noninherited defects in genes and chromosomes will be discussed in this chapter. Problems caused by environmental influences will be described in Chapter 4.

Rather than describe every known chromosomal or genetic abnormality, we have selected examples that allow us to discuss issues relevant to genetic counseling, to detection in infancy, or to treatment during infancy. Many of these examples involve mental retardation, as is true of chromosomal and genetic defects in general, but there are instances of physical and medical disorders as well.

Background Information About Genetics

To understand the discussions of these issues, it will be helpful to review briefly some basic concepts of genetics and to describe techniques by which genetic defects can be identified. The **genotype** is the basic genetic make-up of an individual—that which is transmitted from parents to their offspring. The **phenotype** refers to the observable characteristics of an organism, both biological and behavioral. The phenotype always results from the interaction of the genotype with the environment.

The basic units that transmit the information of heredity are the **genes.** The genes in turn are arranged in linear order on the **chromosomes,** long, thread-like structures in cell nuclei. Humans have 46 chromosomes, 23 from each parent. When the 23 chromosomes from the father's sperm meet the 23 chromosomes from the mother's ovum, they form pairs. The resulting fertilized egg has 23 pairs of chromosomes (Figure 3–1). Each pair has one chromosome from the mother and one from the father. In 22 of the pairs, the two members of the pairs have the same structure; they are called **autosomal.** The remaining pair consists of the sex chromosomes (discussed in Chapter 2). All genes on autosomal chromosomes come in pairs, one on each member of the pair of chromosomes. The combination of the pairs of genes determines the genotype.

The first technique developed to study the actions of genes was to observe the inheritance patterns of traits. In the 1800s Gregor Mendel, a monk of peasant origins, first demonstrated that inherited characteristics are carried from generation to generation as discrete units. By careful, extensive experiments with pea plants, he discovered that various characteristics, such as color and form of seeds, flowers, and pods, all varied in subsequent generations in similar proportions. For example, when he bred red-flowered plants with white-flowered plants, three quarters of the resulting plants were red and one quarter were white. Such a pattern of transmission is characteristic of traits of a particular genetic mechanism, in which the red color is determined by a dominant gene and the white color by a recessive gene. There are different frequency patterns of transmission for traits that are governed by a single recessive gene, by a single dominant gene, or by a single gene on a sex chromosome (the most common of which are X-linked).

We will not attempt an exhaustive description of genetic mechanisms here, but will discuss only those relevant to the examples later in the chapter. Mendel's ratios can be used to trace genetic mechanisms in humans as well as peas. Tracing family histories or pedigrees has allowed identification of many hu-

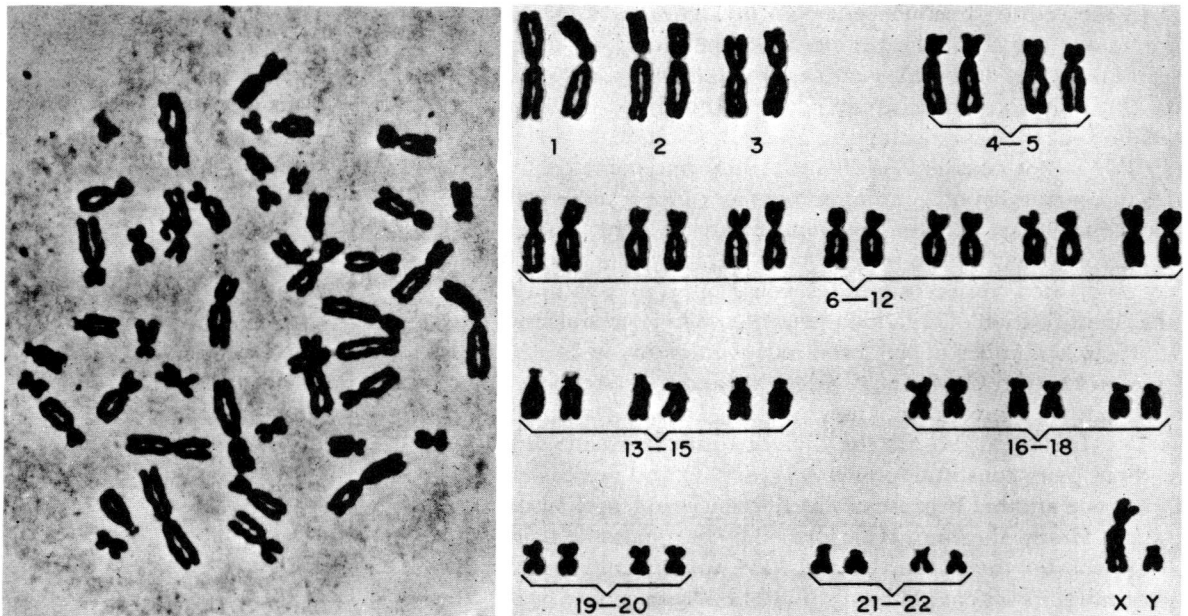

FIGURE 3–1. Analysis of a human chromosome complement. At the left are the spread out chromosomes from a cell. At the right, the chromosomes are arranged into a standard karyotype, numbered as shown. The sex chromosomes, labeled X and Y, are at lower right. (Original furnished by Dr. J.J. Biesele. From An Introduction to Human Genetics *by H. Eldon Sutton. New York: Holt, Rinehart & Winston, 1965. Used by Permission.)*

man genetic defects. For example, hemophilia (bleeder's disease) was shown to be an X-linked disease by its pattern of occurrence in the descendents of Queen Victoria of England, who was a carrier. Notice that the presence and nature of the genotypes were inferred from the distributions among relatives of the traits they produced. Only the phenotypic traits were observed. Similarly, phenylketonuria (PKU) was originally identified as a genetic trait from a study of family histories, although the type of inheritance was different from that found in hemophilia.

As geneticists learned more about genetic mechanisms, they discovered that many genetic defects result in missing or defective **enzymes.** Enzymes are substances that help the body convert one substance to another, as for example in the transformation of nutrients (food) to chemicals usable by the cells. The absence of, or a defect in, one of these enzymes leads to unusual levels of particular chemicals in the body. Levels of an enzyme itself or of the related chemicals can often be detected by laboratory analysis. Thus, the unusual level of particular chemicals in the body is a phenotypical trait that can be used to infer the associated genotype or genetic trait. This method of determining genetic traits provides several advantages over pedigrees. It not only eliminates the necessity of tracking down relatives, but can lead to detection before the more overt phenotypic expression of the trait develops. This is the case for PKU, in which the chemical imbalance occurs and can be detected before overt signs of abnormal behavior, including mental retardation, occur. Early detection allows doctors to intervene before the defects (retardation and hyperactivity in the case of PKU) develop in their worst form. In some other cases of inborn errors of metabolism, as they are called, there is hope that this kind of prevention may be achieved.[1] In many cases, although the phenotypic expression of the metabolic errors cannot be prevented, amniocentesis can be used to detect whether some of them are present prenatally. Affected fetuses can then be aborted. Most inborn errors of metabolism are the result of the action of a single pair of genes.

Geneticists are making tremendous advances in the understanding of the biochemistry of genes and genetic transmission. It is likely that new techniques for identifying genetic disorders will be developed and that ultimately new treatments, including actual modification of the genes, will be possible.

Disorders of single genes are not the only defects that babies may have. Many known disorders are defects in the chromosomes rather than in one gene on a chromosome. Chromosomal defects can be detected by means of a procedure called **karyotyping.** In this procedure some cells from a person are first grown in a culture medium, then chemically stopped in the middle of cell division (mitosis), and treated and stained. The chromosomes are then photographed, enlarged, and arranged according to size. Figure 3–1 shows a typical karyotype. Many chromosomal abnormalities can be detected by inspection of such karyotypes. Do not be misled, however, into thinking that a picture of chromosomes is a picture of a genotype. Chromosomal analysis is directly analogous to the analysis of the chemical byproducts of metabolism. The state of the chromosomes in the developing embryo and fetus is a joint outcome of heredity and development. Although chromosomal abnormalities are sometimes direct expressions of genotypes, often they are not. The best evidence available today suggests that environmental agents, such as irradiation and certain drugs, and environmental events, such as aging of eggs (which are already present in a female's body by the time she is born), may lead to chromosomal abnormalities. Thus, even chromosomes are affected by the environment, and this means they are phenotypic, not genotypic.

Two things should be clear from this discussion. First, the genotype refers only to the inherited potential of individuals. Second, that inherited potential is never directly transmitted to offspring. It is always mediated by the environment. Environmental influences act on sperm and ova and so begin to have effects even before an egg is fertilized, and they continue to act throughout development. During early differentiation of the potential baby, the immediate chemical environment of the cells influences whether and how they will differentiate, as we saw in the last chapter. In the next chapter we will give examples of foreign substances that affect both early stages of differentiation and later prenatal development. Thus, every aspect of a baby's constitution is a result of the interaction between heredity and environment.

Importance of Gene and Chromosome Disorders

Before we discuss some of the dreadful things that can go wrong even before a baby is born, we would like to reassure you that the percentage of babies born with serious genetic defects is very small. We would also like to show you that these babies are a serious problem worthy of consideration.

Chromosome abnormalities and gene defects are rather rare when we consider the general population. Of all the adults and children in the United States, only 1–2% have some sort of gene defect and another 0.5% have a major chromosomal defect. About half of the latter involve abnormalities of the sex chromosomes, many of which are not as serious in their effects as those of other chromosomes. These figures underrepresent the importance to society of genetic and chromosomal abnormalities for three basic reasons. (1) Many of the victims of such disorders die before birth or during their childhood and therefore are not represented in statistics for the general population. (2) While the overall rates may be low, gene defects and chromosomal abnormalities are quite frequent among babies with birth defects. This means that a sizable proportion of patients in hospitals and institutions for the retarded have gene and chromosome abnormalities. (3) In certain racial and ethnic groups, particular genetic effects are much more frequent than in other groups and hence are a

---

[1] There are some case studies indicating successes, but no confirmed results. The case studies include treatment of an afflicted fetus by alteration of maternal intake.

greater source of worry for members of that group. We will consider the first two reasons in turn. The third reason will be alluded to in our discusion of Tay-Sachs disease, Beta thalassemia, and sickle cell anemia.

INCIDENCE AND MORTALITY BEFORE, DURING, AND AFTER BIRTH

Determining prenatal mortality from any one cause is not at all straightforward. The most frequent figure given for the rate of spontaneous abortions and miscarriages is around 10% of conceptions. This figure represents only a fraction of the total rate, however, because spontaneous abortions early in pregnancy are reabsorbed into the mother's body rather than aborted, so even though the mother thinks she was pregnant, she has no way of determining that she has lost her potential offspring. Estimates of the percentage of all human conceptions that are spontaneously aborted run as high as 40–60% (Boue & Boue, 1974; Boue, Boue, & Lazar, 1975). Every stage of pregnancy contributes to this loss rate. We can give you a sense of this by considering some estimates of mortality at various stages due to bad eggs (Witschi, 1970, estimating from the data of Hertig, Rock, Adams, & Menken, 1959; Hertig & Rock, 1949; see also Carr, 1963, 1971). According to these estimates, 16% of bad eggs in contact with sperm fail to fertilize and an additional 15% that have been fertilized are lost prior to implantation (at the cleavage stage). By the second week, or about when the first menses are missed (in the implantation stage) another 27% are lost; and by the second missed menses (in the embryological stage) another 8% are lost. These are all absorbed into the mother's body. Thus, of the grossly abnormal potential infants that might result from bad eggs, 66% have been lost before most women know they are pregnant. At present there is no way to learn about these early pregnancy losses.

How many later prenatal losses are due to gene and chromosome abnormalities? This question can be answered only for chromosomal abnormalities in spontaneous abortions, since these can be detected by karyotyping cells from the aborted embryos and fetuses. It appears that 50–60% of the spontaneous abortions that occur in the first three months of pregnancy have chromosomal abnormalities (Boue et al., 1975). Many later fetal losses are also due to chromosomal abnormalities. Bauld, Sutherland, and Bain (1974) found abnormal karyotypes in 40% of the abortions or miscarriages that occurred between 20 and 28 weeks after conception. The percentage of abnormal karyotypes decreases for deaths during labor and delivery, but abnormalities are still found in 6–7% of these deaths (Bauld et al., 1974; Machin, 1974; Sutherland, Bauld, & Bain, 1974). As these figures indicate, a large portion of prenatal deaths are due to chromosomal anomalies, and—perhaps fortunately—most individuals with chromosomal abnormalities die before birth.

By the time of birth, then, the rates of chromosomal abnormalities have reached the low level we noted earlier. Among unselected newborns, 0.5 to 0.75% have chromosomal abnormalities (Bauld et al., 1974; Hamerton, Manoranjan, Abbott, Williamson, & Ducasse, 1972; Lubs & Ruddle, 1970a, 1970b, as cited in Lubs, 1970; Ratcliffe & Keay, 1973, as cited in Lubs, 1970; Ratcliffe, Melville, Steward, Jacobs, & Keay, 1970, as cited in Lubs, 1970; Sergovich, Valentine, Chen, Kinch, & Stout, 1969).

Comparable rates are much more difficult to produce for specific gene disorders, since a single clear test such as karyotyping is not available. Nevertheless, estimates are possible. Lubs (1977, as cited in National Institutes of Health: *Antenatal Diagnosis*, 1979) estimated that 1–2% of all infants born alive suffer from a single-gene defect. An additional 1–2% of newborns have some condition that is related to genetics (involving multiple genes or interactions between genes and the environment or both). These include club foot, cleft lip and palate, and neural tube defects (estimate from Bernirschke, 1976, cited in NIH: *Antenatal diagnosis*, 1979). Thus, 3–5% of live-born infants in the United States are affected by genetically-based defects. That's 100,000 to 150,000 newborns each year.

Another perspective on the frequency of gene defects and chromosomal abnormalities is obtained by examining infants with birth defects such as those cited above. These defects, which are detectable at birth, are mostly physical, since psychological functioning cannot be evaluated at birth. About 6% of all infants born alive have some sort of birth defect (Shapiro,

Ross, & Levine, 1965). Of these, approximately 20% have defects of known genetic transmission and another 3–5% have defects due to chromosomal abnormalities.

The fetus with chromosomal abnormalities or gene defects who makes it to birth is still at risk. Such babies are much more likely to die during infancy than are other babies. Although they constitute only 3–5% of all live births, they account for 17.3% of infant deaths. In fact, as medical care has improved and led to an over-all decline in infant mortality (see Table 3–1), the percentage of infant deaths due to congenital malformations has increased. In 1915 the infant mortality rate due to congenital malformations was only 6.4%. This means that as the treatment of other medical problems improves, by means of obstetrical care, improved nutrition and environmental conditions, and antibiotic therapies, then birth defects account for a larger proportion of the infant mortality rate.

The proportion of deaths in the population due to genetic causes is markedly underestimated by the rate of 17.3% for infant deaths. Genetic conditions, such as cystic fibrosis and galactosemia, are often not identified early in life, although they may cause death in infancy or later. Other genetic problems such as Huntington's Disease only surface in midlife and cause death in mid to late life. Even for infant deaths the total rate is likely to be at least 20%. This makes genetic disorders the third leading cause of infant death, after immaturity and birth injuries. They are the second leading cause in the 1- to 4-year age range, and the third leading cause in the 15- to 19-year age group. (The figures given here are from 1978 data of the National Center for Health Statistics.)

FREQUENCY OF GENETIC AND CHROMOSOMAL DISORDERS IN SPECIAL POPULATIONS

We have already seen that many birth defects are the result of genetic or chromosomal abnormalities. Genetic-related disorders are also overrepresented in hospitalizations and in residents in institutions for the mentally retarded.

Conditions that have genetic origins (single-gene disorders, chromosomal and developmental anomalies, and malformations) account for 25–30% of children in major acute

TABLE 3–1
Relation of Birth Defects to Infant Mortality in the United States in 1915 and 1976

	1915	1976
Overall infant mortality rate (per 10,000 live births)	1,000	150
Infant deaths due to birth defects (per 10,000 live births)	64	26
Contribution of birth defects to death rate	6.4%	17.3%

NOTE. From *Antenatal Diagnosis:* Report of a Consensus Development Conference, sponsored by the National Institute of Child Health and Human Development. NIH Publication No. 79-1173. Bethesda, Md.: U.S. Dept. of Health, Education, & Welfare, April 1979, p. I-27.

care hospitals (Childs, Miller, & Bearn, 1972; World Health Organization Report No. 497, 1972). Even for adults such conditions account for 13% of hospitalizations (Childs et al., 1972). Translated into numbers, this means 1.2 million persons with genetically-influenced problems are hospitalized each year at a cost of over $800,000,000 (1971 dollars and 1971 prices; Stickle, 1971).

Figures for mental retardation are similar. Of 210,000 individuals institutionalized for mental retardation in 1970, approximately 20–25% of the cases could be ascribed to genetically influenced factors. Furthermore, such disorders are even more disproportionately represented among the most severely retarded. Of individuals with IQs below 50 (the most severe retardation), at least 40% have a chromosomal disorder, a single-gene defect, or a severe developmental malformation syndrome such as spina bifida. The institutionalization of individuals whose retardation is caused by genetic or genetically influenced factors cost $315,000,000 per year in 1970, which is over $630,000 in 1984.

SPECIFIC DISORDERS

Four points are important to the discussion of specific chromosomal and genetic defects. First, the defects described in this chapter (problems of genes and chromosomes) and those described in the next chapter (environmentally-caused constitutional defects) are all mistakes or problems. Information that would enable us to look at the genetics of interesting, positive characteristics, such as high intelligence or positive personality traits, is sparse. Second, it is very important to remember that although we can make a long catalog of unpleasant outcomes of pregnancy, most babies that survive the newborn period do not have these afflictions. Third, not all birth defects are as dramatic and devastating as those we will describe. Finally, some birth defects can be either hereditary or nonhereditary.[2]

There are at least three ways to organize material in the area of genetics. (1) We could, and will, start with defects caused by the largest genetic unit (the chromosome) and proceed to those caused by the smaller genes, which are located on the chromosomes and which determine the inheritance of specific traits. (2) It might seem logical to organize the material in terms of numbers of people affected, but this scheme has no logical structure otherwise. (3) We could organize the discussion in terms of defects that are inherited versus those that involve genetic material but are not inherited. The fact that some defects can be either destroys the beauty or simplicity of this approach. Hence we have chosen the first ordering.

Chromosomal Abnormalities

Chromosomal defects can result from heredity or can be the result of **mutations**—permanent changes in the chromosomes that result in inheritable gene changes. Chromosomal changes usually are incompatible with life and are aborted early. If the total effect of the chromosomal abnormalities is not lethal, the resulting infant is likely to have a large number of abnormalities produced by the disruption of gene functioning. Chromosomal abnormalities usually involve either an extra or a missing chromosome or part of a chromosome, as will be explained for Down's syndrome.

DOWN'S SYNDROME
Down's syndrome or **"mongolism"** is a good starting point for the discussion of chromosomal abnormalities for a number of

reasons. (1) It is one of the most common causes of mental retardation; (2) it is one of the most frequent chromosomal abnormalities; (3) it demonstrates several genetic complexities; and (4) it provides a good example for discussion of some of the social issues involved in dealing with abnormalities.

Characteristics. This syndrome used to be called Mongolism because most persons afflicted with it have a flat face and upward slanting eyes with an epicanthic fold on the eyelid similar to that of Asians or Mongols, and there may be a yellowish cast to the skin. This term is avoided today because of its negative reference to an ethnic group whose members certainly do not resemble victims of this syndrome in any essential way. Instead, it is called Down's syndrome, after the man who originally described it in 1866. It can also be called trisomy 21, because its most frequent cause is an extra or third chromosome, number 21.[3] Some of the other physical stigmata that may be present include an enlarged tongue and finger ridge and palm line patterns that differ from those in normal babies. An example of the latter is the so-called simian crease (a line that goes straight across the palm like the line on the palm of a monkey or ape rather than curving down as it does in most humans).[4] Figure 3–2 shows a relatively mild case of Down's syndrome.

In addition to these externally visible signs, congenital heart disease is common, and many die in the first few years from cardiac complications. Among other mostly invisible characteristics of Down's syndrome are frequent hypothyroidism in adulthood and numerous other metabolic and biochemical problems. Of particular importance are immunological problems that lead to a high level of susceptibility to infections. All of these factors led to an average life expectancy of 15 years in the 1940s. With the advent of better heart surgery, antibiotics, and better metabolic

---

[2] Cleft palate and club foot are examples for points 3 and 4. Surgical correction is quite possible for both problems.

[3] The chromosomal cause of Down's syndrome was suggested as early as 1932, but was only proven in 1959 after the development of electron microscopy and appropriate staining techniques enabled identification of the chromosomes.

[4] Down's victims are not the only humans who have a Simian crease. It is found in about 10% of the human population.

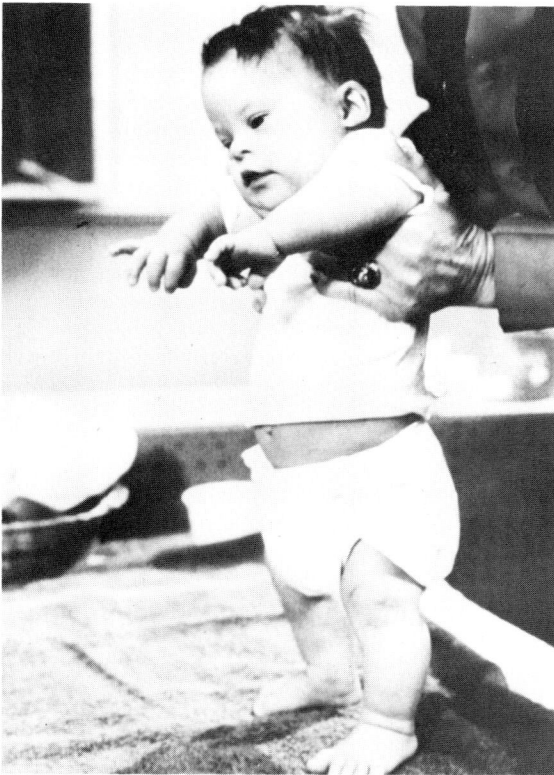

FIGURE 3–2. This is a very "good" Down's baby. Although the baby needs more support in maintaining an erect posture than would be expected at this age, there are few of the physical traits that usually characterize a Down's infant. (Photo courtesy of the Office of Research Reporting, National Institute of Child Health and Human Development, Bethesda, MD.)

mothers of normal infants. Indeed, a greater percentage scored in the more difficult temperament categories, although no mother assigned a difficult rating to her infant (Bridges & Cicchetti, 1982). Six months later fewer than half of the Down's infants scored in the same category as earlier, which shows that their temperaments were not immutably fixed by their chromosomal abnormality. Other findings in this and another study (Emde, Katz, & Thorpe, 1978) suggest that Down's infants demonstrate less frequent and less intense affective expression but not more negative behaviors than do normal infants.

Frequency. Down's syndrome is the most frequent chromosomal anomaly, accounting for 1 in 800 to 1000 births (Fraser, 1984; NIH *Antenatal Diagnosis,* 1979). It appears that trisomy 21 may actually occur in 1 in every 200 conceptions. Thus some 75% of trisomy 21 zygotes are spontaneously aborted (Polani, 1966). From 10 to 20% of all moderately and severely retarded children (the second and third most severe categories of retardation) are Down's cases.

The frequency data need to be broken down by age of the mother in order for the risks to be understood properly. Down's babies are rarely born to young mothers (the risk is 1 in 2400 for mothers 15 to 19), but the rates start to rise dramatically after the mother reaches 30. By the maternal age of 40 years the risk is 1 in 109, by 45 it is 1 in 32, and by 49, 1 in 12. Fathers are the source of the extra chromosome in 25% of the cases, however, and paternal age does not appear to be related to the frequency of occurrence.

Forms and Mechanisms. The complexities of genetic mechanisms are well illustrated by the several forms of Down's syndrome. Although all forms have some abnormality involving the 21st chromosome, the nature of the abnormality varies somewhat and there are different causes for the abnormalities. The most common cause, called **nondisjunction** (failure to divide properly), accounts for 95% of all cases. Nondisjunction occurs during **meiosis,** the cell division that results in the formation of germ cells (ova and spermatozoa). When a pair of chromosomes fails to separate during meiosis, then both chromosomes may

diagnosis and monitoring, Down's children who survive until the age of 5 years are now likely to live to age 40 (Pueschel, 1983) and their long-term life expectancy is not yet known.

The most prominent behavioral characteristic of Down's syndrome is mental retardation. Another behavioral feature commonly described is a pleasant, placid disposition, although the limited available evidence suggests that such an attribution is not entirely accurate for Down's children during infancy. Mothers filling out Carey's Infant Temperament Questionnaire did not describe their Down's infants as easier than did a sample of enter one germ cell. When the abnormal germ cell from one parent joins a normal germ cell from the other parent, the resulting zygote (fertilized egg) has three chromosomes. In Down's syndrome, it is chromosome number 21 that has not separated. The technical description of the karyotype (or description of the physical appearance of the chromosomes of a single cell) for such people is 47,XX,21+ or 47,XY,21+ (for females and males respectively). The three parts of the description identify: (1) the total number of chromosomes (47, not the normal 46); (2) which sex chromosomes are present (XX or XY); and (3) the chromosome that has become a triplet (pair 21).

Nondisjunction is usually not inherited. After a mother has a child with a nondisjunction, she is not at increased risk for having another. Rather, her risk is about the same as that for any mother of her age. Nondisjunction is, however, markedly affected by the age of the mother.

A rarer form of Down's syndrome, which accounts for only 4% of all cases, is the result of a mechanism called **translocation** because extra material from the 21st chromosome is attached to some other chromosome. One-third of these cases are inherited; the others, like the cases of nondisjunction, result from spontaneous errors in the formation of the egg or sperm. In translocation the chromosome breaks during meiosis and a piece becomes attached to another chromosome or wrongly attached to chromosome 21 (for example, tops and bottoms are inverted). Women who carry a translocated chromosome 21 (45, XX, 21−) may be normal, but about 1 in 5 of their offspring has Down's syndrome (the rates vary from 1 in 1 to 1 in 60, depending on which of the other chromosomes has the extra material attached to it). Other offspring will appear to be normal, but may be carriers like their mother. When young mothers give birth to Down's children, they or their husbands are likely to be carriers.[5] Because the risk of having another Down's syndrome child may differ for parents of a nondisjunction Down's baby and for those of a translocation Down's child, karyotyping of the

Down's syndrome infant can help the parents make plans about future child bearing.

A third chromosomal abnormality that results in Down's syndrome is called **mosaicism.** Normally all cells in an organism have the same chromosomal makeup (except the germ cells, which have 23 rather than 46 chromosomes). In some persons, however, cells vary as do the stones in a mosaic. Some cells have the normal number of chromosomes and others do not. Mosaicism may result from nondisjunction occurring after the egg has been fertilized, in other words, during **mitosis**, the form of cell division found in all nongerm cells in which both the original and the offspring cells have 46 chromosomes. If the nondisjunction happens early in development it has widespread effects. Even if only one of the abnormal cells lived and reproduced, its descendents would be distributed widely through the body. Mosiacism involving the 21st chromosome may result in Down's syndrome. Individuals who are mosaic for Down's syndrome tend to have fewer of the symptoms that normally characterize the disorder. They might, for example, have a simian crease and epicanthic folds, but not have thick tongues or heart abnormalities or any other combination of the stigmata associated with Down's syndrome. They may suffer less severe retardation and may even appear normal in intelligence. When a mosaic mother is pregnant it is a good idea to determine whether the fetus has normal chromosomes by karyotyping its cells, which can be obtained by amniocentesis.

Social Issues. Now let us turn to the social issues that can be illustrated using Down's syndrome. In the past, many infants with this syndrome were institutionalized at birth or shortly after. This was true even before genetic analysis was available because Down's infants can usually be recognized or diagnosed at birth on the basis of physical characteristics. Because the outlook (or prognosis) for intellectual development was poor for these babies, their parents were often advised to institutionalize them quickly in order to avoid becoming too attached and to prevent problems for present or anticipated brothers and sisters. More recently, it was found that the intellectual growth of Down's babies who were kept at home was often better than that of those in institutions. Subsequently, experts encouraged parents to

---

[5] The mother is about twice as likely to be the carrier as the father, presumably because spermatozoa with an aberrant chromosome complement are less likely to succeed in fertilizing an egg.

keep their afflicted child at home as long as possible.

As is frequently the case, the pendulum may have swung too far. It is all well and good to advise parents to keep a child with Down's syndrome at home and to provide a maximally stimulating environment for that child, but this advice is often not accompanied by sufficient help in dealing with the inherent problems. This advice may even increase the guilt feelings parents have, especially if they find they cannot cope with the problems and later want to institutionalize the child. Even if the Down's infant can be kept at home fairly easily, increasing age brings increasing problems. When the child reaches adolescence the problems of sexuality and pregnancy arise (incidentally, more females than males have Down's syndrome). As parents get older, they find it increasingly difficult to cope with the burden, and other family members are seldom ready and willing to assume the responsibility. What is to be done then? Will adults with Down's syndrome adapt to institutions as readily as they would have as children? Will the parents feel any less guilty having to institutionalize their offspring because of their inability to care for them?

Parents must weigh the potential stress that coping with these problems might create for themselves and other family members against the potential advantages to the afflicted child. People who advocate home rearing are impressed because (1) Down's syndrome children raised at home may have an IQ (intelligence quotient, a standard measure of intelligence) that is 15 points higher than that of those raised in institutions and (2) a relatively large proportion of home-reared children (13 to 34%, depending on the study) are only mildly retarded (have IQs of 50 to 69), whereas only 1 to 4% of institutionalized cases have IQs that high. Although the difference between institutionalized and home-reared Down's children is sizable, it is probably exaggerated because the more seriously retarded children are more likely to be institutionalized and to be institutionalized earlier. In addition, Down's children raised at home are still likely to be quite retarded. In Cornwell and Birch's (1969) sample of home-reared Down's children, the majority were moderately or severely retarded (their IQs were between 24 and 49). Further-

more, because the IQs of both institutionalized and home-reared cases decline with age, children whose IQs are in the middle 50s in the preschool years may have IQs in the 30s by their teens. Thus rearing Down's children at home will not eliminate retardation. Nevertheless, it is possible that for relatively bright Down's individuals, home rearing could make the difference between being completely dependent on others and being able to function in a sheltered workshop as an adult.

Although institutionalized Down's children in general have lower IQs than those who are home reared, some institutions have been able to improve intellectual performance in their Down's children by special programs. One state hospital worked with a group of Down's children who were 8 years old and had mental ages of 2 or 3. These children had been hospitalized since they were 3 to 5 months old. The workers stressed language skills and dealt with the children both individually and in groups of five. The IQs of these children stopped dropping, they began to talk and use names, and some even learned to read (Stedman & Eichorn, 1964). These results show that intellectual development can be stimulated in institutions as well as in homes. They do not tell us whether institutions can equal homes in intellectual stimulation. Under current conditions, however, it is probable that the average home environment provides better intellectual stimulation than the average institution. Note, however, that home care is not necessarily stimulating. Some parents are not stimulating to either normal or abnormal infants. Some normally stimulating parents react to their infant's handicap by providing lots of tender loving care but little stimulation and few demands. Strong demands accompanied by love may be needed for optimal development.

So far we have focused on intellectual development in children reared in institutions as compared to that of those reared at home. We can make the same comparisons with respect to emotional development. Although people might assume that the loving warmth of a family is the only adequate environment for emotional well-being, it is not clear that living in institutions is necessarily worse for the emotional well-being of Down's children. The quality of the institution is crucial, of course, but it appears that Down's individuals adapt well to institutional life. This general statement does not hold true for every individual and may depend in part on the age at which Down's individuals are placed in an institution. Home life, which is usually less regular or predictable than institutional life, may produce emotional problems, particularly if family members feel resentful toward the child.

Whether or not home rearing is an appropriate alternative for a Down's child also depends on the kind of support the primary caretaker, usually the mother, has. Some families can afford to hire help to ease the 24-hour burden of a relatively dependent child. Others must depend for support on society, which is only beginning to move toward solutions to such problems. There are, for example, some sheltered apartments, homes, and workshops, and at least one entire community that is sheltered. Community placement of formerly institutionalized cases can be at various levels of care, and as in all such matters, quality can vary widely.

Another kind of societal support is found in preschool programs designed to enable Down's syndrome children to reach optimal levels of functioning. One such program is the Multidisciplinary Preschool Program for Down's Syndrome Children at the University of Washington Model Preschool Center in Seattle. Its philosophy is that early education and work with parents is essential. The preschool program starts almost at birth. There are four levels in the program: (1) an Infant Learning Program that meets once a week for 30 minutes of parent training in early motor and sensory development (children from 5 weeks through 18 months); (2) an Early Preschool Program that meets 2 hours a day, 4 days a week with mothers participating for 1 day (18 months to 3 years); (3) an Advanced Preschool Program for children from 3 to 5; and (4) a kindergarten for those 4½ to 6 (Hayden & Dmitriev, 1975). It is not possible to reach any firm conclusions on the basis of the small sample, which contains a wide range of ages and children who entered the program at very different ages. Their results to date appear to be impressive. For example, the developmental lag on the Peabody Picture Vocabulary Test for children already in the program is about 6.5 months compared to 21 months for children of

the same ages who have just entered the program. In addition, children in the program were still showing IQ gains rather than losses and the average IQ was in the low 80s, which is high for those with Down's syndrome. The children lag more in language than in other areas, but some of them were making progress in learning to read. A variety of factors such as size of the sample, age, and varying length of time in the program make adequate determination of the long-term outcomes difficult. Subsequent publications by this group have not provided data that answer the questions about long-term outcomes. A very different effect of the program, which is relevant to our general discussion, is that parents who have been in it and who have left the area have started programs in their new communities.

Sheltered workshops, preschool programs, and other sorts of community support for home-reared retarded do, of course, cost money. However, because the cost of institutionalizing a single Down's victim for an entire lifetime is estimated to run between $200,000 and $250,000, it is likely that community support that would allow more families to keep their Down's children at home would cost society less. Nevertheless, in the current era of cutbacks in human services and in behavioral science research, such cost effectiveness does not seem to be a factor in governmental calculations and a slowdown in the development of public support systems has already occurred.

The best environment for a given Down's child depends of course on individual circumstances. These include the characteristics of the child as well as the psychological strengths of parents and other children in the family, the financial capabilities for providing caretakers, and the community's resources for aiding both the parents and the child. For many Down's children and their families the best solution undoubtedly still is an institution, but only those in the lowest IQ ranges will currently be accepted in many state institutions.

We have discussed the questions of the handling of infants with Down's syndrome in considerable detail because they illustrate the more general issues that apply to a number of the severe problems that are seen either at birth or in infancy. Clearly these issues are present beyond infancy, and indeed the problems may become greater as the child grows older.

OTHER ABNORMALITIES OF AUTOSOMAL CHROMOSOMES

If trisomy 21 exists and causes problems, what about trisomies of other chromosomes? What about the other egg cell that received no chromosome 21 at all and would, if fertilized, result in a person with a missing chromosome? Monosomic zygotes, with the exception of those missing one sex chromosome, do not survive embryonic life. Trisomic individuals also have high intrauterine mortality and only those from the smallest chromosomes (see Figure 3–1) survive infancy with any frequency. Most of those, as we have already seen, constitute the most common form of Down's syndrome (trisomy 21). The next most frequent is trisomy 18, which is sometimes viable. It is the most frequent chromosomal abnormality among late pregnancy abortions and deaths during labor and delivery, occurring in over 25% of such cases (Bauld et al., 1974; Machin, 1974). As is true for trisomy 21, the frequency of trisomy 18 increases greatly with maternal age. It occurs in less than 1% of infants born to mothers under 20 years of age but in 30–40% of infants whose mothers are over 40. For a brief description and pictures of the other gross chromosomal anomalies, see Fraser (1984).

ABNORMALITIES OF SEX CHROMOSOMES

Abnormalities of the sex chromosomes occur in several forms. The one viable case of a person with a totally missing chromosome is a person with a single sex (X) chromosome. This anomaly is called Turner's syndrome and the karyotype is 45,X0 (the zero stands for the missing chromosome). Even though persons with this abnormality sometimes survive, it is estimated that 95% of all such conceptions are aborted. There are also individuals with extra sex chromosomes. These include 47,XXX; 47,XXY; and 47,XYY. Even more Xs are sometimes found. These abnormalities are caused by nondisjunction during meiosis of either the sperm or egg. Variations in the number of sex chromosomes involving extra Xs appear to be more viable than those in other chromosomes

because in the later stages of development and after birth all Xs in excess of 1 become inactive. This theory is not fully confirmed, but appears likely and is attractive to many experts since it would explain a number of other genetic puzzles as well.

Although problems from abnormal complements of sex chromosomes do not create particular treatment problems in early infancy, we include them because these abnormalities are detected during karyotyping. As prenatal karyotyping becomes more and more common, more and more parents will learn of their offspring's chromosomal anomalies before birth. It is thus important to understand the implications of these disorders for development, particularly when controversial allegations about personality characteristics are made, as they have been for the XYY anomaly.

Most abnormalities of the sex chromosomes affect reproductive functioning and physical development. Some are also considered to involve intellectual deficiency or behavioral problems or both, but these characteristics are often questionable. Most of our knowledge of chromosomal anomalies comes from examinations of individuals who are brought to the attention of the medical establishment because of a physical, intellectual, or behavioral problem. This kind of study suffers from two kinds of sampling biases. First, those who might have the chromosomal abnormality without any other detectable abnormalities would not be studied. Second, those typically studied are already adults and many of the abnormal group would have died, been put into institutions for the retarded, or in other ways been lost from the population under study. To ascertain whether a given chromosomal anomaly actually plays a role in a given problem, it must be determined that people with that anomaly are more likely to have a particular problem than a comparable sample of chromosomally normal individuals. This could be done only in a **prospective study,** in which the subjects are selected before the problem manifests itself and are studied longitudinally. In this section, when methodologically rigorous data are available, we will note it. We will also discuss the controversial allegations about the XYY anomaly, since that controversy was created by the dissemination of unjustified conclusions drawn from methodologically unacceptable data.

Turner's Syndrome. Infants born with a 45,X0 chromosomal complement (monosomy) appear to be normal females at birth, although a karyotype would of course reveal the abnormality. Their abnormality often becomes apparent during childhood because they experience abnormally early sexual development (called infantile sexual development), although they never commence menstruation. At maturity they are shorter than average, have webbed necks and poor mammary development, and their external genitalia appear immature. Internally they either lack ovaries or whatever tissue there is fails to produce ova, so they are sterile. Most Turner's individuals have normal intelligence and no neurological defects have been found. The nine cases in a prospective study by Pennington, Bender, Puck, Salbenblatt, and Robinson (1982) did have the commonly found visual–spatial problems, and performance IQs were lower than verbal. They also exhibited problems with handwriting in school. This abnormality occurs about once in every 2500 to 5000 births. Lubs (1970) accumulated data from a group of studies that had used appropriate sampling procedures in newborns, and these data suggest that 1 in 2500 births is the most accurate rate. Unlike most other nondisjunction syndromes, the frequency of births of Turner's babies does not increase with maternal age.

Current treatment of Turner's syndrome consists of administration of female hormones to lessen the symptoms of infantile sexual development. Turner's individuals often have psychological difficulties because of their appearance and because of parental attitudes. These are called **indirect effects** because the chromosomal abnormality does not directly cause the psychological problems; rather it causes some other problems (such as appearance) that cause the psychological problems.

Trisomy X. Females with three X chromosomes (47,XXX) apparently do not characteristically have the physical abnormalities typical of other sex chromosome abnormalities, although Lubs (1970) did find major physical anomalies in two of the nine cases found in a large unselected group of karyotyped infants.

Unlike Turner's syndrome, the sexual structures of trisomy X individuals develop normally and they are fertile. Menstrual irregularities and early menopause (this anomaly has sometimes been called the early menopause syndrome) have been reported, but there is little evidence to demonstrate that trisomy X individuals differ from normal XX women in these respects (Hsia, 1968). Intellectual development does appear to be affected by trisomy X. Lubs (1970) reported that 3 of his 9 cases had borderline IQs. The 11 cases found in the Pennington et al. (1982) study tended to show global delay in intellectual development without being actually retarded and they tended to need speech therapy in school. Furthermore, the incidence of trisomy X in institutions for the retarded is 39 per 1000 but that in the general population is 14 per 1000 (McClearn & DeFries, 1973). There are conflicting reports concerning the relation of frequency of trisomy X to parental age.

Klinefelter's Syndrome. Infants born with an extra X chromosome (47,XXY) are males who have small and immature testes, which means they will be sterile. At maturity they have little facial or body hair and lack other secondary sexual characteristics. To make matters worse, they have female-like breast development. Mental retardation or lower intelligence apparently is part of this syndrome. A particularly large and impressive chromosomal study of Danish men (Witkin et al., 1976) found that Klinefelter's men had significantly lower scores than normal men on the intelligence test given Danish army inductees, and had less education. Whether these data represent a higher proportion of mentally retarded individuals, generally lower but mostly normal intelligence, or differences in related skills such as perseverance or motivation, is not clear. Studies of various non-randomly selected groups have found rates of retardation of from 25–50%, but Lubs' (1970) review of prospective data found that only 1 in 15 cases was below normal intelligence as measured by standard IQ tests. The 15 cases found in the study by Pennington and colleagues (1982) exhibited verbal deficits (with performance IQ higher than verbal), attention problems, reading difficulties, and tended to need speech therapy.

Klinefelter's syndrome has also been associated with a variety of personality and emotional problems. For example, Jarvik, Klodin, and Matsuyama (1973), who accumulated the data from several earlier reports, found that XXY men constituted a higher proportion of residents in mental hospitals than in the general population. These and other available data do not necessarily lead to the conclusion that the chromosomal abnormality produced the psychological abnormalities. Many such problems are likely to be indirect effects due to the physical appearance of the affected individuals.

Klinefelter's is somewhat more frequent than Turner's syndrome; it occurs in from 1 to 1000 to 1 in 2200 births, according to the prospective studies cited by Lubs (1970). Like most nondisjunction syndromes (other than Turner's), it does increase in frequency with maternal age. Incidentally, it occurs with about equal frequency in Blacks and whites. As with Turner's syndrome, sex hormones can be used therapeutically. Androgen can be used to stimulate development of secondary sex characteristics and thereby alleviate some of the indirect effects due to the negative influence of appearance.

XYY Anomaly. The chromosomal defect that has perhaps attracted the most controversy is the one involving an extra Y chromosome. This defect was discovered accidentally in 1961 when a man was karyotyped because he was the father of a child with Down's syndrome. Subsequently several other cases were discovered accidentally when males with some sort of physical abnormality (often undescended testes or genital abnormalities) were examined. In 1965 seven men who were XYY and one who was XXYY were found among a group of 197 hard-to-manage retarded men. The XYY pattern was then found to occur rather frequently among highly aggressive criminals in penal institutions. Even though there were no data at that time to demonstrate that the XYY rate was higher in these aggressive populations than in the general population, many people concluded that an extra Y chromosome causes abnormally high aggressiveness. In spite of several articles discussing the methodological problems of this research (Kessler & Moos, 1970; Kivowitz, 1972), the press widely disseminated the belief that XYY males are hyperaggressive. An Australian court of law even ruled that an XYY murderer could not be held responsible for his actions and should not receive the maximum penalty. Presumably the extra Y chromosome should have!

The first step in evaluating these claims is to determine the **base rate** (the rate of occurrence in the general population). Although early estimates of frequency of XYY males in the general population varied widely (from 1 in 250 to 1 in 2000 in studies reviewed by Jarvik et al. in 1973), enough newborn screening studies have been done to make a reliable estimate. When Jarvik and colleagues combined the data of such studies, they found an incidence of 0.13% (approximately 1 per 1000). There may also be a race difference, although the evidence is contradictory. Walzer, Breau, and Gerald (1969) reported a frequency of 1 in 862 among 10,817 Caucasians, but no cases among 2756 Blacks. In contrast, another study reported no race difference in newborn rates, which should provide the most accurate estimate. No differences were found according to socioeconomic status (SES) or maternal age in the large-scale Walzer and Gerald study (1975).

XYY anomaly has been associated with low intelligence, above-average height, and emotional difficulties of various sorts as well as with unusually high aggressiveness. The large chromosomal study of Danish men by Witkin and colleagues (1976) found that the XYY cases, like the XXY cases, performed significantly below normal on an army intelligence test and had not achieved as high educational levels as had normal men. Jarvik and colleagues (1973) found six earlier studies of the incidence of XYY individuals in mental hospitals, and the cumulative results indicated that the proportion of XYY persons in mental hospitals (compared to other patients) is higher than the base rate of XYY in the general population. Both studies included comparisons with Klinefelter's (XXY) males. The rates for intelligence and level of education and for presence in mental hospitals were the same for these two anomalies of male sex chromosomes. This suggests that it is not the extra Y or extra X that produces mental disturbance. It may be that any disturbance in the XY chromosome balance predisposes one to intellectual and emotional difficulties, but such difficulties may also result from indirect effects, such as those noted in discussions of the effects of other sex chromosome anomalies.

The question of whether unusually high aggressiveness is associated with the XYY chromosomal pattern has received particular research attention. Jarvik and colleagues (1973) found 25 studies of XYY males in criminal populations. When all the samples were considered together (5066 subjects), the total frequency of XYY was 1.9%, which is 15 times that found in either newborn males or the general adult male population.[6] Although such results from a large sample seem to support the hypothesis that an extra Y increases the risk of hyperaggressiveness, other studies suggest alternative interpretations. An important factor is that the XYY anomaly is associated with other characteristics. There is a clear excess of XYY karyotypes among tall men who are antisocial to the extent of needing to be restrained and who are also mentally subnormal (Casey, Blank, & Street, 1969). Thus, it may not be the extra Y chromosome that causes high aggressiveness. The extra Y chromosome might cause men to be tall and of low intelligence, and these factors might indirectly cause aggressiveness. This would be true if (1) tall men are likely to be more effective in their aggressiveness than short men, and (2) less intelligent persons are more likely to get caught than more intelligent ones. Indeed, any picture that shows large groups of male prisoners is likely to contain a preponderance of large muscular men and relatively few short skinny men. Likewise, if we obtain data on their intelligence we will find a large proportion who are below normal.

Research since 1965 also suggests that

aggressiveness may not be the appropriate target characteristic. The studies just cited used criminality or antisocial personality as the measure of aggressiveness. While antisocial persons are often criminals and commit aggressive acts, their primary characteristics are impulsivity, inability to delay gratification, lack of planning ability, and a tendency not to learn from past punishment. The large study by Witkin and colleagues of Danish males (1976) directly compared criminality to aggressiveness. It found that XYY individuals committed more criminal offenses, but they did not commit violent crimes more frequently than normal XY males or than XXY (Klinefelter's) males.

These research data on the relationship of height, antisocial behavior, and XYY provide an example of one of the major problems of correlational research. The research itself does not tell us about causation. Subjects cannot be randomly assigned to be XY or XYY. In addition, supporting data that would make causal inference more reasonable are lacking. For example, the base rate of XYY for tall men who are not in institutions is not known. Without such evidence concerning causality, there is no way to decide between the direct cause and indirect cause interpretations.

A study that would resolve the controversy and shed light on the interactions just mentioned would be one that follows the development of XYY and closely matched XY boys from birth. If the XYY boys were to exhibit greater aggressiveness in early infancy when their environments after birth had had little chance to have an effect, we would be more inclined to give credence to the causal role of the Y chromosome. If virtually all the XYY infants were aggressive, we might conclude that the extra Y chromosome produced the hyperaggressiveness or antisocial personality. If only an excessive number of XYYs were aggressive, we might talk about its predisposing role. If aggressiveness or antisocial personality were to develop later, but was totally unrelated to the kind of child care, the role of the extra Y would also be more certain.

Such results would also be of great interest to those who would like to be able to counsel parents of XYY males. It is a curious twist of fate that a study designed to do just that was aborted as a result of a challenge to the ethics

---

[6]Racial differences in the incidence of XYY types have been found among highly aggressive populations. A report issued in 1974 showed that whites in institutional "security settings" were three times as likely as Blacks in the same institutional settings to have an XYY karyotype. This would presumably be congruent with an interpretation that genetics plays a greater role in this type of crime for whites than for Blacks. It would obviously also be tempting to conclude that social or environmental forces play a greater role in this type of crime for Blacks. Nevertheless, it is difficult to come to any conclusion about the reasons for this reported race difference in incidence of XYY among criminals until we know for sure whether there are race differences in the frequency of XYY in the general population.

of the study. Some of the challengers believed that parents were being told their boys were XYY cases and the researchers wished to follow them. If true, that would have posed serious problems, both ethical and scientific. The ethical problems are that (1) because of the publicity surrounding the study, parents might expect their child to become aggressive, perhaps even criminal, and might communicate that expectation to the child in such a way as to encourage him to become deviant; and (2) on the basis of current knowledge, such parents would be frightened without sufficient evidence and without being offered a way out of the dilemma—that is, a cure. The first ethical problem also poses a scientific dilemma in that the parents' expectation that their sons might be hyperaggressive might affect their son's behavior. Therefore, it would be impossible to tell whether any differences found between the XYY boys and XY boys were related to the extra Y chromosomes or to their parents' expectations. In fact, the investigators told parents that their son had a little piece of chromosome that was broken off and that the possible significance of this was unknown. They were told that they could call the hospital for help if any problems arose. This explanation eliminated the first, but not the second, ethical problem, because it is hardly clear that the doctors would have known how to help.

The publicity brought about by the attacks on the project enabled parents to figure out that their children might be in that project, and ultimately the investigators had to disband it. Hence, efforts to protect the rights of subjects in scientific studies actually prevented the acquisition of the desired prospective data. This in itself led to a controversy. The researchers represented one side, who felt that the issues being studied were important enough to warrant their identifying XYY babies, particularly because they had worked out a reasonably ethical procedure. They were understandably distraught that misconceptions about their procedure forced the project's early demise. Opponents of the research, although also unhappy about the course of this particular incident, argued that such a study should only be undertaken if no feasible alternative approach would suffice and if the problem was of great societal importance. The XYY research, they argued, failed on both counts. First, other types of studies, although requiring more cases to be studied, could yield the same information. Second, the XYY anomaly is extremely rare; it represents fewer than 2% of the prison population. Since this study was terminated, enough evidence has accumulated to make the original hypothesis that the extra Y produces aggression seem unlikely. Nevertheless, this type of ethical debate is repeated over and over in various areas of research with humans.

Abnormalities Resulting From Gene Defects

Now that we have surveyed some kinds of damage resulting from chromosomal abnormalities, let us turn to problems that are caused by the genes on the chromosomes. Genes are the units of the chromosomes that carry specific genetic information. A number of physiological conditions result from specific gene defects. We will discuss a few that are relevant to issues of genetic counseling and/or intervention during infancy. Because most of the disorders we will discuss are caused by a single autosomal recessive gene, we will briefly explain the mechanism first. The word "autosomal" indicates that the problem lies on one of the 22 paired chromosomes other than the sex chromosomes. Genes work in pairs, at corresponding sites of a pair of chromosomes. Each site can be in one of two states (technically, one of two alleles).[7] If one state or allele is dominant, the trait it governs will be expressed in the phenotype. The other possible state (allele) is recessive. A **recessive** trait will only be expressed in the phenotype when both genes in the pair have the recessive allele. Because one chromosome comes from the mother and one from the father, both parents must have passed on a recessive allele to an afflicted baby. In the gene defects we will be discussing, the parents rarely suffer from the same defect. Rather, they are **heterozygous carriers.** This means that both have one dominant (normal) gene and one recessive (non-normal) gene, and both of them passed that defective recessive gene on to their offspring in the sperm and ovum. Because each parent's domi-

---

[7]The states at each site are like the two positions of a toggle switch, on or off.

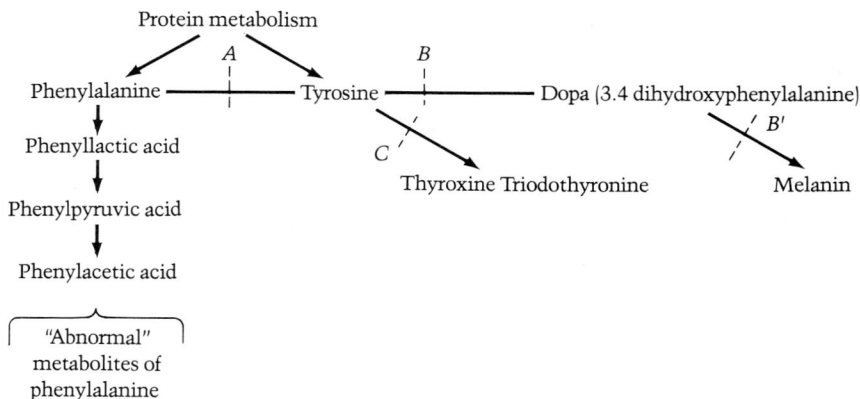

FIGURE 3–3. *Steps in the metabolism of the amino acids phenylalanine and tyrosine. Blocks at the lettered points result in certain disorders. A block at A, caused by an enzyme deficiency, results in a build-up of phenylalanine and the resulting mental retardation syndrome known as phenylketonuria (PKU). The column extending downward from phenylalanine represents other chemicals that result when the normal metabolic pathway is blocked. A block at B or B′ prevents the formation of melanin, the pigment that gives color to hair, skin, and eyes, and thus produces albinism. A block at C leads to a low level of the hormones thyroxine and tri-iodothyronine, which produces goiterous cretinism with its associated mental retardation and small stature. (Adapted with permission from J.R. Vale,* Genes, Environment, and Behavior: An Interactionist Approach. *New York: Harper & Row, 1980, p. 223.)*

nant gene dominates their recessive gene, parents usually do not show signs of the defect. Nevertheless, the recessive gene of a heterozygous carrier does occasionally have some detectable effects (called intermediate or incomplete dominance).

Single gene recessive traits are not the only kind of genetic disorders, although they are the most frequent of the known disorders. Some traits are carried by dominant genes; some are carried on the sex chromosomes and have their own pattern of inheritance (called X-linked); and some traits (called polygenic) result from the action of many genes. Indeed, most of the traits that psychologists are interested in are probably polygenic. Nevertheless, we will concentrate on those traits with single recessive inheritance patterns, because they have been the source of much of the current understanding of genetic mechanisms. Many of them are related to the lack of an enzyme that is crucial for the metabolism of food. The diagram in Figure 3–3 should help you understand the examples we will discuss. The diagram also shows where some treatment efforts using enzymes

might lie. We will discuss other types of treatment later in our discussion of genetic counseling.

TAY-SACHS DISEASE

Tay-Sachs disease is a result of an enzyme deficiency caused by a single autosomal recessive gene. The enzyme hexosamidase A is missing, and this causes various fatty substances to build up in body cells, including those of the brain. The parents, who are heterozygous carriers, each have only about half the normal amount of this enzyme, an amount that is sufficient to make them appear normal (this is one of many examples of built-in biological safety factors in humans and other animals).

Tay-Sachs infants appear normal at birth, but the nervous system is gradually destroyed because of the effects of the missing enzyme. The effects are seen starting at around 3 to 6 months after birth. Tay-Sachs babies gradually lose motoric abilities, such as the abilities to sit up and to roll over. They become deaf and blind and deteriorate intellectually. Death is inevitable, occurring by 4 to 6 years of age. The psychological tragedy of watching what was apparently a healthy baby deteriorate and die in this fashion can hardly be overestimated. In addition to the psychological costs, medical costs are great. The costs of caring for one of these children during its brief lifetime can come to $150 thousand.

Tay-Sachs disease is rare in general, but not equally so in all ethnic groups. Among non-Jews it occurs in only 1 out of 300,000 pregnancies. Among Ashkenazic Jews (those from eastern Europe, which includes about 90% of American Jews), 1 in 30 persons is a carrier. This means that the likelihood that both parents will be carriers is 1 in 900, and because it is an autosomal recessive trait, one of every four offspring of two carriers will have the disease. Therefore, 1 in every 3600 pregnancies among Ashkenazic Jews will result in a Tay-Sachs child. In mixed marriages this frequency becomes 1 in 30,000.

Fortunately, the level of the enzyme hexosamidase A can be measured. This permits prenatal screening of the amniotic fluid to detect Tay-Sachs disease. Carriers also have decreased activity of hexosamidase A compared to healthy or homozygous dominant individuals, and thus carriers can also be detected. Prospective parents who are both carriers then know that they have a 25% chance of giving birth to a Tay-Sachs baby. They can decide not to conceive, to conceive and abort the fetus if it has Tay-Sachs, or they can at least psychologically prepare themselves for the risk they are taking in reproducing.

PHENYLKETONURIA (PKU)

PKU is a particularly interesting disease to examine, not only because it is in the news and dramatic in its effects (though early death does not occur), but also because it was the first of the inborn errors of metabolism whose effects doctors have learned to deal with by environmental manipulation. Like Tay-Sachs disease and most of the other inborn errors of metabolism, PKU is inherited as a simple autosomal recessive characteristic. The problem again is the inability to produce a crucial enzyme that is normally produced by the liver and is necessary for the proper digestion of phenylalanine, a substance that is a constituent of natural proteins. Most food proteins, including milk, contain 4 to 6% phenylalanine. PKU infants will build up large concentrations of phenylalanine and other abnormal metabolic products (see Figure 3–3). These abnormal metabolites affect the central nervous system, especially the brain, in ways that are not fully understood.

The primary symptoms of the disease are severe retardation, often accompanied by hyperactivity and other behavioral problems. In general the infant appears normal at birth and shows normal progress for the first 1 to 3 months. Between then and about 6 months the infant is likely to become unresponsive and listless or, in contrast, extremely irritable. Developmental milestones such as sitting up and turning over aren't accomplished on schedule. Progressive retardation occurs and by 4 years of age the afflicted children are characteristically very retarded. Minor physical characteristics or stigmata are associated with the disease, but they are not very obvious early in infancy. The primary ones involve pigmentation, with skin, hair, and eye color being light. Some PKU infants tend to have vomiting or other feeding difficulties or both. Some cases show excessive irritability or overactivity early and others develop these symptoms more slowly (Berry, 1976).

Importance. Although PKU does not occur frequently, it is the metabolic disorder that is tested for most often in major screening programs. It is also of practical importance because of the substantial numbers of institutionalized retarded who result from PKU. After evidence accumulated that its expression (effects) could be controlled environmentally by providing a diet with very little phenylalanine, its early detection became important in order to avoid wasted lives, parental heartbreak, and the costs of institutionalization.

Frequency. Estimates for rates of occurrence range from 1 in 10,000 to 1 in 40,000 births. A statewide screening program in Massachusetts tested 97–98% of all babies born in the state. It found 54 PKU babies in 747,000 births, and 46 atypical PKU babies (Levy, Karolkewicz, Houghton, & MacCready, 1970). These are by far the most frequently identified disorders in their neonatal screening. The atypical or mild form is not associated with retardation, but the classical type is rarely found with normal intelligence unless it is treated (Levy et al., 1970). British studies have found about the same rate (Smith & Wolff, 1974).

Screening. The substantial numbers combined with a potential treatment led to wide-scale pressures to make neonatal screening for PKU mandatory. As of 1974, 36 states had laws requiring it and another seven had laws recommending screening. The error rate with initial screening procedures, at least in this country, raised serious questions. Much of the error stemmed from the fact that the urine test used initially did not become accurate until a few weeks after birth when the infant had been carrying on its own metabolism separate from the maternal system. In the health care system that exists in the United States, many infants would be lost to testing if it were not done during the brief hospital stay.

The blood test used today is accurate earlier than the urine test was, but still depends on the infant's postnatal processing of its food intake. It appears to be 92% effective (Holtzman, Meek, & Mellits, 1974), and the misses are often related to too early testing. This problem doesn't exist in Great Britain where every baby is seen at home within 14 days of birth by a health visitor who tests any babies that were not born in the hospital or who left the hospital prior to 7 days of age.

Although a blood test at 4–6 weeks used to be advocated for all cases where feasible, so few additional cases are found that the usefulness of this practice is questionable. The Massachusetts screening program has replaced the blood test with a urine test. The mother is given a filter paper that she is to soak in urine on a diaper at 4–6 weeks and mail in for testing. This specimen can also be used to test for a wide range of defects in amino acid metabolism and transport (Levy et al., 1970).

Dietary Treatment. The dietary treatment for PKU poses its own issues and problems. The Committee on Nutrition of the American Academy of Pediatrics noted that dietary treatment of all hereditary metabolic diseases, including PKU, is simpler in theory than it is in fact (Lowe et al., 1967). It suggested that three questions be answered before dietary treatment for any given disorder is instituted: (1) Is

the untreated disease harmful? (2) Is the treatment useful? (3) Can the dietary treatment cause harm either to actual cases of the disease or to those treated by mistake? We will consider each of these questions in turn.[8]

The first question is of course easy in the case of PKU. The effects of not treating PKU are strong and undesirable. The answer to the second question is also quite clear. Research has demonstrated the effectiveness of proper dietary treatment, although some questions have been raised concerning this conclusion (see for example, Hsia, 1968). Proper treatment has a rigorous set of requirements—that the treatment be started early enough and that the diet be carefully enforced and monitored both to prevent too high a level of phenylalanine and to see that the level of phenylalanine is not kept so low as to interfere with normal growth (Smith, Lobascher, & Wolff, 1973; Smith & Wolff, 1974; Steinhausen, 1974). Let us consider this evidence.

The age at which the diet is started is very important in determining the outcome. There is clearly a critical or sensitive period for the effects on the brain of the inappropriate metabolic products found in PKU (see Kaplan's 1962 review). Infants treated prior to 6 months of age had IQs in the range of 70 (borderline retardation) to 100 (normal). This means that almost all of these children are able to attend normal schools (Smith & Wolff, 1974). To be maximally effective, the diet should be started in the first or second month of life (Berman, Waisman, & Graham, 1966; Hudson, Mordaunt, & Leahy, 1970; Steinhausen, 1974). Those who were started on the diet at 7 to 18 months of age had IQs in the 50 to 70 range (mild and borderline retardation), and those who were not started until after 2 years had IQs below 30 (severe or profound retardation). Motor development follows the same pattern as IQ. Late treatment does have some positive effects, however. It reduces the aggressive and listless behaviors that are also found in PKU children.

One of the reasons there have been questions concerning the effectiveness of the treatment is that there may be some reason other

---

[8] An excellent review of this complex area is to be found in Chapter 3 of the book *Genetic Screening: Programs, Principles, and Research,* published by the National Academy of Sciences in 1975.

than diet for the relatively better outcomes for babies treated earlier, because PKU babies are not randomly assigned to dietary treatment or no treatment groups. For example, parents who are conscientious about following up on screening results, and thereby detecting the PKU condition early, and who seek and follow medical treatment for their children might be generally more conscientious, or be better child rearers in other ways. Their offspring might thereby have higher IQs because they had more effective parents. Smith and Wolff (1974) provided data that make this alternative explanation unlikely. They studied families in which one PKU child was treated early and another was not. Untreated or late-treated siblings had lower IQs.

The third question raised by the Committee on Nutrition of the American Academy of Pediatrics demonstrates the difficulties of dietary treatment for PKU babies. The dietary treatment must be carefully monitored to avoid harm to the child. It is a very restrictive diet, because phenylalanine is part of so many protein foods. In addition, care must be taken to avoid restricting phenylalanine (an essential building block) too severely, because growth is then impaired. Thus, careful enforcement of the diet and monitoring of levels of phenylalanine are needed for optimal results. Relatively few centers in the United States are equipped to help parents do this job well. Furthermore, errors in identification are unavoidable because some people who have elevated levels of phenylalanine do not have PKU, at least in its recognized drastic form. Since they can't be distinguished from children who will suffer irreparable harm, all must be given the diet. The fact that those who started treatment in the second month appear to be as well off as those who started in the first month suggests there is adequate time to allow confirmation of diagnosis. However, the current health care delivery system does not really make this a reality in many places.

Social Implications. Successful treatment of PKU babies means that a large proportion of children with this genetic defect are likely to grow up to be productive members of society and to reproduce. Their potential for reproduction raises two problems for the next generation. First, eugenicists, who argue that genetic

weaknesses should be eliminated from the population by preventing reproduction in genetically inferior people (for example, by sterilization), are concerned that the gene pool is being weakened by allowing treated PKU individuals to reproduce. We should point out, however, that although successful reproduction by treated PKU persons will increase the incidence of the defective gene, sterilizing them would not eliminate the disorder. PKU has been and will be maintained in the population by two mechanisms. First, the disease occurs about as frequently as a result of spontaneous mutations of the genes as it does from inheritance. Second, there are many carriers—estimates range from 1 in 50 to 1 in 100 persons. This high frequency of carriers ensures that PKU will remain in our genetic makeup. Even extreme eugenicists would not wish to sterilize all carriers.

A second problem that is raised by the potential for reproduction by mothers who were successfully treated for PKU as infants is that these women are almost certain to have mentally retarded children. This is true even if the child has not inherited the second defective gene from the father. Lenke and Levy (1980) reviewed world-wide data covering 524 pregnancies of 155 women who had been successfully treated for PKU. Virtually all of their offspring were retarded and 73% were microcephalic if phenylalanine levels were high. Congenital heart defects were also prevalent. If maternal levels of phenylalanine were low, fewer infants were retarded, but even at very low levels 25% were microcephalic. The abnormal metabolism of PKU individuals apparently produces an intrauterine environment that negatively affects development of the fetus. This is true regardless of the offspring's genotype. Some evidence exists that resumption of the diet prior to or during pregnancy, or both, will alleviate these effects on the offspring. But even close compliance with the diet before and during pregnancy may not ensure normality (Lenke & Levy, 1982). This is yet another example of the complex interplay between genetics and environmental events.

In order to improve genetic counseling, Massachusetts and Maryland screen all pregnant women for PKU since the current childbearing generation was not screened in infancy and some persons with milder cases of PKU may have achieved pregnancy. The American College of Obstetricians and Gynecologists has gone still further and advocated PKU screening for all retarded mothers and other "at risk" groups.

CRETINISM

Cretinism is a mental retardation syndrome produced by several different mechanisms, all of which cause inadequate functioning of the thyroid gland. One form, familial goiterous cretinism, is inherited as a single recessive trait through several possible metabolic dysfunctions; one of these mechanisms is diagrammed in Figure 3–3. Other forms are environmentally caused or of unknown origin. Whatever the cause of the insufficiency of thyroid gland hormones, the results for the baby are the same (see also Chapter 4).

The signs appear within a few weeks of birth. Growth is stunted; the body is consequently short, but the head is relatively large; the neck is short and thick; the hands broad and short; the abdomen is enlarged. The face takes on a characteristic pattern of low forehead, puffy and wrinkled eyelids, scanty eyebrows, large depressed nose, thick lips, and large protruding tongue. The skin is dry and the body flabby. Motor and language development is delayed and intellectual retardation is severe. In addition, these babies are inactive and slow to respond.

Fortunately, there is a substitute for thyroid hormone. If administration is started early in infancy and continued with regularity, many of the characteristics of this disorder can be avoided. Treatment late in life is only palliative. Before the development of the desiccated thyroid substance, cretinism accounted for sizable numbers of the institutionalized mentally retarded.

OTHER DISORDERS CAUSED BY GENES

We have discussed only a few of the most common gene disorders, those that are of particular relevance to infancy or infancy-related issues such as prevention and treatment of retardation. For example, the Massachusetts 4-week urine test identifies four other inborn metabolic diseases that occur with about the same frequency as PKU. We have not considered them because they are not associated with retardation. The other retardation syndromes identified by this 4-week urine test are much rarer than PKU (Levy et al., 1970).

Although the gene defects we have discussed in detail are caused by autosomal recessive genes, they are not the only kind. There are also autosomal dominant gene defects and defects carried on the sex chromosomes. We will discuss the latter, X-linked traits, in the section on genetic counseling.

There are five genetic disorders that result from mutant genes each of which causes a different deficiency, but all of which lead to accumulation of toxic levels of ammonium. In the normal case, ammonium would be transformed into urea and excreted in the urine. Toxic levels can cause seizures, brain damage, and even death. About 1 in 2500 newborns has one of these five disorders and most die within 1 year. A group of Johns Hopkins researchers (Brusilow & Batshaw, as cited in the NIH *Record*, April 28, 1981, p. 5) is pioneering an attempt to treat them by increasing the excretion of nitrogen in compounds other than urea, thus reducing the accumulation of ammonium. Dietary therapy providing low protein intake to reduce nitrogen waste works only in mild cases (and requires amino acid supplements because the body lacks the building blocks to produce its own). Bypassing the normal metabolic pathways plus dietary therapy is seen as providing hope for prolonging life and preventing brain damage.

RH Factor: A Complex Gene–Environment Interaction

This discussion of the Rh factor appears here, after the section on genetics and ahead of the section on environmental effects on the fetus, for a very good reason. The fetus has not inherited a defect, but it has inherited a factor in the make-up of its blood that may create an environmental problem for it. Another way of looking at this problem is to view it as an interaction between the genetics of mother and of the fetus. Some people have red cell antigens in their blood. This factor is called Rh because rhesus monkeys have it. Humans who have the antigen are called Rh+ and those who do not are called Rh−. When a mother is Rh−, her baby may inherit RH+ blood from the father.

The baby's chance of inheriting Rh + is 100% if the father is homozygous, 50% if he is heterozygous.[9] If the baby's blood is Rh + and the blood of the baby and mother mix in the uterus, the mother's body will consider the Rh + factor a foreign substance and will produce antibodies.[10] Those antibodies cross the placenta and in effect attack the baby's blood, which leads to a chemical substance in the blood called bilirubin. At birth, the baby appears to have severe jaundice (looks very yellow), a condition that causes kernicterus, a form of brain damage that can lead to death.

The first Rh + baby of an Rh − mother will often be spared any obvious negative effects, since the placental circulation system keeps the mother's and child's blood separate. Problems arise for what appears to be the first baby only if there has been a previous abortion or tubal pregnancy that has led to the mixing of fetal and maternal blood, or a previous transfusion with Rh + blood, or an injury during pregnancy that has led to the mixing of maternal and fetal blood.[11] In the birth process, itself, however, some mixing usually occurs and the mother's body starts to produce the antibodies, so the next Rh + child would be expected to have a problem. The severity would depend on the number of antibodies the mother had developed, which in turn depends on the amount of maternal and infant blood that had mixed. Each succeeding baby would be more likely to be affected, and to be more severely affected. (See Figure 3–4 for an illustration of what happens to the brains of such babies.) Finally the effects would be so severe that the mother would not be able to carry an infant to term. As is often the case with hereditary traits, the troublesome characteristic (Rh −) is unequally distributed in the world. The Rh − genotype occurs in 15% of Caucasians and 5% of Blacks in the United States. It is rare or absent in many populations, especially in eastern Asia,

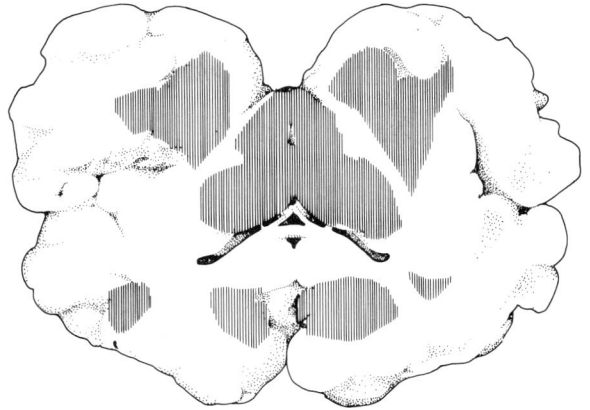

FIGURE 3–4. Cross section of the brain of a baby who had kernicterus. The shaded portions show the damaged parts of the brain that turn yellow.

the Pacific, and among natives of the Americas.[12]

The first step in efforts to conquer this disorder was to test the prospective mother and father to determine whether there was an incompatibility, that is, whether the mother was Rh − and the father was Rh + . If so, they could decide to limit their family size. Next it became possible to test the mother to determine her antibody level during later stages of pregnancy. If it was high and the fetus was viable (mature enough to live outside the womb), it could be delivered then, before it became more affected.

The next improvement in treatment was exchange transfusions. At birth, a longer section of umbilical cord than usual was left attached to the baby and whole blood genetically compatible with its own was pumped in until

---

[9] Actually the Rhesus blood group is not the result of a single gene, but rather of multiple genes, which produce 36 possible combinations in the new organism. Nevertheless, the two combinations relevant to our discussion (Rh + and Rh −) account for 91% of persons in western Europe or North America.

[10] This is the same basic mechanism that is involved in the rejection of skin grafts or organ transplants.

[11] Such injury may result from the implantation process itself.

[12] There are many other possible blood incompatibilities. ABO incompatibility, which is much more frequent but has much less severe effects, results from the same type of autoimmune reaction where the mother has type O blood and the fetus has either A or B. ABO incompatibility may actually protect the fetus from Rh problems because any blood crossing the placental barrier is destroyed before it can produce maternal Rhesus antibodies (Beck, Moffat, & Lloyd, 1973).

all the baby's blood with the damaging bilirubin had been replaced. It might be necessary to do this several times in the newborn period if the baby had high levels of bilirubin as measured by tests rather than the yellow appearance of the skin. Development of a technique to do exchange transfusions while the fetus was still in the uterus further improved treatment.

In the 1950s, third trimester amniocentesis became a useful diagnostic technique. Analysis of the amniotic fluid permitted a direct assessment of the blood type of the fetus and the amount of bilirubin in the fluid, which indicates the severity of the effects of incompatibility. The outcome of these tests helps doctors determine when prenatal blood tranfusions are necessary.

Before effective diagnosis and treatments such as these were developed, some 10,000 babies born in the United States each year either died or suffered brain damage because of Rh incompatibility. By the middle 1960s about 95% of these babies were saved by postnatal exchange transfusions, although not all of those saved from death escaped some residual brain damage because that damage can commence in utero. Of those who would otherwise die in utero, 40% could be saved by prenatal exchange transfusions. Thus, by the 1960s most victims of Rh incompatibility could survive if proper medical treatment were provided.

These techniques were palliative rather than curative, since they did not prevent the attack by the maternal antibodies on the blood of the fetus. Now there is a treatment that does just that: Rhogam injections given to Rh− mothers within 72 hours after the birth of their first child will prevent her Rh+ immunization.[13]

Rh incompatibility is a particularly interesting problem among disorders of development before and during birth. First, it demonstrates that a normal hereditary trait can become maladaptive when the fetus is exposed to a destructive environment. In the next chapter we will see additional examples of subtle interactions between genetics and the environment. Second, effective treatment modes for babies with Rh incompatibility could be developed only to the extent that the basic mechanisms of the disorder were understood. Thus, the key to curing this disorder was basic research into the nature of the problem rather than applied research on various trial-and-error treatments.

GENETIC COUNSELING

With the decrease in perinatal mortality that accompanies better prenatal care and delivery services, the genetic component in the remaining mortality has become of increasing significance. The next question that arises is what, if anything, can be done about reducing the incidence of genetic abnormalities that lead either to death or to some of the crippling disorders we have surveyed.

Genetic counseling is not new. Even before advances in understanding genetics and in the technology for studying the chromosomes it was possible to study the family trees of a couple whose families showed certain well-known genetic disorders and determine the likelihood of the couple's having a child with that handicap. However, initially all that the couple could do on the basis of this information was to decide not to have children. More recently we have greatly improved our ability to diagnose some genetic diseases prior to birth through amniocentesis.[14]

X-linked Traits

The first disorders to be analyzed by amniocentesis were X-linked. Such a defect occurs when a particular recessive gene is carried on the X chromosome of a male. In such traits the X chromosome does not have a matching allele

---

[13] This does not mean that there are no babies with unsafe levels of bilirubin. Other problems can cause this condition, some of which are also related to blood incompatibilities, for example, ABO incompatibility. A transfusion team must still always be on call. Milder levels of kernicterus are often treated by placing the baby under lights, the effectiveness and side effects of which are still controversial.

[14] For an over-all look at the techniques, potential, and problems associated with prenatal diagnosis see one or both of two recent, excellent reviews written for the nonspecialist: Epstein & Golbus, 1977; Fuchs, 1980. An entire book on the subject is Milunsky (1973).

on the Y chromosome and the trait will be expressed. The mother is a heterozygous carrier and therefore the dominant gene on her other X chromosome (the one she did *not* pass on to her son) protects her from the defect. The father, who of course contributed the Y chromosome to his son, does not influence the outcome. The daughters of a mother who is a known carrier and a normal father who has a dominant gene on his X chromosome will be normal since they would require recessive genes on both their X chromosomes to acquire the trait. They might, however, receive the recessive gene from their mother and be carriers. The sons of a carrier mother and normal father, in contrast, have a 50–50 chance of having the trait, since their mother will pass on either her normal or her defective gene.

Genetic counseling began when a method for detecting sex from cells in the amniotic fluid developed. In 1949 Barr determined that female, but not male, cells have a piece of chromosomal material on the membranes of the cell nucleus that stains darkly (now called Barr bodies). Thus, if the mother's family had a history of an X-linked disease, the parents could decide to abort male fetuses and raise only girls. Such an abortion was possible even before the federal law allowing all first trimester abortions because most states allowed abortion if the birth endangered the mental health of the mother. It was argued tht having a child with some of the X-linked disorders could affect the mother's mental health. More recently, more precise tests for some X-linked traits have made it possible to identify whether a given male fetus has the trait.

Perhaps the best known example of a sex-linked trait that might warrant genetic counseling is hemophilia, the "bleeder's disease." It is caused by a deficiency of the substances that lead to blood clotting. Because hemophiliacs are at risk of bleeding to death from even the most minor injuries, they must lead extremely restricted lives. There are treatments that reduce the restriction, but they are difficult and expensive. The incidence in males is about 1 in 10,000 births. For females, who would have to inherit two recessive genes, the incidence is 1 in 50 million births. A precise blood test for detecting the deficiency as early as the sixteenth week after conception was recently developed (Firshein et al., 1979).

Lesch–Nyhan syndrome is another example of an X-linked trait. It results in a neurological condition that develops in infancy. The gene defect leads to the absence or inactivity of an enzyme controlling purine metabolism. The compounds that are not metabolized are converted to uric acid, which builds up and affects neurological development. The effects typically develop before 1 year of age. They include neurological signs of mental retardation, cerebral palsy, and spasmodic, involuntary motor movements. By the age of 3, the child begins to display the behavioral syndrome of compulsive biting and self-mutilation of the lips and hands, head banging, and aggressive behavior toward others. Most cases show severe retardation, little language development, and poor motor development. Most patients die before adulthood.

Lesch–Nyhan syndrome is another X-linked trait for which recently developed techniques have removed the onerous prospect of aborting all male fetuses. The abnormal levels of enzymes and uric acid that characterize it can be detected in both carrier mothers and in victims in utero through amniocentesis. Thus, only affected fetuses need be aborted. Although this disorder is quite rare (1 in 50,000) genetic counseling is quite helpful to families at risk.

Amniocentesis

In the 1950s amniocentesis in the third trimester was found to be a useful technique to assess blood group incompatibility and to measure the severity of the effects of Rh incompatibility (Figure 3–5). As tissue culture techniques developed and expanded to include cultivation of fetal tissue in the 1960s it became possible to use amniocentesis done in the 15th to the 19th week of pregnancy to detect chromosomal abnormalities, the by-products of inborn errors of metabolism, and the presence of alpha fetoprotein, which indicates the presence of neural tube defects. Currently some 40 diseases can be detected prenatally using amniocentesis and an additional 35 are approachable with current data, although positive diagnoses are not yet possible. A good review of the problems of all types of prenatal diagnosis is found in Latt (1984). In more than 6000 amniocenteses per-

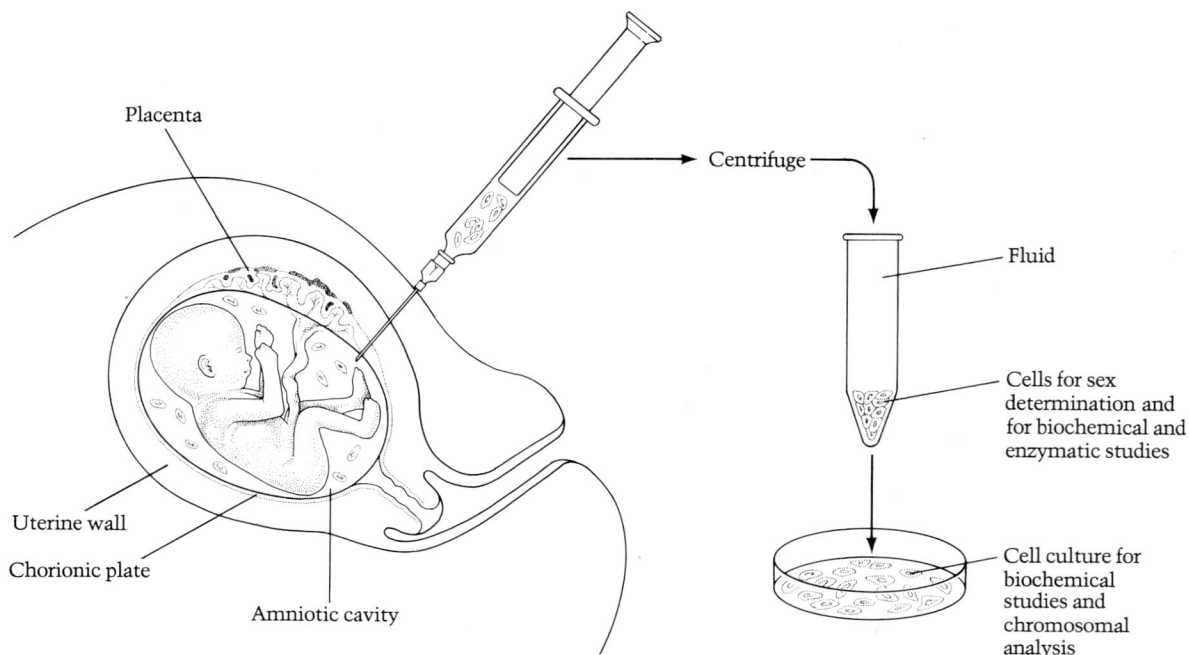

FIGURE 3–5. Amniocentesis. A needle is used to withdraw a small amount of fluid containing fetal cells from the amniotic cavity. The cells and fluid are separated in a centrifuge and the cells are cultured for a variety of tests.

formed in North America between 1967 and 1974, diagnostic accuracy was close to 100% and about 5% of the fetuses were shown to be abnormal (NIH: *Antenatal Diagnosis,* 1979). A genetic screening program that includes amniocentesis allows parents to continue a pregnancy without the fear that the child will have one of these serious handicaps. As automation makes biochemical assays and karyotyping increasingly practical, we must increasingly face the legal, moral, and ethical decisions about their use (see, for example, National Academy of Sciences, 1975).[15]

---

[15] A new technique of tissue sampling considerably earlier in pregnancy is now being given nationwide testing to determine its safety and accuracy. If successful, it would enable earlier decisions about termination of pregnancy, which would be medically easier and safer, and ethically and psychologically less difficult for many. This technique is only for detecting chomosomal abnormalities.

SAFETY

Amniocentesis itself poses significant risks, such as fetal damage or spontaneous abortion, and maternal infection or hemorrhage. Several nationwide studies of amniocentesis have been carried out. In two of these done in the United States and Canada, no significant differences between the amniocentesis samples and the control samples were found in prenatal deaths, problems in labor, delivery, the newborn period, birth weights, birth defects, or development at 1 year of age. The only increase in complications from the procedure occurred when large-gauge needles (18 gauge or over) were used or when two or more needle insertions were required. A third large study, in Great Britain, did find a higher rate of fetal loss, an apparent increase in certain abnormalities, particularly respiratory difficulties and orthopedic postural deformities, and increased complications in late pregnancy and delivery. This study has been criticized on a number of methodological grounds. For example, many more amniocentesis mothers than controls were over 40 years of age, and rates for the types of problems found do increase with age. When adjustments are made for that difference alone, the statistical differences disappear (NIH: *Antenatal Diagnosis*, 1979).

ETHICAL ISSUES

Amniocentesis obviously raises ethical problems. Many parents and doctors do not like to be in the position of making life and death decisions for the fetus. The dilemma is particularly difficult in the X-linked diseases in which all males, both the affected and unaffected, must be aborted if one is to avoid having a handicapped child.

For parents who are willing to abort malformed fetuses, amniocentesis and the associated genetic testing has become a great boon. Women carrying X-linked traits who would refuse to have children for fear that they might give birth to a child with such a disastrous condition as Lesch–Nyhan syndrome can now give birth without fear. Older women, particularly those who have never given birth before, can now become pregnant without the fear of having a Down's syndrome baby.

As amniocentesis becomes more widely available, families who are not convinced of the advisability of aborting fetuses with severe defects are more likely to undergo amniocentesis. If they discover a defect they can learn more about it and its nature by visiting hospitals and mental institutions to see what these children are like, and by interviewing parents, doctors, and others who care for children with that condition. Such knowledge will enable parents to make the best choice for themselves. Indeed, doctors insist that the final decision must be made by the parents.

The limited diagnostic resources for doing the necessary biochemical analyses give rise to another important ethical problem, that of accessibility. Availability of such resources varies both according to geography and pocketbook. Some centers have outreach programs where expert staff is flown to various parts of the state to provide services locally. For example, the University of North Carolina has a program supported by the March of Dimes[16] ("Genetic Clinics Fly," 1974–1975). Until facilities for antenatal diagnosis are available to all who want them, many people feel that parents who are not willing to contemplate abortion if the fetus has a major defect should not undergo amniocentesis because their using the facility may deprive another person of its use.

Balanced Polymorphic Systems

Another problem in genetic counseling is raised by the existence of what geneticists call a balanced polymorphic system. Some serious defects are part of such a system. We will explain it by using sickle cell disease as an example.

SICKLE CELL ANEMIA

This disability is a hemoglobinopathy (disorder of the blood's hemoglobin). It, like another hemoglobinopathy—thalassemia[17]—is an autosomal recessive trait. The person who is homozygous for the problem is said to have sickle cell anemia. In this disorder the red blood cells contain a form of hemoglobin (HbS) that crystallizes when there is inadequate oxygen, as happens at high altitudes or with overexertion. The red blood cells are shaped like sickles and tend to clump together, so they are more likely to block off blood vessels. They live only half as long as normal red cells (those with HbA). Victims suffer from reduced growth, delayed puberty, neurological impairment, and blindness, as well as damage to many other organ systems. While exact mor-

---

[16] The March of Dimes was founded to raise money for research on poliomyelitis but turned its attention to birth defects after polio was virtually wiped out by vaccines. It was recently put under great pressure to abandon funding projects such as the one described here, but resisted the pressure.

[17] Thalassemia syndromes are not known to be balanced polymorphic systems. They are found at different frequencies in different regions (or ethnic stocks). Alpha thalassemia is particularly frequent and severe in Asians. Beta thalassemia is most frequent in Mediterranean countries and the homozygous condition is catastrophic (Glader, 1984). These syndromes, like sickle cell anemia, can be detected prenatally (Leonard & Kazazian, 1978). Active screening programs exist in both Italy and England (for immigrant populations).

bidity and mortality rates are not known, it is estimated that 50% of such individuals do not reach the age of twenty (or the likely age of reproduction) and that most do not live to 40 (Scott, 1970). This condition is rather frequent among Blacks. Although estimates vary from study to study, they converge around a figure of 1 in 500 being affected.[18]

It is reasonable to ask why this trait does not simply disappear by natural selection, because sickle cell anemia victims, with their two recessive genes, are less likely to pass their genes on to offspring than are healthy individuals who have no or one recessive gene. The answer is that this is a balanced polymorphic system: Another trait in this gene system is advantageous. The sickled cells are a poor host for a kind of malaria parasite that spends part of its life cycle in red blood cells. Therefore, the sickle cell anemia victim is protected from malaria. More important for the next generation, in the heterozygous carrier 20–40% of the red blood cells are sickle shaped and they are therefore less likely to contract malaria than the individual with no gene for sickling. They are not likely to develop problems from their sickled cells unless they are subjected to extreme environmental pressures, such as flying at very high altitudes in a plane that is not pressurized or that loses pressure, or extreme exertion. Hence, it is an advantage to be a heterozygote in areas of the world that have malaria, even though heterozygotes are carriers of the sickling gene and are likely to produce offspring who develop sickle cell anemia if they marry a victim or a carrier. Overall, heterozygotes are more likely to survive.

This system is polymorphic because there are two possible consequences of the presence of the gene, sickle cell anemia and malaria resistance, and it is balanced because the biological advantages of malaria resistance offset the maladaptiveness of sickling. Such a balance, however, obtains only in parts of the world (such as equatorial Africa) where malaria exists. Sickling genes are not needed in temperate climates, and white citizens of the United

States do not have them. If a population that has the sickling gene moves to a temperate climate, the advantage of the gene should disappear and its frequency should drop. The time span for such a genetic response is not known, but there may be some signs of it among North American Blacks, who do have a markedly lower incidence of sickle cell anemia than is found in equatorial Africa. Whether selection pressures or mixing of Black with white genotypes plays the principal role in bringing this about is far from clear.

Despite this downward shift in incidence, sickle cell anemia is one of the most important genetic problems in the United States. It is much more frequent than PKU or cystic fibrosis, which we shall discuss shortly. We might say it is of limited concern in an infancy course, since most infants born with the disease do not show signs of it until after 2 years of age. Infants are, however, affected by having mothers with sickle cell anemia. Their mothers are more likely to die when they are born, or to become physically unable to care for them, or to die while they are still infants. In Memphis, Tennessee, in a hospital serving a virtually all-Black population, some 1 in 2000 obstetric patients have sickle cell anemia, but they account for 1 in 6 patient deaths, and only 50% of the sickle cell mothers who survive have a live baby to take home with them. Heterozygous women, who have only a minority of their cells sickled, are not at greater risk for perinatal mortality, but they tend to have more premature births and more babies who are low in weight for their gestational age.

The problem is one for which genetic counseling could play an extremely important role. However, not only are large portions of the Black population less likely to receive optimal medical advice, but the complications resulting from racial and political issues are of profound importance. Further, access to optimal help for coping with a child with sickle cell anemia is often lacking in Black communities, and less money is spent on this problem than on other less frequent disorders (see Wright, Schaefer, & Solomons, 1979 for further discussion and additional references).

CYSTIC FIBROSIS
Cystic fibrosis, another single recessive trait, may also be an example of a balanced

[18]As for PKU, environmental treatments for sickle cell anemia are currently being advocated, especially a drug that would make HbS hemoglobin hold adequate oxygen. Approaches that would lead to more water in the cell and less rigidity have also been suggested but are not yet in the testing stage.

polymorphic system. Children with cystic fibrosis only rarely survive until they become reproductive, so there is strong selection pressure against the homozygous recessive state (the victim). Yet 1 in 20 persons possesses one gene for this trait (is a carrier or heterozygous). Roughly one child in every 1500 live births has the disease (Wright et al., 1979). It is thought that this frequency is much too high to be maintained by spontaneous mutations, and that the heterozygous state must provide some advantage to those individuals.

Balanced polymorphic systems present a dilemma to genetic counsellors. If carriers of such genes are advised not to have offspring, this is a strong selection against that trait. The heterozygous state may provide a stronger reason for maintaining certain genes for serious disorders than the advantages conferred by avoiding having those offspring. At this point these considerations are more speculative than practical, since few balanced polymorphic systems have been identified. Such systems illustrate the kind of unintentional problems that arise as a result of partial knowledge. This is not an argument against studying genetic defects or against genetic counseling, but an argument for thorough and intelligent research before the development of widespread practical application. Currently, a large proportion of the parents of cystic fibrosis children are not receiving adequate genetic counseling with respect to the risks for future children (Wright et al., 1979).

Genetic Diagnosis and Treatment: State of the Art

Because of giant advances in genetics and the development of sophisticated new techniques such as amniocentesis, karyotyping, and automated biochemical analyses, it is possible to identify the potential and actual development of many defects of genes and chromosomes. In addition, for at least one defect, PKU, a treatment exists that prevents the phenotypic expression of the most severe forms of the disorder.

Much of the work that has been done concerns single-gene defects or gross chromosomal abnormalities that result in specific syndromes that are easily identified by their physical stigmata. Although there are variations in the number and severity of symptoms, these variations are merely modifications of the basic genetic patterns.

The ability to detect and treat genetic problems is still in its beginning stages. Remember that 65–70% of all birth defects are of unknown origin. Why should that figure be so high?

First, the vast number and rarity of genetically based disorders make it hard to identify them. Scientists have so far identified more than 2500 human diseases caused by defects in the content or expression of the genetic code and most of them are very rare. This rarity means that the average doctor or hospital has little or no experience in recognizing these defects; hence, correct diagnosis is difficult. This difficulty is currently being tackled by the development of centralized computer systems that enable doctors to provide information about an infant to a computer that can then request further observations about the baby. This back-and-forth dialog between doctor and computer continues until the computer, on the basis of all the information programmed into it, can match the doctor's description with a probable diagnosis. If there is no match, the computer reports that the doctor's description does not fit any of the diagnostic descriptions in the program.

A second difficulty in detecting genetic disorders is that the disorders are extremely complex. This complexity stems from the complexity of development itself. In our discussion of the embryological development of the ear in Chapter 2, for example, we showed the structures of the human ear and the complex way in which they develop from the three primary germ layers (endoderm, mesoderm, ectoderm). It is obvious that in this complex structure there are many ways that development could go wrong. Hearing loss has been found in nine known genetic syndromes in addition to trisomies of chromosomes 21–23, 13–15, and 17–18 (Gluck, 1971). There are, however, more than 60 types of hereditary deafness (Konigsmark, 1971). These include 17 unknown types of severe neural deafness syndrome, which account for over half of the cases of congenital deafness. These syndromes may result from dominant, recessive, or sex-linked transmission and may or may not be associated with other disorders. Among those that are associated with other disorders, the particular systems that have defects vary.

A third reason it is difficult to study genetically related characteristics is that many of the traits that most of us (students, parents, or psychologists) are interested in, such as intellectual and temperamental traits, are polygenic; that is, they are determined by the action (and interaction) of several genes. This means that both the aspects of phenotypic traits due to genetic variation and the action of the causative genes are difficult to detect. In polygenic traits individuals vary widely with respect to that trait. In fact, such traits are usually continuously distributed and the distribution has the familiar form of the bell-shaped curve. If a large number of individuals is measured, virtually all of them will fall between some minimum and maximum. This variation is produced by the combined action of two or more genes that in turn interact with variations in the environment to determine the final phenotypic variation. It is thus difficult to determine when two people differ genetically on a trait (for example, is an IQ of 100 genetically different from an IQ of 110?) because the action of the genes in producing the phenotypic variation is unknown.

DISCUSSION ISSUES

Heredity and Environment

In this chapter we discussed constitutional abnormalities that are produced by genes and chromosomes, an extremely complex topic. We can come to two general conclusions about the relation between genetic mechanisms and environment. First, it is clear that an individual's constitution can never be said to be purely inherited. The genes, as the mechanisms of inheritance, only determine potentials. The outcome is always a complex interaction between that potential and the events that occur as that genetic potential becomes a reality, a process that begins long before conception. The extent to which this is true is nowhere more evident than in chromosomal abnormalities. Even though chromosomes are the carriers of the genes, they themselves are not the genetic potential

but are the result of the relationship between that genetic potential and the environment during meiosis and mitosis.

A second major conclusion about the complex relation between heredity and environment is that gene–environment interactions are complex multistepped affairs, in which each false step affects quite disparate areas of development. PKU is a good example of this. Retardation is not a direct effect of the recessive gene, but rather an indirect effect produced by abnormal metabolites that are the result of the inborn error of metabolism carried by the single recessive gene. Another example is Rh incompatibility. The genetic factor (Rh + or Rh −) is in itself not a defect. It produces an abnormality only because the mother's body treats the Rh − factor of the baby's blood as a foreign invader. In both PKU and Rh incompatibility the abnormality produced can be prevented by changing an environmental step in the sequence from genetic potential to phenotypic expression. Thus the phenotypic expression of genetic traits can be prevented, but only if we understand the mechanisms by which these traits are expressed in the phenotype.

This chapter also gives the first example of a critical period in which the external environment (outside the infant's body) interacts with physical maturation: In PKU the brain damage caused by the abnormal metabolites occurs during a critical period in early infancy. The mechanism is exactly the same as that in embryology, which we discussed in Chapter 2. Thus, we can generalize the notion of critical periods to instances in which the external environment affects physical characteristics of the infant.

Research Issues

SAMPLING

At first, it might seem that studying individuals with specific genetic or chromosomal anomalies would be rather clear cut and factual. In this chapter we have seen that the research enterprise is in no way easy or straightforward. There is not only disagreement about whether a certain abnormality produces a particular problem (for example, does trisomy X produce mental retardation?) but even disagreement about how often a particular anomaly occurs. The latter disagreements stem from various problems of sampling. Most of our knowledge of these disorders has been gained by examining individuals who have come to medical authorities for help with physical, sexual, or psychological problems. They are not necessarily a representative sample of people with that anomaly. Rather they fall into the category of **case studies,** studies of individual cases, usually of a particular physical or psychological problem.

In the study of genetic and chromosomal abnormalities, there are two significant problems with case studies. First, individuals with a given abnormality may not seek medical attention because they don't have the same medical problems others with the disorder have, or because the problems they have don't disturb them, or because they cannot afford or do not believe in medical attention. The second problem is that case studies often fail to compare the incidence of a problem associated with a given anomaly (for example, menstrual irregularity in trisomy X) with the incidence of that problem (menstrual irregularity) in the general population. For example, doctors seeing trisomy X girls would expect sexual problems and so would be likely to assume that the extra X caused any problem they found. Such a conclusion is unwarranted unless the frequency for menstrual irregularity in the general population is known and it is less frequent than that in trisomy X girls.

This problem is exacerbated by the low frequency of trisomy X cases. If a doctor sees three trisomy X patients and one has menstrual irregularities, the doctor is likely to consider this a significant rate since $\frac{1}{3}$ is higher than the base rate in other patients. As we pointed out in Chapter 1, the results of studies with small sample sizes are extremely unstable and often misleading. It might well be that if that doctor saw 10 or 20 more trisomy X patients, not one of them would have menstrual irregularities. If so, then the doctor would have been misled because one individual with menstrual difficulties was one of the first several trisomy X patients she or he saw. The low frequency problem is often solved by adding across a number of studies, as was done for the data from Jarvik and colleagues (1973) on XYY. This practice, however, does not eliminate the need for base rates based on unbiased samples of adequate size.

The best way to attain an unbiased sample is to study sequential births in a population. Those with abnormal karyotypes can be identified and those with normal karyotypes (or a randomly selected subgroup of all the normal births) become the comparison or control group. Researchers then follow the subjects and their controls as they develop. This prospective technique, which we discussed in the section on sex-chromosome anomalies, is the only technique that solves all the selection problems we discussed. It also solves the problems of **retrospective** accounts, in which parents or the subjects themselves have to remember past events (for example, when did you first notice that your daughter's breasts were developing?). We will see several examples of research in which prospective studies are necessary.

STUDYING CAUSALITY WITH CORRELATIONAL RESEARCH

Solving the sampling problems discussed above solves the problems attendant on determining frequencies for a given disorder, but only opens the door to the methodological solution of questions about the effects of these disorders. The basic problem is that we are dealing with correlational research. Since we cannot randomly assign subjects to abnormal and normal groups, any observed differences between these groups may be due to the abnormality or to some associated characteristics, such as tallness or low IQ in the XYY–aggressiveness hypothesis. To compensate for this inherent methodological problem, we must always be alert for alternative causal hypotheses, such as the possible tallness–low IQ cause for aggression in XYY cases, and be willing to expend the extraordinary care necessary to test these alternative hypotheses. In this chapter we have discussed a number of instances of alternative hypotheses. Several were hypotheses of indirect effects in contrast to the main hypotheses of direct effects. The hypotheses of direct effects were that abnormalities in the number of sex chromosomes often produce personality difficulties. The alternative hypotheses of indirect effects were that the chromosomal abnormalities produce differences in appearance and the abnormal appearance causes people to react differently to the afflicted individuals. These reactions produce the psychological differences. Thus the effect of the chromosomal abnormality on personality is indirect (mediated through the effects of the individual's appearance on the way others act toward him or her).

Another alternative hypothesis that we discussed in this chapter is that the combination of tallness and low intelligence may produce aggressiveness in the XYY individual. If this alternative hypothesis is correct, the mechanism is likely to be an indirect effect, because the combination of tallness and low intelligence produces certain reactions from the environment (for example, aggression is rewarded because it achieves the desired effect from other people).

Two other major examples of alternative hypotheses appeared in the material in this chapter. One was with respect to PKU babies and their diet. PKU babies who have been fed the special diet are less retarded than nondiet PKU babies. We'd like to believe that this difference is due to the diet (the independent variable), but it might be due to parental characteristics such as greater conscientiousness and effort on the part of mothers who provide the diet. To rid PKU studies of these extraneous variables, we would like to make sure that mothers in the two groups do not differ in any systematic fashion on important maternal characteristics. A good way of doing this is to use the same mothers in both infant groups, that is, to use as subjects siblings (brothers and sisters), one of whom was treated and one not. This is known technically as using the mothers as their own control. If this technique is used, it is unlikely that differences in offspring IQ (the dependent variable) would be due to differences in mothers of treated and untreated children. An example of this technique appeared in Chapter 2 in the discussion of prematurity, and we shall see additional examples in studies of other prenatal problems in the next chapter. This technique also helps to control for genetic expectations with respect to IQ in any particular family.

One last example of alternative interpretations was the role expectations may play in the outcome of research, an issue we discussed in Chapter 1. If the individuals who measure the behaviors expect to see particular phenomena, they are more likely to see them than individuals who are not thus biased or are biased in the opposite direction. In the XYY situation, the expectations of the parents might also affect the outcome of the research. To do research on such children, children must be identified as XYY individuals. If parents are told this information about their children, they may expect their children to be aggressive and to have poor impulse control. These expectations may encourage the children to become more aggressive than they would have if the parents had other expectations. Thus, if the research findings were that XYY individuals became more aggressive adults than did XY individuals, it might be either because of the extra Y chromosome or because of the parents' expectations. In other words, the parents' expectations serve as an alternative cause—in the same way that an experimenter's expectations can. Parents' expectations are a potential confounding variable whenever a longitudinal study involves telling the parents of the experimental group something that might influence their behaviors toward their children.

ETHICAL AND PRACTICAL ISSUES

The research controversy over XYY prospective studies exemplifies typical ethical and practical issues researchers face. Should parents be told their sons have an extra Y chromosome? Telling parents would surely be morally reprehensible if it contributed to children's hyperaggressiveness. Not telling parents violates their right to know the medical truth about their children. Thus, as is often the case in ethical problems, the course chosen can only be the lesser of two evils.

The particular situation with XYY research also shows that the decision about how to study a given problem or indeed whether to study that problem is a complex mixture of scientific, ethical, and practical issues. Judgments of scientific rigor must be tempered by considerations not only of ethical appropriateness, but also of whether alternative, more ethical but more expensive and time-consuming, approaches might yield the necessary knowledge. In addition, questions of cost are also important but are too little considered. Is the problem important enough to society to warrant the emotional cost to the participants, the monetary price to society? In the XYY situation the monetary and emotional cost of criminals to their victims and to society at large must be weighed against the emotional cost to the participants and the monetary cost to the society that supports the research (often the taxpayers). Another example of monetary issues in research occurred in the section on Down's syndrome. Is it worth society's money to do research on alternative methods of educating and caring for Down's children, when the long-term outcome of such research is to save money on institutionalization of Down's victims? In the case of Down's syndrome, the question is whether society at large could save money in the long run by investing money in the short term in research or in educational facilities, or in both. The possibility that families, and society at large, may be able to avoid the costs of the total dependency of Down's victims is very real and makes such investment programs potentially cost effective.

Parenting

There are several parenting issues inherent in the topics of genetic abnormalities and genetic counseling. Potential parents should know whether they belong to a subpopulation that is at special risk. Some examples of such populations are Mediterraneans for beta thallassemia, Blacks for sickle cell anemia, Ashkenazic Jews for Tay-Sachs disease, older women for Down's syndrome, and persons with family histories containing genetic disorders such as PKU. Couples may also wish to know whether they have a potential Rh problem prior to or early in pregnancy.

Given prior knowledge of their risk for any genetic disorders, a couple has three options: (1) to avoid pregnancy, (2) to take their chances, (3) to have antenatal screening and decide whether to abort a seriously defective fetus. In the vast majority of cases the third choice actually enables couples to continue a pregnancy free from fear. In high-risk communities where genetic screening and abortion are available, the birth rate has risen, since parents no longer feel forced to avoid pregnancy. It is also interesting that in some Mediterranean areas with a high incidence of carriers, the screening centers for beta thalassemia are sponsored by the local archbishop.

Because we have frequently advocated the importance of choosing options for yourself, you may think that we find the second option to be as good as the first and third. After all, there are many aspects of having an infant where taking your chances *is* the only option. The genetic characteristics any one infant will have and how they will interact with prenatal environment to determine the infants' phenotypic characteristics is always a gamble. Nevertheless, when it comes to serious genetic defects—the heartbreaking, financially disastrous ones that lead to relatively early death or severe life-long handicaps—the option of taking your chances should not be chosen lightly. To choose it responsibly you should do two things. First, through a doctor or hospital you should try to talk to the parents of such an infant to see what they are going through and, if possible, to see such an infant. Second, you should contemplate the likely medical costs in making a decision. If you cannot hope to meet them, which is likely since they run into the hundreds of thousands of dollars, you should ask yourself whether it is appropriate or fair to ask society to meet them for you. Although we would strongly oppose having society legislate such matters for anyone, people need to be responsible and take the financial factor as well as the human suffering into account when making a decision.

Parents who have children with birth defects have many varying problems. In the most serious degenerative disorders there is little parents can do other than to ameliorate their infants' suffering and to provide adequate medical care. In serious, but not life-threatening, disorders such as Down's syndrome, parents face the problems of how to provide optimal environments in infancy and beyond. The problems actually are mildest in infancy. The longer range questions of what support systems are available in the community are of great concern and parents need to be alert to them very early. Families may even choose to move to a location that has better support systems or institutions or both, or to join other parents of handicapped children to try to get better facilities in their community. While it does not need to be found in infancy, a solution for the long-range problem of what will happen when the parents die or are too feeble to care for their handicapped offspring needs to be planned for well in advance of its happening.

In disorders that have less serious outcomes, caring for a defective child may still be difficult. For example, PKU need not result in any long-range problem for your offspring, other than a possible inability for a female to produce a normal baby of her own. However, the problems of keeping children on the appropriate diet and having it closely monitored so that they receive enough phenylalanine for relatively normal growth but not enough to accumulate harmful metabolic by-products is far from simple. Keeping PKU children on the diet becomes increasingly difficult after early infancy when they will want to eat what others eat. Unless the family is lucky enough to live near one of the few centers that can provide the monitoring, there will be a great deal of commuting and some relatively long-term stays near the center. The strains on the family can thus be rather severe despite the good prognosis for the infant.

There is also a parenting–grandparenting issue involved in a proper understanding of genetic defects. Most of them involve a recessive gene received from each parent. In the past, there has been a great deal of blame casting associated with genetic defects. In the far past, blame was often cast on witches or persons with the "evil eye." More recently (and probably in many families even today), parents and grandparents have tended to blame the "other side" of the family. This is not only false, but can lead to tremendous tensions in the family. We trust that all of you have learned that it not only takes "two to tango," but also to produce most genetic defects.

Fortunately, while most of you will never have to face these problems, a finite percentage of you (the percentage depends on your ethnic and familial heritage) will, and hence we have felt it important to discuss them.

SUMMARY

A brief and basic review of genetic mechanisms was presented. Conceptions involving most chromosomal and many other genetic defects do not survive to be born alive, and a large proportion of those that do do not live to full maturity. The very small proportion of infants born with genetic defects accounts for a large proportion of hospitalizations and for staggering sums in hospital costs.

Chromosomal abnormalities were discussed, and the mechanisms by which they can occur (nondisjunction, translocation, and mosaicism) were illustrated using Down's syndrome, the most frequent chromosomal disorder. One third of the translocation type (which account for only 4% of Down's cases) are inherited. The relation of the occurrence of trisomy 21 to maternal age is strong and the risk is very high after 40 years of age. Issues involving the benefits and hazards of home versus institutional care were presented, and the question of whether society provides adequate support systems to help families cope with a Down's child was raised.

Trisomies other than Down's occur but most are aborted during the embryonic stage. One that sometimes survives is trisomy 18. It accounts for many deaths in late pregnancy and around childbirth, and is also strongly related to maternal age.

Most of the various syndromes involving abnormal numbers of sex chromosomes are caused by nondisjunction during meiosis of either sperm or egg cells. Turner's syndrome (45,X0) is the only viable case of a totally missing chromosome. Extra X chromosomes are found in two syndromes, XXX (trisomy X) and XXY (Klinefelter's syndrome). Both sexual systems and behavior depart from normal in such persons, but much less seriously than in trisomy 21. An extra Y chromosome is found in the XYY syndrome. The behavioral consequences of this syndrome are very much in question and their study has aroused a great deal of controversy. There are important methodological questions that are raised in the study of such problems.

Defects caused by specific genes are usually recessive; that is, the trait is expressed only when each parent contributes the particular gene to the new organism. Often neither parent has the phenotype of the defect but the infant does. Disorders caused in this way may be fatal early in life, as Tay-Sachs is, or fatal later in life, as cystic fibrosis is, or not fatal.

Those that are not fatal often produce substantial mental retardation, as PKU and cretinism do. The phenotypic expression of mental retardation in both PKU and cretinism can be controlled by special environmental intervention. In cretinism the appropriate therapy is administration of thyroid; in PKU it is a special diet started very early in life and continued for a number of years. The control of the phenotypic expression is not perfect. For example, the offspring of mothers who have been treated for PKU are retarded whether or not they inherit the defect.

Rh factor is an interesting interaction of genetic and environmental influences. If a baby inherits Rh + blood type from its father and its mother is Rh −, then the mother's blood, if and when it mixes with that of her fetus, produces antibodies that attack the baby's blood cells. This causes a dangerous condition (kernicterus) that can damage the brain and even kill the fetus. The history of the increasingly successful efforts to avoid this source of damage is detailed.

Genetic counseling was first feasible with respect to X-linked diseases such as hemophilia. The use of antenatal diagnosis combined with abortion of affected fetuses actually operates to allow many parents who would not otherwise have children to do so.

Some genetic disorders are part of what are called balanced polymorphic systems. An example is sickle cell anemia. While this disorder is very dangerous, the heterozygous carrier condition is an advantage in tropical areas of the world because it greatly reduces the chances of getting malaria. It would appear from prevalance data that cystic fibrosis might also be a balanced polymorphic system, but knowledge about this is uncertain. Such systems pose a potential hazard for genetic counselors. If we try through genetic counseling to eliminate a genetic defect that is part of a balanced polymorphic system we might inadvertently also eliminate the advantage carried by the heterozygous condition.

Unlike the case for chromosomal abnormalities and those arising from defects in single genes, most of the human characteristics psychologists and parents are interested in are polygenic, and the mechanisms of their inheritance are not understood.

REFERENCES

Bauld, R., Sutherland, G.R., & Bain, A.D. (1974). Chromosome studies in investigation of stillbirths and neonatal deaths. *Archives of Disease in Childhood, 49,* 782–788.

Beck, F., Moffat, D.B., & Lloyd, J.B. (1973). *Human embryology.* Oxford, England: Blackwell.

Berman, P.W., Waisman, H.A., & Graham, F.K. (1966). Intelligence in treated phenylketonuric children: A developmental study. *Child Development, 37,* 731–747.

Berry, H.K. (1976). Hyperphenylalaninemias and tyrosinemias. *Clinics in Perinatology, 3,* 15–40.

Boue, A., & Boue, J. (1974). Chromosome abnormalities and abortion. *Basic Life Sciences, 4,* 317–339.

Boue, J., Boue, A., & Lazar, P. (1975). Retrospective and prospective epidemiological studies of 1,500 karytyped spontaneous human abortions. *Teratology, 12,* 11–26.

Bridges, F.A., & Cicchetti, D. (1982). Mothers' ratings of the temperament characteristics of Down syndrome infants. *Developmental Psychology, 18,* 238–244.

Carr, D.H. (1963). Chromosome studies in abortuses and stillborn infants. *Lancet, ii,* 603–606.

Carr, D.H. (1971). Chromosome studies in selected spontaneous abortions and early pregnancy loss. *Journal of Obstetrics and Gynecology, 37,* 570–574.

Casey, M.D., Blank, C.E., & Street (1969). Letter. *Lancet, ii,* 859–860.

Childs, B., Miller, S., & Bearn, A. (1972). Gene mutation as a cause of human disease. In H. Sutton, & M. Harris (Eds.), *Mutagenic effects of environmental contaminants.* New York: Academic.

Cornwell, A.C., & Birch, H.G. (1969). Psychological and social development in home-reared children with Down's Syndrome (Mongolism). *American Journal of Mental Deficiency, 74,* 341–350.

Emde, R., Katz, E., & Thorpe, J. (1978). Emotional expression in infancy: Early deviations in Down's Syndrome. In M. Lewis & L. Rosenblum (Eds.), *The development of affect.* New York: Plenum.

Epstein, C.J., & Golbus, M.S. (1977). Prenatal diagnosis of genetic diseases. *American Scientist, 65,* 703–711.

Firshein, S., Hoyer, L., Lazarchick, T., Forget, B., Hobbins, J., Clyne, L., Pitlick, F., Muir, W.A., Merkatz, I., & Mahoney, M. (1979). Prenatal diagnosis of classic hemophilia. *New England Journal of Medicine, 300,* 937–941.

Fraser, F.C. (1984). Gross chromosomal aberrations. In M.E. Avery & H.W. Taeusch Jr. (Eds.), *Schaffer's diseases of the newborn* (5th Ed.). Philadelphia: Saunders.

Fuchs, F. (1980). Genetic amniocentesis. *Scientific American, 242,* 47–53.

Genetic clinics fly closer to families. (1974–1975). *Developments from the Child Development Institute of the University of North Carolina at Chapel Hill, 2,* 2–3.

Glader, B.E. (1984). Erythrocyte disorders in infancy. In M.E. Avery & H.W. Taeusch, Jr. (Eds.), *Schaffer's diseases of the newborn* (5th Ed.). Philadelphia: Saunders.

Gluck, L. (1971). *Neurosensory factors in newborn hearing.* Paper presented at the Conference on Newborn Hearing Screening, California State Dept. of Public Health, San Francisco, CA.

Hamerton, J., Manoranjan, R., Abbott, J., Williamson, C., & Ducasse, G. (1972). Chromosome studies in a neonatal population. *Canadian Medical Association Journal, 106,* 776–779.

Hayden, A.H., & Dmitriev, V. (1975). An intervention program for atypical infants. In B.Z. Friedlander, G.H. Sterritt, & G.E. Kirk (Eds.), *Exceptional infant: Vol. 3, Assessment and intervention.* New York: Brunner/Mazel.

Hertig, A., & Rock, J. (1949). A series of potentially abortive ova recovered from fertile women prior to the first missed menstrual period. *American Journal of Obstetrics and Gynecology, 58,* 968–993.

Hertig, A., Rock, J., Adams, E., & Menken, M. (1959). Thirty-four fertilized ova, good, bad, and indifferent from 210 women of known fertility. *Pediatrics, 23,* 202–211.

Holtzman, N.A., Meek, A.G., & Mellits, E.D. (1974). Neonatal screening for phenylketonuria I. Effectiveness. *Journal of the American Medical Association, 229,* 667–670.

Hsia, D. Y-Y. (1968). Nutritional management in hereditary metabolic disease. "Annotations." *Developmental Medicine and Child Neurology, 10,* 103–104.

Hudson, F.P., Mordaunt, V.L., & Leahy, I. (1970). Evaluation of treatment begun in first three months of life in 184 cases of phenylketonuria. *Archives of Disease in Childhood, 45,* 5–12.

Jarvik, L.F., Klodin, V., & Matsuyama, S.S. (1973). Human aggression and the extra Y chromosome. *American Psychologist, 28,* 674–682.

Kaplan, A.R. (1962). Phenylketonuria: A review. *Eugenics Quarterly, 9,* 151–160.

Kessler, S., & Moos, R.H. (1970). The XYY karyotype and criminality: A review. *Journal of Psychiatric Research, 7,* 153–170.

Kivowitz, J. (1972). The XYY syndrome in children: A review. *Child Psychiatry and Human Development, 2,* 186–194.

Konigsmark, B.W. (1971). *Hereditary and congenital factors affecting newborn sensorineural hearing.* Paper presented at the Conference on Newborn Hearing Screening, San Francisco.

Latt, S.A. (1984). Prenatal genetic diagnosis. In M.E. Avery & H.W. Taeusch Jr. (Eds.), *Schaeffer's diseases of the newborn* (5th Ed.). Philadelphia: Saunders.

Lenke, R.R., & Levy, H.L. (1980). Maternal phenylketonuria and hyperphenylalinemia: An international survey of untreated and treated pregnancies. *New England Journal of Medicine, 303,* 1202–1208.

Lenke, R.R., & Levy, H.L. (1982). Maternal phenylketonuria—Results of dietary therapy. *American Journal of Obstetrics and Gynecology, 142,* 548–553.

Leonard, C., & Kazazian, H. (1978). Prenatal diagnosis of hemoglobinopathies. *Pediatric Clinics of North America, 25,* 631–642.

Levy, H.L., Karolkewicz, V., Houghton, S.A., & MacCready, R.A. (1970). Screening the "normal" population in Massachusetts for phenylketonuria. *New England Journal of Medicine, 282,* 1455–1458.

Lowe, C.R., Coursin, D.B., Heald, F.P., Holliday, M.A., O'Brian, D., Owen, G.M., Pearson, H.A., Scriver, E.R., Filer, L.J., & Kline, O.L. (1967). Nutritional management in hereditary metabolic disease. *Pediatrics, 40,* 289–304.

Lubs, H.A. (1970). Cytogenetic problems in antenatal diagnosis. In M. Harris (Ed.), *Early diagnosis of human genetic defects: Scientific and ethical considerations* (HEW-NIH publication 72-25). Washington, DC: U.S. Government Printing Office.

Lubs, H.A. (1977). Occurrence and significance of chromosome variants. In R.S. Sparkes, et al. (Eds.), *Molecular human cytogenetics.* New York: Academic.

Lubs, H.A., & Ruddle, F. (1970a). Applications of quantitative karyotypy to chromosome variation. In P. Jacobs, W. Price, & P. Law (Eds.), *Human population cytogenetics.* Baltimore: Williams and Wilkins.

Lubs, H.A., & Ruddle, F. (1970b). Chromosomal abnormalities in the human population: estimation of rates based on New Haven newborn. *Science, 169,* 495–497.

Machin, G. (1974). Chromosome abnormality and perinatal death. *Lancet, i,* 549–551.

McClearn, G.E., & DeFries, J.C. (1973). *Introduction to behavioral genetics.* San Francisco: Freeman.

Milunsky, A. (1973). *Prenatal diagnosis of hereditary disorders.* Springfield, IL: Thomas.

National Academy of Sciences. (1975). *Genetic screening: Programs, principles, and research.* Washington, DC: National Academy Press.

National Institutes of Health. (1979). *Antenatal Diagnosis: Report of a consensus development conference.* Bethesda, Md.: U.S. Dept. of Health, Education, & Welfare, Publication No. 79-1173.

NIH *Record,* citation of Brusilow & Batshaw, April 28, 1981, p. 5.

Pennington, B.F., Bender, B., Puck, M., Salbenblatt, J., & Robinson, A. (1982). Learning disabilities in children with sex chromosome anomalies. *Child Development, 53,* 1182–1192.

Polani, P.E. (1966). Chromosome anomalies and abortions. *Developmental Medicine and Child Neurology, 8,* 67–70.

Pueschel, S.M. (1983). The child with Down's syndrome. In M.D. Levine, W.B. Carey, A.C. Crocker, & R.T. Gross (Eds.), *Developmental behavioral pediatrics.* Philadelphia: Saunders.

Ratcliffe, S.G., & Keay, A.J. (1973). Chromosome studies on 11,000 newborn infants. *Archives of Disease in Childhood, 48,* 407.

Ratcliffe, S.G., Melville, M.M., Steward, A.L., Jacobs, P.A., & Keay, A.J. (1970). Chromosome studies on 3500 newborn male infants. *Lancet, i,* 121–124.

Scott, R.B. (1970). Health care priority and sickle cell anemia. *Journal of the American Medical Association, 214,* 731–734.

Sergovich, F., Valentine, G.H., Chen, A.T.L., Kinch, R.A.H., & Stout, M.S. (1969). Chromosome aberrations in 2,159 consecutive newborn babies. *New England Journal of Medicine, 280,* 851–855.

Shapiro, S., Ross, L.J., & Levine, H.S. (1965). Relationship of selected prenatal factors to pregnancy outcome and congenital anomalies. *American Journal of Public Health, 55,* 268–282.

Smith, I., Lobascher, M., & Wolff, O.H. (1973). Factors influencing outcome in early treatment of phenylketonuria. In J.W.T. Seakins, R.A. Saunders, & C. Toothill (Eds.), *Treatment of inborn errors of metabolism.* London: Churchill Livingstone.

Smith, I., & Wolff, O.H. (1974). Natural history of phenylketonuria and influence of early treatment. *Lancet, ii,* 540–544.

Stedman, D.J., & Eichorn, D.H. (1964). A comparison of the growth and development of institutionalized and home-reared mongoloids during infancy and early childhood. *American Journal of Mental Deficiency, 69,* 391–401.

Steinhausen, H.C. (1974). Psychological evaluation of treatment in phenylketonuria: Intellectual, motor, and social development. *Neuropadiatrie, 5,* 146–155.

Stickle, G. (1971). *Health is indivisible.* Paper presented at National Foundation–March of Dimes conference for community leaders, Boston, MA.

Sutherland, G., Bauld, R., & Bain, A. (1974). Chromosome abnormality and perinatal death. *Lancet, i,* 752.

Vale, J.R. (1980). *Genes, environment, and behavior: An interactionist approach.* New York: Harper & Row.

Walzer, S., Breau, G., & Gerald, P.S. (1969). A chromosome survey of 2,400 normal newborn infants. *Journal of Pediatrics, 74,* 438–448.

Walzer, S., & Gerald, P.S. (1975). Social class and frequency of XYY and XXY. *Science, 190,* 1228–1229.

Witkin, H.A., Mednick, S.A., Schulsinger, F., Bakkestrom, E., Christiansen, K.O., Goodenough, D.R., Hirschhorn, K., Lundsteen, C., Owen, D.R., Philip, J., Rubin, D.B., & Stocking, M. (1976). Criminality in XYY and XXY men. *Science, 193,* 547–555.

Witschi, E. (1970). Teratogenic effects from overripeness of the egg. In F.C. Fraser, & V.A. McKusick (Eds.), *Proceeding of Third International Conference of Congenital Malformations.* Excerpta Medica International Congress Series 204. Amsterdam: Excerpta Medica.

Witschi, E. (1971). Overripeness of the egg as a possible cause in mental and physical disorders. In I.I. Gottesman & L. Erlenmeyer-Kimling (Eds.), Differential reproduction in individuals with mental and physical disorders. *Social Biology,* Vol. 18 Supplement.

World Health Organization. (1972). *Genetic disorders: Prevention, treatment, and rehabilitation* (Report of World Health Organization scientific group, Technical Report Series No. 497). Geneva, Switzerland: Author.

Wright, L., Schaefer, A.B., & Solomons, G. (1979). *Encyclopedia of pediatric psychology.* Baltimore: University Park Press.

INFLUENCE OF
PRENATAL
ENVIRONMENT
ON CONSTITUTION

CHAPTER 4

What aspects of the environment affect the growth and development of the embryo and fetus and hence help to determine the constitution of an infant at birth? As was true in the discussion of genetic effects, the answers to the question posed here are based primarily on investigations of problems. Something goes wrong and observers look for preceding events or influences that could have caused the problem. Babies with no problems or with good constitutions are not studied. Today it is known that in at least some cases, diseases, drugs, radiation, and maternal stresses can affect fetal development (see, for example, Wilson, 1972). Blood incompatibilities were mentioned in Chapter 3 as an interesting case of prenatal influence that involves an interaction between genetics and the environment. Further study may show that the effects of increasing maternal age are in fact caused by some environmental agent, such as radiation. Very young maternal age is also associated with higher risks to the fetus in ways that will be discussed in this chapter. It is likely that some of these risks also stem from environmental causes.

The known causes of birth defects, one of the principal causes of death, disease, and disability in infancy and childhood, include the genetic and chromosomal abnormalities discussed in Chapter 3 and the environmental agents discussed in this chapter. Of the two classes of causes, the former account for the larger proportion, but by far the largest class of causes is that of "unknown," which accounts for 60% of birth defects (Kalter & Warkany, 1983). Thus, a perfect baby is not guaranteed even if all environmental agents and conditions known to produce birth defects are avoided.

For many years, doctors and psychologists have tried to convince mothers that the old wives' tales about "marking" an unborn infant are false, as indeed they are. If a pregnant woman is frightened by a horse, the baby won't be marked by a horseshaped birthmark; nor will it have hare lip if a mother is startled by a rabbit; nor will a mother's attendance at many concerts during pregnancy cause her baby to be musical or even a music lover. This is not to say that musical ability and interest does not run in families; it does, but probably for reasons other than prenatal exposure. For example, mothers who expose their unborn children to music may both carry genes that predispose to musical ability and provide a **postnatal** (after birth) environment that offers many opportunities for the development of musical talent.

In getting rid of these old superstitions, experts tried to convince parents that the uterine environment and the system of placental exchange of food and wastes between mother and fetus provide almost total protection for the fetus. That protection is not complete, however. As one group of authors has written: "There is no doubt that covert extrinsic factors (probably multiple) in combination with a genetic predisposition (in many cases polygenic) are able to push the developing organism beyond a critical threshold in the direction of malformation" (Beck, Moffat, & Lloyd, 1973, p. 292).

The environmental factors (those extrinsic to the embryo or fetus) that can damage the fetus can be put into several broad categories: (1) maternal diseases or chronic conditions, (2) malnutrition and oxygen deprivation, (3) drugs, (4) direct effects of the external environment, and (5) prenatal stress. These factors are called **teratogens:** anything that produces congenital malformations.

Before we discuss these categories, we wish to comment on the types of effects caused by teratological factors. The most common measures of these effects are death rates: deaths early in pregnancy (resorption or spontaneous abortion), deaths later in pregnancy (miscarriage or still birth), and deaths after delivery (neonatal or newborn deaths). When these are combined into one overall measure, it is called **pregnancy wastage.** Death rates are of course important in themselves, but they probably represent only a small portion of total negative effects. Death rates are also an important indicator of stress. In other words, babies who die as a result of a particular teratogen are either those who have been exposed to the most massive doses or those who are most vulnerable, a condition affected by heredity. Many babies who survive may also be harmed, but the harm (for example, to the brain) is not so obvious and therefore is more difficult to determine.

Physical effects are a second commonly

used measure of teratological effects. Examples are blindness, limb defects, and heart problems. A third effect that is often measured is birth weight. Babies who weigh less than 5½ pounds at birth are usually considered low birth weight (LBW) babies. In addition, studies often measure how small babies are for their gestational age (age since conception or, occasionally, time since the mother's last menstrual period). Babies who are particularly small within their prenatal age class are called small for gestational age (SGA) and are believed to be at particular risk. To be maximally precise, we should say "small for their ethnic group and family characteristics." In general, small babies seem to be more vulnerable to a variety of postnatal problems than are larger babies, although there are many individual exceptions. The most clearcut problem associated with low birth weight is neonatal death. Low birth weight babies account for 70% of all neonatal deaths. Hence it seems clear that any environmental event or condition that increases the probability of having a low birth weight infant is undesirable.

A final measure of teratological effects that is frequently used is intelligence as measured by IQ tests. An amazing array of teratogens affect IQ, probably because the brain experiences its greatest growth before birth.

MATERNAL DISEASES AND CHRONIC CONDITIONS

Two kinds of maternal diseases affect the embryo, fetus, or newborn: infectious diseases and noninfectious chronic diseases.

Infectious Diseases

Maternal infections reach infants either by crossing the placental barrier or during the birth process.[1]

---

[1] Much of the material that follows is based on the work of Alford, Reynolds, and Stagno (1974), which is much more complex than what we can present, and on a review by Sever (1982).

RUBELLA

An early demonstration that the placenta does not provide an impermeable barrier against infections was the discovery of the effects of rubella (German measles). Congenital deafness used to occur in spurts, often in such high numbers as to be virtual epidemics. Such a pattern of occurrence led medical investigators in the mid-1960s to search for an environmental event that also occurred in spurts. They found that the spurts of deaf babies followed epidemics of rubella. Although many mothers of congenitally deaf infants knew that they had had German measles during pregnancy, some only vaguely remembered having a mild rash and others were totally unaware of having "been ill." Because rubella often results in very mild symptoms, and because the relation to neonatal defects seemed clear, investigators next studied the history and characteristics of the infants more intensely. It became clear that deafness was not the only handicap these infants had. A larger proportion than normal had heart defects and were retarded. In addition, these babies were likely to have been small for their gestational age, have cataracts or abnormal retinas, be autistic, and have defects in their immunological systems that left them prone to unusual infections (McIntosh, 1984). Doctors refer to such a cluster of problems as a **syndrome.** When rubella was confirmed as the cause of these problems, these became the "rubella syndrome." As more and more defects were identified it came to be called the "expanded rubella syndrome." It is important to note that in 85% of the cases the defects are not detected in the immediate postbirth period.

This syndrome provides examples of critical periods in embryological development. During the embryonic period (or during organogenesis) the negative effects are both more frequent and more profound. They continue even into the second trimester, however. The organ systems affected differ at different stages of development. Fifty percent of fetuses that survive the mother's infection in the first month are damaged. Growth is most likely to be permanently stunted if infection was in the first 8 weeks, but only about 20% of babies infected in the second month are born with defects. Cataracts occur only if the infection is prior to the 60th day post conception, and heart defects occur up to 80 days (or to the end of the first trimester). Overall some 15 to 25% of first-trimester infections will result in damage. Both deafness and disorders of the retina may occur in either the first or second trimesters, but in the second only 10% of fetuses are affected. Deafness occurs both as a result of damage to structures of the ear (Organ of Corti) and as a result of damage to the central nervous system (see, for example, the review by McIntosh, 1984).

Rubella epidemics thus pose a significant threat to developing offspring. The epidemic in the mid-1960s left between 20,000 and 30,000 damaged infants, 16,000 of whom were deaf. Because of this epidemic, Gallaudet College for the Deaf announced in 1983 that it is necessary to expand greatly its facilities to deal with the current influx of students.

Now that the dangers of rubella in early pregnancy are known, extensive attempts to control it are made. Parents and doctors try to make sure that girls have had rubella or have been immunized against it before they reach reproductive age. Vaccination should not be done when there is a chance of pregnancy occurring, however, because maternal infection in the month prior to pregnancy also affects the fetus. If a woman who has not had rubella becomes pregnant, every effort should be made to protect her from exposure. If she is exposed, gamma globulin or immune serum globulin shots will be given, although their effectiveness is currently being questioned. If, despite all efforts, she contracts the disease in the first trimester, a serum antibody test can be used to help assess the risk to the fetus (McIntosh, 1984). If the results are unclear, amniocentesis can be used to provide a positive diagnosis (that is, to tell whether the rubella virus has reached the amniotic fluid) and she can decide whether to have an abortion. All these measures together have reduced cases of rubella to between 23 and 77 per year during the 1970s (a rate of 1.33 per 100,000 live births). This is a real epidemiological success story.

SYPHILIS

Syphilis is a venereal disease produced by the bacterium *Treponema pallidum* (also called *Spirocheta pallida*). Transmission of syphilis to the fetus, unlike the case of rubella,

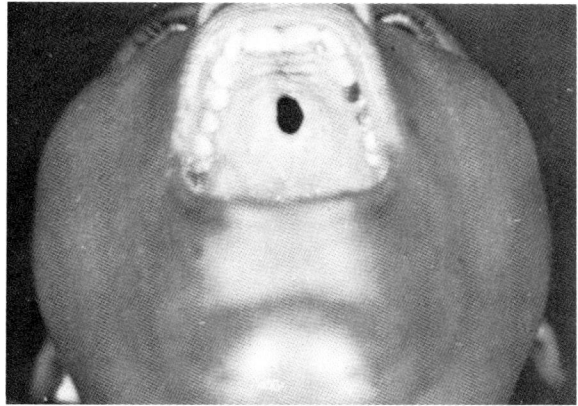

FIGURE 4–1. This victim of congenital syphilis exhibits pegged teeth, discolored molars, and a cleft palate. Much of the damage done by syphilis, to bones for example, is internal. (From Atlas of Mental Retardation Syndromes by S.S. Gellis & M. Feingold (1968). U.S. Dept. of Health, Education, and Welfare, Washington, D.C.)

is more likely later in pregnancy, and it appears that syphilis affects the potential baby only after the 16th to 18th week of gestation. Thus syphilis is not associated with defects in organogenesis, but with defects caused by destructive **lesions** (abnormal changes in structure) of already developed organs. Lesions have been found on the cornea of the eye, producing blindness, and on the skin and mucous membranes. Infants with **congenital** (present at birth or constitutional) syphilis are also likely to suffer problems with their livers, inflammation of the lining of the abdomen (peritonitis), anemia, central nervous system problems, and pegged teeth (see Figure 4–1). These are the defects of those who survive. Twenty-five percent die before birth and another 33% of those who survive birth subsequently die early in life, often from the effects of their congenital syphilis.

Antibiotics became available to the public after World War II and the Public Health Service aggressively pursued policies to eradicate venereal diseases. As a result, syphilis virtually disappeared in the 1950s and 1960s. Unfortunately the Public Health Service budgets implementing these policies were cut shortly before the "sexual revolution" in the late 1960s and the number of cases has increased since the early 1970s. Thus syphilis is a significant problem for pregnant women again, because the organisms causing syphilis remain active even after the symptoms disappear. Fortunately, most states require that all pregnant women reporting to a doctor or hospital be given the simple blood test that detects syphilis. If it is detected and cured before the 16th to 18th week of gestation, serious defects to the fetus will be avoided, although some of the long-term effects, such as the stigmata affecting the skin and teeth, may still occur. If all women got adequate prenatal care, the effects of syphilis on the unborn could be eliminated.

ORGANISMS THAT INFECT THE BABY AT BIRTH

We now turn to four infections that are transmitted primarily at the time of delivery. They are both infections and perinatal events, but because the resulting problems are not directly related to the birth process, we will discuss them here. By putting them here we also stress the point that environmental agents affect the potential baby at various times during gestation.

The first two infections, cytomegalovirus (CMV) and herpes virus hominis (HVH), are both members of the herpes simplex virus family and both produce chronic or recurrent infections. CMV affects one or more of the genitalia, urinary tract, and breasts. It is usually silent; that is, it does not produce symptoms about which the woman complains. It becomes latent but can be reactivated and frequently is during pregnancy. CMV is especially prevalent in the sexually active, the young, and the poor, though 60% of all women have antibodies to CMV. It is active or reactivated in 3% of women in their first trimester and in about 12% near term (McIntosh, 1984). The virus most often affects the **cervix** (the opening from the uterus to the vagina) and the infant contracts it when passing through the cervix during birth. The baby does not always become infected; about 0.5–1.5% of newborns in the United States are infected and 5–10% of these may later be found to be deaf or mentally retarded (Sever, Larsen, & Grossman, 1979).

Relatively few fetuses are afflicted with CMV prior to delivery, and only some of those who are have obvious symptoms. The evidence for those few who have symptoms at birth is both clear cut and depressing. One fourth are dead by three months of age and some two thirds of the remainder are developmentally or intellectually impaired. In contrast, those few who do not have obvious symptoms or defects may be at risk with respect to hearing and intellectual development, though the evidence is not clear.

In general, CMV is the leading cause of sensory neural damage in children in the United States (Stagno, 1980). CMV has also been implicated in 7% of a series of 70 deaths from congenital heart disease occurring shortly after birth.

HVH is the type of herpes that is primarily transmitted venereally. It usually affects the vagina or cervix and, if active at the time of birth, may infect the fetus. HVH is found more frequently among women who are sexually active, and it is more frequent among the poor and the young. It is less prevalent than CMV, but in 1974 it occurred in 1% of obstetric patients in the practice of some doctors or hospitals (Alford et al., 1974). Since that time the epidemic nature of herpes has become considerably more serious with 300,000 new cases per year and more middle class persons affected.

Babies can become infected as they pass through the cervix and vagina (or even by the use of scalp electrodes for fetal monitoring). This is a rare but very serious occurrence. If the mother's infection is in its active stage (that is, if she has symptoms), 50% of exposed babies contract the virus. Infants who do are likely to die if they have either the disseminated (or whole body) type or a localized type that involves the CNS. Death occurs in over 90% or over 50% of these cases, respectively. These death rates can be lowered to 50% and 10%, respectively, by proper diagnosis and treatment, but half of the survivors will develop microcephaly, spasticity, paralysis, seizures, deafness, or blindness (Whitly, Nahmias, Visintine, Fleming, & Alford, 1980, as cited in McIntosh, 1984).

Whether HVH affects earlier prenatal development is not clear. Signs of fetal disease are rare, but there may be an increased abortion rate in early pregnancy among women with genital herpes, perhaps because the virus crosses the placenta. If this is so, then the rates of fetal disease may be low only because many HVH victims have already died.

Prevention of infection of babies is clearly of critical importance, but this is not easy because in two thirds of the cases of maternal infection, there are no active lesions. Because there is no cure for HVH, even if a mother knows that she has had it the safety of her potential offspring is not ensured. Nevertheless, she can reduce the chances that the infection will be active during late pregnancy because medications currently available appear to reduce the re-occurrence of active infections. Active re-occurrences are also dangerous to the baby, though less so than primary infections. When a mother is diagnosed as having an active case of HVH close to delivery time, a **Caesarean section** (removal of the infant by cutting surgically through the mother's abdomen) prior to or shortly after the breaking of the waters can be used with reasonable success to protect the fetus.

The third infectious agent transmitted primarily at the time of delivery is *gonococcus* (plural gonococci), the bacterium that produces gonorrhea. Gonorrhea is a venereal disease that often produces no symptoms or such mild symptoms in women that they do not seek medical attention; hence, it often becomes chronic. As a result, there is a rather great risk that pregnant women are unaware that they have gonorrhea. It used to account for a large proportion of congenitally blind infants. All states have long had laws that mandate the use of drops of silver nitrate or penicillin in the eyes of the newborn. These will destroy the gonococci and prevent the development of the infection that can lead to blindness. Other surfaces of the newborn do not provide a sufficiently warm moist environment to permit the organisms to live long enough to cause infection.

The fourth infectious agent transmitted primarily at delivery is group B streptococcus, a group of bacteria that produce puerperal sepsis (a genital tract infection after childbirth), septic sore throat, scarlet fever, and other infections. It affects from 1 to 30 in 10,000 and can lead to rapid death or meningitis if not detected and treated with antibiotics (Desmonts, 1982).

OTHER INFECTIOUS DISEASES

Although the infections we have discussed—rubella, syphilis, CMV, HVH, gonorrhea, and group B streptococcus—are the most widespread and best understood of teratogenic infectious agents, other infectious diseases are either known to be or thought to be dangerous. Most prevalent among these is toxoplasmosis, an infection by the protozoan (simplest animal) *Toxoplasma gondii*. Humans most frequently contract the disease through contact with cats, particularly with cat feces. It has been tentatively linked to epidemics of congenital hydrocephalus (Carter, 1965), as well as to **microcephaly** (abnormal smallness of the head) and damage to eyes, brain, lungs, and liver (Sever, 1982). Its frequency is highly varied, from 1 to 24 per 10,000 live births. Only one case in ten is serious (Desmonts, 1982).

Chicken pox (another form of herpes, *herpes varicella*) also affects the baby if it is contracted by the mother in the last 4 days of pregnancy or by the baby in the first 2 days after birth, but this is extremely rare.

Viruses that are suspect but have not been proven damaging are Epstein-Barr and hepatitis B. The latter is very prevalent in mothers in some parts of the world, though not in the United States. Vaccines are being developed and treatment is possible for the infant. Hence, it would not seem of great importance, except that it may produce the chromosomal abnormality that results in Down's syndrome. In the state of Victoria, Australia, the infectious hepatitis rates over a 12-year period (Collman & Stoller, 1962) showed a strong relation to the rates of Down's syndrome nine months after the same period.

Finally, the most common viral infection, influenza, may affect prenatal development. Although there is no clear evidence linking it to birth defects, it has been implicated in a five-fold increase in childhood leukemia Fedrick & Alberman, 1972).

IMPLICATIONS OF OUR KNOWLEDGE OF INFECTIOUS AGENTS

The discovery that rubella, a viral disease, affects the fetus demonstrated that viruses can cross the placental barrier. Most bacteria, which are usually much larger than viruses, cannot. Since then, investigations of the role of infectious diseases on prenatal development have focused on viral diseases, which affect approximately 5% of pregnancies. The placenta does not, however, filter out all bacteria. The causative organism in syphilis is bacterial and it evidently reaches the fetus by means of placental exchange between the maternal and fetal bloodstreams. It is thought that in all the diseases we have discussed, placental infection is a precursor to fetal infection.

Timing is important in fetal infections. Rubella clearly operates according to a critical period. The infection is harmful only when it reaches the fetus at the time the vulnerable organ is developing. Syphilis has a different timing that is not associated with organogenesis. CMV, HVH, and gonorrhea, in contrast, are dangerous at the time of birth.

The practical applications of such knowledge are obvious. With good prenatal care, starting even before pregnancy, most of the dangers we have discussed can be prevented or alleviated. In spite of this progress, future research is likely to find other infectious agents that are capable of harming the embryo, fetus, or newborn.

Chronic Disorders or Conditions of the Mother

We now turn to noninfectious chronic diseases or conditions a woman may have that may affect the fetus.

HORMONAL DISORDERS

Hormonal disorders are one class of chronic maternal conditions that can affect the development of a growing fetus. We will describe three common hormonal diseases: hypothyroidism, hyperthyroidism, and diabetes.

Hypothyroidism is a condition in which the mother does not produce enough thyroid hormone. It can be successfully treated by giving hormones to the mother to replace or supplement her own. Unfortunately, not all mothers are adequately treated and their conditions may create problems for their offspring. These mothers have a high incidence of spontaneous abortions, premature deliveries, stillbirths, and infants with major anomalies (Jones & Man, 1969). Those infants that escape a more serious fate are likely to have poorer than average development in infancy and beyond.

Both mental and motor development at 8 months is lower for infants whose mothers had inadequate treatment than for those whose mothers had adequate treatment (Man & Jones, 1969). At 4 and 7 years they are also deficient (Man, Holden, & Jones, 1971; Man, Jones, Holden, & Mellits, 1971). The average IQ of normal controls at 4 years was 100 and that of offspring of adequately treated mothers was 103, compared to 94 for those whose mothers were inadequately treated. Three of these mothers had two pregnancies during the study and had adequate treatment in one but not in the other. The 4-year IQs of the 3 offspring born when the mothers were adequately treated were 94, 100, and 117. Their respective siblings born when the mothers received inadequate treatment had IQs of 72, 76, and 101 (Man & Serunian, 1976).

These three pairs also illustrate an important methodological problem. If any one of these three pairs were investigated by itself, the IQs of pair one (92 and 72) might lead to the conclusion that treatment helps but does not lead to full normality, and the IQs from pair three (117 and 101) to the conclusion that maternal abnormality does not lead to a problem for the infant. In fact, all three cases taken together show that adequate treatment of hypothyroid mothers always leads to higher IQs in the children as compared to siblings born when the mothers were not adequately treated (by 20, 24, or 16 points, which are not trivial amounts). This example shows the dangers of reasoning from individual cases, or **case studies.** It also reaffirms the importance of studying adequate control groups.

Maternal hyperthyroidism (overactive thyroid), also affects the developing fetus. The problems found in a study of 41 pregnancies among 31 women with hyperthyroidism included 5 fetal deaths, 3 cases of goiter, and 1–2 cases each of hypothyroidism, hyperthyroidism, Down's syndrome, and undescended testes (Burrow, 1965). Unlike the situation for hypothyroidism, the drugs used to treat hyperthyroidism may themselves be harmful to prenatal development, because it is known that they cross the placental barrier. Thus the effects of the disease cannot be separated from those of the drug, or the effect of either from genetic inheritance.

Another hormonal disease that can affect

fetal development is diabetes. As in the case of thyroid deficiency, management of diabetes is possible, although it is generally only ameliorative. Women with diabetes frequently have spontaneous abortions or miscarriages. They also have a relatively high incidence of stillbirths. The death of a wanted infant is always a tragedy, but the trauma is particularly great for a woman who has had several miscarriages and finally carries an infant to term only to find that it is not alive at birth.

Surviving infants of diabetic mothers are much more likely to suffer nontrivial abnormalities than are infants of nondiabetic mothers: from 6% to 9% compared to 2% for a control group (Kitzmiller, Brown, Philippe, et al., 1981; Pederson, Tygstrup, & Pederson, 1964). These abnormalities include cardiac, skeletal, and kidney problems. The defects occur during the highly vulnerable first 8 weeks of gestation (Kitzmiller et al., 1981), a period during which women have not normally sought medical care for their pregnancies. The major project with which Kitzmiller is associated tried to contact every diabetic woman in New England who might have any interest in becoming pregnant. If a woman agreed to join the project, she was taught to monitor body temperature to determine probable pregnancy and to seek early confirmation. Unlike other projects that have provided steady insulin maintenance in the hospital during the last months of pregnancy, Kitzmiller's project hospitalized the pregnant woman immediately in order to teach her home use of two new devices, a glucose meter and a portable insulin pump. These devices should enable her to maintain a much more steady biochemical state during the critical early period of pregnancy than is possible with insulin injections. Indeed, a German study (cited in Avery & Taeusch, 1984) has shown that in over 200 women who had such vigorous control started prior to pregnancy and maintained throughout pregnancy there was not a single offspring with a congenital anomaly. Although benefits are derived from late hospital monitoring, they do not affect organ structures.

The stage of the mother's diabetes or degree of its progression is also important to fetal development. Major abnormalities occur three times as often in infants of women with vascular complications of diabetes as in infants of normal mothers. Infants of mothers whose disease had progressed to affect the kidneys or the retina (the part of the eye that transforms light into nerve impulses) had eight times as many major abnormalities as normal babies. These findings raise some question as to whether diabetes itself or other problems associated with diabetes cause teratogenic effects.

In addition to the problems associated with developmental (embryogenic) errors, diabetic mothers are at greater risk of giving birth to both SGA babies and very heavy or large-for-gestational-age (LGA) babies that are maturationally retarded. Babies weighing 10 to 13 pounds are not infrequent among diabetic mothers.

All these effects are poorly understood. They appear to be environmental rather than genetic because diabetes in the father is not a factor. The National Institute of Child Health and Human Development is supporting major efforts to learn more about how these problems are caused and how they can be avoided.

NONHORMONAL DISORDERS

Women who suffer from heart disease, high blood pressure (hypertension), and kidney disorders are themselves at risk during pregnancy. In addition, their condition may impose problems on the fetus they are carrying. For example, such women are more likely to give birth to infants who are small for gestational age (SGA).

In women who have severe cases of one of these diseases, the mother and doctor may discuss abortion as an option because of the mother's health. If they decide to continue the pregnancy, the baby is sometimes delivered early by Caesarean section, either to avoid further strain on the mother or because there are indications that the fetus is having problems and has developed sufficiently to be more likely to survive on its own.

MATERNAL AGE

Another condition of the mother to consider is her age. Increasing maternal age is related to a sharp increase in chromosomal abnormalties, as we discussed in Chapter 3. Very young mothers are also at much greater risk than are mothers in their twenties. Very young mothers are primarily at risk for having premature or SGA babies rather than babies with chromosomal abnormalities. It has been thought for some time that very young mothers were physiologically too immature to provide a proper growing environment for the embryo and fetus. More recently, data have shown that if young mothers receive good diets and good prenatal care, their infants are not at greatly increased risk for prematurity or low birth weight. Thus, the associated factors of poor prenatal care and diet appear to be the primary causal factors in the increased risk for prematurity and low birth weight in this group. Note, however, that in our society a good diet and good prenatal care are not the norm for adolescents, especially not for those from underprivileged environments. To avoid these handicapping conditions, ways of improving prenatal diet and health care for adolescents must be found. In addition, prenatal physical care is not the only problem to be solved by young mothers. They and their babies are at risk because of the social, economic, and psychological disadvantage of teenage pregnancy, and the babies may be socially handicapped by being raised by immature parents.

MALNUTRITION AND OXYGEN DEPRIVATION

Maternal Malnutrition

In our discussions of the effects of various maternal disorders on fetal development, we mentioned the possible mediating role of nutrition several times. The developing baby is entirely dependent upon the mother for its nutrition because it is nourished entirely by means of the mother's blood. Thus, maternal nutrition is an important factor in the nutrition of the developing embryo and fetus, despite the old wives' tale (often supported by doctors) that the fetus will "rob" the mother to further its own development. While the fetus can indeed be described as a parasite, it is far from a perfect one.

Nutritional status is not determined by any single aspect of diet. The principal components used to describe nutritional status are: total number of calories, number and type of protein calories, and appropriate amounts of the various vitamins and important minerals.

Good nutrition consists of a proper balance of all of these, and poor nutrition may result from a lack of any one of them.[2] Poor nutrition can also result from a woman's inability to utilize a given substance or class of substance; this means malnutrition may occur because of the woman's metabolic system rather than because of a poor diet.

The nutritional status of a woman affects all aspects of her reproductive life. The age of onset of menstruation, the onset and regularity of ovulation, and the likelihood of conception are all influenced by her nutritional status.[3] Both chronic nutritional status and acute periods of malnutrition have their effects. The effects of acute malnutrition are startling: loss or marked disruption of menstrual cycles, failure to become pregnant even when no birth control is practiced, high spontaneous abortion rates, high fetal and neonatal death rates, and high proportions of premature and SGA babies. These effects are well documented for war-imposed famine conditions as, for example, in the long siege of Leningrad during World War II when no food could be brought in. When short-term acute famine occurs in a population that is well nourished before and after the acute famine, the long-range effects of surviving offspring have been reported to be minimal. Nevertheless, a statistically significant increase in neurological consequences was found even for this population, however, if the acute malnutrition occurred early in pregnancy (Stein & Susser, 1975a, 1975b; Stein, Susser, Saenger, & Marolla, 1975).

The increase in neurological consequences as a result of malnutrition is consistent with research on the development of the brain itself. Some parts of the CNS develop rather rapidly

---

[2] Serious reading of studies in this field demands careful differentiation between lack of sufficient calories compared to lack of sufficient *and appropriate* protein calories. Most of the work on vitamin deficiencies is less available to students than is the research on calorie or protein–calorie deficiencies. Information on the relevance of trace elements such as zinc, manganese, and copper is even less available and less documented, though these elements are now thought to interact with drugs and with genetic factors in the production of teratologic effects (Hurley, 1982).

[3] A list of references documenting these relations can be found in many sources. We used the 1975 booklet *Nutrition and Fertility, Interrelationships: Implications for Policy and Action* published by the National Academy of Sciences, Washington, D.C.

in late pregnancy and in early infancy (see Chapter 2). Advances in brain physiology and biochemical techniques for measuring cell populations[4] have enabled more direct study of the brain. Studies of rats by Winick and his colleagues (Winick, 1969, 1976; Winick & Noble, 1966) indicate that malnutrition in utero and up to 17 days after birth (rats are less mature at birth than humans) leads to an apparently permanent decrease in the number of brain cells. The most severe decreases from normal occur in rat pups deprived both before and after birth (Winick, 1976). Moreover the harmful effects are greater and longer lasting when malnutrition occurs during pregnancy than during the nursing period (Chow & Sherwin, 1965; Winick, 1976).

Some correlational research with humans corroborates important aspects of the research with rats. Using the same brain assay techniques used with rats, Winick and Rosso (1969) found that the brains of children who died of malnutrition in their first year of life had fewer cells than those of children the same ages who died accidental deaths. Other research corroborates the findings with rats that pregnancy is the crucial time to supplement diet to improve infants' performances on psychological tests in the first 3 years of life (Klein, Forbes, & Nader, 1976; Werner, 1979).

Practically speaking, of course, most women cannot choose when they will suffer malnutrition. Chronic malnutrition before, during, and after pregnancy is a common problem in large parts of the world, including sizable segments of the population of the United States (see, for example, Naeye, Blanc, & Paul, 1973).[5] Even if chronically deprived mothers obtained adequate nutrition during pregnancy and nursing through prenatal and well-baby

programs, malnutrition effects would probably not be eliminated. Indeed, even the birth weights of mothers are related to their pregnancy outcomes (Hackman, Emanuel, van Belle, & Daling, 1983). Children who are sufficiently malnourished suffer permanent growth retardation. When malnourished girls mature, their stunted growth becomes a pregnancy risk factor. For example, in a Scottish study of 26,000 births (Thomson & Billewicz, 1963), decreasing stature was related to increasing rates of perinatal deaths, prematurity, and delivery complications. These outcomes were all affected by parity (number of infants born to a particular mother), age of mother, and social class, but decreasing stature affected the rates of problems independently of these other factors. In other words, the relation between stunted growth and the problems described above was found for each parity and each age group. In addition, Werner (1979) has similar findings for very different ethnic groups. On the island of Kauai, the incidence of LBW babies was 16% for women under 4 feet 9 inches (1 m 52 cm) but only 3% for those who were 5 feet 7 inches or over (1 m 70 cm). The same pattern holds not only for the different ethnic groups (with different expected-genetic-heights) in her study (Japanese, Filipino, Polynesian) but in many other studies in varied settings and with varied populations. As Werner summarizes: ". . . Women whose growth environment has been poor are at a greater risk in childbearing than are those whose opportunities for growth and development have been adequate" (p. 39).

Because the outcome of a pregnancy is related to maternal nutritional status before as well as during pregnancy, and even to maternal birth weight, those who are concerned with infant health have a large stake in advocating adequate nutrition and adequate nutritional education in general as well as during pregnancy. This may be even more important now that the lives of more low birth weight babies are saved, allowing them to become future parents.

Adequate nutrition can be attained even by those from cultures with very different dietary habits. For example, Blacks, Asians, and hispanic Americans are more likely than Caucasians to be lactose intolerant and hence be unable to use dairy products. In these cultures (or subcultures), milk is—not suppris-

---

[4] These techniques depend on the fact that all cells contain the same quantity of DNA. Thus the number of cells in any given tissue or organ can be estimated from its total DNA content. Average cell size and RNA content can also be calculated.

[5] Chronic lack of specific substances is also important as, for example, iodine deficiency. Before recognition of its role in producing goiter in adults and cretinism in infants, the rate of occurrence of the latter was very high, especially in areas where drinking water had little iodine. The use of iodized salt to prevent iodine deficiency is probably the best example there is of the use of a nutritional supplement to prevent a problem (Hurley, personal communication, October 1982).

ingly—less likely to be a regular part of the diet. With proper consideration, alternative sources of calcium can be recommended to mothers with these backgrounds. Special care also needs to be taken to see that pregnant vegetarians get adequate iron supplements and calcium intake. Fad diets are rarely concerned with adequate nutritional balance. Thus, they may be responsible for the increased frequency with which neonatologists see vitamin and trace mineral deficiencies in newborns (National Academy of Sciences, 1975).

Prenatal Fetal Malnutrition and Oxygen Deprivation

Poor nutrition of the infant can result from factors other than poor nutrition of the mother. Several aspects of development discussed in Chapter 2 also affect the nutrition of the developing organism, such as implantation at a part of the uterus where the blood supply is not good and placental inadequacy, which may occur even in well-nourished mothers. Multiple fetuses to be nourished is another source of poor nutrition. Furthermore, maternal diseases that affect prenatal development sometimes do so by cutting down on nutrients or oxygen or both available to the fetus. We will concentrate on multiple births and maternal diseases.

Twins, triplets, and larger groups obviously require more nutrients than a single fetus. All multiple births are more likely to be premature (the more fetuses, the more premature) than are singletons. This may, at least in part, be due to the mother's inability to meet the nutritional demands placed on her system. In general, multiple-birth babies are also SGA. Identical twins who share a single placenta are particularly affected, and often one is much more stunted in growth than the other; in extreme cases one does not survive. For those twins who have two placentas, one may be placed better than the other, resulting in quite different birth weights. In the case of identical twins, nutritional differences produce environmental differences in persons of identical genetic make-up. The neonatal differences in weight and strength often persist into adulthood.

Thus, constitutional differences due to nutrition are one source of differences between

genetically identical individuals. This is another example of the effect of environmental events or circumstances on the phenotype.

The location of implantation, placental inadequacy, and multiple fetuses are all conditions that interact with the mother's nutritional status in affecting the fetus. A well-nourished mother is better able to nourish two or more fetuses than a poorly-nourished mother. In addition, a poorly-located implantation in a well-nourished mother may result in a better outcome than a well-located implantation in a mother who is a long-term victim of malnutrition.

Maternal diseases may interfere with the normal growth of the placenta, which in turn deprives the fetus of needed nutrients and oxygen. The blood supply may be affected directly as happens in chronic heart disease, with high blood pressure, or in severe, prolonged toxemia. The question that can be asked is, Why can reduced blood flow have such a marked influence upon the growth of the fetus? Though many nutrients are adequate in this situation, researchers believe there are one or more factors that limit the ability of the fetus to grow, especially toward the end of gestation. The most important nutrient limited by blood flow problems may be oxygen.

Oxygen is an extremely important nutrient, although it is different from nutrients such as protein, vitamins, and total caloric energy. There are serious effects of oxygen deprivation that are independent of, but parallel to, the effects of nutritional deprivation. One demonstration of such effects is seen in the differences in babies born at different altitudes. Numerous studies have found that babies born to mothers who live at high altitudes during pregnancy tend to have low birth weights or be SGA. For example, nearly 24% of babies in Lake County, Colorado, at 3200 meters (about 10,000 feet) above sea level, were low in birth weight. This rate is far above that for other areas of the United States. In areas where people have lived for many generations at high altitudes, the effects do not appear to be as great despite the fact that their diet and prenatal care may be worse there than in Lake County. For example, in Cuzco, Peru, at 3416 meters (over 11,000 feet) babies are about 400 grams (or 14 ounces) heavier than those in Lake County and only 10% of the infants are of low birth weight

(Haas, 1970). Researchers suggest that biological responses acquired as a result of life-long residence at high altitudes or as a result of genetic selection may account for these differences. In spite of the smaller effects in some populations, there are consistent birth weight differences between groups living at low and high altitudes in the same country and of the same ethnic group. At least some of these studies have controlled for social class, maternal smoking, parity, and parental stature. Hence it is highly likely that oxygen levels account for the results (Haas, 1970, 1973). Furthermore, exposures of rats to anoxia equivalent to altitudes of 33,000 to 46,000 feet have resulted in both weight and behavioral changes (Vierck, King, & Ferm, 1966). These data have led to some concern about the effects of travel to extremely high altitudes on pregnant women who are not adapted to such an environment.

FIGURE 4–2. This armless victim of thalidomide has learned to use his toes and feet as fingers and hands. (UPI/Bettmann-news Photos.)

DRUGS

Another class of substances that produce abnormalities of development is drugs, both prescribed and illicit. Many drugs, in large doses, are known to cause malformations in animals. In November of 1961 Warkany and Kalter's review (1961a, 1961b) of the causes of congenital malformations appeared. They warned that despite the inaccuracies that may occur when data from animal experiments are extrapolated and applied to humans, drugs might cause teratogenic risk in humans. In the same month the first suspicions about thalidomide were voiced in Germany and in the following month in England. Kalter and Warkany (1983) credit the thalidomide tragedy with putting teratology on the map.

Thalidomide

As was the case with rubella, the effects of thalidomide were discovered because of an epidemic of children born with a well-defined set of developmental abnormalities. The most publicized of these were arms or legs or both that were "flipper like" or almost totally absent (Figure 4–2). Medical detective work found that all the mothers of these infants had

taken a mild sedative prescribed by their doctors for morning sickness or anxiety—namely, thalidomide. Few cases occurred in the United States because thalidomide had not been licensed for use here, but some 4500 thalidomide babies were born in West Germany, not including those who died soon after birth.

After thalidomide was identified as the cause of the limb abnormalities, other effects were discovered. Many thalidomide infants suffered malformations of the eyes, ears, heart, intestines, or urogenital tract. It now appears that both mental subnormality and epilepsy are more frequent in thalidomide babies than in the population at large, thus indicating that the central nervous system might also have been affected (McFinn & Robertson, 1973; Stephenson, 1978).

The effects of this drug, like those of rubella, occur during a critical period between the 20th and 35th days after conception. If taken for only a few days, or even for only one day at the most sensitive period, thalidomide can produce defects. The seriousness of the defects, as well as the number of defects, is variable, and may depend on when within the sensitive period the mother took the drug. Indeed, it has been said that the thalidomide syndrome is really a series of syndromes that depend on the time of taking the drug (Fraser, 1984). The period of susceptibility (between the 20th and 35th days after conception) is the time when mothers are likely to suffer from morning sickness and hence to have had this supposedly mild tranquilizer prescribed for them. It has been hypothesized that the wide variety of deformities must result from a toxic factor acting on the initial nerve impulses to muscles that direct growth and development in the organogenetic phase of development, and that the deformities are the result of minor degrees of resorption (Gordon, 1966).

The psychological and financial problems of having a "thalidomide baby" are great. In England parents won a lawsuit holding the drug company responsible for many of the expenses. This decision, however, was relatively recent and came long after the birth of these babies. Physicians, psychologists, therapists of many types, and engineers together with parents were faced with the challenge of how to enable these children to have maximum interaction with their world. Engineers developed arm and leg devices, and the Institute of Mechanical Engineers in London published a special volume, *Basic Problems of Prehension, Movement, and Control of Artificial Limbs*, in which several of the papers were especially directed toward the thalidomide child.

How did medical authorities allow such a powerful teratogen to be licensed for use in any country? The answer to this question demonstrates the complexity and difficulty of doing research on new drugs. The general procedure in testing a new drug is to test it experimentally on animals before it is given to humans. If animals are not harmed by the substance, it is usually given to humans in large, well-controlled studies known as **clinical trials.** Clinical trials are basically nonexperimental because the drug is given only to patients, who therefore are not a random sample of the whole population. Good clinical trials have an experimental component in that patients of equivalent status are randomly assigned to treatment and control groups. The control group may consist of those given other standard drugs, those given a **placebo** (nonactive substance), or both. In cases of severe problems, the use of a placebo would be unethical unless there were no drug of proven value against which to compare the experimental drug. To ensure that a new drug has no teratogenic effect, studies with both lower animals and humans need to be conducted on pregnant females. The reason that both animal and human studies are required is that drugs may not have the same effects in different species because there are real differences in susceptibility among species. In addition, it is difficult both to match dosage levels in different species and to establish equivalent gestational stages. Aspirin is an example of a drug for which there is a difference between species: It is highly teratogenic in rats but not clearly teratogenic in humans. The reverse is true for thalidomide. What happened in the thalidomide disaster is that many Western European countries licensed thalidomide before clinical trials of its teratogenic effects were conducted. While this seems terrible from our current point of view, remember that in the 1960s many experts still thought that the placental barrier was impermeable. One reviewer has stated that the thalidomide episode made the safety of drugs taken during pregnancy a nonacademic question: "The placenta was finally dethroned as a 'barrier'. . . ." (Hutchings, 1978, p. 197).

Even when animal research does not predict the effects with humans, or when the effects are different, it is not useless. Well-controlled studies with lower animals can uncover the mechanisms by which teratogens produce their effects. For example, animal studies can determine whether certain teratogens, such as viruses or drugs of a given chemical nature, act upon the mother and through her on the potential baby, or whether they affect the maternal–fetal interchange, or whether they affect the unborn infant directly. The more that is known about these mechanisms, the better are the predictions about the effects of new drugs and the easier it is to ferret out potentially harmful environmental agents.

Steroid Hormones

Steroid hormones are the sex hormones and those produced by the adrenal glands. Some members of this class of drugs are known to be teratogens.

SEXUAL HORMONES

As long as 30 years ago researchers recognized that treating pregnant mammals, including monkeys, with male sex hormone could produce a condition called pseudohermaphroditism (a condition in which an individual's sex is not clear from external characteristics) in female offspring. This condition occurs in human infants as a result of certain medical conditions. It was also shown as early as 1960 that pregnant women given androgenic (male) hormones prior to the 12th week of pregnancy for the treatment of breast cancer had female infants that were masculinized (recall the material on sexual differentiation in Chapter 2). One important question is: Are systems other than the sexual one affected? Androgen has been shown to affect aspects of the CNS other than those controlling sexual cycles and behavior. Whether androgen is the responsible agent, or whether it is metabolized in the brain to form estrogen and the estrogen acts on the brain to produce the brain differentiation is still being argued (Reinisch, 1974; Reinisch & Gandelman, 1978; Reinisch, Gandelman, & Spiegel, 1979). This argument introduces an important aspect of the steroid hormones. Chemically they are very similar to each other and can be metabolized to yield other steroids. In short, the drug that is ingested may not be the drug that has the effect!

Diethylstilbestrol (DES) is a synthetic estrogen that has been widely publicized because of the occurrence of cancer in the female offspring of women who have taken it during pregnancy to help prevent miscarriages.[6] It also increases the rate of fetal death, miscarriages, and premature births (Herbst, Hubby, Blough, et al., 1980, as cited in Avery & Taeusch, 1984). It is estimated that 30% of male offspring of mothers who took DES are infertile (Bibbo et al., 1977, and Gill, Schumacher, Bibbo, Straus, & Schoenberg, 1979, as cited in Avery & Taeusch, 1984).

The female hormone progesterone has been used medically to treat pregnant women who either have a history of previous spontaneous abortions or who are showing signs of aborting. The synthetic hormone progestin

(norethisterone) is now used for this purpose. Use of the progestins to maintain pregnancy has occurred in the United States and Europe for the past 40 years. In addition, progestins are a major component of birth control pills and are sometimes used to bring on menstruation if it is late. Women may expose their embryo or fetus to this hormone in two ways. They may not realize they are pregnant and continue birth control pills or they may use progestin to bring on menstruation and fail because they are pregnant. Hence some millions of infants have been exposed to some dosage of either natural or synthetic progestins.

The first evaluation of the effects of these exposures occurred less than two decades ago. Although proper experimental controls have been lacking in many studies, the evidence suggests that development is affected by exposure to exogenous progestins during gestation. Progestins act as teratogens in producing an excess of cardiovascular birth defects, and possibly of other defects that are found with such teratogenic agents as thalidomide. In addition, there is evidence that progestins affect sexual differentiation. The effects of natural progesterone are different in this respect from the effects of synthetic varieties. Natural progesterone has been shown to antagonize the masculinizing action of testosterone in infrahuman animals. In contrast, the synthetic progestins appear to have some androgenic potential, as evidenced by the masculinization of the genitalia in a small percentage of the female offspring of mothers who took them during pregnancy. Behavioral effects, especially tomboyism and high IQ, are also indicated by some studies, but this conclusion is not definitive because of problems of sample selection, lack of proper controls, or sometimes both (for example, Dalton, 1968; Ehrhardt & Money, 1967, 1973). The latter study found that the effects were dose dependent and related to the time of administration. More recently, Dalton (1976) has shown that children of mothers given progesterone, usually to avoid toxemia, were more likely to gain entry to a university in England. This is true whether they were compared to normal controls or to controls whose mothers had toxemia but were not treated with progesterone. The methodological weaknesses of the human studies render them inconclusive with respect

---

[6] A number of agents that are teratogenic are also carcinogenic. Which effect occurs may depend on the susceptibility of the target organ at the time of exposure.

to effects on intelligence and personality. Nevertheless, they do agree in finding some effects.

A more careful study compared infants exposed to synthetic progestin alone or together with estrogen or DES, to siblings who had not been exposed (Reinisch, 1977; Reinisch & Karow, 1977). Subjects and controls were evaluated by testers who knew neither the purposes of the study nor the treatment category of the child. This study also yielded differences. As compared to their siblings, exposed children were more independent, individualistic, self-assured, and self-sufficient, both as tested and as reported by their mothers. However, the average of their IQs (121) did not differ from that of their unexposed siblings (120). The lack of IQ difference may have been produced by the use of siblings as controls, but it may also have been a result of (1) the lower potency progestins given in this study, (2) the combination of progestins and estrogens given, or (3) a ceiling effect; that is, the IQs of the exposed siblings are so high that their unexposed siblings could hardly score higher.

ADRENAL HORMONES (CORTICOSTEROIDS)

These hormones have also been used in the treatment of a number of medical conditions, especially rheumatic, allergic, and endocrine disorders, and have been used to induce ovulation and support pregnancy. Cortisone and prednisone, which is five times as potent, are the synthetic compounds. For a time they were considered highly suspect for use in pregnant women because in mice they produced a high rate of **resorptions** (reabsorption of zygotes, blastulas, or embryos into the maternal system), stillbirths, and prematurity. Human evidence did not bear out the dire predictions based on the animal data. It was assumed that the higher dosage levels in animal studies compared to human treatments or species differences might account for the different results. However, recent work in which siblings who had not been exposed to corticosteroid treatment in utero were used as controls (Reinisch, Simon, Karow, & Gandelman, 1978) found an increase in the proportion of SGA infants as compared to the controls. Furthermore, among the babies who could not be classed as SGA, those exposed to corticosteroid treatment were

smaller at birth than their nontreated siblings. These effects on the developing fetus may be either direct effects on growth, because corticosteroids cross the placental barrier readily and young children treated with them for asthma show severe growth retardation, or the effects of placental abnormalities such as prednisone has been shown to produce. In addition, mice given dosages comparable to those used medically with humans show behavioral effects.

Other effects of corticosteroids have been found recently. One is that they change the offspring's sensitivity to male hormones (Simon & Gandelman, 1977), which results in behavioral changes similar to those produced by androgen itself, such as an increase in aggressive behavior. Administration of corticosteroids also has produced permanent effects on the CNS in mice and defects such as cleft palate.[7]

The available research makes it clear that excessive doses of corticosteroids are dangerous to humans, even though adequate amounts are necessary for proper development of the embryo and fetus. Better evaluation of particular effects on humans is clearly mandatory.

Psychotropic Drugs

People take psychotropic drugs for the psychological effects they produce. Examples are heroin (and methadone), lysergic acid diethylamide (LSD), amphetamines, and marijuana. These drugs primarily affect the behavior and physiological functioning of the baby rather than producing physical defects. They are the clearest instances of behavioral teratogens as opposed to physical teratogens.

The most is known about the effects of heroin and of methadone, which is often used to replace it. Heroin passes the placental barrier so that infants of addicted women are born addicted. The withdrawal symptoms they suffer after birth can kill them. Only after doctors

---

[7] Cleft lip, palate, and similar errors in head and face fusion occur in 1 in 500 births in the United States (Pratt, 1982). Pratt has also shown that such defects occur most often when both the mother and the embryo have genetic predispositions *and* are exposed to chemicals or drugs that have teratogenic potential.

recognized that this was what was wrong with relatively large numbers of babies did they learn to manage them appropriately and spare their lives. Even so, survivors suffer from a number of behavioral difficulties (for example, motoric behaviors, soothability, sleep cycles), though it is not known whether these last beyond infancy.

Many heroin addicts have been treated by switching them to methadone maintenance. Unfortunately, it appears that the effects of methadone on the newborn are, if anything, worse than those of heroin and may include physiological damage. The children are born small and are subject to high perinatal mortality (Finnegan, Reeser, & Connaughton, 1977; Zelson, Sook, & Casalino, 1973). The babies suffer more seizures and hence CNS damage, and there is more severe elevation of bilirubin levels (hyperbilirubinemia) than in babies of heroin addicts, but the severity of withdrawal is less. The breathing responses of newborns whose mothers were on methadone are altered, and this persists some 20 to 40 days after methadone can no longer be detected in their systems. Thus these effects may contribute to the larger than usual number of sudden infant deaths (see Chapter 5) of infants born to mothers maintained on methadone (Ostrea, Chavez, & Strauss, 1975). It is reasonable to suspect some CNS damage even in those methadone babies who do not have seizures, because methadone babies have been exposed daily while in utero to an increased level of carbon dioxide and therefore a decreased level of oxygen. The methadone-induced CNS damage seems clearly to affect motoric maturation (Johnson, Diano, & Rosen, 1984; Marcus, Hans, & Jeremy, 1982; Ostrea et al., 1975). The data of Johnson and colleagues (1984) also show differences between methadone babies and controls on the Bayley Mental Development index at both 12 and 24 months. Although this could be due to postnatal environment, the fact that the methadone babies more often have very small head circumferences at birth and at 12 and 24 months of age argues for a possible biological component. Researchers disagree, however, on whether methadone alters state behaviors or produces decreased visual alerting (Marcus et al., 1982; Strauss, Lessen-Firestone, Starr, & Ostrea, 1975; Strauss, Starr, Ostrea, Chavez, & Stryker, 1976). Several studies found the sexes to be affected differently, and males to be more affected than females.

Methadone exposure does not end at birth for infants who are nursed by mothers on methadone maintenance. They receive some methadone, although very much less than the amounts they received in utero, and hence will have a more prolonged narcotic dependence. It is conservatively estimated that 3,000 babies per year are born to narcotic dependent mothers in New York City alone (Carr, 1975), many or most of them on methadone.

Another well-known psychotropic drug is LSD. There has been a great deal of discussion about whether this drug causes chromosomal damage to those who take it, and whether this damage can be transmitted to their offspring. The authors of a comprehensive review of more than 100 articles on the subject (Dishotsky, Loughman, Mogar, & Lipscomb, 1971) concluded that pure LSD in moderate doses does not produce chromosomal damage. LSD has also failed to produce consistent teratogenic effects in rodents, and the several instances of malformation in babies born to women who had taken LSD during pregnancy may be coincidental or due to other drug abuse problems.

Amphetamines belong to a group of drugs called neurotropic-anorexogenic. Drugs in this group are often abused, and may be taken to suppress appetite during pregnancy. Some findings indicate an increase in heart defects in the offspring, but the data are not conclusive. Certainly they are not powerful teratogens like thalidomide.

The last psychotropic drug we will discuss is marijuana. Its prenatal effects have not been well studied in humans, but a handful of studies with animals suggest that it may have a teratogenic effect. Its constituents can cross the placental barrier in rats (Vardaris, Weisz, Fazel, & Rawitch, 1976) and thus at least have teratogenic potential. In addition a direct effect has been demonstrated in rhesus monkeys: Abnormally high fetal loss has been produced by high doses of its active ingredient, delta-9-tetrahydrocannabinol (THC) (Sassenrath, Chapman, & Goo, 1979), perhaps as a result of problems in chromosome segregation during cell division. Although no conclusive evidence of teratogenicity exists for humans, some evidence points to the possibility of subtle effects on birth weight and length and nervous system abnormalities (Fried, 1980). Given the widespread usage of this drug, studies either to establish or to rule out negative effects are very much needed (Institute of Medicine, 1982).

Another health risk from smoking marijuana is similar to the risk from cigarette smoking. Marijuana contains 70% more benzopyrene and more tars, both cancer-causing agents, than tobacco. Marijuana also weakens the antibacterial defense systems of the lungs. In the next section we will discuss the possible effects of cigarette smoking on prenatal development. Until it is known whether and how (by nicotine, tars, or other variables) cigarette smoking acts as a teratogen, it is best to assume that the effects are similar for marijuana smoke.

It is difficult to assess the factors that cause problems in offspring born to drug abusers. Drug abusers typically take many drugs; the drugs they take are often impure; and abusers are likely to be malnourished and are unlikely to get adequate prenatal care. It is even possible that the drugs given to treat postnatal withdrawal could cause or contribute to subsequent behavioral difficulties in these exposed infants. One or more of these factors may contribute to the babies' problems, and there are no data to identify which ones or which combinations are crucial. The problems of sorting out operative causal factors are less likely to occur in studies of the effects of methadone, which is given to replace other drugs, but of course, some women on methadone still take other drugs.

Cigarette Smoking

We include cigarette smoking under the heading of drugs, although it is certainly not clear that the effects of smoking are due to absorption of its drug, nicotine. Changes in oxygen level, changes in carbon monoxide level, poorer nutrition, or other associated life-style variables may contribute to the effects that have been attributed solely to cigarette smoking. There are even data that question whether smoking as such has any effect. These latter data are not cited very often today, because smoking in general is quite appropriately under heavy attack for health reasons.

We will first describe the data that link maternal smoking to negative outcomes of pregnancy. Second, we will examine the issue of causality by describing some data that suggest that smoking itself is not the causal factor, as well as some that suggest it is. Finally, we will discuss other differences between smokers and nonsmokers that might influence or account for the correlations between smoking and infant problems.

PROBLEMS CORRELATED WITH SMOKING

When a pregnant woman smokes, it affects her fetus's heartrate (Sontag, 1941) and breathing and movements (Thaler, Goodman, & Davies, 1980). Such findings raise the issue of whether these effects have long-term consequences.

Birth Weight; Prematurity. Birth weight and prematurity have been the most often studied outcomes. These two measures are closely related because prematurity has often been judged only on the basis of birth weight (see Chapter 2). Both birth weight and prematurity have consistently been found to be related to smoking. The U.S. Department of Health, Education, and Welfare (1979) reported more than 45 studies that confirmed the relation of smoking to birth weight and prematurity (see, for example, Silverman, 1977). This relation has been found in prospective as well as in retrospective studies, in studies of Blacks as well as of whites, and in studies of lower class as well as of middle class and of representative samples. Studies have failed to agree on whether: (1) prematurity or SGA (small for gestational age) is the more important result; (2) LBW (low birth weight) babies of smoking mothers are as likely to die as equivalent weight babies of nonsmoking mothers; (3) there are long-lasting disadvantages for those who survive.

Having thus summarized the complex evidence, let us look at some of it in more detail. Perhaps the first prospective study was done in Baltimore (Frazier, Davis, Goldstein, & Goldberg, 1961). The sample was 2,736 Black women seen at city prenatal health clinics and delivered of single live infants in city hospitals. The investigators found that the rate of births under $5\frac{1}{2}$ pounds went from 11.2% for nonsmokers to 18.4% for smokers, and the increase was in proportion to the amount smoked. They also found fetal and neonatal death rates to be higher for smokers than for nonsmokers. Age, education, work history, and other factors were comparable in smoking and nonsmoking mothers; hence these factors cannot account for the results. The study also examined "nervousness" and found that it was not related to LBW babies in nonsmokers, but was related in smokers (23% LBW babies among "nervous" smoking mothers, 17% among the rest). Although this study found no difference other than smoking between the groups, it did not examine many variables that other studies have found to be correlated with smoking such as drinking.

Another prospective study (Yerushalmy, 1971) was larger and dealt with a broader sample that generally had a higher socioeconomic status (SES). Participants were in a prepaid health care plan and would be expected to have better general health and nutrition, since all had incomes (hence could afford adequate diets) and were entitled to health care without additional cost. There were 9,793 whites and 3,290 Blacks in this sample. The data confirm the relation of smoking to birth weight: There were twice as many LBW babies among smokers. Nevertheless, the investigators did not find the increase in mortality that would be expected with low birth weights. Indeed, LBW babies born to smoking mothers were only about half as likely to die as those born to mothers who never smoked (Yerushalmy, 1964).

A very recent study (Dowler & Jacobson, 1984) found that the amount smoked during pregnancy was significantly related to birth weight and length in a sample of 186 middle class women. The most significant relation was to birth weight, where smoking accounted for less than 6% of the variance. The gestational ages of the infants varied from 35 to 44½ weeks. No infants were SGA, which suggests that in middle class women (presumably well nourished and medically cared for), the effects of smoking on the infants' prenatal growth are minimal.

Other Problems During Infancy. We have already discovered that infants of smoking mothers are more likely to die both before and around birth, although perhaps not so likely as other low weight babies. Many other outcomes are also related (Naeye, 1979b). These babies are more likely to have malformations of the heart and other organs and to suffer respiratory and prenatal infections. Finally, deaths from **Sudden Infant Death Syndrome (SIDS** or "crib death"), the leading cause of death from one month to one year, increased by 52% in the offspring of smokers.

Long-term Outcomes. Some of the outcomes associated with smoking occur later in infancy or childhood. The longer the time since birth that the effects are measured, the greater are the problems of inferring that the prenatal exposure was causal. Nevertheless long-range outcomes are of great interest.

The outcome measure that has been most frequently used is IQ. In a very large prospective study (50,000 pregnancies from the Collaborative Perinatal Research Project), Naeye (1979b) found no IQ differences in babies whose mothers smoked during pregnancy from babies whose mothers did not in this sample of predominantly lower class subjects. His results agree with those of Hardy and Mellitts (1972) in a similar study. They are also corroborated by a recent retrospective study by Lefkowitz (1981) of a much smaller sample of 241 predominantly middle class children (72% white, 20% Black, 8% other) at about 11 years of age. The offspring of smokers did not differ from those of nonsmokers on any of the following sets of variables: (1) height or weight, (2) four measures of intellectual status (including reading and IQ determined by figure drawing), (3) five measures of happiness or depression, or (4) five measures of personal and social functioning (including one of movement assessment). Although Lefkowitz relied on the mothers to report their smoking during the long ago pregnancy, their reliability seems plausible because the birth weights of their infants not only were lower than average, but were lower in the expected amount: 196 grams lower compared to the average of 222 grams lower reported by the Surgeon General (U. S. Department of Health, Education, and Welfare, 1979). The mothers did not differ on social or economic variables, parity, or family size.

Although these studies all agree that smoking during pregnancy does not result in decreased IQ, that conclusion must be qualified, because what is true for children in general is not necessarily true for all subgroups. Broman and Nichols (1981), using data from the same project that Naeye studied, found that for those children who had high or moderately high IQs, there was a negative correlation between their later IQ and their mothers' smoking during pregnancy. The IQ scores were linearly related to the amount of maternal smoking.

Other studies also suggest that smoking during pregnancy does result in long-term outcomes for the offspring. Some of the outcomes measured in these studies are the same as those used by Lefkowitz, and some are different. In one of the largest prospective studies, Britain's Birthday Trust Prenatal Survey of 16,000 children born throughout the United Kingdom in one week in March, 1958, Davie, Butler, and Goldstein (1972) found a number of differences at age 7 in the offspring of mothers who had smoked *heavily* during pregnancy. They were an average of $\frac{1}{2}$ inch shorter, 4 months behind the average in reading level, less well adjusted at school, generally clumsy, and had apparent spatial problems (in the bottom 10% of the class in copying simple designs).

Another, fairly large, retrospective study (Stott & Latchford, 1976) developed a composite measure called the Morbidity Ratio (MR), which measures the occurrence of any handicapping condition. The handicaps include malformations, physical defects, neurological symptoms, retardation in developmental milestones, behavior disturbances, and nonepidemic illness. The 439 offspring of smokers had a 55% higher morbidity ratio than the 739 offspring of nonsmokers. It was also true that the offspring of nonsmokers had fewer handicapping conditions than might be expected from population figures. The investigators also reported that the MR rose in proportion to the amount the mother smoked.

Drawing conclusions from these studies is difficult. The bulk of the available evidence suggests that prenatal smoking does not affect the IQ of the offspring, although it may for higher IQ children. The data for other long-term effects must be considered inconclusive because some of the findings (reading level, adjustment, spatial problems) failed to replicate

in the two studies in which they were measured and because all long-term effects are potentially confounded by postnatal experiences. This is particularly problematic with smoking and the Morbidity Ratio, because postnatal smoking may cause some of the problems (for example, upper respiratory infections; Colley, Holland, & Corkhill, 1974) incorporated into the Morbidity Ratio.

DOES SMOKING CAUSE THESE EFFECTS?

The research we have just described is all correlational, and it is important to remember that correlations do not prove causality. This means that correlations between smoking and infant problems do not prove that smoking causes the difficulties. It would be impossible to conduct an experiment in which pregnant women were randomly assigned to smoking and nonsmoking conditions, so we need to find indirect ways of assessing causality. One way is to allow women to serve as their own controls. This can be done by finding women who smoked during one pregnancy and didn't smoke during another. If smoking is the causal factor, then the offspring who were subjected to smoking prenatally should differ from those offspring who were not. Yerushalmy (1972) found (in the very large sample already discussed) 210 white infants born to mothers who had not yet started to smoke and who later started to smoke and had another infant. The percentage of low birth weight infants born to these mothers before they started to smoke was 9.5 and of infants born to those same mothers after a pregnancy during which they smoked it was 8.9. Furthermore, for mothers who had an infant while smoking and who later quit smoking and had another infant the same similarity in the proportion of low birth weight infants emerged. Yerushalmy concluded, ". . . the reproductive performance of future smokers is much like that of smokers even in the period before they started to smoke and that past smokers' reproductive performances before they quit smoking is much like that of women who never smoked" (p. 283). He continued,

. . . these findings raise doubt and argue against the proposition that cigarette smoking acts as an exogenous factor which interferes with the intrauterine development of

the fetus. Rather, the evidence appears to support the hypothesis that the higher incidence of low birth weight infants is due to the smoker, *not the* smoking. *(Yerushalmy, 1972, p. 283)*

The data from infants whose mothers did not smoke during an earlier pregnancy but did smoke during a later one are particularly impressive, since older mothers have higher perinatal mortality rates. In fact, the risk of infant mortality is greater for a nonsmoking mother 35 or over than for a smoking mother under 35 and of the same parity (Butler & Alberman, 1969).

Although Yerushalmy's data seem convincing, other evidence suggests that smoking itself does have an effect. Using the Morbidity Ratio as their dependent measure of infant problems, Stott and Latchford (1976) found that in cases where the mother gave up smoking when she became pregnant the health risk for her infant was like that of infants whose mothers had not smoked, and much lower than the health risk for babies whose mothers smoked during pregnancy.

Clearly the issue of what problems are caused by smoking is not yet resolved. Yerushalmy has unusually good data in that he compares the same mothers when they smoked and when they didn't. Even more impressive, he finds the same results regardless of whether the women went from nonsmoking pregnancies to smoking pregnancies or from smoking pregnancies to nonsmoking pregnancies. This is important because mothers who change in one direction may share some other characteristics, but it is less likely that those characteristics would be the same for the women who moved in the other direction. For example, women who smoked in an earlier pregnancy but not in a later pregnancy are likely to be a sample of concerned, health-conscious women. Thus, they may have made other special efforts to ensure good prenatal care even in the pregnancy where they smoked and those efforts may have compensated for the harmful effects of smoking. Even if this is so, it is unlikely that women who start smoking in a later pregnancy do so because they are concerned about health. Thus, any extraneous variables that may explain the results for women who became nonsmokers would not be

likely to explain the finding for women who became smokers.

We do not mean to argue that Yerushalmy's data are right and Stott and Latchford's are wrong. As Yerushalmy himself points out, he was unable to control for many variables that might have accounted for his results. Thus the seemingly contradictory findings of these two studies may not really be inconsistent. Notice also that the dependent variables used in the two studies were different. Yerushalmy used low birth weight and Stott and Latchford used their composite measure of a variety of outcomes, present anywhere from the neonatal period through four years. Such a composite would be more sensitive than a single measure if smoking has very small effects on a number of infant problems. Each problem alone might not be detectable, but when all are put together a measurable effect would be obtained. In contrast, the validity of the Morbidity Ratio can be questioned because it can be influenced by experiences after birth. For example, smoking in the family after the baby is born might cause some of the problems incorporated in the Morbidity Ratio (Colley et al., 1974). Thus, the relationship of prenatal smoking and the Morbidity Ratio might be due to postnatal experiences rather than to prenatal smoking. Each of these studies, therefore, has both strengths and weaknesses, and resolution of the issues must await future research. Nevertheless, the two studies are important to know about because they provide evidence crucial to the question of whether prenatal smoking causes the effects commonly associated with it.

POSSIBLE CONTAMINATING FACTORS

Despite our uncertainty as to whether smoking itself is deleterious, there are factors associated with smoking that may contribute to the difficulties observed in the offspring of smokers. One such factor is maternal weight gain, which in turn may reflect malnutrition. Rush (1973, 1974; Rush, Davis, & Susser, 1972; Rush & Kass, 1972) found that mothers who smoke during pregnancy gain less weight, and that the more cigarettes they smoked, the less weight they gained. A lower maternal weight gain is in turn associated with lower birth weight of the offspring, and, to a lesser extent, with shorter length and smaller head circumferences at birth (Luke, Hawkins, & Petrie,

1981). Rush argued that the reduced maternal weight gain associated with smoking may actually represent a malnutrition effect, since malnourished women also gain less weight during pregnancy and have lower weight babies. Smokers may be less well nourished, since most people report that smoking suppresses their appetites. Other social habits associated with smoking might also contribute to poor nutrition.

A second factor is placental abnormalities. Naeye (1978, 1979a) in the massive study referred to earlier found that *placenta previa* (areas of dead tissue on the placenta) were more common in smokers and in women who had previously smoked than in nonsmokers during the studied pregnancy. Placental problems were also strongly implicated in the data of Meyer, Jones, and Tonascia (1976), especially for those who smoked more than one pack a day. The placental abnormalities presumably result in decreased nutrition and poorer oxygen supplies to the fetus. These correlational findings do not indicate whether the smoking or some other characteristic of women who smoke produces the placental abnormalities, which in turn produce the negative outcomes. For example, women who smoke also drink more coffee and more hard liquor and beer than nonsmokers; thus, their consumption of these substances might be the causal factor. To decide whether smoking itself produces the abnormalities would require studies (such as Yerushalmy, 1972) that use mothers as their own controls. Until researchers can isolate the exact cause of the placental abnormalities, it is useful to know that women who smoke are at increased risk for placental abnormalities. Their doctors can then determine whether they experience placental insufficiency during pregnancy.

Let us summarize the arguments we have presented. Fetal malnutrition, including oxygen deprivation, caused by placental abnormalities or low maternal weight gain, or both, have been suggested as correlates of smoking. Both of these factors are known to lead to low birth weights and short gestations. Therefore, it is thought that these factors may produce the negative outcomes for babies of smoking mothers. What is not known is whether smoking directly produces the placental abnor-

malities and low maternal weight gain or whether these are indirect effects.

Other variables that correlate with maternal smoking and poor outcomes for infants have been identified. Two that affect only a small proportion of pregnant women who smoke are lead accumulation and twinning. The causal role of smoking is not clear cut, and insufficient oxygen supply or nutrition are again implicated.

During pregnancy, cigarette smoking is related to an increased accumulation of lead in both mother and fetus among urban dwellers in industrial areas, a group which may include a larger proportion of Blacks than whites. This increase is sufficient to inhibit production of an enzyme that helps the red blood cells make hemoglobin, which is essential for the nutrition and oxygenation of the fetus. While the lead levels in the fetal blood are lower than in the maternal blood, they rise in direct proportion to those of the mother. It is not known what other effects the raised lead levels might have and whether they are sufficient to cause brain damage (Kuhnert, Erhard, & Kuhnert, 1977).

The twinning rate is twice as high in smokers as in nonsmokers (Yerushalmy, 1972), but varies markedly according to race. To be at increased risk of twinning, white women had to smoke only 5 or more cigarettes a day, but Blacks had to smoke 15 or more a day. Because twinning itself leads to an increased risk of prematurity and low birth weight, and because twin births are often excluded in studies of the effects of smoking, it is quite possible that the data underestimate the overall effects of smoking.

In addition to the four factors already discussed, Yerushalmy (1971) found several other differences between smoking and nonsmoking pregnant women that might contribute to their infants' problems. There were differences in the kinds of beverages they drank: A higher proportion of smoking mothers drank coffee, beer, and whiskey and a lower percentage drank tea, wine, and milk. No study has yet examined the effects of these beverages on offspring, but some relevant studies are underway. Smoking mothers also had started to menstruate earlier than nonsmoking mothers, and were less likely to use contraceptives or to plan their pregnancies.

FIGURE 4–3. This poster, widely distributed by the American Cancer Society, dramatizes the dangers of smoking during pregnancy. (Courtesy of the American Cancer Society.)

WHAT SHOULD SMOKING WOMEN DO DURING PREGNANCY?

Should women stop smoking during pregnancy or not? Should they smoke less and if so, how much less? Each woman, faced with the prospect of giving up a very strong habit for the sake of her unborn child, must make that decision herself. It is easy to say that it is better to be safe than sorry and to recommend that all women completely give up smoking while pregnant (Figure 4–3). After all, there clearly is a relation between smoking and serious health problems for women and clear evidence that birth weight is lower in babies of smokers, and there is a possibility that smoking itself is the cause.[8] We have already seen, however, that it

may be the smoker and not the smoking that leads to lower birth weight. Another factor to consider is that giving up smoking may also create problems for the unborn. Pregnant women who give up smoking may be resentful of their offspring. There may be physiological and psychological concomitants of giving up smoking that future research will find to be harmful to the infant. A compromise solution might be for a pregnant smoker to cut down on smoking and to make sure to get adequate prenatal medical care and nutrition in an attempt to eliminate other risks. How much to cut down on smoking is also difficult to determine. The amount of smoking that appears to be related to the poorest outcomes differs in different studies, and differs for Blacks and whites. Over all it appears that a total of less than 14 cigarettes per day for Blacks and fewer for whites might be helpful. For women who decide to continue smoking during pregnancy, it appears that higher weight gain during pregnancy may help to compensate for the growth retardation and thus decrease the risk of low birth weight. (Those seriously interested should read *Smoking for Two* by Fried and Oxorn (1980).)

Alcohol

Alcohol is the drug which, after nicotine, is the most likely to be consumed or abused in American society. Alcohol can cross the placental barrier. Although there is some evidence that there are critical periods during development when its effects are maximal, these are not well documented by current research. Indications are that binge drinking as well as chronic consumption may have effects. As with other drugs, alcohol withdrawal may play a role in the effects, but because alcohol withdrawal is much milder than that from heroin or methadone, it may go unnoticed. It also appears that the adverse effects of alcohol interact with the genetic characteristics of the embryo and fetus to determine whether and to what degree it is affected. In our discussion, we

---

[8] Actually, although this information is not directly relevant to events during pregnancy that affect the embryo or fetus, it is worth noting that the National Collaborative

Perinatal Research Project has shown that the length of time *prior* to pregnancy a woman had smoked was related to minimal brain damage in her offspring at age 7 (Nichols & Chen, 1981).

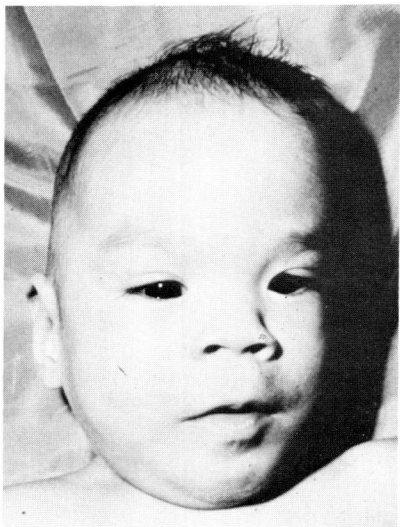

FIGURE 4–4. This FAS baby exhibits facial asymmetry and unusual shape of the eyes. (Photograph courtesy of Dr. Ann P. Streissguth.)

will first consider the better documented effects: fetal alcohol syndrome, pregnancy loss, decreased size, lowered intelligence, and other behavioral effects. Then we will compare the effects of moderate and heavy drinking and discuss other factors associated with alcohol consumption that may contribute to the negative effects.

EFFECTS OF ALCOHOL

Fetal Alcohol Syndrome. Doctors and psychologists have identified what is called Fetal Alcohol Syndrome (FAS). The characteristics include pre- and post-natal growth deficiencies, microcephaly, short palpebral fissures, small cheek bones, congenital heart defects, anomalies of the joints and limbs, and behavioral and cognitive problems (see Figure 4–4). Mental retardation is now seen as the most serious defect, as well as the most sensitive indicator of alcohol abuse. FAS has been described as probably the "most frequent known teratogenic cause of mental deficiency in the Western world" (Clarren & Smith, 1978, p. 1066, as cited in Abel, 1980).

Despite this dramatic view of the importance of alcohol as a teratogen, studies of FAS have appeared in the United States literature only in the last decade. English, French, and German studies had called attention to this syndrome much earlier (Heuyer, Mises, & Dereux, 1957; Lemoine, Haronsseau, Borteryll, & Menuet, 1968; Sullivan, 1899; Uhlig, 1957). In dramatic contrast to the earlier neglect of FAS in the United States, it is now seen by some as one of the most common congenital neurological disorders, together with Down's syndrome and spina bifida. It has been said to occur in some degree in 1 in 750 infants born in the United States (Mukherjee & Hodgen, 1982). Kalter and Warkany (1983) conclude, however, that these views "have been widely publicized and uncritically accepted by many individuals and organizations, including government agencies" (p. 492). It has been noted that even among heavy drinkers only a small proportion have babies characterized by FAS (Rosett, Weiner, Lee, Zuckerman, Dooling, & Oppenheimer, 1983).

Unlike the case for some other teratogens, the effects of alcohol in producing FAS seem to occur in many species, including chickens, rats, mice, guinea pigs, zebra fish, and beagles. For reviews of these data and appropriate references see Abel, 1980; Streissguth, 1977; and Streissguth, Landesman-Dwyer, Martin, and Smith, 1980. A variety of behavioral effects are found in the different species in addition to the physical effects (Jones, Smith, Ulleland, & Streissguth, 1973).

Pregnancy Loss. As is usually the case for a factor that can lead to an obvious birth problem, FAS may represent a very small proportion of alcohol effects. That is, alcohol may have negative effects other than FAS. We will discuss a number of them.

Spontaneous abortions and miscarriages have been found to be related to the use of alcohol. One massive study (Harlap & Shiono, 1980) has shown marked increases in spontaneous second trimester abortions for regular, but not for occasional, drinkers. The effects of drinking were greater than those for smoking, and the two factors were additive. Another large prospective study found increased risk of abortion at a level of drinking one ounce of absolute alcohol twice a week (Kline, Shrout, Stein, Susser, & Warburton, 1980). The mechanisms that produce these effects are not yet clear. On the one hand, these studies suggest that these effects of alcohol are due to its action as a poison, not as a teratogen. This is because the timing of abortions found in both studies fails to support the conclusion that they were a result of malformations. On the other hand, McLaren (1982) demonstrated that female mice given alcohol prior to ovulation produced larger numbers than normal of monosomic and trisomic ova. Because such ova are more likely to be aborted, this chromosomal change may be the mechanism by which alcohol produces abortions. Nevertheless, Kalter and Warkany (1983) in their exhaustive review call for caution in accepting this effect for any but heavy drinkers in view of the conflicting evidence.

Low Birth Weight; Prematurity. As with other teratologic agents, data from both human and animal studies indicate that prenatal growth may be affected by prenatal alcohol exposure. Rat fetuses grown in a culture and exposed to alcohol were not only stunted in growth, but their organ differentiation was retarded (Brown, Goulding, & Fabro, 1979). The degree of retardation was directly related to the amount of alcohol to which the fetuses were exposed. In humans the effects of alcohol cannot be so clearly separated from those of associated factors such as nutritional disturbances and deficiencies. These extraneous factors have also been shown to produce both growth retardation and malformations of the CNS (Abel, 1980). Hence it is likely that in humans both alcohol and nutrition may be involved. Nevertheless, two large-scale studies have found birth weight effects that were statistically independent of nutritional variables such as maternal anemia, weight, and weight gain. Sokol, Miller, and Reed (1980) found their effects for birth weight regardless of preterm status. In contrast, the second study, a large-scale prospective study in Germany (Mau & Netter, 1974, as cited in Streissguth, 1978), did find shorter gestations in mothers who were moderate or heavy drinkers. Thus, these data, though not extensive, do suggest the strong possibility that exposure to alcohol may produce growth retardation and possibly also preterm birth. However, note that in a prospective study (Rosett, Weiner, Lee, Zuckerman, Dooling, & Oppenheimer, 1983) alcohol use was not related to birth weight in a low SES sample. Alcohol together with the mother's prepreg-

nancy weight, race, smoking habits, and education and the baby's sex accounted for only 11% of the variance in birth weight. In addition, Sokol, Miller, and Reed (1980) found the same additive relation between smoking and alcohol consumption and SGA and prematurity that has been found for pregnancy loss, described earlier. SGA infants were 24 times as likely among those who abused alcohol, 18 times as likely among those who smoked, and 39 times as likely among those who did both as among those who did neither. Other studies have found similar patterns, both for chronic alcoholics and for moderate drinkers (Kaminski, Funeau, & Schwartz, 1978; Little, Schultz, & Mandell, 1976; Streissguth, 1977).

Lowered Intelligence. In his review covering studies in France, Belgium, and Germany as well as the United States, Abel (1980) notes that nearly all studies of FAS report retardation. A number of studies agree in finding this effect, but the exact magnitude of the effects is uncertain because of the small number of children who have been followed systematically. In one study, 5 of 12 children of alcoholics followed until age 7 had IQs of 79 or below compared to 9% of a matched control group (Jones, Smith, Streissguth, & Myrianthopoulis, 1974). The degree of retardation appears to be related to the severity of the physical signs of FAS (Streissguth, Herman, & Smith, 1978b). The average IQ for 10 cases with severe or moderate-to-severe physical effects was 57, that for six with moderate effects was 68, and that for four with mild effects was 82. However, not only were the numbers small, but the ages of the cases varied widely, with the result that several different IQ tests had to be used. The apparent relation of retardation to physical stigmata is even more interesting, though, in light of the fact that the physical stigmata appeared to decrease over time, while the intellectual deficit did not. It also is consistent with a study of mice whose mothers were given two small doses of alcohol during the gastrulation phase of embryogenesis (Sulick, Johnston, & Webb, 1981). The offspring developed both CNS malformations (which would be expected to underlie mental retardation in humans) and facial anomalies similar to those of FAS.

It is important to remember that all of the studies using IQ measured some years after birth are potentially confounded by the effects of environment after birth, which is often less than ideal for the children of alcoholics. Studying the effects of postbirth environment is also important as a guide for social action. If the IQs of FAS children improve when they are raised by someone other than their alcoholic mothers, it would strengthen the argument that social service agencies should provide such alternative care. Unfortunately, studies that explore whether home environments with alcoholic mothers themselves lead to lower IQs are not much help. One study found a 10-point higher IQ (84 instead of 74) for 6 children of alcoholics who had lived at least part of the time with relatives or in a foster home as compared to 6 who remained at home (Jones et al., 1974). In another study the mean IQs of 17 children who did not live with their alcoholic mothers was 66 (Streissguth, Herman, & Smith, 1978a). Their IQs did not improve over the next 4 years and did not vary with changes in the home care situation (for either better or worse). With only two studies, very small numbers of subjects, and the large range of ages (which meant that different IQ tests had to be used), it is impossible to reach any conclusion with confidence. It may be possible that good home environments could compensate for the effects of prenatal exposure to alcohol for children with IQs that are closer to normal but not for children who are more severely handicapped. If this is true, the studies of very severely affected children are not confounded by postbirth environments, but those of less severely damaged are. Nevertheless, it is clear that future studies need to include children who are raised by nonalcoholic mothers, both to resolve this methodological problem and to ascertain the best postbirth environment for FAS children.

Other Behavioral Effects. Recent research has focused on the effect prenatal alcohol exposure has on the behaviors of newborns. In one well-controlled prospective study newborns showed poorer habituation (the tendency to respond less and less when a stimulus is presented repeatedly) (Streissguth, Barr, & Martin, 1983) and poorer operant learning (Martin, Martin, Lund, & Streissguth, 1977). These are the two primary response systems that allow newborns to take in information about the world around them (they will be discussed in

Chapter 7). In addition, newborns of mothers who drank during pregnancy have been found to have generally lower levels of arousal,[9] lower levels of vigorous bodily activity, more frequent state changes, and disturbed sleep states (Landesman-Dwyer, Keller, & Streissguth, 1978; Rosett et al., 1979; Streissguth et al., 1983).

A variety of other behavioral effects have been linked to prenatal exposure to alcohol, but the evidence for each is sparse and inconclusive. Prenatal drinking has been linked to state regulation in the newborn (Rosett, Ouellette, Weiner, & Owens, 1978), and to the rather vague group of disorders labeled "childhood hyperactivity" or "minimal brain dysfunction," which are characterized by high levels of activity, difficulty in concentrating, and distractibility. The data for the latter do not seem as compelling as those for impaired intelligence or for newborn behavioral effects. Nevertheless, recent evidence suggests that attentional behaviors in 4-year-olds are affected by their mothers' alcohol consumption during pregnancy (Streissguth, Martin, Barr, Sandman, Kirchner, & Darby, 1984). In addition, many animal studies have shown one or another behavioral differences, but they do not agree on the type of difference (Abel, 1980).

MODERATE VERSUS HEAVY DRINKING

Most of the effects we have described were found in babies of chronic alcoholics or heavy drinkers. An important question is whether moderate or light drinking also affects the embryo or fetus. As in the case for smoking, the evidence from studies done in France, Germany, and the United States shows quite clearly that moderate drinking is related to low birth weight. In a study of several hundred pregnant women in a prepaid health plan in Seattle, this effect remained even when factors known to be related to birth weight (mother's age, height, parity, and smoking and the sex of the infant) were controlled (Streissguth, Martin, Martin, & Barr, 1981). In contrast, several studies in humans (Harlap & Shiono, 1980; Rosett, Ouellette, & Weiner, 1976; Rosett & Sander, 1979) and in dogs (Ellis & Pick, 1980) seem to indicate no excess of anomalies or of

---

[9] Lower levels of arousal means that they were easy to console, not excitable, and that they self-quieted readily, characteristics that have advantages for parents.

growth retardation in mild or occasional drinkers.

A prospective study in which mothers were interviewed during pregnancy on their alcohol intake and 163 high-risk cases were identified (Hanson, Streissguth, & Smith, 1978) indicated that low dosages may produce milder effects similar to those found in FAS. Eleven cases of FAS were identified and 9 of these were from the mothers at highest risk. Only 2 were severely enough affected to be classed as FAS, and both of their mothers were heavy drinkers. The seven more mildly affected babies had mothers who drank an ounce or more of absolute alcohol in the month prior to recognition of pregnancy. Extrapolation from the mouse data (Sulik et al., 1981) indicate that the third week of gestation might be critical. Since drinking before knowledge of pregnancy was most related to outcome, these data would argue for planned pregnancies where drinking is lowered prior to becoming pregnant.

If we look at the data the other way around to define the risk for the potential mother of having a baby with some problem, it would be almost 10% if she drank 1 to 2 ounces of absolute alcohol per day but 19% if she drank 5 ounces (the estimate for chronic alcoholics is 40%). Unfortunately, the long-term significance of detectable problems that are less severe than those labeled FAS is not known (Ouellette, Rosett, & Rosman, 1977; Rosett et al., 1976).[10]

POSSIBLE FACTORS OTHER THAN MATERNAL ALCOHOL

Maternal Factors During Pregnancy. Smoking, poor nutrition, and abuse of other substances are possible confounding variables in the relation between alcohol consumption and poor infant outcomes. We would like to discuss the combination of smoking and drinking because it is so frequent. Studies have found that from 36–60% of women categorized as heavy drinkers smoke more than a pack of cigarettes a day (Cahalan, Cissin, & Crossley, 1969; Rossett et al., 1976, respectively). A number of studies have found evidence that

the combination is worse than either alone. We have already described such evidence for spontaneous abortions and for low birth weight. Similar findings have been made in two other domains. First, an increase in stillbirths has been reported for women who both smoked and drank compared to those who drank the same amounts but did not smoke (Kaminski et al., 1978). Second, behavioral differences in newborns have also been demonstrated (Landesman-Dwyer et al., 1978; Martin et al., 1977; Martin, Martin, Sigman, & Redow, 1978). The behavioral effects range from those of clear importance, such as sucking inefficiency and poor learning, to those whose meaning is unclear, such as atypical sleeping postures. Behavioral differences were also found for infants born to mothers who only drank moderately but also smoked.

At the very least these data indicate the importance of controlling for the amount smoked in any attempt to assess the effects of alcohol. The effects of combinations of alcohol and other drugs, including prescribed medicines, that are examined in some studies (for example, Kline et al., 1980) need to be studied further.

Prepregnancy Factors. Three prepregnancy factors have been identified. One is the possible role that alcohol consumption by the father might have on his genetic contribution to the embryo. The second is the prepregnancy alcohol consumption of the mother. The third is the role of the genetic susceptibility of the offspring.

The possible role of the genes contributed by alcohol-consuming fathers has been identified only by animal studies. It is unfortunate that human studies seem not to have addressed this question at all, because in many families both parents tend to drink (or not to drink) and thus the father's drinking is a potential confounding or contributing factor. Although the animal studies have not addressed directly the relative role of father's and mother's alcohol consumption, they have studied the effects of the fathers' alcohol consumption in isolation, by using as mothers nonalcohol-consuming females. Early studies of guinea pigs (Stockard, 1913; Stockard & Papanicolaou, 1916) indicated that males who were chronically intoxicated from alcohol

[10] For a very reasonable review of this topic we recommend the Guest Editorial by Rosett in the journal *Alcoholism: Clinical and Experimental Research* (1980).

fumes sired offspring that were frequently abnormal and had grandchildren who were less often viable (see also Heuyer et al., 1957). Matings of mice fathers that were injected with alcohol (Badr & Badr, 1975) to normal females produced more resorptions and stillbirths. The mates of rat males who drank alcohol for their liquid had fewer pups (more resorptions) than the mates of those who drank water (Pfeifer, MacKinnon, & Seiser, 1977). Their pups were slightly heavier at birth as is common with smaller litter size, but became lighter at a later age. Rat pups with "alcoholic" fathers were less likely to survive than those of water drinking fathers (78% compared to 93%). There were pronounced sex differences both for body weights and for several tested behaviors, in which females and not males were affected. Further, the female offspring of alcohol-drinking fathers preferred higher concentrations of alcohol when they were older. Male offspring showed the opposite tendency. If these data are extrapolated to the human case, it would seem possible that differences in the occurrence of FAS and related symptoms in babies whose mothers consumed a given level of alcohol may be related to paternal drinking habits.[11]

The second factor, prepregnancy drinking by the mother, was alluded to in our review of the evidence. We noted there that prepregnancy drinking could not be separated from that done early in pregnancy. Hence it is impossible to draw conclusions about the possible importance of this factor. It is unfortunate that the animal studies we cited have not manipulated both paternal and maternal prepregnancy alcohol exposure in ways that allow a clear-cut separation of their effects.

The important role of genetic susceptibility in its interaction with exposure to alcohol and other drugs is dramatized by the occasional findings of differences in the effects on one twin as compared to another. Fraternal twins have been seen where one is severely affected and the other is affected so slightly that it might not have been detected had the other twin not been an obvious victim of FAS (Christoffel & Salofsky, 1975). Similar differences between twins have been found for other drugs, including thalidomide (Lenz, 1966; Loughnan, Gold, & Vance, 1973).

The data described in this section make it mandatory that studies measure the prepregnancy alcohol intake of both father and mother if the teratologic potential of alcohol is to be understood. In addition, they indicate that careful consideration of offspring sex differences is essential. Most studies, at least in the United States, have not had large enough samples to include such comparisons. Finally, the role of genetic susceptibility of the offspring needs to be considered, although current techniques allow only rough methods of studying it in humans.

MECHANISM OF ACTION

Studies with pregnant monkeys (Mukherjee & Hodgen, 1982) suggest a possible mechanism for the action of maternal alcohol intake on the fetus. Five monkeys in their third trimester of pregnancy had incisions made into the uterus to allow direct examination of umbilical and placental functioning (including chemical analysis of blood samples) for 90 minutes after the mothers were injected with alcohol solutions. In all cases the blood vessels in the umbilical cord collapsed within 15 minutes. Circulation between the placenta and fetus gradually recovered during the next hour. All five fetuses developed severe oxygen deficiency (hypoxia) and acidosis (another indication of abnormality).[12] Repeated episodes of hypoxia and acidosis could have a damaging effect on the brain, which is in a stage of marked growth in the third trimester. Note, however, that permanent changes in the placenta did not appear to occur (Sokol et al., 1980).

Such research is, of course, impossible to do with humans. Nevertheless, there is some indication that factors related to the placental exchange system do operate in humans. Palmer, Ouellette, Warner, and Leichtman (1974) found a pair of monozygotic twins who did not

---

[11] Paternal effects on developmental outcomes have been studied for other agents and for genetic contributions. On the whole the data are insufficient to draw clear-cut conclusions. The student wishing to pursue this topic further is referred to Gunderson and Sackett (1982).

---

[12] Two control monkeys received injections of sugar and salt and two received the surgical and other procedures but no injections. No such changes occurred in these fetuses.

exhibit identical characteristics of FAS, although both had it. Such differences cannot be caused by genetic differences because monozygotic twins have the same genes, and differences in prenatal environment between twins are most likely to relate to factors of placental exchange.

Other Drugs

FOLIC ACID ANTAGONISTS AND FOLIC ACID DEFICIENCY

Folic acid antagonists almost always kill the embryo in laboratory animals, hence they were used experimentally to produce abortions in humans in the 1950s and early 1960s. The combined figures for several studies indicate that about 70% of women treated with one of these compounds, usually aminopterin, did abort. Of the fetuses that did not abort and were born at a viable age, between 20% and 30% had defects. There is no one pattern of malformations, which may mean that the drug has different effects at different ages. Which organs are affected would depend on which critical period was disrupted.

Folic acid deficiency, produced by improper diet or by anticonvulsant drugs, apparently predisposes the fetus to malformation, especially of the CNS, including spina bifida (Gordon, 1968). Dietary manipulation in animals has been found to produce teratogenic effects, especially **hydrocephalus** (literally "water head," or "water on the brain"), a syndrome resulting in a very large head and severe brain damage (Kalter, 1968). In addition, folic acid deficiency may increase the risk of neural tube defects such as spina bifida. There is suggestive evidence that giving folic acid during pregnancy to women who have had a baby with neural tube defects may reduce the likelihood of their having another such child. One study of 123 mothers found no cases among 44 treated mothers, but 6 cases among 79 untreated ones (Laurence, 1982). Neural tube defects have declined sharply in certain areas of the world in recent years (for example, by 50% in South Wales), perhaps because women in these areas are eating more green vegetables (a primary source of folic acid) and eating them for larger portions of the year.

ASPIRIN

Aspirin, one of the most commonly used drugs, has been found to be teratogenic in animals when high doses are given. Humans do not typically take such high doses. In both animals and humans, however, aspirin acts in conjunction with benzoic acid, a widely used preservative in such foods as catsup, to increase the level of teratogenic effects. That this combination may be dangerous to humans is indicated by several retrospective studies that found more malformed infants among mothers who took aspirin in the first trimester than among control groups.

Aspirin has a definite but different effect on newborn humans. It diminishes the clotting ability of the blood, which is normally low in newborns, especially in prematures. Hence, aspirin taken shortly before delivery could be dangerous for the baby. For both these reasons, physicians often recommend that pregnant women avoid aspirin unless it is absolutely necessary.

EXCESS VITAMINS

Vitamins can be considered in the same category as drugs. An excess of certain vitamins has teratological effects. An excess of vitamin A leads to defects of closure of structures, for example, of facial structures, resulting in cleft palate, or of the neural tube, resulting in spina bifida. An excess of vitamin D has been shown to cause congenital defects (Seelig & Roemheld, 1969).

INHALANT ANESTHETICS

Long-term exposure to the inhalant anesthetics used in operating rooms appears to lead to pregnancy wastage. Cohen, Belleville, and Brown (1971) have shown that operating room nurses, as compared to general duty nurses, had a higher miscarriage rate—30% compared to less than 9% over a five-year period. Their miscarriages also tended to occur earlier in pregnancy, at eight compared to ten weeks. Female physicians whose practice was limited to anesthesiology had a 38% loss over a six-year period compared to 10% for other female doctors. There is also some evidence that there are increased abortion rates and more congenital defects when the father has worked around inhalant anesthetics (Gunderson & Sackett, 1982).

OTHER POSSIBLE TERATOGENIC DRUGS

A number of additional drugs may be teratogenic, but conclusive evidence does not yet exist. Among them are the antibiotics. Some studies have shown high degrees of pregnancy wastage or defects whereas other studies have not. There is also some indication that the effects of the antibiotic tetracycline may be prevented by vitamin B. These are animal data, and the evidence on whether tetracycline is teratogenic in humans is not clear.

Quinine has long been used to produce abortions by lay people, albeit with uncertain success. In the high dosages used for such purposes, but not in the lower dosages used to combat malaria, there is some, relatively unclear, evidence for visual or auditory defects in humans. In animal studies death and retardation of growth are found, but few malformations.

Several drugs used to treat psychological difficulties are also suspect. Imiprimine and other antidepressants have been implicated with a form of limb deformity not unlike that caused by thalidomide, but the evidence is quite tenuous. Insulin was formerly used in large doses to produce shock in psychiatric patients. When this occurred in the first 14 weeks of pregnancy, the effects were quite startling. In one study of 14 cases, 4 deaths, 4 malformed infants, and 2 mentally defective children resulted. Electrical stimulation has replaced insulin as a way of inducing shock in psychiatric patients, so this particular danger seems past. Insulin appears to be only mildly teratogenic in the lower doses used for treatment of diabetics.

Other drugs used for treatment of specific diseases may also be teratogenic. The following drugs are suspect at this time: oral hypoglycemic drugs (not insulin) used in the treatment of diabetes, alkylating agents used in the treatment of cancer, and drugs used in the treatment of tuberculosis. Establishing the teratogenic effects of such drugs is very difficult. Animal studies don't provide conclusive answers for humans. Drugs that may harm a fetus cannot ethically be given to a woman who doesn't have the disorder for which the drug is relevant. Hence clinical trials must be conducted with women who have the condition that is helped by the drug. It therefore becomes very difficult to separate the effects of the drug from those of the disorder.

Pesticides contain a number of drugs whose damaging effects on the fetus are not yet clear, but they do reach the fetus at least as early as 22 weeks. Other drugs in the environment, such as some agricultural agents and household cleansers, are under suspicion but adequate data for any firm conclusion is lacking for most of them.[13]

DIRECT EFFECTS OF THE EXTERNAL ENVIRONMENT

Many of the "old wives' tales" regarding pregnancy involve claims that the external environmental events directly affect the embryo or fetus, such as if the mother is startled by a rabbit, the baby will have a "hare lip." Such beliefs are problematic. In all the prenatal effects of drugs and diseases that we have studied, the external cause has directly touched the infant by way of the mother and the placenta. The harmful agent either crosses the placenta, or the mother's insufficiency results in something not passing through the placenta, or the functioning of the placental interchange system itself is affected adversely. Such an event as a rabbit startling a pregnant woman could affect the offspring only if it produced a physiological reaction in the mother that affected the potential baby, or if the baby could see it and be startled.

Because embryos and fetuses are cut off from the environment outside their mothers' bodies, they are generally well protected from direct environmental effects. Nevertheless, we can discuss two classes of direct effects. The first includes truly direct effects. The only firmly established example is radiation, which passes through the mother's body to affect the egg, embryo, or fetus directly, but noise and very strong blows may also directly affect the fetus. The second class includes the effects of stress. They are direct effects in that external environmental events, such as physical labor and extreme grief, may affect the organism developing in the uterus, but they are like other teratogens in that the effects are a result of physiological reactions in the mother.

[13] See Gots and Gots, *Caring for Your Unborn Child* (1977), for reviews of these data written for the general reader.

Radiation

Radiation is often called the "universal teratogen." In animals it has been shown to produce malformations or improper development in all organ systems, including the central nervous system. The effects depend upon both dosage and length of exposure, but the pattern of effects is not necessarily the same in different species, or in different studies of the same species. Effects can result from exposure prior to conception, prior to implantation, or during embryological and fetal development. Effects induced prior to fertilization could result from chromosomal damage to either sperm cells or ova by irradiation. Both chromosomal breakage and translocations (see Chapter 3) may occur. The mother is likely to be the crucial parent in such cases. The effects on her ova appear to be cumulative over time, since her ova are present even prior to her own birth and hence are particularly vulnerable to the effects of long-term low levels of radiation. Her ova are continually affected by every X ray she receives and perhaps even by the background radiation where she lives. Indeed, these factors may be part of the reason older mothers have increased numbers of offspring with genetic problems involving the chromosomes. In contrast, the male produces new sperm cells throughout his life; hence any effects of radiation (below the dosage that damages the whole sperm production mechanism) have to be very short term. Among the effects of both high single dosages and chronic low doses of X rays are lowered fertility in both males and females. This may in part represent failure of damaged cells to give rise to conception or to the likelihood of early abortion or miscarriage. In any event, most of the teratogenic effects of X radiation appear to be due to the irradiation of the ovum, embryo, or fetus. Some 30 anomalies, many of which involve the central nervous system, have been reported following fetal irradiation. Microcephaly, often seen in mental retardation, is most frequent, but hydrocephalus and other brain malformations, skull defects, and Down's syndrome are all increased. Clearly human experiments using X rays or other irradiation cannot be used to test the validity of these case study results. We do have corroborating data on humans from the "natural experiment" resulting from the atomic bombings of Hiroshima and Nagasaki during World War II. Women who were pregnant at the time the bomb was dropped showed an enormous increase in the likelihood that their offspring would have one or more birth defects. There was also a dose relation in that the closer the pregnant women were to the place the bomb dropped, the higher the probability of birth defects (Blot & Miller, 1973). Moreover, there was evidence of critical periods. A re-analysis of the radiation data from Japan (Snow, 1982) showed that those exposed in the first 2 weeks after conception had infants with small heads who were not retarded, whereas those who were 8 to 16 weeks into gestation at exposure had babies that were severely retarded.

Data from naturally occurring levels of radiation, such as that given off by certain rock formations, also exist. Pregnant women who live near such rock formations have a greater probability of giving birth to a malformed baby (Gentry, Parkhurst, & Bulin, 1959). In India, Down's syndrome and other genetic forms of severe mental retardation have been found to be four times as high in an area of relatively high background radiation levels as in the control population. Similar findings exist for parts of Brazil (Mauss, 1983).

The relation between irradiation and Down's syndrome has been further documented by a study of 216 families with a Down's infant and a comparable control group of families with a normal child of the same sex born in the same hospital at the same time. The Down's mothers had had seven times as much exposure to radiation. The fathers also had had more exposure to radar, which involves low-level radiation (Cohen & Lilienfeld, 1970). Contradictory findings regarding irradiation and increases in Down's syndrome are cited in Peuschel (1983).

Another effect of X radiation, found in rats and mice, is reduced learning ability. A report on human victims of in utero exposure to atomic radiation from the Hiroshima and Nagasaki atomic bombs showed that, in general, the risk of mental retardation rose directly with increasing dose (Blot & Miller, 1973).

One of the classic books on teratology states:

Prenatal irradiation produces death, decreased size, and congenital malformations.

Preimplantation, preorganogenetic, and undifferentiated embryos are killed or retarded in growth, but not usually malformed, whereas those undergoing differentiation or organogenesis are malformed as well as stunted and killed. (Kalter, 1968, p. 137)

These findings imply that unnecessary X rays are unwise, especially for women during their childbearing years and during pregnancy. In the past, a number of practices such as using X rays to fit shoes or to determine pelvic size in pregnancy could raise total exposure to X rays by women of childbearing age to harmful levels.[14] Today, the primary source of X radiation strong enough to be a major teratogen is its therapeutic use (Kalter & Warkany, 1983). Some dentists may still use inadequate equipment or take inadequate precautions (or both) and take more X rays than necessary, but their technicians are probably more at risk than their patients. Many states that required chest X rays for employees in positions that involve contact with many young people, such as teachers, have allowed job holders to substitute skin tests for tuberculosis and require X rays only if the skin test is positive.[15]

Other Possible External Agents

Other direct effects of the environment are also possible. Potential babies float in the amniotic fluid and thus are protected from many blows, jars, and sounds. Nevertheless, they can hear very loud sounds and they can be affected by very strong blows. It is known that very strong blows can bring on premature labor, and it is even possible that such events in early development might be responsible for club feet.

It has long been known that fetal activity level changes after exposure to loud sounds.

There is also evidence that infants born to mothers who have lived near a jet airport during their pregnancies are more likely to be stillborn, or have relatively low birth weight (Ando & Hattori, 1970, 1973), and have more birth defects (Jones & Tauscher, 1978). In most studies it is impossible to say whether the noise directly affected the developing organism or whether extraneous variables associated with the noise, such as pollutants or stress to the mother caused by noise, caused the differences in the infants. There is also suggestive evidence that infants born to mothers who lived near airport noise throughout their pregnancies react less to the noise of the jets than those whose mothers moved near a jet airport late in pregnancy or right after the infant was born. Scientists are now trying to establish whether these impressionistic data are true. If they are, then it is necessary to find out why the differences occur. It may be that while still in utero the infants suffered hearing loss from long-term exposure in the same way that people of any age do when they are exposed repeatedly to loud noises such as jets, rock music, and noisy factories. Alternatively, it may be that the offspring of mothers who lived near airports throughout their pregnancies became used to hearing airplane noises while in utero and simply did not respond as much to this very familiar noise. It is, of course, possible that the airplane noise did not affect the babies in utero at all and the effect was mediated through the mother. For example, air pollutants from jet exhaust may have entered the fetuses' bodies through the placental exchange system and affected their hearing or their ability to respond to the sounds they heard.

If the effects of prenatal exposure to airplane noise on auditory response after birth are verifiable and if they really are due to the noise itself, they would constitute a direct effect on the fetus rather than an indirect effect, that is, one that operates through or is mediated by the mother. This is a particularly good candidate for a direct effect because the dependent measure of interest, infants' response to auditory stimulation, is a direct response to the independent variable, the airplane noise, rather than a nonspecific effect such as prenatal mortality, which has many disparate causes. Thus, the research on whether prenatal exposure to noise has an effect on infants' response to noise after birth has the potential to provide clear evidence of a direct external environmental effect on prenatal development.

[14] Although formerly almost routine, use of X rays to determine whether pelvic size would permit vaginal deliveries never made sense. The female pelvis is built to stretch during delivery, and an X ray cannot determine stretchability. Today ultrasound imaging has replaced X rays to determine the relation of the fetus to the mother's structures. There are no known negative effects, but its safety is not yet fully documented.

[15] A positive skin test for tuberculosis indicates exposure to it at some time in the past, not necessarily a case of the disease.

In spite of the intriguing nature of the issues of the effects of high levels of noise on prenatal development, the basic phenomenon is not yet firmly established. The Committee on Hearing, Bioacoustics, and Biomechanics of the National Research Council (1982) examined all available evidence and concluded: "There is no conclusive evidence of detrimental effects of high-intensity sound in higher mammals" (p. 10). With respect to human data they noted the limited amounts of data, inadequate samples, and lack of appropriate control populations. Nevertheless, they suggested that "Until better information is available it would appear prudent for pregnant women to avoid exposures of long duration (several hours per day) to loud noises" where loud noises are defined as sounds of 90 dB sound pressure level (SPL) and above (p. 10).

The brevity of this section is an accurate reflection of the limited body of knowledge about external environmental effects. The only firmly established direct effects are those of radiation, which are certainly in a different class than exposure to loud noises, being startled by a rabbit, or being introduced to music prenatally. No research has yet demonstrated unequivocally that environmental events *outside* the mother's body (other than radiation) affect the developing embryo or fetus. Thus, if there are effects from airport noise, they are important not only because they identify one more factor that could be controlled to help prevent prenatal problems, but also because they have far ranging implications for the general issue of whether the external environment can directly affect prenatal development.

PRENATAL STRESS

Although all the prenatal environmental factors we have discussed so far produce stress, there are other environmental conditions that are more commonly given the label of stress. We will discuss two, physical work and psychological stress.

Physical Stress

The role of physical work during pregnancy is one that has long interested people. Indeed, the degree to which pregnancy has been considered an illness, and pregnant women treated with tender loving care and protected from physical labors, changes with time and place. In pioneer days, society could ill afford to lose the work done by its women; hence, they worked throughout most of their pregnancies. This has been true in many cultures and is still true in many, especially where life is lived under substandard conditions. In the United States and many other western cultures, this century prior to the 1960s or 1970s was generally characterized by what might now be considered overprotection of pregnant women. For example, in the 1940s when one of the authors was having her children, mothers were advised not to swim after six or seven months or drive a car after seven months. She was able to talk her doctor into allowing her to drive for eight months, and then she continued to drive against her doctor's orders, including in a blizzard the night before her delivery at full term. In the 1970s most doctors had a more moderate outlook on the physical stresses a mother can safely undergo. In the mid-1970s, the other author was allowed to continue running during pregnancy until it became painful, in her ninth month.

Relatively little data exist about the dangers of hard physical labor during pregnancy. Older studies reported greater numbers of malformations and problems in infants of mothers who worked at extremely hard jobs. However, these studies included jobs that led to the mother's suffering from toxemia (at least when work combined with her generally poor physical condition) and frequently involved exposure to various chemical pollutants and frequent illness on the job.

Stott also studied the effects of work (1972). In his Glasgow sample, which was a random sample of births, he found 153 mothers who worked hard and 26 who worked at heavy work and also had to stand a great deal and complained of feelings of tiredness. As a measure of effects he used his morbidity ratio (MR, discussed in relation to smoking), which includes malformations, physical defects, neurological symptoms, retardation in developmental milestones, behavior disturbances, and nonepidemic illness.

For the hard-working mothers the effects on the children were hardly impressive. Half were in the lower half on the MR, as would be expected by chance, though the average MR for these children was slightly higher than normal. The 26 mothers with the greatest degree of physical stress did have children at greater risk for high morbidity. Stott and Latchford (1976) made similar analyses on their Canadian sample and found a 17% increase in the MR for mothers who worked and a 30% increase for those who stood nearly all day and carried heavy loads. As early as 1958, McDonald (cited in Stott and Latchford) found that mothers who did heavy pulling or carried heavy loads during pregnancy had infants with a significant increase in congenital defects. Greater incidences of prematurity and perinatal death have also been shown in some studies (Stewart, 1955; Stewart, Webb, & Hewitt, 1955). However, women who do such work are likely to have many other factors that operate to make their childbearing more hazardous, such as poor nutrition, poor living conditions, and illnesses. Hence caution is needed in interpreting the differences as due to physical labor.

This section has focused on the effects of hard physical labor as a teratogen. Work environments may have teratogenic effects for very different reasons. Workers may be exposed to agents, such as X rays, that are known to be potentially harmful to the embryo or fetus. More often, workers may be exposed to substances or conditions that are *thought* to have the potential to harm the embryo or fetus, such as noise and pesticides. The evidence is not yet available to determine which of these agents actually are dangerous or how dangerous they are. None of the evidence indicates that holding a job in itself threatens the well-being of developing organisms.

Psychological Stress

The influence of psychological stress during pregnancy on the physiological and behavioral responses of the offspring in humans was first investigated by Sontag and his colleagues in the 1930s and 1940s (see Sontag, Steele, & Lewis, 1969, for a summary). In the late 1950s experimental studies of such effects were conducted using animal models. Although many of the mechanisms that through the ages were thought to account for such effects have been

magical, there are two biologically sound mechanisms by which psychological stress might be transmitted to the offspring. First, stress elicits hormonal reactions and the hormones may pass the placental barrier. Second, anxiety during labor and delivery may increase the risk of complications that can affect the infants.

ANIMAL STUDIES

Early research on prenatal psychological stress was begun by Thompson and his collaborators (Thompson, 1957; Thompson, Watson, & Charlesworth, 1962), who studied animals so that they could control many aspects of experience that are impossible to control in humans. They tried to control for direct effects on the fetus and tried to make sure that any effects of the stimulus were mediated by the mother and her "anxiety." To achieve this, rats were trained to avoid shock when a conditioned stimulus (CS) was presented. After their training was completed they were mated. During their pregnancy the CS, but no shock, was presented in a situation where they could not make the response that had previously permitted them to avoid the shock. This procedure allowed the experimenters to manipulate the pregnant rat's stress without giving shock, which might have had a direct effect on the fetus or on the fetal–maternal system. Thus, it was assumed that any effects on the fetus would come from the effects of "psychological" stress.

The other type of control that these studies imposed that would be impossible in human studies was to separate the effects of prenatal exposure to maternal anxiety from those of being reared by a mother who might be generally anxious and care for her pups in an atypical way. This was achieved by mating the shock-trained rats at the same time as rats that had not been trained (or shocked). Then when the two rats gave birth, half of the pups from the trained ("anxious") mother were given to the other mother and vice versa, a procedure known as cross fostering. Still other litters were left with their own mothers. The results showed behavioral differences between those pups that gestated in the "anxious" mothers and those that gestated in the "normal" mothers regardless of which mothers reared them. The tests used to show differences were behavior in an open field, a fear-arousing situation to rats, and in an alley. The differences were increased defecation, decreased activity, and longer latencies to run in the alley, all behaviors that can be said to be indices of emotionality in rats. Effects were relatively long lasting. They were found at $18\frac{1}{2}$ to 20 weeks of age but not after $25\frac{1}{2}$ to 30 weeks (Hockman, 1961; Thompson, 1957; Thompson et al., 1962).

Later researchers added controls for some extraneous influences, but didn't catch them all. The chief unanswered criticism is that the stimulus used as a CS might itself be aversive.[16] The many interactions between the prenatal treatment and the rearing mother (or fostering procedures) make it clear that the prenatal treatment does affect the mother's behavior after her pups are born, and that cross fostering procedures are thus absolutely necessary to understand the effects of the prenatal exposure on the fetus. Further studies have examined when during pregnancy the animals were stressed and many other variations that don't need to concern us here. (A thorough review of studies until the late 1960s can be found in Joffe, 1969.)

Taken in their totality these studies raise another question of great interest: the role of genetic differences. Some of the early replications of Thompson's work failed to produce the same results. In these replications, it turned out that either different species had been used (mice instead of rats) or that different strains of rats had been used. In the study of stress it is possible that there are differences among strains in both hormonal and behavioral reactions to stressful experiences. It is also possible that the same maternal disturbance could have different effects on fetuses with different genotypes. In fact, it is likely that the maternal and fetal genotypes would interact and that the genotypes of both, as well as their interaction, would lead to phenotypic differences. Unfortunately, experiments that have examined strain crosses in ways that would help to separate these effects have neglected to use the control of cross fostering.

Such controls are necessary because other research has shown that the rearing practices of mothers of different strains or species affect the phenotypic behaviors of the young.

Strain and species differences are of particular relevance to the issues of this book because they may be highly analogous to individual differences in humans. Research with strain crosses shows that the effects of any given stress or strain on a particular body depends both on the genotype of the mother exposed to the stress and on the genotype of the infant exposed to the mother's stress reactions during intrauterine life.

HUMAN STUDIES

Much of the available research on the effects of prenatal stress in humans comes from studies of women who have a child with some abnormality and who have reported their pregnancy histories from memory. Such studies almost invariably show more unusual or abnormal factors or stresses in histories than would be expected. However, mothers of cerebral palsied or retarded children understandably try to find some plausible explanation and they may selectively remember or invent events in ways that differ from the recollections of mothers whose children have no abnormalities. Indeed, the latter mothers may have had similar untoward events but have forgotten them since nothing resulted from them. Because of these problems, prospective studies, which start with pregnant women and then determine the stresses they are subject to prior to their giving birth, are much more convincing. No long-term memory is required and the mothers have nothing to try to explain. We shall first describe prospective studies, then one that is only partly retrospective. Then we shall add some data from retrospective studies.

Davids and colleagues (Davids & DeVault, 1962; Davids, DeVault, & Talmadge, 1961) explored the relation between abnormalities or complications of delivery and responses on an extensive battery of psychological tests that had been given to 53 women during pregnancy. They found that on the basis of two responses on projective tests (in which subjects are given unstructured tasks such as drawing pictures or making up stories about pictures and their responses are interpreted by trained judges) those women who seemed accepting of their preg-

---

[16]The original study used a loud buzzer that may indeed have been noxious or affected the pups in a more direct manner than intended (consider the effects of noise in the previous section).

nant state were less likely to have complications or abnormalities. Unfortunately some conditions the authors classified as complications have no known connections with any problem for infants.

In a second study of the same women, Davids and DeVault (1962) found that the babies of mothers who were highly anxious during pregnancy, as measured by the Taylor Manifest Anxiety Scale, scored lower on an infant intelligence test at 8 months of age (102.5 versus 109.5 on mental performance for offspring of mothers with high and low anxiety, respectively;[17] and 100.5 versus 107.5 on motor performance for the two groups). Unfortunately, at the time the babies were tested, the mothers differed in a variety of ways that make it highly plausible that differences in rearing rather than in the prenatal period may have accounted for the differences in the offspring. The mothers with high anxiety scores during pregnancy were higher on measures of hostility and control on a test given them when their infants were eight months old (the Parent Attitude Research Instrument or PARI), higher on dissatisfaction with the role of mother, and on being irritable in their relations with their husbands and children. They also received less favorable ratings from those who examined their babies on their relations with their infants during the testing procedures (Davids, Holden, & Gray, 1963).

Another prospective study (Ottinger & Simmons, 1964) administered an anxiety test to mothers in each trimester of pregnancy. Babies of mothers in the high anxiety group cried more when hungry than babies of mothers in the low anxiety group. Because they did not cry more after feedings, the interpretation was that babies stressed by maternal anxiety during pregnancy are less able to cope with the stress of hunger. However, not everyone would agree that more crying is maladaptive, because it might serve to get food more quickly.

The final prospective study we shall dis-

cuss is one by Stott (1973) who studied 200 randomly-sampled Scottish pregnancies and followed the delivery and development of the offspring. He used a morbidity score to describe the overall health of the children that was similar to his mobidity ratio, which we described earlier. His major finding was that stress was related to infant outcomes only when it involved personal tension in the mother. He found this pattern in three kinds of stress. First, deaths and illnesses in the family and similar events led to higher morbidity scores only if the circumstances were traumatic and involved direct participation of the pregnant woman, for example, helping an accident victim or helping after an attempted suicide. Second, situational stresses led to higher morbidity scores only when they included personal tensions, and then the relation was particularly high when the stress was continuous, likely to erupt at any time, or incapable of resolution. Third, when unfavorable surroundings or low socioeconomic status were not accompanied by personal tensions, these were related to child morbidity to only a small degree.

Every single aspect of child morbidity that Stott examined, except physical defects, was associated with personal tensions during pregnancy. A case-by-case analysis of the 14 mothers who had scored high on personal tensions during pregnancy shows twice as large a proportion of infants who were late or poor walkers as in the group at large. Ten of the 14 children had one or more indications of congenital hyperactivity.

Stott engaged in extensive comparisons and analyses to bolster the conclusion that other factors, especially postnatal factors, cannot account for the relations he found. Although his study was correlational, he makes the point that it is plausible to consider personal tensions to be a causal factor.

The data from one study that is not quite prospective and yet is only partly retrospective are worth citing (Cohen, 1981). Mothers responded to a standardized interview while still in the hospital after giving birth and before they had any extended contact with their infants. The interview could be scored for physical, psychological, and total stress during pregnancy. Mothers also rated themselves on their anxiety in general and their anxiety during

---

[17]Davids and DeVault showed that the mother's anxiety scores were not related to her IQ scores. Had such a relation existed, the developmental differences in the infants would be assumed to be a result of either the nature of the stimulation the mothers provided their children or of the genetic potential of the children.

pregnancy. All infants had previously been assessed on the Graham/Rosenblith neonatal tests (see Chapter 8), and all were judged healthy to the degree that they were not receiving any special care in the nursery. Low psychological stress scores were related to low irritability during the neonatal examination, and moderate physical stress scores were related to good motor performance. Mothers' self-ratings of the stress they felt were less related to their babies' behaviors than were the scores based on their answers in their interviews. Nevertheless mothers with low self-ratings for anxiety during pregnancy were more likely to have babies with optimal scores on the neonatal subtest most related to outcomes at 4 and 7 years of age (Rosenblith 1979a, 1979b, 1979c). Although the above data are based on only 32 mother–infant pairs, they are not only significant, but impressive. Of the 8 babies whose mothers scored in the lowest quartile for psychological stress during pregnancy, 7 were in the lowest quartile on irritability. And, at the other extreme, of the 7 babies whose mothers were in the highest quartile, only 1 was in the lowest quartile on irritability.

Stott and Latchford's much larger retrospective study (1300 subjects; 1976) confirmed many of the findings of Stott's smaller prospective study (1973). Temporary physical stresses such as operations, accidents, and falls were not related to morbidity. Morbidity was increased by moving to a new locale in what appeared to be a direct relation to the personal tensions associated with the move. Moves in the same locale increased the MR by 20%, those to new localities increased it by 31%, and those that took the family away from the mother's mother, when this was reported as disturbing, by 47%. Economic worries, such as a husband out of work or being in debt during pregnancy, were related to morbidity. Interestingly, fear of job loss during pregnancy had more deleterious effects than actual job loss. Illnesses and deaths during pregnancy were related to later morbidity, but the effects were small compared to those related to tensions with husband, family, or outsiders. Examples of increased morbidity associated with these tensions are: 57% for those whose mothers reported fears about their marriages, 94% for those reporting marital discord, and 137% for those mothers reporting being short of money

but having husbands who spent freely. Note, however, that many of the personal tensions experienced during pregnancy continued during the child's postnatal life and presumably contributed to morbidity. (Cross fostering in humans is rare.)

One form of possible prenatal psychological stress that is of special interest is that occasioned by premarital conception or illegitimate birth or both. Stewart (1955) showed that there was twice as much prematurity and three times as many perinatal deaths in women who conceived while unmarried. This was true even though three quarters of these infants were born in wedlock. In fact, she also showed (Stewart et al., 1955) that the proportion of fetal deaths was even higher among the premaritally conceived than among the illegitimate. Stott and Latchford (1976) showed a 44% increase in the morbidity ratio for the illegitimate or premaritally conceived. Among those illegitimate that were adopted (a form of cross fostering), the MR was only 37% higher, but it was 66% higher for those kept by their mothers. Although it is true, as he pointed out, that the data are biased in favor of those adopted by the fact that unhealthy babies had a poorer chance of being adopted, the question of postnatal influence again looms large.

The sort of stress that results from unwelcome pregnancy is not limited to premarital or illegitimate pregnancies. Those mothers in Stott and Latchford's study (1976) who reported that they had not intended the pregnancy had children with a 24% increase in MR, and those who reported feeling desperate about the pregnancy had children with a 46% increase. Premarital and even unwanted pregnancies showed greater effects in families that were also inadequately housed.

Stott did not present data on deaths or pregnancy loss. Drillien had shown earlier (Drillien, Jameson, & Wilkinson, 1966) that there are increased prenatal deaths in pregnancies when the mother is emotionally distressed. This finding provides a possible explanation for an earlier finding (Eckhoff, Gawsha, & Baldwin, 1961) that families with high amounts of stress have more girls than boys, because boys are more likely to die perinatally. There are other data that make this explanation plausible, though it is still unproven.

The effects of stress on the prenatal maternal and embryonic and fetal systems are presumably mediated by hormonal reactions in the mother. In this chapter we have seen that excess hormones, either administered from outside (exogenous) or produced by a mother with a hormonal disorder (endogenous), are harmful to the developing embryo and fetus. In the case of stress, the increased levels of hormonal production are presumably lower than those required to produce obvious damage, but great enough to have some deleterious effects on the embryo or fetus. Better prospective studies, and prospective studies linked with hormonal studies, are necessary for a fuller understanding of the effects of psychological stress during pregnancy. As techniques of hormonal assay improve, it will be possible to deal directly with hormonal levels during pregnancy in relation to both psychological stressors and outcomes for infants. Genetic differences in reactions to stress (which we discussed in relation to work with animals) may be mediated by differential reactivity of the hormonal systems. Such differences in both the maternal and fetal genotype may be important.

CONCLUSIONS

The methodological difficulties, the relative sparseness, and the noncomparability of studies of psychological stress during pregnancy make it difficult to decipher the research in this area. Nonetheless, considering both the relatively well-controlled experimental animal research and the human studies with their varying methodological problems, it seems likely that babies of women who feel stressed during pregnancy are adversely affected. Exactly how they are affected is difficult to tell, because the dependent measures vary greatly across studies. If we put the effects into two major classes, emotionality and physical outcomes, then we can find consistencies across variations in experiment designs and operational definitions. Increased emotionality is the major effect found in the animal research and may be roughly comparable to the measures of irritability and crying-when-hungry found to correlate with psychological stress in the human studies. Birth complications and morbidity ratio have been used to assess physical outcomes, and correlations with psycholog-

ical stress during pregnancy have been found in both cases.

The positive conclusions derived from this analysis need to be tempered by the knowledge that the methodological controls are often inadequate. Adequate research requires prospective rather than retrospective studies, cross fostering controls (adoption in humans) for experiences after birth, hormonal assays to measure directly the hormonal concomitants of stress, new and better manipulation of stress in animal research, and clearly defined outcome measures of some practical importance. The research done to date is more tantalizing than conclusive.

ISSUES IN TERATOLOGY

Teratology is the study of the causes of congenital malformations. It could have been discussed in Chapter 3 because teratologists also study problems with genes and chromosomes that cause congenital defects. In a strict sense teratology has concerned itself primarily with major congenital malformations (Kalter & Warkany, 1983). However, the concept has been broadened by some workers to include more minor malformations and behavioral differences (see Fein, Schwartz, & Jacobson, 1983; Hutchings, 1978; Werboff & Gottlieb, 1963).

We agree with the behavioral teratologists that behavioral differences are important and may exist for more agents and with less exposure than gross malformations. We also agree with Kalter and Warkany (1983) when they say that: "The ascertainment of minor structural blemishes and aberrations, which are usually of little or no medical importance, of reduced birth weight at term [we would add, if within approximately normal range], spontaneous abortion, and of mental retardation is often liable to biases; and only with circumspection can they be subjects of epidemiologic and comparative studies" (p. 425). We believe that the study of teratology in its broader conceptualization is important if it meets the following criteria: (1) the outcomes are of long-term importance for the medical or psychological functioning of the child, as would be the case for mental retardation; and (2) close attention is paid to the methodological problems.

Complexities of Teratology

We have seen that a given teratological agent may have very different effects depending on timing, dosage or severity, genotype, and unknown factors. Another way to make clear the complexities of teratology is to examine all of the different teratological agents or events that have been accused of leading to one single problem. We will choose hearing problems. These may be genetically caused as well as caused by prenatal or **perinatal** (around birth) environmental events. Maternal diseases, diseases contracted by the baby during delivery, and drugs may all affect the newborn's hearing. Not only is rubella in the mother a frequent cause of hearing problems, but diabetes, syphilis (5% of offspring), Asian flu, and infectious mononucleosis appear to result in occasional cases. In addition, CMV (cytomegalovirus) contracted from the mother at the time of delivery may lead to hearing defects. The drugs that have been implicated range from the so-called ototoxic antibiotics (those that can destroy otoliths or hair cells, such as streptomycins, neomycin, kanamycin) and thalidomide to those for which the evidence is not clear, such as quinine, aspirin, various aniline dyes, and carbon monoxide (Gluck, 1971). In addition severe hyperbilirubinemia at birth, from whatever cause, may produce hearing loss, probably due to a specific type of brain damage, namely loss of neurons in the cochlear nuclei (Gerard, 1952, cited in Konigsmark, 1971).

Ways Teratogens Can Affect Development

Many environmental factors can operate to affect the developing embryo or fetus, and many of them have similar effects. In this chapter, we have grouped them according to the nature of the environmental agent (for example, drugs, diseases). It might be more logical, though less obvious to the lay person, to group the environmental agents that can affect viability and constitution in terms of the mechanisms that may be the direct cause of the problems suffered by the developing organism: (1) Environmental agents may operate at a genetic level, causing damage to chromosomes or genes that affect the instructional map for development; (2) they may cause destruction in organ systems at the time of the system's rapid growth and differentiation; (3) they may slow down or stunt normal growth and development.

The first two modes of operation may give rise to physically obvious problems (teratological effects), although these effects may be in internal structures and only become obvious after death or as a result of special examination procedures, such as X rays, electroencephalograms (EEGs), and CAT scans. Other effects may be biochemical, analogous to those of inborn errors of metabolism. The third class is visible when total growth is affected and is often indexed by low birth weight. As for the other two classes, the effects on internal organs can only be detected by special examination or autopsies.

The brain is the organ of special interest to our discussion. Damage to it can occur through any of the three mechanisms. Because only gross defects in the brain can be detected, even with special techniques, and because its gross characteristics are not closely related to its function, behavioral teratology tries to assess damage to function.

Much of the work we have reviewed concentrated on easily measured characteristics, such as proportions who die or who have low birth weights. These measures are not only crude indices of the underlying problem but they are a result of many different influences. When the effects of a teratogen are startling, clear cut, and distinctive, as is the case with thalidomide and rubella, it is possible to pinpoint the primary causative agent. When the effects are limited to low birth weight or slightly lowered behavioral functioning, it is difficult to assign primary responsibility to any one of its many potential causes.

DISCUSSION ISSUES

Early Experience

This chapter gives a number of examples of critical periods in embryological development. In general the developing organism is at greatest risk to damage from teratogenic agents in the period from differentiation of the germ layers through organogenesis. Death rather than malformation is a likely result earlier, and relative resistance to damage is the norm later. Some of these critical periods are extremely well documented. For example, the critical period for thalidomide is pin-pointed at between the 20th and 35th day after conception. Even within this short period the effects depend on timing, and more severe effects are found at the peak of the critical period. Also, even in teratological critical periods, not all babies are affected. In the case of rubella, for example, only 10–30% of infants exposed to the virus are affected. The examples of thalidomide and rubella also make clear that the mechanism of critical periods in teratology is the same as that in development of the lens and development of male sexual structures, discussed in Chapter 2. The abnormal environmental agent (the drug thalidomide or the rubella virus) interferes with the initial development (organogenesis) of the affected organs—limbs in the case of thalidomide and ears, eyes, heart, and brain in the case of rubella.

Not all critical periods in teratology occur during organogenesis. The spirochetes that cause syphilis produce destructive lesions in the eyes, skin, liver, and central nervous system only after the sixteenth to eighteenth week of gestation.

In brain development there are several critical periods. Dobbing (1976) found two periods of vulnerability, both after organogenesis—one during neuronal multiplication in the twelfth to eighteenth week after conception, and one during dendritic branching and synapse formation in the third trimester and after birth. In addition, the finding that drinking alcohol before the mother knows she is pregnant is correlated with negative outcomes suggests that the brain is also vulnerable during organogenesis.

Remember that not all teratogens operate during critical periods. Some, such as X rays, operate on the genes and chromosomes directly, and hence can operate at any time in the life of the ovum or during spermatogenesis.

This chapter has produced another good example of the complexity of the route from genotype to phenotype. Identical twins, who share the same genotype, must share nutritional resources while in the uterus, and one twin often suffers from this competition. This is particularly true of identical twins who share a placenta. Their phenotypes differ even at birth, although they have identical genotypes.

Research Issues

This chapter provides another example of the problems inherent in making inferences from case studies: the study of three women with hypothyroxinemia who had two pregnancies, only one of which was treated. If any one of those cases had been considered alone, the researchers might have come to an incorrect conclusion. Examination of additional cases allowed confirmation that the conclusions were indeed incorrect because they did not hold for all cases. The additional cases also allowed the researchers to isolate the conclusion that did hold for all three cases: offspring of mothers who received prenatal thyroid treatment had higher IQs than offspring of the same untreated mothers.

We should point out that three subjects is really too small a sample to make such a conclusion very convincing. In this study, however, the three cases in which the subjects served as their own controls corroborated the findings obtained with a larger group of women who had only one pregnancy included in the study. Thus, the small, better-controlled sample supplemented the larger, less well-controlled sample. The technique of corroborating findings with the results of studies using different methods is a common one. In this case one study with good control of extraneous variables related to maternal characteristics (same mothers) but with a small sample size is supplemented by a study with weaker controls but larger sample size. A different use of complementary studies occurs frequently when experimental research with animals supplements correlational research with humans. In both instances the studies with the better controls have a problem in the degree to which their findings can be generalized. In the first case the small sample size does not permit us to assume that the results would hold for all mothers. In the second case the fact that most of the data come from another species does not permit us to assume they hold for humans. Thus, in both cases, there is a trade-off between greater methodological control and increased difficulty in generalization.

Studies of the teratogenic effects of drugs are a good example of the second kind of complementary study. Generalization from other animals to humans is sometimes unwarranted because effects of drugs on prenatal development are not always the same in humans and in other animals or even in different species of rodents (for example, mice and rats). Because of this imperfect match in teratogenic effects from one species to others, potentially useful drugs must eventually be tested directly with humans in clinical trials. Clinical trials are not experimental in that the drugs can ethically be given to pregnant women only if they need them for treatment and thus the disease in need of treatment is an extraneous variable. The dangers of this design are reduced when all the members of the patient sample are randomly assigned to treatment conditions. Then if the negative outcomes are more frequent in the drug group than in the control group, it is possible to conclude that the drug is at least partially responsible for the effect. Even so, it is impossible to determine whether the results would be the same in another population, for example, women with a different form of diabetes. Furthermore, in many clinical trials subjects are not randomly assigned to treatment groups, but the assignment is based on other criteria, such as the willingness of the subject to try an experimental drug.

The complexities of correlational research were well demonstrated in this chapter, particularly in the sections on smoking, alcohol, and noise. In all three areas, the research endeavor began with the discovery of a correlation between the occurrence of the environmental event during pregnancy and negative infant outcomes. Such correlations naturally raise the question of whether the environmental event produces the outcome, but causality cannot be inferred from correlational research and in none of these cases is experimental research with humans possible. Nevertheless, there are a number of techniques available to help determine causality. Using corroborative experiments with animals is one good technique, because it establishes causality in a similar context, and the reasonableness of generalizing from infrahuman species to humans is in-

creased by similarities of results with two or more species. A second technique discussed in Chapters 2 and 3 is using the mother as her own control. This technique eliminates a variety of extraneous variables that are necessarily present when one group of mothers is compared to another. Examples of such extraneous variables that are likely to influence outcomes in prenatal development are social class, living conditions, and care of oneself during pregnancy. Less effective ways to control for the same sorts of extraneous variables are also often used. Groups can be matched so that they do not differ on the extraneous variables. This is of limited usefulness because the extraneous variables have to be identified in advance and matching on more than a few extraneous variables becomes cumbersome. Matching was used effectively in the smoking and alcohol research to control for nutritional variables.

Another group of related techniques are statistical. Once the data are collected, the effects of the extraneous variables are separated from the effects of the independent variable. This requires only that the researchers measure the extraneous variables of interest while they are collecting their data, which in turn requires that (1) the extraneous variables be specified, (2) valid measures of the variables be available, and (3) there is enough time and money to gather the data on the extraneous measures.

All of these techniques were used in various studies described in the sections on smoking, alcohol, and noise. Although all are useful and make the findings of a study more believable, researchers generally consider the techniques differentially convincing. We have discussed them in order from the most convincing (corroborative experimental research with animals) to the least convincing (statistical control during data analyses).

The effectiveness of these methodological solutions is determined by the ingenuity of the researchers who use them. They must ferret out the potential alternative causes as well as devise means by which to test the alternative causal hypotheses against the original. The process of devising alternative causal hypotheses, testing them out, eliminating some and revising and honing others is demonstrated well in the smoking and alcohol sections. Often at the beginning of this long progression from correlational finding to causal explanation, the goal of the researchers is to eliminate extraneous variables that potentially confound the results. In showing that the extraneous variable does not affect the results, they can strengthen the likelihood that the original causal hypothesis is true. This simple solution is often inadequate because the extraneous variable turns out to influence the results. Then the research question becomes whether the extraneous variable and not the original independent variable produces the effect (which makes it a confounding variable) or whether both the extraneous and independent variables are operating. In the smoking and alcohol research, the latter more often appears to be the case. In some instances, the extraneous variable **contributes** (adds) to the effect of the independent variable. For example, the effects of alcohol are exacerbated by smoking—the extraneous variable (smoking) contributes to the effects of the independent variable (alcohol). The same is likely to be true for paternal prepregnancy drinking and for drug abuse. In other cases the extraneous variable **moderates** the independent variable; that is, the extraneous variable sets the conditions under which the independent variable operates. We discussed this kind of interaction between independent and extraneous variables in the Research Issues in Chapter 2. An example from this chapter is that the genetic susceptibility of the offspring may determine whether prenatal exposure to alcohol has an effect. Such exposure may cause defects in susceptible offspring, but not in invulnerable offspring.

Another research strategy is to clarify the causal relation by searching for the **mediating** effects (that is, the mechanisms of action). Researchers ask how smoking or alcohol might produce the effects that are correlated with it. One answer they've proposed is that smoking or alcohol produces difficulties in the placental interchange system and the placental problems produce the negative effects in the offspring. This hypothesis was supported in the smoking literature by the finding that the frequency of placental abnormalities was higher in smoking than in nonsmoking mothers. This is still correlational, but begins to establish a pattern of correlations among smoking, placental dysfunction, and outcomes that would make the explanation feasible. In the alcohol literature

the same hypothesis was tested experimentally in monkeys and thereby a causal hypothesis was established. If research can establish the mechanism by which the independent variable produces the dependent variable, then the likelihood that the original correlational finding reflected a causal hypothesis is strengthened.

The correlational research in this chapter not only provided good demonstrations of how researchers attempt to find causal relations when experiments with humans are impossible, but it also demonstrates the influence of social pressures in research. Whether prenatal smoking itself causes problems for the offspring is quite unclear, but people are so emotionally involved in the conclusions from this research that causality is assumed. In fact, there are campaigns to encourage women to stop smoking during pregnancy at both federal and local levels. Such imposition of social pressure on the conclusions drawn from research is most problematic when the research is inconclusive, contradictory, or against the biases of social policy makers. In the prenatal smoking research all three of these conditions hold true.

Parenting

This chapter reviewed many of the specific drugs, diseases, and conditions that can affect the developing offspring. Much of the value of good prenatal care lies in its ability to reduce the influence of these teratogens. It is important to anticipate pregnancy and to seek medical attention as early as possible, because most teratogens operate early in pregnancy. In fact, some measures are best taken before pregnancy, such as testing for rubella immunity and vaccination, if necessary; testing for toxoplasmosis and avoidance of cats, particularly their fecal matter; and establishment of a healthy diet, even though that will not eliminate effects of long-term inadequate nutrition. An early visit to a doctor will allow the doctor to identify substances including medications, alcohol, and over-the-counter drugs that may be among the myriad potentially teratogenic agents, and to outline steps the pregnant woman may take to protect her developing offspring.

A growing number of women, however, are reluctant to take advice from a doctor unquestioningly, particularly if that advice is to give up a strong habit such as smoking or drinking, or a drug that has been relied upon, such as aspirin for arthritis or severe, chronic headaches. This is understandable because the evidence is often unclear, as we have seen. Conservative medical practice is that when consistent correlational findings in humans or strong experimental evidence in animals exists, the appropriate advice is to stop using that substance while pregnant. When it is not clear that a particular drug is harmful, as is true for nicotine and aspirin, then women with strong habits may find it difficult to follow the doctor's advice. In the case of smoking, each woman must assess the degree of uncertainty of the research, the strength of her own needs, and the degree of harm likely to result to her child. A woman to whom smoking is extremely important might judge that the probability of serious defect is too low to warrant her giving up smoking completely, but a woman to whom smoking is less important might find that giving up smoking is easier than worrying about whether her smoking is harming her offspring. The same argument can be made for other teratogens for which conclusions from research are still unclear.

It is important to understand that the risks discussed in this chapter are small in terms of the number of people who will be affected by them or the proportions of the total number of serious defects they account for.[18] Maternal infections of all the types we discussed account for less than 2% of major congenital malformations (Kalter & Warkany, 1983), or affect fewer than 6 out of every 10,000 live births. Maternal illnesses other than diabetes account for only very few, and diabetes accounts for 1.4% of gross malformations. Keeping a sense of proportion is important because the thalidomide tragedy, which focused attention on birth defects, also convinced many people that the causes of all birth defects could be determined and they could then be prevented by avoiding all potentially harmful agents in diets and environments. This chapter should make clear that this is not the case.

---

[18] The numbers of problems involved nation-wide or world-wide are great, but that is primarily a societal problem rather than a personal problem for the parent-to-be.

This was not intended to be a chapter on pregnancy care, although it contained much information relevant to that topic. Many important pregnancy care topics are not covered, such as weight gain, effects of exercise, and sexual relations. For a complete treatment of pregnancy care, we suggest Hotchener's *Pregnancy/Childbirth* (1979), an engaging and reasonably accurate book of this type. Another book for the general reader is *Caring for Your Unborn Child* (Gots & Gots, 1977).

SUMMARY

Various external agents can cause abnormalities in the development of the embryo or fetus, including infectious agents, drugs, alcohol, and irradiation. These agents are called teratogens. The effects of teratogens are pregnancy wastage, premature birth, low birth weight, obvious physical problems, or more subtle problems. The more subtle problems may include hidden physical defects with related health consequences. More important, from the standpoint of behavior, they may include subtle forms of brain damage. Most teratogens reach the fetus by being in the mother's system and then passing across the placental barrier to the fetus.

Maternal Diseases and Chronic Conditions

Rubella, or German measles, if contracted by the mother in early pregnancy during critical periods of embryogenesis or organ development, can result in significant damage to ears, eyes, heart, and brain. Other infections can cause profound damage. The time at which they act to harm the organism ranges from early in embryogenesis (rubella), to late pregnancy (syphilis), to during delivery (*herpes simplex* or gonorrhea).

Hormonal disorders in mothers can affect the fetus. The effects on the fetus can be at least partially controlled (as in hypothyroidism) if mothers are adequately treated during pregnancy. Diabetes is currently less well controlled, but progress in control appears to be imminent. Women with severe heart and kidney problems must decide with their doctors whether a pregnancy should be continued. Both the effects on the mother and on the potential baby need to be considered.

Maternal age can be a factor in prenatal development. As noted in Chapter 3, older mothers have a higher risk of producing babies with chromosomal abnormalities. Very young mothers may not provide adequate nutrition.

Malnutrition and Oxygen Deprivation

Because the nutritional status of the mother affects all aspects of her reproductive functions as well as the health of her baby, a proper balance of calories, especially protein calories, vitamins, and minerals is essential both before and during pregnancy. Infant malnutrition, for reasons other than maternal malnutrition, is most likely to occur because of multiple fetuses, implantation of the fertilized egg on a less favorable area of the uterine wall, or placental inadequacy. Serious effects from oxygen deprivation may occur as a result of certain maternal illnesses or from exposure to unaccustomed high altitudes. Other possible teratogens may have their effects by affecting nutrition or oxygen levels.

Drugs

The discovery that thalidomide produces severe defects in limb development and other effects demonstrated beyond doubt that drugs can pass the placental barrier. It also demonstrated the necessity of conducting extensive clinical trials with humans before licensing a drug for use.

A number of steroid hormones, both natural and synthetic, have been found to affect prenatal development. In addition to pregnancy loss, prematurity, and low birth weights, sexual differentiation may be affected. Evidence for behavioral differences is more complex and controversial.

Psychotropic drugs such as heroin and methadone affect the behavior of the newborn. The effects of methadone may be worse than those of heroin and may include neurological damage. Studies on the prenatal effects of any psychotropic drug are complicated by the fact that other life-style variables such as poor nu-

trition go with drug usage; often more than one drug is used; and often the drugs used are contaminated by impurities that may also be harmful. When behaviors for the postnatal period are examined, the total child rearing pattern may also affect the infant's behavior and thereby confound the results.

Cigarette smoking is related to a number of infant characteristics. These include increased fetal and neonatal death rates, higher prematurity rates, and lower birth weight. In addition, morbidity is increased. The exact degree of danger to those who survive the neonatal period is unclear, however. The evidence of long-range effects on intelligence is somewhat divided. Because the research is correlational, it is hard to be sure that smoking is a direct cause of the effects found. As with psychotropic drugs, associated variables may be responsible. In addition, it is not clearly established whether the drug (nicotine), or possibly even tars, directly causes the problems or whether the link between smoking and malnutrition and periodic inadequate oxygen may cause the problems. Further, not only child rearing variables but also postnatal exposure to smoking may add to the differences found.

Alcohol may be one of the most important drugs that affects fetal development, both in terms of frequency and severity of effects. Fetal Alcohol Syndrome is the most dire outcome. It includes a number of physical problems as well as mental retardation. As with other teratogens, pregnancy loss and prematurity and low birth weight are more frequent among drinkers. Both binge drinking and chronic alcohol consumption may have negative effects on the embryo and fetus. Moderate drinking appears to be related primarily to low birth weight. When combined with smoking it appears to have worse effects than either alone. Moderate drinking prior to pregnancy may be handicapping. The role of placental abnormalities as a mediator of the effects of smoking has been shown. They may also be related to effects of alcohol. Their role needs to be further studied. The effects of paternal drinking need further exploration in view of animal data. The influence of genetic susceptibility on the effects of alcohol or other drugs is an important topic for additional investigation.

A number of other drugs also have teratogenic effects: folic acid antagonists, anticonvulsant drugs, aspirin in conjunction with benzoic acid, and inhalant anesthetics. There is a long list of other possible teratogenic drugs. Among them are antibiotics, quinine, antidepressants, insulin, oral hypoglycemic drugs, alkylating agents, drugs used in the treatment of tuberculosis, and pesticides.

Radiation

This is often called the "universal teratogen." It passes through the mother's body to affect the eggs, embryo, or fetus directly. Every X ray received by the mother, plus possible constant background radiation, is cumulative over time and affects the mother's ova. Among potential effects are lowered fertility, increased likelihood of miscarriage, brain malformations, Down's syndrome, various other birth defects, and mental retardation.

Direct blows to the fetus or unusual noise levels, as happens close to airports, may have a direct effect on the fetus, although current knowledge suggests that embryos and fetuses tend to be well protected from direct effects of the environment outside their mother's body. Further study of factors such as noise may lead to revised understanding of the role of the external environment.

Prenatal Stress

Little conclusive data exists for determining the degree of physical labor, in athletics or in work settings, that is optimal for fetal development. Negative effects on the mother or fetus or both are found from heavy work, but the studies do not take into account confounding factors such as nutritional status, poverty, and illness. Psychological stress has been studied experimentally with animals and correlationally with humans. These studies find that psychological stress during pregnancy may affect complications during delivery, and affects the developing offspring. Babies from stressed pregnancies have been found to exhibit greater emotionality or irritability or both, lower infant test scores, and an increased morbidity ratio. It appears that potential stresses are harmful to infants only when the mother has experienced personal tension. The probable mechanism for these effects on the offspring is stress-produced hormones in the mother. These hormones then cross the placental barrier and affect the embryo or fetus. Techniques for measuring hormones are now available that should permit future researchers to clarify their role and the effects of stress during pregnancy.

REFERENCES

Abel, E.L. (1980). Fetal alcohol syndrome. *Psychological Bulletin, 87,* 29–30.

Alford, C.A., Reynolds, D.W., & Stagno, S. (1974). Current concepts of chronic perinatal infections. In L. Gluck (Ed.), *Modern perinatal medicine.* Chicago: Year Book Medical Publishers, Inc.

Ando, Y., & Hattori, H. (1970). Effects of intense noise during fetal life upon postnatal adaptability. *Journal of the Acoustical Society of America, 47,* 1128–1130.

Ando, Y., & Hattori, H. (1973). Statistical studies on the effects of intense noise during human fetal life. *Journal of Sound Vibration, 27,* 101–110.

Avery, M.E., & Taeusch, H.W. (1984). Maternal conditions and exogenous influences that affect the fetus/newborn. In M.E. Avery & H.W. Taeusch (Eds.), *Schaffer's diseases of the newborn* (5th Ed.). Philadelphia: Saunders.

Badr, F.M., & Badr, R.S. (1975). Induction of dominant lethal mutation in mice by ethyl alcohol. *Nature, 253,* 134–136.

Beck, F., Moffat, D.B., & Lloyd, J.B. (1973). *Human embryology.* Oxford, England: Blackwell.

Bibbo, N., Gill, W.B., Azizi, F., Blough, R., Fang, V.S., Rosenfield, R.L., Schumacher, G.F.B., Sleeper, K., Sonek, M.G., & Wield, G.L. (1977). Follow-up study of male and female offspring of DES-exposed mothers. *Obstetrics and Gynecology, 49,* 1–8.

Blot, W.J., & Miller, R.W. (1973). Mental retardation following in utero exposure to atomic bombs of Hiroshima and Nagasaki. *Radiology, 106,* 617–619.

Broman, S.H., & Nichols, P.L. (1981, August). *Predictors of superior cognitive ability in young children.* Paper presented at the meeting of the American Psychological Association, Los Angeles.

Brown, N., Goulding, E., & Fabro, S. (1979). Ethanol embryotoxicity: Direct effects on mammalian embryo in vitro. *Science, 31,* 573–575.

Burrow, G. (1965). Neonatal goiter after maternal propylthiouracil therapy. *Journal of Clinical Endocrinology, 25,* 403–408.

Butler, N.R., & Alberman, E.D. (Eds.). (1969). *Perinatal mortality.* Edinburgh: E. and S. Livingstone, Ltd.

Cahalan, D., Cissin, I.H., & Crossley, H.M. (1969). *American drinking practices: A national study of drinking behavior and attitudes.* New Brunswick, NJ: Rutgers University Press.

Carr, J.N. (1975). Drug patterns among drug-addicted mothers: Incidence and effects on children. *Pediatric Annals, 4,* 65–77.

Carter, M.P. (1965). A probable epidemic of congenital hydrocephaly in 1940–1941. *Developmental Medicine and Child Neurology, 7,* 61–64.

Chow, B.F., & Sherwin, R.W. (1965). Fetal parasitism? *Archives of Environmental Health, 10,* 395–398.

Christoffel, K.K., & Salofsky, I. (1975). Fetal alcohol syndrome in dizygotic twins. *Journal of Pediatrics, 87,* 963–967.

Clarren, S.K., & Smith, D.W. (1978). The fetal alcohol syndrome. *New England Journal of Medicine, 298,* 1063–1067.

Cohen, B.H., & Lilienfeld, A.M. (1970). The epidemiological study of Mongolism in Baltimore. *Annals of the New York Academy of Sciences, 171,* 320–327.

Cohen, E.N., Belleville, J.W., & Brown, B.W. (1971). Anesthesia, pregnancy, and miscarriage: A study of operating room nurses and anesthetists. *Anesthesiology, 35,* 343–347.

Cohen, L. (1981). *The effects of maternal psychological stress during pregnancy on subsequent postnatal behavior in 2 day old infants.* Unpublished senior honors thesis, Wheaton College, Norton, MA.

Colley, J.R.T., Holland, W.W., & Corkhill, R.T. (1974). Influence of passive smoking and phlegm on pneumonia and bronchitis in early childhood. *Lancet,* 1031–1034.

Collman, R., & Stoller, A. (1962). A survey of mongoloid births in Victoria, Australia. *American Journal of Public Health, 52,* 813–829.

Committee on Hearing, Bioacoustics, and Biomechanics, National Research Council. (1982). *Prenatal effects of exposure to high-level noise.* Washington, DC: National Academy Press.

Dalton, K. (1968). Ante-natal progesterone and intelligence. *British Journal of Psychiatry, 114,* 1377–1383.

Dalton, K. (1976). Prenatal progesterone and educational attainments. *British Journal of Psychiatry, 129,* 438–442.

Davids, A., & DeVault, S. (1962). Maternal anxiety during pregnancy and childbirth abnormalities. *Psychosomatic Medicine, 24,* 464–470.

Davids, A., DeVault, S., & Talmadge, M. (1961). Anxiety, pregnancy, and childbirth abnormalities. *Journal of Consulting Psychology, 25,* 74–77.

Davids, A., Holden, R.H., & Gray, G.B. (1963). Maternal anxiety during pregnancy and adequacy of mother and child adjustment eight months following childbirth. *Child Development, 34,* 993–1002.

Davie, R., Butler, N., & Goldstein, H. (1972). *From birth to seven: The second report of the child development study* (1958 cohort). London: Longman and National Children's Bureau.

Desmonts, G. 1982, October). Report of workshop on infectious diseases at the World Conference on Prevention of Physical and Mental Congenital Anomalies, Strasbourg, France.

Dishotsky, N.I., Loughman, W.D., Mogar, R.E., & Lipscomb, W.R. (1971). LSD and genetic damage. Is LSD chromosome damaging, carcinogenic, mutagenic, or teratogenic? *Science, 172,* 431–440.

Dobbing, J. (1976). Vulnerable periods in brain growth and somatic growth. In D.R. Roberts (Ed.), *The biology of the human fetus.* London: Taylor & Francis.

Dowler, J.K., & Jacobson, S.W. (1984, April). *Alternative measures of maternal smoking and caffeine consumption as predictors of neonatal outcome.* Paper presented at the biennial meeting of the International Conference on Infant Studies, New York.

Drillien, C.M., Jameson, S., & Wilkinson, M.E. (1966). Studies in mental handicap: I. Prevalence and distribution by clinical type and severity of defect. *Archives of Diseases of Childhood, 41,* 528–538.

Eckhoff, E., Gawsha, J., & Baldwin, A.L. (1961). Parental behavior towards boys and girls of preschool age. *Acta Psychologia, 18,* 85.

Ehrhardt, A.A., & Money, J. (1967). Progestin induced hermaphroditism: IQ and psychosexual identity in a study of 10 girls. *Journal of Sex Research, 3,* 83–100.

Ehrhardt, A.A., & Money, J. (1973). Prenatal hormones and human behavior. *Illinois Medical Journal, 141,* 386–389.

Ellis, F.W., & Pick, J.R. (1980). An animal model of the fetal alcohol syndrome in beagles. *Alcoholism: Clinical and Experimental Research, 4,* 123–134.

Fedrick, J., & Alberman, E.D. (1972). Reported influenza in pregnancy and subsequent cancer in the child. *British Medical Journal, 2,* 485–488.

Fein, G.G., Schwartz, P.M., Jacobson, W.S., & Jacobson, J.L. (1983). Environmental toxins and behavioral development. *American Psychologist, 38,* 1188–1197.

Finnegan, L.P., Connaughton, J.F., & Schut, J. (1975). Infants of drug-dependent women: Practical approaches for management. In *Proceeding of the 37th Annual Scientific Meeting of the Committee on Problems of Drug Dependence of the National Research Council.* Washington, DC: National Academy of Sciences.

Finnegan, L.P., Reeser, P.S., & Connaughton, J.F. (1977). The effects of maternal drug dependence on neonatal mortality. *Drug and Alcohol Dependence, 3,* 131–140.

Fraser, F.C. (1984). Other congenital defects involving bones. In M.E. Avery & H.W. Taeusch (Eds.), *Schaffer's diseases of the newborn* (5th Ed.). Philadelphia: Saunders.

Frazier, T.M., Davis, G.H., Goldstein, H., & Goldberg, I.E. (1961). Cigarette smoking and prematurity, a prospective study. *American Journal of Obstetrics and Gynecology, 81,* 988–996.

Fried, P.A. (1980). Marihuana use by pregnant women: Neurobehavioral effects in neonates. *Drug and Alcohol Dependence, 6,* 415–424.

Fried, P.A., & Oxorn, H. (1980). *Smoking for two: Cigarettes and pregnancy.* New York: Free Press.

Gentry, J.T., Parkhurst, E., & Bulin, G.V. (1959). An epidemiological study of congenital malformations in N.Y. state. *American Journal of Public Health, 49,* 1–22.

Gerrard, J. (1952). Kernicterus. *Brain, 75,* 526–570. As cited in Konigsmark, B.W. (1971).

Gill, W.B., Schumacher, G.F.B., Bibbo, M., Straus, F.H., II, & Schoenberg, H.W. (1979). Association of diethylstilbestrol exposure in utero with cryptorchidism, testicular hypoplasia, and semen abnormalities. *Journal of Urology, 122,* 36–39.

Gluck, L. (1971). Neurosensory factors in newborn hearing. In *Conference on newborn hearing screening: Prodeedings summary and recommendations.* Sacramento, CA: California State Department of Public Health.

Gordon, G. (1966). The mechanisms of thalidomide deformities correlated with the pathogenic effects of prolonged dosage in adults. *Developmental Medicine and Child Neurology, 8,* 761–767.

Gordon, G. (1968). Folic acid deficiency from anticonvulsant therapy. *Developmental Medicine and Child Neurology, 10,* 497–504.

Gots, R.E., & Gots, B.A. (1977). *Caring for your unborn child.* New York: Stein & Day.

Gunderson, V., & Sackett, G.P. (1982). Paternal effects on reproductive outcome and developmental risk. In M.E. Lamb & A.L. Brown (Eds.), *Advances in developmental psychology* (pp. 85–123). Hillsdale, NJ: Erlbaum.

Haas, J.D. (1970). Prenatal and infant growth and development. In P.T. Baker & M.A. Little (Eds.), *Man in the Andes.* Stroudsburg, PA: Dowden, Hutchinson, & Ross.

Haas, J.D. (1973, December). *Biocultural factors relating to infant growth and motor development in Peru.* Paper presented at the annual meeting of the American Anthropological Association, New Orleans.

Hackman, E., Emanuel, I., van Belle, G., & Daling, J. (1983). Maternal birth weight and subsequent pregnancy outcome. *Journal of American Medical Association, 250,* 2016–2019.

Hanson, S.W., Streissguth, A.P., & Smith, D.W. (1978). The effects of moderate alcohol consumption during pregnancy on fetal growth and morphogenesis. *Journal of Pediatrics, 92,* 457–460.

Hardy, J.B., & Mellitts, E.D. (1972). Does maternal smoking during pregnancy have a long-term effect on the child? *Lancet, ii,* 1332–1336.

Harlap, S., & Shiono, P.H. (1980). Alcohol, smoking and incidence of spontaneous abortions in the first trimester. *Lancet, i,* 173–176.

Herbst, A., Hubby, M., Blough, R., et al. (1980). A comparison of pregnancy experience in DES-exposed and DES-unexposed daughters. *Journal of Reproductive Medicine, 24,* 62.

Heuyer, C., Mises, R., & Dereux, J.F. (1957). La descendance des alcooliques. *La Presse Medicale, 29,* 657–658.

Hockman, C.H. (1961). Prenatal maternal stress in the rat: Its effects on emotional behavior in the offspring. *Journal of Comparative and Physiological Psychology, 54,* 679–684.

Hoffman, D., Felton, R., & Cyr, W. (1981). *Effects of ionizing radiation on the developing embryo and fetus.* Publication FDA 81-8170. Washington, DC: United States Department of Health and Human Services.

Horner, J.S. (1972). *The health of Hillingdon.* Uxbridge, Middlesex, U.K.: The Health Department.

Hotchner, T. (1979). *Pregnancy/Childbirth.* New York: Avon.

Hurley, L.S. (1982, October). *Trace elements and their interactions as causes of congenital defects.* Paper presented at the World Conference on Prevention of Congenital Anomalies: Physical and Mental. Strasbourg, France.

Hutchings, D.E. (1978). Behavioral teratology: Embryopathic and behavioral effects of drugs during pregnancy. In G. Gottlieb (Ed.), *Various influences on brain and behavioral development.* New York: Academic.

Institute of Medicine. (1982). *Marijuana and health.* Washington, DC: National Academy of Sciences Press.

Joffe, J.M. (1969). Prenatal determinants of behavior. In *The International Series of Monographs in Experimental Psychology* (Vol. 7). Oxford: Pergamon Press.

Johnson, H.L., Diano, A., & Rosen, T.S. (1984). 24-Month neurobehavioral follow-up of children of methadone-maintained mothers. *Infant Behavior and Development, 7,* 115–123.

Jones, F.N., & Tauscher, J. (1978). Residence under an airport landing pattern as a factor in teratism. *Archives of Environmental Health, 35,* 10–12.

Jones, K.L., Smith, P.W., Streissguth, A.P., & Myrianthopoulis, N.C. (1974). Outcome in offspring of chronic alcoholic women. *Lancet, ii,* 1076–1078.

Jones, K.L., Smith, P.W., Ulleland, C.W., & Streissguth, A.P. (1973). Patterns of malformations in offspring of chronic alcoholic women. *Lancet, i,* 1267–1271.

Jones, W.S., & Man, E.B. (1969). Thyroid function in human pregnancy, VI: Premature deliveries and reproduction failures of pregnant women with low serum butanol-extractable iodines. *American Journal of Obstetrics and Gynecology, 104,* 909–914.

Kalter, H. (1968). *Teratology of the central nervous system.* Chicago: University of Chicago Press.

Kalter, H., & Warkany, J. (1983). Congenital malformations: Etiologic factors and their role in prevention. *The New England Journal of Medicine, 308,* 424–431.

Kaminski, M., Funeau, C., & Schwartz, D. (1978). Alcohol consumption in pregnant women and the outcome of pregnancy. *Alcoholism: Clinical and Experimental Research, 2,* 155–164.

Kitzmiller, J., Brown, E., Philippe, M., et al. (1981). Diabetic nephropathy in perinatal outcome. *American Journal of Obstetrics and Gynecology, 141,* 741–751.

Klein, P.S., Forbes, G.B., & Nader, P.R. (1976). Letter: Short term starvation in infancy re subsequent learning disabilities—A proven relationship? *Journal of Pediatrics, 88,* 702–703.

Kline, J., Shrout, P., Stein, Z., Susser, M., & Warburton, D. (1980). Drinking during pregnancy and spontaneous abortion. *Lancet, i,* 176–180.

Konigsmark, B.W. (1971). Hereditary and congenital factors affecting newborn sensorineural hearing. Publication of Conference on Newborn Hearing Screening, San Francisco, CA. San Francisco: State Department of Public Health.

Kuhnert, P.M., Erhard, P., & Kuhnert, B.R. (1977). Lead and delta-aminolevulinic acid dehydrastase in RBC's of urban mothers and fetuses. *Environmental Research, 14,* 73–80.

Landesman-Dwyer, S., Keller, L.S., & Streissguth, A.P. (1978). Naturalistic observations of newborns: Effects of maternal alcohol intake. *Alcoholism: Clinical and Experimental Research, 2,* 171–177.

Laurence, K.M. (1982, October). *Prevention of neural tube defects by improvement in a maternal diet and preconceptional folic acid supplementation.* Paper presented at the meeting of the World Conference on Prevention of Physical and Mental Congenital Anomalies, Strasbourg, France.

Lefkowitz, M.M. (1981). Smoking during pregnancy: Long-term effects on offspring. *Developmental Psychology, 17,* 192–194.

Lemoine, P., Haronsseau, H., Borteryll, J.P., & Menuet, J.C. (1968). Les enfants de parents alcooliques: Anomalies observées à propos de 127 cas. *Quest Medical, 25,* 476–482.

Lenz, W. (1966). Malformations caused by drugs in pregnancy. *American Journal of Diseases in Children, 112,* 99–105.

Little, R.E., Schultz, F.P., & Mandell, W. (1976). Drinking during pregnancy. *Journal of Studies of Alcohol, 37,* 375–379.

Loughnan, P.M., Gold, H., & Vance, J.C. (1973). Phenytoin teratogenicity in man. *Lancet, ii,* 70–72.

Luke, B., Hawkins, M.M., & Petrie, R.H. (1981). Influence of smoking, weight gain, and pregravid weight for height on intrauterine growth. *Amer-*

ican Journal of Clinical Nutrition, 34, 1410–1417.

Man, E.B., Holden, R.H., & Jones, W.S. (1971). Thyroid function in human pregnancy, VII: Development and retardation of 4-year-old progeny of euthyroid and of hypothyroxinemic women. *American Journal of Obstetrics and Gynecology, 109,* 12–19.

Man, E.B., & Jones, W.S. (1969). Thyroid function in human pregnancy, V: Incidence of maternal low serum butanol-extractable iodines and of normal gestational TBG and TBPA capacities; retardation of 8-month-old infants. *American Journal of Obstetrics and Gynecology, 104,* 898–908.

Man, E.B., Jones, W.S., Holden, R.H., & Mellits, E.D. (1971). Thyroid function in human pregnancy, VIII: Retardation of progeny aged 7 years; relationships to maternal age and maternal thyroid function. *American Journal of Obstetrics and Gynecology, 111,* 905–916.

Man, E.B., & Serunian, S.A. (1976). Thyroid function in human pregnancy IX: Development or retardation of 7-year-old progeny of hypothyroxinemic women. *American Journal of Obstetrics and Gynecology, 125,* 949–957.

Marcus, J., Hans, S.L., & Jeremy, R.J. (1982). Differential motor and state functioning in newborns of women on methadone. *Neurobehavioral Toxicology and Teratology, 4,* 459–462.

Martin, J.C., Martin, D.C., Lund, C.A., & Streissguth, A.P. (1977). Maternal alcohol ingestion and cigarette smoking and their effects on newborn conditioning. *Alcoholism: Clinical and Experimental Research, 1,* 243–247.

Martin, J.C., Martin, D.C., Sigman, P., & Redow, B. (1978). Offspring survival, development and operant performance following maternal ethanol consumption. *Developmental Psychobiology, 10,* 435–446.

Mau, G., & Netter, P. (1974). Kaffee und Alkoholkonsum—Riskfaktoren in der Schwangerschaft? [Are coffee and alcohol consumption risk factors in pregnancy?]. *Gebürtshilfe und Frauenheilkunde, 34,* 1018–1022.

Mauss, E.A. (1983). Health effects of ionizing radiation in the low-dose range. *Annals of the New York Academy of Sciences, 403,* 27–36.

McDonald, A.D. (1958). Maternal health and congenital defect. *New England Journal of Medicine, 258,* 767–773.

McFinn, J.H., & Robertson, J. (1973). Psychological-test results of children with thalidomide deformations. *Developmental Medicine and Child Neurology, 15,* 719–727.

McIntosh, K. (1984). Viral infections of the fetus and newborn. In M.E. Avery & H.W. Taeusch, Jr. (Eds.), *Schaffer's diseases of the newborn* (5th Ed.), Philadelphia: Saunders.

McLaren, A. (1982, October). *Early stages of development of mammalian embryos.* Paper presented at the meeting of the World Conference on Prevention of Physical and Mental Congenital Anomalies, Strasbourg, France.

Meyer, M.B., Jones, B.S., & Tonascia, J.A. (1976). Perinatal events associated with maternal smoking during pregnancy. *American Journal of Epidemiology, 103,* 464–476.

Mukherjee, A., & Hodgen, G. (1982). Ethanol exposure induces transient impairment of umbilical circulation and severe fetal hypoxia in monkeys. *Science, 218,* 700–702.

Naeye, R.L. (1978). Effects of maternal smoking on the fetus and placenta. *British Journal of Obstetrics and Gynaecology, 85,* 732–737.

Naeye, R.L. (1979a). The duration of maternal cigarette smoking and fetal and placental disorders. *Early Human Development, 3,* 229–237.

Naeye, R.L. (1979b). Relationship of cigarette smoking to congenital anomalies and perinatal death. *American Journal of Pathology, 90,* 289–293.

Naeye, R.L., Blanc, W., & Paul, C. (1973). Effects of maternal nutrition on the human fetus. *Pediatrics, 52,* 494–503.

National Academy of Sciences. (1975). *Nutrition and fertility.* Washington, DC: National Academy of Sciences Press.

Nichols, P.I., & Chen, T. (1981). *Minimal brain dysfunction: A prospective study.* New Jersey: Lawrence Erlbaum Associates.

Ostrea, E.M., Chavez, C.J., & Strauss, M.E. (1975). A study of factors that influence the severity of neonatal narcotic withdrawal. *Addictive Diseases, 2,* 187–199.

Ottinger, D.R., & Simmons, J.E. (1964). Behavior of human neonates and prenatal maternal anxiety. *Psychological Reports, 14,* 391–394.

Oullette, E.M., Rosett, H.L., & Rosman, N.P. (1977). Adverse effects on offspring of maternal alcohol abuse during pregnancy. *New England Journal of Medicine, 297,* 528–530.

Palmer, R.H., Ouellette, E.M., Warner, L., & Leichtman, S.R. (1974). Congenital malformations in offspring of a chronic alcoholic mother. *Pediatrics, 53,* 490–494.

Pederson, L.M., Tygstrup, I., & Pederson, J. (1964). Congenital malformations in newborn infants of diabetic women. *Lancet, i,* 1124–1126.

Pfeifer, W.D., Mackinnon, J.R., & Seiser, R.L. (1977). *Adverse effects of paternal alcohol consumption on offspring in the rat.* Paper presented at the annual meeting of the Psychonomic Society, Washington, DC.

Pratt, R.M. (1982, September 28). As cited in *NIH Record*, p. 6.

Pueschel, S.M. (1983). The child with Down syndrome. In M.D. Levine, W.B. Carey, A.C. Crocker, & R.T. Gross (Eds.), *Developmental behavioral pediatrics.* Philadelphia: Saunders.

Reinisch, J.M. (1974). Fetal hormones, the brain, and human sex differences: A heuristic integrative review of the recent literature. *Archives of Sexual Behavior, 3,* 51–90.

Reinisch, J.M. (1977). Prenatal exposure of human foetuses to synthetic progestin and estrogen affects personality. *Nature, 266,* 561–562.

Reinisch, J.M., & Gandelman, R. (1978). Human research in behavioral endocrinology: Methodological and theoretical considerations. In G. Dorner & M. Kawakami (Eds.), *Hormones and brain development.* Amsterdam: Elsevier North Holland Biomedical Press.

Reinisch, J.M., Gandelman, R., & Spiegel, F. (1979). Prenatal influences on cognitive ability: Data from experimental animals and human genetic and endocrine syndromes. In M.A. Wittig & A.C. Petersen (Eds.), *Determinants of sex-related differences in cognitive functioning.* New York: Academic Press.

Reinisch, J.M., & Karow, W.G. (1977). Prenatal exposure to synthetic progestins and estrogens: Effects on human development. *Archives of Sexual Behavior, 6,* 257–288.

Reinisch, J.M., Simon, N.G., Karow, W.G., & Gandelman, R. (1978). Prenatal prednisone exposure in humans and animals retards intrauterine growth. *Science, 202,* 436–438.

Rosenblith, J.F. (1979a). The Graham/Rosenblith behavioral examination for newborns: Prognostic value and procedural issues. In Osofsky, J. (Ed.), *Handbook of infant development.* New York: Wiley & Sons.

Rosenblith, J.F. (1979b, April). *Relations between Graham/Rosenblith neonatal measures and seven year assessments.* Paper presented at the meeting of the Eastern Psychological Association, Philadelphia.

Rosenblith, J.F. (1979c). *Relations between behavior in the newborn period and intellectual achievement and IQ at seven years of age.* Paper presented at the meeting of the International Society for the Study of Behavioral Development, Lund, Sweden.

Rosett, H.L. (1980). Guest Editorial: A clinical perspective on the fetal alcohol syndrome. *Alcoholism: Clinical and Experimental Research, 4,* 119–122.

Rosett, H.L., Ouellette, E.M., & Weiner, L. (1976). A pilot prospective study of the fetal alcohol syndrome at the Boston City Hospital: Part I. Maternal drinking. *Annals of the New York Academy of Science, 273,* 118–122.

Rosett, H.L., Ouellette, E.M., Weiner, L., & Owens, E. (1978). Therapy of heavy drinking during pregnancy. *Obstetrics and Gynecology, 51,* 41–46.

Rosett, H.L., & Sander, L.W. (1979). Effects of maternal drinking on neonatal morphology and state regulation. In J. Osofsky (Ed.), *Handbook of infant development.* New York: Wiley.

Rosett, H.L., Snyder, P., Sander, L.W., Lee, A., Cook, P., Weiner, L., & Gould, J. (1979). Effects of maternal drinking on neonate state regulations. *Developmental Medicine and Child Neurology, 21,* 464–473.

Rosett, H.L., Weiner, L., Lee, A., Zuckerman, B., Dooling, E., & Oppenheimer, E. (1983). Patterns of alcohol consumption and fetal development. *Obstetrics and Gynecology, 61,* 539–546.

Rush, D. (1973). A correction by author: "Maternal smoking: A reassessment of the association with perinatal mortality." *American Journal of Epidemiology, 97,* 425.

Rush, D. (1974). Examination of the relationship between birthweight, cigarette smoking during pregnancy and maternal weight gain. *The Journal of Obstetrics and Gynecology of the British Commonwealth, 81,* 746–752.

Rush, D., Davis, H., & Susser, M.W. (1972). Antecedents of low birthweight in Harlem, New York City. *International Journal of Epidemiology, 1,* 375–387.

Rush, D., & Kass, E.H. (1972). Maternal smoking: A reassessment of the association with perinatal mortality. *American Journal of Epidemiology, 96,* 183–196.

Sassenrath, E.N., Chapman, L.F., & Goo, G.P. (1979). Reproduction in Rhesus monkeys chronically exposed to moderate amounts of delta-9-tetrahydrocannabinol. In G.G. Nahas & W.D. Patton (Eds.), *Marijuana: Biological effects.* Elmsford, New York: Pergamon Press.

Seelig, H.P., & Roemheld, R. (1969). Untersuchungen zur histochemischen lokalisation der leucin-un cystinamino-pepidase (oxytocinase) in der placente. *Histochemie, 18,* 30–39.

Sever, J.L. (1982, October). *Frequency of infection*

during pregnancy. Paper presented at the meeting of the World Conference on Prevention of Physical and Mental Congenital Anomalies. Strasbourg, France.

Sever, J.L., Larsen, J.W., Jr., & Grossman, J.H., III. (1979). *Handbook of perinatal infections.* Boston: Little, Brown.

Silverman, D.T. (1977). Maternal smoking and birth weight. *American Journal of Epidemiology, 105,* 513–521.

Simon, N.G., & Gandelman, R. (1977). The estrogenic arousal of aggression eliciting properties of estrogen in male mice. *Hormones and Behavior, 10,* 118–127.

Snow, M.H.L. (1982, October). *Restorative growth and its problem in morphogenesis.* Paper presented at the meeting of the World Conference on Prevention of Physical and Mental Congenital Anomalies, Strasbourg, France.

Sokol, R.J., Miller, S.I., & Reed, G. (1980). Alcohol abuse during pregnancy: An epidemiological study. *Alcoholism: Clinical and Experimental Research, 4,* 135–145.

Sontag, L.W. (1941). Significance of fetal environmental differences. *American Journal of Obstetrics and Gynecology, 42,* 996–1003.

Sontag, L.W., Steele, W.G., & Lewis, M. (1969). The fetal and maternal cardiac response to environmental stress. *Human Development, 12,* 1–9.

Stagno, S. (1980). Comparative study of diagnostic procedures for congenital cytomegalovirus infection. *Pediatrics, 65,* 251–255.

Stein, Z.A., & Susser, M.W. (1975a). The Dutch famine, 1944/45 and the reproductive process: I. Effects on six indices at birth. *Pediatrics Research, 9,* 70–76.

Stein, Z.A., & Susser, M.W. (1975b). The Dutch famine, 1944/45 and the reproductive process: II. Interrelations of caloric rations and six indices at birth. *Pediatrics Research, 9,* 75–83.

Stein, Z.A., Susser, M.W., Saenger, G., & Marolla, F. (1975). *Famine and human development: The Dutch hunger winter of 1944–1945.* New York: Oxford University Press.

Stephenson, J.B.P. (1978). Epilepsy: A neurological complication of thalidomide embryopathy. *Developmental Medicine and Child Neurology, 18,* 189–199.

Stewart, A.M. (1955). A note on the obstetric effects of work during pregnancy. *British Journal of Preventative and Social Medicine, 9,* 57–61.

Stewart, A.M., Webb, J.W., & Hewitt, D. (1955). Observations on 1,078 perinatal deaths. *British Journal of Preventive Social Medicine, 9,* 57–61.

Stockard, C.R. (1913). The effect on the offspring of intoxicating the male parent and the transmission of the defects of subsequent generations. *American Naturalist, 47,* 641–682.

Stockard, C.R., & Papanicolaou, G. (1916). A further analysis of the hereditary transmission of degeneracy and deformities by the descendants of alcoholized mammals. *American Naturalist, 50,* 65–88.

Stott, D.H. (1972). The congenital background to behavior disturbance. In L.W. Robbins & M. Pollack (Eds.), *Life history research in psychopathology* (Vol. 2). Minneapolis, MN: University of Minnesota Press.

Stott, D.H. (1973). Follow-up study from birth of the effects of prenatal stresses. *Developmental Medicine and Child Neurology, 15,* 770–787.

Stott, D.H., & Latchford, S.A. (1976). Prenatal antecedents of child health, development, and behavior. *Journal of the American Academy of Child Psychiatry, 15,* 161–190.

Strauss, M.E., Lessen-Firestone, J.K., Starr, R.H., Jr., & Ostrea, E.M. (1975). Behavior of narcotics addicted newborns. *Child Development, 46,* 887–893.

Strauss, M.E., Starr, R.H., Jr., Ostrea, E.M. Jr., Chavez, C.J., & Stryker, J.C. (1976). Behavioral concomitants of prenatal addiction to narcotics. *The Journal of Pediatrics, 89,* 842–846.

Streissguth, A.P. (1977). Maternal drinking and the outcome of pregnancy: Implications for child mental health. *American Journal of Orthopsychiatry, 47,* 422–431.

Streissguth, A.P. (1978). Fetal alcohol syndrome: An epidemiologic perspective. *American Journal of Epidemiology, 107,* 467–478.

Streissguth, A.P., Barr, H.M., & Martin, D.C. (1983). Maternal alcohol use and neonatal habituation assessed with the Brazelton scale. *Child Development, 54,* 1109–1118.

Streissguth, A.P., Herman, C.S., & Smith, D.W. (1978a). Stability of intelligence in the Fetal Alcohol Syndrome. A preliminary report. *Alcoholism: Clinical and Experimental Research, 2,* 165–170.

Streissguth, A.P., Herman, C.S., & Smith, D.W. (1978b). Intelligence, behavior, and dysmorphogenesis in the fetal alcohol syndrome: A report on 20 patients. *The Journal of Pediatrics, 92,* 363–367.

Streissguth, A.P., Landesman-Dwyer, S., Martin, J.C., & Smith, D.W. (1980). Teratogenic effects of alcohol in humans and laboratory animals. *Science, 209,* 353–361.

Streissguth, A.P., Martin, D.C., Barr, H.M., Sandman, B.M., Kirchner, G.L., & Darby, B.L. (1984). Intrauterine alcohol and nicotine exposure: Attention and reaction time in 4-year-old children. *Developmental Psychology, 20,* 533–541.

Streissguth, A.P., Martin, D.C., Martin, J.C., & Barr, H.M. (1981). The Seattle longitudinal prospective study of alcohol and pregnancy. *Neurobehavioral Toxicology and Teratology, 3,* 223–233.

Sulik, K.K., Johnston, M.C., & Webb, M.A. (1981). Fetal alcohol syndrome: Embryogenesis in a mouse model. *Science, 214,* 936–938.

Sullivan, W.C. (1899). A note on the influence of maternal inebriety on the offspring. *Journal of Mental Science, 45,* 489–503.

Thaler, I., Goodman, J.D.S., & Davies, G.S. (1980). Effects of maternal cigarette smoking on fetal breathing–fetal movements. *American Journal of Obstetrics and Gynecology, 138,* 282–287.

Thompson, W.R. (1957). Influence of prenatal maternal anxiety on emotionality in young rats. *Science, 125,* 698–699.

Thompson, W.R., Watson, J., & Charlesworth, W.R. (1962). The effects of prenatal maternal stress on offspring behavior in rats. *Psychological Monographs, 76* (whole No. 38).

Thomson, A.M., & Billewicz, W.Z. (1963). Nutritional status, maternal physique and reproductive efficiency. *Proceedings of the Nutrition Society, 22,* 55.

U.S. Department of Health, Education and Welfare. (1979). *Smoking and health: A report of the surgeon general.* CDHEW Publication No. PNS 79-50066. Washington, DC: U.S. Government Printing Office.

Uhlig, H. (1957). Missbildungen unerwunschter Kinder. *Arztlische Wochenshrift, 12,* 61–66.

Vardaris, R.M., Weisz, D.J., Fazel, A., & Rawitch, A.B. (1976). Chronic administration of delta-9-tetrahydrocannabinol to pregnant rats: Studies of pup behavior and placental transfer. *Pharmacology and Biochemistry of Behavior, 4,* 249–254.

Vierck, C., King, F.A., & Ferm, V.H. (1966). Effects of prenatal hypoxia upon activity and emotionality of the rat. *Psychonomic Science, 4,* 87–88.

Warkany, J., & Kalter, H. (1961a). Congenital malformations. *New England Journal of Medicine, 265,* 993–1001.

Warkany, J., & Kalter, H. (1961b). Congenital malformations (concluded). *The New England Journal of Medicine, 265,* 1046–1052.

Warkany, J., Lemire, R.J., & Cohen, M.M. (1981). *Mental retardation and congenital malformation of the central nervous system.* Chicago: Year Book Medical Publishers.

Werboff, J., & Gottlieb, J.S. (1963). Drugs in pregnancy: Behavioral teratology. *Obstetrical and Gynecological Survey, 18,* 420–423.

Werner, E.E. (1979). *Cross cultural child development: A view from planet earth.* Monterey, CA: Brooks/Cole.

Whitly, R.J., Nahmias, A.J., Visintine, A.M., Fleming, C.L., & Alford, C.A. (1980). The natural history of herpes simplex virus infection of mother and newborn. *Pediatrics, 66,* 489–494.

Wilson, J.G. (1972). Environmental effects on development—Teratology. In N.S. Assali (Ed.), *Pathophysiology of gestation,* Vol. 2. New York: Academic.

Winick, M. (1969). Malnutrition and brain development. *Journal of Pediatrics, 74,* 667–679.

Winick, M. (1976). *Malnutrition and brain development.* New York: Oxford University Press.

Winick, M., & Noble, A. (1966). Cellular response in rats during malnutrition at various stages. *Journal of Nutrition, 89,* 300–306.

Winick, M., & Rosso, P. (1969). Head circumferences and cellular growth of the brain in normal and marasmic children. *Journal of Pediatrics, 74,* 774–778.

Yerushalmy, J. (1964). Mother's cigarette smoking and survival of the infant. *Journal of Obstetrics and Gynecology, 88,* 505–518.

Yerushalmy, J. (1971). The relationship of parents' cigarette smoking to outcome of pregnancy—Implications as to the problem of inferring causation from observed associations. *American Journal of Epidemiology, 93,* 443–456.

Yerushalmy, J. (1972). Infants with low birth weight born before their mothers started to smoke cigarettes. *American Journal of Obstetrics and Gynecology, 112,* 277–284.

Zelson, C., Sook, J.L., & Casalino, M. (1973). Neonatal narcotic addiction: Comparative effects of maternal intake of heroin and methadone. *New England Journal of Medicine, 289,* 1216–1220.

NOTE: Papers by Desmonts, Hurley, Laurence, McLaren, Sever, and Snow, presented at the Strasbourg conference in October, 1982, are available in *Prevention of Physical and Mental Congenital Defects: A. The Scope of the Problem* (M. Marois, Ed.), New York: Allan R. Liss (in press).

PERINATAL EVENTS THAT AFFECT CONSTITUTION AND DEVELOPMENT

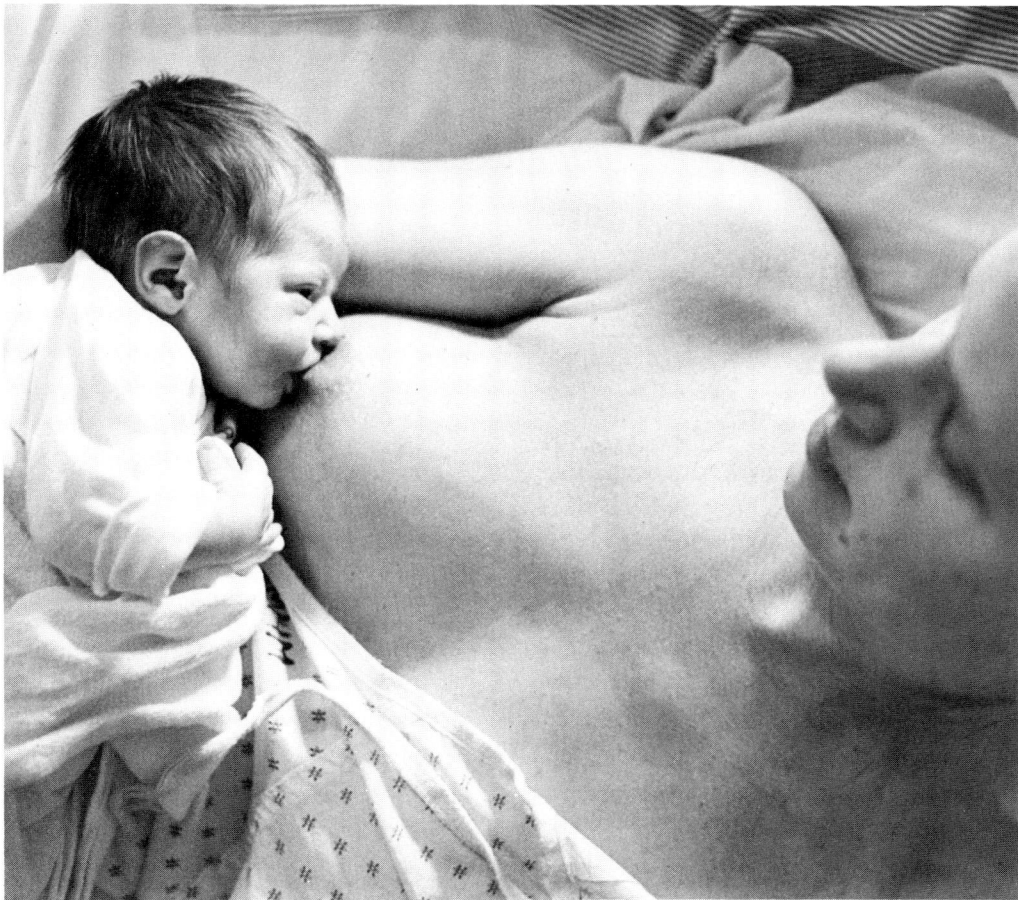

CHAPTER 5

In Chapters 2–4 we discussed the development of the infant that takes place before birth and the genetic and environmental problems that may occur then. Another set of environmental determinants of the constitution of the baby are associated with the birth process itself and with the immediate postnatal events in the baby's life.

A number of factors associated with the delivery process are clearly capable of harming the infant. Others are thought to be harmful or are considered less than optimal from the standpoint of the infant's current health or later development. Still others may hinder mother–infant interactions or the interactions of other family members with the infant. We will discuss the possible influences in the following categories: complications of delivery and ways to avoid or counteract them, drugs used during delivery, childbirth practices, and mother–infant bonding.

Before we discuss these topics, however, we will give a brief overview of the process of labor and delivery. "Labor" is a very appropriate name for what goes on in childbirth; it is hard physical work. There are three stages of labor. In the first, the cervix expands or dilates so that it will be large enough to allow the infant to pass through it. This normally takes 8 to 10 hours in first pregnancies. In the second stage the baby passes through the birth canal and is born (Beynon, 1975). This stage usually lasts 1 to 2 hours in first pregnancies. In the third stage the placenta, or so-called "afterbirth," is delivered or "born," a matter of 15 or 20 minutes.

COMPLICATIONS OF DELIVERY

Speed of Delivery

As is true of many things, too much or too little speed in delivery is bad. Labors that are too long or too short are more likely to result in problems than are those of moderate length. The length of the second stage of labor, in which the baby's head is passing through the birth canal, is most crucial. If the baby is squeezed through very rapidly (in less than 10 minutes according to most views), the delivery is called precipitate. There are two dangers in precipitate delivery: (1) There may not be enough time between contractions (which prevent the normal flow of blood) to allow the blood to provide adequate oxygen for the fetus, and (2) the head may be subjected to such pressure that blood vessels in the brain hemorrhage and cause injury to the brain. Babies whose heads have been squeezed often look rather peculiar. Normally the different bones of the skull meet smoothly, except for the fontanelle (the soft spot at the top of the skull). However, there are joints between all the skull bones, which are still soft, and babies who have been subjected to a lot of pressure during delivery may be born with each bone at a level very different from that of its neighbor. Because the joints or sutures between the bones are flexible, the odd appearance goes away and the bones level out in a matter of days or weeks, but this recovery does not indicate whether any minor damage has been done to the brain cells. It is thought that very small hemorrhages that are not severe enough to be detected in the newborn period may occur and may cause problems in later life such as poor motor coordination, learning disabilities, mental retardation, or, in more severe cases, even cerebral palsy or epilepsy. The strength of contractions, or the amount of pressure on the baby when it is in the uterus, has some of the same potential for causing minor brain damage.

A long, drawn-out delivery is also considered undesirable. As in a precipitate delivery, a long delivery can lead to brain damage. In this case it is usually caused by **anoxia** (lack of sufficient oxygen) rather than by hemorrhaging. Anoxia can be caused by long-term squeezing of the umbilical cord during delivery or by a decrease in maternal blood pressure.

Presentation at Delivery

The normal way for the baby to "present" (that is, the part of the baby that enters the birth canal first) is the crown of the head. Sometimes the face presents first, but this is not common and it is not desirable because the possibility of damage to the neck and spinal cord is greater in such presentations. About 4% of babies don't arrive head first at all. Some come buttocks first (breech deliveries), others feet first (footling breech), and still others have one or both hands coming first (see Figure 5–1). All the un-

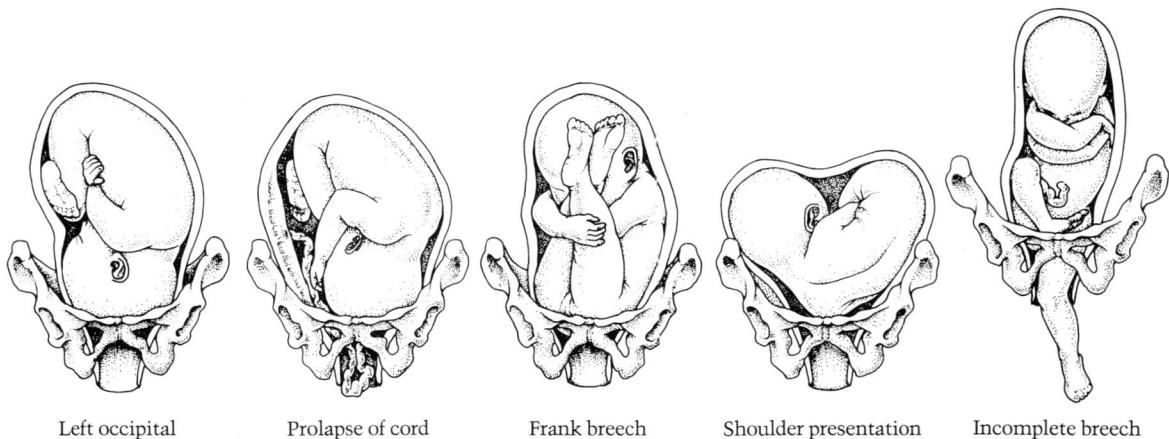

FIGURE 5–1. *Various deviations from the most optimal vertex presentation. The first drawing on the left shows a minor deviation in which the head is first but is turned to the side. The next shows a prolapsed cord. The more extreme presentations are shown in the three drawings on the right.*

Left occipital   Prolapse of cord   Frank breech   Shoulder presentation   Incomplete breech

usual presentations are more dangerous for the baby. When it is known that a baby's head is not engaged at the exit of the uterus and that the buttocks or some other part is, doctors may attempt to manipulate the fetus. If such attempts fail, a Caesarean section may be used.

All of these presentations make physical injury more likely and raise the probability that umbilical circulation may be cut off at some point during the delivery, depriving the baby's brain of adequate oxygen. Babies that are born buttocks first usually have quite abnormal patterns of muscle tonus after birth. These tend to disappear in a matter of weeks to months. Nevertheless, lasting damage may be done. Recently a group of babies who were breech deliveries, of which some were vaginal deliveries and some were by Caesarean section, were compared over a period of from 1 to 5 years. Not only was mortality lower for those delivered by Caesarean, but neurological and developmental outcomes were more optimal for them as well (Ingemarsson, Westgren, & Svenningsen, 1978).

Entangling Alliances

Another variable in deliveries is whether the umbilical cord has become wrapped around the baby's neck during intrauterine growth or the processes culminating in delivery. The cord may be wrapped around the neck one, two, or three times, and the wrapping may be loose or quite tight. Some deaths in late fetal development (stillbirths) are caused by this form of strangulation. Fetuses who do not die prior to birth are still at risk, particularly if the cord is multiply or tightly wrapped or if it passes through the cervix before the baby does (technically, a prolapsed cord). Other complications of delivery may have very different effects in a baby that has become entangled.

WAYS TO AVOID OR COUNTERACT COMPLICATIONS

Fetal Monitoring

There are a number of levels of fetal monitoring. The nurse, midwife, or doctor who listens to the fetal heart beat is monitoring the fetus, but the term usually refers to continuous electronic monitoring. This may be done externally using electrodes around the mother's abdomen or, more invasively, using electrodes put through the vagina and cervix and attached to the baby. Other aspects of the baby's condition may also be monitored using invasive techniques. Scalp needles may be inserted to measure blood gasses and acid–base balance (or pH). These give information not only about the degree of anoxia the fetus is suffering, but also about the physiological responses to it, which are even more crucial for determining possible effects of the anoxia.

Fetal monitoring is valuable because it can give direct information about the state of the infant. We mentioned the dangers of anoxia occurring in deliveries that are too short or too long, or where there are difficulties with the umbilical cord or with unusual presentations. However, the length of labor is not a good predictor of whether the baby is in trouble or suffering fetal distress, nor is position during delivery or knowing the cord is wrapped around the neck. Direct information on the state of the fetus is what is crucial for deciding whether interventions are needed. Unfortunately, the direct information does not always clearly indicate the degree of fetal distress. Diagnosing a normal heart rate pattern and hence avoiding possible interventions is quite possible; determining whether an abnormal heart rate pattern really indicates fetal distress is more difficult. Rules of thumb are adopted that are not always tested. The interpretation of the cause of a lowered pH may also be difficult.

In addition to problems with using the information obtained from fetal monitoring, the invasive kind has other problems of its own. The risks of infection to both mother and fetus are increased. One type of fetal infection that could result (as we mentioned in Chapter 4) is the type where the fetus is infected with a disease present in the mother's vagina or cervix. General infections are also increased (Gassner & Ledger, 1976). Furthermore, the mother's delivery is disturbed, which may result in her needing more drugs or in a slowing down of the process even if extra drugs are not used. The question of whether either the psychological or monetary costs are worth the possible benefits to the baby has been raised in a review of the existing information on the effectiveness of invasive monitoring (Banta & Thacker, 1979). Questions have even been raised as to the effectiveness of fetal monitoring in lowering neonatal death rates (Neutra, Fienberg, Greenland, & Friedman, 1978). And finally, there is a question of whether doctors' choices to monitor are based on patient need or on fear of a malpractice suit if something happens and monitoring was not used. We agree with Banta and Thacker (1979) and others that invasive monitoring should only be used in high risk pregnancies and deliveries, or where there are signs of problems during the delivery.

The sections on delivery complications and this one on fetal monitoring have stressed the importance of the fetus receiving enough oxygen. In the extreme, oxygen deficiency leads to asphyxiation and death, but the danger that less severe degrees of anoxia will damage the infant's brain is a more frequent concern. Although a large body of data on anoxia in humans indicates that it leads to a greater risk for various problems, including cerebral palsy, these data provide no satisfactory picture of the results of anoxia itself. There are a number of reasons for this. (1) The definitions of anoxia differ greatly from study to study, even those done after sophisticated chemical measures were available. (2) The behavioral studies are primarily retrospective and have numerous methodological flaws. One of the better ones, which used sibling controls, showed that neonates with severe anoxia were 8 times more likely to show intellectual retardation than their siblings, but there were no differences on other psychological tests. The researchers noted that relatively few of the anoxic newborns became abnormal (about 20%), and some of them had superior intelligence compared to their siblings (Benaron et al., 1960). A prospective study with very well defined levels of anoxia at birth (Ernhart, Graham, & Thurston, 1960)[1] also found lowered average intelligence, but no evidence for improved intelligence in some children compared to matched, but unrelated, controls. At 7 years of age the same children no longer showed differences in IQ, but the anoxics showed impairment in abstract verbal ability, perceptual skills, and social competence (Corah, Anthony, Painter, Stern, & Thurston, 1965).

The animal data are more clear cut. For example, Windle, one of the principal students of the effects of anoxia, experimentally induced it in monkeys. He noted (1966) that the neurological symptoms tended to become less severe over time. Some animals appeared able to compensate for their early deficits whereas others did not. Even in monkeys who had developed cerebral palsy but who had improved behaviorally, brain autopsies showed progressive atrophy, with more damage in those

---

[1] Note that anoxia at birth includes both that caused by delivery factors and that caused by other factors operative prior to delivery. For a review of the causes, detection, and results of anoxia, see Adamsons and Myers (1973).

whose brains were studied at 5 years of age than there was in those whose brains were studied in the first months. Myers (1972), also working with monkeys, showed that more babies who have suffered asphyxia die as a result of failure of the heart and circulatory system than survive less severe heart damage to exhibit brain damage later.

It is too bad that researchers have not heeded the call for more studies using more accurate definitions of the degree, duration, and clinical features of asphyxia or anoxia, a call made by Graham and her colleagues in the late 1950s (Graham, Caldwell, Ernhart, Pennoyer, & Hartman, 1957). Certainly much greater knowledge of the mechanisms that produce individual differences in reactions are needed to understand why deprivation of oxygen (or exposure to harmful agents as discussed in Chapter 4) has such different effects in different individuals (monkey or human).

Aids for the Delivery Process

Despite any reservations about the inevitability of bad outcomes for babies who have suffered relatively severe anoxia at birth, it is clear that mothers and doctors would like to avoid this risk factor when possible. If fetal distress is indicated, what can lessen its duration? In the case of precipitate deliveries, little can be done during labor and delivery, although there are treatments that can be used with the baby after birth to lessen the damage done by hemorrhaging.

For other complications, three major interventions or aids can be used to speed up delivery: administration of oxytocin, use of mechanical aids for speeding delivery (forceps and vacuum extraction), and performing a Caesarean section (or C. section) to deliver the fetus surgically. We will discuss oxytocin in the section on drugs; discussions of the others follow.

FORCEPS

In a forceps delivery, the doctor clamps the infant's head with a tong-like instrument much like that used to lift corn on the cob from boiling water. These are called forceps. They are applied while the infant is in the birth canal. There are three types of forceps: high, medium, and low. The type used depends on how far into the birth canal the infant is and how much and which parts of the infant's head can be grasped. High forceps are used when the baby is still high in the birth canal. They require more pressure on the infant's head and on a softer part of the head, so there is more likely to be hemorrhaging in the brain and consequent brain damage. In addition, high forceps may cause a precipitate delivery with its usual hazards. Furthermore, the amount of pressure used and its sudden release when the baby comes out may fracture, rupture, or tear the baby's spinal cord, resulting in death or severe handicap.[2] Fortunately, the use of high forceps has been all but abandoned in favor of C. sections and other aids, including oxytocin and vacuum extraction.

Low forceps are applied when the infant's head is almost through the birth canal, and medium forceps are used in intermediate placements. Low or medium forceps do not pose the problems that high forceps do. They may produce superficial bruises, but these pass and are not likely to produce internal hemorrhaging. Both are still in use, though the use of medium forceps seems to be declining markedly, mostly in favor of Caesarean sections. There is little evidence concerning the long-term consequences of low and medium forceps delivery. One recent study by Murray, Dolby, Nation, and Thomas (1981) compared 28 low forceps babies, whose mothers also received regional anesthetics, to babies with normal, unmedicated deliveries. As newborns, the forceps babies were more disorganized in terms of their motoric, physiological, and state behaviors. At 1 month they were fed less often and seen by their mothers as more bothersome and more poorly organized, as measured by the Maternal Assessment of Behavior Inventory. Whether these differences are due to forceps or anesthetics and whether they would remain at later ages and in different samples is not clear.

VACUUM EXTRACTION

Currently, a number of doctors and hospitals have substituted vacuum extraction for forceps. The technique involved is the same as

---

[2]Old-time obstetricians delight in telling of the "terrible old days" when doctors frequently used high forceps. Each seems to have a tale of seeing a doctor pull so hard that when the baby came out the doctor flew across the room as a result of the release of pressure.

that used in extracting menses or in abortions, but the scale is larger. It is generally thought that properly used vacuum extraction has less potential for harming the brain than either precipitate delivery or medium forceps, *if* the head is low enough and *if* there are no other risk factors. Distortion of the shape of the skull may result from vacuum extraction, but it is often less unsightly than forceps bruises and passes relatively quickly.

There are sharp differences in the western world about the value of vacuum extraction. Experience in Sweden and Germany in the 1960s indicated that it might be safer than forceps, except for preterm fetuses, and it was widely used. The technique did not become popular in Britain or the United States. Subsequent long-term follow up (Bjerre & Dahlin, 1974) suggested no long-term negative consequences of using vacuum extraction. Short-term effects seemed to be related to the conditions that led to intervention, but present data do not permit distinguishing the problems caused by either medium forceps or vacuum extractions from those caused by the conditions that led to their use.

CAESAREAN SECTION

The other basic type of delivery that an infant may experience is surgical delivery by Caesarean section. This procedure appears to be replacing many high forceps and some medium forceps deliveries. In it the mother is normally given general anesthesia, the abdomen and uterus are opened, and the baby and placenta are removed. With the development and use of anesthesia and sterile surgical practices, the modern Caesarean section represents a tremendous advance in obstetrics for mothers and infants. In the past when delivery by the vaginal canal had been impossible, as it is when the infant's head is too large to pass through the pelvic opening, death for both mother and baby often resulted. When this surgery became relatively safe and pain free, it became attractive to some for reasons other than saving lives, however. There were both mothers and doctors who found it convenient in order to plan the time of birth. Some women even found it attractive because it would make their childbirth less "animal like." Caesareans became something of a fad, despite their disadvantages.

Today Caesarean sections are not usually done for the convenience of mother or doctor for several reasons. First, although the chances that the mother may die are small, they are 3 to 30 times that for women who are vaginally delivered (Benaron & Tucker, 1971; Case, Corcoran, Jeffcoate, et al., 1971; De La Fuente, Hernandez-Garcia, Escalante, et al., 1971; Evrard & Gold, 1977). This difference in rate is, of course, partly because women who are at high risk are more likely to have a Caesarean. Nevertheless, some of the higher maternal mortality stems from the method of delivery itself. Evrard and Gold (1977) found that four of the nine deaths in their sample could be attributed to the method itself. Second, other problems associated with surgery, such as operative trauma and sepsis (or infection of other organs), are risks for Caesarean section mothers. Third, the risks of uterine infections are greater for Caesareans than for vaginal deliveries (Gassner & Ledger, 1976; Ledger, Norman, Gee, et al., 1975). For example, Petrie (1981) cited a 38% infection rate in a major New York City teaching hospital (a hospital in which medical students and interns are taught), and 4% of those women failed to respond to treatment. Fourth, it takes longer to recover from abdominal surgery than from childbirth. Fifth, for many years women who had one child by Caesarean were told that they would have to have all future children that way, and thus the number of children they could have was limited. At present more and more obstetricians are willing to allow women who have had a Caesarean to try to deliver subsequent children vaginally, and a recent national conference at which all concerned disciplines were represented has supported an effort to increase this practice.

In spite of the disadvantages of Caesareans and the decrease in those done for convenience, the rates for this method of delivery have been rising sharply in the United States in the last two decades. Medical research indicates that the reasons given for doing Caesareans in first births have increased in the following ways: cephalopelvic disproportion, in which the baby's head is too big for the mother's pelvis, a two-fold increase; breech delivery, a fifty-fold increase; and fetal distress, a seventy-fold increase (Haddad & Lundy, 1978). The increase in fetal distress is probably related to increased fetal monitoring, but fetal distress cases are not a major contributor to the total number of Caesareans. Why Caesarean rates for breech and cephalopelvic disproportion, which constitute the vast majority of such deliveries, should rise is more difficult to explain because they are relatively rare occurrences and presumably are not becoming increasingly frequent in the population of childbearing women. Many people, including large segments of the women's movement, have become suspicious of the increased rate of Caesarean sections. They argue that doctors are becoming more inclined to intervene and to intervene more drastically in the birth process when it may be unnecessary, and that this deprives parents of their rights to participate in the meaningful experience of the vaginal delivery of their babies.

The result has been a controversy between doctors and parents over whether a Caesarean section promotes the best health of the baby and mother. It would be easy to agree with those against Caesareans if in fact doctors chose them because they were tired or wanted to get away to other commitments or to make more money. It would also be easy to agree if doctors chose them because they were unconsciously motivated to maintain control of the birth process rather than share it with their patients. The truth of such assertions would, however, be extremely difficult, if not impossible, to test. The real questions probably arise when the medical advantages and disadvantages for performing a Caesarean section are weighed. Because the procedure is relatively safe, doctors argue that the best medical practice is to use it if there is the slightest doubt about the infant's or mother's safety. In response, it can be argued that doctors are too conservative, that they overrespond to situations that have very little risk, and that they may be more worried about malpractice suits than they are about the quality of the birth experience for the woman and her family.[3] As more women become more insistent on plan-

ning their own deliveries and argue for vaginal deliveries, doctors may have to become less conservative. This issue is part of the more general one of hospital childbirth practices, which we will discuss later in this chapter.

Although the controversy over Caesarean sections has focused on the medical indications versus the childbirth experiences of the parents, another question is whether babies so delivered are adversely affected. In studies of humans it is difficult to separate the effects of the C. section from those of the anesthetics, which are of different types and amounts than in vaginal deliveries. It is also impossible to separate the effects of the Caesarean from those of the medical problem that led to doing it.

Some studies have found that children delivered by Caesarean develop lower IQs and some have found higher IQs. Several studies of outcomes for babies were reported at the 1980 International Conference on Infant Studies. They failed to agree on what, if any, effects they had on the babies' development, but did agree in showing effects on father–infant interactions. The fathers of C. section babies not only did more caretaking, but they felt better about themselves as fathers (Grossman, 1980; Pederson, Zaslow, Cain, & Anderson, 1980; Vietze, MacTurk, McCarthy, Klein, & Yarrow, 1980).

To give a flavor of the complexity and inconsistency of results in this area, we will describe two studies—one an experiment with monkeys and the other a correlational study with humans—that used some of the same outcome measures. Meier (1964) experimentally delivered monkeys by C. section, that is, in the absence of medical reasons for doing so. Those delivered by Caesarean, compared to vaginally-delivered monkeys, had lower total activity, fewer vocalizations, and showed later acquisition of learning (that is, fewer conditioned responses). Field and Widmayer (1980) compared low income Black babies delivered by C. section to controls matched for variables other than obstetric complications. They failed to find any disadvantages for C. section babies in the newborn period. In fact, they found that the C. section babies vocalized more and showed more contented facial expressions during feeding interactions at 4 months of age than did vaginally-delivered babies. Differ-

---

[3] A 1983 poll of Florida physicians showed that over 20% of them had stopped doing deliveries and a similar percentage were considering doing so because of the risk of being sued for various errors of omission or commission that might have led to the brain damage of an infant they delivered. Minimal malpractice insurance now costs $27,000 per year, and the coverage a doctor might need to settle such a case would cost $54,000 per year.

ences between the groups at 4 or 8 months were few and those that were found were sometimes in favor of the vaginally-delivered babies and sometimes in favor of the C. section babies. This failure to corroborate the findings of the study with monkeys is particularly striking, because the extraneous variables should increase the probability of finding negative outcomes for C. section babies compared to vaginally-delivered babies, not decrease them. Certainly a simple view that Caesarean deliveries handicap babies is hard to hold in the face of all these data.

DRUGS USED DURING DELIVERY

During hospital delivery mothers are often, even usually, given drugs to reduce pain, to relieve anxiety, or both. Sometimes drugs are given to speed up delivery, and in specific instances some other type of drug might also be given. Here we shall concern ourselves only with drugs given for the first two major purposes.

Types of Drugs

The most universally used drugs are those used for pain or anxiety, or both. In the earlier stages of labor, tranquilizers, sedative-hypnotics, narcotic analgesics (drugs that do not kill all pain but do make it more tolerable), and drugs that are narcotic antagonists (drugs designed to reduce the bad side effects of the narcotics) are often given. Many different tranquilizers are used, such as (by trade name) Thorazine, Vistaril, Phenergan, and Largon. The sedative-hypnotics include various barbituates (for example, Nembutal, Seconal, Amytal) and nonbarbituates (for example, Valium and scopolamine). The narcotic analgesics include morphine, Demerol, and Nisintil. In later stages of labor anesthetics (drugs designed to eliminate or greatly reduce pain) are often given as are antihypotensive drugs. The latter combat low blood pressure in the mother and protect the fetus from its effects. Low blood pressure may be brought on by drugs used during delivery and may be exacerbated by the **lithotomy** position (the typical delivery position in which the woman lies on her back, of-

ten on a hard surface, with her legs drawn up to the sides of her abdomen and sometimes fastened by supports; see Figure 5–2).

Anesthetics are sometimes local in action. Again there is a whole family of drugs (drugs with some chemical similarity) that are given in this way. They are given by injection, and the place where they are injected as well as the quantities injected varies (see Figure 5–3). How high up the spinal cord they are injected determines the area of the body that has no pain sensations, and over which the patient has no voluntary control. In general, this area includes all points below the site of injection. Other anesthetics are used so as to be general or affect the entire body. These include the inhalant anesthetics and anesthetics given by intravenous injection, the latter including barbiturates as well as some nonbarbiturate agents. The inhalants include nitrous oxide, cyclopropane, and ether compounds such as Penthrane and Fluorthane, which have replaced the ether and chloroform used earlier. (A comprehensive review of anesthetics is in Brackbill (1979b).)

Before discussing the possible effects of these drugs, let us consider some of the reasons it is appropriate to be concerned about them. Drugs given the mother during labor and delivery may have an effect on the fetus and newborn, and possibly at later stages of development, for a number of reasons. First, most of these drugs cross the placental barrier, so the fetus is not protected from them (see the discussion in Chapter 4). Second, another barrier they can cross that makes it likely that they can directly affect the brain of the fetus is the blood–brain barrier. It consists of the membranes between the circulating blood and the brain. Third, the dosage of a drug given the mother is determined by her size or body weight. If anything like this concentration of the drug gets into the fetal system, it is an incredibly large dose. Fourth, the liver of the fetus or newborn, a principal organ for metabolizing drugs, and the kidneys, principal agents for excreting them and their metabolic products, are quite immature. Once the drugs are in the infant's system, they will stay there much longer than they would stay in an adult's system. The actual amounts of a drug that will remain in the newborn's system depend not only on the amount given the mother but also on the time at which it is given in relation to

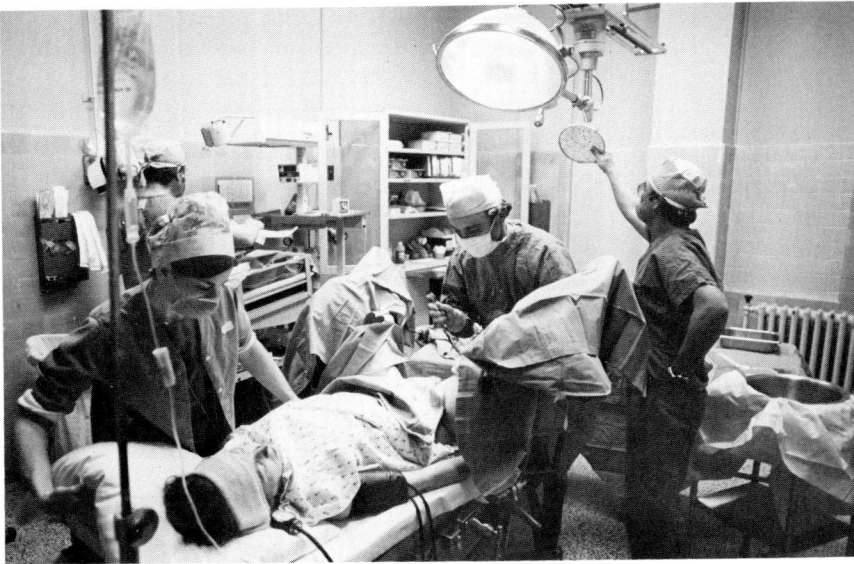

FIGURE 5–2. *The standard hospital delivery is represented in this picture. The woman is on an operating type table in the lithotomy position.*

birth. More exactly, it is the time in relation to when the umbilical cord is cut that matters. Drugs differ markedly from each other in the time they take to cross the placental barrier and in how rapidly they are metabolized by the mother's system. Consequently, a drug that acts rapidly but is also rapidly metabolized by the mother's body may be effectively removed from the infant's system if it is given substantially prior to birth. If that same drug is given shortly before the cord is cut, it will remain in the infant's system because the baby can only metabolize and excrete substances very slowly.[4]

A fifth, and very different, reason for concern about the effects of drugs on the infant is the prevalence of their use. Although many people think that drug use in delivery is diminishing in the United States, there is some evidence that this may not be so. Brackbill (1974) polled 18 American teaching hospitals and found that only 5% of their deliveries were accomplished without anesthesia. Comparable figures for deliveries in which no analgesics

were used are not available, but it is likely that they are even fewer in number. (Note that the amounts of drugs and the timing of administration are not taken into account in these results.) Brackbill did report that some drugs, such as barbiturates and scopolamine, may be less used today than formerly. Nonetheless scopolamine, at least, appears to be in frequent use in some places or under some circumstances. In Field and Widmayer's (1980) study of Caesarean deliveries, 12 of 20 Caesarean mothers, but no vaginally-delivered mothers, had received scopolamine.

Difficulties of Establishing Effects

Doing research to determine whether drugs administered during labor and delivery harm the newborn infant is extraordinarily difficult. We have already described some of the reasons: a large number of different drugs are used and they are administered in different amounts, at different times in relation to birth, and by different methods. It is particularly hard to assess the effects of a single drug, because most women are given analgesics or sedative-hypnotics in combination with anesthetics. Furthermore, because so few deliveries in the

[4]Although it is not directly relevant to the effects of drugs used during delivery, the fact that drugs taken after delivery may be excreted in the breast milk and thus affect nursing infants should be noted here.

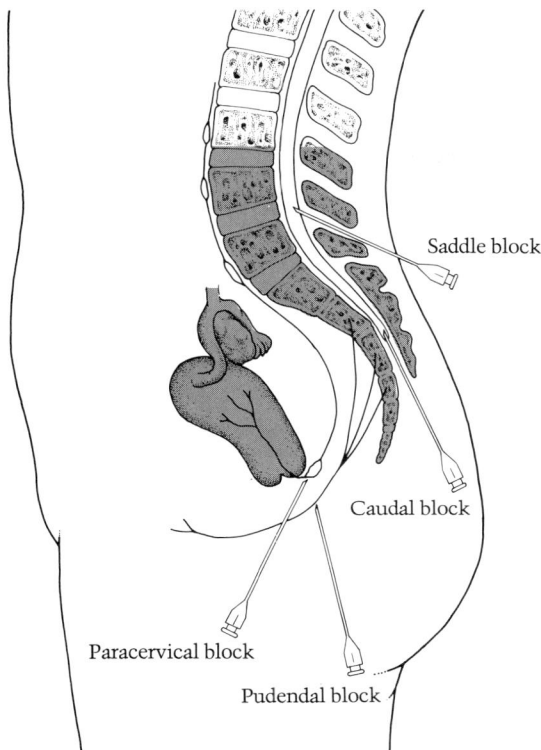

FIGURE 5–3. Diagram of the spine with needles inserted at various points to illustrate where drugs used to block pain are injected.

In a lumbar epidural block a woman can feel pressure but no pain. Her contractions may slow down and she loses the urge to push. This is often considered the most desirable form of regional anesthetic. Spinals and saddle blocks are injected approximately at this place. A spinal not only numbs sensation but also paralyzes a woman to her waist. Contractions lose full force and the pushing urge is stopped, but trained women can still push on command. It is not administered before the second stage of labor, and therefore is used primarily when there is a medical reason to shorten the second stage. A saddle block deadens the area that a saddle touches and to some extent the legs. Spinals and saddle blocks are used less frequently than caudals and epidurals. A caudal block cuts off sensations and stops the urge to push, but trained women can be instructed to push. With proper doses, it does not affect contractions. A pudendal block is considered a local anesthetic and numbs the vagina and perineum (the region from the vagina to the anus). Women lose the urge to push, but can do so on command. It is a good choice for forceps delivery. A paracervical block, considered a local anes-

United States are undrugged, and because many of these are at the insistence of mothers who may be atypical in other ways, it is difficult to establish the characteristics of undrugged babies as a basis for comparison. Finally, none of these variables can be controlled experimentally, that is, by random assignment of subjects to groups. Because of the possible dangers of drugs used in delivery, it is ethically difficult to assign mothers at random to receive particular drugs or drug combinations. Also, many mothers would not be willing to be assigned randomly to a drugged or drug-free delivery. Thus, researchers are limited to correlational studies that explore the relation between drug experiences during labor and delivery and behaviors of the offspring in the newborn period or later. The outcomes of such studies are likely to be influenced by a variety of extraneous variables. Mothers who receive no anesthetic and little or no other drugs are likely to be better educated, to receive better prenatal care, to come from better social and economic circumstances generally, to have attended childbirth preparation classes, and to have different ideas about how they want to interact with their babies than mothers who are more heavily drugged. In addition, drug-free deliveries may be more likely in easy labors, which are more likely to occur in second and subsequent births. The potential influence of these variables would have to be controlled for in the less adequate ways available to correlational research, such as matching or statistical techniques.

Measuring the dependent variable in studies of obstetric medication is also complex. The effects are always multiple, never single. Effects may be measured at various ages: at birth, 1 month, 1 year, 4 years, 7 years, adolescence. The type of effect also varies. First, physiological effects can be measured and are usually assessed only in early life. Second, psy-

thetic, stops pain in the pelvis from the uterus and cervix. It can temporarily decrease intensity and frequency of contractions, but rarely slows labor. Infiltration of the perineum is also commonly used to numb the region so the doctor can surgically cut the perineum to facilitate delivery and prevent tearing of the tissues (the procedure called an episiotomy).

chological and psychophysiological effects may be assessed at birth using various infant tests (see Chapter 8) or in infancy or childhood. We know of only one study that goes beyond 7 years in its follow-up assessments, and it is not yet published in detail.

Effects of Drugs

Methodological problems have certainly not prevented researchers from doing studies, especially of the effects of drugs on some aspect of behavior in the neonatal period (Aleksandrowicz & Aleksandrowicz, 1974, 1976; Brackbill 1979b; Brumitt & Dowler, 1984; Conway & Brackbill, 1970; Friedman, Brackbill, Caron, & Caron, 1978; Moreau & Birch, 1974; Murray, Dolby, Nation, & Thomas, 1981; see also Federman & Yang, 1976, for a critique). Indeed, the number of studies and the complexities involved would require a chapter (or better, a book) to review adequately. Most of these studies have used 20 to 30 infants per group and have not been able to control for agents other than the one or two under study. Medically-oriented studies have used larger numbers of subjects, but more limited measures of effects. The fetal respiratory and circulatory systems are particularly vulnerable (see Chapter 2) to injury during labor and delivery; hence, much medical research has focused on neonatal depression (the slowing of physiological functions, especially of respiratory and heart functions) and on mobility.

PRE-ANESTHETICS

The effects of tranquilizers are particularly hard to assess because they are almost always used in conjunction with other drugs. Clearly some of them augment the effects of the analgesics and hence make it possible to get good pain relief with smaller doses. Several studies (Moya & Thorndike, 1962; Potts & Ullery, 1961; both as cited in Bowes, Brackbill, Conway, & Steinschneider, 1970) have shown that tranquilizers appear to have little or no depressant effect on the fetus. One study (Brower, 1974, as cited in Brackbill, 1979b) that used changes in the EEG to assess the drug effects compared groups that received the narcotic-analgesic meperidine alone or with Valium or Phenergan. There were no differ-

ences between these groups, but all differed from a group receiving no meperidine.

A study done in the early 1960s looked for the effects of the tranquilizer Largon (propriomazine). Controls were used for placebo effects (water injections), for effects of narcotic analgesics (all mothers also received Demarol (meperidine), and for type of anesthesia (almost all mothers received spinals). There were no medical side effects that could be attributed to the Largon. The only advantage it had over other tranquilizers was a shorter duration of action. Behavioral differences were assessed for a subsample of 47 babies using the Graham/Rosenblith scales (to be discussed in Chapter 8). The examiner did not know whether the mother had received Largon or water. There were no differences between the groups for those babies examined at from 6 to 16 hours after birth. However, babies examined at 16 to 36 hours after birth whose mothers had received water were more variable in the General Maturation scores than those whose mothers had Largon. This suggests that this tranquilizer masks some individual differences otherwise present.

By far the largest study of the effects of drugs was done by Brackbill and Broman (unpublished). It drew on the data of the Collaborative Perinatal Research Project, a major study done under the auspices of the National Institutes of Health.[5] Brackbill and Broman studied all the full-term, singleton infants born to healthy mothers, aged 16 to 40, with low-risk pregnancies and uneventful vaginal deliveries (3,528 of the 50,000 deliveries studied in the Project). The data on two frequently used tranquilizers, promazine and promethazine (Sparine and Phenergan), used on one-fifth and one-seventh of the sample, respectively, produced some strange results. The use of one of these tranquilizers was related to half of the items on the pediatric-neurological examination done at 4 months, but it was not always related to poor outcomes. For promazine half of the significant relations were to what are presumed to be better outcomes. For promethazine only one-fifth were. The relations to items from the 12-month pediatric-neurological examination do not form a clear-

---

[5] For a description of the Project, see Niswander and Gordon (1972).

cut pattern, nor are those found psychologically meaningful.

Broman and Brackbill (unpublished) also studied the relation between use of tranquilizers and infant performance on standard tests of motor and mental development (Bayley scales, described in Chapter 8) at 8 months, and the results were similarly inconclusive. Promazine was related only to items from the Motor scale, and again half the significant relations were to presumably better outcomes. Promethazine was related to items on both the Mental and Motor scales and was seldom related in a positive direction. The size of the effects found, however, generally was not large enough to be of practical significance. Overall, then, the pattern of findings in this study does not suggest that the use of tranquilizers during labor is harmful. Furthermore, a highly-controlled subsample of the Collaborative Project institutions (2 hospitals) is currently being investigated (Broman, 1981, 1983; Broman & Brackbill, 1980). This sample is all white, and all babies were born after uneventful pregnancies, weighed over 2500 g, and had vaginal, vertex deliveries. Although detailed analyses have not yet been published, reports giving overall results do not indicate harmful effects for the tranquilizers.

The narcotic-analgesic that has been most studied is probably meperidine (Demarol). It had been found to be related to response decrement in the newborn period by Brackbill and her colleagues (Brackbill, Kane, Manniello, & Abramson, 1974). In the Collaborative Project data it, like one of the tranquilizers, was related to outcomes of a positive nature as often as to those of a negative nature, and the strength of the relations was low.

A recent study of the behavioral effects of meperidine (assessed using the NBAS or Brazelton test described in chapter 8) shows that effects differ both as a function of which other drugs were administered with it and as a function of whether it was administered intravenously or intramuscularly (Brumitt & Dowler, 1984). Intravenous meperidine led to better muscle tone at 3 days of age, but intramuscular use had no effect. When it was combined with the tranquilizer hydroxyzine, it was associated with poorer muscle tone. When it was administered together with oxytocin used to induce or strengthen labor it did have the effect

found by Brackbill and colleagues. Here is another instance of the difficulties in deciding on the effects of one drug when they depend on how it was administered as well as on which drugs were administered with it. This study did not consider timing, which would almost certainly also have affected the results.

Secobarbital (Seconal), like some of the tranquilizers, was shown in the Collaborative Project data to be related to positive outcomes for nearly half of the measures (43%).

The sedative-hypnotic drug that has been most studied is scopolamine. In the original Collaborative Project sample it had been given to 36% of the sample, but the negative results were not striking. In the current analyses (Brackbill & Broman, unpublished; Broman, 1981, 1983) it appears that exposure to scopolamine is associated with slightly lower scores on some cognitive tasks at both 4 and 7 years. Among all the pre-anesthetic agents it is the drug that appears most suspect. Many mothers find it very upsetting not to remember that their baby has been born or anything about the birth, another effect of scopolamine. Thus there are both infant-related and mother-related reasons to question its use carefully as well as to try to obtain more data on its effects.

The results for the other drugs used to relieve pain or make it less bothersome do not seem to be consistent enough or strong enough to make us question their safety with respect to the future behavioral development of the infant. We have not tried to review all of the data on physiological or medical effects, and we do not make any generalizations about them.

REGIONAL ANESTHETICS

Regional anesthetics are controversial because many of them interfere with a woman's contractions or her ability to push or both. This not only affects the woman's birthing experience but it increases the possibility that forceps, vacuum extraction, or Caesarean delivery will be needed. For example, in one study 12 of the 20 infants whose mothers were given epidural anesthetics were delivered by low forceps (Murray et al., 1981). In addition, the mother's blood pressure may drop precipitously, which endangers the oxygen supply to the fetus. Thus, both the mother's blood pressure and the baby's heart rate (and perhaps blood oxygen level) are usually monitored when regional anesthetics are used. Whether the relief from pain afforded the mother is worth the costs to her and her infant's birthing experience, including the added inconvenience and discomfort of the medical interventions required, is obviously an individual decision.

The question concerning regional anesthetics that is of most concern in this book is whether they harm the baby. One major review (Bowes et al., 1970) concluded that their overall safety record in terms of medical criteria is well established, whereas another (Brackbill, 1979b) concluded that such medication affects the behaviors of infants up to at least 1 year of age. Aleksandrowicz, in his 1974 review, suggested that all obstetric drugs add to the demands of the birth process on the newborn's functioning. We will describe a few assorted studies to give a flavor of the kind of effects found.

Mepivicaine and lidocaine (Xylocaine), both used in epidurals and caudals, cross the placenta rapidly and are relatively stable in the blood (Bowes et al., 1970; Morishima & Adamson, 1967). They were found to affect newborns' muscle strength and muscle tone, but such effects wore off rapidly in the first day (Scanlon, 1976; Tronick, Wise, Als, Adamson, Scanlon, & Brazelton, 1976). Mepivicaine was also shown to lead to depression in about 20% of the 56 infants in another study (Morishima, Daniel, Finster, Poppers, & James, 1966). When accidentally injected directly into the fetus, it led to death in 2 of 4 cases and to survival only after exchange transfusions in the other 2 cases (Sinclair, Fox, Lentz, Field, & Murphy, 1965). Maximum effects of this agent occur if the infant was born 20 to 30 minutes after administration of the drug.

Bupivicaine, which is chemically similar to mepivicaine and lidocaine and is also used for caudal and epidural blocks, has been shown to have effects that persist for at least several days after birth (Lieberman et al., 1979; Murray et al., 1981). In the study by Murray and her colleagues, babies whose mothers had epidurals with bupivicaine exhibited poorer overall scores on a newborn assessment test of behavioral functioning (the NBAS or Brazelton; see Chapter 8), and on the motor, state control, and physiological response clusters of the same test. The state control differences persisted into the fifth day of life. The epidural babies

also cried more in the neonatal period. By 1 month of age there were no differences on the test of behavioral functioning, but there were differences on other measures. Medicated mothers spent more time stimulating their babies to suck, yet fed them less often, and reported less prompt responses to their cries. Finally, they exhibited less affectionate handling, although the actual size of the difference was very small. The medicated babies were seen by their mothers as less adaptable, more intense, having less good interactive capacities, poorer state control, and as more "colicky" (Murray et al., 1981; see also Broussard & Hartner, 1971). This study, then, unlike most of the others described in this section, found some effects that persisted at 1 month of age.

Evidence for negative effects on babies of giving their mothers other regional anesthetics is even less convincing for drugs other than mepivicaine, lidocaine, and bupivicaine. Procaine (Novocaine) and tetracaine (Pontaine), used in spinal and saddle blocks, are inactivated more rapidly than lidocaine and mepivicaine and thereby may have less effect. A study of 261 women who had paracervical blocks with low doses (Freeman & Arnold, 1975) showed no increased risk to the mothers, although the intensity of uterine contractions decreased. The risk to the infants appeared to be minimal because their Apgar scores (an index of physiological status or depression at birth) were not affected, although in 6% of the 104 cases that used fetal monitoring their heart rates were affected. The doctors doing the study recognized that they could not exclude the possibility of minor or subtle fetal damage resulting from lack of oxygen related to the heart rate changes. Nevertheless they judged that the potential fetal risks from this type of anesthesia were acceptable given the ease of the procedure and the degree of pain relief obtained.

One recent study directly attacked the problem that women who choose to give birth without anesthetics differ in factors such as age, education, and financial security from those who choose medicated births. Standley (1974) introduced statistical controls for parental characteristics and orientation to the pregnancy. She found no influence of regional anesthetics on neonatal behaviors (as measured by the Brazelton scales), specifically not on items that assess motor maturity and irritability (Standley, 1976).

GENERAL ANESTHETICS

These produce a lack of sensation throughout the entire body as opposed to locally or only below a certain level of the body. General anesthesia can be produced by intravenous injection or by inhalation of anesthetic agents. It is indicated in cases where intrauterine manipulation of the fetus is required and when the woman feels she cannot cope with being awake during delivery. These two needs can also be met by regional anesthesia combined with sleep-inducing drugs, as can the requirements for a surgical delivery.

Anesthetists tend to prefer the intravenous anesthetics, primarily barbiturates, which act quickly and allow rapid recovery of consciousness. This is fortunate because there is more evidence that inhalants may be harmful. As a class the inhalants are more often related to the outcomes at each age studied, and the relations are predominately negative (Brackbill & Broman, unpublished; Broman, 1981, 1983). In particular, their results suggest "that inhalants are associated with defects in psychomotor and neuromotor functioning in the first year" (Broman, 1981, p. 134). Most studies that have shown negative effects from inhalants or general anesthesia have either not included nitrous oxide ("laughing gas"), which is the most frequently used inhalant in the United States, or have included it only if it was used in combination with other inhalation anesthetics that are known to have a medically depressing effect on infants (Cosmi & Marx, 1968; Horowitz, Ashton, Culp, Gaddis, Levin, & Reichmann, 1977; Moya & Thorndike, 1962).

Nitrous oxide is not considered to have a significant depressive effect medically (Moya & Thorndike, 1962). Furthermore, as long ago as 1961, Brazelton suggested that it might provide protection against the effects of other medications. This idea has never been seriously tested, to our knowledge. However, a study by Field and Widmayer (1980) found results that might possibly be accounted for by such a protective action of nitrous oxide. In a study of the effects of Caesarean deliveries, they found much less effect of drugs on Brazelton scores than they anticipated. Given the

high levels of drugs and judging from previous studies, they would have expected much less optimal Brazelton scores than those they obtained. Field and Widmayer speculate that the lack of effects in babies whose mothers had high levels of narcotics and barbiturates, and frequently had had oxytocin as well, may have resulted from the ability of nitrous oxide to provide an antagonistic or protective effect.

Were nitrous oxide to have such an effect the results obtained for inhalant anesthetics in the Brackbill and Broman studies may underestimate their harm inasmuch as nitrous oxide was included with all other inhalants in their analyses.

OVERALL LEVEL OF MEDICATION

Although the thrust of most research has been to identify whether particular drugs are harmful, another valid question is whether a certain level of medication regardless of kind is harmful. We are considering overall level of medication at the end of the section that deals with drugs given to reduce pain or change the mother's reactions to it despite the fact that many studies have included oxytocin among the drugs included in arriving at an overall level of medication. The inclusion of oxytocin in the overall levels of medication seems unfortunate to us, given both the different purpose and the different nature of the drug, and we shall discuss it separately in the next section.

Horowitz and her collaborators have attempted to answer the question of harmful level of medication in three different studies. They had to go to different countries to find a wide range of medication levels. In the United States they found that among medicated mothers, higher levels of medication were correlated with negative outcomes in the neonatal period, but there were not enough unmedicated cases to compare drugged to no-drug groups (Horowitz et al., 1977).

In Israel they compared a moderately-medicated group (one that had no anesthetics) and a completely drug-free group. Israel was a particularly fortunate choice because there the reasons women choose drugs do not seem to be associated with extraneous variables such as education and social class, as they are in the United States. The infants were tested with the Brazelton scales (Kansas version) for the first 4 days and at 1 month and with the Bayley scales at 3 months. Only two items on the Brazelton scales differentiated the drug group from the nondrug group: (1) a measure of the lability of the infant's states (see Chapter 6 for a discussion of state) and (2) defensive response to cloth being placed over the face. The latter is particularly interesting because defensive responses on another neonatal behavioral test (the Graham/Rosenblith) were lower for infants who subsequently died of Sudden Infant Death Syndrome (see Chapter 8 for a fuller description of this relation). Unfortunately both the finding itself and the possible link to SIDS are difficult to interpret because of the difference in tests used, the small magnitude of the differences between groups, and because Horowitz's third study, in Uruguay, found the opposite difference between medicated and nonmedicated groups: there drugged babies did better.[6]

These three studies taken together suggest that low levels of medication are less likely to result in problems in the neonatal period than are higher levels. Whether drug-free labors and deliveries are safer for newborns than those with low levels of medication is not yet clear. It has been suggested that too little use of drugs to relieve anxiety and pain may increase the risks of anoxia in the fetus or newborn because both may affect hormone secretions in the mother in a way that may lead to reduced blood flow to the uterus (Shnider, 1981).

Effects of Oxytocin

We have mentioned this drug several times in previous sections. It has been used widely to induce labors or to speed up labors that are not progressing, but its effects have only recently been subject to close scrutiny. Murray and colleagues' 1981 study of bupivicaine, already described, also studied 20 mothers who had both bupivicaine and oxytocin. By comparing the women who had bupivicaine alone and the women who had both bupivicaine and oxytocin, the effects of the oxytocin itself can be estimated (although the same effects might not be obtained with oxytocin used alone or with

other anesthetics). The interpretations must also take account of the ways in which the groups differed on other variables related to delivery that could affect infant outcomes. These are shown in Table 5–1. Bupivicaine appears to decrease labor time, presumably due to greater relaxation. Note also that one or both drugs were more likely to be used when there was malposition of the fetus. Differences in the frequency of use of low forceps are partly to be expected in the oxytocin group. Zero use in the no drug group presumably reflects the mother's better muscle control, but may also be related to the length of labor. Doctors who gave bupivicaine may have intervened earlier with forceps, leading to shorter labor time.

Thus we see that even in a "relatively clean" study there are many complications to making interpretations with confidence. Nevertheless, let us look at the development of these babies.

On the newborn behavioral assessment (NBAS), babies whose mothers had received oxytocin (and bupivicaine) had lower scores than either the bupivicaine only or the unmedicated groups on overall results and on the motor, state control, and physiological response clusters. They were tense and hypertonic, which interfered with their motor activity. The state control differences persisted in the fifth day of life. In contrast to the other two groups, the oxytocin babies rarely woke for feedings. Furthermore, 5 of the 20 oxytocin babies received phototherapy for jaundice, whereas only 1 of the bupivicaine only babies and none of the unmedicated babies did. At 1 month of age there were no longer any differences on the NBAS, but the feeding situation elicited even more differences than at 5 days. The greatest difference was that mothers who had had oxytocin spent more time stimulating their babies as compared to the other groups. Their babies also exhibited the other differences relative to unmedicated babies that were reported earlier, although those differences are presumably not due to the oxytocin as such.

The Collaborative Project data provide some evidence for negative effects of oxytocin at ages beyond 1 month, but the information is limited because information on its use was not routinely collected during the entire period. It would appear from the available data that its use is related to some items on the 4- and 8-

---

[6]In general the differences between the groups in the three different locales were much greater than the differences between the different levels of medication.

TABLE 5–1
Characteristics of Infants Whose Mothers Received Different or No Drugs

	No drugs (15 cases)	Bupivicaine (20 cases)	Oxytocin and bupivicaine (20 cases)
Length of second stage labor	100 min	84 min	48 min
Malposition of fetus	0 cases	5 cases	8 cases
Use of low forceps	0 cases	12 cases	6 cases
Mother–infant separation[a]	0 cases	4 cases	6 cases
Phototherapy for jaundice	0 cases	1 case	5 cases[b]

[a]Done for observation of the newborn.
[b]There were other cases of jaundice in this group but they did not require therapy.

month pediatric neurological and psychological assessments. Most of these relations are in the negative direction, but their magnitude is not very great. The current analyses (Broman, 1981) indicate that oxytocin is related to psychomotor deficit in the early period and that at school age it is associated with lower achievement test scores.

Although the published details of these analyses do not allow us to assess the strength of the relations, it does appear that there is more unanimity of findings of negative effects of oxytocin than for most of the pain-related drugs. Between these data and those related to optimal strength of contractions in relation to producing fetal anoxia, it would seem that considerably more caution might be exercised in elective use of oxytocin. In this connection it is interesting that a study that has found oxytocin-induced labors to be related to unexplained language and motor delays at four years did not find such an association for prostaglandin-induced labors. None of the data we have discussed here have separated the use of oxytocin to induce labor (see Friedman, Sachtleben, & Wallace, 1979, for evidence with respect to induced labor) from its use to speed labor, and this is a topic for which more research might be productive.

Conclusions

Strong conclusions about the effects of obstetrical drugs are difficult to reach because of the methodological problems intrinsic to research in this field, the sparseness of the data, and the inconsistencies and conflicts in the available

information. Nevertheless, we can make some tentative conclusions. First, all drugs do not have similar effects. Some drugs have not been shown to have long-term negative consequences and parents can compensate for many of the short-term consequences, such as increased crying and decreased feeding. Tranquilizers, most of the sedative-hypnotics, analgesics, and regional anesthetics are in this category. Other drugs are more suspect with respect to long-term disadvantages. Oxytocin, used to induce or augment labor, scopolamine, and inhalant anesthetics other than nitrous oxide are in the latter category.

Second, the magnitude of drug effects is usually small. The effects of birth weight, parity (particularly the first versus subsequent deliveries), and SES, for example, are usually much larger.

Third, a given drug often has an effect on some, but not other, outcomes, and sometimes the medicated group is advantaged and sometimes disadvantaged. Such seeming inconsistencies may reflect the operation of chance factors. If the drug had no consistent effect and the investigators calculated many statistical tests, some results would be significant merely by chance. Half of those significant findings should favor the drug group and half the non-drug group. Some of the findings we have reported were like this. In other studies, more than a chance number of significant findings occurred or most of the significant findings were in one specific direction (that is, were good or bad). Although most investigators have assumed that drugs have only negative effects, positive effects are not an unreasonable possibility. Drugs may reduce stress during labor and delivery, thus reducing the probability of constitutional effects; or they may increase stress, which may inoculate the baby against future stress. Research on animals has demonstrated the existence of such inoculation effects.

Fourth, the overall amount of medication may be an important variable. Drugs that do not have effects singly or in moderate dosages may have effects when used in combination with several other drugs. High total dosage or interaction effects among specific drugs might account for this.

Fifth, not all babies respond in the same way to a given drug at a given dosage. Individual differences in babies' abilities to metabolize or otherwise cope with a given drug undoubtedly contribute to the conflicting findings. Babies' capacities in this regard cannot be known before birth, so a mother's personal decision regarding drugs during delivery cannot be influenced by this factor.

CHILDBIRTH PRACTICES

We have discussed the known and potential impacts of various perinatal factors—obstetrical medication and type of delivery—on the physical well-being of infants. Another set of potentially important variables revolves around the impact of labor and delivery upon the mother's feelings toward her infant and their possible effects upon the quality of her subsequent mothering.

Standard Delivery Practices

There is currently considerable controversy over hospital practices with respect to childbirth. This controversy stems from several sources: (1) the various movements for childbirth reform that have focused on the delivery itself, such as those of Dick-Read, Lamaze, and Leboyer; (2) the feminist movement, which has been concerned with the impact of delivery practices on the family unit; and (3) doctors and researchers concerned with the maternal bond to the infant.

Before these influences had any effect, the standard childbirth in the United States took place in a hospital with a doctor in charge of the delivery. The woman was admitted to the hospital, "prepped" or prepared for labor (this did not mean she was instructed or given counsel, but had her pubic hair shaved and was given an enema). When labor was well under way she was separated from the father and any relatives by being placed in a "labor room," often with several other women in labor, some of whom might be screaming or crying. Then, when she was about to deliver, she was taken to the "delivery room" where she was placed on her back on a hard table with her knees in the air over metal supports (the lithotomy position), and the obstetrician delivered the baby with appropriate help from an anesthetist and a nurse or nurses. The whole setting was like an operating room (see Figure 5–2). We shall first describe criticisms of these standard practices and then describe other approaches to childbirth.

Criticisms of Standard Delivery Practices

There are three major criticisms of the so-called standard hospital practices. They are: the exclusion of persons significant to the mother from the whole delivery process; the separation of the mother from her newborn baby in the first minutes and hours after birth; and the notion that giving birth should be treated like a disease and women in labor like sick patients.

To understand all these criticisms, it is important to put current American childbirth procedures into some anthropological and historical perspective. Unfortunately, popular literature on these topics contains much romantic lore about the superiority of the methods used in other cultures or at other times, or on what is "natural," so it is essential to know something about the origins of current practices.

The standard procedures used in today's hospital delivery resulted from efforts to make childbirth as safe as possible for both mother and infant. Infant and maternal death rates dropped remarkably with the advent of modern hospital practices; that is, after the roles of germs and infection were understood. Few would want to return to practices that result in the higher mortality rates that are aspects of the "good old times" or of doing what is "natural." At the same time, it is clear that many hospitals have been reluctant to accept newer techniques for avoiding infections and keeping infants well that would allow the presence of others. Instead, they have maintained customs that are for the convenience of their staff rather than for the safety of the mother and infant.

EXCLUSION OF SIGNIFICANT OTHERS

Most of the controversy about the exclusion of significant persons centers on the exclusion of the father from labor and delivery rooms. Some persons are also concerned about the exclusion of children, relatives, and friends. These practices are decried by some proponents of alternative childbirth systems as going against nature, but an examination of practices in various cultures demonstrates that there is no one norm. Although fathers are allowed at deliveries in some cultures, throughout history other cultures, both literate and preliterate, have excluded all men (including husbands, doctors, and medicine men). Some continue the exclusion for weeks or even months after birth because the mother is considered to be unclean during this time. There are cultures where the father is not present but where he takes to a labor bed himself and acts as if he is in labor while his wife is (a practice known as couvade). In another culture the father is reportedly chained in the sea so that the tide will drown him if his wife does not have a suitably rapid delivery. Mothers in both of these cultures are separated from their husbands, but the impact of couvade on the mother must be rather different from the impact of having the father chained in the sea! In our own culture the exclusion of fathers was common long before hospitals were invented. The father pacing outside the room where his child was being born is an old and widespread image. Here, too, the wife was often attended only by women.[7]

Whether fathers are excluded from labor and delivery thus depends largely on cultural traditions, although there are often practical realities lying behind the cultural practices. For example, where population densities were low, fathers relatively often had to help at their wives' deliveries, as they still do when labor moves faster than the mother can get to the hospital. We even know of one case where the mother, a doctor, delivered herself in the back seat of a car while the father drove, and the parents together provided commentary for a young sibling for whom there had been no available baby sitter. The controversy in our culture arose because the cultural norm was to exclude fathers and the most popular alternative childbirth techniques include the father. Today substantial numbers of hospitals allow fathers to be present throughout labor, delivery, and most of the immediate postdelivery period, and allow fathers unlimited visiting of their wives. Not every hospital allows all of these, and sometimes they are allowed only if the father fulfills certain conditions such as attending childbirth classes.

Cultural norms concerning the exclusion of other people important to the mother also vary widely. Such "others" include siblings of the infant being born, male or female relatives, and friends. Some cultures allow siblings or other children, some allow only one sex, some only those below a certain age, and some only those above a certain age. In some cultures birth takes place with all the relatives and friends present, but in others the mother is isolated from all but one or two special persons. In still other cultures, she is expected to deliver herself while working in the fields with no one present.[8]

In our culture, siblings usually have been cared for by relatives or friends for a period of time around birth and they were long banned from obstetrical units even for visits to their mother who often was there for 10 days. Hospitals now vary widely in their practices. Children are often allowed to visit their mothers in the hospital (a safer procedure now that vaccines have conquered many childhood diseases) and are sometimes allowed to touch and hold the newborns as well. In contrast, recently a family had to get a court order in order to allow their male child to attend his mother's hospital delivery.

---

[7] A good book for historical background is *Lying-in: A History of Childbirth in America*, by R. W. Wertz and D. C. Wertz (1979).

[8] Konner (1980) discussed a culture in which this was the cultural ideal, but where it was acknowledged that the ideal was reached only in higher parities (not for first or second children).

SEPARATION OF MOTHER AND NEWBORN

The second major focus of attack on standard hospital procedures for deliveries and mother–child care involves the separation of the mother from her newborn infant. The initial separation can result from the mother's being so deeply anesthetized that she is unable to respond to her infant (a condition found with general anesthesia), but is not limited to those cases. In the past, all babies were removed to another room or another part of the room as soon as the umbilical cord was cut so that some people in the delivery room could concentrate on the newborn's well-being while the obstetrician concentrated on the mother's well-being. When the procedures of the delivery room were completed, babies usually were taken to the nursery and the mother to the recovery room (or to her own room, depending on hospital practice and the characteristics of the delivery, such as use of anesthetics or Caesarean section).

In addition to the initial separation of the mother from her infant right after birth, it was standard to allow the infant in the mother's room only during feeding time (or at the normal feeding time if that occurred before the infant was "due" to receive a first feeding). From the 1940s to the 1960s, when very few American mothers were nursing their infants, feeding periods were quite short. Although in general strict scheduling no longer prevailed by the 1960s, hospitals still adhered rather strictly to schedules (whether for the good of the infant or of the hospital staff may be debatable). These practices, which extended through the hospital stay of 10 days to 2 weeks, were supposed to enable the mother to rest and recover, and to allow her to receive visitors without exposing her baby to their germs. Many would argue that the more important effects were to make the mother feel incapable of caring for her own infant, especially if she was having her first baby and had had little previous experience caring for infants (as is common in cultures in which small nuclear families are the norm). A capable nurse was needed for this chore.

The perception of the appropriateness of having people other than the mother provide primary care for newborns varies greatly across cultures and history. In some cultures the mother is the primary caregiver from the time her baby is born. In others she is thought to be able to care for her newborn only if other women take over her other responsibilities (from cooking and cleaning to having intercourse with her husband). In some cultures the mother is considered incapable of doing anything for her newborn, other than nurse it, for weeks and often for months. It is rare, however, to separate infants from their mothers to the extent that occurs in standard hospital practices, because until 75 years ago infants had to be breast fed[9] and that requires frequent interactions. The sooner and more frequently a baby nurses after birth, the sooner the mother's milk comes in. A baby who is nursed on demand will nurse every 2 to 3 hours. If the mother's breasts are not stimulated in the first few days after she gives birth, her milk production system will turn off. Thus, nursing mothers and their infants must have more frequent access to each other in the newborn period than has been standard hosital practice. In fact, the desire to have mothers nurse was part of the impetus for the movement in the 1940s to have newborns "room in" with their mothers in the hospital. Today the desire to encourage breast feeding is one of the major reasons for the objection to hospital practices that separate mothers from infants.

A second basis for objection to the separation of mother and infant is the psychological well-being of the pair. Proponents of rooming in the 1940s argued that such contact promoted the development of the mother–infant relationship. Although the evidence gathered to support this belief was inconclusive, the basic hypothesis has resurfaced in the bonding hypothesis, which in its strongest form proposes that there is a critical period in the first few hours after birth during which the mother establishes a bond to her infant. Separation from her baby during that time will interfere with the development of her maternal love. We will discuss the evidence for this hypothesis later in the chapter.

---

[9] Among the upper classes in Western cultures, women called wet nurses often have been hired to nurse babies and thus relieve the mother of the (animal-like?) chore of nursing. For a discussion of the effect of this practice on the infants of the women hired, see Piers's book, *Infanticide* (1978).

PREGNANCY AS ILLNESS; DELIVERY AS SURGICAL

The third major criticism of current standard practices is related to the perception of pregnancy as an illness and delivery as a surgical procedure. Since the development of modern medicine in our culture, doctors have managed pregnancy and birth and usually have taken the medically safest route, arguing that if there is a potential danger it is best to avoid it. This has led them to require women to restrict their activities in substantial ways during pregnancy. Before the women's movement and modern childbirth movements began to challenge the concept of pregnancy as an illness, doctors commonly forbad many activities during the latter part of pregnancy (for example, intercourse and exercise ranging from driving an automobile to running). Many women object to such restrictions, but have been afraid to go against the doctor's advice, because the doctor's word has often been considered law. Thus women have been made to feel helpless in the face of their doctors' demands (social psychologists have a subfield that deals with such "learned helplessness").

Cultural norms influence pregnancy practices as they do other human endeavors, and doctors are not immune to such influence. In some cultures pregnant women are considered much more delicate than they are in others. The same is true of different economic levels within cultures. Women in the upper classes are much more likely to be treated as ill and to be pampered during pregnancy than are those in the lower classes, who usually have to work throughout pregnancy. Attitudes toward intercourse during pregnancy provide a good example of cultural variation in activities permitted during pregnancy. Some cultures ban intercourse for much of pregnancy, whereas others permit it throughout. There is at least one culture in which the husband is urged to have intercourse frequently throughout pregnancy because it is thought that his ejaculation is necessary to nourish the growing child (this certainly gives the father a role in the pregnancy).

The treatment of women during labor and delivery in a hospital (including maternity hospitals) as if they were surgical patients contributes to the depersonalization and loss of control women in that situation often experience.

We will discuss four practices that have fallen under attack: fetal monitoring, delivery position, episiotomies, and length of hospital stay.

Fetal monitoring, which has been discussed earlier, has come under attack because it interferes with the woman's freedom of movement during labor, because it has been overused, and because, particularly with the most invasive techniques, it conveys an aura of medicine and surgery.

The standard lithotomy position on a hard table in a setting similar to an operating room (see Figure 5–2) has been attacked because women find it uncomfortable, they feel very helpless in this position, and it is a very surgical setting. It is also medically suspect; we will discuss the medical evidence in the section on alternative childbirth techniques.

Episiotomies are surgical incisions of the perineum (the area between the vagina and anus) that doctors make during delivery to prevent the perineum from tearing and to facilitate the delivery. Doctors in the United States (but not in Europe) do them in 90% of all deliveries. They consider them good preventive medicine because cuts are easier to repair than jagged tears (Banta, 1981; Thacker & Banta, 1980) and because a tear that reaches to the anus is dangerous. Many women object to episiotomies because they are done routinely rather than only when there is danger of extensive tearing, because techniques used to reduce the probability of tearing in other countries (a vertical or semivertical delivery position and massaging with warm compresses and oil) are not commonplace in the United States, and because episiotomies are uncomfortable (even more so than repaired tears) during the healing and often interfere with sexual intercourse for many months after birth.

When delivery is considered to be like surgery, the patient needs to recuperate for a considerable period of time—10 days to 2 weeks. Such a long period of recuperation encourages women to see themselves as ill and in need of medical care. Today many women go home from the hospital between 2 and 5 days after childbirth, although this may have more to do with rising hospital costs than with changes in doctors' perceptions caused by women's objections to being treated as patients. In any case, with shorter hospital stays women certainly have less time to feel ill (or pampered).

Other Approaches to Childbirth

Let us turn to some of the movements for alternative childbirth practices that are followed by substantial numbers of people in western cultures. The several methods of prepared childbirth, also called "educated" or "natural" childbirth, were developed to teach women to deal with the pain and discomfort of labor and childbirth and therefore to reduce or eliminate obstetrical medication.

CHILDBIRTH WITHOUT FEAR

The British obstetrician Grantly Dick-Read began the first modern movement toward natural childbirth. He believed that such a natural process as childbirth should not be full of pain. He decided that the source of the pain was not labor itself, but was women's fear of it, a fear instilled by other women and even by so authoritative a source as the Bible. The natural implication of his belief was that if fear could be eliminated, then the pain would be reduced or eliminated also. His classic book, *Childbirth Without Fear* (1944), was designed to convince women that childbirth could be a positive experience if only they weren't fearful. Dick-Read did not provide any techniques for reducing pain other than positive thinking, and many other obstetricians who attempted this form of childbirth with their patients were much less successful than he was. The role of hypnosis and self-hypnosis came to be questioned as a possible basis for Dick-Read's successes.

Russian obstetricians, in contrast, provided techniques for dealing with pain in childbirth. Their system, called "psychoprophylaxis" (mind-prevention), applied the classical conditioning paradigm to labor.[10] The unconditioned stimulus, the labor contraction, leads to the unconditioned responses of pain and tension. The therapeutic technique involves conditioning women to respond positively—through breathing and muscular relaxation responses—to the signals of onset of contraction. The conditioned relaxation then competes with the tension associated with the pain of the contractions and the relaxation responses of women who are well practiced win the battle and reduce the pain.

LAMAZE TECHNIQUE

The Russian techniques were adopted and further developed in France by Lamaze, and then were subsequently modified and spread throughout much of the United States. We will briefly describe the Lamaze system as it is usually practiced in the United States. The Lamaze technique and others based on it have been widely accepted by much of the medical establishment, probably for two reasons: (1) nurses have often been its advocates and teachers, and (2) it accepts many of the standard hospital practices. It is conceived of as a way for women to control and deal with the pain of childbirth actively and positively so as to avoid or reduce medication, and to maximize the participation of parents in childbirth. Unlike Dick-Read advocates, Lamaze parents are usually taught that medication may become desirable (to the mother) or required (by the physician) and that such eventualities should not be interpreted as failure. If a Caesarean section becomes advisable, Lamaze parents are encouraged to accept that as an unfortunate, but acceptable, outcome.

Lamaze classes are widely available in the United States. They usually involve six weekly sessions in which the childbirth process is described and the relaxation and breathing exercises are introduced and practiced. The goal of the classes is to enable the woman to deal with her pain. Only 3–14% of women in general report no pain compared to 10–20% of prepared childbirth women. Several techniques are used in addition to the conditioning techniques derived from the Russians. Lamaze parents are taught to focus cognitively on relaxing thoughts. They are encouraged to select and take to the hospital an object or picture that is relaxing to them to focus on during contractions. Lamaze classes also provide detailed information about the labor process so that the mother can estimate the time between contractions, during which she can relax, and can estimate how much longer and how intense the pain is likely to get. Knowing how much is still to come can help to promote relaxation. These techniques taken together can max-

---

[10]It is interesting to note that this method was developed in conjunction with, or in response to, the lack of available drugs in Russia in World War II because they were used to treat soldiers.

imize the likelihood that mothers-to-be will be awake and alert and in a positive frame of mind to enjoy the birth of their babies.

An interesting historical accident has resulted in a major component of Lamaze deliveries as they are now practiced in the United States. In France, trained women called "montrices" assist the women in labor. In the United States, such assistants are not available and fathers largely assume that function. Fathers thus become necessary as well as desirable participants in the labor and delivery process. They attend childbirth classes with their mates, learn the techniques, and help in such practical matters as timing contractions, massaging the mother, and providing emotional support. The father's involvement is now seen as one of the major desirable features of Lamaze childbirth.

Prepared childbirth techniques may affect the relations between mothers and fathers and their infants. Mother and infant receive a reduced amount of obstetrical medication, so the mother is more alert and more able to enjoy the birth experience, and perhaps she is more likely to form an early attachment to her infant. Reduced medication makes it likely that the infant will also be more responsive, whereas more medication may decrease the baby's responsiveness so that it may be harder for the mother to relate to her infant. Babies groggy from medication are less likely to nurse with sufficient vigor to stimulate the mothers' milk production, which may lead to difficulties in etablishing a successful nursing relationship, especially because nursing is often either discouraged or given little or no encouragement in many hospitals. Finally, Lamaze deliveries provide an explicit and necessary role for the father. He not only gets to watch his child aborning, in a context where his emotional bond to his spouse may well be strengthened, but his initial bonding to the baby may also be facilitated.

To evaluate the desirability of Lamaze childbirth, it is necessary to consider the effects on the family separately from those on the baby. It is one thing to engage in prepared childbirth for the sake of the parents' emotional experience. That decision is one that is properly up to each family. It is quite another thing to argue that prepared childbirth will lead to advantages for the offspring.

LEBOYER: "BIRTH WITHOUT VIOLENCE"

Another set of alternative delivery practices is known as "birth without violence," derived from the title of Leboyer's book (1975), or as Leboyer delivery. These practices assume an alert, awake mother at delivery, and in fact they are most often paired with the Lamaze type of preparation and delivery. The focus, however, is on the infant's birth experience. The techniques derive from the theories of Reich, Rank, and Janov, all of whom argued that birth is the prototypical emotional trauma, which leads to emotional difficulties later in life. Leboyer developed techniques designed to minimize this birth trauma. Bright, glaring operating room lights are replaced with dim, indirect lighting so as not to shock the infant. The temperature in the room is raised to be closer to that of the mother's body, to which the infant has been adapted. After delivery and before the umbilical cord is cut, the naked baby is put on the mother's bare belly, thus providing skin-to-skin contact. The people in the room refrain so far as possible from talking loudly and making noise[11] and they handle the baby gently and slowly, which is presumably the way he was jostled in the womb. After the cord stops pulsating, it is cut and the infant is given a warm bath, presumably to recreate his experiences of the womb.

Leboyer deliveries are extremely controversial for many reasons. They are very intrusive on hospital staff and nonbelievers are not likely to be amenable to such disruptions of procedures. More theoretically, some authorities argue that the shock of bright lights and noise may help to establish regular breathing. If there is a positive outcome, it should show up in the research on infant outcomes. Early reports were enormously positive. For example, Rappoport (1976) found that 120 Leboyer-delivered babies walked sooner than average, were unusually adept with their hands, toilet trained easily, and learned to feed themselves early. Unfortunately, she made no direct comparisons with traditionally-delivered infants. Most important, the parents chose a Leboyer delivery. It is likely that these women differ from women who chose other methods of childbirth in ways that may be im-

---

[11] In some places music selected by the parents may be played throughout labor and delivery.

portant to infant outcomes. Parents who are concerned with the delicate sensibilities of their newborns may be generally sensitive to their infants' emotional needs, and, as we shall see in Chapter 12, this apparently is a major variable in child rearing. More generally, people who choose a new experimental procedure may differ in important ways from those who stick with tradition. Studies of Leboyer babies in which subjects are not randomly assigned to Leboyer versus standard techniques will never determine the effects of the delivery technique itself unconfounded by the possible influence of differences between parents who choose Leboyer deliveries and those who do not.

One recent well-done study did attempt to do this (Nelson, Enkin, Saigel, Bennett, Milner, & Sackett, 1980). Low-risk pregnant women who were interested in the Leboyer approach, intended to attend prenatal classes, and would be available for follow ups 3 days and 8 months after giving birth formed the subject pool. Mothers who met these criteria and were willing to be randomly assigned (56 out of 153) were stratified according to whether it was their first pregnancy or a later one and according to social class. Within these groupings they were randomly assigned to the Leboyer delivery group or the control. Conventional deliveries (the control group) took place in a cool, well-lit delivery room, with the cord cut within 60 seconds and the baby wrapped in a blanket and returned to the mother. Leboyer deliveries were in the mother's bed in a warm, dimly-lit labor room. The baby was placed in skin-to-skin contact with the mother and massaged by her. The cord was cut only after it stopped pulsating and a warm bath was given by the father.

Both groups were the same in that fathers participated actively, no prepping was done (no shaving or enemas), and no medication other than epidurals were used. Bulb suctioning of the nasopharynx was done as needed for both groups and infants in neither group were weighed or given silver nitrate drops in the eyes in the first hour. The groups also did not differ significantly in actual medications used, use of labor induction, spontaneous rupture of membranes, or on rooming in (all had at least part time) or feeding practices (most breast fed). All Caesarean (5) and forceps (8) deliveries in both groups were excluded from the study. The Leboyer group had significantly shorter first-stage labor (median 7.5 hours compared to 14 hours for the control group). Although the study does not report on it, it would seem plausible that the absence of the lithotomy position and the more relaxed setting could have produced the shorter labors in the experimental group. The authors discussed another possible explanation for the difference in length of labor, that of a placebo effect. Specifically, the Leboyer mothers may have expected easier births and that belief may have made their labors easier. Mothers in the two groups did not differ in their ratings of the birth experience, their psychological adjustment, or their perceptions of their babies as difficult (as compared to the average baby). At 3 days and 6 weeks they did not differ in their perceptions of the delivery's effect on their babies, but at 8 months the Leboyer mothers were more likely to think the delivery had influenced their baby's behavior.

Maternal perceptions, however, may be influenced by mothers' beliefs about the effects of delivery practices. Nelson and colleagues (1980) also measured infants' behaviors and did not find the advantages predicted by Leboyer proponents. Proponents have reported that babies born in this fashion are quieter, more alert, and cry less, but in this study the infants in the two groups did not differ along any of these dimensions. The calming effect of the bath was also not obvious because 9 of the 19 babies observed in it reacted with irritable crying. Brazelton's newborn assessment, done at both 24 and 72 hours by examiners with no knowledge of the baby's method of delivery, showed no statistically significant differences in interactive or motor processes, state control, or response to stress. The Bayley tests of development at 8 months also failed to show differences on either the motor or mental scales. Finally, no differences between groups were found on the Carey assessment of temperament.

From this research, it appears that the claimed superiority of Leboyer delivered babies does not exist in an experimental study in which all mothers have some prenatal education, are delivered with a significant other present, receive little anesthesia or other drugs, and participate in several other features of the various systems that have challenged conventional procedures. Note, however, that only one third of the mothers approached agreed to random assignment. In any event, the lack of significant differences in morbidity and negative outcomes should be reassuring to doctors and patients who desire a Leboyer delivery.[12]

The research just described deals with Leboyer deliveries as a package. As in most real-life applications, there are several different aspects of this package that might influence later development of the infant.[13] The Leboyer movement has focused on infant outcomes. The effect of such practices on the mother has intrigued other researchers. As we will describe in the next section, one of the aspects, early tactile contact between mother and infant, is thought by some to be an important ingredient for the maternal bonding process.

VERTICAL DELIVERY POSITION

A movement to permit women a choice of a vertical or semivertical delivery position (in a birthing chair, propped up against pillows or another person, or squatting on a floor or in a wading pool) has grown out of the reexamination of standard hospital practices inspired by the objections raised by advocates of alternative childbirth techniques and of women's rights. There is much historical and cultural precedent for vertical delivery positions. In many preliterate societies, women gave birth in a squatting position. Throughout history, women in various cultures have used semi-upright positions. As a teenager, one of the authors discovered that an English obstetrician had invented a delivery chair.[14] It made good sense to her then, and still does, and she wondered why it had gone out of favor. She later learned that this was a reinvention of the obstetrical chair. The Old Testament refers to an obstetrical chair; the walls of the tomb of Queen Hatshepshut of Egypt (who died in 1468 B.C.) show its use for the delivery of her son; and it was part of a midwife's equipment until the nineteenth century.

More recently, Caldeyro-Barcia built an obstetrical chair modeled after a sixteenth century French one, all of whose parts were adjustable. All of his mothers chose the chair in preference to the lithotomy position. Figure 5–4 shows a currently available obstetrical chair, but it is not as adjustable as Caldeyro-Barcia's.

Other forms of vertical deliveries are also becoming common. In many hospitals in the United States women may choose their birthing position, which may be squatting, sitting in a chair, or propped against pillows (see Figure 5–5). In Odent's obstetrical service in the hospital at Pithiviers, France, women may choose one of these options or they may squat in a wading pool (Odent, 1982, 1984). Most women who are offered a choice choose a vertical position.

There is growing medical evidence that lying down is not a good position for either labor or delivery. A vertical position and movement both strengthen contractions (Mendez-Bauer, Arroyo, Garcia-Ramos, et al., 1975) and shorten labor. Caldeyro-Barcia (1981) found first-stage labor to be 25% shorter for 40 patients who were primarily vertical (median 147 minutes compared to 225 minutes for 5 who were horizontal; all were having their first babies and had had normal pregnancies). Rates of assisted and Caesarean deliveries are reportedly much lower. Caldeyro-Barcia reports that even breech deliveries do not require maneuvers. Odent reports a Caesarean rate of only 8% among 1800 deliveries in 1977 and 1978. The mother's circulatory system may be stressed

---

[12] One measure did differentiate the groups, but was not considered sufficiently deviant to be a real problem. Underarm temperature in the first hour of life was lower than normal for the Leboyer babies, but not dangerously low. It could be that the procedures led to less shock, hence to less adaptive responses to achieve self-regulated temperature, a hypothesis that would find some support from the literature on the responses to cold stress. It could also be that Leboyer babies were simply more exposed to relatively cool air.

[13] For example, the babies are placed in a prone (front down) position on their mothers' abdomens. Most infants in western societies are placed in the supine position (on their backs). At least one study (Anderson, Fleming, & Vidyasagar, 1980) shows that the heart rate is lower and the respiratory rate higher for infants in the prone position than it is for supine infants in the first hours of life. Both rates may be related to the increased crying found in supine babies. There were 99 instances of abnormal heartbeats in supine babies and only 18 in prone babies. Feeding behavior was also affected. Twice as many babies in the prone group took over 15 cc in their first feeding. Whether the head was elevated or not made no difference in the measures.

[14] She learned this from a book by H. W. Haggard called *Devils, Drugs, and Doctors* (1929). The first two parts of it surveyed the history of practices surrounding childbirth. She highly recommends it.

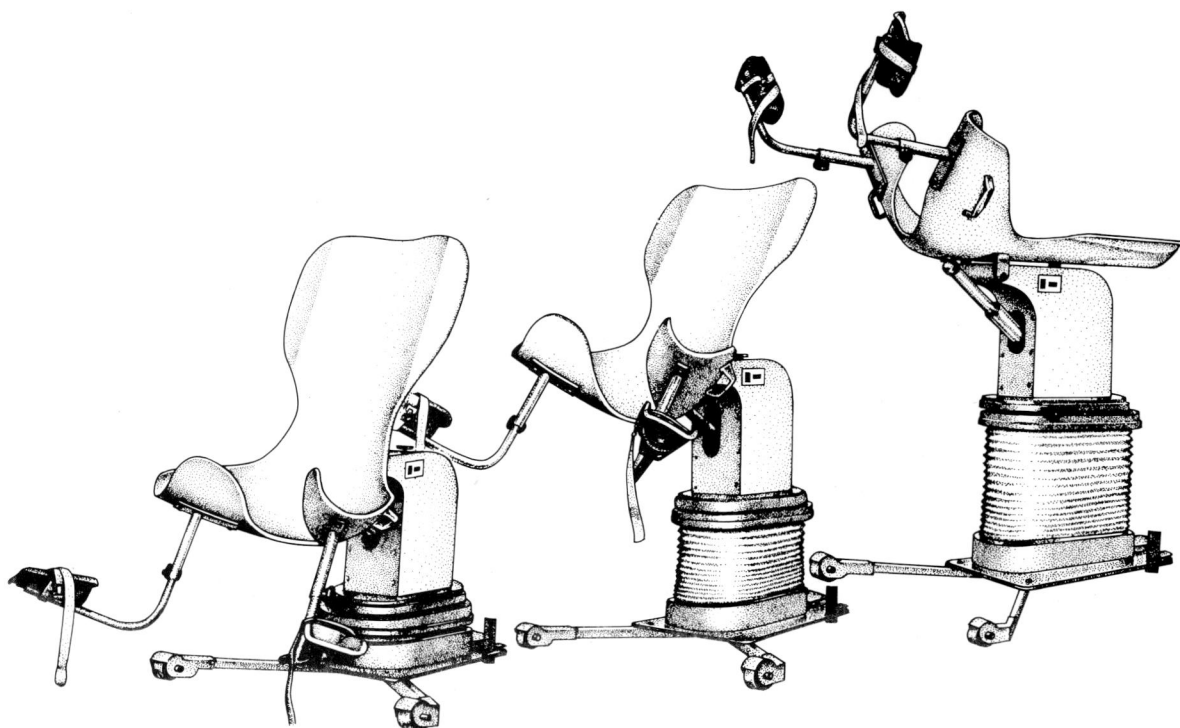

FIGURE 5–4. An obstetrical chair that is currently available commercially in the United States. We understand it is being modified to be more adjustable.

by a horizontal delivery, because the lungs and the major blood vessels are compressed when she is lying down. This affects the amount of oxygen the mother and her infant receive. In long deliveries (over 200 minutes), the carbon dioxide pressure (PCO_2), an index of anoxia, does not rise in sitting up deliveries, although it rises after only 50 minutes in horizontal deliveries. Oxygen levels are also better in mothers in a sitting position compared to mothers in the standard lithotomy position (Wood et al., 1965).

Infants born in vertical deliveries appear to be either at no increased risk or at reduced risk compared to those born in horizontal deliveries. Odent found a perinatal death rate of only 9 per 1,000 compared to 20 per 1,000 for all infants. Only 1.7% of the babies had to be transferred to intensive care hospitals. In addition, infections in babies and mothers were infrequent even though mothers wore their own clothes, used the wading pool, and had fathers present. Drs. Claudio and Moyses Paciornik (1976) found fewer neurological problems in Indian babies in Brazil whose mothers squatted during delivery than in their "civilized" counterparts delivered with their mothers lying on their backs.[15]

The lithotomy position stretches the perineum because the feet are apart. Thus the perineum is less elastic and the likelihood of tears or episiotomies is increased. In vertical deliveries both tears and episiotomies are much less frequent (Caldeyro-Barcia, 1981; Odent, personal communications, 1981, 1982).

In sum, giving birth in a sitting or squatting position seems to be at least as safe or safer for both mothers and infants than delivering in

---

[15] A film by the Paciorniks, "Birth in the Squatting Position," is available from Polymorph Films, 118 South Street, Boston, MA 02111.

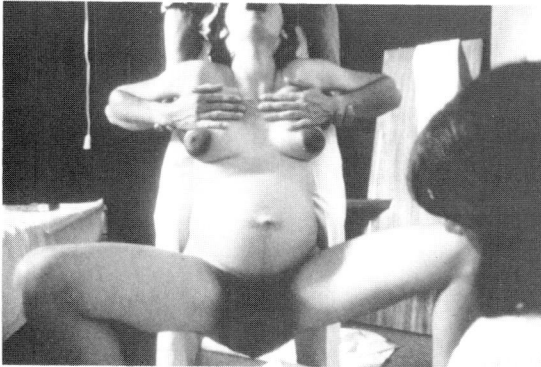

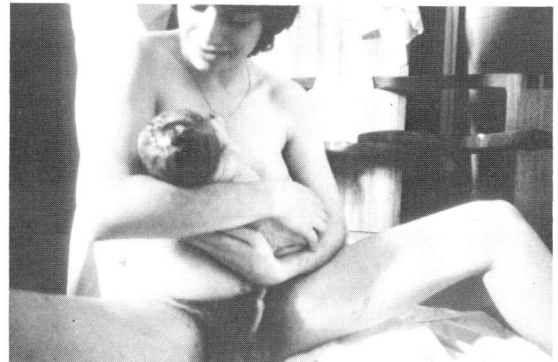

FIGURE 5–5. One kind of alternative birthing experience. (a) The mother in a squatting position. She is attended by a midwife, the back of whose head is visible. The midwife monitors the delivery and calls on the doctor only if necessary. The baby's head is crowning, as can be seen in the bulge at the vaginal opening. (b) A mother nursing her newborn. The umbilical cord is still attached and the placenta has not yet been delivered. This illustrates some of the bonding practices we will discuss in the next section: skin-to-skin contact, early suckling, no early separation. In fact, all mothers in this hospital have rooming in, including those whose babies must be in incubators but do not require intensive care. (Photos courtesy of Dr. Michel Odent.)

the lithotomy position. If future research replicates these findings, these positions should become popular.

HOME DELIVERIES

The movement to give birth at home has gathered strength in the United States in the last few years. It is another response to the objections to standard hospital practices, especially to the perception of pregnancy as illness and childbirth as a semisurgical procedure. The home birth movement could also be seen as a response to the resistance by doctors and hospitals to modify standard practices. Home deliveries permit parents to control the process and thereby design a birth experience according to their own ideas. Indeed, most women who deliver at home, usually with prepared childbirth techniques, report their deliveries as peak experiences. Nevertheless, Brazelton (in Klaus & Kennell, 1976) wondered whether such euphoria was merely relief at having made it intact.

Home deliveries are standard practice in some western countries. In the Netherlands, for example, women who are at minimal risk deliver at home, but others go to the hospital.

Those delivered at home are assisted by professional midwives, an honored profession in the Netherlands, most of Scandinavia, and many other countries. The midwife is also in attendance at a hospital delivery but will be joined by a doctor at any sign of a problem. The neonatal death rate for all deliveries in Holland is lower than that for the United States.

We cannot, however, conclude from the Dutch experience that home deliveries in the United States would be as safe as hospital deliveries, for three basic reasons. One is the selection process that determines who is delivered at home; the second is the type of medical attention available at home deliveries; and the third is that there is very little poverty in the Netherlands and substantial numbers of people who live in poverty in the United States. Selection in the United States is largely made by the individuals themselves. Although books supporting home deliveries invariably recommend them only for low-risk women, there is no one to determine who is at risk. In Holland there is a very wide net for screening out risk cases. A woman is defined as at risk if she is very young or relatively old, if she is unmarried, or if she is of relatively low SES. In addition she is, of course, considered at risk if she has any chronic illness, has had any problems during the pregnancy, or has had any previous pregnancy losses or complications, and even if she has not had regular prenatal care.

In the United States, home deliveries are often not attended by medical professionals. This is true for several reasons: (1) Most doctors refuse to attend home deliveries. (2) Trained midwives are in relatively short supply and are even illegal in most states.[16] (3) Some persons opting for home delivery are rejecting the medical model and so do not wish to have any medical personnel present. In Holland, a midwife is routinely present.

Social differences between the two countries are also very important. Holland is a small country with a relatively homogeneous population with respect to both social class status and ethnic origins. Even the lower SES mothers (considered at risk in Holland) are considerably better off in social and economic terms than what is considered to be lower SES in the United States. In the United States, maternal and neonatal death rates are very different for different ethnic and social class groups. In 1976, for example, 9 white mothers died in every 100,000 live births but 26.5 Black mothers died. Hence, the rates in the United States may be quite comparable for comparable social groups in Holland, and possibly even better, but many more American women are at risk because there are so many more disadvantaged mothers.

Although the overall question of the safety of home deliveries in the United States is still in some dispute, some conclusions can be made. If a very careful assessment of risk is made, if an adequately trained midwife or a doctor is present, and if hospital facilities are not too far away should they be needed by mother or infant, we can see no reason why home deliveries would not be as safe as in other countries. Home deliveries that do not have all of these safeguards would seem unnecessarily risky to us.

An incident in a TV documentary on home delivery dramatizes the dangers of unattended home deliveries. A family in which both parents are college professors, and who live near a hospital, chose home delivery for their second child. The birth was attended by family friends, the sibling, and children of friends. The husband served as the midwife. After the delivery, the mother, husband, and many of the others experienced the euphoria commonly described in home deliveries. Unfortunately, in their euphoria and absorption with the infant they failed to notice that the placenta had not been delivered. By the time this was noticed and the mother was rushed to the hospital, she was in a state of medical shock. A very few more minutes and she would have died. This story had a happy ending, but there are some that don't. The family planned to have a third child at home, but the husband seemed very lukewarm about the idea, agreeing only because it was what his wife wanted.

MOTHER–INFANT BONDING

Many people believe that the emotional attachment of mothers to their infants is set in a profound way during the first hours, days, or weeks after birth. Circumstances related to delivery that prevent, or make more difficult, the establishment of a bond to the infant at that time may make its later establishment harder, and this may result in suffering for the infant. This argument has been applied particularly in the case of premature infants who are isolated from their mothers to a greater extent and for a longer period than are full-term infants. Nevertheless, it is argued that term infants may also be at risk because most western deliveries take place in hospitals where it is common practice to remove infants from their mothers for considerable periods of time right after birth. In hospitals it may also be common practice to give the mother enough drugs during delivery to result in her being less responsive to her baby in the period immediately after birth than would presumably be optimal for her attachment to the infant.

Although most psychologists are delighted to see humanizing changes in hospital practices, many disagree with the notion that experiences during the immediate postnatal period are crucial to the mother's ability to mother

---

[16]An increasing number of schools in the United States now offer nurse–midwife degrees; 25 of them in early 1983.

her child. That is, they doubt that there is a critical or sensitive period for maternal bonding to infants. We will first provide some background and outline the pros and cons of the issues; then we will proceed to the detailed research evidence.

There are two bases for recent thinking about the mother's attachment to her infant. One is the impact of the field of **ethology** (a branch of zoology that studies animal behavior in its evolutionary and developmental context) on behavioral scientists and students of infancy in particular. Research inspired by ethological concepts has demonstrated that when mothers of some mammalian species are separated from their offspring for relatively short periods of time, it becomes difficult to get them to accept the baby again and provide normal mothering for it. This is particularly true with cows, sheep, and goats (all of which are ungulates). In the case of goats, the data are particularly clear that the mother will not reaccept her kid and mother it, even though rejection will lead to its death unless the experimenters intervene. The second basis for the current interest in this topic stems from a number of clinical observations of infants who have failed to thrive after being sent home from the hospital as presumably healthy. While a number of clinicians, usually pediatricians, have made such observations, the work that is most often cited is that by Klaus and Kennell (1976), which we will discuss in detail shortly.

Before we turn to a detailed discussion of the research evidence, let us cite a few important considerations that might lead to some skepticism about a critical period for human mothers to form attachments to their infants. First, ungulates are mammals but they are not human, and we have already discussed the dangers of extrapolating from one species to another. Second, many mammals do not show any strong rejection of their offspring after **postpartum** (after delivery) separation. Many species will even accept and nurture the offspring not only of other mothers but of other species, although they may require a little extra time to accept them. Furthermore, primates have been shown to provide compensatory care for experimentally damaged infants (Berkson, 1974; Rosenblum & Youngstein, 1974). Third, to the extent that original work has focused

primarily on premature infants and been extrapolated to term infants, it is necessary to note that many factors other than the mother's lack of contact with her infant in the newborn period may operate to reduce the effectiveness of her bonding to (or forming a strong attachment to) her infant. The infant may be less physically attractive; the mother may regard her preemie as made of egg shells and be afraid to handle or express love toward her baby; the infant's behavior at home may be more difficult than that of other infants and hence less likely to trigger affectionate responses (and, in extreme cases, may trigger hostile ones); even if the behavior is not difficult in some absolute sense, it may be so different from what is expected from the mother's previous experience and reading that the mother may react negatively. There may also be physical reasons, not just psychological ones, that sometimes play a role in failure to thrive. All of these factors may be considered as alternatives to lack of early contact as an explanation for failure of maternal bonding or for producing poor outcomes for infants. It is nevertheless possible that procedures to enhance bonding may help some mothers deal more adequately with these factors and thus lead to lower risk for their infants. Fourth, another fact that leads to skepticism about the criticality of early contact is that for many centuries, the world over, there have been cases of successful adoption. These occur not only with "mothers" who have not given birth to this baby or child, but also with "mothers" who have never given birth to any baby.

The following discussion of the research in this important area shows that the outcomes are not yet clear and the methodological problems are great. In this section it is important to notice problems of mis- or over-application of results that might be made by the popular press or others, and to be alert to the possible dangers to parents who may question the adequacy of their attachment to their children if they were born without an opportunity for immediate bonding experiences. It is also important to be aware of the possible negative effects on mothers if they are made to feel that they must opt for and attain these procedures if they are not to deprive their child.

The issue that we will discuss in the rest of this section is whether differences in childbirth practices affect the infant through the mechanism of maternal bonding. In other words, if the process of the mother's attaching to the infant is disrupted by hospital practices, will this disruption affect the well-being of the infant? Although the hospital practices discussed in this chapter have primarily dealt with the birth of full-term babies, we will start our discussion of bonding with a consideration of the premature infant. One reason for doing this is historical because the original studies and the impetus for them came from clinicians' experiences with prematures. Further, it is wise to separate the discussion of bonding with prematures from that with term infants because hospital practices differ so much for the two groups, and because prematures may be more vulnerable to any deficiencies in the quality of their mother's bond to them.

Bonding to Premature Infants

The experiences pediatricians had with premature infants raised many questions in their minds. Babies whose lives had been saved, often by heroic efforts, and who were developing very well in the hospital often returned to the hospital after a period at home with what is known as "failure to thrive"; that is, they did not gain weight or develop appropriately at home, and there seemed to be no physical reason for this. Indeed, they often began to develop normally again after nothing more than routine hospital care. Studies of failure to thrive and of battering found that many more premature or LBW babies were abused than would be expected by chance. Klaus and Kennell, and others, hypothesized that the mothers of these infants might be inadequate because they had been separated from their infants in the immediate post-birth period. The standard hospital practices for such babies have been to isolate them in special nurseries, never take them to their mothers, and often not allow the mother to touch or feed her infant until weeks or even months after birth.

Klaus and Kennell have pointed out that had hospital practice followed the advice given in the first textbook on neonatology (Budin, 1907), some of these problems might have been avoided. Budin reported that some mothers of prematures lost all interest in their babies and subsequently abandoned them. He advised that mothers of prematures should breast-feed their infants and be allowed to visit and look at them (he invented the glass-walled incubator), and care for them, even though they might have to be in the hospital for considerable periods of time.

Unfortunately Budin's pupil and disciple, Cooney, who publicized the methods for care of prematures, left out the factors of maternal care and feeding. Indeed, his publicity techniques seem quite astounding today; they certainly dictated against involvement of the mothers. From 1896 through 1940, Cooney exhibited premature infants in glass incubators at major fairs and expositions in Berlin, London, and various parts of the United States, offering the mothers free passes to the fairs. At the Chicago World's Fair in 1932, the receipts from Cooney's exhibit were second only to those for Sally Rand, the famed fan dancer (Liebling, 1939, cited in Klaus & Kennell, 1976). At the New York World's Fair in 1940, he exhibited and successfully cared for 5,000 prematures!

In the 1920s hospitals began to establish nurseries and to run them in ways that derived from the need to avoid infections. Practices for nursery management, like those for maternal care, did not change as techniques for prevention and cure of infections improved. Nor did they change as a result of demonstrations in England in the late 1940s and early 1960s that maternal care and even home maternal care (Miller, 1948, cited in Klaus & Kennell, 1976) did not increase infections or substantially raise mortality rates.[17] As Klaus and Kennell noted: "Standard textbooks on the care of the newborn from 1945 to 1960 continued to reflect the traditions and fears of the early 1900s, recommending only the most essential handling of the infants and a policy of strict isolation [exclusion of visitors]" (Klaus & Kennell, 1976, p. 6). These recommendations were in part based on a desire to protect prematures from overstimulation, which was seen as overtaxing their limited resources.

Klaus was among the colleagues of Barnett (Barnett, Grobstein, & Seashore, 1972) who started the first study in the United States (in 1964 at the Stanford University Hospital) of

---

[17] Current procedures for monitoring and controlling fluid levels and acid–base balance used with very small or sick prematures could not, of course, be instrumented at home.

the effects of permitting parents in the premature nursery. It established that parent visitation was safe because not only were there no cases of viral or bacterial infections but there were fewer potentially dangerous organisms either on the infants or on objects in their environment. Nurses who had originally been quite skeptical about the innovation found that their routines were not interfered with and that most mothers were a real help in caring for their infants. In fact, nurses became enthusiastic. Nevertheless, nurseries in the United States were slow to change. In 1970 only one third of some 1400 premature nurseries answering a questionnaire allowed mothers to enter. Only 12% allowed mothers to touch their premature babies in the first few days (Barnett et al., 1972, cited in Klaus & Kennell, 1976).

RESEARCH THAT SUPPORTS THE BONDING HYPOTHESIS

What were the actual effects of early contact on the mothers and their premature infants? First, 2 of the 13 mothers selected for the study actually refused to enter the nursery. They feared becoming more attached to their babies and then having to suffer more if they should die. Neither of these 2 families named their baby for a month, though the babies had been declared out of danger well before that.[18]

The 11 mothers who did enter the nursery touched, explored, fed, diapered, and talked and cooed to their babies despite the plastic barrier between them. The investigators felt that the mothers were more committed to their babies, had more confidence in their mothering abilities, and showed greater skill in stimulating and caring for their infants than the mothers who were in the group who did not visit their infants. Although the investigators do not present objective data and may well have been biased, the outcomes seem highly reasonable. The investigators did provide data on the way in which the mothers

touched and explored their babies' bodies. The mothers of full-term babies explored and touched their babies more, and more actively, than the mothers of prematures. Mothers of prematures began to behave more like the mothers of full-term babies by their third visit. Specifically, they increased fingertip contacts, the number of times they touched the trunk as opposed to the extremities,[19] and the proportion of time spent in the *en face* (face-to-face) position. Despite these changes, the mothers of prematures were far behind those of term infants in first contacting their babies. On the third visit they spent about half as much time in contact, and about one third as much time contacting with the palm or contacting the baby's trunk, as mothers of full-term infants on their first visit.

The first two major long-term studies of the effects of separation on mother–infant interaction and development of premature infants were done at Stanford University (Leifer, Leiderman, Barnett, & Williams, 1972) and at Case Western Reserve University (Klaus, Jerauld, Kreger, McAlpine, Steffa, & Kennell, 1972; Klaus & Kennell, 1970, 1976). At both places one group of mothers was allowed in the Intensive Care Unit (ICU) in the first 5 days after birth and the other group was allowed only visual contact for the first 21 days. In the Stanford study, a comparison group of mothers of full-term infants had the usual contacts at feeding time for the 3 days they were hospitalized. In both places the early and late contact groups were run at separate times. The investigators found it impossible to run them simultaneously because the staff would not allow only some mothers to have contact and not others. Although subjects were thus not randomly assigned, there is no reason to assume that the population was different in one year than in another. The Stanford groups were all middle class and the Case Western Reserve groups covered a range of social classes.

Let us look at each study separately. In the Stanford study (Leifer et al., 1972), the early contact mothers were free to visit their babies in the intensive care unit as frequently as they wished, yet they actually visited only once every 6 days on the average. Thus this group

---

[18] It is interesting that in a number of cultures where infant mortality is high it is the custom not to name infants for considerable periods of time after birth. For example, in Egypt, Rosenblith was told that it is difficult to get good infant mortality figures because parents do not register the birth of a baby for several weeks or until they feel it is sure to live for some months. When neonatal mortality was higher, births were registered even later.

[19] Anyone familiar with a premature nursery will readily understand why the mother may be inhibited from touching the baby's trunk.

made only 3 to 4 more visits than the low contact group did. Either the privilege was not seen as one, or the practical difficulties of arranging a visit to the hospital did not permit parents to take advantage of the privilege. It is thus not surprising that there were few differences between early and late contact mothers of prematures, although the late contact mothers did feel less capable. In contrast, mothers of preterm babies differed from those of full-term babies in that they had less physical and social contact with their infants.

There was, however, one incidental difference between early and late contact mothers that impressed the investigators. At the start of the study, all mothers in both groups were married and intended to keep their infants. Despite this there was a large differential in divorce rates by the study's end: one divorce out of 22 mothers in the early contact group and 5 out of 22 in the late contact group (Leifer et al., 1972). Although one cannot put much faith in uncontrolled incidental findings, the role of the stress of coping with a premature baby is a reasonable factor in the increased divorce rate, and is supported by the findings of Rosenfield (1980) who found serious marital disturbances centered on conflicts related to the infants in several families in her study. Perhaps it is plausible that even such limited early contact, given its relation to greater feelings of competence, did help.

The mother–infant pairs in the Case Western Reserve study, like those at Stanford, were assigned to treatment groups (early or late contact) on the basis of when the delivery occurred. In this study, time-lapse movies[20] were made of the mothers feeding their infants. The films were made just before discharge from the hospital and one month later when the babies were brought back. In addition, Bayley developmental examinations were given to the babies just before their discharge from the hospital and at 9, 15, and 21 months of age. A Stanford–Binet IQ test was given the infants at 42 months of age. Differences related to treatment groups were few whether maternal or infant behaviors were examined. Mothers with

early contact looked more at their babies during feeding. IQs were higher for the 18 out of 53 early contact babies who were available for testing at 42 months (by 14 points on the average). The degree to which these 18 were representative of the total sample cannot be determined; hence it is impossible to interpret the finding.

A separate study at Case Western Reserve (Fanaroff, Kennell, & Klaus, 1972, cited in Klaus & Kennell, 1976) found that low frequency of visiting was related to a number of the negative outcomes that first stimulated those working with premature infants to study the effects of contact (or "bonding"). Only 2% of the mothers who visited their babies more than 3 times in 2 weeks battered, abandoned, or fostered their babies, but 25% of mothers who visited less than 3 times did so. This was in a nursery where mothers could telephone and visit as often as they wished. Although these differences are impressive, they are open to two quite contrasting interpretations because, as is the case with all correlational studies, extraneous variables may influence the findings. Specifically, the *reasons* some parents visit more than others rather than the *number* of visits may be what influenced the outcomes. Those who favor the bonding hypothesis would be inclined to assume that the differences in frequency of visits were due to a variety of reasons that are not relevant to the outcomes, such as distance from home to the hospital and transportation difficulties. If this were so, the correlation of frequency of visiting with outcome variables could reasonably be attributed to better bonding among high-frequency visitors. In contrast, those skeptical of the bonding hypothesis would point out that high-frequency visitors might differ from low-frequency visitors in ways that do influence outcome. For example, mothers who are unstable prior to delivery would be likely to visit less and also more likely to abuse, abandon, or foster their babies regardless of the frequency of visits to the hospital. Likewise, if the mother found her newborn baby unattractive[21] or unrewarding, she would probably visit the

---

[20] Movies made in extremely slow motion so that frames are exposed after longer lapses of time than are needed for natural movement. They require less film to shoot, and less time is needed to watch and analyze them.

[21] Nurses who are experienced in caring for prematures, and those not so experienced, have been shown to be able to rate reliably the differential attractiveness of premature infants (Corter, Trehub, Boukydis, Celhoffer, & Minde, 1978).

baby less frequently and also (and independently) be more likely to abuse it. Rosenfield (1980) has found evidence that indirectly supports this hypothesis. She found that mothers of low-birth-weight babies in an experimental program of extra stimulation gradually increased their frequency of visiting over the course of the study to a greater degree than did mothers of control babies. The data in Chapter 2 support the likelihood that the stimulated babies became more appealing to their mothers, thus stimulating the more frequent visits. A third important difference between high- and low-frequency visitors might be marital stress. In the same study, Rosenfield found incidental evidence in favor of this hypothesis. Three of her families were experiencing serious marital stress and all three exhibited unusual visiting patterns.

Thus, the findings of both Fanaroff and colleagues (1972) and Rosenfield (1980) are consistent with the hypothesis that the characteristics of the mother that influence her behavior during the postpartum period, including her frequency of visits, also affect her child rearing behaviors at later ages. If this interpretation is correct, researchers should look for continuing, long-term influences of mother and baby on each other rather than for strong effects of critical experiences in the first few hours or days after birth.

RESEARCH THAT CHALLENGES THE BONDING HYPOTHESIS

Neither these studies nor the literature as a whole allow us to determine which of these two positions is correct. The evidence in favor of the bonding hypothesis has been sporadic at best, and evidence that disconfirms or fails to support the bonding hypothesis has been growing in recent years. We will separate these studies into two groups: (1) those that explored mothers' bonding responses themselves, and (2) those that explored the long-term consequences for the offspring of their mothers' hypothesized failure to bond properly.

Remember that the bonding hypothesis includes the theory that mothers of preterm infants should have more difficulty bonding than mothers of term infants because preterm infants are separated from their mothers during the hypothesized critical period for bonding. A

number of recent studies have suggested that infants at risk (premature or otherwise) receive more, not fewer, favorable interactions. Compared to normal infants they have been found to receive more interaction, holding, and affection from their mothers (Campbell, 1977; Crawford, 1982; Field, 1977). Their cries elicit more tender and effective responses from adults (Zeskind, 1980). Furthermore, among high risk babies, those whose obstetrical and postnatal course was less optimal received more interactions from their mothers despite the fact that they could be described as less rewarding. They cried and fussed more, slept more, and made fewer nondistress vocalizations. Good sample sizes and controls and the partial replications of these results (true for various of the studies cited) make it likely that these results are replicable. In addition, all the results are in the same direction, so that although the size of the relations between risk and maternal interaction is not great, they strongly suggest that most mothers of nonoptimal babies provide compensatory care for them rather than neglect or abuse them.

The second group of studies that challenge the bonding hypothesis deals with infant outcomes. In the two studies we will describe, the major finding was that experience in the neonatal period was not related to infant behaviors at later times. The first study was a longitudinal study of premature or ill babies who had been separated from their mothers at birth and for prolonged periods thereafter (Rode, Chang, Fisch, & Sroufe, 1981). According to the bonding hypothesis such separation should mean that the babies' mothers could not bond properly. If so, the infants' bonding (or attachment) to their mothers should also be affected. In spite of their early separation, the study showed that they were not more likely than other babies to be insecurely attached to their mothers (security of attachment is discussed in Chapter 12). In addition, other neonatal factors—birth weight, gestational age, number of days spent in neonatal intensive care units, and parental visiting patterns—were also unrelated to security of attachment. These data fail to confirm the bonding hypothesis and support the notion that preterm babies are resilient with respect to their neonatal experiences.

Note that the babies in the study by Rode

and her colleagues were from a relatively privileged group: infants being reared in intact, middle class families. In these circumstances, caring for a sick or premature infant is less stressful than would be the case in families with greater economic and family stresses. Deficits in bonding might be expected to have their strongest effects when the mother–infant pair is under stress. It is therefore reassuring to look at a second study of infant outcomes that has disadvantaged babies as its subjects. In this study, Bakeman and Brown (1980; Brown & Bakeman, 1980) studied the relation between mother–infant interactions and subsequent development in both preterm and term babies. The preterm babies in this study were all healthy enough to be out of intensive care by 24 hours of age. Standard hospital practices were followed and thus the term babies had not been separated from their mothers as long as the preterm babies. Interactions were assessed in three 30-minute sessions devoted primarily to feeding. There were profound differences between the two groups in the nature of their interactions during the neonatal period. Nevertheless, there were no relations between the interaction scores (taken one at a time or together) and the Bayley Mental Development Index at either 12 or 24 months, or to the Stanford–Binet IQ at 3 years of age. Furthermore, although knowing whether the baby was preterm or term helped to predict later IQ, adding knowledge about the nature of early feeding interactions with their mothers did not improve the prediction. These data clearly do not support the hypothesis that the neonatal period is critical for later infant development. In fact, they suggest that the opposite may be true. Because striking differences in early mother–infant interactions had no long-term effect on subsequent development, the neonatal period might in fact be a time in which infants are "buffered" against any long-term consequences of their early interactions.

CONCLUSIONS

We have seen both evidence that suggests that early contact experiences influence mother–infant outcomes and evidence that suggests that they are not important determinants of later maternal behaviors or infant outcomes. Finding apparently contradictory results often means that research questions are inappropriate or are being asked in an inappropriate fashion. One problem is that the original hypothesis was formulated as a critical period hypothesis, that is, that the necessity for bonding at birth is biologically based and therefore crucial for all mother–infant pairs. The research we have described renders that formulation unlikely, but it may be that lack of early contact has deleterious effects in some contexts or with some women. For example, it may be that certain mothers, such as those who avoid visiting their infants in the hospital even though it would be feasible, have trouble dealing with the fact that they have given birth to an at-risk infant. The lack of early contact may intensify their difficulties in accepting their babies; alternatively, early contact and other early support services may help them to overcome their difficulties. Klaus and Kennell designed a new study to try to answer some of these problems. They were attempting to control for the number of visits and give support for touching and caretaking as well as special guidance in understanding needs and responsiveness (or lack of it) in prematures. Unfortunately, they were not able to maintain the study (Kennell, personal communication, Spring, 1984).

Regardless of the research data's lack of clarity, it is clear that there are many changes in the practices of neonatal intensive care units and that parents in many hospitals are no longer told not to touch their premature or sick infant unless absolutely necessary, and may be encouraged to visit frequently. Indeed, these changes make it impossible to do experimental studies in many hospitals.

Bonding to Term Infants

If the evidence on the importance of immediate and continuing postpartum contact to maternal bonding is tenuous for premature infants, the evidence and experimental data for bonding to term infants is even more so. Generalizations from samples that are fairly modest in size and not very representative are being used as support for a sensitive period immediately after birth for the formation of the maternal bond to the infant. Although the personal preference of the authors would be to choose the type of contact that is advocated as a result of the sensitive period hypothesis, we would not feel guilty if for some reason this type of contact were not possible. Let us look at the evidence to see why we believe that personal preference rather than the hypothesized sensitive period is the appropriate criterion for choosing how much contact a mother has with her newborn.

The first study done by Klaus and colleagues on bonding to term infants (Klaus et al., 1972) included 28 mothers of term babies. The mother–infant pairs were randomly assigned to experimental and control groups and the groups were matched on parity (all mothers having their first infant), age (average age about $18\frac{1}{2}$ years), marital status (about 65% unmarried), race (all but 1 in each group were Black), and SES (very low). The mean birth weights and sex distributions for the two groups did not differ, nor did the amount of nursing care received or length of time spent in the hospital (almost 4 days). In short, the study is a true experiment with random assignment of subjects, but the subjects are not representative of the population at large.

The control groups in this study received the routine treatment for that hospital: a glimpse of their baby at birth, another brief contact at 6 to 8 hours, and then every 4 hours for feeding. The experimental group had their nude babies in bed with them for 1 hour in the first 2 hours after birth and then had their babies for an extra 5 hours on each of the next 3 days. Hence the experiment does not test the hypothesis of a critical period immediately after birth. Rather, it asks whether exposure to infants in the first 2 hours *coupled with* greater than average exposure throughout the hospital stay will affect the dependent variables assessed.

When the babies were 28–32 days of age, their mothers answered a questionnaire concerning their behaviors toward and feelings about their babies. Their interactions during a feeding session and during the physical examination of the baby were videotaped and then scored **blind**, that is, by persons who did not know which group a pair belonged to. The extra contact mothers spent more time during feedings either fondling their babies or in the *en face* position or a combination of the two. They also had higher scores on the question-

naire items presumed to index attachment, a finding that is difficult to interpret because they could also be claimed to describe overinvolvement.

The mother–infant pairs were assessed again during the infants' physical checkups at 1 year of age. Of the 25 behaviors measured, only 2 yielded significant differences between the extended contact group and the controls. These were that the extended contact mothers spent more time near the examining table and soothing their infants (Kennell et al., 1974), behaviors that Brazelton suggested (in comments included in Klaus & Kennell, 1976) might be interpreted as overprotective rather than loving. Follow ups on 5 children when they were 2 years old (Ringler, Kennell, Jarvella, Navjosky, & Klaus, 1975) and of a few more (a total of 9) at 5 years of age (Ringler, Trause, Klaus, & Kennell 1978) yielded some additional differences between the groups, although some findings were contradictory to earlier ones.

Klaus and Kennell (1976) concluded: "These findings suggest that just 16 extra hours of contact within the first three days of life affect maternal behavior for one year and possibly longer, and they offer support for the hypothesis of a maternal sensitive period soon after birth" (p. 59). They also call attention to the idea that the effects might have been stronger had the infants been placed with the mother immediately after birth and left with her continuously, and had the mothers not received any medication.

These data are impossible to interpret with respect to the original hypothesis of a sensitive period for bonding, because the extended contact group were given extra contact throughout their hospital stay, not just in the first 24 hours after birth. Furthermore, the mothers studied were lower class, young, Black, and usually unmarried. Hence, at best the findings could be generalized only to a similar sample.

In another study, Klaus and Kennell (1976), with Guatemalan colleagues, did test the critical period hypothesis directly because only immediate contact was varied. Mothers in the experimental group had their babies and privacy for 45 minutes on the delivery table (nude, under a heat panel) immediately after delivery. Mothers in the control group had their babies taken away immediately after birth. Six months after giving birth, more mothers from the immediate contact group were still breast feeding their babies; their babies had gained 1½ pounds more than those of the controls; and they had fewer infections. The differences in weight gain and frequency of infections may actually reflect the advantages of breast feeding over bottle feeding. Mothers' milk provides better immunity and avoids the contamination in bottled milk preparation that is common in the very low SES population sampled in this study. Thus all the differences found in this study may have been due to the early contact's facilitation of breast feeding rather than to bonding effects. Other studies have also found that contact immediately after birth helps to establish breast feeding (Souzea et al., 1974; Winters, 1973; both cited in Klaus & Kennell, 1976). However, early contact was confounded with rooming in and special aid for breast feeding in Souzea and colleagues' study. The mechanism by which this early contact affects nursing may be hormonal rather than psychological. The results of that study were not replicated in a Guatemalan hospital that served a higher SES population (Klaus & Kennell, 1976). It may be that early contact operates more powerfully in groups that are at risk in terms of socioeconomic factors.

Since the first studies by Klaus, Kennell, and their associates, other laboratories have conducted similar studies to try to replicate their results. The outcomes of the first round of such studies are similar to those of the original group, and they do not permit a clear-cut resolution of the controversy.

Two series of studies in Sweden, one by Schaller, Carlsson, and others at the University of Göteborg and one by de Chateau and colleagues (Carlsson et al., 1978, 1979; de Chateau, 1977a, 1977b, 1980a, 1980b, 1980c; de Chateau, Holmberg, & Jakobsen, 1977; de Chateau & Wiberg, 1977a, 1977b; Schaller, Carlsson, & Larsson, 1979), gave some confirmation for the bonding hypothesis. Both groups (Carlsson et al., 1978; de Chateau & Wiberg, 1977a) found an increase in affective aspects of nursing behavior in the immediate postpartum period for mothers who had extended body contact with their newborns in the first 2 hours. However, the study by Carlsson and colleagues (1979) found no effects

at 6 weeks of age, in contrast to de Chateau and Wiberg who found differences at 3 months, 1 year, and 3 years (de Chateau, 1980b, 1980c; de Chateau & Wiberg, 1977b, 1982).

Although these findings provide some support for the influence of extended contact during the critical postpartum period, they are sporadic, as were those of Klaus and colleagues, who had found differences in only 2 of 25 observational categories (Kennell et al., 1974). For example, de Chateau and Wiberg (1977a) found differences in only 3 of their 35 observational measures in the newborn period, and only 1 of those had any connotation of affection. In their assessment at 3 months, de Chateau and Wiberg (1977b) found differences in only a few of the 61 behavior categories, and none of those was the same for both sexes. Another study that found few differences among many variables tested is that by Vietze and his colleagues (Vietze, O'Connor, Falsey, & Altemeier, 1978). This study also permitted separation of the effects of early contact from those of extended contact. Furthermore, the actual behaviors that differed were rarely the same in different studies, and the differences are not even in the same direction from one age to another. An example of the differences between studies can be found with respect to findings about *en face* contact. Klaus and his colleagues (1972) found that mothers who had received extended contact spent more time *en face* with their babies at 1 month, but Schaller and colleagues (1979) found no differences between experimental and control subjects in *en face* contact either in the first week of life or at 6 weeks of age, and Svedja, Campos, and Emde (1980) found *en face* differences at 36 hours of age only for males. The language findings at 2 years of age were often in the opposite direction from those at 1 year (Ringler et al., 1975, 1978).

Other studies provide even less support for either the critical period view of bonding or for the more general early contact hypothesis. The study by Svedja and colleagues (1980) is particularly notable because it introduced a number of excellent methodological controls. For example, in addition to random assignment of subjects to groups, they used a **double blind** procedure, which means that neither the subjects nor the experimenters knew who was in what group. They also chose response measures that were closely tied to the construct of attachment. Nevertheless, only when the data were analyzed by sex were any significant differences found. There were a higher number of touches to female babies and more *en face* interactions with males in the high contact group. A pooled group of behaviors considered to be affectionate did occur more often in the 10 minutes of free interaction in the experimental group. Entwisle and Doering (1981) found that the amount of contact mothers had with their infants in the first 3 days did not predict nurturant behavior even 3 to 4 weeks later *if* pre-existing differences among mothers were statistically controlled for.

Svedja and colleagues (1980) argue that the positive findings of other studies (for example, de Chateau & Wiberg, 1977a, 1977b; Hales, Lozoff, Sosa, et al., 1977; Klaus et al., 1972) may have been due to the fulfillment of experimenter expectations. Others, who favor the bonding or early contact hypothesis, argue that population differences might account for the differences in results. The subjects in the study by Svedja and colleagues (1980) were high school graduates from middle class, intact families, and the fathers had been present at most deliveries, whereas the original Klaus and Kennell research was based on mothers from deprived circumstances. It is easy to assume that both experimenter expectations and differences in maternal contact could have some profound effects in a deprived population. Klaus and Kennell's associates in Central America found results congruent with this idea. The positive effects of early contact were found in a lower class population but not in a separate study of a more middle class population. Social class cannot account for all positive findings, however. The Swedish study that included long-term follow up found some positive effects, of about the same strength as those found by Klaus and Kennell's associates, in their middle class sample. Thus the inconsistency of findings is not wholly a result of early contact being more important for mothers from deprived circumstances.

To make this complex topic even more complex, a recent German study of middle class, stable families (Grossmann, Thane, & Grossmann, 1981) found effects largely for mothers whose pregnancies were planned and not for those whose pregnancies were unplanned. According to the social class hypothesis, middle class women with planned pregnancies would not be expected to be more like women in deprived circumstances than like middle class women with unplanned pregnancies. In this study, the ethological or bonding variable was manipulated separately from the more general early-contact variable: One group had their nude babies with them for at least 30 minutes after birth (bonding group), one group had rooming in for 5 hours on each of the 10 days in hospital (extended contact group), one group had both the bonding experience and extended contact thereafter, and one group had the standard hospital practice. The primary measure of interest was the amount of cuddling and tender touching that occurred at times other than during caretaking tasks.

Mothers with early contact were highest in tender touching and mothers with extended contact were lowest. But it had been found that an extraneous variable—whether or not the pregnancy had been planned—affected these outcomes. About twice as many mothers in the extended contact group had not planned their pregnancies. When planning was controlled for statistically, there was no longer an effect of extended contact. The effect of early contact was highest for early contact groups who said they had planned their pregnancies. Thus early contact was most helpful for those who seemed least likely to need it.

The positive effects for mothers with planned pregnancies were temporary. By 7 to 9 days after giving birth, the frequency of tender touches by the experimental mothers had decreased and those of the control mothers had increased, with the result that there were no longer any significant differences between them. When the attachment behaviors of the infants were tested at 12 months, no differences were found to result from either early postpartum contact or extended contact. Bonding advocates would point out that the effects might have been stronger if only first-time mothers were considered (half the sample), because Klaus and Kennell's mothers had all been first-time mothers. One bonding advocate has suggested (Anderson, 1977) that a major weakness of almost all studies of bonding is that contact is given according to an experimental protocol and not according to the mothers' wishes or the baby's demands. More technically, contact is on a scheduled, not a self-regulatory, basis and this would be expected to weaken any positive effects.

Summary of Bonding Research

It is clear from the research on maternal bonding that strong conclusions are unwarranted. If the validity of the hypotheses were determined by counting the findings for or against them, the bonding hypothesis would surely be invalid. In virtually every study there have been more similarities than differences between extended contact and control groups. In fact, in most of the studies the proportion of positive findings (differences) to negative findings has been so small that many of the positive findings are likely to be chance events. If the criterion for significance is a *p* level of .05, then 5 of every 100 findings will be significant by chance. Therefore, if 50 differences were tested, as was typical in these studies, 2 or 3 of them would be significant by chance alone.

Although our review may seem harsh, note that in two recent reviews of this literature by psychologists, one (McCall, 1982) has conclusions very like those presented here and the other (Lamb, 1982) is even harsher. The abstract of Lamb's review states: ". . . these [bonding] conclusions are shown to have been based on equivocal findings obtained in methodologically impoverished studies. . . . No positive long-term effects have been demonstrated" (p. 763).

Science does not, however, proceed entirely by tallying scores for and against a hypothesis. Inconsistent findings sometimes mean that the research question has not been properly asked. In the case of bonding, the strong form of the hypothesis—that there is a biologically-based universal critical period during which mothers *must* have contact with their babies in order to develop a strong emotional bond to them—is clearly *not* correct. Nevertheless, early or extended or enriched contact may be an important variable in some contexts. Restricting access to their babies may have deleterious effects on some mothers and not on others. Greater difficulties in bonding might be expected in mothers who feel a

high degree of stress and have limited resources to deal with it, who feel inadequate because of inexperience or for other reasons, or who have at-risk babies, a factor which could contribute to both previous problems. Effects of bonding practices may be found only in mother–infant pairs in which the mothers are at the extremes with respect to one or more of these variables. Further research would be necessary to determine whether there are particular kinds of mothers (or even pregnancies) who could be helped.

Another factor that might limit the finding of bonding effects is that early contact might only influence certain areas of maternal behaviors, or certain mother–infant relationships, or certain children's behaviors. The clearest effects found to date have been those related to nursing, where early contact seems to result in a better (or at least longer) nursing relationship. Certain areas of infant development may also be more likely to be affected. A logical place to look for them would be in the nature of toddlers' attachments to their mothers, because in other research contexts attachment has been shown to be related to mothers' emotional responses to their babies. At least two studies have failed to find a relation between neonatal contact and later attachment. However, because many other influences may have affected the mother–infant relationship between birth and the time attachment is measured (typically at around 1 year) and because the standard measures of attachment leave out important areas of infant love (see Chapter 12), the existence of a relation between bonding practices and a baby's love for mama is not ruled out.

Let us conclude by returning to practical applications relevant to bonding. On the basis of the bonding research alone, there is no compelling reason to force all mothers to have early or extended contact with their babies. Most mother–infant pairs seem to compensate easily for any negative effects stemming from being separated during the postpartum period. Grossmann, Thane, and Grossmann (1981) have data that suggest such a compensatory mechanism. Nevertheless, separation may have a negative influence on some mothers. Other mothers may avoid early contact because they are having difficulty accepting their newborn, and additional contact and help during the immediate postpartum time might enable these mothers to work through their negative feelings and thereby reduce the chances of later neglect or battering.

Looking at the opposite side, we would like to repeat our hope that the weakness of the findings on the effects of maternal bonding will not be used as an excuse to keep mothers and their infants separated in the hospital. Although the separation may do no permanent harm for most mother–infant pairs, providing contact in a way that is acceptable to the mother surely does no harm and gives much pleasure to many mothers. Anything that may make the postpartum period more pleasurable surely is worthwhile, a conclusion much like that reached by McCall (1982).

DISCUSSION ISSUES

Vulnerability in the Perinatal Period

In this chapter, as in Chapters 2 and 4, the issue of fetal vulnerability and relative invulnerability arises. Why do some fetuses suffer great damage, some moderate damage, and others no apparent damage from a given environmental stress? For any given causal factor, there are a wide range of effects.

In our discussion of the effects of prematurity in Chapter 2, we pointed out that some infants are more affected by a given degree of prematurity than others. We indicated that the postnatal environment might play a major role in whether or not, or to what degree, infants might be handicapped because of their prematurity. For example, whether they suffer growth retardation may depend on the adequacy of their diet, and whether they suffer intellectual deficits may depend on diet, intellectual stimulation, and adequacy of emotional relationships. In addition, the biological constitution of the infant prior to and at birth may play a role in determining the outcome. Each of these factors may make infants more vulnerable to prematurity.

In Chapter 4 we saw that a disease transmitted to the fetus could have greater or lesser effects. We speculated that the varying degrees of vulnerability were caused by differences in the severity of the disease. This could be due to a lesser exposure, or to the fetal immune system's ability to provide protection, an aspect of biological makeup.

In Chapter 5 we have discussed the effects of stresses such as (1) drugs transmitted to the fetus just prior to or during birth, (2) partial or total loss of oxygen supply during delivery, and (3) too much compression of the head during delivery. We emphasized that it is difficult to determine the effects of a given delivery factor on the fetus because of the complex network of factors in which any one is entwined. Nevertheless, when all factors are equal—to the greatest degree that can be measured—for a group of neonates, they are not all equally affected. Of 3 infants of the same sex, birth weight, gestational age, SES, and ethnic group whose oxygen supply was interrupted for the same number of minutes, one may be clearly damaged and remain so, one may be clearly damaged and appear to recover fully, and the third may not be detectably damaged. It is possible that different parts of the brain are more affected in one than in another and this may determine some differences in outcome. It is also clear that some babies seem able to withstand any given stress better than others.

Although most of the vulnerability factors we have discussed are biological, the social–cognitive environment is just as important. Social class and its related environmental factors appear to affect the extent to which prematurity affects IQ. Maternal variables may influence the degree to which separation in the immediate postpartum period affects the mother–infant relationship. In the remainder of this book we will discuss many more instances of the effects of the social and cognitive environment on vulnerability.

Researchers in the field of infancy have made and continue to make good progress in ferreting out causes of vulnerability, but that does not mean that individual differences can be eliminated. Some infants are invulnerable to one or another of the causal factors in either the biological or social environments. The example of asphyxiation during delivery is a good biological example; a social example follows. Some teen-aged, poor, unmarried mothers without extensive family support and whose medical care leaves much to be desired become adequate or good mothers of their infants. Why were they so invulnerable to their social and health stresses? Are there hidden protective factors in their social life histories, or are they constitutionally (biologically) different? We are a long way from knowing the answers to these fascinating questions.

Studying invulnerability is a difficult enterprise that involves many conceptual, procedural, and statistical complexities. For example, outcome is measured by number and degree of defects, but children who show no defects may not be invulnerable. Rather they may have had the genetic potential to achieve a superior level of attainment that was thwarted by environmental experiences such as delivery difficulties or poor prenatal nutrition. Thus the dependent measure is necessarily always inaccurate. Determining whether children have been affected is helped by comparing children exposed to a potential damaging factor with siblings who were not. Because of the difficulties of doing such research and because researchers in these areas typically are more concerned with learning how to prevent defects or help infants cope with them, little research on invulnerability as such has been done.[22]

The emphasis on individual differences throughout this book is meant to stress the role of the organism that reacts—to a drug, or to being talked to, or to being cared for by many or a few persons. This is one way to avoid oversimplistic models in which exposure to factor *A* is taken to lead inevitably to bad condition *B*, but it also emphasizes the fact that each fetus, baby, infant is a unique organism—unique genetically (unless there is an identical twin) and phenotypically. The interaction of these unique characteristics with any causal event will produce varied results as long as the factor is not lethal for all cases; indeed even the amount of poison needed to produce death differs for different people of the same weight and sex.

---

[22] We have mentioned the National Perinatal Research Project as a source for some of the prospective information on the effects of factors discussed in Chapters 4 and 5. Its original name was the Collaborative Project for the Assessment of Perinatal Factors in Cerebral Palsy, Mental Retardation, and Related Neurological Disorders. In its planning stages the hope was often expressed that it would not only shed light on the relations between events in pregnancy and delivery and outcomes for the baby, but would also explain why some babies exposed to negative factors do not seem to show negative effects. Unfortunately, we have not yet seen any analyses of these data addressed to this issue.

Research Issues

We dealt with two topics on which the research was limited to correlational studies because subjects could not be assigned to groups. The first was the effects on the offspring of medication given to the mother during labor and delivery. Randomly selected mothers cannot be asked to undergo labor and delivery without medication, and therefore samples are limited to mothers who choose to use or to forego medication. These two groups of mothers, at least in the United States, are likely to be different in several ways, examples of which were given in the chapter. Researchers could conceivably use the technique of using the mother as her own control (as described in Chapters 3 and 4) and might find a sample of women who used medication in one pregnancy but not in another and whose deliveries were otherwise comparable. However, detailed data on the development of the first child would usually not be available.

The second example of the limits of correlational research was the topic of Leboyer deliveries. Without random assignment of subjects to groups, parents' expectations about the superiority of the Leboyer techniques or other parental personality and motivational variables may confound the results. This research also demonstrated the problems of attempting to assign subjects randomly to groups in a situation in which strong preferences are the rule. Only one third of the women the researchers asked agreed to participate in a study that tried to do this. Thus the resulting findings of no differences between Leboyer deliveries and more standard deliveries can only be generalized to women who have no strong preexisting preferences.

The section on obstetric medication presented an example of a variable that caused short-term deficits but not long-term deficits. In the study of psychological effects, one can never assume that just because there are short-term effects there will be long-term effects. We will see more examples of this later in the book. We will also see the opposite kind of situation: no short-term effects but subsequent long-term effects. Such effects are called sleeper effects, because they initially lie dormant, only to pop up later. Such discontinuities of effects also pose problems of generalization. It is impossible to assume that long-term effects will occur just because there are short-term effects, or that the absence of short-term effects indicates there will be no long-term effects.

The sections on obstetrical drugs and on bonding provide examples of the role statistics play in reaching conclusions from data. In studies of long-term effects of obstetric medication, Brackbill and Broman (unpublished) repeatedly found that a large proportion of the significant effects of a given drug were in the opposite direction from what was expected. In each study in the bonding research, only a small proportion of the measured outcome variables were significantly related to contact immediately after birth in the expected direction. Such patterns of results may indicate that the true situation is that there are no differences between groups. This would occur in two types of circumstances: (1) The number of significant effects, both in favor of and counter to the predicted direction, are a small proportion of the total number of tests conducted; and (2) there are approximately equal numbers of results in each direction. The first type exists because of the significance level of statistical tests. An effect is significant at a p level (probability level) of .05 or .01. That means that 5 of 100 or 1 of 100 statistical tests will show a significant effect *merely by chance*. In many exploratory studies that use a large number of dependent variables or need to control for many variables, it is not unusual to run dozens or hundreds of tests and thereby to obtain some spurious findings (ones that appear to be valid but are really due to chance). The second type, that the significant findings are half in one direction and half in the opposite direction, is also based on chance. If there are truly no differences between groups and the significant findings are an accident, then the direction of the differences would be due to chance also. Just as would happen in flips of a coin, half the time the medicated group would be superior and half the time the unmedicated group would be. The only conclusive way to determine whether the results are a statistical artifact or not is to replicate the findings; that is, to conduct another study measuring the same variables in the same way and finding the same relation between causal and outcome variables.

This chapter also provided a number of examples in which results were not consistent in two or more studies. The studies of bonding varied in a variety of ways: the operational definitions of early contact, the characteristics of the babies (preterm versus full term), the pre-experimental characteristics of the mother–infant pairs (such as social class, education, and whether the mother had previous children), the ages at which outcomes were measured, the particular outcomes assessed, and the measures used to assess them. When many such differences exist, it is difficult to conclude whether the inconsistencies in results mean that the hypothesis is wrong or whether they mean that the hypothesis is true under some conditions and not under others. To determine which of these alternatives is correct, future research may vary these parameters within the same experiment. In bonding studies to date, this has been done only with respect to the operational definition of early contact. Recent studies have independently varied contact in the first hours after birth (the presumed critical period for bonding) and extended contact throughout the hospital stay. Unfortunately, this clarification through careful use of operational definitions of the experimental contact variables did not clarify the inconsistencies in the results of the research, but it did eliminate one possible explanation for the inconsistencies. Future studies will have to follow the same procedure for other inconsistencies. For example, one step would be to compare directly, in the same experiment, mothers who are more likely to suffer from lack of early contact (such as first-time mothers who are uneducated and under stress) to those who are less vulnerable (such as experienced, educated mothers under minimal stress).

The discussion of the problems of ferreting out causes for inconsistencies in findings makes it clear that it often takes great care to make studies comparable enough to produce consistent findings. Such problems lead some researchers to design studies that are as comparable to earlier research as possible. Unfortunately, this strategy is not always possible in research in real-world environments. For example, hospital practices have changed, even though they may not have changed rapidly enough to suit some. Thus, effects may not replicate because certain conditions have changed; for example, the number of different drugs and the dosage of each drug used may have declined since earlier research was done.[23] Given the almost fad-like quality of some aspects of childbirth and infant care, this problem is particularly important in the research described in this chapter. In Chapter 8 we will see that studies re-establishing norms for physical and motor development found that the norms had substantially changed over the years, presumably due to better nutrition and health care.

Several examples of the influence of experimenter and subject expectations arose in this chapter. We discussed the role of expectations in Chapter 3 when we described a study of XYY boys in which parents were not told that their boys were XYY for fear that the parents would then expect the boys to be more aggressive, and those expectations might become self-fulfilling prophecies. Parental expectations may strongly influence the outcome in many childbirth practices, such as Leboyer deliveries, birthing position, and even obstetrical medication. In other circumstances, the parents may not bring such biases to the study, but they may develop expectations if the experimenter informs them of the hypotheses of the study.

Experimenter expectations may also influence the results, and this is a more common problem for research. In the bonding research, the original research by Klaus and Kennell and their colleagues suffered from this potential bias because they believed in the importance of early contact. In later research, theirs and others, a control for one form of experimenter expectation was introduced by having the outcome behaviors coded blind; that is, the coding was done by people who did not know what groups the subjects were in. This removed the possible influence of bias on the part of the coders (often a potent source of bias), but other potential expectation effects were not controlled.

---

[23] Sometimes the study itself influences practices. For example, many doctors have commented that in hospitals where the National Perinatal Research Project was being run, the use of obstetric drugs declined during the course of the study. They thought this was due to the presence of someone in the delivery room monitoring the baby, which made medical personnel more aware of "dopey" sluggish babies who needed considerable resuscitative efforts.

A better procedure would be to use a double blind procedure. In such a procedure, neither the subjects nor the experimenters know the experimental predictions so that the expectations of both are no longer potential confounding variables. Svedja and colleagues (1980) used a double blind procedure and found no effects of early contact. It is no surprise, then, that that study attributed earlier positive findings to such expectations. Of course, other researchers disagree with their conclusions because of another methodological problem; that is, there are other differences, especially sampling differences, between the confirming studies and Svedja and colleagues' study that might account for the differences in results.

Parenting: Childbirth

The customs surrounding childbirth have varied widely in different cultures and at different points in history. Hence, it is next to impossible to talk about the "natural" or correct way to give birth to a child. At present, fads associated with childbirth and with people's attitudes toward it may lead to extreme positions on both sides of what might seem an attractive middle ground.

We, personally, are concerned about some of the customs associated with birth, and in some instances we have not provided enough historical background to give both extremes. For example, western cultures have swung between extreme reactions with respect to the use of anesthetics in childbirth. When Queen Victoria received chloroform for a delivery, ministers and others decried its use. According to them, God had ordained that Eve should bring forth children in sorrow; hence women "in travail" should not be given pain relievers. In the second quarter of this century, many women were delivered under general anesthesia. Today most doctors and mothers are shifting away from both general anesthesia and other pain killing drugs. We hope that this chapter has shown that women should not be compelled to return to the Victorian theory that they should not be allowed any pain killing drugs.

In the United States, childbirth has shifted from a midwife-attended event in the home to a medically-attended event in the hospital, frequently with marked usage of drugs. Many doctors used to promise their pregnant patients, who were happy to have the promise, that anesthesia would prevent them from experiencing any of the birth process—they "wouldn't know a thing." The pendulum has swung and now many mothers not only demand to know everything, but to know it in a totally unmedicated state.

Today parents in many places have many options open to them. Maternity hospitals and the maternity wings of general hospitals have become much more flexible. Hence prospective parents should inform themselves about the variety of options available so that they can choose those that will make the birth of their child as positive an experience as possible. To make such decisions, parents must weigh the medical arguments against their own desires. The first step in such decision making should be to assess the effectiveness of various procedures in saving lives and in preventing biological and psychological damage to both mother and infant. Much of the research described in this chapter was designed to do just that. Some form of preparation and education for childbirth is also desirable, especially because women growing up in today's world have much less experience with childbirth than their ancestors may have had. Childbirth classes are widely available, as are books on pregnancy and childbirth (see, for example, Boston Women's Health Book Collective, 1979; Hotchner, 1979). Discussion with the mother's obstetrician or midwife about their attitudes toward the various options and their general attitude toward the birthing experience is important. It is also important to determine the practices of the hospital and its options for styles of birthing. It is even more important to discuss the doctor's attitude toward who is to be saved in the highly unlikely event that a choice between the survival of the infant or the mother has to be made.

This chapter has presented ways to examine research findings in this field and has suggested the sorts of questions to ask as a basis for making choices where possible. In the absence of data to indicate dangers associated with a choice, a mother should choose what is most satisfying to her. She should also feel free to reject any practice that is fashionable at the time in the absence of good data to support its safety if she finds it personally undesirable.

SUMMARY

Complications of Delivery

A number of aspects of the birth process may affect the well-being of the newborn. The speed of delivery, presentation at delivery, and whether and how the umbilical cord is entwined around the fetus all may influence the neonatal outcome. They may lead to death, to oxygen deprivation, brain hemorrhages, or to damage to the spinal cord.

Ways to Avoid or Counteract Complications

Fetal monitoring by a belt on the mother's abdomen or an electrode on the baby's scalp is often used to determine heart rate and thus indicate whether sufficient oxygen is reaching the fetus. If any indication of abnormality arises, blood samples are often taken from the baby's scalp. If fetal distress is indicated, the baby is often delivered by Caesarean section. The use of monitoring is controversial because fetal distress is often detected when none exists, because it poses some risk, and because it prevents the mother from moving around, which may lengthen labor.

There are three major interventions or aids that can be used to speed up delivery when that is considered desirable. They are: administration of oxytocin, use of mechanical aids (forceps and vacuum extraction), and Caesarean sections. High forceps are known to be dangerous and have been replaced by C. sections. Low forceps and vacuum extractions are less invasive and are often used, particularly when the mother has been anesthetized. Caesareans are widely used because they are relatively safe for the mother and often safer for the fetus than other methods of delivery when labor or delivery is complicated. The evidence concerning long-term effects of a C. section on the baby is conflicting and inconclusive.

Drugs Used During Delivery

Several types of drugs are used in connection with childbirth. We focused on those used early in labor to reduce pain or anxiety or both (analgesics, tranquilizers, and sedative-hypnotic agents), anesthetics used during delivery, and drugs used to speed up delivery by increasing the strength of the contractions. There are substantial numbers of drugs in each of the first two categories and the effects of each are likely to differ.

The complexities of determining the effects of drugs were discussed. The chief factors to be considered are the many combinations of drugs, the dosages, and the timing with respect to the separation of the infant from the mother. One very serious methodological problem stems from using as controls mothers who had no drugs in a culture in which that is not the norm, so that such women are likely to be atypical. Because of these complexities, the data on drug effects are far from conclusive. It is hard to draw firm conclusions other than that inhalant anesthetics, other than nitrous oxide, should probably be avoided. It is also evident that the effects of oxytocin, used to speed up labor, need to be assessed much more carefully, especially because it is used very frequently.

Childbirth Practices

The standard delivery in the United States from the 1940s through the 1960s was in a medical context of illness and surgery. Objections to standard practices have focused on the mother's separation from significant others during labor and delivery, her separation from the newborn after delivery, and the attitude of medical personnel that pregnancy is like an illness and delivery is like a surgical procedure. Infant and maternal mortality rates declined during this period, but the necessity for or even the desirability of many of the practices associated with standard deliveries has been questioned. This type of delivery has been challenged by doctors proposing alternate systems, by feminists challenging the doctor's role, and by many women who want their giving birth to be more psychologically meaningful to them and to the fathers of the babies. One of the first challengers was Dick-Read in England, whose book *Childbirth Without Fear* appeared in 1944. In France, Lamaze developed techniques for controlling the pain of labor and delivery based on the Russian technique of psychoprophylaxis. His techniques and variants thereof are widely followed today, and in the

United States they have increased the involvement of fathers in labor and delivery. Leboyer's technique of birth without violence is designed to make the birthing experience less stressful for infants and, by extension, to promote maternal bonding. Although hard data on the benefits of these systems for mothers or infants are sparse, there is little evidence that they are harmful and it seems clear that these approaches are psychologically meaningful and satisfying to many couples.

A number of doctors in various countries practice deliveries that do not use the standard lithotomy position. Birthing chairs, squatting deliveries, deliveries while seated in wading pools, or while reclining on pillows or the father's lap fit this group. Research indicates that the labor is easier and faster in these positions, so there is less chance for fetal damage and less need to resort to medical interventions.

The home birth movement, which may have any assortment of the features of the other systems, is more controversial. There is a definite chance that harm could come to the mother or fetus in the absence of emergency medical equipment. The chance is markedly increased unless there is careful assessment of risk and good supervision available for the low risk cases for whom it is suitable.

Mother–Infant Bonding

Many people have investigated the hypothesis that there may be a critical period immediately after birth for maternal bonding. The belief stemmed from later problems of babies who had been unusually separated from their mothers (premature and sick babies) and was bolstered by reference to animal behavior. Species that will not accept or nurse their young if separated immediately after birth were used as models. Species that not only do not reject their own young, but accept and nurse other young (and even young of other species) were not considered as models. Generalization from any species to man is always hazardous, but given the prevalence of adoption in preliterate cultures and our own, the latter model seems more appropriate.

Cultures vary in the amount of mother–infant contact they promote, yet healthy children are reared in all of them. Lasting and effective bonds are established between nonbiological parents and their adopted offspring. Thus it is hardly surprising that the research on the importance of immediate post-birth contact has failed to yield clear-cut results in its favor.

REFERENCES

Adamsons, K., & Myers, R.E. (1973) Perinatal asphyxia: Causes, detection and neurologic sequelae. *Pediatrics Clinics of North America, 20,* 465–480.

Aleksandrowicz, M.K. (1974). The effect of pain relieving drugs administered during labor and delivery on the behavior of the newborn: A review. *Merrill-Palmer Quarterly, 20,* 121–141.

Aleksandrowicz, M.K., & Aleksandrowicz, D.R. (1974). Obstetrical pain-relieving drugs as predictors of infant behavior variability. *Child Development, 45,* 935–945.

Aleksandrowicz, M.K., & Aleksandrowicz, D.R. (1976). Obstetrical pain-relieving drugs as predictors of infant behavior variability: A reply to Federman and Yang's critique. *Child Development, 47,* 297–298.

Anderson, G.C. (1977). The mother and her newborn: Mutual caregivers. *Journal of Gynecological Nursing, 6,* 50–57.

Anderson, G.C., Fleming, S., & Vidyasagar, D. (1980, April). *Effect of position on infant behavior and physiologic stabilization during the first four hours postbirth.* Paper presented at the International Conference on Infant Studies, New Haven, CT.

Bakeman, R., & Brown, J.V. (1980). Early interaction: Consequences for social and mental development at three years. *Child Development, 51,* 437–447.

Banta, H.D. (1981, October). *The risks and benefits of episiotomy.* Paper presented at the conference on "Obstetrical management and infant outcome 1981: Implications for future mental and physical development," sponsored by the American Foundation for Maternal and Child Health, Inc., New York.

Banta, H.D., & Thacker, S.B. (1979). *Costs and benefits of electronic fetal monitoring: A review of the literature* (NCHSR Research Report Series, DHEW Publication No. (PHS) 79-3245). Washington, DC: U.S. Government Printing Office.

Barnett, C.R., Grobstein, R., & Seashore, M. (1972).

Personal communication to Klaus & Kennell, cited in Klaus and Kennell, 1976.

Benaron, H.B.W., Tucker, B.E., Andrews, J.P., Boshes, B., Cohen, J., Fromm, E., & Yacorzynski, G.K. (1960). Effect of anoxia during labor and immediately after birth on the subsequent development of the child. *American Journal of Obstetrics and Gynecology,* 1129–1142.

Benaron, H.B., & Tucker, B.E. (1971). The effect of obstetric management and factors beyond clinical control on maternal mortality rates at the Chicago Maternity Center from 1959 to 1963. *American Journal of Obstetrics and Gynecology, 110,* 1113–1118.

Berkson, G. (1974) Social responses of animals and infants with defects. In M. Lewis & L.A. Rosenblum (Eds.), *The effect of the infant on its caregiver.* New York: Wiley-Interscience.

Beynon, C.L. (1975). The normal second stage of labor. *Journal of Obstetrics and Gynecology, 64,* 815–820.

Bjerre, J., & Dahlin, K. (1974). The long-term development of children delivered by vacuum extraction. *Journal of Developmental Medicine and Child Neurology, 16,* 378–381.

Boston Women's Health Book Collective. (1979). *Our bodies, ourselves.* New York: Simon & Schuster.

Bowes, W.A., Jr., Brackbill, Y., Conway, E., & Steinschneider, A. (1970). The effects of obstetrical medication on fetus and infant. *Monographs of the SRCD, 35,* (4, Serial No. 137).

Brackbill, Y. (1974). Unpublished study, cited in Brackbill, 1979a.

Brackbill, Y. (1979a, November). *Effects of obstetric drugs on human development.* Presentation at the American Foundation for Maternal and Child Health, Inc., Symposium, New York.

Brackbill, Y. (1979b). Obstetrical medication and infant behavior. In J. Osofsky (Ed.), *Handbook of infant development.* New York: Wiley.

Brackbill, Y., & Broman, S.H. (Unpublished). Obstetrical medication and development in the first year of life.

Brackbill, Y., Kane, J., Manniello, R.L., & Abramson, D. (1974). Obstetrical meperidine usage and assessment of neonatal status. *Anesthesiology, 40,* 116–120.

Brazelton, T.B. (1961). Psychophysiologic reaction in the neonate. II, The effects of maternal medication on the neonate and his behavior. *Journal of Pediatrics, 58,* 513–518.

Broman, S.H. (1981). Risk factors for deficits in early cognitive development. In G.G. Berg & H.D.

Maillie (Eds.), *Measurement of risk*. New York: Plenum.

Broman, S.H. (1983). Obstetric medications. In C.C. Brown (Ed.), *Childhood learning disabilities and prenatal risk*. Skillman, NJ: Johnson & Johnson Baby Products Co.

Broman, S.H., & Brackbill, Y. (Unpublished). Analysis of obstetrical data from the National Institutes of Health Collaborative Perinatal Study. Unpublished reports based on this have been circulated and are available under the Freedom of Information Act.

Broman, S.H., & Brackbill, Y. (1980). *Obstetric medication and early development*. Paper presented at the annual meeting of the American Association for the Advancement of Science, San Francisco.

Broussard, E.R., & Hartner, M.S.S. (1971). Further consideration regarding maternal perception of the first born. In J. Hellmuth (Ed.), *Exceptional infant: Studies in abnormalities*, Vol. 2. New York: Brunner/Mazel.

Brower, K.R. (1974). *Effects of intranatal drugs on the newborn EEG*. Unpublished master's thesis, University of Hawaii, Honolulu.

Brown, J.V., & Bakeman, R. (1980). Relationships of human mothers with their infants during the first year of life. In R.W. Bell & W.P. Smotherman (Eds.), *Maternal influences and early behavior*. Jamaica, NY: Spectrum.

Brumitt, G.H., & Dowler, J.K. (1984). *Behavioral effects of obstetrical medication on the newborn*. Paper presented at the Fourth Biennial International Conference on Infant Studies, New York.

Budin, P. (1907). *The nursling*. London: Caxton.

Caldeyro-Barcia, R. (1981, October). *The scientific bases for preserving the normal physiology of labor and birth through non-intervention*. Paper presented at the Conference on Obstetrical Management and Infant Outcome, New York.

Campbell, B.K. (1977). An assessment of early mother–infant interaction and the subsequent development of the infant in the first two years of life. *Dissertation Abstracts International, 38,* 1856–1857.

Carlsson, S.G., Fagerberg, H., Horneman, G., Hwang, C.P., Larsson, K., Rodholm, M., Schaller, J., Danielsson, B., & Gundewall, C. (1978). Effects of amount of contact between mother and child on the mother's nursing behavior. *Developmental Psychobiology, 11,* 143–150.

Carlsson, S.G., Fagerberg, H., Horneman, G., Hwang, C.P., Larsson, K., Rodholm, M., Schaller, J., Danielsson, B., & Gundewall, C. (1979). Effects of various amounts of contact between mother and child on the mother's nursing behavior: A follow up study. *Infant Behavior and Development, 2,* 209–214.

Case, B., Corcoran, R., Jeffcoate, N., et al. (1971). Caesarean section and its place in modern obstetric practice. *Journal of Obstetrics and Gynaecology of the British Commonwealth, 78,* 203–214.

Conway, E., & Brackbill, Y. (1970). Delivery medication and infant outcome: An empirical study. In W.A. Bowes, Jr., Y. Brackbill, E. Conway, & A. Steinschneider (Eds.), *The effects of obstetrical medication on fetus and infant* (pp. 24–34). *Monographs of the Society for Research in Child Development, 35* (Serial No. 137).

Corah, N.L., Anthony, E.J., Painter, P., Stern, J.A., & Thurston, D.L. (1965). The effects of perinatal anoxia after seven years. *Psychological Monographs, 79* (Whole No. 596).

Corter, C., Trehub, S., Boukydis, L.F., Celhoffer, L., & Minde, K. (1978). Nurses' judgments of the attractiveness of premature infants. *Infant Behavior and Development, 1,* 373–390.

Cosmi, E.V., & Marx, G.F. (1968). Acid–base status and clinical condition of mother and fetus following methoxythrane anesthesia for vaginal delivery. *British Journal of Anesthesia, 40,* 94–98.

Crawford, J.W. (1982). Mother–infant interaction in premature and full-term infants. *Child Development, 53,* 957–962.

de Chateau, P. (1977a). The influence of early contact on maternal and infant behavior in primiparae. *Birth and the Family Journal, 3,* 149–155.

de Chateau, P. (1977b). The importance of the neonatal period for the development of synchrony in the mother–infant dyad: A review. *Birth and the Family Journal, 4,* 10–23.

de Chateau, P. (1980a). Early post-partum contact and later attitudes. *International Journal of Behavioral Development, 3,* 273–286.

de Chateau, P. (1980b). Effects of hospital practices on synchrony in the development of the infant–parent relationship. In P.M. Taylor (Ed.), *Parent–infant relationships*. New York and London: Grune & Stratton.

de Chateau, P. (1980c). Parent–neonate interaction and its long-term effects. In E.G. Simmel (Ed.), *Early experience and early behavior*. New York: Academic.

de Chateau, P., Holmberg, H., & Jakobsen, K. (1977). A study of factors promoting and inhibiting lactation. *Developmental Medicine and Child Neurology, 19*, 575–584.

de Chateau, P., & Wiberg, B. (1977a). Long-term effect on mother–infant behavior of extra contact during the first hour post-partum, I. First observation at 36 hours. *Acta Paediatrica Scandinavia, 66*, 137–144.

de Chateau, P., & Wiberg, B. (1977b). Long-term effect on mother–infant behavior of extra contact during the first hour post-partum, II. Follow-up at three months. *Acta Paediatrica Scandinavia, 66*, 145–151.

De La Fuente, P., Hernandez-Garcia, J.M., Escalante, J.M., et al. (1971). Caesarean operation: Indications and maternal and fetal mortality. *Contributions to Gynecology and Obstetrics, 3*, 135–141.

Dick-Read, G. (1944). *Childbirth without fear.* New York and London: Harper & Bros.

Entwisle, D.R. & Doering, S.G. (1981). *The first birth: A family turning point.* Baltimore: Johns Hopkins University Press.

Ernhart, C.B., Graham, F.K., & Thurston, D. (1960). Relationship of neonatal apnea to development at three years. *Archives of Neurology, 2*, 504–510.

Evrard, J.R., & Gold, E.M. (1977). Caesarean section and maternal mortality in Rhode Island. *Obstetrics and Gynecology, 50*, 594–597.

Fanaroff, A.A., Kennell, J.H., & Klaus, M.H. (1972). Follow-up of low birth-weight infants—The predictive value of maternal visiting patterns. *Pediatrics, 49*, 288–290.

Federman, E.J. & Yang, R.K. (1976). A critique of "Obstetrical pain-relieving drugs as predictors of infant behavior variability." *Child Development, 47*, 294–296.

Field, T.M. (1977). Effects of early separation, interactive deficits, and experimental manipulation on mother–infant face-to-face interaction. *Child Development, 48*, 763–771.

Field, T.M., & Widmayer, S.M. (1980). Developmental follow up of infants delivered by Caesarean section and general anesthesia. *Infant Behavior and Development, 3*, 253–264.

Freeman, D.W., & Arnold, N.I. (1975). Paracervical block with low doses of chloroprocaine. *Journal of the American Medical Association, 231*, 56–57.

Friedman, E.A., Sachtleben, M.R., & Wallace, A.K. (1979). Infant outcome following induction. *American Journal of Obstetrics and Gynecology, 133*, 718–722.

Friedman, S.L., Brackbill, Y., Caron, A.J., & Caron, R.F. (1978). *Obstetric medication and visual processing in 4- and 5-month-old infants. Merrill-Palmer Quarterly, 24*, 11–128.

Gassner, C.B., & Ledger, W.J. (1976). The relationship of hospital-acquired maternal infection to invasive intrapartum monitoring techniques. *American Journal of Obstetrics and Gynecology, 126*, 33–37.

Graham, F.K., Caldwell, B.M., Ernhart, C.B., Pennoyer, M.M., & Hartmann, A.F., Sr. (1957). Anoxia as a significant perinatal experience: A critique. *Journal of Pediatrics, 50*, 556–569.

Grossman, F.K. (1980, April). *Psychological sequelae of Caesarean delivery.* Paper presented at the International Conference on Infant Studies, New Haven, CT.

Grossmann, K., Thane, K., & Grossmann, K.E. (1981). Maternal tactual contact of the newborn after various postpartum conditions of mother–infant contact. *Developmental Psychology, 17*, 158–169.

Haddad, H., & Lundy, L. (1978). Changing indications for Caesarean section. *Obstetrics and Gynecology, 51*, 133–137.

Haggard, H.W. (1929). *Devils, drugs, and doctors.* New York: Harper & Bros. (Reprinted by Pocket Books, 1946, 1953, 1959.)

Hales, D.J., Lozoff, B., Sosa, R., et al. (1977). Defining the limits of the maternal sensitive period. *Developmental Medicine and Child Neurology, 19*, 454–461.

Horowitz, F.D., Ashton, J., Culp, R., Gaddis, E., Levin, S., & Reichmann, B. (1977). The effects of obstetrical medication on the behavior of Israeli newborn infants and some comparisons with Uruguayan and American infants. *Child Development, 48*, 1607–1623.

Hotchner, T. (1979). *Pregnancy and childbirth: The complete guide for a new life.* New York: Avon Books.

Ingemarsson, I., Westgren, M., & Svenningsen, N.W. (1978). Long-term follow-up of preterm infants in breech presentation delivered by Caesarean section: A prospective study. *Lancet, ii*, 172–175.

Kennell, J.H., Jerauld, R., Wolfe, H., Chesler, D., Kreger, N.C., McAlpine, W., Steffa, M., & Klaus, M.H. (1974). Maternal behavior one year after early and extended post-partum contact. *Developmental Medicine and Child Neurology, 16*, 172–179.

Klaus, M.H., Jerauld, R., Kreger, N.C., McAlpine, W., Steffa, M., & Kennell, J.H. (1972). Maternal attachment: Importance of the first post-partum days. *New England Journal of Medicine, 286*, 460–463.

Klaus, M.H., & Kennell, J.H. (1970). Mothers separated from their newborn infants. *Pediatric Clinics of North America, 17*, 1015–1037.

Klaus, M.H., & Kennell, J.H. (1976). *Maternal–infant bonding.* St. Louis, MO: Mosby.

Konner, M.J. (1980, April). *Functional consequences of nursing frequency among hunter-gatherers.* Paper presented at the International Conference on Infant Studies, New Haven, CT.

Lamb, M.E. (1982). Early contact and maternal–infant bonding: One decade later. *Pediatrics, 70,* 763–768.

Leboyer, F. (1975). *Birth without violence.* New York: Knopf.

Ledger, W.J., Norman, M., Gee, C., et al. (1975). Bacteremia on an obstetric-gynecologic service. *American Journal of Obstetrics and Gynecology, 121,* 205–212.

Leifer, A.D., Leiderman, P.H., Barnett, C.R., & Williams, J.A. (1972). Effects of mother–infant separation on maternal attachment behavior. *Child Development, 43,* 1203–1218.

Lieberman, B.A., Rosenblatt, D.B., Belsey, E., Packer, M., Redshaw, M., Mills, M., Caldwell, J., Notarianni, L., Smith, R.L., Williams, M., & Beard, R.W. (1979). The effects of maternally administered pethidine or epidural bupivicaine on the fetus and newborn. *British Journal of Obstetrics and Gynaecology, 86,* 598–606.

Liebling, A. (1939). Profile: Patron of the preemies. *New York Magazine* (June 3), 20–24.

McCall, R.B. (1982). A hard look at stimulating and predicting development: The cases of bonding and screening. *Pediatrics in Review, 3,* 205–212.

Meier, G.W. (1964). Behavior of infant monkeys: Differences attributable to mode of birth. *Science, 143,* 968–970.

Mendez-Bauer, C., Arroyo, J., Garcia-Ramos, C., et al. (1975). Effects of standing position on spontaneous uterine contractility and other aspects of labor. *Journal of Perinatal Medicine, 3,* 89–100.

Miller, F.J.W. (1948). Home nursing of premature babies in Newcastle-on-Tyne. *Lancet, ii,* 703–705.

Moreau, T., & Birch, H.G. (1974). Relationship between obstetrical general anesthesia and rate of neonatal habituation to repeated stimulation. *Developmental Medicine and Child Neurology, 16,* 612–619.

Morishima, H.O., & Adamson, K. (1967). Placental clearance of mepivicaine following administration to guinea pigs. *Anesthesiology, 28,* 343–348.

Morishima, H.O., Daniel, S.S., Finster, M., Poppers, P.J., & James, L.S. (1966). Transmission of mepivicaine hydrochloride (Carbocaine) across the human placenta. *Anesthesiology, 27,* 147–154.

Moya, F., & Thorndike, V. (1962). Passage of drugs across the placenta. *American Journal of Obstetrics and Gynecology, 84,* 1778–1798.

Murray, A.D., Dolby, R.M., Nation, R.L., & Thomas, D.B. (1981). Effects of epidural anesthesia on newborns and their mothers. *Child Development, 52,* 71–82.

Myers, R.E. (1972). Two patterns of perinatal brain damage and their conditions of occurrence. *American Journal of Obstetrics and Gynecology, 112,* 246–276.

Nelson, N.M., Enkin, M.W., Saigel, S., Bennett, K.J., Milner, R., & Sackett, D.L. (1980). A randomized clinical trial of the Leboyer approach to childbirth. *New England Journal of Medicine, 302,* 655–660.

Neutra, R.R., Fienberg, S.E., Greenland, S., & Friedman, E.A. (1978). Effect of fetal monitoring on neonatal death rates. *New England Journal of Medicine, 299,* 324–326.

Niswander, K.R., & Gordon, M. (Eds.). (1972). *The women and their pregnancies.* Philadelphia: Saunders.

Odent, M. (1982). The milieu and obstetrical positions during labor: A new approach from France. In M.H. Klaus & M.O. Robertson (Eds.), *Birth, interaction, and attachment: Exploring the foundations for modern perinatal care* (pp. 23–28). Skillman, NJ: Johnson & Johnson Baby Products Co.

Odent, M. (1984). *Birth reborn.* New York: Pantheon Books.

Paciornik, M., & Paciornik, C. (1976). Do not disturb the deliverance of Indians. The squatting deliverance confronting the dorsal decubitus deliverance. Annals: III Paraguayan Congress of Gynecology and Obstetrics.

Pederson, F., Zaslow, M., Cain, R., & Anderson, B. (1980, April). *Caesarean childbirth: The importance of a family perspective.* Paper presented at the International Conference on Infant Studies, New Haven, CT.

Petrie, R.H. (1981, October). *The challenge of the 80's: Balancing medical education and humanistic obstetrics in a teaching hospital.* Paper presented at the Conference on Obstetrical Management and Infant Outcome, New York.

Piers, M. (1978). *Infanticide: Past and present.* New York: Norton

Potts, C.R., & Ullery, J.C. (1961). Maternal and fetal effects of obstetric analgesia. Intravenous use of promethazine and meperidine. *American Journal of Obstetrics and Gynecology, 81,* 1253–1259.

Rappoport, D. (1976). Pour une naissance sans violence: Resultats d'une première enquête. *Bulletin Psychologie, 29,* 552–560.

Ringler, N.M., Kennell, J.H., Jarvella, R., Navojsky, B.J., & Klaus, M.H. (1975). Mother-to-child speech at 2 years—Effects of early postnatal contact. *Journal of Pediatrics, 86,* 141–144.

Ringler, N.M., Trause, M.A., Klaus, M.H., & Kennell, J. (1978). The effects of extra postpartum contact and maternal speech patterns on children's IQs, speech, and language comprehension at five. *Child Development, 49,* 862–865.

Rode, S.S., Chang, P., Fisch, R.O., & Sroufe, L.A. (1981). Attachment patterns of infants separated at birth. *Developmental Psychology, 17,* 188–191.

Rosenblum, L.A., & Youngstein, K.P. (1974). Developmental change in compensatory dyadic response in mother and infant monkeys. In M. Lewis and L.A. Rosenblum (Eds.), *The effect of the infant on its caregiver.* New York: Wiley-Interscience.

Rosenfield, A.B. (1980). Visiting in the intensive care nursery. *Child Development, 51,* 939–941.

Scanlon, J.W. (1976). Effects of local anesthetics administered to parturient women on the neurological and behavioral performance of newborn children. *Bulletin of the New York Academy of Medicine, 52,* 231–240.

Schaller, J., Carlsson, S.G., & Larsson, K. (1979). Effects of extended post-partum mother–child contact on the mother's behavior during nursing. *Infant Behavior and Development, 2,* 319–324.

Shnider, S. (1981). Choice of anesthesia for labor and delivery. *Journal of Obstetrics and Gynecology, 58* (5 Suppl.), 24S–34S.

Sinclair, J.C., Fox, H.A., Lentz, J.F., Field, G.L., & Murphy, J. (1965). Intoxication of the fetus by a local anesthetic. A newly recognized complication of maternal caudal anesthesia. *New England Journal of Medicine, 273,* 1173–1177.

Souzea, P.L.R., Barros, F.C., Gazalle, R.V., Begeres, R.M., Pinheiro, G.N., Menezes, S.T., & Arruda, L.A. (1974, October). Attachment and lactation. Paper presented at the Fifteenth International Congress of Pediatrics, Buenos Aires.

Standley, K. (1974, August). *Prenatal and perinatal correlates of neonatal behaviors.* Paper presented at the meeting of the American Psychological Association, New Orleans.

Standley, K. (1976, April). *Sources of variation in the behavior of normal newborns: Consequences of obstetric medication.* Paper presented at the meeting of the Eastern Psychological Association, New York.

Svedja, M.J., Campos, J.J., & Emde, R.N. (1980). Mother–infant "bonding": Failure to generalize. *Child Development, 51,* 775–779.

Thacker, S.B., & Banta, H.D. (1980). Benefits and risks of episiotomy: An interpretive review of the English-language literature, 1860–1980. *Obstetrical and Gynecological Survey, 34,* 627–642.

Tronick, E., Wise, S., Als, H., Adamson, L., Scanlon, J., & Brazelton, T.B. (1976). Regional obstetric anesthesia and newborn behavior: Effect over the first ten days of life. *Pediatrics, 58,* 94–100.

Vietze, P.M., MacTurk, R.H., McCarthy, M.E., Klein, R.P., & Yarrow, L.J. (1980, April). *Impact of mode of delivery on father– and mother–infant interaction at 6 months.* Paper presented at the International Conference on Infant Studies, New Haven, CT.

Vietze, P.M., O'Connor, S., Falsey, S., & Altemeier, W.A. (1978, August). *Effects of rooming-in on maternal behavior directed towards infants.* Paper presented at the annual meeting of the American Psychological Association, Toronto.

Wertz, R.W., & Wertz, D.C. (1979). *Lying-in: A history of childbirth in America.* New York: Schocken.

Windle, W.F. (1966). An experimental approach to prevention or reduction of brain damage of birth asphyxia. *Developmental Medicine and Child Neurology, 8,* 129–140.

Winters, M. (1973). *The relationship of time of initial feeding to success of breast feeding.* Unpublished masters's thesis, University of Washington, Seattle.

Wood, C., et al. (1965). Effects of meperidine on the newborn infant. *Collaborative Project Reporter,* Winter 1964–1965, *33,* 1–8.

Zeskind, P.S. (1980). Adult responses to cries of low and high risk infants. *Infant Behavior and Development, 3,* 167–177.

PART TWO

BIRTH TO TWO YEARS

THE DEVELOPMENT OF BASIC CHARACTERISTICS OF INFANTS

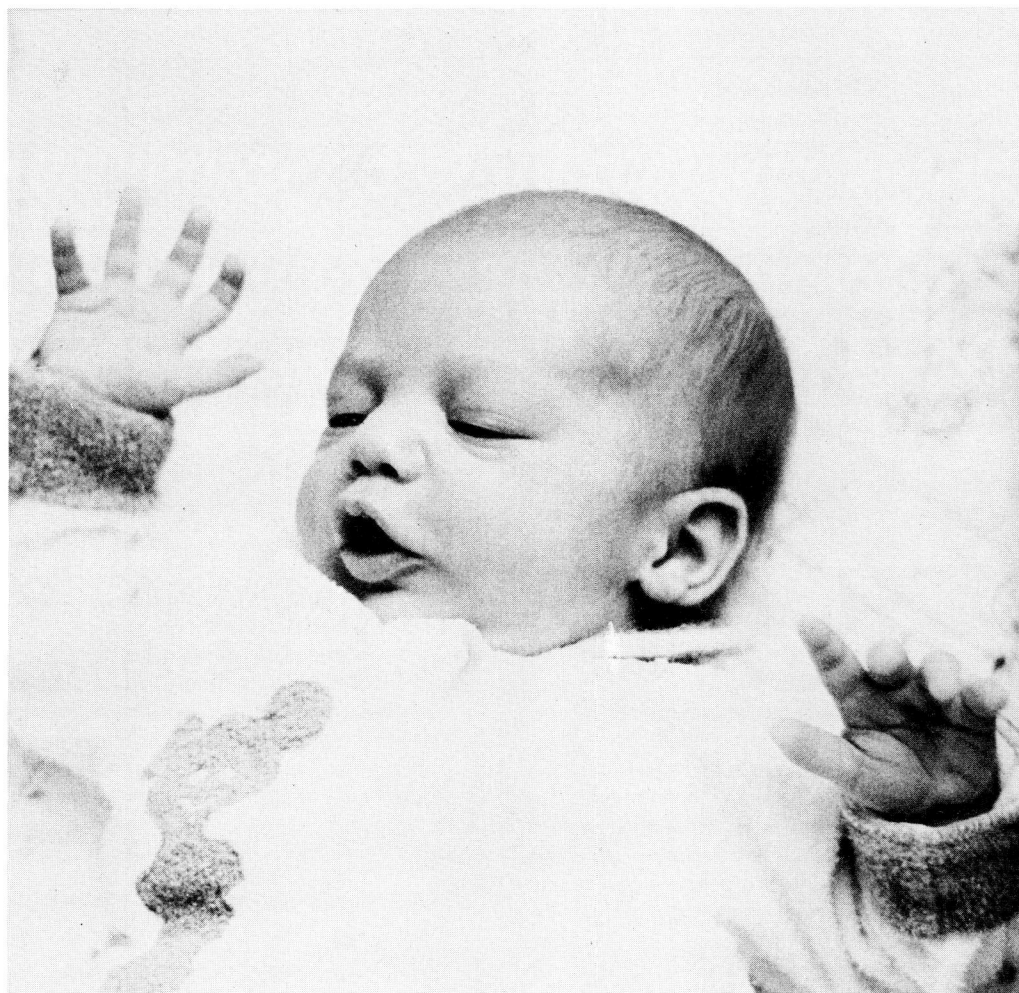

CHAPTER 6

ewborns are often described as creatures who only eat, sleep, and cry. Although babies do spend much of their time in such activities, this description by no means fully represents their abilities. In this chapter we will explore the basic response systems of young babies. First we will discuss three aspects of the young baby's activities: sleep, activity, and attention. These, and crying which we will consider later in the chapter, are all aspects of what is called state. Studies of learning, perception, and cognition, and the testing of infants, especially young ones, are all dependent on state.

Next we shall consider sucking, a behavior of primary importance to infant survival and one that is the focus of a major theoretical debate in the field of child development.

Finally, we will look at three affective behaviors of infants that also serve important communicative functions for both biological survival and social development. These are crying, smiling, and laughing.

The research relevant to these topics focuses on whether and how these basic response systems operate in newborns. This permeates the study of infants, since one of the major purposes in studying infants is to discover when and how human characteristics get started. In addition, knowing the basic responses of normal infants helps in the recognition or diagnosis of abnormality. Although we discuss development of the basic response systems when information about their development is available (our best example is sucking), this kind of information is sporadic at best. It is important to realize that all these systems undoubtedly change radically as infants grow.

HOW BABIES SPEND THEIR DAYS

Sleep

Sleep is a behavior that interests parents and researchers alike. It starts during fetal life and its patterns change throughout infancy. Parents are generally interested in how long babies sleep and in the variability of their sleep patterns. Researchers are interested in specific types of sleep, and in sleep patterns and their variability, both within and among babies. They are also interested in such questions as what proportion of sleeping time is spent in quiet versus active sleep (Dreyfus-Brissac, 1968). In quiet sleep the baby shows little or no motor activity, the eyes are firmly closed and motionless, and respiration is relatively slow and constant in depth. In active sleep a wide range of motor activity may be seen. The eyes are usually closed, but brief eye-opening may accompany rapid eye movements (REMS). Respiration is more rapid and less regular in deep than in quiet sleep. There is also a transitional stage that is a mixture of these two.

Parents are interested in both the amount of time their baby will spend sleeping, and when during the twenty-four-hour day this will occur. A good starting point for examining this question would seem to be to study the naturally occurring sleep patterns in newborns (see Figure 6–1). Such studies are complicated by the fact that in most hospitals, and even in many homes, babies are awakened for feedings at regular intervals so no accurate picture of spontaneous sleep patterns can be obtained. Within this limitation, however, researchers can systematically explore the sleeping patterns of newborns. One of the best studies of sleep in the neonatal period is that by Parmelee, Schulz, and Disbrow (1961). They obtained a sample of 100 babies approximately evenly divided between breast- and bottle-fed babies and between boys and girls. Adequate records were obtained from 75 mothers and these showed average sleeping times of 17 hours in the first day, 16.5 hours in the second, and 16.2 in the third. The average number of feedings increased from fewer than five to six or more in this 3-day period. The total sleeping time averaged 17 hours for all the babies, but it varied among the babies from 10.5 to 23 hours on the second day and from 11.4 to 21 on the third. Babies who slept most on the first day tended to sleep most on the next two days, but the difference between the long and short sleepers was no longer as great. A study that followed the sleeping times of 19 infants over the first months of life (Kleitman & Engelmann, 1953) found an average of under 15 hours for babies from 3 through 15 weeks of age.

The data of Parmelee, Schulz, and Disbrow (1961) confirm something parents have often

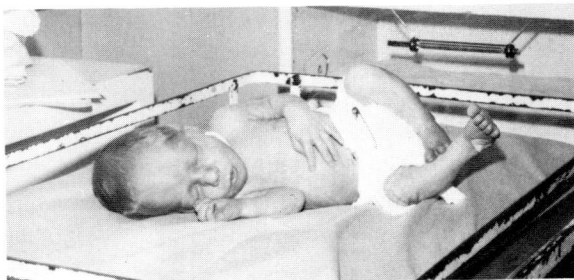

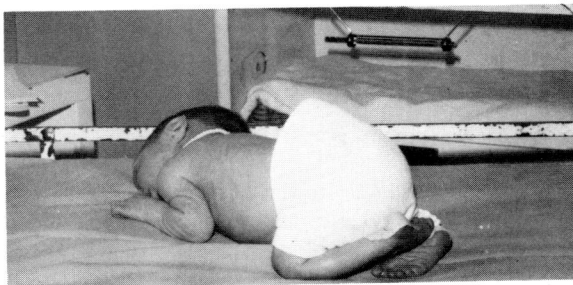

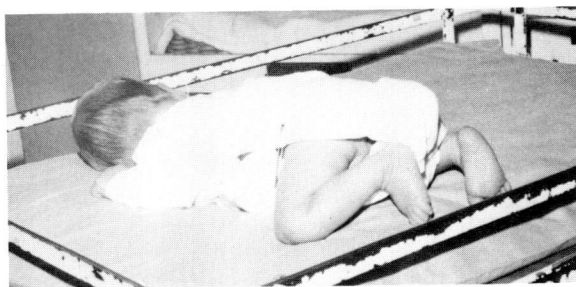

FIGURE 6–1. Some common postures of newborns during sleep. Most babies sleep better on their sides or on their tummies (prone). The baby on his back is in a more active stage of sleep—he has just kicked his foot.

noticed during their long walks in the middle of the night. Many babies (43%) do not have their longest period of sleep between 11 P.M. and 7 A.M., and many babies do not have any long periods of sleep. The lengths of the longest periods of sleep varied from 2 to 10 hours. These sleep patterns do not seem to be affected by the sex of the infant or the type of feeding. Although total sleep stays about constant, it tends to change from 3- to 4-hour periods evenly distributed throughout the day and night to 2 such periods entrained into a night diurnal cycle. (Entrainment refers to the ways

in which the external environment affects basic biological rhythms.) Parmelee stated:

One would like to conclude that some fundamental biological rhythms are present very early in life and remain relatively invariant with maturation of the nervous system, while the behavioral patterns of sleep and wakefulness that develop around them change dramatically in character and reflect the rapid maturation of the central nervous systems interactional processes, particularly controlling mechanisms. (Parmelee, 1974, p. 309)

Scientists and pediatricians have also been interested in the distribution of the amounts of time spent in quiet versus active sleep. Stern, Parmelee, Akiyama, Schultz, and Wenner (1969) reported on the cyclic fluctuations between quiet and active sleep of newborns and of older infants (3 and 8 months old). This study involved recording eye and body movements, respirations, and EEGs (electroencephalograms, records of the electrical activity of the brain). The quiet–active cycles in the sleep of the full-term infants lasted only 47 minutes compared to 90 minutes in adult sleep. The length of these cycles did not change rapidly. They only increased to 49 minutes at 3 months and only to 50 minutes by 8 months. Although there was no change in the length of the cycles over this age range, there was a change in the proportion of each cycle that was composed of total quiet sleep. At birth, quiet sleep time equaled active sleep time, but by 3 months quiet sleep was twice as long as active sleep (compared to three times as long in adults) and remained so at 8 months. The investigators wondered whether quiet sleep had any analogy to quiet attentiveness in the awake state. In premature infants that used to be considered nonviable (24 to 27 weeks of conceptional age), the primitive sleep state that exists has no cyclic organization (Dreyfus-Brissac, 1968).

There has been much research on the sleep patterns of premature infants. Studies comparing the development of sleep patterns in prematures to that in term babies have identified an interesting pattern of features. Prematures show greater maturity than term infants of the same age since conception for some aspects of sleep and less maturity for others (see, for example, Booth, Leonard, & Thoman, 1980). Prematures do not simply lag behind their term peers by a factor that reflects their age since conception, a fact that leads to intriguing research questions. What experiences or environmental factors lead to these differences in state organization? Are there long-range consequences of such differences?

We cannot begin to do justice to the literature on sleep and its development, but we hope we have presented enough of it to demonstrate the importance of individual differences in sleep behaviors.

Activity

Activity is an aspect of behavior that varies in the awake state as well as in sleep. It is one characteristic of infants' behavior that is noted even before birth. The levels of activity displayed by different newborns and by different fetuses vary markedly. This variation has led people to wonder whether the activity level of an infant is indicative of a life-long or enduring constitutional or temperamental trait. Babies differ not only in the amount of activity they show spontaneously, which is what is usually studied, but also in the ways in which their activity changes in response to stimulus situations (Figure 6–2).

BACKGROUND ISSUES

History of Debates on the Nature of Activity in Newborns. Let us begin with a discussion of the history of the arguments about the nature of activity. Preyer (1880/1888) questioned the relation between early general activity and later adaptive behaviors. He even proposed a mechanism resembling what is now called reinforcement that operated to determine the aspects of activity that were stable or kept by the baby. His view can be seen as fitting either of the opposing positions about the nature of activity that developed later. One of these positions is represented by Watson (1937) and Dennis (1932) who saw the infant's "stream of activity" as made up of unlearned responses (that is, of discrete activities) that quickly became conditioned. At the opposite extreme were those like Coghill (1929a, 1929b), Irwin (1930), and Weiss (1929) who believed that the infant's activity was better described by the phrase "mass activity" than as

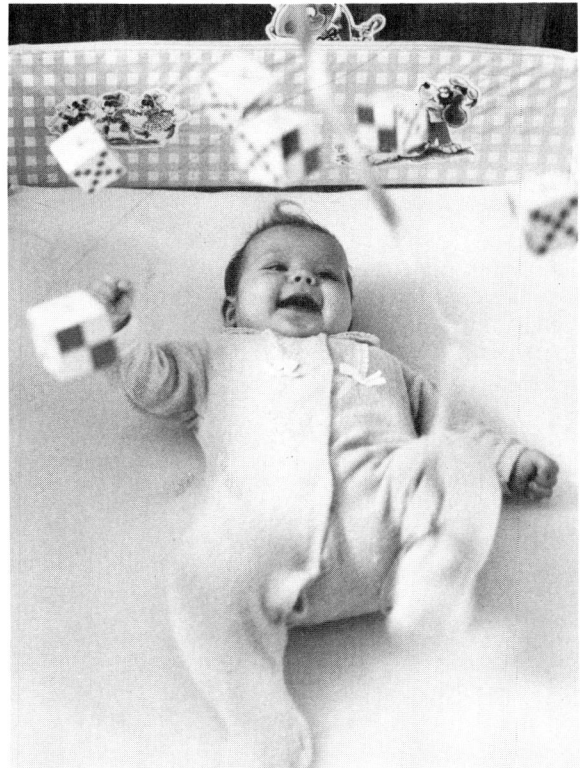

FIGURE 6–2. An active baby, responding to the stimulus of a mobile. (Photograph courtesy of Carolyn Rovee-Collier.)

reflexes or discrete behaviors. Weiss, for example, found that 30–40% of newborns' movements were rapid, unorganized, and involved the entire body. Irwin (1930) and Coghill (1929a, 1929b) proposed that growth proceeded by differentiation of specific movements out of this mass activity, rather than by the conditioning of specific responses. Since that time, researchers have generally not concerned themselves with this issue as such, but with using measures of activity to study other aspects of infant behavior.

Measurement of Activity. Let us now consider some of the ways in which activity is measured. Many observational schemes have been used. Some are directed toward assessing mass activity, others toward specific movements, some towards both. There is even one attempt at a choreographic description of "rhythms of movement" (Kestenberg, 1965). As in all observational techniques, the problems of definition are great and always involve some judgment. What constitutes a specific movement? How much activity constitutes "mass activity?" How many different kinds of activity are there? Thus, it is crucial that workers establish **reliability** in scoring.[1] This requires careful descriptions of categories, considerable training and experience, and avoidance of an excessive number of categories (that demand that excessively fine distinctions be made). Given these conditions, the human observer may be a rather good instrument for measuring activity. Becoming such a skilled observer is a rather demanding task, however, and investigators searched for more objective and less demanding ways to record activity. The result was the early development of methods using various kinds of apparatus to aid in measurement.

A number of devices called stabilimeters have been developed for this purpose. They involve some system for measuring movements of the mattress on which an infant is lying, and they usually enable analyses of different directions of the motions, in other words, left–right or up–down (see Weiss, 1929). Photoelectric cells and spring suspensions are among the systems that have been used to provide information that can be fed into computers (for example, see Crowell, Yasaka, & Crowell, 1964). Studies using such devices are more likely to study mass activity, because that is what the device records best, although some systems have allowed recording of a finite number of specific responses (see, for example, Lipsitt & DeLucia, 1960). Changes in the amount of activity from before to after administration of a stimulus can be assessed by any of the systems. Unfortunately, differences among the stabilimeter systems used to study activity are so great that it is hard to compare results from one study to another.

There have been many attempts to return to schemes that use direct observations. Vari-

ous techniques have been used to increase the precision of observational measurement. For example, Gordon and Bell (1961) observed the movements of each body part and used these movements to arrive at activity levels only after the movements were scored in relation to the normal amount of movement for that body part.

Film has been used for some time to measure infant activity, and today videotape is frequently used. Film and videotape combine observational methods with the ability to check and recheck observations as often as necessary. Gesell and his colleagues in the 1930s developed objective methods for scoring filmed records (Gesell & Thompson, 1934; Gesell, 1948) and used them to study individual differences in activity (Ames, 1942, 1949) as did Bell (1960). The films or tapes can be projected onto a screen with a superimposed grid and the number of times a given body part crosses a grid line, or the number of grid lines it crosses, can be scored. Because it is possible to count these features any number of times, and because any number of people can count them, the observational scheme can be refined repeatedly until reliability is achieved. This process is tedious, but the tedium can be reduced by having the camera only take (or the rater only rate) one picture every so many seconds. This technique has been used to record movements of a baby wearing a wrist band to enable easy scoring of its crossings of grid lines (Robertson, 1982). Haith (1966) has described an efficient system for reducing film and videotaped records to manageable size.

The relation between activity level and crying is another problem in activity measurement. Korner, Thoman, and Glick (1974) showed that all measures of total infant activity are badly contaminated by the amount of time infants spend crying. Their study showed that a crying baby produced about 12,000 movements per hour compared to about 2,000 for a noncrying baby. Because some babies practically never cried and others cried as much as 22% of the time, measures of over-all activity levels that did not take crying into consideration could be grossly misleading. When the investigators measured noncrying activity alone, babies still showed strong individual differences, ranging from 1100 to 4500 movements per hour. Activity in noncrying pe-

[1]Reliability means that two (or more) persons scoring behaviors agree most of the time. Agreement is measured by determining the correlation coefficients for their two sets of scores (or ratings), or the percentage of all instances of the behavior on which they agree. A more complete discussion of reliability appears in the Research Issues section of this chapter.

riods was fairly highly correlated with activity when crying (r = .62), which suggests that babies who are more active than most when quiet are likely to be more active when crying as well. Thus measuring activity during either quiet or crying periods may provide a valid measure of activity level, but measures taken when both quiet and crying occurred may be confounding.

Not all measures of activity are based on direct observation and quantification of the number or location of movements. Data from various neonatal and infant tests have also been used to arrive at activity measures or ratings (see Chapter 8).

ACTIVITY LEVEL IN RESPONSE TO STIMULATION

The previous discussion focused on spontaneous activity. We will now discuss the kinds of stimuli, both internal and external, that affect activity.

Internal Stimuli. The activity level of newborns clearly is responsive to internal stimuli, but in complicated ways. Hunger is the only stimulus that has been, or can reasonably be, studied because it can be operationally defined as time since last feeding or can even take account of the amount consumed at that feeding. In general, hunger increases activity level, but the pattern of activity changes differs in different babies. Wolff (1966) observed 5 infants who showed a sharp increase in activity from the period just after feeding to the middle of the time between feedings and then a slight drop just before a feeding, though this drop was to a level higher than that in the postfeeding period. In contrast, 6 infants showed a small increase between the periods immediately after feeding and midway between feedings and a sharp rise in the period just before feeding. It would be interesting to know whether these two activity patterns are related to differences in total consumption (or in total consumption in relation to weight) or differences in metabolic rates. Clearly, individual differences in the relations between hunger and activity level are marked.

External Stimuli. Young babies also become more active in response to external stimuli, and they show large individual differ-

ences in this response. Some events that stimulate changes in activity level are rubbing the forehead with a soft cloth, holding a nipple (without food) in the mouth, and removing a nipple from the mouth (McGrade, 1968).

ACTIVITY LEVEL AS A PREDICTOR OF LATER DEVELOPMENT

Prenatal Activity. Early on, researchers asked whether prenatal activity level is related to later outcomes. Richards and Newberry (1938) studied 12 pregnant women for 5 to 6 hours every week or two. The number of minutes the mothers-to-be reported the fetus to be active in any way was determined and an activity rate (number of minutes of activity per 10 minutes of observation) was obtained. This rate in the last 2 months of pregnancy was correlated with the babies' total Gesell scores (see Chapter 8 for a description of this test) at 6 months, and for half of the subjects again at 12 months. The resulting correlations were positive, that is, the higher the activity level, the better the Gesell scores. The correlations were highly significant, leading the authors to conclude that 30–70% of the variance in developmental level at 6 months is accounted for by the fetal activity levels (see the Research Issues section for an explanation of variance).

This study was replicated by Walters (1965) with a larger sample of 35 mothers, most of whom were educated. Seven babies were eliminated from the main sample used to test the hypothesis because of pregnancy or delivery factors that might have affected either prenatal activity level or postnatal development or both. Activity levels were recorded by mothers during the last 3 months of pregnancy (1½ hours each week, averaged to provide a monthly score). Babies were tested on the Gesell scale at 12, 24, and 36 weeks after birth by investigators with no knowledge of the babies' activity scores. Fetal activity scores for each month were correlated with those for total development and for each area of the Gesell scale.

Direct correlations between the activity scores and Gesell scores and correlations taking account of birth weight were calculated. Activity in each of the last three prenatal months was related to the total Gesell score (see Table 6–1), thus replicating the previous findings even to finding similar strengths of re-

TABLE 6–1
Correlations Between Fetal Activity and Gesell Scores[a]

Prenatal Month	Gesell Motor Score at:			Gesell Total Score at:		
	12 wks	24 wks	36 wks	12 wks	24 wks	36 wks
Seventh	.29	.54	.53	.29	.44	.51
Eighth	.32	.33	.38	.35	.31	.23
Ninth	.26	.37	.51	.40	.40	.40
Average	.53	.44	.53	.40	.31	.51

[a] Adapted from Walters (1965).

lationships. Activity in each of the last three prenatal months was also related to motor development at all three postnatal ages. Other aspects of the Gesell scale were not related to activity at all the prenatal ages, and the 8-month measures were less related than those at 7 or 9 months or than the average for the three months. An important aspect of these data is that the strength of the relations did not decline as postnatal age increased. Fetal activity was as much or more related to development at 36 weeks as it had been at 12 or 24 weeks.

Examined separately, the data for the 7 babies eliminated because of prenatal or delivery problems show that their activity levels appear to be negatively (but not significantly) correlated with the total Gesell scores. Had these cases been kept in the main study, this negative relation would have affected the results, possibly making it appear that there were no significant relations between pre- and postnatal activity. Because the main study was limited to babies born to middle or upper middle class families after normal pregnancies and deliveries, the results can only be generalized to such families and births. For these babies, the data suggest that fetal activity would be positively correlated with development in the first 8 months of life. However, given the modest sizes of the correlations, this prediction would only hold for the group, and a good prediction could not be expected for individual cases.

Postnatal Activity. If activity level is a **trait** (that is if there are stable individual differences in it), then spontaneous postnatal activity scores should have the measurement characteristics that are typical of traits such as height, weight, and IQ. And they do. Measures of postnatal activity exhibit a wide range of scores and an approximately normal distribution of scores. For example, in one study (Brownfield, 1956) scores ranged from 34 to 134, with an average score of 80 and a standard deviation of 19, with no sex differences. Because activity level has these measurement characteristics, it is plausible to conceive of activity level as a trait.

Although activity level has some of the measurement characteristics of a trait, evidence that spontaneous activity is a stable trait is sporadic and inconsistent. The strongest evidence that activity over at least the first month of life period predicts later activity is data from a study by Lancione, Horowitz, and Sullivan (1980). They found stability over the first month of life, using as activity measures the Kansas version of Brazelton's Neonatal Behavioral Assessment Scales (see Chapter 8). In fact, of all the characteristics measured, activity showed the greatest evidence of stability over the first month of life. However, even this stability was modest even though it was based on a sample of 106 infants who were assessed five times during the first month, of which three times were in the first 3 days. Korner, Thoman, and Glick (1974) found very modest correlations of noncrying activity from one feeding interval to another (in the mid .30s range), which certainly does not suggest strong stability even in such short intervals. These studies give little indication that individual differences in spontaneous activity in the newborn constitute a highly stable trait. It is thus not surprising to find that newborn spontaneous activity level was not related to performance at 8 months on the Bayley tests of infant development (McGrade, 1968).

It is possible that measures that include both spontaneous activity and activity in response to stimulation might be more stable or a better predictor of later development. McGrade (1968) measured activity in response to three external stimuli—the forehead being rubbed with a soft cloth, having a nipple without food held in the mouth, or having a nipple removed from the mouth—and then calculated the differences between baseline activity and each responsive activity. She correlated those differences with 8-month ratings of activity, tension, fearfulness, and happiness (from the Infant Behavior Profile of the Bayley test). Neonates who had responded with high activity to nipple withdrawal (a stressor) were significantly more active, happier, and less tense at 8 months of age. She concluded that it was the reaction to stress in the neonatal period that was related to reactions to stress at 8 months. Her conclusion is consistent with one of the findings in the Lancione and colleagues (1980) study cited above. Defensive movements (high activity plus a focus) in response to a cloth over the face were as stable over the period from birth to 1 month as was activity itself.

Another study (Goldsmith & Gottesman, 1981) also found some evidence that activity level is a trait, if both spontaneous and reactive activity are included. This study used a research strategy different from the studies considered so far. The first step was to demonstrate that a broad set of behaviors from the Bayley examination at 8 months cluster into an activity factor. The cluster included speed of response, active manipulation, response duration, pursuit persistence, and activity level. Thus, it involved both spontaneous activity and activity in response to stimulation. The second step was to demonstrate that there is a genetic component to this activity factor. This was done by comparing identical and fraternal twins. The investigators found that identical twins, who share the same set of genes, were more similar to each other than were fraternal twins, who are no more genetically alike than two siblings of different ages. Although this finding demonstrated a genetic contribution to activity level, it accounted for less than 35% of the variance in the activity factor scores, leaving 65% of the variance to be accounted for by other influences.

Thomas, Chess, Birch, Hertzig, and Korn (1963) have described stability over the period from birth to age two, but we conclude that the degree of stability demonstrated in their studies is too low to give strong support to the theory that activity level is a stable genetic or constitutional trait. We hasten to add, however, that it is premature to conclude that activity level is *not* an important predictor of later development.

CONCLUSION

Activity is clearly a characteristic that shows strong individual differences from prenatal life throughout infancy, differences about which parents, caretakers, and scientists can agree. There is less agreement about whether activity is a stable trait. Data from twin studies seem to show that there is some genetic basis for individual differences in activity. In contrast, the lack of impressive evidence for the long-term stability of individual differences in activity level makes its status as a biological trait somewhat questionable. Whether or not it is a stable trait, at least prenatal activity level is related to more general later outcomes.

Attention

Attention is another topic of importance in the study of infants. In the following discussions of state, each system of descriptions has one or two categories in which attention is most likely (or which describe an attentive state). Attentiveness is an important topic for our knowledge of infancy; it is while infants are awake and attentive that they can best perceive and process their world.

Attention has been relatively ignored in the study of infancy. In disguised form it is frequently found in the description of the numbers of infants that had to be excluded from a study because their state was inappropriate (that is, they were sleeping or crying or inflexibly focused) or because they failed to attend to the stimuli although they were apparently awake. Eliminating babies from studies because they are not paying attention can be a serious source of bias because the babies who have been eliminated may differ in important ways from those who have not.

ATTENTION GETTING AND ATTENTION HOLDING

Attention is the focus of many studies of infants' responses to particular stimuli. Cohen (1972) distinguished between what he called "attention getting" and "attention holding." Attention getting refers to how readily the infant will turn toward (orient to) a stimulus. Attention holding refers to how long the infant looks at a stimulus (Cohen was studying vision). Attention getting is the response most often measured in neonatal tests (see Chapter 8). It is an attending response, but one that can be elicited even in sleeping infants (for auditory stimuli) or in drowsy ones. Cohen originally hypothesized that attention getting is a reflexive response, but subsequent work by Cohen and his colleagues (Cohen, DeLoache, & Rissman, 1975; DeLoache, Rissman, & Cohen, 1978) has indicated that attention getting is a more active process in which orienting is partially a function of prior experience, at least in 16-week-old infants.

Attention holding is often used as a dependent variable in studies of infant perception and cognition. For example, if infants look longer at one of two geometric shapes presented side by side, then we can conclude that the infants can perceive the difference between the two (see Chapter 9 for more examples). It is also used as a measure of individual differences in attentiveness. Such differences have been related to variables such as prematurity, perinatal events (including obstetric medication), Apgar scores, and maternal caretaking behaviors. For example, term infants who are less attentive are likely to have more neurological problems than those who are more attentive (Sigman, Kopp, Parmelee, & Jeffrey, 1973). Full-term infants who are more attentive to visual and auditory stimuli during neonatal testing are likely to have mothers who are more attentive and sensitive to them (Osofsky, 1976; Osofsky & Danzger, 1974; Sigman & Beckwith, 1980), presumably because more attentive babies elicit more positive caretaking responses from their mothers.

ATTENTION IN FULL-TERM AND PRETERM BABIES

Visual attentiveness in preterm infants is quite different from that in full-term infants. Specifically, babies who are alert and process information efficiently as newborns may become children and then adults who are more intelligent and better thinkers. To begin with, preterm infants tested at 40 weeks postconceptional age (that is, when they should have been born) show much longer fixation times (attention spans) than full-term babies do at birth (Sigman et al., 1973; Kopp, Sigman, Parmelee, & Jeffrey, 1975; Sigman & Beckwith, 1980). Furthermore, the relations between attentiveness and maternal caregiving behaviors are generally in opposite directions for prematures and full-term infants. Although the pattern of results was complicated by sex differences (Sigman & Beckwith, 1980), it is generally fair to say that the more attentive preterm babies receive less caregiving from their mothers. Since high attentiveness in the preterm babies was negatively related to later Bayley scores in girls, Sigman and Beckwith concluded that in preterm infants high attentiveness reflects an inability to turn off stimulation rather than a state in which the ability to process information is maximal.

ATTENTION AS A PREDICTOR OF LATER DEVELOPMENT

Researchers are beginning to attend more to attention, especially to its possible predictive value. In both healthy term babies and in prematures attention has been shown to be related to some later developmental outcomes. Sustained attention in 8-month-old preterm, male infants is related to cognitive competence at 2 years of age as measured by both the Gesell and Bayley tests (Kopp & Vaughn, 1982).

Attention at 4 months of age as measured by habituation rate or frequency (see Chapter 7) was related to Bayley test results at 12 months of age for a small sample ($N = 20$) of middle class healthy babies (Ruddy & Bornstein, 1982). It was also related to the size of the babies' vocabulary.

Because deficits in attentive behaviors are found in learning disorders and other problems in the school years, research in the development of attention in infancy seems a promising area.

State

CLASSIFICATION OF STATE

Close observation of newborns reveals that there are a number of gradations of sleep and waking in addition to those already discussed that can be accurately identified by researchers or parents. These states reflect both the babies' needs and their availability for contact with the external environment. This last aspect is very important to many types of research as well as to parents. For example, when an infant is brought in for a feeding, the state of the infant appears to be the main factor in whether or not the mother greets the baby (Levy, 1958). Of 19 mothers studied, all greeted their babies when they were brought in in an awake, quiet state; one third greeted them if they were crying or whimpering; and only one sixth greeted them if they were asleep.

Researchers also have to take the state of the infant into account in any study of them. For discussions of these issues, see, for example, Bell, 1963; Escalona, 1962; Hutt, Lenard, and Prechtl, 1969. Infants are differentially responsive to various stimuli depending on their state. Numerous workers have been interested in the question of unusual state patterns in infants, such as babies who cry a lot and sleep little, that might affect mother–infant interaction. To study any of these state patterns successfully, it is necessary to describe them in such a way that two observers working independently can judge the same infant to be in the same state. A variety of schemes for classifying states have been proposed, and all of them can be used reliably by researchers. We will describe Brown's in greater detail and present those of three other researchers in Table 6–2 to illustrate the differences among the classifications of different workers.

TABLE 6–2
Four Systems for Classifying States

Brown	Wolff	Korner	Prechtl
1. S_3, deep sleep	1. Regular sleep. Comparable to Brown's S_3, but low muscle tone is a descriptor and eye movements visible under lids is not.	1. Regular sleep	I. Eyes closed, regular respiration
2. S_2, regular sleep	2. Periodic sleep. Respiration is periodic with bursts of rapid shallow and deep slow breathing.		II. Eyes closed
3. S_1, disturbed sleep	3. Irregular sleep. Some irregularities in respiration; better muscle tone than in state 1. Frequent grimaces and occasional REMs (rapid eye movements).	2. Irregular sleep	
4. A_1, drowsy	4. Drowsiness	3. Drowsiness	III. Eyes open, no gross movement
5. A_2, alert activity	5. Waking activity. Frequent spurts of diffuse motor activity; no auditory or visual pursuit.	4. Waking activity (diffuse), eyes open, not alert	IV. Eyes open, gross movements, no crying
6. A_3, alert and focused	6. Alert inactivity. Eyes open, alert; has conjugate focus.	5. Alert inactivity	
7. A_4, inflexibly focused	7. Crying. Does not include sucking or inflexibility.	6. Crying; vigorous diffuse movements	V. Crying, eyes open or closed
		7. Indeterminate	

SOURCES. Brown, J.L. (1964). States in newborn infants. *Merrill Palmer Quarterly, 10*, 313–327. Prechtl, H.F.R. (1965). *Advances in the study of behavior*, 75. Sigman, M., Kopp, C.B., Parmelee, A.H., & Jeffrey, W.E. (1973). Visual attention and neurological organization in neonates. *Child Development, 44*, 461–466. Wolff, P.H. (1966). The causes, controls, and organization of behavior in the neonate. *Psychological Issues, 5* (1, Whole No. 17).

Brown (1964) used three stages of sleep and four of wakefulness to describe the states that encompassed the range of observed behaviors. A brief description of her seven states follows.

S_3, deep sleep. Motionless, eyes closed, regular respiration (breathing), no vocalizations, unresponsive to external stimulation.

S_2, regular sleep. Very few movements except for periodic discharges (a topic we will return to), skin may be mottled or pale, breathing may be raspy or wheezing, respirations may be regular or pass from regular to irregular.

S_1, disturbed sleep. Variable amounts of movement, eyelids closed but may flutter, breathing regular or irregular, squawks, sobs, and sighs.

A_1, drowsy. Eyes open or partly open and glassy, little movement (startles or free movements may occur), breathing regular, skin mottled or pale, more regular vocalizations than in S_1 and with transitional sounds.

A_2, alert activity. The state commonly seen by the parent as awake. Eyes open and bright, many free movements, possible fretting, skin reddening and irregular respirations as tension mounts.

A_3, alert and focused. Comparable to attention in an older child but quite uncommon in the newborn. Eyes open and bright. The little motor activity that occurs is integrated around a specific activity. (In Brown's study, this state occurs in listening or auditory focus and in looking or visual focus; see Figure 6–3.)

A_4, inflexibly focused. Awake but nonreactive to external stimuli; found in concentrated sucking and wild crying. In sucking, all motor reactivity is integrated around it and the eyes are closed or glassy. In crying there is a lot of free activity (thrashing); the eyes are often squeezed shut and the skin reddens as the baby screams.

The various states reflect different kinds of organization in the central nervous system. Crying might appear to be the least organized state to the lay observer, but in fact irregular sleep is the least organized state. Regular sleep demands the strongest organization (or ho-

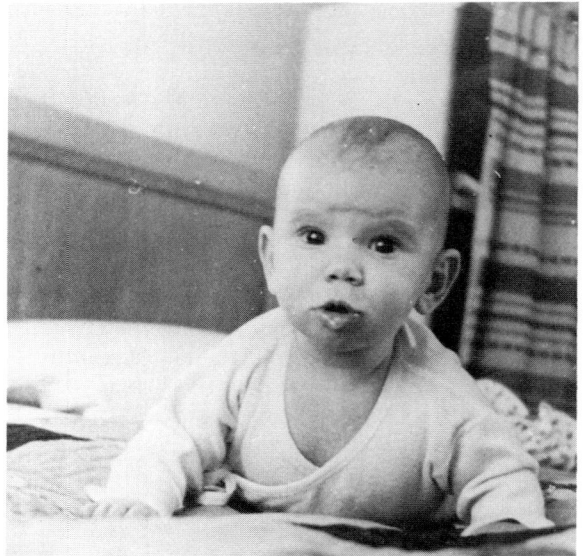

FIGURE 6–3. A 3-month-old infant in a quiet, alert state, showing fixed visual regard. (Photograph by J.F. Rosenblith.)

meostatic control). Infants with CNS damage seem unable to achieve it (Hutt et al., 1969).

STATES AND THE BABY'S DAY

Using the classification schemes in Table 6–2, a large number of researchers have mapped out how babies spend their time. As already noted, newborns spend most of their time asleep (17 to 20 hours a day, three quarters of it in regular sleep). Newborns are awake and quiet for 2 to 3 hours, awake and active for 1 to 2 hours, and cry or fuss for the remainder of the time, which would be from 0 to 4 hours based on the extremes of the other figures. These figures do not tell the whole story, however, because individual differences among babies are so striking. For example, in an intensive observational study of only 6 full-term babies, these wide variations were found: (1) Alert receptive states were attained only 4% of the time by one infant but 30% or more of the time by two. (2) One baby slept 56% of the time and cried only 17% of the time, but the baby with only 4% alert receptive periods slept 37% of the time and cried 39% of it (Brown, 1964). Some babies seemed to have a better capacity to lower their own arousal, from crying to alert inactivity for example, than others, a point featured in Brazelton's neonatal examination (see Chapter 8). These differences did not appear to be related to delivery factors and they tended to be consistent from the first three to the second three days of life. The environment also affects babies' states. For example, both temperature and relative humidity affect the length of time spent in regular sleep.

The tremendous variations in the ways babies spend their days can be expected to have profound effects upon parents. The amount and pattern of babies' sleep influences the amount of rest their parents get. The amount of time the baby spends crying determines how much of their parents' time is spent trying to soothe their bawling newborn. Parents who are unable to soothe their babies are likely to feel that they are incompetent. Since pleasant social interactions are most likely when the baby is in an alert, focused state, babies who spend much time in that state will be more engaging to parents than babies who rarely achieve it. Because babies vary in the patterns of states they exhibit, some babies seem much more rewarding than others. The baby who sleeps for long, regular periods during the night, cries little, and spends a lot of time in an alert, focused state is a very easy baby. One who sleeps irregularly, and not at night, cries a lot, is not easily soothed, and spends little time in an alert, focused state is likely to have tired, irritable parents who feel incompetent and who get little pleasure or reward from their newborn.

Luckily, parents and other adults are not helpless and can often help infants to change states. The actions found to lower arousal are, from most to least effective, picking up, auditory stimulation, restraint of limbs, and position changes. Auditory stimulation and position changes were also effective in arousing the infants, but were far less arousing than undressing. Individual differences are important. Different babies responded differently to the stimulation of these different soothing techniques, and the differences between them were stable from one testing to another. Thus, parents need to find the techniques that work best for their baby. Ways parents can soothe crying babies will be discussed in more detail in the section on crying.

It is clear that the individual differences discussed above mean something to parents, but do they mean anything for the subsequent development of the infant? One example of research that seeks to answer that question is that of Moss and Robson (1970). They hypothesized that infants who tended to spend more time in an awake, alert, nonirritable state would be likely to have more advanced visual behaviors. The states of 42 infants (21 of each sex) were assessed during home observations at 1 and 3 months of age and from maternal reports. As might be expected, the babies were awake more and drowsy or crying less at 3 months than at 1 month. The amount of fussing stayed about the same, with boys fussing more than girls. The only relations between state and visual behaviors were for boys. Those who spent more time in an awake state at 1 month fixated on social stimuli longer at 3 months ($r = .59$, $p < .01$). In addition boys whose mothers described them as fussy or demanding spent less time looking at geometric designs. Boys who enjoyed or were quieted by visual stimuli (according to their mothers) tended to look more at both geometric and social stimuli. There were no significant relations among any of these variables for girls.

STATES AND RESPONSIVENESS

The states of newborns clearly affect the kind and degree of responsiveness they will show. This is true even at the most basic level of reflex behaviors, those that involve only one **synapse** (nerve junction) at the spinal level and that do not need to be transmitted all the way to the brain. Different groups of reflexes can be obtained in different states. The very simple one-synapse reflexes such as the knee jerk and Moro reflexes occur stongly during regular sleep and wakefulness (Prechtl's states I and III; see Table 6–2), but are absent or weak in irregular sleep (Prechtl's state II). Other reflexes that involve many synapses, such as the grasp reflex, can be elicited in their strongest form only during wakefulness. A third group, made up of reflex responses to stimuli that cause pain or damage (for example, a pin scratch), can be obtained in all states (Lenard, Von Bernuth, & Prechtl, 1968; Hutt et al., 1969). Notice that this third group is the only one in which infants are responsive in all states, and even then they may not be equally responsive.

Other studies of responses that are less clearly reflexive have also found that only a few stimuli, whose responses have adaptive significance, are effective in a wide variety of states. Lamper and Eisdorfer (1971) examined the relation of prestimulus state to the intensity of response to stimuli of 3 sensory modalities (sound, cold, and touch) and found that state affected all responses except those to cold (applied to the thigh). It appeared that this stimulus was so intense that it overrode the effects of state. Covering the nostrils with a cotton ball also triggers responses in a fashion that tends to override state. Rosenblith and Anderson-Huntington (1975) have shown that responses to covering both nostrils with cotton do not appear to be dependent on state when testing is done in the context of an examination in which efforts are made to keep the baby's state as appropriate as possible. However, when babies are tested in their cribs without special efforts to control their state, their responses to cotton (or cellophane) over their nostrils do depend to a considerable degree on their state during the testing. Thus, evidence from three different kinds of threatening stimuli (pain, cold, and those threatening the air supply) suggest that responses that are of special adaptive value may be less dependent on state than others.

When stimuli do not override state or trigger pure reflexes, responses to them are influenced by state. For example, Brown (1964) found that infants are least responsive in deep sleep (S_3) and in the inflexibly focused state (A_4), are relatively unresponsive in regular sleep and alert inactivity (S_2 and A_2), are somewhat responsive in disturbed sleep and in the drowsy state (S_1 and A_1), and are most responsive in the alert focused state (A_3).

Responsivity to stimulation must be clearly distinguished from arousal. Most of the schemes in Table 6–2 represent a continuum from low arousal (deep sleep) to high arousal (crying). Prechtl's states, for example, range along a continuum from I (low arousal) to V (highest arousal). Nevertheless, babies are not least responsive to external stimulation in state I and most responsive in state V. Lenard and his colleagues point out that if there were such a continuum, reflexes would be more or less strongly elicited as an infant goes from sleeping to waking states or vice versa, and that is not what they found. Brown's characterization of responsivity to external stimuli also does not fit a single dimension of arousal. Figure 6–4 shows Brown's states arrayed around the outside of a circle and the Prechtl states on the inside. The state in which babies are most responsive, alert focused (A_3), is at the top of the circle, and those in which they are least responsive, deep sleep and inflexibly

FIGURE 6–4. The relations among responsivity to stimulation, wakefulness, and arousal. The states represented by the letters A (awake) and S (sleeping) are found to be related to responsivity to external stimulation (Brown, 1964). The roman numerals represent the corresponding states according to Prechtl's scheme, which ranges from I (low arousal) to V (high arousal). (Scheme developed by J.F. Rosenblith.)

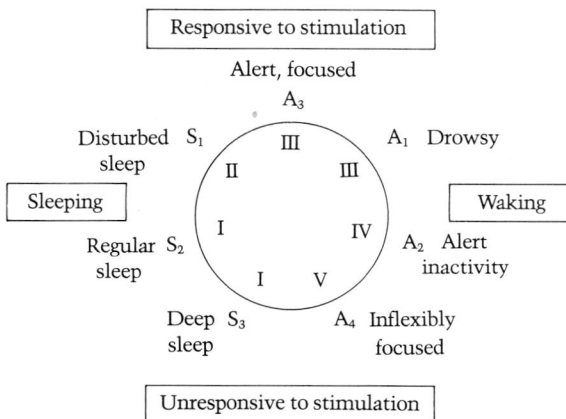

focused (S_3 and A_4), are at the bottom. The states of intermediate responsivity are appropriately arranged in between so that the upper half of the circle represents responsive states and the lower half relatively unresponsive states. The states on the left side of the circle are sleep states and those on the right are waking states. Notice that the unresponsive states include the highest, lowest, and moderate arousal states. Responsivity does not correspond to a continuum from waking to sleeping. From the top of the circle to the bottom, except for the most responsive state (A_3), all levels of responsivity are found in both sleeping and waking states. As the arrangement in Figure 6–4 shows, states can be conceived of as qualitatively different systems or organizations rather than as a simple continuum of arousal, responsivity, or wakefulness.

As complex as this description of the relation of state to responsivity is, it is oversimplified. Brown (1964) also showed that the relation between state and responsivity differed somewhat for different sensory modalities (for example, to visual versus auditory stimuli). In addition, babies differ somewhat from each other in respect to the state in which they are most responsive.

STATES: A PROBLEM IN THE STUDY OF NEWBORNS

The amount of time spent in an awake, alert state is very small for most newborns, but this state is assumed by many to be optimal or even necessary for carrying out certain types of studies. Although infants may be responsive in light or active sleep, they will be unresponsive if they are too deeply asleep. If they are very active, the experimenter may not be able to detect a response to a stimulus in the midst of all the other activity. Babies are also unresponsive when they are in the state that Brown (1964) called inflexibly focused, that is, when they are deeply involved in crying or sucking. Different states do not simply result in responses or no responses. Babies may respond in two different states, but the responses may be different. Thus, responses obtained in different states can lead to markedly different views of the functional capacities of young babies.

Physicians have typically examined newborns in ways that lead to their rapid arousal and crying. This, combined with the fact that the physician rarely has time to calm the infant, means that during most of their examination the infant is inflexibly focused. When researchers began to devise "tests" that measured infants' abilities to respond to stimuli, they typically tried to use less aversive techniques or techniques that enabled them to observe the babies' responses in different states (Brazelton, 1973; Graham, Matarazzo, & Caldwell, 1956; Rosenblith, 1961a, 1961b).

The same problems arise in other research contexts. Whether the topic is the general level of functioning in the newborn as determined by a "test" (see Chapter 8), or learning abilities (see Chapter 7), or perceptual abilities (see Chapter 9), the state of the infant must be taken into account. The problem is compounded when the same infant is examined on several occasions. Particularly for newborns, the reproducibility of responses at different times of the day or on different days may be influenced more by fluctuations in state than by changes in the babies' behavioral capacities or qualities. To assess truly developmental changes in infants, or stable individual characteristics, it is necessary to make sure that results are not inadvertently produced by changes in state.

Before we describe some solutions to the state problem, we wish to point out that this problem exists for all dependent variables. Not only are reflexes and behavioral responses to sensory stimuli dependent on state, but so are the more physiological responses such as heart rate, respiration rate, electroencephalograms (EEGs), and the galvanic skin response (GSR).[2] Thus, the approaches we are about to describe must be applied to all types of measures.

One approach to solving the problem of state is to wait for the infant to be in the desired state for the study, which may be very time consuming. Another technique is to try to manipulate the state. An example of state manipulation to produce a sleep-like state is to swaddle babies and keep them in a monotonous environment, such as in constant temperature and light. Wolff (1966) has pointed out, however, that there are differences between "normal" quiet sleep and that induced by

---

[2] The galvanic skin response (or reflex) is the name given to changes in the skin's conductivity to electrical stimulation. It usually indicates emotional reactions or arousal.

sound, and it would be nice to see a study comparing the sleep induced by swaddling with normal sleep.[3] Another way to manipulate state is to use soothing and rousing manipulations designed to keep the baby in an appropriate state for the desired observation.

If researchers don't wish to manipulate state, and they don't have time to wait for optimal states, they can simply assess or measure state in addition to measuring the behaviors of central interest. Then they can relate the infants' behaviors to their states, or they can consider only those results obtained in the most appropriate states. This can be done at the observational level by using any of the state classification schemes in Table 6–2, or by using physiological measures of state. In general, physiological measures may appear simple and objective, but in practice they do not necessarily enable a simpler solution. EEG is often used either to assess state in order to time the presentation of simuli or to judge state at the time the stimulus was presented. The first use probably does not represent much improvement over behavioral observations; the second may.

All of this leaves researchers with a lot of complexities to deal with. Whether a study controls for state by waiting for the desired one to occur, by special techniques such as swaddling, or by assessing it, may influence the research outcomes (dependent variables). Furthermore, when researchers control by assessing state by observational or physiological techniques, they will find different results depending on which observational scheme or which physiological index (heart rate, respiration, EEG patterns) is used.[4] It is also the case

that different dependent variables may be differently affected by the way the state problem is addressed.

STATES IN PRETERM BABIES

States and state organization are very different in preterm as compared to full-term babies. This indicates the importance of maturation of physiological systems (including the CNS) for state organization and emphasizes the warning (Prechtl, Fargel, Weinman, & Bakker, 1979) that the characteristics used to define behavioral states in term neonates are not applicable to preterm neonates. We have already discussed this fact for sleep and attention.

Aylward (1981) has provided a very useful series of state observations showing state both before being disturbed and after various arousing manipulations in the course of a modified Prechtl neurological assessment. In Aylward's study unstimulated Black infants of 29 to 30 weeks conceptional age were all in Prechtl's state II. As they approached normal term age they were increasingly in other states, especially state III. The youngest infants moved into state III after moderate amounts of manipulation and the older ones showed moderate amounts of state IV (30%). Stronger stimulation such as that provided by a pin prick did not rouse the youngest to more than state III. Crying, which occurred 75% of the time in 40-week-olds, was only present 33–40% of the time at 34 to 38 weeks, and did not appear prior to 31 weeks. Prematures respond to gravitational changes (such as from raise to sit, suspend in prone, or spinning manipulations) at younger ages and with greater arousal than they respond to other types of stimulation. Aylward's prematures, like those studied in a different manner by Prechtl et al., were all healthy, so his data, though based on only 58 babies, provide a basis for judging how typical (or normal) the state change responses of prematures from 31 to 38 weeks conceptional age are. His data should be replicated for white babies to be certain there are no ethnic differ-

[3] This is like the problem in animal work when, for example, brain signals or electrical activity in response to a sensory stimulus are studied to determine the animal's sensory capacities. Before computers and computer averaging techniques were available (see Figure 9–1 for an illustration of computer averaging), this had to be done in anesthetized animals so that the background activity of the brain would be low and the electrical response to the simulus could be observed. The comparability of these responses to those in an awake animal were suspect.

[4] Individual physiological measures have their own special problems. For example, a range of heart rates cannot be used as an index of state across a group of infants because a given heart rate may be associated with different states in different infants: with active awake in one, drowsiness in another, and quiet sleep in still another. Thus, if initial heart rate is used to control for state, as is common in studies of perception (see Chapter 9), the control is not

fully adequate unless the relation of heart rate to state is determined separately for each infant. Some specific examples of problems such as these may be found in Campos and Brackbill (1973), Lewis, Bartels, and Goldberg (1967), and Schachter, Bickman, Schachter, Jameson, Lituchy, and Williams (1966).

ences, but because many of the prematures seen in big city hospitals are Black, his data are currently useful.

RHYTHMIC ACTIVITIES

An Overview

Several of the behavior systems we will cover show strong rhythmic characteristics, such as sucking and crying or Piaget's circular reactions. Certain rhythmic behaviors (rocking and head banging) have long attracted the attention of clinicians, but rhythmic behaviors in their totality (which would include eating and sleeping rhythms) have been little studied. Thelen (1981) has made a natural history and an ethological catalog of all rhythmical stereotyped motor behavior bouts from 4 weeks to 1 year. Over 16,000 bouts were recorded. There were great individual differences. Some infants spent only 5% of their time in such behaviors and others spent 40%. Most of the bouts were associated with either a change in stimuli or with a nonalert state.

There were developmental (or age) changes both in the amounts of rhythmic behaviors and the type of stimuli that elicited them. Rhythmic movements of given body systems appear to increase just before the infant achieves voluntary control of that system. Indeed, maturational level seems to be the primary determinant of these behaviors. Evidence for this is that no differences were found between normal term infants and prematures who had respiratory distress, or between normals and postmatures when they were at the same gestational ages (Field, Ting, & Shuman, 1979).

The CNS mechanisms governing the rhythmic patterns of motor behaviors are little known. Robertson (1982) has found rhythmic or periodic spontaneous wrist movements in the awake infant similar to those found in movements and startles during sleep. Normative data might allow detection of abnormal patterns or abnormal amounts of these behaviors even if the mechanisms are not understood.

It is to be hoped that more research in these areas will enable testing of some of the hypotheses arrived at by Thelen (1981), who related these behaviors to a wide range of other

observations in developmental psychology, both human and animal.

Sucking

GETTING STARTED

Sucking is a rhythmic activity that is actually one of a group of feeding reflexes that include the rooting reflexes, the lip and sucking reflexes, and the swallowing reflexes.

The Rooting and Sucking Reflexes. The rooting reflex is the name given to a reflexive response to touch stimulation of the area around the mouth (the perioral region). It has been described by Kussmaul (1859) as well as detailed by Prechtl (1958), who differentiated a side-to-side head-turning reflex from a directed head-turning response. In the former the head turns first one way, usually toward the stimulus (gentle tapping or stroking of some perioral area), and then the other way. The swings become progressively smaller until the mouth is sufficiently oriented toward the stimulus to bring the lips into contact and allow sucking to follow. This reflex disappears or gradually becomes the directed head-turning response by 3 weeks of age in normal newborns. The directed head-turning response involves a single well-directed or apparently purposeful head movement that brings the infant's mouth into contact with the stimulus. It can only be elicited from areas close to the mouth, but can include up, down, or rotational movements of the head in response to stimulation of the middle of either lip or at an angle from the corners of the mouth. While the directed reflex is usually present at birth, it is more difficult to elicit and is often found together with the more predominant side-to-side reflex.

In the normal course of feeding, the rooting reflexes lead to contact with the nipple, especially in breast feeding babies whose rooting response is said to be better developed after the first two or three weeks than that of bottle-fed babies (Ingram, 1962). Even though rooting is unnecessary for bottle-fed babies, unless they are left with propped bottles, they often root when the nipple is inserted in their mouth.

Although the strength of the rooting reflexes varies from time to time, we know of no systematic studies linking these variations to changes in hunger. In general, rooting seems to be more easily obtained when infants are hungry or drowsy and when they are in the normal feeding position (Ingram, 1962). Some parents feel that ease in eliciting the rooting response and its strength can be used to determine whether their infant's fussing is related to hunger.

The rooting reflexes have not been found to be useful for neurological diagnosis (Ingram, 1962) because of the wide range of individual differences in the ease of eliciting them and because they are relatively invulnerable to neurological deficit. For example, they have been found in babies with severe cortical damage and even been found temporarily in **anencephalics** (babies who lack a cortex). This invulnerability seems sensible from an evolutionary perspective. The reflexes necessary to ingest food would be expected to be among the most built in, or most resistant to damage.

There is a lip reflex, sometimes called the "cardinal point sign," that is similar to the head movement reflexes. It can be elicited by touching or stroking. This causes the lips to move toward the stimulus when the head does not (Thompson, 1903; André-Thomas & Dargassies, 1952). In the newborn the mouth opens and the tongue protrudes, and at the end of the motion the tongue retracts, the lips close, and swallowing and sucking movements follow. Occasionally there is an inverted response in which the movements are away from the stimulus. These responses are similar to those found in the 3- to 4-month fetus (Minkowski, 1922, 1928; Prechtl, 1958).

The behavior of sucking itself—the sucking reflex—is triggered by an object (especially a nipple-like one) touching the lips, gums, hard palate, or front of the tongue. Repetitive sucking usually follows such a touch, often after an initial swallow. If it doesn't, gentle movements of the object within the mouth will usually produce sucking. This is, of course, the time-honored technique by which mothers encourage their babies to nurse (Figure 6–5) or to suck their bottle nipples.

Thus far we have discussed the sucking part of this whole complex of reflexes as if it were a unitary process. It actually contains two separate processes by which milk is obtained. One is the squeezing of the nipple between

FIGURE 6–5. In some cultures, nursing is a casual affair.

tongue and palate, called expression, and the other is the suction or negative pressure generated in the mouth cavity (Ardran, Kemp, & Lind, 1958, cited in Sameroff, 1968). The two components are normally linked; in other words, when one occurs so does the other. Nevertheless, they can be separated under experimental conditions. There are stable individual differences in both suction pressure and expression amplitude, as well as in the number of responses (Sameroff, 1968).

Sucking and Eating. Sucking (or the whole complex of feeding behaviors) is often described as a reflex or an innate response, but many mothers know that these reflexes do not always work well. There are great individual differences in the efficiency with which normal term newborns take to sucking or feeding. For efficient feeding, not only must all these reflexes be present and coordinated, but they must also be coordinated with another reflex in the complex of feeding reflexes, the swallowing reflex. It is less studied than the sucking reflex, probably because it is less visible and because it is less likely to need any special stimulation. Indeed, reflex swallowing is produced by many stimuli that have no relation to feeding. In addition, the pattern of sucking and swallowing in the newborn makes it hard to differentiate the swallowing from the sucking.

The sucking and swallowing reflexes must also be coordinated with breathing or respiratory activity. Although each reflex can be tested separately, the coordinated presence of all of them is necessary for successful feeding. In particular, the coordination of sucking and swallowing with breathing is necessary if the baby is to avoid getting food into the lungs instead of the stomach. Lack of this coordination, more often than the absence of reflexes, leads to the necessity to feed premature infants by gavage, a tube inserted directly into the stomach or esophagus.

Although the individual feeding reflexes are not useful for neurological diagnosis, spontaneous feeding behavior, which involves their integration, does help identify infants with physiological and motor problems and with retardation. For example, there is evidence showing that high bilirubin levels (severe jaundice) lead to a disintegration of the sucking pattern (Kazmeier, 1973; Kazmeier, Keenan, & Sutherland, 1977). This relationship is dramatically evident in infants who receive exchange transfusions in which all of the blood in their bodies is replaced by new blood with normal bilirubin levels. The degree to which the sucking pattern is organized is directly related to the bilirubin levels. There is a gradual decrease in the level of organization as bilirubin levels build up, followed by a dramatic increase in organization after the exchange transfusion, followed by a gradual decrease again, for as many times as it takes to stabilize the infant's bilirubin at a normal level.

Changes in Sucking Pressure During the Perinatal Period. A variety of data (Anderson, McBride, Dahm, Ellis, & Vidyasagar, 1982; Gaulin-Kremer, Shaw, & Thoman, 1977; Koepke & Barnes, 1982) suggest a very early readiness to suck in both premature and term infants. Sucking pressures do not increase gradually but, in fact, decline by 6 to 8 hours of

age. Note that this is before many hospitals provide feeding or nonnutritive sucking (the latter occurs in breast-fed babies). In the discussion of maternal bonding (Chapter 5), the importance of putting the infant to the breast in the first hours after birth was stressed. The maximal pressures in those hours may improve the establishment of the maternal milk supply (remember that long-range effects of "bonding" practices were found almost entirely in nursing variables). The data presented above also emphasize that what happens in the maternal–infant interaction in the immediate post-birth period is partly the result of infant behaviors, not just maternal behaviors or maternal bonding.

Sucking and Experience. We have already shown that sucking reflexes change rapidly, even before sucking experience could do much to modify them. It is also important to note that early sucking responses are modified by experience. Sameroff (1968) systematically studied the influence of learning on the two components of the sucking response. He used the technique of operant conditioning in which newborns were rewarded (given milk) if they sucked (one condition) or if they expressed milk (another condition). He found that the sucking component was governed largely by the reward: when sucking got them milk, the babies sucked more; when it didn't get them milk, their sucking fell off. Expression movements were also responsive to the reward, but less so than sucking. The expression pressure increased when that was necessary to get milk, but expression continued even when it was not rewarded. These results suggest that sucking is governed in part by basic biological mechanisms and is in part a response to environmental events.

Because sucking develops so rapidly in the first three weeks of life, partly in response to the environment, the lack of opportunity to suck may be disadvantageous to infants. This reasoning has led several investigators to question common hospital practices for prematures. Although prematures at all stages of development show some sucking behaviors, many nevertheless are fed by tubes down the esophagus in order to make certain that the liquid reaches their stomachs and is not breathed into the lungs where it can cause pneumonia. The tubes remove the necessity for the premature infants to coordinate sucking with swallowing and breathing movements, and deny them the opportunity to establish their sucking patterns during the immediate postpartum period. In three studies reported in a symposuim at the 1980 International Conference on Infant Studies, prematures were given sucking experience in the hospital. Anderson, Burroughs, Measel, Afone, and Vidyasagar (1980) described the soothing effects of giving nonnutritive sucking to prematures. When allowed to keep a pacifier in their mouths, many sucked as much as an hour at a time. A variety of indices showed these prematures to be physiologically and neurologically in better condition and better organized than those who were not given pacifiers. Anderson reported another study (Anderson, Fleming, & Vidyasagar, 1980) in which the second-born of twins, who are usually more at risk, were given nonnutritive sucking together with their tube feeding. Compared with the first-born of these twin pairs, who received routine procedures, the second-born (or experimental) twin was ready to suck for food three days earlier, had fewer complications in general, and was discharged for home many days earlier. Another study (Ignatoff, 1980; Ignatoff & Field, 1982), compared an experimental group of 16 prematures (under 1800 grams and less than 35 weeks gestational age but with no genetic or physical abnormalities) with 17 control prematures with the same characteristics. Infants had been assigned to the groups by stratified random sampling. Both the experimental and the contol groups received pacifiers according to the normal practice of the unit they were on, but the pacifier was only linked with food intake for the experimental group. They were given the largest pacifier they could tolerate with each tube feeding.[5] They showed better weight gain and were considered ready to be sent home earlier. Hence their separation from their parents was shorter and their postnatal care cost much less. The evidence with respect to long-term differences is not available, so it is not yet known whether there are any subsequent advantages or harmful side effects.

Over all, the preliminary evidence seems to indicate that both nonnutritive sucking in general and nonnutritive sucking that is linked to the delivery of food is good for prematures.

THE SOCIALIZATION OF SUCKING

As we mentioned above, the individual reflexes in the feeding behaviors can be elicited without feeding the infant. Even if sucking isn't elicited, both newborns and older infants will suck things that do not lead to obtaining nourishment or food. This is commonly described as nonnutritive sucking. Babies even do nonnutritive sucking prior to birth as has been often illustrated by a photo showing a fetus in utero sucking its thumb. Some newborns have damaged fingers or thumbs that appear to be the result of excessive sucking prior to birth. Sucking is another behavior that shows strong individual differences. Nonnutritive sucking persists as is shown in Figure 6–6.

Nonnutritive sucking is an important dependent variable in research with young infants because they stop sucking when they at-

FIGURE 6–6. Nonnutritive sucking in a toddler.

---

[5] This is possible because the tubes used to feed prematures are usually put down the nostril, not the mouth.

tend to a stimulus. Thus it can be used to detect when an infant is attending to a stimulus such as a picture or a speech sound.

Nonnutritive Sucking: Good or Bad? Nonnutritive sucking has aroused a great deal of interest throughout history, both in relation to practical questions of infant management and with respect to theoretical questions. Most infant management questions center around nonnutritive sucking (whether to allow thumb or finger sucking or to give pacifiers). Nutritive sucking is central only to the management problem of when and how to wean infants (except for some newborns who need to be taught to suck). Attitudes toward nonnutritive sucking found in different cultures, and in our own, at different points in history have varied widely, as have opinions about the proper age at which to wean babies from nutritive sucking. Babies suck fingers, fists, pacifiers, blankets, toys, or anything that is available. Such sucking has been perceived as a tool by which the infant can achieve self-quieting; as a form of self-gratification or indulgence; or as a nasty habit that should not be allowed to develop, or, at least, should be stopped as soon as possible. When experts in the United States considered nonnutritive sucking to be a nasty habit, they advised the following steps, to be taken in the order given, for preventing its continuation: (1) Paint the baby's hands with iodine or other unpleasant tasting substances. (2) Fasten cuffs over the baby's arms so the hands cannot get to the mouth. (3) Tie the sleeves of the baby's clothes to the sides of the crib.[6]

It is tempting to explain the view of nonnutritive sucking as bad as a reflection of a puritan heritage that essentially held that any pleasure is necessarily sinful. Superimposed on this was the Watsonian behaviorist view that the more pleasure (reward) an infant got from undesirable behaviors, the harder it would be

to cure these "bad" habits. Thus, parents should prevent the habit of nonnutritive sucking from getting started. Subsequently, Freudian theories began to have a major impact on some parents and on the advice given to parents in women's magazines, government booklets, and newspapers. To oversimplify, Freudian theory saw sucking as a normal need that could only be dealt with satisfactorily by gratifying it. That is, Freud considered sucking to be a psychological need, analogous to the physical need for food, which must be satisfied if growth is to proceed normally. If properly gratified, this need would be outgrown in a healthy way. If gratified too little or too much, the baby would not outgrow the need and would develop emotional problems such as oral addictions (liquor, pills, cigarettes, talking).

The Clash of Theories About the Role of Sucking. The contrast between Freudian views and the "learned bad habit school" led to the theoretical emphasis on the role of nonnutritive sucking. One debate was over the question of whether sucking was innately pleasurable or became so only after being associated with feeding (that is, as the result of learning). Indeed, a whole chapter of a book on the history of selected problems in psychology (McKee & Honzik, 1963) is devoted to the sucking of mammals as an illustration of the nature–nurture issue. The authors of that chapter point out that Darwin had suggested that both learning (habit) and an "inherited or instinctive tendency" might be necessary for sucking. They comment on the preoccupation with the single behavior of sucking, especially thumb sucking or pleasure sucking, that characterized the period from the early 1920s until the early 1960s. They discuss the controversy between psychoanalysis and behaviorism in greater detail than is possible here, but we would like to illustrate the issue by describing several classic studies on both sides.

The first is a study by David Levy, an important child psychiatrist (1892–1977). Having interviewed mothers and found that thumb suckers had had less opportunity to suck in nursing, a finding that would be expected from Freudian theory (Levy, 1928), he designed a study to test the Freudian hypothesis further. A litter of 6 puppies was separated into three

---

[6] Much of the advice given to parents earlier in this century treated both sucking and masturbation (another rhythmic behavior) as nasty habits. The techniques described to cope with sucking were similar to those prescribed to prevent infants from "handling themselves." Boy babies who moved their thighs to produce genital stimulation were to have their legs tied to the bars of the crib to prevent masturbation. Babies who both sucked their fingers and masturbated might have both hands and legs tied to the bars of their cribs, if parents followed this advice.

pairs at 10 days of age. One pair continued to nurse from the mother, one pair was bottle fed from very slowly-flowing nipples, and the third was fed by tube for 3 days. Because this pair was losing weight, they were subsequently fed from very fast-flowing nipples. When all the pups were later tested for sucking on a nipple-covered finger (that is, for nonnutritive sucking), the pair fed on rapidly-flowing nipples (who had had the least chance to suck) sucked the most. That pair also appeared to be more restless and required more formula to achieve normal weight gain than the others. This study was replicated in 1957. Thus, this research supported the Freudian notion that infants need a certain amount of sucking or gratification from sucking, and that infants who were denied it during nutritive sucking would do more nonnutritive sucking.

The second study stemmed from learning theory, although at least one of its authors (Sears) was trained both in learning theory and in psychoanalytic theory. In this study (Davis, Sears, Miller, & Brodbeck, 1948), a group of infants were fed by cup from birth. Because they got little nutritional sucking from which they could develop a learned drive to suck, learning theory would predict that they should show less nonnutritive sucking than the control groups who were fed by breast or bottle. According to Freudian theory, the cup-fed infants should show more nonnutritive sucking because they had not experienced adequate oral (sucking) gratification. Twenty newborns in each group (cup fed, bottle fed, and breast fed) were studied. All infants were observed in non-nutritive sucking test behaviors (as in Levy's study) for 10 days. The breast-fed group showed increased nonnutritive sucking, as learning theory predicts. The bottle-fed group, however, was like the cup-fed group, which was not what learning theory predicts. The authors' explanation after the study was that the nipples were so easy that bottle feeding was like cup feeding in the amount of oral gratification received. Indeed, bottle-fed babies, like cup-fed babies, consumed their food in half the time taken by breast-fed babies. If this explanation is correct, then the bottle- and cup-fed babies both fulfilled the learning theory's expectations that they would engage in less nonnutritive sucking than the hard-sucking breast-fed babies. A replication study designed to test this

interpretation (Brodbeck, 1950) both confirmed the earlier results and made the explanation more plausible.

These two sets of studies support opposing theoretical positions. Other studies have also yielded inconsistent results. The Freudian oral drive view that adequate sucking during feeding leads to little nonnutritive sucking has been supported by Fleischl (1957) and Ross (1951). The learned habit view has been supported by Blau and Blau (1955), Brodbeck (1950), and Sears and Wise (1950).

Let us look at a well-designed study of infant monkeys (Benjamin, 1961) to see what light it can shed on this argument. The results are limited by the fact that monkeys still are not humans and by the fact that the monkeys in the study were being raised on artificial mothers. (Artificial mothers enabled easier control of sucking experiences, but may limit generalizability of the results, even for monkeys). The sex of the infant monkeys was controlled, as was their exposure to nonnutritive sucking, and experimental conditions were balanced between infants with stationary mothers and those with rocking mothers. Not only was nonnutritive sucking examined as an outcome measure, but weight gain, the time taken in feeding, and the degree of post-feeding disturbance (crouching and rocking) were noted. The study was longitudinal, looking at the outcome measures for about 6 months, equivalent to a much longer time in humans. The experimental conditions were that one group had no experience sucking for food (they were cup fed), and the second group experienced sucking for food (from a bottle with the smallest holes that the infants would feed from).

During the first three months of life, differences in oral activity were found between these two groups of animals, although the direction of the effects on nonnutritive sucking were opposite to those for nonsucking oral activity. The bottle-fed infants engaged in more nonnutritive sucking than the cup-fed ones, thus supporting the learning theory prediction that the sucking habit would be strengthened by sucking experience. Nonnutritive sucking, however, also showed various changes over the course of the study that cannot be interpreted easily in terms of either theory. Nonnutritive sucking increased in both groups over the first

70 days. It started to wane for the bottle-fed group at that point, and somewhat later for the cup-fed group. The differences between the groups in nonnutritive sucking waxed and waned during the first three months, but became very small after 90 days. In contrast, oral behaviors other than nonnutritive sucking were higher for cup-fed than for bottle-fed infants, a finding that supports Freudian theory. Again, the differences between the groups decreased after 90 days. The fact that groups fed in both ways engaged in nonnutritive oral behaviors during the first three months and then decreased in both sucking and other forms of oral activity suggests the existence of an underlying oral responsiveness (orality or oral drive) that waxes and wanes during infancy. The finding that nonnutritive sucking was the preferred form for the bottle-fed group and that other nonnutritive oral behaviors were the preferred form for cup-fed infants suggests that the form that oral behaviors take depends on the kind of experience the baby has had.

Benjamin's study might resolve the discrepancies of the previous studies, if we could generalize the results to humans. It suggests that researchers must include both sucking and other forms of nonnutritive oral behaviors. Because the previous studies failed to measure nonsucking oral activity, they may have failed to uncover nonnutritive orality in infants with little sucking experience. Benjamin's study also leads to the conclusion that the Freudians were incorrect in their claim that early sucking experience has long-lasting effects. After 90 days of age even monkeys who experienced no nutritive sucking were no different in oral behaviors from those with adequate nutritive sucking experience.[7]

All the studies we have discussed so far have focused on nonnutritive sucking during infancy. The crucial Freudian hypothesis, however, is that inappropriate sucking experiences during infancy have permanent effects on personality. Thus, the inconclusive findings on the effects of nursing variables on sucking during infancy are interesting, but they do not invalidate Freudian theory. Unfortunately, adequate tests of the Freudian hypothesis with respect to long-term outcomes are rare. Most Freudian studies are retrospective; in other words, they find subjects with certain behavior (for example, high orality as measured by addiction to nicotine, alcohol, or other drugs) and then ask these people or their relatives to recall the subject's early experiences. This is an extremely problematic procedure because everyone's memory of long ago events is extremely faulty. We know of only one long-term prospective study of the development of oral behaviors. Skard (1966) followed the development of children and their parents from their prenatal months to 9 years of age. On the basis of interviews with the parents and observations and tests of the children, she determined feeding practices, finger sucking, hand–mouth reactions, and other oral activity during free play when they were babies and during school class sessions and sandbox play when they were older. Her sample was so small that statistical analyses would not be helpful; therefore, we will describe the data for her strongest findings in terms of the individual children.

During infancy most of the babies sucked their fingers, so there was no relation between feeding practices and whether babies sucked their fingers. The age of onset of finger sucking and age of weaning appeared to be related. This suggests that the finger sucking was a compensation for their loss of nutritive sucking, which is consistent with Freudian theory and the conclusions we drew from Benjamin's study of monkeys. Skard also found that babies who were allowed to regulate their own food intake or sucking time, or both, were not likely to finger suck early: only 1 in 7 did. In contrast, babies whose food intake or sucking time, or both, was regulated by their mothers were likely to finger suck early: 7 of 9 did.[8] This

---

[7]Benjamin also indicated that the data provided indirect support for the suggestion that masturbation and thumbsucking enhance each other, that is, that both are forms of sexual gratification, a Freudian notion. The finding they refer to is that the only masturbators in the group studied were four males who were thumbsuckers and who also had rocking mothers. We would like to remark that this finding equally suggests that rocking mothers may enhance both thumbsucking and masturbation. In other words, the pleasures of rhythmic activity, learned from a rocking mother, may produce a secondary drive for rhythmic activity such as sucking and masturbating in at least some monkey infants.

[8]The same relations were found between the mother's attitudes toward the infant's need for gratification and finger sucking, but unfortunately the influence of maternal attitudes was not separated from that of maternal behaviors.

result agrees with an earlier finding (Yarrow, 1954) based on a larger sample. Both findings are consistent with some of the others discussed in this section: Babies who were allowed to suck enough to meet their needs had less need to suck their fingers.

The long-term outcomes in Skard's study of humans generally support and extend Benjamin's conclusion that early sucking experiences in monkeys had no long-term consequences. There were no definite relations between the outcome measures of oral activity at 3½ years and any of the following: amount of orality in the first year, weaning age, self-demand food intake, or mothers' attitude toward need gratification in the first year. The relations between early sucking experience and oral behaviors at 6, 7, 8, and 9 years were only slightly more impressive. The only apparent relation of orality in infancy to later orality was found between the duration of breastfeeding and oral activity at 7 years. This relation was curvilinear, but in the direction opposite to what would be predicted by Freud. Those who received only a short experience with breastfeeding (less than 1 month) or who had a very long experience by western cultural standards (7 months or more) exhibited less oral activity at 7 years than those breastfed for from 2½ to 5 months. Specifically, only 2 of 7 in the extreme categories showed high oral activity but all of the 8 children in the middle category did. This finding of long-term oral consequences for children weaned in the middle age range (2½ to 5 months) is similar to Childers and Hamil's (1932) finding that children weaned at between 1 and 5 months of age were over-represented in behavior problem groups. Sewell and Mussen (1952), however, found no outcome differences for such children at ages 5 and 6. If it is true that children weaned between 1 and 5 months are at risk for later problems—and the data are by no means conclusive—then this would support Freud's general claim that feeding practices during infancy have long-term consequences, but clearly disconfirms his hypothesis that moderate levels of oral gratification produce optimal outcomes. A reasonable explanation of the findings is that infants' sucking needs (or their needs for the other comforts provided by breastfeeding, that is, longer and more frequent intimate interaction) are highest during the 1- to 5-month period, so that denial

of oral needs in that period has more impact than denial when the needs are less strong.

Skard's study provided additional evidence consistent with the conclusion that Freud was correct in his hypothesis concerning long-term effects of early experience but wrong in his beliefs concerning oral gratification and later behavior. Parents' attitudes and behaviors toward crying in the first year were related to oral behaviors at 3½ years. Of the 6 children who were usually picked up when they cried, only 1 showed much finger sucking at 3½ years, but 7 of the 10 who were usually left to cry showed a lot. It could be argued that both this finding and the relation between the length of breastfeeding and oral behaviors at 7 years show the long-term negative effects of lack of comfort during infancy. Skard points out that failure to provide comfort, at least in the case of crying, is likely to be a general parental characteristic that lasts beyond their child's infancy, and that the 7-year finding may be a cumulative effect rather than a result of treatment in infancy.

To make matters more complicated, Skard's data provide indications of still other possible influences on orality. Children who came from very warm, accepting homes showed more orality, a result also found by McFarlane, Allen, and Honzik (1954). Somewhat in contrast is Skard's finding that only 1 of 10 children from homes with low conflict between parents showed high orality whereas 4 of the 5 children from homes with high conflict showed high orality.

Taken in their entirety, Skard's data show that the factors that determine later orality are complex. Freud may be correct that experiences during infancy affect later orality, but if so, they are not the experiences proposed by Freud. Some Freudians might still object to this conclusion, however, because the outcome behaviors measured by Skard were not the ones Freud was trying to predict for adults, such as pathological orality, drug addiction, or personality characteristics such as passive dependency. It is possible that future research may show that sucking experiences during infancy do influence the development of these other dependent variables.

Skard's findings that parental warmth and responsivity and low conflict in the home are related to later behaviors are consistent with much research in the last 15 years. These variables have been found to be relatively more important in explaining development in several domains than are sucking and feeding experiences during infancy. We will discuss some of the infancy-related research on such variables in Chapters 12 and 13.

Because earlier research did not find profound effects of early sucking experiences on orality and because later work (to be discussed in Chapter 12) showed that nursing variables were not important determinants in the development of infants' attachment to their mothers, few researchers today are exploring the role of sucking in personality development. Instead, there is increased emphasis on using sucking as a tool to find out about some other aspect of the child's behavior (see Chapter 9) and to indicate something about the medical status of newborns. The recording of sucking behavior has become automated and computerized so that objective records of the behavior are now relatively easy to obtain.

Practical Issues. As for the practical problems of nonnutritive sucking (thumbs, fingers, pacifiers), the research in this area suggests that parents' personal decisions will probably have no serious long-term consequences for the later personality of their child. The issues to consider, then, are more immediate and practical. Most babies suck their fingers at some time during infancy (Simsarian, 1947; Skard, 1966) and that seems to be because babies do have a basic need to suck. Both nutritive and nonnutritive sucking have immediate quieting effects that are innate[9] (Kessen, Leutzendorff, & Stoutsenberger, 1967). Allowing upset babies to suck can thus be a boon to baby and parent alike. Furthermore, finger sucking shows a normal developmental progression of waxing and waning, so parents do not condemn their children to a difficult habit if they allow them to finger suck. Many parents worry about the difficulty of "breaking the habit" later if they allow their babies to suck. It is true that about 40% of children continue to suck their thumbs even after they start school (Kessen, Haith, &

Salapatek, 1970). Note, however, that this late sucking need is at least as likely to be from constitutional individual differences as it is to be due to parental behaviors. One small study of infants found great individual differences in the length of time and degree to which 5 babies sucked their fingers even though they all had similar experiences in that they were breast fed on demand (Simsarian, 1947). It is not likely that differences in sucking experience alone produced these individual differences. If parental behaviors are important in preventing school-age fingersuckers, it is not known what those behaviors are. Whether parents' decisions about sucking-related issues in infancy have long-term effects on oral behaviors, and what role other parental behaviors play, is not clear.

AFFECTIVE BEHAVIORS

Three emotionally expressive behaviors—smiling, laughing, and crying—have received a great deal of attention from infant researchers because they are so prominent in infants. The more general issues of whether infants exhibit emotional expressions that can be recognized by adults and whether infants can recognize adults' emotional expressions have been only sporadically studied. In this section we will first review research on the communicative nature of emotional expressions in infancy, and then we will describe the particular research on crying, smiling, and laughing that focuses on the development of these responses and the environmental stimuli that elicit them.

Communicative Aspects of Emotional Expressions

Darwin made observational studies of the expression of emotion in animals and humans (1872), and he included observations of these expressions in his infant diary (see Chapter 1). Recently, a spate of studies have appeared that demonstrate that it is possible for adults to identify accurately the emotional expressions of babies in the first year of life (Izard, Huebner, Risser, McGinnes, & Dougherty, 1980; Izard, Hembree, Dougherty, & Spizziri, 1983; Hiatt,

---

[9]Benjamin (1961) found that frustrating monkeys by delaying and interfering with their getting at preferred food items increased their nonnutritive sucking during the frustration. For 2 males, the sucking was sexual (1 penis, 1 scrotum).

Campos, & Emde, 1979; Stenberg, Campos, & Emde, 1983). In all of these studies the labels given to the emotional expressions are adult labels; that is, the stimuli used to produce the expressions are those adults deem likely to lead to the emotions whose labels are used. In these studies both experienced health professionals and college students, as well as trained and untrained judges, have reliably judged facial expressions of interest, joy, surprise, anger, disgust, sadness, and fear. The primary effect of training was to improve the observers' identification of negative (not positive) emotions and to improve the performance of those that were least accurate initially. Raters were equally accurate judging video tapes and slides.

Let us give just one example of concrete data. The sort of emotional response infants have to a given stimulus changes with age. Izard and colleagues (1983) found that distress reactions to "shots" declined from 2 months to 18 months, whereas anger responses increased dramatically after 6 months of age.

If adults can discriminate the affective expressions of infants, can infants discriminate emotional expressions of adults or peers? Work in this area has just started and no major conclusions should be drawn from it. We would like to describe three studies that indicate the direction of this research. The first (Field, Woodson, Greenberg, & Cohen, 1982) explored newborns' responses to various expressions made by a single model. The adult model first attracted the newborns' attention. Then, when the infants were looking, the model made a happy, sad, or surprised face. The newborns did discriminate among the various expressions. The discriminations were detected by an experimental technique known as the habituation–dishabituation paradigm, which we will describe in Chapter 7. The technique shows only that babies could discriminate perceptually among the various expressions. It does not show that the newborns knew that these expressions indicated different emotional states.

The second study also explored infants' abilities to discriminate among visual representations of expressions (Caron, Caron, & Myers, 1982). In contrast to Field and colleagues (1982), Caron and colleagues included a condition that required the infants to detect the similarities of an expression, happy for instance, in four different faces and then to de-

tect the difference between that expression and another, say surprise. They found that 30-week-old infants, but not 18- or 24-week-olds, were able to differentiate between happy and surprised expressions. This is a more complex perceptual task than that studied by Field and colleagues, and so it is reasonable to expect that it develops later. Caron and colleagues had a second task in which the infants could discriminate between two faces with the same expression. Babies at all the ages studied (18 weeks or older) were able to do this. Girls were substantially better at these tasks than boys.

In the third study, infants 10 to 29 months old, most of whom were under 2 years, were studied in naturalistic settings (Cummings, Zahn-Waxler, & Radke-Yarrow, 1981). The infants responded with distress to high-intensity anger expressed by a parent to someone other than themselves (in 69% of the episodes that involved hitting, usually of a sibling, and in 41% of episodes of anger without hitting). Exposure to such angry behaviors did not lead to angry responses on the part of the infants, but the more fights between parents the infants had been exposed to, the more likely they were to respond with affectionate/prosocial behaviors, anger, or distress, and the less likely they were to respond unemotionally.

Positive emotional expressions of affection towards others most often elicited affectionate/prosocial behaviors from infants (61% of instances), but jealous affection and anger were also relatively frequent responses. In specially-staged incidents of expression of affects, negative responses were much less frequent, suggesting that the infants could discriminate these from the real thing.

After this glimpse of infants' ability to discriminate among and respond to affective displays, we now turn to the infant expression of affect that has always had powerful effects on parents: crying.

Crying

The most important mechanism newborns have for communicating with their world is crying. This is true from the first cry, a signal that tells the mother, doctor, or whoever is present or even outside the room, that the baby's lungs have been filled with air. It is also

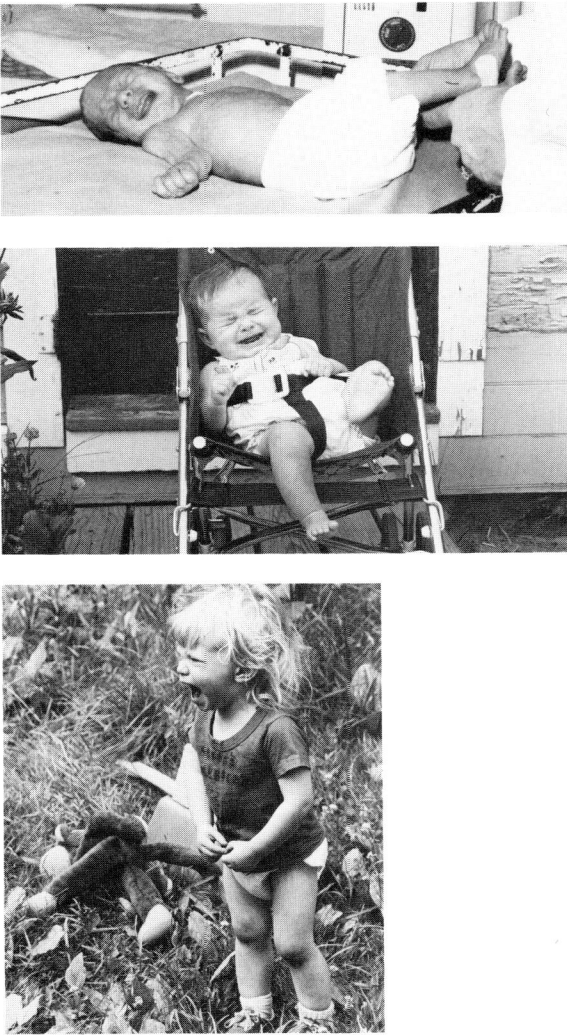

FIGURE 6–7. Crying babies. (a) is a neonate, (b) is about 8 months old, and (c) is a toddler. Notice that the oldest child shows the least body involvement.

true of the cries weeks and months later that often are quite accurately interpreted by caretakers. Cries may also tell a doctor or scientist something about the state of the baby's central nervous system (see Figure 6–7).

CHARACTERISTICS OF CRIES

As long ago as 1832 different types of cries were described in terms of musical notation (Gardiner, 1838). Darwin (1872) studied the facial grimaces associated with crying in chil-

dren. By 1906 it was possible to use early recording discs to study the **acoustical** (or sound) properties of cries. Even then researchers noticed that the pitch of the cries of an infant with breathing problems was about an octave higher than that of normal infants. With the development of the sound spectrograph, which allows visual presentation of acoustic characteristics of sounds (see Chapter 11), it became possible to analyze cries in more detail. In 1965 a series of papers describing the sounds and movements involved in newborn cries were published as a supplement to the Scandinavian pediatric journal (Lind, 1965).[10] The cry of the newborn is described as "a vivid manifestation." It is both a vocalization containing acoustic information and a complex motor act in response to some stimulus, starting with the stimulus provided by the birth experience. Taken in its entirety, including actions of the pharynx, soft palate, tongue, larynx, and even the trunk as it participates in respirations, the performance pattern of the cry may be the infant's most distinctive motor activity. Indeed, just as infants are footprinted for identification, the concept of a "cryprint" was introduced in 1960 (Truby, 1959, 1960, cited in Lind, 1965). Thus, it is not surprising that mothers often report (correctly) that they are able to tell when their baby is crying in the hospital nursery, even though they cannot see the baby.

The cries of newborns also vary in different circumstances. Wasz-Hockert, Lind, Vuorenkoski, Partanen, and Valaane (1968) measured a variety of acoustic characteristics in cries obtained in different circumstances. On the basis of these characteristics they were able to differentiate among cries obtained in four situations: birth, hunger, pain, and pleasure. Wolff (1969) described three types of cries: basic, anger, and pain. He believes it is wrong to talk about a hunger cry, because it is really the basic cry and is not specifically caused by hunger. The basic cry is a rhythmical pattern that typically consists of the basic cry followed by a briefer silence, a shorter inspiratory whistle that is of somewhat higher pitch than the cry proper, and another brief rest period before the

---

[10] For some reason workers in Finland and Sweden have led the way in such studies.

next cry. The anger cry, so called because most mothers infer exasperation or rage from it, is a variation of the basic cry, differing in that excess air is forced through the vocal cords. The pain cry, which is elicited by high-intensity stimuli, differs from the others in that it has a sudden onset of loud crying without preliminary moaning and a long initial cry followed by an extended period of breath holding. Even this cry gradually subsides into the basic cry.[11]

Wolff (1966) also found that crying before feeding differed from that after feeding, based on observing 3 infants for 16 to 18 hours a day. Before feeding, crying was rhythmical, had a braying quality, and was accompanied by kicking that seemed governed by the same rhythm. Crying after meals tended to be less rhythmic, more shrill, and not synchronized with kicking. The extent to which individual babies differed in amount of crying also seemed to be specific to the type of crying. Wolff found relatively little variation in the amount of time spent crying before meals but great variation after meals. One infant cried only 4 minutes after a meal, one 89 minutes, and the third, 361 minutes.

The pitches that make up hunger cries differ from those of attention-getting cries (Lynip, 1951). Distress cries are also louder and last longer than hunger cries and tend to be more irregular. There is less variability in cries in response to a pinch than in those in response to mild discomfort.[12]

Both diary studies (Brazelton, 1962) and tapes of infant vocalizations (Rebelsky & Black, 1972) have followed the developmental course of crying. They agree that it increases over the first six weeks of life and then decreases; that maximum crying occurs in the evening in the first weeks of life, then shifts toward feeding times; and that there are marked differences among babies. There are also differences in the same baby from day to day or week to week.

DIAGNOSTIC VALUE OF CRIES

What about the neurological or medical information to be found in the cry? The booklet edited by Lind (1965) contains a chapter on the cries of infants with physical abnormalities of the mouth area. We are more interested, however, in the question of whether an infant's cry can help diagnose neurological abnormality. Infants diagnosed at birth as normal, but noted by nurses or others to have an unusual cry, are often later found to have CNS abnormalities, even to the extent of lacking a cerebral cortex.

Aspects of the timing of infant cries in normal and abnormal samples have been studied (Prechtl, Theorell, Gramsbergen, & Lind, 1969). These researchers found marked and stable individual differences in the duration of the cry over the first 8 days of life, from 0.4 to 0.9 seconds. The duration of spontaneous crying rises over the first 3 days, stays high until day 5, and then declines from day 5 to day 8. The crying time of infants with neurological problems, however, does not decline. Furthermore, the duration of their cries in response to a pinch is markedly longer than that of normals. Indeed, there is practically no overlap between the two groups in the length of that response.

Ostwald and Peltzman (1974) studied the pitch of cries in small samples of normal (5), possibly abnormal (5), and abnormal (3) infants. They found that the pitch patterns of both latter groups were higher than those of the normal group.

Computers have recently been added to the array of devices used to study abnormal patterns of cries. Eighty-eight characteristics of the cries produced by heel sticking (used to get routine blood samples) were extracted and used to provide a "cry model" (Golub & Corwin, 1980, 1982). From the model, Golub and Corwin selected 8 abnormal cry patterns. They then analyzed the cries of 55 normal term infants and compared their patterns with those found in the cries of 17 infants with multiple or severe abnormalities and 12 infants who had only elevated bilirubin levels (that is, they were moderately to very jaundiced). The tapes of 3 other infants who later died of Sudden Infant Death Syndrome (SIDS), but whose tapes were not necessarily recorded in the neonatal period, were also analyzed. Of 55 normal, term infants, only 10 had any of the 8

---

[11] The actual sound characteristics used to identify cries and the ways they are measured are well described in Lester and Zeskind (1982).

[12] The infant has a remarkable capacity to produce varied sounds. The pitches in a single infant's hunger cries may span a range of from two octaves below middle C (a note sung by bassos) to three octaves above middle C (higher than the top notes sung by a coloratura (Fairbanks, 1942).

abnormal patterns and none had more than one abnormal pattern. In contrast, every one of the 17 abnormal infants had at least one abnormal pattern and 14 of them had two or more. The cry model predicted that infants with respiratory distress would have the pattern called abnormal respiratory efforts. In fact, 10 of the 12 infants with respiratory distress had this pattern and only 4 of the 77 infants that did not have respiratory distress had it. Only 1 of the 12 jaundiced babies had no abnormal pattern. The others all had the pattern called glottal instability, but no other abnormal pattern. Because muscle tonus and state are both affected by jaundice, this pattern may be related to them. The group with multiple abnormalities also contained babies with moderate jaundice. If all jaundiced babies are considered, 22 out of 24 had glottal instability, but only 8 of 63 without jaundice had this pattern. The three infants who died of SIDS all had cry patterns associated with constriction of the vocal tract. If these data can be replicated, the move to refine the analysis of cry characteristics for use in diagnosis will be well on its way.

EFFECTS OF CRIES ON ADULTS

Much of the evidence on adult reactions to crying is anecdotal, common sense, or derived from inferences from naturalistic observations of mothers and infants. Some relevant research questions are:

1. Do parents and other adults react differently to cries than to other expressions of affect, and do they react differently to different types of cries?
2. Do parents distinguish the different cries of their own baby better than those of a strange baby?
3. Do parents respond differently to cries than people who are not parents?
4. Do fathers or other men respond differently than mothers or other women?
5. Do the cries of abnormal infants affect adults differently than those of normal babies?
6. Do child abusers respond differently to cries than nonabusers?

We will discuss the research with respect to each of these questions.

Frodi and colleagues (Frodi, Lamb, Leavitt, & Donovan, 1978; Frodi, Lamb, Leavitt, Wil-

berta, Donovan, & Sherry, 1978) investigated parents' physiological responses to smiles and cries and answers to a mood adjective check list. The 48 couples who watched 6-minute tapes of a baby who either cried or smiled in the middle 2 minutes did show different physiological responses as measured by diastolic blood pressure and skin conductance, as well as different moods in response to crying as compared to smiling. Parents have also been shown to respond differently to tapes of cries as compared to tapes of pure tones (Wiesenfeld, Malatesta, & DeLoache, 1981). Sixteen mothers and sixteen fathers listened to tapes of anger and pain cries. Physiological indices of stress (skin conductance and EKG) differed on the two types of cry as did parents' ratings of the tapes for pleasantness and unusualness, and of their own tension while listening. Both parents found the pain cries of their own child to be the most unpleasant and to cause the most tension. Not all of the dependent measures showed the same results in this study and some of the differences depended on the type of cry; we shall discuss these when we discuss question 4. Zeskind and colleagues (Zeskind & Lester, 1978; Zeskind, Sale, Maio, Huntington, & Weiseman, 1984) have shown that both inexperienced and experienced adults can distinguish cry sounds. The latter study showed that even for very brief segments of cry tapes, pain cries were more aversive and arousing and seemed more urgent than hunger cries. Berry (1975) showed that children as young as 7 years of age could distinguish cry types. This research all supports the conclusion that babies' cries do communicate to others, even to young others.

The answer to question 2 also appears to be positive. In Wiesenfeld and colleagues' study cited above (1981), the cries parents heard were either of their own or of another baby. Both parents were good at identifying cries as taped from their own baby, but when tapes were from another baby they were less accurate in distinguishing the cries of a strange baby.

The question of whether parents respond differently to cries than do nonparents (question 3) has been addressed by Zeskind (1980). In his study, adults (parents or nonparents) chose from a list of six caretaking behaviors (feed, cuddle, pick up, clean, give pacifier, wait and see) one that they would use in response to the cry they had just heard. At the end of the study participants were asked to rate each of the caretaking behaviors as to "how tender and caring the response is" and "how immediately effective the response would be in terminating the crying." Thus, the researchers were actually measuring respondents' interpretations of their psychological reactions, not their actual behaviors. No differences were found between parents and nonparents in responses to low-risk infants, but there were differences in response to the cries of infants at greater risk. Although adults' perceptions of the nature and effectiveness of caretaking behaviors are important, they are of course not the same as behaviors, and it is the caretaking behaviors themselves that affect babies, not their parents' beliefs about those behaviors. To answer the question of whether parents have learned to respond more appropriately to their babies' cries than nonparents, both kinds of responses must be measured. There is reason to suggest (Boukydis & Burgess, 1982; Lounsbury & Bates, 1982) that the amount of experience with infants is a more meaningful distinction than parental status.

The fourth question on our list really is derived from the hypothesis that women are biologically preprogrammed by evolution to respond to the cries of babies in ways that men are not (see, for example, Klaus, Trause, & Kennell, 1975; Money & Tucker, 1975). The answer to this question is not clear cut. In the Frodi studies already described (Frodi, Lamb, Leavitt, & Donovan, 1978; Frodi, Lamb, Leavitt, Wilberta et al., 1978) both mothers and fathers were studied. Although they did not differ in their responses on the physiological measures, the mothers did use somewhat more extreme mood ratings. Nevertheless, the same pattern of effects in relation to the nature of the stimulus held for both mothers and fathers. In view of the common acceptance of the idea that women are encouraged more than men to give expression to emotions, this one difference doesn't seem to constitute much support for the evolutionary view. In addition, a study using college students (Freudenberg, Driscoll, & Stern, 1978) did not show any sex differences in the responses.

Zeskind and colleagues have found little evidence for sex differences. Zeskind (1980) does not report separate analyses, but the strength of the findings makes such differences unlikely, and Zeskind and colleagues (1984) found very minimal differences. Boukydis and Burgess (1982) also found no differences between men and women in skin potential responses to different types of cries. They did find that fathers were more likely than mothers to judge cries as indicating that an infant was spoiled and to react with irritation rather than caregiving responses.

One study that did show quite a few sex differences (or differences between mothers and fathers) had the greatest number of complexities in its design (Wiesenfeld et al., 1981). There were cries and pure tones. The cries were of anger or pain, of the subjects' own baby or another baby, and the dependent measures were of both physiological responses (skin conductance and EKG) and ratings. Each parent listened to six tape segments (two of which were pure tones) and judged whether the cry segments were their own or another baby and whether they were cries of pain or anger. A number of sex differences were found.

Fathers and mothers were alike in showing orienting type heart rate responses (ones that indicate that the stimulus is heard and attended to) to the cries of other infants. They differed in that fathers did this for the cries of both their own and the other infant, whereas mothers showed defensive type heart rate responses to the cries of their own infants. Mother's skin conductance responses (galvanic skin reflex or GSR) differed according to whether the cry was her own infant or not, with responses to her baby's pain cry being strongest. Both mothers and fathers found pain cries more unpleasant and tension evoking than anger cries. Fathers, however, differed from mothers as to which stimuli elicited the next highest degree of affective reaction. For fathers it was the pain cries of the other infant, but for mothers it was the anger cries of her own infant.

Mothers were better than fathers at identifying cries as not coming from their own baby, as being anger cries, and as being anger cries of their own baby. Their accuracy at these judgments varied from 63% to 81%. Pain cries were only slightly better recognized by mothers than fathers, and were much less well recognized by either. Mothers were right 50%

of the time for their own baby and 25% for other babies; fathers were right 38% and 31% of the time, respectively.

Thus, several of the findings showed that mothers are somewhat better than fathers at recognizing cry stimuli. Although the differences weren't great, these findings could be taken as support for the view that women, but not men, are preprogrammed to respond to stimuli that are relevant to survival. The fact that pain cries were less well recognized than anger cries by either parent, however, would seem directly counter to any evolutionary hypothesis, because response to pain is most important in guaranteeing the survival of babies. Considering all of these studies, there is little consistent evidence to support the hypothesis that females, but not males, are innately programmed (or at least predisposed) to respond in a nurturing way to infant signals.

The fifth question may possibly have some relevance to evolutionary thinking, but since it is possible to make quite opposite arguments as to what evolution might have programmed into the species, no findings can be interpreted in relation to evolutionary theory.[13]

The answers to question 5 are further complicated by the great variety of stimuli used to study the question, including pain cries of high-risk babies compared to low-risk term infants (Zeskind, 1980); cries of Down's syndrome babies compared to those of normal babies (Freudenberg et al., 1978); cries of prematures compared to those of term infants (Frodi, Lamb, Leavitt, & Donovan, 1978; Frodi, Lamb, Leavitt, Wilberta et al., 1978); cries of normal babies that were labeled as coming from normal, difficult, or premature infants (Frodi, Lamb, Leavitt, & Donovan, 1978; Frodi, Lamb, Leavitt, Wilberta et al., 1978); and cries of babies rated as difficult, average, or easy (Boukydis & Burgess, 1982; Lounsbury & Bates, 1982). In some studies the cries were

considered to be hunger cries and in others they were pain induced. In only a few of these studies were the actual acoustic properties of the cries analyzed to enable determination of how they relate to outcomes.

These research difficulties are compounded by the fact that different studies use different measures of the adults' responses or use more than one measure and get different results depending on which of their measures they use. The most frequently used measures are: (1) various physiological responses, especially heart rate and GSR; (2) statements of what they would do in response to cries; and (3) ratings of their mood when listening to the cries. In some studies of responses to the cries of "difficult" infants, whether the mother has a difficult infant herself is also a variable (see Bates, Olson, Pettit, & Bayles, 1982), and whether listeners are nonparents, first-time parents, or multiparous parents is often varied. It is not surprising that researchers have reached different and even opposite conclusions from these studies, and that the data are hard to integrate to provide answers to our questions.

To answer question 5, it seems imperative to use acoustic analyses of the pitch, intensity, and rhythmic pattern, especially the pattern of pauses, of cries, and to use cries from babies with a wide range of abnormalities. At present there is some evidence to support almost *any* answer to questions about whether problem babies elicit more TLC (tender, loving care) or are aversive to caretakers and elicit avoidance, abuse, or both. In addition, because the characteristic cries vary for different abnormalities, the answers to this question may well depend on the particular abnormality or cry pattern.

Various persons have hypothesized that child abusers may abuse infants whose emotional expressions are different from normal. Another hypothesis is that child abusers may react differently than nonabusers to the communicative signals their infants provide. These hypotheses are of interest in relation to question 6. There are relatively little data of a controlled sort on this topic. Frodi and Lamb (1980) have used the same techniques as in the other Frodi studies already described (Frodi, Lamb, Leavitt, & Donovan, 1978; Frodi, Lamb, Leavitt, Wilberta et al., 1978) to study responses of child abusers (recruited from Par-

---

[13]It is possible to argue that the human species might be preprogrammed to respond more to the cries of abnormal or at risk infants. Conversely, it could also be argued that over most of history societies have not had enough resources to allow spending them on abnormal or difficult infants. Indeed, many cultures have had practices to ensure against such a waste of resources, such as abandoning sickly infants (and old people) and one member of twin pairs, and survival tests.

ents Anonymous) in comparison to those of a control group (recruited from a YWCA and a Well Baby group). We will consider the responses of the abuser to both the smile and the cry stimuli. Responses of abusers were markedly different from those of the controls or from the participants in the earlier Frodi and colleagues studies. The abusers, as compared to controls, showed greater arousal as indexed by both heart rate and GSR, but they showed less blood pressure increase. They reported less sympathy toward and were more annoyed by the crying baby than were control parents. Abusers rated a smiling baby as less pleasant than did the control group, and they reported themselves as less attentive and less willing to interact with the smiling baby than did nonabusers. They also were more indifferent toward the smiling baby, though their blood pressure and skin conduction responses to the smiling baby were greater than those of nonabusers. In short, their responses to the smiling baby were very like their responses to the crying baby.

Frodi and Lamb (1980) theorize that this response pattern where any social solicitation by an infant (specifically, crying or smiling) is seen as aversive by abusers has developed through their transactions with children who, "because of their temperament or their parents' incompetence, are difficult to care for" (p. 243). They point out the need for studies that would directly link behavior patterns of abusive and nonabusive parents to their physiological responses.

Lamb (1978) has argued, as has Bowlby (1969), that the responses to smiling and crying should be sharply differentiated, but that both have evolutionary survival value. Although some of the data seem to support their position, there is a very real question as to whether the aversive nature of the cry that leads to attention and care might be (or become) so aversive that it hinders care or leads to avoidance or abuse. Clearly, much more work is necessary to determine with any certainty what features of cries adults respond to and how they respond to them.

HOW TO SOOTHE CRYING BABIES

The aspect of crying that is of most concern to parents is how to soothe crying babies.

There has been a fair amount of work exploring the relative effectiveness of various soothing responses. In study after study it has been found that picking up a baby is the most effective method of getting the baby to stop crying (Bell & Ainsworth, 1972; Brown, 1964; Wolff, 1969). A high, front-to-front position, so the baby looks over the adult's shoulder, appears to be the most effective holding position (Korner & Thoman, 1972). In fact, Bell and Ainsworth found that this technique was effective in stopping crying in 85% of the cry episodes in both the first and the last quarter of the first year.

Other techniques are also effective. Among stimuli that were effective more than half of the time were sucking (Bell & Ainsworth, 1972; Wolff, 1969), rocking (Gordon & Foss, 1966; Kopp, 1971), and auditory stimulation (Bell & Ainsworth, 1972; Brown, 1964; Kopp, 1971; Wolff, 1969). The particular kind of auditory stimulation that is most effective depends at least in part on the age of the infant. For newborns, nonsocial auditory stimuli seem to be most effective. For example, Kopp (1971) found that white noise soothed 1-month-old babies 56% of the time and their mother's voice soothed them only 6% of the time. The most effective nonsocial auditory stimuli are low pitched continuous sounds (see Chapter 9). It is no wonder, then, that for generations mothers have sworn by such soothing techniques as turning on music, or putting babies on top of or next to machinery such as clothes washers or dryers or vacuum cleaners. Recent fads include a machine that reproduces the human heartbeat for the purpose of soothing babies and a record that reproduces the intrauterine sounds to which the baby was exposed before birth.

The most effective soothing stimuli change rapidly in the first months of life. Although nonhuman auditory stimulation seems to soothe newborns best, the human voice quickly becomes a more effective stimulus. By 3 months of age the mother's voice is more effective than white noise (Kopp, 1971). Visual stimulation, initially rather ineffective as a soother, becomes increasingly effective and by the age of 3 to 4 months it works about half the time (Kopp, 1971; Wolff, 1969). Giving a toy to babies of this age, who do not yet reach, is actually presenting visual, and sometimes auditory, stimulation. It is no surprise, then, that it is an effective soother (Ainsworth, 1972). By 4 months of age the combination of visual and auditory stimulation seems more effective than either is alone.

Certain forms of tactual (touching) and kinesthetic (movement and balance) control, other than rocking and holding, are often effective infant soothers. Sometimes these techniques decrease stimulation and sometimes they provide stimulation. Swaddling or restraining the limbs of very young infants often quiets them effectively (Wolff, 1969; Brown, 1964). Touching soothes successfully 50% of the time, according to Bell & Ainsworth (1972). Kopp (1971) found that rhythmic patting was effective, but only 15–20% of the time. Brown (1964) found that changing the baby's position sometimes reduces arousal. In none of these studies is the reason for the baby's crying considered independently. Clearly, babies that are crying because they are hungry can, at best, only be quieted temporarily by these techniques.

Virtually all of this information deals with infants in the first three months of life. It would have to be modified considerably for older infants, as Bell and Ainsworth (1972) demonstrated. They found that in the first three months crying was less frequent when the mother was in close physical contact and was most frequent when the mother was out of sight or earshot. When they studied the same babies in the last three months of the first year, they found that crying was *more* frequent when the mother was physically close. This supports the view that crying has become a true communication; that is, it is under the infant's control and is not just a response to stimulation.

All this information can help caregivers deal with infants in several ways. It provides a number of alternative soothing techniques and a knowledge of which ones are most likely to work. It shows that running through several different techniques is a good idea because no one technique will work all the time. It focuses the caretaker's attention on the fact that babies change rapidly. Therefore, techniques that were maximally effective for newborns will have to be changed with older infants, even within the first three months of life. There is much truth in mothers' complaints that as soon as they figure out how to handle their babies, the babies change and the mothers have to figure them out all over again.

There are great individual differences in what will soothe a baby. For example, babies who are less active in the first quarter of life are more soothed by visual or tactile-kinesthetic techniques (Kopp, 1971). Even more important, babies differ greatly in how soothable they are by any technique, a fact that is related to the concept of the "difficult" baby. Parents of babies who cry a lot or who have very unpleasant cries may wear themselves out trying to soothe their children. Trying many different techniques may yield one or more that successfully quiet a particular child, but it may also be that intractable crying is physiologically produced and cannot be controlled by parental soothing techniques. In such cases parents must find ways to cope with the situation. They may wear ear plugs or turn on the stereo or TV loud enough to drown out the sounds of the cries or they may put the baby in a room at the far end of the house and close all the doors between, or drug the baby (or themselves), or beat the baby. We know very little about what happens in these circumstances, but at least one study (Dunn, 1975) has suggested that mothers whose babies cry frequently and for long periods of time have decreased affectionate contact with their babies at later ages. This was probably not a result of the mothers' inability to respond appropriately to the crying itself, because there was no relation between the babies' crying and their mothers' affectionate contact at the same age, only with maternal affectionate contact later on. This pattern held for the first 30 weeks of life. These data suggest that regardless of mothers' immediate responses to high levels of infant crying, eventually such high levels may lead to decreased contact.

TO SOOTHE OR NOT TO SOOTHE

The idea that prompt, efficient response to babies' crying is optimal has been implicit, if not explicit, in our discussion of adult responses to cries. Nevertheless, whether such prompt responsiveness is a good idea has been the center of intense theoretical debate. According to the Freudian-influenced ethological school, represented by Ainsworth and others (Bell & Ainsworth, 1972; Ainsworth & Bell, 1977), prompt response to crying makes infants feel secure and promotes their sense of efficacy and their attachment (to be discussed in Chapter 12). Thus, it should lead to less crying, fussing, and other manifestations of frustration and insecurity. In support of this position, Bell & Ainsworth (1972) reported that the babies of mothers who responded promptly to their babies' cries in the first 3 months of their lives cried *less* in assessments made later in their first year. These babies were also more likely to exhibit clear and varied noncrying modes of communication later in their first year of life.

Learning theorists from Watson to the present day counsel that if parents reinforce crying (attend to it positively or negatively), it will increase in frequency. Gewirtz (Gewirtz, 1977; Gewirtz & Boyd, 1977a, 1977b) has critiqued the methodology of the Ainsworth findings from this perspective. In addition, Etzel and Gewirtz (1967) have shown that crying and fussing can be decreased through procedures in which they are ignored (not reinforced) and a competing response (smiling) is reinforced.

Two studies that found prompt response to babies' crying early in their first year to be associated with greater amounts of fussing later in the first year may be interpreted as more supportive of learning theory than of the Freudian-influenced ethological school, if crying and fussing are assumed to be different aspects of the same complex. Moss (1967) found that prompt response to crying in the first 3 weeks of life led to higher rates of fussing at 3 months. Landau (1982) examined responses to crying in four different child rearing settings in Israel, including the Bedouin. Infants at four ages from 2 to 11 months of age were observed for crying and other relevant behaviors for substantial periods of time. The contrast between the Bedouin and the other cultural settings provides an interesting theoretical contrast because in the Bedouin environment infants are always with their mothers and are not allowed to fuss, being fed as soon as they begin to fuss. Of the four groups studied, the Bedouin infants fussed the most in the presence of familiar people and showed the highest rates of fussing when their mothers attempted to elicit smiling behavior from them.

The available evidence clearly does not permit a resolution of the controversy. It is likely that such a resolution will require a more complex formulation. For example, although prompt response to crying may reinforce crying, it is likely to reinforce only mild crying. In contrast, when a mother is slow to respond to her infant's cries, the cries are likely to become stronger and more noxious. The mother may respond only when they have become too unpleasant for her to bear. She would then be reinforcing noxious crying, and it is this sort of crying that Etzel and Gewirtz (1967) successfully reduced through learning procedures. More sophisticated research is needed to test hypotheses such as this.

Aside from this contemporary argument, different cultures (and the same culture at different times) have had very different attitudes about appropriate responses to a crying infant. The Dutch, for example, tend to feel that crying is good for the infant; it provides necessary exercise and thus strengthens them. Even those who are not oriented toward learning theory, such as Brazelton (1962) and Emde, Gaensbauer, and Harmon (1976), have noted that a certain amount of crying is necessary for infants' organization. The question then becomes how much, at what ages, and in what circumstances? We have no answers to these questions.

Smiling

Smiling is perhaps the earliest clearly social and positive behavior in very young infants. Like crying, it is a behavior that communicates affect, or is seen to do so. All baby books give ages at which parents can expect their infants to smile. Parents who think they see their infant smiling earlier than this are usually politely told that what they saw was an expression due to gas pains. This response does not, however, jibe with what is now known about smiling. There is a form of smiling during the neonatal period that is called reflex smiling to differentiate it from "real" or "social" smiling that develops later. The characteristics of this early reflex smile have been explored by Wolff (1959, 1963, 1966) and Korner (1969).[14] Reflex

---

[14] Although Wolff's and Korner's observations agree on the characteristics of reflex smiles, Wolff found much higher frequencies of smiling than Korner did. Wolff observed babies in incubators, while Korner observed babies in bassinets. Korner discusses the ways these differences in observational situation may have resulted in different amounts of smiling.

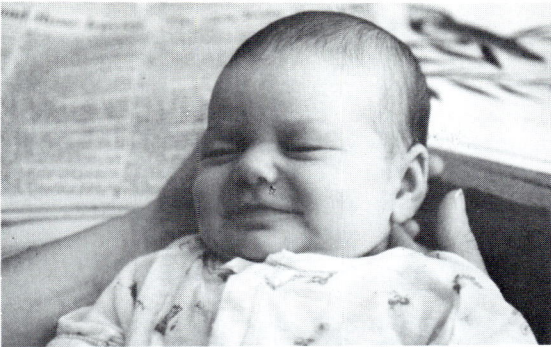

FIGURE 6–8. A sleep or reflexive smile. Only the mouth is smiling; the eyes are not.

smiling involves only the muscles of the lower face, but later smiling involves the eye muscles as well. Early smiling occurs when the baby is in different states than those for later smiling, and often occurs without outside stimulation. Reflex smiles occur most often in irregular sleep, occasionally in a drowsy state, and never in deep sleep or in alert states (see Figure 6–8). Those who have cared for very young babies (or observed them) may recall having seen them "smile" as they were falling asleep, and might describe them as looking as if they were having a pleasant dream. The smiles occur in bursts and do not come soon after a startle, but are similar to the muscle jerks or startles that sometimes reawaken adults as they are falling asleep.[15] There is a marked difference between sexes in the number of spontaneous smiles per hour. Girls have twice as many as boys, but only half as many startles.

These reflex or spontaneous smiles occur without obvious external stimulation, but they can also be elicited by gentle stimulation or by high-pitched sounds in 30–40% of tries.[16] It is

easy to understand how a mother, cooing or talking gently to her baby as she soothes the baby to sleep, sees these smiles "in response" and might consider them to be social.

There is clearly a difference between these early spontaneous smiles and later "social" smiles, as researchers starting with Darwin have noted (Darwin, 1872; Emde & Harmon, 1972; Emde et al., 1976; Sroufe & Waters, 1976; Wolff, 1966), but whether early spontaneous smiles can be considered to be social or not depends on what is meant by "social." Early smiles are generally not considered to be social because: (1) they occur spontaneously (without external stimulation), (2) when they are elicited by an auditory stimulus, they are as likely to be elicited by high-pitched sounds that are not voices as they are by voices, and (3) they seem particularly nonsocial when compared to later smiling in which alert babies selectively smile to purely social stimuli, such as the reappearance of a familiar person. Despite all this, early smiles can be considered social in the sense that they serve as social stimuli to mothers.

Smiling rapidly changes into a more responsive form (see Table 6–3). In the second week it is not unusual to see smiling movements when the eyes are partially open. These usually occur at the end of a feeding when the baby is drowsy and the mother is making soft sounds. At this age visual stimuli are not effective in producing smiles. After the second week smiling gradually shifts to periods when the infant is awake and in a state of alert inactivity. Smiles are still triggered best by sounds, and a high-pitched voice is more effective than a low-pitched one, whether live or taped.[17] This may explain the fact that some studies have shown fathers to be less effective in eliciting smiles than mothers (but see Figure 6–9).

Toward the end of the fourth week the combination of a visual and an auditory stimulus is more effective than the auditory stimulus alone. Silent nodding of the head is sometimes effective and pat-a-caking is, even if there is no previous experience with it. Indeed, pat-a-cake can get 20 to 30 smiles but other stimuli can get only 8 to 10. By 28 days (or one

---

[15] These behaviors occur spontaneously (without obvious stimulation) as the infant falls asleep and are considered to be discharge behaviors "released" or triggered by the sudden absence of afferent inputs. Technically this is called deafferentation or deprival of afferent (or incoming) inputs to the nervous system.

[16] If the smiles are elicited repeatedly, a phenomenon similar to that for elicited startles occurs. If the infant responds to the first one or two stimulus presentations, there is no response to the subsequent presentations. This quick cessation of response is called habituation. The latency for the appearance of the smile is in the middle of the range of that for responses generally, averaging 7 seconds compared to 3 to 11 seconds for other types of responses.

[17] One of Wolff's incidental observations was that the ears work in a smiling response. It is possible to speculate that this is related phylogenetically to the prepotency of auditory stimuli in the early elicitation of smiles.

TABLE 6–3
The Development of Smiling and Laughter

Age	Response	Stimulation	Latency	Remarks
		SMILING		
Neonate	Corners of the mouth	No external stimulation		Due to central nervous system fluctuations
Week 1	Corners of the mouth	Low level, modulated	6–8 sec	During sleep, boosting of tension
Week 2	Mouth pulled back	Low level, modulated; voices		When drowsy, satiated
Week 3	Grin, including eyes	Moderate level, voices	4–5 sec	When alert, attentive (nodding head with voices)
Week 4	Grin, active smile	Moderate, or moderately intense	Reduced	Vigorous tactile stimulation effective
Weeks 5–8	Grin, active smile, cooing	Dynamic stimulation, first visual stimulation	3 sec or less	Nodding head, flicking lights, stimulation that must be followed
Weeks 8–12	Grin, active smile, cooing	Static, visual stimulation, moderately intense	Short	Trial by trial effects, effortful assimilation, recognition; static at times more effective than dynamic
		LAUGHTER		
Month 4	Laughter	Multimodal, vigorous stimulation	1–2 sec	Tactile, auditory
Months 5–6	Laughter	Intense auditory stimulation, as well as tactile	Immediate	Items that may have previously caused crying
Months 7–9	Laughter	Social, visual stimulation, primarily dynamic	Immediate	Tactile, auditory decline
Months 10–12	Laughter	Visual, social	Immediate or anticipatory	Visual incongruities, active participation

NOTE. From "The ontogenesis of smiling and laughter: A perspective on the organization of development in infancy" by A. Sroufe and E. Waters, 1976, *Psychological Review, 83,* p. 175. Copyright 1976 by the American Psychological Association. Reprinted by permission.

month), visual stimuli tend to become more effective than auditory ones. Vocalizations now tend to elicit gurgling (inexact imitation) rather than smiling. Human faces are effective stimuli, but a change in a rhythmic visual stimulus also evokes a smile. Masks or glasses evoke smiles, but mirror glasses tend to evoke a crying type of face.

After the first month smiling appears to become almost an obligatory response. A crying infant will stop crying to smile at an effective stimulus and resume crying when the smile is completed. By another month the response becomes selective. This selectivity of the smile is part of what people mean when they consider these later smiles to be truly social. Babies by this age respond clearly to humans and do so differentially (see Chapter 9 for descriptions of the development of differential responsivity to faces compared to other visual patterns and to mothers' faces compared to those of others; see Chapter 12 for a description of the development of social relationships). This selectivity continues to develop and change during infancy. For example, Hetzer and Tudor-Hart (1927) found that at 6–8

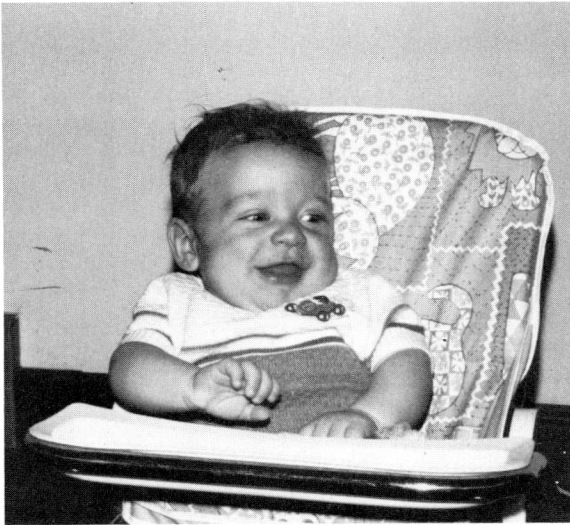

FIGURE 6–9. A social smile. This baby is responding to a stimulus from his (off-camera) father. Notice that the whole face is smiling.

weeks babies smiled to humans regardless of the person's expression or voice tone, but by 5 to 7 months the baby would adopt the adult's facial expression, angry or friendly, and cry at a scolding voice with an angry face.

Smiling is studied from a wide variety of perspectives: (1) as an innate indicator of emotion or pleasure as Darwin did (for example, in the work of Sroufe); (2) as a stimulus for adult responses (Frodi, Lamb, Leavitt, & Donovan, 1978; Frodi, Lamb, Leavitt, Wilberta et al., 1978); (3) as a response that can be learned, that is, can be enhanced and diminished in accordance with learning principles (Brackbill, 1958; Gewirtz, 1965; Rheingold, 1961);[18] and (4) as an indicator of cognitive processing (e.g., Kagan, 1971; Lewis, Sullivan, & Brooks-Gunn, 1981; McCall, 1972; Sroufe & Wunsch, 1972; Schultz & Zigler, 1970; Zelazo & Komer, 1971). Despite all of this interest, a coherent view of smiling in its developmental aspects does not currently exist. Sroufe and Waters (1976) have attempted to survey much of the work on smiling and on laughter, and to order it in terms of a

[18] Even Preyer in 1881 and Bühler and her colleagues in the late 1920s (Bühler, 1930, 1931) discussed the possibility that smiling to the mother and others might be a conditioned reflex, especially since they noted conditioned sucking at about the same age as smiling became strong.

theory of excitation (arousal or tension) and tension release. We highly recommend their article.

Laughing

Laughter is not present in the newborn and usually follows infant smiling by at least 1 month (Rothbart, 1973). Some infants in home situations apparently exhibit laughter as early as 5 to 9 weeks of age, as has been observed by baby biographers (Church, 1966; Darwin, 1872; Major, 1906). Parents and many other adults call these early responses laughter, but researchers are more hesitant to do so (Wolff, 1963). Washburn (1929) obtained clear instances of laughter in the strange situation of the laboratory only at 12 to 16 weeks, but even then not in all babies. In her study, although 4 babies laughed at one or more stimulus situations as early as 12 weeks, 1 baby did not laugh until 52 weeks of age. She found no developmental changes between 16 and 52 weeks of age (a combination cross-sectional and longitudinal design was used).

Washburn asked the parents to make their babies laugh. Parents most frequently tickled their babies to achieve this, and it was effective for infants between the ages of 24 and 52 weeks of age. Washburn, however, was successful eliciting laughter by tickling only once; in other instances the babies either responded negatively or smiled. Wilson (1931) had 14 mothers keep records of what made their babies laugh when they were between 1 and 29 months of age. The effective stimuli reported were boisterous play; tickling; surprising sounds, sights, or movements; and motor accomplishments, such as rolling over or standing up.

More recently Sroufe and Wunsch (1972) studied laughter and its eliciting stimuli systematically in a series of studies (one longitudinal and two cross-sectional). The infants were 4 to 12 months of age. A strong pattern emerged, despite differences in frequency of laughing related to differences in the experimental situations. Tactile and kinesthetic stimuli were most potent in producing laughter. Seven- to 9-month-olds laughed more and to more things than did 4- to 6-month-olds. When the younger babies laughed, it was more likely to be in response to items with a tactile or auditory component. Visual stimuli (such as mother covers face, makes object disappear, sucks baby bottle) and social stimuli (such as mother plays tag, "gonna get you," or peek-a-boo) elicited increasing responses with increasing age. The social items peaked in effectiveness earlier than the visual ones.

There are a number of similar theories concerning what produces laughter (Ambrose, 1963; Berlyne, 1960; Rothbart, 1973). We will describe Rothbart's. Sudden, intense, or discrepant stimulation arouses individuals. They then attend to and evaluate the stimulus. If they perceive it to be dangerous, they become fearful, and babies often cry. If it is not dangerous but is difficult to understand, they attempt to figure it out. Once they understand it (either with or without problem solving at the time), their arousal decreases and they either smile or laugh. Rothbart hypothesizes that the more arousing the nondangerous stimulus is, the more likely it is to evoke laughter rather than smiling.

If this arousal theory is true, fear and laugh responses would be expected in similar situations. Several studies with infants have supported this relation between fear and laughter. Sroufe and Wunsch (1972) found that an object coming straight toward the infant (looming), which is an arousing stimulus, led to both laughter and fear. One of their stimulus situations produced laughter while a very similar situation in another study (Scarr & Salapatek, 1970) produced fear. In Sroufe and Wunsch's laughter-producing situation, masks were put on by the infants' mothers while the infants were watching. In the situation in the study that produced fear, the experimenter put on a mask out of the infants' sight and then appeared before them. A similar result was found by Lewis and Brookes-Gunn (cited in Rothbart, 1973) in a study of responses to strangers, mothers, and selves in a mirror. Both positive (smiling and laughing) and negative (crying) reactions were most likely when the stimulus person was near the child and least likely when the stimulus person was on the other side of the room. In addition, the direction of the affect depended on the stimulus. The mother and mirror self generally elicited positive reactions, while adult strangers elicited negative reactions.

The arousal theory involves cognitive processes in several ways. First, the theory proposes that laughter should occur only to stimuli that are understood. Sroufe and Wunsch (1972) found that more cognitively complex stimuli evoked laughter in older infants, but not in younger ones. They also found that younger infants laughed only after the stimulus, while older infants often laughed before the stimulus ended. It takes more cognitive capacity to understand an event well enough to anticipate its end from its beginning. Only the older infants apparently had the necessary understanding to anticipate and therefore laugh before the stimulus ended. Second, the theory proposes that achieving understanding of something initially not understood should produce laughter. For example, babies laugh when they achieve mastery (Rothbart, 1973; Wilson, 1931). Stimuli that are moderately difficult to figure out should be more likely to elicit laughter according to the theory; stimuli that are too easy to process may not be arousing enough; and stimuli that are too difficult will either be ignored or responded to with fear. This is also in keeping with White's (1959) effectance concept and his conclusion that ". . . children enjoy most that which lies at the growing edge of their capacities" (p. 335). It is also possible that laughter may be evoked by a violation of an expectation, perhaps because such a situation is arousing.

The arousal model of laughter explains a large body of research in both infants and other organisms, but it is not the whole story. Rothbart (1973) points out that laughter serves a very useful role in giving infants control over their environment. When babies cry, their caregivers respond to them. If the babies continue to cry, their caregivers change behaviors, over and over again until the baby stops crying or the caregiver gives up. When babies laugh, their caregivers tend to repeat whatever they just did; in other words, the babies' laugh is reinforcing to the caregiver and to others, such as big brothers and sisters. Thus, through their laughter babies learn that they can affect other people, an important aspect of White's concept of effectance motivation. In the same situation babies also learn about their world. Consider the contingencies in a laughter "game." An older person does something. If the baby laughs, the person repeats; if the baby does not laugh, the person does not repeat. Therefore, the stimulus is repeated only if it is at an appropriate cognitive level for the infant. The repetition itself may be important. As we will see in our discussions of perception and cognition, babies often need long or repeated presentations of a stimulus in order to process it. The "power" of the rewarding properties of their laughter helps to keep the stimulus around.

TRAITS OR TEMPERAMENT

At several points in this book we have mentioned the relation of some pre- or postnatal characteristic to later aspects of behavior. These aspects are sometimes considered to be the precursors of personality or are labeled temperamental characteristics. Activity level and possibly attentiveness, both of which we discussed earlier in this chapter, are such characteristics. The finding of presumably stable temperamental characteristics by the New York Longitudinal Study (Thomas, Chess, Birch, Hertzig, & Korn, 1963) generated renewed interest in questions about the characteristics of temperament: What are they? How stable are they? How can they be measured? To what degree do they have genetic or constitutional determiners?

Current Status of Research

It is our general feeling that because the evidence varies so greatly from study to study, and because the amount of variation in measurements at later ages is so little accounted for by those made at earlier ages (made when the baby has had less experiential molding), it is highly premature to address these questions in a textbook. We also feel that the measures designed to assess temperament leave a great deal to be desired. This is not surprising because it is such a difficult task. Nevertheless, we would like to give a flavor of the status of the research on one of the most popular hypothesized types of temperament, that of the difficult child.

The concept of the "difficult" child grew out of the New York Longitudinal Study (see, for example, Thomas & Chess, 1977) and was more or less accepted until very recently. Today researchers question whether current evidence is strong enough to conclude that such a personality type exists. In a recent series of articles in the *Merrill-Palmer Quarterly* (1982), prominent researchers in the field expressed the differing opinions that are characteristic of the field. Thomas, Chess, and Korn (1982) made their case for the reality of the concept and its usefulness. Kagan (1982) cited some evidence that supports their view. Rothbart (1981, 1982), who has developed one of the scales used to measure temperament, called attention to the lack of evidence for stability of "difficultness" prior to 3 or 4 years of age. She also noted the dangers of labeling infants with difficult temperaments as being "at risk," inasmuch as there is a large chance that an infant may be incorrectly labeled as difficult. This provides another situation in which adults' expectations may lead to a self-fulfilling prophecy. Plomin (1982), who is interested in genetic components of temperament, cautioned that the concept of temperament is difficult and that it is too much to hope that eclectic approaches will lead to "prompt improvement and final recovery" from these difficult problems. Echoing Plomin's sentiments, Thomas (1982) concluded that the difficult study of temperament has a bright future. It is easy to agree with this statement, but it is a statement about the future, not about the current status of the field.

To give a flavor of the kind of evidence currently available, we shall describe part of a broader study by Bates and colleagues (1982) that examined the role of mothers in the development of their infants' difficultness. They found a significant, but very modest, correlation (about .30) between a mother's perception of her 6-month-old infant as difficult and the infant's fussy behaviors seen in home observations. This finding is in close agreement with earlier work by the same group (Bates, 1980). Bates and colleagues (1982) also related the difficultness of the child to maternal behaviors in order to test the hypothesis that a child perceived as "difficult" may "turn off" the parent. This hypothesis was not confirmed; there were no correlations between the infant's difficultness and negative aspects of maternal behaviors. Instead, there were modest relations to positive aspects of maternal behaviors. The authors conclude that if the difficult infant becomes the difficult child as a result of negative interactions with the mother, the crucial interactions must occur later than infancy. A learning theorist might conclude that the positive maternal behaviors reward undesirable behaviors that over the long run dominate the child's behaviors.

For further consideration of individual differences in temperament and their development see Rothbart and Derryberry (1981), and for a look at theories of temperament see Goldsmith and Campos (1983).

Assessment of Temperament

There are a number of tests used to assess temperament, and we have already noted that there are problems with them. In a review (Hubert, Wachs, & Peters-Martin, 1982) of the instruments designed to assess temperament from infancy into the school-age period, the authors found 26 such instruments, at least 16 of which were designed for use in some portion of infancy. While most of these showed good interjudge reliability and moderate-to-good test–retest reliability, the stability data were found to be inconsistent. When validity data were available they were inconsistent and not similar from one instrument to another. The categories assessed lacked internal consistency in at least some tests (Huitt & Ashton, 1982). Hubert and colleagues (1982) called attention to the fact that the theories of temperament are rather controversial, so that only operational definitions of the construct of temperament are possible. This fact makes it imperative to pay attention to the measuring instruments used.

Most of the measures of temperament are based on questionnaires filled out by the mother. If studies using such measures do find continuity (and thus support for the existence of some trait), the similarity over time may be in the parent rather than in the infant. This issue is addressed in some of the papers cited, but we would like to discuss two studies that are relevant to this issue.

Data relevant to the question of whether the trait is in the adult assessing the infant or in the infant is found in studies by Sameroff and his colleagues (Sameroff, Seifer, & Elias, 1982; Sameroff, Seifer, & Zax, 1982). They found that more of the scales on Carey's Infant Temperament Questionnaire (ITQ; Carey & McDevitt, 1978) were related to maternal characteristics than to child variables (6 compared

to 4). In addition, 4 of the 6 ITQ scales that were related to maternal characteristics were still related after all effects of the children's behaviors were removed (partialled out statistically). Only 1 of the ITQ scales was still related to children's characteristics after maternal characteristics were partialled out. Thus we see that maternal characteristics have more effect on mothers' ratings of their infants' temperaments than do the infants' behaviors.

A different kind of study, which also bears on the issue of stability or its source, is that by Field and Greenberg (1982). They examined the degree to which different persons (and persons in different settings) rated infants and older preschoolers similarly. Again they used the ITQ. The scores of mothers and fathers correlated significantly for 4 traits: activity, rhythmicity, approach, and the summary score. However, parent–teacher ratings did not agree, although the two teachers making ratings each had more than 4 months of experience with the infant. Mothers' scores were not related to teachers' on a single ITQ scale, and fathers' scores were related only for mood. Thus there seems to be no stability of perceptions of temperamental traits across settings. In contrast with these findings on temperamental traits, the same study found good agreement if the same sets of adults were asked how many behavior problems the children had (correlations ranged from .50 to .80), and the setting in which children were observed was no longer a large influence on the outcomes.

Taken together, these studies suggest that much that is measured by infant temperament questionnaires is either in the eye of the beholder or in the setting in which the child is observed. Both of these are contrary to the idea that the stable characteristics of the child are being assessed. In contrast, childrens' behavior problems seem to be stable across settings and are seen similarly by different adults (both parents and teachers).

DISCUSSION ISSUES
Continuity of Development

A fundamental issue that underlies much of this chapter is that of whether there is continuity of development. Can knowing something about an infant's (or fetus's) characteristics predict something about that individual as a school-aged child or adult? Do the vast individual differences we have described in early patterns of sleep, activity, attention, crying, and other behaviors relate to similar differences in older infants, children, or adults? If so, these would constitute traits, and clusters of traits might identify types.

These questions, in turn, are much involved with the whole history of humankind, which shows that classifying "things" into types is a fundamental human characteristic. Most sciences have begun by making classifications, and long before psychology appeared as a discipline philosophers and men of medicine classified humans into types. Early psychologists joined this tradition, which flourished until well into this century. Somewhere between the 1930s and the 1960s typologies went out of style, together with many notions of fixed traits. It became clear from research that life was not so simple. In the field of intelligence testing, for example, the notion of one general trait of intelligence was replaced first by that of seven primary mental abilities (Thurstone) in the 1930s, then by that of 120 traits organized into a structure of intellect (Guilford) in the 1960s, and then by the theory that there are multiple intelligences (Gardner) in the 1980s. Politics probably helped make typologies unpopular, because Hitler was a fervent typologist and typologies have not infrequently been misused.

In this chapter we reviewed evidence about whether spontaneous activity level is a stable trait and found that it is unlikely to be one. We also showed that activity level at certain periods of infant life does help predict later development in some areas. We looked at evidence about whether enduring behavior traits were determined by early sucking experiences, and found that although short-term effects could be found, lasting effects did not seem to be indicated by the research findings.

We noted that longitudinal research is needed to address some of these questions, and only hinted at what some of its special problems are. For a detailed, but still brief, account of this issue see Chapter 2, "Research Strategies Old and New," of Tyler (1978); Moss and Susman (1980); and for a broad overall perspective, Kagan (1980). The data from the Berkeley and Fels longitudinal studies (which readers will encounter in later portions of this book) have contributed a great deal to knowledge in this area. Kagan and Moss (1962) devoted a book specifically to looking for long-term consistency in development from the Fels data. More recently, Kagan wrote a book examining consistency and change just in the period of infancy (1971). Brim and Kagan (1980) have edited a book that addresses this duality for many aspects of development (physical, physiological, and several psychological systems). In addition, the more clinically oriented longitudinal studies of the Menninger clinic looked for normative patterns in infancy (Escalona, 1968), as well as ways to group individual behavior characteristics into adaptational syndromes (Escalona, 1973). These syndromes have been examined in relation to the impact that different environmental conditions have on infants. We have, and will frequently, call attention to the fact that no matter what environmental impact we talk about, it never affects all babies the same way. For example, there is research (Schaffer, 1966), indicating that at least one determiner of reaction to deprivation is the baby's activity level.

It is clear that psychology has not lost its interest in traits and typologies. The New York Longitudinal studies, which we discussed in this chapter, stopped seeking continuity in traits and clustered them into a three-way typology. As we noted, the "difficult baby" portion of that typology gained wide acceptance, but is currently coming under fire. The problems of findings and methodologies that led to this have been discussed. The same points are largely relevant to the work with the Carey ITQ, which was based on the New York studies.

The same questions about the assessment of continuity and change have been raised in development past infancy. For an excellent and even-handed review of this topic in relation to personality, see Moss and Susman (1980).

Research Issues

It is appropriate that in this chapter that deals with infants' behavior after birth, we immediately face the problem of how to measure behaviors accurately. In Chapter 1 we discussed the very large problem of separating observed behaviors from interpretations. Whenever observers wish to make an objective measurement of the ongoing flow of infants' interactions with the world, they confront a very ambiguous and, to the observer's eye, unknown phenomenon. The very act of putting order into such observations necessarily involves the preconceptions of the observer. Historically, the first real scientific solution to this problem came from the behaviorists, Pavlov, Thorndike, and Watson. These men argued that to observe humans or animals objectively, scientists must limit themselves to observing discrete behaviors. Behaviors are objective because they are publically observable; that is, people can agree on what has occurred. Therefore, two judges observing independently, without interacting with each other, can agree whether an infant's eyes are closed or whether the infant is clasping a nipple placed in its mouth. In principle this is easy. In practice, observing behaviors is more complex than it first appears. Observers may use different criteria for including an act in a behavioral category. For example, if a baby's eyes are three-quarters closed, the eyes may be judged as closed by one observer but not by another. Thus, researchers must give precise behavioral descriptions of the response categories they wish to measure. Once the researchers define behaviors to their satisfaction, then they can make certain that their descriptions are adequate by assessing the agreement between two judges. The simplest kind of agreement measure is the percentage of acts that both observers categorized in the same way. For example, a simple computation could be made of the number of times both observers rated the infant as having closed eyes divided by the total number of instances in which judgments were made by either observer. More sophisticated statistics are often used, but they all assess the same general concept. These procedures assess interjudge reliability and are required in any behavioral study that uses observational data.

Another problem with observational data is choosing the behaviors to include. For example, should sleep be assessed by observing whether eyes are opened or closed, by muscular activity, by lack of response to external stimulation, or by some combination of behaviors?

Researchers studying the same phenomenon often devise quite different category systems, and the system they choose to use often influences their results. That this happens indicates that researchers' judgments influence how they define behavioral categories even when the categories seem to be based on simple, straightforward behaviors. For example, in Table 6–2, which describes different systems for measuring state, some researchers use two alert states and others use only one. If one of the two state categories is related to a given outcome variable and the other isn't, researchers using the two-category system will find a relation between one of them and the outcome whereas those using a one-category system may not find any relation between it and the outcome.[19] This does not mean that the two-state system is necessarily better. If the distinction between these two alert states does not make a difference, then the system that combines them will be more likely to yield significant results. Furthermore, one system may work better for one outcome measure and the other for a different outcome.

There is a particular form of sampling bias that is a large factor in studies of young infants. Many times, about half of the infants who start the procedures are eliminated from the sample because they are sleeping, crying, or simply inattentive to the experimenter's game. Can we assume that the same results would be obtained with these eliminated subjects? Recently, techniques have been developed (see particularly Horowitz, Paden, Bhana, & Self, 1972) that result in the loss of far fewer subjects than formerly. It is important to evaluate studies on the basis of sample loss, particularly when findings of two or more studies disagree.

Another sampling problem arises when newborns whose deliveries were not optimal are eliminated. In Walters' (1965) study of the relation between activity level and later development, opposite results were obtained with babies of optimal and of nonoptimal deliveries. If both kinds of babies were in a single group, the researchers would probably not have found any significant results, because the results for nonoptimal babies would have canceled the findings for optimal babies. And if they had not

---

[19] They will find a relation if by chance most of their alert babies were in fact in the state for which there is a relation.

included analyses of the data for the nonoptimal babies, no one would have known whether it was appropriate to generalize from the optimal to nonoptimal babies. It was clear in Walters' study that such a generalization was not appropriate.

A third research problem, which arose in the section on prenatal activity level, is that of the interpretation of the size of correlations. In the results described there, the correlations were all of statistical significance, which means that a correlation as large as the one obtained is unlikely to have occurred simply by chance. Thus, it is appropriate to consider the finding "real" or valid, particularly when it has been replicated. A statistically significant correlation does not, however, mean that the relation is strong enough to be of practical significance; that is, it may be of such a small magnitude that it adds little to the understanding of a particular outcome or the ability to predict it. Researchers can assess the importance of the magnitude of a correlation by calculating the proportion of variance accounted for by it. The calculation is simple: it involves squaring the correlation coefficient. For example, if the correlation coefficient is .30, the proportion of variance accounted for by that correlation is .09 or 9%. The interpretation of this calculation is based on the notion of variance, which reflects the influence of all the variables that together determine the scores of the individuals measured. The variance in the outcome variable is what we want to explain. The specific correlation in our example (.30) accounts for some part of the total variance to be explained. In this case it is less than 10%. That portion left unexplained by the correlation is 1.00 minus the proportion accounted for (.09); in our example .91 or 91% is unexplained variance. Thus, many statistically significant correlations are of minor importance in explaining a given outcome. Worse, even correlations that are quite high for a given area of research may not be large enough to be of practical predictive value. Even the highest correlation between fetal activity level and Gesell scores (Table 6–1) is $r = .54$, which when squared indicates that the proportion of variance accounted for is only .29 and the proportion unexplained is .71.

Our discussion so far has been based on predicting a group of scores. Thus, in our ex-

ample, in a sample of 100 babies those with high prenatal activity scores are likely to have higher Gesell scores than those with low prenatal activity. Unless the correlation is perfect (1.00), the correlation does not mean that every baby with a high prenatal activity level will have higher Gesell scores than every baby with a low prenatal activity score. Thus, readers of such research should refrain from concluding that all children with low prenatal activity levels will have low Gesell scores. As the proportion of variance statistic tells, there are usually a large number of other variables that also contribute to the particular outcome variable, in this case the Gesell scores.

Parenting

In this chapter we discussed many of the behavioral systems that have the greatest impact on parents. We focused on their beginning— the neonatal period, which of course is also the time of greatest change for parents. The information in this chapter can be applied to parenting in several ways.

First, a description of infants' characteristics helps parents to develop accurate expectations concerning their babies. The information about how babies spend their days shows that newborns are not terribly responsive creatures. They sleep most of the day and spend only part of their waking time in an alert, responsive state. Even when they are alert and awake, their attention is not sustained. Although they may smile occasionally, it is not the sustained smile in response to social stimulation that develops later. Babies change rapidly, of course, as they develop. During the second month of life they sleep less, are alert more, attend better, and develop the social smile. No wonder parents often describe their 6-week-old babies as "waking up" or "becoming human." There are comparable changes during this period in their learning, perceptual, and cognitive abilities, as we will discuss later.

Second, an appreciation of the great variability of babies can help parents put their own babies' behaviors in perspective, and should reassure them that the variations are normal and that the parents did not produce their infants' patterns.

Third, research on infants' basic characteristics can also help parents be more sensitive to their babies' signals. For example, researchers have described different cries that babies exhibit at different times, and parents can learn to recognize these differences. We will discuss the general issues of maternal sensitivity and early mother–infant interaction in Chapter 12.

Fourth, the research on basic characteristics has identified the relative effectiveness of various soothing techniques. Parents can use the relatively more effective techniques and can experiment with various techniques to find those that best soothe their babies.

One soothing technique has been the focus of much controversy: thumb, fist, or finger sucking. In general, experts' and parents' tolerance for nonnutritive sucking has changed as fads in child rearing changed. Today parents vary greatly in the amounts of nonnutritive sucking they allow and in the form in which they permit it (such as a thumb or a pacifier). This is perhaps appropriate. The available research suggests that the need to suck waxes and then wanes during infancy. After the need diminishes there are no longer any differences attributable to the extent and manner in which babies' sucking needs were met. While there may be long-term effects stemming from some aspects of experience during infancy, variations in parental treatment of sucking needs do not seem to be part of that set of important variables. Hence decisions about nonnutritive sucking—whether to provide a pacifier, whether to fight thumbsucking, whether and when to try to wean children from the habit—seem to be primarily the parents' decision. They should take into account how strong their particular infant's needs are and how much energy they are willing to devote to finding other ways of quieting their infants and to trying to stop their children from sucking nonnutritively.

Fifth, the research that has examined whether individual differences in traits such as activity or attentiveness, or in a temperamental characteristic such as difficultness, are stable over development has to a great extent failed to find correlations large enough to be of practical predictive value. Thus, parents need not be fearful that they will have to endure characteristics they find unattractive in their newborns. Newborns who are very active and sleep little in the first month of life are not

destined to be hyperactive as preschoolers, or even overly active at 6 months. In fact, they are only slightly more likely to be above average in activity at 6 months than less active newborns.

SUMMARY

The most basic characteristics of newborns and something about their development in the period after birth are discussed in this chapter.

Sleep is the activity in which most very young babies spend the greatest proportion of their time. Nevertheless, there are large individual differences in the length of time babies sleep, when during the day they sleep, and how long their longest period of sleep is. Sleep can be divided into quiet and active sleep. The relative proportion of each changes with age.

Although babies vary in the amount of active sleep they have, most baby watchers are apt to be more interested in the different amounts of activity they show when awake. Theoretical arguments about the nature of newborn activity were once an active focus of research. The methods for measuring activity have become more sophisticated over time. They provide good examples of measurement problems in infant studies. In comparing results of different studies, it is important to see that measures are comparable and that they are reliable.

Babies are highly variable in the amounts of spontaneous activity they show. This is true even in the fetal stage. These differences in healthy babies have been found to be related to later motor development and even to general development. Spontaneous activity level after birth also varies widely among infants, but those individual differences do not seem to be stable even for relatively short periods of time. Identical twins are more alike than fraternal twins, but their similarities are not that great. Activity in response to external stimuli is mixed with spontaneous activity in some studies. Activity in response to external stimuli, especially to stresses, may have more potential as a possible trait. This research question has been explored very little.

One of the most dramatic changes in behavior from birth to 2 years is the increasing ability of infants to be attentive to things in their environment. What catches the infant's attention is not necessarily what keeps it. It is thus important to distinguish between stimuli that can catch the attention and those that are better at holding it. The baby whose attention is most easily caught is not necessarily the one who will pay sustained attention to stimuli, a behavior necessary for certain kinds of cognitive processing. Attention is affected by other variables such as prematurity, and by perinatal events such as exposure to drugs, so it is used as a dependent measure. One of the marked differences between full-term and preterm infants is in their visual attentiveness. A baby's attentiveness also appears to affect the behavior of the mother. Just as early researchers wanted to know whether differences in activity level were related to later development, so today researchers are beginning to study whether early differences in attentive behaviors have long-range meaning.

Sleep, activity, and attention all have to do with the broader topic of state. The classification of states for the purposes of research and for the diagnosis of problems is very important. States appear to differ qualitatively from one another. They can be conceived of in two ways that are *not* identical. One is in terms of sleep (or arousal) and the other is in terms of availability to external stimuli. Most stimuli will only be responded to when the baby is in certain states. Only intense, noxious stimuli may be at least partially exempt from the rule that state determines responsivity.

Because states determine responsivity, methods used to control state or to control for state in infant studies are extremely important. In doing research it is very difficult to achieve comparable states and this may lead to excessive subject loss and biasing of the sample for whom results are reported. Artificial means of manipulating states may not produce the same effects on behavior as the naturally occurring states do. Techniques used to determine states are both observational and electrophysiological and each has its own problems. There is no neat solution to the problems of dealing with state in research with young infants.

Predominant states and state changes in response to stimulation are sharply different in premature babies still less than 38 weeks conceptional age. Infants vary widely in the ways their days are divided between the various states, and these variations may have profound effects on parents.

Another aspect of infant behaviors that attracts attention is their rhythmic behaviors. The amount of time babies spend in rhythmic activities varies greatly. These behaviors include sucking, kicking, arm swaying, head banging, rocking, crying, and all of Piaget's circular reactions. Which rhythmic behaviors are most frequently found changes with age, as do the stimuli that evoke them.

Sucking is a primary behavior system on which life normally depends. It involves the coordination of a whole group of reflexes, including those of swallowing and breathing, for feeding to be assured. Sucking develops rapidly after birth as a result of both experience and maturation. Sucking may help to organize the development of babies, including prematures.

The role of innate as opposed to learned behaviors has been much debated with respect to sucking. Cultural attitudes about whether nonnutritive sucking is good or bad change over time and differ from one culture to another. Freudian and learning theories predict very different outcomes from different feeding and weaning experiences. The Freudian view is that sucking is an innate need that must receive adequate gratification, and learning theorists propose that the more sucking reinforcements an infant gets, the more sucking they will want. A variety of studies, both human and animal, provide data some of which supports and some of which disconfirms the views of both schools. Taken as a whole, the research fails to provide evidence for long-term differences as a result of different early feeding and sucking patterns.

Affective behaviors have been studied from several points of view. Starting with Darwin, both the built-in nature of certain expressions and the abilities of persons to judge the meaning of expressions has interested many people. Adults and even children are good at identifying emotions from facial expressions and the meanings of cries. We examined a little evidence on infants' differential responses to expressions and looked briefly at research on infants' reactions to different affective behaviors.

The very first affective behavior is crying. Cries communicate to adults about the baby. They may communicate to doctors or researchers about the neurological status of the infant, and to parents and others about the distress of the infant. Cry sounds are highly varied in nature, differing according to the nature of the stimulus for crying and as a function of physiological and neurological conditions. The specific aspects of the sounds that vary include frequency (or pitch), intensity, and pause patterns.

The effects of cries on adults are the subject of a number of recent studies. Most adults react differently to cries that communicate different affects (for example, anger or pain). Parents can distinguish their own baby's cries from those of other babies quite well, and they are somewhat better at distinguishing different cry meanings for cries of their own babies than for strange babies. Although there is evidence that parents sometimes respond differently to cries than do nonparents, actual experience with infants seems the more important source of such differences. The evidence for differences in the responses of males or fathers from those of mothers or females is complex but tends to show few differences. The cries of abnormal infants tend to elicit different responses from those of normal infants; these cries, however, vary markedly according to the nature of the abnormality.

All of these studies suffer from the fact that physiological and questionnaire responses have been studied, not actual caretaking responses. Only recently have cries been studied for their acoustic properties to determine what factors in the physical stimulus seem to trigger the observed differences in responses.

The question has been raised as to whether child abusers respond differently to cries than do nonabusers. What little research exists suggests that abusers find crying babies more aversive than do nonabusers. Abusers also appear to react differently and less positively to smiling babies. Thus it appears that reactions to a number of aspects of infant behavior should be examined for differences between abusers and nonabusers.

What can be done to soothe crying babies and how this changes with age is discussed, as is the fact that babies vary greatly in how much they cry. As with sucking, the theoretical and value-laden arguments over whether to soothe crying babies, or under what circum-

stances to do so, are vigorous. The major controversy over whether and how quickly to soothe was presented very briefly. We do not feel that the answer is clear or that the positions are as antithetical as their proponents believe.

Cries are soon joined by smiles as a different form of affective communication, and one that communicates a different affect. Smiles are present in primitive (reflex?) form from birth and quickly become social. The stimuli that elicit smiles change markedly with age. Laughter appears somewhat later and is elicited by rather different stimuli. These two positive affective behaviors are linked to both cognitive processing and emotional arousal, laughter perhaps more clearly so than smiling.

REFERENCES

Ainsworth, M.D.S. (1972). Attachment and dependency: A comparison. In J.L. Gewirtz (Ed.), *Attachment and dependency*. Washington, DC: Winston & Sons.

Ainsworth, M.D.S., & Bell, S.M. (1977). Infant crying and maternal responsiveness: A rejoinder to Gewirtz and Boyd. *Child Development, 48,* 1208–1216.

Ambrose, J.A. (1963). The concept of a critical period for the development of social responsiveness in early infancy. In B.M Foss (Ed.), *Determinants of infant behaviour* (Vol. 2, pp. 201–225). London: Methuen.

Ames, L.B. (1942). Supine leg and foot postures in the human infant in the first year of life. *Journal of Genetic Psychology, 61,* 87–107.

Ames, L.B. (1949). Bilaterality. *Journal of Genetic Psychology, 75,* 45–50.

Anderson, G., Burroughs, A., Measel, C., Afone, U., & Vidyasagar, D. (April, 1980). *Non-nutritive sucking opportunities: A safe and effective treatment for premature infants.* Paper presented at the Second International Conference on Infant Studies, New Haven, CT.

Anderson, G.C., Fleming, S., & Vidyasagar, D. (April, 1980). *Effect of position on infant behavior and physiologic stabilization during the first hours postbirth.* Paper presented at the Second International Conference on Infant Studies, New Haven, CT.

Anderson, G.C., McBride, M.R., Dahm, J., Ellis, M.K., & Vidyasagar, D. (1982). Development of sucking in term infants from birth to four hours postbirth. *Research in Nursing and Health, 5,* 21–27.

André-Thomas & Dargassies, S.S.-A. (1952). *Etudes neurologiques sur le nouveau-né.* Paris: Masson.

Ardran, G.M., Kemp, F.H., & Lind, J. (1958). A cineradiographic study of bottle feeding. *British Journal of Radiology, 31,* 11–22.

Aylward, G.P. (1981). The developmental course of behavioral states in pre-term infants: A descriptive study. *Child Development, 52,* 564–568.

Bates, J.E. (1980). The concept of difficult temperament. *Merrill-Palmer Quarterly, 26,* 299–319.

Bates, J.E., Olson, S.L., Pettit, G.S., & Bayles, K. (1982). Dimensions of individuality in the mother–infant relationship at six months of age. *Child Development, 53,* 446–461.

Bell, R.Q. (1960). Relations between behavior manifestations in the human neonate. *Child Development, 31,* 463–477.

Bell, R.Q. (1963). Some factors to be controlled in studies of the behavior of newborns. *Biologia Neonatorum, 5,* 200–214.

Bell, S.M., & Ainsworth, M.D.S. (1972). Infant crying and maternal responsiveness. *Child Development, 43,* 1171–1190.

Benjamin, L.S. (1961). The effect of frustration on the nonnutritive sucking of the infant rhesus monkey. *Journal of Comparative and Physiological Psychology, 54,* 700–703.

Berlyne, D. (1960). *Conflict, arousal, and curiosity.* New York: McGraw-Hill.

Berry, K.K. (1975). Developmental study of recognition of antecedents of infant vocalization. *Perceptual and Motor Skills, 41,* 400–402.

Blau, T.J., & Blau, L.R. (1955). The sucking reflex: The effects of long feeding vs. short feeding on the behavior of a human infant. *Journal of Abnormal and Social Psychology, 51,* 123–5.

Booth, C.L., Leonard, H.L., & Thoman, E.B. (1980). Sleep states and behavior patterns in preterm and full term infants. *Neuropediatrie, 11,* 354–364.

Boukydis, C.F.Z., & Burgess, R.L. (1982). Adult physiological response to infant cries: Effects of temperament of infant, parental status, and gender. *Child Development, 53,* 1291–1298.

Bowlby, J. (1969). *Attachment and loss. Vol. 1. Attachment.* London: Hogarth; New York: Basic Books.

Brackbill, Y. (1958). Extinction of the smiling response in infants as a function of reinforcement schedule. *Child Development, 29,* 115–124.

Brazelton, T.B. (1962). Crying in infancy. *Pediatrics, 29,* 579–588.

Brazelton, T.B. (1973). *Neonatal behavioral assessment scale. Clinics in developmental medicine,* No. 50. Philadelphia: Lippincott.

Brim, O.G., & Kagan, J. (1980). *Constancy and change in human development.* Cambridge, MA: Harvard University Press.

Brodbeck, A.J. (1950). The effect of three feeding variables on the non-nutritive sucking of newborn infants. *American Psychologist, 5,* 292–293.

Brown, J.L. (1964). States in newborn infants. *Merrill-Palmer Quarterly, 10,* 313–327.

Brownfield, E.D. (1956). An investigation of the activity and sensory responses of healthy newborn infants. *Dissertation Abstracts, 16,* 1288–1289.

Bühler, C. (1930). *The first year of life* (Translated by P. Greenberg & R. Ripin from 3 German publications appearing in 1927, 1928, & 1930.) New York: Day.

Bühler, C. (1931). The social behavior of the child. In C. Murchison (Ed.), *A handbook of child psychology.* Worcester, MA: Clark University Press.

Campos, J.J., & Brackbill, Y. (1973). Infant state: Relationship to heart rate, behavioral response and response decrement. *Developmental Psychobiology, 6,* 9–20.

Carey, W.B., & McDevitt, S.C. (1978). Revision of the infant temperament questionnaire. *Pediatrics, 61,* 735–739.

Caron, R.F., Caron, A.J., & Myers, R.S. (1982). Abstraction of invariant face expressions in infancy. *Child Development, 53,* 1008–1015.

Childers, A.T., & Hamil, B.M. (1932). Emotional problems in children as related to duration of breastfeeding in infancy. *American Journal of Orthopsychiatry, 2,* 134–142.

Church, J. (1966). *Three babies: Biographies of cognitive development.* New York: Random House.

Coghill, G.E. (1929a). *Anatomy and the problem of behavior.* Cambridge: Cambridge University Press.

Coghill, G.E. (1929b). The early development of behavior in amblystoma and in man. *Archives of Neurology and Psychiatry, 21,* 989–1009.

Cohen, L.B. (1972). Attention-getting and attention-holding processes of infant visual preferences. *Child Development, 43,* 869–879.

Cohen, L.B., DeLoache, J.S., & Rissman, M.W. (1975). The effect of stimulus complexity on infant visual attention and habituation. *Child Development, 46,* 611–617.

Crowell, D.H., Yasaka, E.K., & Crowell, D.C. (1964). Infant stabilimeter. *Child Development, 35,* 525–532.

Cummings, E.M., Zahn-Waxler, C., & Radke-Yarrow, M. (1981). Children's responses to expressions of anger and affection by others in the family. *Child Development, 52,* 1274–1282.

Darwin, C. (1872). *Expressions of the emotions in man and animals.* London: John Murray.

Davis, H.V., Sears, R.R., Miller, H.C., & Brodbeck, N.J. (1948). Effects of cup, bottle, and breast feeding. *Pediatrics, 2,* 549–558.

DeLoache, J.S., Rissman, M.D., & Cohen, L.B. (1978). An investigation of the attention-getting process in infants. *Infant Behavior and Development, 1,* 11–25.

Dennis, W. (1932). Discussion: The role of mass activity in the development of infant behavior. *Psychological Review, 39,* 593–595.

Dreyfus-Brissac, C. (1968). Sleep ontogenesis in early human prematurity from 24 to 27 weeks conceptional age. *Developmental Psychobiology, 1,* 162–169.

Dunn, J.F. (1975). Consistency and change in styles of mothering. In *Parent–infant interaction. Ciba Foundation Symposium 33 (New Series).* Amsterdam: Elsevier.

Dunn, J.F. (1976). Mother–infant relations: Continuities and discontinuities over the first 14 months. *Journal of Psychosomatic Research, 20,* 273–277.

Emde, R., & Harmon, R. (1972). Endogenous and exogenous smiling systems in early infancy. *Journal of the American Academy of Child Psychiatry, 11,* 177–200.

Emde, R.N., Gaensbauer, T.G., & Harmon, R.J. (1976). Emotional expression in infancy: A biobehavioral study. *Psychological Issues Monograph Series, 10* (37).

Escalona, S. (1962). The study of individual differences and the problem of state. *Journal of the American Academy of Child Psychiatry, 1,* 11–37.

Escalona, S.K. (1968). *The roots of individuality: Normal patterns of development in infancy.* Chicago: Aldine.

Escalona, S.K. (1973). The differential impact of environmental conditions as a function of different reaction patterns in infancy. In J.C. West-man (Ed.), *Individual differences in children.* New York: Wiley.

Etzel, B.C., & Gewirtz, J.L. (1967). Experimenter modification of caretaker maintained high-rate operant crying in a 6- and a 20-week old infant (infans tyrannorearus): Extinction of crying with reinforcement of eye-contact and smiling. *Journal of Experimental Child Psychology, 5,* 303–317.

Fairbanks, G. (1942). An acoustical study of the pitch of infant hunger wails. *Child Development, 13,* 227–232.

Field, T.M., & Greenberg, R. (1982). Temperament ratings by parents and teachers of infants, toddlers, and preschool children. *Child Development, 53,* 160–163.

Field, T.M., Ting, G., & Shuman, H.H. (1979). The onset of rhythmic activities in normal and high-risk infants. *Developmental Psychobiology, 12,* 97–100.

Field, T.M., Woodson, R., Greenberg, R., & Cohen, D. (1982). Discrimination and imitation of facial expressions by neonates. *Science, 218,* 179–181.

Fleischl, M.F. (1957). The problem of sucking. *American Journal of Psychotherapy, 1,* 86–87.

Freudenburg, R.P., Driscoll, J.W., & Stern, G.S. (1978). Reactions of adult humans to cries of normal and abnormal infants. *Infant Behavior and Development, 1,* 224–227.

Frodi, A.M., & Lamb, M.E. (1980). Child abusers' responses to infant smiles and cries. *Child Development, 51,* 238–241.

Frodi, A.M., Lamb, M., Leavitt, L.A., & Donovan, W.L. (1978). Fathers' and mothers' responses to infant smiles and cries. *Infant Behavior and Development, 1,* 187–198.

Frodi, A.M., Lamb, M.E., Leavitt, L.A., Wilberta, L., Donovan, C.M., & Sherry, D. (1978). Fathers' and mothers' responses to the faces and cries of normal and premature infants. *Developmental Psychology, 14,* 490–498.

Gardiner, W. (1838). *The music of nature.* Boston: Wilkins & Carter.

Gaulin-Kremer, E., Shaw, J.L., & Thoman, E.B. (1977). *Temporal course of sucking responsiveness in the earliest hours of life.* Paper presented at the biennial meeting of the Society for Research in Child Development, New Orleans.

Gesell, A. (1948). *Studies in child development.* New York: Harper & Brothers.

Gesell, A., & Thompson, H. (1934). *Infant behavior: Its genesis and growth.* New York: McGraw-Hill.

Gewirtz, J.L. (1965). The course of infant smiling in four child-rearing environments in Israel. In B.M. Foss (Ed.), *Determinants of infant behaviour* (Vol. 3). London: Methuen.

Gewirtz, J.L. (1977). Maternal responding and the conditioning of infant crying: Directions of influence within the attachment—acquisition process. In B.C. Etzel, J.M. LeBlanc, & D.M. Baer (Ed.), *New developments in behavioral research: Theory, method, and application.* Hillsdale, NJ: Erlbaum.

Gewirtz, J.L., & Boyd, E.F. (1977a). Does maternal responding imply reduced infant crying? A critique of the 1972 Bell and Ainsworth report. *Child Development, 48,* 1200–1207.

Gewirtz, J.L., & Boyd, E.F. (1977b). In reply to the rejoinder to our critique of the 1972 Bell and Ainsworth report. *Child Development, 48,* 1217–1218.

Goldsmith, H., & Campos, J. (1983). Toward a theory of infant temperament. In R. Emde & R. Harmon (Eds.), *Attachment and affiliative systems.* New York: Plenum.

Goldsmith, H.H., & Gottesman, I.I. (1981). Origins of variation in behavioral style: A longitudinal study of temperament in young twins. *Child Development, 52,* 91–103.

Golub, H.L., & Corwin, M. (1980). *A physioacoustic model of the infant cry and its use for medical diagnosis and prognosis.* Paper presented at the meeting of the Society for Pediatric Research.

Golub, H.L., & Corwin, M.J. (1982). Infant cry: A clue to diagnosis. *Pediatrics, 69,* 197–201.

Gordon, N.S., & Bell, R.Q. (1961). Activity in the human newborn. *Psychological Reports, 9,* 103–106.

Gordon, T., & Foss, B.M. (1966). The role of stimulation in the delay of onset of crying in the newborn infant. *Quarterly Journal of Experimental Psychology, 18,* 79–81.

Graham, F.K., Matarazzo, R.G., & Caldwell, B.M. (1956). Behavioral differences between normal and traumatized new-borns. I. The test procedures. *Psychological Monographs, 70* (20, Whole No. 427).

Haith, M.M. (1966). The response of the human newborn to visual movement. *Journal of Experimental Child Psychology, 3,* 235–243.

Hetzer, H., & Tudor-Hart, B.H. (1927). Die Frühesten reactionen auf die menschliche stimme. *Quellen und Studien, 5,* 103–124.

Hiatt, S., Campos, J., & Emde, R. (1979). Facial patterning and infant emotional expression: Happiness, surprise, and fear. *Child Development, 50,* 1020–1035.

Honzik, M. (1965). Prediction of behavior from birth to maturity, a book review of *Birth to maturity. Merrill Palmer Quarterly, 11,* 77–88.

Horowitz, F.D., Paden, L.Y., Bhana, K., & Self, P. (1972). An infant control procedure for studying infant visual fixations. *Developmental Psychology, 7,* 90.

Hubert, N.C., Wachs, T.D., & Peters-Martin, P. (1982). The study of early temperament: Measurement and conceptual issues. *Child Development, 49,* 571–600.

Huitt, W.G., & Ashton, P.T. (1982). Parents' perception of infant temperament: A psychometric study. *Merrill-Palmer Quarterly, 28,* 95–109.

Hutt, S.J., Lenard, H.G., & Prechtl, H.G.R. (1969). Psychophysiological studies in newborn infants. In L.P. Lipsitt & H.W. Reese (Eds.), *Advances in child development and behavior* (Vol. 4, pp. 128–172). New York: Academic.

Ignatoff, E. (April, 1980). *Effects of nonnutritive sucking on clinical course and Brazelton performance of ICU neonates.* Paper presented at the Second International Conference on Infant Studies, New Haven, CT.

Ignatoff, E., & Field, T.M. (1982). Effects of nonnutritive sucking during tube feedings on the behavior and clinical course of ICU preterm neonants. In L.P. Lipsitt & T.M. Field (Eds.), *Infant behavior and development: Perinatal risk and newborn behavior.* Norwood, NJ: Ablex.

Ingram, T.T.S. (1962). Clinical significance of the infantile feeding reflexes. *Developmental Medicine and Child Neurology, 4,* 159–169.

Irwin, O.C. (1930). The amount and nature of activities of newborn infants under constant external stimulating conditions during the first ten days of life. *Genetic Psychology Monographs, 8,* 1–92.

Izard, C.E., Hembree, E.A., Dougherty, L.M., & Spizzirri, C.C. (1983). Changes in facial expressions of 2- to 19-month-old infants following acute pain. *Developmental Psychology, 19,* 418–426.

Izard, C.E., Huebner, R.R., Risser, D., McGinnes, G.C., & Dougherty, L.M. (1980). The young infant's ability to produce discrete emotion expressions. *Developmental Psychology, 16,* 132–140.

Kagan, J. (1971). *Change and continuity in infancy.* New York: Wiley.

Kagan, J. (1980). Perspectives on continuity. In O.G. Brim & J. Kagan (Eds.), *Constancy and change in human development.* Cambridge, MA: Harvard University Press.

Kagan, J. (1982). The construct of difficult temperament: A reply to Thomas, Chess, and Korn. *Merrill-Palmer Quarterly, 28,* 21–24.

Kagan, J. & Moss, H. (1962). *Birth to maturity: A study in psychological development.* New York: Wiley.

Kazmeier, K.J. (March, 1973). *Non-nutritive sucking patterns of jaundiced infants.* Paper presented at the sixth annual meeting of the Gatlinburg Conference on Research and Theory in Mental Retardation, Gatlinburg, TN.

Kazmeier, K.J., Keenan, W.J., & Sutherland, J.M. (1977). Effects of elevated bilirubin and phototherapy on infant behavior. *Pediatric Research, 11,* 563.

Kessen, W., Haith, M.M., & Salapatek, P.H. (1970). Infancy. In P.H. Mussen (Ed.), *Carmichaels' manual of child psychology* (3rd ed., Vol. 1, pp. 287–445). New York: Wiley.

Kessen, W., Leutzendorff, A., & Stoutsenberger, K. (1967). Age, food deprivation, non-nutritive sucking and movement in the human newborn. *Journal of Comparative Physiology and Psychology, 63,* 82–86.

Kestenberg, J.S. (1965). The role of movement patterns in development: I. Rhythms of movement. *Psychoanalytic Quarterly, 34,* 1–36.

Klaus, M.H., Trause, M.A., & Kennel, J.H. (1975). Does human maternal behaviour after delivery show a characteristic pattern? In *Parent–infant interaction. Ciba Foundation Symposium 33.* Amsterdam: Elsevier.

Kleitman, N., & Engelmann, T.G. (1953). Sleep characteristics of infants. *Journal of Applied Physiology, 6,* 269–282.

Koepke, J.E., & Barnes, P. (1982). Amount of sucking when a sucking object is readily available to human newborns. *Child Development, 53,* 978–983.

Kopp, C.B. (April, 1971). *Inhibition of crying: A comparison of stimuli.* Paper presented at the biennial meeting of the Society for Research in Child Development, Minneapolis.

Kopp, C.B., Sigman, M., Parmelee, A.H., & Jeffrey, W.E. (1975). Neurological organization and visual fixation in infants at 40 weeks conceptional age. *Developmental Psychobiology, 8,* 165–170.

Kopp, C.B., & Vaughn, B.E. (1982). Sustained attention during exploratory manipulation as a predictor of cognitive development in preterm infants. *Child Development, 53,* 174–182.

Korner, A.F. (1969). Neonatal startles, smiles, erections, and reflex sucks as related to state, sex, and individuality. *Child Development, 40,* 1039–1053.

Korner, A.F., & Thoman, E.G. (1972). Relative efficacy of contact and vestibular stimulation on soothing neonates. *Child Development, 43,* 443–453.

Korner, A.F., Thoman, E.B., & Glick, J.H. (1974). A system for monitoring crying and noncrying, large, medium, and small neonatal movements. *Child Development, 45,* 946–952.

Kussmaul, A. (1859). *Untersuchungen über das seelenleben des neugeborenen menschen.* Tübingen, Heidelberg, and Leipzig: Moser and C.F. Winter.

Lamb, M.E. (1978). Qualitative aspects of mother- and father–infant attachments. *Infant Behavior and Development, 1,* 51–59.

Lamper, C., & Eisdorfer, C. (1971). Prestimulus activity level and responsivity in the neonate. *Child Development, 42,* 465–473.

Lancione, G.E., Horowitz, F.D., & Sullivan, J.W. (1980). The NBAS-K: I. A study of its stability and structure over the first month of life. *Infant Behavior and Development, 3,* 341–359.

Landau, R. (1982). Infant crying and fussing: Findings from a cross-cultural study. *Journal of Cross-Cultural Psychology, 13,* 427–444.

Lenard, H.G., Von Bernuth, H., & Prechtl, H.F.R. (1968). Reflexes and their relationships to behavioral state in the newborn. *Acta Paediatrica Scandinavica, 55,* 177–185.

Lester, B.M., & Zeskind, P.S. (1982). Biobehavioral perspective on crying in early infancy. In H.E. Fitzgerald, B.M. Lester, & M. Yogman (Eds.), *Theory and research in behavioral pediatrics* (Vol. 1). New York & London: Plenum.

Levy, D.M. (1928). Finger sucking and accessory movements in early infancy: An ethological study. *American Journal of Psychiatry, 7,* 881–918.

Levy, D.M. (1958). *Behavioral analysis.* Springfield, IL: Charles C. Thomas.

Lewis, M., Bartels, B., & Goldberg, S. (1967). State as a determinant of infant's heart rate response to stimulation. *Science, 155,* 486–488.

Lewis, M., Sullivan, M.W., & Brooks-Gunn, J. (April, 1981). *The emotional concomitants of contingent stimulation in early infancy.* Paper presented at the annual meeting of the Eastern Psychological Association, New York.

Lind, J. (Ed.). (1965). Newborn infant cry. *Acta Paediatrica Scandinavica* (Suppl. 163).

Lipsitt, L.P., & DeLucia, C. (1960). An apparatus for the measurement of specific responses and general activity of the human neonate. *American Journal of Psychology, 73,* 630–632.

Lounsbury, M.L., & Bates, J.E. (1982). The cries of infants of differing levels of perceived temperamental difficulties: Acoustic properties and effects on listeners. *Child Development, 53,* 677–686.

Lynip, A. (1951). The use of magnetic devices in the collection and analysis of the preverbal utterances of an infant. *Genetic Psychology Monographs, 44,* 221–262.

Major, D.R. (1906). *First steps in mental growth.* New York: Macmillan.

McCall, R. (1972). Smiling and vocalization in infants as indices of perceptual cognitive processes. *Merril-Palmer Quarterly, 18,* 341–347.

McFarlane, J.W., Allen, L., & Honzik, M.P. (1954). A developmental study of the behavior problems of normal children between 21 months and 14 years. *University of California Publications in Child Development, 2,* 1–122.

McGrade, B.J. (1968). Newborn activity and emotional response at eight months. *Child Development, 39,* 1247–1252.

McKee, J.P., & Honzik, M.P. (1963). The sucking behavior of mammals: An illustration of the nature–nurture question. In L. Postman (Ed.), *Psychology in the making: Histories of selected research problems.* New York: Knopf.

Minkowski, M. (1922). Ueber frühzeitige bewegungen reflexe und muskulare reaktionen beim menschlichen fötus und ihre beiziehungen zum totalen nerven- und muskelsystem. *Schweizer Medizinische Wochenschrift, 52,* 721–751.

Minkowski, M. (1928). Neurobiologische studien am menschlichen fötus. *Abderhalden's Handbuch der Biologishe Arbeitsmethoden, 5.*

Money, J., & Tucker, P. (1975). *Sexual signatures.* Boston: Little, Brown.

Moss, H.A. (1967). Sex, age and state as determinants of mother–infant interaction. *Merrill-Palmer Quarterly, 13,* 19–36.

Moss, H.A., & Robson, S. (1970). The relation between the amount of time infants spend at various states and the development of visual behavior. *Child Development, 41,* 509–517.

Moss, H.A., & Susman, E.J. (1980). Longitudinal study of personality development. In O.G. Brim & J. Kagan (Eds.). *Constancy and change in human development.* Cambridge, MA: Harvard University Press.

Osofsky, J.D. (1976). Neonatal characteristics and mother–infant interaction in two observational situations. *Child Development, 47,* 1138–1147.

Osofsky, J.D., & Danzger, B. (1974). Relationships between neonatal characteristics and mother–infant interaction. *Developmental Psychology, 10,* 124–130.

Ostwald, P.F., & Peltzman, P. (1974). The cry of the human infant. *Scientific American, 230* (3), 84–90.

Parmelee, A.H. (1974). Ontogeny of sleep patterns and associated periodicities in infants. In F. Falkner, N. Kretchmer, & E. Rossi (Eds.), *Modern problems in Paediatrics* (Vol. 13). Basel.

Parmelee, A.H., Jr., Schulz, H.R., & Disbrow, M.A. (1961). Sleep patterns of the new-born. *Journal of Pediatrics, 58,* 241–250.

Plomin, R. (1982). The difficult concept of temperament. A response to Thomas, Chess, and Korn. *Merrill-Palmer Quarterly, 28,* 25–33.

Prechtl, H.F.R. (1958). The directed head turning response and allied movements of the human baby. *Behavior, 13,* 212–242.

Prechtl, H.F.R. (1965). Problems of behavioural studies in the newborn infant. In D.S. Lehrman, R.A. Hinde, & E. Shaw (Eds.), *Advances in the study of behavior* (pp. 75–96). New York: Academic.

Prechtl, H.F.R., Fargel, J.W., Weinman, H.M., & Bakker, H.H. (1979). Postures, motility and respiration of low-risk pre-term infants. *Developmental Medicine and Child Neurology, 21,* 3–27.

Prechtl, H.F.R., Theorell, K., Gramsbergen, A., & Lind, J. (1969). A statistical analysis of cry patterns in normal and abnormal newborn infants. *Developmental Medicine and Child Neurology, 11,* 142–152.

Preyer, W. (1888). *The mind of the child. Part I: The senses and the will* (N.W. Brown, Trans.). New York: Appleton. (Original work published in 1880.)

Rebelsky, F., & Black, R. (1972). Crying in infancy. *The Journal of Genetic Psychology, 121,* 49–57.

Rheingold, H. (1961). The effect of environmental stimulation upon the social and exploratory behaviour in the human infant. In B.M. Foss (Ed.), *Determinants of infant behaviour* (Vol. 1, pp. 143–177). London: Methuen.

Richards, T.W., & Newberry, H. (1938). Studies in fetal behavior: III. Can performance on test items at 6 months postnatally be predicted on the basis of fetal activity? *Child Development, 9,* 79–86.

Robertson, S.S. (1982). Intrinsic temporal patterning in the spontaneous movement of awake neonates. *Child Development, 53*, 1016–1021.

Rosenblith, J.F. (1961a). *Manual for behavioral examination of the neonate as modified by Rosenblith from Graham.* Unpublished manuscript, Brown University Institute for Health Sciences, Providence, RI. (Available from J.F. Rosenblith, Wheaton College, Norton, MA 02766.)

Rosenblith, J.F. (1961b). The modified Graham behavior test for neonates: Test–retest reliability, normative data, and hypotheses for future work. *Biologia Neonatorum, 3*, 174–192.

Rosenblith, J.F., & Anderson-Huntington, R.B. (1975). Defensive reactions to stimulation of the nasal and oral region in newborns: Relations to state. In J. Bosma & J. Showacre (Eds.), *Development of upper respiratory anatomy and function: Implications for Sudden Infant Death Syndrome.* Washington, DC: DHEW Publications.

Ross, S. (1951). Sucking behavior in neonate dogs. *Journal of Abnormal and Social Psychology, 46*, 142–149.

Rothbart, M. (1973). Laughter in young children. *Psychological Bulletin, 80*, 247–256.

Rothbart, M. (1981). Measurement of temperament in infancy. *Child Development, 52*, 569–578.

Rothbart, M. (1982). The concept of difficult temperament: A critical analysis of Thomas, Chess, and Korn. *Merrill-Palmer Quarterly, 28*, 35–40.

Rothbart, M., & Derryberry, D. (1981). Development of individual differences in temperament. In M. Lamb & A. Brown (Eds.), *Advances in Developmental Psychology.* Boston: Erlbaum.

Ruddy, M.G., & Bornstein, M.H. (1982). Cognitive correlates of infant attention and maternal stimulation over the first year of life. *Child Development, 53*, 183–188.

Sameroff, A.J. (1968). The components of sucking in the human newborn. *Journal of Experimental Psychology, 6*, 607–623.

Sameroff, A.J., Seifer, R., & Elias, P.K. (1982). Sociocultural veriability in infant temperamental ratings. *Child Development, 53*, 164–173.

Sameroff, A.J., Seifer, R., & Zax, M. (1982). Early development of children at risk for emotional disorder. *Monographs of the Society for Research in Child Development, 47* (7).

Scarr, S., & Salapatek, P. (1970). Patterns of fear development during infancy. *Merrill-Palmer Quarterly, 16*, 53–90.

Schacter, J., Bickman, L., Schacter, J.S., Jameson, J., Lituchy, S., & Williams, T.A. (1966). Behavioral and physiologic reactivity in human neonates. *Mental Hygiene, 50*, 516–521.

Schaffer, H.R. (1966). Activity level as a constitutional determinant of infantile reaction to deprivation. *Child Development, 37*, 595–602.

Schultz, T.R., & Zigler, E. (1970). Emotional concomitants of visual mastery in infants: The effects of stimulus movement on smiling and vocalizing. *Journal of Experimental Child Psychology, 10*, 390–402.

Sears, R.R., & Wise, G. (1950). Relation of cup feeding in infancy to thumb sucking and the oral drive. *American Journal of Orthopsychiatry, 20*, 123–138.

Sewell, W.H., & Mussen, P.H. (1952). The effects of feeding, weaning and scheduling procedures on childhood adjustment and the formation of oral symptoms. *Child Development, 23*, 185–191.

Sigman, M., & Beckwith, L. (1980). Infant visual attentiveness in relation to caregiver–infant interaction and developmental outcome. *Infant Behavior and Development, 3*, 141–154.

Sigman, M., Kopp, C.V., Parmelee, A.H., & Jeffrey, W.E. (1973). Visual attention and neurological organization in neonates. *Child Development, 44*, 461–466.

Simsarian, F.P. (1947). Case histories of five thumb-sucking children breast fed on unscheduled regimes, without limitation of nursing time. *Child Development, 18*, 180–184.

Skard, A.G. (1966). Orality in the first nine years of life. *Nordisk Psykologi Monografiserien No. 20.*

Sroufe, L.A., & Waters, E. (1976). The ontogenesis of smiling and laughter: A perspective on the organization of development in infancy. *Psychological Review, 83*, 173–189.

Sroufe, L.A., & Wunsch, J.P. (1972). The development of laughter in the first year of life. *Child Development, 43*, 1326–1344.

Stenberg, C.R., Campos, J.J., & Emde, R.N. (1983). The facial expressions of anger in seven-month-old infants. *Child Development, 54*, 178–184.

Stern, E., Parmelee, A.H., Akiyama, Y., Shultz, M.A., & Wenner, W.H. (1969). Sleep cycle characteristics in infants. *Pediatrics, 43*, 65–70.

Thelen, E. (1981). Rhythmical behavior in infancy: An ethological perspective. *Developmental Psychology, 17*, 237–257.

Thomas, A. (1982). The study of difficult temperament: A reply to Kagan, Rothbart, and Plomin. *Merrill-Palmer Quarterly, 28*, 313–315.

Thomas, A., & Chess, S. (1977). *Temperament and development.* New York: Brunner/Mazel.

Thomas, A., Chess, S., & Korn, S.J. (1982). The reality of difficult temperament. *Merrill-Palmer Quarterly, 28,* 1–20.

Thomas, A., Chess, S., Birch, H.G., Hertzig, M.E., & Korn, S. (1963). *Behavioral individuality in early childhood.* New York: New York University Press.

Thompson, J. (1903). On the lip-reflex (mouth phenomenon) of newborn children. *Review of Neurological Psychiatry, 1,* 145.

Truby, H.M. (1959). Acoustico-cineradiographic analysis considerations. *Acta Radiologica, Supplements, 182, No. 69.* Stockholm.

Truby, H.M. (1960). *Some aspects of acoustical and cineradiographical analysis of newborn infant and adult phonation and associated vocal-tract activity.* Paper presented at the annual meeting of the Acoustical Society of America.

Tyler, L.E. (1978). *Individuality: Human possibilities and personal choice in the psychological development of men and women.* San Francisco: Jossey-Bass.

Walters, C.E. (1965). Prediction of postnatal development from fetal activity. *Child Development, 36,* 801–808.

Washburn, R.W. (1929). A study of the smiling and laughing of infants in the first year of life. *Genetic Psychology Monographs, 6,* 397–535.

Wasz-Hockert, O., Lind, J., Vuorenkoski, V., Partanen, T., & Valaane, E. (1968). *The infant cry. Clinics in developmental medicine.* London: Spastics International Medical Publications.

Watson, J.B. (1937). *Behaviorism.* Chicago: University of Chicago Press.

Weiss, A.P. (1929). The measurement of infant behavior. *Psychological Review, 36,* 453–471.

White, R. (1959). Motivation reconsidered: The concept of competence. *Psychological Review, 66,* 297–333.

Wiesenfeld, A.R., Malatesta, C.Z., & DeLoache, L.L. (1981). Differential parental response to familiar and unfamiliar infant distress signals. *Infant Behavior and Development, 4,* 281–295.

Wilson, C.D. (1931). *A study of laughter situations among young children.* Unpublished doctoral dissertation, University of Nebraska, Lincoln.

Wolff, P.H. (1959). Observations on newborn infants. *Psychosomatic Medicine, 21,* 110–118.

Wolff, P.H. (1963). Observations on the early development of smiling. In B. Foss (Ed.), *Determinants of infant behaviour* (Vol. 2, pp. 113–138). London: Methuen.

Wolff, P.H. (1966). The causes, controls, and organization of behavior in the neonate. *Psychological Issues, 5* (1, Whole No. 7).

Wolff, P.H. (1969). The natural history of crying and other vocalizations in early infancy. In B.M. Foss (Ed.), *Determinants of infant behaviour* (Vol. 4, pp. 81–109). London: Methuen.

Yarrow, L.J. (1954). The relationship between nutritive sucking experiences in infancy and non-nutritive sucking in childhood. *Journal of Genetic Psychology, 84.* 149–162.

Zelazo, P.R., & Komer, M.J. (1971). Infant smiling to nonsocial stimuli and the recognition hypothesis. *Child Development, 42,* 1327–1339.

Zeskind, P.S. (1980). Adult responses to cries of low-risk and high-risk infants. *Infant Behavior and Development, 3,* 167–177.

Zeskind, P.S., & Lester, B.M. (1978). Acoustic features and auditory perception of the cries of newborns with prenatal and perinatal complications. *Child Development, 49,* 580–589.

Zeskind, P.S., Sale, J., Maio, M.L., Huntington, L., & Weiseman, J.R. (April, 1984). *Adult perceptions of pain and hunger cries: A synchrony of arousal.* Paper presented to the biennial meeting of the International Conference on Infant Studies, New York.

CONDITIONING, IMITATION, HABITUATION, AND MEMORY

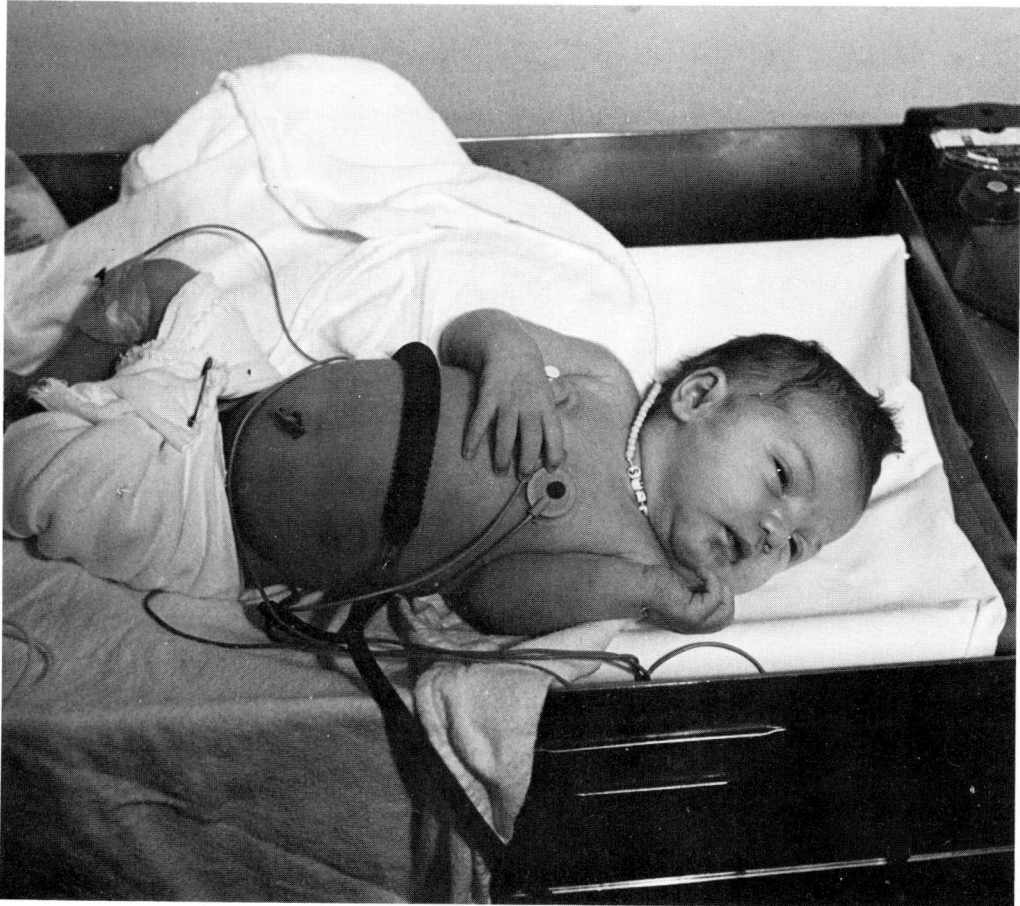

CHAPTER 7

In this chapter, we will discuss research that attempts to determine the extent to which young babies are able to learn about and remember their world. Research in this area has focused primarily on when babies can first use a particular mechanism to acquire knowledge about the world. Researchers have explored the onset in infants of some of the processes that operate in learning and memory in older humans and in many other species. These processes are conditioning, imitation, habituation of the orienting response, and memory.

LEARNING

The big question that has long intrigued many people is: Are newborns equipped to learn immediately after birth, or do they develop learning abilities only at later ages? If they develop these abilities later, how much later? What kinds of things can newborns learn earliest and what sorts of learning must wait for later development? These questions have occupied many infant researchers over the past decades, and the orientations of particular researchers have influenced the way they have asked these questions. Most topics in infant development involve learning in the broad sense of some relatively permanent changes in behavior as a result of environmental events. Learning psychologists, however, have made a unique contribution in that they have asked what the specific mechanisms are by which learning can occur. They have focused on the infants' ability to form new associations, between stimuli and responses or between two stimuli, rather than on their ability to make sense of the world (for example, to recognize faces or to categorize objects). They have used the paradigms of conditioning to ask these questions about learning:

1. When (at what age) can classical conditioning be obtained? What kinds of unconditioned and conditioned stimuli are effective? What responses can be conditioned?
2. When (at what age) can operant conditioning be obtained? What responses can be conditioned? What events can serve as reinforcers?

Classical Conditioning

Classical conditioning, developed by Pavlov early in this century, begins with a naturally occurring stimulus–response connection. The stimulus, an environmental event, **elicits** (produces) a response from the organism. In infant studies an innate stimulus–response connection such as the rooting reflex (stroking the infant's cheek stimulates head turning) is typically used. This stimulus–response connection occurs before conditioning takes place, so it is called unconditioned. The stroking is the **unconditioned stimulus** (UCS) and the head turning is the **unconditioned response** (UCR). The purpose of classical conditioning is to train a new stimulus–response connection, the conditioned association. This is done by pairing a neutral stimulus with the UCS. For example, a buzzer is often used as the neutral stimulus, called the **conditioned stimulus** (CS). The CS and UCS are repeatedly presented together, with the CS always preceding the UCS. If classical conditioning occurs, the subject eventually responds to the CS alone. In the rooting reflex example, after a number of trials in which the buzzer is sounded (CS) and the baby's cheek is stroked (UCS), the baby should turn its head when only the buzzer is sounded. This head-turning response is called the **conditioned response** (CR). Even though the UCR and CR are similar (both are head turning), subtle differences as, for example, in intensity or duration, can be demonstrated, so they are given different names. The process of classical conditioning is diagrammed in Figure 7–1.

What is learned in classical conditioning is an association between two events: that the CS always occurs before the UCS. A further demonstration that the subjects have learned such an association is to reverse the process and break the association after it has been learned. This procedure, called **extinction,** occurs after initial testing for conditioning. The CS is presented alone again and again and subjects gradually cease to make the CR. At that point their responses are said to have extinguished.

CAN NEWBORNS BE CLASSICALLY CONDITIONED?

The purpose of much of the research on classical conditioning in infancy is to discover whether newborns can learn associations that

Before training

UCS ————————————————————→ UCR
    (stroking infant's cheek)   (head turn)

CS – – – – – – – (does not) – – – – – – → head turn
   (tone)

Training (one of many trials)

CS
   (tone)

    UCS ————————————————————→ UCR
        (stroking)   (head turn)

When classical conditioning has occured

CS ————————————————————————→ CR
                                              (head turn)

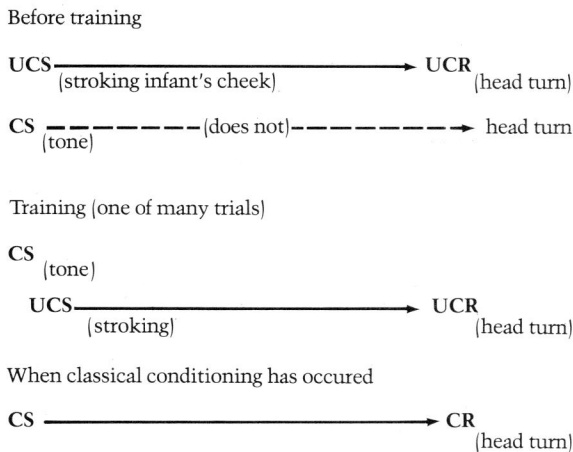

FIGURE 7–1. The course of classical conditioning. Before conditioning infants make no association between the CS and the UCS–UCR sequence. After conditioning the CS acts as a signal that the UCS will follow and hence triggers the CR.

are new to them. There is a long history of attempts to demonstrate such conditioning in newborns, which is understandable because classical conditioning was the earliest form of learning demonstrated experimentally. In 1931, Marquis tried to condition newborns to suck a nipple in response to a buzzer. During each session a buzzer sounded for 5 seconds, followed by the insertion of the milk bottle into the baby's mouth. Marquis found conditioning effects; that is, babies learned to start sucking when the buzzer sounded. Later studies, however, demonstrated that such a result may really be due to other phenomena. This sort of apparent, artifactual conditioning is now called **pseudo-conditioning.** The first study to demonstrate the existence of pseudo-conditioning was done by Wickens and Wickens (1940). Their UCS–UCR sequence was another newborn reflex: mild electric shock (UCS) produces foot withdrawal (UCR). They paired a buzzer with the shock in the effort to get the CS–CR sequence, buzzer–foot withdrawal. And it worked: the sound of the buzzer came to elicit foot withdrawal. Wickens and Wickens would have concluded that conditioning had taken place except for the fact that they had a control group in which the shocks alone were given during conditioning. During the

subsequent test procedure the buzzer, which the babies in the control group had not experienced, was presented alone. It elicited foot withdrawal even though it had never been paired with shock. Although the babies may have learned something, it was not the association of the buzzer with shock. Because Marquis did not have control groups that would have eliminated alternative interpretations of her results, they have not been accepted as evidence that classical conditioning occurs in newborns.

Subsequent attempts to demonstrate classical conditioning in newborns have been equally problematic. The choice of a UCS–UCR connection is difficult. Such connections in newborns are all reflexes, and not all reflexes are appropriate. The response must be one that can come under voluntary control. The foot withdrawal reflex chosen by Wickens and Wickens is not a good candidate for study. Because development proceeds from head to foot (the cephalocaudal principle of development), foot withdrawal would not be expected to win a race to be conditionable earliest. By the late 1960s most investigators had begun to use responses at the head of the body—sucking (also used by Marquis in 1931) and head turning. Since then it has become clear that choosing prepotent responses presents its own problems. Sucking, for example, is such a strong response that it often occurs naturally in response to what are supposed to be CSs. For example, auditory stimuli innately elicit sucking responses (Keen, 1964; Semb & Lipsitt, 1968). Therefore, complex controls are necessary in studies of classical conditioning of sucking.

The states of the infants being tested have been shown to be powerful variables in their conditionability. There is a clear relation between the state of wakefulness and the probability of obtaining even the UCR in response to the UCS (Clifton, Siqueland, & Lipsitt, 1972). Because newborns drift in and out of sleep, even in experimental situations, state has to be carefully controlled.

In spite of improved methodology, based on increased sophistication both in experimental design and in electronic technology, it is not yet clear whether newborns can be classically conditioned in the purest sense of that term; that is, that any CS can be associated with any UCS through a gradual process of "stamping in" the association. It does appear, however, that there are three circumstances under which classical conditioning or a variant can be achieved in newborns. The first is when the behaviors and the contingencies between CS and UCS are biologically adaptive ones that newborns are "prepared" to learn (see a recent example by Blass, Ganchrow, & Steiner, 1984; and discussions by Fitzgerald & Brackbill, 1976; Lipsitt, Mustaine, & Zeigler, 1977; Rovee-Collier & Lipsitt, 1982; Sameroff, 1971; Sameroff & Cavanagh, 1979). There is ample evidence from conditioning studies in other domains that such associations are more easily conditioned than ones that are not biologically prepotent (Seligman, 1970). One classic example is that rats learn to associate taste with poisoned food in one trial rather than learning the association slowly over repeated trials. Fitzgerald and Brackbill (1976) argued that tactile, auditory, and visual CSs are more readily conditioned to motoric responses (such as head turning), whereas temporal CSs are more readily linked to autonomic responses (such as the pupillary reflex).

The second circumstance is found in three recent methodologically sophisticated studies that show evidence of learning within a classical conditioning paradigm, but not in the classical sense of a gradual increase in the strength of the conditioned response followed by a gradual decrease during extinction, when the CS is no longer paired with the UCS (Clifton, 1974; Crowell, Blurton, Kobayashi, McFarland, & Yang, 1976; Stamps & Porges, 1975). All of these studies did find evidence that newborns sometimes reacted differently to the CS during extinction (after they had been conditioned) than they did before. In two of the studies (Clifton, 1974; Stamps & Porges, 1975) the response shown on extinction was heart rate deceleration rather than conditioned acceleration. Heart rate deceleration is a typical response mammals make to a change in the environment; that is, it is a response indicating interest or orienting to a novel stimulus. That these infants showed this response, called the orienting response, means that they noticed the change in stimuli. In other words, they must have learned to expect the UCS. When it was no longer presented, it violated their expectation and they responded to the change. To call this kind of learning classical conditioning may be misleading, however, because it is clearly different in kind.

The third circumstance under which something like classical conditioning has been demonstrated in newborns involves a paradigm developed by Papoušek (1961, 1967a, 1967b) that uses components of both operant and classical conditioning. His UCS was a tactile stimulus to the side of the mouth, which elicits the UCR of a head-turning response about 25% of the time (the rooting response). An auditory stimulus was used as the CS and was paired in standard classical conditioning fashion with the UCS. Papoušek's innovation was to reward the head-turning response with milk. This introduces operant conditioning (to be discussed next), in which a reward increases the probability that the subject will make a future response. Thus, success at conditioning might be due to the influence of the reward. Papoušek's procedure did succeed with newborns, but only after an average of 177 trials over a 3-week period. The interpretation of these results is clouded in two ways. First, as we already mentioned, the results might be due to the effectiveness of the reward or to the specific combination of operant and classical techniques. Second, by the time the newborns had learned the response they were no longer newborns. Subsequent attempts to demonstrate conditioning in one session using Papoušek's techniques have met with some success (Clifton, Meyers, & Solomons, 1972; Clifton, Siqueland, & Lipsitt, 1972; Siqueland & Lipsitt, 1966), but alternative interpretations are still possible (see Sameroff & Cavanagh, 1979). At best it is possible to conclude that a combination of classical and operant conditioning is possible at birth; at worst that even this combined conditioning is not clearly demonstrated until 3 weeks of age.

LATER DEVELOPMENT

The bulk of the research on classical conditioning has been designed to discover the earliest age at which it is possible. Explorations of classical conditioning in older infants are extremely limited. Papoušek (1967a) is one of the few researchers who has used the same procedure with babies of different ages. He used the combined procedure described above with newborns and with 3- and 5-month-old babies. He found that the older babies learned more rapidly. The number of trials to criterion decreased from 177 for newborns, to 42 for 3-month-olds to 28 for 5-month-olds. Once babies learned the response, they showed the same resistance to extinction regardless of their age. That is, they all took the same amount of time to stop responding when the CS was presented alone. This indicates that what develops with age is the speed of learning, not the nature of the response once it is learned (Papoušek would call the latter "the neurological mechanisms"). Perceptual studies of babies' ability to recognize their mothers show a similar phenomenon in that young babies need a longer time to examine the faces, but given that time, they can distinguish their mother from a stranger.

Operant Conditioning

Operant conditioning starts with a spontaneous or **emitted** response; that is, one that the subject makes or emits rather than one the experimenter instigates. The subject's response is followed by a **reinforcer** (reward or desirable environmental event). The consequence of reward is that the subject is more likely to emit the response again. We say that **operant conditioning** has occurred if the probability of the subject's response increases when it has been followed by a reward. During extinction the subject's response is no longer rewarded and the probability of it occurring decreases.

DEVELOPMENT OF OPERANT CONDITIONING
Operant conditioning of newborns has been well demonstrated, most often with two response systems. The first is sucking, which we described in the last chapter. The second is head turning, which has been demonstrated and replicated (reported in Sameroff & Cavanagh, 1979). In these head-turning studies a band that allowed continuous recording of head turns was placed on the newborns' heads. Any turn greater than 10 degrees in any direction was followed by insertion of a nonnutritive nipple to suck on for 5 seconds. Head turning quickly increased.

Although these studies demonstrate that newborn infants clearly respond to reward in some instances, caution must be exercised in generalizing the results. Newborns do not condition easily. They are most likely to respond during active awake periods, which constitute a small proportion of their day. As babies mature, they spend more and more time in active awake periods and are thereby more often available to learn.

Young babies also condition relatively slowly. Babies 8–9 weeks of age often require two sessions before conditioning is evident, whereas babies 12 weeks of age exhibit reliable conditioning in the first 3–6 minutes of training (Gekoski, 1977; Davis & Rovee-Collier, 1983; Sullivan, 1982). A similar development has been found in preweanling versus postweanling rats (Spear & Parsons, 1976).

The variety of responses that can be operantly conditioned in newborns is also limited. The responses most likely to be conditioned—sucking and head turning—involve a natural relation between the response (sucking or head turning) and the reward (milk or nonnutritive sucking). Thus, these appear to be biologically prepotent associations that newborns are "prepared" to learn.

Studies of operant conditioning in older infants have been successful in a greater range of situations (see Figure 7–2), but they still show that some response–reward pairings are easier to condition than others. Social responses, such as vocalization, are more effectively conditioned by social reinforcement, such as mommy saying "peek-a-boo," than they are by comparable nonsocial reinforcement (Ramey & Watson, 1972; Weisberg, 1963). Social reinforcement works better for social than for nonsocial responses (Millar, 1976). Nonsocial responses (auditory localization) are learned more easily when the reinforcer is a complex nonsocial stimulus (animated toy) than when it is either social or a simple nonsocial stimulus (a blinking light).

RESPONSE ELICITATION
In many, but not all, operant conditioning studies, some aspect of the situation results in an increase in the frequency with which the infant makes the target response, even when that response has not been paired with reward. This phenomenon, called **response elicitation,** is both a methodological problem, in that it represents a form of pseudoconditioning, and an interesting phenomenon in its own right.

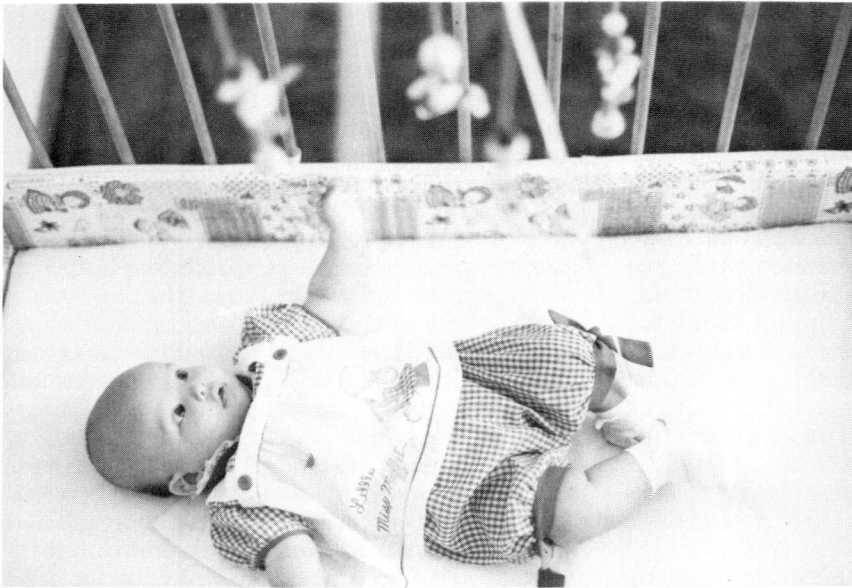

FIGURE 7–2. An infant participating in the operant conditioning developed by Rovee-Collier and described in the section on memory later in this chapter. A ribbon is attached to the infant's leg. She has learned that when she kicks her leg, the mobile moves. The intent look on her face as she watches the mobile shows how rewarding it is to her. (Photograph courtesy of Carolyn Rovee-Collier).

Response elicitation can be demonstrated by the use of a **noncontingent reinforcement** control condition, in which the environmental event that serves as reinforcer in the experimental group is presented to the control group, but not in relation to the subject's responses. A good example of the use of a noncontingent reinforcement control to demonstrate response elicitation is found in a study by Cavanagh and Davidson (1977). Six-month-old infants who pressed a clear plexiglass panel were rewarded by seeing a multicolored light display behind the panel and hearing a bell. The contingent reinforcement (experimental) group received the reward only after they had pressed the panel whereas the noncontingent reinforcement group received the reward on random occasions—sometimes after they had pressed the panel and sometimes when they had not pressed the panel. Each infant in the experimental group was **yoked** to one in the noncontingent control group such that the control infant received the same number of rewards distributed similarly in time during the experi-

mental session as the experimental group. In every other way each pair of babies was treated exactly the same. The frequency of panel pressing increased for both groups during training (when they were experiencing "reinforcement"), although the contingent group showed a greater increase. That the noncontingent group increased the frequency of their panel pressing even though they were not rewarded for those responses demonstrates response elicitation. Conditioning was also demonstrated in this study because the frequency of response increased more in the contingent reinforcement group than it did in the noncontingent reinforcement group. In methodological terms, response elicitation is a form of pseudoconditioning. That is, the infants' responses change *as if* they were being conditioned, but the cause is response elicitation, not conditioning. To determine whether true conditioning has occurred, it must be shown that contingent reinforcement results in greater response change than noncontingent reinforcement.

Response elicitation is also an interesting phenomenon in its own right. It is adaptive because it keeps infants actively interacting with the environment so that eventually they are more likely to make the response that is rewarded. Thus response elicitation can provide the basis on which reward contingencies can be learned. It is also a very general phenomenon. It may result from an innate connection (such as an auditory stimulus that elicits sucking) or from a learned connection. An example of the latter is that babies may kick when they see an interesting event because in their experience prior to the present situation, they learned that kicking was followed by (reinforced by) interesting events. Response elicitation also occurs with social responses such as vocalization (Bloom & Esposito, 1975) and smiling (Zelazo, 1971).

The operant conditioning paradigm has become a powerful technique for studying other aspects of infant development. Later in this chapter we will describe how it has been used to study memory, and in Chapter 9 we will describe how it is used to study perception.

IMITATION

One of the more frequent and more noticeable behaviors of older babies and young children is their tendency to imitate. In this section we will focus on the issues of whether babies imitate in the first two months of life, how such early imitation develops, and how imitation facilitates learning, problem solving, and parent–infant relationships. In Chapter 10 we will discuss in greater detail the development of increasingly sophisticated forms of imitation during infancy and its relation to cognitive development.

Development of Imitation

As with many other infant behaviors, the predominant question studied about imitation is, What is the earliest age at which babies can imitate? To address this question we must first discuss how babies may mislead observers into thinking they are imitating when they are not. Next we will describe research on imitation

with very young babies. Although demonstrations of neonatal behaviors that could be interpreted as imitation do exist, whether they truly represent imitation is hotly contested. Researchers who believe that imitation is an innate ability are likely to accept such behaviors as demonstrating imitation, whereas those who believe that imitation develops gradually through a series of increasingly sophisticated forms, as delineated by Piaget (1945/1962), do not.

The Piagetian perspective not only provides an alternative view to the hypothesis that imitation is innate, it also provides predictions about later development. In Chapter 10 we will discuss in detail the sequence of development of imitation and research relevant to that sequence; in this section we will just summarize those aspects of Piaget's developmental progression that have received the most support.

DO VERY YOUNG BABIES IMITATE?

Study of this question seems very straightforward. A researcher presents a behavior to be imitated to newborn infants and records how frequently the infants imitate. Studies using this technique have demonstrated that the phenomenon is much more complex than this simple-sounding description would indicate. It is not easy to determine whether infants' responses are truly imitative. Two kinds of pseudo-imitation occur. In one kind, children make a response that is of the same general class as the model's, and this is called **inexact,** or **same-class,** imitation. For example, a parent may make a particular sound such as "ahh" and the infant may respond with a vocalization such as "ehh." The response is the same class of behavior that the parent has modeled, but does not exactly match it. In the course of a number of same-class imitations an exact imitation may occur by chance. If researchers pay attention only to the exact match and ignore the same-class imitations, they will falsely conclude that the infant is capable of exact imitations.

Another kind of pseudo-imitation may occur when a desired infant behavior (say cooing or smiling) is reinforced by an adult (say by smiling or going "kitchy-coo"). Other behaviors of the infants are not responded to or reinforced. Once the infant repeats (emits) the desired behavior frequently, the adult rewards the behavior only when it is in response to the adults' performance of the act, which then serves as a conditioned stimulus. The sequence of adult behavior followed by the infant's same behavior looks like imitation, but it is not, for two reasons. First, the same identical procedure could be used when the behaviors of the adult and those of the infant are different, as, for example, reinforcing the baby for cooing when the adult smiles. Here it is clear that a specific response rather than an imitative one is being learned through reinforcement. Second, true imitation is a general skill; it should occur with various unrelated behaviors (for example, both in facial expressions and in hand movements). If infants have been reinforced for imitating a facial expression but then imitate a hand movement only after they have been trained to make the hand movement in response to the adult's model, we must conclude that the infants are not truly imitating.

Researchers studying imitation in very young babies not only have to be careful to distinguish imitation from pseudo-imitation, they also have to take care to select behaviors that answer the questions they are asking. Different kinds of behaviors have different theoretical implications. First, studies of newborn imitation have all used behaviors that babies can exhibit spontaneously, such as crying, sticking out their tongues, and opening and closing their hands. Demonstrating imitation of familiar actions answers the question of whether very young babies imitate, but it does not demonstrate their ability to learn new actions by imitation; only their imitation of unfamiliar actions would show that. Second, the theoretical implications of a successful demonstration of imitation differ depending on whether the babies can see or hear their own actions. Babies cannot see their faces, so to imitate a facial gesture they must have a mental representation of that gesture that permits them to recognize the similarity between their facial gesture and that of the model. In contrast, they can match hand gestures externally by watching their hands and the model's hands. If newborns can imitate actions they can't see themselves perform, this would be evidence that their innate cognitive equipment is much more sophisticated than many psychologists believe it is.

The first behavior used to investigate neonatal imitation was crying. Newborns in hospital nurseries cry in response to the cries of other newborns. As long ago as 1928, Bühler and Hetzer found that 84% of babies in their first 2 weeks of life cried when exposed to another crying infant. When researchers again became interested in imitation in the 1970s, they introduced conditions that have demonstrated that this sort of crying is not simply a response to a noxious noise. Several studies have now found that newborns cry more in response to cries of other newborns than they do to cries of older infants, synthetic cries, cries of a chimpanzee, or silence (Martin & Clark, 1982; Sagi & Hoffman, 1976; Simner, 1971). They also respond differently to the cries of other newborns than they do to their own cries. A tape of another newborn crying increased crying both when the target infants were calm and when they were excited; a tape of their own crying had no effect when they were calm and almost completely stopped their crying when they were already crying as the tape of their cry started (Martin & Clark, 1982).

If imitative crying were simply part of the newborn's basic tendency to cry at loud noises, then all of the situations mentioned should increase crying similarly. In fact, a newborn's own crying would be expected to elicit crying better because to the baby itself it should be as loud or louder than that of other babies. The cries of a chimpanzee or an older baby would also be expected to be more effective stimuli because adults rate these cries as more aversive than the crying of a neonate.

It seems clear that newborns respond to something rather specific when they cry in response to the cries of other newborns, but whether this indicates that newborns imitate is still open to question. It is clearly exact imitation in the sense that the response is triggered by the specific stimulus of another crying newborn, but the research does not indicate whether the response is specific. Studies have not compared the response of crying to other responses. For example, other arousal responses, such as activity level, might increase as much as crying responses. That would suggest that crying in response to crying is not imitation. The imitation explanation also does not explain why distress is part of the response. Several researchers (Martin & Clark, 1982; Sagi & Hoffman, 1976) have argued that a better

TABLE 7–1
Imitative Responses of Young Infants[a]

Scored responses	Gestures shown to infants:			
	Lip protrusion	Mouth opening	Tongue protrusion	Sequential finger movements
Lip protrusion	<u>27</u>	17	15	19
Mouth opening	11	<u>24</u>	17	19
Tongue protrusion	21	20	<u>30</u>	26
Sequential finger movements	14	13	16	<u>27</u>
Hand opening	22	24	28	24
Finger protrusion	18	19	10	8
Passive hand	18	16	18	13

[a]Distribution of responses across the four gestures shown to the infants. The figures in the first four rows are from Figure 2 of Meltzoff and Moore (1977). The rest of the figures were obtained from A.N. Meltzoff. The underlined entries indicate matching responses. NOTE. From Anisfeld, M. (1979). Interpreting "imitative" responses in early infancy. *Science, 205,* 214–215.

explanation for this phenomenon is that it is a rudimentary empathic response to distress.

Other researchers have explored facial and hand responses. Meltzoff and Moore (1977) claimed to have demonstrated imitation of lip and tongue protrusions, mouth openings, and sequential finger movements in 12- to 21-day-old babies, but their claim has been disputed on a number of grounds, both methodological and theoretical (Anisfeld, 1979; Cohen, 1981; Koepke, Hamm, Legerstee, & Russell, 1983a; Masters, 1979; McKenzie & Over, 1983a; see also Meltzoff & Moore's responses to some of these criticisms, 1979, 1983a). Although Meltzoff and Moore (1983b) did replicate their own original findings, several attempts by others to replicate them have failed (Hayes & Watson, 1981; Koepke, Hamm, Legerstee, & Russell, 1983b; McKenzie & Over, 1983b). The actual data from Meltzoff and Moore's main experiment are presented in Table 7–1, in the restructured form Anisfeld provided. The table demonstrates one of the major problems with that study: that is, whether the babies' responses look like imitation or not depends on which aspects of the data are focused on. Meltzoff and Moore compared the underlined numbers (the diagonals) to the other entries in the same row and found, for example, that the infants were more likely to protrude their lips immediately after the adult protruded his lips

than they were to protrude their lips after the other adult gestures. The same was true for the other three imitative responses. In contrast, the vertical columns that list infant responses to each adult gesture show that in many instances the infant did something different from what the adult modeled. In fact, only 20 of the scored responses were imitative. Arguments can be made for both criteria of whether imitation has occurred (Anisfeld, 1979, argues for the column comparison; Meltzoff & Moore, 1979, for the row comparisons). Nevertheless, the column comparisons make it clear that exact imitation is not a common response.

Field, Woodson, Greenberg, and Cohen (1982) studied facial expressions (happy, sad, surprised) rather than isolated facial gestures. Adults first stimulated the babies to get their attention and then made a happy, sad, or surprised face (see Figure 7–3). By Meltzoff and Moore's criterion, these newborns imitated; for example, they were more likely to widen their eyes and mouths to surprised models than to other modeled expressions. The researchers did not report whether the babies were more likely to exhibit the appropriate facial expression than they were to make other facial expressions or to do something else, which is necessary to demonstrate exact imitation, as Anisfeld argued with respect to Meltzoff and Moore's data.

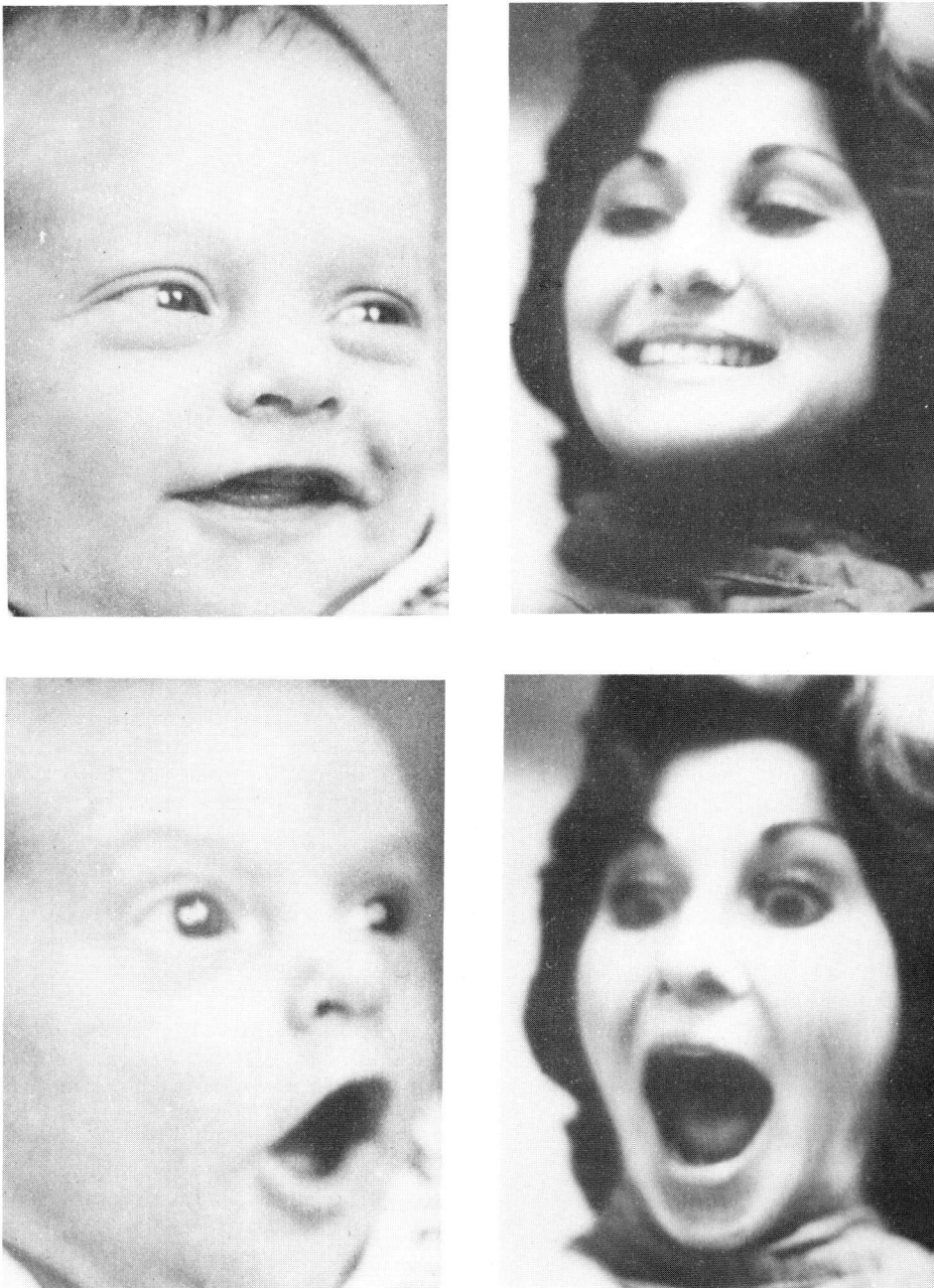

FIGURE 7–3. Newborns imitating happy and surprised facial expressions in the experiment by Field and her colleagues (1982). The controversy over neonatal imitation does not hinge on whether such sequences ever occur; rather, the question is whether this is true imitation rather than a striking coincidence. (From "Discrimination and imitation of facial expressions by neonates," by T. Field, R. Woodson, R. Greenberg, & D. Cohen. Science, 1982, 218, 179–181. Reproduced by permission.)

Studies similar to Meltzoff and Moore's have also been done with 6-week-old babies with specific attention to the question of whether such imitation is exact (Abravanel & Sigafoos, 1984; Gardner & Gardner, 1970; Jacobson, 1979; see also Jacobson & Kagan, 1979, for a slightly different description of the same study). These studies suggest that imitation even in somewhat older infants is imitation in the same general class rather than exact imitation. Gardner and Gardner, in a case study of one 6-week-old infant, found that the response of protruding or opening might be made with a different organ than that modeled (for example, model opens hand, infant opens mouth). Jacobson found that other objects moved toward and away from 6-week-old infants elicited tongue protrusions as effectively as modeled tongue protrusions. She also showed that the babies' protrusions were to a class of protruding stimuli and not just part of general arousal, because other stimuli (hand-grasping movements and a ring dangling) did not elicit as high a level of clear tongue protrusions (those lasting over $\frac{1}{2}$ second).

Even same-class imitations in 6-week-olds may be limited to certain response dimensions. Jacobson found no pattern of responses indicative of same-class imitation for hand movements in her 6-week-old infants, although there was such a pattern for tongue protrusions. Maratos (1973) also found that early imitations were limited to behaviors infants would make spontaneously. Several studies (Abravanel & Sigafoos, 1984; Jacobson, 1979; Maratos, 1973) have found imitative tongue protrusions to be less frequent in babies 3 months and older than in younger babies, except in Jacobson's experimental group of babies whose mothers regularly modeled tongue protrusion. These patterns of results suggest that imitation in very young infants is extremely limited and tied to behaviors that are prepotent. Such behaviors may be part of the newborns' repertoire of reflex behaviors that, if not subjected to special training, drop out.

These conclusions for babies 6 weeks of age appear to contrast sharply with the claims for imitation in newborns, but that is partly due to the differences in criteria employed by different researchers. If the criterion for same-class imitation used by Jacobson were applied to Meltzoff and Moore's data in Table 7-1, it is not clear that even inexact imitation has occurred for either seen or unseen actions. For example, in modeled tongue protrusion, an action infants cannot see themselves perform, hand opening (not the same class) was a much more frequent response than lip protrusion (same class). In sequential finger movements, an action infants can see themselves perform, tongue protrusions were essentially as frequent as exact imitations. The more conservative explanation of the newborn research, particularly in light of the studies of somewhat older babies, is that adult modeling of both seen and unseen familiar actions produces nothing more than response elicitation. An alternative argument is that it is possible to be too conservative and that some rudimentary imitative ability does exist in the newborn period. Which of these positions researchers accept often depends on their theoretical biases. Those who believe that babies are born with a set of well-developed cognitive structures are likely to believe that newborns are imitating, whereas those who believe in Piaget's theory of cognitive development are more likely to believe that newborns are exhibiting response elicitation and that 6-week-olds are exhibiting same-class imitation (we will examine this research from Piaget's developmental viewpoint in Chapter 10).

Notice that whatever conclusion is accepted, it holds only for actions newborns spontaneously emit. It has not been demonstrated that newborns will imitate unfamiliar actions, that is, that imitation forms a major basis for learning new actions in the newborn period.

LATER DEVELOPMENT

Most of the research on imitation in infancy has focused on imitation in very young babies. Only in Piagetian research, which examines imitation as the development of increasingly sophisticated steps toward mature imitation, has imitation later in the first year of life been studied. Our major discussion of Piaget's theory of imitation and the research designed to test these developmental forms is best discussed in the context of his overall theory, so at this time we will give only a brief summary of those developmental phenomena that have received some research support beyond Piaget's own studies.

As we have just noted, same-class imitation of actions already in their behavioral repertoire develops during 1 to 4 months of age. By 4 to 8 months infants can imitate actions that are familiar to them and do so frequently (Abravanel, Levan-Goldschmidt, & Stevenson, 1976). By 8 to 12 months they are able to imitate actions that are unfamiliar to them. Over the period from 6 to 12 months babies' imitation becomes increasingly exact (Kaye & Marcus, 1981).

All of the research we have reviewed thus far has studied **immediate** imitation, in which the imitative response is made immediately after the modeled act. **Delayed** imitation, in which the imitation occurs at a later time, appears to be a more sophisticated form of imitation. It is characteristic only of highly intelligent animals, such as chimpanzees, monkeys, and humans (Yando, Seitz, & Zigler, 1978). Consistent with this, it develops only at the end of the second year of life in humans (Piaget, 1945/1962; Uzgiris & Hunt, 1975).

The Mechanism by Which Imitation Develops

Reinforcement psychologists (such as Baer, Peterson, & Sherman, 1967; Gewirtz, 1971a, 1971b; Gewirtz & Stingle, 1968) believe that imitation develops by means of reinforcement training. They argue that infants' imitative-like responses are reinforced in many different situations, and that through this repeated training a general tendency to imitate develops. The basic mechanism by which such general response tendencies develop through specific training with a large number of exemplars (learning sets) was demonstrated many years ago by Harlow (1949). It is also known that even very young infants can be trained to imitate, so the basic mechanism has been demonstrated in infants. Generalized imitation has even been painstakingly developed in severely retarded children (Baer & Sherman, 1964).

Other psychologists argue that just because it would be possible to develop a generalized imitative tendency by means of reinforcement, this does not mean that it normally develops this way. They believe that imitation is as much a natural characteristic of humans as is the tendency to respond to rewards. We will present four arguments used to defend this position. First, some imitation occurs within the first month or two of life, when there is little or no reinforcement history. Second, the course of development of imitation follows closely the course of development of cognition (see Chapter 10). Third, even when external reinforcers are present, their significance becomes submerged in favor of apparent intrinsic satisfaction. Bruner described this tendency in the following way: "The play aspect of tool use (and indeed, complex problem solving in general) is underlined by the animal's loss of interest in the goal of the act being performed and by its preoccupation with means—also a characteristic of human children" (1972, p. 695). A good example of this is Rumbaugh's account (1970) of the chimpanzee, Lana, who saved her banana reinforcements and then returned them to the experimenter in the next part of the experiment, one per trial. If the bananas had been rewards in the traditional learning sense of that term, Lana would have eaten them. Rather she became preoccupied with the means—the use of bananas as rewards. Fourth, reinforcement is evidently not necessarily involved in imitation. Waxler and Yarrow (1975) found that while reinforcement operates in a straightforward way in some children's imitation, similar imitation occurs in children who do not experience reinforcement.

Roles Imitation Plays in Infant Development

Imitation plays important roles both in learning about the world and in social development. Both psychologists who focus on learning as a result of reinforcement and those who focus on children's abilities to solve problems agree that much learning results from imitation. Indeed, one of the characteristics of the profoundly retarded is that they do not imitate adult behaviors to anything like the degree that normal or mildly retarded children do. Hence we can conceive of imitation as one of the very fundamental human abilities.

Imitation plays a crucial role in learning through reinforcement, because it is an important mechanism by which behaviors may be initially elicited. Remember that in operant conditioning the behavior must first occur before it can be reinforced. Some infant behaviors are highly likely to occur (be emitted) or are easy to elicit for biological reasons (such as sucking), and these behaviors can easily be controlled by reinforcement. Other behaviors are rarely emitted spontaneously. Learning psychologists have developed some techniques to encourage individuals to produce (emit) such behaviors, but they tend to be either very time consuming or rather unpleasant. It is, however, usually easy for adults to model a desired response. Because infants and young children have a great tendency to imitate, they are likely to mimic the response. Voila! The behavior occurs and the adult can now reinforce it. Thus, imitation is a powerful method by which children can be induced to behave in a particular way, and that behavior can then become subject to control through reinforcement.

This technique forms an important part of Brazelton's technique for toilet training (1974). He suggests that an older child or parent demonstrate to the 2-year-old the correct procedure for using a toilet. Then, when the child imitates the toilet-going behaviors, this performance can be reinforced. Learning by modeling plus reinforcement is very common throughout childhood. It is used by parents in child rearing (see, for example, Mussen & Eisenberg-Berg's 1977 review of its role in the development of prosocial behaviors) as well as in the development of such diverse skills as tennis, spear throwing, and American Sign Language. In fact, Cole and Scribner (1974) report that imitation is the major form of teaching in non-technological cultures.

Because imitation evidently develops through a series of different forms, one can ask at what age imitation can first become an effective mechanism by which to elicit behaviors to be reinforced. Immediate imitation clearly provides such a mechanism. Inexact imitation may also sometimes be useful to the person who wishes to train through reinforcement; it can provide a basis for **shaping,** the process whereby reinforcement is initially given for a crude approximation of a desired behavior and subsequently is given only for behaviors that are nearer and nearer to the desired behavior. For example, consider teaching an infant to play "so big," the game where the parent says, "How big is the baby?" and the baby responds

by raising his hands at the same time the adult says "so big." The parent models the hand raises. On the first trial any hand movement is rewarded. After several trials the parent stops rewarding any movement and rewards only movements toward the ceiling. The process is repeated; again the parent ceases to reward the previously acceptable response, and rewards only responses closer to the desired arm raises. After several cycles of this procedure, the infant raises his arms in response to the parent's query and model of the arm raise. In this way inexact imitations may be used as the basis for developing exact imitations. Shaping can also be used effectively to teach an unfamiliar action on the basis of a familiar action provided the shaper can build successive approximations from the familiar action to the unfamiliar action. Thus, imitation can be an effective learning device for some activities at least by 6 weeks of age, when it is clear that babies exhibit same-class imitation of familiar actions. Imitation may become even more effective later in infancy, when infants exhibit exact imitation of unfamiliar actions.

Psychologists interested in the development of reasoning and problem solving have identified a second role imitation plays in the acquisition of knowledge. Imitation of unfamiliar actions is considered by Piaget to be a primary way children incorporate new behavior patterns into their cognitive structures. This imitative learning may occur while the infant is trying to solve a problem or it may occur in the context of play, in which no obvious problem is being solved. An example of the latter is when an older sibling may move a stool to the sink and stand on it to brush her teeth. The toddler, imitating, takes the stool and carries it from place to place. At each place he puts it down, steps on it, then steps off, picks it up, and takes it to another place. Never during this entire sequence does the toddler use this action to reach something. At some later time, however, the toddler wishes to reach a light switch that is too high and fetches the stool to stand on. Bruner (1972) reports an identical pattern for chimpanzees. This pattern, in which a behavior develops through imitation and later is applied to a problem-solving situation, is an example of a more general relation between play and problem solving that has been found repeatedly in psychological research. Animals from rats to chimps to humans will engage in exploratory play when they are not hungry. Later when they have a problem (for instance, they are hungry and want to obtain food) they will use the knowledge of their environment gained in play to solve the problem (find the food). Acquiring problem solutions through imitation, either in intentional problem solving or in the context of play, should occur only when the infant can imitate unfamiliar actions, an ability that first develops between 8 and 12 months of life. Research that tests the relation between imitation and problem solving will be disussed in Chapter 10.

Imitation also plays a role in the development of the caretaker–infant relationship. Adults like and are warmer toward children who imitate them (Bates, 1975), and children find being imitated by an adult rewarding (Fouts, 1972, 1975; Thelen, Dollinger, & Roberts, 1975). Infants need not exhibit true imitation for it to facilitate the caretaker–infant relationship. Parents are typically delighted with any response from young infants, and they are likely to be rewarded by inexact imitation and by response elicitation as well as by exact matches. Likewise, if parents can successfully train their infants to imitate, the mutually rewarding interaction should occur even though it is not true imitation. Indeed evidence exists that mothers and infants do engage in prolonged reciprocal imitation that involves inexact and trained imitations as well as true imitations. In these sequences the infant and mother trade similar responses back and forth in a sort of dance (Papoušek & Papoušek, 1975, 1977; Stern, 1977). It is also clear from this research that both participants enjoy the interaction; the sequence is continued so long as both participants continue to imitate, which may be a long time, and is stopped when one participant makes another kind of response. Such interactions might serve as an important mechanism in the development of attachment, a topic we will discuss in Chapter 12.

HABITUATION OF THE ORIENTING RESPONSE

All mammals have a very general response to a change in stimulation, which is called the **orienting response** (OR). Whenever stimulation changes—whether it is from no stimulation to stimulation (stimulus onset), from stimulation to no stimulation (stimulus offset), or from one kind of stimulation to another, and regardless of whether the level of background stimulation is high or low—we orient to the change; that is, we look and listen and our heart rate (HR) becomes slower. The orienting response is the most general attention-getting mechanism (see Chapter 6 for a further discussion of attention). If the changed stimulation continues unchanged for a while, we gradually stop paying attention to it. This decrease in response is called **habituation** of the orienting response. If a new response is then presented, we will again orient; this renewed OR to a newly-changed stimulus is called **dishabituation** (because it reverses the previous habituation). In evolutionary terms, the orienting response is a very adaptive characteristic, for it causes us to attend to any change in the world around us. We can then investigate the cause of the change and respond appropriately.

Many responses have been used to measure the OR. Some of them are internal responses, such as heart rate and respiration rate, which are measured by electrophysiological apparatus. Others are externally observable responses, such as the length of time babies look at a stimulus and cessation of sucking (infants stop sucking when they orient to a change in stimulation, and gradually resume sucking as they habituate).

Development of the Orienting Response and Its Habituation

Early researchers investigated when the OR, measured by changes in heart rate, developed (Graham & Clifton, 1966; Lipton, Steinschneider, & Richmond, 1966). Their results suggested that the OR developed at around 2 months of age. Younger babies' heart rates speeded up when they were presented with a novel stimulus, whereas the HR of babies 2 months and older slowed down, the typical OR response. Severe methodological problems led many researchers to seek better procedures and solutions to the problems. It now seems clear that newborns can exhibit the

OR, although they do it under very circumscribed conditions. For older infants and adults, however, the OR is a very general and frequent response. Almost all the successful demonstrations of OR in newborns have used samples limited to alert infants. In addition, HR deceleration is most consistently found when babies are alert for more than a few minutes. This is true both for newborns and older infants. Furthermore, if newborns are sucking, they do not exhibit HR deceleration. Even more limiting are the findings that deceleration only occurs in response to some kinds of stimuli; for example, to pulsed sounds (sounds that go on and off repeatedly) but not to continuous sounds (see Berg & Berg, 1979; Von-Bargen, 1983, for reviews of this research). Because the OR as measured by cardiac deceleration is so difficult to obtain before 2 months of age, we might expect habituation of it to be difficult to obtain as well. That is the case. Although some studies have demonstrated such habituation, many others have failed to do so (see Berg & Berg's 1979 review).

Habituation and dishabituation of responses other than heart rate have also been studied. Newborns stop sucking when they see a new visual stimulus or hear a new sound, and habituation of this response can be reliably obtained with newborns, although it is less successfully obtained with older infants. Habituation of looking responses to visual stimuli is easily found with older infants. Whether it occurs in very young infants has been unclear (see Werner & Perlmutter's 1979 review), although a recent study has resolved some of the earlier inconsistencies by identifying circumstances under which it can be obtained in newborns (Slater, Morison, & Rose, 1984). Recently habituation and dishabituation of movements of eyes, mouth, head, and arms has been demonstrated in newborns (Kisilevsky & Muir, 1984).

Does the Orienting Response Reflect Cortical Function?

One of the reasons the OR has generated so much interest is that Sokolov (1963) hypothesized that it represents processing of information in the cortex. There are three important implications of this hypothesis. First, this would make the OR an important mechanism by which mammals learn about the world. Second, study of the OR could yield information about the development of cortical functioning in newborns. Third, the OR might serve as a marker variable for cortical dysfunction in infants.

Soon after the publication of his book, Sokolov's hypothesis was countered by Lipton, Steinschneider, and Richmond (1966) who argued that the OR reflected the operation of the autonomic nervous system. In spite of almost 20 years of subsequent research, this disagreement is still not resolved. Perhaps the research most often cited in support of the cortical interpretation is Brackbill's (1971) study of a 3-month-old infant with no cortex (anencephalic). This infant exhibited no habituation of the OR. More recently Graham, Leavitt, Strock, and Brown (1978) tested another anencephalic infant when the baby was 3 to 6 weeks of age. This infant did exhibit habituation of the OR, and in fact the pattern of response appeared to be precocious (more like that of a normal 2-month-old). The incompatibility of the results of the study of these two cases makes it impossible to come to any conclusions about cortical involvement in the OR, and they clearly indicate that its use as a marker for cortical dysfunction in newborns is suspect.

A second way of determining whether the OR is cortical or autonomic is by the state in which it occurs. Most research demonstrating the OR and its habituation has involved infants in awake alert states, which is the optimal state of functioning of the central nervous system. Nevertheless, two recent studies (Field, Dempsey, Hatch, Ting, & Clifton, 1979; Kisilevsky & Muir, 1984) have demonstrated habituation of the OR by newborns during sleep, which is the optimal state for autonomic nervous system functioning because metabolic demands are minimal.

A third argument remains. Variations in type of stimulation affect the OR and do so increasingly with age, as would be expected for a cortical function, but not for an autonomic function (Berg & Berg, 1979).

Those who favor the cortical interpretation ask the subsequent question of exactly what cortical functioning is involved. Most answers are psychological; that is, they attempt to describe the kinds of knowledge the infant must have to exhibit a particular pattern of habituation and dishabituation (for example, Cohen, 1973; Lewis, 1971; Olson, 1976). Dannemiller and Banks (1983) argue that these models, which require higher processing (presumably involving the association areas), fit well the evidence concerning older babies, but that habituation in the first 3–4 months of life may operate by a different mechanism. The mechanism they propose is that single neuronal cells in the visual cortex (the first place in the cortex reached by signals from the visual receptors) may stop responding (fatigue or adapt) as a result of repeated presentations. This explanation, which they call selective sensory adaptation, fits in well with what is known about the behaviors of such cells in other contexts. It is also congruent with evidence about the development of visual perception (which we will discuss in Chapter 9): Newborns appear to see primarily as a function of the activity of single cells in the visual cortex, and more complex bases for visual perception develop only after the first several months of life. As they readily acknowledge, Dannemiller and Bank's hypothesis about the changing basis of habituation in the first several months of life at this point is consistent with the available evidence, but has yet to be validated by research designed specifically to test it against alternative hypotheses.

Use in Research

Habituation of the OR is probably the most widely used experimental technique in infant research today. It is not only of interest for its own sake, but it is also used to test memory, which we will discuss in the next section, and perception, which we will discuss in Chapter 9. In perceptual studies the habituation–dishabituation phenomenon can be used to test infants' ability to discriminate between two similar stimuli. The subjects are habituated to the first stimulus and then the second is presented. If they perceive the new stimulus as different, they will dishabituate. If they do not perceive the new stimulus as different, they will continue to show little or no response (that is, to exhibit habituation). For example a red square can be presented re-

peatedly until babies habituate (stop responding) and then a blue square of the same size and brightness can be presented. If the infants dishabituate (that is, respond anew) to the blue square, this response indicates that they discriminate red from blue.

As is true with conditioning paradigms, the habituation paradigm requires careful attention to methodology. First, different dependent variables are appropriate for different ages. For newborns, cessation of sucking is an excellent response to use, but it becomes less good as babies grow older. In contrast, heart rate and looking times are not always reliable measures in newborns but can be used effectively with babies older than two months.

Second, each dependent variable has a set of measurement problems that have to be attended to. We will illustrate this by describing some of the problems of measuring heart rate. The amount of change depends in part on the rate prior to the presentation of the stimulus (Steinschneider, Lipton, & Richmond, 1966). Heart rate also reflects movement. Movements such as startle responses or sucking may be triggered by the stimulus or may be mere random arm or leg movements. Perhaps most important, heart rate and heart rate changes are both related to behavioral state, as we discussed earlier.

Third, it is important to include dishabituation even when, as in memory studies, the focus is on habituation. What appears to be habituation (that is, a response decrement) might actually be sensory fatigue (in the sense of receptor cells themselves), or fatigue in the motor system, or changes in state, but then one should not expect to find dishabituation as well. Thus care must be taken to demonstrate that infants do dishabituate in the experimental situation, so as to eliminate these alternative hypotheses.

Fourth, the way in which the habituation procedure is instituted makes a tremendous difference in how cooperative babies are while being habituated. Horowitz, Paden, Bhana, and Self (1972) developed what has come to be known as "the infant-controlled habituation technique." In the traditional method, experimenters determined how long the stimulus was presented and they often chose to present the stimuli for relatively short periods (for example, 30 seconds) to avoid fatiguing the babies. Horowitz and colleagues let young babies (3 to 14 weeks of age) control the length of presentation: The stimulus was turned off only when an infant had not looked at it for 2 consecutive seconds. When the infants controlled the presentation rates, they cried and fussed less. The experimenters were able to complete 93% of the testing sessions compared to 70% in the fixed-presentation mode, and only 28% of the subjects were lost to the study compared with 40% in fixed-presentation studies. In addition, babies often looked longer at the stimulus than most researchers would have believed. The longest single look was 1073 seconds (over 17 minutes) and times over 2 minutes were very common. Subsequent research (Slater, Morison, & Rose, 1984; see also our description of face perception in Chapter 9) suggests that infants in the first several months of life can process stimuli much better than had previously been thought, but can do so only after much longer inspection times.

MEMORY

In the most general sense, memory is the characteristic of living organisms through which past experience is recorded. Thus all learning implies memory.

Neonatal Memory

The answer to the question of the age at which memory can first be demonstrated can be found in the research on conditioning and habituation discussed above. This research clearly demonstrates that newborns can remember for a few minutes. During conditioning, newborns can change the characteristics of their sucking and can turn their heads in response to changing environmental events. Thus, they must be storing that information in some way. Likewise, newborns under some circumstances habituate over a number of trials. It can be concluded from this that babies are remembering the stimulus during the few minutes that the experiment lasts so long as they also exhibit dishabituation, which demonstrates that the habituation is not due to fatigue in either the sensory or the motoric response system under study nor to state change.

This memory is, however, extremely limited. First, as we discussed in the conditioning and habituation sections, newborns condition and habituate only in limited situations. Second, memory for longer periods of time, such as several hours or a day, has not been demonstrated in newborns. Sameroff (1968), for example, explicitly tested whether there was any evidence that conditioning of sucking in one feeding session carried over to the next and found that it did not. This outcome is particularly convincing because Sameroff used a response that is presumably biologically prepotent and because conditioning involves many repeated trials. Thus his procedure should have been optimal to produce long-term memory.

Memory over only a few minutes is a fairly primitive beginning, yet it is an important beginning. It allows infants time to process the information their receptors are receiving. Presumably, it thereby forms the basis for memory over a longer period of time.

Memory That Lasts at Least 24 Hours

WHEN DOES IT DEVELOP?

Although newborns apparently do not remember events for more than a few minutes, longer-term memory develops fairly rapidly. How early depends on the situation. Long-term memory in very young babies has been demonstrated only when the stimulus is made very familiar to the baby or when the stimuli are very simple. For example Ungerer, Brody, and Zelazo (1978) had mothers repeat a single word 60 times a day for 13 days to their 2–4-week-old babies. By the end of the 13 days the babies exhibited recognition of the familiar stimulus (primarily by moving or widening their eyes or both) after delays of 15 hours and 42 hours. Thus, babies 4 weeks of age are capable of remembering for over 24 hours. Beware, though, of overgeneralization. These authors provided a neat demonstration of just how unusual their situation was. They also tested recognition of the infants' own names, which the babies presumably heard rather frequently during this same period. The infants exhibited no recognition of their own names. Thus it appears that infants of this age are unlikely to exhibit 24-hour memory for most of the events they normally experience.

By 8 weeks of age babies can remember a single learned event when they have not re-experienced it for 2 weeks, but only under special circumstances. Rovee-Collier and her collaborators have studied memory for previously learned operant responses in babies 2 and 3 months old (see the review of this work in Rovee-Collier & Fagen, 1981). In their paradigm infants first learn to move an overhead mobile by kicking their legs, which are attached to the mobile by a ribbon, as shown in Figure 7–2. The babies are then brought back to the experimental situation 1 or 2 weeks later. The mobile is visually present, but remains still. If the babies resume kicking, they demonstrate that they have remembered the situation. This is analogous to the **cued recall** technique used with older children and adults, in which part of a to-be-remembered stimulus is presented at the time of the memory test.

A more sensitive technique to measure memory, called **reactivation** or **reinstatement**, can also be used. A day before the long-term memory test, the babies are put back into the experimental crib but the ribbon is not attached to their feet. Rather, the experimenter (hidden from view) makes the mobile move by pulling the ribbon so that the babies experience part of the experimental situation. If this experience reactivates their memories, they will exhibit that by kicking their feet when the ribbon is reattached at the memory test the next day.

Using this technique, Rovee-Collier and her collaborators have found that 2- and 3-month-old babies exhibit memory for the response that they had learned 2 weeks earlier, but did so consistently only if their memories had been reactivated (Davis & Rovee-Collier, 1983; Rovee-Collier, Sullivan, Enright, Lucas, & Fagen, 1980; Sullivan, 1982; Sullivan, Rovee-Collier, & Tynes, 1979). They have also found reactivated memory in 3-month-olds tested 4 weeks after initial conditioning.

Another method that has been used to study infant memory is the habituation paradigm. Such studies measure memory for events that are much less frequently experienced than in Ungero's study of repeated words or in conditioning studies. These studies typically expose the subjects to the stimuli for one session, until the infants habituate, and then they test the infants for long-term memory by rehabituating the babies at a later time.

If they habituate faster than they did originally, the hypothesis is that they must have retained something of their earlier experience. This is a measure of **savings,** one of the classic measures of memory for past learning. By $3\frac{1}{2}$ months babies have been shown to exhibit savings through rehabituation for more than 24 hours after the stimulus had been experienced in a single habituation session (Martin, 1975; Topinka & Steinberg, 1978). By $5\frac{1}{2}$ months they can retain comparable information up to 48 hours, and can retain photographs of faces, which are presumably easier because they are more familiar, for up to 2 weeks (Fagan, 1973). By $7\frac{1}{2}$ months babies exhibit memory for previously unexperienced stimuli for between 1 and 2 weeks (Topinka & Steinberg, 1978).

Memory for what has been learned in an habituation session does not last as long as memory for a conditioned response. Sullivan, Rovee-Collier, and Tynes (1979) found that 3-month-olds remembered their contingent kicking for 1 week even without a reactivation session. This may be because conditioning involves considerably longer initial training than habituation and requires a more active motoric response.

These data considered together provide fairly convincing evidence that 2–4-month-old babies show evidence of memory over a matter of days or weeks. They also demonstrate that memories at a given age can be elicited after longer delays when the experimenters help them along.

WHAT YOUNG BABIES REMEMBER

Although the focus of our discussion of memory so far has been on how long memory lasts (for example, a few minutes versus more than 24 hours), this focus should not obscure the importance of the nature of the stimulus situation. The role of familiarity with the to-be-remembered stimuli has already arisen. Ungerer, Brody, and Zelazo (1978) found that babies 4 weeks of age were able to remember for 24 hours, but only with a highly familiar experimental word. Babies remember photographs of strange faces longer than they do abstract black and white patterns (Fagan, 1973; Rose, 1981), presumably because infants have greater experience with faces. Although length of time of familiarization within a single session has not been widely studied in the context of long-term memory, there is some evidence that it also facilitates long-term memory. Retention is better after the longer training involved in conditioning than in habituation, although the role of familiarization has not been isolated from the other differences between the two procedures. Rose (1981) found that if unfamiliar stimuli were presented only long enough to be minimally encoded, then even infants as old as 6 months failed to remember them after only a few minutes of delay. These findings are consistent with those found for processing within a single experimental session. As we noted in our discussion of habituation, the length of time the infant spends encoding has been shown to affect memory over the few minutes of a habituation session.

Most stimulus situations are complex, that is, there are many separable aspects to them. Rovee-Collier, Fagen, and their collaborators have conducted a number of studies that explored the conditions under which 2- to 4-month-old babies remember specific aspects of their conditioning situation. When they compared infants' memories for the exact same mobiles to their memories for mobiles with certain visual characteristics changed (form of the objects, color of the objects, or number of objects), they found that the babies kicked less in recognition of the changed mobiles for the first few days after testing (Fagen, 1984; Fagen, Yengo, Rovee-Collier, & Enright, 1981; Mast, Fagen, Rovee-Collier, & Sullivan, 1980; Rovee-Collier & Fagen, 1976; Rovee-Collier & Sullivan, 1980). This demonstrated that the infants had encoded these visual aspects of the stimulus situation. The magnitude of the reduction in kicking produced by the changed mobiles decreased when the infants were tested more than 3 days later (Fagen, 1984; Rovee-Collier & Sullivan, 1980), suggesting that after sufficiently long periods of time they forgot the details of the stimulus situation, although they remembered the general situation well enough to resume their conditioned kicking response.

These researchers have also found that infants of this age can remember the details of a stimulus situation in a much more abstract sense (Fagen, Morrongiello, Rovee-Collier, & Gekoski, 1984). They demonstrated that babies could learn to expect a new mobile (with different colored and shaped objects) on each day of training. These babies showed less 24-hour memory when tested on the mobile they experienced their first day of conditioning than they did when tested with still another new mobile. Thus, these babies learned to expect a new mobile and remembered that expectation at testing.

In their research Rovee-Collier and Fagen have asked whether babies remember various aspects of the conditioning situation, but they have not asked whether some comparable details of the stimulus are easier to remember than others. The latter question has been studied by presenting a stimulus with multiple aspects and then testing for memory of particular components by changing one aspect of the stimulus at a time. Strauss and Cohen (1980) found that 5-month-old babies remembered the form (the shape) of a stimulus after 24 hours whereas they remembered the color of the same stimulus for 15 minutes but not for 24 hours.[1] This result may be because the shape of a stimulus is a more important cue to its identity than its color for a 5-month-old baby. Although the relative importance of various aspects of stimuli has not been studied extensively in infant memory research, it has been of greater interest in perception, that is, in studies of the initial encoding of stimuli. This topic will be discussed in Chapter 9.

Productive Memory

None of the research we have discussed so far has measured pure **productive memory,** which involves remembering a previous event without the reappearance of that event. The standard measure of productive memory is usually verbal recall, which is of course not an appropriate measure to use with infants. Piaget (1968) argued that productive memory depended on mental representation (mental imagery and language), which develops around 2 years of age. This is true by definition for verbal recall (saying out loud the items to be remembered), because it required language. It is,

---

[1] Fagen (1984) found longer-duration memory for color in 3- to 4-month-olds, but because his conditioning procedure typically led to memory of longer duration than that obtained in habituation procedures and because he did not compare color to shape, his findings do not necessarily conflict with those of Strauss and Cohen.

however, at least possible to conceive of a non-verbal form of productive memory: memory through actions. If action-based productions could be measured adequately, it would be possible to determine whether infants can manifest productive memory. The failure of such an enterprise would be consistent with Piaget's belief that productive memory requires mental representation and that infants lack mental representation.

Nonverbal productive memory would be extremely difficult to elicit in a laboratory situation, so Ashmead and Perlmutter (in press) decided to study naturally-occurring incidents. They had parents keep diaries of memory behaviors of 11 infants who were 7 to 11 months of age at the beginning of the 6-week recording period. Although the parents reported an average of fewer than 1 episode per day that demonstrated memory, all infants did exhibit behaviors that clearly required retrieval. They all searched for absent objects or people and initiated social interactions based on previous experiences (such as peek-a-boo games), even though the latter incidents were rare among the youngest infants. Unfortunately the researchers apparently did not differentiate between cued and spontaneous productive responses. Such a differentiation is important because in research with adults cued recall is easier than spontaneous recall. Ashmead and Perlmutter's examples of both search and initiated social interactions were of cued retrieval; for example, the child sees and picks up a toy bottle and then goes to the bedroom and gets a doll. Piaget would probably call such cued productive actions **reconstructive** (reproductions from elements of the situation) rather than productive memory (products arising entirely from memory). The distinction is of some theoretical importance because Piaget believed that reconstructive memory is grounded in imitation (in his terminology, imitation is the figurative aspect of reconstructive memory), whereas he believed that productive memory is based on mental imagery. Thus reconstructive memory should develop in the middle and end of the first year of life, whereas productive memory should not develop until the end of the second year of life.

If one accepts this extension of Piaget's formulations concerning memory, then one sees Ashmead and Perlmutter's results as supporting Piaget's theory. In contrast, Rovee-Collier's demonstration of reactivation in 2-month-old babies may be a disconfirmation of Piaget's conceptualization, because it too is a form of cued recall and it develops earlier than Piaget believes imitation develops.

The Role of Context in Infant Memory

One of the popular trends in adult memory research demonstrates that events are remembered not as isolated instances, but rather as part of the larger whole provided by the context. Presenting a to-be-remembered stimulus within a context facilitates memory for that stimulus relative to one presented with no context. The context, when presented at the time of test, serves as a retrieval cue. Memory is best if the context of the situation is the same at the time of encoding (when it is first remembered) and at the time of the test (when the stimulus is remembered). If the context is changed between the initial experience and the time of remembering, adults are less likely to remember the event.

Although there is little research with babies designed to test context effects directly, several disparate avenues of research carried out to test other hypotheses demonstrate that context is an important variable in infant memory. In both conditioning and habituation studies designed to demonstrate memory lasting over 24 hours in babies 2 to 3 months of age, it has been found that re-experiencing the laboratory situation facilitated memory (Sullivan, Rovee-Collier, & Tynes, 1979; Topinka & Steinberg, 1978).

The role of similarity of the contexts at encoding and at test has been demonstrated in two recent studies (MacKay-Soroka, Trehub, Bull, & Corter, 1982; Ruff, 1981). In them the context was manipulated by the types of exploration permitted. The context was the same when the babies were allowed to explore both visually and manually at both encoding and test, or when they were permitted only to explore visually at both times. Changed context occurred when the infants explored both visually and manually at either encoding or test, but not at both times. Infants in the second half of their first year exhibited memory only when the mode of exploration was the same at initial presentation and at test. In a subsequent study, Ruff (1982) demonstrated why changing the type of exploration permitted at the time of test interferes with memory in this experimental situation. She found that when infants explored manually they were more likely to process shape and texture information, whereas when they explored only visually they were more likely to process only the two-dimensional visual characteristics. Thus when the context was the same, the infants were being tested for the same types of information they had encoded, but when the context was changed they were being tested for aspects of the stimulus they had not encoded.

Research using delayed search tasks provides another example that the context of the memory plays an important role in infants' memory, as it does in the memory of older humans. In addition, it demonstrates a developmental trend in both the kind and the range of context cues that facilitate memory. This research has used variations of a basic hide-and-seek game. While the infant watches, the experimenter hides a toy. After a given delay, the infant is allowed to search for it. When the cuing context is meaningful to them, babies as young as 18 months can successfully search for hidden objects after substantial delays. De-Loache and Brown (1979, 1983) found performance in such search tasks significantly higher when the objects were hidden in obvious spots in the infants' home than when the objects were hidden in metal boxes. Similarly, the memory of 24-month-olds in a search for objects hidden in metal boxes was improved when there was a picture of the hidden object on the box (Ratner & Myers, 1980), but not when there was a picture of an unrelated object (Horn & Myers, 1978). It also improved when the boxes were of different sizes (Daehler, Bukatko, Benson, & Myers, 1976). There appears to be rapid development in the range of contextual cues that facilitate memory between the ages of 18 months and 3 years (De-Loache & Brown, 1983; Horn & Myers, 1978). By 3 years children can use rather arbitrary contextual cues such as unrelated pictures on the boxes or the location of the box in the room.

Considering all that is known about the role of contextual effects in infants' memory, it seems fair to conclude that they are important determinants of long-term memory throughout development and that the basic principles by which they operate are recognizable in infants. What develops is the nature of effective cues. The earliest effective cues seem to be ones that require little or no extra processing themselves—aspects of the environment that are extremely familiar, meaningfully related, or easily processed. Cues that became effective only after the age of 2 years require additional processing themselves.

Conclusions

The explicit study of infant memory has just begun, and, as is true of all good research, creates more questions than it answers. The research has demonstrated several important points. First, when babies as young as 2 months learn about a visual stimulus or a stimulus response contingency, they retain this knowledge over relatively long periods. Second, although their access to such memories is limited, it can be tapped by reactivation or renewed exposure. Third, the nature of the context plays a large role in the ability to remember. Fourth, both recognition and reconstructive memory (and possibly productive memory) develop during the first year of life.

Much more needs to be known about how infant memory is similar to and different from memory in older people. For example, the relative roles of interference and decay may differ (Cohen, DeLoache, & Pearl, 1977; Fagan, 1973, 1977; McCall, Kennedy, & Dodds, 1977; Rose, 1981). It is safe to say, however, that the mysteries of memory development are intertwined with those of cognitive development in general. Memory is always the memory of something, and the most comprehensive theories of memory acknowledge the influence of the general knowledge base, the nature of the concepts to be remembered, and the form of representation (for example, see Jenkins, 1980). Future research on the development of memory in infancy will undoubtedly focus on these topics.

DISCUSSION ISSUES

Biology and Experience

This chapter has more to do with the influence of environment and less to do with the influence of biology than any of the others in this book. The definition of learning itself specifies that it is a relatively permanent change of behavior as a function of experience. Nevertheless, even in learning and memory, the quintessential experiential mechanisms, biology plays a role. For example, all of the newborns' responses are not equally conditionable and those that are conditionable are those that are likely to be biologically prepotent responses. In the phenomena we have explored in this chapter, the biological influence is most obvious during the first weeks of life. Both conditioning and imitation seem to depend more heavily on biologically-based behaviors early in life than they do later in infancy and childhood. Although in later development one would expect some responses to be more easily conditioned than others, the biological limitations on conditioning seem far less restrictive.

Research Issues

The development of the research on conditioning and imitation gives two good examples of how scientific research develops by means of testing alternative interpretations. Almost as soon as an interesting phenomenon is demonstrated, researchers ask whether there are alternative interpretations that could explain the phenomenon just as well. We discussed two such alternative explanations for apparently conditioned responses, pseudo-conditioning and response elicitation. In each case researchers had to devise procedures that would allow them to differentiate between the original hypothesis, that of conditioning, and the alternative interpretations, pseudo-conditioning or response elicitation. In each case the additional procedures demonstrated that changes in behavior may occur even when there is no conditioning. To demonstrate that conditioning as such is the mechanism involved, it is necessary to demonstrate that conditioning produces greater changes in behavior than the control procedure, just as in drug studies the drug is expected to produce greater effects than the placebo. Thus, in every experiment researchers should use sufficient controls to demonstrate that the conditioning procedure actually produces learning.

Imitation provides a parallel example. Two forms of pseudo-imitation and response elicitation have been identified. To avoid possible confounding, care must be taken to avoid reinforcing imitative responses, an everpresent possibility in studies in which the adult models an action repeatedly. If researchers wish to demonstrate exact imitation, they must be careful to show that same-class imitation or response elicitation are not equally valid explanations of the data.

This discussion of pseudo-conditioning, pseudo-imitation, and response elicitation has treated these alternative interpretations as methodological problems rather than as theoretical problems. As is often the case, however, alternative interpretations that were first introduced in a research area as methodological problems are of interest in their own right. We found this to be true in Chapter 2 when we discussed the role of extraneous variables in research on prematurity. In Chapter 3 we discussed alternative interpretations of the effects of anomalies of the sex chromosomes, and found that some of the behavioral effects probably result from indirect effects of the individual's experience and not from the influence of the anomalies themselves. In these cases the investigation of the alternative explanation clarifies the issue at hand in a theoretically meaningful fashion. This is also true of the phenomenon of response elicitation. It is one of the general response characteristics of infants that facilitates interaction with their world. It facilitates conditioning—it increases the probability that a response will be emitted, which is, of course, a prerequisite for operant conditioning—but it must be differentiated from conditioning itself.

Although we defined same-class imitation as pseudo-imitation and thus an alternative hypothesis, it can also be conceived as a particular operational definition of imitation. As discussed in the Research Issues of Chapter 2, differences in operational definitions may produce differences in research findings. Several important differences in operational definitions arose in imitation and memory. Imitation may be immediate or delayed; it may be exact or same-class. Memory may be measured by more rapid rehabituation or by a reactivated response, each of which are different measures of a more general type of memory called recognition (that is, noticing familiarity). Or memory may mean productive memory, the ability to reproduce verbally or motorically a previously experienced event, with or without a cue. These disparate operational definitions may not relate to the conceptual definition in the same way because the different operational definitions may tap different steps in a developmental sequence. For example, immediate imitation develops before delayed imitation, and memory over the course of minutes develops before memory over days. That different forms of imitation and memory develop at different ages means that it is not appropriate to conceive of them as one general ability. Rather each consists of a number of sub-abilities that develop at different ages.

The choice of a behavioral domain may also affect the findings. The behaviors used most successfully to elicit imitation in newborns (for example, crying, tongue protrusions, and facial expressions) may be specific biologically prepotent responses. The same may be true of sucking and head turning in conditioning. It would be an inappropriate generalization to assume that other, less biologically prepotent, responses can be conditioned.

The last research issue we wish to discuss here is the effect of experimenters' beliefs on their interpretations of research findings. In previous chapters we have discussed the influence of such biases on collection of data and the necessity for blind controls. In this chapter the influence of researchers' opinions occurs after the data have been collected. No one argues that the data in Table 7–1 are wrong; Meltzoff and Moore have replicated their findings and similar results have been found in other studies. The conflict arises in the interpretation of the data: what aspects of the data are crucial and whether, taking all the data together, one should conclude that newborns imitate. Such conflicts are at an impasse and must be resolved by future advances in knowledge, which often occur in one of two ways. First, new data about the phenomenon in question may resolve the controversy. Second, knowledge from other related domains may

suggest a likely resolution. For example, the discovery that newborns automatically connect information from different sensory modalities would make neonatal imitation of unseen actions a more likely interpretation of the currently available data.

Parenting

Conditioning and imitation have obvious applications in the care of infants. The infants' responses that parents like can be rewarded and others can be ignored. It is also highly desirable for babies to have good models of appropriate behavior, as Brazelton suggests for toilet training. Nevertheless, applying these principles is not always as straightforward as it appears. One use of such methods that has been highly controversial is with respect to the control of crying, as we discussed in Chapter 6. Reinforcement psychologists argue that rewarding babies when they cry will increase the probability of crying and that parents should ignore crying and reinforce more appropriate (from the parents' point of view) ways of seeking attention. Others feel that prompt parental response to crying allows babies some control over their environment and thus allows them to develop a sense of trust in their mother, thereby leading to less crying in the long run. It is beyond the scope of this book to discuss in detail how learning principles may be applied in practical situations. This chapter does demonstrate, however, that the techniques most often used in practical applications—conditioning, extinction, generalization, shaping, modeling—develop at very young ages, and can be applied to some degree by the second month of life.

An adjunct to this conclusion is that learning principles may control infants' behavior whether or not parents consciously choose to use them. For example, research with older children has demonstrated that aggression is often rewarded in nursery schools (children get their way), which increases its frequency. Young children imitate their parents, both good and bad behaviors. Some research even suggests that children are less likely to imitate task-relevant behaviors (usually what the parents model intentionally) and are more likely to imitate task-irrelevant behaviors (including parents' unintended emotional expressions).

The processes described in this chapter are also important because they affect adult-infant interactions. This has been discussed most thoroughly in the context of imitation. Even very young infants respond when their parents imitate them, and when their parents exhibit particular responses, the babies make imitative-like responses. These responses help to maintain parent–infant interactions, which presumably form the basis for the establishment of parent–infant emotional attachments.

Conditioning also plays a role in parent–infant interactions. When an infant exhibits a response the parents like, such as a smile or a vocalization, the parents respond positively. This acts as a reinforcement and the baby will be more likely to respond in the future. Although several experts in mother–infant interactions (Papoušek & Papoušek, 1975, 1977; Thoman, 1981) argue that these sequences occur so rapidly that they must be unlearned, this argument does not imply that all such sequences are unlearned. Particularly as infants develop a history of mother–infant interactions, such a conditioning history will develop as well.

Habituation also plays a role in parent–infant interactions, and knowing how it works can help parents to interact more effectively with their infants. Babies will respond to change in stimulation; if the stimulation is repeated frequently, their responses will decrease until they no longer respond. In mother–infant interactions, mothers often do something novel and repeat it frequently until the baby stops responding and then they change their behavior. Experienced parents will often repeat a stimulus even if the infant only responds by staring (an orienting response). These adults know that the orienting response indicates interest, and that many repetitions are often necessary for the infant to process the stimulus. The adult's cue to stop or change behaviors is when the baby turns its attention away.

Infants' memory capacity also influences the parent–infant relationship. Once babies develop memory over hours and days, they remember their mothers' faces and the games that they and their mothers like to play, and they become more patient as they learn their feeding and sleeping schedules.

SUMMARY

This chapter explored several mechanisms by which infants acquire knowledge of their world. For each mechanism we focused on the question, At what age does it first develop? At birth infants' capacities in these realms are quite primitive. Newborns can be conditioned, but only under circumscribed circumstances and with biologically prepotent responses. It is not yet clear whether newborns can imitate. There is some evidence that they imitate crying, tongue protrusion, and facial expressions, but in none of these cases is the evidence conclusive. Newborns do exhibit the orienting response and it does habituate, but only under very limited circumstances.

Memory also shows primitive beginnings at birth. A newborn who exhibits operant conditioning or habituation is also exhibiting memory over the few minutes of the experimental session. Memory over a matter of hours or days has not been demonstrated.

Later development of these processes has been less systematically explored. State becomes less important, but this may be entirely due to the fact that older babies spend more of their time in states appropriate to researchers' needs. Older infants process information more quickly in all ways. They need less time to look at a stimulus to process it, they take fewer trials to be conditioned, and they habituate more rapidly. As infants develop, their responses become more general. More kinds of responses can be conditioned and babies imitate a broader range of stimuli. They can remember for longer and longer periods of time and can use a wider variety of cues. These summary statements are only part of the story, however. In this chapter we have dealt with only a few of the variables that influence the age at which infants will condition, imitate, habituate, or remember. Much of the study of perception and cognition, which we will discuss in Chapters 9 and 10, is concerned with these variables.

REFERENCES

Abravanel, E., Levan-Goldschmidt, E., & Stevenson, M. B. (1976). Action imitation: The early phase of infancy. *Child Development, 47,* 1032–1044.

Abravanel, E., & Sigafoos, A. D. (1984). Exploring the presence of imitation during early infancy. *Child Development, 55,* 381–392.

Anisfeld, M. (1979). Interpreting "imitative" responses in early infancy. *Science, 205,* 214–215.

Ashmead, D. H., & Perlmutter, M. (in press). Infant memory in everyday life. In M. Perlmutter (Ed.), *New directions in child development: Naturalistic approaches to children's memory.* San Francisco: Jossey Bass.

Baer, D. M., Peterson, R. F., & Sherman, J. A. (1967). The development of imitation by reinforcing behavioral similarity to a model. *Journal of Experimental Analysis of Behavior, 10,* 405–416.

Baer, D. M., & Sherman, J. (1964). Reinforcement control of generalized imitation in young children. *Journal of Experimental Child Psychology, 1,* 37–49.

Bates, J. E. (1975). Effects of a child's imitation versus nonimitation on adult's verbal and nonverbal positivity. *Journal of Personality and Social Psychology, 31,* 840–851.

Berg, W. K., & Berg, K. M. (1979). Psychophysiological development in infancy: State, sensory function, and attention. In J. D. Osofsky (Ed.), *Handbook of infant development* (pp. 283–343). New York: Wiley.

Blass, E. M., Ganchrow, J. R., & Steiner, J. E. (1984). Classical conditioning in newborn humans 2–48 hours of age. *Infant Behavior and Development, 7,* 223–235.

Bloom, K., & Esposito, A. (1975). Social conditioning and its proper control procedures. *Journal of Experimental Child Psychology, 20,* 51–58.

Brackbill, Y. (1971). The role of the cortex in orienting: Orienting reflex in an anencephalic human infant. *Developmental Psychology, 5,* 195–201.

Brazelton, T. B. (1974). *Toddlers and parents: A developmental perspective.* New York: Dell.

Bruner, J. S. (1972). Nature and uses of immaturity. *American Psychologist, 27,* 687–708.

Bühler, C., & Hetzer, H. (1928). Das erste Verständnis von Ausdruck im Ersten Lebensjahre. *Zeitschrift für Psychologie, 107,* 50–61.

Cavanagh, P., & Davidson, M. L. (1977). The secondary circular reaction and response elicitation in the operant learning of six-month-old infants. *Developmental Psychology, 13,* 371–376.

Clifton, R. (1974). Heart rate conditioning in the newborn infant. *Journal of Experimental Child Psychology, 13,* 43–57.

Clifton, R., Meyers, W. J., & Solomons, E. (1972). Methodological problems in conditioning the headturning response of newborns. *Journal of Experimental Child Psychology, 13,* 29–42.

Clifton, R., Siqueland, E. R., & Lipsitt, L. P. (1972). Conditioned headturning in human newborns as a function of conditioned response requirements and states of wakefulness. *Journal of Experimental Child Psychology, 13,* 43–57.

Cohen, J. S. (May, 1981). *Neonatal imitation: A critical analysis of its implications for Piagetian theory.* Paper presented at the meeting of the Jean Piaget Society, Philadelphia.

Cohen, L. B. (1973). A two-process model of infant visual attention. *Merrill-Palmer Quarterly, 19,* 157–180.

Cohen, L. J., DeLoache, J., & Pearl, R. A. (1977). An examination of interference effects for infants' memory for faces. *Child Development, 48,* 88–96.

Cole, M., & Scribner, S. (1974). *Culture and thought: A psychological introduction.* New York: Wiley.

Crowell, D. H., Blurton, L. B., Kobayashi, L. R., McFarland, J. L., & Yang, R. K. (1976). Studies in early infant learning: Classical conditioning of the neonatal heart rate. *Developmental Psychology, 12,* 373–397.

Daehler, M., Bukatko, D., Benson, K., & Myers, N. (1976). The effects of size and color cues on the delayed response of very young children. *Bulletin of the Psychonomic Society, 7,* 65–68.

Dannemiller, J. L., & Banks, M. S. (1983). Can selective adaptation account for early infant habituation? *Merrill-Palmer Quarterly, 29,* 151–158.

Davis, J. M., & Rovee-Collier, C. K. (1983). Alleviated forgetting of a learned contingency in 8-week-old infants. *Developmental Psychology, 19,* 353–365.

DeLoache, J. S., & Brown, A. L. (1979). Looking for Big Bird: Studies of memory in very young children. *Quarterly Newsletter of the Laboratory of Comparative Human Cognition, 1,* 53–57.

DeLoache, J. S., & Brown, A. L. (1983). Very young children's memory for the location of objects in a large-scale environment. *Child Development, 54,* 888–897.

Fagan, J. F., III. (1973). Infant's delayed recognition memory and forgetting. *Journal of Experimental Child Psychology, 16,* 424–450.

Fagan, J. F., III. (1977). Infant recognition memory: Studies in forgetting. *Child Development, 48,* 68–78.

Fagen, J. W. (1984). Infants' long-term memory of stimulus color. *Developmental Psychology, 20,* 435–440.

Fagen, J. W., Morrongiello, B. A., Rovee-Collier, C., & Gekoski, M. J. (1984). Expectancies and memory retrieval in three-month-old infants. *Child Development, 55,* 936–943.

Fagen, J. W., Yengo, L. A., Rovee-Collier, C. K., & Enright, M. K. (1981). Reactivation of a visual discrimination in early infancy. *Developmental Psychology, 17,* 266–274.

Field, T. M., Dempsey, J. R., Hatch, J., Ting, G., & Clifton, R. K. (1979). Cardiac and behavioral responses to repeated tactile and auditory stimulation by preterm and term neonates. *Developmental Psychology, 15,* 406–416.

Field, T. M., Woodson, R., Greenberg, R., & Cohen, D. (1982). Discrimination and imitation of facial expressions by neonates. *Science, 218,* 179–181.

Fitzgerald, H. E., & Brackbill, Y. (1976). Classical conditioning in infancy: Development and constraints. *Psychological Bulletin, 3,* 353–376.

Fouts, G. T. (1972). Imitation in children: The effect of being imitated. *Catalog of Selected Documents in Psychology, 2,* 105.

Fouts, G. T. (1975). The effects of being imitated and awareness on the behavior of introverted and extroverted youth. *Child Development, 46,* 296–300.

Gardner, J., & Gardner, H. (1970). A note on selective imitation by a six-week-old infant. *Child Development, 41,* 1209–1213.

Gekoski, M. J. (1977). Visual attention and operant conditioning in infancy: A second look. *Dissertation Abstracts International, 38,* 875B. (University Microfilms No. 77-17,533.)

Gewirtz, J. L. (1971a). Conditional responding as a paradigm for observational, imitative learning and vicarious reinforcement. In H. W. Reese (Ed.), *Advances in child development and behavior* (Vol. 6). New York: Academic.

Gewirtz, J. L. (1971b). The roles of overt responding and extrinsic reinforcement. In R. Glaser (Ed.), *The nature of reinforcement.* New York: Academic.

Gewirtz, J. L., & Stingle, K. G. (1968). Learning of generalized imitation as the basis for identification. *Psychological Review, 75,* 374–397.

Graham, F. K., & Clifton, R. K. (1966). Heart-rate change as a component of the orienting response. *Psychological Bulletin, 65,* 305–320.

Graham, F. K., Leavitt, L. A., Strock, B. D., & Brown, J. W. (1978). Precocious cardiac orienting in a human, anencephalic infant. *Science, 199,* 322–324.

Harlow, H. F. (1949). Formation of learning sets. *Psychological Review, 56,* 51–65.

Hayes, L. A., & Watson, J. S. (1981). Neonatal imitation: Fact or artifact. *Developmental Psychology, 17,* 655–660.

Horn, H., & Myers, N. A. (1978). Memory for location and picture cues at ages two and three. *Child Development, 49,* 845–856.

Horowitz, F. D., Paden, L. Y., Bhana, K., & Self, P. (1972). An infant control procedure for studying infant visual fixations. *Developmental Psychology, 7,* 90.

Jacobson, S. W. (1979). Matching behavior in the young infant. *Child Development, 50,* 425–430.

Jacobson, S. W., & Kagan, J. (1979). Interpreting "imitative" responses in early infancy. *Science, 205,* 215–217.

Jenkins, J. J. (1980). Can we have a fruitful cognitive psychology? *Nebraska Symposium on Motivation, 28,* 211–238.

Kaye, K., & Marcus, J. (1981). Infant imitation: The sensory-motor agenda. *Developmental Psychology, 17,* 258–265.

Keen, R. (1964). Effects of auditory stimuli on sucking behavior in the human neonate. *Journal of Psychology, 1,* 348–354.

Kisilevsky, B. S., & Muir, D. W. (1984). Neonatal habituation and dishabituation to tactile stimulation during sleep. *Developmental Psychology, 20,* 367–373.

Koepke, J. E., Hamm, M., Legerstee, M., & Russell, M. (1983a). Methodological issues in studies of imitation: Reply to Meltzoff and Moore. *Infant Behavior and Development, 6,* 113–116.

Koepke, J. E., Hamm, M., Legerstee, M., & Russell, M. (1983b). Neonatal imitation: Two failures to replicate. *Infant Behavior and Development, 6,* 97–102.

Lewis, M. (1971). Individual differences in the measurement of early cognitive growth. In J. Hellmuth (Ed.), *Exceptional infant* (Vol. 2, pp. 172–210). New York: Brunner/Mazel.

Lipsitt, L. P., Mustaine, M. G., & Zeigler, B. (1977). Effects of experience on the behavior of the young infant. *Neuropadiatrie, 8,* 107–133.

Lipton, E. L., Steinschneider, A., & Richmond, J. B. (1966). Autonomic function in the neonate: VII. Maturational changes in cardiac control. *Child Development, 37,* 1–16.

MacKay-Soroka, S., Trehub, S. E., Bull, D. H., & Corter, C. M. (1982). Effects of encoding and retrieval conditions on infants' recognition memory. *Child Development, 53,* 815–818.

Maratos, O. (April, 1973). *The origin and development of imitation in the first six months of life.* Paper presented at the annual meeting of the British Psychological Society, Liverpool, England.

Marquis, D. (1931). Can conditioned responses be established in the new born infant? *Journal of Genetic Psychology, 39,* 479–490.

Martin, G. B., & Clark, R. D., III. (1982). Distress crying in neonates: Species and peer specificity. *Developmental Psychology, 18,* 3–9.

Martin, R. M. (1975). Effects of familiar and complex stimuli on infant attention. *Developmental Psychology, 11,* 178–185.

Mast, V. K., Fagen, J. W., Rovee-Collier, C. K., & Sullivan, M. W. (1980). Immediate and long-term memory for reinforcement context: The development of learned expectancies in early infancy. *Child Development, 51,* 700–707.

Masters, J. C. (1979). Interpreting "imitative" responses in early infancy. *Science, 205,* 215.

McCall, R. B., Kennedy, C. B., & Dodds, C. (1977). The interfering effects of distracting stimuli on the infant's memory. *Child Development, 48,* 79–87.

McKenzie, B., & Over, R. (1983a). Do neonatal infants imitate? A reply to Meltzoff and Moore. *Infant Behavior and Development, 6,* 109–111.

McKenzie, B., & Over, R. (1983b). Young infants fail to imitate facial and manual gestures. *Infant Behavior and Development, 6,* 85–95.

Meltzoff, A. N., & Moore, M. K. (1977). Imitation of facial and manual gestures by human neonates. *Science, 198,* 75–78.

Meltzoff, A. N., & Moore, M. K. (1979). Interpreting "imitative" responses in early infancy. *Science, 205,* 217–219.

Meltzoff, A. N., & Moore, M. K. (1983a). Methodological issues in studies of imitation: Comments on McKenzie & Over and Koepke et al. *Infant Behavior and Development, 6,* 103–108.

Meltzoff, A. N., & Moore, M. K. (1983b). Newborn infants imitate adult facial gestures. *Child Development, 54,* 702–709.

Millar, W. S. (1976). Social reinforcement of a manipulative response in six and nine month old infants. *Journal of Child Psychology and Psychiatry, 17,* 205–212.

Mussen, P., & Eisenberg-Berg, N. (1977). *Roots of caring, sharing, and helping: The development of prosocial behavior in children.* San Francisco: W. H. Freeman and Company.

Olson, G. M. (1976). An information-processing analysis of visual memory and habituation in infants. In T. J. Tighe and R. N. Leaton (Eds.), *Habituation: Perspectives from child development, animal behavior, and neurophysiology.* Hillsdale, NJ: Erlbaum.

Papoušek, H. (1961). Conditioned head rotation reflexes in infants in the first months of life. *Acta Pediatrica, 50,* 565–576.

Papoušek, H. (1967a). Conditioning during postnatal development. In Y. Brackbill & G. G. Thompson (Eds.), *Behavior in infancy and early childhood* (pp. 259–284). New York: Free Press.

Papoušek, H. (1976b). Experimental studies of appetitional behavior in human newborns and infants. In H. W. Stevenson, E. H. Hess, & H. L. Rheingold (Eds.), *Early behavior: Comparative and developmental approaches* (pp. 249–78). New York: Wiley.

Papoušek, H., & Papoušek, M. (1975). Cognitive aspects of preverbal social interactions between human infants and adults. In *Parent–infant interaction. Ciba Foundation Symposium 33 (new series).* Amsterdam: Elsevier.

Papoušek, H., & Papoušek, M. (1977). Mothering and the cognitive head-start: Psychobiological considerations. In H. R. Schaffer (Ed), *Studies in mother–infant interaction.* London: Academic Press.

Piaget, J. (1962). *Play, dreams and imitation in childhood* (C. Gattegno & F. M. Hodgson, Trans.). New York: Norton. (Original work published 1945).

Piaget, J. (1968). *On the development of memory and identity.* Barre, MA: Clark University Press.

Ramey, C. T., & Watson, J. S. (1972). Nonsocial reinforcement of infants' vocalizations. *Developmental Psychology, 6,* 538.

Ratner, H. H., & Myers, N. A. (1980). Related picture cues and memory for hidden-object location at age two. *Child Development, 51,* 561–564.

Rose, S. A. (1981). Developmental changes in infants' retention of visual stimuli. *Child Development, 52,* 227–233.

Rovee-Collier, C. K., & Fagen, J. W. (1976). Extended conditioning and 24-hour retention in infants. *Journal of Experimental Child Psychology, 21,* 1–11.

Rovee-Collier, C. K., & Fagen, J. W. (1981). The retrieval of memory in early infancy. In L. P. Lipsitt (Ed.), *Advances in infancy research.* Norwood, N.J.: Ablex.

Rovee-Collier, C. K., & Lipsitt, L. P. (1982). Learning, adaptation, and memory in the newborn. In P. Stratton (Ed.), *Psychobiology of the human newborn*. New York: Wiley.

Rovee-Collier, C. K., & Sullivan, M. W. (1980). Organization of infant memory. *Journal of Experimental Psychology: Human Learning and Memory, 6*, 798–807.

Rovee-Collier, C. K., Sullivan, M. W., Enright, M., Lucas, D., & Fagen, J. W. (1980). Reactivation of infant memory. *Science, 208*, 1159–1161.

Ruff, H. (1981). Effect of context on infants' responses to novel objects. *Developmental Psychology, 17*, 87–89.

Ruff, H. (1982). Role of manipulation in infants' responses to invariant properties of objects. *Developmental Psychology, 18*, 682–691.

Rumbaugh, D. M. (1970). Learning skills of anthropoids. In L. A. Rosenblum (Ed.). *Primate behavior: Developments in field and laboratory research*. New York: Academic Press.

Sagi, A., & Hoffman, M. L. (1976). Empathic distress in the newborn. *Developmental Psychology, 12*, 175–176.

Sameroff, A. J. (1968). The components of sucking in the human newborn. *Journal of Experimental Child Psychology, 6*, 607–623.

Sameroff, A. J. (1971). Can conditioned responses be established in the newborn infant? *Developmental Psychology, 5*, 1–12.

Sameroff, A. J., & Cavanagh, P. J. (1979). Learning in infancy: A developmental perspective. In J. D. Osofsky (Ed.), *Handbook of infant development* (pp. 344–392). New York: Wiley.

Seligman, M. E. P. (1970). On the generality of the laws of learning. *Psychological Review, 77*, 406–418.

Semb, G., & Lipsitt, L. P. (1968). The effects of acoustic stimulation on cessation and initiation of non-nutritive sucking in neonates. *Journal of Experimental Child Psychology, 6*, 585–597.

Simner, M. L. (1971). Newborn's response to the cry of another infant. *Developmental Psychology, 5*, 136–150.

Siqueland, E. R., & Lipsitt, L. P. (1966). Conditioned head-turning in human newborns. *Journal of Experimental Child Psychology, 3*, 356–376.

Slater, A., Morison, V., & Rose, D. (1984). Habituation in the newborn. *Infant Behavior and Development, 7*, 183–200.

Sokolov, E. N. (1963). *Perception and the conditioned reflex*. New York: Macmillan.

Spear, N. E., & Parsons, P. G. (1976). Analysis of reactivation treatment: Ontogenetic determinants of alleviated forgetting. In D. L. Medin, W. A. Roberts, & R. T. Davis (Eds.), *Processes of animal memory*. Hillsdale, NJ: Erlbaum.

Stamps, L. E., & Porges, S. W. (1975). Heart rate conditioning in newborn infants: Relationships among conditionability, heart rate variability, and sex. *Developmental Psychology, 11*, 424–431.

Steinschneider, A., Lipton, E. L., & Richmond, J. B. (1966). Auditory sensitivity in the infant: Effect of intensity on cardiac and motor responsivity. *Child Development, 37*, 233–252.

Stern, D. (1977). *The first relationship: Infant and mother*. Cambridge, MA: Harvard University Press.

Strauss, M. S., & Cohen, L. B. (April, 1980). *Infant immediate and delayed memory for perceptual dimensions*. Paper presented at the Second International Conference on Infant Studies, New Haven, CT.

Sullivan, M. W. (1982). Reactivation: Priming forgotten memories in human infants. *Child Development, 53*, 516–523.

Sullivan, M. W., Rovee-Collier, C. K., & Tynes, D. M. (1979). A conditioning analysis of infant long-term memory. *Child Development, 50*, 152–162.

Thelen, M. H., Dollinger, S. J., & Roberts, M. C. (1975). On being imitated: Its effects on attraction and reciprocal imitation. *Journal of Personality and Social Psychology, 31*, 467–472.

Thoman, E. B. (1981). Early communication as the prelude to later adaptive behaviors. In M. J. Begab, H. C. Haywood, & H. L. Garber (Eds.), *Psychosocial influences in retarded performance. Volume II, Strategies for improving competence*. Baltimore: University Park Press.

Topinka, C. V., & Steinberg, B. (March, 1978). Visual recognition memory in $3\frac{1}{2}$- and $7\frac{1}{2}$-month-old infants. Paper presented at the First International Conference on Infant Studies, Providence, RI.

Ungerer, J., Brody, L. R., & Zelazo, P. R. (1978). Long-term memory for speech in 2- to 4-week-old infants. *Infant Behavior and Development, 1*, 127–140.

Uzgiris, I. C., & Hunt, J. McV. (1975). *Assessment in infancy*. Urbana, IL: University of Illinois Press.

VonBargen, D. M. (1983). Infant heart rate: A review of research and methodology. *Merrill-Palmer Quarterly, 29*, 115–150.

Waxler, C. Z., & Yarrow, M. (1975). An observational study of maternal models. *Developmental Psychology, 11*, 485–494.

Weisberg, P. (1963). Social and non-social conditioning of infant vocalizations. *Child Development, 34*, 377–388.

Werner, J. S., & Perlmutter, M. (1979). Development of visual memory in infants. In H. W. Reese & L. P. Lipsitt (Eds.), *Advances in child development and behavior* (Vol. 14, pp. 1–56). New York: Academic.

Wickens, D. D., & Wickens, C. (1940). A study of conditioning in the neonate. *Journal of Experimental Psychology, 25*, 94–102.

Yando, R., Seitz, V., & Zigler, E. (1978). *Imitation: A developmental perspective.* New Jersey: Erlbaum.

Zelazo, P. R. (1971). Smiling to social stimuli: Eliciting and conditioning effects. *Developmental Psychology, 41*, 32–42.

CHAPTER 8

DEVELOPMENTAL MILESTONES

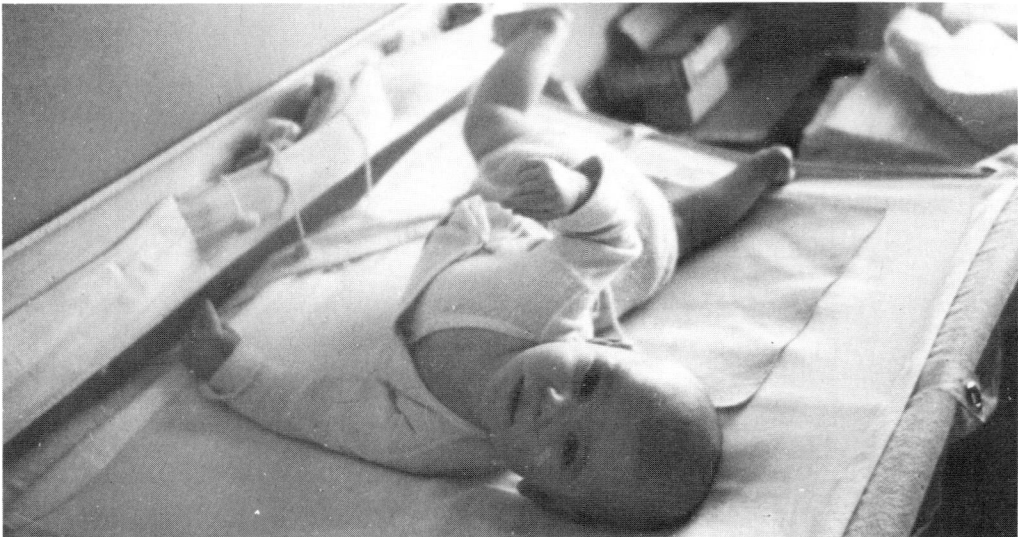

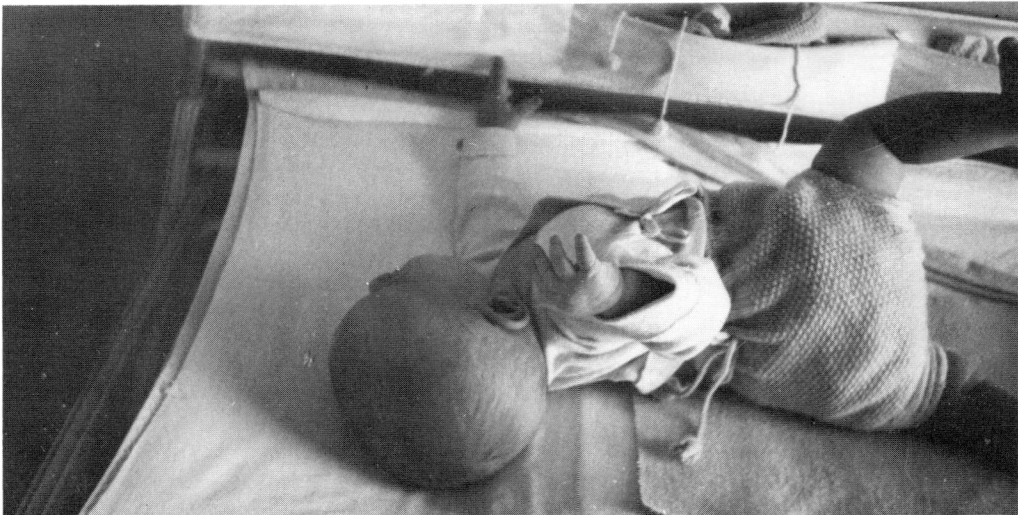

CHAPTER 8

In this chapter, we will take up some conventional topics of growth and development throughout the period of infancy. We start with the least psychological: physical growth. Next come aspects of motor development and developmental milestones. Finally, we will discuss the neurological and psychological assessment of newborns and infants.

PHYSICAL DEVELOPMENT

Introduction

The beginning of this chapter is a continuation of the discussion of physical growth in Chapter 2. The most rapid growth of all life occurs prior to birth, but this growth is not seen and so must be admired in the abstract. The growth that takes place after birth is visible to one and all. Indeed, infancy is the next most rapid period of physical growth, particularly during the first year. In it the birth weight of the average baby triples and length increases 9 to 10 inches. This rate of growth is higher than that of any subsequent period, including the so-called adolescent growth spurt.

Why do we devote a section to physical growth and development in a text on infancy? One obvious reason is that parents and those who work with children are interested in the physical growth and development of infants. Another is that professionals are interested in physical growth because it often indexes problems in development. James M. Tanner (Professor of Child Health and Growth at the Institute of Child Health of the University of London), one of the world's experts in this field, elaborated this thesis at the end of his book *Foetus Into Man* (1978):

Provided always that parental size is known, growth emerges as the prime measure of a child's physical and mental health. The study of growth emerges also as a powerful tool for monitoring the health and nutrition of populations, especially in ecological and economic circumstances that are sub-optimal. It is equally powerful for studying the effect of political organization upon the relative welfare of the various social, cultural and ethnic groups which make up a modern state. Thus the study of growth has a very direct bearing upon human welfare. At the same time it gives us valuable lessons on the way in which our biological heritage and our technological culture interact. It warns us that all too soon we shall be technically capable of creating monstrously specialized, monstrously similar children. It points to our need to be reconciled with our origins, to see ourselves once again as a part of the natural order; not foetus into angel, nor foetus into monster, but foetus into Man. (p. 219)

To give a concrete example, in rural Guatemala, length and weight are the indices most strongly correlated with behavioral development over the first two years (Lasky, Klein, Yarbrough, Engle, et al., 1981). These relations were not accounted for by gestational age, food intake, prevalence of disease, or characteristics of the family.

The timetables of growth are largely genetically determined and an infant's genetic make up has a large influence on ultimate height and body type and even weight. In interaction with genetic factors, living standards, nutrition, general health, and emotional health all have a lot to do with optimal growth, as Tanner implies. We will devote considerable attention to final or adult height because differences in adult height represent the joint action of genetic and environmental factors in development.

Several important longitudinal studies that involved physical growth were started in the United States a century after the pioneer studies of Quetelet (1835). These include the Berkeley Growth Studies and the Fels Institute studies. These and other studies, usually cross sectional, were used to provide norms by which pediatricians and parents could judge the development of a given child. They were usually based on samples from limited geographic areas and from only a narrow portion of the socio–economic range, primarily middle or upper-middle class. Only recently have normative data based on representative samples of the population of the United States become available for older children, but unfortunately infancy was neglected in the two major national studies that produced these data.[1] Nevertheless, they led to an assessment of existing norms and the combining of the Preschool Nutrition Survey (Owen, Kram, Garry, Lower, & Lubin, 1974) and the Fels longitudinal data to provide norms for the period from birth to 36 months of age. We will refer to the data for the first two years in the section that gives normative data on height and weight in infancy.

It is important to have up-to-date norms for physical development because of the so-called **secular trends** in growth. These are changes in heights and weights of given populations over time that are thought to be related to environmental influences; that is, upward secular trends are thought to reflect improved diet and health care that enable more infants more nearly to reach their genetic potentials. Secular trends are especially obvious in the more developed countries where such diets and health care are more prevalent. Height in the United States, Sweden, Japan, and Holland have all increased markedly in this century, especially since World War II. The sex or racial groups that had been more disadvantaged within these countries had the greatest increase in height. This indicates that these people had previously been prevented from reaching their genetic potential to a greater degree than their more advantaged counterparts. In Japan after World War II, children could not use the school desks that their parents used, and young adults in the United States today are, on the average, 1 inch taller than their parents who, in turn, were 1 inch taller than *their* parents.

These secular trends in average heights and weights appear to have nearly ceased, at least in the United States, according to the National Center for Health Statistics Growth Charts (1976). This relatively representative data base indicates that this cessation, which had earlier been shown for advantaged Harvard students (Damon, 1968), may now extend to most of the population. The report of the National Center for Health Statistics states:

Whatever complex factors had been producing the secular trend to increasing body size of children (and adults) from the prenatal period onward had ceased to be of sufficient magnitude by 1955 or 1956 to affect these rather sensitive data across most socioeconomic levels of the American [United States] population. When the stragglers will finally achieve their genetic potential to full stature can probably be better predicted by economic and social factors than by biologic ones *[emphasis added]. (p. 19)*

A more detailed discussion of secular trends and the issues associated with assessing them is available in Roche's monograph (1979).

The secular trends affecting adult heights and weights are also found in the data on birth weights and heights. Both have increased over the time spans discussed. There is less regularity over time in these changes, due in part to changing fashions about the appropriate amount of weight for a pregnant woman to gain during pregnancy.

Methodology

Any given set of figures on birth weight or birth height requires very cautious interpretation because of the difficulties of making standardized measurements of these physical characteristics. For weight this is only a question of whether the baby was weighed with a diaper (wet or dry) or blanket or not, and whether the baby was quiet for the weighing, a problem some modern digital scales can solve. For height, however, the problems are greater. Because a newborn cannot stand, the measurement is made on the horizontal; it is hard to have the head at the correct angle with respect to the head board; the head may be out of shape due to delivery; and it is hard to extend fully the legs of a newborn. Thus in comparing any figures it is important to know that the same techniques were used to make the measurements. People often think that psychological data are peculiarly messy because of the problems of standardization of measurement techniques, but we want to make sure that you

---

[1] The Health Examination Survey and the Health and Nutrition Examination Survey of the National Center for Health Statistics are the studies. They were done to assess the health and nutritional status of noninstitutionalized people in the United States, not to provide growth norms.

understand that measurement problems are not limited to psychological variables for which there are no accepted yardsticks (or metrics); they exist even in areas where such metrics exist.

To use birth weights for comparative or diagnostic purposes, it is important to know not only whether similar measurement techniques were used, but also how soon after birth the weighing was done, the conceptual age of the baby, birth order, whether it was a multiple birth or not, and the heights and weights of the parents.

Now that we have stressed the hazards of measurement and interpretation of data on size, let us turn to another important methodological issue concerning this type of data. One of the chief ways the contribution of heredity to any characteristic is assessed is by examining the degree to which characteristics are related for different groups of target persons (children and relatives of varying degrees of closeness of relationship). The degree of relation between any two groups on some trait (height, weight, IQ, and others) is assessed by the statistical technique of correlation coefficients (see Chapter 1). In general, the closer the relationship of the people, the higher the correlation (where 1.00 is a perfect correlation). The highest correlation is found for identical twins, who are most closely related inasmuch as they are genetically identical (have the same genotype). The correlations between the heights of children and their parents are substantial and even those for weight are moderate. Correlations between characteristics such as the heights of children and their parents do not, however, preclude a substantial difference in actual heights. In fact, even if the correlations were perfect there could be marked differences in actual heights as long as the ordering of the heights remains the same in both groups. The hypothetical example in Table 8–1 illustrates such a situation. This example also illustrates what happens in the case of a rather extreme secular change.

TABLE 8–1
Father–Son Pairs Whose Heights Differ but Are Perfectly Correlated

	Father's Height	Son's Height
Pair 1	5 ft 6 in.	5 ft 8 in.
Pair 2	5 ft 7 in.	5 ft 9 in.
Pair 3	5 ft 8 in.	5 ft 10 in.
Pair 4	5 ft 9 in.	5 ft 11 in.
Pair 5	5 ft 10 in.	6 ft 1 in.
Pair 6	5 ft 11 in.	6 ft 2 in.
Pair 7	6 ft 0 in.	6 ft 3 in.

Nature of Physical Growth

In this section we will give several examples to show how one system in the body would develop if it were to grow at the same rate as other systems. Each such comparison is a dramatic illustration of the uneven rates of growth of different body parts, organs, or tissues.

HEIGHT

At birth, full-term babies average 19 to 21 inches in length and boys are slightly longer than girls. Firstborns are slightly shorter than later borns. The growth curves for length published by the National Center for Health Statistics (1976) are shown in Figure 8–1, (a) and (b). Although height is highly influenced by genetic factors, the length of infants at birth has little relation to their heights as adults. By the end of the first year there is a moderate correlation (.50 for boys and .60 for girls in the Berkeley Growth Study data). By the second year these correlations rise to the mid or high .70s (Tanner, 1978).

One way of looking at growth in this period is in terms of the proportion of adult height that infants have reached at a given age. By 2 years boys have reached 50% of their mature height and girls 53% (Harvard data, cited by Bayley, 1954). Another way of looking at it

FIGURE 8–1. Charts (produced by the National Center for Health Statistics) showing length and weight development by age percentiles from birth to 36 months. (a) Girls' length; (b) boys' length; (c) girls' weight; (d) boys' weight.

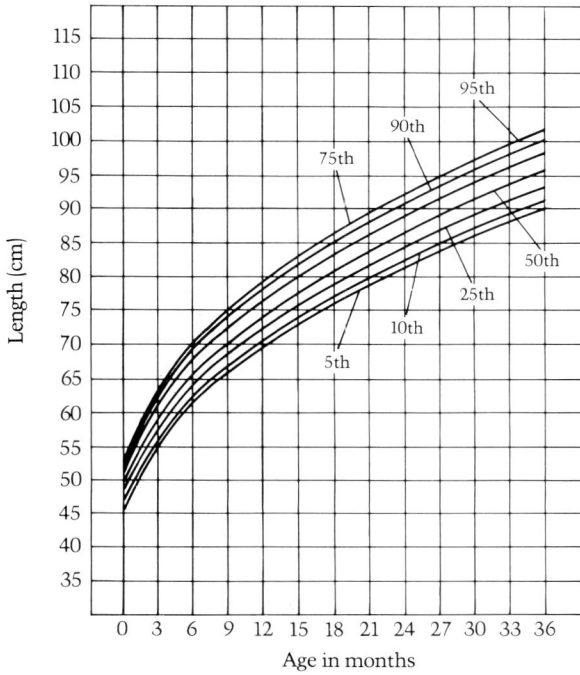

(a) Girls' length by age percentiles: Birth—36 months

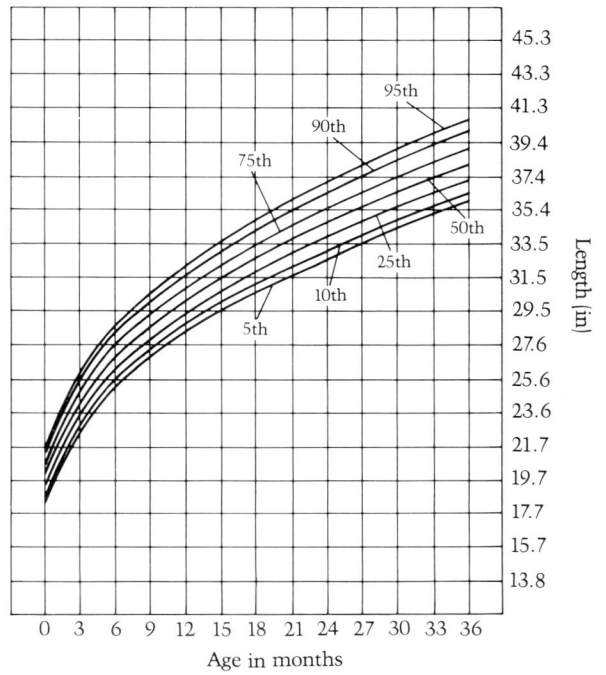

(b) Boys' length by age percentiles: Birth—36 months

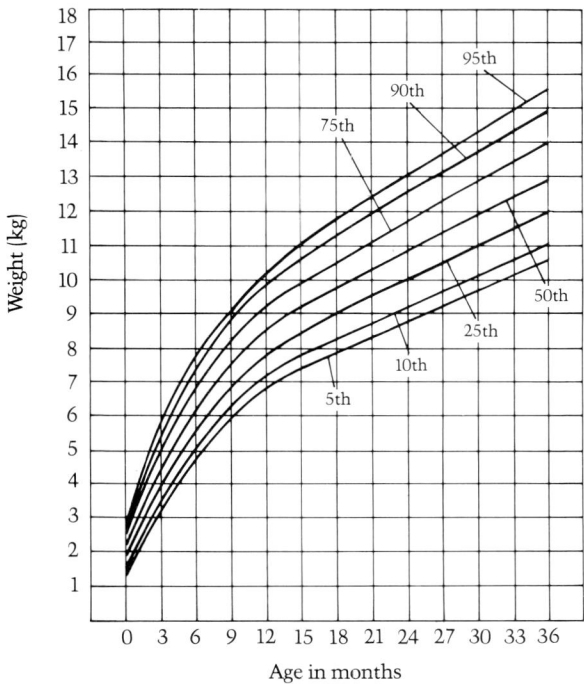

(c) Girls' weight by age percentiles: Birth—36 months

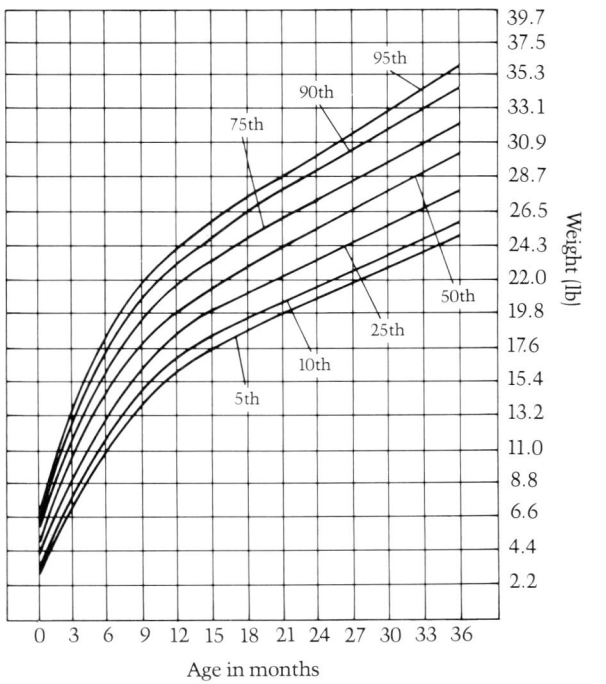

(d) Boys' weight by age percentiles: Birth—36 months

is in terms of the proportion of their birth length that infants grow over a given time period. By one year infants have grown by 50% of their birth height, and by two years by 75% of it (Stuart & Meredith, 1946).

WEIGHT

Term Infants. At birth boys average 3.3 kg in weight and girls 3.2 kg (National Center for Health Statistics, 1976). Tanner's figures for British children (1970) are about 0.1 kg higher. The curve of weight growth is not so smooth as that of height growth (Figure 8–1, (c) and (d)). Weight is more affected than height by health and environmental factors, including even the seasons. Birth weight is actually slightly more related to adult weight than is birth length to adult height. Indeed, it is not much more related to weight at age two than it is to adult weight and then only for boys ($r = .51$; Tanner, Healy, Lockhart, MacKenzie, & Whitehouse, 1956; Tanner, Whitehouse, Marshall, Healy, & Goldstein, 1975). Birth weight is also less correlated with parental weight than is height. In fact, a girl is 6 years old before her weight is significantly correlated with that of her mother (Bayley, 1954).

Birth weight normally doubles in the first five months, triples in the first year, and quadruples by 2½ years. If height did the same, 1 year-olds would be 5 feet tall! Between 2 and 5 years of age, however, the average child will increase less in weight than during the first year of life.

Premature Infants. All of the above figures are for full-term newborns. It is very important to distinguish between premature babies and those who are small for their gestational age because the weight of the premature is particularly important in assessing how much at risk the infant is. Tanner and Thomson (1970) provided charts of weight norms for babies born at between 32 and 42 weeks of gestational age. These charts show the average weights and the 5th, 10th, 25th, 75th, 90th, and 95th percentiles for both boys and girls. Figures are given separately for first-born and later-born boys and girls, and a correction factor based on the mother's height and weight is given. All of these factors need to be taken into account when the status of the infant is being interpreted.

HEAD CIRCUMFERENCE

Another physical measurement that is of great interest to physicians and that has potential meaning for the psychologist is head circumference. Again, the problems of standardizing the measurement are considerable, but the effort is useful because infants who are outside the normal range on either the large or small side are at risk. Infants with unusually large heads are likely to have hydrocephaly, a condition in which the cerebrospinal fluid that normally bathes the brain doesn't drain out of the skull properly. This results in pressure on both brain and skull, which leads to brain damage and a large head. If hydrocephaly is identified, the excess fluid in the head can often be drained or shunted to other parts of the body. This can even be done when a baby is still in utero. Both the degree of the problem and how early it is corrected affect the outcome. A large head is sometimes the result of enlargement of the brain and is then called megalencephaly.

Babies whose heads are abnormally small may have microcephaly, in which the small size of the skull reflects a small brain, or craniostenosis, a condition that results from premature closure of one or more of the sutures between the bones of the skull. In the past the two were not clearly distinguished, which led to confusion about the success of surgery to separate the sutures (Menkes, 1984). Microcephaly is either the result of anomalous development in the first 7 months of gestation or of an insult in the last 2 months or perinatally. Anomalous development is sometimes a result of chromosomal or inherited problems (as was discussed in Chapter 3), and it is sometimes a result of intrauterine causes such as rubella, CMV, toxoplasmosis, maternal PKU, irradiation, or drugs (as was discussed in Chapter 4). Perinatal insults and those of the last 2 months of gestation include infections, trauma, and metabolic and anoxic destruction of brain tissues.

If microcephaly is part of general growth retardation it appears to be less serious than when only the head is affected. In general the outlook for intellectual development in microcephalics is poor. Even if an infant's head circumference is smaller than normal, but above the microcephalic range, intellectual development is more likely to be handicapped (Broman, 1981).

BRAIN

Let us examine the changes taking place in the brain. The brain, the largest part of the central nervous system, develops earlier than most other organs, so that from early fetal life its weight is closer to its adult level than any other organ except perhaps the eye (Tanner, 1978). The brain's weight at birth is 25% of its adult weight. By 6 months it weighs 50% as much as that of an adult, and at two years 75% as much. In contrast, at birth the body as a whole weighs only 5% of an adult's and doesn't reach 50% of adult weight until 10 years. If the rates of growth for height and weight after birth were as slow as that for the brain, boys and girls would both only grow to be about 4 feet 3 inches tall as adults and would weigh only about 40 pounds. This means that the brain does not increase in its proportion of total body weight as the infant develops from birth to adulthood.

The cortex at birth is very poorly developed, which suggests that little cortical function is possible. By one month the appearance of the cells in the primary motor area of the brain that controls the upper limbs and trunk suggests that this area may be functional. By 3 months all primary areas are relatively mature, with the motor areas most advanced, especially those controlling the hands, arms, and upper trunk. Their development earlier than the areas controlling the lower trunk and legs emphasizes the postnatal importance of the cephalo–caudal principle of development; that is, that development proceeds from head (ceph) to tail (caud).

Development of the primary sensory areas of the brain lags behind that of the primary motor areas, but by 2 years they have caught up. The association areas develop more slowly than the motor and sensory areas, but they develop in the same order. At 2 years some of these areas are still immature.

The maturation of these areas of the cortex does not mean that brain development is complete. Other aspects of brain development, such as myelination and development of neural processes, continue after cell division has ceased (see Chapter 2). Some illustrations of myelination in various areas are: Fibers linking the cerebellum to the cortex that are necessary for precise control of voluntary movement are not fully myelinated until 4 years of age;

auditory system fibers begin to myelinate in the 6th fetal month and continue until the 4th year; visual system fibers start to myelinate just before birth, but complete the process rapidly; and still other structures continue to myelinate until puberty or beyond.

UNEVENNESS OF GROWTH

Although growth measured by height, weight, or head circumference is important and of interest to parents and pediatricians, one of the most striking features about growth is that different body parts grow or change at such different rates. We have already noted that height and weight do not change at the same rate. One of the most striking results of differential growth is seen in the great difference in the relative proportion of length that is accounted for by the length of the head compared to that of the legs (Figure 8–2). On the average, the head accounts for one-quarter of a baby's length at birth compared to one-eighth of adult height. In contrast, the legs are only one-third of the total length at birth, but one-half of adult length. The head doubles in length between birth and adulthood, whereas the trunk triples, the arms quadruple, and the legs quintuple.

Another, less obvious aspect of growth is the fact that weight is made up of varied proportions of the different types of tissue that make up the body. For example, at birth 25% of weight is accounted for by muscle, 16% by vital organs, and 15% by the central nervous system. In the adult, by contrast, 43% of weight is accounted for by muscle, 11% by vital organs, and 3% by the central nervous system. From this point of view, "growing up" physically seems to be disproportionately a matter of developing more muscle. Another big change that occurs rather quickly after birth is in the proportion of the body weight that is accounted for by water. At birth the body is 75 to 80% water, but by one year it is only 59% water (Tanner, 1962). Despite the separate weight norms shown for boys and girls, the differences are slight in the first year. Starting at age one the differences increase. From 1 to 6 years, girls lose fat more rapidly than boys. At 6 this reverses, but large individual differences in the amount of fat in relation to bone and muscle overwhelm the average differences between the sexes.

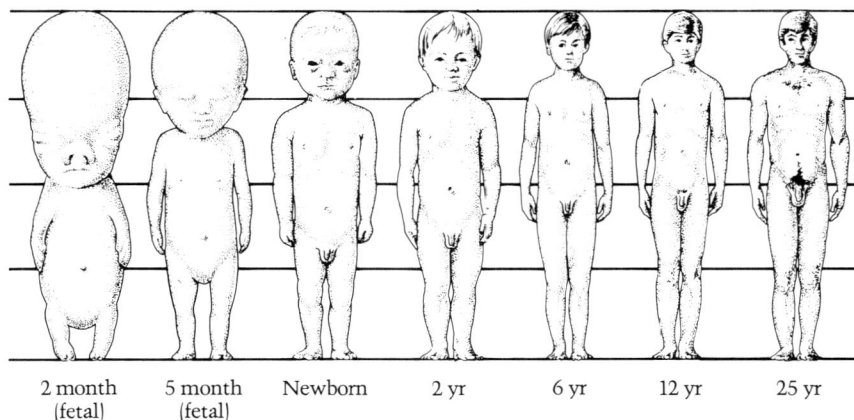

|2 month
(fetal)|5 month
(fetal)|Newborn|2 yr|6 yr|12 yr|25 yr|

FIGURE 8–2. The very different proportions of body length accounted for by the head, trunk, and legs at different ages or stages of development. The disproportion is greatest in fetal life: The head decreases from 50% of total body length at 2 months post conception to only 25% at birth and 12% in adulthood.

MOTOR DEVELOPMENT

Second to watching and charting physical growth and development, parents, pediatricians, and grandparents probably most often look for the milestones of motor development. When does the baby hold its head up steadily? Sit up? Stand up? Walk? Run? These motor accomplishments are aspects of gross motor development and are among the developmental milestones parents record in "baby books." Parents also read books on development, and ask their parents or friends or pediatricians when they can expect their baby to sit up, crawl, walk, and so forth. Parents also compare notes with friends about the ages at which their respective babies accomplish these skills. Parents then may feel good or bad because their baby is early or late to achieve the given skill.

Psychologists, pediatricians, and parents are also sometimes attentive to behaviors that are aspects of fine motor development. The ability to grasp objects with the hands and with ever greater smoothness and precision of movement, and to grasp very small objects with neat pincer movements of thumb and one finger, are aspects of fine motor development. These are probably less often carefully ob-served or charted by parents, but are of great importance for development.

Background of the Study of Motor Development

Much of the early data describing the course of motor development came from infant testers. Hence, although we discuss developmental tests in the next section, we need to mention them here as well. We wish, nevertheless, to discuss motor development separately from tests not only because of the parental interest mentioned above, but also because motor behaviors are a crucial element in Piaget's theory of sensorimotor stages of development. An additional reason to discuss motor development separately from tests is that in contrast to tests, where the focus is diagnostic, our focus on motor behavior is not. Some of the pioneer students of motor behaviors were certainly interested in the processes of motor development (see, for example, Shirley, 1931) and not just in normative data on developmental milestones or in diagnosis. This aspect of their work, however, was not always what was picked up by and accentuated for pediatricians or parents, or even by other researchers.

Let us start by discussing Gesell, one of the pioneers of the detailed study of infants. In his infant tests, he originally used seven categories to cover the total development of the infant. Three of these—postural, locomotive, and prehensive behaviors—were relevant to motor development. The first two are gross motor behaviors. It may seem strange to see posture listed as behavior. Here is what Gesell said about this:

Posture is behavior. Postural patterns are behavior patterns. To be sure, these patterns are influenced by bodily size and proportions, by joints and ligaments, and even by abdominal viscera. But primarily they are determined by the maturity and organization of the infant's central neural equipment. The positions, the stances, the motor attitudes which he assumes are net resultants of a complicated system of reflexes and reaction trends which vary from age to age. Posture is not the manifestation of a discrete set of abilities which increase as the child grows stronger. (Gesell, Thompson, & Amatruda, 1934, p. 44)

Locomotion, or the ability to move from one place to another, is clearly a motor act and is clearly important in infant development. In the very first normative study known, Feldman (1833) gave average ages of walking for his sample.

Prehension, or the ability to grasp things with the hands, is a fine motor behavior. It may be important not only for the developmental stages described by Piaget, but also has been said to be one of the important features that differentiate humans from other animals, enabling the precise use of tools. We shall return to it later.

Although Gesell created one of the most used infant tests, he was also interested in process. He and other early pioneers of the study of various aspects of motor development (including McGraw, 1935, and Shirley, 1931) used observational techniques to study such motor behaviors as grasping, crawling or creeping, swimming, and walking. Gesell also pioneered the use of motion pictures which allow frame-by-frame analysis of the movement sequences.

By comparing films made at different ages, a view of the process of development of motor skills is possible.[2]

Although many perceived Gesell as providing normative data on the age of achievement of various skills, caution is needed in accepting the data from these early studies as providing norms for when to expect a normal infant to achieve any given skill. For one thing, because these observations were highly detailed, they were often made using relatively small numbers of infants, and often these infants were not representative of the population at large. Furthermore, the infants were studied some time ago. As is true of physical growth and development, there have been changes over time in actual motor skills and the age at which a skill normally develops, changes that are probably related to those for physical growth.

A number of factors affect the age at which motor skills are achieved. For example, appropriate motor development appears to depend not only on physical characteristics and growth factors, but also on the appropriate functioning of other systems. A large proportion of congenitally blind children, for example, are hypotonic and have slow motor development. (There is some suggestion from head shape that these infants may be left too much in the supine position and that this rather than blindness may be the cause). These children also tend to walk before they crawl (Fraiberg, 1971, as cited in Jan, Robinson, Scott, & Kinnis, 1975).

Since that early research, unfortunately psychologists in general have concentrated on the average age and normal range of ages for the appearance of various motor skills. Medical specialists, especially neurologists, interested in diagnostic problems have complained about the lack of detailed knowledge of normal motor performance that would enable them to be better judges of departures from it. (See Neuhauser, 1975, for a review of this topic.) Most techniques used to assess motor development after infancy require cooperation from

---

[2] The student whose library has a copy of Gesell's *An Atlas of Infant Behavior* (Vols. I and II, 1934) is urged to look at these books with their detailed pictures of the development of various motor acts.

the subject and hence are not readily applicable to either infants or highly disturbed children. As a result, knowledge of motor development lacks some of the precision and detail that are available for other systems such as sensory/perceptual development, for which techniques have been developed to surmount the inability of the baby to cooperate or communicate verbally (see Chapter 9). Neuhauser (1975) has this to say about the need for better data:

While available motometric tests are able to give a global impression of motor skills and motor functioning, further investigations and new methods are necessary to achieve a more valid recording of various motor components involved in motor skills. Further, motometric tests insufficiently assess all the various phenomena and signs of movement disorders in children, because they are used in particular to assess the motor task achievement and give a motor behavior age of the child. They do not record the quality of the successive motor phenomena used in performing a given task; . . . For recording of the quality of movement patterns, more details and specified analyses are necessary. (p. 373)

McGraw, one of the pioneer students of motor development, noted in her 1977 address to the Society for Research in Child Development that researchers (herself in her earlier work included) have not paid enough attention to differences in the quality of motor performance. For example, three toddlers who can walk on a raised board may do so very differently. One may do it with what might be described as finesse, another with competence, and the third clumsily, often appearing to be about to fall off. They would all pass the item, but they are not all functioning at the same level. The psychological consequences of such qualitative differences are just beginning to be studied.

Nature versus Nurture

Gesell assumed that postural, locomotive, and prehensile skills were biologically determined and depended primarily on the passage of time to unfold. Others working in the 1930s certainly agreed (see Dennis, 1938, 1940, 1943;

McGraw, 1935). In fact, that era was characterized by a number of studies that attempted to assess the relative contributions of nature and nurture to motor skills, including those used as developmental milestones as well as advanced or specialized ones such as climbing, swimming, and roller skating.

Dennis, for example, studied the age of walking in Hopi infants who were reared on the traditional cradle board compared to those who were not and to non-Indian children (Dennis & Dennis, 1940). He concluded that the age of walking was not affected by experiences or by the opportunity for practice. The postural experience of being upright, which may be important for walking, was much more prevalent for his babies on cradle boards than for those with "Western" rearing. McGraw made a famous study of twins in which one twin was given early practice on some motor skill such as roller skating and the other twin got no training until the first was proficient at the skill. The twin without the early practice caught up rapidly when given practice later.[3]

Many ideas current in the United States about waiting to teach a skill until a child is ready to learn to swim or skate or read (which requires a great deal of motor skill, much of it fine motor skill) came from these studies. Even after learning theory dominated developmental psychology in the United States, the basic motor skills were still largely thought of as primarily maturational, or as the result of genetic and constitutional factors in development. The view that special coaching of the types attempted did not greatly affect the time at which skills universally acquired by the human species developed was widely held, even by those with a strong interest in learning.

The pendulum of opinion has now begun to swing back and psychologists are again exploring the role of experience as it interacts with maturation in motor development. Even McGraw (1977), who returned to developmental psychology after a considerable hiatus, has had some second thoughts about her earlier conclusions that maturation was all important for motor development. She has noted that the

---

[3] Unfortunately, McGraw's twins turned out to be nonidentical, which rather spoiled the method of co-twin control. This method was initiated by Gesell so that experience could be separated from genetic endowment.

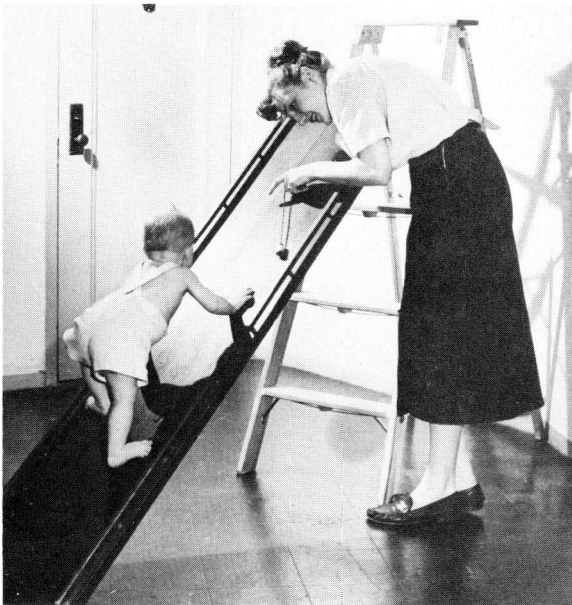

FIGURE 8–3. McGraw's early work, showing that babies need to be encouraged to learn unusual skills such as going up or down inclined boards. The first two pictures (top) show that as the baby's other motoric skills increase, the locomotor methods used to get down become more advanced. With encouragement the slightly older infant can make it up a much steeper incline (bottom), a highly unusual performance for infants of this age. Although much older children may master similar feats on their own, a certain fearlessness may be learned by the young infant, in addition to the motor accomplishment itself. (Photographs courtesy of Dr. Myrtle McGraw.)

twins did differ in the quality of their motor performance as adolescents and young adults. Furthermore, as she now reflects on the total body of her work on motor development (McGraw, 1977, and personal communication 1983), she is convinced that if a function can be detected just as it is ready to emerge, and if it is then continuously challenged, its performance can be expanded. An example of this from her earlier studies can be found in crawling behavior. She placed a baby who was just starting to crawl on a slightly inclined surface. When the baby could crawl up this incline, it was made a little bit steeper. In a steady continuation of this process, a 6-month-old baby developed the ability to crawl up a 70-degree incline (Figure 8–3). Later in his life, Dennis too had a very different view of the role of experience, as we will see in Chapter 13.

More recent work from the field of cross-cultural psychology has provided another look at both the question of experience versus maturation and the question of genetic influences on motor development. When Geber reported (1958; Geber & Dean, 1957) that African infants learned motor skills well in advance of children in the United States or France, the debate about the causes for the differences became a lively one. Many psychologists accepted the differences without much question, others speculated about possible environmental differences, but still others built the differences into their theoretical structures for the genetic inferiority of some racial groups (see, for example, Jensen, 1973).[4] More careful analysis of the data on African precocity questions any genetic basis for it. Geber's own data had shown that westernized Africans from the same genetic stock as that she found to be precocious were not motorically precocious. Warren systematically reviewed 30 articles with some relevant data (1972). He found so many serious flaws that he could not conclude with certainty that there even was such a thing as African locomotor or postural precocity.[5] This makes the arguments as to whether the precocity is genetically based rather meaningless.

Super has tried to get around some of the problems of comparing apples and oranges[6] that has featured much of the work on motoric precocity. He did this by systematic study not only of the motor behaviors of infants but also of the child-rearing practices of the mothers across 14 African groups and one American group. A preliminary report on part of his results (1976) is certainly not incompatible with an environmental explanation for the differences found. His main study was on all the children born between 1972 and 1975 in Kokwet, a community that is prosperous, has good nutrition (they produce maize and milk), and is high enough in altitude to escape most of the worst tropical diseases. These children were

tested with some Bayley test items once each month and observed at random times of day once a week to get a view of their everyday life. Mothers were interviewed about their babies' motor development. These babies of the Kipsigis tribe were in fact able to sit, stand, and walk well in advance of their counterparts in the United States—about 1 month earlier as judged by Bayley norms. But they were not advanced in all motor behaviors. Those involving motor control in the prone position, head control, and crawling were behind the American norms. These differences in infant skills are directly parallel to differences in maternal teaching practices. The Kipsigis consider it important to teach sitting and walking as is illustrated by the fact their language has special words for the teaching of these skills.

The proportion of mothers who said they taught their babies to crawl in each of the six samples analyzed by Super in this paper (1976) was quite directly related to the age at which babies in those samples did crawl ($r = .77$). Ninety-three percent of the agricultural Teso mothers said they taught their babies to crawl, and their babies learned to crawl at about $5\frac{1}{2}$ months of age. Only 13% of the desert Boran mothers thought it was important to teach their babies to crawl, and their babies did not crawl until they were 8 months old.[7] Mothers in each group did not vary enough in teaching sitting and walking to allow relating the teaching of these skills to the age of the achievement. Super (1976) wrote, "Viewed in a cultural context, however, which includes a broad range of naturally occurring environments, these skills (which have so long been accepted by Western psychologists as genetically determined) look much more like other species-specific behaviors in the human." The basic structures may be in (our) genes, "but the environment contributes to *how* and *how fast* they develop" (p. 565).

A related theoretical issue concerns the relation between early reflexes and later similar voluntary behaviors. In western cultures many reflexes, including crawling, swimming, and walking, drop out long before infants learn to do these things voluntarily. In cultures like

---

[4] Precocious attainment of motor skills was seen as genetically determined and as providing a limit to intellectual growth.

[5] Studies of psychomotor development in the first 2 years have also been reviewed for infants from around the world by Werner (1972). For a fuller picture of similarities and differences among infants from a wide variety of cultures, we recommend this survey.

[6] Groups compared have differed not only in their genetic pools, but also in their nutritional status, the altitude at which they live, their health or disease patterns, the amount of sun received, and last, but not least, the child-rearing practices to which they were exposed.

[7] The correlation of the combination of teaching and opportunity to practice (amount of time awake, lying down) with the age of crawling is .97.

FIGURE 8–4. Encouragement for walking in Bali. This Balinese baby uses a rail built specially to help walking. In western cultures aids take the form of furniture; special rails are not needed. (Photograph from the Library of Congress.)

that in Kokwet there is little or no discontinuity between the reflexes and voluntary behaviors; that is, the standing, stepping, and placing reflexes do not disappear at around 2 months as they do in European and United States babies. Indeed, Super found that other motor skills (such as sitting) were advanced in cultures that taught them, although the relation to reflexes was not specifically addressed. One United States study has looked at what happened when special exercise was given to the walking reflex (Zelazo, Zelazo, & Kolb, 1972; see also Figure 8–4). The answer was that the reflex stayed in infants' behavior repertoires longer and walking occurred earlier.

We know of no advantage in modern western culture to having infants walk early. Indeed, there is a great disadvantage associated with their being able to get into things before they can learn what to avoid. However, there may be a practical question of interest. Could the training techniques of Kokwet mothers be used with infants whose early motor development is at risk for neurological or other reasons? For example, would they serve any purpose with congenitally blind infants?

Developmental Norms

We have chosen the Bayley Motor Scale (Psychomotor Development Index or PDI) for our

presentation of developmental norms for two reasons. (1) The standardization sample on which it is based is closer to being representative of babies in the United States than that of any other test. (2) The data for the PDI show not only the usual age at which the behaviors are achieved, but also the youngest and oldest ages at which any baby in the standardization sample demonstrated the behavior. These extremes illustrate the extreme nature of individual differences. It is possible that babies who achieve a skill at the latest ages may have suffered damage. The rest of the variability is accounted for by an inextricable mixture of genetic and experiential factors.

The ages at which these motor milestones are now reached compared to earlier in this century seem to indicate secular trends similar to those found for height and weight. For example, babies appear to walk earlier than they did 50 years ago, based on a comparison of the norms found by Bayley in 1969 with those based on the work of Gesell and his colleagues in the 1920s and 1930s (Gesell & Amatruda, 1941; Gesell, Thompson, & Amatruda, 1934). The Bayley norms also show a lower age for achieving a number of motor acts than did her earlier (1935) norms, despite the fact that her earlier sample, like Gesell's, represented a narrower range that was higher in SES. In all probability, better health care and nutrition and changed ways of caring for children all contribute to the observed changes over time. It may be that unknown factors in the sampling or other unknown factors also contribute to secular changes.

In presenting the normative data from the Bayley test we have reorganized them according to the postural position or stimulus situation in which the behaviors are found at the earlier ages, and by the type of motor behavior at later ages. (On the test, items are ordered according to the age at which they are normally passed.)

Two developmental principles previously discussed are again illustrated in these tables. The first is that development tends to proceed cephalo-caudally. Head control is achieved before trunk control (sitting) which is achieved before leg control (walking). The second is the proximo-distal (or center out) characteristic of development. It is illustrated in motor development by the fact that head control is achieved

TABLE 8–2
Motor Milestones

Behavior	Average age (approximate)	Range of ages
A. HEAD CONTROL WHEN HELD TO SHOULDER		
Lifts head	Neonatal period	
Makes postural adjustment	Neonatal period	
Head erect—vertical	3 weeks	9 days–3 months
Head erect—steady	7 weeks	3 weeks–4 months
Holds head steady	2½ months	1 month–5 months
Head balanced	4 months 1 week	2 months–6 months
B. MOTOR BEHAVIORS IN PRONE POSITION		
Lateral head movements	Neonatal period	
Crawling movements	By 2 weeks	Neonatal period–3 months
Elevates self by arms	Just after 2 months	3 weeks–5 months
Able to progress (move) in some fashion	Just after 7 months	5 months–11 months
C. MOTOR BEHAVIORS IN SUPINE POSITION OR ON SIDE		
Thrusts arms in play	3½ weeks	9 days–2 months
Thrusts legs in play	3½ weeks	9 days–2 months
Holds on to large plastic ring	3½ weeks	9 days–3 months
Lifts head (dorsal suspension)	1 month 3 weeks	3 weeks–4 months
Turns from side to back	By 2 months	3 weeks–5 months
Turns from back to side	2½ months	2 months–7 months

NOTE. Tables 8-2–8-5 are adapted from the Collaborative Perinatal Research Project form of the Bayley tests.

before arm control, which is achieved before hand control, which in turn precedes finger control.

We will not try to describe everything in the tables but will comment on one or two highlights from each. First, let us look at the behaviors that index head control and postural adjustment when the infant is held to the shoulder. Table 8–2A shows that the final stage of holding the head balanced is achieved after 4 months, on the average, but by some babies at 2 months and by others only at 6 months. The next table, Table 8–2B, shows those behaviors exhibited when the baby is in the prone position (lying on the stomach). Both crawling and head control are involved here. The ability to move is achieved on the average at just over 7 months, but the range is from 5 to 11 months. The third table in this sequence, Table 8–2C, shows the motor behaviors that

take place when the baby is supine (on the back) or on the side. In this position the baby is free to move the arms and to move the legs in a different fashion than when prone, and can turn over. Actually, turning over is achieved earlier in the prone position. Once babies can use just their arms to elevate their heads and shoulders and thus get the head well above the rest of the body, they can accidentally move in such a way that their center of gravity and momentum will result in their turning over. Usually, but not always, this is followed in a relatively short time by the baby appearing to carry out the sequence intentionally. Perhaps this is why turning over was not included in prone position behaviors, but is included in the supine behaviors, because intentionality is more clearly demanded here. Turning over is the capstone achievement of this sequence.

Sitting behaviors when the baby is placed

TABLE 8–3
Sitting Behaviors and Efforts to Achieve a Vertical Position

Behavior	Average age (approximate)	Range of ages
	A. PLACED BY ADULT	
Sits with support	2 months 1 week	1 month–5 months
Sits with slight support	3 months 3 weeks	2 months–6 months
Sits alone, momentarily	5 months 1 week	4 months–8 months
Sits alone, 30 seconds or more	6 months	5 months–8 months
Sits alone, steadily	6½ months	5 months–9 months
Sits alone, good coordination	7 months	5 months–10 months
	B. HELPED BY ADULT	
Makes effort to sit	4 months 3 weeks	3 months–8 months
Pulls to sitting	5 months 3 weeks	4 months–8 months
Pulls to standing	8 months +	5 months–12 months
	C. HELPED BY FURNITURE	
Raises self to sitting	8 months 1 week	6 months–11 months
Stands up alone	8½ months	6 months–12 months
Stands up, level I	12½ months	9 months–18 months
Stands up, level II	By 22 months	11 months–30 + months
Stands up, level III	30 + months	22 months–30 + months

in the sitting position by an adult are shown in Table 8–3A. Sitting behaviors that involve the babies' own efforts, but with some adult help, are shown in Table 8–3B, and Table 8–3C deals with efforts to gain a vertical position without the help of others, but using furniture as an aid, and with independent efforts to stand up.

Many different levels of a given behavior are charted in the tables. It is impossible to say at what age a baby sits alone without specifying for how long and in what situation. Note that the differences between the earliest and latest age for achieving the various sitting behaviors range from 3 to 5 months. For the different standing behaviors they range from 6 to over 19 months.

The behaviors relevant to the development of grasp and manipulation will not be presented here. They are related to fine motor development, so they will be considered in the next section.

The last table in this sequence based on Bayley's Motor scales covers walking, balance, and stair climbing (Table 8–4). The tables as we have presented them omit a few behaviors that may occur by the end of the second year, but not many. The Bayley scales themselves extend beyond 2 years with a considerable number of items that are achieved, on the average, at 30 + months of age.

In Table 8–4, again note the very great range of ages at which infants attain motor skills. Achievement of balance seems to be extremely variable. We know of no studies that explain the factors in this variability. The role of the mechanisms of balance relative to other physiological factors or relative to experience is an interesting but unexplored terrain.

Fine Motor Development

A large proportion of the behaviors charted in the Bayley Motor Development sequences are gross motor behaviors. Infants have relatively little control over fine motor acts at birth, yet they have surprisingly many components of what later become finely coordinated arm, hand, and finger movements. The sequences of

TABLE 8–4
Walking,[a] Standing Balance, and Stair Climbing Behaviors

Behavior	Average age (approximate)	Range of ages
A. WALKING		
Early stepping movements	7 months 2 weeks	5 months–11 months
Stepping movements	8 months 3 weeks	6 months–12 months
Walks with help	$9\frac{1}{2}$ months +	7 months–12 months
Sits down	$9\frac{1}{2}$ months +	7 months–14 months
Stands alone	11 months	9 months–16 months
Walks alone	11 months 3 weeks	9 months–17 months
B. BALANCE		
Stands on right foot with help	16 months	12 months–21 months
Stands on left foot with help	16 months +	12 months–23 months
Stands on left foot alone	22 months 3 weeks	15 months–30+ months
Stands on right foot alone	$23\frac{1}{2}$ months	16 months–30+ months
Jumps off floor, both feet	By $23\frac{1}{2}$ months	17 months–30+ months
C. STAIR CLIMBING		
Walks up stairs with help	16+ months	12 months–23 months
Walks down stairs with help	By $16\frac{1}{2}$ months	13 months–23 months
Walks up stairs alone, both feet on each step	25+ months	18 months–30+ months
Walks down stairs alone, both feet on each step	25 months 3 weeks	19 months–30+ months
Walks up stairs alternating forward foot	30+ months	23 months–30+ months

[a]Includes motor control in standing position.

these developments were studied in detail by early workers and pictured in detail in Gesell's *An Atlas of Infant Behavior* (1934). This two-volume work contains 3,200 action photographs of infant behaviors. An example of one of his sequences is given in Figure 8–5.

Halverson published seven studies of grasping responses (or prehension) using systematic movie records between 1931 and 1937. In his 1931 study he describes this development:

The development of reaching and grasping affords excellent examples of the progress of maturation from the coarser to the finer muscles. The early approach patterns consist largely of crude shoulder and elbow movements in which slow and somewhat angular action predominates, while the later approach patterns employ better directed shoulder and elbow action, in addition to wrist movements and hand-rotation, under the dominating influence of the forefinger and thumb. The early approach reveals a crudely functioning hand at the end of a poorly directed arm, while the later approach reveals a well coordinated arm under the directing influence of a pretty well developed prehensile organ. (p. 279)

He also pointed out (1931) that both maturation and learning were involved in these developments.

This developmental sequence is also included in Bayley's Motor scale, and the average age for achieving each item is shown in Table 8–5. Figure 8–6 illustrates in more detail the development of the grasping behaviors listed in part A of the table.

At birth the infant has a grasp reflex. Any

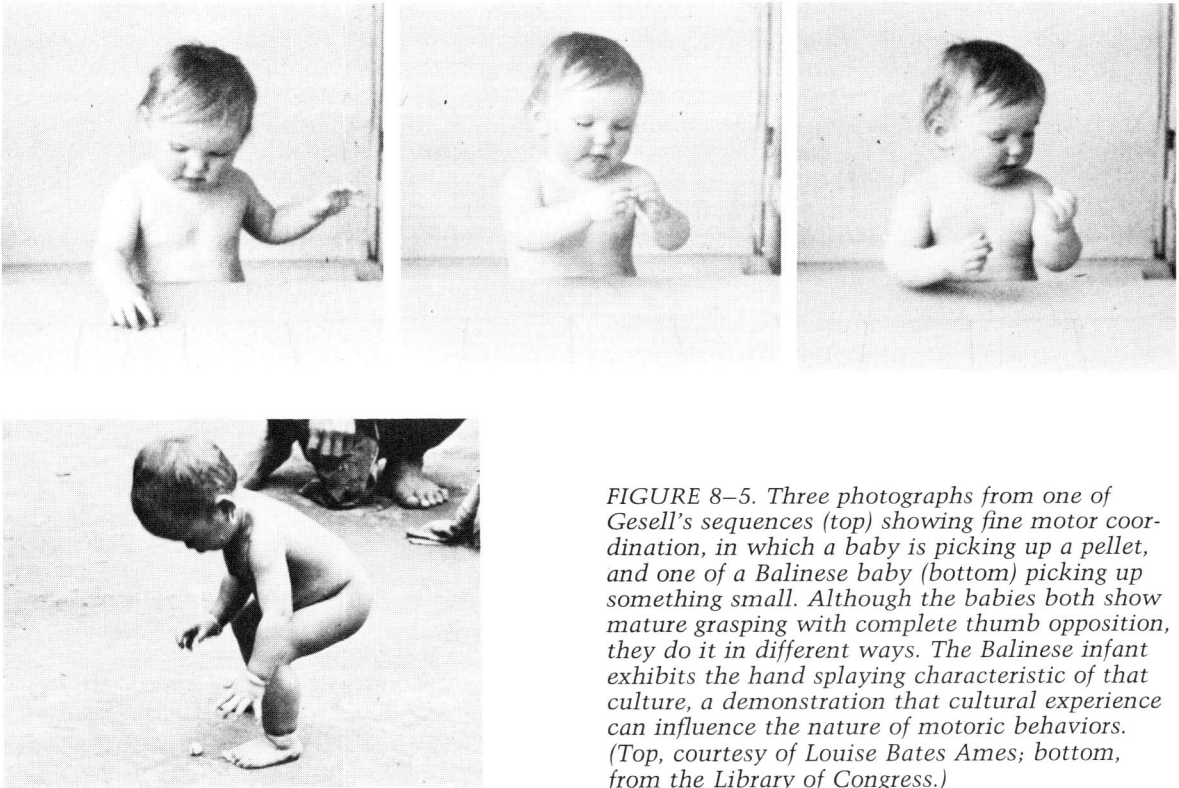

FIGURE 8–5. Three photographs from one of Gesell's sequences (top) showing fine motor coordination, in which a baby is picking up a pellet, and one of a Balinese baby (bottom) picking up something small. Although the babies both show mature grasping with complete thumb opposition, they do it in different ways. The Balinese infant exhibits the hand splaying characteristic of that culture, a demonstration that cultural experience can influence the nature of motoric behaviors. (Top, courtesy of Louise Bates Ames; bottom, from the Library of Congress.)

small rod-like object (including a finger) that is placed against the palm of the hand will be grasped. This reflex can be used to measure the strength of pull, as was shown by early workers who demonstrated that babies could support their full weight by hanging from a rod by two hands (28% of 97 infants tested at less than 24 weeks of age, but fewer of those tested after this age when the reflex has usually dropped out). More recently, neonatal tests use this reflex to measure the strength of pull of the supine newborn. In the normal course of events this reflexive response is replaced by intentional object manipulation.

It is not known precisely how the grasp reflex is related to later development. Because other reflexes are at least potentially related to later motoric development (such as the stepping reflex to walking), the same might be expected to be true of the grasp reflex. Unfortunately, there has been little research exploring the relation between the grasp reflex and more voluntary reaching and grasping. There has,

however, been quite a bit of research exploring the nature of grasping in response to something seen, which in its mature form is called visually guided reaching, and the effects of experience on the development of this behavioral sequence.

First, let us describe what is known about the development of visually guided reaching. Newborns not only grasp, but they also reach (their arms are extended forward in space), and grasping does often follow reaching in much the same way it does for adults (Trevarthen, 1974). When the newborn's eyes are fixated on an object, the reaching movement is generally aimed in the direction of the object (Alt, in Bruner, 1973; Hofsten, 1982), but these primitive responses are not highly coordinated. Newborns only infrequently succeed in grasping the object (Dodwell, Muir, & DiFranco, 1976; Ruff & Halton, 1978; Trevarthen, 1974) and they are unlikely to reach unless their trunks are supported in such a way that their arms are free of postural constraints (Bower,

TABLE 8–5
Grasping or Hand Usage in Sitting Position, and Fine Hand Control

Behavior	Average age (approximate)	Range of ages
A. GRASPING		
Grasps cube with ulnar–palm prehension (1-inch cube)	3 months 3 weeks	2 months–7 months
Grasps cube with partial thumb opposition	By 5 months	4 months–8 months
Grasps cube with complete thumb opposition (radial–digital)	By 7 months	5 months–9 months
B. MANIPULATIVE CAPACITY		
Reaches for object, one hand only	By 5½ months	4 months–8 months
Rotates wrist	5 months 3 weeks	4 months–8 months
Combines objects at midline (spoons or cubes)	8½ months	6 months–10 months
Plays pat-a-cake with midline skill	9 months 3 weeks	7 months–15 months
C. SMALL PELLET SKILLS		
Attempts to secure	5½ months	4 months–8 months
Scoops	6 months 3 weeks	5 months–9 months
Grasps, partial finger prehension (inferior pincer)	7 months 2 weeks	6 months–10 months
Grasps, fine prehension (neat pincer)	By 9 months	7 months–10 months

FIGURE 8–6. Grasping behaviors listed in part A of Table 8–5.

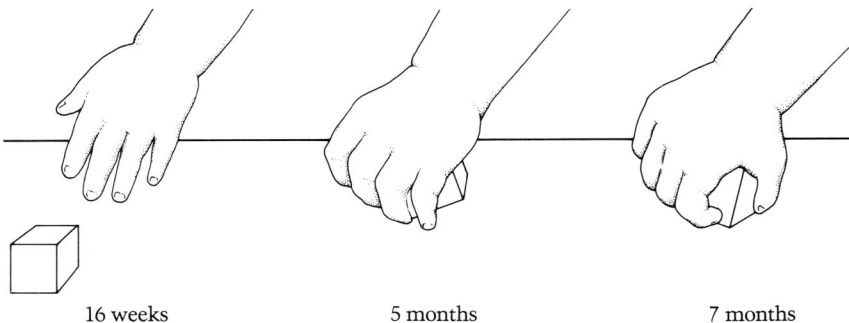

16 weeks   5 months   7 months

1982). The extent to which the object itself plays a role in neonatal reaching is unclear. Some research has suggested that it doesn't matter whether there is an object or not (see Chapter 9 for a fuller discussion of this issue). Furthermore, neonatal reaching is apparently not guided by feedback during the grasp. Newborns make one straight-line grasp. If they happen to touch the object and if their hand happens to close at the right time, their grasp will be successful. They appear to be unable to make corrections during reaching (Dunkeld & Bower, 1981; McDonnell, 1975) and they immediately withdraw their hand after reaching rather than making adjustments (Trevarthen, 1974). Because it has these characteristics, newborn reaching has been called **visually** *initiated* reaching (see Figure 8–7) as opposed to **visually** *guided* **reaching,** the form that appears at 4 months of age.

In visually guided reaching, the object is usually grasped successfully. Both the reach and the grasp are more modulated; that is, the infant is more likely to take the characteristics of the object (for example, whether it is graspable, its size, distance) into account.

There is less research exploring development of reaching behaviors that occur between the first and twentieth week of life than there is research on reaching in the first weeks of life. The research that is available has focused on the roles of maturation and experience in such development. Hofsten (1984) has traced the development of reaching and grasping movements longitudinally, seeing 23 infants every 3 weeks from their first week of life to 16 weeks of age. The pattern of reaching changed at around 7 weeks of age. The number of reaches decreased from the first to the seventh week and then increased substantially and at each successive test period. Hand movements during reaches also changed around the same age. At 7 weeks the percentage of reaches during which fists were clenched increased dramatically and then decreased at later ages. The babies were as likely to clench their fists when they were not looking at the stimulus object as they were when they were looking at it. After 7 weeks of age the percentage of reaches where the hand opened during the reach increased but only for those instances in which the infant looked at the stimulus. Hofsten argued on the

basis of these and other findings that reaching in the first 2 months is reflexive and that, after that time, through maturation, it becomes reorganized and governed by cortical mechanisms. This reorganization produces more adaptive reaching, that is, reaching that is more responsive to the environment.

This decrease in a newborn form of a response at 2-3 months of age followed by the development of a more mature form is like that found with other motoric reflexes (discussed earlier in this chapter). Also like them is what apparently happens when babies are given opportunities for practice: the neonatal components of reaching and touching do not drop out, but are practiced and form the components from which visually guided reaching develops (Bower, 1982; Bruner, 1973).

Another aspect of the development of reaching between 1 and 4 months that may reflect brain development are changes in the manner in which reaches occur. In the first weeks, reaching and grasping are limited mainly to **ipsilateral** reaching (reaching for an object with the hand that is on the same side as the object). Provine and Westerman (1979) charted the development of visually directed reaching that resulted in either grasping or touching in infants 9 to 20 weeks of age. At 9 weeks all infants touched objects on the ipsilateral side, one-third reached for objects at the midline, but none reached for objects on the **contralateral** side (the side opposite the hand that is reaching). This limits infants' ability to explore, particularly because they are less likely to reach with their left hands (Hofsten, 1982), which means that they are not likely to reach for things on their left side. Contralateral and midline reaching develop gradually so that by 20 weeks of age all infants contacted objects in all three positions (Provine & Westerman, 1979).

At about the same time that infants reach to all positions, they change their preferred reaching mode from a one-handed to a two-handed reach in the midline (White, Castle, & Held, 1964). This opens the door to the explosion of exploration that occurs at about 4 months. Now infants explore multiple aspects of objects in a single sequence that involves looking at, grasping, fingering, and mouthing. This does not, however, mark the final develop-

(a)

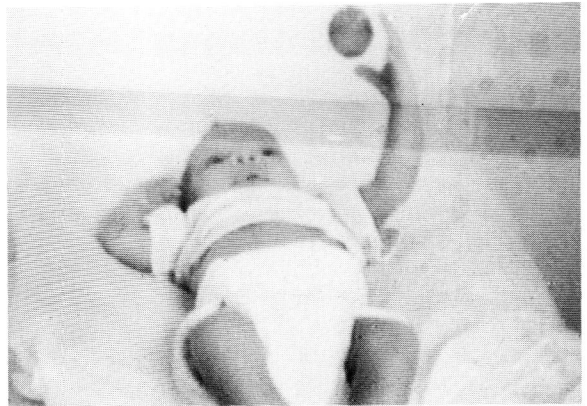

(b)

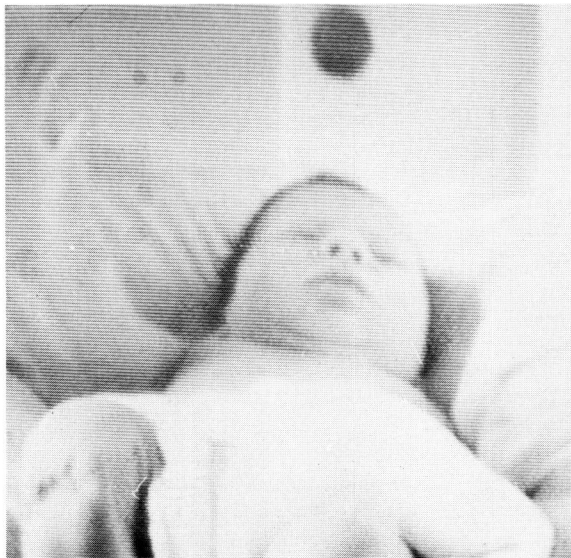

(c)

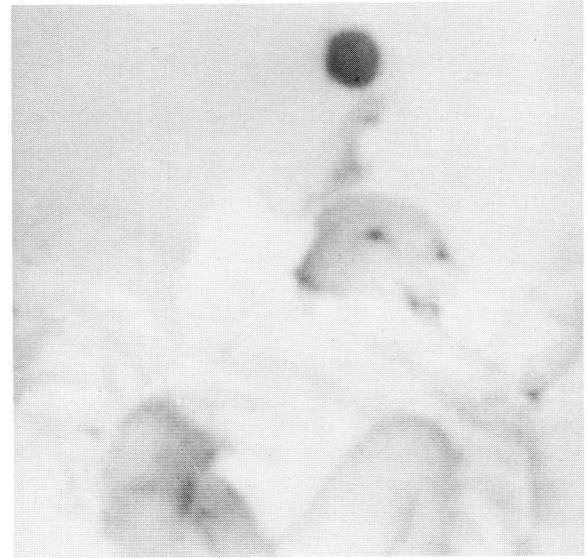

(d)

FIGURE 8–7. Four photographs of varying reaching responses of newborns, made from Ruff's videotaped records (hence their poor quality).
(a) The infant gazes at the object, but makes no attempt to reach.
(b) The infant successfully reaches and grasps the object.
(c) and (d) These infants are making arm and hand movements similar to those of the infant in part (b), but the ball is in the background and out of the infant's sight. This is a control condition. It demonstrates that movements that might be interpreted as reaching and grasping are part of the repertoire of spontaneous activities in newborns. (Photographs courtesy of Holly Ruff.)

ment of visually guided reaching. In more complex situations, such as when an object is held in one hand and another object is presented to the same side, 4- to 5-month-olds will not reach with the contralateral hand. Crossing the midline in this situation occurs several months later (Bruner, 1969, 1971). This achievement obviously further increases the exploratory capacity of babies.

The development of midline coordination and contralateral reaching apparently reflects important brain development. A preference for ipsilateral over contralateral reaching exists for young children, but normally drops out with age. Older handicapped children and adults with brain damage often show ipsilateral preference. Thus, the development of laterality in reaching might be an index of normal versus abnormal development.

Thus far in our discussion of the development of visually guided reaching we have not considered the mechanism by which visually initiated and visually guided reaching develops. Most experts in the field consider the neonatal visually initiated form to be automatic and biologically organized and therefore to require little experience to develop. For example, Bruner (1973) considers it a released action pattern in the ethological sense, which means that it is a response that needs only to be exposed to the appropriate environmental stimulus in order to emerge full blown. This position is supported by research on a similar visually triggered response (called placing) in kittens. Kittens need only to be exposed to unpatterned light to develop the response. If the kittens have been raised in the dark, only a very little experience in diffuse light will begin to trigger placing (Ganz, 1975).

The role of experience in the development of visually guided reaching is clearly much more extensive than it is in visually initiated reaching. Documentation of this can be found in the work of White and his colleagues (White, 1971; White & Held, 1966). They provided different forms of enrichment to orphanage babies who were moderately deprived of social and visual stimulation in an attempt to facilitate the development of their visually guided reaching. The dependent variable of concern to us was the age at which the infants developed visually guided reaching. The most effective

form of enrichment was two pacifiers ringed by two disks (one was patterned) attached to the side of the crib. In fact, it was more effective than a massive enrichment condition that included tactile stimulation from extra handling, improved mattresses that enabled easier movements, and a variety of visual stimuli that included a large, complex stabile, patterned crib sheets and bumpers, and removal of crib bumpers three times a day to enable babies to see the rest of the ward. Although less effective than the simpler enrichment, this program did accelerate development. The extra stimulation provided by adults who handled the infants for a longer time did not, by itself, facilitate development of visually guided reaching, though it did increase visual attentiveness. The effective enrichments were those that allowed the infant to reach and touch the stimuli, accidentally or otherwise, and to see both the stimuli and their hands simultaneously. Comparable research with animals has also indicated that experiencing visual feedback from reaching is necessary for the development of visually guided reaching (Hein & Diamond, 1971; Hein & Held, 1967; Walk & Bond, 1971).

We do not wish to give the impression that visually guided reaching must be laboriously taught or that parents must worry about providing the appropriate environmental stimulation. First, virtually all homes provide a stimulating environment. Second, the animal data indicate that recovery from even the most restrictive deprivation conditions occurs after very short periods of normal visual experience. No enrichment or special therapy was needed to overcome the deprivation-induced deficit (Hein, 1972). The human data are congruent, because White's (1971) orphanage infants, who were in a visually deprived environment compared to home-reared infants, did develop visually guided reaching within a reasonable time even if they received no enrichment. The importance of these studies is that they show the interrelation between experience and development. They show that coordinated sensorimotor experience is necessary for the development of visually guided reaching, in contrast to the visually initiated reaching in newborns.

Except for the research on the development of visually guided reaching, there has been little research on the development of fine motor development. This is unfortunate, in our opinion, because fine motor development appears to be related to later developmental outcomes to a much greater degree than is gross motor development. Even though fewer items on the Bayley scales assess fine motor development than gross motor development, 8-month performance on fine motor development items is more related to IQ at 4 years of age than is performance on the gross motor items or the Bayley Mental scales (Kangas, Butler, & Goffeney, 1966). Recent work by Kopp (1974) may provide a possible explanation for this relation. She studied infants who demonstrated the same level of development of grasp pattern and assigned them to coordinated or clumsy groups on the basis of five characteristics of their approach to objects, five characteristics of the grasp itself, and two aspects of extraneous motor activity. She found that coordinated babies explored more frequently and for longer periods of time. The way in which the two groups explored also was different. Clumsy infants spent about half their time in some type of visual exploration, whereas coordinated infants spent only one-third of their time this way, but more than half of their time in manipulation. Mouthing, an important form of exploration at 8 months was shown by 85% of coordinated infants but by only 40% of clumsy ones. Unfortunately, the clumsiness variable was confounded with prematurity. Of the 36 infants studied, 10 were preterm and they made up the bulk of the clumsy group (7 out of 12). Nevertheless, both groups of infants showed age-appropriate grasp patterns. Although the conclusions that can be drawn from this study are limited by the confounding variable, the findings are very provocative. They suggest that the reason fine motor development is related to later IQ is that it influences the quantity and quality of cognitive exploration.

DEVELOPMENTAL TESTING

We will discuss neonatal testing, which is done quite soon after birth, in some detail, and then examine testing done during infancy.

Neonatal Testing

NEUROLOGICAL TESTING

Pediatric neurologists have devised standard examination schedules for neurological functioning in the neonatal period. These batteries include tests of a variety of reflexes as well as some responses that are not clearly reflexive (for example muscle tonus). Some examples of reflexes are shown in Figure 8–8. Some reflexes disappear in short periods of time, others after longer periods of time, and some never. Pediatric neurologists have made careful catalogs of which reflexes should be present at which times in development. The absence of an expected reflex or the presence of one for longer than expected can indicate damage to the central nervous system. The presence or absence of reflexes must be determined with due consideration of the baby's state when the reflex is being tested for, a fact that has made pediatric neurologists very concerned with state and its assessment (as noted in Chapter 6). For example, the Moro reflex and elicited nystagmus have especially long histories of being useful in assessing infant neurological status (articles appeared in 1910, 1921, 1927, 1941, 1953, 1961). The Moro reflex is an infantile startle response in which an infant's arms spread wide in a curve and then slowly come together, while the legs are brought up in a similar fashion. It is typically elicited by a loud noise, by dropping the infant's head for a short distance, or by banging the side of the baby's bassinet or crib. Nystagmus, an oscillation of the eyeballs from one side to the other with a series of jerking movements by which the eye returns to the original side, is obtained by rotating the infant, and occurs after rotation ceases.

The best known test in the United States is that devised by Prechtl and his colleagues (Prechtl, 1977; Prechtl & Beintema, 1964; Prechtl & Dijkstra, 1960). This battery meets the criteria for good test development: (1) detailed, exact procedures for eliciting responses; (2) quantification of responses; (3) consideration of state of the infant (their definition of state was given in Chapter 6); (4) reliability of administration; and (5) standardization on a large sample that included 1500 infants. Prechtl and Beintema also developed a shorter version of their test for screening purposes. Other neurological examinations popular in

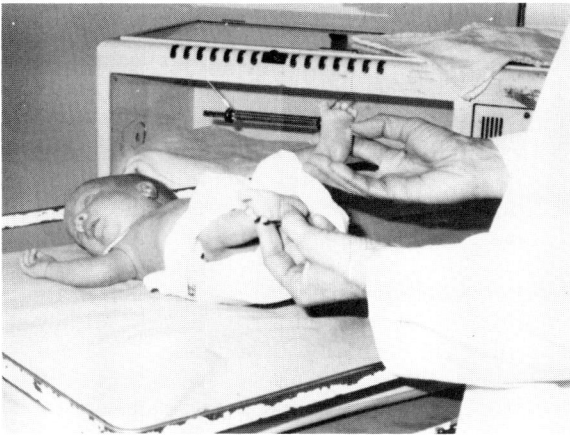

(a)

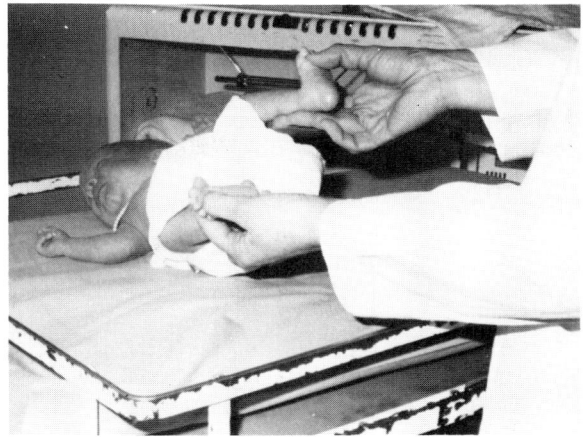

(b)

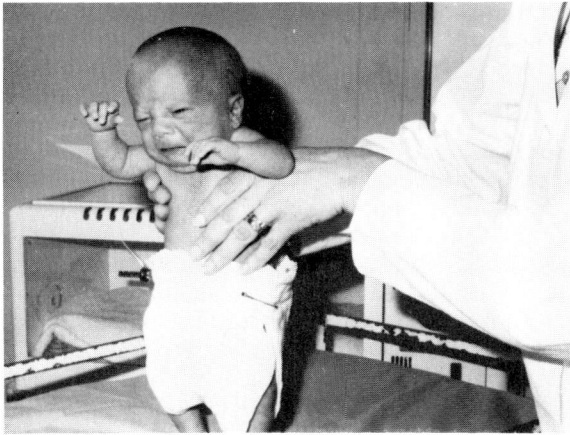

(c)

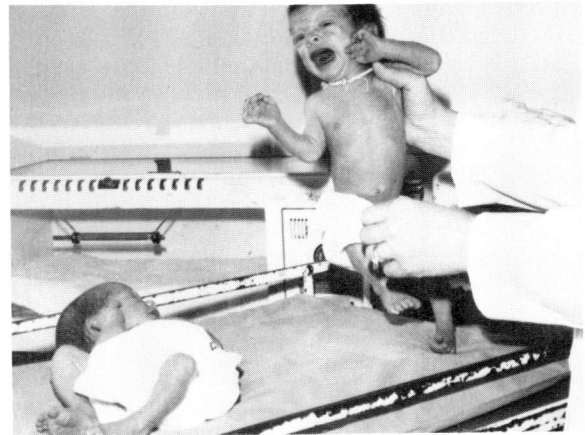

(d)

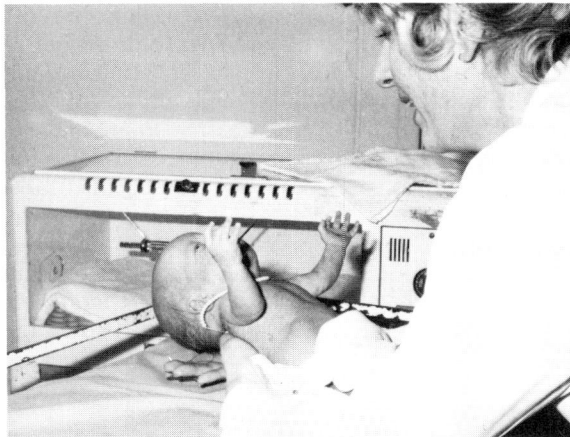

(e)

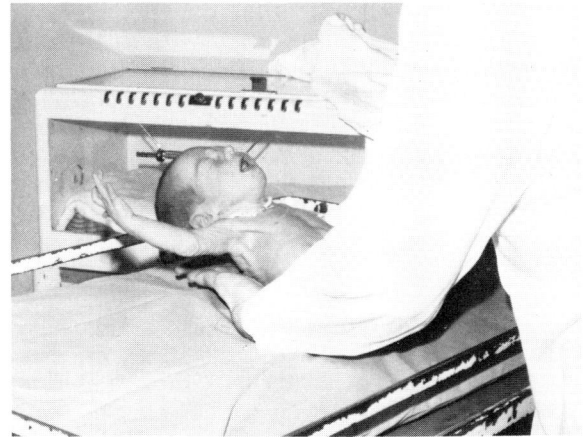

FIGURE 8–8. Some of the neonatal reflexes. (a) Babinski; (b) plantar; (c) weight support; (d) stepping; (e) Moro reflexes.

Europe are those of the French workers André-Thomas and Saint-Anne Dargassies (André-Thomas & S.-A. Dargassies, 1960; S.-A. Dargassies, 1972, 1977a, 1977b, 1983) and Amiel-Tison (1976, 1982), and the German, Peiper (1963). For a review of these European examinations, see Parmelee (1962) and Prechtl (1982). Parmelee himself (1974) has developed a neurological examination based on his and his colleagues' extensive work with premature, term, and at-risk babies.

RESEARCH USING NEUROLOGICAL TESTS

These tests were developed for the purpose of identifying neurological problems that might presage difficulties in later development. To determine whether they meet that goal, it is necessary first to assess whether they actually are related to neurological status. Prechtl has used his test to identify three patterns or syndromes in newborns. One is the apathy syndrome, found frequently in infants with a history of prenatal or perinatal complications. The second is the hyperexcitability syndrome, the most important aspect of which is tremor. Whereas apathy is associated with severe complications in the prenatal or perinatal period, hyperexcitability is associated with only moderate complications. The third syndrome, the hemisyndrome, is characterized by multiple lacks of symmetry between the left and right sides. It is associated with obstetrical complications, including forceps deliveries. Both hyperexcitability and the hemisyndrome are found more often in boys. Prechtl has also found that the thresholds (strength of the stimulus needed to elicit the response) of the Moro and elicited nystagmus reflexes were related to neurological status.

Whether Precthl's test will have long-term diagnostic significance is not yet clear. Performance on his test by high-risk infants predicted outcomes at between 2 and 4 years and at 8 years of age (Prechtl, 1965). Nevertheless, only one-fourth of the 285 infants showed stability of diagnostic categories for the entire period and one-fourth of the sample failed to show any stability. Other studies have failed to replicate the long-term findings (Prechtl, personal communication, 1972).

Saint-Anne Dargassies (1983) has also presented evidence that indicates that assessment of a newborn as neurologically abnormal does not mean that that baby will necessarily have long-term difficulties. She found that infants whose normal developmental functions had resumed by 15 days of age very gradually became normal. She also found that among prematures the degree of prematurity was more important to their later intellectual development (to age 10 years) than the amount of neonatal abnormality. In addition, prematures were more likely to suffer long-term intellectual impairment than were full-term babies who had neurological problems as newborns.

It is interesting to note that scores on Parmelee's examination have been shown to be related to visual fixation in term infants (Kopp, Sigman, Parmelee, & Jeffrey, 1975), but not in premature infants tested at 40 weeks of gestational age (Sigman, Kopp, Littman, & Parmelee, 1975; Sigman, Kopp, Parmelee, & Jeffrey, 1973). These findings again indicate that both nature and environmental factors influence these behaviors. That had also been indicated by the fact that (as was shown in Chapter 5) these behaviors were affected by drugs used during delivery.

Long-term predictability (or stability) may be difficult to show for reasons other than those imposed by the limitations of the particular test. If functioning is not sufficiently impaired to appear suspicious or abnormal on several different tests, it also may not seriously affect long range development. An example of this is seen in the work of Rubin and Balow (1980) relating IQ at 4 and 7 years and neurological abnormalities at age 7 to the number of tests in infancy on which the children had been classified as abnormal or suspect neurologically. As Table 8–6 shows, those who were classified as abnormal or suspect only once were not more likely to have low IQs at 4 or 7 years than those always diagnosed as normal. In sharp contrast, the relatively few children (22) who had been classified as neurologically abnormal or suspect on 2 or 3 of the infant testings were very likely to have low IQs at age 7 (14 times as likely as would be expected by chance). If neurological problems were seen at 2 or 3 periods of infancy, they were very likely to continue to be present at age 7 (about 64% were either neurologically abnormal or suspect). Nevertheless, note that even infants with strong evidence of neurological impair-

TABLE 8–6
Percentage of Infants with Negative Outcomes as a Function of Their Infant Neurological Functioning

	Number of tests on which abnormal or suspect		
	0	**1**	**2 or 3**
Number of cases	1066	156	22
Outcomes:			
IQ below 70 at 4 years	1.0	1.9	31.8
IQ below 70 at 7 years	0.7	1.3	21.1
Neurologically abnormal at 7 years	1.1	9.3	50.0[a]

[a] Another 13.6% were neurologically suspect.

ment (that is, on 2 or 3 tests) in the first year of life were not necessarily doomed to later deficit. Fewer than one third of them scored in the retarded IQ range and at least 35% of them showed no neurological problems at age 7. The fact that the percentage who had IQs below 70 declined between age 4 and age 7 is congruent with the data on recovery of function after anoxia that was discussed in Chapter 5 or recovery after prematurity that was discussed in Chapter 2.

Note, however, that Rubin and Balow (1979) were working with a population that could be considered as at relatively low risk: It was a white, middle class sample representative of an area with a relatively low neonatal death rate. Because the three risk groups differed on both birth weight and SES, these factors were controlled for in looking at the later outcomes. Thus, it is important to be aware that a sample from a less optimal environment (pre- and post-natally) might produce a higher proportion of infants who continued to show deficits into middle childhood or later.

We cannot attempt any comprehensive review of the efficacy of neurological tests in early infancy, but these examples give some background that should be useful as we consider the structure and effectiveness of the behavioral tests used to assess newborns. In general, neurological examinations in the newborn period seem to be useful in predicting long-term outcomes, but in very modest ways. It may be that they are of practical use only when the evidence for nontransient neurological abnormality is very strong (Prechtl, 1982). Even then, it does not mean that prediction

will work for the individual case or that all infants with such evidence of abnormality will have later deficits.

BEHAVIORAL TESTING

Several of the neurological examinations of newborns, long in existence, were formalized in the period subsequent to the 1950s when the current wave of research interest in newborns and young infants began. Behaviorally oriented examinations for newborns and young infants also were developed and standardized at that time. They owe more of a debt to the infant examinations developed earlier by Gesell and Bayley than to those developed by pediatric neurologists.

Graham Behavioral Test. The first behavioral examination was developed by Graham and her collaborators in the 1950s (Graham, 1956; Graham, Matarazzo, & Caldwell, 1956). She adapted items from Gesell's and Bayley's earlier scales, quantified them, and organized them into a battery called the Graham Behavior Test for Neonates. This provided a general maturation score, a visual following score, and a threshold of reaction to electrical or electrotactual stimulation. (The latter test finds the weakest amount of stimulation to the skin just below the knee that the baby will respond to.) It also provided a rating of irritability and of muscle tonus. Graham's test helped spawn two other neonatal batteries, the Graham/Rosenblith Behavioral Test for Neonates (G/R) and the Brazelton or Newborn Behavior Assessment Scale (NBAS).

Graham/Rosenblith Behavioral Test. Rosenblith spent almost two years studying the Graham tests in the early 1960s. She revised them to provide a score for muscle strength and coordination (the Motor score), a score for adaptive (or defensive) responses to stimulation of the nose and mouth areas (the Tactile-Adaptive or TA score), a score for reactions to sounds (rattle and bicycle bell),[8] and a score for visual following. The techniques and specific responses of newborns are illustrated in Figure 8–9. The ratings of muscle tonus uses a differ-

---

[8] All of these were part of Graham's general maturation score.

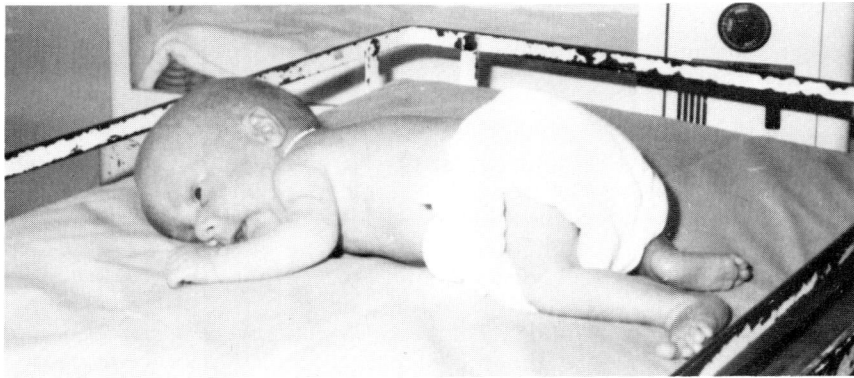

(a)

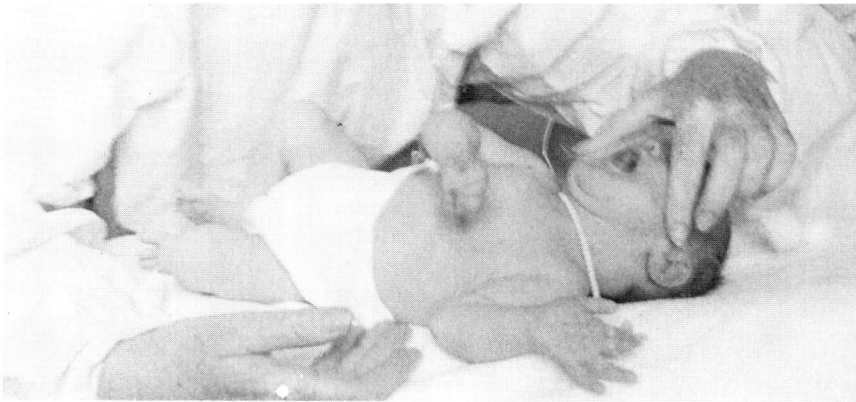

(b)

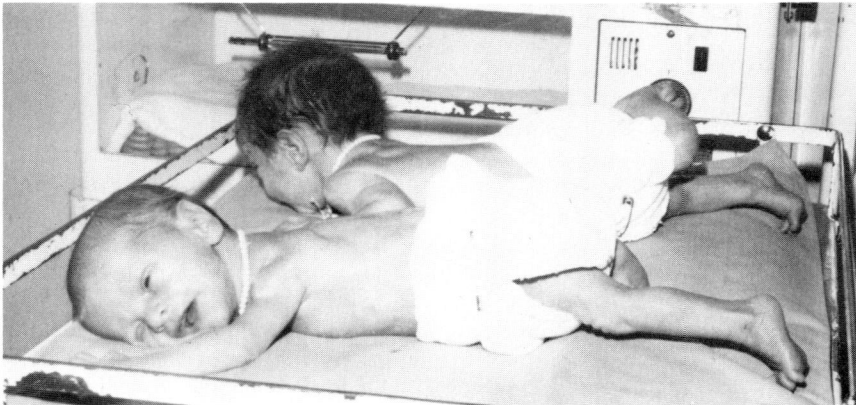

(c)

FIGURE 8–9. Items from the Graham/Rosenblith neonatal assessment. (a) Freeing nose after being placed flat on face; (b) responding to stimuli used to assess tactile–adaptive reactions; (c) muscle tonus assessment. In (c), twins are shown; the one on the right tends slightly toward hypertonicity.

ent system of quantification from that used by Graham. The Graham/Rosenblith (G/R) also has ratings of actual irritable behavior as well as of irritability.[9] Rosenblith excluded the pain or electo-tactual threshold, which required more elaborate instrumentation than was appropriate for a screening test (Rosenblith, 1961a, 1961b).

Brazelton or Newborn Behavior Assessment Scales (NBAS). This examination borrows from Prechtl (1974, 1977) as well as from Graham in that it has a section devoted to reflexes and is very concerned with the states of the infant. Its purpose is less neurological, however, because it is not primarily oriented towards detecting CNS immaturity or malfunction. Rather, it is oriented towards detecting behaviors that affect mother–infant interaction. It is designed for use with the normal newborn.[10] This test was used in several forms prior to its publication in a standardized form in 1973.

The NBAS considers state the single most important element and attempts to track "the pattern of state change over the course of the examination, its lability and its direction in response to external and internal stimuli" (Brazelton, 1973, p. 2). The variability in state is seen as indicative of infants' abilities for self-organization and hence as important for behavior. The babies' abilities to quiet themselves after experiencing aversive stimuli (as contrasted to needing external help to quiet)[11] is another aspect of self-organization measured by the NBAS. External procedures are used to calm infants only after a 15-second period during which the infants' self-calming is noted. Calming procedures are done in a set order: talking, hand on belly, restraint, holding, and rocking.

Response to animate or human stimuli (face, voice, cuddling) are compared with responses to inanimate auditory (rattle and bell) and visual (red ball and white light) stimuli and to what is described as temperature change associated with uncovering. Note that the latter always has tactile components as well. Habituation is assessed for three modalities: auditory, visual, and pain (light pin prick to heel of foot).

Although the G/R scored hand-to-mouth activity, trembling, startles, and general activity across the entire examination, these were not among the scores analyzed in relation to follow-up (though some of the information was used in scoring muscle tonus). On the NBAS these items have the same status as any other scored item. The reflexes are scored from 0 to 3 (not elicited, low, medium, high responses). All other scored items are scored on nine-point scales with behavioral definitions provided for each point. The differences between behaviors is very small for some items. We will not describe the examination in detail, but we would like to describe the cuddliness scale as an example. (This scale will also be important to a discussion of the NBAS in relation to neonatal–maternal interactions in Chapter 12.) The infant is held against the chest and shoulder of the examiner, who judges the extent to which the infant cuddles in response to the examiner's cuddle. The NBAS assumes that this response is a linear (straight line) dimension, ranging in nine equal steps from "very resistant to being held" to "extremely cuddly and clinging." The nine steps of the scale are listed in Table 8–7. Notice that the differences between 5, 6, and 7 are rather small. The decision to score all behaviors in the finalized NBAS on a nine-point scale made such small distinctions necessary.[12]

Different approaches to scoring are illustrated by comparing the scoring for defensive movements on the NBAS (Figure 8–10) and that for responses on the tactile–adaptive responses on the G/R. Table 8–8 describes the

[9]Irritability ratings attempt to exclude irritable behavior due to such reasonable causes as the baby being sleepy, hungry, or suffering from gas, from the examiner's judgment of irritability.
[10]Als, Brazelton, and their colleagues have recently developed an examination specifically for use with prematures (Als, Lester, Tronick, & Brazelton, 1982).
[11]Four manipulations are considered by Brazelton to be moderately aversive (uncovering, undressing, being pulled to sit, and being placed in prone position) and four are considered to be strongly aversive (elicitation of pain reflex, tonic neck reflexes, Moro reflexes, and of defensive reactions to cloth on the face).

[12]An alternative approach to scoring is to find the optimal number of steps needed to describe each behavior. It is interesting that the adaptation of the NBAS for use by mothers, called the Maternal Assessment of the Behaviors of her Infant (MABI) does all ratings on four-point scales. It has been shown to yield scores that are related to those obtained on the NBAS by experienced testers (Field, Dempsey, Hallock, & Shuman, 1978).

TABLE 8–7
Cuddliness

Score	Behavior
1	Resists being held; continuously pushes away, thrashes, or stiffens.
2	Resists being held most of time.
3	Doesn't resist, doesn't participate (passive; rag doll).
4	Eventually molds into arms after lots of nestling and cuddling efforts by examiner.
5	Usually molds and relaxes when first held, nestling into examiner's neck or crook of elbow. Turns toward body when held horizontally; seems to lean forward when held on examiner's shoulder.
6	Always molds initially, as above.
7	Always molds initially with nestling, and turns toward body, and leans forward.
8	Molds and relaxes. Nestles and turns head, leans forward on shoulder, fits feet into cavity of other arm. All of body participates.
9	All of 8, plus baby grasps examiner and clings.

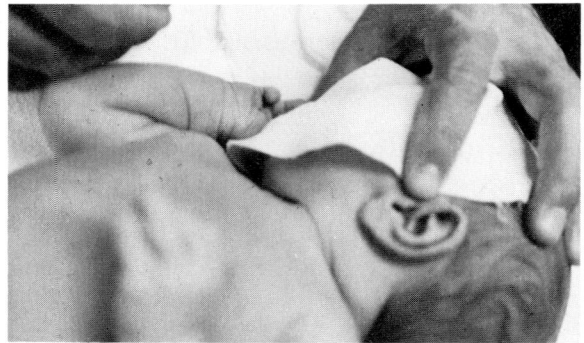

FIGURE 8–10. The stimulus situation for the defensive movement item on the NBAS. This can be contrasted with the similar tactile-adaptive item on the G/R shown in Figure 8-9(b). (Photograph courtesy of T.B. Brazelton.)

specific stimuli used in both scales and the methods of scoring. Note that the G/R has fewer and less specific categories that are more clearly ordered along the single dimension of effectiveness in getting rid of the stimulus.

Although the NBAS was not originally structured to yield a small number of scores, Brazelton's colleagues and he have devised an a priori group of clusters based on their conceptualizations of the organism. They assign the 26 nine-point scales and the whole group of reflex items to 1 of 4 dimensions, physiological, motoric, state, or interaction (Adamson, Als, Tronick, & Brazelton, 1975; Als, 1978; Als, Tronick, Lester, & Brazelton, 1977) and describe the baby as "worrisome," "normal," or "superior" on each. Despite their conceptual ideas about the importance of these clusters, they accept the probability that different studies with different specific goals may find different clusters useful.

Other workers using the NBAS have applied statistical techniques to arrive at factors. These analyses have yielded 5 to 10 factors, with considerable similarity in the various different studies (see, for example, Kaye, 1978;

Lasky et al., 1983; Mitchell, Abbs, & Barnard, 1977; Strauss & Rourke, 1978).

RELIABILITY OF NEONATAL TESTS

All of these tests attempt to describe a neonate's or young infant's developmental status or behaviors by a few scores or ratings and all have resisted the temptation to try to describe it with a single score such as the IQ or developmental quotient (DQ).[13] All have been shown to demonstrate satisfactory test characteristics. The interscorer agreement of two testers on the Graham and G/R has been shown to be satisfactory (Bench & Parker, 1970; Graham et al., 1956; Rosenblith & Lipsitt, 1959). The NBAS has been shown to be reliably scored by trained examiners (Horowitz & Brazelton, 1973; Brazelton & Tryphonopoulou (unpublished), as cited in Brazelton, 1973). Nevertheless, some work has shown that despite good interscorer reliability throughout a year of data collection, there are large effects due to different examiners (Mitchell, Abbs, & Barnard, 1977; Streissguth, personal communication, 1982; Streissguth & Barr, 1977). Equivalent data do not exist for the Graham or G/R. Nevertheless, these findings pose serious questions as to whether any neonatal examination should be considered as a standardized test in

---

[13] The DQ, used by Gesell, is analogous to the IQ in that it describes whether infants do more or less than expected at their age. Average for age is represented by 100. For a fuller description, see the next section.

TABLE 8–8
Defensive Response Items of the NBAS Compared to the Tactile–Adaptive Scale of the G/R

	NBAS Defensive movements	G/R Tactile–adaptive responses
Stimulus	Cloth over entire face	Cotton over nostrils, cellophane over nose and mouth
How held	Light pressure on upper part of face toward side of head, in front of ears with one finger but other fingers touching head	Firm pressure against nostrils and upper lip Firm pressure against side of face or head, in front of ears, one finger each side only
Length of application	1 minute or until a series of responses	20 seconds
Scoring categories	1 No response 2 General quieting 3 Nonspecific activity increase, long latency 4 Same as 3 but short latency 5 Rooting and lateral head turning 6 Neck stretching 7 Nondirected swipes of arms 8 Directed swipes of arms 9 Successful removal of cloth with swipes	0 No response 1 Any movement within 2 seconds 2 Specific movements of head or mouth, including rooting, neck stretching, head turning, back arching 3 Specific movements more than half of time (10 sec.) 4 Responses of head and mouth and coordinated arm movements all present, and one or more for more than 10 of the 20 seconds. An additional one-half point was given if the infant responded persistently across trials for all but 4 seconds of each stimulus period on one-half of the 6 trials; a full point was given if persistent response occurred on at least two-thirds of the stimulus presentations.[a]
Number of trials	Not specified	Three with each stimulus
Scoring	Best score	Best score based on sum for each stimulus Worst score based on sum for each

[a]In Rosenblith's revision (in progress) this is 2 or 1 points thus eliminating half-point scores.

the way in which tests given to older children or adults are.

Another characteristic that testers consider necessary in a good test is what is called **test–retest reliability.** That is, a person (here, a newborn) tested on two occasions should, in general, have similar scores. All testers of newborns know that the newborn is making profound adaptations to extrauterine life and hence is in an unstable condition. They have therefore sought to determine stability of scores over a period of days or weeks. While the stabilities found for the Graham and G/R have been only modest to moderate, they have been considered acceptable for newborns (Bench & Parker, 1970; Graham et al., 1956;

Rosenblith, 1961b). The NBAS has also been shown to have reasonable test–retest reliability (Horowitz et al., 1971; Horowitz et al., 1973; Lancione, Horowitz, & Sullivan, 1980). In an Israeli sample of babies whose mothers had received little or no medication, the reliabilities were higher (Horowitz et al., 1977).

Kaye (1978) repeatedly tested newborns with the NBAS. Some of his data seem to accent the expected instability of behavior in newborns. The point has been made that those critical of the reliability of the individual items on the NBAS from day to day (such as Horowitz, Sullivan, & Linn, 1978; Sameroff, Krafchuk, & Bakow, 1978) tend to ignore the stability over the entire item set for at least some individual infants (Linn & Horowitz, 1983). This occurs in testing older infants as well, where they "accidentally pass items" and fail others they have previously succeeded at in ways that balance out their total scores.

VALIDITY

Once it has been established that a test consistently measures a domain by one or more reliability measures, the next question is whether the test measures something important or stable (or both) about infant functioning. If it does, the test is said to have **validity.** The two classic types of validity are concurrent and predictive validity. To have **concurrent validity** a test measure must be significantly related to some other aspect of behavior (or medical status) measured at the same point in time. To have **predictive validity** a test should predict the same or related characteristics in the future. The lines between the two are not always sharp because what is considered to be either the same point in time or the future varies for different researchers and in relation to different research goals.

RELATION OF NEONATAL TEST PERFORMANCE TO INFANT VARIABLES

The Graham tests had been developed as part of a project to study newborns with anoxia. The researchers were interested in determining whether anoxic babies could be identified on the basis of their behaviors as well as on the basis of medical judgments or biochemical measures, or both. The Graham battery did differentiate babies who had had anoxia from those who hadn't (Graham et al., 1956). Different degrees of anoxia were related to different levels of performance on these scales. This means there was concurrent validity. The scores for babies with problems other than anoxia also differed from those of normal term babies. These tests can thus be seen as indicative of the functional integrity of the CNS. Rosenblith was not interested in the relation of neonatal tests to concurrent status, hence did not focus on relations to other neonatal measures.[14]

The NBAS was designed to assess neonatal characteristics that might be related to mother–infant interaction. Concurrent relations beween scores on the Kansas version of the NBAS (NBAS-K) and ratings of behaviors during mother–infant interaction during feedings have been studied recently (Linn & Horowitz, 1983). Healthy infants (28) were tested twice and observed twice during the first 5 days of life (always by different persons). Several NBAS-K summary scores were significantly related to infant state during the feeding interaction. These seemed to reflect different measures of the same type of behavior. This similarity based on similarities of behavior in the test and interaction situations does not always occur. Cuddliness on the NBAS-K was not at all related to cuddling during the mother–baby interaction. Several NBAS-K items were related to maternal behaviors that reflect her interaction with the baby. These were failing to interact and keeping the baby (bassinet) more than 3 feet from her. Both the best and average orientation scores were negatively related to these failures of the mothers to interact with their babies. In addition, the NBAS-K examiners' ratings of the reinforcing value of the baby during the exam were negatively related to these behaviors and positively related to the baby being in a positive alert state and looking at the mother during the interaction.

Linn and Horowitz also looked at whether babies whose scores were stable from one NBAS-K testing to another tended to elicit less responsiveness from the mother than those who were more variable. This hypothesis had been suggested by Emde (1978).[15] There was a significant tendency in this direction.

Another study of mothers interacting with their 51 newborn infants during feeding was done by Osofsky and Danzger (1974). Like the subjects in the Linn and Horowitz study, all were Black and of lower SES, and all mothers had fed their babies at least four times before the observation. There were a number of NBAS behavior measures that were related to the ratings of the newborn's behaviors in the feeding

---

[14] Both the G/R and the NBAS have been used to compare the neonatal behaviors of different ethnic groups. All of these studies are faced with such serious methodological questions of numbers studied, types of variables controlled for, and so forth, that they will not be considered here.

[15] The point is currently being made by some that the question of infant stability, rather than the traditional question of test stability or reliability, is more appropriate in infancy research.

interaction. The babies' state at the start of the NBAS, cuddliness, self-quieting, and hand-to-mouth activity during the NBAS were related to the largest number of infant behaviors during the mother–infant interaction (four or five each). The NBAS measures were related to behaviors such as predominant state, characteristic amount of eye contact, and auditory responsiveness during the feeding, characteristics that are, in fact, quite similar to those assessed by the NBAS itself.

A later and larger study (Osofsky, 1976) further examined the mother–infant interaction and the relation of NBAS scores to the infants' behaviors in other situations. The same procedures were used as before except that interactions during a semistructured situation as well as those during feeding were studied. One hundred thirty-four Black, lower SES mother–infant pairs were studied. Almost 60% of this sample were first-time mothers (primiparas). The semistructured situation was designed to approximate NBAS assessments. Again there were relations between infant behaviors on the NBAS and those during the feeding interaction and the maternal stimulation situations (patterned on NBAS procedures).

The magnitude of the relations, however, was somewhat smaller than that for the mother–infant feeding interaction of the first study. This seems surprising because the greater similarity between the NBAS test and maternal stimulation based on it might lead to an expectation of higher correlations. Although there were many significant correlations between infant and maternal behaviors in the structured interaction, they too tended to be low. Nevertheless there was similarity in the pattern of relations. Maternal sensitivity was related to infant responsiveness for four of the five stimuli presented by the mother.

Vaughn and his colleagues (Vaughn, Taraldson, Crichton, & Egeland, 1980) related the NBAS (both the 4 Als cluster scores and scores on 5 factors derived by factor analysis of the NBAS items) to variables assessed during mother–infant interactions at 3 and 6 months of age. Neither cluster scores nor factor scores were related to any of the 3 factors derived from 33 ratings of the feeding interaction at 3 months. Two of the feeding interaction factors reflected maternal behaviors and 1 reflected the babies' sociable behaviors. The same 3 factors occurred based on behaviors during feeding interactions at 6 months. Two of the Als a priori clusters of the NBAS, motoric processes and muscle tonus, did distinguish babies who were at the extremes in terms of social behavior during feeding and during play. Three of the 5 factor analytically derived NBAS scores (arousal, tonus, and quieting) discriminated the extreme group on the 6 month feeding factors. Hence for this population of 243 low SES mothers and their first-born babies, the aspects of their babies' behaviors assessed by the NBAS did not seem related to later maternal behaviors assessed during interaction with their babies during feeding or play. NBAS scores were related (significantly, but weakly) to the babies' later behaviors.

Ploof (1976), in a study primarily focused on maternal attitudes toward and perceptions of their infants, also examined mothers' perceptions in relation to their infants' performance on the NBAS scales. At birth the infants' characteristics as assessed by the NBAS did not relate to their mothers' perceptions of them except for alertness. This would seem reasonable in view of the lack of much contact between mothers and infants at that period. The newborn NBAS behaviors were related to the mothers' assessment of their babies' temperaments at 4 months of age. Although the size of the relations was generally not great, several correlations were substantial (r about .50, or 25% of the variance accounted for). Activity, alertness, ease of arousal, difficulty of habituation, and self-quieting were related to similar characteristics at 4 months, but they were related more to the mothers' perceptions of their 4-month-olds than to the latter's actual behaviors. These data could be taken as providing some support for the idea that the NBAS taps temperamental or personality characteristics of infants, at least as they are seen by their mothers.

It would be nice to draw some neat set of conclusions with respect to the question of whether the NBAS scores help to improve predictions of mother–infant interactions. Because the different studies we have cited have used different measures and measured different things at different times, and sometimes in different sorts of samples, this is not possible. In general it does appear that state and alertness and orientation variables are related to each other, whether they are assessed during the NBAS or during mother–infant interactions. Relations for other variables such as cuddliness to maternal responsiveness are contradictory. Much more data and longitudinal data are needed to be able to determine an answer to this question.

NEONATAL TESTS AS DEPENDENT VARIABLES

Neonatal tests are also used to provide a dependent measure of the effects of experimental treatment variables, and as outcome measures in correlational studies of the effects of pre- and perinatal factors. Although we know of no such use of the Graham test, we do know cases where the G/R has been used to assess the effects of stimulation programs of various types.

Neal (1968) used the G/R to assess the effects of a stimulation program in which small premature infants (1 lb 1 oz to 3 lb 9 oz) received a period of rocking in a hammock daily from the fifth day after birth until they reached 36 weeks gestational age. The experimental groups (tested by persons unaware of their treatment group) scored higher on motor strength and coordination, visual following, and some of the other specific items of the G/R. They also gained more weight.

Another study assessed the effect of patterned auditory stimulation (a tape recording of the mother's voice talking to her infant) on the development of 28- to 32-week gestational age prematures randomly assigned to experimental and control (routine care) groups. When assessed at 36 weeks by the G/R, the experimental group had higher general maturation, visual and auditory scores, and muscle tonus ratings, but did not differ in irritability. The tonus ratings differed according to the particular hospital the babies were in, so they are hard to interpret (Katz, 1970).

The use of the G/R and NBAS as dependent variables was encountered in Chapter 5 in the studies of the effects of maternal medications on babies. Some of the studies cited found differences in relation to medication and some did not. Even in studies that did find differences, the differences were often small, smaller even than the reliability of the scales. The Graham/Rosenblith has sometimes been

used in a similar way (Sostek, Brackbill, Broman, & Rosenblith, 1976) with similar results. The use of the NBAS as a dependent variable to assess the effects of maternal methadone addiction on infant behavior was covered in Chapter 4. We will not review those studies here, nor will we attempt to cover all such instances in this book.

LONG-TERM PREDICTIVE VALUE

To test long-term or predictive validity, Graham and her colleagues tested the infants they had studied as newborns again when they were 3½ years old (Graham, Ernhart, Thurston, & Craft, 1962). In general they found no relations between their newborn measures and various measures of intellectual, perceptual, and emotional functioning at age 3½. However, their analyses were all made within specific medical groups (normal, anoxic, other problems) and used statistical techniques (correlation coefficients) that obscure nonlinear relations, relations where one variables does not increase, or decrease, when the other does.

Rosenblith has shown that the tactile–adaptive (TA) score is related to outcomes at 8 months and at 4 and 7 years of age (Rosenblith, 1973, 1974, 1979a). This score is related to even more outcomes at 7 years than at 4 (Rosenblith, 1979b). It is related in a nonlinear fashion to a number of outcomes. For them, a medium score often has a better outcome than a high score, which in turn has a better outcome than a low score. The motor score is related to outcomes at 8 months and to a few at 7 years, but not to as many outcomes as are related to the TA score.[16] The TA score that is discussed here is based on the best of 3 responses to each stimulus, as discussed in the description of the tests. A low tactile–adaptive (LTA) score based on the poorest performances has been shown to be related to the occurrence of Sudden Infant Deaths (Anderson-Huntington & Rosenblith, 1971, 1976).

---

[16] The G/R is different from the original Graham test because Rosenblith decided, after a year of testing newborns with the Graham test, that Graham's General Maturation score encompassed two quite separate aspects of maturation as well as one aspect of sensory functioning. The score made by summing all the scores on the G/R, which is more analogous to Graham's General Maturation score, is not as related to outcomes at any age as are the more specific scores.

The muscle tonus rating is the most powerful predictor of development at 7 years. Indeed, it is the most powerful predictor of any aspect of the examination (Rosenblith & Anderson, 1968; Rosenblith, 1979a, 1979b). It is strongly related to a number of intellectual, perceptual, and behavioral outcomes for term infants. In addition, it is strongly related to reading achievement test scores at 7 years for premature babies. Pediatric neurologists have also been very interested in muscle tonus; however, none of them has identified (to our knowledge) the specific pattern of tonus that has the poorest outcomes. In this pattern, the arms are relatively flaccid or hypotonic and the legs are relatively hypertonic or tense. The usual pattern is that the arms are more tense than the legs and the difference in tonicity between arms and legs is smaller than in this "at risk" pattern.

Scores obtained on examinations done in the first two days of life generally tend to be more related to later outcomes than those obtained in days 3 or 4. This finding is contrary to what would be expected if behaviors in the immediate post-birth period reflected only the rapid adaptations being made. A possible interpretation is that responses during a period of stress can reflect problems in adaptation and these may be related to problems during later stressful adaptations (as, for example, the stresses of adapting to school at 7–8 years of age).

A surprising finding in the follow-up studies with the G/R is that although irritable behavior and ratings of irritability were generally not related to developmental outcomes at the earlier ages (8 months or 4 years), irritability was related to outcomes at 7 years for premature infants.

As was the case for neurological tests, although test scores and ratings were significantly related to later outcomes, they cannot be used to predict the outcome for an individual baby.[17] However, in the course of studying over 1500 newborns, one behavior that was incidental to the examination and that was observed in only a small number of cases, did predict the outcome for every case. All newborns are very sensitive to light compared to older infants and especially compared to children or adults. However, every newborn who was abnormally sensitive compared to other newborns showed later neurological abnormalities and intellectual retardation (Anderson & Rosenblith, 1964; Anderson-Huntington & Rosenblith, 1972; Rosenblith, Anderson, & Denhof, 1970).

In general, the NBAS was not designed to predict later developmental outcomes. Nevertheless, it has been used this way in some studies. For example, Tronick and Brazelton (1975) compared the predictive value of the NBAS to that of a standard neurological examination in a sample of infants that had been diagnosed as neurologically suspect or abnormal. They found that their diagnoses appeared to have greater long-range validity than the neurological tests given the suspect infants. This was true in the sense that babies identified by neurologists as suspect or abnormal and who later were found actually to be normal were less likely to have been called abnormal on the NBAS. These results utilized overall diagnoses based on two or more administrations of the NBAS.

There are also studies showing that the NBAS related to performance on the Bayley scales (described in the next section) at 6 weeks (Sostek & Anders, 1977) and at 8 months (Field et al., 1978). One summary type score (motoric process) derived either from the MABI or the NBAS is significantly related to the 8 month Bayley physical development scores in both normal and post-mature babies.

More recently, Vaughn and colleagues (1980) looked at relations between the NBAS and the Bayley scales, both mental and motor, as well as the Infant Behavior Record (IBR) at 9 months of age. The neonatal exams were done on day 7 for 243 infants and again on day 10 for most of them. The infants were all first babies, of low SES, and predominately white. Testing was done in the home, which resulted in less well-standardized test conditions. The babies' best performances were used to score the Als a priori cluster. A factor analysis that yielded five factors was also performed on both sets of scores. The factors were similar to those found by others (for example, Sameroff et al., 1978). Three of these five factors were significantly

---

[17] These statements are based on analyses of specific scores and ratings of neonatal test behaviors. The latter have not been combined into risk indices or used to provide a global diagnosis.

correlated with the Bayley mental scales, but the largest r was .19 (less than 4% of variance accounted for). None of the factors was significantly correlated with the motor scores on the Bayley, a finding replicated by Sostek and Anders (1977). A rating of "worrisome" on the a priori dimensions of motor processes and state control was related to significantly lower mental scores than a rating of average or optimal. Sostek and Anders (1977) had also found state control to be related to 10-week Bayley mental scores. The worrisome group (Vaughn et al., 1980) scored at or above the norm (IQs 99 to 118), however.

These are the same babies whose maternal interaction data at 3 and 6 months will be reported in that section in Chapter 12. Vaughn and colleagues called attention to the fact that the later the follow-up assessment, the greater the number of significant relations. However, that relation is confounded with the types of behaviors measured at the different ages. Vaughn and colleagues (1980) conclude: "It is our conclusion that individual differences assessed shortly after birth, using the NBAS, do account for a modest but significant proportion of the variance of infant behavior assessed later in the first year of life" (p. 63). They suggest that infants in the worrisome clusters on the first 3 Als dimensions are at greater risk (domain still unspecified). The authors caution that these results are limited by the nature of the sample (young, uneducated, often unmarried, and poor). All 157 infants born from January, 1971, to February 28, 1973, in 4 villages in rural Guatemala were assessed using an earlier version of the NBAS (the NAS) as part of a larger study (Lasky, Klein, Yarbrough, & Kallio, 1981). They were assessed on a battery of tests at 6, 15, and 24 months, and at 3 and 4 years of age. The researchers reported (Lasky, Klein, Yarbrough, & Kallio, 1981), "The correlations between the NBAS variables and all later assessments of intellectual performance were generally nonsignificant (only 13 of the 294 correlations were significant at the .05 level with no pattern evident)" (p. 851). It had previously been shown (Brazelton, Tronick, Lechtig, & Lasky, 1977) that the NBAS variables did have concurrent validity because they did correlate with birth weight and other indices of risk in this population. It was also shown (Lasky, Klein, Yarbrough, Engle, et al., 1981)

that neonatal length and weight were significantly related to behavioral development in this population, although the NBAS was not. In a middle class but highly varied sample of infants in the United States, a sample that included premature (in intensive care) and term infants (healthy and hospitalized because of the illness of their mothers), even less evidence of predictive value of the NBAS for later IQ was found. Neither obstetric nor postnatal complications, nor the NBAS, nor a combination of these, predicted IQ at age 3 (Reich, Holmes, Slaymaker, Lauesen, & Gyurke, 1984).

Infant Testing

We will now turn to the infant tests that had been developed before the neonatal tests and to which the latter owed a great debt. The infant tests, in turn, were an outgrowth of the testing movement that had started with school-age children. To understand the infant tests, then, a brief overview of the school-age testing is necessary. At the beginning of this century, Binet and Simon (1905) developed tests to screen children to determine who could profit from schooling. Terman and Merrill (1937, 1960) adapted these tests for use in the United States. They were both at Stanford University at the time and their adaptation became known as the Stanford Binet Test. Terman, like Gesell, was a student of G. Stanley Hall, whom many regard as the first American developmental psychologist.

Tests for school-age children (the Binet-Simon and a number of subsequent ones) examined a wide variety of behaviors, all thought to indicate intelligence. They were designed to sample all intellectual functions through "the sinking of shafts at critical points" (Terman & Merrill, 1937, p. 4). In fact, the variety of behaviors is strongly biased toward verbal behaviors. These tests of intellectual function arrived at a single score that summarized the child's status. At first this status was expressed as a mental age (MA), which was the age at which the average child performed as well as the child being tested. For example, if Samantha passed as many test items as the average 8-year-old, she would be given an MA of 8 years (regardless of her chronological age).

The MA allows comparisons of children's mental functioning and permits actions based on functioning. For example, all children functioning at an MA of 8 years can be put into the same classroom, thereby creating a presumably homogeneous group to teach. The functioning of 2 individuals can also be compared. For example, if Samantha has an MA of 8 and Julia an MA of 6, Samantha is functioning at a higher level than Julia. If Samantha and Julia are of the same chronological age (say 6 years), then we can say that Samantha is brighter. If, however, Samantha is much older (or younger) than Julia, then such comparison becomes more difficult and MA does not tell which is brighter. To solve this problem, the intelligence quotient (IQ) was developed early in the history of intelligence testing (Kuhlman, 1912; Stern, 1914/1924). It compares MA to chronological age (CA) and provides a measure of intellectual functioning that is independent of age; that is, that permits comparisons of the brightness or so-called intelligence of children of different ages. In the original IQ measure, MA was divided by CA and the product multiplied by 100. If Samantha were 10, her IQ would be $(8/10) \times 100 = 80$. If Julia were 4, her IQ would be $(6/4) \times 100 = 133$. Thus, although Samantha is functioning at a higher level than Julia, Julia is brighter; Julia is functioning ahead of her years and Samantha is functioning behind hers.

More recently the formula for the IQ has been changed to reflect better the statistical nature of the distribution of scores.[18] For tests scored the new way (such as the various Wechsler tests) and for the Binet tests it is substantially correct to say that the average IQ is between 85 and 115 (or the mean of 100 plus or minus one standard deviation). This means that about 68% of persons tested will have IQs in the average range.

The infant and preschool testing movement grew out of both the school-age testing movement and out of the enthusiasm for the

study of growth and development that characterized the 1930s and led to longitudinal studies of physical and psychological development. In contrast with the tests for school-age children, infant and preschool tests cannot be primarily verbal; indeed, tests in early infancy can only examine sensory, perceptual, and motor development and their linkages, and social interactions. They can include more symbolic material after one year.

We will describe briefly some of the infant tests that have been used extensively in both research and practical settings. Then we will describe the Bayley test in detail, because it is probably the most widely used test in infant research in the United States.

GESELL

First we will consider one of the key figures in understanding the sequencing of development and in the development of infant tests, Arnold Gesell. He has been largely neglected by psychologists in recent years. At first this neglect was probably triggered by many of the same factors that led child psychologists in the United States to neglect the work of Piaget (see Chapter 10). Gesell's work was criticized for lack of rigor and control. However, the data on the developmental sequences of responses to certain stimulus situations that he and his colleagues produced have withstood the test of time. The theories he derived from his data, especially with respect to continuity of development and the biological nature of the growth spiral, are more subject to criticism. For a single source that gives his own presentation of his views and work at a relatively late stage in his life, see Gesell (1954).

Gesell was also a pioneer in the use of the moving picture camera to study infant behavior. The film provides a record that others can study to determine whether they see the same sequences or not. Gesell used motion pictures (which had only recently become available) because, he said (1934), "The wealth and complexity of infant behavior are beyond human description" (p. 20). Movies supplemented by other forms of investigation and inventory are needed to chart such behavioral complexity systematically.

The Sunday supplements of the mid-1930s not only published articles and reviews of Gesell's books, but pages and pages of his pic-

---

[18] The resulting IQ scores can be interpreted in the same way as the original formula, and with greater confidence. Such scores take account of several flaws in the Binet IQs that derived from the facts that the range of scores around the 100 that represented normal varied at different ages tested and that standard deviations were different at different ages.

tures. After his initial scientific books, he and his colleagues wrote books designed specifically for parents and child workers (a pattern followed earlier by Preyer, see Chapter 1). Many generations of American children (at least from upper educational levels) were raised by parents who used Gesell norms to see whether their baby was behaving appropriately (normally) or was farther ahead of the norms than their friends' babies.

After a 1919 study charting behavior from birth to age six, Gesell (1925) codified his developmental schedule and in 1926 started a normative study using movies. Unlike intelligence testers, he did not try to represent the population as a whole in a standardization sample. Rather, he attempted to represent the "most normal" by choosing only full-term infants born after normal pregnancies and from what he considered to be a "homogeneous middle class population." This population was both considerably varied and rather different from current perceptions of the middle class. For example, sound sources in the home included radios (62% of homes), victrolas (old version of record player, in 40%), and pianos (19%). Only 35% had a car but 52% sent their laundry out.

Detailed observations, including some physiological measures, and extensive movies and history taking took a full half day.[19] Because mothers were asked to choose an optimal time of day and as a result of Gesell's remarkable skill, only 1 out of 524 examinations of the 107 infants studied had to be continued to another day.

The first form of his examination used 7 groups of behaviors to describe the infant. This was later reduced to 4 major groupings of behaviors: motor, adaptive, language, and personal–social. Maternal reports were largely used for the latter two areas. The Gesell test can be used with separate evaluations for each of the 4 areas of performance[20], or those scores can be combined into one and a developmental quotient (DQ) obtained. The latter was to provide an infant evaluation analogous to that of the IQ. Numerically, it works like the IQ. The average score is 100 and 68% of all babies score between 85 and 115. The DQ is, however, psychologically quite different from the IQ. Many of the behaviors that go into the DQ score are decidedly nonintellectual; postural and locomotor behaviors (discussed in the earlier section on motor development) are perhaps the best examples. The DQ and comparable scores on other infant tests are not, in fact, highly related to IQ scores; that is, babies who have relatively high or low DQs may or may not have similarly high or low IQs. Gesell's belief that the DQ and the IQ were highly related is one reason that psychologists have ignored his work in recent decades. Nevertheless, with the exception of quick screening tests such as the Denver Developmental Screening Test (Frankenburg, Camp, & VanNatta, 1971; Frankenburg & Dodds, 1967; Frankenburg, Goldstein, & Camp (1971), the Gesell has been, and probably continues to be, the infant examination most used by pediatricians. A relatively recent revision has been issued (Knoblock & Pasamanik, 1975).

OTHER EARLY TESTS

Another early test, by Bühler & Hetzer (1935), included items that assessed phenomena that have not been used in other standardized infant tests until recently when Uzgiris and Hunt (1975a, 1975b) developed tests based on Piaget's research. A good example is an ingenious item that could be said (in current terms) to assess memory or cognitive processing or object constancy, but that can also be well described as a form of delayed reaction test. The infant was given a rubber ball out of which a chicken pops when the ball is squeezed. After playing with this toy for 1 minute, the infant is engaged by the examiner in other activities from 1 to 15 or 20 minutes. The infant is then given a ball that looks and feels just like the first one, but nothing pops out when it is squeezed. Expressions of astonishment, questioning looks at the tester, and exploration of the hole from which the chicken "should have popped" are scored as passing the item. At 10 or 11 months of age this item can be passed after a 1-minute interval and at 15 to 16 months children usually pass after a delay of 8 minutes. Delays of 15 minutes are tolerated

---

[19] The stenographic reports dictated during the examinations occupy 5,504 pages!
[20] Some IQ tests for older children now have more subscales. For example, the Wechsler Intelligence Scale for Children has two major sections, verbal and performance, and each of those has several subscales.

at 19 to 20 months, and 17 minutes at 21 to 24 months.

Other early infant tests included the following:

1. Mental measurement of Preschool Children by Stutsman (1931).
2. Bayley scales, 1933.
3. Measurement of Intelligence in Infants and Young Children, by Cattell (1940). This test attempts to achieve an infant format more like that of the Stanford-Binet. The age range is 2 to 30 months. It is still used, but has never been properly standardized. It does have the advantage of being relatively short and interesting to infants.

Infant tests developed and primarily used in other countries (that are cited in the literature in the United States) include:

1. The Abilities of Babies, developed by Griffiths in England (1954). It has 5 subtests: locomotor, personal–social, hearing and speech, hand–eye functions, and performance. It uses a motor and mental DQ. The performance scale is interesting in that it attempts to assess the infant's readiness and ingenuity over a variety of test situations. Like most infant tests it borrows heavily from the Gesell. Unlike Gesell, Griffiths not only did not feel that her test should predict later IQ, but she did not understand why psychologists should expect this to be the case.
2. Brunet–Lézine Test. This French test (Brunet & Lézine, 1951) follows the Gesell scheme of dividing items into 4 categories, as well as the Binet–Simon (Cattell) scheme of having set numbers of items at each age level. It also asks a set number of questions of the mother (caretaker) at each age level. Scoring is based on both the test items passed and the mother's reports. The test is widely used in Europe.

THE BAYLEY SCALES

Now we will take up the test that is most widely used in the United States today and consider it in greater detail. This test was developed by Bayley in connection with the Berkeley Growth Study, which she helped initiate in the late 1920s. It was one of several longitudinal studies of development. The test was originally called the California First-Year Mental Scale (Bayley, 1933a), but was extended to cover ages from 1 to 30 months. It had originally been standardized on a sample from the Berkeley–Oakland area that was not chosen to be representative and that later turned out to have average IQs of 120. This sample of 61 infants was tested monthly from 1 to 15 months, and at least 46 subjects were tested at each age level.[21] The Bayley scales received a new standardization in the 1960s. The 1969 revision (Bayley, 1969) was standardized on a stratified sample of 1262 infants. It includes both new items and changes in the order of items. Its current norms are quite representative of babies in the United States. The normative samples were cross-sectional, which is probably a good thing. The Gesell, Cattell, and original Bayley tests all tested the same babies every few weeks or months, so the babies were highly practiced. The examiners were also the same and thus might remember and have expectations of the babies that could well affect both their perceptions of the infants' future behaviors and even the infants' actual behaviors (based on examiner interactions with them). On the Hunt–Uzgiris scales, infants tested longitudinally, compared to those the same age but tested in a cross-sectional design, were advanced 2 to 3 steps in an 8-step sequence (Jackson, Campos, & Fischer, 1978).

The current form of the test has a Mental scale, a Motor scale, and an Infant Behavior Profile based on the examiners' observations during administration of the scales. The Motor scale is scored separately from the Mental scale, and has been described in our earlier section on motor development. The procedure used for the Mental scale attempts to elicit the following adaptive responses: attending to stimuli (visual and auditory), manipulation (grasping, manipulating, combining objects, shaking a rattle, and ringing a bell), interaction with the examiner (smiling, cooing, babbling, imitation, following directions), relating to toys in meaningful ways (putting cubes in a cup, banging spoons together), showing memory or awareness of object constancy (looking for a fallen object, uncovering a hidden toy, search-

---

[21] This is in contrast to Cattell's sample, which was studied less frequently and sometimes had only 20 subjects at a given age.

ing for a hidden toy in a small box), goal-directed tasks requiring perseverance (putting pegs in a peg board, forms in a form board), and ability to follow a complex set of directions that demand knowledge of object names and the meaning of prepositions as well as the concept of "one."

The number of items passed on each scale is converted to either a Mental Development Index (MDI) or a Psychomotor Development Index (PDI), based on the standardization sample. At the end of each complete examination the examiner fills out a series of ratings called an Infant Behavior Record (IBR). The usefulness of these ratings seems to depend more on the individual examiners (or teams of examiners) than do the MDI or the PDI (Bayley, personal communication). Although the Bayley is really two tests, the MDI and the PDI, it does not have a large variety of subscores as the Gesell does, even though the Gesell is often reported by the single DQ score.

Many of the studies reported in this book make use of this test, largely because it has the best standardization, but partly because it covers the ages for which much infancy work is done, and partly in the desire to make new research results comparable with those already published using this test. In addition, its use with about 50,000 8-month-olds during a national collaborative project investigating pre- and perinatal factors in development means that there are many trained testers in various parts of the United States.

ORDINAL SCALES

Other developments in infant testing include an emphasis on what are called **ordinal** scales. Test items that form an ordinal scale must show a progression in difficulty. An infant who can pass the third item should be able to pass the first two. One who passes the fifth item should have passed the first four. In terms of age, the infant should pass the first item at an earlier age than any of the later items.

There are two examples of tests based on ordinal scales. One (Kohen-Raz, 1967) is based on 67 of the 163 items on the Bayley test. These items formed five ordinal scales: eye–hand, manipulation, object relation, imitation–comprehension, and vocalization–social contact–active vocabulary. These scales

worked equally well (that is, they were equally ordinal) in the three subpopulations studied by Kohen-Raz; hence it is reasonable to assume that the ordinal character of the scales may be generalized to other populations. It was his hope that such ordinal scales would be more effective in predicting later outcomes than the more global measures of the Bayley. We shall return to this question later.

The second example of ordinal scales in infant testing are those developed by Uzgiris and Hunt (1975a, 1975b). They are the only tests that started with a theory (that of Jean Piaget, see Chapter 10). All others are **empirically based**; that is, their items were selected purely on the basis that they discriminated between what older and younger infants (or children) can do. Because Piaget's theory says that the order of achieving skills is always the same, the tests take the form of ordinal scales. The potential advantage of a theory-based test is that it may select behaviors that are more relevant to intellectual development, and hence could predict later intellectual behaviors better. The possible disadvantage is that the test will only be as good as the theory. Theories may lead a test constructor either to omit aspects of behavior that do not fit the theory or to include items that fit but are in fact not important.

RELIABILITY

The questions that we addressed in connection with neonatal tests can also be asked about the reliability of infant tests and their uses. Indeed, a book could be written on the answers to these questions. We shall take a very brief look at them. Two reviews that address these issues for infant tests generally are those by Thomas (1970) and St. Clair (1978). The latter is historical, as is ours to a limited degree.

The reliability of the Bayley tests of mental and motor abilities was assessed by her in her original work (Bayley, 1933a, 1933b, 1935). In addition, in connection with the large-scale national collaborative project already referred to, this question was again addressed on a rather large scale (Werner & Bayley, 1966). Agreement in scoring between well-trained testers and observers was high, indicating good reliability of this type. In addition, 8-month-old infants who were retested after a week's time tested very similarly. When these results were broken down according to the individual items on the tests, they showed that items from the mental scales that had relatively poor reliabilities were the ones involving social interactions, but even for these items the reliabilities were relatively high compared with neonatal tests. For the motor scale items the poorest reliabilities were for items involving assistance from an adult.

DIAGNOSTIC VALUE

As is the case for neonatal tests, infant tests are also used as diagnostic aids or as predictors of later development. This was an important aim of Gesell. Because infants were either tested by persons who knew their histories or tested repeatedly by the same person in much of his work, people came to mistrust his findings or at least his strong opinions about the very great predictive value of his tests. Other infant testers such as Griffiths and Uzgiris and Hunt have not expected test scores to be predictive. Both Cattell (1940) and Bayley (1955) considered predictability an empirical question to be answered from their longitudinal studies. Both concluded that variability was marked and that the test should not be relied on for long-range prediction. Indeed, even at 2 years of age the Bayley results from the Berkeley Growth and Berkeley Guidance studies showed that there were very low correlations (about .30) with IQ at 8 years. Data based on a Stockholm study using the Brunet–Lézine tests are similar (cited in Honzik, 1976). The closer together in time the tests are given (years, not weeks), and the older the child, the closer the correlation between an earlier and a later assessment (Bayley, 1955; Honzik, 1976), but even at 5 years of age IQ tests did not correlate with 8 year IQ tests more than .70.

Other studies showed greater predictive value for the infant tests. These studies included larger proportions of damaged or handicapped infants and children or predicted for the retarded portions of their samples (Broman & Nichols, 1975; Honzik, 1962; Illingworth, 1960; Knoblock & Pasamanick, 1960; MacRae, 1955; Reich et al., 1984). Drillien (1961) directly demonstrated that developmental tests, especially in prematures, do a very good job of predicting mental dullness. Of 16 children found unsuitable for ordinary school education at 5 years (IQ less than 70), 12 had performed at this level at 6 months and at all ages up to 5 years. Not a child in this group had scored higher than very dull on any test at any age. Even among the 16 children whose IQs were borderline (70–79) at 5 years, 12 had performed at this level or lower from 6 months on. Werner and colleagues (Werner, Bierman, & French, 1971; Werner, Honzik, & Smith, 1968) have shown that Hawaiian infants with Cattell IQs below 80 at 20 months are very likely to have low IQs at age 10.

Another support for the predictive usefulness of infant tests comes from tests of muscular–motoric development. Although there is little in common between what would be called intelligence in infancy and what would be called intelligence in later childhood, there may be some infant behaviors that are indicators of general biological or maturational functioning. (Recall our discussion of muscle tonus in relation to neonatal testing, for example.) Kangas and colleagues (1966) rescaled the Bayley into three scales: mental, fine motor, and gross motor. They found that the 8-month performance on the fine motor scale had by far the highest correlation to 4-year Stanford-Binet IQ scores. In fact, the fine motor scale alone correlated as well as the fine motor combined with the mental scales.

One study looked directly at the question of which of several infant tests provides the greatest predictive validity. Siegel (1981) administered both the Bayley and the Uziris–Hunt scales to 148 infants, 80 of whom were preterm (less than 1501 grams). The preterm infants were matched with the full-term ones on SES, parity, sex, and maternal age. The 10 preterm and 1 full-term infant that were discovered to have serious disabilities (cerebral palsy, blindness, severe developmental delay) were excluded. The scales were administered at 4, 8, 12, and 18 months. The Bayley was scored both traditionally and by the Kohen-Raz ordinal scaling referred to earlier.

At 24 months the infants were tested again and had a standardized test of language expression and comprehension (the Reynall). These constituted the criterion measures to be predicted. All of the testing was done blind by testers who had no knowledge of the infants' prenatal history or performance on previous tests.

In this varied sample, the Bayley Mental and Motor indices showed impressive stability. Both were related to language comprehension and expression at 2 years. The Kohen-Raz scoring shows that different scales are related to the Bayley Motor and Mental indices depending on which of the earlier test ages are examined. It is impressive to note that the eye–hand coordination and manipulation scale at 4 months is about as much related to the 2 year indices as the Bayley at 18 months is. By 8 months his conceptual ability scale is also related to the 2 year measures and is more strongly related than any other scale. By 12 months all five of Kohen-Raz's ordinal scales are related to the 2 year Bayley outcomes and account for 15–36% of the variance. The pattern is similar when the language scores are used as the criteria.

The Uzgiris–Hunt scales also show impressive relations from 4 months to 2 years, except for the gestural imitation scale (which assesses a skill that is poorly developed at 4 months). In general, the 8-month Uzgiris–Hunt scales were not more correlated with the 2-year motor and mental indices than the 4-month results were (except for gestural imitation). At later ages the Uzgiris-Hunt scales do not become more predictive, a fact that might be attributed to an insufficient range at the older ages. Again, a similar pattern holds when the language scores are the criteria. It is interesting to note that the vocal imitation scale from the Uzgiris–Hunt is not related to either language expression or comprehension.

Considering all of Siegel's data (that described here as well as some that is not), we can conclude that which tests will predict better depends on the age at testing, and, to a lesser degree, on whether the goal is to predict Bayley performance or language scores. The Kohen-Raz scaling of the Bayley does seem to have achieved some of the better prediction he was hoping for. The results for the Uzgiris–Hunt seem to indicate that they were correct not to expect long-term prediction.

The diagnostic worth of infant tests is not limited to their predictive power. Illingworth (1960) showed their effectiveness in assessing the effects of various damaging conditions such as anoxia, head damage, and viral diseases capable of affecting the brain. Honzik (1962, 1976) has shown that infants diagnosed as having neurological problems are well differentiated from controls at 8 months of age on both the mental and the motor scales of the Bayley. Suspect infants were less well identified, but did differ from controls. The Cattell has also been shown to be a useful supplement to pediatric diagnosis at 20 months (Bierman, Connor, Vaage, & Honzik, 1964; Werner et al., 1968; Werner et al., 1971).

We have not mentioned the rather widely used Denver Developmental Test because information on its diagnostic efficiency is rather mixed. Early reports indicated that it did rather well, but more recent evidence indicates that it may not be so useful (Solomons & Solomons, 1975; Wacker, 1980).

INFANT TESTS AS DEPENDENT VARIABLES

In our examination of the usefulness of neonatal tests we looked at their use as a dependent variable to measure the effects of some other factor such as obstetric medication or anoxia. To some extent the work of Illingworth (1960) and Honzik (1976) discussed above follows this model. Infant tests are also used to assess the effects of such variables as malnutrition, institutional life, maternal deprivation, various aspects of parent–child interaction, and aspects of the nature of the home (such as the stimulating factors in it). Siegel's study (1981) that assessed the comparative value of infant tests also in effect used the infant test at 2 years to look at the effects of various home and maternal factors as measured by the Caldwell Inventory of Home Stimulation (HOME) at 12 months. Siegel found that maternal responsiveness, avoidance of restriction or punishment, and organization of the environment at 12 months were not related to the 2-year outcomes. The provision of stimulation and its variety were related. To a lesser degree maternal involvement was related to performance on the test but not to the infant's language expression. Indeed, a total score based on all aspects of the HOME inventory was not as highly related to performance as was the single subscale provision of play materials.

DISCUSSION ISSUES

Research Issues

The four major criteria to consider in evaluating a test are reliability, validity, sampling, and test bias.

Reliability in its most general sense refers to consistent, accurate measurement. All good scientists have to spend a great deal of their time eliminating or reducing errors in their measurement techniques so that the techniques will be accurate and the measurements will be consistent. Unfortunately, there is no way to be sure that all errors will be eliminated, so techniques are needed to evaluate consistency of measurement. In Chapter 6 we discussed perhaps the most widely used technique in developmental psychology for assessing reliability, interobserver agreement. In this technique two observers both watch the behavior—for example, newborns' responses to an object being presented out of their reach. They independently judge whether the baby reached for the object, swiped at the object, "waved" at the object, and so forth. The extent to which they agree on the category they used to describe the behavior represents the reliability of that measurement. Unless such reliability is obtained, a measurement cannot be considered to be objective. Generally speaking, the more reliable a measure is, the more likely it is to work when it is used to test hypotheses. Therefore, researchers have to try to make certain their measures are reliable. Although we have chosen to discuss the meaning of reliability in the context of testing where it is most commonly used, issues of reliability occur throughout this book whenever we talk about errors of measurement. For example, systematic experimenter biases can be eliminated by having those who make the observations or measurements be unaware of the nature of the hypotheses and of what study group the subjects are in. Lack of awareness of group memberships and hypotheses generally should serve to reduce bias. Interjudge reliability needs to be established whenever a measurement includes a judgment. Neonatal and infant tests usually include observations that require such judgments, as for example in scoring the NBAS or the Hunt–Uzgiris tests. The greater the numbers of categories to which a behavior can be assigned, the more difficult it is to achieve observer agreement.

A second way reliability is assessed is consistency over time, which is known as test–retest reliability. If a measurement is accurate and objective, the same result should be obtained each time the measurement is made providing the time lapse between tests is not great and no great changes have occurred. In the design of a measurement device, be it a machine or a test, the procedures for its use must be selected and specified in great detail. Otherwise it is unlikely that similar results will occur when a given infant (or adult) is measured on two occasions. The measurement of length and weight of newborns provides a good example. The conditions must be constant (for example, the angle of the head, position of the feet, presence of diaper, and so on) if the same results are to occur on 2 occasions.

When researchers construct a test, they must consider reliability from the very beginning, when they are first considering how to measure their variable. The cleanest procedure is to construct items that involve little judgment. For example, "Did the infant pick up the ball when requested to do so?" involves little judgment whereas "Did the infant indicate any recognition of a request to pick up the ball?" involves substantial judgment when the infant makes ambiguous responses (for example, judges often disagree on whether the infant looked at the ball). Unfortunately, data are often desired that can be gathered only by having people make judgments. Then it is crucial to obtain interjudge reliability. Test–retest reliability ensures that the behaviors measured are not ephemeral, but rather reflect subjects' consistent response tendencies. The standards of reliability that are accepted for neonatal tests are much lower than those for tests of older children because of the great instability of newborn organisms. Infancy tests are also less stable (reliable) than those for older children. There are additional ways of assessing reliability, but they are not often used for infant tests.

Once a test has sufficient reliability, its validity can be tested. Validity, like reliability, is a general term that also has a specific meaning in the context of the statistics of test construction. In the general sense it means that an argument or theory is true. In the specific sense it means the extent to which a test measures what it is designed to measure; for example, does an infant intelligence test measure intelligence? Historically, the concept of validity included a predictive element. A valid intelligence test would predict future performance in intellectual domains, such as school. For infant intelligence tests, the criterion for validity usually was a later intelligence test. By this criterion, infant intelligence tests failed, although they have been proved valid by other criteria. The Graham/Rosenblith Behavioral Test for Newborns has demonstrated long-term predictive validity. This means that the test is useful; it also means that the test measures some true component of infant functioning, even though its nature is not altogether clear. The same holds for fine motor coordination: It predicts later development and therefore taps some real behavioral characteristic (one that varies among individuals).

A test may be valid even if it lacks predictive validity. In fact, the purpose of some tests (such as the NBAS and the Uzgiris–Hunt scales) is to achieve concurrent validity. As with predictive validity, concurrent validity is measured by correlating performance on the test with a criterion. The criterion for predictive validity is future behavior (for example, intellectual performance at age 8 years); the criterion in concurrent validity is measured at the same time as the test. For example, neonatal tests can be said to have concurrent validity because babies with medical problems do more poorly than babies who do not.

Most of the research we have reviewed in this chapter has a practical aim of distinguishing those who are at risk for future problems from those who are not. In theory the predictor variable or the items on a predictive test could be anything. For example, if length of the big toe was one item on a predictive test, and if it was correlated with future risk, it would be kept on the test. A test with such items would be an empirically derived test: a test that is valid if it is correlated with the criterion, regardless of whether formal or informal theories hypothesize the correlation. Nonetheless, most researchers are also interested in the nature of the construct being measured. For example, the Bayley does not predict intelligence test results in middle childhood, except at the extremes. Thus, the conclusion is that the Bayley does not measure intelligence of the sort

that develops after infancy. It does, however, correlate with other measures of intellectual behaviors in infancy and it correlates with a number of other infant variables (such as medical risk). It also has become a major dependent variable or outcome variable in many studies of the effects of early experience. All these data together support the conclusion that the Bayley measures something real in infants: It may measure infant intelligence or perhaps infant adaptive competence. This process of gathering data that relates a test to a variety of other variables in a theoretically meaningful fashion establishes what is called its **construct validity.** Strictly speaking, construct validity requires a well-developed theory with a variety of testable hypotheses. If a number of different hypotheses regarding the test are supported by empirical research, the test has construct validity. Historically, however, the criterion of a priori hypotheses very often is *not* met. The volume of research findings just grows as different researchers use the test for different reasons. When all the findings are examined together, however, a pattern may become clear, as it has for the Bayley. Nevertheless, to support confident claims about the Bayley measures, additional research is needed. For example, to claim that it measures infant intelligence and not general adaptive competence requires a demonstration that it correlates with variables that are related to intelligence, such as problem solving, and not to nonintellectual variables, such as social competence.

The third major issue in validating and interpreting a test is the nature of the samples used in the studies that establish the norms (called the normative samples) and those used to validate the test. The most typical samples in behavioral research are urban, middle class, and normal individuals. In infancy research low-income, low-education minority group samples are also common. Even when the sample is carefully selected and of adequate size, the results of a study with such a sample can be generalized only to that specific population, that is, to other babies of the same sort— urban, middle class, and normal. A more representative method of sample selection is stratified sampling. In stratified sampling, the sample population is divided into strata representing the major divisions of the general population. Thus, the lower SES stratum in the sample would comprise the same proportion of the sample as that stratum does in the society. The same would be true for other social classes and other subgroups of interest (urban, rural, Black, white). Random sampling then takes place within each stratum. This procedure allows the test to be used appropriately for all subgroups of the society, although it does not eliminate the problem of test biases, which we will discuss shortly.

Another sampling problem stems from longitudinal sampling, which was characteristic of many of the early infant tests. The effects of repeat testing on the test or the performance of the subjects has to be considered. Cross-sectional testing (testing each child at only one age) eliminates this problem, but of course it cannot be used to study continuity of development. If tests are used to look for continuity in development (as Gesell used his) then longitudinal testing needs to be done by different persons when the subjects are different ages; otherwise continuities that are found may lie in the examiners' perception of the infant (a criticism frequently leveled at Gesell's work).

The fourth major issue in using tests is test fairness. Even in infant tests, some babies will have had more experience with the stimulus situations (that is, with having problems posed and posed by strangers) and some will have had more experience with the materials used to pose the problems (that is, with peg boards, pull toys, blocks, or whatever). Differences in both of these types of exposure are frequently related to social class, race, or ethnic origin. Fairness is also affected by whether the subjects have been appropriately represented in the standardization sample for the test. The problem of lack of representation in standardization samples (from which the norms for the test are derived) is behind our decision not to discuss the use of neonatal tests to compare babies from different ethnic and cultural groups.

Proper representation in the standardization sample does not fully adjust for a given infant's unfamiliarity with test materials or situations. One way to deal with this problem is to establish separate normative samples for the different groups in a study. This may adjust for different types of maternal care and child-birth procedures in the case of neonatal tests, or for different types of relevant experience in the case of older babies and infants. The disadvantage of this approach is that there then is no way infants from two different populations can be compared. This could only be accomplished if the long range meanings of the subjects' position with respect to the norm for their culture were known and could be compared across cultures or subcultures.

Parenting

We could omit a parenting section, but we want to point out a few implications of various portions of this chapter. Those readers who become parents should be much better prepared for growth changes and for the unevenness of physical growth, and should be aware of the tremendous individual differences in when various motor milestones are achieved. Thus some may be spared from senselessly bragging about an infant's early achievements and some from senselessly worrying about an infant who is late to walk or whatever.

More important, parents should understand that although it is possible to train some early motor developments, this may not be an advantage for the child or the parents. Early walking, for example, is likely to enable infants to get into trouble before they can understand reasons to avoid it. This in turn may force parents to adopt various practices that they may find difficult or unpleasant. They may deal with the problem by childproofing the house, by exercising unusually close supervision, by utilizing restraints such as gates and playpens, or by resorting to punitive techniques to teach the child to avoid dangers or absolute no—nos.

If a baby is tested as a newborn (either neurologically or behaviorally) and the results indicate no problems, parents can be happy, but not 100% sure there will be no later problems. If, in contrast, various problems are identified, parents should understand that the likelihood of long-term problems is really very low, especially if these problems are not confirmed at a number of ages in infancy.

If a child is tested as an infant, much the same story holds. However, if there is a profound lag behind the norms at 1 or 2 years of age, this is a matter of considerable concern, especially if the lag is on the fine motor or so-called mental portions of tests.

For parents who, for one reason or another, are anxious to produce a physical activity super-kid, McGraw and other early workers showed that providing opportunities and encouragement for activities may indeed greatly accelerate the age at which skills are mastered. If parents do this for many types of activities, *perhaps* infants will be more physically adventurous. However, great patience and care to avoid pressure are needed. One currently popular (in some circles at least) form of this is teaching very young babies to swim. This practice, like those of Africans who teach their babies to walk, sometimes tries to build on a pre-existing reflex activity. We say "sometimes" because not all infant swim coaches start that early (but usually early enough to avoid fear responses). Some people in our culture probably stress early performance more than is necessary for optimal later growth and development.

SUMMARY

Physical Development

Knowledge of physical growth and development of the infant is interesting to parents and professionals both to give a picture of normal growth and to provide an index of potential problems. It also can lead to deeper understanding of historical and social trends, of health and nutritional changes within populations, and of the relationship between genetic inheritance and environmental experiences.

Diet and improved health care over the last 100 years has led to an average increase in height (in developed countries) ranging from 2.9 cm (young white males in the United States) to 10.8 cm (Swedish conscripts over a period of 122 years). Both height and weight at birth have also increased. Difficulties in determining exact measurements and in interpreting the data for such comparative figures were also discussed.

The aspects of growth most often measured in the infant are height, weight, and head circumference. One of the most striking features about growth is that different body parts

grow or change at different rates. The head doubles in length between birth and adulthood, the trunk triples, the arms quadruple, and the legs quintuple.

The brain develops earlier than most other organs and its weight at birth is closer to the adult level than that of other organs (except the eye). However, development of major functional areas within the brain continues until puberty and beyond.

Motor Development

Most development occurs cephalo-caudally (from the head down) and from the center to the periphery of the body (proximo-distally). Developmental milestones for both gross and fine motor development have been identified. The age at which a baby holds up its head, sits, stands, walks, reaches for or grasps objects, is of great interest to parents and researchers.

One important theoretical issue is the relative roles of experience and maturation on motor development. Gesell studied various aspects of motor development and created a widely used test. He also pioneered the use of motion pictures, which enabled frame-by-frame analysis of the movement sequences of children. Gesell assumed that motor development was biologically determined and depended primarily on the passage of time to unfold. Most researchers now believe that there may be wide age differences in the acquisition of particular motor skills, depending on a number of factors that include health, nutrition, genetic background, environmental stimulation, and opportunities for learning and practice.

Further improvements are needed in the assessment of motor tasks to reveal the quality of motoric behavior; that is, whether or not the task has been accomplished with ease or difficulty, whether the infant is in general coordinated or clumsy, and so forth. Tests of motor behavior should take degrees of competence into account, not just success or failure. Cross-cultural studies add information to the discussion of the effect of different child-rearing patterns on motor development.

The Motor scale of the Bayley test was summarized to show the normal ages at which various motor behaviors are achieved. The youngest and oldest ages at which any baby in a standardization sample demonstrated the behavior were also shown; such ranges emphasize the fact that there are large individual differences among infants.

At birth infants exhibit little that could be called fine motor behavior. They do show many of the gross motor components that will later become coordinated into finely tuned arm, hand, and finger movements.

The infant is born with numerous reflex movements, some of which may fade before reappearing as parts of newly developed skills. Reflex grasping and stepping are examples. The discontinuity found in western culture between the reflex and the later coordinated behavior may be a function of the type of experiences babies have.

One of the most important aspects of fine motor coordination that develops during infancy is visually-guided reaching. It develops around 4 months of age and allows infants to explore their world much more effectively and thereby to occupy themselves for much longer periods of time. A more primitive neonatal form, visually initiated reaching, is largely governed by biological factors and is relatively impervious to environmental deprivation, whereas the 4-month form requires that infants experience visual feedback of their reaching movements. Fine motor development deserves more research attention because it appears to be more related to later outcomes (for example, IQ at age 4) than is gross motor development.

Developmental Testing

NEONATAL TESTING

The presence or absence of expected reflex responses in newborns can be useful for diagnostic purposes. Various reflexes appear and disappear on varied time schedules. Some never disappear in normal people. The assessment of muscle tonus is also used for diagnostic and predictive purposes. Several neonatal neurological examinations have been developed to identify neurological problems that might presage difficulties in later development, and to determine which sick babies should have a good prognosis. Prechtl's test identifies apathy, hyperexcitability, and the hemisyndrome, but the diagnostic stability of

his tests for long-term predictions has not been demonstrated. Saint-Anne Dargassies, in France, has presented evidence that neurological difficulties in infancy do not necessarily mean long-term difficulties.

Several behavioral tests were discussed in detail: the Graham Behavioral Test for Neonates, the Graham/Rosenblith Behavioral Test for Neonates, and the Brazelton or Newborn Behavioral Assessment Scales (NBAS). The first two are primarily oriented toward detecting CNS immaturity or damage, and the NBAS is concerned with behaviors that might affect mother–infant interaction.

Interscorer agreement has been shown to be satisfactory on these tests. Test–retest reliability is considered adequate given the fact that newborns make rapid and profound changes during the first days of their lives. It is nevertheless doubtful that any neonatal exam should be considered a standardized test in the way that tests given to older children and adults are.

Although the evidence for the relation of the NBAS to other neonatal variables is complex and sometimes contradictory, there is some support for the idea that the NBAS taps temperamental characteristics of infants.

Neonatal tests have also been used successfully as dependent variables in experimental treatment programs. For example, the effects of stimulation activities for prematures have been evaluated with the Graham/Rosenblith.

The Graham/Rosenblith has demonstrated some long-term predictive validity, although it does not enable predictions to be made for an individual baby. Muscle tonus is strongly related to a number of intellectual, perceptual, and behavioral outcomes. The day on which a baby is tested is relevant to the predictive usefulness of the test, but varies for different behaviors tested.

INFANT TESTING

The history of tests for intellectual ability (IQ) and developmental level (DQ) was reviewed briefly. The infant and preschool testing movement grew out of the IQ testing movement. However, infant tests must necessarily be less verbal and therefore they test primarily sensory, perceptual, and motor development, their linkages, and social interaction. The historical role of the Gesell test in the development of all other tests designed to assess infants was acknowledged. The Bayley tests were discussed in detail because they are best standardized and most widely used.

Other recent developments in infant testing include an emphasis on ordinal scales, which show a regular progression in difficulty on a variety of tasks. The Bayley scales have been scored in ways that produce ordinal scales. Ordinal scales based on Piagetian theory have been developed by Uzgiris and Hunt. The Kohen-Raz ordinal scales based on the Bayley appear to have greater predictive validity than the Bayley itself, but this has not been replicated. The authors of the Hunt–Uzgiris ordinal scales have a more Piagetian outlook and are less concerned with prediction.

Neonatal and infant tests do not have long-range accuracy, except for those who have been badly damaged. The tests are useful for assessing the effects of factors such as malnutrition, drugs, institutional life, maternal deprivation, environmental stimulation, or parent–child interaction.

REFERENCES

Adamson, L., Als, H., Tronick, E., & Brazelton, T.B. (1975). *A priori profiles for the Brazelton Neonatal Assessment.* Unpublished manuscript. (Available from Child Development Unit, Children's Hospital, Boston.)

Als, H. (1978). Assessing an assessment: Conceptual considerations, methodological issues, and a perspective on the future of the Neonatal Behavioral Assessment Scale. In A.J. Samaroff (Ed.), *Organization and stability of newborn behavior: A commentary on the Brazelton Neonatal Behavior Assessment Scale. Monographs of the Society for Research in Child Development,* 43 (5–6, Serial No. 177).

Als, H., Lester, B.M., Tronick, E.Z., & Brazelton, T.B. (1982). Toward a research instrument for the assessment of preterm infants' behavior (APIB). In H.E. Fitzgerald, B.M. Lester, & M.W. Yogman (Eds.), *Theory and research in behavioral pediatrics.* New York and London: Plenum.

Als, H., Tronick, E., Lester, B.M., & Brazelton, T.B. (1977). The Brazelton Neonatal Behavioral Assessment Scale (BNBAS). *Journal of Abnormal Child Psychology, 5,* 215–231.

Amiel-Tison, C. (1976). A method for neurologic evaluation within the first year of life. In L. Gluck (Ed.), *Current problems in pediatrics.* New York: Year Book Publishers.

Amiel-Tison, C. (1982). Neurological signs, aetiology, and implications. In P. Stratton (Ed.), *Psychobiology of the human newborn.* New York: Wiley.

Anderson, R.B., & Rosenblith, J.F. (1964). Light sensitivity in the neonate: A preliminary report. *Biologia Neonatorum, 7,* 83–94.

Anderson-Huntington, R.B., & Rosenblith, J.F. (1971). Sudden unexpected death syndrome: Early indicators. *Biology of the Neonate, 18,* 395–406.

Anderson-Huntington, R.B., & Rosenblith, J.F. (1972). Report on newborns with questionable light sensitivity. *Biology of the Neonate, 20,* 81–84.

Anderson-Huntington, R.B., & Rosenblith, J.F. (1976). Central nervous system damage: A possible component of the Sudden Infant Death Syndrome. *Developmental Medicine and Child Neurology, 18,* 480–492.

André-Thomas, Chesni, C.Y., & Saint-Anne Dargassies, S. (1960). Neurological examination of the infant. In *Clinics in Developmental Medicine, No. 1.* London: Spastics International Medical Publications.

Bayley, N. (1933a). *The California first-year mental scale.* Berkeley: University of California Press. (U.C. Syllabus Services, No. 343.)

Bayley, N. (1933b). Mental growth during the first three years. A developmental study of 61 children by repeated tests. *Genetic Psychology Monographs, 14,* 1–92.

Bayley, N. (1935). The development of motor abilities during the first three years. *Monographs of the Society for Research in Child Development, 1* (Serial No. 1).

Bayley, N. (1954). Some increasing parent–child similarities during the growth of children. *Journal of Educational Psychology, 45,* 1–21.

Bayley, N. (1955). On the growth of intelligence. *American Psychologist, 10,* 805–818.

Bayley, N. (1969). *Manual for the Bayley Scales of Infant Development.* New York: Psychological Corporation.

Bench, J., & Parker, A. (1970). On the reliability of the Graham/Rosenblith behavior test for neonates. *Journal of Child Psychology and Psychiatry, 11,* 121–131.

Bierman, J.M., Connor, A.M., Vaage, M., & Honzik, M.P. (1964). Pediatricians' assessments of the intelligence of two-year-olds and their mental test scores. *Pediatrics, 34,* 680.

Binet, A., & Simon, T. (1905). Upon the necessity of establishing a scientific diagnosis of inferior states of intelligence. *L'Annèe Psychologique, XI,* 163–190. (English version: Kite, E.S. (1916). *The development of intelligence in children.* Baltimore: Williams and Wilkins.)

Bower, T.G.R. (1982). *Development in infancy* (2nd ed.). San Francisco: Freeman.

Brazelton, T.B. (1973). *Neonatal Behavioral Assessment Scale.* National Spastics Society Monograph. Philadelphia: Lippincott.

Brazelton, T.B., Tronick, E., Lechtig, A., & Lasky, R. (1977). The behavior of nutritionally deprived Guatemalan infants. *Developmental Medicine and Child Neurology, 19,* 364–372.

Brazelton, T.B., & Tryphonopoulou, Y.A. (Unpublished). A comparative study of the Greek and U.S. neonates. Cited in Brazelton (1973).

Broman, S. (1981). Risk factors for deficits in early cognitive development. In G.G. Berg & H.D. Maillie (Eds.), *Measurement of risks.* New York: Plenum.

Broman, S., & Nichols, P.L. (1975, September). Early mental development, social class, and school-age IQ. Paper presented at the annual meeting of the American Psychological Association, Chicago.

Bruner, J.S. Eye, hand, and mind. (1969). In D. Elkind & J.H. Flavell (Eds.), *Studies in cognitive development: essays in honor of Jean Piaget.* New York: Oxford University Press.

Bruner, J.S. (1971). The growth and structure of skill. In K.J. Connolly (Ed.), *Motor skills in infancy.* New York: Academic.

Bruner, J.S. (1973). Organization of early skilled action. *Child Development, 44,* 1–11.

Brunet, O., & Lézine, P.U. (1951). *Le développement psychologique de la première enfance.* Issy-les-Moulineaux: Editions Scientifique et Psychotechniques.

Bühler, C., & Hetzer, H. (1935). *Testing children's development from birth to school age* (H. Beaumont, Trans.). New York: Farrar and Rinehart.

Cattell, P. (1940). *The measurement of intelligence in young children.* New York: Psychological Corporation.

Damon, A. (1968). Secular trend in height and weight within old American families at Harvard, 1870–1965, I: Within twelve four-generation families. *American Journal of Physical Anthropology, 29,* 45–50.

Dennis, W. (1938). Infant development under conditions of restricted practice and of minimum social stimulation: A preliminary report. *Journal of Genetic Psychology, 53,* 149–158.

Dennis, W. (1940). Does culture appreciably affect pattern of infant behavior? *Journal of Social Psychology, 12,* 305–317.

Dennis, W. (1943). Is the newborn infant's repertoire learned or instinctive? *Psychological Review, 50,* 330–337.

Dennis, W., & Dennis, M.G. (1940). The effect of cradling practices upon the onset of walking in Hopi children. *Journal of Genetic Psychology, 56,* 77–86.

deVries, M., & Super, C.M. (1978). Contextual influences on the Neonatal Behavioral Assessment Scale and implications for its cross-cultural use. *Monographs of the Society for Research in Child Development, 43* (Serial No. 177).

Dodwell, P.C., Muir, D., & DiFranco, D. (1976). Responses of infants to visually presented objects. *Science, 194,* 209–211.

Drillien, C.M. (1961). A longitudinal study of the growth and development of prematurely and maturely born children. *Archives of Disease in Childhood, 36,* 233–240.

Dunkeld, J., & Bower, T.G.R. (1981). The effect of wedge prisms on the reaching behavior of infants. Manuscript in preparation. Department of Psychology, University of Edinburgh.

Emde, R.N. (1978). Commentary on "Organization and stability of newborn behavior: A commentary on the Brazelton Neonatal Behavior Assessment Scale." *Monographs of the Society for Research in Child Development, 43* (Serial No. 177).

Feldman, H. (1833). *Observations on the normal functioning of the human body.* Bonne, C. Georgie.

Field, T.M., Dempsey, J.R., Hallock, N.H., & Shuman, H.H. (1978). The mother's assessment of the behavior of her infant. *Infant Behavior and Development, 1,* 156–167.

Fraiberg, S. (1971). Interaction in infancy: A program for blind infants. *Journal of the American Academy of Child Psychiatry, 10,* 381–405.

Frankenburg, W.K., Camp, B.W., & VanNatta, P. (1971). Validity of the Denver Developmental Screening Test. *Child Development, 42,* 475–485.

Frankenburg, W.K., & Dodds, J.B. (1967). The Denver Developmental Screening Test. *Journal of Pediatrics, 71,* 181–191.

Frankenburg, W.K., Goldstein, A.D., & Camp, B.W. (1971). The revised Denver Developmental Screening Test: Its accuracy as a screening instrument. *Pediatrics, XX,* 988–995.

Ganz, L. (1975). Orientation in visual space. In A.H. Riesen (Ed.), *The developmental neuropsychology of sensory deprivation.* New York: Academic.

Geber, M. (1958). The psycho-motor development of African children in the first year, and the influence of maternal behavior. *Journal of Social Psychology, 47,* 185–195.

Geber, M., & Dean, R.F.A. (1957). Gesell tests on African children. *Pediatrics, 20,* 1055–1065.

Gesell, A. (1925). *The mental growth of the preschool child.* New York: MacMillan.

Gesell, A. (1934). *An atlas of infant behavior* (Vols. I and II). New Haven: Yale University Press.

Gesell, A. (1954). The ontogenesis of infant behavior. In L. Carmichael (Ed.), *Manual of child psychology* (pp. 335–373). New York: Wiley.

Gesell, A., & Amatruda, C.S. (1941). *Developmental diagnosis.* New York: Hoeber.

Gesell, A., & Amatruda, C.S. (1947). *Developmental diagnosis.* New York: Harper & Row.

Gesell, A., & Thompson, H. with Amatruda, C.S. (1934). *Infant behavior: Its genesis and growth.* New York and London: McGraw-Hill.

Gesell, A., & Thompson, H. (1938). *The psychology of early growth.* New York: MacMillan, 1938.

Graham, F.K. (1956). Behavioral differences between normal and traumatized newborns: I. Test procedures. *Psychological Monographs, 70:* 20 (whole No. 427).

Graham, F.K., Ernhart, C.B., Thurston, D., & Craft, M. (1962). Development three years after perinatal anoxia and other potentially damaging newborn experiences. *Psychological Monographs, 76:* 3 (whole No. 522).

Graham, F.K., Matarazzo, R.G., & Caldwell, B.M. (1956). Behavioral differences between normals and traumatized newborns: II. Standardization, reliability and validity. *Psychological Monographs, 70:* 21 (whole No. 428).

Griffiths, R. (1954). *The abilities of babies: A study in mental measurement.* New York: McGraw Hill.

Halverson, H.M. (1931). An experimental study of prehension in infants by means of systematic cinema records. *Genetic Psychology Monograph, 10,* 107–286.

Halverson, H.M. (1932). A further study of grasping. *Genetic Psychology Monograph, 7,* 34–64.

Hein, A. (1972). Acquiring components of visually guided behavior. In A. Pick (Ed.), *Minnesota symposia on child psychology* (Vol. 6) Minneapolis: University of Minnesota Press.

Hein, A., & Diamond, R.M. (1971). Contrasting development of visually triggered and guided movements in kittens with respect to interocular and interlimb equivalence. *Journal of Comparative and Physiological Psychology, 76,* 219–224.

Hein, A., & Held, R. (1967). Dissociation of the visual placing response into elicited and guided components. *Science, 158,* 390–391.

Hofsten, C. von (1982). Eye–hand coordination in the newborn. *Developmental Psychology, 18,* 450–461.

Hofsten, C. von (1984). Developmental changes in the organization of prereaching movements. *Developmental Psychology, 20,* 378–388.

Honzik, M. (1962). *The mental and motor test performance of infants diagnosed or suspected of brain injury.* Unpublished manuscript.

Honzik, M. (1976). Value and limitations of infant tests: An overview. In M. Lewis (Ed.), *Origins of intelligence: Infancy and early childhood.* New York: Plenum.

Horowitz, F.D., Aleksandrowicz, M., Ashton, L.J., Tims, S., McCluskey, K., Culp, R., & Gallas, H. (1973, March). *American and Uruguyan infants: Reliabilities, maternal drug histories and population difference using the Brazelton scale.* Paper presented at the biennial meeting of the Society for Research in Child Development, Philadelphia.

Horowitz, F.D., Ashton, J., Culp, R., Gaddis, E., Levin, S., & Reichmann, B. (1977). The effect of obstetrical medication on the behavior of Israeli newborns and some comparisons with American and Uruguyan infants. *Child Development, 48,* 1607–1623.

Horowitz, F.D., & Brazelton, T.B., (1973). Research with the Brazelton Neonatal Scale. In T.B. Brazelton (Ed.), *Neonatal Behavioral Assessment Scale.* National Spastics Society Monograph. Philadelphia: Lippincott.

Horowitz, F.D., Self, P.A., Paden, L.Y., Culp, R., Boyd, E., & Mann, M.E. (1971, April). *Newborn and four-week retests on normative population using the Brazelton Newborn Assessment pro-*

cedure. Paper presented at the biennial meeting of the Society for Research in Child Development, Minneapolis.

Horowitz, F.D., Sullivan, J.W., & Linn, P. (1978). Stability and instability in the newborn infant: The quest for elusive threads. In A.J. Sameroff (Ed.), *Organization and stability of newborn behavior: A commentary on the Brazelton Neonatal Assessment Scale. Monographs of the Society for Research in Child Development, 43* (5–6, Serial No. 177).

Illingworth, R.S. (1960). *The development of the infant and young child: Normal and abnormal.* London and Edinburgh: Livingston.

Jackson, E., Campos, J., & Fischer, K. (1978). The question of décalage between object permanence and person permanence. *Developmental Psychology, 14,* 1–10.

Jan, J.E., Robinson, G., Scott, E., & Kinnis, C. (1975). Hypotonia in the blind child. *Developmental Medicine and Child Neurology, 17,* 35–39.

Jensen, A. (1973). *Educability and group differences.* London: Methuen.

Kangas, J., Butler, B.V., & Goffeney, B. (1966, March). Relationship between preschool intelligence, maternal intelligence, and infant behavior. Paper presented at the second Scientific Session, Collaborative Study on Celebral Palsy, Mental Retardation, and Other Neurological and Sensory Disorders of Infancy and Childhood (U.S. Department of Health, Education, and Welfare, Public Health Service), Washington, DC.

Katz, V. (1970). The relationship between auditory stimulation and the development behavior of the premature infant. Unpublished doctoral dissertation, New York University.

Kaye, K. (1978). Discriminating among normal infants by multivariate analysis of Brazelton scores: Lumping and smoothing. *Monographs of the Society for Research in Child Development, 43* (Serial No. 177).

Knoblock, H., & Pasamanick, B. (1955). A developmental questionnaire for infants 40 weeks of age. *Monographs of the Society for Research in Child Development, 2* (Serial No. 61).

Knoblock H., & Pasamanick, B. (1960). An evaluation of the consistency and predictive value of the 40-week Gesell Development Schedule. *Psychiatric Research Reports, 13,* 10–31.

Knoblock, H., & Pasamanik, B. (1975). *Gesell and Amatruda's developmental diagnosis* (3rd ed., revised and enlarged). Hagerstown, MD: Harper & Row.

Kohen-Raz, R. (1967). Scalogram analyses of some developmental sequences of infant behavior as measured by the Bayley Infant Scale of Mental Development. *Genetic Psychology Monographs, 76,* 3–22.

Kopp, C.B. (1974). Fine motor abilities of infants. *Developmental Medicine and Child Neurology, 16,* 629–636.

Kopp, C.B., Sigman, M., Parmelee, A.H., & Jeffrey, W.E. (1975). Neurological organization and visual fixation in infants at 40 weeks conceptional age. *Developmental Psychobiology, 8,* 165–170.

Kuhlman, F. (1912). A revision of the Binet–Simon system for measuring the intelligence of children. *Journal of Psycho-Asthenics,* Monograph Supplement.

Lancione, E., Horowitz, F.D., & Sullivan, J.W. (1980). The NBAS-K. I: A study of its stability and structure over the first month of life. *Infant Behavior and Development, 3,* 341–359.

Lasky, R.E., Klein, R.E., Yarbrough, C., Engle, P.L., Lechtig, A., & Martorell, R. (1981). The relationship between physical growth and infant behavioral development in rural Guatemala. *Child Development, 52,* 219–226.

Lasky, R.E., Klein, R.E., Yarbrough, C., & Kallio, K.D. (1981). The predictive validity of infant assessments in rural Guatemala. *Child Development, 52,* 847–856.

Lasky, R.E., Tyson, J.E., Rosenfeld, C.R., Priest, M., Krasinski, D., Hartwell, S., & Gant, N.F. (1983). Principal component analyses of the Bayley Scales of Infant Development for a sample of high-risk infants and their controls. *Merrill-Palmer Quarterly, 29,* 25–32.

Linn, P.L., & Horowitz, F.D. (1983). The relationship between infant individual differences and mother–infant interaction during the neonatal period. *Infant Behavior and Development, 6,* 415–428.

MacRae, J.M. (1955). Retests of children given mental tests as infants. *Journal of Genetic Psychology, 87,* 111–119.

McDonnell, P.M. (1975). The development of visually guided reaching. *Perception and Psychophysics, 19,* 181–185.

McGraw, M.B. (1935). *Growth: A study of Johnny and Jimmy.* New York: Appleton.

McGraw, M.B., (1977, March) *Theories and techniques of child development research during the 1930s.* Invited address at the biennial meeting of the Society for Research in Child Development, New Orleans.

Menkes, J.H. (1984). Malformations of the central nervous system. In M.E. Avery & H.W. Taeusch, Jr. (Eds.), *Schaffer's disease of the newborn* (5th Ed.). Philadelphia: Saunders.

Mitchell, S.K., Abbs, M., & Barnard, K. (1977, August). *Intercorrelations between Brazelton Scale scores, perinatal indices, and early behavior.* Paper presented at the annual meeting of the American Psychological Association, San Francisco.

National Center for Health Statistics. (1976). *Monthly Vital Statistics Report, 25* (3, Supplement (HRA)).

Neal, M.V. (1968). Vestibular stimulation and developmental behavior of the small premature infant. *Nursing Research Report, 3,* 1 and 3–5.

Neuhauser, G. (1975). Methods of assessing and recording motor skills and movement patterns. *Developmental Medicine and Child Neurology, 17,* 369–386.

Osofsky, J.D. (1976). Neonatal characteristics and mother–infant interaction in two observational situations. *Child Development, 47,* 1138–1147.

Osofsky, J., & Danzger, B. (1974). Relationships between neonatal characteristics and mother–infant interaction. *Developmental Psychology, 10,* 124–30.

Owen, G.M., Kram, K.M., Garry, P.J., Lower, L.E., & Lubin, A.H. (1974). *A study of status of preschool children in the United States* (pp. 597–646), *53* (Part II, Supplement).

Parmelee, A.H., Jr. (1962). European neurological studies of the newborn. *Child Development, 33,* 169–180.

Parmelee, A.H., Jr. (1974). *Newborn Neurological Examination.* Unpublished manuscript.

Peiper, A. (1963). *Cerebral function in infancy and childhood* (3rd ed.; H. Nagler & B. Nagler, Trans.). New York: Consultants Bureau Enterprises. (Original work published in 1961).

Ploof, D. (1976, April). *The reciprocal effects of maternal perceptions and infant characteristics in the early mother–infant interaction.* Paper presented at the meeting of the Eastern Psychological Association, New York.

Prechtl, H.F.R. (1965). Prognostic value of neurological signs in the newborn infant. *Proceedings of the Royal Society of Medicine, 58,* (3).

Prechtl, H.F.R. (1974). The behavioral states of the newborn infant (A review). *Brain Research, 76,* 185–212.

Prechtl, H.F.R. (1977). The neurological examination of the full-term newborn infant (2nd ed., revised and enlarged). *Clinics in Developmental Medicine, No. 63.* London: Heinemann.

Prechtl, H.F.R. (1982). Assessment methods for the newborn infant, a critical evaluation. In P. Stratton (Ed.), *Psychobiology of the human newborn.* New York & Chichester, England: Wiley.

Prechtl, H.F.R., & Beintema, D.J. (1964). The neurological examination of the full-term infant. *Clinics in Developmental Medicine, No. 12.* London: Heinemann.

Prechtl, H.F.R., & Dijkstra, J. (1960). Neurological diagnosis of cerebral injury in the newborn. In B.S. ten Berge (Ed.), *Prenatal care.* Gröningen: Noordhoff.

Provine, R.R., & Westerman, J.A. (1979). Crossing the midline: Limits of early eye–hand behavior. *Child Development, 50,* 437–441.

Quetelet, L.A.J. (1835). *Sur l'homme et le developpement de ses facultès ou essai de physique sociale.* Paris: Bachdier.

Reich, J.N., Holmes, D.L., Slaymaker, F.L., Lauesen, B.F., & Gyurke, J.S. (1984, April). *Infant assessments as predictors of 3-year IQ.* Paper presented at the Fourth International Conference on Infant Studies, New York.

Roche, A.F. (1979). Secular trends in human growth, malnutrition, and development. *Monographs of the Society for Research in Child Development, 44* (Serial No. 179).

Rosenblith, J.F. (1961a) *Manual for behavioral examination of the neonate.* Published privately by Brown University; available from the author.

Rosenblith, J.F. (1961b). The modified Graham behavior test for neonates: Test–retest reliability, normative data, and hypotheses for future work. *Biologia Neonatorum, 3,* 174–192.

Rosenblith, J.F. (1973). Prognostic value of neonatal behavioral tests. *Early Child Development and Care, 3,* 31–50.

Rosenblith, J.F. (1974). Relations between neonatal behaviors and those at 8 months. *Developmental Psychology, 10,* 779–792.

Rosenblith, J.F. (1979a). The Graham/Rosenblith behavioral examination for newborns: Prognostic values and procedural issues. In Osofsky, J. (Ed.), *Handbook of infant development.* New York: Wiley.

Rosenblith, J.F. (1979b, June). *Relations between behaviors in the newborn period and intellectual achievement and IQ at 7 years of age.* Paper presented at the International Society for the Study of Behavioral Development, Lund, Sweden.

Rosenblith, J.F., & Anderson, R.B. (1968). Prognostic significance of discrepancies in muscle tonus. *Developmental Medicine and Child Neurology, 10,* 322–330.

Rosenblith, J.F., Anderson, R.B., & Denhoff, E. (1970). Hypersensitivity to light, muscle tonus discrepancies: A follow-up report. *Biology of the Neonate, 15,* 217–228.

Rosenblith, J.F., & Lipsitt, L.P. (1959). Interscorer agreement for the Graham Behavior Test for Neonates. *Journal of Pediatrics, 54,* 200–205.

Rubin, R.A., & Balow, B. (1979). Measures of infant development and socioeconomic status as predictors of later intelligence and school achievement. *Developmental Psychology, 15,* 225–227.

Rubin, R.A., & Balow, B. (1980). Infant neurological abnormalities as indicators of cognitive impairment. *Developmental Medicine and Child Neurology, 22,* 336–343.

Ruff, H.S., & Halton, A. (1978). Is there directed reaching in the human neonate? *Developmental Psychology, 14,* 425–426.

Saint-Anne Dargassies, S. (1972). Neurodevelopmental symptoms during the first year of life. *Developmental Medicine and Child Neurology, 14,* 235–246.

Saint-Anne Dargassies, S. (1977a). *Neurological development in the full term and premature neonate.* Amsterdam: Elsevier. (Original work published 1974).

Saint-Anne Dargassies, S. (1977b). Neuro-developmental symptoms during the first year of life. Part I: Essential landmarks for each rey-age. Part II: Practical examples and the application of this assessment method to the abnormal infant (analytical charts, synthetic evolutive profiles). *Developmental Medicine and Child Neurology, 19,* 462–478.

Saint-Anne Dargassies, S. (1983). Developmental neurology from the fetus to the infant: Some French works. In W. Hartup (Ed.), *Review of child development research* (Vol. 6). Chicago: University of Chicago Press.

Sameroff, A.J., Krafchuk, E.E., & Bakow, H.A. (1978). Issues in grouping items from the Neonatal Behavioral Assessment Scale. In A.J. Sameroff (Ed.), *Organization and stability of newborn behavior: A commentary on the Brazelton Neonatal Assessment Scale. Monographs of the Society for Research in Child Development, 43* (5–6, Serial No. 177).

Shirley, M.M. (1931).*The first two years: A study of twenty-five babies. Vol. 1, Postural and locomotor development.* Minneapolis: University of Minnesota Press.

Siegel, L.S. (1981). Infant tests as predictors of cognitive and language development at two years. *Child Development, 52,* 545–557.

Sigman, M., Kopp, C.B., Littman, B., & Parmelee, A.H. (1975, April). *Infant visual attentiveness in relation to birth condition.* Paper presented at the biennial meeting of the Society for Research in Child Development, Denver.

Sigman, M., Kopp, C.B., Parmelee, A.N., & Jeffrey, W.E. (1973). Visual attention and neurological organization in neonates. *Child Development, 44,* 461–466.

Solomons, G., & Solomons, H.G. (1975). Motor development in Yucatecan infants. *Developmental Medicine and Child Neurology, 17,* 41–46.

Sostek, A.M., & Anders, T.F. (1977). Relationships among the Brazelton Neonatal Scales, and early temperament. *Child Development, 48,* 320–323.

Sostek, A.M., Brackbill, Y., Broman, S.H., & Rosenblith, J.F. (1976). *Effects of barbituates on newborn behavior—Short and long term effects on the offspring.* Part of symposium on maternal medication presented at the annual meeting of the American Psychological Association, Washington, DC.

St. Clair, K.L. (1978). Neonatal assessment procedures: A historical review. *Child Development, 49,* 280–292.

Stern, W. (1924). *Psychology of early childhood: Up to the sixth year of age.* (3rd ed. revised and enlarged; A. Barwell, Trans.). New York: Holt. (Original work published in 1914.)

Strauss, M.E., & Rourke, D.L. (1978). A multivariate analysis of the Neonatal Behavioral Assessment Scale in several samples. In A.J. Sameroff (Ed.), *Organization and stability of newborn behavior: A commentary on the Brazelton Neonatal Behavioral Assessment Scale. Monographs of the Society for Research in Child Development, 43* (5–6, Serial no. 177).

Streissguth, A.P., & Barr, H.M. (1977, August). *Neonatal Brazelton assessment and relationship to maternal alcohol use.* Paper presented at the annual meeting of the American Psychological Association, San Francisco.

Stuart, H.C., & Meredith, H.V. (1946). Use of body measurements in school health programs. *American Journal of Public Health, 36,* 1365–1386.

Stutsman, R. (1931). *Mental measurement of preschool children; With a guide for the administration of the Merrill-Palmer Scale of Mental Tests.* Yonkers-on-Hudson, NY: World.

Super, C.M. (1976). Environmental effects on motor development. *Developmental Medicine and Child Neurology, 18,* 561–567.

Tanner, J.M. (1962). *Growth at adolescence* (2nd ed.). Oxford: Blackwell.

Tanner, J.M. (1970). Physical Growth. In P.H. Mussen (Ed.), *Carmichael's manual of child psychology* (Vol. 1). New York: Wiley.

Tanner, J.M. (1978). *Foetus into man.* Cambridge, MA: Harvard University Press.

Tanner, J.M., Healy, M.J.R., Lockhart, R.D., MacKenzie, J.D., & Whitehouse, R.H. (1956). Aberdeen growth study, I. The prediction of adult body measurement from measurements taken each year from birth to 5 years. *Archives of Diseases in Childhood, 31,* 372–381.

Tanner, J.M., & Thomson, A.M. (1970). Standards for birth weight at gestation periods from 32 to 42 weeks allowing for maternal height and weight. *Archives of Diseases in Childhood, 45,* 566–569.

Tanner, J.M., Whitehouse, R.H., Marshall, W.A., Healy, M.J., & Goldstein, N. (1975). *Assessment of skeletal maturity and prediction of adult height.* London: Academic.

Terman, L.M., & Merrill, M.A. (1937). *Measuring intelligence.* Cambridge, MA: Houghton Mifflin.

Terman, L.M., & Merrill, M.A. (1960). *Stanford–Binet Intelligence Scale.* Cambridge, MA: Houghton Mifflin.

Thomas, H. (1970). Psychological assessment instruments for use with human infants. *Merrill-Palmer Quarterly, 16,* 179–223.

Trevarthen, C. (1974). The psychobiology of speech development. In E. Lennenberg (Ed.), *Language and brain: Developmental aspects. Neurosciences Research Program Bulletin, 12,* 570–585.

Tronick, E., & Brazelton, T.B. (1975). Clinical uses of the Brazelton Neonatal Behavioral Assessment. In B. Friedlander, G.M. Sterritt, & G.E. Kirk (Eds.), *Exceptional Infant* (Vol. 3). New York: Brunner/Mazel.

Uzgiris, I.C., & Hunt, J. McV. (1975a). *Assessment in infancy.* Champaign/Urbana, IL: University of Illinois Press.

Uzgiris, I.C., & Hunt, J. McV. (1975b). *Toward ordinal scales of psychological development in infancy.* Champaign/Urbana, IL: University of Illinois Press.

Vaughn, B.E., Taraldson, B., Crichton, L., & Egeland, B. (1980). Relationships between neonatal behavioral organization and infant behavior during the first year of life. *Infant Behavior and Development, 3,* 47–66.

Wacker, D. (1980, September). *Diagnostic efficiency of the Denver Developmental Screening Test.* Paper presented at the annual meeting of the American Psychological Association, Montreal.

Walk, R.D., & Bond, E.K. (1971). The development of visually guided reaching in monkeys reared without sight of the hands. *Psychonomic Science, 23,* 115–116.

Warren, N. (1972). African infant precocity. *Psychological Bulletin, 78,* 353–367.

Werner, E.E. (1972). Infants around the world: Cross-cultural studies of psychomotor development from birth to two years. *Journal of Cross-cultural Studies, 3,* 111–134.

Werner, E.E., & Bayley, N. (1966). The reliability of Bayley's revised scale of mental and motor development during the first year of life. *Child Development, 37,* 39–50.

Werner, E.E., Bierman, J.M., & French, F.E. (1971). *The children of Kauai: A longitudinal study from the prenatal period to age 10.* Honolulu: University of Hawaii Press.

Werner, E.E., Honzik, M.P., & Smith, R.S. (1968). Prediction of intelligence and achievement at 10 years from 20 month pediatric and psychological examinations. *Child Development, 39,* 1063–1075.

White, B.L. (1971). *Human infants: Experience and psychological development.* Englewood Cliffs, NJ: Prentice-Hall.

White, B.L., Castle, P., & Held, R. (1964). Observations on the development of visually-directed reaching. *Child Development, 35,* 349–364.

White, B.L., & Held, R. (1966). Plasticity of sensorimotor development in the human infant. In J.F. Rosenblith & W. Allinsmith (Eds.), *The causes of behavior: Readings in child development and educational psychology* (2nd ed.). Boston: Allyn & Bacon.

Zelazo, P.R., Zelazo, N.A., & Kolb, S. (1972). "Walking" in the newborn. *Science, 176,* 14–15.

SENSORY AND
PERCEPTUAL ABILITIES

CHAPTER 9

In this chapter we will explore infants' abilities to see, hear, taste, touch, and smell. Three major questions have been asked in the research. The first is, What is the state of the sensory systems at birth? All of them function at birth, and in many ways they are remarkably mature. Each system will be considered in turn.

Given that the sensory systems function, the second major question is, What do infants perceive from the information their senses provide? It is possible that infants may see, hear, touch, and so forth, in a purely reflex fashion. Alternatively, they may be able to attach some meaning to the information their senses process, and it is even possible that babies at birth are biologically preprogrammed to attach meaning to some stimuli. For example, if babies reach for something they see, does this imply that they know the object is at some point distant from themselves? Do they know that the thing that makes soft, appealing noises (the female voice) is part of the same object that has a peculiar configuration of what adults would call eyes, nose, and mouth? If they recognize the configuration of the human face, do they recognize that it belongs to one of their own kind?

The third major question is, What is the course of development of the sensory and perceptual systems over the first months and years of life? Although all five senses function at birth, none is totally mature; all undergo subsequent development. For example, if newborns are not able to recognize their mothers, when do they develop this ability, and what do they need to learn in order to accomplish this goal?

IMPORTANCE OF STUDYING PERCEPTUAL DEVELOPMENT

Scientists explore the three questions outlined above for four important reasons. One is that the information is of practical use in medicine. Data about normative development, and about the amount and kind of perceptual development typical of infants of a given age, is needed to assess when development goes awry. Knowing the normal status of perceptual development at birth allows medical researchers to as-

sess the influences of various prenatal factors and provides a way to predict later outcomes of development on the basis of the status at birth. Because the perceptual capacities are so highly developed at birth they may be a good measure of general level of maturation, and may become better measures as new and better techniques by which to assess them are developed. Later perceptual development may also serve as an outcome measure of earlier development and as a predictor of still later behavior (of course, with later development it is not possible to separate prenatal influences from postnatal influences in determining outcomes).

A second reason to study perceptual development is its relevance to traditional issues in psychology and philosophy concerning the basic nature of knowledge. For example, research on perception has been used to test empirically whether the basic ways humans structure the world (for example, as objects that exist in a three-dimensional space) is innate or learned. **Empiricists** believe that everything humans know has to be learned, including depth perception and the understanding of what an object is. They argue that newborn babies are not able to perceive depth and do not know that the red, round thing they see is an object that adults call a ball. Newborns do not, therefore, know that what they see can be grasped and what they grasp can be seen, or that what they hear can be seen. In contrast, **nativists** believe that humans do not gain knowledge of spatial relations and objects through experience. They believe that humans directly perceive depth and that, without having to learn, know that objects have both visual and tactual aspects. Much research on perception in newborns is designed to see whether newborns act as if they already organize the world into objects in a three-dimensional space.

A third reason to do research in perceptual development is to assess the influences of environment on development. One of the most popular beliefs in all of developmental psychology is that the period of infancy is particularly important for the development of later functions. Some investigators focus on whether inadequate stimulation results in deficiencies in psychological development, while others are more interested in whether enriched environments improve development. Regardless of the focus, it is important to be able to identify appropriate kinds of stimulation. To identify appropriate stimulation for perceptual development, it is necessary to know the nature of perceptual development. For example, many middle-class families in the United States provide a mobile for their very young infants to watch. We now know enough about perceptual development to know that newborns look much longer at patterned stimuli than at plain stimuli and at objects with many contours (for example, a many-sided figure) than objects with little contour. If a study to assess the effects of the presence of mobiles on subsequent development used a mobile with plain squares and circles, the results might indicate that there were no effects. It would be wrong to conclude from this that stimulation had no effects. If the mobile had been more interesting to the infants, they might have looked longer at it and this might have had positive consequences. In fact, only when the basic perceptual capacities of infants are understood can stimuli be designed that will adequately test the hypothesis of the role of environmental stimulation on development.

The fourth reason to do research on perceptual development is to understand more about other aspects of development—namely affective, language, and cognitive development. The so-called older senses (ones that are highly represented in the older parts of the brain), such as smell, tactile sensitivity, and taste, clearly play an important role in our emotional lives. Although there is currently a great increase in research interest in affective behaviors, few links to perceptual data have been forged. It is our hope that the current research in affective development will stimulate more work on the older senses. The functioning of the auditory system is also important for emotional development because it is a primary means of social interaction, but little research to date has focused on its role in social interactions. Audition is also normally the means by which language is learned. The development of auditory capacities to process language begins at birth and continues throughout infancy even though infants do not start producing words before the end of their first year (this developmental sequence will be described in Chapter 11). Perceptual development is also important for cognitive development, because all of infants' knowledge of the world must be obtained through their senses. Vision, the most widely studied sense, is the most important for the achievement of the Piagetian stages of infancy (to be discussed in Chapter 10). Audition is also important for cognitive development, although research on its influence has focused on language and has relatively rarely explored the role of nonlanguage auditory stimuli.

RESEARCH TECHNIQUES

To understand the research that explores infants' sensations and perceptions, it is necessary to know how researchers study and learn about infants' abilities, particularly about newborns' abilities. They cannot talk or answer questions, they cannot move themselves about, and they have poor motor coordination. How do researchers find out what infants can see, hear, and so forth? Historically, the standard technique was naturalistic observation of the limited responses infants can make. Babies can move their eyes, pull their feet back, blink, startle, cry, suck, turn their heads, and so forth. If babies make these responses immediately after some event occurs in the environment, people infer that they are responding to that event and that therefore they perceive it. Such simple techniques are limited in three ways. We discussed the first two ways in Chapter 6: First, the observations may be unreliable—that is, observers may not always agree that the response in question has occurred. Second, the responses are not easily quantified. The third limitation is that it is impossible to tell what the infants have responded to. They may have responded only to the change from no stimulation to stimulation, or to aspects of the stimulus that differ from those noted by the adults. That leaves unanswered questions such as, Do they perceive color? Can they discriminate sweet from sour?

It became possible to study unseen responses such as heart rate in the 1930s, and the 1960s brought further methodological advances. It is now possible to study many aspects of sensation and perception that could not be studied before. Three basic techniques are commonly used to study babies' sensory and perceptual abilities. We will discuss each in turn and then compare them.

The simplest technique is the **preference technique.** It is used primarily in the study of visual stimuli. Two stimuli are presented side by side. Infants, even newborns, look from one to the other of these stimuli. Both the number of times they look at each stimulus and the length of time they spend looking at each stimulus can be measured. Basically this involves a sophisticated use of observational techniques combined with an experimental design for stimulus presentation. Researchers have developed very sophisticated ways of determining when infants are actually looking at a stimulus, using photographic techniques to measure the reflection of the stimulus on the infants' eye and to time this very accurately (see Maurer's 1975 review of techniques). If they look at one stimulus longer (or more times) than they look at the other stimulus, then it is possible to conclude that they can discriminate between those two stimuli and that for some reasons they find one more intriguing. If infants fail to show a visual preference, no clear interpretation can be made. They may either be unable to discriminate between the stimuli or they may find them equally interesting.

Because this technique requires simultaneous presentation of two stimuli, it is most appropriate for visual stimuli. Nevertheless, preference techniques can also be used with other senses. For example, in taste discrimination infants can be offered two substances in alternation (with a pause between) and the amounts they consume of each can be used as a measure of their preference for it. One half of the infants should have one substance offered first and the other half should have the second substance first, to control for satiation effects. The preference technique can also be used to study responses to smell and sounds, although measuring infants' tendencies to turn toward or away from the stimulus are more crude than the response measures for visual and taste stimuli.

The second technique is the habituation–dishabituation paradigm discussed in Chapter 7. It can be used to test infants' ability to discriminate between two similar stimuli by habituating the infants to one and presenting the other as a dishabituation stimulus. If they perceive the difference between the two stimuli, they will dishabituate. If they do not perceive the new stimulus as different, they will continue to show habituation; that is, they will exhibit little or no response. Since the two stimuli are presented successively, the habituation–dishabituation paradigm is a good choice for studies of hearing and smelling.

The third technique is operant conditioning, also discussed in Chapter 7. In **discrimination learning,** operant conditioning is used to train infants to discriminate between two or more stimuli. In one method, subjects are trained to respond when one stimulus is present and not to respond when that stimulus is absent. In another, they are trained to make one response in the presence of a certain stimulus and another response in the presence of a different stimulus. If the training to respond differentially to two stimuli is successful, then it is possible to conclude that the infant can discriminate between the two stimuli.

Training infants to make discriminative responses is a time-consuming task. Luckily, conditioning also provides another, easier, technique for testing infants' discriminative ability. It uses an aspect of the conditioning paradigm called **generalization.** Once infants are conditioned to respond to a particular stimulus by operant conditioning, they will also respond to stimuli that are similar to the original stimulus. If, for example, they are trained to turn their heads when they see a square, they are also likely to turn their heads when they see a rectangle. The tendency to generalize in this way is so strong that subjects' responses form a generalization gradient such that the more similar a stimulus is to the training stimulus, the stronger the subjects' responses. Thus, generalization provides two kinds of information. First, it tells whether infants perceive two stimuli to be similar or different, just as the preference and habituation–dishabituation paradigms do. Second, it can tell which among several stimuli are perceived by infants to be most similar to the training stimulus.

Conditioning is probably the least popular of the three measurement techniques, primarily because establishing the basic conditioned response is time consuming, particularly with young infants. It is, however, the best technique to use to show that some stimuli are perceived to be similar and others are perceived to be different.

TACTILE SENSITIVITY

We will begin our examination of the senses with tactile sensitivity or sensitivity to touch, partly because we believe it to be important to the emotional development of the child, but chiefly because it has been relatively neglected. We will also consider the presence or absence of any differences between the sexes in their sensitivity to stimuli in this domain. We do this because many people believe that there are such differences and some people have built them into their theories of sex differences of older children and adults.

Response to stimulation of the skin (or cutaneous sensitivity) is what might be called a very old sense. It is present by the eighth week of intrauterine development in the area around the mouth (perioral region). Cutaneous responses are also old in the sense that they have been studied since early in the scientific study of infancy. Renewed interest in these responses occurred as part of the wave of neonatal and infancy studies that started in the 1920s (Dockeray & Rice, 1934; Pratt, as cited in Kessen, Haith, & Salapatek, 1970; Sherman & Sherman, 1925; Sherman, Sherman, & Flory, 1936).

Responsivity to Aversive Stimulation

Much of the early research on tactile sensitivity explored pain responses. One of the major motivations for this research was the desire to determine whether newborns experience pain. Many doctors and nurses have been taught that newborns don't feel pain, and as a result they have assured mothers that various medical procedures (including circumcision) do not hurt the infant. Other people have expostulated on the wonderful design of nature that makes the fetus and newborn insensitive to pain, hence unresponsive to the pain of being born (or circumcised). Others remain unconvinced. Why do baby boys scream so violently when they are circumcised? Why are they so hard to rouse from sleep afterward? And why are they so irritable when roused that researchers give up trying to get them into a state suitable for neonatal testing?

Unfortunately, the research conducted on tactile sensitivity does not clearly answer these questions. The aversive stimuli used in the studies were not sufficiently strong to elicit crying or other signs of bodily discomfort from the infants. Thus, the results from these studies may not be appropriately generalized to situations of more intense pain, as measured by crying or grimacing.

Research in this area has used two kinds of stimuli. Three early studies used pinpricks on the skin at different regions of the body and counted the number of pricks necessary to obtain a withdrawal or avoidance response (Dockeray & Rice, 1934; Sherman & Sherman, 1925; Sherman, Sherman, & Flory, 1936). These studies found exactly opposite effects. Sherman and Sherman (1925; Sherman, Sherman, & Flory, 1936) found a rapid increase in sensitivity following birth with the head area being most sensitive and all extremities less sensitive, whereas Dockeray and Rice (1934) found no change in sensitivity with increasing age and found that sensitivity was the inverse of what would be expected from cephalocaudal development; that is, the legs were more sensitive than the arms or head.

More recent work on pain thresholds has used mild electric shock, which in principle can be much better controlled than pinpricks.[1] Graham, Matarazzo, and Caldwell (1956) stimulated the area just below the kneecap and found increased sensitivity with age over the first 5 days of life.

Lipsitt and Levy (1959) replicated Graham et al.'s findings using an improved electrode that was designed to minimize different degrees of contact with the skin. They then did another study to eliminate a possible confounding factor: Because the same infants had been tested on each day, the increased sensitivity might be due to experience in the testing situation (resulting either in sensitization or conditioning) rather than to age or maturation. In their second study, 20 boys and 20 girls were tested on the first day and a different 15 boys and girls tested on each subsequent day, from

---

[1] In fact, different degrees of contact of the electrode with the skin, different amounts of fat under the skin where the electrode is placed, and the possibility that different babies may have slightly different locations of nerve endings and that the electrode may accidentally be closer to or farther from relevant nerve endings may all act to reduce the apparent precision obtained by setting the dials on electronic stimulators.

the second through the fourth day. These data showed a less regular increase in sensitivity with age. The babies tested on the third day were somewhat more sensitive than the groups tested on the second or the fourth day.

Kaye (1964; Kaye & Lipsitt, 1964) tested the influence of another extraneous variable: skin conductance, the mechanism by which the electric current is transmitted. It is directly related to sweat gland function, which in turn is affected by a wide variety of other factors including activity level and state of wakefulness.[2] Since both of the latter increase in the first few days of life, they could lead to changes in sweat gland activity, which would be related to an apparent increased sensitivity. Kaye did find the apparent increase in sensitivity with age whether or not one group was studied longitudinally or different groups were tested on each day. However, there were marked individual differences in the patterns of change over age. The presence of anoxia and drugs used during delivery, both of which affect sweat gland functioning, affected the developmental course of sensitivity. He concluded, after an analysis of the research related to these factors, that the developmental change in sensitivity to aversive stimulation was produced by a developmental change in skin conductance resulting from an increase in general arousal level. It is unfortunate that Kaye did not analyze his own data according to sex or to the state of the infant at the time the measurement was made, because these factors may also have influenced his findings.

In summary, a number of well-done, increasingly technical, studies have failed to find strong evidence that sensitivity to aversive tactual stimulation increases during the first several days of life, or that newborns are impervious to pain.

The search for sex differences has also yielded inconclusive evidence. In both studies reported in their 1959 paper, Lipsitt and Levy found that girls were more sensitive than boys, but the differences (on each day) were sig-

nificant only in the first study. Even these weak sex differences might be an artifact. Male babies are on the average heavier than females, so they may have more subcutaneous fat, which would interfere with the electric current and thus make them appear to be less sensitive.

Another type of aversive stimulus has been used in two of the neonatal assessment batteries, the Neonatal Behavior Assessment Scale (NBAS) and the Graham/Rosenblith Test (G/R). Both involve stimulating newborns to remove something that covers their faces. In the NBAS, the Defensive Responses item assesses movements of the body that appear to be directed towards getting rid of a cloth over the face. The tactile-adaptive (TA) scale of the G/R examination involves defensive responses directed towards two stimuli: (1) cotton that is held over the nostrils and reaches just to the top of the lip; and (2) cellophane that is held across the baby's face from just above the nostrils (but not touching the eyes) to just below the mouth. These stimuli combine tactile stimulation with partial blocking of air supply, and so do not provide pure measures of tactile sensitivity. Newborns usually respond vigorously with various movements that would normally get rid of the sitmulus. Some of these are withdrawal responses analogous to withdrawal from mild electrical stimulation.

Rosenblith and DeLucia (1963) found no sex differences in the TA scale between 76 females and 88 males, all of whom were grossly normal and who were examined at from 2 to 96 hours of age.

Responsivity to Nonaversive Stimuli

Trying to find appropriate stimuli for testing tactual sensitivity is not straightforward. Bell and Costello (1964) tried three different stimuli: removal of a covering blanket, an air puff, and an aesthesiometer. Removing the blanket was unsatisfactory in two ways. It failed to give test–retest stability, and as a stimulus it involved temperature reduction and friction as well as tactile stimulation.

They then tried air puffs to the abdomen and various parts of the face. Each stimulus was presented only when the baby was in quiet sleep, and the flow was gradually increased un-

[2] Some of these problems had also been studied in the earlier wave of work with infants (Richter, 1930; Wenger & Irwin, 1936, and more recently Eichorn, 1951) but many problems were left unresolved by those studies. One way in which Kaye took account of their work was to use a variety of electrode placements in areas with different amounts of fat pad and of sweat glands.

til the infant showed a response. Although the observations were not highly reliable, they did suggest that newborns do respond to the tactile stimulation of an air puff to these areas.

The third stimulus was an aesthesiometer, which is a series of filaments of carefully measured bending force.[3] Under carefully limited conditions and with a larger sample, Bell and Costello were able to obtain high observer agreement on responses to tactile stimulation to the foot. On retest, but not on the initial test, there was a consistent relation of threshold to age. Greater sensitivity was shown by babies who were older when they were tested.

Bell and Costello argued from this complex set of data that the aesthesiometer is the most reliable way to assess tactile sensitivity because it yielded much greater observer agreement as to whether a response had occurred than the air puff did. They also argued that interactions and other complexities made it necessary to use complex research designs and control for large numbers of variables (see also Bell, 1963).

Clear demonstrations of tactile sensitivity have been obtained using tactile stimulation of the tongue. Weiffenbach (1972a, 1972b, 1977) discovered a stereotyped reflex response to tactile stimulation of the tongue, in which the tongue moves toward the side on which it is stimulated. The response is easily identified, reliably observed, consistent from test to test, and can be elicited by several different types of stimulation of the tongue near its tip. Thach and Weiffenbach (1976) used the same filament aesthesiometer used by Bell. All newborns responded to this form of stimulation and they exhibited an orderly increase in responses as a function of the stimulus intensity. They were, however, much less sensitive than adults. The sensitivity of newborns' tongues (Thach & Weiffenbach, 1976) was about equal to the sensitivity of the upper arm of adults (Ghent, 1961). The responsivity of the infants was a function both of their gestational age and of their postnatal age. Sensitivity decreased between the testing at 96 hours and that at 1 week, but increased again at 2 weeks postnatally.

Sex differences have been found only occasionally in reactions to these nonaversive stimuli. Bell and Costello found sex differences in responsivity to the removal of a blanket and to air puffs to the abdomen, but not to air puffs to the face or in responses to the aesthesiometer.

Most research on tactile responses to nonaversive stimuli has focused on whether newborns respond to tactile stimuli and how sensitive such responsivity is. Little research has addressed questions of their ability to discriminate a particular tactile stimulus from other stimuli. Recently Kisilevsky and Muir (1984), using a habituation-dishabituation technique, found that newborns can discriminate between brush strokes on the ear and ones on the lips, and between brush strokes and the sounds of a rattle. Their study not only demonstrates that newborns have a basic ability to discriminate tactile stimuli from other stimuli, but it also provides effective methodology for future explorations of tactile perception in young infants.

Summary

To summarize this rather complex area of tactile sensitivity, it seems clear that newborns do respond to a wide variety of tactile stimuli, including stimuli that are purely tactile (that is, that do not include temperature changes or other sorts of stimulation). Changes in sensitivity to tactual stimuli occur over the first few days of life, but perhaps not because of changes in sensitivity as such. Furthermore, the developmental changes found with different kinds of stimuli often differ in unanticipated ways. Tactile responses frequently have been found to vary as a function of other characteristics of the infants, such as activity level and kind of feeding. Most of these have been studied so infrequently that general conclusions about them are impossible. Sex differences, however, have been studied quite frequently, and on the basis of the existing data, we must conclude that they are not consistent, particularly when birth weight is controlled. Finally, newborns can discriminate between tactile stimuli on two different places on their bodies and between a tactile and an auditory stimulus.

---

[3]Thirteen filaments were used from 2.44 to 5.46 log of bending force.

TASTE

Two of the important nineteenth century infant researchers concluded that the sense of
taste was well developed at birth. Kussmaul, in
1859, observed facial expressions and sucking
movements of prematures in response to various solutions. Acid, salt, and quinine evoked
grimaces, but sugar led to sucking movements
(except in a few infants). Indeed, quinine was
rejected and sugar accepted as much as two
months before the normal time of birth. Preyer
(1881/1893) found much the same pattern of
reactions to similar classes of stimuli, but was
able (still on the basis of facial expressions) to
differentiate expressions in response to bitter
from those to sour, as well as to see that both
differed from those to sweet. He also found individual differences and rapid development of
sensitivity over the first few days of life. In
fact, his observations led him to conclude that
the gustatory (taste) sense was one of the most
highly developed in the newborn. Early in this
century, workers were somewhat more cautious about newborns' abilities in this domain
and cautioned against confusing responses to
smell, temperature, and intensity of stimulation with those to taste, a problem that is still
pertinent today. At the turn of the century people also began to measure responses other than
observed facial expressions and sucking reactions. Canestrini (1913) recorded pulse and respirations and found different responses to different stimuli (controlled for temperature). Salt
disrupted respirations and disrupted and increased pulse rate. The effects of sour and bitter were the same but more profound, whereas
sweet solutions lowered pulse and respiration
rates, producing a calming effect. He was not
able to show differences in response to cow's
milk versus that of the mother.

Pratt, Nelson, and Sun (1930) in their
classic monograph on infant behavior added
another response: stabilimeter readings that recorded bodily movements. Sucking reactions
and facial movements were also monitored.
They found that over the first 15 days of life
infants made some response to all stimuli except water on 85% of trials and engaged in
sucking on 30%. They also noted differential
responses to the classic sugar, salt, bitter, and
acid stimuli. Age-related changes also occurred
over this period. Sucking in response to sugar

and water increased, while that to quinine and
acid decreased. In the same time period Jensen
(1932) recorded sucking responses to various
solutions, using an early automated nipple. Infants showed differential responses to the substances, and those differential responses were
not accompanied by marked differences in facial expressions. If facial expressions changed,
however, they were always accompanied by
changes in sucking. Thus, sucking was a more
sensitive response measure. Infants also exhibited marked and stable individual differences.
Inasmuch as Jensen tested infants both 15 minutes before and 15 minutes after feeding, he
was able to note that moderately satiated infants were better discriminators of taste than
were very hungry infants.

Steiner (1977) has returned to facial expressions as a way to study the affective dimension of food-related stimuli. This methodology has also improved over that of the
earlier workers because records (videotape,
movie, or still photos) are made of the facial
expressions and these records are judged by
persons who do not know what substance is
being used to stimulate the baby. Steiner found
that observers of these records can reliably
classify the expressions, even when the taste
stimuli were presented before the newborn had
received any feeding. His conclusion was that
discriminative taste sensitivity is present at
birth; hence it cannot depend on life experience. The strength of this conclusion is
mitigated slightly by the fact that the infant
has swallowed (hence tasted) amniotic fluid for
long periods prior to birth, and this may provide an adaptation level against which new
stimuli are judged. Nevertheless, the fact that
Steiner also showed that two anencephalics
and two hydro-anencephalics (infants born
without cortexes) exhibited similar reactions
certainly supports the conclusion that the gus-
tofacial response is a low-level reflex-like response that does not involve cortical structures. In addition, the fact that adults can
interpret these responses means that they do
communicate to adults or that they are part of
the catalogue of nonverbal communicational
patterns broadcast by the infant to his mother.

The genesis of preference for sweet tastes
has intrigued several researchers. Desor,
Maller, and Greene (1977) measured infants'
preference for sweet versus other tastes. Prefer-

ence was assessed by the amounts of different liquids the infants consumed. Newborns (1 to 3 days old) were tested with different sugars and at different concentrations. All were tested midway between feedings in a schedule that alternated water and the particular sweet solution. All of the sugars were preferred to water, but glucose was preferred least of the sugars. Desor and colleagues concluded that responsiveness to sweetness is innate. Indeed, in another test they found that infants preferred a sucrose solution to milk. When older infants who had varied amounts of experience with milk and other foods were tested, essentially the same results were found, both at 5 to 11 weeks and at 20 to 28 weeks. The preferences were the same, although the infants were now able to consume larger quantities. Again these authors concluded that preference for sweet is characteristic of the human species. They noted that there are, nevertheless, large individual differences in the level (or degree) of sweetness preferred. Because the species preference indicates that this is an inherited trait, they studied older twins to determine whether the individual preference seemed to be inherited. There was no evidence that either inheritance or living in the same households led to similarity of taste preference, either for sweet or saltiness. These authors conclude that sweetness is a unique sensory quality, because similar universal preferences do not exist for other senses.

Another current approach to the study of sweet preferences, that of Lipsitt and his collaborators, utilizes advances in technology that enable simultaneous and highly sophisticated recording of respiration and heart rate, as well as sucking. The latter two measures are also simultaneously converted to digital information that can be fed directly to computers. The computer picks up information from the sucking on an automatic nipple and gives sucking response rates for each condition of testing for each child. The number of sucks per minute and the average interval between sucks are available (see Lipsitt, 1977). In several studies (Ashmead, Reilly, & Lipsitt, 1980; Crook & Lipsitt, 1976; Lipsitt, Reilly, Butcher, & Greenwood, 1976) Lipsitt and his collaborators have found that human newborns respond differently to sweet solutions than they do to water or to nonnutritive sucking; they suck more

slowly but more continuously, and their heart rates increase for sweet stimuli. These researchers interpret these reactions as reflecting pleasure.

Newborns also show evidence of adaptation of their responses to taste stimuli (Kobre & Lipsitt, 1972). The mean rate of sucking for very small drops of water or sucrose is stable over a 20-minute period and is about the same for both, about 55 per minute. If water is alternated with sucrose, however, the rates change. With repeated alternations the rates for sucrose increase slightly to about 60 per minute. They conclude that this represents an early effect of experience. They call it the negative contrast effect and say that it may represent an early and rudimentary learning phenomenon.

Thus, we can conclude that newborns do discriminate among tastes and that this responsivity is found for several different kinds of responses. It is interesting that some of them (like facial expressions) are obvious to the observer; some, like sucking, cannot be easily quantified by simple observation; and others, like heart rate, are not directly observable. Both of the latter appear to be more sensitive measures.

SMELL

A sense that is closely related to taste as experienced in the process of eating is smell (Figure 9–1). In evolutionary terms, smell is one of the oldest senses, and it is one of the most important senses for many adaptations of other mammals. Eating behaviors, avoidance of predators, sexual behaviors, and maternal behaviors are all strongly influenced by the sense of smell. It is true that the portions of the brain devoted to smell appear to be much smaller in humans than in most other mammals. Nevertheless, it is surprising that so little infancy research has dealt with the infant's capacities in this sensory domain. Some reasons for the lack of studies may be scientific, such as the difficulty of controlling the presentation of the stimuli and the problems of adaptation and interactions between stimuli. The fact that many newborns do not indicate displeasure at the sour milk smells of their own regurgitation or the smells of their own diapers may lead par-

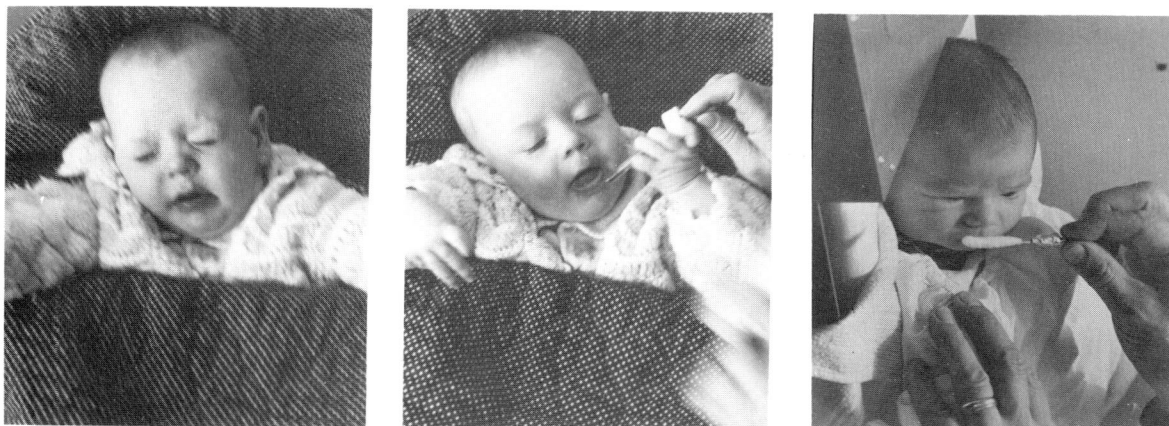

FIGURE 9–1. *Babies responding to taste and smell stimuli: (left) lemon juice; (center) a sweetened medicine; (right) an odorant on a cue tip. (Photograph on right courtesy of T. Engen. From* The Perception of Odors *by T. Engen. © 1982 by Academic Press. Used by permission.)*

ents (who sometimes are also scientists) to think that smell is not very important to the newborn.

Early scientific researchers did look at newborns' reactions to different odors. They found that not only did they react to odors, but differentiated among some of the same odors that adults discriminate. Responses indicative of displeasure or avoidance or both were found to odors such as asafetida (which adults find nauseatingly bad), and responses indicative of pleasure were found to odors that adults find pleasant.

There are a few studies from the 1960s and early 1970s that reconfirm what the early workers found: Newborns smell and discriminate between different smells, and they improve somewhat over the first few days of life (Engen & Bosack, 1969; Engen & Lipsitt, 1965; Engen, Lipsitt, & Kaye, 1963; Lipsitt, Engen, & Kaye, 1963; Self, Horowitz, & Paden, 1972; Steiner, 1977[4]).

Subsequent work (Guillory, Self, Francis, & Paden, 1979; Guillory, Self, & Paden, 1980) has challenged the existence of olfactory discrimination in the newborn period while confirming its existence at 1 month of age. The control stimulus in much of the earlier work lacked humidity and these workers used a paradigm in which habituation to a moist stimulus (cue tip in distilled water) was obtained. The dishabituation stimuli were 4 moist odorants and a dry cue tip. Any behavioral response (gross or fine motor or facial movements) was considered evidence of dishabituation. A large proportion of the 30 infants tested in light sleep responded differentially to all test stimuli other than lavender. In deep sleep only the noxious asafetida led to dishabituation responses in about half the infants. Guillory and colleagues concluded that previous researchers had confounded smell with humidity and thus that they may actually have been measuring discrimination of humidity and not of smells. Although their point about humidity is interesting, some earlier studies (for example, Engen & Bosack, 1969) examined mixtures of stimuli and the effects of moist adapting stimuli, and this tempers our acceptance of the new view. We are led by these considerations and by personal experience to retain the current view that newborns can detect odors until replications of the new findings, the longitudinal data the authors of these studies are pursuing, and a resolution of the conflicting data become available.

Recently, research on smell that has **ecological validity** has begun to appear. This

---

[4] Some researchers, most notably Steiner, have used facial expressions to gauge neonatal responses to different tastes and odors. There are some unpublished studies of failures to replicate that make us cautious of interpreting those data.

term describes research that attempts to study psychological phenomena that are as close to real life as possible. MacFarlane (1975) explored newborns' responses to breast pads their mothers had been wearing, most of which were dry. At 6 days of age the babies turned toward their own mothers' breast pads significantly more than towards another mother's pads. This is apparently a developmental phenomenon because 2-day-olds did not discriminate, although MacFarlane points out that younger infants might show a discrimination if a different response were used.

AUDITION

For hearing, as for all the other senses, the first question that has always been asked is, Can newborns respond to sound? Can they respond before the normal time of birth (prematurely delivered or in utero)? If the answers to these questions are No, then the question is, How soon are they able to do so? If they can respond, the second question becomes, What aspects of the sound stimuli are they able to respond to? To answer this question, it is necessary to consider the various aspects of sounds. Sounds are characterized by loudness (intensity, in physical terms), by pitch (determined by the frequency of the sound waves), by duration, and by where in space they originate (localization). In addition, there are differences in complexity. There are pure tones, combinations of pure tones, combinations of tones with a wide or narrow band of frequencies, noises, noises with different frequency components, and speech sounds (the last will be discussed in Chapter 11).

As in all studies of sensory and perceptual abilities in preverbal organisms, the particular responses of the organism used to judge the presence or absence of responses has a profound influence on the answer obtained. The responses most often used by the earliest workers were startles, the eye-blink reflex, turning toward the sound (which means that the babies not only heard the sound but also knew, at least in general, where it came from), and quieting. All of these responses are still studied, and with advancing technology there are a number of additional responses that per-

mit observation of activities inside the organism, such as changes in the electrical activity in the parts of the brain that process auditory stimuli. The interruption of sucking (often an orienting response) has also been used to indicate hearing. These new techniques have been automated, and so the role of human judgment in determining responses is reduced. Measurement of some of the externally observable responses, such as activity and blink reflexes, has also been automated with the consequent elimination of the necessity for human judgment (Figure 9–2).

In addition to the general question of understanding the functioning of infants, there is the more applied or clinical question involving the normalcy of the infant. In the case of hearing, the question has a particular relevance to infancy, because a large proportion of students in special education programs for the hearing impaired (77% in the United States in 1971) were deaf at birth. The hearing loss in over one third of these children was not discovered until after they were 3 years old. By this age it is almost impossible to begin good speech training. To detect deafness early it is necessary to identify the hearing capacities of normal infants to provide a standard for comparison.

Loudness (Intensity)

We shall start with perhaps the most fundamental characteristic of a sound stimulus, its loudness or intensity. There are two questions about intensity that are of interest. The first is how intense a sound has to be to elicit a response from an infant, and the second is whether the infant can detect differences in intensity (that is, respond differently to different intensities), and if so, how large the differences have to be.

Studying infants' responses to intensity is not simple, because responsivity to intensity of sounds depends both on the kind of sound being used and the response measure. For example, infants respond differently to noises than they do to pure tones. They respond differently to different pitches and to different speeds with which a sound begins (technically, speed of onset). These characteristics interact with the particular response chosen for study.

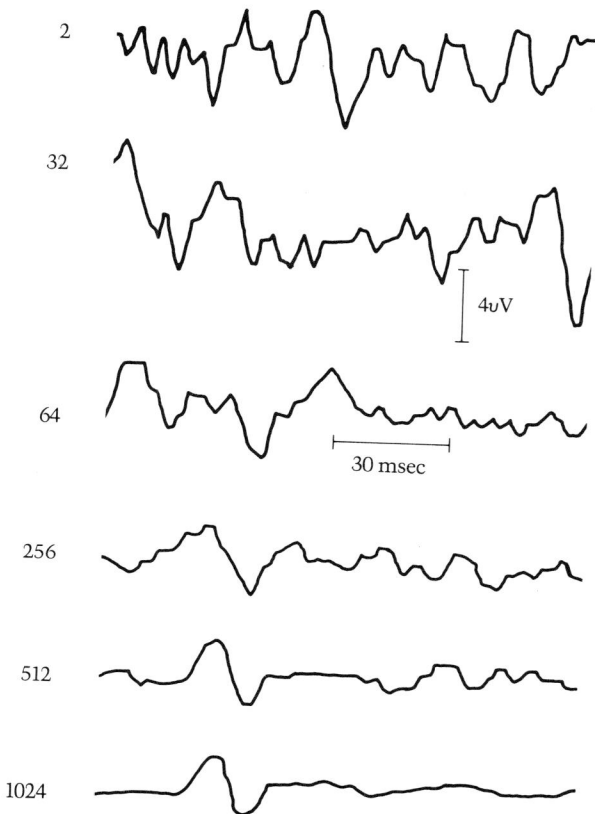

FIGURE 9–2. Graphs showing how information can become clear as a result of using computer averaging, and showing the form that an auditory evoked potential takes. The numbers on the left show the number of responses that were averaged. The amount of amplification was increased four fold between the top and the second graph. This figure is modified from Figure 1 of Geisler and Rosenblith (1962), who were the first to use this technique. (From "Average responses to clicks recorded from the human scalp," by C.D. Geisler and W.A. Rosenblith. The Journal of the Acoustical Society of America, 1962, 34, 125–127.)

Greater intensity is required to elicit startle than to elicit an eyeblink, which in turn requires greater intensity than that required to elicit a quieting response (which can only be elicited by soft sounds), or a heart rate response or an auditory evoked response in the electroencephalogram (EEG).

Researchers in the nineteenth and early twentieth centuries did not agree on whether babies could hear from birth. Tiedeman (1897/1927) reported that his son paid attention to those who spoke to him by 13 days, and that his crying could be somewhat hushed by soothing speech. Prior to that he had often startled to sudden sound and blinked his eyes to sudden sounds. Kussmaul (1859), in contrast, was convinced that newborns did not hear. Preyer (1881/1893) reported that his son could not hear for the first three days, but heard handclaps on the fourth and responded to a whisper and was quieted by his father's voice on the eleventh and twelfth days. Genzmer (1882) had already repeated Kussmaul's experiments with a bell and had concluded that infants heard on the first or at least the second day of life.

All of these workers were using complex sounds (bells, rattles, human voices, handclaps) to obtain or judge responses. The responses noted were attentive or quieting responses (related to what would be called orienting responses today), startles and eyeblinks (both are reflexes, the latter technically known as the auropalpebral reflex), and various bodily movements, especially of the face and eyes.

As early as 1881 the questions of the infant's state and the variability of responses had been noted. In the early 1900s it had been shown that newborns respond to a rattle within 10 to 360 minutes after birth (Peterson & Rainey, 1910), that movements in the fetus occur in response to an automobile horn (Peiper, 1924), in response to a glass struck on a metal bathtub in which the mother is sitting (Forbes & Forbes, 1927), and even in response to pure tones (Bernard, 1946). Heart rate changes were shown for the 7- to 9-month fetus in response to a wide range of relatively pure tones (Bernard & Sontag, 1947).

The auropalpebral reflex (eyeblink) has been used in recent years to detect malingering in persons who claim they cannot hear, but it has long been applied to another class of verbally uncooperative subjects—infants—to get answers to researchers' questions. Genzmer and Preyer both used it. In 1960 Fröding established that within one-half hour of birth 96% of infants showed this response to a gong that produced sounds of 126 to 132 dB (dB is the abbreviation for decibel, the unit by which loudness or intensity is measured; loud thunder is about 120 dB).

Starting in the 1920s, after Pavlov's work, conditioned responses were used to study the ability to respond to sound. Marquis (1931) established that 7 out of 8 neonates responded by sucking to the sound of a buzzer that had been paired with food during the first 10 days of life. While much argument exists as to whether this was conditioning, it clearly demonstrates that the infants did respond to sound.

Newborns have been shown to respond differentially to different intensities of sounds. Both the number of startles and the latency of the motor responses are related to intensity. Heart rate accelerations are also related to intensity, as has been found by both early and more recent studies (Bartoshuk, 1964; Bridger, 1961; Canestrini, 1913; Eichorn, 1951; Steinschneider, Lipton, & Richmond, 1966). It has also been shown that the size of the auditory evoked responses to clicks in sleeping infants varies in a linear fashion with the intensity of the clicks (Barnet & Goodwin, 1955).

Several studies have attempted to measure newborns' absolute threshold for sound (the softest sound they can hear). Estimates vary depending on the response used by the researchers. Responses to softer tones can be detected using auditory evoked potentials rather than heart rate responses, which in turn are more sensitive than the blink or startle response. The estimate for the threshold also depends on the stringency of criteria used. Most studies yield estimates of around 40 dB (sound of a quiet office) to 60 dB (the level of a conversation; see review by Berg & Berg, 1979). Wedenberg (1956) has shown what noise levels wake babies: They are awakened from deep sleep by 70–75 dB sounds (the noise of a busy street) and from light sleep by 55 dB sounds (a quiet car). In contrast, he found that it took sounds of over 105 dB (the sound of a boiler shop) to elicit the eyeblink response.

Thus, babies are able to hear a wide range of sounds, including that stimulus of great interest, the human voice. They are not, however, able to hear as well as adults (who can hear approximately 0 dB). Infants improve rapidly. Taguchi, Picton, Orpin, and Goodman (1969) found that hearing improves markedly over the first few days of life (about 16 dB), which is apparently *not* due to loss of extra tissue in the middle ear as has often been supposed. Sharp decreases in the threshold have also been shown between 3 and 8 months

(Hoversten & Moncur, 1969). Nevertheless, for infants in the second half year of life thresholds for sounds in the frequency range of speech (fundamental frequencies of 200–500 Hz) are still 15 to 30 dB higher than those for adults (Moore & Wilson, 1978; Sinnott, Pisoni, & Aslin, 1983; Trehub, Schneider, & Endman, 1980).

Localization

Head turning or eye movements toward a sound were interpreted by the early baby biographers as a sign of responding to sound. They observed these behaviors occasionally in the first few weeks of life. Since that time, some researchers have found that newborns fairly consistently turn toward a sound (for example, Crassini & Broerse, 1980; Field, Muir, Pilon, Sinclair, & Dodwell, 1980; Leventhal & Lipsitt, 1964; Mendelson & Haith, 1976; Muir & Field, 1979; Turkewitz, Birch, Moreau, Levy, & Cornwell, 1966; Wertheimer, 1961), but others have found no neonatal responsiveness (for example, Butterworth & Castillo, 1976; Chun, Pawsat, & Forster, 1960; McGurk, Turnure, & Creighton, 1977). These discrepancies in findings are apparently produced by differences in the kinds of sounds used by various researchers. For example, soft sounds appear to be more likely to produce head and eye movements toward the stimulus (Muir & Field, 1979; Turkewitz et al., 1966) and continuous sounds may be more effective, perhaps because newborns' responses are quite slow (Muir & Field, 1979). With optimal stimuli, Muir and Field (1979) found that of 12 infants who had optimal characteristics at birth (no birth complications, limited obstetric medication, high Apgar scores, and so forth) and who could be maintained in an alert state for the necessary 10 to 15 minutes, 11 showed consistent orientation responses. Two additional studies using similar procedures found that infants around 2 months of age were less responsive (there were more trials in which no head turn occurred), but that infants 3 to 4 months of age were again more responsive (Field, Muir, Pilon, Sinclair, & Dodwell, 1980; Muir, Abraham, Forbes, & Harris, 1979). By 3 to 6 months this response is so robust that head turning in the direction of a sound from an invisible source appears on infants' tests (Bayley, 1969; Cattell, 1940).

It has also been shown that a sound can be used to help alert infants to attend visually. Both in newborns (in the Graham/Rosenblith tests; Mendelson & Haith, 1976) and in 2-month-old infants (Culp, 1971; Self, 1971) sound has been used to get infants' eyes to midline so visual following can be measured. Mendelson and Haith (1976) argue that sound initiates a scanning routine that increases the likelihood the newborn will find a visual change, and that this is not just a function of arousal but rather is part of the basic information-processing equipment of humans.

Turning in the direction of a sound is a very primitive form of localization. It does not necessarily mean that newborns can look precisely toward the source of sounds coming from various places around them. Indeed, the animal literature suggests that precise looking appears to require cortical control whereas a simple head turn in the direction of sound does not (Clifton, Morrongiello, Kulig, & Dowd, 1981b). There is little evidence about newborns' abilities to localize more precise positions in space. In the Graham/Rosenblith a slightly more precise measure of localization is given. A rattle and a bell are sounded at each of four points around the supine infant (to the left of the left ear, the right of the right ear, in the midline above the head, and in the midline below the ears or over the belly button). Rosenblith and Anderson-Huntington tested large numbers of newborns using this procedure. Although some repeatedly localized correctly by head or eye turning or both, they were a minority of all newborns tested (the sound stimuli are relatively intense—80 dB—and the infants' mothers had been relatively highly medicated). In testing a smaller number of babies of different ethnic groups, whose mothers had received less medication, Rosenblith found a higher proportion who localized (turned correctly) toward one or both of these stimuli.

Another localization phenomenon that is also more complex than a simple head turn to a sound is the precedence effect. If a sound is fed through two loudspeakers on opposite sides of the adult listener and the sound in one speaker is delayed by several milliseconds, the listener hears the sound as if it were coming from the first speaker and suppresses the information from the second speaker. It is thought that this is the organism's way of suppressing interfering echoes and that it is a cortical mechanism. In two studies (Clifton et al., 1981b, Morrongiello, Clifton, & Kulig, 1982), newborns did not show the precedence effect even though they did show localization to a single source. In another study they found that the precedence effect had developed by 5 months of age (Clifton, Morrongiello, Kulig, & Dowd, 1981a). These two studies are further evidence that newborns' ability to localize sound is rudimentary at birth.

Among the major reasons for researchers' interest in auditory localization are the potential epistemological implications (that is, implications concerning the nature of human knowledge). Adults who consistently turn their heads toward a sound expect to see an object making the sound. In other words, for an adult a sound emanates from an object. The epistemological question is whether newborns also know that sounds emanate from objects. Some people would argue that turning toward a sound demonstrates that newborns have that knowledge, even though they are probably unaware of it. Other researchers argue that the simple localization phenomenon found in newborns may not require the knowledge that an object has visual and auditory characteristics. Rather, they argue, it appears to be a primitive reflex-like mechanism, which drops out and is replaced by a more mature, cortically-mediated mechanism. Only in the latter, more mature, form will infants understand that objects have both visual and auditory characteristics. There is evidence that babies 3 to 4 months of age do understand the intermodal nature of objects (Broerse, Peltolta, & Crassini, 1983; Goldenberg, Starkey, & Morant, 1984; Spelke, 1976; Spelke & Owsley, 1979) whereas the evidence that younger infants do so is inconclusive (Aronson & Rosenbloom, 1971, found evidence that they do, but Condry, Haltom, & Neisser, 1977, and McGurk & Lewis, 1974, failed to replicate these findings). Furthermore, research has consistently found that not until 9 to 12 months of age can infants use sound to search for a hidden object (Bigelow, 1983; Freedman, Fox-Kolenda, Margileth, & Miller, 1969; Uzgiris & Benson,

1980), thereby demonstrating that they expect a sound to emanate from an object even when they cannot see it.

Pitch (Frequency) and Complexity

Sounds also vary in pitch (high versus low tones) and in complexity (pure versus multi-toned sounds). These characteristics affect responsivity to sound, as we mentioned in our description of the research on thresholds and localization. Now we will examine infants' responses to these specific characteristics. The physical dimension underlying pitch is the frequency of sound waves, given in units called Herz (Hz). For example, the range of a baritone voice is about 96 to 320 Hz; of a violin, 190 to 3000 Hz; and of a tuba, 45 to 350 Hz. Adults generally can hear sounds from 20 to 20,000 Hz. Complexity refers to how many frequencies a sound has. The flute makes an almost pure tone; it sounds almost exclusively at a single frequency. Most other sounds, including music from other instruments, voices, and noises, are complex; they include several frequencies. White noise is a particularly interesting complex sound. In its pure case, which sounds like a waterfall, all frequencies are present and of equal intensity. Figure 9–3 demonstrates the differences between simple and complex sounds.

Early studies, which used complex sounds, found that young infants were responsive to stimuli of various frequencies. As laboratory equipment and methods have become more sophisticated, researchers have confirmed that newborn infants do respond to sound of various frequencies, but only in certain circumstances. They respond to white noise (Lenard, Bernuth, & Hutt, 1969; Turkewitz, Birch, & Cooper, 1972a, 1972b) and to square-wave tones (selected fundamental tones with superimposed high frequencies of various fundamental frequencies, which result in a broader band of frequencies, not a single one as in the case of a pure tone sine wave, particularly for low frequencies (Bench, 1973; Hutt, Hutt, Lenard, Bernuth, & Muntjewerff, 1968; Lenard et al., 1969). They are much less likely, however, to demonstrate consistent responses to sustained pure tones (such as those produced by tone generators or a well-played flute) than to other

stimuli (Clarkson & Berg, 1978; Hutt et al., 1968; Lenard et al., 1969; Turkewitz et al., 1972b).

Some studies have compared newborns' sensitivity to soft sounds (absolute threshold) at various frequencies (pitches). The results of such studies are not consistent. Some find different thresholds at different frequencies (Ashton, 1971; Hutt et al., 1968; Hutt, Lenard, & Prechtl, 1969; Lenard et al., 1969) and others do not (Ashton, 1971; Clarkson & Berg, 1978; Crowell, Jones, Nakagawa, & Kapuniai, 1971; Taguchi et al., 1969). Nevertheless, when such differences are found, the direction of differences is consistent. Newborns exhibit greater sensitivity to moderately low tones (100–1000 Hz) than to higher or very low frequencies.

Other studies have addressed the question of whether young babies can discriminate among sounds of different frequencies. The outcomes of these studies are also inconsistent and the inconsistencies are difficult to interpret because the various studies use different stimuli and procedures. Two studies exemplify the problem. Wormith, Pankhurst, and Moffitt (1975) found evidence for such discrimination in 1-month-olds, using continuous pure tones of 200 and 500 Hz in a conjugate reinforcement procedure, whereas Trehub (1973) found no evidence for discrimination in 1- to 4-month-olds using discrete square wave tone bursts of 100 versus 200 Hz and 1,000 versus 2,000 Hz, or among pure tone bursts of 200 versus 1,000 Hz in a habituation procedure.

Other research exploring newborns' responsivity to frequency of sounds has taken an approach that has more ecological validity by examining responsiveness to stimuli that have more meaning than isolated tones. Two such ecologically valid avenues of study are responsivity to human voices and differential emotinal responses to various sounds. Newborns are apparently especially responsive to sounds in the frequency range of the human voice (see review by Eisenberg, 1970b). They even prefer music when voices accompany it (Butterfield & Siperstein, 1974). In addition, human voices quickly take on emotional meaning for babies. DeCasper and Fifer (1980) found that 3-day-old babies clearly showed a preference for their own mothers' voices over those of strange women.

Nonhuman sounds can also affect babies

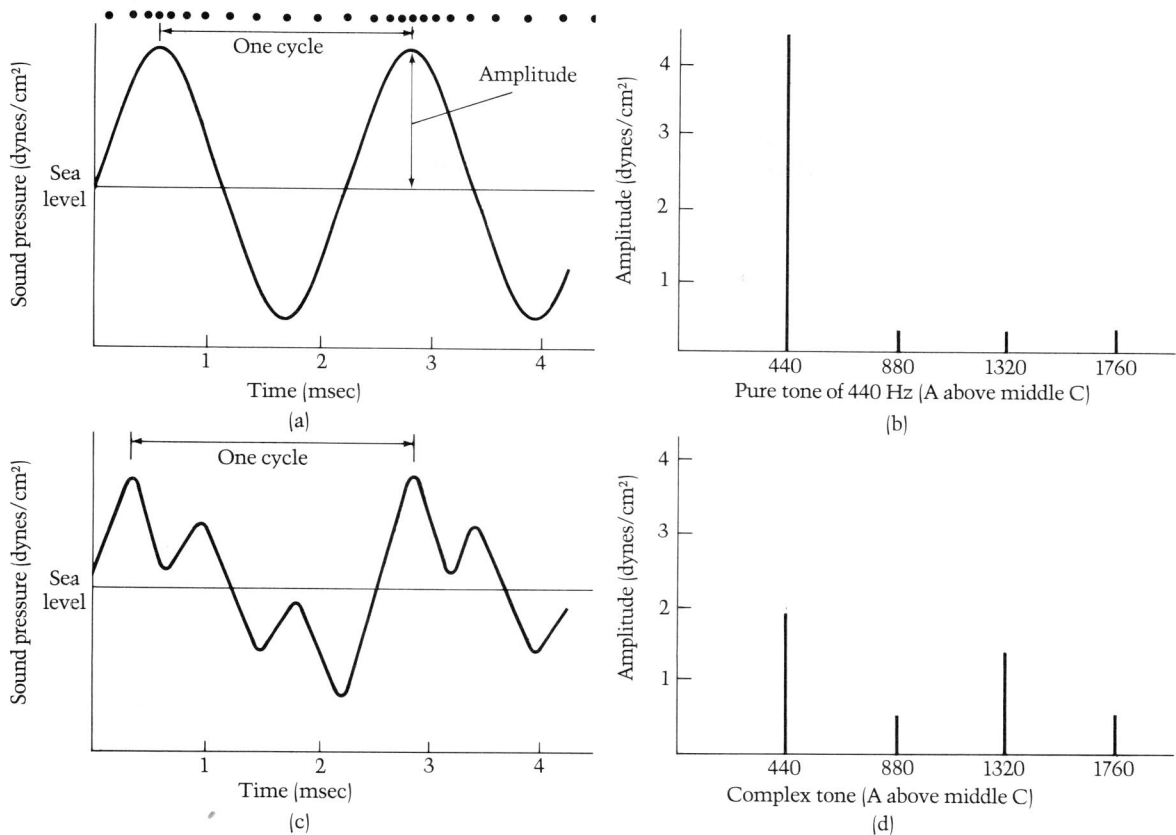

FIGURE 9–3. Sound waves are disturbances in air molecules caused by vibrating objects. The vibrations alternately push the air molecules together (compression, or increasing sound pressure) and allow the air molecules to spread out (expansion, or decreasing sound pressure). The number of such waves in a second (the frequency) determines the pitch of the tone. (a) The waves of compression and expansion of a pure tone such as that of a tuning fork or a flute. The dots above the tone represent the air molecules. The wave form is called a sine wave. This tone is the first A above middle C on the piano. The figure represents two waves; there will be 440 such waves in 1 second in a tone of this pitch. (b) A pure tone with just one frequency. This figure, which represents the same tone as in part (a), shows that its fundamental frequency is 440 Hz. (c) A complex tone, typical of most sounds. Voices, bird songs, and most musical instruments produce complex tones. The fundamental frequency of this tone is also 440Hz, which means that it will sound the same pitch as in part (a). (d) Unlike pure tones, complex tones exhibit frequencies in addition to the fundamental frequencies. The fundamental frequency of complex tones is always their lowest frequency. The number of additional frequencies may vary from a few, as in this figure, to 20 to 30. (Adapted with permission from Psychology: Its principles and meanings (4th Ed.), by L.E. Bourne, Jr., and B.R. Ekstrand. New York: Holt, Rinehart, & Winston, 1982.)

emotionally. They can soothe, alert, or distress infants. Very high frequencies (above 4,000 Hz; Haller, 1932) or very low frequencies (70 Hz; Hutt et al., 1968) appear to distress newborns. Complex sounds that are in the low frequency range appear, in contrast, to be soothing to infants (Birch, Belmont, & Karp, 1965; Bench, 1969). These responses are similar to those of adults (Eisenberg, 1970a, 1970b). In music and everyday life adults use high frequencies to communicate alarm, excitement, or disturbance, and low frequencies to communicate relative calm. That newborns have different emotional or affective responses to high- and low-pitched sounds demonstrates that they can discriminate between them.

Although most of the research on pitch perception has focused on newborns, a spate of studies exploring its development in older infants has appeared. Trehub, Schneider, and their colleagues (Schneider, Trehub, & Bull, 1980; Trehub, Schneider, & Endman, 1980) have found, using broad-band sounds, that by 6 months of age infants are more sensitive (relative to adults) to higher frequencies than to low frequencies. For the highest sounds they tested (19,000 Hz), infants 24 months of age were just as sensitive as adults and infants 6–18 months old were only 5–10 dB less sensitive. For lower, but still high, tones (10,000 Hz), all infants tested (6–24 months) were slightly (12–16 dB) less sensitive than adults. In contrast, response to low-pitched sounds (200 to 400 Hz) developed more slowly. Babies 6 months old were 5–8 dB less sensitive than 12-month-olds and 20–30 dB less sensitive than adults.

Olsho (1984) found similar results in a study of sensitivity to differences between two tones (difference threshold). Infants discriminated between tones of high frequencies (4,000 and 8,000 Hz) as well as adults did, but they were inferior to adults at lower frequencies (250 Hz and 2,000 Hz). A study by Berg and Smith (1983), however, failed to find better high-frequency sensitivity in 6- to 18-month-old babies, and the reasons for the inconsistent findings have not yet been demonstrated.

The findings that older babies are more sensitive to high-frequency sounds contrast sharply with those studies that have found newborns to be more sensitive to low-frequency sounds. Because the research results with both newborns and older infants are in-

consistent, it is perhaps premature to try to reconcile them. Nevertheless, both conclusions can be valid. Sensitivity to high-frequency sounds may be very inadequate in newborns but may develop rapidly, and sensitivity to low-frequency sounds may be greater at the time of birth but may increase relatively slowly after birth. Trehub, Schneider, and their colleagues review physiological data that suggest that the part of the ear responsible for detecting high-frequency sounds is mature at birth and begins to deteriorate during infancy, which fits with the facts that (1) hearing loss first manifests itself in high-frequency sounds and (2) children are more sensitive to high-frequency sounds than adults. Further, they suggest that environments noisy in high-frequency sounds might affect the hearing of infants and children.

Continuity or Repetitiveness of Stimulation

The soothing effect of low-frequency sounds is especially pronounced if the sound is continuous or rhythmic. Brackbill (1970) studied the effects of continuous sound as compared with intermittent sound or silence on infants 1 month of age. She found that there was no crying at all under the continuous sound condition and that the highest levels of arousal occurred in the intermittent sound condition (in the latter condition infants spent one-fourth of the time crying). In another study (Brackbill, 1971) she compared continuous stimulation in the auditory sense modality with other forms of continuous stimulation (light, warmth, and swaddling).[5] All of the forms of continuous stimulation had soothing effects and often led to quiet sleep. There was also some tendency for the effects of the different modalities to be cumulative.

This phenomenon has been put to practical use in various ways. Long before any of these data or devices were available, Rosenblith (and probably countless other mothers) found that the sound of the vacuum cleaner could lead her fussy infant to be quiet or go to

---

[5] Swaddling is probably not as good an example of the effects of continuous stimulation as are constant light or temperature.

sleep. She also found that it worked for visiting infants. Today, manufacturers make devices that produce continuous sounds advertised to help babies sleep. Whether such devices are optimal as soothing techniques is unclear. Wolff (1966) found that the quiet (or non-REM) sleep induced by a continuous sound differs from normal quiet sleep in the pattern of the spontaneous startles and mouthings. Wolff also noted that from the second week on, the internal biological clocks of infants seemed to determine that quiet, non-REM sleep periods rarely last longer than 21 minutes; and that this was true of periods occurring with continuous sound stimulation whether or not the sound had been turned on at the beginning, middle, or end of the cycle. Because he considered his data tentative and no further findings are available, it is difficult to draw practical conclusions regarding the use of such devices.

The research interest in rhythmic auditory stimulation probably started when Dr. Lee Salk, a pediatrician who writes for parents, reported (1962) that recordings of a mother's heartbeat played in a newborn nursery led to less crying and faster weight gain. Consistent with popular ideas at that time in the history of child psychology, he considered the possibility that infants were biologically set to respond to their mothers' heartbeats. He also speculated on the significance of mothers usually holding their infants on the left side where they can best hear the mother's heartbeat, and even on the artistic depictions of mothers and infants in this position. This seems rather weak evidence for the heartbeat hypothesis because mothers may hold their infants on the left side to free their right hands (the preferred hand for almost 90% of adults) for other uses. A better test of Salk's hypothesis is to test newborns' responses to heartbeats in comparison to other stimuli. In one such study responses to a heartbeat were compared to responses to the sounds of a metronome beating, a lullaby being sung, and silence (Tulloch, Brown, Jacobs, Prugh, & Greene, 1964). All three sounds led to quieting (less crying, less activity, less variable respiration, and a lower and less variable heart rate) compared to the condition of silence. No one of the sounds was any more effective than the others. This means, of course, that there was no innate special responsivity to mother's heartbeat. More recently, Detterman (1978) has attacked the heartbeat hypothesis on methodological grounds and Salk (1978) has defended his position.

VISION

People have long been interested to know whether babies see when they are first born, or how soon they see. As we noted in Chapter 1, both early baby biographers and the early scientists studying newborns concluded that babies do see, a conclusion that later became unfashionable. Early workers relied primarily on two responses to infer that babies see: (1) Whether they turned toward light or objects, and (2) whether they followed the course of a moving object with their eyes.

The current cycle of interest in visual perception in infancy was stimulated by Fantz's (1961) development of the visual preference technique, described at the beginning of this chapter. It and the other new techniques described there have permitted researchers to ask much more sophisticated questions concerning the nature of what infants might see—whether they discriminate colors, brightness, patterns, depth, and so forth. This research has also raised questions about the way infants explore visually—the nature and meaning of eye movements, how they scan stimuli, and how these abilities develop.

We shall begin with a discussion of the research on visual exploration, which has focused on development in early infancy. Then we will consider research on various sorts of visual information. We will ask our standard questions about the age of onset of vision and its subsequent development to a mature form.

Visual Exploration

To process visual information, humans need to look at a stimulus. Even newborns have some capacity to find and look toward stimuli although they are much more limited in such abilities than are older people. We have already discussed the ability to turn toward a sound, which is present in limited form at birth. In this section we will discuss infants' abilities to find visual stimuli and keep them before their eyes.

EYE MOVEMENTS THAT MAINTAIN FIXATION ON LARGE MOVING TARGETS

The first eye movement that we will discuss is **optokinetic nystagmus** (OKN). OKN occurs when a large target with a repetitive pattern on it moves past a stationary observer (for example, vertical black and white stripes) and when an observer moves past a large pattern (for example, a person in a moving car watching telephone poles pass by). In either case the person's eyes typically fixate on some part of the pattern (a particular telephone pole, for example), follow that part with a smooth movement in the direction of the motion, then make a quick, jerky movement (called a saccade) back toward the center of the visual field (in the direction opposite that of the motion). OKN seems to a certain extent to be involuntary, although a similar nystagmus can be started voluntarily. OKN is easily found in newborns. Although it includes both the smooth pursuit and the jerky, saccadic movements we will discuss next, OKN is apparently more mature at birth than saccadic movements are, and is more easily elicited.

SACCADES: LOOKING TOWARD STIMULI IN THE CORNER OF THE EYE

When a stimulus appears in **peripheral** vision (anywhere outside the field of focus), a **saccadic** movement may occur. A saccade consists of a very rapid, usually accurate, movement that is ballistic (that is, it goes in a single motion from its origin to a predetermined end point). Saccades bring peripheral stimuli into central focus, where adults' vision is most acute. The eliciting stimulus may be small and nonrepetitive (unlike that which elicits OKN). Motion is best detected in peripheral vision and thus saccadic movements play an important role in detecting potentially dangerous missiles. Consider, for example, a driver who sees a car out of the corner of her or his eye. The driver automatically—and very rapidly—turns her or his eyes (and head, if the approaching car is very far to the side) toward the car so that it comes into central vision. The same happens if a rock or ball is detected in peripheral vision.

Saccades not only save lives by helping people process danger signals, they also help process visual materials, both pictures and reading. Perusal of visual information takes place by a series of fixations and saccades. In reading, for example, saccades occur approximately every 250 msec and each one takes 25–40 msec.

The most striking thing about newborn saccades is that they exist. Infants evidently do not have to learn or practice for their eyes to move toward a peripheral target. Young infants look toward stimuli in the periphery even when they are already looking at something in their central vision, but saccades are less likely to occur when the infant is looking at an object in central vision. Infants are much more likely to make saccades to relatively near targets than to far objects and are more likely to make horizontal than vertical saccades.

The form of the saccade differs from that of adults in several ways that make it less efficient and perhaps less accurate. It also is slower to start, at least compared to the most rapid responses of adults, but it is still rapid—usually within 2 seconds of the onset of the peripheral target. It is not known when the mature form develops, but it is after 7 weeks of age (see review by Salapatek, 1975).

That newborns make such saccadic movements shows that they can detect the presence of a peripheral stimulus, but it does not tell whether infants perceive the nature of the peripheral stimuli. It is known that adults can process information in the periphery and apparently do so better than young children (see Rayner, 1978, for a discussion). To find out how this ability to process peripheral stimuli develops in infants, researchers can study their ability to discriminate among stimuli presented in the periphery. Maurer and Lewis (1979) found that infants at least as young as 3 months do discriminate between stimuli in the periphery. They selected pairs of stimuli such that one would be preferred and then presented them peripherally, one on each side of the infants' midline. Infants made a saccade to the side with the preferred stimulus on the first trial, thereby demonstrating that they saw both stimuli and discriminated between them.

In summary, the research on saccadic eye movements shows that the basic physiological mechanism for detecting and responding to stimuli in the periphery is present in newborns and develops rapidly in the early months of life, which means that newborns are well equipped to locate visual events in this world.

It also indicates that at 3 months of age, infants can discriminate between peripherally presented patterns.

DO NEWBORNS SEARCH FOR VISUAL STIMULI?

The research on saccadic movements that we have just described has established the existence of captured attention in the neonatal period. Nevertheless, there is disagreement over whether saccadic movements also are part of active visual exploration. Tronick and Clanton (1971) found that very young infants are likely to make saccades even when no peripheral stimulus is presented. They interpreted this as searching for a stimulus. This interpretation has been challenged by Salapatek (1975), who suggested that there may have been very peripheral stimuli unnoticed by Tronick and Clanton, and the infants were simply making the first of multiple saccades to such stimuli.

Haith and his colleagues (Haith, 1978, 1980; Haith & Goodman, 1982; Mendelson & Haith, 1976) attacked this question in a quite different fashion. They had observers judge whether infants' eye movements were controlled or were broad uncontrolled jerks. The observers were able to make these judgments very reliably. In darkness newborns exhibited frequent and controlled eye movements, which were not dependent on visual sensory feedback signals. Haith believes that they did this to search for visual contours. In patterned light, visual exploration was also controlled, as would be expected. Surprisingly, however, in light without patterns (a homogeneous field), the eye movements of newborns were uncontrolled, which suggests that they were not searching for visual information. Taking all three situations together, Haith concluded that newborns are active visual explorers and that lack of control will be found only when there is no contour to explore or if the visual information is uninteresting or unattended.

TRACKING MOVING STIMULI

From birth, infants attend to and track moving stimuli, as Graham and colleagues had shown in the 1950s (Graham, 1956). We have already described optokinetic nystagmus, which has been found in newborns in response to moving vertically striped patterns. Newborns also track single moving objects for a

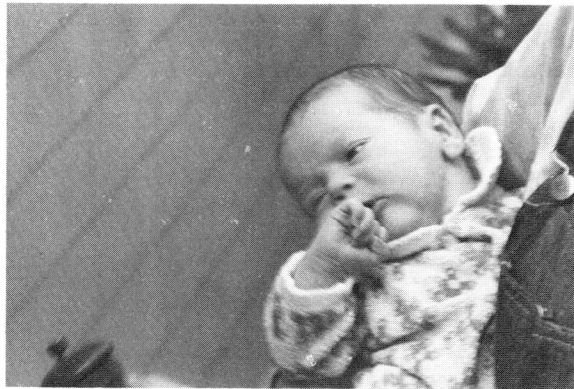

FIGURE 9–4. A newborn making a saccadic movement toward a stimulus.

wide distance (up to 90 degrees of a circle; Gregg, Clifton, & Haith, 1976; White, 1971). Their tracking is quite immature, however, and is rarely a sustained smooth pursuit. Kremenitzer, Vaughan, Kurtzberg, and Dowling (1979) found smooth tracking in less than 15% of the exposure time. During the rest of the time pursuit was jerky: The infants' eyes were stationary for a time and then a saccade occurred in the direction of the moving object. They also responded at their maximum to much more slowly moving targets than do adults (14 deg/sec and 40 deg/sec, respectively), which is consistent with many other findings that newborns require longer exposure times than older infants. Pursuit is often far less frequent when the stimulus is a single target than when it is vertical stripes (OKN stimuli; Kremenitzer et al., 1979; see also Figure 9–4).

Smooth pursuit develops at 6–8 weeks of age, at least for some speeds of stimulus movement (Aslin, 1981; Dayton & Jones, 1964; White, 1971). The infant now anticipates the movement of the object and in a smooth, continuous head and eye movement keeps the target in central vision. The ability to track stimuli moving at various speeds continues to develop in the first half year of life (Aslin, 1981; Ames & Silfen, 1965).

Thus, the research suggests that infants respond to movement of visual stimuli from birth and become more responsive to it as they develop. The shortness of this section may give the impression that perception of moving objects is not very important in early infancy.

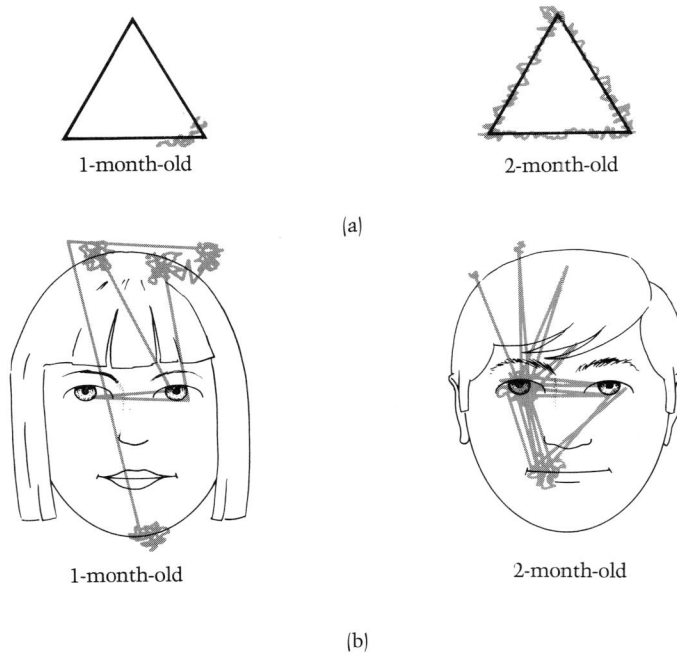

(a)

(b)

FIGURE 9–5. *Schematic plots of visual scanning by representative 1- and 2-month-old babies. Infrared lights are placed behind the stimulus and reflect off the babies' eyes when they look at a picture. When their eyes change position to look at a new place, the infrared reflection changes position too. The tracings are drawn by observers who watch the videotape (but do not see the stimulus and thus cannot be biased by it). The tracings consist of zigzag lines because of the infants' saccades: their eyes jerk from one location to another.*
(a) Triangles. The 1-month-old fixates primarily on one corner of the triangle, while the 2-month-old scans all three corners. (b) Faces—pictures with internal contour. The younger infant scans mostly those external contours that have high contrast (the chin and hairline) and the older infant scans primarily internal contours. (Adapted from "Pattern perception in early infancy" by P. Salapatek, in Infant perception: From sensation to cognition. *Volume 1, Basic visual processes. Copyright 1975 by Academic Press. Used by permission.)*

Such an impression is certainly false. Movement seems to play a very important role in the development of early social responsiveness (Moltz, 1960; Rheingold, 1961; Stern, 1977). It also appears to be of fundamental importance in learning about objects. We will discuss the role of movement in perceiving objects later in this chapter.

SCANNING STATIONARY PATTERNS

In addition to studying the way infants get and keep visual events in their center of vision, researchers can study how infants look at an object once they have focused on it. Newborns generally look at a single feature or contour of an object; for example, one corner of a triangle. By 2 months of age infants begin to scan more broadly; for example, along the sides and other corners of a triangle (see Figure 9–5). Salapatek, in his 1975 review of this literature, points out that 2 months is also the age at which infants become able to exhibit complex visual discriminations.

Another developmental trend in scanning in this age range is a shift from looking at external contours to examination of internal contours. Salapatek and Moscovich (unpublished study reported in Salapatek, 1975) presented squares embedded within squares to 1-month- and 2-month-old infants. The 1-month-olds looked at a corner of the big square, while the 2-month-olds typically selected the internal features. Similar results have been obtained with other geometric patterns (Bushnell, Gerry, & Burt, 1983), and with faces (see the section on face perception later in this chapter). Infants younger than 2 months look at the external contours (the hairline and chin, or an ear) while 2-month-olds look at the eyes.

Independent evidence that the scanning of patterns reflects infant processing has been presented by Milewski (1976), who habituated 1-month- and 4-month-old infants to a compound figure similar to that used by Salapatek and Moscovich. The older infants dishabituated (showed evidence of discriminating) in response to changes in shape of either the external or the internal contour. In contrast, younger infants dishabituated only to changes that involved the external contour. This suggests that 1-month-old infants not only ignore the internal contours in scanning but also fail to remember anything about those internal contours.

Detecting Visual Information

We have discussed how babies explore their visual world; let us examine what they see. Some of the information visual stimuli provide comes from their brightness and color. Most of the information, however, is carried by the pattern of the visual stimuli. Pattern includes external contour (shape) and internal features, as well as the more subtle and complex information that tells what the object is and where it is in space.

The most basic question asked about pattern perception was whether newborns detect patterns at all. Fantz's seminal work (for example, 1961, 1963) demonstrated that they do; they consistently look longer at patterns than at homogeneous fields. Perhaps the next logical steps were to ask how well they see (acuity) and what kind of patterns they see. Researchers have been particularly interested in discovering whether infants can perceive the visual patterns that signify human faces.

Visual patterns give one crucial kind of information about an object, but other kinds of information are just as important. Objects exist in three-dimensional space, and visual information provides the cues that tell that an object is three dimensional and how far away it is. Infant researchers are interested in the questions of when such object perception develops and how it develops. We will first describe what is known about infant perception of brightness and color and then proceed to the various issues of pattern perception.

BRIGHTNESS (INTENSITY) OF LIGHT

It seems clear that young infants are very good at discriminating among lights that vary in brightness. Hershenson (1964) found that infants 2 to 4 days of age looked longer at lights of medium intensity than they did at bright or dim lights. Peeples and Teller (1975) found that somewhat older babies could discriminate brightness almost as well as adults. Their 2-month-old subjects could distinguish a bar of light from its background when the brightness of the two stimuli differed by only 5%. The smallest difference adults can discriminate is 1%. In both of these studies the two lights were presented at the same time. When lights are presented one after the other, infants as old as 4 months are very poor at discriminating differences in brightness (Kessen & Bornstein, 1978), probably because of memory limitations.

The ability to discriminate among lights of different brightness or intensity is clear. What about the question of sensitivity to light in a more absolute sense? Gross observational methods suggest that newborns are more sensitive to light than older infants or children (or adults). They blink, close or squint their eyes, and turn away from lights of lower intensity (or brightness) than would cause this reaction in older children. Greater extremes of hypersensitivity than are normally found in newborns are very rare but are associated with neurological damage (Anderson & Rosenblith, 1964). However, we know of no systematic studies in which responses to intensity have been examined in a systematic and fine-grained way.

COLOR

It might seem a simple matter to determine whether infants can discriminate among

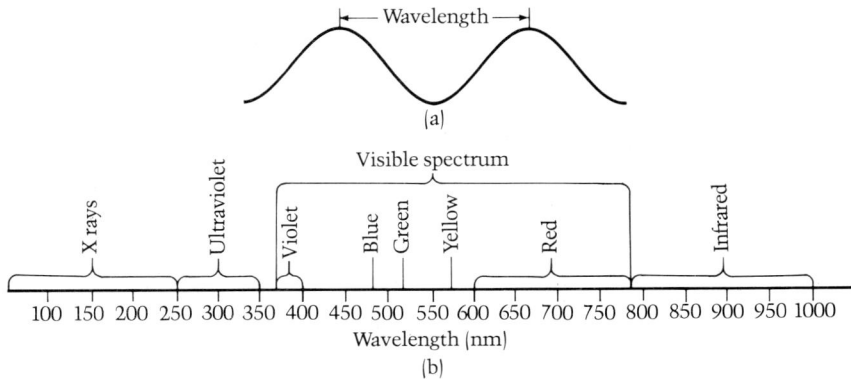

FIGURE 9–6. Light waves. (a) Like pure tones, the wave forms of light waves are sine waves, but they are measured by the distance between two crests rather than by time. The unit of measurement is a nanometer (nm), which is one billionth of a meter (m; 1 m = 39.37 in.). (b) Wavelengths for the visible spectrum and those near the visible spectrum. Only wavelengths from about 380 to 780 nm are visible to humans. From 380 nm and up, humans see colors change from violet to blue to green and so forth through the colors of the rainbow, ending with red. The range of wavelengths both longer and shorter than those of visible light is much greater. This figure shows ultraviolet light (~300 nm), X rays (~10 nm), and infrared waves (≡1000 nm). There are even shorter and longer wavelengths: gamma rays (~0.001 nm) and cosmic rays (~0.00001 nm) are much shorter, and microwaves (~0.001 ft), TV waves (~10 ft), and radio waves (~100 ft) are much longer.

colors, but in fact it is not. The reason for this is that some colors are brighter than others and so any ability to discriminate may be on the basis of brightness rather than hue or color. Attempts to make colors equally bright have come to grief because researchers had no basis for equalizing the brightness between pairs of colors except from results on visual studies of adults, and the interaction between color and brightness differs for adults and babies (see Cohen, DeLoache, & Strauss, 1979, for a nice discussion of these problems). Recently, several ingenious researchers (Bornstein, 1976; Oster, 1975; Peeples & Teller, 1975; Schaller, 1975) all hit upon the technique of purposely varying brightness across color discriminations rather than trying to equalize it. In this technique infants are presented the same pairs of colors (such as yellow and red) many times, but sometimes one is brighter and sometimes the other is. If infants consistently look longer at the red stimulus, the response must be on the basis of hue rather than brightness. These studies all found that infants 8-12 weeks old could dis-

criminate colors. The conclusions that can be reached from these studies are limited, however, because they have used only a limited range of hues and the babies were all 2 or 3 months old. There is, for example, evidence that babies younger than 3 months of age are not capable of discriminating all colors (see review by Banks & Salapatek, 1983). Thus, the full developmental history of infants' ability to discriminate color is far from clear.

The physical stimulus for color is determined by its wavelength. Wavelengths vary continuously from infrared (too long for humans to see) through red, yellow, green, and blue, to ultraviolet (wavelengths too short for humans to see; see Figure 9–6). Although people can discriminate among stimuli that differ by only a few wavelengths, they tend to give stimuli of many different similar wavelengths a single name. These naming practices reflect what is often called **categorical** or **discontinuous perception**. In categorical perception similar wavelengths are grouped together as a single color, whereas wavelengths that are slightly longer or shorter are excluded from the category. This difference in naming occurs even though the physical differences between two wavelengths within a category and two other wavelengths that are on two sides of a category boundary may be the same size. For example, light of wavelengths 570 nm and 580 nm both appear to be yellow to adults, whereas light of wavelength 560 nm, also a 10-nm difference from 570, appears to be green.[6] Categorical perception of colors appears to be based on the physiology of the visual system and not to be a product of learning, because humans of other cultures and animals with similar color vision systems exhibit the same sort of categorical perception.

Bornstein and his collaborators (Bornstein, 1976; Bornstein, Kessen, & Weiskopf, 1976) found that infants 3 and 4 months of age exhibited categorical perception, except in one red-yellow test. The investigators hypothesized that the failure to show categorical perception to red was due to infants' strong preference for this color. Others have questioned these conclusions (Banks & Salapatek, 1983; Werner & Wooten, 1979; but see also Bornstein's reply (1981) to Werner & Wooten), so that it is necessary to await the outcome of further research to conclude with confidence that young infants have categorical perception of color.

PATTERN VISION

Acuity of Pattern Vision. In determining whether infants see patterns, the first question to be answered is, How accurately can infants see? This is equivalent to asking what their visual acuity is. The most familiar test of visual acuity is probably the Snellen chart, which has a big E at the top and lines of successively smaller letters below. Patients read down the chart until the print is too small for them to read. The results are reported in terms of what a person with unimpaired vision can see at 20 feet. Thus 20/20 is considered to be the norm. People's vision can vary in either direction from this. A person with 40/20 vision can see at 40 feet what the normal person can see at 20 feet, but a person with 20/400 vision can see at 20 feet what the normal person can see at 400 feet (that is, the best this person can do on the Snellen chart is to read the big E). We will use these equivalents in our discussion of infants' acuity.

Preference tests are the most widely used measures of infants' visual acuity. Even newborn infants will look longer at a striped stimulus than at a plain gray stimulus. A striped pattern can be made with thinner and thinner stripes until the stripes appear to blend with each other and do not seem to a viewer to be different from the homogeneous gray field. If such striped and grey stimuli are shown to infants, they will cease to show a preference for the striped pattern when it looks like a grey blur. This technique has shown that the visual acuity of infants under 2 months of age is somewhere between 20/300 and 20/800. These estimates coincide with those which result when stripes are moved across the infants' visual field and acuity is measured by the width of stripe required to elicit optokinetic nystagmus (OKN; see Cohen et al., 1979, for a review). Acuity estimates are quite variable, however, both across different studies and for different individuals. The most acute vision found in young infants has been about 20/150. This value was found for some babies when the stimuli were stripes (Dayton et al., 1964) and as a general finding when the stimulus was a single line (Lewis, Maurer, & Kay, 1978). Other studies suggest that newborns' acuity is lower. In their recent review, Aslin and Dumais (1980) concluded that 20/500 is the best estimate for newborns.

Acuity develops rapidly during the first six months of life (see review by Banks & Salapatek, 1983). Some methods estimate that acuity reaches maturity by 6 months whereas others indicate that the vision of 6-month-olds is still much less acute than that of adults. It has been argued that these differences are due to the different methods, stimuli, and criteria for performance, but two studies (Goldblatt, Strauss, & Hess, 1980; Gwiazda, Brill, Mohindra, & Held, 1978) have shown that even when a single procedure is used, acuity continues to develop in the second half year of life. The reasons that acuity increases during the first year of life are not known. Banks and

---

[6] Some researchers (see Werner & Wooten, 1979) believe that the term "categorical perception" should be limited to situations in which subjects cannot discriminate among stimuli within a category. By this definition categorical perception would be characteristic of speech perception but not color naming.

Salapatek argue that development of neural mechanisms of the visual system is the most likely explanation. Although this explanation has not been directly confirmed experimentally, it is consistent with available evidence and there is direct evidence that the explanation, at least for development in the first 12 weeks, is maturational rather than experiential (Dobson, Mayer, & Lee, 1980; Miranda, 1970). These studies compared full-term infants to prematures matched on conceptional rather than postbirth age. The acuities of the two groups of infants were similar, even though the preterm infants often had had 4 weeks more experience than the full-term infants.

Acuity is maximal only under certain conditions. When there is little contrast between the brightness of a target and that of its background, the target is more difficult for infants to see (Atkinson, Braddick, & Moar, 1977; Banks & Salapatek, 1978; Gwiazda et al., 1978). Infants' sensitivity to contrast is not mature at birth. Indeed it shows a twofold increase between 1 and 3 months of age (Atkinson et al., 1977; Banks & Salapatek, 1978).

Infants' acuity may also depend on the distance from the babies' eyes to the stimulus. When adults focus on a target at different distances, special eye muscles (called interocular to distinguish them from the extraocular muscles that move the eyeball) automatically change the shape of the lens to bring the object into focus. This is called visual accommodation. A procedure called dynamic retinoscopy allows measurement of the effects of lens changes by observing the focus of objects on the retina without cooperation from the subject except that the eyes must remain open. Haynes, White, and Held (1965) used this technique to demonstrate that infants show no accommodation in the first month. This means that the eyes of infants under 1 month are fixed at one distance (like a fixed-focus camera). This distance was, on the average, 19 cm (7.5 in.). By the fourth month accommodative ability had nearly reached adult levels.

This distance limitation was taken very seriously by infant researchers and almost all the subsequent studies of visual perception presented stimuli at around 19 cm from the infants' eyes. Furthermore, researchers studying infant–mother interaction emphasized the fact that the mother's and infant's heads are approximately that distance apart in the normal nursing position and argued that this provides an ideal situation for the infant to recognize the mother.

Such acceptance of the conclusions of Haynes, White, and Held may have been premature. Their conclusions have been questioned on two grounds. First, re-examination of their method suggests a possible confounding factor. Their targets may have been too small for infants' acuity when placed at the far distances but of sufficient size when placed close to the infants. If this were true, the drop in acuity at long distances might be due to loss of acuity and not to lack of accommodation. Two recent studies using different measurement techniques have found accommodation developing earlier than Haynes et al. did (Banks, 1980; Braddick, Atkinson, French, & Howland, 1979). They found that accommodation is nearly as good as that of adults at 2 months and that even 1-month-old babies show partial accommodation.

The second reason for questioning Haynes et al. involves their implications. In adults, failure to accommodate produces an out-of-focus image and thereby loss of acuity. It was naturally assumed that the same is true of infants, but this need not be so. Two studies of visual perception, one done before the Haynes, White, and Held study (Fantz, Ordy, & Udelf, 1962) and one done since then (Salapatek, Bechtold, & Bushnell, 1976) have found that young babies' visual acuity does not vary at distances from 12.7 cm (5 in.) to 150 cm (59 in.) even though adults' acuity would. This is presumably because small errors in accommodative focus will produce a greater loss of acuity in adults' more finely tuned systems. Thus, it appears that young babies can see at their maximal acuity across a substantial range of distances and that the nursing position is no more ideal for learning to recognize mother than many other positions.

Is There Foveal Vision at Birth? Adults' vision is most acute in the **fovea,** that part of the **retina** (the part of the eye with the nerve cells that transform light patterns into nerve impulses) that is most packed with sense receptors. The measures of acuity used with infants do not require that the subjects use foveal vision because their heads are free to move and thus the stimulus may fall on areas outside the fovea. Indeed, in the optokinetic nystagmus measure, peripheral vision must be involved. The sense receptors in the periphery of the retina are almost mature at birth, while those of the fovea are very immature. This has led some researchers to suggest that newborns lack foveal vision altogether. Recently, however, Lewis and Maurer (1980) found evidence that newborns can perceive foveally. They found that newborns exhibit longer total duration of central fixation to a small dot than to a blank field. The total duration of fixation is a good measure, they argue, because it indicates that the infant is maintaining fixation in the fovea.

What Patterns Do Newborns Detect? We have noted that newborns prefer to look at patterned stimuli rather than plain stimuli. That preference is the basis for many studies of acuity. This basic finding has given rise to a large and complex literature exploring the kinds of patterns young infants discriminate, whether these early discrimination abilities mean that infants are "prewired" to perceive certain meaningful patterns, and whether changing preferences among visual stimuli mean that young infants are rapidly learning to extract information from their world.

This enterprise is extremely difficult. There is an incredible number of two-dimensional patterns, both those in the natural world and those that can be created. Consider how difficult it is to select a few to present to newborns in the paired preference technique. Because of the complexities involved, we will not attempt to present the research in an historical context, but will summarize the most widely accepted findings. This presentation will leave out many possibly important results that have not yet been replicated or corroborated by other kinds of research.

It is quite clear that newborn infants look longer at figures with a high **contour density** (the total length of edges or contours in a given area). For example, a square with its four edges has higher contour density than a line, which has only one edge. Checkerboards with small squares have higher contour density than those with large squares. Contour density can account for infants differentiating between a large number of patterns that were at one time thought to test more advanced abilities, such as the ability to perceive meaningful form or

the ability to process large amounts of information (for discussions of this, see Fantz, Fagan, & Miranda, 1975; Karmel & Maisel, 1975; Salapatek, 1975). Detecting differences in contour density does not suggest such advanced abilities because human visual systems are physiologically structured to detect such changes, as we shall see shortly.

Not only do newborns respond to contour density, they also respond to the sharpness of contours. Under 2 months of age infants look longer at stimuli that have high contrast: black and white rather than muted (for example, gray on white or yellow on orange); sharp rather than blurred edges; bright, flat surfaces rather than softer, textured ones (Fantz et al., 1975). This preference for sharp contrast (large differences in brightness), unlike that for contour density, disappears after 2 months of age.

Another pattern preference that seems clear is that young infants, including newborns, prefer patterns with circular elements to patterns with straight elements (Fantz et al., 1975). This is true whether the circular elements are incorporated into a configuration (such as a bull's eye or face) or are randomly placed segments.

There are a few other dimensions that infants respond to, but investigators disagree on whether the infant is cued by that dimension itself or is really cued by other dimensions such as contour density, which also vary. Newborns prefer large to small patterns (2-in. squares versus 1 in.), while 2-month-old infants are less sensitive to size and are more sensitive to differences in number: They look longer at stimuli with many elements (Fantz et al., 1975). There may also be a basic preference for irregular over regular figures, but this preference disappears for certain stimuli, such as those with circular elements, and at certain ages (Fantz et al., 1975). Finally, infants at 2 months of age seem to look longer at vertical than at horizontal lines (Salapatek, 1975).

These pattern preferences and the developmental changes they exhibit can be explained better by physiological maturation than by learning for several reasons. First, the human visual system seems wired to respond to characteristics of visual stimuli such as straight and curved edges, which are involved in contours. To explain this, let us examine some research on physiological responses in the visual system in animals. The technique used in this research is to record the firing of single nerve cells by means of a very small needle-like instrument called a microelectrode. These electrodes are so small that their tips are usually less than one micron (one one-thousandth of a millimeter) in diameter. They can record the firing of single cells in the optic nerve (the bundle of nerve fibers that conduct the visual impulses from the eyes to the higher centers of the brain) and in the visual cortex (the cortex is the outer layer of the brain where the more complex processes occur; the visual cortex is the part of the cortex devoted to perception of complex visual events). We will concentrate on research with cats because (1) it is the most extensive, (2) cats' and humans' visual systems are similar, and (3) the results of research with humans using both microelectrodes and other techniques is consistent with the results obtained with cats.

The microelectrode research addresses two questions: Is pattern perception an integral part of the structure of the visual system? If so, is this wiring innate? If a single nerve cell fires only to specific complex stimuli, then the conclusion is that the visual system is physiologically structured to detect that pattern. If this single cell fires in newborn animals, it is possible to conclude that the anatomical wiring is innate. Briefly, the answers to these questions are that perception of some patterns is structurally wired and is at least partly innate.

Many different kinds of detectors have been found in cats and, directly or indirectly, in humans. In the visual cortex there are cells that fire in response to a border or edge (light on one side, dark on the other), others that respond to straight lines (dark line with light on either side), and still others to slits (lines of light with dark on either side). Two levels of edge, line, and slit detectors have been found. One kind, called simple cells, responds to edges, lines, and slits only in a particular orientation in a particular place in the visual field. For example, one detector might fire for horizontal lines in the lower right of a cat's visual field, but not to vertical lines or to horizontal lines in other parts of the visual field. Complex cells, in contrast, fire for all stimuli of the particular pattern and orientation to which they are responsive, regardless of where in the visual field they are located.

Thus, a horizontal line in the lower right corner of a cat's visual field would cause a simple horizontal-specific line detector and its comparable complex line detector to fire. A horizontal line in the upper right of the visual field would cause the same complex line detector to fire, but the particular simple cell referred to in the previous sentence would remain silent, and a different simple cell would fire. Both simple and complex cells can be divided into two subclasses, those that respond optimally to bars or edges of one particular length and those that respond to a wider range of lengths. This combination of types of detector cells allows cats to be sensitive to shape, size, and position of stimuli, and presumably to learn to respond appropriately to any of them.

The existence of these various kinds of receptors are firmly established in cats. Although additional kinds of detectors are likely to be found, it is unlikely that the roles of ones already found will be disputed by later research. Furthermore, both direct and indirect research with adult humans suggests that the detectors found in cats exist in similar fashion in humans (for reviews of this research, see Sekuler, 1974; Leibowitz & Harvey, 1973). Thus, we can say that the visual system is physiologically structured to detect the kinds of patterns described above. Many of the single-cell detectors in cats also seem to be present in primitive form at birth or shortly thereafter (see, for example, Bonds, 1979; Hubel & Wiesel, 1963; Pettigrew, 1974), although we will see that these cells must receive visual stimulation to stay alive.

Let us now return to our main line of argument, that many of the early visual responses in human infants are due to neural functioning. Notice that single-cell detectors are designed to respond to edges (contours), bars, and slits, all of which are kinds of light–dark patterning. Many of the dimensions of discrimination found in newborns, such as contour density and contrast, are also functions of light–dark patterning and thus may reflect firing of such detectors. A good example of a specific visual discrimination that is consistent with this hypothesis is from a study by Cohen and Younger (1984). They habituated young infants to an angle and tested dishabituation to various transformations of the habituated angle. Their results indicated that 6-week-old infants process specific line segments in specific orientations, whereas infants 3 months of age respond to an angle as a unit. Because single cells respond to individual lines in specific orientations, it is likely that the younger infants responded on that basis. Responses of the older infants, in contrast, evidently involved additional kinds of processing.

Karmel and Maisel (1975) found direct evidence for the functioning of single-cell detectors by measuring infants' brain wave responses (electroencephalograms, or EEGs) to visual patterns. Their research indicated that newborns' ability to distinguish contours is based on the early firing of these contour-receptive cells and that stimulation must occur if these cells are to continue to respond.

Another reason that pattern perception in young infants seems due to physiological maturation comes from a study by Fantz and colleagues (1975) that pitted conceptional age against experience. They studied premature infants as well as full-term infants and found that conceptional age predicted the developmental changes better than post-birth age. In other words, the number of weeks of experience the infants had in the visual world was not an important determinant of their changing patterns of preference, but the number of weeks since they had been conceived was.

This picture of young infants' pattern perception has not yet provided any indication that they perceive meaningful patterns. The ability to discriminate among stimuli that vary in brightness, color, or contour density does not mean that these are perceived as meaningful. Furthermore, young infants seem to perceive stimuli piecemeal rather than as integrated figures. They scan only external contours (before 2 months) or internal features (2–3 months), but not both. Their preference for circularity does not require a complete configuration such as a circle or bull's eye; they also prefer scattered curved line segments to scattered straight line segments (Fantz et al., 1975). Even early face recognition, as we shall see shortly, seems to be on the basis of a few pertinent features. None of these phenomena require that the babies perceive the stimuli as meaningful.

We have not yet discussed preferences for form or shape itself, for example, preference for

X versus O, or triangles versus squares. To claim that young infants can detect meaningful figures, it is necessary to demonstrate first that they perceive either shapes or configurations of groups of elements (such as dots). Although early research on infant pattern perception was interpreted as a positive indication of such ability, we know now that those early findings were due to differences in such characteristics as contour density and brightness. Salapatek (1975) directly tested the influence of shape differences compared to brightness and contour density differences. He found that 2-month-olds do not show preferences based on shape alone. In fact, his results suggest that infants of that age do not even necessarily look preferentially at central figures rather than at background figures, which is one of the most basic characteristics of visual perception. Not until around 5 months of age do infants perceive compound figures (figures made up of more than one simple figure such as a cross within a circle) as integrated single figures rather than two separate figures (see Cohen et al., 1979, for a review). These findings strengthen the notion that perception in young infants is of a piecemeal nature, is largely governed by the firing of single neurons in the visual system, and is controlled by the physiological maturation that naturally occurs in babies exposed to normal visual experiences.

Development of Face Perception. Although the research using abstract patterns as stimuli has failed to find any clear evidence that newborns can perceive meaningful patterns, it is possible that infants innately perceive certain biologically important patterns. These particularly important configurations might then provide the basis from which infants learn the meaning of other visual stimuli. Certainly the face is a highly likely candidate for such a configuration. The ability to recognize the configuration of a face early in infancy *and* to know (or learn rapidly) that the face is associated with food, warmth, safety, and other positive factors, would be extremely adaptive in an evolutionary sense. Thus, ethologists as well as perception psychologists are interested in finding out the nature of early face perception. Ethologists, however, are not primarily interested in whether face perception is similar to or a precursor of perception of meaningful forms in general. Rather, they wish to explore the importance of face perception as a basis for early attachment to the mother. In this section we will focus on the relevance of face perception to the general issue of what infants can perceive. We will examine research relevant to the questions of whether perception of the human face is innate and, if it is not completely developed at birth, when and how it does develop.

Researchers studying face perception have usually used either of two kinds of stimuli. One kind tests infants' ability to discriminate line drawings of faces from various other configurations of similar complexity, often faces with the features scrambled. The other kind compares two different faces, particularly the mother's versus a stranger's. Success on the latter sorts of discriminations obviously requires memory as well as perceptual ability.

It is clear that newborns prefer drawings of faces to less complex stimuli such as plain ovals, bull's eyes, and newsprint (Fantz, 1963, 1966). The problem with such findings is, of course, that these results may be due to stimulus differences unrelated to the stimulus being a representation of a face, such as differences in contour density, brightness, and so forth. Studies in the 1960s and 1970s that controlled for these confounding variables found consistant discrimination of faces at 4 months and not earlier (Haaf, 1974; Haaf & Bell, 1967; Haaf & Brown, 1975; Kagan, Henker, Hen-Tov, Levine, & Lewis, 1966; Koopman & Ames, 1968). At that age babies could also discriminate their mother's face from that of a stranger (Ambrose, 1961, 1963).

More recently researchers have been successful in demonstrating face perception in younger infants. All of these studies have used Horowitz, Paden, Bhana, and Self's (1972) infant-control procedures (described in Chapter 7). It is important to point out that these procedures typically result in infants spending longer times fixating the stimuli than was the case in earlier studies. For example, the 2-month-old babies in Maurer and Barrera's (1981) study usually fixated for longer than 40 seconds per trial whereas previous research usually presented stimuli for set periods typically no longer than 30 seconds. These procedures also result in a higher proportion of infants making it through the experimental

procedures. Research using these techniques has established that face perception develops earlier than 4 months of age.

Several studies of infants' scanning the reflection in a mirror of real faces (Haith, Bergman, & Moore, 1977; Maurer & Salapatek, 1976) have found development comparable to that of scanning geometric figures. One-month-old babies do not attend much to the faces at all, and when they do, they primarily scan borders that have high contrast, such as the hairline. Consistent with this, they look longer at Caucasian faces with dark hair (higher contrast) than they do Caucasian faces with light hair (Melhuish, 1982). At 2 months infants attend much more to the faces (almost 90% of their time in the apparatus) and primarily scan internal features, such as the eyes.

Maurer and Barrera (1981) reasoned from these data that 2-month-olds should be capable of discriminating faces, but because their scanning is still fairly primitive, they would need more time. Using the procedures of Horowitz and colleagues that provide more time, they found that 2-month-old infants did discriminate faces from scrambled faces (Figure 9–7). Their conclusion was especially strong because use of both the visual preference and the habituation–dishabituation paradigms achieved the same results. To support further their interpretation that the development of scanning is the basis for the development of facial discrimination, Maurer and Barrera (1978) presented facial features (eyes, nose, and mouth) without the external contours of a surrounding oval to 1-month-olds. As expected, babies of this age were able to discriminate these faces from scrambled ones (also lacking an external contour) although they could not distinguish the standard schematic face with a border from scrambled ones with borders. These results suggest that the reason very young babies do not discriminate between regular and scrambled faces is that they look primarily at the external contour (the boundary between face and hair), which does not provide them with enough information to enable them to make such discriminations.

Similar research has demonstrated that babies 3 months of age make more subtle discriminations among real faces. They can discriminate the photographed faces of their own mothers and fathers from those of strangers

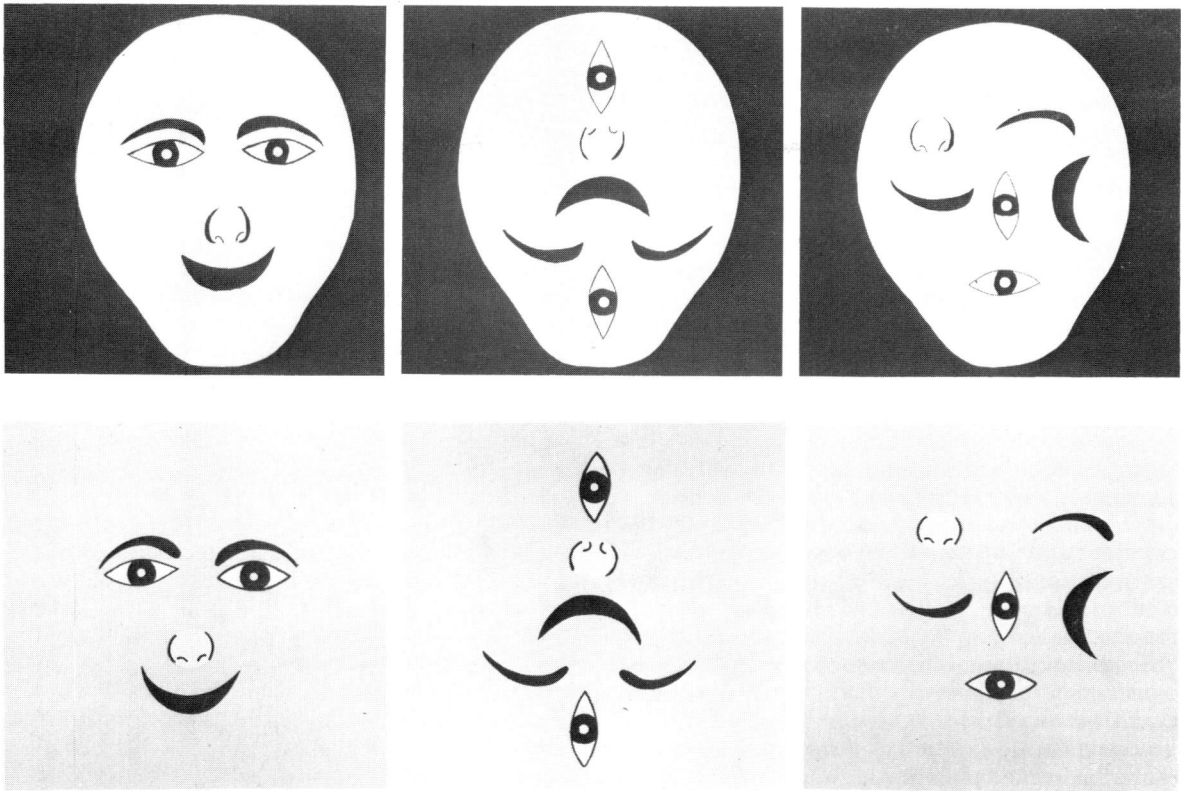

FIGURE 9–7. Diagrams of faces—scrambled and unscrambled, without external contours and with contours—used by Maurer and Barrera. (Photographs courtesy of Daphne Maurer.)

(Barrera & Maurer, 1981b; Maurer & Heroux, 1980). They can discriminate between photographs of two strangers (female strangers, Barrera & Maurer, 1981a; male strangers, Maurer & Heroux, 1980).

This research shows that babies' ability to perceive faces apparently develops as a function of their general perceptual development. Babies 1 month old attend primarily to regions of high contrast and do not process the internal features of a stimulus. Thus they will fail to identify the features of a face (eyes, nose, mouth) and any rearrangements of these features. By 2 months they attend to internal features and thus can discriminate scrambled from regularly arranged features. By 3 months they process those internal features well enough to identify their mother and to discriminate between some facial expressions.

Subsequent development of face perception also seems consistent with general perceptual development (see Fagan, 1979, for a good review). The earliest age at which infants have been found to identify the equivalence between a photograph of a strange person and the actual person is 5 months (Dirks & Gibson, 1977), although their ability, developed earlier, to recognize a photograph of their mother implies some equivalence between mother and her picture. Even at 5 months infants' abilities to discriminate faces is still based on rather gross features. In the Dirks and Gibson study, the babies recognized as similar to the live person they had seen both photographs of that person and photographs of a person with similar hair and features. Present data show that 7-month-old babies are able to make more subtle identifications: They recognize the same person from different perspectives such as full face versus profile (Cohen & Strauss, 1979; Fagan, 1976); they can identify as similar the same facial expression on different faces (Caron, Caron, & Myers, 1982); and they can discriminate male from female faces (Cornell, 1974; Fagan, 1976). All of these require the perception of faces as integrated configurations of internal and external contours, an ability that develops with the ability to perceive compound patterns at 5 months.

The studies discussed above all indicate that true identification of faces occurs at the earliest at 2 months, but a few studies have found face perception in even younger infants (Carpenter, 1974a; Field, Cohen, Garcia, & Greenberg, 1984; Goren, Sarty, & Wu, 1975; Thomas, 1973). Replications of the studies by Goren and colleagues and by Carpenter using stricter methodology have failed to support the original conclusions (Maurer & Young, 1983; Melhuish, 1982, respectively). It is difficult to reach conclusions concerning the validity of the studies that found early identification because (1) none has yet been successfully replicated, (2) all are vulnerable to alternative interpretations, and (3) their findings are at variance with the description of the development of pattern and face perception provided by most of the research in the field. Nevertheless, they indicate that face perception may develop earlier than is currently thought by most researchers.

In summary, the best guess based on currently available evidence is that recognition of faces is not innate and that infants' abilities to perceive faces appears to develop gradually as part of the general development of visual perception. It is clear, however, that this conclusion is not accepted by all and that psychologists will continue to try to find evidence for the ability to identify faces in the neonatal period or very shortly thereafter.

Abstraction of Perceptual Invariants. Among the major influences on the field of perception have been the related theories of E.J. Gibson (1969) and J.J. Gibson (1966, 1979). They believe that humans learn to perceive objects by abstracting that which is unchanging or **invariant** in a stimulus. For example, a face always has a particular configuration of eyes, nose, and mouth. A set of invariants uniquely specifies an object; for example, all closed

plane figures with three angles are triangles. One object may represent a class (all men) or a particular object (my Daddy). In either case it has a set of invariant features that differentiate it from all other stimuli.

The developmental question for infancy that Gibsonian theory raises is when and how the perception of invariants develops. Based on the discussion of pattern perception, a reasonable guess would be that infants younger than 2 months probably do not abstract invariants although they can make many of the discriminations that form the basis of distinctive features. By 2 to 3 months of age babies do recognize unchanging configurations in stimuli that vary in other ways. Milewski (1979) demonstrated this by habituating 3-month-old infants to one of two patterns. Both patterns were made of 3 dots, one in a triangular configuration and the other in a straight line. The crucial test of perception of invariance is whether the infants dishabituate to stimuli that have the same configuration as the habituation stimuli, but differ in other attributes. The infants in Milewski's study did not do this, which indicates that they detected the pattern that was invariant. The infants did, however, dishabituate to stimuli with a new configuration but with the familiar size and position, which further strengthens the interpretation that they abstracted the perceptual invariant.

If the development of face perception is analyzed in terms of perceptual invariants, then the research is consistent with Milewski's findings. By 3 months of age babies recognize photographs of their mothers' faces, which means that they have abstracted some invariant characteristics of their mothers' faces. This ability, however, is not yet fully developed. Dirks and Gibson (1977) showed that 5-month-old babies did not differentiate between photographs of faces of like sex, hair color, and hair style when they were habituated to the live version of one of those faces. Only at 7 months of age did infants abstract the perceptual invariants of a strange face in a way expected of an older child or adult.

OBJECTS IN SPACE
Most of the research on pattern perception that we have just discussed uses two-dimen-

sional stimuli, either line drawings or photographs, but the world is made up of three-dimensional objects situated in three-dimensional space. That humans perceive visual patterns as objects at all is one of the great mysteries to be unraveled in psychology. The eyes are similar to a camera in that the image that is recorded on the retina (analogous to the film of the camera) is essentially two dimensional. Yet on the basis of these two-dimensional images humans perceive three-dimensional objects in space. Whether this three-dimensional perception is innate or learned is one of the focuses of the empiricist–nativist argument. Do humans perceive three dimensions innately or do we learn to do so?

We have selected three specific topics from the larger topic of perception of objects in space because they have been the focus of concentrated interest in infancy research. They are: (1) the role of movement in perceiving objects, (2) the implications of visually initiated and visually guided reaching for infants' knowledge of objects, and (3) the development of depth perception.

The Role of Movement in Perceiving Objects. Most laboratory studies of visual perception have used static (nonmoving) displays. Outside the laboratory, however, objects move a lot. The Gibsons have been instrumental in analyzing the role of kinetic information and in providing a basis from which infant researchers can explore the development of sensitivity to such information. They argue that continuous motion of both target objects and the viewer with respect to stationary objects provides the most fundamental mechanism for the extraction of information about objects. The simplest case is when a rigid object moves across a field, an action called translation. During such a movement the texture elements on the object remain in the same (invariant) relation to each other because they move together. At the same time the relation of the object to texture elements of the background changes. Thus, by specifying characteristic patterns of invariance and change, movement helps to differentiate the expanse of the object from the background and from other objects and thereby helps to specify the nature of the object. Theoretically, similar patterns of invariance and change specify objects regardless of the kinds

of motions they undergo. In addition, particular motions can be identified by their characteristic patterns of variance and invariance, regardless of the particular object that is moving.

Motion is evidently important from birth. Even newborns track moving stimuli, although the kind of information picked up by their jerky, immature eye movements may be different from that resulting from the later-developing continuous smooth tracking. There is also evidence that babies as young as 2 weeks of age prefer moving stimuli to the same stimuli when stationary (Carpenter, 1974b, with 2-week-olds; Kaufmann & Kaufmann, 1980, with 4-month-olds), although whether that is true for 5-month-old babies is unclear (Nelson & Horowitz, 1983).

Three distinct theoretical questions about kinetic information have been addressed in the infant research:

1. Does movement provide a better basis for object recognition than static displays of the same object?
2. What kinds of movements provide the best information for object recognition?
3. Can babies detect different kinds of kinetic cues that carry various kinds of information?

We will discuss each question in turn.

The first question is perhaps the most basic. When objects move, their various parts move together and the invariant configurations so produced provide a cue that they are parts of the same object. Three disparate studies have recently demonstrated that movement often provides the information necessary for babies to recognize an object where a stationary pattern does not. We will discuss them in the order of the age of the subjects. Kellman and Spelke (1983) were interested in whether 4-month-old babies perceive an object when it is partly hidden behind another object. They found that babies 4 months old only perceived the partly hidden object as a single, continuous object rather than two discontinuous objects when they saw the object move behind its occluding object. When the pattern was stationary, the babies acted as if they did not know whether the hidden pattern was one or two objects. The second study (Owsley, 1980) explored the relative effectiveness of continuous movement (as in a movie) versus a series of static displays of the same movement (as in a selection of individual frames of the movie). Continuous motion is hypothetically more effective because it provides overlapping information that specifies the invariance. Owsley demonstrated that a moving object was effective in producing recognition in 4-month-old infants whereas a set of still views of the object in different orientations was not. In the third study, Ruff (1982a) presented complex objects moving in various ways (see Figure 9–8) to 6-month-old babies. After familiarizing the infants with one object, she presented the familiar object with a novel one and measured whether they looked longer at one of the stimuli. She found that infants exposed to moving objects did exhibit recognition, whereas infants exposed to objects that were primarily stationary (they moved a little) did not.

These studies demonstrate that movements that specify the perceptual invariants of objects are effective cues to object recognition. In addition, movement appears to be necessary for object perception for young infants in some circumstances. Nevertheless, it is clear that with older babies and adults, stationary cues are sufficient. Kellman and Spelke (1983) demonstrated that adults use either movement cues or stationary cues in their object perception. Likewise, it is known that, unlike Owsley's 4-months-olds, 7-months-olds do abstract invariance from different discrete views (Cohen & Strauss, 1979; Fagan, 1976; McGurk, 1972). Thus there may be a developmental progression from primary reliance on movement to reliance on the visual characteristics of an object. Both Kellman and Spelke (1983) and Bower (1974) found that babies under 5 months of age relied only on movement cues. Bower also demonstrated that at about 5 months of age they start using visual characteristics to identify objects.

Ruff (1982a) also explored the second question, that of the effect of different kinds of movements on promoting recognition. She found that simple translations (moving stimuli across the field) were more effective than more complex rotations (see Figure 9–8). She further demonstrated that a simple rotation condition moderately facilitated recognition if infants were given more familiarization than they needed for equivalent effects of translational

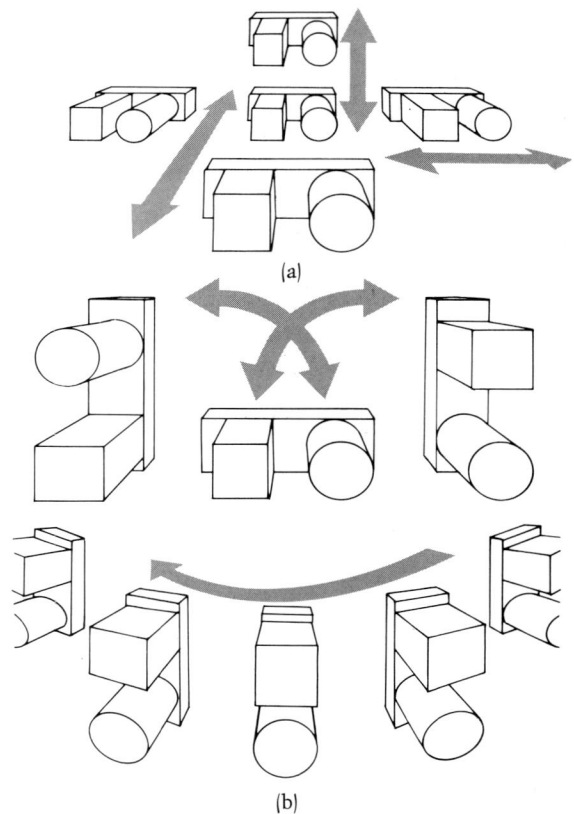

FIGURE 9–8. *Two distinct kinds of continuous movement used by Ruff in her study of 6-month-old infants (Ruff, 1982a). Arrows show the direction of movement. (a) A simple translation movement. The object stays facing the same way and is moved up, down, left, right, forward, and back. Watching these movements helped infants to recognize the object, whereas watching the same object when it moved just slightly (2.54 cm) in these directions (the control condition) did not. (b) Two of the three movements in a simple rotation condition. In the top drawing the object rotates in a frontal plane. In the bottom drawing the object rotates on its vertical axis and is in translational motion. This rotation condition moderately facilitated recognition, but only when infants were given more trials than was necessary for the translation condition to work. A more complex rotation condition did not facilitate recognition. (From "Effect of object movement on infants' detection of object structure," by H.A. Ruff,* Developmental Psychology, *1982, 18, 463–472. Copyright 1982 by the American Psychological Association. Reprinted by permission.)*

motion. This pattern of results would be expected because in translation movements the object undergoes less change and hence the changing relations of the object to the background are clearly highlighted, whereas in rotation there is more internal change in the object and the relation of object to background changes more.

The third question, identifying the sorts of kinetic cues babies respond to, is vast and largely uncharted territory. The most widely studied type of kinetic stimuli, that of looming (objects that look as if they are going to hit the observer), will be discussed in the section on depth perception, because it has most often been studied in that connection. In the past few years several studies demonstrating that infants 3–6 months of age discriminate among other kinds of moving stimuli have appeared (Bertenthal & Proffitt, 1982; Fox & McDaniel, 1982; Gibson, Owsley, & Johnston, 1978; Kaufmann-Hayoz & Jäger, 1983; Ruff, 1982b). We will describe two of these. The first examined whether babies can tell the difference between a rigid object and one that is elastic (changes shape when deformed). The cues that differentiate these two classes of objects are given only by the ways the object changes when it is moved in particular ways (for example, rotating a rigid object versus squeezing a sponge). Gibson and colleagues (1978) found that 5-month-olds do discriminate between these two movements.

The second is Ruff's recent (1982b) work on infants' ability to detect different motions regardless of the object. She demonstrated that 5-month-olds differentiated between translation movements and rotation movements and between full rotations (repeated 360-degree turns in one direction, a spinning motion) and oscillating rotations (180-degree rotations back and forth). Ruff also explored in more depth exactly what changes in the stimulus the babies were responding to. (We recommend that students interested in Gibsonian theory read Ruff's study in its entirety.)

The research we have described in this section has used infants 4 to 6 months of age and it is clear that by that age they are quite sensitive to kinetic information. This research does not imply, however, that younger babies are incapable of picking up such information. In fact, in the research using looming stimuli we will see that younger babies do respond to kinetic information. It is likely that research in this area will soon demonstrate other early-developing skills.

The Role of Visually Guided Reaching in Perceiving Objects. The research on the development of visually guided reaching that we described in Chapter 8 was done primarily to discover what infants know about objects and space. The description of the research that we gave there is generally acceptable to experts in the field, but that description masks a hot controversy over what the research reveals about what infants know about their world. The existence and nature of visually guided reaching can elucidate three related epistemological issues. One is the infants' appreciation of three-dimensional space (depth). If they reach for objects they see, two kinds of knowledge can be inferred: (1) knowledge that there is an object in three-dimensional space and (2) knowledge that the object they see is graspable; that is, that it has three-dimensional mass. This is part of the issue of coordination of senses (we discussed the coordination of vision and audition in the section on auditory localization). Knowing that sensations in separate modalities come from the same object is an important part of knowing what an object is. When infants develop visually guided reaching at 4 months of age, they presumably have this knowledge. That conclusion is generally accepted. What is controversial is whether the neonatal form, visually initiated reaching, also requires that knowledge.

The subtleties of the reaching response can potentially resolve the controversy. Babies who succeed in grasping objects and who behave differently when there is a graspable object than they do when there is either no object or an object that is not graspable can be said to have this underlying knowledge. If neonates do not possess this underlying knowledge, then a different pattern of responses should obtain. They should exhibit a variety of behaviors—looking, mouth opening and closing, hand movements, arm pumping, and leg kicking—which are made both in response to a stimulus and spontaneously (that is, when adults cannot detect a specific stimulus). On some occasions just the right combination of these responses and of a stimulus object will occur and the neonate will successfully grasp the object (see Figure 8–7 for an illustration of such responses).

Let us describe the research designed to test these alternative hypotheses about what newborns know. First, there is disagreement over how frequently successful grasping responses occur. Bower (1982) found that neonates succeeded in grasping the object on 40% of their reaches, whereas Ruff and Halton (1978) found only 7% of neonatal reaches to be successful. At least some, if not all, of such discrepancies are demonstrably due to differences in the criteria used for reaching (Rader, Opaluch, & Johnson, as cited in Rader & Stern, 1982). The researchers' choice of criteria is a matter of their judgment and usually reflects their biases. Researchers who believe neonatal reaching to be a general phenomenon reflecting innate knowledge are likely to use criteria that result in relatively higher frequencies of reaching. Thus, such data are not likely to resolve the controversy.

Second, studies that have compared neonatal reaching when a stimulus object is present to when no stimulus is present have yielded conflicting results (Hofsten, 1982; Rader & Stern, 1982; Ruff & Halton, 1978). These studies do, however, consistently report that there is some reaching when there is no object. The most we can say is that a pattern in the baby's visual field is more likely to elicit a reach than a patternless field, and even that may be overstating the case.

Third, there are conflicting results in studies that compare graspable to nongraspable stimuli. Bower (1972) found that newborns were more likely to reach for three-dimensional objects than they were for two-dimensional objects (pictures), as they should be if they know that objects have mass and pictures do not. Two attempts to replicate that finding, however, have failed (Dodwell, Muir, & DiFranco, 1976; Rader & Stern, 1982).

Fourth, slightly older infants have been found to reach differentially to a graspable object than to a nongraspable object or to the absence of an object (Brazelton, Koslowski, & Main, 1974; Bruner & Koslowski, 1972; Trevarthen, Hubley, & Sheeran, 1975). These findings may, however, reflect development since birth rather than innate knowledge of objects in space, a conclusion supported by the developmental findings of Hofsten (1984).

How these results are interpreted depends partly on how the various studies are weighed. Bower (1982) is willing to accept the research that shows the more sophisticated abilities in newborns on the grounds that it is easy to find no results (that newborns can't do something) and difficult to demonstrate a subtle ability. It is no surprise then that Bower is more willing to accept visually initiated reaching as evidence that for newborns, objects have multisensory attributes and mass and exist in three-dimensional space. In contrast, other researchers are more conservative. They are very aware that a given study often produces positive results that subsequent research shows to be due to methodological flaws or to be better explained by alternative interpretations. The solution such researchers apply to conflicting studies is to find the methodologically more sophisticated studies and to look for findings that replicate within that subset. On this basis they would conclude that newborns do not know that there are three-dimensional objects in three-dimensional space: They do not know the difference between a picture and an object, they reach when there is no object, and in the majority of instances they do not reach even when there is an object. The most that such researchers will conclude is that newborns come equipped with the rudiments with which to acquire that knowledge—they respond to visual patterns with increased activity of their hands and arms that sometimes result in successful grasps.

Depth Perception. This topic has been a favorite in epistemology since long before scientists ever studied infants. For example, Bishop Berkeley, the 18th-century British associationist, argued that people do not perceive depth directly. Rather, they must learn to perceive depth through associating varying sizes of objects with their varying distances. We all know that if we are very far away from what we look at—for example, on top of a tall building looking down to ground level—what we see looks very tiny and people on the ground look like ants. Berkeley believed that we had to learn that human beings that looked like mere specks could nevertheless be real, full-sized, human beings that were far away. He argued that we discover that those very small images are really very far away because images get larger and larger as they get closer and closer, and we associate the changing visual image with the movements of our eye muscles as they converge to focus on the images. Other philosophers such as Immanuel Kant argued that knowledge of space is innately given. Sense impressions are not the bases by which we detect depth. They only serve as material for the organizing principles. The perception of depth is given to us from elsewhere. Philosophers often argue that it was given to us by God or by an abstraction of the notion of God. Those psychologists who are nativists tend to argue that it is given to us by our biological inheritance. In other words, the human biological optical system is so organized that we see depth. The obvious way to resolve this nature–nurture argument is to study the development of depth perception in infants. The nativist position would be supported if newborns perceive depth when they are first exposed to patterned light. If the ability to perceive depth develops, then the situation is more complex. Such development may proceed as a function of experience or it may be governed primarily by a biological timetable in much the same ways as motoric skills.

We have already discussed the evidence provided by studies of visually guided reaching. We can safely conclude from these studies that 4-month-olds act as if they perceive depth, but we cannot conclude with confidence that younger babies do so. In this section we will describe four additional areas of research. We will examine them in the order of the age at which they demonstrate evidence for depth perception, from the earliest to the latest. This ordering will facilitate comparison of the various methods and help speculations both about what each technique measures and about when various components of depth perception develop.

First we will examine the research on **looming.** A looming object is something that comes closer and closer as if it is going to hit you, such as a ball thrown at your face. The physical cue to depth is the apparent size of the ball. The ball seems small (subtends a smaller area on the retina) when it is far away and large when it is close up, and the change is marked by magnification of the contours corresponding to the edges of the object. The rate of magnification increases as the object ap-

proaches at a constant rate, and becomes explosive just before contact. This accelerated expansion and the associated filling of the visual field (as the ball becomes larger, it becomes all that can be seen) specifies imminent collision (Gibson, 1958).

A looming stimulus obviously carries depth information, and thus charting the development of responses to it can reveal something about the development of depth perception. Interest in this area of research is not new. The earliest studies were conducted by Raehlman (1891), Preyer (1881/1893), and other German researchers at the beginning of this century (see Peiper, 1961/1963, for summaries of these early papers), and the topic attracted the attention of Gesell (1925) and some of his contemporaries. The goal of this early research was to ascertain whether there was a blink reflex to looming stimuli. The results of these early studies were quite consistent. Babies under 2 months of age stared at an approaching object and did not blink. They began to blink in response to such stimuli around 2 months of age and the response was found to be virtually universal by 4 months.

Interest in looming then subsided until the explosion of work on infant perception in the 1960s and 1970s. It reappeared with the publication of two studies that reported defensive reactions in infants younger than 2 months (Ball & Tronick, 1971; Bower, Broughton, & Moore, 1971). These studies, however, did not use blinking to indicate a response. Their measure was an integrated avoidance response involving the eyes opening wide, the head going back, and both hands coming up between the object and the face. Notice that in this avoidance response the eyes open wide rather than blink, which means that a failure to blink would not be interpreted as a failure to respond to the looming stimulus (Figure 9–9).

Yonas and colleagues (1977) repeated the Ball and Tronick procedure with additional controls. They did not find an integrated avoidance response, but they did find that 1–2-month-olds made more backward head movements to looming than to nonlooming stimuli. They noted that there is a viable alternative interpretation of this finding. The infants may have been following the upper contour of the object as it moved upward. Young babies, who do not have much motoric control of their

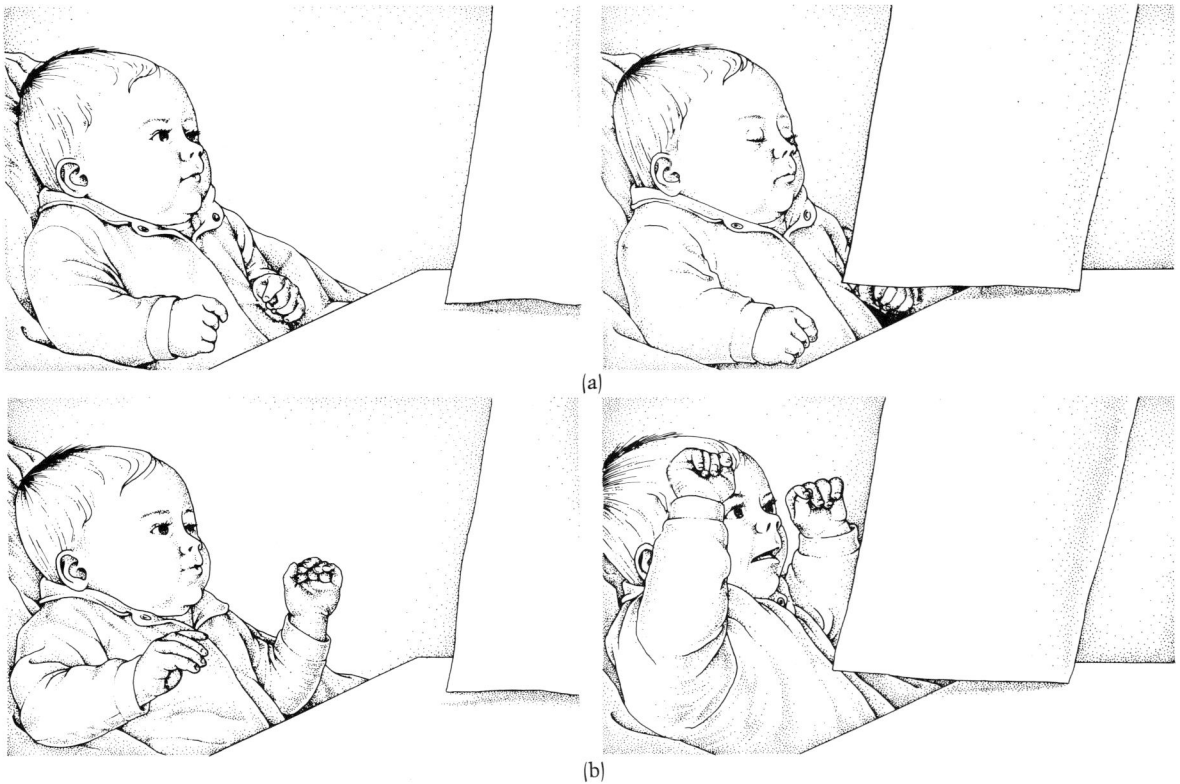

(a)

(b)

FIGURE 9–9. Responses to a looming stimulus. Whether researchers believe that young babies react defensively to impending collision depends in
part on the dependent measures (infants' responses) they use. (a) Blinking,
the response first used to explore response to a looming stimulus. It is a
reliable measure, and studies using it show a developmental progression in
the first 3 to 4 months of life. (b) An integrated avoidance response: eyes
opening wide, head going back, both hands coming up between the object
and the face. This response has been found in newborns in two studies, but
not until 8 months in another. (Drawing in part (b) adapted from photographic sequence in Development in infancy (2nd Ed.), by T.G.R. Bower.
San Francisco: Freeman. Used by permission.)

heads, would be likely to jerk their heads backward as they tried to follow the upper contour.
In several different manipulations, Yonas and
his collaborators (Yonas et al., 1977; Yonas,
Pettersen, & Lockman, 1979) found that backward head movements occurred only when an
upper contour moved upward and did not occur
when the stimulus loomed but had no upward
moving contours. They did not find the integrated avoidance response until 8 months of
age.

In contrast, these researchers found that

blinking responses were elicited by the visual
information of impending collision regardless
of whether there was an upward-moving contour. In addition, Yonas, Petterson, Lockman,
and Eisenberg (1980) showed that 3-month-old
babies consistently blink (66% of the trials)
only when the conditions specified by Gibson
are met: explosive magnification and filling
the visual field (100 degrees of arc, which is
56% of the total visual field). Younger babies (1
month of age) responded both to the impending
collision stimulus and to one in which the ob-

ject appeared (to adults) to be slowing. Thus, the responses of younger babies can be said to be more general and less exact. They are also much rarer. The frequency of responses to approaching objects is about 16% at 6 weeks and increases with age, reaching 75% by 10 weeks (Yonas, 1981). Such development may, of course, reflect either maturation or experience. One research technique that can help to distinguish between maturationally-based and experientially-based development is to compare babies with different gestational histories. Pettersen, Yonas, and Fisch (1980) compared the blink response to approaching stimuli in full-term infants (born within 1 week of their expected delivery date) to postmature infants (born at least 3 weeks after their expected delivery date). At 6 weeks of age the full-term babies blinked to the approaching stimulus only 16% of the time, whereas the postmature babies blinked on 37% of the trials. Because the amount of postnatal experience was held constant in the two groups, the difference between them was attributable to maturation. Pettersen and colleagues also varied experience while holding maturation constant by comparing babies who were 3–6 weeks premature and tested 13–14 weeks after birth to full-term and to postmature babies who were tested at 10 weeks after birth. The frequency of blinking was not different in the premature group compared to the full-term or postterm groups. Thus, the number of weeks of experience, as operationally defined in this study, did not influence the development of blinking to a looming stimulus. It is likely, however, that if experience had been operationally defined as no experience (deprivation of normal binocular experience) versus normal experience, experience would have had an effect. The latter pattern of results is typical of research on the development of binocular responsivity of cortical cells, which we will discuss later in this section.

The second area of depth perception research that we will discuss is **binocular perception** (the cues to depth given by the joint functioning of two eyes). Because the eyes of humans are separated but are both directed ahead, a slightly different view of the visual field is seen by each eye. To see what we mean, look at something close up; then close first one eye and then the other. The two different views

of the two eyes will be obvious. These are the strongest cues to depth for objects that are relatively close to the viewer (beyond 30 feet the two images do not differ). The development of two binocular phenomena in humans has been demonstrated and replicated. They are convergence and stereopsis.

When a visual target is moved from a far to a near distance, the eyes maintain fixation by moving inward toward the nose. When a person follows a moving target coming toward the eyes, the two eyes move inward or **converge.** When objects move away from the eyes, the eyes move to a straight-ahead position—they **diverge.** Convergence and divergence together are called **vergence.** It appears that even newborns under some conditions exhibit convergence: They show binocular fixation to stationary targets when they are at certain distances from the target (Hershenson, 1964; Slater & Findlay, 1975), but they do not consistently exhibit appropriate vergence movements to moving stimuli. By 2 to 3 months of age, babies do make reliable vergence movements (Aslin, 1977; Ling, 1942).

The second binocular phenomenon we wish to discuss is **stereopsis,** which is the perception of depth based solely on the information provided by the two different images of the two eyes. The difference in the two images is called **retinal disparity.** Stereopsis is difficult to study in infants because the perception of depth is a subjective experience. Nevertheless, it is possible to discover whether young infants detect the underlying cues given by changes in the degree of overlap between the two images (that is, by the difference in retinal disparity). This is done by presenting stimuli stereoptically, the same procedure used to make the 3D movies that require goggles for proper viewing. Two overlapping images are presented, one to each eye. The goggles are actually filters that allow one image to reach one eye and the other image to reach the other eye. Experimental procedures necessary to produce a convincing demonstration of this phenomenon have been developing in the last decade (see Aslin & Dumais, 1980, for a review). Three recent studies using these highly developed procedures demonstrated that babies under 10 weeks of age do not detect the difference in retinal disparity and therefore do not experience stereopsis, the strongest single cue for depth. This ability develops during the period between $3\frac{1}{2}$ and 6 months and by the end of that period is close to mature (Fox, Aslin, Shea, & Dumais, 1980; Held, Birch, & Gwiazda, 1980; Petrig, Julesz, Kropfl, Baumgartner, & Anliker, 1981). Thus it appears that divergence develops somewhat earlier than the ability to detect retinal disparity.

The ability to detect differences in retinal disparity is a prerequisite for binocular depth perception, but it is not sufficient to demonstrate that perceptual ability. Infants may be able to detect disparity cues but not perceive them as depth cues; that is, they may not perceive the stereoptic image as nearer to them than the background. Fox and colleagues gathered additional evidence to bolster the interpretation that their older infants really perceived depth. They presented a series of stereograms that adults found relatively more or less effective in producing a fused image of an object in depth. Infants 3–5 months old detected the depth cues only with the stimuli that were the most effective producers of depth for adults. The authors suggest this means infants of this age truly perceive depth binocularly.

The roles of maturation and experience in the development of binocular depth perception have been investigated by studying cortical neurons in cats. Pettigrew (1974) discovered that most cortical neurons in newborn kittens were binocular (they fired from stimulation in both eyes), but each responded to a broad range of disparities. Thus, newborn cortical neurons in cats apparently are structured to develop binocularity, but at birth they detect binocular disparity only in a very coarse fashion. By 5–6 weeks of age each neuron becomes finely tuned to a narrow range of disparities and thus together the neurons provide very sensitive depth information. This description, based on neuronal development, has been confirmed behaviorally (Timney, 1981). If binocular experience is disrupted in the first 5 weeks of life, disparity detection does not develop normally (see Banks & Salapatek, 1983, for a timely review). Thus, detection of disparity apparently has an underlying maturational base, but requires appropriate experience (exposure to patterns that are concordant and synchronous in both eyes) to develop.

The third area of depth perception research that we will present uses an apparatus called

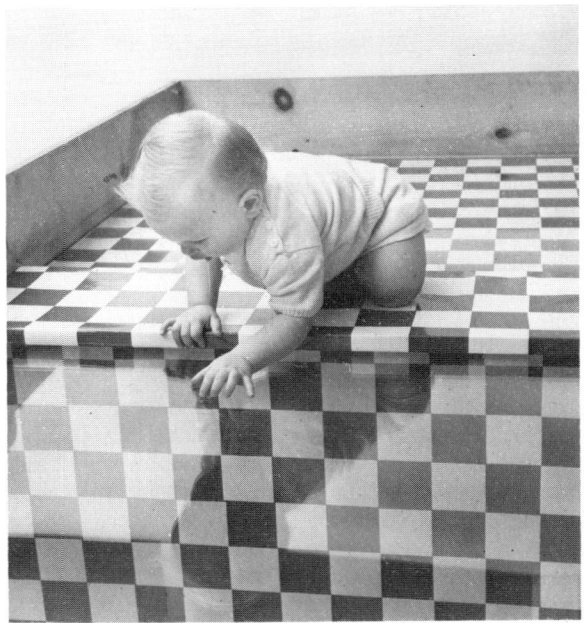

FIGURE 9–10. A baby on the visual cliff apparatus. The baby is intently exploring the glass surface above the deep side. (William Vandivert and Scientific American.)

the visual cliff, developed by E.J. Gibson and Walk (Gibson & Walk, 1960; Walk & Gibson, 1961). It is essentially a table divided into two halves (see Figure 9–10). The entire table top is covered by glass. One half has an opaque surface immediately underneath the glass and the other half has a drop of several feet to an opaque surface like the other. Down the center of the table, dividing the two halves, is a board raised slightly above the surface of the glass. The infant is put on the board. The mother stands across the table and tries to coax her baby to cross either the shallow or the deep side. If the infant refuses to cross to the mother on the deep side but crosses to the mother on the shallow side, this would demonstrate that the baby perceives depth. Gibson and Walk found that when babies first crawled, at 6–9 months of age, most avoided the deep side, so long as the depth cues were made obvious by putting patterns on the floor of the visual cliff. This finding, however, cannot be considered clear support for innate depth perception because so much development occurs in the first 6 months of life. Although babies do not have the experience of moving themselves through space before they start crawling, they clearly have the experience of being moved through space and of correlating this sensory experience with their reaching movements.

A recent series of studies by Campos and his collaborators has modified the visual cliff procedure so it can be used with younger infants (Campos & Langer, 1971; Campos, Langer, & Krowitz, 1970; Schwartz, Campos, & Baisel, 1973). They placed infants on the visual cliff so that the infants looked at either the deep or the shallow side and measured responses such as heart rate, looking, and motor quieting. They found that babies between 1½ and 3 months of age oriented more to the deep side than to the shallow side, which means that babies could discriminate between the two sides. It is possible, however, that the babies were simply discriminating between two visual patterns without knowing that one of those patterns was farther away than the other.

Campos, Hiatt, Ramsay, Henderson, and Svejda (1978) studied infants' placing responses by holding them horizontally above the surface of the cliff and slowly lowering them. Infants were scored as exhibiting the placing response if they extended their limbs and fanned their fingers outward before touching the surface of the cliff. At 7 months of age infants exhibited placing on the shallow, but not on the deep side, which demonstrates that they perceived depth. This may be an overestimate of the age at which depth perception by this measure develops, because they did not test younger babies.

Several studies have explored the role of the development of crawling on visual cliff behavior. The results of such research differ considerably depending on the dependent variable used. Using the original measure of avoidance (crossing the shallow side but not the deep side), Rader, Richards, and their collaborator (Rader, Bausano, & Richards, 1980; Richards & Rader, 1981) gathered evidence that indicates that maturation and not experience predicts infants' responses. They found that the only variable that predicted avoidance responses was the age at which the baby started crawling: Babies who started crawling earlier than 6.5 months of age crossed the deep side whereas those who started crawling later than 6.5

months of age avoided the deep side. This is exactly the opposite of what would be expected if experience determined avoidance responses, because babies who crawled early would have the most experience at the time of testing and yet they were the ones who failed to avoid the deep side. Other variables that index experience—age of the baby and number of days crawling—failed to predict avoidance behaviors if the influence of age of onset of crawling was controlled for. Why should babies who crawl early fail to avoid the deep side? The authors argue that early crawlers learn to crawl during a maturational period in which they are dependent on tactual information and so their later crawling continues to be guided primarily by tactual information. By the time later crawlers learn to crawl, they have matured enough to coordinate visual information with their crawling.

Other response measures suggest that experience moving about underlies performance on the visual cliff. Campos and his colleagues demonstrated this for two measures, the number of seconds it took to start (or to finish) crossing the two sides of the cliff and fear (measured by acceleration of heart rate). We will concentrate on the evidence for the fear response, because it is more extensive. They first demonstrated a relation to age, which is correlated with crawling experience. They found that babies 5–6 months of age (who generally were not yet crawling) did not show fear of the deep side whereas babies 8–9 months of age (most of whom were crawling) did (Campos et al., 1978; Schwartz et al., 1973). They also studied the role of experience in locomoting directly. They first studied the relation of crawling experience with performance on the visual cliff and found that babies the same age who had already started crawling showed fear of the deep side whereas those who hadn't started crawling did not (Campos et al., 1978). Next they tested their interpretation experimentally by exposing one group of noncrawling infants to a walker (a chair on wheels that allows infants to move around). This experience accelerated the development of the fear response (Campos, Svejda, Bertenthal, Benson, & Schmid, 1981).

Let us summarize the research on the visual cliff. This research demonstrates that by 6–7 months of age at the latest infants perceive

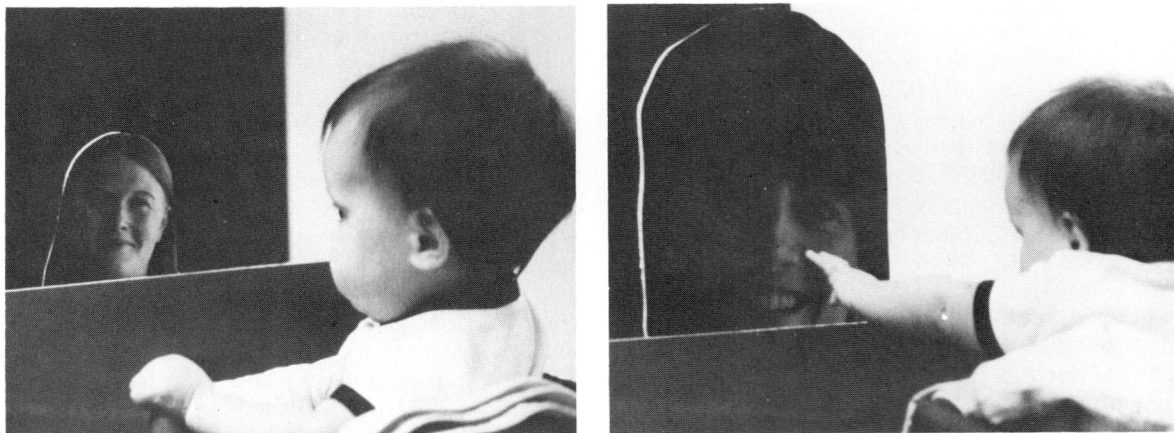

FIGURE 9–11. An example of the procedure used by Yonas to explore sensitivity to pictorial cues. The baby reaches for the larger face. (Photographs courtesy of Dr. Albert Yonas.)

the depth cues of the visual cliff, although they do not exhibit fear until later. Babies as young as 1½–3 months of age can discriminate the difference between the shallow and deep sides of the cliff, but they may not perceive those differences as differences in depth.

Maturation and experience contribute to different aspects of performance on the visual cliff. Maturation appears to underlie the development of the avoidance response itself whereas experience influences the speed of the avoidance response and the development of the fear response. Thus, it seems that fear of the deep side must be learned through crawling—and presumably falling. It is more difficult to reach conclusions about the determinants of the depth perception involved in performance on the cliff. Current research suggests a maturational component, but further evidence is needed both to specify the nature of the maturational underpinning and to explore the determinants of the earlier developing components of performance.

The fourth area of depth perception we will discuss is a set of depth cues known as **pictorial** cues because they are the cues that produce a sense of depth in two-dimensional arrays. For example, if two cars known to be of comparable size are drawn different sizes, and placed side by side in a picture, the smaller one is perceived to be farther away. The same cues also provide information concerning depth in three dimensions. In fact, persons looking at a three-dimensional scene under conditions that eliminate other cues (they look through one eye only and don't move their heads or eyes and the stimuli do not move) would still perceive depth because of pictorial cues.

While there have been numerous sporadic attempts to explore the development of infants' knowledge of pictorial cues, only recently has a systematic program of research been undertaken by Yonas and his collaborators (see Yonas & Owsley, in press, for a review). This research suggests that sensitivity to pictorial cues develops between 5 and 7 months. We will describe one study that exemplifies this research program. Yonas, Pettersen, and Granrud (1982) presented cut-outs of photographs that were either larger or smaller than life size. The 7-month-old infants, when looking with one eye only, were more likely to reach to the larger face than they were to the smaller face (see Figure 9–11). This is what they should do if they are responding to the size of the face. They know what size faces normally are and so respond to the larger face as if it were nearer than it actually was (it was out of reach) and to the smaller face as if it were too far to be reached. Yonas and colleagues included two other conditions to make certain that the infants were responding to the perceived distance. First, they presented the faces to the infants with both eyes uncovered, which destroys the illusion of depth for adults because of the availability of binocular cues.

Second, they created an analogous condition with checkerboard patterns: Such a condition should not produce an illusion of depth because there is no standard size for checkerboards, so a larger checkerboard would be perceived as larger rather than as closer to the observer. In these two control conditions there were no differences in reaching; that is, the infants did not perceive the size differences as cues to depth.

This study and several others from Yonas' laboratory demonstrate that by 7 months of age infants respond to pictorial cues, which are a major source of depth information in the three-dimensional world, particularly at distances greater than 10 feet (when binocular cues become less effective), and which are the only source of depth information in pictures. They also demonstrate that the knowledge 7-month-old infants have gathered in their brief lives influences their depth perception.

The study of the development of depth perception is such a dynamic and rapidly changing field that it is difficult to draw any firm conclusions. We have confined ourselves for the most part to phenomena that have been replicated at least once. We also have taken a conservative position with respect to early development. Doing so allows us to suggest a consistent developmental progression.

Newborns show only very rudimentary abilities in the perception of depth. They occasionally reach for and grasp objects in space, but this neonatal visually elicited reaching is inaccurate and automatic and so does not indicate a knowledge of how far away in space the seen object exists. Newborns also change the relative position of their eyes to stimuli at 10 versus 20 inches away, but not to closer stimuli (Slater & Findlay, 1975), thus showing rudimentary binocular skills.

By 1 to 3 months the depth perception mechanisms are developing rapidly. By 2–3 months of age infants are exhibiting clear vergence and accommodation. They blink in response to the visual information of impending collision. Infants of this age also detect the differences between the deep and shallow sides of the visual cliff, although more evidence is needed to determine that this discrimination is between objects differing in depth.

By 4–6 months sophisticated depth perception develops. The mature forms of visually guided reaching and binocular perception are developing. In the sixth and seventh month of life sensitivity to pictorial depth cues develops.

What can we conclude about the influences of nature and nurture on the development of depth perception? First, if we interpret the nativist position as arguing that depth perception is present at birth, we can conclude that depth perception is not innate. Few of the components of adult depth perception can be demonstrated in newborns, even in areas such as looming, in which procedures appropriate for newborns are possible. Such an interpretation of nativism, is, however, naive. Just because a behavior develops does not mean that the development is determined only by experience. Maturation clearly influences the development of the blinking response to a looming stimulus, as was demonstrated by Pettersen and colleagues (1980). Maturation has also been implicated in the development of binocular responsivity of cortical neurons and in avoidance responses to the visual cliff. Thus the development of several aspects of depth perception is at least in part determined by biological development. This does not mean, however, that experience plays no role. Maturation requires a substrate of experience. The research on cortical neurons in kittens is the clearest example of this. Given normal experience with patterned light, the cortical cells will develop binocularly. If, however, the kitten is deprived of binocular experience, the cortical cells will become unresponsive to binocular information. Thus, as we have demonstrated repeatedly in this book, when maturation is involved in development, it interacts with experience.

Critical Periods in Visual Perception

It is clear that newborn infants are capable of perceiving their world. It is also clear that their perceptual abilities develop dramatically during infancy. These findings raise the question of the role of early experience in perceptual development, a question that underlies much of the chapter, in that we have repeatedly asked what kinds of experiences affect various perceptual functions. In this section, however, we are going to look specifically at the question of whether there is a critical period for the development of perceptual abilities. This question has primarily been explored in the visual domain. For this sensory domain the hypothesis is as follows. Normal visual development requires that the organisms' visual system be used; that is, that organisms experience visual stimulation during a particular period of development. If they are deprived of that stimulation, normal visual development cannot occur and permanent deficits in vision will result. Note that in accord with our general use of the critical periods hypothesis, there must be a particular circumscribed period in which these environmental events must occur; the same events should not have the same effect outside of that critical period; and the effects should be permanent.

The development of microelectrode techniques and the subsequent understanding of the operation of single visual cells have provided a powerful technique for exploring critical periods. The effects of deprivation can be assessed both physiologically and psychologically. Research of this nature has demonstrated a clear period in the infancy of cats in which deprivation of patterned light has profound effects. This period begins at around 1 month of age and ends between 2 and 4 months of age (it seems to taper off gradually; Dews & Wiesel, 1970). Light deprivation during this period produces abnormalities in the response of the cortical cells to the appropriate patterns. Light deprivation before or after this period results in no abnormalities. Even one hour of exposure to the appropriate patterned light will result in functioning cells (Blakemore & Mitchell, 1973), although not in complete normalcy. Indeed, at the height of the critical period (2–3 months for cats), the longer cats are exposed to patterned light, the closer to normal they appear (Dews & Wiesel, 1970; Hubel & Wiesel, 1970).

These effects have been found both in neuronal responses (the firing of the cortical cells) and in perceptual behavior (Blakemore & Cooper, 1970; Dews & Wiesel, 1970; Hirsch, 1972; Hubel & Wiesel, 1970). Blakemore and Cooper found that cats who had been exposed only to horizontal or only to vertical stripes were functionally blind to patterns involving the orientation they had been deprived of. They would not play with rods held in that orientation, they would not extend their paws

in anticipation of reaching a surface (visual placing) if it were striped in the "wrong" direction, and they did not even startle to the plexiglass striped stimulus when it approached them rapidly. Dews and Wiesel found that all of their cats who had been deprived of all light in one eye for varying periods suffered a decrease in acuity, and that cats deprived for the entire critical period also failed a visual placing test. They were, however, able to find their way down a runway to press a lighted panel rather than a darkened panel, so they retained both the ability to distinguish light from dark and minimal sensorimotor coordinations.

The effects of experiences during a critical period are by definition supposed to be permanent. In general, permanent effects, both behavioral and physiological, were found in this research. Nevertheless, the differences in permanence between the two kinds of dependent measures are extremely interesting. Cortical cells measured after long periods of recovery (for example, a year of exposure to normal visual environments) tended to show the same abnormalities as earlier. There is recovery of function in a minority of cells, but those that recover are not the ones that were specifically deprived (Hirsch, 1972; Hubel & Wiesel, 1970).[7]

Behavioral measures, in contrast, show much more recovery (Dews & Wiesel, 1970; Hirsch, 1972). This is most clearly shown in the Dews and Wiesel study. They sutured one eye shut during the critical period. When they opened that eye, they did either of two things. For some cats, they simply exposed both eyes to a normal visual environment. For the other cats, they sutured the nondeprived eye shut for the recovery period (the reversed group). This meant that the latter cats could use only their deprived eye. In all cases the reversed cats recovered more than the nonreversed cats. One reversed cat who had been deprived for the entire critical period (and was therefore the most deficient) was allowed to recover (experience a

[7]We may have to qualify this conclusion in the future. It appears that such cells may not have completely died. Injections of a neural chemical into such animals were sufficient to get the deprived cells to fire again. Whether they would subsequently fire normally to visual stimuli cannot be ascertained at present because the chemical injection kills the organism.

normal visual environment) for 5 years. That cat passed the most difficult acuity test, one that other reversed cats who had been deprived for as long a period were unable to pass. These data suggest that if the deprived animal is allowed (forced) to function in the world and is given extensive experience it can overcome the functional effects of deprivation. Although it is not known how this is achieved, Hirsch thinks that the visual system is so competent that other parts of it can take over the functions that the cortical cells damaged by deprivation cannot perform.

This research calls attention to a very important concept: The permanent effects of deprivation during a critical period may be overcome by compensating mechanisms. In this case it is possible, fortunately, to measure the neuronal effects separately from the behavioral effects, something that is not possible in most research on the usefulness of the critical periods hypothesis in understanding development. Nevertheless, that compensation happens in one domain establishes the general principle and thus makes it more reasonable to argue that it happens in other instances.

Can the conclusions from this experimental research with animals other than humans be generalized to humans? In this instance, there are a few studies that directly test the implications of this work. Experiments with humans that involve deprivation are ethically out of the question, but it is possible to study the later visual development of children who suffer visual defects. Astigmatism and disturbances in the development of binocular vision have been investigated. Astigmatism is a defect in the optics of the eye that results in acute vision in only one orientation and blurring in other orientations. Many astigmatic adults suffer loss of acuity (called meridional amblyopia) even when their astigmatism (that is, the blurring) is corrected optically. The loss of acuity is specific to the blurred orientations, which suggests that it is produced by the experience of habitual blurring prior to optical correction. One way of testing whether the permanent loss of acuity is due to experience is to study the relative courses of development of the astigmatism and the amblyopia. During infancy astigmatism is very common. About half of the infants sampled by Mohindra, Held, Gwiazda, and Brill (1978) had significant astigmatism,

which is five times that found in adulthood, but most infants lose their astigmatism during the first year or two of life. During infancy acuity is restored when the astigmatism is corrected optically, which suggests that the period of susceptibility for the permanent defect does not begin before the second year of life. The earliest a child has been found to suffer loss of acuity even when the astigmatism is corrected is 2 years 10 months of age (Held, 1979). This suggests that the deprivation of visual experience produced by astigmatism causes the later-developing amblyopia and that the period of susceptibility begins in the second year of life.

Research on the development of other defects also is consistent with a critical periods notion, although the age of onset is earlier than has been found for the permanent loss of acuity caused by astigmatism. The data of Held and his collaborators suggest that infants who use only one eye, either because they suffer from strabismus (crossed or wall eyes) in which only one eye focuses on objects or because they have one eye patched (usually done to strengthen the unpatched eye), suffer losses of acuity in the deprived eye as early as 4–6 months of age, but not earlier (Held, 1979; Held, Birch, & Gwiazda, 1980). Banks, Aslin, and Letson (1975) studied children who had developed strabismus at various ages and who had had corrective surgery at different ages. They concluded from these data that there is a critical period for the onset of binocular vision beginning around 4 months of age and peaking between 1 and 3 years of age. There is also evidence for an end to the critical period: Children who develop defects after 3–4 years of age or who have corrective surgery in the first few years of life are not likely to suffer permanent deficiencies in binocular vision (Banks et al., 1975; Hohmann & Creutsfeldt, 1975).

Thus, the research on the development of visual defects in humans is consistent with the experimental findings with cats; that is, deprivation of certain kinds of visual experience at certain developmental periods results in permanent losses. No direct evidence exists that in humans these critical periods are due to maturation of cortical cells, but at present that seems a reasonable conclusion.

The discussion of critical periods may give the impression that all visual functioning may be vulnerable to the strong sorts of deprivation effects we have just mentioned. That is clearly untrue. Visual–motor behaviors, including locomotion and visually guided reaching, seem much less vulnerable to deprivation effects. Even when organisms are raised in complete darkness for rather extended periods of time, these functions recover rapidly. It is possible to deprive an organism for so long that such spatial orientation disappears permanently as a consequence of retinal atrophy, but that has only occurred with periods of deprivation of the order of 2 years (see Ganz, 1975, for a review).

DISCUSSION ISSUES

Research Issues

Although the issues of interest in this chapter are quite different from most of the other topics we have discussed so far in this book, the research issues are similar. That is, an understanding of the phenomena of interest proceeds in a number of discrete steps. (1) A hypothesis is generated either as a part of an overall theory or from informal observations. (2) The hypothesis is tested and the results may or may not confirm the hypothesis. (3) If they do not confirm the hypothesis, they may suggest an alternative hypothesis or the results may simply be unclear. Each of these three possibilities requires further research. If the results are unclear, investigators try to figure out what has produced the inconsistency and then try another study (or give up). When the results form a consistent but unanticipated pattern, researchers typically try to generate an explanation for the pattern. This is called a **post hoc** (after the fact) explanation. It is not as convincing as an **a priori** (before the fact) hypothesis (the hypothesis a study is designed to test), because it has not been subjected to the rigors of the scientific method. For any given finding human ingenuity can generate a variety of explanations. Accepting one over another as the best post hoc explanation for some set of results is a personal rather than a scientific decision. A post hoc explanation achieves scientific respectability only when it is subsequently tested as an a priori hypothesis and predicts specific outcomes that other explanations fail to predict. Because it is also possible that the original results might simply have occurred by chance, the ability of a post hoc explanation to predict new outcomes ensures that it was not just making sense of error.

Corroboration of a hypothesis is of course the most straightforward outcome, because it means that the investigators have been able to predict the results. Nevertheless, it is still only a first step. Alternative hypotheses can almost always be found. It is then the job of the investigators to disconfirm the alternative hypotheses. Some philosophers of science (such as Popper, 1959) believe that science progresses through the disconfirmation of alternative hypotheses.

This chapter provided two good examples of testing interpretations that challenged an a priori hypothesis. One was research on whether newborns can perceive colors. Early research showed discrimination between colors but later researchers pointed out that colors often vary in brightness. It took several methodological advances before a conclusive way of separating color and brightness was developed. By this technique it was confirmed that newborns discriminate among many colors independent of brightness differences among those colors.

The second example was the hypothesis that over the first several days of life infants improve greatly in their sensitivity to tactual stimulation. Again, early studies led to this conclusion, but later researchers suggested that extraneous variables, such as amount of body fat, conductivity of the skin, and the placement of electrodes, might produce the effect. Careful attention to the influences of these alternative interpretations has led to the conclusion that there is an apparent increase in sensitivity over the first few days but it is probably due to an increase in conductivity. In this case, an alternative interpretation was the one eventually supported.

The second kind of alternative interpretation does not attack the a priori hypothesis directly, but rather challenges the implications of that hypothesis. For example, the failure of young infants to accommodate (to change their focus as a function of viewing distance) suggested that they could only focus clearly on objects at distances of around 19 cm from their eyes. This implication was derived from knowledge of adults' perception. The alternative hypothesis is that what is true for adult perception does not necessarily apply to infant perception. When infants' ability to focus was directly tested, it was found that they did focus at different distances even though they could not accommodate. Thus, the research finding itself—no accommodation in the newborn period—was solid, but the implication drawn from it was invalid.

This chapter also gives several more examples of the problems of operational definitions, both those of the stimulus dimensions and those of the responses. A simple example of both is the study of auditory thresholds. How well a baby responds to auditory stimulation depends on the kind of sound. Continuous sounds are more effective stimuli than single sounds. Complex sounds are often more responded to than pure tones. Thus, there will be different estimates of thresholds depending on the kind of sound used as a stimulus. In the same way, estimates of infants' responsivity to auditory stimuli depend on the response measures used. For example, it takes a louder sound to elicit a heart rate response than it does to elicit an auditory evoked potential response. Thus, threshold values will depend on both the stimuli and the response measures.

Parenting

Although the goal of most research in perceptual development is not practical, some of it has practical implications. Good examples are applications to abnormalities in perceptual capacities. Two examples of this were given in audition and in vision. Language researchers have established that children must experience oral language in order to learn to talk in a normal fashion. If they are identified early enough, children who are hard of hearing can be given hearing aids and increased language stimulation (for example, loud TVs and radios). Research in normal perception has played a crucial role in permitting early identification. Techniques have been developed to test auditory capacities in young babies as well as to show how babies with normal hearing hear at various ages. Such norms serve as a baseline against which to compare hearing-impaired infants.

A similar case exists for deficiencies in vision. The research on the development of single-cell detectors in kittens suggested that there may be a critical period in humans, and there now is evidence that this is so. This means that it is important to identify such visual problems early in infancy and to correct them before the critical period ends. Correction sometimes takes the form of surgery, as in strabismus or cross eyes. Sometimes it takes the form of special environmental intervention, as when glasses are worn to correct astigmatism.

Studies of the influence of infants' responsivity to different kinds of auditory stimulation also have yielded practical implications for soothing babies. Stimuli in the pitch range of human voices have a soothing effect, and continuous stimulation has a soothing effect relative both to other sounds and to silence, although sleep so induced may differ both in quality and in length from other forms of sleep. The popular notion that human heartbeats are more soothing than other stimuli is not true. Babies respond in the same way to other repetitive or continuous stimulation, such as that of a metronome or a lullaby.

A final tidbit of a practical nature stems from studies of taste. Sweet solutions seem to be innately pleasurable and to be preferred over more nutritious substances such as milk. This fits in with research with older babies that suggests that babies will select a well-balanced diet from a cafeteria of choices over a week's time, but only if sugar is not included among their choices.

SUMMARY

One of the major focuses of this chapter is the question of how sophisticated or mature the perceptual abilities of newborn babies are. Although at various times in history newborns were considered to be nonfunctioning vegetables, it is now known that in normal babies every sense is operative at birth. Newborns respond to a wide variety of tactual stimuli, and they can differentiate the four basic tastes (sugar, acid, salt, and bitter). They can discriminate among various pleasant and unpleasant smells and they agree with adults' judgments as to what smells are pleasant and what smells are unpleasant. In all the three so-called minor senses, newborns improve rapidly in their ability to discriminate over the first days of life.

The major senses—audition and vision—also function at birth. Newborns' hearing is functional, although less sensitive than that of adults. The softest sounds they can hear are about the same intensity as those of a quiet office or a low conversation. Newborns have a basic ability to localize sounds, although they become more consistent and more sophisticated in this ability by 3 to 6 months of age. They can discriminate among pitches at birth although not as well as older infants and children, and are more restricted in the kinds of sound they respond to. The kinds of sounds that stimulate newborns most easily are complex sounds and continuous sounds.

The development of visual perception was the longest and most complex portion of the chapter, which is not surprising: Vision is the most highly developed sense in humans. We divided the discussion into two sections, visual exploration and detection of visual information. In visual exploration we asked questions relating to how newborns search for and examine visual stimuli and how such exploration develops.

Newborns do look for visual stimuli in at least two respects. First, they look toward stimuli that they see out of the corner of their eyes; that is, they exhibit saccadic movements. Second, evidence is mounting that their eye movements are organized, both endogenously and in response to stimuli in the field. Newborns also can track a moving stimulus, although they are limited in such abilities. Their tracking is frequently jerky and discontinuous rather than smooth and continuous, and the target must move more slowly than is true for adults. By 6 to 8 weeks of age their tracking becomes smooth and sustained, although still more limited than that of adults. Finally, when presented with a stationary stimulus, newborns do not adequately examine all parts of the stimulus. Rather, their attention tends to remain focused on one area, usually of high contrast and part of an external contour. By 2 months of age babies' scanning has improved greatly. They scan multiple features of a stimulus, internal as well as external. They do

so well enough to detect and remember meaningful stimuli.

The second major question about visual perception in infancy is what aspects of the stimuli newborns can detect. We divided kinds of visual information into four categories: color, brightness, pattern, and objects. It is clear that newborns detect patterns and they can discriminate brightness differences. It is probable that they can discriminate color differences, although the only studies that controlled adequately for brightness confounding used infants 8 weeks of age and older. Researchers have also found that the way in which infants detect color is categorical as it is in adults. This suggests that categorical perception of colors is a biologically mediated structure rather than a learned one. (In Chapter 11 the same argument is used for the perception of speech sounds, which are also perceived categorically.)

Knowing that newborns detect patterns (that is, they discriminate between a patterned and a homogeneous field) is only the first step to exploring pattern perception. Subsequent steps have been made in several directions. One has been to assess the acuity of newborns' vision. It appears that newborns are decidedly nearsighted. Some estimates suggest that they could not see the big E on an eye chart, whereas other estimates of acuity, at least under optimal conditions, have them seeing considerably better. There has been some serious question of whether newborns can see foveally at all, but recent research suggests that they can.

Another step to exploring pattern perception is to ask what kind of pattern infants can detect. This has been done primarily in the context of the issue of whether newborns perceive meaningful stimuli. If they do perceive meaningful stimuli, one could conclude that humans have some innate knowledge of the world, an idea that has been very controversial in philosophy for thousands of years. So far, although several researchers have produced evidence that they consider supportive of perception of meaningful patterns in newborns, there has been no body of evidence that convinces the majority of researchers in the field. Rather, it appears that pattern perception in the first month or two of life is governed primarily by the operation of single-cell detectors. Thus, newborns respond to contours, particularly those with high contrast, but they respond equally when those contours are not part of a meaningful pattern and when they are. By 2 months of age infants begin to perceive meaningful patterns. The best evidence comes from studies of face perception. At 2 months of age babies can discriminate between faces with features in their normal arrangement and faces with features in a scrambled arrangement. By 3 months babies can discriminate their mothers from strangers and can discriminate some facial expressions, although it is not clear on what basis those facial expressions are discriminated. This may be part of a more general ability to detect invariant perceptual configurations, which also develops at this age. By 5 months babies discriminate between photographs of two strangers, which indicates that they are becoming more adept at processing facial stimuli. These abilities are still limited, however, because 5-month-old infants still discriminate on the basis of gross physiognomic features. By 7 months it is clear that babies can detect subtle differences among faces.

Many aspects of perception of objects cannot be studied with static, two-dimensional patterns. One of these aspects is the movement of objects. Although exploration of infant development in this area is just beginning, it is clear that by 4–6 months, and probably earlier, babies both can distinguish between kinds of kinetic information and can extract information about objects by movement of those objects.

Another aspect of objects is their solidity; that is, that they are graspable. By the time mature visually guided reaching develops, at 4 months, babies act as if they know this. It is not yet clear whether such knowledge is innate and, if not, how it develops.

The third aspect of knowledge of objects we discussed was depth perception. There have been a few demonstrations of depth perception with babies as young as newborns, but they have not been sufficiently precise or replicable to convince the majority of researchers. In addition there is evidence that suggests that components of depth perception develop sequentially during the first seven months of life.

Our final section discussed the evidence that there is a critical period for the development of vision. The evidence, primarily from the study of kittens, indicates that there is a strong critical period during maturation of single-cell detectors. If kittens are deprived of the appropriate kind of patterned light during this period, the cells will atrophy, a permanent effect. Unlike the embryological critical periods discussed in Chapter 2, the functional effects are not equally permanent. Given extensive amounts of appropriate stimulation, kittens exhibit substantial recovery of their visual functioning, presumably because other areas of the cortex take over for the atrophied cells. Several studies with humans indicate that critical periods for visual development exist in humans as well.

REFERENCES

Ambrose, J.A. (1961). The development of the smiling response in early infancy. In B.M. Foss (Ed.), *Determinants of infant behaviour* (pp. 179–196). New York: Wiley.

Ambrose, J.A. (1963). The concept of a critical period for the development of social responsiveness. In B.M. Foss (Ed.), *Determinants of infant behaviour* (Vol. 2, pp. 201–225). New York: Wiley.

Ames, E., & Silfen, C. (1965). *Methodological issues in the study of age differences in infant's attention to stimuli varying in movement and complexity.* Paper presented at the biennial meeting of the Society for Research in Child Development, Minneapolis.

Anderson, R.B., & Rosenblith, J.F. (1964). Light sensitivity in the neonate: A preliminary report. *Biologia Neonatorum, 7,* 83–94.

Aronson, E., & Rosenbloom, S. (1971). Space perception in early infancy: Perception within a common auditory–visual space. *Science, 172,* 1161–1163.

Ashmead, D.A., Reilly, B.M., & Lipsitt, L.P. (1980). Neonates' heart rate, sucking rhythm, and sucking amplitude as a function of the sweet taste. *Journal of Experimental Child Psychology, 29,* 264–281.

Ashton, R. (1971). State and the auditory reactivity of the human neonate. *Journal of Experimental Child Psychology, 12,* 339–346.

Aslin, R.N. (1977). Development of binocular fixation in human infants. *Journal of Experimental Child Psychology, 23,* 133–150.

Aslin, R.N. (1981). Development of smooth pursuit in human infants. In D.F. Fisher, R.A. Monty, & J.W. Senders (Eds.), *Eye movements: Cognition and visual perception.* Hillsdale, NJ: Erlbaum.

Aslin, R.N., & Dumais, S.T. (1980). Binocular vision in infants. In H.W. Reese & L.P. Lipsitt (Eds.),

Advances in child development and behavior (Vol. 15). New York: Academic.

Atkinson, J., Braddick, O., & Moar, K. (1977). Development of contrast sensitivity over the first 3 months of life in the human infant. *Vision Research, 17*, 1037–1044.

Ball, W., & Tronick, E. (1971). Infant responses to impending collision: Optical and real. *Science, 171*, 818–820.

Banks, M.S. (1980). The development of early infancy. *Child Development, 51*, 646–666.

Banks, M.S., Aslin, R.N., & Letson, R.D. (1975). Sensitive period in the development of human binocular vision. *Science, 190*, 675–677.

Banks, M.S., & Salapatek, P. (1978). Acuity and contrast sensitivity in 1, 2, and 3-month-old human infants. *Investigative Ophthamology, 17*, 361–365.

Banks, M.S., & Salapatek, P. (1983). Infant visual perception. In P.H. Mussen (Ed.), *Handbook of child psychology: Vol. 2. Infancy and developmental psychobiology* (4th ed., pp. 435–571). New York: Wiley.

Barnet, A.B., & Goodwin, R.S. (1965). Average evoked electroencephalographic responses to clicks in the human newborn. *Electroencephalography and Clinical Neurophysiology, 18*, 441–450.

Barrera, M.E., & Maurer, D. (1981a). Discrimination of strangers by the three-month-old. *Child Development, 52*, 558–563.

Barrera, M.E., & Maurer, D. (1981b). Recognition of mother's photographed face by the three-month-old infant. *Child Development, 52*, 714–716.

Bartoshuk, A.K. (1964). Human neonatal cardiac responses to sound: A power function. *Psychonomic Science, 1*, 151–152.

Bayley, N. (1969). *Bayley scales of infant development: Birth to two years.* New York: Psychological Corp.

Bell, R.Q. (1963). Some factors to be controlled in studies of the behavior of newborns. *Biologia Neonatorum, 5*, 200–214.

Bell, R.Q., & Costello, N.S. (1964). Three tests for sex differences in tactile sensitivity in the newborn. *Biologia Neonatorum, 7*, 335–347.

Bench, J. (1969). In discussion of: Heron, T.G. & Jacobs, R. Respiratory responses of the neonate to auditory stimulation. *International Audiology, 8*, 77.

Bench, J. (1973). Square-wave stimuli and neonatal auditory behavior. Some comments on Ashton

(1971), Hutt et al. (1968) and Lenard et al. (1969). *Journal of Experimental Child Psychology, 16*, 521–527.

Berg, W.K., & Berg, K.M. (1979). Psychophysiological development in infancy: State, sensory function, and attention. In J.D. Osofsky (Ed.), *Handbook of infant development* (pp. 283–343). New York: Wiley.

Berg, W.K., & Smith, M.C. (1983). Behavioral thresholds for tones during infancy. *Journal of Experimental Child Psychology, 35*, 409–425.

Bernard, J. (1946). Human fetal reactivity to tonal stimulation. *American Psychologist, 1*, 256.

Bernard, J., & Sontag, L.W. (1947). Fetal reactivity to tonal stimulation: A preliminary report. *Journal of Genetic Psychology, 70*, 205–210.

Bertenthal, B.I., & Proffitt, D.R. (1982, March). *Development of infant sensitivity to biomechanical motion.* Paper presented at the Third International Conference on Infant Studies, Austin, TX.

Bigelow, A.E. (1983). Development of the use of sound in the search behavior of infants. *Developmental Psychology, 19*, 317–321.

Birch, H.G., Belmont, I., & Karp, E. (1965). Social differences in auditory perception. *Perceptual and Motor Skills, 20*, 861–870.

Blakemore, C., & Cooper, G.F. (1970). Development of the brain depends on the visual environment. *Nature, 228*, 477–478.

Blakemore, C., & Mitchell, D.E. (1973). Environmental modification of the visual cortex and the neural basis of learning and memory. *Nature, 241*, 467–468.

Bonds, A.B. (1979). Development of orientation tuning in the visual cortex of kittens. In R.D. Freeman (Ed.), *Developmental neurobiology of vision.* New York: Plenum.

Bornstein, M.H. (1976). Infants are trichromats. *Journal of Experimental Child Psychology, 21*, 425–445.

Bornstein, M.H. (1981). "Human infant color vision and color perception" reviewed and reassessed: A critique of Werner and Wooten (1979a). *Infant Behavior and Development, 4*, 119–150.

Bornstein, M.H., Kessen, W., & Weiskopf, S. (1976). The categories of hue in infancy. *Science, 21*, 425–445.

Bower, T.G.R. (1972). Object perception in infants. *Perception, 1*, 15–30.

Bower, T.G.R. (1974). *Development in infancy.* San Francisco: Freeman.

Bower, T.G.R. (1982). *Development in infancy* (2nd ed.). San Francisco: Freeman.

Bower, T.G.R., Broughton, J.M., & Moore, M.K. (1971). The development of the object concept as manifested by changes in the tracking behavior of infants between 7 and 20 weeks of age. *Journal of Experimental Child Psychology, 11,* 182–193.

Brackbill, Y. (1970). Acoustic variation and arousal level in infants. *Psychophysiology, 6,* 517–526.

Brackbill, Y. (1971). Cumulative effects of continuous stimulation on arousal level in infants. *Child Development, 42,* 17–26.

Braddick, O., Atkinson, J., French, J., & Howland, H.C. (1979). A photorefractive study of infant accommodation. *Vision Research, 19,* 1319–1330.

Brazelton, T.B., Koslowski, B., & Main, M. (1974). The origin of reciprocity in the mother–infant interaction. In M. Lewis & L. Rosenblum (Eds.), *The effect of the infant on its caregiver.* New York: Wiley.

Bridger, W.H. (1961). Sensory habituation and discrimination in the human neonate. *American Journal of Psychiatry, 117,* 991–997.

Broerse, J., Peltolta, C., & Crassini, B. (1983). Infants' reactions to perceptual paradox during mother–infant interaction. *Developmental Psychology, 19,* 310–316.

Bruner, J.S., & Koslowski, B. (1972). Visually preadapted constituents of manipulatory action. *Perception, 1,* 3–14.

Bushnell, I.W.R., Gerry, G., & Burt, K. (1983). The externality effect in neonates. *Infant Behavior and Development, 6,* 151–156.

Butterfield, E.C., & Siperstein, G.N. (1974). Influence of contingent auditory stimulation upon non-nutritional suckle. In J.F. Bosma (Ed.), *Proceedings of Third Symposium on Oral Sensation and Perception: The mouth of the infant.* Springfield, IL: Thomas.

Butterworth, G., & Castillo, M. (1976). Coordination of auditory and visual space in newborn human infants. *Perception, 5,* 155–160.

Campos, J.J., Hiatt, S., Ramsay, D., Henderson, C., & Svejda, M. (1978). The emergence of fear on the visual cliff. In M. Lewis & L. Rosenblum (Eds.), *The origins of affect.* New York: Plenum.

Campos, J.J., & Langer, A. (1971). The visual cliff: Discriminative cardiac orienting responses with retinal size held constant. *Psychophysiology, 8,* 264–265.

Campos, J.J., Langer, A., & Krowitz, A. (1970). Cardiac responses on the visual cliff in prelocomotor human infants. *Science, 170,* 196–197.

Campos, J.J., Svejda, M., Bertenthal, B., Benson, N., & Schmid, D. (1981). *Self-produced locomotion and wariness of heights: New evidence from training studies.* Paper presented at the biennial meeting of the Society for Research in Child Development, Boston.

Canestrini, S. (1913). Ueber das sinnesleben des neugeborenen. *Monographien aus dem Gesamtgebiete du Neurologie und Psychiatrie, 5,* 1–104.

Caron, R.F., Caron, A.J., & Myers, R.S. (1982). Abstraction of invariant face expressions in infancy. *Child Development, 53,* 1008–1018.

Carpenter, G.C. (1974a). Mother's face and the newborn. *New Scientist,* 742–744.

Carpenter, G.C. (1974b). Visual regard of moving and stationary faces in early infancy. *Merrill-Palmer Quarterly, 20,* 181–194.

Cattell, P. (1940). *The measurement of intelligence in young children.* New York: Psychological Corporation.

Chun, R.W.N., Pawsat, R., & Forster, F.M. (1960). Sound localization in infancy. *Journal of Nervous and Mental Diseases, 130,* 472–476.

Clarkson, M., & Berg, W.K. (1978). Cardiac deceleration in neonates is influenced by temporal pattern and spectral complexity of auditory stimuli. *Psychophysiology, 5,* 284 (Abstract).

Clifton, R.K., Morrongiello, B.A., Kulig, J.W., & Dowd, J.M. (1981a). Developmental changes in auditory localization in infancy. In R.N. Aslin, J.R. Alberts, & M.R. Petersen (Eds.), *Development of perception: Psychobiological perspectives: Vol. 1. Audition, somatic perception, and the chemical senses* (pp. 141–160). New York: Academic.

Clifton, R.K., Morrongiello, B.A., Kulig, J.W., & Dowd, J.M. (1981b). Newborns' orientation toward sound: Possible implications for cortical development. *Child Development, 52,* 833–838.

Cohen, L.B., DeLoache, J.S., & Strauss, M.S. (1979). Infant visual perception. In J.D. Osofsky (Ed.), *Handbook of infant development* (pp. 393–438). New York: Wiley.

Cohen, L.B., & Strauss, M.S. (1979). Concept acquisition in the human infant. *Child Development, 50,* 419–424.

Cohen, L.B., & Younger, B.A. (1984). Infant perception of angular relations. *Infant Behavior and Development, 7,* 37–47.

Condry, S.M., Haltom, M., & Neisser, U. (1977). Infant sensitivity to audio-visual discrepancy: A failure to replicate. *Bulletin of the Psychonomic Society, 9,* 431–432.

Cornell, E. (1974). Infants' discrimination of photographs of faces following redundant presentations. *Journal of Experimental Child Psychology, 18,* 98–106.

Crassini, B., & Broerse, J. (1980). Auditory-visual integration in neonates: A signal detection analysis. *Journal of Experimental Child Psychology, 29,* 144–155.

Crook, C.K., & Lipsitt, L.P. (1976). Neonatal nutritive sucking: Effects of taste stimulation upon sucking rhythm and heart rate. *Child Development, 47,* 518–522.

Crowell, D.H., Jones, R.H., Nakagawa, J.K., & Kapuniai, L.E. (1971). Heart rate responses of human newborns to modulated pure tones. *Proceedings of the Royal Society of Medicine, 64,* 8–10.

Culp, R. (1971). *Looking response, decrement, and recovery of eight- to fourteen-week-old infants in relation to presentation of the infant's mother's voice.* Unpublished master's thesis, University of Kansas, Lawrence.

Dayton, G.O., Jr., & Jones, M.H. (1964). Analysis of characteristics of fixation reflexes in infants by use of direct current electrooculography. *Neurology, 14,* 1152–1156.

Dayton, G.O., Jr., Jones, M.H., Aiu, P., Rawson, R.A., Steele, B., & Rose, M. (1964). Developmental study of coordinated eye movements in the human infant: I. Visual acuity in the newborn human: A study based on induced optokinetic nystagmus recorded by electrooculography. *Archives of Opthalmology, 71,* 865–870.

DeCasper, A.J., & Fifer, W.P. (1980). Of human bonding: Newborns prefer their mothers' voices. *Science, 208,* 1174–1176.

Desor, J.A., Maller, O., & Greene, L.S. (1977). Preference for sweet in humans: Infants, children and adults. In J.M. Weiffenbach (Ed.), *Taste and development: The genesis of sweet preference* (DHEW Publication No. (NIH) 77-1068). Bethesda, MD: National Institute of Dental Research.

Detterman, D.K. (1978). The effect of heartbeat sound on neonatal crying. *Infant Behavior and Development, 1,* 36–48.

Dews, P.B., & Wiesel, T.N. (1970). Consequences of monocular deprivation on visual behavior in kittens. *Journal of Physiology, 206,* 437–455.

Dirks, J., & Gibson, E. (1977). Infants' perception of similarity between live people and their photographs. *Child Development, 48,* 124–130.

Dobson, V., Mayer, D.L., & Lee, C.P. (1980). Visual acuity screening of preterm infants. *Investigative Ophthalmology and Visual Science, 19,* 1498–1505.

Dockeray, F.C., & Rice, C. (1934). Responses of newborn infants to pain stimulation. *Ohio State University Studies, Contributions to psychology, 12,* 82–93.

Dodwell, P.C., Muir, D., & DiFranco, D. (1976). Responses of infants to visually presented objects. *Science, 194,* 209–211.

Eichorn, D. (1951). *Electrocortical and autonomic response in infants to visual and auditory stimuli.* Unpublished doctoral dissertation, Northwestern University, Evanston, IL.

Eisenberg, R.B. (1970a). The development of hearing in man: An assessment of current status. *Journal of the American Speech and Hearing Association, 12,* 119–121.

Eisenberg, R.B. (1970b). The organization of auditory behavior. *Journal of Speech and Hearing Research, 13,* 453–471.

Engen, T., & Bosack, T.N. (1969). Facilitation in olfactory detection. *Journal of Comparative and Physiological Psychology, 68,* 320–326.

Engen, T., & Lipsitt, L.P. (1965). Decrement and recovery of responses to olfactory stimuli. *Journal of Comparative Physiology and Psychology, 59,* 312–318.

Engen, T., Lipsitt, L.P., & Kaye, H. (1963). Olfactory responses and adaption in the human neonate. *Journal of Physiology and Psychology, 56,* 73–77.

Fagan, J.F., III. (1976). Infants' recognition of invariant features of faces. *Child Development, 47,* 627–638.

Fagan, J.F., III. (1979). The origin of facial pattern perception. In M.H. Bornstein & W. Kessen (Eds.), *Psychological development from infancy: Image to intention* (pp. 83–113). Hillsdale, NJ: Erlbaum.

Fantz, R.L. (1961). A method for studying depth perception in infants under six months of age. *Psychological Record, 11,* 27–32.

Fantz, R.L. (1963). Pattern vision in newborn infants. *Science, 140,* 296–297.

Fantz, R.L. (1966). Pattern discrimination and selective attention as determinants of perceptual development from birth. In A.H. Kidd & J.L. Rivoire (Eds.), *Perceptual development in children.* New York: International University Press.

Fantz, R.L., Fagan, J.F., III, & Miranda, S.B. (1975). Early visual selectivity as a function of pattern variables, previous exposure, age from birth and conception, and expected cognitive deficit. In L.B. Cohen & P. Salapatek (Eds.), *Infant perception: From sensation to cognition: Vol. 1. Basic visual processes.* New York: Academic.

Fantz, R.L., Ordy, J.M., & Udelf, M.S. (1962). Maturation of pattern vision in infants during the first six months. *Journal of Comparative and Physiological Psychology, 55,* 907–917.

Field, J., Muir, D., Pilon, R., Sinclair, M., & Dodwell, P. (1980). Infants' orientation to lateral sounds from birth to three months. *Child Development, 51,* 295–298.

Field, T.M., Cohen, D., Garcia, R., & Greenberg, R. (1984). Mother–stranger face discrimination by the newborn. *Infant Behavior and Development, 7,* 19–25.

Forbes, H., & Forbes, H. (1927). Fetal sense reaction: Hearing. *Journal of Comparative Psychology, 7,* 353–355.

Fox, R., Aslin, R.N., Shea, S.L., & Dumais, S.T. (1980). Stereopsis in human infants. *Science, 207,* 323–324.

Fox, R., & McDaniel, C. (1982). The perception of biological motion by human infants. *Science, 218,* 486–487.

Freedman, D.A., Fox-Kolenda, B., Margileth, D.A., & Miller, D.H. (1969). The development of the use of sound as a guide to affective and cognitive behavior. *Child Development, 40,* 1099–1105.

Fröding, C.A. (1960). Acoustic investigation of newborn infants. *Acta Oto-laryngolica, 52,* 31–40.

Ganz, L. (1975). Orientation in visual space. In A.H. Riesen (Ed.), *The developmental neuropsychology of sensory deprivation.* New York: Academic.

Genzmer, A. (1882). *Untersuchungen über die Sinnes wahrnehmungen des neugeborenen Menschen* (National Institute of Health, Trans., for J.F. Bosma). Halle: Max Niemeyer.

Gesell, A. (1925). *Mental growth of the preschool child.* New York: Macmillan.

Ghent, L. (1961). Developmental changes in tactual thresholds on dominant and nondominant sides. *Journal of Comparative and Physiological Psychology, 54,* 670–673.

Gibson, E.J. (1969). *Principles of perceptual learning and development.* New York: Appleton-Century-Crofts.

Gibson, E.J., Owsley, C.J., & Johnston, J. (1978). Perception of invariants by five-month-old infants: Differentiation of two types of motion. *Developmental Psychology, 14,* 407–415.

Gibson, E.J., & Walk, R.D. (1960). The "visual cliff". *Scientific American, 202,* 64–71.

Gibson, J.J. (1958). Visually controlled locomotion and visual orientation in animals. *British Journal of Psychology, 49,* 182–194.

Gibson, J.J. (1966). *The senses considered as perceptual systems.* Boston: Houghton Mifflin.

Gibson, J.J. (1979). *An ecological approach to visual perception.* Boston: Houghton Mifflin.

Goldblatt, A., Strauss, S., & Hess, P. (1980). A replication and extension of findings about the development of visual acuity in infants. *Infant Behavior and Development, 3,* 179–182.

Goldenberg, I., Starkey, D., & Morant, R.B. (1984). *Auditory–visual integration: Face–voice mismatch.* Manuscript submitted for publication.

Goren, C., Sarty, M., & Wu, P. (1975). Visual following and pattern discrimination of face-like stimuli by newborn infants. *Pediatrics, 56,* 544–549.

Graham, F.K. (1956). Behavioral differences between normals and traumatized newborns: I. The test procedures. *Psychological Monographs, 70*(20, Whole No. 427).

Graham, F.K., Matarazzo, R.G., & Caldwell, B.M. (1956). Behavioral differences between normals and traumatized newborns: II. Standardization, reliability, and validity. *Psychological Monographs, 70*(21, Whole No. 428).

Gregg, C., Clifton, R.K., & Haith, M. (1976). A possible explanation for the frequent failure to find cardiac orienting in the newborn infant. *Developmental Psychology, 12,* 75–76.

Guillory, A.W., Self, P.A., Francis, P., & Paden, L.L. (1979, April). *Odor perception in newborns.* Paper presented at the annual meeting of the Southwestern Psychological Association, San Antonio, TX.

Guillory, A.W., Self, P.A., & Paden, L.L. (1980, April). *Odor sensitivity in one month infants.* Paper presented at the International Conference on Infant Studies, New Haven, CT.

Gwiazda, J., Brill, S., Mohindra, I., & Held, R. (1978). Infant visual acuity and its meridional variation. *Vision Research, 18,* 1557–1564.

Haaf, R.A. (1974). Complexity and facial resemblance as determinants of response to face-like stimuli by 5 and 10 week old infants. *Journal of Experimental Child Psychology, 18,* 480–487.

Haaf, R.A., & Bell, R.Q. (1967). A facial dimension in visual discrimination by human infants. *Child Development, 38,* 893–899.

Haaf, R.A., & Brown, C.J. (1975). *Developmental changes in infants' response to complex facelike patterns.* Paper presented at the biennial meeting of the Society for Research in Child Development, Denver.

Haith, M.M. (1978). Visual competence in early infancy. In R. Held, H.W. Leibowitz, & H.L.

Teuber (Eds.), *Handbook of sensory physiology* (Vol. 8, pp. 311–356). New York: Springer.

Haith, M.M. (1980). *Rules that infants look by.* Hillsdale, NJ: Erlbaum.

Haith, M.M., Bergman, T., & Moore, M.J. (1977). Eye contact and face scanning in early infancy. *Science, 198,* 853–855.

Haith, M.M., & Goodman, G.S. (1982). Eye movement control in newborns in darkness and in unstructured light. *Child Development, 53,* 974–977.

Haller, M. (1932). The reactions of infants to changes in the intensity and pitch of pure tones. *Journal of Genetic Psychology, 40,* 162–180.

Haynes, H., White, B.L., & Held, R. (1965). Visual accommodation in human infants. *Science, 148,* 528–530.

Held, R. (1979). Development of visual resolution. *Canadian Journal of Psychology, 33,* 213–221.

Held, R., Birch, E., & Gwiazda, J. (1980). Stereoacuity of human infants. *Proceedings of the National Academy of Sciences USA, 77,* 5572–5574.

Hershenson, M. (1964). Visual discrimination in the human newborn. *Journal of Comparative and Physiological Psychology, 58,* 270–276.

Hirsch, H.V.B. (1972). Visual perception in cats after environmental surgery. *Experimental Brain Research, 15,* 405–423.

Hofsten, C. von. (1982). Eye–hand coordination in the newborn. *Developmental Psychology, 18,* 450–461.

Hofsten, C. von. (1984). Developmental changes in the organization of prereaching movements. *Developmental Psychology, 20,* 378–388.

Hohmann, A., & Creutsfeldt, D.D. (1975). Squint and the development of binocularity in humans. *Nature, 254,* 613–614.

Horowitz, F.D., Paden, L.Y., Bhana, K., & Self, P. (1972). An infant control procedure for studying infant visual fixations. *Developmental Psychology, 7,* 90.

Hoversten, G.H., & Moncur, J.P. (1969). Stimuli and intensity factors in testing infants. *Journal of Speech and Hearing Research, 12,* 687–702.

Hubel, D.H., & Wiesel, T.N. (1963). Receptive fields of cells in striate cortex of very young, visually inexperienced kittens. *Journal of Neurophysiology, 26,* 994–1002.

Hubel, D.H., & Wiesel, T.N. (1970). The period of susceptibility to the physiological effects of unilateral eye closure in kittens. *Journal of Physiology (London), 206,* 419–436.

Hutt, S.J., Hutt, C., Lenard, H.G., Bernuth, H.V., & Muntejewerff, W.J. (1968). Auditory responsivity in the human neonate. *Nature, 218,* 888–890.

Hutt, S.J., Lenard, H.G., & Prechtl, H.F.R. (1969). Psychophysiological studies in newborn infants. In L.P. Lipsitt & H.W. Reese (Eds.), *Advances in child development and behavior* (Vol. 4, pp. 128–172). New York: Academic.

Jensen, K. (1932). Differential reactions to taste and temperature stimuli in newborn infants. *Genetic Psychology Monographs, 12,* 363–479.

Kagan, J., Henker, B.A., Hen-Tov, A., Levine, J., & Lewis, M. (1966). Infants' differential reactions to familiar and distorted faces. *Child Development, 37,* 519–532.

Karmel, B.Z., & Maisel, E.B. (1975). A neuronal activity model for infant visual attention. In L.B. Cohen & P. Salapatek (Eds.), *Infant perception: From sensation to cognition. Vol. 1. Basic visual processes.* New York: Academic.

Kaufmann-Hayoz, R., & Jäger, B. (1983, April). *Infants' perception of a face revealed through motion.* Paper presented at the biennial meeting of the Society for Research in Child Development, Detroit.

Kaufmann, R., & Kaufmann, F. (1980). The face schema in 3- and 4-month old infants: The role of dynamic properties of the face. *Infant Behavior and Development, 3,* 331–339.

Kaye, H. (1964). Skin conductance in the human neonate. *Child Development, 35,* 1297–1305.

Kaye, H., & Lipsitt, L.P. (1964). Relation of electrotactual threshold to basal skin conductance. *Child Development, 35,* 1307–1312.

Kellman, P.J., & Spelke, E.S. (1983). Perception of partly occluded objects in infancy. *Cognitive Psychology, 15,* 483–524.

Kessen, W., & Bornstein, M.H. (1978). Discriminability of brightness change for infant. *Journal of Experimental Child Psychology, 25,* 526–530.

Kessen, W., Haith, M.M., & Salapatek, P.H. (1970). Human infancy: A bibliography and guide. In P.H. Mussen (Ed.), *Carmichael's manual of child psychology* (3rd ed.; Vol. 1, pp. 287–445). New York: Wiley.

Kisilevsky, B.S., & Muir, W. (1984). Neonatal habituation and dishabituation to tactile stimulation during sleep. *Developmental Psychology, 20,* 367–373.

Kobre, K.R., & Lipsitt, L.P. (1972). A negative contrast effect in newborns. *Journal of Experimental Child Psychology, 14,* 81–91.

Koopman, P., & Ames, E. (1968). Infants' preferences for facial arrangements: Failure to replicate. *Child Development, 39,* 481–487.

Kremenitzer, J.P., Vaughan, H.G., Jr., Kurtzberg, D., & Dowling, K. (1979). Smooth-pursuit eye movements in the newborn infant. *Child Development, 50,* 442–448.

Kussmaul, A. (1859). *Untersuchungen über das seelenleben des neugenborenen menschen.* Tübingen: Moser.

Leibowitz, H.W., & Harvey, L.O., Jr. (1973). Perception. *Annual Review of Psychology, 24,* 207–240.

Lenard, H.G., Bernuth, H.V., & Hutt, S.J. (1969). Acoustic evoked responses in newborn infants: The influence of pitch and complexity of the stimulus. *Electroencephalography and Clinical Neurophysiology, 27,* 121–127.

Leventhal, A.S., & Lipsitt, L.P. (1964). Adaptation, pitch discrimination, and sound localization in the neonate. *Child Development, 35,* 759–767.

Lewis, T.L., Maurer, D., & Kay, D. (1978). Newborn's central vision: Whole or hole?. *Journal of Experimental Child Psychology, 26,* 193–203.

Lewis, T.L., & Maurer, D. (1980). Central vision in the newborn. *Journal of Experimental Child Psychology, 29,* 475–480.

Ling, B.C. (1942). A genetic study of sustained visual fixation and associated behavior in the human infant from birth to six months. *Journal of Genetic Psychology, 61,* 227–277.

Lipsitt, L.P. (1977). Taste in human neonates: Its effects on sucking and heart rate. In J.M. Weiffenbach (Ed.), *Taste and development: The genesis of sweet preference* (Publication No. (NIH) 77-1068). Bethesda, MD: National Institute of Dental Research.

Lipsitt, L.P., Engen, T., & Kaye, H. (1963). Developmental changes in the olfactory threshold of the neonate. *Child Development, 34,* 371–376.

Lipsitt, L.P., & Levy, N. (1959). Electrotactual threshold in the neonate. *Child Development, 30,* 547–552.

Lipsitt, L.P., Reilly, B.M., Butcher, M.J., & Greenwood, M.M. (1976). The stability and interrelationships of newborn sucking and heart rate. *Developmental Psychobiology, 9,* 305–310.

MacFarlane, J.A. (1975). Olfaction in the development of social preferences in the human neonate. In *Parent–infant interaction. Ciba Foundation Symposium 33 (new series).* Amsterdam: Elsevier.

Marquis, D. (1931). Can conditioned responses be established in the newborn infant? *Journal of Genetic Psychology, 39,* 479–490.

Maurer, D. (1975). Infant visual perception: Methods of study. In L.B. Cohen & P. Salapatek (Eds.), *Infant perception: From sensation to cognition: Vol. 1. Basic visual processes* (pp. 1–76). New York: Academic.

Maurer, D., & Barrera, M. (1978). *Infants' perception of the natural and distorted arrangements of the human face.* Paper presented at the Second International Conference on Infant Studies, New Haven, CT.

Maurer, D., & Barrera, M. (1981). Infants' perception of natural and distorted arrangements of a schematic face. *Child Development, 52,* 196–202.

Maurer, D., & Heroux, L. (1980). *The perception of faces by three-month-old infants.* Paper presented at the Second International Conference on Infant Studies, New Haven, CT.

Maurer, D., & Lewis, T.L. (1979). Peripheral discrimination by three-month-old infants. *Child Development, 50,* 276–279.

Maurer, D., & Salapatek, P. (1976). Developmental changes in the scanning of faces by young infants. *Child Development, 47,* 523–527.

Maurer, D., & Young, R.E. (1983). Newborn's following of natural and distorted arrangements of facial features. *Infant Behavior and Development, 6,* 127–131.

McGurk, H. (1972). Infant discrimination of orientation. *Journal of Experimental Child Psychology, 14,* 151–164.

McGurk, H., & Lewis, M. (1974). Space perception in early infancy: Perception within a common auditory–visual space? *Science, 186,* 649–650.

McGurk, H., Turnure, C., & Creighton, S.J. (1977). Auditory–visual coordination in neonates. *Child Development, 48,* 138–143.

Melhuish, E.C. (1982). Visual attention to mother's and stranger's faces and facial contrast in 1-month-old infants. *Developmental Psychology, 18,* 229–231.

Mendelson, M.J., & Haith, M.M. (1976). The relation between audition and vision in the human newborn. *Monographs of the Society for Research in Child Development, 41*(4, Serial No. 167).

Milewski, A.E. (1976). Infants' discrimination of internal and external pattern elements. *Journal of Experimental Child Psychology, 22,* 229–246.

Milewski, A.E. (1979). Visual discrimination and detection of configural invariance in 3-month infants. *Developmental Psychology, 15,* 357–363.

Miranda, S.B. (1970). Visual abilities and pattern preferences of premature infants and full-term neonates. *Journal of Experimental Child Psychology, 10,* 189–205.

Mohindra, I., Held, R., Gwiazda, J., & Brill, S. (1978). Astigmatism in infants. *Science, 202,* 329–331.

Moltz, H. (1960). Imprinting: Empirical basis and theoretical significance. *Psychological Bulletin, 57,* 291–316.

Moore, J.M., & Wilson, W.R. (1978). Visual reinforcement audiometry (VRA) with infants. In S.E. Gerber & G.T. Mencher (Eds.), *Early diagnosis of hearing loss.* New York: Grune & Stratton.

Morrongiello, B.A., Clifton, R.K., & Kulig, J.W. (1982). Newborn cardiac and behavioral orienting responses to sound under varying precedence-effect conditions. *Infant Behavior and Development, 5,* 249–259.

Muir, D., Abraham, W., Forbes, B., & Harris, L. (1979). The ontogenesis of an auditory localization response from birth to four months of age. *Canadian Journal of Psychology, 33,* 320–333.

Muir, D., & Field, J. (1979). Newborn infants orient to sounds. *Child Development, 50,* 431–436.

Nelson, C.A., & Horowitz, F.D. (1983). The perception of facial expressions and stimulus motion by two- and five-month old infants using holographic stimuli. *Child Development, 54,* 868–877.

Olsho, L.W. (1984). Infant frequency discrimination. *Infant Behavior and Development, 7,* 27–35.

Oster, H.S. (1975). *Color perception in ten-week-old infants.* Paper presented at the biennial meeting of the Society for Research in Child Development, Denver.

Owsley, C.J. (1980). *Perceiving solid shape in early infancy.* Paper presented at the Second International Conference on Infant Studies, New Haven, CT.

Peeples, D.R., & Teller, D.Y. (1975). Color vision and brightness discrimination in two month old human infants. *Science, 189,* 1102–1103.

Peiper, A. (1924). Sinnesempfindungen des kindes vor seiner Geburt. *Monatschrift Kinderheilkunde, 29,* 236–241.

Peiper, A. (1963). *Cerebral function in infancy and childhood* (3rd ed.; B. Nagler & H. Nagler, Trans.). New York: Consultants Bureau. (Original work published in 1961.)

Peterson, F., & Rainey, L. (1910). The beginnings of mind in the newborn. *Bulletin of Living-In Hospital, City of New York, 7,* 99–122.

Petrig, B., Julesz, B., Kropfl, W., Baumgartner, G., & Anliker, M. (1981). Development of stereopsis and cortical binocularity in human infants: Electrophysiological evidence. *Science, 213,* 1402–1405.

Petterson, L., Yonas, A., & Fisch, R.O. (1980). The development of blinking in response to impending collision in preterm, full-term, and postterm infants. *Infant Behavior and Development, 3,* 155–165.

Pettigrew, J.D. (1974). The effect of visual experience on the development of stimulus specificity by kitten cortical neurons. *Journal of Physiology, 237,* 49–74.

Popper, K.R. (1959). *The logic of scientific discovery.* New York: Basic Books.

Pratt, K.C., Nelson, A.K., & Sun, K.H. (1930). The behavior of the newborn infant. *Ohio State University Studies, Contributions to Psychology,* No. 10.

Preyer, W. (1893). *The mind of the child: Part I. The senses and the will* (3rd ed., H.W. Brown, Trans.). New York: Appleton, (Original work published 1881.)

Rader, N., Bausano, M., & Richards, J.E. (1980). On the nature of the visual cliff avoidance response in human infants. *Child Development, 51,* 61–68.

Rader, N., & Stern, J.D. (1982). Visually elicited reaching in neonates. *Child Development, 53,* 1004–1007.

Raehlmann, E. (1891). Physiologisch-psychologische studien über die entwickelung der gesichtswahrnehmungen bei kindern und bei operierten blindegeborenen. *Zeitschrift für Psychologie und Physiologie der Sinnesorgane, 2,* 53–96.

Rayner, K. (1978). Eye movements in reading and information processing. *Psychological Bulletin, 85,* 618–660.

Rheingold, H.L. (1961). The effect of environmental stimulation upon social and exploratory behavior in the human infant. In B.M. Foss (Ed.), *Determinants of infant behaviour* (pp. 143–177). New York: Wiley.

Richards, J.E., & Rader, N. (1981). Crawling-onset age predicts visual cliff avoidance in infants. *Journal of Experimental Psychology: Human Perception and Performance, 7,* 382–387.

Richter, E.P. (1930). High electrical resistance of the skin of newborn infants and its significance. *American Journal of Diseases of Children, 40,* 18–26.

Rosenblith, J.F., & DeLucia, L.A. (1963). Tactile sensitivity and muscular strength in the neonate. *Biologia Neonatorum, 5,* 266–282.

Ruff, H.A. (1982a). Effect of object movement on infants' detection of object structure. *Developmental Psychology, 18*, 462–472.

Ruff, H.A. (1982b). *Infants' detection of information specifying the motion of objects.* Paper presented at the Third International Conference on Infant Studies, Austin, TX.

Ruff, H.A., & Halton, A. (1978). Is there directed reaching in the human neonate? *Developmental Psychology, 14*, 425–426.

Salapatek, P. (1975). Pattern perception in early infancy. In L.B. Cohen & P. Salapatek (Eds.), *Infant perception: From sensation to cognition: Vol. 1. Basic visual processes.* New York: Academic.

Salapatek, P., Bechtold, A.G., & Bushnell, E.W. (1976). Infant visual acuity as a function of viewing distance. *Child Development, 47*, 860–863.

Salk, L. (1962). Mother's heartbeat as an imprinting stimulus. *Transactions of the New York Academy of Science, 24*, 753–763.

Salk, L. (1978). Response to Douglas K. Detterman (The effect of heartbeat sound on neonatal crying). *Infant Behavior and Development, 1*, 49–50.

Schaller, M.J. (1975, April). *Chromatic vision in human infants: Conditioned fixation to "hues" of varying intensity.* Paper presented at the biennial meeting of the Society for Research in Child Development, Denver.

Schneider, B., Trehub, S.E., & Bull, D. (1980). High frequency sensitivity in infants. *Science, 207*, 1003–1004.

Schwartz, A.N., Campos, J.J., & Baisel, E.J., Jr. (1973). The visual cliff: Cardiac and behavioral responses on the deep and shallow sides at five and nine months of age. *Journal of Experimental Child Psychology, 15*, 86–99.

Sekuler, R. (1974). Spatial vision. *Annual Review of Psychology, 25*, 195–232.

Self, P.A. (1971). *Individual differences in auditory and visual responsiveness in infants from three days to six weeks of age.* Unpublished doctoral dissertation, University of Kansas, Lawrence.

Self, P.A., Horowitz, F.D., & Paden, L.Y. (1972). Olfaction in newborn infants. *Developmental Psychology, 7*, 349–363.

Sherman, M.C., & Sherman, I.C. (1925). Sensory motor responses in infants. *Journal of Comparative Psychology, 5*, 53–68.

Sherman, M.C., Sherman, I.C., & Flory, C.D. (1936). Infant behavior. *Comparative Psychology Monographs, 12*(4).

Sinnott, J.M., Pisoni, D.B., & Aslin, R.N. (1983). A comparison of pure tone auditory thresholds in human infants and adults. *Infant Behavior and Development, 6*, 3–17.

Slater, A.M., & Findlay, J.M. (1975). Binocular fixation in the newborn baby. *Journal of Experimental Child Psychology, 20*, 248–273.

Spelke, E. (1976). Infants' intermodal perception of events. *Cognitive Psychology, 8*, 553–560.

Spelke, E.S., & Owsley, C.J. (1979). Intermodal exploration and knowledge in infancy. *Infant Behavior and Development, 2*, 13–27.

Steiner, J.E. (1977). Facial expressions of the neonate infant indicating the hedonics of food-related chemical stimuli. In J. M. Weiffenbach (Ed.), *Taste and development: The genesis of sweet preference* (DHEW Publication No. (NIH) 77-1068). Maryland: National Institutes of Health.

Steinschneider, A., Lipton, E.L., & Richmond, J.B. (1966). Auditory sensitivity in the infant: Effect of intensity on cardiac and motor responsivity. *Child Development, 37*, 233–252.

Stern, D. (1977). *The first relationship.* Cambridge, MA: Harvard University Press.

Taguchi, K., Picton, T.W., Orpin, J.A., & Goodman, W.S. (1969). Evoked response audiometry in newborn infants. *Acta Oto-laryngologica Supplementum, 252*, 5–17.

Thach, B.T., & Weiffenbach, J.M. (1976). Quantitative assessment of oral tactile sensitivity in premature and term neonates, and comparison with adults. *Developmental Medicine and Child Neurology, 18*, 204–212.

Thomas, H. (1973). Unfolding the baby's mind: The infant's selection of visual stimuli. *Psychological Review, 80*, 468–488.

Tiedemann, D. (1927). Tiedemann's observations in the development of the mental faculties of children (S. Langer & C. Murchison, Trans.). *Pedagogical Seminary and Journal of Genetic Psychology, 34*, 205–230. (Original work published 1897.)

Timney, B. (1981). Development of binocular depth perception in kittens. *Investigative Ophthalmology and Visual Science, 21*, 493–496.

Trehub, S. (1973). Infants' sensitivity to vowel and tonal contrasts. *Developmental Psychology, 9*, 91–96.

Trehub, S.E., Schneider, B.A., & Endman, M. (1980). Developmental changes in infants' sensitivity to octave-band noises. *Journal of Experimental Child Psychology, 29*, 282–293.

Trevarthen, C., Hubley, P., & Sheeran, L. (1975). Les

activités innée du nourrison. *La Recherche, 6,* 447–458.

Tronick, E., & Clanton, C. (1971). Infant looking patterns. *Vision Research, 11,* 1479–1486.

Tulloch, J.D., Brown, B.S., Jacobs, H.L., Prugh, D.G., & Greene, W.A. (1964). Normal heartbeat sounds and the behavior of human infants: A replication study. *Psychosomatic Medicine, 26,* 661–670.

Turkewitz, G., Birch, H.G., & Cooper, K.K. (1972a). Patterns of response to different auditory stimuli in the human newborn. *Developmental Medicine and Child Neurology, 14,* 487–491.

Turkewitz, G., Birch, H.G., & Cooper, K.K. (1972b). Responsiveness to simple and complex auditory stimuli in the human newborn. *Developmental Psychobiology, 5,* 7–19.

Turkewitz, G., Birch, H.G. Moreau, T., Levy, L., & Cornwell, A.C. (1966). Effect of intensity of auditory stimulation on directional eye movements in the human neonate. *Animal Behavior, 14,* 93–104.

Uzgiris, I.C., & Benson, J. (1980, April). *Infant's use of sound in search for objects.* Paper presented at the Second International Conference on Infant Studies, New Haven, CT.

Walk, R.D., & Gibson, E.J. (1961). A comparative and analytic study of visual depth perception. *Psychological Monographs, 75* (Whole No. 519).

Wedenberg, E. (1956). Auditory tests on newborn infants. *Acta-Oto-laryngologica, 46,* 446–461.

Weiffenbach, J.M. (1972a). Discrete elicited motion of the newborn's tongue. In J.F. Bosma (Ed.), *Third Symposium on Oral Sensation and Perception* (pp. 347–361). Springfield, IL: Thomas.

Weiffenbach, J.M. (1972b). Infants with clefts of lip and palate: Observations of touch elicited oral behavior. In J.F. Bosma (Ed.), *Third Symposium on Oral Sensation and Perception* (pp. 391–399). Springfield, IL: Thomas.

Weiffenbach, J.M. (1977). Sensory mechanisms of the newborn's tongue. In J.M. Weiffenbach (Ed.), *Taste and development: The genesis of sweet preference* (DHEW Publication No. (NIH) 77-1068, pp. 205–212). Bethesda, MD: National Institute of Dental Research.

Wenger, M.A., & Irwin, O.C. (1936). Fluctuations in skin resistance of infants and adults and their relation to muscular processes. *University of Iowa Studies of Child Welfare, 12,* 141–179.

Werner, J.S., & Wooten, B.R. (1979). Human infant color vision and color perception. *Infant Behavior and Development, 2,* 241–274.

Wertheimer, M. (1961). Psychomotor coordination of auditory and visual space at birth. *Science, 134,* 1962.

White, B.L. (1971). *Human infants: Experience and psychological development.* Englewood Cliffs, NJ: Prentice-Hall.

Wolff, P.H. (1966). The causes, controls and organization of behavior in the neonate. *Psychological Issues, 5,* 1–105.

Wormith, S.J., Pankhurst, D., & Moffitt, A.R. (1975). Frequency discrimination by young infants. *Child Development, 46,* 272–275.

Yonas, A. (1981). Infants' responses to optical information for collision. In R.N. Aslin, J. Alberts, & M. Petersen (Eds.), *Development of perception: Psychobiological perspectives: The visual system* (Vol. 2, pp. 313–334). New York: Academic.

Yonas, A., Bechtold, A.G., Frankel, D., Gordon, F.R., McRoberts, G., Norcia, A., & Sternfels, S. (1977). Development of sensitivity to information for impending collision. *Perception and Psychophysics, 21,* 97–104.

Yonas, A., & Owsley, C. (In press). Development of visual space perception in infants. In P. Salapatek & L. Cohen (Eds.), *Handbook of infant perception.* New York: Academic.

Yonas, A. Pettersen, L., & Granrud, C.E. (1982). Infants' sensitivity to familiar size as information for distance. *Child Development, 53,* 1285–1290.

Yonas, A., Pettersen, L., & Lockman, J.J. (1979). Sensitivity in 3- and 4-week-old infants to optical information for collision. *Canadian Journal of Psychology, 33,* 268–276.

Yonas, A., Pettersen, L., Lockman, J.J., & Eisenberg, P. (1980, April). *The perception of impending collision in 3-month-old infants.* Paper presented at the Second International Conference on Infant Studies, New Haven, CT.

COGNITIVE DEVELOPMENT

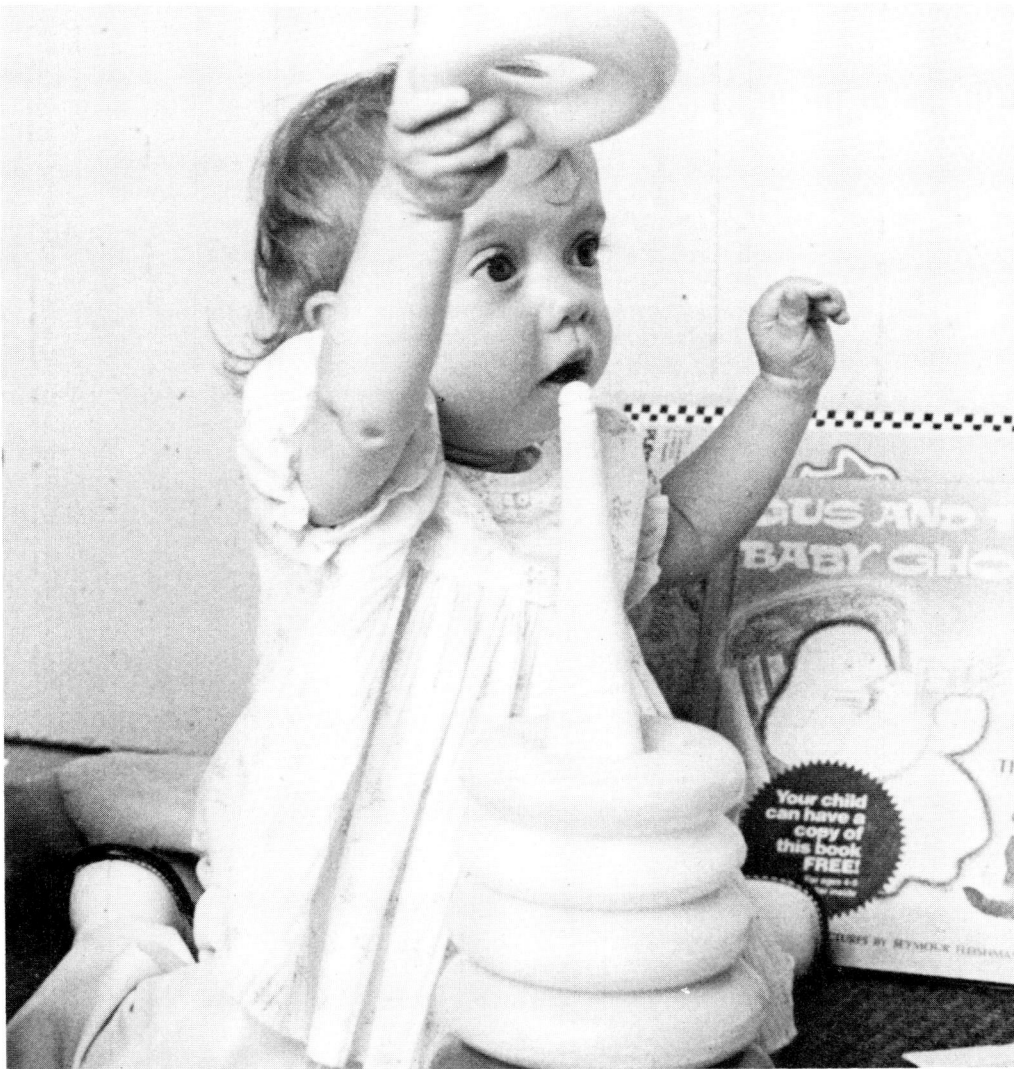

CHAPTER 10

OVERVIEW

In this chapter we will examine what and how infants understand about their world and how that understanding develops. We will first examine the historical context from which the research developed. Next we will study in some detail the theory of Jean Piaget, who developed what is currently the most extensive theory of cognitive development, and who has been the major impetus for research in this area over the last two decades. Piaget's theory is a very broad, complex theory with many interpretations that go far beyond the data. We have several goals in writing about his work. First, we want to describe the phenomena Piaget identified in terms of everyday behaviors of infants so that readers can identify these behaviors in informal observations. Second, we want to describe the theory and phenomena in a way that shows how he arrived at his highly inferential theory. Third, we want to evaluate the theory in a way that will enable students to cope with the complexity of the issues and the research. Our strategy to accomplish these goals is as follows. We will first present Piaget's theory more or less as he developed it, sprinkling our description liberally with "homey" examples. We decided to include both those aspects of his theory that have been replicated and those about which there is a lot of controversy. We will mention the controversial aspects as we go through the general description, but will not attempt to deal with them at that time. After we have presented the theory, we will examine some of the work it has inspired. We will first describe the large-scale studies that replicated the behavioral sequences described by Piaget and studies of sensorimotor development in other species. Next we will evaluate two of the areas that have generated the most research: imitation and the object search tasks of the object permanence sequence. After that we will review Fischer's theory, designed to incorporate the best of both Piagetian and learning theory. Finally, we will examine the research on categorization, to which Piaget contributed little, but which psychologists with other orientations have explored.

Consider what perception researchers have learned about the ability of babies to take in information about their world. Even newborns can see, hear, taste, smell, and feel—not always as well as an adult, but surely well enough to be able to learn about the world. That immediately raises the question, What do the environmental events that infants see, hear, and so forth, mean to them? For example, infants can detect light–dark contours, but does that mean they can know what a rattle, a breast, a newspaper, or a human being is? Infants have biologically adaptive responses such as avoidance responses to looming objects and rooting responses to a touch on the cheek, but what do such responses imply about the infants' knowledge about the stimuli that trigger them? Adults have an astounding understanding of the world. We take for granted most of this information and are unaware of our knowledge. We know, for example, that objects are objects. To know this requires an understanding of what separates one object from another; for example, that the features of a face all belong to one object and that the hat above the face is an object in its own right rather than part of the face object. Adults also know that objects are stable and enduring and exist even when people are not interacting with them, that is, when people cannot see, hear, touch, smell, or taste them. In addition, adults know that certain objects are similar to each other and different from others and that those patterns of similarities and differences identify the object—what its function is, how it is related to other kinds of objects, which aspects of it are important and which unimportant.

HISTORICAL PERSPECTIVE

How humans come to know all this about their environment has been the object of speculation at least since the time of the ancient Greeks. Philosophers who study epistemology have subjected these issues to reasoned arguments that form the context from which much of the psychological research in infant cognition has developed. Indeed, Jean Piaget, one of the foremost cognitive researchers, called himself a **genetic epistemologist**—that is, one who studies the basis of knowledge by studying development. The epistemological questions that have been most often pursued through infant research are the two related questions: (1) Are infants born with knowledge about the world, and (2) How is knowledge structured or organized?[1] To understand the research on these questions, it is important to know something about the historically important philosophical positions.

The Associationist View

In a very real sense, the associationist theory is the traditional theory of knowledge, against which all others argue (Bolton, 1972). Aristotle first formulated it; it flowered again among the British associationist school of the seventeenth and eighteenth centuries—Hobbes, Locke, Hume, James Mill, and John Stuart Mill; and it was reborn in psychology in the learning theories of the twentieth century. To understand infancy research, it is necessary to understand two basic principles common to most associationistic theories. First, they reflect a belief in empiricism (see Chapter 8). Babies at birth know nothing and have no preconceived notions such as what an object is or who mother is. The second basic principle, which gives associationism its name, is that humans learn who mother is, what time is, and how to reason logically by associating sense impressions. Aristotle argued for three principles of association: (1) contiguity: things are associated because they are experienced at the same time and place; (2) similarity: things are associated because they are alike; and (3) contrast: things are associated because they are opposites. It is easy to see how learning psychology fits in. Both classical and operant conditioning occur when two events, previously not associated by an organism, become associated. Imitation also fits into associationism if an imitation is assumed to be an association of another's behavior with one's own. The only mental ability that is innate in associationism is the ability to receive sense impressions and to form associations among them.

Nativism

Nativism is the belief that certain structures of knowledge exist independent of sensations and thus of experience. (They may also exist independent of minds, but we will not consider that aspect of the issue.) We described this view in Chapter 9, but to understand the issues in this chapter we need to describe the historical development in psychology a bit more. This position also has a long, illustrious past, starting with Plato, continuing with Kant, and currently represented by Gestalt psychologists, ethologists, and those linguists and psychologists who follow Chomsky's views about language. Kant, for example, believed that the concepts of objects, space, time, and causality are given a priori; that is, they don't have to be learned. Gestalt psychologists believe that people automatically impose organization on their perceptual world. For example, if they see dots arranged in a circle, they perceive a circle. Ethologists believe that through evolution animals have become biologically prepared to recognize certain classes of things that have survival value for them. For exmple, precocial birds (those that can walk at birth, such as geese, chickens, and ducks) appear to recognize their predators at their first exposure to them or to a reasonable facsimile. A baby chick will avoid a hawk-like figure even though it has never seen, let alone been attacked by, a hawk. Chomsky argues that human knowledge of the structure of language is innate, and that young children need only hear language in order to actualize that knowledge.

PIAGET'S INTERACTIONIST THEORY

Piaget was unhappy with both the associationist and the nativist solutions to the question of how humans know. He wished to reconcile the two approaches by demonstrating that the laws of logic and the Kantian categories can be derived from experience, something that associationists were never able to do convincingly. To do this he adopted an empirical approach; that is, he used the scientific method to investigate how humans' knowledge actually develops rather than using argumentation as the sole

---

[1] This is not to imply that all philosophers would accept such research as an appropriate way to approach epistemological questions. Many philosophers consider questions about the basis of knowledge to be independent of questions about how humans think.

basis for his opinion.[2] This approach motivated him to engage in intensive naturalistic studies of his own three babies, which we described in Chapter 1. He concluded that babies are born with the potential to form Kantian categories, but they must construct their knowledge of the world from their interactions with the world beyond themselves. Newborns are equipped with reflex structures that permit them to act upon the world, for example, to suck, look, and grasp. Those reflex structures develop (by the process of adaptation) into cognitive structures. These cognitive structures form the basis both of knowledge of the physical world and of understanding of general principles. Let us see how Piaget proposes this comes about.

Model of Adaptation

The concept of adaptation is Piaget's model to explain the process whereby children come to know about their world. Rather than proposing that people make associations among events (stimuli and responses, or two stimuli, in learning terms) Piaget believed that people incorporate each new event into the structure of what they already know, so that experiencing new events enlarges and changes what they know. At the core of the model is what children understand. Children assimilate (take in, understand) new information when it fits what they already know. When they can't fit it into what they already understand (or, in the case of infants, when they don't know how to act upon it), then they will do one of two things. They will ignore it, if it is just too far from anything they understand, or they will accommodate (modify their understanding) so that they can act upon the stimulus. The latter will presumably happen when some aspect of the environmental event or object is similar enough to their current understanding that they can stretch or modify that understanding to fit the new stimulus.

Assimilation, then, is the name for the process of incorporating an environmental event into one's understanding of the world. **Accommodation** is the name for the process of

modifying one's understanding to embrace novel aspects of an environmental event. It occurs when the event could not be assimilated (directly incorporated into one's understanding) without changing the way one understands things like that object or event. The mutual functioning of assimilation and accommodation is what Piaget calls **adaptation.**

Assimilation and accommodation always occur relative to what a person understands. Piaget believes that a person's understanding of an event is organized into **cognitive structures,** which are structures of the mind analogous to the structures of a building. In other words, the structure provides the framework of understanding on which humans hang information from the world. Infants understand and organize their world through physical acts such as looking, grasping, shaking, and sucking. The motor act itself is the means by which the infant learns about the world. Repetition of these motor acts forms infants' cognitive structure, the framework by which they organize their understanding. The structure is not the act itself but is the residue left from the repetition of actions. The structure is the means by which the meaning of environmental events becomes codified and remembered. These cognitive structures of infancy are called **behavioral schemes** and are individually labelled by the respective acts, such as the sucking scheme or the grasping scheme. Central to Piaget's theory is his belief that infants are active and will use their structures, beginning with reflex structures. Piaget did not believe that reinforcement by the environment was necessary to motivate infants to act.

As an example of how the cognitive system operates in concrete situations, consider a 10-month-old infant who has been given a new rattle. She has played with rattles before and has learned to shake them, which produces the rattle noise. Today she looks at the new rattle, mouths it, feels its contours, and finally shakes it. It rattles and she breaks into a smile and shakes it again and again (see first part of Figure 10–1). She has assimilated this object into her things-that-can-be-shaken-and-make-noise scheme. Next the baby is given a stuffed animal that makes a noise when a key on its back is turned. She mouths the key, feels its contours, shakes the animal—but she doesn't

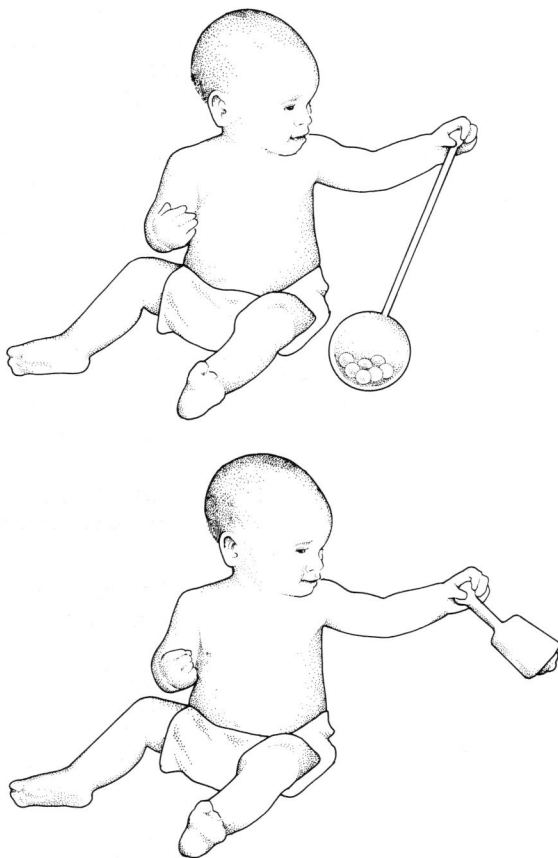

FIGURE 10–1. This baby accommodates her rattle shaking scheme (above) to an object that is only somewhat like the rattles she has previously experienced (below).

turn the key. The object is simply too different to be accommodated into her scheme, because shaking it doesn't produce a noise and she can't change her shaking action to a turning movement. She can, however, accommodate to a less different object. Next she picks up a pull toy that has a long handle attached to an egg-shaped plastic container half filled with marble-like balls. She can't hold the container in one hand and shake it like a rattle because it is too large. She can't hold the handle and shake the toy like an oversized rattle because she lacks the strength. She can, however, accommodate to the object: She grabs the handle (the egg is on the ground) and moves the hand and arm that is holding the handle up and

down. This causes the ball to move back and forth on the floor and it rattles (second part of Figure 10–1). Thus, the baby has been able to accommodate her scheme to the new object—to change her scheme to match the requirements of the new object—and she can then assimilate that object to her scheme. Note that assimilation and accommodation are mutually interacting modes. The child must accommodate to certain environmental events if she is to assimilate them. Likewise, she must have assimilated enough objects to have a smoothly functioning scheme before she can accommodate new things or events to them.

Cognitive change occurs through this mechanism. When the child accommodates to a scheme, that scheme becomes, at the very least, more complex, because it can handle a new kind of object. The scheme does not lose specificity through this process; that is, the distinctions between rattles and pull toys are not masked. Observers know this because in the future the baby shakes rattles and her pull toy in different ways. Other, greater kinds of cognitive change also occur through adaptation. New, differentiated schemes sometimes develop, such as shaking rattles and pulling toys. Schemes also can become intercoordinated: The pull toy can be shaken and pulled.

Finally, adaptation is the process through which the child changes from one kind of functioning to another; that is, moves from one stage of development to the next. Piaget's theory is a stage theory. He divides all of development into three (or four, depending on how they are counted) major stages, which he calls periods. The first period is infancy, or the period of sensorimotor development, and it lasts for the first two years of life. This period is the one we are concerned with in this book on infancy.[3] This sensorimotor period can be divided into six stages, and the infant progresses through the stages in an invariant sequence (that is, Stage I is always before Stage II, which is always before Stage III, and so forth). In each stage the infant's cognitive understanding is

---

[3] The other periods are: II, preparation for and development of concrete operations with subgroups of pre-operational and concrete operational periods, and III, formal operations (or II, pre-operational, III, concrete operational, and IV, formal operations).

distinctly different from that in the other stages. Through adaptation the infant's behavioral schemes (the structures of the sensorimotor period) begin, become more complex, and gradually change into the next, more sophisticated form.

Before describing the infant at each of these stages, we should note that although Piaget gave ages for each stage, they are only approximate. Humans are the most variable of creatures and will only sometimes progress at specified ages. Piaget noted:

In considering the problems of duration or rate of succession of the stages, we can readily observe that accelerations or delays in the average chronological age of performance depend on specific environments (e.g., abundance or scarcity of possible activities and spontaneous experiences, educational or cultural environment), but the order of succession will remain constant. (Piaget, 1970, p. 713)

Underlying the above statement is Piaget's belief that children actively construct their cognitive structures through their interactions with the environment. He does not believe that each stage unfolds according to fixed biological laws, as did Gesell. This is clear in the following quotation:

. . . the stages always appear in the same order of succession. This might lead us to assume that some biological factor such as maturation is at work. But it is certainly not comparable to the hereditary neurophysiological programming of instincts. Biological maturation does nothing more than open the way to possible constructions (or explain transient impossibilities). It remains for the subject to actualize them. (Piaget, 1970, p. 712)

This means that children must interact with the environment to develop, and that the speed with which they move through the cognitive stages depends on the quality of the environment. It does not mean that poor environments will permanently prevent cognitive development, at least not in the infancy period. All except the most profoundly retarded (who lack the biological prerequisite) do proceed through all six stages of infancy.

Stage I. Reflex Structures (0–1 Month)

Piaget believes that infants are born with the potential to develop complex cognitive structures culminating in the understanding of formal logic at around 14 years of age. At birth, however, they have no cognitive structures. They do have precursors to cognitive structures, which Piaget calls reflex structures. They are sucking, grasping, crying, looking, and so forth. These reflex structures exhibit the tendency to function spontaneously and repeatedly. People who watch newborns when they are awake quickly become convinced that they do use these reflex structures and that they use them with increasing frequency as the first month passes.

Piaget always asked what infants of a certain stage of development know and how they know it. We will provide Piaget's answer to those questions for each of the six stages of infancy. Stage I infants know very little. True, they can see, hear, grasp, suck, taste, and smell, but these provide them with little meaningful information. Even though infants have a number of innate responses to environmental events, this does not mean that they understand those events the way adults do. Consider auditory localization. That infants look in the direction from which a sound emanates does not mean that they know objects have both visual and auditory characteristics. It is just as reasonable to conclude that infants have a biological predisposition to orient toward sounds and that they don't make the inference that the sound-making object is seeable. Although either view might be correct, it is safer to conclude that the infant is unaware that the noise-producing stimulus is an object because it doesn't require as many assumptions about what the newborn innately knows (this is an example of the principle of parsimony, sometimes known as "Occam's razor"). Such additional assumptions—that newborns know what an object is, that they know how to differentiate among objects, that they know that objects exist in three-dimensional space, and so forth—would be reasonable only if there were additional evidence that suggested they are likely. Piaget saw no evidence to support these assumptions but other investigators have gathered some. We discussed in Chapters 7 and

9 the evidence that newborns can imitate, can perceive patterns, particularly faces; have intersensory coordination; and perceive objects in three-dimensional space. While the results of the research in all these areas are still controversial, in none of these areas have researchers been able to convince the majority of experts in the field that newborns know what objects are.

Stage II. Primary Circular Reactions: The First Acquired Adaptations (1–4 Months)

Gradually, through repeated use, reflex structures are transformed into sensorimotor cognitive structures called behavioral schemes. Piaget identifies these first cognitive structures by a new kind of behavioral sequence. In this sequence, called a **circular reaction,** a baby does something (such as sucks or looks), repeats the behavior several times rapidly, gradually slows down the frequency of repetition, and finally stops altogether. An example from one of Piaget's observations of his children illustrates this reaction:

Observation 53—From 0;2(3)[4] Laurent evidences a circular reaction which will become more definite and will constitute the beginning of systematic grasping; he scratches and tries to grasp, lets go, scratches and grasps again, etc. On 0;2(3) and 0;2(6) this can only be observed during the feeding. Laurent gently scratches his mother's bare shoulder. But beginning 0;2(7) the behavior becomes marked in the cradle itself. Laurent scratches the sheet which is folded over the blankets, then grasps it and holds it a moment, then lets go, scratches it again and recommences without interruption. At 0;2(11) this play lasts a quarter of an hour at a time, several times during the day. At 0;2(12) he scratches and grasps my fist which I placed against the back of his right hand. He even succeeds in discriminating my bent middle finger and grasping it separately, holding it a few moments. At 0;2(14) and 0;2(16) I note how definitely the spontaneous grasping of the sheet reveals the characteristics of circular

reaction—groping at first, then regular rhythmical activity (scratching, grasping, holding and letting go), and finally progressive loss of interest.

But this behavior grows simpler as it evolves in that Laurent scratches less and less, and instead really grasps after a brief tactile exploration. Thus already at 0;2(11) Laurent grasps and holds his sheet or handkerchief for a long time, shortening the preliminary scratching stage. So also at 0;2(14) he pulls with his right hand at a bandage which had to be applied to his left. (Piaget 1936/1963, pp. 91–92)

Other typical Stage II circular reactions are pumping the arm up and down, sucking the thumb, and sticking out the tongue. Remember, to be a circular reaction these behaviors must be repeated in an almost rhythmical fashion. Piaget concluded that infants must be learning something through circular reactions because they repeat the reactions at various times with different objects and because the circular reactions change as they become more practiced, as described in the observation of Laurent's grasping.

Piaget observed circular reactions in infants beginning at about one month of age. Papoušek's studies of conditioning (see Chapter 7) found that newborns could be conditioned, but it took about a month to do so and infants already one month old conditioned much more rapidly. A convergence such as this, using two disparate kinds of evidence (experimental and naturalistic observation), strengthens the conclusion that a real development in learning ability occurs around this time.

The circular reaction in Stage II marks the beginning of learning ability, but it is a very primitive beginning. Piaget identified three levels of circular reactions—primary, secondary, and tertiary. In Stage II, when circular reactions first appear, they are, naturally enough, of the primary type (see Figure 10–2). Primary circular reactions are distinctive in that infants focus on the action itself; in later versions they focus more and more on the object. In fact, primary circular reactions often do not involve objects at all. Babies can be seen opening and closing their hands on thin air as well as on blankets or shoulders or any available object.

---

[4]This is Piaget's age notation. Laurent was 0 years, 2 months, and 3 days old.

FIGURE 10–2. Humans are not the only primates to exhibit the behavioral sequences described by Piaget. Gorillas develop in very similar ways to humans, although stumptail macaque monkeys do not. Here, in three frames of a sequence, an infant gorilla, Mkumbwa, repeatedly grasps his foot with his hand. It is a circular reaction in that it is repetitive; it is primary in that the infant focuses on the actions of his own body. (Photographs courtesy of Dr. Suzanne Chevalier-Skolnikoff.)

Furthermore, they don't explore characteristics of the object involved in circular reactions, such as size, shape, or differences from other objects. When they are no longer acting upon (looking, grasping, sucking, and so forth) the object, Stage II babies act as if the object no longer exists. They do not search for objects when they drop them, for example. These three characteristic behaviors suggest that infants of this age know objects only as extensions of their actions and not as independent things-in-the-world.

When a circular reaction begins, infants often appear to be concentrating intensely. After the repetitions become rapid and smooth (it is tempting to say "After they get the problem firmly in hand"), their expressions often become more relaxed. They are full of smiles and often laughter and gleeful screams ensue. Such expressions strengthen Piaget's interpretation that circular reactions are the way cognitive structures develop. He also notes that this is the earliest kind of play. He calls it functional play because through it infants develop the means to operate intellectually (adapt).

Two other major advances occur during Stage II. First, Piaget believed that Stage II marks the very beginnings of imitation. For example, when someone coos (makes vowel sounds), infants of this age will also coo. Piaget

believed this response to be a very primitive approximation to imitation because (1) infants will only imitate behaviors if the model has just imitated them (that is, the sequence is: baby emits behavior, adult imitates, baby imitates adult), and (2) the infants' responses do not usually match the adults' behaviors exactly. Piaget believed that infants are assimilating the modeled behavior to their own schemes, thus sparking their own circular reactions. This means that imitation at this stage is a learning device in the same sense that circular reactions are: a means of assimilating. Later imitation will become a way of changing, expanding, and differentiating schemes: a way of accommodating. This interpretation of imitation in young infants is controversial, as we saw in Chapter 7. Some researchers believe that neonatal imitation is exact imitation, which requires more innate knowledge than Piaget was willing to attribute to young infants.

Finally, during Stage II the various schemes—looking, sucking, grasping—become coordinated. The last intercoordination is visually guided reaching (discussed in Chapter 8), which develops around 4 months of age. Piaget used the development of these intercoordinations as crucial evidence that young infants construct their understanding of objects through actions. He argued that through the gradual intercoordination of schemes, Stage II infants learn that a single object can be explored in all modalities (visual, oral, and so forth) at the same time, and thereby they learn that these multimodal characteristics inhere in one object. Thus, the object is no longer merely an extension of one action. As an object becomes distinct from any particular action, a step is taken toward its becoming one object with an existence separate from the infant and his actions. In Chapter 9 we noted that this aspect of Piaget's theory is controversial, and that Bower (1982) has presented evidence, also controversial, to support an alternative theory of innate intersensory coordination.

The increase in exploratory skills and the intercoordination of schemes that occur at 4 months of age (or reintercoordination, in Bower's view) has implications for parents and others who play with babies. One of the first coordinations is between hand and mouth, which allows infants to find their fingers to suck. Those babies who suck their fingers or thumbs have a ready means to calm themselves. Visually guided reaching provides infants with a marvelous means by which they can entertain themselves and also get into trouble—they can grab everything in sight. Babies who can reach for things to explore also seem to become more human to many parents.

Mouthing is an extremely important exploratory tool for infants that seems to develop at the time the schemes are being coordinated. Before this time babies tend to suck vigorously at every object put into their mouths (unless they're hungry; at that time they refuse non-nutritive objects), but once visually guided reaching develops, the sucking changes to mouthing (the mouth is not pursed and no vacuum is created) and for months afterward exploration includes putting all possible objects into the mouth.

Stage III. Secondary Circular Reactions (4–8 Months)

Two effects of the accomplishments of Stage II are that (1) infants' abilities to explore their world are vastly improved because they can look at what they grasp, and (2) objects thereby become things that have visual, auditory, and tactile features and thus are pried loose from their original position as mere extensions of a single action. These developments mark the onset of the secondary circular reactions. Secondary circular reactions are quite striking behaviors, perhaps because the object plays such a much more important role than it did in Stage II. A good example is dropping and picking up. Infants in this stage often drop toys they have grasped and this action often results in a secondary circular reaction in which they grasp and then drop the toy repeatedly. Such sequences have all the characteristics of circular reactions: The first several repetitions are done slowly and with expressions of intense concentration; they increase in speed and are often accompanied by smiles and gleeful squeals; the repetitions are rather rhythmical; and they peter out gradually. Secondary circular reactions are more advanced than primary ones in that the infants seem to be repeating or maintaining an interesting environmental event. In the above example, the dropping of the object is the interesting event. Other such interesting events that secondary circular reaction repeat or maintain are the sounds of rattles being shaken, objects being rubbed against others, objects being swung in the air, and of course that all-time favorite called dump the bowl (this last can only be a circular reaction with the patient help of an older human who must refill the bowl so that it can be dumped again).

Notice that the infants' actions in producing these events are necessary for the descriptions of the events. Although the object or event plays a larger role than in primary circular reactions, Piaget believed that infants' understanding of the world is still firmly tied to their own actions. Notice also that the first instance of the secondary circular reaction occurred by chance. That is also characteristic.

One reason Piaget believed that secondary circular reactions are attempts to reproduce interesting events is that infants attend more to the objects they are manipulating than they did in primary circular reactions. The circular reaction of dropping is a good example of this because the babies' eyes follow the falling object, which is direct evidence of their interest in the object. In some circular reactions, there is no direct evidence of attention to the object. For example, in a circular reaction such as rattle-shaking, we can't see the babies listen. Nevertheless there are behaviors that suggest that they are attending to the environmental result of their actions. They continue the circular reaction when they are successful; that is, when they make noise, they often smile and squeal when the sound occurs.

A second behavioral phenomenon that led Piaget to conclude that Stage III infants are more aware of and interested in environmental events is a special case of the secondary circular reaction that he called "procedures for making interesting spectacles last." These procedures occur when babies of this stage are confronted with a new event that they find interesting. Rather than attending to the novel aspects of the object or event (which would lead older infants to play with the object appropriately), Stage III infants simply apply their habitual schemes. This sometimes results in procedures that would have to be magical to be effective. As an example, consider a Stage III infant who knows how to pump his arms up and down to shake rattles. An adult stands beyond his reach with a string of bells. The adult shakes the bells and the infant looks toward the bells and reaches for them. When he fails to grasp them, he immediately starts pumping his arm up and down. He stops when the adult rings the bells again and repeats the action when the bells stop ringing.

During the course of Stage III these procedures become more and more obviously magical and look less like actual circular reactions (circular reactions differ from procedures for making interesting spectacles last in that in circular reactions the babies' actions do make the environmental event occur). Here is an example from Piaget's observations of his son Laurent, which shows the procedures at their colorful, magical best:

At 0;7(7) he looks at a tin box placed on a cushion in front of him, too remote to be grasped. I drum on it for a moment in a rhythm which makes him laugh and then present my hand (at a distance of 2 cm. from his, in front of him). He looks at it, but only for a moment, then turns toward the box; then he shakes his arm while staring at the box (then he draws himself up, strikes his coverlets, shakes his head, etc.; that is to say, he uses all the 'procedures' at his disposition). He obviously waits for the phenomenon to recur. Same reaction at 0;7(12), at 0;7(13), 0;7(22), 0;7(29) and 0;8(1) in a variety of circumstances. . . . (Piaget, 1936/1963, p. 201)

The procedures for making interesting spectacles last indicate clearly that Stage III infants are aware of environmental events and wish to perpetuate them.

Secondary schemes are also infants' first system for classifying and relating objects. When infants of this age are given a familiar object, they can immediately comprehend its uses because of their secondary schemes. They know whether it can be shaken, thrown, mouthed, and so forth. They can explore possible classifications of a new object by mouthing it, fingering it, kicking it, and so forth. Thus, Stage III infants demonstrate that objects are similar—to them—by acting upon them in the same way. Thus all objects that can be put into their mouths are assimilated to the mouthing schemes and therefore can be said to be in the same class. Piaget believed that this primitive organization develops many years later into that most basic intellectual pursuit, logical classification. Two aspects of this description have been widely investigated. One is the general question of how infants' abilities to form concepts develop, and the second is whether early concepts of objects are based on action schemes. We will discuss research in both of these areas later in this chapter.

In describing how Stage III marks the onset of the ability to form relations among events, Piaget focuses on relations between means and ends. Stage III infants repeat behaviors that are the means to reach an end, such as pulling a cord to make an attached object move. These are the earliest instances Piaget found (and he was looking hard to find them) in which infants relate two events (for example, a pull and the subsequent movement of a toy). This is not true means–end problem solving, however, because they discovered the means to the end by chance and have simply become able to repeat the means action.

Piaget futher noted that infants seem to

vary the intensity of their actions and the intensity of the subsequent reaction in a systematic way. For example:

Jacqueline, too, at 0;9(5) shakes while holding a celluloid rattle in the form of a parrot which she has just been given. She smiles when the noise is slight, is anxious when it is too loud and knows very well how to gradate the phenomenon. She progressively increases the noise until she is too frightened and then returns to the soft sounds. Furthermore, when the rattle is stuck at one of the ends, she shakes the parrot by turning it in another direction and thus knows how to reestablish the noise. (Piaget, 1936/1963, pp. 166–167)

Piaget infers from such examples that Stage III infants not only relate two events, but also discover quantitative relations. This is another first in Stage III, and Piaget claimed that this primitive forming of relations provides the basis from which all later relation-making comes. Included in the later forms are Piaget's famous seriation tasks (making sequential orderings along a dimension, such as ordering ten sticks by size) and understanding of number (which is based on understanding "greater than" and "less than")

Early signs of object permanence also appear in Stage III. The sequence of behaviors describing the development of object permanence is one of the most reproducible parts of Piaget's infancy work, yet his theoretical conclusions from them are among the most challenged portions of his infancy work. The topic of object permanence includes two questions: (1) Do infants know that an object exists when they are not acting upon it? (For Piaget, this is equivalent to the question, Can they mentally represent an absent object?) (2) How do infants conceive of objects? (For Piaget, this means, Do objects exist as entities in the world separate from the infants' actions and separate from other objects?) Piaget inferred that for infants of Stages I and II, objects do not exist when the infants are not acting upon the objects (his answer to the first question), and that the object is merely an aspect of their action, not separable in any way (the second question).

Stage III infants have made progress toward both aspects of object permanence. When infants of this age drop objects, they look at the place where the object disappeared for a few moments. If an object they were playing with is partly, but not wholly, covered, they will reach for it; that is, the part signals the presence (and the existence) of the whole object. Piaget used these behaviors to argue that infants of this age have a primitive notion that an object continues to exist when they are not acting upon it.

Another phenomenon that Piaget found to appear first in Stage III is motor recognition. Here babies perform their secondary schemes, but in abbreviated form and with no apparent attempt actually to act upon the object. For example, he concluded that Lucienne shook herself in recognition of events involving shaking, because he saw her do so when she was presented with several objects that she had previously shaken in circular reactions (spools hanging on elastic bands, two celluloid parrots). These movements were always abbreviated and always in response to situations that in the past had elicited more extensive shaking of the objects.

Piaget believed that imitation in Stage III acts as a procedure to make interesting events last. If, for example, the model makes a sound, infants will go through several verbal schemes to maintain the event. If the model requires exact imitation, infants can provide it, with the limitations that (1) they must have a scheme that closely corresponds to it, and (2) it must be an act they can see themselves make (which eliminates facial gestures). Thus, while exact imitation is possible, it has no interest for the infant other than as a way to maintain an interesting event. As we discussed in Chapter 7, this conclusion is challenged by the research on neonatal imitation.

Although secondary schemes are a great cognitive advance, they are still quite limited. The secondary scheme is an unanalyzed action–object sequence in which the particular characteristics of the object are not noticed. Given a new object, infants run through their habitual schemes in habitual fashion. By so doing, they must ignore novel features. This characteristic is very obvious to adults when they give babies of this age a marvelous toy and watch the baby play with it "all wrong"—such as mouthing the handle of a pull toy rather than pulling it or fingering the various protuberances of a toy truck rather than pushing it along the ground (see Figure 10–3).

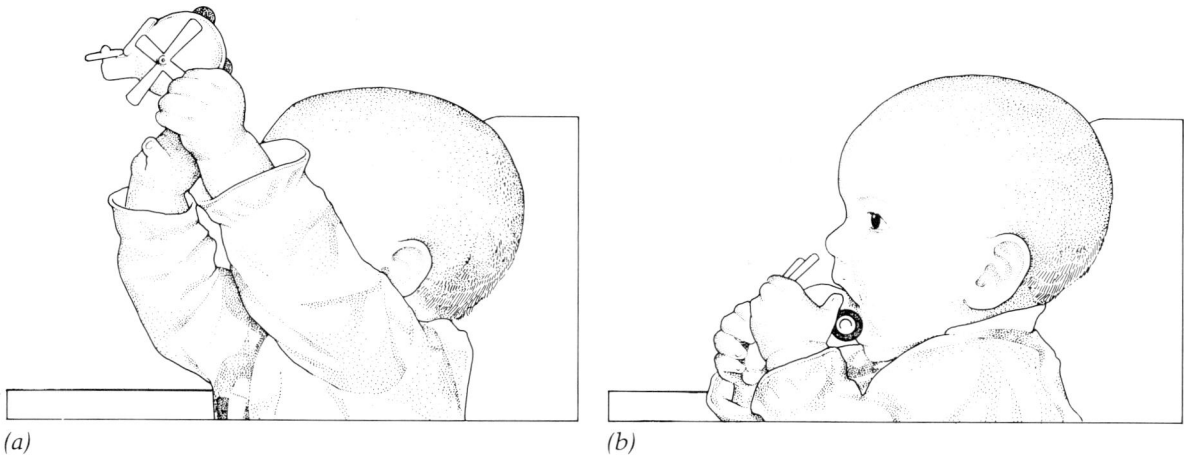

(a)   *(b)*

FIGURE 10–3. Two examples of typical secondary circular reactions. They were exhibited during a single interaction with the toy. The actions are very different from the ones an older infant would exhibit with this toy. (a) Lifting the arm. This develops from a primary circular reaction of moving the arm up and down repeatedly. In its reappearance as a secondary scheme it is part of the baby's exploration of the object. If this were a rattle, it would shake during this response and the baby would recognize it as a thing-that-can-be-shaken-and-make-noise. (b) Mouthing the object. This is part of the typical exploration sequence of look-reach-grasp-put-into-mouth. Most objects are explored in this way. Notice that the baby is mouthing the wheel rather than running the wheel along the table top as would be appropriate for the toy.

This tendency to ignore novel characteristics of an object in favor of applying habitual schemes (Piaget would call this more assimilation than accommodation) also limits the quality of classification. Because objects are so undifferentiated from actions in Stage III, the precision of classification must also be extremely rough. As the object becomes more differentiated from action in later stages, infants can better judge when two objects are in equivalent classes (for example, two toys are for shaking). The tendency to ignore novel characteristics of an object prevents infants from being able to abstract from the totality of the situation the characteristics of the object that make an action appropriate.

Finally, what is represented in the infants' cognitive structures is the undifferentiated action–object scheme. This limits their ability to conceive of an object independent of their own action. Looking for an object that has disappeared is possible only because the search immediately follows the infants' action, and uncovering a hidden object is possible only when part of it is visible.

Stage IV. Coordination of Secondary Schemes (8–12 Months)

The major development in Stage IV is that babies become able to coordinate secondary schemes. Thus they are able to use one scheme as a means of obtaining their desired goal (of using another scheme). Such means–end behaviors are the prototypes of all problem solving. These are the first infant behaviors that Piaget called truly intelligent. Here is an example of Laurent during this stage:

Observation 130.—Laurent, at 0;10(3) utilizes as a "means" . . . a behavior pattern which he discovered the previous day . . . By manipulating a tin of shaving cream he learned, at 0;10(2), to let this object fall intentionally. Now, at 0;10(3) I give it to him again. He at once begins to open his hand to make it fall and repeats this behavior a certain number of times. I then place, 15 cm. from Laurent, a large wash basin and strike the interior of it with the tin in order to make Laurent hear the sound of the metal against this object. It is noteworthy that

FIGURE 10–4. Means-end behavior. This 40-week-old baby pulls a string to get the ring toy attached to it. (From Atlas of Infant Behavior *by A.L. Gesell, Yale University Press, 1934. Used by permission.)*

Laurent, already at 0;9(0), had, while being washed, by chance struck a small pot against such a basin and immediately played at reproducing this sound by a simple circular reaction. I therefore wanted to see if Laurent was going to use the tin to repeat the phenomenon and how he was going to go about it.

Now, at once, Laurent takes possession of the tin, holds out his arm and drops it over the basin. I moved the latter as a check. He nevertheless succeeded, several times in succession, in making the object fall on the basin. Hence this is a fine example of the coordination of two schemes of which the first serves as "means" whereas the second assigns an end to the action: the schema of "relinquishing the object" and that of "striking one object against another." (Piaget, 1936/1963, p. 225)

Other common means–end behaviors seen at this stage are pushing an obstacle away to get at a goal object; pulling a string to get the object attached to it (Figure 10–4); and trying to reproduce an interesting event by having the person who first produced that event repeat it (such as putting a whistle in a parent's mouth to be blown).

Means–end behaviors are the first behaviors that Piaget thought were intentional beyond a doubt. Two advances convinced him of this. First, in Stage III Laurent could not have abstracted the means (dropping the tin) from its original context and applied it to a new goal (making the metallic clink against the basin). Second, Stage III infants often get caught by the means behaviors and forget the original goal.

(For example, once they pick up the cloth covering a desired toy, they play with the cloth, not the toy.) Stage IV infants, in contrast, typically return to their goal after performing the means scheme. Thus by using a scheme as a means in a new situation, Stage IV infants demonstrate that they have produced the means behavior on purpose rather than by accident. Also by consistently stopping the means scheme when it has served its purpose and by engaging in the goal behavior they demonstrate that they really were interested in that goal. This is a conservative use of the term intentional. In contrast, Bruner (1973) called visually guided reaching intentional because infants make anticipatory adjustments in order to reach accurately.

Understanding that a behavior can be the means to an end is a major step toward understanding causality. For example, Jacqueline must attribute a causal role to Piaget's hand when she places it against a swinging doll that she wishes to activate (Piaget, 1937/1954, p. 260). She is now free from her earlier magical assumption that her actions upon an object were responsible for all environmental events, including procedures for making interesting spectacles last, which would entail action at a distance. Furthermore, Stage IV babies begin to discover that other objects (in addition to themselves) can act as causal agents, an achievement that helps infants to conceive of one independent force acting upon another. Their notion of causality is not yet mature, however, because they still appreciate an external causality only when their own actions intervene (as when Jacqueline placed Piaget's hand on the doll).

Also appearing in Stage IV is the ability to anticipate actions of objects and of other people on the basis of a sign. For example, babies of this age often cry when they see the white-coated doctor who has inflicted pain on them in the past or protest when parents put their coats on to go out. Piaget considered these true signs compared to the more primitive signals (which first appear in Stage II), because a sign is an anticipation of an event that is independent of the infant, whereas a signal forms part of an undifferentiated action scheme. Signs can be distinguished from signals in that signs become independent of their original contexts. Piaget gave the example of a creaking chair being a sign for a person's disappearance. This occurred first at the dinner table, but was quickly generalized to Piaget's creaking his desk chair (1936/1963, p. 252). This development is important theoretically because signs are another indication that infants are separating actions of objects from their own actions to a greater extent than in previous stages.

The coordination of secondary schemes makes other advances possible. When schemes are coordinated they are extracted from their original circumstances. They can then be applied to all sorts of new situations, so they are more effective instruments of exploration. Through this more extensive exploration, Stage IV children become able to attend more closely to the characteristics of objects and thus can apply their schemes more appropriately.

An advance in object permanence is also related to the coordination of secondary schemes. Infants can now search for an object that has disappeared and can remove a screen that completely covers an object. These are both means–end behavioral sequences (doing something to retrieve an object the infant is interested in acting upon). Because all means–end sequences require that infants know that they will be able to execute their goal (such as touching, shaking, dropping the object) before they actually do it, they must know something about the object even when the object is completely absent (and they are not engaged in acting upon it in any way, not even looking at it). This means that Stage IV infants possess some incipient representation of objects, but, Piaget argues, that representation is still tied to the infants' actions. His evidence for this interpre-

tation is the AB̄ (read "A, not B") error. This error occurs when an object is put first under one cover (A) and then under a second (B). Stage IV babies often look under the first cover rather than the second even though from an adult point of view the object is clearly under the second. Everyday examples are also easy to find. For example, if an infant is playing with a ball and it rolls under a chair, she can retrieve it (a single cover). If she continues to play with it and it now rolls out the door of the room and out of sight, she is likely to look under the chair for it (see Figure 10–5). Piaget interprets the error as indicating that:

> . . . there would not be one chain, one doll, one watch, one ball, etc., individualized, permanent, and independent of the child's activity, that is, of the special positions in which that activity takes place or has taken place, but there would still exist only images such as "ball-under-the-arm-chair," "doll-attached-to-the-hammock," "watch-under-a-cushion," "papa-at-his-window," etc. Certainly the same object reappearing in different practical positions or contexts is recognized, identified, and endowed with permanence as such. In this sense it is relatively independent. But, without being truly conceived as having several copies, the object may manifest itself to the child as assuming a limited number of distinct forms of a nature intermediate between unity and plurity, and in this sense it remains a part of its context. (Piaget, 1937/1954, pp. 62–63)

This phenomenon has been replicated many times over, although babies only sometimes make the error. Whether Piaget's interpretation needs modification is a matter of opinion, as we will see later.

The ability to imitate also takes a giant step forward in Stage IV. For the first time infants are able to imitate behaviors of others that are not already in their repertoire. They can also imitate behaviors of another person when that person is matching actions of the infants that the infants cannot see themselves perform (for example, biting the lip). (See Figure 10–6.) This is accomplished by the same mechanism as that of means–end behaviors. Infants first run through the familiar schemes that are similar to the model's behavior (for

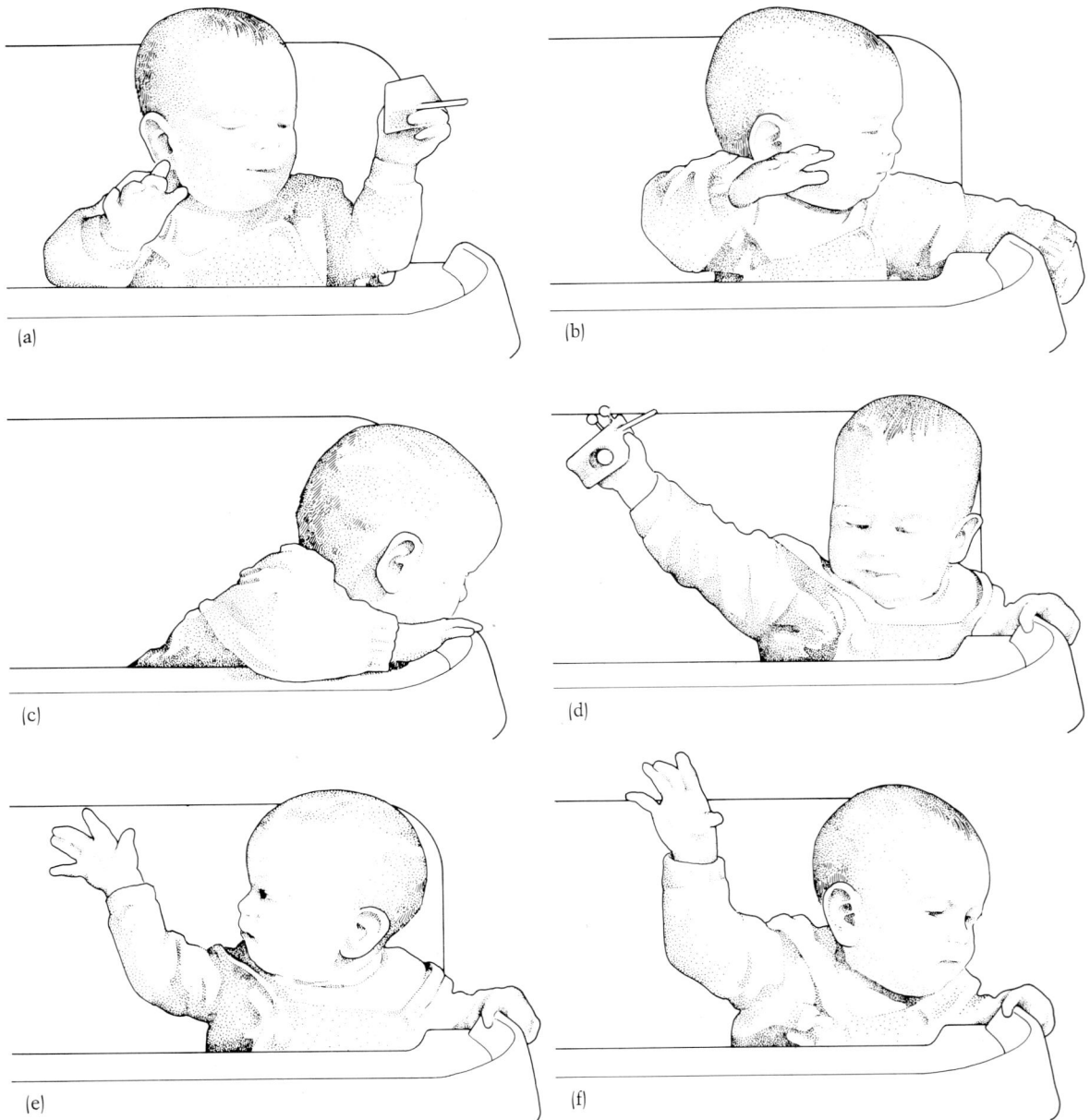

FIGURE 10–5. An A$\bar{B}$ error in spontaneous play behavior. These pictures are drawn from a movie sequence of an infant playing with his toys in his home. (a) and (b) He drops the toy car over the right side (A) of his high chair. (c) He looks after the toy he has just dropped. (d) He drops the car over the left side (B) of the high chair. (e) He looks at his empty hand as if noting the absence of the car. (f) He looks over the right side (A$\bar{B}$) of the high chair.

FIGURE 10–6. The Piagetian sequence of imitative development is also seen in gorillas. Here Koko shows Stage IV imitation of body parts she is unable to see on herself. This sort of behavior first develops in gorillas at about the same age as it does in human infants, but Koko is much older in this photograph. (Photograph courtesy of Dr. Suzanne Chevalier-Skolnikoff.)

example, all the ways of moving their mouth). Then, if the modeled behavior is new to them they combine (coordinate) schemes in their attempt to match the new behavior. Thus imitation becomes intentional, albeit limited. This stage marks the beginning of the use of imitation as a means of accommodation, a development that fits in with the general characterization of Stage IV as the first stage in which assimilation and accommodation become differentiated. Such a mechanism for learning new things provides an important impetus to cognitive growth.

Although Stage IV advances are quite impressive, they of course have their limitations. Means–end behaviors do represent truly intelligent behavior, but the efficiency of the Stage IV version is quite limited because these infants can only employ familiar schemes as means in their problem solving. If a habitual way of interacting is not successful, they simply can't solve the problem. Because they are limited to applying familiar schemes, their exploration of a new object is limited to a search for ways in which it operates in the same way as familiar objects. Likewise, they are only able to imitate new behaviors that are very similar to familiar behaviors, and then only through

a rather lengthy process of trying familiar schemes and combinations of familiar schemes. Finally, their understanding of objects and events is still tied to their actions.

Stage V. Tertiary Circular Reactions (12–18 Months)

Piaget calls Stage V the stage of the elaboration of the object because infants' interactions with objects are much more reality-oriented than in earlier stages. Stage V babies actively investigate the novel properties of objects rather than running roughshod over unusual features in their attempts to assimilate the objects to their familiar schemes. They can learn accurately the spatial and causal relations among objects. In short, objects have become conceptually separated from and independent of infants' actions upon them.

The mechanism of these advances is the tertiary circular reaction. As with all circular reactions, Stage V reactions are repetitions of an action upon an object with the apparent goal of reproducing the effect. As in earlier forms of circular reactions, the new goal is always discovered by chance. Unlike earlier forms, however, in tertiary circular reactions infants vary their actions upon the object to explore its nature. (Piaget concludes that their purpose is exploration because they attend carefully to the object during their varying actions.) A classic example is dropping things:

At 0;10(11) Laurent is lying on his back but nevertheless resumes his experiments of the day before. He grasps in succession a celluloid swan, a box, etc., stretches out his arm and lets them fall. He distinctly varies the positions of the fall. Sometimes he stretches out his arm vertically, sometimes he holds it obliquely, in front of or behind his eyes, etc. When the object falls in a new position (for example on his pillow), he lets it fall two or three times more on the same place, as though to study the spatial relation; then he modifies the situation. At a certain moment the swan falls near his mouth; now, he does not suck it (even though this object habitually serves this purpose), but drops it three times more while merely making the gesture of opening his mouth. (Piaget, 1936/ 1963, p. 269)

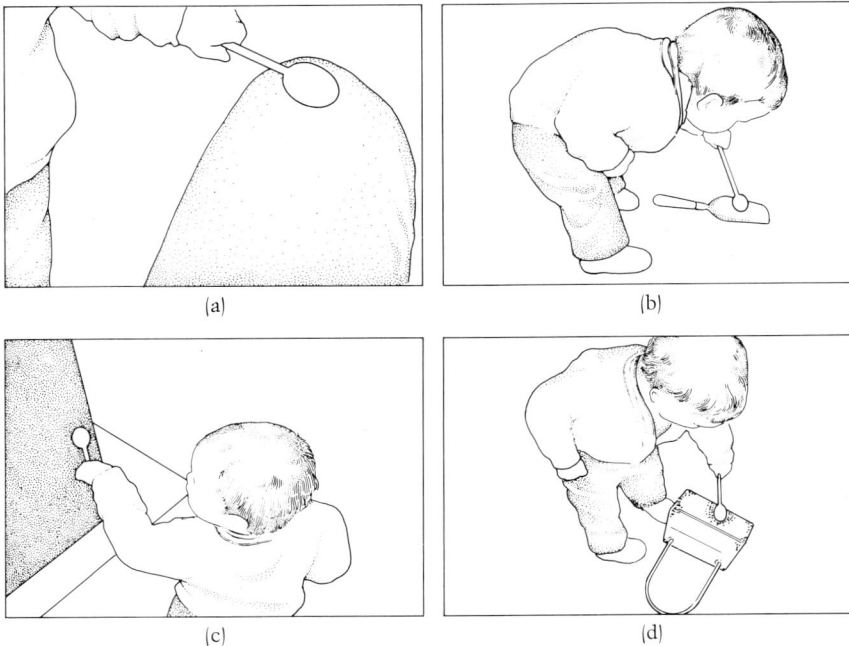

FIGURE 10–7. An experiment in order to see, which occurred during spontaneous play. These pictures are drawn from a movie sequence. This toddler is playing with a "banger" (to adults, a honey dipper) for the first time. She explores what objects are "bangable" and what the consequences of this banging are. (a) On Daddy's knee the banger makes little noise and doesn't bounce much. (b) In a scoop the banger makes a tinkling noise and sets the scoop rocking. (c) On a loudspeaker the banger produces a thud, a moderate give and bounce back, and a parental admonition. (d) On a purse the banger sinks in and makes little noise.

The net effect of such exploration is that infants can discover properties of objects that they could not discover in earlier stages. They also discover relations among objects. Stage V babies spend hours putting objects into, on top of, and beside other objects. They explore how spoons fit into certain containers and not others, how tops fit onto certain containers, fall into other containers, and fall off still other containers. They find out that some objects make loud noises when they are thrown on the ground, some objects bounce or roll, and some objects make the most satisfying splat (Figure 10–7).

At first it may seem difficult to distinguish tertiary circular reactions from the secondary version because in both cases infants systematically vary the effects. Recall the example of Jacqueline in Stage III shaking her parrot rattle with different degrees of vigor, which produced rattle sounds of varying intensities. Such gradations of secondary circular reactions produce variations of a single effect (in this case the rattle sound), but those of the tertiary circular reactions produce different effects. Contrast the parrot rattle example with the following example of a tertiary circular reaction:

Observation 146.—At 1;2(8) Jacqueline holds in her hands an object which is new to her: a round, flat box which she turns all over, shakes, rubs against the bassinet, etc. She lets it go and tries to pick it up. But she only succeeds in touching it with her index finger, without grasping it. She nevertheless makes an attempt and presses on the edge. The box then tilts up and falls again. Jacqueline, very much interested in this fortuitous result, immediately applies herself to studying it.— Hitherto it is only a question of an attempt at assimilation analogous to that of Stage IV and of the fortuitous discovery of a new result, but this discovery, instead of giving rise to a simple circular reaction, is at once extended to "experiments in order to see."

In effect, Jacqueline immediately rests the box on the ground and pushes it as far as possible (it is noteworthy that care is taken to push the box far away in order to reproduce the same condition as in the first attempt, as though this were a necessary condition for obtaining the result). Afterward Jacqueline puts her finger on the box and presses it. But as she places her finger on the center of the box she simply displaces it and makes it slide instead of tilting it up. She amuses herself with this game and keeps it up (resumes it after intervals, etc.) for several minutes. Then, changing the point of contact, she finally again places her finger on the edge of the box, which tilts it up. She repeats this many times, varying the conditions, but keeping track of her discovery: now she only presses on the edge! (Piaget, 1936/1963, p. 272)

In this Stage V example, when Jacqueline discovered by chance that the box sometimes tilted and sometimes slid, she was interested in both effects and experimented to see what action caused each effect. In Stages III or IV she would have been unable to understand that variations of her actions could lead to two different kinds of movement of the boxes.

Piaget called tertiary circular reactions "experiments in order to see" for two reasons. First, infants in tertiary circular reactions are pursuing novelty for its own sake—in order to see—because they attend closely to the varying results and repeat the actions that lead first to one outcome and then to another. Younger babies do not actively investigate novelty. Stage III babies competely ignore aspects of objects that cannot readily be assimilated to their secondary schemes. Stage IV babies discover novelties only because during their persistent attempts to explore objects and events, they must cope with the novel aspects of those objects and events (that is, they must accommo-

date in order to assimilate). In contrast, Stage V infants seek out the novelty; that is, accommodation becomes an end in itself.

The second reason Piaget calls tertiary circular reactions "experiments in order to see" is that they are experiments. Infants of this age explore the nature of objects by trying them out. For example, they explore the nature of chalk by writing first on a chalkboard, then on the floor, then on the wall, their clothes, their friend's face, and so forth.

Tertiary circular reactions provide the mechanism for another advance, the discovery of new means through active experimentation. Means–end behaviors in Stages IV and V are very similar. They occur when babies want to play with an object or reproduce an interesting event, and that goal can be reached only by an intermediate action. They reach the goal by forming a new coordination between behaviors that serve as the means and as the goal action. Stage IV infants are limited to using familiar schemes as means, but Stage V infants can find new means through tertiary circular reactions, that is, by varying their behaviors and observing the effect upon the goal.

There are really two steps to discovering new means. First, infants must realize that the familiar means are not adequate, and second, they must be able to discover the new means. Younger infants try to do something to maintain interesting events (procedures to make interesting spectacles last in Stage III and familiar means in Stage IV), but they do not really understand the physical principles involved and so they don't know exactly how their behaviors are related to the goal.

Piaget describes quite a few examples of discovery of new means through active experimentation. Babies discover how to use a stick to nudge objects toward them; this is the earliest tool use Piaget observed. They learn that when an object rests on a support such as a blanket or cardboard, they can reach the object by pulling the support. They discover how to tilt long, skinny objects to bring them in between the bars of their playpens or cribs. They discover how to open various containers and how to put peculiar objects, such as watch chains, into small receptacles. To solve all these problems requires that infants understand the relation between variations of their actions and the differing effects so that they can discard ineffective actions, improve upon partially effective actions, and repeat successful actions.

Infants' notion of causality thus takes a giant step forward in Stage V because they can explore the nature of the physical relations among objects in a much more precise way than before. Another advance in the understanding of causality is that babies of this age begin to treat themselves as objects and therefore they can serve as effect as well as means. Piaget gives the example of Jacqueline at 1;3(10) letting herself fall down in a sitting position. Her goal is the dropping of herself. This was a new behavior for her at this time; before that she would not let go of the bars of her playpen until she was seated (Piaget, 1937/1954, p. 291).

Imitation of new behaviors becomes much more extensive and systematic in Stage V. As with the discovery of new means, infants grope through various new actions in their attempts to imitate. Thus they can imitate behaviors that are much more unfamiliar than those they could imitate in Stage IV, when they were limited to familiar schemes and combinations of familiar schemes. Notice also that the success of Stage V groping towards accurate imitation requires that infants be able to decide when they have produced a behavior that matches the model's action. Doing so requires that the infants assimilate their new actions to the framework provided by their schemes. Piaget gives the example here of Jacqueline recognizing that she has correctly imitated Piaget touching his hair by touching her own hair and recognizing it by its texture (a previously learned tactual scheme).

Recall that Piaget calls this the stage of the elaboration of the object. Let us review our discussion of tertiary circular reactions to see how those phenomena demonstrate maturation of the object concept. First, because Stage V infants focus on novel aspects of objects and can investigate novel effects of objects, they can find out how a new object differs from familiar objects as well as how it is similar. Stage IV babies' interactions with novel aspects of objects are limited to searching for ways in which those novel aspects are assimilable to familiar schemes. For example, Stage IV infants presented with a toy car notice those peculiar protuberances adults call wheels and run through

their typical action patterns of shaking, touching, mouthing, and so forth to find out how the wheels look, feel, taste, sound, and so forth. Stage V infants do not stop there because novelty itself fascinates them. They vary their action patterns while paying close attention to the resulting behaviors of the wheels. Through such experimentation they discover that the wheels go around in a unique fashion, and eventually they rub those wheels along the floor and the car moves in its conventional fashion. Thus, experimentation leads to a more accurate understanding of the object. A second way that tertiary circular reactions lead to the elaboration of the object is the advance in the precision of understanding causal behaviors. Consider how Stage V babies learn about the properties of sticks by trying to pull them through the bars of playpens or cribs. Finally, a third indication of the maturation of the object concept is found in the infants' ability to treat themselves as objects of causal actions. This indicates that they are able to consider themselves one object among other objects.

The next step in the object permanence sequence demonstrates additional aspects of the elaboration of the object. In Stage V the AB error disappears. Infants at this stage can watch an object being hidden successively under three screens and will pick up the last screen to find the object underneath. This ability shows that infants no longer consider the object to be imbedded in the global action–object sequence. They now know that the object is a thing that is different from themselves, although their ability to conceptualize movements of objects independent of themselves is still limited. Piaget hypothesized this because infants of this age can follow an object through three displacements only if the examiner makes the object visible to the infants between each screen. Infants will look under the first screen if the disaplacements are invisible. This phenomenon suggests that Stage V infants' ability to represent an absent object is still limited.

The nature of tertiary circular reactions also supports Piaget's interpretation of the object permanence sequence limitation in terms of limits in mental representation. Children of this age can solve problems only through actions. In both experiments to see and discovery of new means, infants try different behaviors and observe the effect. For example, when trying to fit a stick through the bars of a playpen, they must actually try all physical displacements that occur to them—horizontal and vertical, with or without tilt—until they hit upon one that works. They cannot simply examine the stick and the playpen bars and after some pause execute the correct movement. Solution of problems by thinking rather than acting has not yet developed.

Stage VI. Invention of New Means Through Mental Combinations (18 Months)

Mental representation finally develops in Stage VI. Piaget considers this achievement so important that he describes Stages I–V as five parts of one large stage characterized by the absence of representation.

Problem solving in Stage VI involves the same process as in Stage V except that the actual experimentation is absent. Instead, the infant pauses for a brief period and then solves the problem.

The following description is of Jacqueline discovering through Stage V active experimentation how to make a watch chain enter a narrow opening. Notice that after 22 attempts she still achieves success only with some difficulty.

At 1;7(25) Jacqueline holds a rectangular box, deep and narrow whose opening measures 34 × 16 mm. (for this purpose I use the cover of a match box which is three quarters open), and she tries to put my watch chain into it (45 cm. long). During the first fifteen attempts, she goes about it in the following way: First she grasps the chain about 5 cm. from this end and thus puts a second segment into the box. She then gets ready to do the same with a third segment when the chain, no longer supported by the child's hand, slides out of the box and falls noisily. Jacqueline recommences at once and fourteen times in succession sees the chain come out as soon as it is put in. It is true that, around the tenth attempt, Jacqueline has tired of it and was about to give up; but I placed the chain in the box (without the child's seeing how) and then she regained

hope by noting that such a result was not impossible.

At the sixteenth attempt, a new phenomenon: Jacqueline having grasped the chain nearer the middle, the chain no longer lengthened as before at the time when the child raises it but takes the form of two entwined cords. Jacqueline then understands the advantage she can take of this new presentation and tries to make the two ends enter the box together (more precisely, one immediately after the other, the second following shortly after the first). She no longers lets the chain go after putting one of the ends into the box, as was the case in attempts 1–15, but tries to put all of it in. But, as always occurs when a child of this age manipulates flexible objects, Jacqueline considers the chain as being rigid and lets go the whole of it when both extremities have been put in the box. The chain then comes out again somewhat, but Jacqueline gently reintroduces the part that hangs (the middle part).

Attempt 17: Jacqueline distinctly tries to repeat the preceding movement. At first she does not grasp the chain at one end but pulls it together somewhat and grasps the middle part (without of course trying to find the actual middle).

Attempt 18: resumes the initial procedure and fails.

Attempt 19: rediscovers the procedure of attempts 16 and 17.

Attempt 20: same reaction, but this time Jacqueline encounters some difficulty in putting the second end in. Not succeeding, she recommences trying to put in a single end first. But as the chain slides out, she resumes the procedures of attempts 16, 17 and 19.

Attempts 21–22: same hesitations, but with ultimate success. (Piaget, 1936/1963, pp. 318–319)

Lucienne solved the same problem in Stage IV through mental combinations. She is trying to put the chain in the box:

She begins by simply putting one end of the chain into the box and trying to make the rest follow progressively. This procedure which was first tried by Jacqueline, Lucienne finds successful the first time (the end put into the box stays there fortuitously), but fails completely at the second and third attempts.

At the fourth attempt, Lucienne starts as before but pauses, and after a short interval, herself places the chain on a flat surface nearby (the experiment takes place on a shawl), rolls it up in a ball intentionally, takes the ball between three fingers and puts the whole thing in the box.

The fifth attempt begins by a very short resumption of the first procedure. But Lucienne corrects herself at once and returns to the correct method.

Sixth attempt: immediate success. (Piaget, 1936/1963, pp. 336–337)

Problem solving in Stage VI often happens very rapidly and without distinctive behaviors. The above examples demonstrate that the absence of behavioral experimentation marks the advance. This makes it difficult for adults to detect when Stage VI infants are solving problems, particularly because they are often solving problems of such an elementary nature that adults often fail to see it as a problem. Sometimes the only indication that a child is solving a problem rather than engaging in habitual actions is a brief pause before their problem-solving action. Occasionally, however, Stage VI children give a positive indication that they are actually thinking through a problem. Here is an example:

I put the chain back into the box and reduce the opening to 3 mm. It is understood that Lucienne is not aware of the functioning of the opening and closing of the matchbox and has not seen me prepare the experiment. She only possesses the two preceding schemes: turning the box over in order to empty it of its contents, and sliding her finger into the slit to make the chain come out. It is of course this last procedure that she tries first: she puts her finger inside and gropes to reach the chain, but fails completely. A pause follows during which Lucienne manifests a very curious reaction bearing witness not only to the fact that she tries to think out the situation and to represent to herself through mental combination the operations to be performed, but also to the role played by imitation in the genesis of representations. Lucienne mimics the widening of the slit.

She looks at the slit with great attention; then, several times in succession, she opens and shuts her mouth, at first slightly, then wider and wider! Apparently Lucienne understands the existence of a cavity subjacent to the slit and wishes to enlarge that cavity. The attempt at representation which she thus furnishes is expressed plastically, that is to say, due to inability to think out the situation in words or clear visual images she uses a simple motor indication as "signifier" or symbol. . . .

Soon after this phase of plastic reflection, Lucienne unhesitatingly puts her finger in the slit and, instead of trying as before to reach the chain, she pulls so as to enlarge the opening. She succeeds and grasps the chain. (Piaget, 1936/1963, pp. 337–338)

In this example Lucienne used a motoric symbol to represent the solution to the problem. This is a positive sign that she is really able to represent an absent object mentally. She does so with a motoric gesture because she is not yet able to use language. Infants often use private symbols, both motoric and verbal, before they are able to use conventional language. Piaget's observations indicate that these private forms of representation nevertheless fulfill the criterion for mental representation: They act as referents for absent objects or events.

Obviously the advent of mental representation means that objects have achieved permanence. Stage VI infants can follow an object as it is hidden sequentially under three screens even when it is hidden in the examiner's hand between screens. This indicates that Stage VI infants assume objects exist even when the objects are not visible. They therefore assume that the object is not annihilated during its displacements and they infer its movement from the movements of the hand of the examiner.

The ability to represent the world by mental images clearly represents an extraordinary advance in problem solving and in children's understanding of objects. It is, however, equally important in the development of other domains. We will describe advances in three other areas, causality, imitation, and play.

Mental representation makes possible two advances in infants' ability to understand causality. First, they can infer causes when they see

FIGURE 10–8. Delayed imitation. This child has previously been shown how to use the hammer on the xylophone. This is also inexact imitation because the ball end of the hammer is held in the palm of the hand and the stick extends out between two fingers.

effects. Piaget gives the example of Laurent being able to remove an armchair that was holding a gate closed. He experienced the effect, that the gate would not open, and inferred the cause, that something must be blocking its path (1937/1954, p. 296). Second, they can infer effects when given causes. Piaget described an example in which Jacqueline infers the effect of expressing a need to go to the bathroom:

> *Observation 160—At 1;4(12) Jacqueline has just been wrested from a game she wants to continue and placed in her playpen from which she wants to get out. She calls, but in vain. Then she clearly expresses a certain need, although the events of the last ten minutes prove that she no longer experiences it. No sooner has she left the playpen than she indicates the game she wishes to resume!*
>
> *Thus we see how Jacqueline, knowing that a mere appeal would not free her from her confinement, has imagined a more efficacious means, foreseeing more or less clearly the sequence of action that would result from it. (1937/1954, p. 297)*

A particularly important advance is that of deferred imitation (Figure 10-8). Stage VI infants for the first time imitate events that occurred in the past. For example, Piaget describes Jacqueline imitating a temper tantrum that she had seen a little boy perform a day earlier (1945/1962, p. 63). She could only do this if she had some way of mentally representing that past event. Note also that deferred imitation demonstrates that infants can now remember specific past events when no sign of the event remains. Imitation that follows right after a model's action also changes in Stage VI. It both becomes more direct and immediate and it is less embedded in a context of other actions. The immediacy results from the fact that external experimentation has been replaced by internal combinations. All in all, imitation at this stage appears even to the untutored eye to be imitation.

Finally, the emergence of mental representation marks the onset of make-believe or symbolic play. Children of this age and older children use broomsticks to represent horses, sand to represent bread dough, and blocks to represent houses. Piaget believes that younger infants do not engage in this form of play because they are unable to abstract their understanding of an object from its basis in an action pattern. Thus they cannot, for example, use a block to represent a house, although they can use a block to stack or to throw.

RESEARCH INSPIRED BY PIAGET'S THEORY

It should be obvious by now that Piaget's analysis of infant development is integrated, complex, and extensive. Piaget's epistemological approach—both a strength and weakness—provided a framework for his investigations. He looked for behaviors relevant to such questions as how infants come to understand causality and whether they are born with certain kinds of knowledge about the nature of the world. Because he was looking for evidence that would resolve these questions, he noticed behaviors and developmental sequences of behaviors that other infant observers had not noticed. The danger of this approach is that a believer is more likely to notice supporting evidence and less likely to notice disconfirming evidence than is a nonbeliever. This is a particularly troublesome problem for Piaget's research because it lacks the kind of controls that would minimize the effect of experimenter bias. Nevertheless, Piaget's observations of his infants are striking because of his search for alternative interpretations.

Replication Studies

It is a tribute to Piaget's skill as a scientist that the behavioral sequences he described have been confirmed by studies using methods far more controlled than his own. There have been several large-scale replications (Corman & Escalona, 1969; Decarie, 1965; Uzgiris, 1973; Uzgiris & Hunt, 1975) and many small-scale studies. The most extensive well-controlled study was that of Uzgiris and Hunt. Their goal was to develop standardized Piagetian infant tests. In so doing they collected data on all the aspects of Piaget's theory that we have described (object relations or the development of schemes, object permanence, means–end behaviors, imitation, and causality) plus one more (spatial relations).

The first step in verifying Piaget's formulations concerning infancy is to establish that the behaviors he described can be reliably observed. Piaget's work clearly fulfills this requirement by two criteria: interobserver agreement and test–retest reliability. Uzgiris and Hunt found that two observers agreed on their

assessments of over 90% of infants' reactions. They also found that on the average 80% of the responses infants gave on one day were the same as those they gave 48 hours later. This demonstrates that Piaget did discover real behaviors and that they are typical and consistent infant behaviors.

The second step in evaluating Piaget's work is to determine whether the behaviors develop in the order described by Piaget. By definition, stage sequences must occur in an invariant order: Stage I must always precede Stage II, which must always precede Stage III, and so on. Although they used a finer analysis than the six stages (their scales had from 7 to 14 levels), Uzgiris and Hunt found remarkable consistency in development within each scale. Other studies, which have used the six stages, have also found the sequences to be as Piaget described. The stages have been corroborated by both cross-sectional and longitudinal studies. Indeed, of dozens of studies that have tested the hypothesis of invariant order of development, only one major study (Miller, Cohen, & Hill, 1970) found clear disconfirmatory evidence (in the object permanence sequence). Even those authors, when repeating their study with a shortened test series (Kramer, Hill, & Cohen, 1975), failed to replicate their original findings: In the second study they found the order predicted by Piaget.[5]

Although it seems clear that infant cognitive development in each domain (such as sensorimotor schemes, imitation, object permanence) does proceed in an invariant order, the domains do not always develop together (Corrigan, 1979; Uzgiris & Hunt, 1975). Thus, a baby may exhibit Stage IV behaviors with respect to object permanence, but Stage III behaviors with respect to imitation. Although Piaget provided a term to describe such uneven development (horizontal décalage), he did not allow it to interfere with his tendency to describe children as if all aspects of their development proceeded in lock step. Such a practice is often inaccurate, given the frequency with which

[5] Keep in mind that these are group data. The majority of infants do show perfect ordinality (58% of the subjects in Kramer, Hill, & Cohen, 1975, showed perfect ordinality over a 6-month period), but there are exceptions. Piaget would claim that the exceptions are either measurement error or anomalies due to particular environmental experiences.

any given baby may be in several stages in different domains. Thus, it is probably preferable to specify the task domain when describing infants' cognitive development; for example, Johnny is in Stage IV of imitation, rather than Johnny is in Stage IV.

Sensorimotor Development in Other Species

The sensorimotor sequence of development has also been demonstrated in primates. The great apes, whose evolution and biology are most like that of humans, show remarkably similar progression through the sensorimotor stages. Chevalier-Skolnikoff has studied gorillas, chimpanzees, and orangutans (1977, 1979) and has found that they progress through each stage sequentially in the same invariant sequences as humans. They do not skip stages nor do two or more stages appear simultaneously (Chevalier-Skolnikoff, 1982). There are also differences in development that seem to reflect the unique biology of each species. We will give two examples, one specific to humans and one to orangutans. Only humans exhibit sensorimotor development in the realm of vocal gestures. If the development of vocal schemes presages language development, this species difference is consistent with the rather extensive research in language training in great apes. Chimpanzees and gorillas seem readily able to learn to use tokens or signs as symbols (a sensorimotor Stage VI achievement), but they have not demonstrated (to the satisfaction of many researchers) that they can master the more specifically linguistic aspects of language, that is, grammar (for example, Premack, 1976; Seidenberg & Petitio, 1979; Terrace, 1979). The second example is the orangutans' use of feet. They use their feet as hands to a greater extent than any of the other great apes, presumably because they are the most arboreal. As a Piagetian might expect, they use their feet in circular reactions much more frequently than gorillas or humans, and this use progresses through the three types of circular reactions.

These variations are in no way inconsistent with the conclusion that the sensorimotor development of great apes is in general quite like that of humans. It is also more similar to humans than it is to monkeys who show many fewer sensorimotor phenomena (stumptail macaques, Chevalier-Skolnikoff, 1977 and Parker, 1977; langurs, Chevalier-Skolnikoff, 1982). Perhaps most importantly, monkeys apparently exhibit tertiary circular reactions only socially and not with objects, which means that their problem solving skills are severely limited, and it is not clear that they reach Stage VI, which is when mental representations develop. If these conclusions hold when more subjects and more species of monkeys are studied, it will suggest that the later sensorimotor skills evolved during the last 10 to 20 million years, after the evolutionary separation of humans from monkeys but before the separation of humans from great apes.

Evaluation of Theoretical Implications

The studies we have just described, both with humans and with other primates, have demonstrated that there are invariant sequences of development within each of the specific behavioral domains such as sensorimotor schemes, imitation, and object permanence. This degree of confirmation is quite impressive in an area in which the methodology is as difficult as it is in infant studies. It is advisable, therefore, not to ignore Piaget's theory of infant development. This research does not, however, demonstrate that Piaget's *theory* is the best explanation of infant cognition. Just because the behavioral sequences exist does not mean that Piaget's interpretation of them is correct. Observers may agree that infants exhibit certain behaviors, but may disagree about their meaning and about the determinants of those behaviors. Furthermore, investigators with different theoretical orientations may notice different behaviors. Piaget may have selected behaviors that fit the interpretations that he favored. Therefore, establishing the validity of Piaget's behavioral sequences is not sufficient. A critical evaluation of a theory of the scope of Piaget's is an extremely complex task. It typically proceeds in saltatory fashion, testing each derived hypothesis or set of hypotheses separately. For each of these separate enterprises researchers must develop clever research designs to differentiate Piaget's theory from alternative explanations. This kind of work is going on for a number of different aspects of Piaget's theory. We will discuss two, imitation and object permanence.

IMITATION

Research on imitation tackles Piaget's major premise that imitative ability is part of and dependent on cognitive development. Two derivatives from that hypothesis have been tested. The first is that imitation must develop in the same sequence and at the same pace as general cognitive development, which it did according to Piaget's account. The second is how imitation is involved in the acquisition of new knowledge. Piaget believed that imitation, once developed, primarily involved accommodation; that is, when one imitates, one must stretch or modify one's understanding to be able to understand the modeled behavior. Thus, imitation is a major mechanism for adaptation. It does have limits in that children should be unable to imitate a behavior that is totally unfamiliar to them because they lack the requisite cognitive basis for understanding. We will first deal with research that challenges Piaget's description of the development of imitation and then describe research on the relation between imitation and acquiring new knowledge.

We noted above that studies of the general sequence of behaviors as described by Piaget have supported his findings (Uzgiris, 1972; Uzgiris & Hunt, 1975). Likewise, research done in other contexts has also generally supported aspects of Piaget's behavioral descriptions. Abravanel, Levan-Goldschmidt, and Stevenson (1976) presented a large number of modeled actions to babies 6 to 15 months of age. The actions the youngest babies were most likely to imitate were familiar schemes—scratching and patting surfaces, placing and shaking objects. Pawlby (1977) found that both the number of imitative acts and the variety of behaviors imitated increase from 4 to 8 months of age (Stage III), which is when such proliferation should occur. Research designed to clarify the nature of early imitative responses, however, has been less supportive. There are three relevant issues. First is the question of whether there is imitation before the onset of primary schemes, which occurs at about one month of age. Second is whether developmental changes in imitation between birth and 4 months reflect the development of primary schemes. Third is whether there is imitation of unseen actions earlier than Piaget claimed. In Chapter 7, we discussed the research on neonatal imitation. Those who believe there is neonatal imitation consider the evidence as tending toward their position, whereas those who are inclined toward a Piagetian position are not convinced by the evidence. This is largely because the two groups have different requirements for establishing the existence of imitation. Those who wish to demonstrate neonatal imitation are impressed by any demonstration that neonates ever exhibit anything akin to imitation. They then focus on the positive findings in Meltzoff and Moore's original (1977) demonstration of imitative tongue protrusion rather than the negative findings. They are impressed that Martin and Clark (1982) found that newborns cry differentially more to crying of other newborns than to other kinds of cries and noises. They are not convinced by the alternative interpretation that the crying represents an innate response to distress. Piagetians, in contrast, require the more stringent criterion for exact imitation and conclude that neither exact nor same-class imitation in newborns has been demonstrated. They are unconvinced that the neonatal crying phenomenon is imitation; alternative interpretations such as the innate response to distress interpretation or several proposed by Piaget (1945/1962) seem more feasible. They do accept the evidence that 6-week-olds exhibit same-class imitation. This fits with Piaget's theory: Same-class imitation is a developmental phenomenon that is contingent on the development of primary schemes and thus should only develop after the first month of life. Piaget described same-class imitation in babies this age for other responses such as vocalization.

The final aspect of Piaget's description of young babies' imitation is his claim that before Stage IV, babies cannot imitate actions of body parts that they cannot see. Abravanel and Sigafoos (1984), Jacobson (1979), and Maratos (1973) all found that babies imitated tongue protrusions (unseen) in Stage II and Kaye and Marcus (1978) showed imitation of mouth opening in Stage III. Although this seems at first glance to be clear disconfirmation of Piaget's theory, it actually is a difference of interpretation. Piaget noted similar phenomena (including tongue protrusions and mouth opening, which are unseen responses), but felt that they were not instances of true imitation. He claimed that these "pseudo-imitations" can be distinguished from "true" imitation because the former cannot be consistently elicited and because they do not last "unless the training is prolonged and consistently kept up" (1945/1962, p. 27). The data support that claim. All three studies found that imitative tongue protrusions became less frequent around 3 months of age, except in Jacobson's experimental group of babies whose mothers regularly modeled tongue protrusions.

In summary, Piaget would consider the research on the early development of imitation to confirm his theory. He considered these early phenomena to be unrelated to what to him were the more interesting later developing forms of imitation, those which he called "true imitation." Of course, he might have been wrong about their lack of importance. To demonstrate that they are important, researchers could show (1) that these early imitative responses are related to later forms; (2) that early forms clearly show greater cognitive competence than Piaget granted them, an argument made by Bower (1976) and by Meltzoff and Moore (1977), and argued against by Anisfeld (1979), Cohen (1981), and Masters (1979); or (3) that Piaget's interpretations of the later forms are wrong.

Today, the studies of early imitation are very intriguing to many workers. Although Piaget himself refused to offer an explanation for such pseudo-imitation (1945/1962, p. 18), others have tried (Bower, 1976; Cohen, 1981; Jacobson, 1979; Meltzoff & Moore, 1977; Smillie, 1980; Trevarthen, 1978). One particularly interesting interpretation is that the early imitation of unseen actions represents the same sort of intersensory unity that has been found with vision–audition and visually guided reaching. As with visually guided reaching, the early form of imitation seems to be distinct from the later form. Early forms wane during Stage II and the later forms wax during Stage III (see Cohen, 1981, for an excellent discussion of this view). In addition, the early forms of imitation are not accompanied by well-formed orienting and vocalizing behaviors, as later forms are (Trevarthen, 1978).

The second aspect of Piaget's account of imitation that has been investigated in some detail by others is the role imitation plays in cognitive development. We will describe three disparate ways in which this relation has been explored. First are two studies of the development of the imitative response itself. Kaye and Marcus (1978, 1981) reasoned that if Piaget's description of imitation is correct, then studies that test imitation of only one or two modeled acts are insufficient to test it. They made a longitudinal study of development of six different imitative responses in babies 6–12 months old by modeling each action repeatedly for periods of up to 10 minutes, stopping each task when the infant cried or turned away permanently. They found that generally the infants' imitations became more and more exact over time. For example, in response to the model clapping her hands 4 times, babies exhibited the following behaviors in a consistent order from less to more exact: touching experimenter's hand, touching own hands together, pulling experimenter's hands together in clapping motion, clapping once own hands, clapping 4 times. Kaye and Marcus interpreted this to mean that the babies successively assimilated features of the modeled behavior until they successfully accommodated to the modeled behavior.

The second research strategy explores the relation of types of imitations to children's cognitive level on other tasks. In Piaget's account, children imitate behaviors at or just above their typical level of cognitive ability. They do not imitate behaviors either too advanced or too primitive with respect to their current cognitive functioning. Watson and Fischer (1977) examined this relation. They elicited pretending behaviors by modeling both less and more cognitively mature instances of the behaviors they wanted. Both the spontaneous and the elicited imitations demonstrated by their toddlers were at or near their highest cognitive capacity and they did not imitate behaviors that reflected skills they had mastered much earlier. In language also imitation reflects the child's cognitive level. When children imitate adults' utterances, they change the utterances into their own more primitive grammatical structures (see Chapter 11).

The other side of this relation between imitation and understanding of modeled acts is that modeling is an effective teaching tool only when children are cognitively ready to learn. For example, it should be impossible to teach a Stage II infant to solve invisible displacements (a Stage VI achievement), but training might be effective for a Stage V infant. This third research strategy of training subjects at different developmental levels has been employed primarily with older children. It suggests that the most effective kinds of training, including that of modeling, are effective with children who are just one step below the level described (see Yando, Seitz, & Zigler, 1978, for a review of this literature). Comparable research with infants would have to be designed to consider their limited imitative ability, but that could be done.

In summary, the research generally supports Piaget's proposal that what children imitate depends on their cognitive skills. It also supports the notion that imitation does develop over time and become more frequent and more exact, although at least some of the details of Piaget's developmental sequence may need revision. The remaining important controversy is whether newborns can imitate. Current evidence is conflicting, but if such imitation is demonstrated in the future, it would seriously question Piaget's major tenet that newborns have no innate epistemological categories and must construct their own reality.

EXPLORATIONS OF THE UNDERLYING PROCESSES INVOLVED IN OBJECT SEARCH TASKS

Piaget's work on object permanence has generated the most voluminous literature of any aspect of his theory of cognitive development in infancy. It also has generated the most sophisticated analyses in Piagetian infant research. As we stated earlier, the behavioral sequence as originally described by Piaget has been replicated both cross-sectionally and longitudinally. Nevertheless, the question of whether Piaget's interpretations are valid still remains. We will describe examples of research that have explored several factors hypothesized to underlie performance on two search tasks—searching under a single screen and the $A\bar{B}$ situation.

Motoric Ability. One factor that might account for performance on object search tasks is

that limitations in motoric ability may prevent infants from exhibiting their knowledge. This is a particularly cogent argument for Stage III infants, who have very limited ability to coordinate their movements. To remove the cover from a completely occluded object requires lifting the cover and either removing the cover before reaching for the object or holding the cover while reaching for the object. Piaget (1937/1954) argued that limitation in motoric ability was not a likely alternative since it could not account for limitations of older infants. For example, Stage IV infants clearly possess the motoric ability to remove a cover and yet are two stages away from mature object permanence. Now direct evidence is available. The role of motoric ability has been tested by comparing infants' performance on object permanence tasks with an opaque and a transparent cover. Both should require the same motoric abilities but the transparent cover should require less cognitive ability. Therefore, if infants who fail to solve the problem with an opaque cover solve it with a transparent cover, the infants' difficulty is not motoric. Gratch (1972) found that 6-month-old infants were more likely to remove a transparent cover from an object they held in their hand than they were to remove an opaque cover. Thus, motoric abilities are not the limiting factor in the development of this ability, which is an early Stage III behavior. Bower and Wishart (1972) conducted a similar study with a later developing behavior. In their procedure the object was placed under the screen when the infant was not grasping it. They found that 5-month-old infants were more likely to reach under a transparent than an opaque cover, although they had trouble with both. These results do not eliminate the possibility that limitations in motoric ability play a role in this task, because the transparent cover was still difficult. They do, however, demonstrate that motoric limitations are not the complete explanation for performance on search tasks.

In addition to studies using transparent covers, research that documents transitional behaviors within a single task demonstrates that motoric limitations cannot be a complete explanation for performance on search tasks. For example, Willatts (1984) demonstrated the existence of a transitional search pattern between the Stage III failure to search for the hidden object and the Stage IV successful search in the single cover task. The transitional pattern, which is still in Stage III, consists of a search that is not yet intentional. In transitional search the infant is likely to play with the barrier, whereas in intentional search the infant removes the barrier, fixates on the toy, and retrieves the toy immediately. In both transitional and intentional search patterns the infant removes the cover, yet in transitional search the infant does not yet have the requisite cognitive abilities to search intentionally. This demonstrates that the motoric ability to remove a barrier develops earlier than the Stage IV intentional search pattern.

Memory. Just because inadequate motoric ability cannot account for the object permanence sequence by itself does not mean that Piaget's cognitive theory must be true. Another possibility is that infants fail these tasks only because their memories are so limited. This hypothesis may seem confusing, because Piaget would certainly agree that memory is a necessary condition for object permanence; that is, that object permanence cannot occur until infants' memories are adequate. He did not believe, however, that memory development is a sufficient explanation for the development of object permanence. Piaget hypothesized that babies make the AB error because their understanding of an object is tied to their actions, and so they will remember incorrectly.

The studies described in the motoric ability section are also relevant to determining the role of memory limitations. A transparent screen eliminates the necessity of remembering the object because it can still be seen. Thus, if memory limitations are responsible for failure to complete object permanence tasks, using transparent covers should permit infants to pass the test. Both the studies using the single cover task (Bower & Wishart, 1972; Gratch, 1972) and others using the AB situation (Butterworth, 1977; Harris, 1974) found that transparent covers were easier than opaque covers but they did not eliminate infants' errors. This demonstrates that memory limitations are involved but that they cannot account for all errors. In research using other variations of the AB situation, Harris (1973) found evidence supporting this conclusion; he demonstrated that when experimental conditions minimized memory requirements, Stage IV infants were less likely to commit AB errors.

Cummings and Bjork (1981a, 1983) also demonstrated that memory limitations are involved in performance on object search tasks. They argued that past research failed to support Piaget's interpretation of the AB error because in many studies the error rate is around 50%, which is what would be expected if babies could not remember where the object was and so chose a position randomly. A greater number of positions in the experimental situation would permit a more adequate test of Piaget's interpretation that babies return to A because their conception of the object is tied to their previous actions upon it. If babies choose to respond to A (the first hiding position) regardless of how many positions away from B (the second hiding position) it is, Piaget's position would be confirmed. If they choose positions close to B regardless of where A is, that would demonstrate that they remember the general location, although they may be unable to remember B specifically. The latter results were found in a series of studies with both Stage IV and Stage V versions of the AB error (visible and invisible displacement tasks). The evidence clearly demonstrates that infants' memory for hiding places is only approximate, but it is not clear whether this constitutes disconfirmation of Piaget's theory of secondary schemes for two reasons, one conceptual and one evidential. First, a situation with five possible hiding places might simply confuse the subjects so much that they would be unable to use their action-based memories of A and so would be limited to their more recent memory of the object at B. Second, infants in a replication study (Schuberth & Gratch, 1981) exhibited AB errors in Bjork and Cummings' situation (but see Cummings & Bjork, 1981b, for their objections to Schuberth and Gratch's article).

What can we conclude about the role of memory in object search tasks? First, memory is clearly involved. Second, memory alone cannot account for all the phenomena exhibited in the research. Third, whether memory is of action–object sequences remains unclear. We will describe additional research relevant to this issue in the next sections.

Action. Piaget claimed that infants construct their cognitive structures through active exploration of the world and that this is the basis of cognitive development. This stance is among the most controversial aspects of his theory. His notion contrasts sharply with that of associationists who believe that connections among stimuli or between stimuli and responses are stamped in only when they are repeatedly experienced together; the organism is the passive recipient of such experiences. His notion also contrasts sharply with the view of nativists such as the Gestaltists, who believe that such knowledge as the sight and sound of an object are innate.

Unfortunately, the experiments designed to disconfirm Piaget's theory of action have not always tested Piaget's notion of action; in fact there is disagreement over exactly what Piaget did mean. Thus researchers' beliefs about whether a particular study has confirmed or disconfirmed Piaget's theory are often influenced by their interpretations of Piaget. When Piaget described the role of action in infancy, many of his examples were specific motoric actions. This is particularly true of the object permanence sequence, which has been widely studied in this context because Piaget interpreted the developmental progression as reflecting the change from an understanding of objects based solely on infants' actions, through an understanding based on action–object sequences, to an understanding of objects independent of actions. In object permanence tasks the specific actions infants exhibit are usually reaching and grasping. Therefore much of the research designed to test Piaget's theory of action has used reaching and grasping as the operational definition of action. Some psychologists have claimed that this operational definition is adequate because Piaget meant motoric movements when he described actions as the basis of the behavioral schemes of infancy. This view is reinforced by Piaget's description of Stage II, in which he devotes more attention to grasping and sucking schemes than he does to visual and auditory schemes. In contrast, considering Piaget's notions about action in the context of his entire theory, including development after infancy, it

is possible to conclude that Piaget meant action in the general sense that infants actively construct their world; that is, the knowledge they acquire through their interactions with toys, people, and events is a function of the understanding they bring to the situation, which develops through adaptation. In fact the behavioral schemes are the only cognitive structures that can be traced to motoric actions, and even then the relation of behavioral schemes to the actions themselves is indirect. Piaget considered the cognitive structures in later childhood and adulthood to be interiorized actions, but only rarely is an actual motoric action involved. Stage VI problem solving demonstrates this. When toddlers solve a problem through mental representation they are not motorically acting upon the objects. The relation between actions and thoughts becomes even more indirect in later childhood.

The two contrasting views of the meaning of action—reaching to grasp a toy under a cover in infancy versus reasoning through mental representation—are considered by some to be consistent because they represent cognitive structures at different periods. Even in that view there is still ambiguity concerning whether Piaget considered actions in infancy to be restricted to motoric acts or whether he also considered other sorts of active exploration of the environment to be actions. This ambiguity is reflected most importantly in how visual exploration is interpreted in regard to Piaget's theory. Some researchers have argued that Piaget's notion of action eliminates any visual exploration. Others have argued that visual exploration of stationary objects does not involve action, although it is motoric when eye muscles move, as occurs in tracking objects moving across the visual field or in adjusting one's eyes to approaching or departing objects. Still others argue that all visual exploration is action based, because it involves active construction of one's world.[6]

We will discuss the research on the role of action as it is relevant to these various interpretations of Piaget. The research is informative with respect to the role of action regardless

---

[6] Some perception researchers also argue that all visual exploration requires motoric activity.

of beliefs about what Piaget proposed. The most extreme interpretation is that action means motoric actions, particularly grasping and sucking, and that looking, hearing, and the other senses are not based in motoric actions. Two conclusions can be reached from such research. First, it is clear that reaching and grasping actions do play a role in performance on object search tasks. This has been most frequently investigated in the context of the $A\bar{B}$ error, because of Piaget's interpretation of the error as reflecting babies' understanding of objects as object–action sequences. Landers (1971) demonstrated that infants in Stage IV made more $A\bar{B}$ errors if they had made previous reaches to the initial hiding place than if they had just observed the object being hidden. Also, when the infants had to choose between making a response consistent with the direction of their previous reach or with the previous place of hiding, they chose the reach (Bremner & Bryant, 1977). Thus, actions do play a role in the $A\bar{B}$ error.

Second, several avenues of research suggest that modes other than grasping and sucking play major roles in the development of Stage IV behaviors. For example, Stage IV infants make the $A\bar{B}$ error even when they are just observing and are not themselves reaching (Butterworth, 1974). Babies born without limbs (primarily victims of their mothers' prenatal use of thalidomide) evidently develop cognitively in a relatively normal fashion even though they obviously have little or no grasping experience (Kopp & Shaperman, 1973). In fact, vision appears predominant in development of the object permanence sequence in Stages III and IV. Blind babies develop reaching behaviors much later than sighted infants, apparently only because they have to rely on auditory cues. Sighted babies generally develop object permanence to the sound of objects later than they do to the sight of objects (Bigelow, 1981, 1983; Freedman, Fox-Kolenda, Margileth, & Miller, 1969; Uzgiris & Benson, 1980). In fact, the general tenor in infancy research that involves sucking, grasping, looking, and hearing is that the visual modality is the primary modality for cognitive development in babies. Although some experts consider this evidence to be a serious challenge to Piaget's theory, others disagree, although they acknowledge that he probably seriously overes-

timated the importance of sucking and underestimated the importance of looking.

If actions are interpreted as including visual exploration involving objects moving through space, but not visual exploration of stationary objects, then infants should not notice anything about the visual features of objects because they base their understanding on action schemes. Psychologists who argue this way typically also argue that action schemes are not the basic building blocks of cognition and that spatial and featural rules are (Bower, Broughton, & Moore, 1971; Clark, 1981; Moore, Borton, & Darby, 1978). Those who accept the broader notion of action schemes would predict that infants' appreciation of the characteristics of objects should develop gradually, beginning with Stage III, but expanding largely in Stage IV and continuing to improve with the development of tertiary schemes. The next section will describe research demonstrating that Stage IV infants do know something about the hidden objects and the characteristics of the barrier.

Other Perceptible Aspects of the Task. Perhaps the conceptually easiest method of determining whether infants have some idea of differences in objects independent of their own actions is to change the object in the middle of the $A\bar{B}$ situation; that is, to hide one toy under cover A in the first hiding and to change toys for the second hiding under B. If the infants' understanding of the situation is entirely in terms of their actions, they presumably should not notice when the object itself changes. In two studies using single-cover tasks, Stage IV babies noticed when the object changed (LeCompte & Gratch, 1972; Ramsay & Campos, 1975). In three similar studies using the $A\bar{B}$ situation two (Moore & Clark, 1979; Schuberth, Werner, & Lipsitt, 1978) found that Stage IV infants were less likely to make the $A\bar{B}$ error if the object changed, whereas the third (Evans & Gratch, 1972) found no differences in the probability of making an error when the object changed and when the object did not.

Infants also process information about the perceptual configuration of the situation. When perceptual aspects, such as distinctive colors of the covers, consistently cue the presence of the object (for example, the object is always under the blue cover), infants are less likely to make the AB̄ error than when no such cues exist (Bremner, 1978; Bremner & Bryant, 1977; Butterworth, Jarrett, & Hicks, 1982). Likewise, when the perceptual cues conflict with the placement of the object, infants do worse than when there is no such conflict (Butterworth et al., 1982). Either the perceptual configuration allows the infants to keep track of the presence of the object or they conceive of the situation as an undifferentiated totality, one in which the object is not separated from the perceptual configuration in which it is moved.

Infants' concepts of the nature of barriers also influence their behaviors in the AB̄ situation. For example, Freeman, Lloyd, & Sinha (1980) hypothesized that whether infants would make the AB̄ error depended on their interpretation of the hiding action, and they conducted a series of studies manipulating various characteristics of the covers. Infants behaved as if they had the following expectations: (1) when an object is hidden *under* a cover (such as under a model house) and the cover is moved, the object should stay in the first position; (2) when the object is inside a container (such as a cup) and the container is moved, the object should stay in its container. Freeman and colleagues also demonstrated that this understanding of covers versus containers is not quite like that of adults. First, model houses turned upside down can be containers to an adult, but evidently are not recognized as such by infants. Most of even the oldest subjects (15 months) committed the AB̄ error in that situation. Second, they acted as if cups were containers even when a cup was used as a screen, that is, when the object was hidden behind the cup. Thus, they have not yet inferred the functional relations that define "inside," "over," and "behind" independent of their experience with particular barriers.

Freeman and collaborators' research suggests that performance on object search tasks reflects infants' current understanding of how objects act in relation to the rest of the environment, which is a more complex and differentiated understanding than early accounts suggested. Nonetheless, their account is still incomplete. Dunst, Brooks, and Doxsey (1982) found partly disparate results using somewhat different containers and mostly younger subjects, which suggests that the complete story of the development of infants' understanding of the occlusion of objects is even more complex.

Coordination of Schemes. According to Piaget, Stage IV infants are able to remove a barrier to reach an object because they can coordinate two schemes (the scheme that governs removing the barrier with the one that governs reaching for the desired object). They commit the AB̄ error because the first coordination they form (remove-barrier-at-A and grasp-object-previously-hidden-at-A) interferes with their being able to form the second (remove-barrier-at-B and grasp-object-previously-hidden-at-B). Frye (1980) tested this interpretation in an ingenious pair of experiments. He argued that if Piaget's interpretation is correct, then having infants form a novel coordination of schemes after they form the coordination involving A and before they form the coordination involving B should help to break the influence of the first coordination (involving A) and prevent its intrusion into the B situation. He found this to be the case for two of three interposed tasks (hiding at a third place and pulling a support to get to an object, but not for pulling a string to get at an object). In addition he included other experimental groups to permit comparisons of the predictive power of several other explanations. Only the intercoordination hypothesis predicted the results.

Evaluation. Research on the object search tasks has clearly confirmed some of Piaget's claims and disconfirmed others. It has confirmed Piaget's argument that performance on these tasks cannot be explained completely by motoric or memory limitations. Any evaluation of the status of Piaget's theory of secondary schemes as action–object sequences depends on the interpretation of Piaget's theory that is used. Perhaps the greatest success of the post-Piagetian literature has been to specify acceptable interpretations of his theory more precisely and to submit them to experimental test. On that basis it is possible to eliminate two interpretations. First, an acceptable action-based explanation cannot define action as reaching movements. Actual reaching is not necessary; in fact, experience in any one modality is unnecessary. Second, reaching actions do affect performance, but they are not the only influence. Thus, reaching actions are neither necessary nor sufficient to explain behaviors in the AB̄ situation. Moreover, it is clear that other aspects of the situation—characteristics of the objects and covers—influence infants' search.

Whether Piaget's theory is adequate to account for these data is controversial. Those who still say it is not adequate are likely to equate action with reaching, whereas those who would say it is adequate are likely to interpret Piaget's use of action in the more general context of actions as active exploration of the environment. Perceptible features are thus incorporated into schemes by active visual exploration. By this interpretation the evidence so far accrued is consistent with Piaget's notion of action. In addition, his explanation of the AB̄ situation in terms of coordination of schemes has received independent validation (Frye, 1980).

Regardless of whether one accepts the research as consistent or inconsistent with Piaget's theory, it is clear that Piaget's theory did not *predict* all the results obtained. The research on the nature of the barrier indicates that additional theoretical principles are necessary to explain infants' performance on object search tasks.

A NEW LOOK IN NORTH AMERICAN COGNITIVE RESEARCH IN INFANCY

In science a new theory takes hold when it proves to be a powerful heuristic device by which research can be guided. Associative learning theory provided such an impetus to the study of infants in the 1950s and 1960s and Piagetian theory did the same in the 1960s and 1970s. As knowledge from research inspired by a theory accumulates, instances in which the data do not fit the theory also increase. This has happened to both these theories. In the last few decades numerous theories of small scope (often called microtheories) have been formulated. Some are direct consequences of research initially undertaken to test some aspects of Piagetian or learning theories.

It is often the case in psychology that the research outcomes are more complex than the

theoretical concepts available. Then researchers often concentrate their subsequent work on identifying and developing their conceptualizations of the processes they have uncovered.

Another source of process-oriented research programs was neither learning nor Piagetian theories, but the information processing approach. In this view, information from the environment (the stimulus in learning theory) is processed by the organism, who then acts upon it. Information processing approaches are derived from analogies to machines. The most popular machine model today is, of course, the computer. This approach has become so popular that many of the process-oriented theories that initially developed in other contexts are now called information processing models. We will consider all such process-oriented theories together since they all attempt to identify and describe the component processes or skills found in a given situation.

Comprehensive theories that attempt to integrate knowledge gained from the more specific, task-related theories are now appearing. We will briefly review that of Fischer (1980), which includes specific attention to infancy. Then we will examine the research exploring the development during infancy of one specific process, classification.

Skills Theory

Fischer (1980) has recently developed a skills theory from the context of American learning theory and Piagetian or Genevan research and theory, and his theory can be classified as a process-oriented theory. As is true of most process-oriented psychologists, Fischer's skills theory assumes that the cognitive structures of the organism interact with the environment to determine the organism's behavior at a given time. Although he acknowledges that the role of the organism includes inherited and constitutional factors, his theory does not focus on the biology–experience issue. In one sense he takes the same interactionist stance with respect to innate ideas as does Piaget: Fischer believes that, rather than being innate, the first sensorimotor structures develop through experience acting upon the reflex structures, and he cites some evidence to support that belief (Bullinger, 1977). In spite of this similarity, Fischer has a different answer to the question of what is the basic nature of the categories of mind, a matter we will return to shortly. His theory also differs from that of Piaget in that he attributes far less of development to maturation. Like learning theories, his theory focuses on the role the environment plays in producing cognitive structures and their development. He starts from the general notion of adaptation in the sense that "the cognitive organism is constantly adapting skills to the world, and this adaptation provides the foundation for cognitive development and learning" (Fischer, 1980, p. 525). The skills mentioned in this quotation are the heart of Fischer's theory. Their role is analogous to that of schemes in Piaget's theory. They develop through the infant acting (motorically or perceptually) on the environment. Like Piaget's schemes, Fischer's skills are the basic cognitive structures for knowing; that is, they are procedures by which infants come to know their world. They are different from Piaget's schemes in two very important ways. First, schemes are organized by particular actions, such as a scheme for scratching versus a scheme for shaking, but skills are developed from initial global situations, such as shaking and hearing a rattle. Whereas for Piaget each scheme develops in its own modality and must be coordinated with the schemes of other senses, for Fischer the set of actions in a particular environmental situation is globally linked in a basic skill set, and later will be differentiated and then interrelated in a more sophisticated fashion. The second way Fischer's skills differ from Piaget's schemes is related to the first. Piaget assumes that the sensory and motoric action patterns derive from the infants' biological substrate and therefore will develop as cognitive structures of wide generality regardless of the particular environment in which the baby grows up. Fischer assumes the opposite. Skills develop from the particular situations infants encounter, and the course of each infant's development may be somewhat different because of the particular situations he or she encounters. This means that (1) babies will not develop at the same rate, (2) they will develop along somewhat different pathways, and (3) individual babies will be more advanced in some task domains than

in others. Fischer's theory here is a response to much data that found unevenness in development both within a given child and from one child to another. Although Uzgiris and Hunt (1975) found clear developmental sequences within a particular domain such as object permanence or imitation, they found only low correlations from one domain to another (some correlation would be expected because development in each domain is correlated with age). Fischer argues that unevenness is the norm in development because the particular skills infants develop are the result of both the particular environment they experience and their own level of understanding with respect to that skill domain.

Skills theory allows for maturation in that each child has an optimal level of skills development. This is the highest level the child can reach at any particular time. For example, if a baby's optimal level is still sensorimotor rather than representational, then that baby is not able to reach mature understanding of object permanence. Fischer does not specify what determines optimal level. It can be governed by maturation or by experience or by both without affecting the theory.

Fischer's theory can also be compared to learning theory. Skills can be conceived of as operants (emitted behaviors that are changed by environmental contingencies). This means that skills are more likely to recur if they have been followed by a reinforcement. It is also consistent with learning theory to suggest that uneven development is normal, because the opportunity to practice skills is what determines whether and how rapidly particular skills develop. Furthermore, starting from the premise that development proceeds within specific domains and the accompanying assumption that under most circumstances development in other domains will be asynchronous is consistent with the learning theory point of view. Skills are unlike operants in one very important way. The concept of operant does not include a system that describes how operants are related to each other or how those relations change with learning and development. Skill theory provides such a system. The baby acquires specific skills; these become more complex, differentiated, and integrated; and they become intercoordinated with other skills.

Fischer accepts Piaget's division of development into three broad periods, which he calls tiers. His first tier corresponds to Piaget's sensorimotor period, and like Piaget's ends when the baby develops mental representations. Within each tier, Fischer identifies four levels of development. The first three levels of the first tier correspond, *roughly*, to Piaget's primary, secondary, and tertiary schemes, and the fourth is equivalent to Piaget's Stage VI. We will use Piagetian phenomena to demonstrate the first four levels of skills theory.

Level 1 skills are simple sets of sensorimotor actions. Actions coalesce in a set because they occur in a certain situation, such as in interaction with particular people, objects, or events. Unlike Piaget's primary schemes, these sets may involve two sensory modalities, such as vision and audition. Fischer argues this way because many of the studies of conditioning in young infants may involve such multimodality sets (see Papoušek, 1967; Sameroff, 1971). This concept also, of course, fits Bower's theory of innate intercoordination of senses.

Level 2 is reached when one sensorimotor set is **mapped** (related element by element) onto another. A good example of a mapping is visually guided reaching, in which looking at an object becomes integrated with grasping it. Many, but not all, of Piaget's secondary circular reactions are Level 2 mappings.

Level 3 involves more complex mappings in which two or more components of one sensorimotor set are mapped onto analogous components of a second set, producing what Fischer calls a system. The tertiary circular reactions, in which variations of infants' actions produce interesting variations in results (see Piaget's description of Jacqueline exploring how the box moves, earlier in this chapter) are an example of Level 3 mapping.

Level 4 is when two systems become intercoordinated. For example, a child's sensorimotor system by which he manipulates a toy car becomes intercoordinated with a system derived from watching his older brother play with the toy car. This final intercoordination of systems frees children from the sensorimotor limitation of objects being tied to specific sets of actions. They can now represent simple properties of objects, events, and people independently of their own actions.

Thus intercoordination of sensorimotor systems produces a simple representational set. The 2-year-old, with these simple representational sets, starts on another tier of development that parallels the first—but that is a story for another book.

Fischer bases his description of sensorimotor development on the phenomena discovered by Piaget, but he provides a different theoretical basis, one that eliminates the following controversial aspects of Piaget's theory: (1) the assumption of general developmental synchrony, (2) Piaget's belief that infants actively invent their understanding of the world rather than learn about the environment, and (3) Piaget's belief that young infants cannot coordinate sensory information from several modalities and therefore have only fragmented knowledge of a single stimulus situation. Most of the evidence Fischer and his coworkers have produced has been related to the issue of asynchrony versus synchrony in development (Bertenthal & Fischer, 1978; Corrigan, 1979; Jackson, Campos, & Fischer, 1978; Watson & Fischer, 1977). It is too soon to know whether aspects of skills theory such as the structure of development will prove to have more heuristic value than Piaget's.

Categorization

The terms category, class, and concept all refer to a group of objects or events that are considered to belong together. The meanings of the three terms vary subtly in the way psychologists use them. Classification is usually operationalized as the act of sorting objects into two or more groups on the basis of some criterion (or criteria) such as animals versus nonanimals. The resulting groups are called classes. The terms concept and category are more often used to refer to a person's understanding of the attributes by which an object or event is identified as such. For example, the term concept is used in discussions of infants' object concept, described in this chapter, and of concepts of common objects and events as evidenced by their developing use of words, which we will discuss in the next chapter. Piaget has said very little about the development of such concepts as cars, animals, and so forth, except to say that behavioral schemes are precursors to classification skills. This is because he was interested in logical classification; that is, the ability to sort objects into consistent and exclusive classes such as all circles, all squares, all triangles. Before Piaget was willing to attribute such ability to a child, that child had to be able to make such a sorting without error and then put all the objects back together and sort them on a different basis, such as all large, all medium, all small. Success in such tasks is usually achieved in the late preschool years. By accepting other less stringent criteria and by using sensitive experimental techniques, researchers have been able to detect categorization much earlier. Much of the research has used the techniques developed in perceptual studies, particularly habituation–dishabituation, conditioning, and tracking of visual stimuli. We will first describe research that uses these techniques to study concepts that can be represented visually. Then we will describe the few studies that have used object sorting, and finally the research that has related developing categorization to development of symbols.

VISUAL CONCEPTS

It is perhaps easiest to grapple with the issues of how concepts and classification develop by starting with newborns and reviewing the discussion in Chapter 9 about infants' ability to discriminate among patterns. It is clear that newborns can make many of the discriminations from which concepts are formed. They can detect contours that demarkate the boundaries between objects. They can discriminate straight lines from curves, vertical lines from horizontals or diagonals, patterns with high density from patterns with low density, and they can detect color and brightness.

With the possible exception of perception of faces, the evidence consistently supports the view that infants younger than 2 months do not use such discriminations to form concepts. The first indication that infants perceive a configuration of such discriminable elements as a unit is found in the research on face perception. Two-month-old infants consistently discriminate between faces and scrambled faces. By 3 months of age infants discriminate their mothers' faces from strangers' faces. This demonstrates that they have learned to recognize a particular configuration in contrast to others.

By 3 months of age infants also perceive an angle as the relation between two lines, whereas infants 6 weeks old perceive the same angles as lines of differing orientation (Cohen & Younger, 1984). Three-month-old babies treat triangular patterns of dots of various sizes and in varying positions in their field of vision as similar to each other and different from dots in a straight line (Milewski, 1979). Thus, it is reasonable to conclude that 3-month-old infants can abstract simple perceptual invariants; that is, they recognize relations among perceptual elements as the same, even when other, irrelevant characteristics vary. This kind of behavior is concept-like in that responses to similar patterns (such as triangular patterns of dots) are similar and responses to dissimilar patterns (line of dots) are different. Of course, babies of this age do not sort these exemplars. Most frequently, they are habituated to one class of patterns (such as triangles in several orientations and patterns) and then are tested for dishabituation (to a new triangle or a straight line). Nevertheless, their patterns of habituation and dishabituation indicate that stimuli that share a perceptual invariant are more similar to them than stimuli that do not have that perceptual invariant. Sugarman (1982) points out that there is no way of knowing whether infants conceive of the habituation stimuli as the same stimulus repeated or as discrete objects that share some similarity. She argues that only infants who conceive of objects as discrete but similar can be said to have a concept. Thus it can be argued that infants at 3 months identify perceptual invariants, but there is no evidence that they classify in the sense of putting discrete objects in the same category. At 4 months infants develop visually-guided reaching, which is the last of the intersensory coordinations (Piaget, 1936/1963). This marks the achievement of the concept of an object as something that has mass in a three-dimensional world and that has visual, tactual, and sometimes auditory attributes.

Let us summarize the developmental sequence we have discussed so far. Newborns can make visual distinctions, but such distinctions apparently have no larger meaning. By 3 months of age infants can detect perceptual invariants and some (at least faces) carry associated meaning. For example, the configuration of mother's face may be a signal for dinner. This does not mean that all aspects of the concept are equivalent to those of adults. It may be that 3-month-old infants conceive that there are many mothers at difference places, even if they all belong in one category. By 4 months of age information from the different senses is apparently unified into a single concept of an object.

Four- and five-month-olds make other perceptual discriminations that demonstrate their increasing knowledge of objects in the world and that could conceivably provide the basis for classification. Five-month-old infants can discriminate between two strange faces and between a photograph of a person or doll and the actual person or doll. This capability evidently reflects, in part, infants' changing abilities to process multidimensional stimuli. Bower (1966) found that 4–5-month-old babies respond to complex patterns as integrated wholes, whereas younger infants seem to respond to complex patterns as collections of separate parts. Five-month-old infants also can detect a single dimension within a complex pattern as well as compounds of such dimensions (Cornell, 1975; Fagan, 1977; Cohen, Gelber, & Lazar, 1971), although these studies did not test younger babies and so have not demonstrated conclusively that such abilities do not develop until this age.

A spate of studies of 6- or 7-month-old infants suggests that the ability to form concepts has improved relative to 5-month-old infants (although not all studies directly compare the two ages). One that does and that also describes well the new achievements is a study of face concepts by Cohen and Strauss (1979). They used a habituation–dishabituation paradigm to test concept formation. They presented several different exemplars of the concept during habituation trials. If babies habituate to these multiple stimuli, it suggests that they might be responding to the exemplars as a class. Dishabituation trials can verify that interpretation. If babies are forming a concept they should dishabituate to stimuli that are not in that class and should fail to dishabituate (that is, continue to show little response) to stimuli that are new instances of the habituated concept. Cohen and Strauss's habituation stimuli (their perceptual concept) were pictures of a particular face (a stranger's) across variations in orien-

tation. Seven-month-old infants were able to form a concept based on a particular face regardless of orientation; that is, they habituated, they dishabituated to new faces, and they failed to dishabituate to the same face in novel orientations. They were also able to form a concept (in the habituation–dishabituation sense) to faces in general. Infants of 4 and 5 months acted as if changing the orientation of the face introduced a new concept. They were not able to form an invariant class based either on a specific face or on faces in general. This is a fairly stunning limitation, for it implies that although 4- and 5-month-old infants are good at visual discrimination they cannot use that ability to form ecologically important concepts from unfamiliar instances. Caron, Caron, and Meyers (1982) have found a similar pattern of results for facial expressions. They also habituated infants to a group of stimuli, in this case to four pictures of different women with happy expressions (or four with surprised expressions). Babies at 7 months of age responded as if they formed a concept of facial expression: they dishabituated to faces with a different expression but generalized to new faces with the same expressions. The 4 and 5$\frac{1}{2}$-month-old infants did not show this pattern. As might be expected from these two studies, 7-month-old infants were also found to form similar concepts of geometric forms across changes in orientation (McGurk, 1972), which demonstrates that their ability to form concepts is not limited to those very familiar, important stimuli, faces.

If all concepts were like the ones we have discussed, the story would be finished. Nevertheless, many concepts are much more complex, so the story continues. Two other major forms of concepts are commonly studied in psychology. In the concepts specified in the research discussed above, there is always a single perceptual attribute or set of attributes that distinguish exemplars of the concept from nonexemplars. This is not always the case. For example, the category "food" is defined by a nonperceptual attribute, "you can eat it." Concepts that cannot be defined by perceptual communalities are often called **abstract** concepts. Most studies of both perceptually based and abstract concepts have used stimuli that form logical classes, that is, classes in which all members of the class share an attribute or set of attributes (for example, every member of the class of all large cats must be both large and a cat). In the past decade or so, researchers have also studied **ill-defined** concepts, in which there is no one common attribute. Instead, each member of the class has some of the class attributes, but not necessarily the same subset of attributes as other members. The member of the class that has all attributes is called the prototype—the most typical case. An example appears in the next paragraph.

Ill-defined concepts have been demonstrated in 10-month-old infants and abstract concepts in 12-month-olds. Several different varieties of ill-defined classes have been demonstrated with 10-month-old babies. We will describe one of these studies to show what they are like. Husaim and Cohen (1981) constructed make-believe animals that varied along four dimensions: body size, neck length, leg length, and number of legs. They trained infants to turn their heads to the left when they saw one class of animals and to the right when they saw a second class. The best exemplar of the first class had a large body, long neck, long legs, and four legs, but each exemplar the subjects saw had only three of those four attributes and each of the four training exemplars had a different set of three attributes. Thus, there was no common attribute among all exemplars. The second category was constructed in much the same way. Infants 10 months of age were able to learn to respond differentially to the two categories and then to generalize to new instances. This study corroborates an earlier study by Strauss (1979) and further demonstrates that infants relied on a combination of dimensions rather than one single dimension. In addition, Younger and Cohen (1982) demonstrated that 10-month-old infants were able to differentiate between attributes that were correlated to form a category and attributes of the same objects that were irrelevant. Ill-defined categories have not yet been studied in younger babies, so it is not yet known whether 10 months is the youngest age at which such concept development is possible.

Likewise, abstract concepts, such as dogs versus antelopes (Cohen & Caputo, 1978) and men versus other animals, and food versus furniture (Ross, 1980), have been demonstrated in babies 12 months of age, but whether younger infants are incapable of comparable perfor-

mance is unclear. Ross found two results that raise interesting questions. First, she studied children 12, 18, and 24 months of age and found no changes across that age range. Because the second year is notable for improvement in communication skills, particularly in language, it is striking that by Ross's technique (habituation–dishabituation), knowledge of concepts in a nonverbal context does not appear to be developing as well. Second, she found that the subjects did not habituate to some concepts, although they still distinguished between novel exemplars and nonexemplars. The exemplars of the concepts for which this was true—animals, food, furniture—were all more varied than for those that habituated—men, the letters M and O. Thus, the more abstract (less perceptually based) concepts elicited different behaviors. Whether this has any important implications for development is unclear.

SORTING STUDIES

None of the studies of conceptual development that we have described so far has used that classic method of testing children's concepts, the sorting task. By 6 months of age infants are good at reaching for objects they see and therefore it is possible to lay out a group of toys and watch what infants do with them. Starkey (1981) has done just that, using a procedure highly congenial to the ages he studied (see Figure 10–9). He found that 6-month-old infants neither sorted into groups nor sequentially touched more than two similar objects. After selecting one or two of a kind, they would start to reach for a third, only to stop in the middle and move to another object that had caught their attention. This may seem surprising, since Starkey's toys were clearly no more complex than Cohen and Strauss's faces, which infants of this age did categorize. The object sorting task, however, is probably more difficult for two reasons. First, it requires that infants maintain their activity with respect to a single category in the face of possibilities of alternative classification criteria. In habituation–dishabituation paradigms there are no alternative categories to be ignored. Throughout development, problems that present a conflict between two alternative solution strategies are more difficult and the ability to solve them develops later than it does for comparable tasks without such conflicts. Second, the grouping

FIGURE 10–9. The stimulus situation and typical responses of infants in object sorting tasks. (This example is adapted from D. Starkey, "The origins of concept formation: Object sorting and object preference in early infancy," Child Development, 1981, 52, 489–497). (a) A tray with the stimuli spread out was placed in front of the infants without verbal instructions or modeling and the infants were permitted to play with them as they wished. Parts (b), (c), and (d) represent infant responses of varying sophistication. (b) Selecting 2 of a kind. About 33% of 6-month-old babies and 80% of 9-month-old infants do this on occasion. (c) Selecting all 4 of a kind. About 40% of 12-month-old babies do this on occasion. (d) Both classes of objects separated into distinct groups. This ability develops between 1½ and 2½ years of age.

task also often involves sophisticated reaching, particularly reaching while already holding an object. Such complex reaching skills develop later than 6 months of age (Bruner, 1969, 1973).

By 9 months infants show signs of overcoming the problems 6-month-olds have. Over 80% of Starkey's 9-month-old babies tended to pick sequentially at least 3 or 4 similar objects from a group of toys and to put at least 2 of them into a separate pile. Infants advance rapidly after this initial achievement. By 12 months around 40% of infants, on at least one occasion, picked out all 4 instances of one class and put those objects together.

Whether this sequential selection requires true classification skills is not clear. Sugarman (1982) argues that infants may successively select objects only because each object interests them, not because they are noting that a similarity relation exists among the discrete objects. Both her data (1981) and Starkey's (1981) support this notion. Infants younger than $1\frac{1}{2}$ years showed successive selection of exemplars in a class primarily when the stimuli in one class were more likely to interest the infants and when the two sets were easily distinguishable.

Sugarman (1981; see also 1982 for additional analyses) argues that infants have established true classes when they select all of one class and then all of a second class. This develops between 18 and 24 months and is soon followed by another advance. At $2\frac{1}{2}$ years infants begin to group into two classes at once; for example, they will pick up two dolls and put them in one place, then put a circle in a second place, next place another doll with the other dolls, and so on.

CONCEPTS AND SYMBOLIZATION

At about the same time the more complex forms of concepts discussed above are apparently developing, the use of symbols (perhaps more accurately called presymbols) is beginning. A **symbol** is an activity or object that can refer to something that is not present. A narrower definition reserves the term symbol for instances in which the signifier and the referent are arbitrarily related. For example, words are arbitrarily related to their referents because they do not in any way resemble the objects to which they refer. We will, however, use the term symbol to include both abstract

signifier–signified relations and those in which the signifier does resemble its referent, because we are focusing on what toddlers' developing symbol use can reveal about their knowledge of concepts. Much of the work that sheds light on this question concerns language development, which will be described in Chapter 11. In this chapter we will deal with some of the burgeoning research that investigates the developing use of symbols through representational systems other than language.

Bates, Bretherton, and their colleagues have been studying the development of gestural schemes in relation to verbal schemes. In gestural schemes infants represent knowledge of an object by involving it in a conventional action in a pretend fashion. For example, infants show by gesture that they know something about a telephone if they put the receiver of a play telephone to their ears. Likewise, they know something about soap if they pretend to wash their hands when they see a bar of soap. Gestural schemes occur frequently by 10 to 12 months of age. When gestural schemes are used with their original objects, they show that the infants know something about the object, but they do not demonstrate that the infant has demarcated a class of objects. When infants also exhibit these schemes with new and similar objects, they can be said to know the concept. In addition, as children develop, they exhibit their gestural schemes with substitute objects that "stand for" the original object. This development was called symbolic play by Piaget and is characteristic of Stage VI. The substitute object serves as a symbol for the object in the gestural scheme, and, according to Piaget, indicates that the scheme has become representational.

When these gestural schemes first develop, they are closely tied to their original context. For example, gestural schemes are less likely to be made when the object is abstract (same basic shape and criterial attribute) than when the object is realistic (Bretherton et al., 1981). Objects used as signifiers in symbolic play are likely to be similar, both perceptually and in function, to the signified object (Ungerer, Zelazo, Kearsley, & O'Leary, 1981).

With time, these schemes become more widely applied, and applied in an increasing number of different circumstances ("decontextualized," in the language of Werner & Kaplan,

1963). For example, a child might develop a telephone gesture in a game with her mother, and first apply it only to that toy telephone, then to other toy telephones, outside game contexts, and later still to a spoon (Bates, Camaioni, & Volterra, 1975; Volterra, Bates, Benigni, Bretherton, & Camaioni, 1979). The same decontextualization occurs with symbolic play. Children 2 years and older are more likely than younger children to use as a symbolic object one that bears little physical resemblance to the referent (Elder & Pederson, 1978; Fein, 1975; Watson & Fischer, 1977; Ungerer et al., 1981). Through decontextualization children's concepts clearly become more refined, because the essential characteristics become abstracted from the original context in which they were learned and can be applied to a range of appropriate exemplars.

These findings about the development of gestural schemes has an interesting parallel in recent evidence concerning the use of what for adults is a shared symbol system, American Sign Language (ASL). Bonvillian and his colleagues (Bonvillian, Orlansky, & Novack, 1983; Bonvillian, Orlansky, Novack, & Folven, 1983) studied the development of the use of ASL in children of deaf parents. Although signs in ASL are gestural, they are quite different from gestural schemes. Gestural schemes develop from the sensorimotor schemes of the babies themselves whereas signs are taught by the parents in the same way language is taught. Therefore ASL might be expected to develop the same way language does. Because the fine motor coordination necessary to sign evidently develops earlier than motoric control of the articulatory apparatus, signing should develop earlier than language, so long as infants' concepts are sufficient. This is the question that such a study investigates: Do infants have the concepts necessary to be able to attach symbols to them at an earlier age than they can in language? Bonvillian and his colleagues answered that they do. The average age at which the children in their study produced their first recognizable sign was 8.6 months when they scored primarily in sensorimotor stages III and IV (by Uzgiris and Hunt norms). Nevertheless these early signs were not necessarily used in a completely symbolic fashion. During their home visits Bonvillian and his collaborators were seldom able to elicit signs for objects that

were not present or for events that had not just happened. They therefore made a separate judgment on the basis of parents' diaries and discussions with them as to when such signs were made in clear symbolic fashion (a procedure often used in assessing language development). The babies did not use their signs symbolically until after they had developed 10 signs (13.2 months) and sometimes not until they had started to combine signs (17.1 months) and had reached Piagetian Stages V or VI.

Thus, ASL signs develop at about the same time gestural schemes develop and significantly earlier than words. Early use, however, is not fully symbolic, in that signs initially occur only in context, as do gestural schemes. This is also consistent with Sugarman's interpretation of sequential selection of same class objects in a display; that is, infants of this age are able to note similarities among objects within a class, but have not yet developed the representational skills necessary to conceptualize classes independent of the particular exemplars in the particular situation.

It is more difficult to draw conclusions from this research with respect to development in the second year. It is clear that concepts become representational: Signs of ASL become true symbols, used when their referents are not present; verbal and gestural schemes become decontextualized, and thereby represent concepts that are more generalized and effective; and object sorting more clearly reflects classification independent of action schemes. Although they will develop in the second year, the time periods within which each of these phenomena develops are not consistent and the relations among the phenomena have yet to be established. In addition, gestural schemes are apparently transitional in their symbol-like use. They start to decline by 20 months of age (Bretherton et al., 1981) and are replaced by a communal symbol system (a language).

SUMMARY

By the end of their first two years, children are still a long way from the sort of mature classification behaviors seen in late preschool and elementary school children. Nevertheless, infants are beginning to form concepts and thereby distinguish between exemplars and nonexemplars of such concepts during these two years. The description of this developmental sequence is still extremely sketchy and care must be used in interpreting the data. Nonetheless, it seems clear that there are several phases. Before 2 months of age babies seem capable only of discriminating among stimuli and show little ability to make similarity judgments in response to repeated patterns. Simple examples of recognizing such similarity in visual configurations appear at 2–3 months. By 5 months it is clear that infants can coordinate various aspects of objects and events such as two or more visual dimensions, or visual attributes with place and movement. At 6 months they can coordinate stimuli in different orientations into a single class. In the last half of the first year, there are examples of infants exhibiting concepts that have the same structures as those of older people. Their use of such concepts is not mature, however, and is still tied to the contexts in which they learned them, so they cannot be considered fully representational. Knowledge of development of concepts during the second year is still quite sketchy, but it is safe to say that by the end of the second year almost everyone would agree that children have the basic abilities necessary to learn symbolic concepts.

DISCUSSION ISSUES AND SUMMARY

The discussion of issues and summary of this chapter follows a format somewhat different from most of the other chapters of this book. Because of our desire to show how knowledge about infants is discovered as well as the knowledge itself, we felt it was important to present the research in its scientific context. The complexities of that context make it difficult to see what a baby at each age is like. We shall therefore first give a chronological summary of the sequence of cognitive development in infancy. In this summary we include the most firmly established and least controversial evidence and not those aspects about which there is substantial disagreement. We also include developmental phenomena from earlier chapters when they elucidate cognitive development. After this chronological summary, we shall summarize some of the interesting and important unresolved issues and the

methodological points made in this chapter. Finally we shall discuss some practical applications of knowledge of infants' cognitive development.

Chronological Summary

At birth infants can respond to limited sorts of changes in their world. They can change their sucking behaviors to meet the world's requirements, such as adapting to fast- or slow-flowing nipples. They also exhibit behaviors such as grasping, sucking, and looking in the absence of an obvious eliciting stimulus: They seem to act just to act.

In the first month of life more sophisticated abilities begin to develop. By the end of that first month babies are able to learn new, previously unknown connections, ones that are not just responses to immediate changes in the environment. They can learn arbitrary associations such as that footsteps in the hall occur just before they receive milk and they can remember the connection so that the next time they hear those footsteps they know food will arrive. Furthermore, babies 1 month old have acquired a primitive means by which to actively explore their world, the primary circular reactions.

During the second and third months of life (Piaget's Stage II) infants advance in several ways. They can detect perceptual invariants, the mark of true perceptual processing (Hershenson, Kessen, and Munsinger, 1967; Hershenson, 1971), and they can distinguish their mothers from strangers. They can imitate in a general, same-class fashion. They can recognize previous events for at least 24 hours without prompting and for several weeks if their memories are reactivated before presentation of the stimulus.

At 4 months infants develop the mature form of visually guided reaching, which greatly improves their ability to explore the world. Infants of this age (entering Stage III) are more responsive to environmental events and objects than are younger infants and they can often make a happening recur through their own actions (secondary circular reactions). They imitate frequently, albeit still with limitations. Their understanding of the world is still very limited.

During the 4–6-month period infants show improved ability to discriminate among multidimensional stimuli. They clearly have intercoordinated an object's visual, auditory, and tactile characteristics, and apparently see objects in depth. These developmental phenomena suggest that babies of this age understand the nature of three-dimensional objects. By 6 to 7 months babies have the sort of concepts that are based on a common visual attribute or configuration.

By 8 months (entering Stage IV) infants have developed truly intentional behaviors. They can set aside an obstacle to reach an object and pull a string to get what is attached to it. They are beginning to develop object permanence in that they search for objects that are out of their sight, including objects that they left in another room several minutes earlier. Their concept of the object, however, is not yet mature. They often commit the $A\bar{B}$ error, looking for an object in a previous hiding place even though they have seen it put into a new hiding place. This error reflects several limitations of infants' minds at this age: limitation of memory, lack of differentiation between infants' action and the movement of the object, and the infants' previous experience with the way hidden objects act. Infants of this age clearly use imitation to learn about their environment, because they imitate unfamiliar actions and their imitation seems intentional. They also show evidence of reconstructive memory. By 10 months infants show evidence that they understand ill-defined concepts. During this period they often use gestures (or signs for those learning ASL) to communicate.

By around 12 months of age (the beginning of Stage V) infants have learned that objects are independent of their own actions on them. Because of this they can focus on the characteristics of an object to a greater degree than in previous stages and they become particularly interested in novel aspects of their environment. They pay close attention to distinctive features of objects. They vary events such as the height from which they drop objects so that they can note the varying actions of the falling object. They can recognize abstract concepts, ones that have no common perceptual attribute or configuration.

The problem solving of infants in Stage V also takes a major step forward. They not only can use means to achieve ends, but they can invent new means, that is, they can figure out how to solve means–end problems by new, untried means. Their problem solving ability is still limited, however, and they have to try out the means behavior to see if they will achieve the desired end.

Although it has been developing gradually throughout infancy, particularly in Stage IV and V, representational thought is not clearly developed until the last half of the second year. By that time infants (1) achieve mature object permanence, (2) can solve problems through mental combinations, (3) classify two classes at a time (Sugarman's 1982 criterion of true representation in classification), and (4) use language symbolically.

Controversies About Infant Cognition

Disagreements concerning infants' conceptions of the world begin at the beginning, with the nativism–empiricism argument about what infants know at birth. Piaget believed that infants know nothing at birth other than their own sense impressions and so they have no notion of what an object is and they do not realize that particular visual, auditory, and tactile impressions come from a single object. In contrast, Bower believes that the notion of an object as a three-dimensional thing with visual, auditory, and tactile components is innate. Fischer believes that characteristics of the object and its environmental context are chunked in a global fashion. He expects that newborns would act as if the auditory, visual, and tactile characteristics were related. This does not mean, however, that he would agree with Bower's interpretation of such behaviors. Since newborns' idea of the situation is global, they would not differentiate between two objects in a situation, or between an object and their own action. Thus, his theory does not have the epistemological implications that Bower's does.

The import of the controversy over early imitation is similar. If newborns can imitate others' actions exactly, particularly actions that involve body parts they cannot see on themselves, then they must have some innate concept of what the action is and can map the action of the model onto their schema of their own action.

Another series of disagreements stems from the controversy concerning how infants (and adults) come to know the world. Piaget believed that infants construct their world, including their knowledge of objects, by acting upon the environment. Other psychologists, particularly the Gibsons and those influenced by them (including Bower), argue that infants come to know the world through perceptual differentiation (detecting perceptual invariants). The research on the role action plays in the $A\bar{B}$ task indicates that both processes are important, but it is not clear how they are related. That means how infants do conceptualize the objects and events in their environment is also not clear. Fischer hypothesizes that their sets begin with concrete situations, which they understand only globally. The research that has shown that performance on the $A\bar{B}$ task depends on the way the object is hidden fits well with this notion. Infants' understanding of a cup is global (they do not understand that hiding an object in a cup has different consequences from hiding an object behind a cup) and specific to their experience (a cup is a container, but an upside-down model house is not). Thus, Fischer's theory might provide a framework whereby action and perceptual differentiation can be integrated.

The third aspect of object concept that is controversial is its relation to mental representation. There is agreement that when symbols—particularly language—develop, representational thought has also developed. Beyond that, there is disagreement even about what abilities indicate that mental representation has developed. The existence of long-term memory over days or weeks at 3 months suggests to some researchers that infants must have representational abilities, but others argue that recognition does not require representation. The recent demonstration that infants as young as 7 months demonstrate understanding of concepts such as a face in different orientations, indicate to some that infants of that age must have mental representation, but others would disagree. The evidence of at least limited object permanence by 12 months also argues to some, but not others, that some representational thought must exist. Such a list of disagreements over the interpretation of data

suggests that the argument about mental representation may be merely a semantic one. Dismissing it with this label would seem to hide the fact that people's understanding of mental representation is extremely primitive.

Research Issues

The study of Piaget brings into focus one of the central methodological controversies in psychology. Most American psychologists, including those who have tested Piaget's theory, employ the experimental method, in which experimenters randomly assign subjects to experimental and control groups, then expose the groups to differing conditions (the independent variable) and measure whether those conditions differentially affected their performance on some relevant task or other measure (the dependent variable). Through this procedure they can ensure that any differences in the final measure (the dependent variable) are due to the experimental conditions. Executing a series of such carefully controlled experiments is an extremely slow, laborious process, as demonstrated by the slowness with which understanding of performance on object search tasks has progressed.

Piaget's approach was very different. He relied on careful observation of infants' naturally occurring behaviors and on informal experiments under relatively uncontrolled conditions. Opponents of the controlled experiment approach argue that only by approaches such as Piaget's can the richness of human experience be appreciated, and that controlled experiments lose sight of interesting phenomena because they reduce, eliminate, or equalize so many aspects of the situation. They would say, for example, that studying infants' ability to turn their heads when a bell rings is so unlike any natural behavior infants exhibit that such studies reveal little of what people want to know about infants. The opposite arguments can be summarized in one general statement: Without rigorous controls, research findings are suspect. Although psychologists always try to be unbiased and objective in their work, they all have pet beliefs and hypotheses that they would like to have supported, and those biases can work in subtle ways. Although it is still unclear whether experimenters' biases influence the outcomes of rigorously controlled experiments (see Barber & Silver, 1968a, 1968b; Rosenthal, 1968), it is clear that such biases can affect observers' judgments of infants' behaviors (Piaget's method). Any naturally occurring behavior can be interpreted in several ways, and if researchers seek behaviors to support a particular belief, they often favor the confirming interpretation and do not look for alternative interpretations. Wason (1960, 1968) demonstrated this experimentally by showing that adults generate one hypothesis and look to see whether subsequent evidence supports that hypothesis and not whether another hypothesis could equally well explain the data.

Piaget attempted to avoid this kind of bias in his observations precisely because he was such a careful scientist. His writings are full of considerations of alternative interpretations. Thus, although he clearly was looking for behaviors that signaled the onset of intention, mental representation, causality, and so forth, he did not accept his favored interpretation of a behavior until he had considered alternative interpretations that did not support his hypothesis. Piaget consistently chose to err on the conservative side until he was quite certain that no plausible alternative interpretations existed. It is a tribute both to Piaget's sensitive observations and to his sophisticated analysis that the behavioral sequences he delineated can also be found when better controlled, more rigorous methods are used.

The replication studies improved on Piaget's method in several ways. They selected larger, less biased samples of subjects, thereby ensuring that Piaget's findings were not specific to the three frequently studied children of a brilliant scientist but doting parent. The materials, surroundings, and procedures were controlled to minimize the influence the examiner might have on the babies, and they were the same for each child.

That these studies did confirm Piaget's naturalistic observations suggests that each method has a role in the development of science. Piaget identified many interesting behaviors that would probably not have been discovered by other methods. Because of the uncontrolled nature of his observations, however, his descriptions remained unconvincing until they had been replicated with more sophisticated methodology. Both approaches were necessary to convince others that the behavioral sequences do occur.

The next step in science is to test alternative interpretations to the originator's theory. Eventually such tests are bound to yield evidence that does not support the theory. Usually, a particular study or set of studies cannot invalidate a theory, in part because the road from theoretical claim to operational definition is never straightforward, as exemplified in the research testing Piaget's interpretation of performance on object search tasks. Research typically proceeds, as it has in this case, by disconfirming particular interpretations or aspects of a theory and by pointing up its inadequacies. In the case of the object search tasks research at the leading edge is focusing more and more on just what infants' concept of the object is, because Piaget's description of action–object sequences cannot predict what other aspects of the situation infants attend to. Eventually a point is reached at which enough new knowledge accumulates to enable someone to devise a new theory that will both incorporate all available evidence and explain how Piaget's theory is wrong.

Practical Uses of Knowledge of Infants' Cognitive Development

Now that we have reviewed what is and is not known about infants, it might be useful to discuss how such knowledge can be put to use. First and foremost, it can contribute to an increased appreciation of that marvelous creature, the infant. People who have frequent contact with infants can hardly help noticing the rapid changes in their physical development, but their equally rapid cognitive progress is not so easily observed. Piaget in particular identified many subtle behaviors (such as motor recognition and procedures for making interesting spectacles last) that might otherwise not be noticed. He also showed that some of babies' more obvious (and often irritating) behaviors, such as dropping and throwing, are really important modes of cognitive exploration. If adults (especially parents) recognize them as such, then they can enjoy such behaviors and spend their time devising related games rather than plotting the baby's immediate demise.

Second, psychologists are beginning to use the Uzgiris and Hunt scales to chart development of individual infants. Some psychologists believe that Piagetian norms may be better than infant intelligence tests such as the Bayley, because they believe that he has identified genuine, consistent dimensions of intellectual development rather than putting together diverse and unrelated tasks by which to assess development.

Third, the research described in this chapter may show how to maximize the environment for intellectual growth. Most parents in the United States and some other developed countries believe that the kind of environment babies live in affects their intellectual growth, and most would like to expose their children to environments that facilitate development. That's easier said than done, however. Parents often feel as if they are in a Kafkaesque world when they seek advice about the best way to foster their child's intellectual development— what toys to buy and what toys not to buy, what sorts of games and novel experiences to provide. They receive expensive advice from toymakers: "Buy our super-duper, deluxe mobile; it's only twice as expensive as any other mobile, but it's good for your child's development." They receive conflicting advice: "Read to your infant"; "don't bother reading to an infant." They receive refusals for advice: "We really don't know" (an honest answer, by the way). They receive advice from other parents: "My baby just loved this truck" (of course, when the beleaguered parents buy the twenty-dollar truck, their infant ignores it).

To understand how the cognitive environment affects infants it is important to understand both what the cognitive world of infants is like and what helps them to grow intellectually. The research in this chapter suggests that different kinds of stimulation are useful to babies at different ages. For example, the best toys for young babies are simple ones that provide visual, auditory, and tactual stimulation to facilitate the development of schemes such as things-to-be-shaken. For older babies toys should provide characteristics to be explored, problems to be solved, and objects or aspects of objects to be classified. This chapter has not dealt with the question of what level and variety of stimulation is necessary for adequate or for maximal cognitive development and whether parents need worry about whether they are providing an adequate environment. These issues are addressed in Chapter 13.

REFERENCES

Abravanel, E., Levan-Goldschmidt, E., & Stevenson, M.B. (1976). Action imitation: The early phase of infancy. *Child Development, 47,* 1032–1044.

Abravanel, E., & Sigafoos, A.D. (1984). Exploring the presence of imitation during early infancy. *Child Development, 55,* 381–392.

Anisfeld, M. (1979). Interpreting "imitative" responses in early infancy. *Science, 205,* 214–215.

Barber, T.X., & Silver, M.J. (1968a). Fact, fiction and the experimenter bias effect. *Psychological Bulletin Monographs, 70,* 1–29.

Barber, T.X., & Silver, M.J. (1968b). Pitfalls in data analysis and interpretation: A reply to Rosenthal. *Psychological Bulletin Monographs, 70,* 48–62.

Bates, E., Camaioni, L., & Volterra, V. (1975). The acquisition of performatives prior to speech. *Merrill-Palmer Quarterly, 21,* 205–226.

Bertenthal, B.I., & Fischer, K.W. (1978). The development of self-recognition in the infant. *Developmental Psychology, 14,* 44–50.

Bigelow, A.E. (1981). Object permanence for sound-producing objects: Parallels between blind and sighted infants. *Journal of Genetic Psychology, 139,* 11–26.

Bigelow, A.E. (1983). Development of the use of sound in the search behavior of infants. *Developmental Psychology, 29,* 317–321.

Bolton, N. (1972). *The psychology of thinking.* London: Methuen.

Bonvillian, J.D., Orlansky, M.D., & Novack, L.L. (1983). Developmental milestones: Sign language acquisition and motor development. *Child Development, 54,* 1435–1445.

Bonvillian, J.D., Orlansky, M.D., Novack, L.L., & Folven, R.J. (1983). Early sign language acquisition and cognitive development. In D. R. Rogers & J. A. Sloboda (Eds.), *Acquisition of symbolic skills* (pp. 207–214). New York: Plenum.

Bower, T.G.R. (1966). Heterogeneous summation in human infants. *Animal Behavior, 14,* 395–398.

Bower, T.G.R. (1971). The object in the world of the infant. *Scientific American, 222*, 30–38 (offprint No. 539).

Bower, T.G.R. (1976). Repetitive processes in child development. *Scientific American, 235*, 38–47.

Bower, T.G.R. (1982). *Development in infancy* (2nd ed.). San Francisco: Freeman.

Bower, T.G.R., Broughton, J.M., & Moore, M.K. (1971). The development of the object concept as manifested by changes in the tracking behavior of infants between 7 and 20 weeks of age. *Journal of Experimental Child Psychology, 11*, 182–193.

Bower, T.G.R. & Wishart, J.G. (1972). The effects of motor skill on object permanence. *Cognition, 1*, 165–172.

Bremner, J.G. (1978). Spatial errors made by infants: Inadequate spatial cues or evidence of egocentrism? *British Journal of Psychology, 69*, 77–84.

Bremner, J.G., & Bryant, P.E. (1977). Place vs. response as the basis of spatial errors made by young infants. *Journal of Experimental Child Psychology, 23*, 162–171.

Bretherton, I., Bates, E., McNew, S., Shore, C., Williamson, C., & Beeghly-Smith, M. (1981). Comprehension and production of symbols in infancy: An experimental study. *Developmental Psychology, 17*, 728–736.

Bruner, J.S. (1969). Eye, hand, and mind. In D. Elkind & J. H. Flavell (Eds.), *Studies in cognitive development: Essays in honor of Jean Piaget*. New York: Oxford University Press.

Bruner, J.S. (1973). Organization of early skilled action. *Child Development, 44*, 1–11.

Bullinger, A. (1977). Orientation de la tête du nouveau né en présence d'un stimulus visuel [Orientation of the head of the newborn in the presence of a visual stimulus]. *L'Année Psychologique, 77*, 357–364.

Butterworth, G. (1974). *The development of object permanence*. Unpublished doctoral dissertation, Oxford University, Oxford, England.

Butterworth, G. (1977). Object disappearance and error in Piaget's Stage IV tasks. *Journal of Experimental Child Psychology, 23*, 391–401.

Butterworth, G., Jarrett, N., & Hicks, L. (1982). Spatiotemporal identity in infancy: Perceptual competence or conceptual deficit? *Developmental Psychology, 18*, 435–449.

Caron, R.F., Caron, A.J., & Myers, R.S. (1982). Abstraction of invariant face expressions in infancy. *Child Development, 53*, 1008–1015.

Chevalier-Skolnikoff, S. (1977). A Piagetian model for describing and comparing socialization in monkey, ape, and human infants. In S. Chevalier-Skolnikoff & F.E. Poirier (Eds.), *Primate bio-social development: Biological, social, and ecological determinants* (pp. 159–187). New York: Garland.

Chevalier-Skolnikoff, S. (1979). Kids: Zoo research reveals remarkable similarities in the development of human and orangutan babies . . . and one very special difference. *Animal Kingdom, 82*, 11–18.

Chevalier-Skolnikoff, S. (1982). A cognitive analysis of facial behavior in Old World monkeys, apes, and human beings. In C.T. Snowdon, C.H. Brown, & M.R. Petersen (Eds.), *Primate communication*. Cambridge, England: Cambridge University Press.

Clark, D.E. (1981, May). *Object permanence development: A comparison between Piaget's schema theory and Moore's identity theory.* Paper presented at the meeting of the Jean Piaget Society, Philadelphia.

Cohen, J.S. (1981, May). *Neonatal imitation: A critical analysis of its implications for Piagetian theory.* Paper presented at the meeting of the Jean Piaget Society, Philadelphia.

Cohen, L.B., & Caputo, N. (1978, March). *Instructing infants to respond to perceptual categories.* Paper presented at the First International Conference on Infant Studies, Providence, RI.

Cohen, L.B., Gelber, E.R., & Lazar, M.A. (1971). Infant habituation and generalization to differing degrees of stimulus novelty. *Journal of Experimental Child Psychology, 11*, 379–389.

Cohen, L.B., & Strauss, M.S. (1979). Concept acquisition in the human infant. *Child Development, 50*, 419–424.

Cohen, L.B., & Younger, B.A. (1984). Infant perception of angular relations. *Infant Behavior and Development, 7*, 37–47.

Corman, H.H., & Escalona, S.K. (1969). Stages of sensorimotor development: A replication study. *Merrill-Palmer Quarterly, 15*, 351–360.

Cornell, E.H. (1975). Infants' visual attention to pattern arrangement and orientation. *Child Development, 46*, 229–232.

Corrigan, R. (1979). Cognitive correlates of language: Differential criteria yield differential results. *Child Development, 50*, 617–631.

Cummings, E.M., & Bjork, E.L. (1981a). The search behavior of 12 to 14 month-old infants on a five-choice invisible displacement hiding task. *Infant Behavior and Development, 4*, 47–60.

Cummings, E.M., & Bjork, E.L. (1981b). Search on a five choice invisible displacement hiding task: A rejoinder to Schuberth and Gratch. *Infant Behavior and Development, 4,* 65–67.

Cummings, E.M., & Bjork, E.L. (1983). Search behavior on multi-choice hiding tasks: Evidence for an objective conception of space in infancy. *International Journal of Behavioral Development, 6,* 71–87.

Decarie, T.G. (1965). *Intelligence and affectivity in early childhood.* New York: International Universities Press.

Dunst, C.J., Brooks, P.H., & Doxsey, P.A. (1982). Characteristics of hiding places and the transition to Stage IV performance in object permanence tasks. *Developmental Psychology, 18,* 671–681.

Elder, J., & Pederson, D. (1978). Preschool children's use of objects in symbolic play. *Child Development, 49,* 500–504.

Evans, W.F., & Gratch, G. (1972). The Stage IV error in Piaget's theory of object concept development: Difficulties in object conceptualization or spatial localization? *Child Development, 43,* 682–688.

Fagan, J.F., III (1977). An attention model of infant recognition. *Child Development, 48,* 345–359.

Fein, G. (1975). A transformational analysis of pretending. *Developmental Psychology, 11,* 291–296.

Fischer, K.W. (1980). A theory of cognitive development: The control and construction of hierarchies of skills. *Psychological Review, 87,* 477–531.

Freedman, D.A., Fox-Kolenda, B., Margileth, D.A., & Miller, D.H. (1969). The development of the use of sound as a guide to affective and cognitive behavior. *Child Development, 40,* 1099–1105.

Freeman, N.H., Lloyd, S., & Sinha, C.G. (1980). Infant search tasks reveal early concepts of containment and canonical usage of objects. *Cognition, 8,* 243–262.

Frye, D. (1980). Stages of development: The Stage IV error. *Infant Behavior and Development, 3,* 115–126.

Gratch, G. (1972). A study of the relative dominance of vision and touch in six-month-old infants. *Child Development, 43,* 615–623.

Harris, P.L. (1973). Perseverative errors in search by young children. *Child Development, 44,* 28–33.

Harris, P.L. (1974). Perseverative search at a visibly empty place by young children. *Journal of Experimental Child Psychology, 18,* 535–542.

Hershenson, M. (1971). Development of visual perceptual systems. In H. Moltz (Ed.), *The ontogeny of vertebrate behavior.* New York: Academic.

Hershenson, M., Kessen, W., & Munsinger, H. (1967). Pattern perception in the human newborn: A close look at some positive and negative results. In H. Wathen-Dunn (Ed.), *Models of the perceptuion of speech and visual form.* Cambridge, MA: MIT Press.

Husaim, J.S., & Cohen, L.B. (1981). Infant learning of ill-defined categories. *Merrill-Palmer Quarterly, 27,* 443–456.

Jackson, E., Campos, J., & Fischer, K.W. (1978). The question of the décalage between object permanence and person permanence. *Developmental Psychology, 14,* 1–10.

Jacobson, S.W. (1979). Matching behavior in the young infant. *Child Development, 50,* 425–430.

Kaye, K., & Marcus, J. (1978). Imitation over a series of trials without feedback: Age six months. *Infant Behavior and Development, 1,* 141–155.

Kaye, K., & Marcus, J. (1981). Infant imitation: The sensory-motor agenda. *Developmental Psychology, 17,* 258–265.

Kopp, C.B., & Shaperman, J. (1973). Cognitive development in the absence of object manipulation during infancy. *Developmental Psychology, 9,* 430.

Kramer, J.A., Hill, K.T., & Cohen, L.B. (1975). Infant's development of object permanence: A refined methodology and new evidence for Piaget's hypothesized ordinality. *Child Development, 46,* 149–155.

Landers, W.F. (1971). Effects of differential experience on infants' performance in a Piagetian Stage IV object concept task. *Developmental Psychology, 5,* 48–54.

LeCompte, G.K., & Gratch, G. (1972). Violation of a rule as a method of diagnosing infants' levels of object concept. *Child Development, 43,* 385–396.

Maratos, O. (1973, April). *The origin and development of imitation in the first six months of life.* Paper presented at the annual meeting of the British Psychological Society, Liverpool.

Martin, G.B., & Clark, R.D., III. (1982). Distress crying in neonates: Species and peer specificity. *Developmental Psychology, 18,* 3–9.

Masters, J.C. (1979). Interpreting imitative responses in early infancy *Science, 205,* 215.

McGurk, H. (1972). Infant discrimination of orientation. *Journal of Experimental Child Psychology, 14,* 151–164.

Meltzoff, A.N., & Moore, M.K. (1977). Imitation of facial and manual gestures by human neonates. *Science, 198,* 75–78.

Milewski, A.E. (1979). Visual discrimination and detection of configural invariance in 3-month infants. *Developmental Psychology, 15,* 357–363.

Miller, D., Cohen, L.B., & Hill, K.T. (1970). A methodological investigation of Piaget's theory of object concept development in the sensory-motor period. *Journal of Experimental Child Psychology, 9,* 59–85.

Moore, M.K., Borton, R., & Darby, B.L. (1978). Visual tracking in young infants: Evidence for object identity or object permanence? *Journal of Experimental Child Psychology, 25,* 183–198.

Moore, M.K., & Clark, D.E., (1979, April). *Piaget's Stage IV error: An identity theory interpretation.* Paper presented at the biennial meeting of the Society for Research in Child Development, Denver.

Papousek, H. (1967). Experimental studies of appetitional behavior in human newborns and infants. In H.W. Stevenson, E.H. Hess, & H.L. Rheingold (Eds.), *Early behavior: Comparative and developmental approaches.* New York: Wiley.

Parker, S.T. (1977). Piaget's sensorimotor series in an infant macaque: A model for comparing unstereotyped behavior and intelligence in human and nonhuman primates. In S. Chevalier-Skolnikoff & F.E. Poirier (Eds.), *Primate biosocial development: Biological, social, and ecological determinants* (pp. 43–112). New York: Garland.

Pawlby, S. (1977). Imitative interaction. In H.R. Schaffer (Ed.), *Studies in mother–infant interaction.* New York: Academic.

Piaget, J. (1954). *The construction of reality in children* (M. Cook, Trans.). New York: Basic Books. (Original work published 1937.)

Piaget, J. (1962). *Play, dreams and imitation in childhood* (C. Gattegno & F.M. Hodgson, Trans.). New York: Norton. (Original work published 1945.)

Piaget, J. (1963). *The origins of intelligence in children* (M. Cook, Trans.). New York: Norton. (Original work published 1936.)

Piaget, J. (1970). Piaget's theory. In Mussen, P.H. (Ed.), *Carmichael's manual of child psychology* (3rd ed., Vol. 1, pp. 703–732). New York: Wiley.

Premack, D. (1976). Language and intelligence in ape and man. *American Scientist, 64,* 674–683.

Ramsay, D.S., & Campos, J.J. (1975). Memory by the infant in an object notion task. *Developmental Psychology, 11,* 411–412.

Rosenthal, R. (1968). Experimenter expectancy and the reassuring nature of the null hypothesis decision procedure. *Psychological Bulletin Monographs, 70,* 30–47.

Ross, G.S. (1980). Categorization in 1- to 2-year-olds. *Developmental Psychology, 16,* 391–396.

Sameroff, A.J. (1971). Can conditioned responses be established in the newborn infant? *Developmental Psychology, 5,* 1–12.

Schuberth, R.E., & Gratch, G. (1981). Search on a five-choice invisible displacement hiding task: A reply to Cummings and Bjork. *Infant Behavior and Development, 4,* 61–64.

Schuberth, R.E., Werner, J.S., & Lipsitt, L.P. (1978). The Stage IV error in Piaget's theory of object concept development: A reconsideration of the spatial localization hypothesis. *Child Development, 49,* 744–748.

Seidenberg, M.S., & Petitto, L.A. (1979). Signing behavior in apes: A critical review. *Cognition, 7,* 177–215.

Smillie, D. (1980). *Evaluating Piaget's theory of the origin of imitation.* Paper presented at the Second International Conference on Infant Studies, New Haven, CT.

Starkey, D. (1981). The origins of concept formation: Object sorting and object preference in early infancy. *Child Development, 52,* 489–497.

Strauss, M.S. (1979). Abstraction of prototypical information by adults and 10 month old infants. *Journal of Experimental Psychology: Human Learning and Memory, 6,* 618–632.

Sugarman, S. (1981). The cognitive basis of classification in very young children: An analysis of object-ordering trends. *Child Development, 52,* 1172–1178.

Sugarman, S. (1982). Developmental change in early representational intelligence: Evidence from spatial classification strategies and related verbal expressions. *Cognitive Psychology, 14,* 410–449.

Terrace, H.S. (1979, November). How Nim Chimsky changed my mind. *Psychology Today,* pp. 65–76.

Trevarthen, C. (1978). Modes of perceiving and modes of acting. In H.L. Pick & E. Saltzman (Eds.), *Modes of perception and processing information.* New York: Erlbaum.

Ungerer, J.A., Zelazo, P.R., Kearsley, R.B., & O'Leary, K. (1981). Developmental changes in the representation of objects in symbolic play from 18 to 34 months of age. *Child Development, 52,* 186–195.

Uzgiris, I.C. (1972). Patterns of vocal and gestural imitation in infants. In F.J. Monks, W.H. Hartup, & J. DeWit (Eds.), *Determinants of behavioral development*, New York: Academic.

Uzgiris, I.C. (1973). Patterns of cognitive development in infancy. *Merrill-Palmer Quarterly, 19*, 181–204.

Uzgiris, I.C., & Benson, J. (1980, April). *Infants' use of sound in search for objects.* Paper presented at the Second International Conference on Infant Studies, New Haven, CT.

Uzgiris, I.C., & Hunt, J.McV. (1975). *Assessment in infancy.* Urbana, IL: University of Illinois Press.

Volterra, V., Bates, E., Benigni, L., Bretherton, I., & Camaioni, L. (1979). First words in language and action: A qualitative look. In E. Bates (Ed.), *The emergence of symbols: Cognition and communication in infancy.* New York: Academic.

Wason, P.C. (1960). On the failure to eliminate hypotheses in a conceptual task. *Quarterly Journal of Experimental Psychology, 12*, 129–140.

Wason, P.C. (1968). On the failure to eliminate hypotheses—A second look. In Wason, P.C. & Johnson-Laird, P.N. (Eds.), *Thinking and reasoning.* Baltimore: Penguin.

Watson, M.W. & Fischer, K.W. (1977). A developmental sequence of agent use in late infancy. *Child Development, 48*, 828–835.

Werner, H. & Kaplan, B. (1963). *Symbol formation.* New York: Wiley.

Willatts, P. (1984). Stages in the development of intentional search by young infants. *Developmental Psychology, 20*, 389–396.

Yando, R., Seitz, V., & Zigler, E. (1978). *Imitation: A developmental perspective.* Hillside, NJ: Erlbaum.

Younger, B.A. & Cohen, L.B. (1982). Infant perception of correlated attributes. *Infant Behavior and Development, 5*, 262.

EARLY COMMUNICATIVE AND LANGUAGE BEHAVIOR

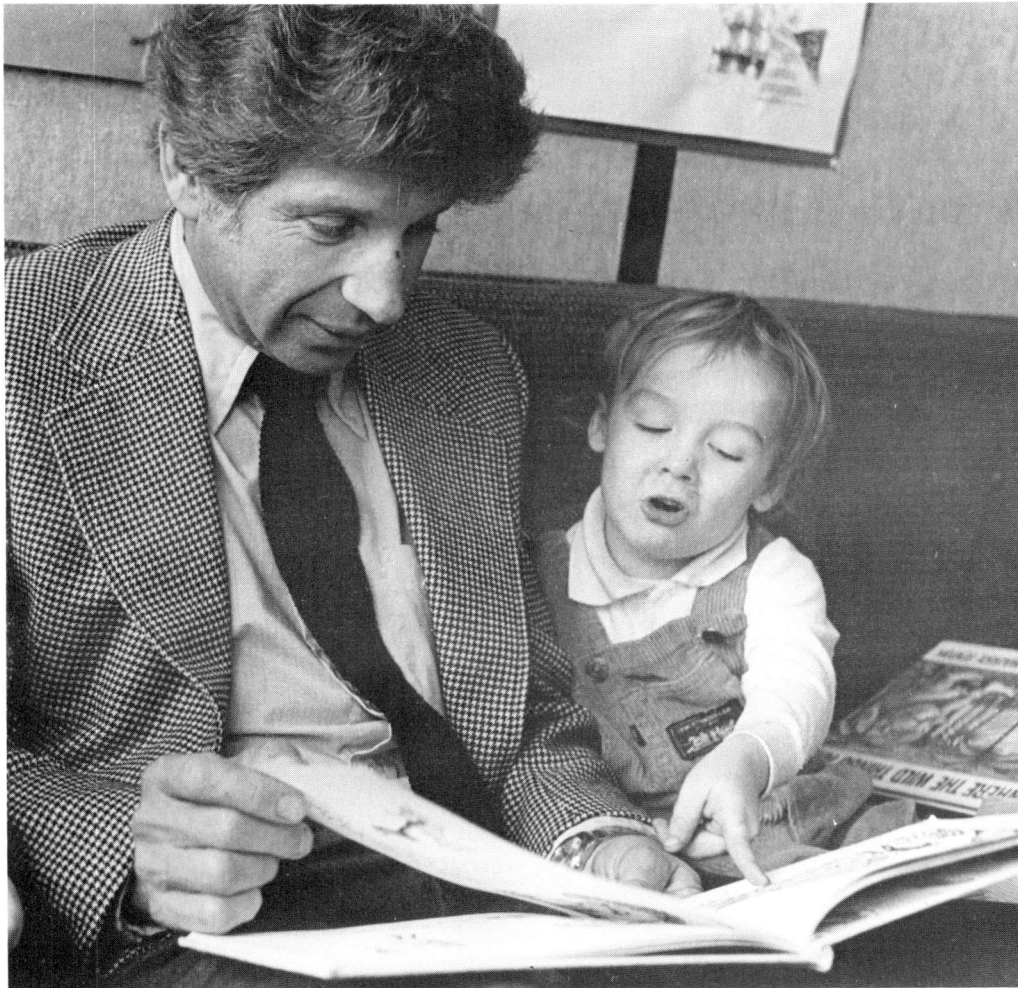

CHAPTER 11

INTRODUCTION AND OVERVIEW

Language development is a topic that has received a great deal of attention over the years but most descriptions of this development, with a few exceptions, were usually only catalogs of the types of sounds, words, sentences, and errors produced by children as they matured (Menyuk, 1971). Simple explanations were provided to account for development and errors. Over the past two decades researchers have attempted both to describe the developmental process more adequately and to explain it. These efforts have resulted in much more information about the details of language development from birth on. This information indicates that the infant is much more linguistically sophisticated than had previously been thought, and this, in turn, has led to many more questions about the behaviors observed in infants.

One of the most exciting developments that takes place during infancy is the child's acquisition of the community's language. Parents greet the production of first words with overt joy and often state, prior to its occurrence, that they wished the child would communicate with them. As we shall see, infants communicate long before the appearance of these words. Further, they learn a great deal about the structure and function of language during the so-called pre-word or babbling period. Many caregivers behave *as if* infants communicate during this period, and this may play a very important role in infants' acquisition of the language of the community. In some instances, the expected first words do not appear during infancy, because of known or suspected physiological causes. In these instances, language acquisition is either delayed or both delayed and different.

In this chapter we will discuss communicative behavior, the perception and production of aspects of language during infancy, and the effect of biological, environmental, and cognitive factors on early acquisition of language. Finally, we will indicate some of the vital unanswered questions about language acquisition during this period of development.

Before these topics are addressed, the general language acquisition accomplishments of the infancy period need to be discussed. The period has traditionally been divided into the prelinguistic and linguistic phases, which were held to be unrelated. The prelinguistic phase—babbling—was thought to end with a period of silence before the onset of the linguistic phase—the production of words (Jakobson, 1968). This view of complete discontinuity between behaviors before and after the use of words is no longer accepted, but the exact relations between the phases are still matters for research.

Language development in infancy can be divided into the cooing and babbling phase and the word and word combination phase. At around 2 years of age most children produce utterances that often are composed of at least two words. A few still produce one-word utterances (holophrases) and some produce lengthier utterances. Comprehension of language over this period cannot be so clearly defined. Studies have indicated that very young infants, 1 to 2 months of age, can discriminate among speech sounds. Observational data indicate that infants can comprehend a small set of words some months before they produce any recognizable words. Some experimental data indicate that infants 8 to 12 months of age can learn to associate objects with words or nonsense syllables if they are specifically taught to do so, and do associate very familiar objects with words at 12 months. Nevertheless, the extent of and the basis for recognition of the meaning of words during these early months is open to question. Babies of this age may also understand a few short sentences but they are probably using the concrete context to interpret the language they hear rather than understanding the language as such. This primitive understanding of short sentences and phrases precedes the ability to produce them.

In general it is thought that comprehension precedes production of both words and sentences, but little is known about the extent and nature of the production lag. There is some agreement that production does not faithfully follow the developmental progression of comprehension. That is, children do not always comprehend an aspect of language before they produce it. This means that the bases for the acquisition of comprehension and production may differ.

COMMUNICATIVE BEHAVIOR

Human Compared to Animal Communication

Many animal species, ranging from the social insects (bees, wasps, ants, and termites) to chimpanzees, have elaborate communication systems. These systems, while extremely complex and effective as communication devices, seem to be different in kind from human language (Fromkin & Rodman, 1974). The most important characteristics of human language that are not true of other communication systems are the following:

1. Creativity or generativity. Rearrangements of parts (sounds, words, and sentences) can create totally new messages. (Example: "The dog chased the cat" and "The cat chased the dog.")
2. Arbitrariness. Words stand for objects and events but are not the objects and events themselves (such as a cry of fear) or graphic representations of them (such as a picture of a tree).
3. Discreteness. Parts are separated into units such as sounds, words, and sentences.
4. Displacement. Language can be used to refer to things that are remote in time or space.

Vocalization during the earliest phases of infancy, when the child does not understand the meanings of words and sentences and does not produce words or sentences, is not generally considered to be language but, rather, communication. The only structured aspects of language present in early infancy are those related to speech sounds. As already mentioned, in their first months of life babies can discriminate among the speech sounds of others and can produce speech sounds themselves. These aspects will be discussed later in this chapter.

The Use of Sounds to Convey Intentions

Very young infants are sensitive to certain communications carried by the sequences of speech sounds. Spoken sentences carry information in addition to the meaning of the individual words and the meaning carried by the relations among the words in the sentence. Information concerning the age, sex, and even the identity of speakers is carried by the tone qualities of their voices. The patterns of rise and fall of pitch and loudness of sentences, which are called **intonation contours,** also carry meaning. Intonation contours differ as a function of the emotion of the speakers (such as anger or friendliness). They also tell whether speakers are making a statement, asking a question, or demanding something. In English statements (narration and assertion), speakers' voices rise gradually and then fall; in requests their voices rise gradually at the end of the sentence; and in commands there is a sharply rising and then falling contour. Speakers also emphasize certain parts of sentences by increasing loudness (called stress). These different kinds of information, all carried by the sequence of speech sounds in sentences but not by the words and relations among words, are called **prosodic** or **suprasegmental** cues.

The ability to use suprasegmental cues to convey needs and feelings and to understand communicative intent develops very early in infancy and remains fairly stable throughout life. It is not, however, a uniquely human characteristic. Other animals who use an auditory–oral system to communicate also use suprasegmental cues. The precise system of signals varies among species, depending on the auditory and vocal mechanisms available to the animal; for humans who can hear, the signal system is speech.

Humans also differ from other animals in the variability of the meaning attached to suprasegmental cues. In nonhuman species the meaning of these cues is typically ritualized and innately determined, but in humans the particular meanings given to a cue can vary across cultures, as can the meanings of many facial expressions and gestures. Despite these differences between humans and animals, the purpose of the communication system during infancy doesn't vary. It is used by all nonhuman animals and by young human infants primarily to convey needs and feelings and to socialize.

Development of Communication

Let us now turn to the development of prelinguistic communication in infants. Most of the information available about communicative behavior during this period is based on data obtained in western, urbanized, primarily middle-class cultures. Further, the infant–caregiver pairs studied are few in number and there are large differences among such pairs. Nevertheless, there are general trends in communication development as well as individual differences, and these general trends will form the focus of our discussion.

From birth infants engage in both cry and noncry vocalizations, although crying is the most frequent vocalization in the first 5 or 6 months. In general, vocalizations are initially only expressions of infants' physiological state, that is, comfort or discomfort. Little control of air flow can be observed. At about 6 to 8 weeks, both cries and noncries begin to take on the structure of human speech. This is the result of the infant's achievement of much greater control of the expenditure of air and movement of parts of the vocal mechanism during vocalizations (Truby, Bosma, & Lind, 1965). Phonation, or sound making, is superimposed on the infant's normal respiratory cycle and one phonation is much longer than one normal respiration (Nakazima, 1962). By about 3 months of age, patterned vocalizations that are vowel-like (ah, ee, and so forth) are produced.

At about the same time, so-called pseudo-conversations between caregiver and infant have been observed (Bateson, 1969). The adult vocalizes, waits for a vocal response from the infant, and then vocalizes again, either in reply to the infant's vocalization or to elicit a response if one is not forthcoming (see Figure 11–1). Although imitation of vocalization and attempts to elicit responses are primarily caregiver behaviors in early conversations, infants occasionally have been observed to attempt to elicit a vocal response to their vocalization if their caregivers do not respond. In urban groups in western cultures, these vocal exchanges are a very frequent occurrence in the interactions between 3-month-old infants and their caregivers, regardless of the socioeconomic status of the **dyad** or mother–infant pair (Lewis & Freedle, 1972). These behaviors have been called "conversational turn-taking."

Sensitivity to cues that mark whose turn it is in a conversation and prompt participation once the cues are given are presumably evidence of mature communicative behavior. Evidence of this behavior appears very early in life.

Conversational turn-taking appears to begin when the infant indicates readiness by the nature of the vocalizations produced and by being quietly alert for longer periods of time. Caregivers appear to be cued by the infant's behaviors to engage them in vocal–social interactions. Thus, both readiness on the part of the infant and caregiver sensitivity to readiness cues contribute to the establishment of communicative interaction at this early period in the child's life.

In addition to taking turns—which, after all, fulfills a social obligation—infants communicate needs and feelings by vocalization, facial expression, and gesture. Crying is one such means of communication, but it is not the only one. Infants modify the intonation contour of their babbles in a manner that is quite similar to the one used by adults. In a study of the vocalizations of infants in American-English and Japanese-speaking environments, Nakazima (1962) found that both groups of infants start to imitate sentence intonation contours (rising or falling patterns) in their babbled utterances at about 6 to 8 months of life. A little later their babbled utterances contain stressed and unstressed syllables. Tonkova-Yampolskaya (1969) found that different adult-like patterns of intonation developed at different times over the first 2 years of life among infants in a Russian-speaking environment. The contours described earlier that are typical of statements appeared during the second month; those of requests, in the seventh month; those of commands, in the tenth month; and those of questions, at the beginning of the second year.

These data are corroborated by data on perception of contours. Infants discriminate between utterances with rising contours and those with falling contours and they respond differently to the emotional qualities of voice alone (that is, without visual cues). Thus, researchers have concluded that the use and knowledge of the meaning of different intonation contours is not only a very early language acquisition but precedes knowledge of any other aspect of language (Kaplan & Kaplan, 1970). The research on turn-taking in conversation and use of suprasegmental features to convey intent and emotion indicates that these basic principles of communicative interaction appear to be well established during the first

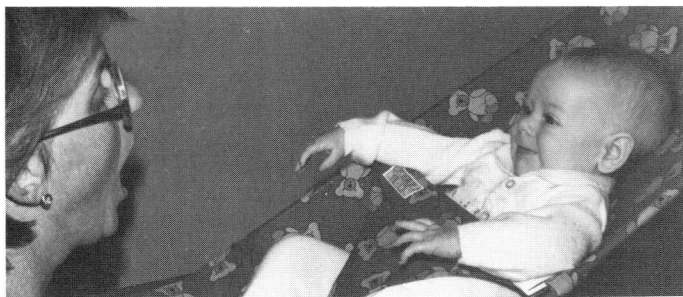

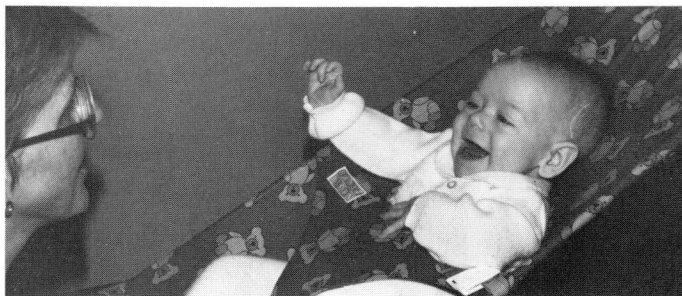

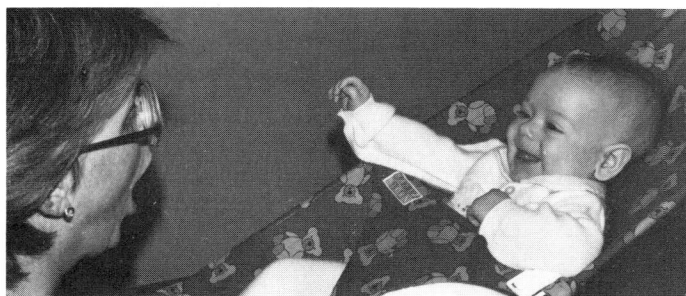

FIGURE 11–1. A pseudo-conversation. The adult says a word and waits. The infant then responds and the adult says the same or another word.

year of life. During the first year, the infant shows behavior that indicates that knowledge of other aspects of language, as compared to comprehension of words, is being acquired as well.

In the post-babbling period, some developmental changes occur in both turn-taking behavior and the use of suprasegmental features. A longitudinal study of conversational turn-taking in four mother–toddler dyads was carried out by Donahue (1978). The toddlers ranged in age from 12 to 19 months at the beginning of the study and were observed at biweekly intervals for 8 months. The principal findings of the study were that patterns of turn-taking behavior change over time and be-

come almost adult-like during the period. The infant develops from merely taking a turn to engaging in true conversation.

Recall that early turn-taking behavior consisted primarily of responding to vocalization with vocalization. In the transition from this behavior to communicative exchanges, Donahue's study showed that particular strategies were used to indicate that a turn was being taken. These went beyond mere vocalization but were different for the girls studied as compared to the boys. The two girls took a turn by imitating the intonational contour of the mother's utterances. The two boys responded with a set question phrase ("wuzzis" or "wuzzat"). Still later in the transition period the girls responded by using intonational contours that contrasted with those of the mothers' utterances (falling to rising or rising to falling), whereas the boys provided acknowledgments ("oh!" "uh huh"). These latter behaviors gave the impression that real understanding was taking place but the behaviors were, in fact, random. The final period was marked by appropriate responses to the content of the mother's utterances. These systematic changes in conversational behavior have led some researchers to conclude that the primary impetus to and basis for further language development stems from interactions between caregiver and infant. However, it is not clear how interaction alone can lead to acquisition of knowledge of language structures since these interactions are not tutorial. Mothers seem to accept whatever the infant provides. What is remarkable is that from a very early age (3 months) infants appear to understand that taking a turn is necessary.

FROM PRELANGUAGE TO LANGUAGE BEHAVIOR

Towards the end of the first year of life, babbling decreases and word-like approximations are more frequently produced. After babbling decreases, a large proportion of the utterances produced are recognizable words or recognizable words in stereotyped or babbled utterances (Branigan, 1976). The different intonational contours used with babbled utterances (assertion, narration, command, and request contours) are now used with words and phrases (Menyuk & Bernholtz, 1969). Thus, there is continuity in development in that strategies developed earlier to convey needs and feelings (gesture, facial expression, and suprasegmental features) continue to be used in the same form during the post-babbling or real word production phase. Turn-taking in communicative interaction is also continuous behavior. In addition, however, there are new developments. Needs and feelings are now specified by references to the particular objects and actions wanted or rejected or liked, because recognizable words and phrases are now being used. Conversational turn-taking is no longer simply participation in an exchange by any vocal response but is a response appropriate to the nonlinguistic context and the content of the utterance heard. In summary, the general purpose of communication and some of the means by which communicative intent is conveyed remain unaltered from the purpose and means established during the very early months of life. It is the content of utterances produced and understood that changes from phase one to phase two in infancy. The infant's ability to understand and produce words and phrases in the language of the community is the basis of the change. These developments will be traced in the next two sections.

Speech Sound Discrimination

The ability to produce speech-like sounds is a function of the human vocal mechanism. Researchers concluded that efforts to teach chimpanzees to speak were doomed to failure not simply because of possible intellectual limitations on syntax acquisition, but also because their vocal mechanisms do not permit the production of speech (Lieberman, 1974). Recent studies of infant speech sound discrimination have raised the question of whether the infant has a species-specific sensitivity to certain sound differences that no other species has. These sound differences make up the features of speech.

A pioneering study using synthetic speech (speech generated by a computer) found that 1- and 4-month-old infants discriminated between speech sounds in an adult-like manner (Eimas, Siqueland, Jusczyk, & Vigorito, 1971). The stimuli used were speech sounds that ranged in a continuum of gradual change from an *unvoiced stop* and vowel (/pa/) to a *voiced stop* and vowel (/ba/). The distinction between /pa/ and /ba/ in terms of sound is the voicing onset time (VOT) of the vowel that follows the burst of the stop consonant. Adults given stimuli that range across a set of VOTs categorize stimuli at one end of the range as /pa/ and at the other end as /ba/ but do not notice sound differences of stimuli that vary in VOT within the range. In like fashion, infants conditioned to suck when presented with a stimulus at one end of the range and habituated to the sound, increase sucking rate only when a second stimulus from the other range is presented and not

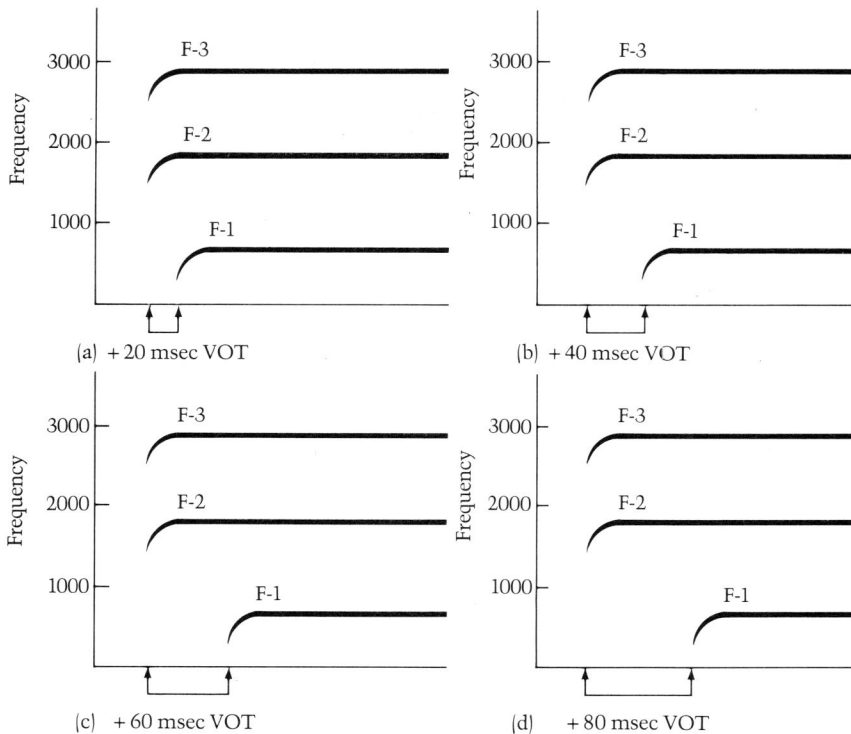

FIGURE 11–2. A visual representation of auditory speech stimuli. The vertical axis represents frequency of sound waves (pitch) and the horizontal axis represents time. As a consonant is uttered, sound is produced in a series of waves, called formants, represented in these figures by thick black lines. The relative time of onset of the first two formants (F-1 and F-2) distinguish between the /b/ and /p/ sounds and is called voice onset time (VOT). (a) If the formants start fewer than 25 msec after the burst (the VOT in the figure is 20 msec), the consonant is voiced and is heard as /b/. (b) If the formants start more than 25 msec after the burst (the VOT in the figure is 40 msec), an unvoiced consonant, /p/, is heard. (c) and (d) Discrimination of speech sounds is categorical, because all differences in VOT within a speech sound category are heard as the same speech sound. Thus, the stimuli in (c) and (d) are both perceived as /p/. Their VOTs (60 msec and 80 msec, respectively) are both greater than 25 msec, the cutoff between /b/ and /p/.

Notice that the difference between the VOTs in parts (c) and (d) (60 and 80) is physically the same as the difference between the VOTs in parts (a) and (b) (20 and 40). Thus, although the physical difference between the two stimuli in (c) and (d) is exactly the same as that between (a) and (b), humans (adults and babies) can hear a difference between (a) and (b) but not between (c) and (d).

when the sound stimulus comes from the same range, even though it is acoustically different from the first. Figure 11-2 shows two stimuli that are differentiated by both infants and adults and two stimuli that infants and adults do not discriminate. Because this behavior is observed in infants at an age when little learning of the phonological or speech sound categories of any language can have occurred, it has been suggested that there are detectors in the human auditory system that are particularly sensitive to only those acoustic differences that mark speech sound differences in any language. This is analogous to findings concerning color perception (see Chapter 9).

Speech sounds vary from each other in a number of acoustic dimensions called distinctive features (Jakobson, Fant, & Halle, 1963). For example, some sounds are consonants and others vowels. Some consonants are nasal (such as m and n) and others are oral (s, t); some are continuants (such as s and sh) and others are stops (p, t, k). These features are determined by particular articulatory movements and produce different acoustic consequences. Some sounds vary from each other in terms of one feature: /p/ is an unvoiced sound and /b/ a voiced sound; /b/ is nonnasal and /m/ is nasal. Some vary in several features: /t/ is unvoiced, noncontinuant, and coronal (made with the tongue tip touching the roof of the mouth), /r/ is voiced, continuant, and noncoronal. Thus, some sounds differ from each other more markedly than others; in addition, some features are presumably more perceptually salient than others because they are more easily detected by the human auditory system. For example, the presence or absence of nasality is easy to detect. Some types of feature distinctions are found in all languages and some in only a subset of languages. For example, Spanish and related languages make voicing distinctions that are not made in English.

Since the initial study of infant speech discrimination in the early 1970s, many studies have examined a variety of speech sound contrasts and have used different response measures to test discrimination. Further discussions of speech sound discrimination can be found in, for example, Yeni-Komshian, Kavanagh, and Ferguson (1980) and Eimas and Miller (1981). The initial study used the haptic sucking response. Cardiac rate change and conditioned head-turning have also been used. In all studies the infant's notice of a change in stimulus is being measured but different methods of determining discrimination apparently yield somewhat different results. Further, it was thought that any speech sound feature contrast that could be found in any human language would be discriminable by infants at a very early age..This would support the notion that there are detectors in the human auditory system that are sensitive to any potential speech sound differences, although not all such speech sound differences can be found in every language. This does not appear to be the case. Certain contrasts are observed before others, an indication that a developmental sequence exists (Eilers, Wilson, & Moore, 1977), and that particular language experience appears to affect the infant's ability to discriminate among speech sounds, even at two months of age (Streeter, 1976). The latter findings challenge the notion that all speech sound differences can be equally discriminated at the same developmental age. Consequently, the notion of innate speech sound feature detectors becomes somewhat questionable, although not entirely. There may be some innate speech sound feature detectors but clearly there are not detectors for all possible features, and these so-called detectors may not be limited to speech sound differences but may detect other classes of sound differences as well. What innate and noninnate feature detectors exist is still an open question because all of the possible contrasts have not been examined with infants who come from a variety of linguistic communities.

Speech Sound Production

What is the relation between early speech sound discrimination and later perception of speech sounds? What is the relation between speech sound discrimination and babbling? At one time researchers thought that infants babbled all possible human sounds randomly throughout the babbling period. Research has now revealed that babies begin to babble some speech sounds earlier than others, and there is evidence that the same developmental sequence in production of sounds is found in children of differing language communities.

The actual content of babbled utterances is difficult to determine. In addition to listening to and coding these utterances into phonetic symbols (such as /pa/ and /ba/), researchers have carried out spectrographic analyses of samples of utterances. Spectrograms provide a graph of a vocalization that can then be analyzed in terms of whether or not particular features of sound formation are present. Examples of the kinds of information spectrograms can provide were given in Figure 11–1 where the between-category characteristics of two speech sounds (+voice /ba/ and −voice /pa/) were shown.

There is a great deal of argument about the validity of both human and spectrographic analysis of speech sounds. Spectrograms can provide more objective information about the speech sound content of an utterance than can the ear of a human coder, because human coders tend to hear their own native speech sound categories when an infant vocalizes regardless of the actual content of the vocalization. It is also sometimes difficult to see characteristics of speech sounds in the spectrograms of infant vocalizations. Researchers often use both techniques and see how each relates to the other.

The pioneering work of Irwin (1947), using phonetic coding of infant utterances, indicated that the infant did not produce all possible sounds in languages with the same relative frequency throughout the babbling period. Irwin found, for example, that consonantal speech sounds that were made with the lips (/p/, /b/, /m/) occurred with much greater frequency at the beginning of the babbling period than did sounds that were made with the tongue tip (/d/, /n/). This difference in relative frequency of production of certain sounds at the beginning of the babbling phase was also observed with stop and nasal sounds (/b/, and /m/), with /m/ occurring more frequently. The proportional representation of different sounds changes over the babbing period so that the different sounds produced accurately reflect their actual frequency of occurrence in the language toward the end of the babbling phase. It has been suggested that these shifts reflect the infant's increasingly greater control of the articulators (Menyuk, 1972) because the shifts seem to reflect differences in ease of articulation of various sounds. Sounds that are easiest to ar-

ticulate are produced with much greater frequency at the beginning of the babbling phase, more difficult sounds begin to occur with increased frequency toward the middle, and the still more difficult ones toward the end. Even at the end not all the sounds of the language occur in babblings, and the missing sounds require very subtle adjustments of the articulators.

It has been hypothesized that because the sequence of speech sound production appears to be a reflection of increasing control of the vocal mechanism and because the general sequence of motor development is a universal development over this period, similarities in the pattern of sounds babbled should be observed in children acquiring different languages. Such a cross-linguistic similarity was found in a study that employed spectrographic analysis to compare the vocalizations of the infants in a Japanese-speaking and an American-English-speaking environment (Nakazima, 1972). Clearly, until data has been collected from many comparative studies no conclusions can be reached about universality in the sequence of babbling. It may be that acquisition of a particular language affects the sequence of sounds babbled (as was the case for some instances of early speech sound discrimination), or that the sequences may be universal, or that such effects do not occur. If the latter is the case, then it might be concluded that the discrimination of speech sounds and the production of speech sounds are not intimately related during the babbling period. Such conclusions must await more data collected in a variety of linguistic settings.

Some fairly sizable studies of infant vocalizations in American-English speaking environments, which have included both spectrographic analysis and phonetic coding, have been carried out recently. One study (Oller, 1978) lists the following changes and the approximate ages at which they occur:

1. Phonation (0–1 month). Nonsyllabic and primarily vocalic.
2. Cooing (2–3 months). Nonsyllabic, partially repetitive, vowel and velar consonant (/g/) productions.
3. Expansion (4–6 months). A variety of vocalizations including vowel-like ele-

ments; raspberries, squealing, growling, yelling, ingressive–egressive sequences, and marginal babbling ("shaky or slow transitions between vowel and consonant").

4. Canonical (7–10 months). Syllabification and reduplication of the same consonant and vowel (/ba/ /ba/ /ba/).
5. Variegated babbling (11–12 months). Variation in consonant and vowel (/babi/, /bada/).

Relation Between Discrimination and Production

Recall that at age 1 month, and more robustly at 4 months, infants discriminate between a number of speech sound contrasts. Not until approximately 6 or 7 months do children reproduce some of the speech contrasts they were able to distinguish much earlier. This fact supports the notion that speech sound perception and speech sound production follow different developmental courses and that these courses are based on differing kinds of capacities. Another group of studies supports the notion of the independence of perception and production (separation between these developments) during this early phase. These studies use delayed auditory feedback. This technique feeds back through earphones, with some delay, the sounds that have just been produced by the speaker. The speaker who is talking hears only what has been said some milliseconds previously. With older children and adults, delayed feedback results in prolongations and repetitions (stuttering) in speech, presumably because immediate auditory feedback is used to monitor on-going speech. When this feedback is out of phase, production is disrupted. This technique appears to have no effect on infants' cry vocalizations except that they stop crying to listen. Increases in phonation time have been observed between the ages of 1 year 9 months and 2 years 2 months. Disruption in production has not been observed until the ages of 2 years 4 months to 2 years 11 months. These data may indicate a gradual convergence of the two processes, perception and production of speech, when words are recognized and produced. (These studies are summarized in Menyuk, 1971).

Perception and Production of Language

Toward the end of the babbling phase, utterances begin to take on the shape of words. Long babbled utterances are reduced to one syllable or reduplicated syllable length. These syllables sound like words because they contain well-formed consonant–vowel sequences. This change occurs at about 1 year. Sometime before this, at about 8 months, the infant has been observed to recognize a small repertoire of words as indicated by head-turning toward or reaching for an object or person named (Murai, 1960). Infants at 13 months of age give evidence of associating a small set of objects with their names (Thomas, Campos, Shucard, Ramsay, & Shucard, 1981). Thus, several months before the infant produces word-like approximations a few words are recognized. There have been few studies of infants' comprehension of words during the latter months of the first year of life, so the average number and types of words recognized is unknown. The infant must be developing understanding of some vocabulary because at about 12 months recognizable words begin to be produced, and some of them are used appropriately to express needs and feelings about particular objects and actions. It is logical to conclude that when the child produces these words, this production is based on the ability to relate speech sound sequences heard and understood to objects and events seen. After the production of words and their use referentially comes the next phase of language development: understanding how words are combined to express relations between objects and actions and attributes of objects and actions.

WHAT MUST BE LEARNED
The functions of language are (1) to express needs and feelings and (2) to describe relations among objects and actions and attributes of both objects (for example, *red* or *funny* hat) and actions (for example, ran *fast* or *into* the house). To develop language, the infant must acquire knowledge of the structural properties of language needed to carry out the above two functions. Because language is composed of several nested structures, the infant must learn to segment a stream of speech into several categories. These categories can then be filled or

combined in different ways to convey different meanings. A basic unit is the sentence and it is composed of phrases. The sentence "The dog chased the cat" is composed of two phrases: the subject phrase (the dog) and the predicate phrase (chased the cat). A different subject and predicate would convey a different meaning as in the sentence "The cat saw the bird." Each sentence and phrase is composed of **morphemes,** the grammatical and meaningful segments of words. The sentence "The dog chased the cat" consists of six (not five) such segments: the five words and the past-tense segment "ed" of "chase." The "ed" conveys the time at which the action took place. Grammatical as well as meaningful morphemes can also be replaced as "The dog chases the cat" or "A dog chased the cat" or "The dogs chased the cats," and the meaning changes each time. Relations can be negated, as in "The dog didn't chase the cat"; questioned as in "Did the dog chase the cat?"; or action commanded as in "Chase that cat!" Morphemes themselves are composed of speech sounds. Changing a single segment in a morpheme can change its meaning as in "boy" versus "toy," "pop" versus "pot," and "big" versus "bag."

During the language acquisition process, children learn the variety of ways in which their language allows morphemes, phrases, and sentences to be formed. This is termed acquisition of knowledge of the rules of language. There are morpho-phonological rules that govern how sounds are put together to create morphemes and semantactic rules that govern how words are put together to create sentences. As the child matures, knowledge of the rules not only grows but also changes. For example, at one period the child may have no rule for making plurals and may say "foot" for one or more feet. Later, plural is marked by generalizing a rule and more than one foot is "foots." Still later the generalization changes and the word may be expressed as "feets" and finally as "feet." Similar changes occur in forming sentence types. To express negation initially the child says "no" then "not" ("no bed" "not go"). Later the negative morpheme is inserted in a sentence ("he no can go") and finally the rules for producing negative sentences in English are applied ("He can't go"). The change is from no rule to express a relational meaning to some rule or rules and finally to the appropriate rule for the language.

WHAT IS PRODUCED IN UTTERANCES

During the early stages of this early period of language development, the child produces utterances that have been labeled "holophrastic." This implies that the single words produced by the child ("mommy," "shoe," "sit") convey more than merely the name of an object or action. As we have seen, children convey different intentions by the use of different intonational contours with the same word. Thus they can request, demand, or state the presence of an object or event using different intonational contours with a single word (Menyuk & Bernholtz, 1969). In addition, children presumably convey a relation among attributes, objects, and events by use of situational context, gesture, and facial expression. Greenfield and Smith (1976) carried out a detailed study of the utterances of two children over a period of several months. During this time the children produced primarily one-word utterances. The technique used to code these utterances was to have two adults (the mother and an observer) indicate the communicative intent of the utterance, that is, the relation intended. When there was agreement, an utterance was coded as expressing a particular relation. On the basis of such clear cases the investigators concluded that after a short initial period in which words are used in imitative routines, naming games, and calls to others (for example, "Mama," called vocatives), all holophrastic utterances express a two-part relation. Although only one part of the relation is expressed, the second part is intended. For example, when the infant says "dirty" and points to an object, the intention is to state that the object is dirty. The relations expressed change with time, and the experimenters suggest that these changes are due to cognitive maturation. The cognitive maturations cited to account for the change are perceptual in nature: observation of action of objects first and then of the state of objects, and the process of decentering or taking the perspective of another person. These cognitive maturations are reflected in the child's expressing the relation action of object before state of object and talking about self as actor before others as actors. The findings of the above study have suggested to some that in addition to expressing needs and feelings by the use of intonation and gesture with a single word, young children can convey semantic relations with single words. A lot of rich interpretation is needed to come to this conclusion.

WHAT IS COMPREHENDED IN UTTERANCES

There is some real evidence that children understand some two-part relations when they themselves produce only holophrases. Sachs and Truswell (1976) studied the ability of holophrastic children to carry out actions that describe a relation (for example, "Kiss Teddy."). It was found that a significant proportion of the children's responses were related to the utterances (70%) and that 75% of the related responses were correct. The older children (1 year 8 months to 2 years) in the group responded more frequently and more correctly than did the younger children.

Children appear to comprehend two-part relations while producing only one word. Additional support for the claim that linguistic relational knowledge is available to the holophrastic child is provided by two studies. One examined perception and the other production during the transition period between single-word and two-word utterances. Branigan (1976) studied successive one-word utterances, those in which children utter two seemingly related words but with a large pause between the two words. Branigan found that such utterances had the intonation contour of a two-word utterance. There was no falling contour on the first word but, rather, a continuation rise. This indicates that the children intended to relate the two words. Horgan (1976) found that during this period children could successfully identify pictures that describe a three-part relation of subject, action, and object. All of these findings indicate that knowledge of semantic relations (how two words are put together to describe relations among objects, actions, and their attributes) gradually builds up over the so-called holophrastic period. Babies in this phase apparently cannot produce a combination of words, so they initially produce one word or an unsegmented phrase and then later two single words with large pauses between the words during the transition period. Never-

theless, babies indicate comprehension of some two-part relations during the one-word period and some three-part relations during the transition period.

The Sachs and Truswell (1976) and Horgan (1976) studies also provide some evidence that children not only acquire knowledge of semantic relations but also have some basic syntactic knowledge during the holophrastic and transitional stages. This is knowledge of such fundamental word-order rules in the English language as: action precedes the object (kiss Teddy), subject precedes the action (Teddy kiss), the attribute comes before the noun (dirty baby), and the actor or subject precedes action which precedes object (daddy kiss Teddy). Unless these ordering rules were understood, incorrect responses would occur such as Teddy kissing daddy in response to "daddy kiss Teddy." At 2 years of age many children produce two-word utterances that describe a range of semantic relations, and some produce utterances with three or more words in which the basic structure of English sentences (actor + action + object) is expressed. A few children at this age produce what are called embedded sentences such as "I want to go" (Limber, 1973). This sentence contains two relations: I want and I go. In addition, the basic sentence types of declaration, negation, question, and imperative are produced with two-word and lengthier utterances. Nevertheless, there are still many structural gaps in the utterances produced. Table 11–1 gives examples of the relations and sentence types produced at the two- and three-word sentence stages. The list shows that three-word utterances represent combinations of relations produced during the two-word phase. Figure 11–3 demonstrates the variety of different relations a single two-word utterance can express. It also shows that adults and older children often have to use the context of the utterance to guess which of these relations a toddler wishes to express.

Word Acquisition

In addition to acquisition of knowledge of how some basic semantic and syntactic relations are expressed in sentences, there is very rapid acquisition of the meaning of words as such

TABLE 11–1
Early Relations and Sentence Types Produced in Two- and Three-Word Utterances

Two Words		Three Words	
Agent + action	Baby run.	Agent + action + present participle	Baby running.
Action + object	Push truck.[a]		
Agent + object	Daddy truck.	Agent + action + object	Mommy push truck.[a]
Possessor + possessed	Daddy hat.		Daddy drive truck.[a]
Demonstrative + noun	That fish.	Demonstrative + possessor + possessed	That daddy hat.
Attributive + noun	Dirty baby.	Location + attributive + object	Here dirty baby.
Location + object	Here ball.	Location + copula + object	Here be ball.
Action + location	Put chair.[a]	Action + object + location	Put sweater chair.[a]
Negation	No/t wash, no/t fish.	Negation	Me no wash, that no fish.
Question	Where daddy?	Question	Where daddy go?

[a]These utterances are either comments on actions observed or commands.

during this period of development. Several aspects of early acquisition of word meaning have been studied. The first words produced appear to be limited to expression of needs and feelings and socialization. For example, action words that can carry out these functions, such as "want," "give," "no," "like," "up," "see," are acquired early. Nelson (1973) found that most of the first 50 words produced by a group of children could be categorized as specific nominals (mamma, pappa), general nominals (toy, doggie), actions (go, up), attributes (more, all gone) and social or affective words (O.K., please; see Figure 11–4).

The meanings of nominals appear to change over time. A number of researchers have found that word usage or production is overgeneralized at first. It has been hypothesized (Clark, 1973) that one word is initially applied to several objects that share certain perceptual features. The word "doggie," therefore, may be applied to all objects that share the features + animal + four-legged (cow, horse, cat.)[1] Thus, some words are first applied in a very general way. As additional features are distinguished in the meanings of words, new words are used to mark this differentiation. This early behavior does not mean that the infant perceives dogs, horses, cows, and cats as having the same observable features; it

merely means that early on only the most salient or general features are associated with the meanings of words. Later the infant appears to observe that different words are used to mark differences that exist between members of a class. Both horse and dog may then be used to mark a difference in size of animal, and cat and dog used to mark a difference in the sound made by an animal. The process is described by Clark as being one of feature addition in the following way: + animal + 4-legged = dog, + animal + 4-legged + large = horse, + animal + 4-legged + meow = cat.

The acquisition of word meaning in production does not appear, however, to be simply a matter of observing additional features that should be associated with a word. Gruendel (1977) video-taped the communicative interaction of two children and their mothers over the age period of approximately 1 to 2 years. Use of words during this period displayed the following developmental progression. Overextension was observed infrequently at first but reached a peak at about 18 months when both children had about 50 words. Specific references were used before class referents (for example, "cup" referred to a specific cup before it was used to denote all cups) and overextension occurred first on the basis of function of referents (for example, "hat" for a Frisbee that was put on the head) and then on the basis of form (shape) of referents. Thus, underextensions occurred before overextensions and the type of features

---
[1] + is used to mark features.

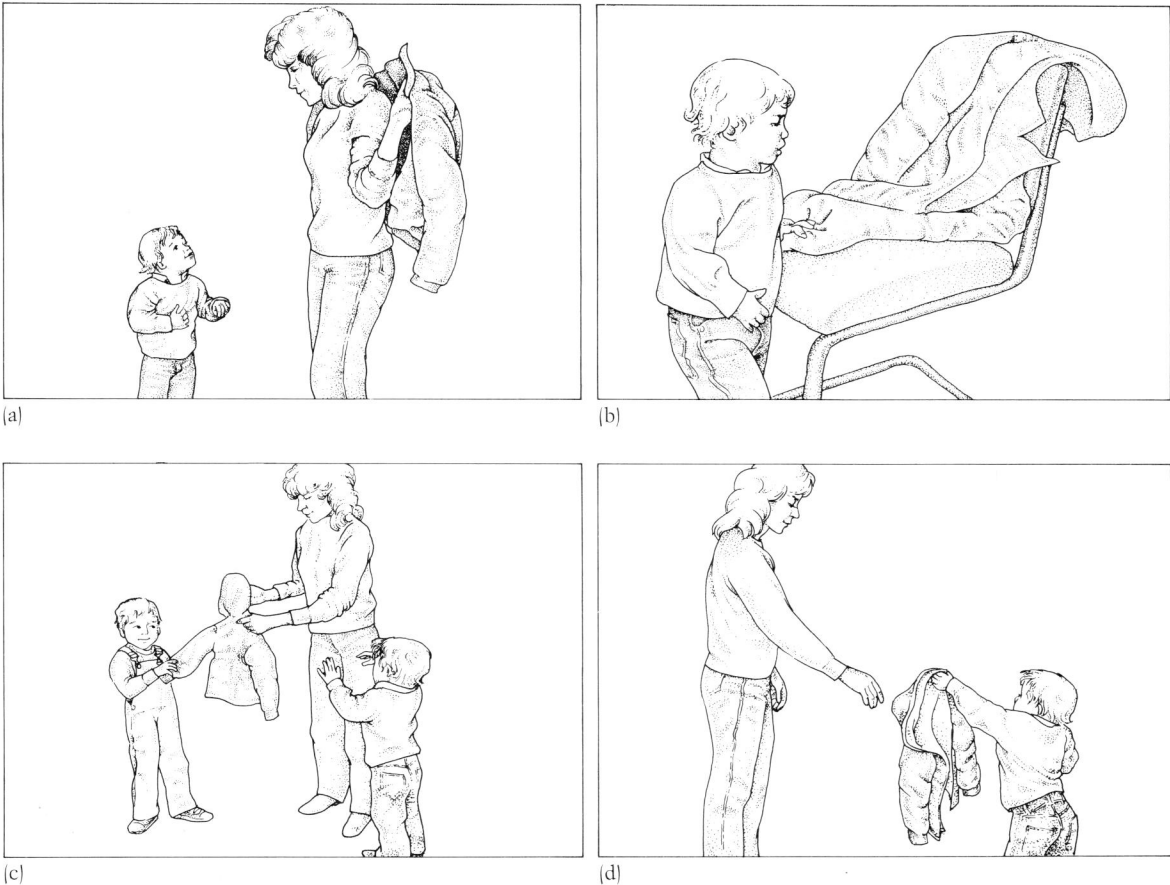

FIGURE 11–3. When a toddler says "Mommy coat," the utterance may have any of a number of meanings. (a) If this is what the child means, the two-word utterance can be described as agent (Mommy) + object (coat). The intent is to describe Mommy's action. (b) If this is what the child means, the two-word utterance is possessor (Mommy) + possessed (coat). (c) If this is what the child means, the two-word utterance would be agent (Mommy) + object (coat). Notice that the sentence type is the same as that in (a), but the implied action is different. The action here is "get," not "put on." A three-word sentence, "Mommy get coat," would make the toddler's intent clear. (d) If this is what the child means, the two-word utterance is again agent (Mommy) + object (coat).
The unuttered action in both (a) and (d) is "put on," so a three-word utterance would not distinguish between the two meanings. The adjective specifying which coat distinguishes (a) from (d): In (a) the action is Mommy putting on her coat and (d) is Mommy putting the child's coat on the child. Notice that in (d) the child's intonation might give a clue as to the meaning of the utterance. The word "Mommy" operates as an appositive, and in adult language would be followed by a pause. If such a pause exists in the toddler's utterance, it would suggest meaning (d) rather than (a) or (c). Likewise, the child's intonation in (d) is likely to be a command rather than a simple declarative.

Mama	Sheep	Picture
Dada	Cup	Book
Baby	Bee	See
Car	Tea	Wa-wa (as in water)
Tree	Shoes	Bye-bye
Bow-wow	Button	Pig
Cow	Tick-tock	Hi
Turkey	Light (pronounced yight)	Hello
Chicken	Cheese	Up
Duck	Choo-choo (as in train)	Cracker

FIGURE 11–4. The first thirty words spoken by one child. The child was 14 months old when the 30th word was added to the vocabulary. At that time the addition of new words became so rapid that keeping track was no longer feasible for the parents. The animals probably represent exposure to picture books as well as to a small town environment. In addition to using "bye-bye" to indicate a desire to go out, this infant would also bring galoshes to indicate that she wanted to go out.

as well as the number of features associated with words changed in time.

All the above observations about the acquisition of word meanings have been based on production of words, not perception. Studies of the development of perception of word meanings during this period are rare. There have been no studies of whether or not an infant would point to a cat, dog, or horse when asked to show the "doggie" during the period when they are using "doggie" to refer to all three animals. The study cited above (Gruendel, 1977) simply noted that comprehension of the meaning of words did not appear to follow the same developmental course as that observed in production. Children appear to understand more than they say but the exact extent of their understanding is unclear. In one of the rare studies of word perception, Nelson (1972) examined comprehension of words by children aged 18 to 24 months. The children were asked to name or point to pictorial examples of familiar words that were either ambiguous (the words shared features with each other or represented many members of a class such as "dog") or unambiguous. The pictured representations varied in detail and included sets of outline drawings, detailed drawings, and photographs. The degree of detail of the pictures affected the number of correct responses, but there were no differences between detailed drawings and photographs. Both the ambiguous and unambiguous pictures of familiar words were recognized less often in their outline representations. Significantly more names were given to familiar and ambiguous items (that is, members of a class) than to unfamiliar and unambiguous objects. Outline drawings of less familiar and unambiguous items were named correctly more frequently than detailed drawings or photographs of the same objects. Nelson concluded that the developmental progression in associating names with concepts is from a few concepts, each unique and for which no perceptual contrasts are utilized in naming, to overspecificity of concept where detail is needed for identification, to complete and well-defined concepts where generalizations have taken place and outlines can be used. Thus, familiar and class items (ambiguous) have already reached the second stage in the progression at 18 to 24 months whereas unfamiliar unique items, when named correctly, are still at the first stage of the recognition progression.

The findings of the above study indicate that how children use words reflects, to some extent, how they understand words. That is, in both processes children appear first to be specific and then to generalize. The one exception to this similarity in progression appears to be overextension in the use of words. This type of behavior apparently does not appear in word comprehension. In a study of older children (Saltz, Dixon, Klein, & Becker, 1977) it was found that 2-year-olds either could not identify representations of a class or only selected "core" representations as exemplars of a class. Older children (4-year-olds) not only had more concepts but also accepted peripheral items (for example, slipper for shoe) as exemplars of a word. The progression of requiring specificity for associating a word with a referent before generalization takes place may be a process that occurs over and over as the child develops and acquires new concepts.

Combining Speech Sounds into Words

Comprehension of words (or utterances) requires relating speech sound sequences to objects and events in the environment. Production requires retrieving from memory and articulating a speech sound sequence that relates to objects and events in the environment. This behavior requires segmentation of the stream of speech and categorization of segments into utterances, words, and speech sounds. The data available on speech sound production in words and utterances indicate that just as in babbling, there are developmental changes that occur in the speech sounds produced over the period of early word acquisition. Some speech sounds are produced more frequently and accurately than others at the beginning of this phase. Indeed, there appears to be a great deal of similarity in the productive sequence observed during the babbling and word production phases (Menyuk, 1972). In contrast to babbling, which produces nonsense syllables, the target for production during this period is a word or phrase that has meaning. Given the speech sound sequences produced during this phase it has been hypothesized that words are intially produced as unsegmented wholes and not as a sequence of speech sound segments. Later behavior indicates that syllables are the target in speech production rather than single sounds or distinctive features of sounds (Menyuk & Menn, 1979). Since the infant's vocabulary is small during the second year of life it is not unreasonable to think that words are initially stored in memory as wholes and not simply retrieved as wholes for production. Once the vocabulary of the child grows into thousands of words, these words *may* be stored in terms of patterns of sequences of sound rather than as wholly different and unique sound sequences.

Evidence of this can be found in the older child's ability to segment a word into separate sounds and relate sounds to symbols in reading.

In contradiction to the above statement about early word storage, it has been suggested that by 2 years of age the child is able to perceive phonetic (or speech–acoustic) distinctions between speech sounds and words the way an adult does (Smith, 1973). To support this notion, some studies (Schvachkin, 1973; Garnica, 1973) which require that children contrast the initial segments of nonsense syllables (for example, /pa/ versus /ba/) and relate these syllables to nonsense objects indicate that all the initial vocalic and consonantal segmental distinctions in the language can be made by about two years. The degree of similarity between this experimental task and what the child does when listening to meaningful speech is unclear. The child may be attending to the whole syllable in the experimental task and not simply the initial segment.

In opposition to the suggestion that all speech sound segments in the language are differentiated at an early age, it has been hypothesized that only some distinctions are made and other sounds are perceived as "noise." (Ingram, 1974). None of the suggestions about what occurs in speech sound perception when meaningful words and phrases are processed indicate that the child's perceptual phonological rules are similar to those of the adult. Further, there is no suggestion that speech sound segments are analyzed in terms of the distinctive features of segments and possible sequences of segments in the language. Thus, the exact basis (that is, whole word, syllable, segment, or distinctive features) of very young children's ability to perceive differences between the words and phrases they hear has not been completely determined.

Summary

The research discussed in this section shows that there is a body of data available on the language structures (semantic, syntactic, and phonological) produced by the child in the second year of life, but there is comparatively little data on what the child perceives. It has been assumed that perceptual development precedes productive development. The productive data indicate that 2-year-olds have at least acquired knowledge of how to express basic semantic relations in the correct syntactic (word order) form of a particular language and that word meanings and phonological realizations are in the beginning stages of acquisition. How far perceptual knowledge exceeds productive knowledge at age 2 is still unclear, but there is some indication that perceptual abilities do exceed the knowledge displayed in production.

Research also indicates that the infant communicates needs and feelings at a very early age by the use of intonation, facial expression, and gesture along with vocalization. These aspects of the communicative situation are also the ones that are understood by the infant long before the meaning of words is understood.

FACTORS THAT AFFECT LANGUAGE DEVELOPMENT

Various theoreticians have taken dramatically opposing views about the effect of environmental factors on the language behaviors observed during infancy and later. In one view, the development of language during infancy is primarily a function of the types of inputs the infant receives from caregivers. From the opposite viewpoint, language developments are primarily a function of the biological structure of the human infant. Similarly, some theorists suggest that language development is a product of cognitive development but others suggest that language development is special and is not dependent on cognitive development. All of these positions highlight important factors in the process of language development but no one of them explains all of language acquisition. What seems to be the case is that there are obvious biological factors that affect the course of development over this period and there are environmental factors that affect it as well. There are general cognitive factors that appear to affect both language and other development (for example, early speech perception and visual perception) and there are aspects of some areas of development that seem to require special types of processing that are not shared with other areas of development. The research concerning biological and environ-

mental factors that might affect development during infancy will be discussed first. Research concerning the relation between cognition and language will be discussed later.

Biological Factors

The biological factors that have been cited as affecting the course of language development in infancy include the special nature of the central nervous system and of the auditory and vocal mechanisms of the human infant (Menyuk, 1971). Structural and functional differences in the two hemispheres of the brain have indicated that the association area of the cortex in the left hemisphere of the neonate is larger than in the right. When speech and nonspeech sounds are presented to an infant there is greater electrical activity in response to speech in the left hemisphere and to nonspeech in the right. These findings have led to the conclusion that the human infant is biologically preprogrammed to acquire language because special left or dominant hemisphere processing has been found to be crucial in speech processing and this specialization appears to be present at birth. Additional evidence cited for biological preprogramming is the structure and functioning of the vocal mechanism. The human vocal tract is different from that of other animals even at birth. The structure of the pharynx, the location of the vocal cords in the pharynx, and the size and shape of the mouth, tongue, and lips and their relation to each other allow for the production of articulated sounds. No other animal's vocal mechanism has the same characteristics, and this is one of the reasons why attempts to teach great apes to talk were doomed to failure. The course of maturation of the vocal tract is said to account for the sequence and organization of vocal behavior during babbling; therefore, these vocal behaviors are presumed to be universal.

The structure of the auditory mechanism of the human infant is not different from that of other animals. Nevertheless, the data obtained from studies of infant speech sound discrimination have led some researchers to the conclusion that the infant is, first, biologically preprogrammed to be sensitive to certain acoustic feature differences and, second, to process the acoustic information in speech in special ways. These acoustic feature differences are just those required to discriminate between the speech sounds in any language. Like babbling, then, the sequence of development of speech sound discrimination should be universal. Nevertheless, some studies show the very early effect of a particular linguistic environment on these discriminations. These data do not exclude the possibility of detectors of universal speech features in the infant because early tuning to environmental sounds is possible even with universal detectors. However, they do raise doubts.

Finally, it is clear that the information processing capacities of the human infant differ from those of other animal infants. This fact has also been cited as evidence for biological preprogramming for language acquisition. There is nothing about these capacities as such, however, that indicates that they are specially designed for language acquisition. They simply allow the acquisition of all types of human knowledge, linguistic and nonlinguistic.

Data obtained in studies of handicapped children shed some light on the biological prerequisites to language acquisition and thus on the role of special biological structures in language acquisition. Children who are born deaf have enormous difficulty in acquiring oral language but not sign language. Children who are deafened after the second year of life have much less difficulty with oral language, although problems still exist. Exposure to language, even if only for the first 2 years, provides a foundation of basic knowledge that allows further, if very slow, development of this knowledge (Lenneberg, 1967). In addition, it has been suggested that deaf youngsters who are not exposed to sign language or to oral language invent a symbol system that is quite similar in structure (that is, in semantic relations and order of gesture) to the system developed by young hearing children (Feldman, Goldin-Meadow, & Gleitman, 1978). The oral language development of blind children has been found to be very similar to that of sighted children, with some minor deviations (Fraiberg & Adelson, 1973). There is no evidence that children who suffer loss of limbs or lack of control of limbs (that is, they cannot walk or even sit up) have any difficulty in acquiring language. All of these findings, which indicate that sensory–motor deficits or losses do not

prevent the acquisition of language, have led to the conclusion that language development is independent from other developmental processes and, therefore, that the human infant is biologically predisposed to acquire language. If this is the case, then the question that still remains is, What structures or functions in the infant cause this predisposition?

Known or suspected lesions in the brain, and not sensory-motor deficits, appear to be the biological factors that can either enormously delay the process of language acquisition (to the point where it is suspected that language knowledge, when acquired, is really different for these children), or cause differences in the acquisition of particular aspects of language (semantic, syntactic, or phonological; Menyuk, 1975). It is not the case that such lesions always, if ever, cause *only* language difficulties. Severely retarded children show enormous delay in language development but they may be delayed in all aspects of development. Children labeled as dysphasic show specific difficulties in either comprehending or producing certain categories and relations in the language rather than overall delay, but it is not clear that they are only deficited linguistically (Menyuk, 1978). Not all mentally retarded children acquire language at an enormously slow rate, and their rate and level of learning development is not wholly reflected by measured IQs in the range of moderate retardation. Dysphasic children vary in their language behaviors and this variation seems quite similar to that observed with adult aphasics who have suffered injury in different parts of the brain (Menyuk, 1978). These findings of differences within these populations in patterns of language behavior lead to a suspicion that different parts and functions of the central nervous system are affected in different children all of whom have been labeled as belonging to the same diagnostic category. Given the above findings of differences in language behavior, it is also reasonable to suppose that different parts of the brain control different aspects of language behavior. It is known or highly likely that such lesions existed prenatally or were caused by birth trauma. This fact also leads to the reasonable assumption that organization of parts and functions of the brain takes place prenatally, at least in terms of readiness to begin processing different types of information in different ways. There is probably a great deal of redundancy in the nervous system, which allows for compensation for some types of damage. In other instances, as in the populations described above, compensation does not take place at all, or not to a sufficient enough degree to allow for normal language development.

In conclusion, data on the language development of handicapped children indicate that such development is highly resistent to peripheral sensory losses and that differing central losses or deviations lead to differences in aspects of language development. All of these data suggest that the biological specialization of the human infant to acquire language lies in the structure and organization of the brain, but whether or not this biological specialization is different for language processing as compared to other types of cognitive processing is still open to question.

Input Factors

A reasonably intact nervous system is a necessary condition for language development, but it is not sufficient. It is clear that communicative interaction with other humans is also necessary for language development (see Figure 11–5). The question is, What role does this interaction play in language development? Some theoreticians suggest that the environment teaches language to the infant by modeling and shaping behavior (Moerk, 1976). Others suggest that simple exposure is all that is necessary to get the presumably innate language acquisition device going. Still others suggest that the environment tunes language input to the capacities of the infant and thus provides the infant with appropriate data to work on (Snow, 1972). Conversely, others suggest that it is the infant who tunes the environment and elicits from adults the appropriate data to keep the language acquisition device going (Menyuk, 1977).

There is clear evidence that caregivers talk to their infants and young children in a different way than they talk to their older children and to adults. When they talk to infants their voices are higher pitched and they use simpler sentences and phrases. They appear to tune their utterances to what they think the child

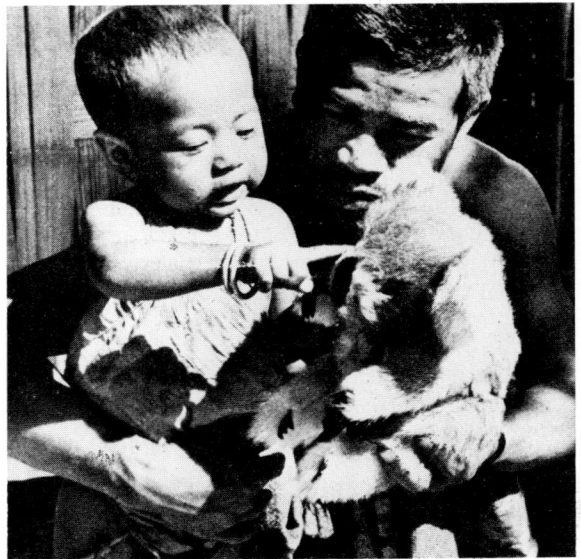

FIGURE 11–5. Games that teach babies comprehension of words are common in many cultures. Here a Balinese baby and an American baby respond to the question "Where is the nose?"

knows about language, but it is also the case that the primary functions of communication to young children are quite limited and simple. Thus, it is not clear whether caregivers speak in simple structures in order to provide appropriate language data or because what they wish to say requires only simple structures.

A number of studies indicate that there is a marked shift in the structure of maternal utterances once the mother believes that her utterances might be at least partially understood. For example, in a study of 4-, 6-, and 8-month-old infants and their mothers' vocal interactions (Sherrod, Friedman, Crawley, Drake, & Devieux, 1977) it was found that the age of the infant had a significant effect on the mean length of utterances (MLU) and on the complexity of the mother's utterances. They were shorter and simpler (often parts of sentences rather than whole sentences) to 8-month-old infants than to 4- and 6-month infants. At a later age when the infant can respond by action, a number of studies indicate that a large proportion of the mother's utterances are simple directions ("Drink your juice") but there are also frequent indirect requests ("Your hands are dirty") that require inferential abilities. It is difficult to see how language input of this kind can teach language structures directly because such differing structures are used to convey similar meanings. It is also not clear that mothers use communicative interaction to teach language. Maternal utterances seem to be a product of what goes on naturally between mothers and infants rather than being designed to teach language.

The most important question about the effect of input on language development is not what caregivers do and why they do it but, rather, what effect what they do has on language development. In a carefully designed longitudinal study that examined correlations between what mothers do and what their infants do linguistically, Newport, Gleitman, & Gleitman (1977) found that what mothers did had little effect on the development of what is called the propositional content of utterances (that is, the number and type of noun phrases and verb phrases in an utterance). There was some effect on the use of auxiliary verbs (*am going*) and plural markers on nouns (cake*s*), which are both grammatical markers. Nevertheless, the way mothers promoted the development of grammatical markers was not direct; that is, they didn't use these aspects of language more frequently than did mothers whose children were slower in acquiring these aspects. Rather, they provided more instances in which these aspects were presented clearly. For example, mothers who asked more yes–no

questions in which the auxiliary verb is fronted (appears at the beginning, as in "Is he going?") had children who developed auxiliary verbs more quickly. Thus, the teaching was very indirect and was limited to specific kinds of grammatical knowledge.

Additional data, which support the finding that mothers' form of talking has little effect on the rate of their children's structural language development, has been found in a study of 53 infants and their mothers (Murphy, Menyuk, Liebergott, & Schultz, 1983). However, the same study found that the number of opportunities that mothers provided for their babies to take a turn in conversations and their degree of acknowledgment of that turn had an effect on how early their children adequately participated in conversation (Chesnick, Menyuk, & Liebergott, 1983). Thus, what mothers do may have an effect on their babies' willingness and ability to communicate.

Children who come from socioeconomically deprived families are often cited as proof of the effect of input (or lack thereof) on language development. There is a long history of research that appeared to indicate language deficit in these children. However, more recent studies do not indicate marked differences in the amount of input provided infants during the early months of life that is dependent on the SES of the family (Lewis & Freedle, 1972; Tulkin & Kagan, 1972). Studies of low SES children's language knowledge do not always indicate deficits, but do show differences in language knowledge that are due to the particular dialects and rules of language that the children are exposed to (Menyuk, 1971). Chapter 12 will present further discussion of this topic.

Role of Imitation

From the research on the effect of language input on language development it is clear that children need to hear language, and that the nature of language children hear is different for babies of different ages and for children of different socio-linguistic backgrounds. The exact relations between type of input and acquisition of linguistic knowledge is still unclear. One aspect of input that has received a great deal of attention is imitation. The notion is that the environment provides the models that the infant imitates and then stores in memory. Some researchers suggest that imitation of a structure in the language is necessary for its acquisition. Several studies have examined the role of imitation in language acquisition and have come up with conflicting conclusions (Menyuk, 1971). In summary, some findings indicate that imitation plays no role because children do not imitate what they do not produce spontaneously. Other findings indicate that imitation may be used to test hypotheses about the production of categories and relations in the language but plays no role in comprehension (Menyuk, 1977).

Two recent studies point up the complexities of assessing the role of imitation in acquisition. Ninio and Bruner (1978) observed one child over a period of 12 months who was provided with the names of objects while being read to. They found that the rate of repetition of words by the child was not increased either by the mother's imitation of the child's utterances or by the mother providing a model. They concluded that participation in ritualized dialogue rather than imitation is the major mechanism through which word acquisition is achieved. Folger and Chapman (1978) studied the effect of types of speech act or purpose of communication on spontaneous imitation by six children aged 1 year 7 months to 2 years 1 month. They found that (1) children imitated when cued to do so, that is, when they heard their own utterance repeated or when the referent was described or talked about; (2) elicited imitation was an infrequent occurrence; (3) spontaneous imitation occurred most frequently in particular speech act situations such as when the mother described referents or when the baby asked for information about a referent; and (4) there was a significant correlation between the percentage of infant utterances imitated by mothers and the percentage of maternal utterances imitated by infants. That is, children who imitated had mothers who imitated.

Both studies indicate that little direct modeling or imitation of a model goes on in acquisition of words. However, the studies differ in terms of their findings concerning indirect modeling in which repetition of the child's utterance by the mother leads to repetition on the part of the child. The first study finds no positive effect; the second does. However, the two studies differ in the situations they observed and in the sampling procedures they used (the first was a longitudinal study, the second was cross-sectional). These conflicting findings underscore the difficulties in making generalizations about the role of imitation in language acquisition. The amount of imitation varies from situation to situation and, indeed, from child to child (Nelson, 1973). Nevertheless, it is clear that mothers do not strive to elicit imitation (that is, to teach words directly by modeling) and that imitation does not play a direct role in the acquisition of even such likely candidates as words. If this is the case, it is highly unlikely that imitation plays a direct role in the acquisition of semantic and syntactic categories and relations.

Cognitive Factors

Research on the role of cognitive development in language acquisition has also led to many more questions than answers, and there are conflicting views on the subject. One view is that each linguistic development is dependent on some cognitive development. For example, object permanence is said to lead to vocabulary acquisition (Bloom, 1973), and internalization of sensory–motor schema to sentence production (McNeill, 1974). These are only hypotheses because in neither instance was evidence obtained on the relation between the language used and the cognitive behaviors cited. A longitudinal study of three infants, aged 9 to 11 months at its beginning and 27 to 29 months at its end, examined the relation between object permanence and word acquisition (Corrigan, 1978). Corrigan found that both abilities matured but that when age was partialed out statistically there were no significant correlations between the two abilities. In a later analysis of the data, Corrigan (1979) notes that statements about the relation between cognition and language (either positive or negative) depend on the particular measures of cognition and language used.

An opposing view is that language is crucial to cognitive development (Vygotsky, 1962). Most researchers who take this position, however, are referring to the cognitive developments that take place after age 2. Prior to that age linguistic and cognitive developments are presumably independent. Still another point of view is that both the cognitive accomplishments that are observed over the first 2 years of life and the linguistic accomplishments discussed in previous sections of this chapter are dependent on developmental changes in infants' ability to process the information that reaches their senses (Menyuk, 1980). The exact nature of these changes is unknown at present. Data from infant visual processing (Haith, 1979) and speech sound processing (Eilers et. al., 1977) indicate that as maturation takes place both the amount and type of information that the infant can process changes. For example, in speech sound perception larger chunks of speech sound sequences (more than one syllable) can be processed and different distinctions within the speech sound stimuli can be detected as the infant matures. These changes in abilities are probably what govern observed developmental changes in linguistic and nonlinguistic behavior rather than behaviors in one domain causing changes in behavior in the other domain, at least during the early months of life. The perceptual salience, simplicity of structure of the information, plus its usefulness (in terms of outcomes for the infant) probably affect, respectively, the rate and sequence of acquisitions in either domain.

DISCUSSION ISSUES

Some Questions and Implications

It should be clear by now that many questions are still unanswered about both the content of language acquisition and the factors that affect it over the first 2 years of life. The most important omissions at present will be noted here, as well as the implications for obtaining further detailed information with better measures in early language development. Three questions that have yet to be examined in depth are the following: What linguistic relations and categories are perceived as well as produced over the first 2 years of life, and what are the relations between the two developmental processes? What is the exact nature of the changes in the information processing capacities and strategies that lead to changes in language be-

havior over this period? What effects do different rates and patterns of language development during this period have on subsequent development? This last question is closely related to the whole content of this book. Recently there has been much greater interest in infancy because of the notion that developments during the period are crucial for later developments. If it is the case that relations can be established between language development during this period and later language behavior, and if differences among children that make a difference in subsequent development can be identified, then intervention strategies that might prevent or ameliorate later language difficulties might be developed. Given the importance of language development for all other areas of development—cognitive, social, affective, and academic—prevention or amelioration of difficulties in language development might prevent or ameliorate difficulties in those areas.

The key phrase in the above paragraph is "if differences among children that make a difference in subsequent development can be identified." The findings of recent studies of early language development all point to variation in the language acquisition process. Thus, although there are universal or general trends in development, there are also individual variations (Nelson, 1980). For example, some children use pronouns to a much greater extent than nouns in early two-word utterances. Some children imitate to a much greater extent than others. Some children use language primarily to express needs and feelings whereas others use language primarily to name actions and objects. Some children produce primarily single words, others use ritualized phrases with words—for example, "wuzzat shoe"— and still others combine the above patterns when they are in the holophrastic stage. Finally, differences in rate of development of all aspects of early language have long been noted. Interestingly, some of these individual differences go together. Infants who use pronouns extensively also use language primarily to express needs and feelings, produce ritualized phrases with words more frequently, and appear to be slower word acquirers. Note that no child does one thing to the exclusion of others. For example, no child uses pronouns exclusively.

These are some examples of differences found in the language development of apparently normally developing children. The phrase "apparently normally developing children" is used here for two reasons. First, some of the differences observed appear to make a difference in later language behavior. Although there appears to be a catch-up period in children who are slow in developing aspects of language (primarily premature infants) between the ages of 2 and 4 years (Menyuk, 1979) some children who do not appear to be markedly different from their age peers in oral language behavior nevertheless have difficulty in processing the verbal material on reading readiness tests when they are of school age. Still others seem to get through the first three grades adequately and then encounter difficulty as academic tasks become more difficult in grades three and four (Menyuk & Flood, 1981). These findings raise the suspicion that important signs of potential problems may have been missed.

Clearly what is needed is better and standardized measures of communication and language development during the first 2 years of life, as well as more longitudinal studies of language development that follow children from infancy into the early school years. Throughout this chapter, the techniques used in the past decade to measure very early language behavior were briefly described and problems or questions about their use discussed. These techniques are promising, but much more time and effort are needed to make them reliable, feasible, and economical. If this were done, then such data could be more widely collected and used to answer the question of which differences make a difference.

Parenting

This chapter was written to describe the universal features of language acquisition and did not go into individual differences, so it poses different problems for the discussion of parenting. On the one hand it gives a reasonable basis for expectations about language development in infancy or of what will follow what as language develops. On the other hand it does not set up timetables that include such facts as that some children use their first words at 7 to 8 months and sentences by 1 year but others (apparently normal) say their first words at 1½ years of age. Despite this wide variation, any serious delay in first words should be a clue to adults to make sure the infant hears (and hears what cannot be seen). There appear to be familial tendencies to talk early or late that are separate from general intelligence, but this is not well documented. Knowledge of the family may thus be useful in helping to interpret any delay in speaking.

Although this chapter stresses the lack of conclusive evidence about the importance of when, how much, and what types of interaction with a baby are optimal for language development, note that some types of interaction appear to be important for communicative development. The next two chapters give data that are relevant to the issue of interaction in other contexts. In particular, note that although cognitive skills improved as a result of stimulation programs in an orphanage, verbal skills did not improve until specific verbal stimulation based primarily on imitation was instituted (see Chapter 13). There are no data to indicate that parents can harm their babies by talking to them, and some to suggest that talking to infants before they can talk leads to improved responsiveness generally; hence we would suggest that this is a good thing to do. That does not mean that adults should bombard infants with constant speech, and it does mean that giving baby a turn is part of the game and can be quite important in the development of the ability to engage adequately in discourse.

General competence in the use of a language seems to occur in what might seem to be conditions of minimal stimulation, and that is one basis for the biological hypothesis. The question of what leads to a superior mastery of language is unanswered, however, and much of the answer undoubtedly lies in development and events that occur beyond infancy.

SUMMARY

It was long held that the period in infancy before words are produced was unrelated to subsequent language development and the term prelinguistic was applied to babies during this time. This view has now changed, largely due to studies that indicate that babies know a great deal about communication and learn a great deal about the structure of language before they have words.

So far as knowledge of the structure of language is concerned, the different phases of language production in infancy can be characterized as the cooing, then babbling, phase followed by word and word combination phases. Perception of speech grows from single-syllable discrimination (/pa/ versus /ba/) to discrimination of larger speech chunks, such as multisyllables. Along with single-syllable discrimination the infant is able to discriminate between rising and falling intonations of these syllables, and along with multisyllable discrimination the infant is able to distinguish between statement and question intonation contours of sentences. At the end of the first year of life there is evidence that babies know what words for a small set of objects mean even when the words are presented in isolation.

Communication between baby and caregiver takes place at a very early age. Because babies and caregivers have different personalities, the exact content of these interactions will vary from dyad to dyad. Nevertheless, some general trends in communication interaction can be observed. Both cry and noncry vocalizations are present from birth. These two types of vocalizations and variations of them reflect the baby's state of comfort or discomfort. By 6 to 8 weeks the baby has achieved some control of the air flow, and vowel-like sounds occur by 3 months. Conversational turn-taking between caregiver and infant occurs at about this time. The infant's readiness, and the caregiver's sensitivity to the cues that indicate the infant is ready, bring about the establishment of this communication interaction.

Infants communicate needs and feelings by different types of vocalizations, facial expressions, and gesture. The different types of vocalizations are achieved by modifying the contours of their babbles. They do this by using modifications of the contours that characterize adult speech: statement, request, and command contours. These different patterns are achieved at different ages. Babies also discriminate among, or at least respond differently to, these contours as well as to the emotional qualities of the voice. Both turn-taking in vocalization and use of suprasegmental features (intonation and stress) to convey intent and emotion are well established in the first year, but the latter ability continues to develop and becomes almost adult-like over the next half year. There is some evidence that boys and girls use different strategies in taking their turn in conversation as they develop although both are equally able to take their turn from the earliest age on. After words appear there is a continuation of turn-taking and of earlier strategies for conveying needs and feelings, but the content of the child's turn changes and it becomes a meaningful response to the caregiver's utterance.

The ability of young infants to discriminate speech sounds in the same fashion as adults has raised the question of whether there are detectors in the auditory system that are particularly sensitive to acoustic differences relevant to speech sounds in any language (as with early sensitivity to color categories). Speech sounds vary in several acoustic dimensions or distinctive features. There is a developmental sequence in the contrasts detected, and the language experience of infants modifies their ability to discriminate between distinctive features as early as 2 months. Further, infants discriminate between sounds on the basis of acoustic dimensions that are not limited to speech sounds, and other animals can be taught to discriminate between speech sounds. Hence the existence of innate speech detectors in the infants' auditory system is questionable.

The production of speech sounds in babbling appears to develop in the same order in children from different language communities. Certain consonant sounds occur earlier than others; for example, those formed by lips ahead of those formed by the tip of the tongue. This order seems to be a reflection of ease of articulation. Unlike earlier views that babbling contained all possible speech sounds of all languages, the current notion is that sounds produced during the babbling period are a reflection of the development of motor skills and that sounds requiring subtle articulatory muscle control have not occurred even by the end of the period. This motor skill aspect of speech sound production would imply a universal pattern of acquisition across all language communities. The data collected thus far support this implication, but they are too scanty for valid conclusions.

The idea that speech discrimination and production follow different courses and are based on different capacities is supported by the time lag between the two abilities and the fact that the order in which speech sounds are perceptually and productively contrasted is different. Delayed auditory feedback of sound production has no effect on infant vocalization, whereas such a delay causes hesitation and stuttering even in young children.

Once children understand that words represent and refer to objects, their discrimination of words is based primarily on meaning rather than speech sound differences. There are data that indicate that comprehension of words out of context begins at about 12 months. At first words are used to express needs and feelings about objects and actions. Next comes their use to describe relations between objects and actions. Finally the attributes of objects and actions are described.

First productions are often holophrases, single words or unsegmented phrases that convey a variety of meanings about an object or event as a result of use of different intonation contours. They are used in particular situational contexts with particular gestures and facial expressions. Several sources indicate that infants may understand relations between objects and actions or objects and attributes while they can produce only one part of the relation. This knowledge reflects understanding of the syntactic rules of word order. Thus, even at this early age infants indicate knowledge of some basic syntactic rules of language as well as semantic knowledge or knowledge of the meaning of words.

Knowledge of word meanings develops in a nonrandom fashion. The types of words used first refer to persons, objects, and actions that are important to all infants. Words are first used in an underextended manner and then are overextended to refer to more than one object in a category. Data on comprehension of word meaning are limited, but it appears that infants are first specific and then generalize in both the processes of perception and production, although overextension does not occur in word comprehension.

The factors that affect language development include biological factors: an intact CNS, appropriate hemisphere specialization of the brain, intact vocal structures (and muscle control mechanisms, not discussed), and a sufficiently intact auditory system to discriminate speech sounds for acquiring oral language. Research indicates, however, that deafness, blindness, and loss of ability to manipulate the vocal mechanism does not prevent or even seriously retard acquisition of language, either oral or signed. Hence, on the one hand language acquisition is independent of peripheral sensory-motor abilities. On the other hand, evidence that damage to the CNS does seriously affect the process suggests that the biological predisposition to acquire language lies in the structure and function of the brain. Whether this specialization for language differs in any meaningful way from that of other forms of cognitive processing is still an open question.

Language acquisition also depends on communicative interaction with other language users. The role of this environmental input is interpreted very differently by different workers. The role of the frequency of varying types of utterances used by caregivers and their linguistic complexity is not well understood. The frequency and complexity change with the age and linguistic competence of the infant, but whether this serves a caregiver need or helps teach is unclear. Evidence for the effect of the teaching role from examples of different kinds of input (specific types of mother input or SES background) on basic knowledge is lacking, though differences in style and use of language do result from these factors. There are data that indicate that providing babies with the opportunity to take a turn has a positive effect on their conversational abilities. The specific role of imitation is not agreed upon, but considerable evidence is cited to indicate that it is not crucial.

The relation of language development to general cognitive development (questioned previously in relation to biological factors) needs more study, and the studies that exist yield conflicting results. Is language crucial to cognitive development or vice versa (at different periods of development), or are language and cognitive development two sides of a single coin?

The question of whether the large individual differences in rate of language development and uses of early language make a difference for subsequent linguistic, cognitive, and social development is not thoroughly answered. Several kinds of evidence suggest that this is not the case except in instances of very evident deficit. Perhaps, however, the wrong things are still being measured.

REFERENCES

Bateson, M. (1969). The interpersonal context of infant vocalization. *Quarterly Progress Reports, Research Laboratory of Electronics, M.I.T.* (100), 170–176.

Bloom, L. (1973). *One word at a time.* The Hague, Holland: Mouton.

Branigan, G. (1976). Organizational constraints during the one word period. Paper presented at the First Annual Boston University Conference on Language Development, Boston.

Chesnick, M., Menyuk, P., & Liebergott, J. (1983). *Who leads whom in language development.* Paper presented at the meeting of the Society for Research in Child Development, Detroit.

Clark, E. (1973). What's in a word? In T. Moore (Ed.), *Cognitive development and the cognition of language* (pp. 65–100). New York: Academic.

Corrigan, R. (1978). Language development as related to stage 6 object permanence development. *Journal of Child Language, 5,* 173–189.

Corrigan, R. (1979). Cognitive correlates of language: Differential criteria yield differential results. *Child Development, 50,* 617–631.

Donahue, M. (1978). Form and function in mother–toddler conversational turn-taking. Unpublished doctoral dissertation, Boston University, Boston.

Eilers, R., Wilson, W., & Moore, J. (1977). Developmental changes in speech discrimination. *Journal of Speech and Hearing Research, 20,* 766–780.

Eimas, P. & Miller, J. (Eds.). (1981). *Perspectives on the study of speech.* Hillsdale, NJ: Earlbaum.

Eimas, P., Siqueland, F., Jusczyk, P., & Vigorito, J. (1971). Speech perception in early infancy. *Science, 171,* 303–306.

Feldman, H., Goldin-Meadow, S., & Gleitman, L. (1978). Beyond Herodotus: The growth of language by linguistically deprived deaf children. In A. Locke (Ed.), *Action, gesture and symbol* (pp. 351–414). New York: Academic.

Folger, J. & Chapman, R. (1978). A pragmatic analysis of spontaneous imitations. *Journal of Child Language, 5,* 25–38.

Fraiberg, S. & Adelson, E. (1973). Self-representation in language and play: Observations of blind children. *The Psychoanalytic Quarterly, 43,* 539–562.

Fromkin, V. & Rodman, R. (1974). *An introduction to language.* New York: Holt, Rinehart & Winston.

Garnica, O. (1973). The development of phonetic speech perception. In T. Moore (Ed.), *Cognitive development and the acquisition of language,* (pp. 215–222). New York: Academic.

Greenfield, P. & Smith, J. (1976). *The structure of communication in early language development.* New York: Academic.

Gruendel, J. (1977). Referential extension in early language development. *Child Development, 48,* 1567–1576.

Haith, M. (1979). Visual cognition in early infancy. In R. Kearsley & I. Sigel (Eds.), *Infants at risk: Assessment of cognitive functioning* (pp. 23–48). Hillsdale, NJ: Erlbaum.

Horgan, D. (1976). Linguistic knowledge at stage I: Evidence from successive single word utterances. Paper presented at Child Language Research Forum, Stanford University, Palo Alto, CA.

Ingram, D. (1974). Phonological rules in young children. *Journal of Child Language, 1,* 49–64.

Irwin, O. (1947). Infant speech: Consonant sounds according to the manner of articulation. *Journal of Speech Disorders, 12,* 397–401.

Jakobson, R. (1968). *Child language, aphasia and phenological universals.* The Hague, Holland: Mouton.

Jakobson, R., Fant, G., & Halle, M. (1963). *Preliminaries to speech analysis.* Cambridge, MA: MIT Press.

Kaplan, E.F. & Kaplan, G.A. (1970). The prelinguistic child. In J. Eliot (Ed.), *Human development and cognitive processes.* New York: Holt, Rhinehart & Winston.

Lenneberg, E. (1967). *Biological foundations of language.* New York: Wiley.

Lewis, M. & Freedle, R. (1972). Mother–infant dyad: The cradle of meaning. Princeton, NJ: Educational Testing Service.

Lieberman, P. (1974). *On the origins of language.* New York: Macmillan.

Limber, J. (1973). The genesis of complex sentences. In T. Moore (Ed.), *Cognitive development and the acquisition of language* (pp. 169–186). New York: Academic.

McNeill, D. (1974). Semiotic extension. Paper presented at the Loyola Symposium on Cognition, Chicago.

Menyuk, P. (1971). *The acquisition and development of language.* Englewood Cliffs, NJ: Prentice-Hall.

Menyuk, P. (1972). *Speech development.* Indianapolis, IN: Bobbs Merrill.

Menyuk, P. (1975). Children with language problems: What's the problem? In D. Dato (Ed.), *Georgetown University Roundtable on Linguistics,* (pp. 129–44). Washington, DC: Georgetown University Press.

Menyuk, P. (1977). *Language and maturation.* Cambridge MA: M.I.T. Press.

Menyuk, P. (1978). Linguistic problems in children with developmental dysphasia. In M. Wyke (Ed.), *Developmental dysphasia* (pp. 135–158). London: Academic.

Menyuk, P. (1979). Methods used to measure linguistic competence during the first five years of life. In R. Kearsley & I. Sigel (Eds.)., *Infants at risk: Assessment of cognitive functioning* (pp. 85–114). Hillsdale, NJ: Erlbaum.

Menyuk, P. (1980). Non-linguistic and linguistic processing in normally developing and language disordered children. In N.J. Lass (Ed.), *Speech and language: Advances in basic research and practice* (Vol. 4, pp. 1–97) New York: Academic.

Menyuk, P. & Bernholtz, M. (1969). Prosodic features and children's language. *Quarterly Progress Reports.* Research Laboratory of Electronics, M.I.T. (93), pp. 216–219.

Menyuk, P. & Flood, J. (1981). Linguistic competence, reading, writing problems and remediation. *Bulletin of the Orton Society, 31,* 13—28.

Menyuk, P. & Menn, L. (1979). Early strategies for the perception and production of words and sounds. In P. Fletcher & M. Gorman (Eds.), *Language acquisition* (pp. 49–70). Cambridge, England: Cambridge University Press.

Moerk, E. (1976). Processes of language teaching and training in the interactions of mother–child dyads. *Child Development, 47,* 1064–1078.

Murai, J.-I. (1960). Speech development of infants. *Psychologia, 3,* 27–35.

Murphy, R., Menyuk, P., Liebergott, J., & Schultz, M. (1983). *Predicting rate of lexical development.* Paper presented at the meeting of the Society for Research in Child Development, Detroit.

Nakazima, S. (1962). A comparative study of speech developments of Japanese and American English childhood. *Studia Phonologica, 2,* 27–39.

Nelson, K. (1972). The relation of form recognition to concept development, intension of concept, properties and attributes. *Child Development, 43,* 67–74.

Nelson, K. (1973). Structure and strategy in learning to talk. *Monographs of the Society for Research in Child Development, 38.*

Nelson, K. (1980). Individual differences in language development: Implications for development and language. Paper presented at the Fifth Annual Boston University Language Development Conference, Boston.

Newport, E., Gleitman, H., & Gleitman, L. (1977) Mother, I'd rather do it myself: Some effects and non-effects on maternal speech style. In C. Snow & C. Ferguson (Eds.), *Talking to children* (pp. 109–149). Cambridge, England: Cambridge University Press.

Ninio, A., & Bruner, J. (1978). The achievement and antecedents of labelling. *Journal of Child Language, 5,* 1–15.

Oller, K. (1980). The emergence of the sounds of speech in infancy. In G. Yeni-Komshian & C. Ferguson (Eds.), *Child phonology: Vol. 1* (pp. 93–112), New York: Academic.

Sachs, J. & Truswell, L. (1978). Comprehension of two-word instructions by children in the one-word stage. *Child Language, 5,* 17–24.

Saltz, E., Dixon, E., Klein, S., & Becker, G. (1977). Studies of natural concepts, III. Concept over-discrimination in comprehension between two and four years of age. *Child Development, 48,* 1682–1685.

Schvachkin, N. (1973). The development of phonemic speech perception in early childhood. In C. Ferguson & D. Slobin (Eds.), *Studies of child language development* (pp. 91–127). New York: Holt, Rinehart & Winston.

Sherrod, H., Friedman, S., Crawley, S., Drake, D., & Devieux, J. (1977). Maternal language to prelinguistic infants. *Child Development, 48,* 1662–1663.

Smith, N. (1973). *The acquisition of phonology: A case study.* Cambridge, England: Cambridge University Press.

Snow, C. (1972). Mothers' speech to children learning language. *Child Development, 43,* 549–555.

Streeter, L. (1976). Language perception of 2-month old infants shows effects of both innate mechanisms and experience. *Nature, 259,* 39–41.

Thomas, D., Campos, J., Shucard, D., Ramsay, D., & Shucard, J. (1981). Semantic comprehension in infancy: A signal detection analysis. *Child Development, 52,* 798–803.

Tonkova-Yampolskaya, R. (1969). Development of speech imitation in infants during the first 2 years of life. In translation in *Soviet Psychology, 7,* 48–54.

Truby, H., Bosma, J., & Lind, J. (1965). Newborn infant cry. *Acta Paediatrica Scandinavica,* Supplement 163.

Tulkin, S. & Kagan, J. (1972). Mother–child interaction in the first year of life. *Child Development, 43,* 31–41.

Vygotsky, L.S. (1962). *Thought and language.* Cambridge, MA: M.I.T. Press.

Yeni-Komshian, G., Kavanagh, J., & Ferguson, C. (Eds.) (1980). *Child Phonology, Vol. 2: Perception.* New York: Academic.

CHAPTER 12

SOCIAL DEVELOPMENT

CHAPTER 12

Our discussion of social development begins with the development of infants' love relationships, called **attachments** by psychologists. This topic has been a strong focus of the field for a very considerable period of time. Most theorists and researchers have considered infants' attachments to their mothers to be of primary importance, so we will take up that topic first. We will then move to mother–infant interactions in early infancy. These are considered by many to be the major determinant of so-called "good attachment." This field has recently become prominent because the research has shown that infant development is a result of a reciprocal relationship in which the infant is a major determiner of caretaker behaviors. Finally, we will describe infants' developing relationships with their fathers, a topic that has only recently begun to receive much research attention.

ATTACHMENT TO MOTHER

History and Theories of the Concept

Psychoanalytic theory is the source of much of the belief that infants' initial attachment to their mothers is of utmost importance. Freud (1905/1938) came to believe that the mother–infant relationship is unique and established unalterably for a lifetime as the prime love-object that serves as the prototype of all later emotional ties to people. According to his theory babies developed what he called their **object relation** with their mother through the feeding relationship. During the first year of life the primary means of gratification available to the infant, according to Freud, is sucking. Thus, the person who provides that gratification becomes a love object (the primary object relation). Weaning, which withholds gratification from the baby, produces a conflict in this all-important relationship. Only if weaning is neither too severe nor too lenient, neither too rapid nor too prolonged, will the baby develop the ability to establish adequate interpersonal relationships later in life.

Because Freud was interested in psychopathology and gathered only case-study data from adults, he contributed little to the verification of this aspect of his theory. Nevertheless, his ideas appealed strongly to psychiatrists, psychologists, and lay people alike and they continue to influence not only the study of attachment, but also the study of infants' separation from and deprivation of their mothers.

Erik Erikson has extended and revised Freud's theory, incorporating much of the new knowledge gained between Freud's time and his own (Erikson, 1963). Erikson hypothesized that children who experience a good mother–infant relationship in infancy develop a basic trust in people and institutions, but children who do not experience a satisfactory attachment develop basic mistrust. The trust-mistrust dimension is the infants' general emotional reaction to events in their world. Trust implies a positive and accepting reaction whereas mistrust is a negative and rejecting reaction. Erikson hypothesized that the relationship is developed both through sucking and through other forms of mother–infant interactions.

For both Freud and Erikson, the prototypical mother–child relationship is believed to set the child's way of interacting with others for life, and inadequate attachment should therefore result in interpersonal difficulties throughout life. This should be reflected, most importantly, in marital and parental difficulties. As if these two dire consequences are not enough to blame on the nature of the attachment relationship, Erikson's notion of basic trust also includes consequences for the development of instrumental competence—competence with things rather than with people. This happens in two ways. The child develops trust in himself and his own competence and trust in institutions, from that of the family to government and religion. The mechanism by which trust in one's own competence might develop from attachment is clear. Mothers of toddlers who are attached serve as a secure base from which they can explore, and toddlers develop competence through exploration. Trust in institutions is somewhat of a generalization from the notion of basic trust, but it does follow reasonably. Basic trust is a pervasive emotional tendency to respond positively and in an accepting fashion, so it would be reasonable to predict that this acceptance would extend to abstract institutions as well as to people and oneself.

The term "attachment" was not used by the early Freudians, but Sears used it to describe children's differential relationships to parents (or, in psychoanalytic terms, their differential cathexes) in his 1943 survey of objective studies of psychoanalytic concepts. Nevertheless, it was not widely used until 15 years later when Bowlby (1958) adopted the term attachment, partly in the effort to avoid the difficulties of doing behavioral studies using the Freudian concept of object relations, partly to get away from the concept of dependency as used by learning theorists,[1] and partly because he thought it better expressed some of the ideas about affectional ties that were being developed by animal ethologists. His efforts provided a reformulation (or updating in his and Ainsworth's view) of psychoanalytic instinct theory in the ethological context, which views behavior, including human social behavior, in terms of Darwinian evolutionary theory. Ethological theory, developed by zoologists rather than by psychologists, focuses on those environmental events and infant response systems that are specific to each species. Many of the original formulations of ethologists were based on studies of **imprinting** in precocial birds (birds that can walk at hatching), such as ducks, geese, and chickens. For these species, attachment develops during a critical period that occurs shortly after birth. The crucial experience is that the mother moves away from the infant and the infant follows her. That which the infant follows "becomes" its mother. For example, Konrad Lorenz, who first documented the phenomenon, became "mother" to many goslings because he, rather than their biological mothers, happened to move away from them during the first few days of life. Thereafter they followed him and not adult geese. When they reached sexual maturity, they attempted to mate Lorenz's leg and not other geese. Since Lorenz's initial work, imprinting has been studied extensively. Researchers have determined that "mother" is a stimulus moving away at a particular rate and that the effects of this early experience typically are long lasting.

Because ethologists appreciate the great differences that exist among species, and because humans cannot follow at birth, ethologists do not claim that following a stimulus that is moving away plays the same unitary and crucial role for the development of attachment in humans that it does in precocial birds. Their accounts do, however, maintain the general flavor of the imprinting phenomenon: that infants are biologically predisposed to learn to recognize their "mother" (analogous to being predisposed to follow an object moving away) and to respond to that "mother" by a strong, enduring bond, such as is found in the birds.

Bowlby searched for and found five behavioral response systems in human infants that he thought functioned to develop the attachment relationship. Following is of course an obvious first choice, derived from imprinting research. Clinging may serve the same function for many primates (monkeys and apes) that following does for precocial birds and therefore is a good second choice. Human newborns, however, do not show the universal and intense clinging to their mothers that monkeys do, and so clinging is not likely to be a predominant response for humans the way following is for precocial birds or clinging for monkeys. Bowlby proposed that three additional response systems play important roles in human infants' development of attachments: crying, smiling, and sucking. All three of these behavioral systems are present in at least primitive form in early infancy (see Chapter 6) and they all have the effect of bringing or keeping the adult in contact. In Bowlby's view, all five of these behavioral systems are initially independent of each other and develop at different times and at different rates, but they become integrated and focused on the mother. They then form the basis of attachment, which develops in humans by about 7 months of age.

Consistent with his ethological viewpoint, Bowlby considered the development of the specific attachment to the mother to be biologically based. That does not mean that it unfolds solely due to maturation or that the envi-

---

[1] This notion was that some children develop a general tendency to seek help, attention, or emotional support from adults. This was conceived to be a generalized individual trait that the child would be expected to exhibit in many situations and with many different adults. It was often hypothesized to develop because the mother reinforced her child for such behaviors during infancy and later childhood.

ronment is irrelevant.[2] Rather, he proposes that each of the five response systems needs environmental stimulation to develop. Thus, each of the response systems depends on both experience and maturation, and attachment depends on the role of experience and maturation in integrating the systems. We find, however, that it is all too frequently true that Bowlby and those who have come after him have talked about behaviors at given stages as if they were entirely dependent on maturation, whereas they depend both for their timing and their very existence on particular environments.

This is sometimes true even in the writings of Ainsworth, whose extensive research has been a major contribution to understanding individual differences in attachment and the antecedent mother–infant interactions that seem to produce these differences.

Much of the early interest in attachment came from studies of the reactions of infants and young children to being hospitalized. This situation involves threats to the infant other than just separation from the mother. The hospital is a very strange environment and many unpleasant things may happen to the infant both for medical reasons and because of the social structure of the environment. Hence the effects of hospitalization on attachment can hardly be expected to be the same as the effects of other types of separation. We will limit our discussion of attachment to its development and expression in the normal North American environment.

Development of a Specific Attachment

Young babies cannot recognize their mothers and hence cannot exhibit different emotional responses to them, but they do show what is called **undiscriminating social responsiveness.** During the first 2 or 3 months infants can use their basic capacities (described earlier) to

orient to people as well as to things. They orient to salient features of the environment, which often are human, by such responses as visual fixation, visual tracking, listening, rooting, and postural adjustments when they are held. They can also gain or maintain contact with other humans in a limited way through sucking or grasping, although they don't exhibit these behaviors in order to maintain social contact (remember from Chapter 10 that they have not yet developed means–ends behaviors). They also have special signaling behaviors, that again presumably are not intentional: smiling, crying, and vocalizing. As we described in Chapters 7 and 9, some stimuli are more attractive than others, including several that commonly emanate from adults. These include faces, voices, and parents' imitations of the infant, particularly vocal imitation. This early experience with humans presumably provides the basis by which young infants can learn to discriminate one human from another. Recall from Chapter 9 that newborn babies probably cannot distinguish faces; by 8 weeks, babies can discriminate faces, but only if given ample time; and only by 3–4 months can they easily and quickly recognize a particular face. Once such discriminative ability develops, the infant has the basis for the next phase, **discriminating social responsiveness,** during which infants respond differently (for example, in their vocalizing, smiling, and crying) to one or a few familiar figures than they do to relative strangers. Ainsworth (1973) subdivides this stage into an early one, in which infants differentiate between the attachment figure and a stranger only when near or in contact with them, and a later subphase, in which infants respond differentially when the attachment figure is close or at a distance, such as when he or she enters or leaves the room.

Babies who exhibit discriminating social responsiveness not only are able to discriminate mother's face from other faces but also have become familiar with their mothers' caretaking and social behaviors. This familiarity has undoubtedly been developing throughout their young lives because (recall Chapter 7) newborns are able to learn at birth, and their learning abilities increase rapidly in the first few months. Thus they are more and more able to learn their mothers' ways of interacting and to respond to their mothers in ways that will

---

[2]Although sucking is one of the behaviors in his group, Bowlby did not consider feeding to play an important role in attachment. This conclusion was concurrently being demonstrated empirically by the Harlows (see Harlow, 1958), who found that in monkeys clinging (contact comfort) was a far more important ingredient for attachment to artificial mothers than was feeding. This research will be discussed later in this chapter.

lead to rewards and will be rewarding to their mothers. Most of the studies known as attachment research have not studied these first two phases. Rather they have focused on the third phase, **active initiative in seeking proximity and contact,** which has been described as follows by Ainsworth:

During this phase all the earlier attachment behaviors are still present and differential, but there is a striking increase in the baby's initiative in promoting proximity and contact. His signals are no longer merely expressive or reactive; they often are intended to evoke a response from the mother or other attachment figure. Locomotion facilitates proximity seeking, and voluntary movements of hands and arms are conspicuous now in attachment behavior. Greeting responses become more active and effective. Following, approaching, clinging, and various other active contact behaviors become significant. The median age for attaining this phase is about seven months. Bowlby suggests that "goal-corrected" sequences of behavior emerge in this phase: sequences guided by a constant stream of feedback so that the baby alters the direction, speed, and nature of his behavior in accordance with that of the figure to whom he has become attached. . . . It also coincides with the period during which psychoanalytic theorists judge "true object relations" to emerge. Further, its onset coincides with Piaget's fourth stage of sensorimotor development, in which the child first begins to search for hidden objects and thus manifests the beginnings of the concept of an object as permanent despite its not being present to perception. (Ainsworth, 1973, p. 12)

Clearly, part of the reason that this phase in attachment develops at this time is that certain motoric and cognitive developments are occurring. Infants are beginning to move on their own, so they can seek proximity to mother much more effectively. Further, as we described in Chapter 10, infants of this age are developing intentionality (means–ends behaviors) and the beginnings of object permanence (successful search for an object hidden under a single screen). An example of the newly developed intentionality is when infants lift their hands to be picked up. A secondary scheme—

hand lifting—has been subordinated to the goal of being picked up. Developing object permanence also means that infants now understand that mother still exists when the infant is not presently interacting with her. In the previous Piagetian stage, part of the object (mother) would have to be present for the infant to initiate any action toward it (her).

Although most of the rest of the material on attachment concerns various responses during this third phase of development, Bowlby (1969) suggested that there is a fourth phase, **goal-corrected partnership.** It probably starts at about 3 years, so it is not really a stage of infancy. During this phase children come to understand the factors that influence their mothers' behaviors and can therefore be more sophisticated in their efforts to modify their mothers' behaviors to fit their own needs.

The first three stages just described are well documented, especially by the work of Ainsworth. All children apparently go through each stage in the same sequence, although not at the same ages. Ainsworth (1967) found this to be true of babies in Uganda as well as in the United States. This invariance of stage development supports the ethological notion of the maturational unfolding of stages, given prior activation of the infant's behavior systems by the environment. Such a formulation is not the only possibility, however. The mechanisms underlying this invariant stage sequence might instead reflect perceptual, motor, and cognitive development. For example, it seems clear that infants are social creatures; that is, they make social responses to social stimuli (see the discussions of smiling in Chapter 6, imitation in Chapter 7, early verbal communication in Chapter 11, and early social responsiveness later in this chapter). They cannot, however, respond differentially to their mothers versus strangers until they can discriminate perceptually between them. Thus, they cannot "pass" from Phase 1 to 2 until they have learned something about mommies and strangers. If perceptual, motor, and cognitive mechanisms determine the development of attachment, then the ethologists are wrong in hypothesizing that attachment is directly controlled by maturation.

Note that although each of these stages is qualitatively distinct from the other, that does not mean that the transitions between them

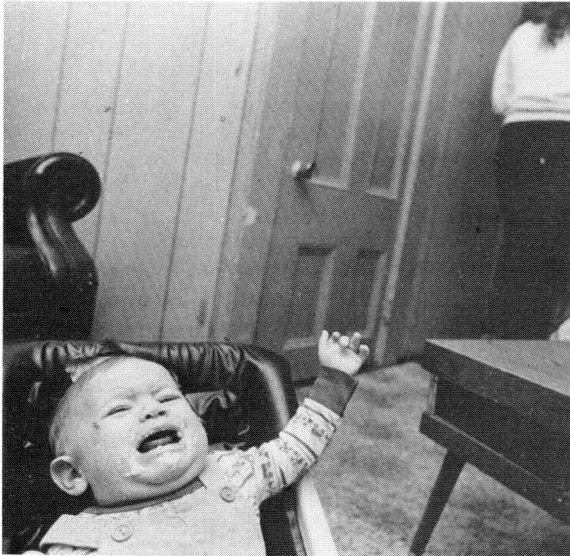

FIGURE 12–1. Aspects of attachment: protest at separation (left) and fear of the strange (right).

are abrupt. Infants develop gradually and there may be occasional signs, say, of preferential looking at mother, long before preferences are expressed in other behaviors (such as smiling and waving) or in more than one context (such as arrival of mother, departure of mother, changes in mother's behaviors). Only at the height of each phase would the phenomena described be strong and clear to the casual observer. Even then babies do not behave consistently in all situations. For example, they are more likely to protest separation in a strange place than at home, after previous separation than at first separation, and when left with a stranger than when left with another attachment figure. In technical language, attachment behaviors are context specific.

What Is This Thing Called Attachment?

Because most of the research on the development of infants' attachment has focused on the phase of active initiative in seeking proximity and contact, the term "attachment" often refers specifically to that phase. The conceptualization underlying the first research in attachment came from the notion introduced by

Sigmund Freud and developed in this context by Spitz (1950), that the underlying motivating force behind attachment is infants' fear of losing their mothers. Thus, the best measures of this love force should be protest (crying and fussing) at separation from the mother, measured either in the laboratory or in natural situations, and fear of strangers (Figure 12–1). The reason protest at separation reflects infants' fear of losing mother is obvious, but the relation to stranger anxiety is more indirect. Spitz suggested that when infants are confronted by a stranger, they realize that the stranger is not mother and fear that mother has been lost.

As research on attachment has developed, researchers have questioned whether degree of protest and stranger anxiety are adequate measures of attachment. Protest at separation is a peculiar measure in several ways. Babies who exhibit intense protest at separation may be less secure in their attachment or may be more insecure in general rather than being more positively attached. Babies who exhibit little separation protest may not be less attached; they may simply be more secure or may have mothers who have discovered specific techniques for solving protest at separation (Weinraub, 1977; Weinraub & Lewis, 1977). In addition to these objections, it has been shown to be a less sensitive measure than the ones we will discuss next; that is, infants will sometimes show equal protest at separation to two attachment figures, but will show greater attachment to one in other ways (see for example Fox, 1977).

In her earliest research on attachment, Ainsworth (1963) became convinced that more positive indications of attachment were needed. She developed a laboratory situation in which the baby remains in the room while the mother and a stranger each enter and leave the room several times. This provided measures of the infant's behaviors before, during, and after separation from the mother, and when with a stranger or alone. This situation, which she called the strange situation, permitted her to measure positive attachment behaviors, such as heightened proximity-seeking and contact-maintaining behaviors when infants were reunited with their mothers after brief separations.

Ainsworth's work in this field has also led her to conclude that stranger anxiety is not a valid measure of developing attachment (1973). Her first reason is that stranger anxiety first develops at a different time than other attachment measures and cannot therefore be part of the same process (and she cites six studies to support her claim). Her second reason is that not all babies who are attached to their mothers display fear of strangers with any consistency. In fact Ainsworth and Wittig (1969), who had a stranger pick up 1-year-olds after the mother had left, found that the stranger was able to comfort some of the infants (the infants cried less or clung tightly, or both, and some protested when put down by the stranger and tried to maintain contact by clinging).

A recent study by Solomon and Décarie (1976) also supports Ainsworth's claim that stranger anxiety is not universal. Their 8- to 12-month-old infants were confronted by three different strangers within a period of 10 days. Fear of strangers was not consistently displayed, although positive responses were (see also Sroufe & Waters, 1977). If fear of strangers is not fear of losing mother, then what is it? A plausible answer is that it is part of the general fear of the strange that is typical of infants. Such general fear seems to be a biologically adaptive response. It is found in chimpanzees (Hebb & Riesen, 1943), rhesus monkeys (Harlow, 1958), and many other species (see Sluckin, 1965; Bronson, 1968). This explanation also provides a reason for the lack of stranger anxiety in some babies. If a baby encounters many strangers daily, strangers will not be strange to that infant and will not elicit fear. For example, one of the authors kept her baby in her office three days a week for the first nine months of his life. He experienced dozens of strangers weekly, both in her office and around a college campus. During this period he never exhibited stranger anxiety. In fact, at a party of around 50 adults in a large room, he spent most of the time surrounded by strangers at the opposite end of the room from his mother. She repeatedly attempted to get him to exhibit stranger anxiety in front of a movie camera so there would be a record for future classes. Only one attempt was successful: He was left with a stranger of more mature years than most college students, in the stranger's yard. Even after that time he exhibited no fear of strangers, even of being left in a stranger's house.

Since the early 1970s, a somewhat different controversy related to the behaviors used to index attachment has arisen. It has been argued that protest at separation and proximity seeking do not index a general individual characteristic or trait called attachment, although they may be valid measures of the *onset* of attachment. If there were a trait of attachment, infants who scored high on one measure (for example, protest at separation) should also score high on other measures (for example, proximity-seeking). Furthermore, infants should exhibit long-term stability; that is, infants who show high proximity-seeking at 10 months should show high proximity-seeking at 18 months. Finally, infants who are strongly attached in one context, such as under the stress of an unfamiliar situation, should show that same strong attachment in other contexts, such as at home. None of these predictions has been supported when the index behaviors we have described have been used to measure attachment. These measures of attachment can be used profitably, but only to study the influence of the environment on specific behaviors within the mother–infant pair (Cairns, 1972; Gewirtz, 1972a, 1972b; Rosenthal, 1973).

In direct opposition are the views of Ainsworth (1972, 1973, 1974) and Sroufe (Sroufe &

Waters, 1977; Sroufe, 1979). They agree that attachment as measured by the behaviors described above is not a stable individual trait (in the way dependency presumably is), but they argue that the failures described above should not lead to the conclusion that there is no such construct as attachment. Attachment does have meaning beyond the specific behaviors studied, they say, but only if one conceptualizes both its meaning and the way one measures it differently from that of an internal personality trait. It is different, first, in that attachment is not something characteristic of an individual, but rather is characteristic of an infant's interactions with a particular individual. Second, the reality of the attachment lies not in specific behaviors, even if positive, but rather in qualitative patterns of behaviors. Ainsworth and colleagues have developed a tripartite classification scheme for patterns of attachment (Ainsworth & Wittig, 1969; Ainsworth, Bell, & Stayton, 1971; Bell, 1970). In this scheme, **securely attached** infants, the largest group, exhibit increased positive reunion behaviors toward their mothers with few proximity-avoiding, angry, or resistant behaviors. **Resistant** (or ambivalently attached) infants show heightened positive reunion behaviors, but in addition display angry, resistant behavior (for example, kicking, hitting, or pushing). When reunited with their mothers, **avoidant** infants avoid and ignore their mothers or mix avoiding behaviors with approach behaviors, for example, move toward their mothers, then stop and look away (see Figure 12–2).

The organizational approach espoused by Ainsworth and Sroufe predicts that these three qualitatively different patterns of reunion behavior should be stable although the more discrete behaviors are not. For example, infants who are securely attached at 12 months should still be securely attached at 18 months, at least when their living situation has been stable. Waters (1978) found that 48 out of 50 infants remained in the same one of the three attachment categories, even though they did not show stability on concrete behaviors. For example, a particular avoidant infant may have turned his head away when he was picked up at 12 months but not at 18 months, and he may have ignored his mother at 18 months but not at 12 months. Nevertheless, he would have

FIGURE 12–2. *The ambivalent reactions some toddlers (12- to 18-month-olds) have when their mothers return after a brief absence. This toddler is approaching his mother (a positive reaction), but his head is turned away (a negative reaction).*

been classified as stably avoidant. Both turning away his head and ignoring mother are avoidant, but in different ways. Although the stability Waters found is truly impressive, it must be interpreted carefully. Waters deliberately selected as subjects babies from advantaged, stable, middle class homes. Vaughn, Egeland, Sroufe, and Waters (1979) tested 100 economically disadvantaged babies of whom only 62 were assigned to the same attachment category at both 12 and 18 months. They also asked mothers to complete a checklist to measure occurrences of stressful events. They found that infants who changed from secure to anxious attachments came from homes with more stress than did those who exhibited stable secure patterns. Thompson, Lamb, and Estes (1982) reported similar findings. They correlated stability in attachment to changes in family circumstances within a broad range of middle class families (from semiskilled workers to professionals). Only 53% of their infants were in the same attachment category at both 12 and 19 months. Changes in attachment classes were more common for babies whose mothers took jobs, although the baby was as likely to go from insecure to secure attachment as vice versa. The authors suggested that maternal employment required renegotiation of the mother–infant relationship, which could be for better or for worse.

These three studies on stability of attachment considered together show that (1) the tripartite classification of babies' *patterns* of attachment leads to more stability of measurement than do measures of individual behaviors, but (2) although there is substantial stability, there is also substantial instability when infants' life situations are changed. This state of affairs is common in the study of stability of children's behaviors, be they those of attachment or those assessed by the DQ. Usually when researchers argue that a behavioral pattern or trait is stable they mean that children show more stability than would be expected on the basis of chance alone. They do not mean that all individuals are stable.

The tripartite classification of quality of attachment also suggests other hypotheses. We will mention a few that have been supported experimentally. First, the negative feelings avoidant infants have toward their mothers interfere with seeking and maintaining contact. Waters, Wippman, and Sroufe (1979) demonstrated that such infants play with their mothers during the initial period before their mothers leave, but this shared play does not include expressions of emotion. Such emotional sharing would be expected in babies who feel securely attached. Second, securely attached infants exhibit more friendly, cooperative behaviors toward peers and adults than ambivalent or avoidant infants (Pastor, 1980). Third, securely attached infants exhibit less fear of strangers (Sroufe, 1977).

All of the measures of reactions to mothers' leaving and return—protest at separation, positive reunion behaviors, and qualitatively different patterns of reunion behaviors—

have been used successfully in research concerning the role of attachment in infants' development and its relation to maternal behaviors hypothesized to be important to the development of the mother–infant relationship. Unfortunately, these different measures of attachment often yield different conclusions about the same hypothesis. We will favor conclusions that have been reached using several different measures, and when we are forced to rely on only one measure, we will always mention the measure used.

The Functions of Attachment

We have discussed what attachment is and how it develops. It is obviously an area of great interest and concern for parents, who find their children's developing love to be exciting and rewarding. Attachment also has a very important role in children's development.

DURING INFANCY

First, attachment functions as a biological mechanism for survival. Let us review the basics of the theory of evolution. Those organisms who manage to produce offspring who in turn survive to reproduce are more successful than those who do not, because their genes will survive across generations. The famous phrase "survival of the fittest" refers to the survival of an organism's genes and therefore its species. Animals who are successful in passing on their genes to subsequent generations are said to adapt effectively to their environment. Successful adaptation, then, requires that organisms survive until they are old enough to mate and then that they mate successfully and nurture their offspring in such a way as to maximize the probability that their offspring will survive.

One important difference among species is the extent to which learning plays a role in the life of the individual. For example, appropriate mating and parenting behaviors must be learned in some species but are instinctive in others. To confirm this generalization, let us look at the effect of deprivation in different species. In some bird species, for example, individuals raised from birth to reproductive age in isolation are able to mate normally and become successful parents. In other species, such as the rhesus monkey, animals raised in isolation are unable to mate and raise young normally, which means that they need to learn something in their own lifespan to be able to engage in these basic functions. Those species for whom extensive learning is necessary typically are born at a quite immature stage of development and have long childhoods. In contrast, those species whose basic behavioral systems are prewired typically are born at a more mature stage, are better able to fend for themselves, and have short childhoods.

It is clear that basic behavioral systems (such as mating and raising young) that can be modified by learning are biologically adaptive traits because many species have so evolved. The long period of immaturity after birth does, however, pose substantial survival risks to the offspring. Perhaps the biggest danger in the wild, for both humans and other animals, is danger from predators. Although predators are not a major problem for most infants living in industrial societies, substantial dangers exist for toddlers in the form of mechanical and electrical monsters such as cars, electrical outlets, stoves, and hot water faucets, and chemical monsters such as lye, bleach, insecticides, pills, and lead paint. One role of caretakers clearly is to protect babies from such dangers. Babies' attachment to their mothers helps their mothers provide such protection. Attached offspring are secure near mother and are afraid when far from mother. Therefore, they tend to stay close to her where she can protect them, particularly in new, strange surroundings. This desire for maintaining proximity develops at the time infants are beginning to move on their own and don't yet know what is dangerous. Thus, it is maximally adaptive.

Second, attachment figures function as secure bases for exploration. Because learning is very important in animals with long childhoods, it is important for babies to explore: That is how they learn. Exploration, however, is at odds with survival. If toddlers were to explore far and wide without supervision, they would encounter increased survival dangers. The attachment relationship is an effective device because it provides a way to balance exploration needs with security needs. As we said earlier, a novel situation typically elicits fear in toddlers. Mothers provide security and therefore reduce that fear, which allows babies to

explore the strange situation. Thus, we would expect toddlers to explore a strange, presumably anxiety-invoking situation much more readily when mother is present than when she is not. This phenomenon has been well established in different contexts and in different groups, including both humans (Ainsworth & Bell, 1970; Arsenian, 1943; Cox & Campbell, 1968; Gershaw & Schwartz, 1971; Lester, Kotelchuck, Spelke, Sellers, & Klein, 1974; Maccoby & Feldman, 1972; Rheingold, 1969; Rheingold & Eckerman, 1970; Schaffer & Emerson, 1964) and monkeys (Harlow & Zimmerman, 1959). This pattern develops in the second half of the first year of human life (Ainsworth, 1974) and is waning by the second birthday (Cox & Campbell, 1968). Furthermore, infants show less wariness of strangers in standard stranger-approach studies when they are near their mothers or on their laps (Bronson, 1972; Campos, Emde, & Gaensbauer, 1975; Morgan & Ricciuti, 1969).

When mother is present, the basic pattern of exploration for both monkeys and humans is an alternation between exploring the environment and a kind of checking in with mother that may involve eye contact, proximity, or clinging. The confidence with which toddlers explore a strange situation when their mothers are present is both delightful and somewhat surprising. As we shall see, toddlers often move away from their mothers immediately after they enter a strange environment; they often leave the room the mother is sitting in to explore neighboring areas; and they may even allow their mothers to go into a nearby room out of sight and sound of the child, especially if they have something interesting to explore.

It seems clear that in such situations infants leave their mothers in order to explore. Rheingold and Eckerman (1969) had mothers sit in a small unfurnished room that adjoined a larger unfurnished room (called the open field room). All 24 of their 10-month-old infants left the mother's room without fussing or crying. When a toy was in the open field room, the children spent less time with their mothers than when there was no toy. Children who had access to 3 toys in the open field room (versus 1 toy) went farther from their mothers and stayed away longer. In short, the more there was to explore, the more time infants spent away from their mothers exploring.

In an interesting variation of this kind of research, Rheingold and her colleagues (Corter, Rheingold, and Eckerman, 1972) had mothers leave the infant in the first room with or without a toy. Infants without a toy followed their mothers virtually immediately and reached the threshold between rooms in an average of 23 seconds. Infants with a toy followed much more slowly and took an average of 215 seconds. When the toy group did go to the mother, however, they more quickly touched her (average latency to touch was 69 seconds for the toy group and 123 seconds for the no toy group). It would appear that the infants' desire to explore the toy was powerful enough to delay following, but when they did follow, they seemed more intent on making contact with the mother; that is, on touching base. The no toy babies seemed, in contrast, to be following mother to find stimulation; they were not eager to establish or to maintain physical contact.

In another study, Rheingold and her colleagues (Ross, Rheingold, & Eckerman, 1972) found that 12-month-old infants preferred going to a room with a novel toy over going to a room with a familiar toy. They spent more time with the novel toy and spent relatively little time in contact with their mothers (averages were 66 and 76 seconds out of 5 minutes for each of two trials). Great individual differences were shown, however; the range was 1 to 198 seconds on the first trial and 15 to 262 seconds on the second trial. It would be interesting to know if these individual differences were related to differences in attachment classifications. Securely attached infants might be expected to spend less time with their mothers.

In these studies, exploration by toddlers seems remarkably courageous. They leave their mothers and even tolerate her moving out of their sight and sound with remarkably little anxiety. The more interesting the environment the more readily they leave her. Nonetheless, these studies show only one side of the coin—the high quality exploration that occurs when mother is nearby or easily reachable. It appears that any condition that emotionally stresses infants decreases their exploration and increases their need for their mothers. For example, in Rheingold's situation (Eckerman & Rheingold, 1974) when a strange person rather than a toy was in the adjoining room, infants

were much less likely to enter that room (5 of 10 infants in the stranger group entered versus 9 of 10 in the toy group). Those infants in the stranger group who did enter the second room did so much more slowly.

In studies with an even more stressful situation, in which a stranger confronts the infants in the same room, 12-month-olds tended to move toward their mothers and to explore the stranger visually from that safe vantage point (Bretherton & Ainsworth, 1974; Feldman & Ingham, 1975). Those few infants who were brave enough to touch the stranger were highly likely to run back to their mothers immediately afterwards (Bretherton & Ainsworth, 1974).

When toddlers experience successive anxiety-arousing experiences, there is a cumulative effect (Ainsworth & Bell, 1970). The amount of exploration 1-year-olds exhibited decreased when a stranger entered the room in which mother and baby had been playing, declined further when mother left the room, revived somewhat when mother returned, but declined to a new low when the mother left for a second time, and did not revive when she returned the second time.

It also seems quite clear that the developed attachment relationship is truly what provides the security. For example, Rheingold (1969) found that when the mother was gone, neither toys nor the presence of a stranger encouraged exploration any more than an empty room. Overt signs of support from the mother are not necessary. Carr, Dabbs, and Carr (1975) found that toddlers 18–30 months of age played with toys more if their mothers were readily in visual contact (seated on the other side of the toys rather than behind the child or behind a screen). They did not actually interact with her more when she was in sight, but having the opportunity evidently gave them the necessary base from which to explore the toys in the room.

The third function attachment figures serve in infancy is to provide a source of stimulation and to be a playmate. For example, in the study by Corter and colleagues (1972) described earlier, the babies in the toy group apparently followed their mothers to touch base—that is, for security reasons—but the no toy babies seemed to be seeking stimulation from her.

Another phenomenon demonstrating that

toddlers' relationships to their mothers is one of playmate is that they share their toys with their mothers. Rheingold, Hay, and West (1976) documented this in a series of studies of 15- and 18-month-old toddlers. They measured three related kinds of behavior: (1) showing by pointing or holding up an object, (2) giving (that is, putting an object in a person's hand or lap), and (3) manipulating an object that the child had given the adult who was still in contact with it. Almost all the children observed exhibited all three behaviors frequently. In a 10-minute period, the children on the average showed and gave objects approximately 6 times and engaged in partner play about 3 times. These data suggest that toddlers use their mothers not only as secure bases for exploration, but also as playmates. It has not yet been clearly demonstrated that such sharing is necessarily an aspect of differential attachment to a particular person rather than simply one facet of social development. Nevertheless, the study by Rheingold and her colleagues provides some limited support for the idea that sharing is related to attachment. In one of their experiments, fathers (to whom specific attachments are also formed) and strangers were present and the children shared more with their fathers than with strangers.

In a later section of this chapter we will describe research that suggests that mother's role as playmate and stimulator is related to the quality and intensity of attachment.

LONG-TERM CONSEQUENCES

We have just discussed three functions of attachment during infancy: (1) it keeps infants close to their mothers who provide safety, (2) it enables babies to explore the inanimate world within that safe context, and (3) it provides the opportunity for the attachment figure to provide stimulation through playful interactions. None of these functions addresses the issues of most fascination to both those interested in evolution and those interested in the development of mental health, issues that revolve around the belief that early maternal–infant relationships form the basis for later interpersonal relationships. For Freud and Erikson, attachment is the prototype for all later personal relationships (of which mating and raising offspring are the most important). For evolution-

ary theorists, attachment is what allows the young to learn the social interactions necessary for these later activities. Bowlby, who integrated Freudian and ethological theory, shared this view, and his work has been extremely important in advancing these beliefs in the present era.

Note that these views all assume a "critical period": Events that occur within a restricted period of infancy (the first year of life for Freud and Erikson; 6 months to $1\frac{1}{2}$ years for Bowlby) have permanent long-term consequences and the period of susceptibility or sensitivity is determined by biological mechanisms. Both Freud and Erikson soften the permanence aspect of the critical period hypothesis somewhat. They believe that reliving the infancy experiences in therapy can undo, or at least ameliorate bad effects. Erikson further believes that although basic trust is most easily developed during infancy, negative outcomes from infancy can be overcome by a good environment in later stages. When the critical periods notion is changed to make it more flexible it is often called a "sensitive period" hypothesis.

Most of the research designed to test hypotheses concerning long-term consequences of attachment has used the strategy of studying children deprived of their mothers and has tested general outcomes rather than specific personality outcomes. This research, along with that designed to test specific critical period hypotheses, will be discussed in the next chapter.

Another line of research has sprouted quickly since Ainsworth developed her tripartite classification of the quality of attachment. The strategy in these studies has been to do follow-up studies of children who have been classified with respect to the quality of their attachment. The assessment of attachment usually occurs between 12 and 18 months and the follow-up 1 to 2 years later. The behaviors measured at the time of follow-up have varied widely across the few studies and at present do not provide a coherent picture of exactly what sorts of cognitive, emotional, and social characteristics are related to quality of attachment. Nevertheless, these studies consistently show relations to quality of attachment.

To demonstrate the kinds of variables for which relations have been found, we will describe several of the findings. Main (1973) found that securely attached infants (measured at 12 months) had higher Bayley scores at 21 months than resistant children (avoidant children were in between). Resistant children also showed less intense play with toys, more restless changing of activity, and less enjoyment than did securely attached or avoidant children. Matas, Arend, and Sroufe (1978) measured 2-year-olds' problem solving involving the use of a standard set of tools. They found that securely attached infants clearly enjoyed the situation, followed instructions easily, and even when frustrated by failure they seldom cried, fussed, or became angry. When they needed help, they asked nearby adults and showed little discomfort in the process. Insecurely attached infants (either avoidant or resistant) became frustrated easily and reacted strongly to the frustration, and quickly gave up trying to solve the problems. They seldom asked for help, even when they needed it, and ignored or rejected directions from adults. Waters, Wippman, and Sroufe (1979) observed children who previously had been classified as to attachment when they were in nursery school at $3\frac{1}{2}$ years. Those who had been securely attached as infants tended to be social leaders; that is, they initiated and participated actively in group activities and were sought out by other children. Teachers rated them as curious and eager to learn and as more self-directed and forceful. Insecurely attached children were more likely to be socially withdrawn and to hesitate about participating in activities. By teachers' ratings they were less curious and less forceful in pursuit of their activities.

Clearly there are many differences between securely and insecurely attached children. Notice, however, that most of the differences found in these studies have been between securely attached infants and the two groups of insecurely attached infants. Few long-term differences have yet been found between avoidant and resistant infants even though as infants and toddlers they appear quite different.

Remember that correlations do not prove causality. Given the findings described above, secure attachment may provide the basis for later positive development, but it is just as likely that mothers whose parenting behaviors produce secure attachment in infancy continue to behave in equally successful ways when their children are preschoolers. Thus, maternal behaviors at the later age may be the cause of the later good development. Of course, it also may be that maternal behaviors are determined by their infants' behaviors. Babies who are easy and rewarding to take care of may encourage responsivity, acceptance, and even sensitivity in their mothers. Thus, the stability of these behaviors might be caused more by infants' stable characteristics or by the interaction of infants' individual characteristics with their mothers' rearing preferences and techniques than by any specific maternal characteristics or infant-care techniques mother or other caretakers may use.

The Mother's Role in the Development of Attachment

Most of the research exploring this question has focused naturally enough on the role mothers play in determining the degree and quality of their infants' attachment. The maternal–infant interaction that has most frequently been hypothesized to be important in the development of infants' love for their mothers is the feeding situation. This may be because young infants spend such a large portion of their waking hours feeding and mothers spend so much of their caretaking time in feeding interactions. At any rate, both Freudian (psychoanalytic) and classical learning theory hypothesize that the feeding situation is crucial to the development of infants' attachment. Two related hypotheses are derived from these theories. One is that she who feeds the infant should be the object of attachment; if mother is not the primary food-provider, then she will not be the primary object of the infant's affection. The second relates to the quality of feeding. In the Freudian version a mother who provides either too much or too little sucking gratification disrupts the quality of her infant's attachment and emotional health. Quality of feeding is important in the everyday feeding situation and in weaning. Weaning, in Freudian theory, is a time of major crisis for infants because the gratification of their sucking need is threatened, and thus the severity and suddenness of weaning should affect the quality of the attachment relationship.

Before we describe the research designed to test these hypotheses relating feeding variables to attachment, we will describe a second variable that has been compared to feeding. **Contact comfort** has been called a major determinant of attachment by people who are ethologically oriented or who have been influenced by Harlow's research with monkeys, which we are about to describe. The ethologists have noticed that infants of many primate species spend much time clinging to their mothers and that this often serves an adaptive purpose in allowing mothers to move around without needing to provide much support for the baby. Although human infants do not need to cling to survive, they nevertheless do cuddle. Indeed, as we discussed in Chapter 5, advocates of Leboyer deliveries and many of those who believe in maternal bonding both emphasize the value of skin-to-skin contact immediately after birth. Advocates of breast feeding also often talk about the importance of the body contact involved. As with feeding, there are two specific hypotheses to be tested. One is that contact comfort is necessary for the development of attachment, and the second is that the quality of contact comfort or cuddling is related to the quality of attachment.

Trying to test these hypotheses or others concerning the role of the mother in attachment is a very difficult proposition, because it is impossible to randomly assign human babies to different maternal rearing conditions and watch the results. It is possible, however, to do experimental animal studies and compare the results with those obtained from correlational studies using humans. Fortunately, in this area of research, the findings from the two kinds of studies fit together nicely and so it is possible to be more confident about the conclusions than is often the case when only correlational studies with humans are available.

The animal research has been done primarily with rhesus macaque monkeys and was begun by Harry and Margaret Kuenne Harlow (Harlow, 1958; Harlow & Harlow, 1966; Harlow & Zimmerman, 1959). Rhesus monkeys are a good choice for this research because, like humans, they are mammals, and their infants are born singly and in an immature state that requires substantial maternal care. Furthermore, their intellectual and emo-

FIGURE 12–3. Surrogate mothers used in Harlow's studies of the development of attachment in baby rhesus monkeys. The baby can choose either the soft nonfeeding mother or the wire feeding mother. She spends most of her time on the soft mother who cannot feed her and becomes attached only to it. (Photograph courtesy of H.F. Harlow, University of Wisconsin Primate Laboratory.)

tional systems are highly complex and vulnerable to environmental deprivation.

To manipulate the role the mother plays in the development of attachment, the Harlows built surrogate monkey mothers, as shown in Figure 12–3. The surrogate mothers are essentially angled stands that were designed so that infants could get food from or cling to their "mothers" or both. The surrogates could have nipples or not, and they could be covered with terry cloth or not. The Harlows first tested whether the provision of nutritive nipples and of contact comfort each influenced the development of attachment independent of the other. They found that both variables played a role. If baby monkeys had access to two surrogates, one with a working nipple and one without, baby monkeys spent more time on the feeding mother. If the babies had available a terry cloth and a wire mother, they spent more time on the terry cloth mother.

The next step was to discover which of these two variables was more important. They provided a wire mother with a nipple and a cloth mother with no nipple. In this case, the babies had to choose between their pleasures— food or contact comfort. The babies overwhelmingly chose contact comfort. They would stay on the nonfeeding cloth mother for most of the time, switching to the wire mother only to feed. If they could reach, they would stay on the cloth mother even when feeding (see Figure 12–3).

Is the amount of time spent clinging an adequate measure of attachment? Even baby monkeys might prefer a soft to a hard seat, and yet that might not be attachment. Luckily, the Harlows and their colleagues did not stop there. They also measured the infants' use of their surrogate mother as a secure base for exploration. They put the infants and the "mothers" into a strange room filled with many scary things, such as a wooden block, a doorknob, and a cootie toy. Monkeys raised with cloth mothers or with both cloth and wire mothers would rush to their cloth mothers and cling, subsequently venturing out to explore. They derived no comfort from the wire feeding mother and would cower in a corner and act as if no mother at all was there, if she was the only one present. Even infants who had known only a nursing wire mother from birth derived no comfort from her in this open-field test. Finally, babies who had both a nursing and a nonnursing terry cloth mother showed no long-term preference between the two, although they did show preference for the nursing mother prior to 100 days of age. Thus, it is clear that the nursing aspect of mothering did not provide an adequate basis for the development of the secure base phenomenon.

The attachment these infant monkeys developed to their cloth mothers was maintained even after long separations. One group was separated from their surrogate mothers at 180 days of life and they still showed positive responses to them at 2 years of age.

Thus, for rhesus monkeys, it appears that nursing plays only a small role in the initial

development of attachment and is of no importance to the longer-term function of attachment as a secure base for exploration. Contact comfort, in contrast, is a powerful and long-term influence in the monkey infants' developing bond. That contact comfort is so powerful a determinant of attachment in baby monkeys should not lead to the belief that there is nothing more to mothering than providing a soft surface. Contact comfort was sufficient to establish attachment and the secure base phenomenon; it was not sufficient to establish appropriate social relationships in adulthood. When cloth-reared monkeys grew up, they were unable to mate properly, and if a female was made pregnant, she was unable to mother properly. Figure 12–4 shows such a mother rejecting her offspring.

The relative importance of feeding and contact comfort, then, is quite clear in the case of monkeys, but what about humans? One of the very early observers of infant development, Tiedemann, noticed a similar relation between feeding and nonfeeding caretakers:

. . . *Whenever the weather permitted, his nurse took him out upon the streets, which gave him inordinate pleasure and a great desire for this type of diversion, despite the cold air. Therefore, he was loathe to leave his nurse, and even preferred her to his mother except when he was hungry. (Tiedemann, 1897/1927, p. 217)*

Schaffer and Emerson (1964) provided good corroborative evidence for the role of feeding. They did a short-term longitudinal study of 60 normal infants from intact working class families in Glasgow, Scotland. The infants were studied every 4 weeks until 1 year of age and again at 18 months. The major measure of attachment was based on mothers' reports of infants' reactions to normally occurring separations in seven situations: (1) left alone in the room, (2) left with other people, (3) left in a baby carriage outside the house, (4) left in a carriage outside shops, (5) left in a crib at night, (6) put down after being held in adult's arms or lap, and (7) passed by while in a crib or chair. Mothers were also interviewed about their socialization practices with respect to feeding, weaning, and toilet training. (In psychoanalytic theory, toilet training is related to develop-

FIGURE 12–4. A monkey mother who had been reared on a surrogate mother. Her baby clings to her, even though the mother tries to push the baby away. (Photograph courtesy of H.F. Harlow, University of Wisconsin Primate Laboratory.)

ment in the second year of life.) In addition to the interview information, fear of strangers was directly observed. The observer made a six-step graduated approach to the infant, starting with appearing in the infant's visual range but doing nothing else and ending with picking up and placing the infant on his knee. Scores on this measure agreed with the mother's report of the infant's behaviors toward strangers 92% of the time.

They found that the feeding and weaning variables were not related to intensity of attachment as indexed by their measures. They also failed to find relations between attachment and toilet training variables. This may be considered to support the evidence against Freudian theory.

Studying contact comfort in humans turns out to be a complex proposition. Before we delve into those complexities, we would like to point out one qualification concerning contact comfort. The Harlows' studies showed that contact comfort is sufficient for the develop-

ment of early attachment, but they did not show that it is the only avenue to attachment. It appears that infants can attach through means other than contact comfort. Cairns and Johnson (1965) have shown that lambs will attach to their mothers even if separated from them by a fence so that they cannot touch the mothers. Lambs will even attach to a television set that provides visual and auditory stimulation (Cairns, 1966). There has also been at least one case of a human who is reported to have developed a normal love relationship with his family even though he had no physical contact with them. He had to exist exclusively inside a set of plastic bubbles in their living room because he had a rare genetic disorder that resulted in his having no resistance to disease.

Exploring the role of contact comfort in humans is complicated, both theoretically and methodologically. On purely theoretical grounds, contact comfort might be expected to be more important in monkeys than in humans. Rhesus monkeys cling to their mothers' bodies strongly enough that their mothers can travel through the trees, using only one limb to support the young infant. In contrast, clinging in humans does not have that kind of survival value. Rather, human mothers provide full support for their infants when the pair moves through space. Also, in contemporary western cultures, infants spend less of their time in contact with their mothers than is true in some other cultures, because western babies typically sleep alone in a crib or carriage. Methodologically, it is difficult to investigate contact comfort in humans, because experimenters would not deny tactile contact to human babies to satisfy their intellectual curiosity.[3] All humans, generally speaking, are soft, so all infants in the normal process of caretaking are exposed to what is probably adequate contact comfort. Therefore, in the study of contact comfort in humans, its presence cannot be compared to its absence. Nevertheless, the amount and quality of contact comfort infants receive can be studied. This has been done experimentally in what is called an ana-

---

[3] Indeed, one of Harlow's samples of isolated monkeys showed rather normal behaviors. It was later discovered that a student caretaker had felt sorry for them and had taken them out at night and played with them.

logue[4] study. Roedell and Slaby (1977) studied the development of 5-month-old infants' relationships with a female stranger during 8 sessions spread out over 3 weeks. Each infant saw three different women, one at a time, who interacted in three distinct ways. The person in one role (called the proximal interacter) patted, rocked, and carried the infant around the room, but she did not smile or speak nor did she play eye-contact games. In the second role, the distal interacter did not touch the infant, but smiled at, talked to, played peek-a-boo with, and in other ways kept eye contact with the infant. The person in the third role was simply present and did not interact with the baby. Each of the women played each of the roles, so that there was no confounding between individual and role (that is, any effects were due to the roles the three women played and not to differences in the women's personalities). The measure of the infant's feelings toward the women was the amount of proximity seeking: Each infant was put in a wheeled walker and the time spent near each of the three women was measured. The amount of time spent near the distal interacter increased over the three weeks, while the amount of time near the proximal interacter decreased. The amount of time near the neutral interacter remained the same.

At first glance, the conclusions from this study seem directly opposite to those from the contact comfort work with monkeys, but the difference in findings might be a result of differences in the manipulations of contact comfort. The human babies were living in a world in which the normal behavior to be expected from their adult toys was that they provide social interaction in a variety of ways, including talking to, looking at, and responding to the infants. Thus, the proximal interacter was only one part of the infants' social world and violated the infants' expectations developed on the basis of their interactions with others. The baby monkeys exclusively experienced surrogates who provided contact comfort but no other form of interaction. Soft, unresponsive

surrogates might be preferred over wire surrogates but would not be preferred over more responsive and stimulating surrogates.

Even if one accepts this explanation of the differences in findings about contact comfort in the monkey studies and the Roedell and Slaby study, it is still necessary to ask whether the latter results can be generalized to infants' real-life situations, a problem for all analogue studies. The contact comfort provided by the experimenters differs in a number of ways from that experienced in real life. Mothers typically interact visually and verbally as well as tactually. Furthermore, in the normal world of human infants, contact comfort takes place under certain circumstances, that is, either when the infants signal their desires for contact or when mothers deem it necessary. Providing proximal contact when babies neither want it nor need it might be aversive to them, at least when they have experienced other kinds of social interactions. It might well be that caregivers who provide contact comfort in the context of responsivity and other forms of stimulation would be preferred over those who provide responsivity and other forms of stimulation without contact comfort.

In summary, this study tells us that distal social stimulation alone is preferred to contact comfort alone. Although generalizing from an analogue study to real-life situations is always problematic, the finding that distal forms of social interaction are effective is consistent with correlational research in natural situations that shows that babies become more (or more securely) attached to mothers who provide social stimulation and who are sensitive and responsive to their infants' needs.

Schaffer and Emerson (1964), in the study discussed earlier, rated mothers on their tendencies to interact and to respond. Interaction referred to the mothers' tendencies to initiate interactions of any sort (not just distal, as in the Roedell and Slaby, 1977, analogue study). Responsivity referred to the consistency and speed with which mothers responded to their infants' crying. Both of these variables were related to infants' intensity of attachment (for example, mothers who were highly responsive tended to have babies who protested strongly to separation). It is interesting to note that the type of interaction did not matter. Whether mothers initiated contact sports such as pick-

---

[4] An analogue (or analog) study is one that is designed to be similar to the desired one. Typically, the analogue study is a practical substitute for the desired study, which is difficult or impossible to conduct for practical or ethical reasons.

ing up, fondling, and kissing, or noncontact social interactions such as talking, cooing, singing, and smiling, or impersonal interactions such as presenting toys, food, and other objects, did not matter. What did matter was that the mother initiated interactions. Thus, it appears that contact comfort was desirable when it provided social stimulation, but it was no more effective than other forms of social stimulation.

Two subsequent studies have confirmed these findings using somewhat different maternal ratings and including quality of attachment as measures. Ainsworth, Bell, and Stayton (1971) rated mothers on four dimensions, all having to do in some way with sensitivity and responsivity.

1. Sensitivity–insensitivity. Sensitive mothers perceive their infants' needs and respond to their signals. Insensitive mothers interact with their babies on the mothers' schedules and according to the mothers' needs.
2. Acceptance–rejection. Accepting mothers in general accept the problems and limitations imposed by the responsibility of having an infant. Although they sometimes get irritated at their babies they generally enjoy the babies' good moods and accept their bad moods. Rejecting mothers feel so angry and resentful that these negative feelings outweigh their affection for their babies. These feelings may be expressed by complaining about the baby's irritating behaviors, by frequently opposing the infant's wishes, by scolding, or all of these.
3. Cooperation–interference. Cooperative mothers allow their babies autonomy and avoid interrupting their activities or exerting direct control. When they have to exert control, they try to do so in a way that will be congenial to the child. Interfering mothers impose their wills on their babies with little concern for the children's moods or current activities. They attempt to force the children to their standard, often doing so in an abrupt manner.
4. Accessibility–ignoring. Accessible mothers pay attention to their infants' signals even when distracted. Ignoring mothers are preoccupied wih their own activities and thoughts. They don't notice their infants'

signals, and tend to their infants only during scheduled times or when the infants demand it.

As would be expected, mothers of securely attached 12-month-old infants scored above average on all four dimensions; they were sensitive, accepting, cooperative, and accessible. Mothers of avoidant infants were rejecting and insensitive; those of resistant (ambivalent) infants were rejecting and either interfering or ignoring.

In the second study, Clarke-Stewart (1973) followed a similar procedure. When the babies in the sample were 11 months old, their mothers' behaviors were rated on three dimensions. Responsiveness was indexed by the proportion of the infants' calls, cries, and other signals to which the mothers responded. Expression of positive emotion was measured by the frequency of affectionate touching, smiles, praise, and social speech per hour of her infant's waking life. Social stimulation was assessed by the average number of times the mother came close to, smiled at, talked to, or imitated the child in an average hour when the child was awake. Thus, the first dimension measured the responsivity of the mother; the second, maternal warmth or acceptance; and the third, mother as playmate.

When the infants were 12 months old they were given Ainsworth's strange situation test and were classified into one of three patterns that were similar to those of Ainsworth. Consistent with the many studies we have discussed, securely attached babies had mothers who scored high on all three dimensions, while mothers of the other two classes of infants (unattached and malattached, in Clarke-Stewart's system) were low on all three dimensions.

Clarke-Stewart also used a measure of attachment intensity such that infants were considered intensely attached if they frequently looked at, smiled at, stayed close to, followed, or gave objects to their mothers. Thus her measure is one of active interaction rather than protest at separation. The results, however, were consistent with the other measures employed: Mothers who received high scores on all three dimensions tended to have intensely attached babies.

The research reviewed above was impressive in that different ways of measuring maternal characteristics and infant characteristics provided similar results. Nevertheless, it is problematic in that all the relationships found are correlational. Although it would be nice to be able to make causal statements such as "mothers who are sensitive provide a good environment in which babies can establish secure attachments," correlational data do not permit this. Researchers cannot do experimental studies with humans, and manipulating maternal sensitivity in monkey mothers would be extremely difficult.[5] Confidence in the causal nature of the relation between maternal sensitivity and infant attachment can be enhanced, however, by examining maternal characteristics or maternal reactions to infants in early infancy (prior to the development of attachment). Ainsworth and her colleagues have done this in several studies (see, for example, her 1973 review) and have consistently found that ratings of maternal sensitivity early in infancy predicted security of attachment when it subsequently developed. Such findings make a causal explanation more plausible, but are not conclusive. It is possible, for example, that some babies have ways of interacting that appeal to their mothers and that other babies' responses do not appeal to *their* mothers. The more appealing babies then get responded to more promptly, more often, and more positively. The ultimate cause of their subsequent secure attachment may then be the babies' ability to reward their mothers rather than the mothers' ability to respond to and stimulate their babies.

If one accepts as a working hypothesis the causal explanation favored by the researchers in this field, one can make some interesting conclusions about the maternal characteristics that are or are not important in the development of attachment. Whether mothers feed their babies and whether they spend a lot of time holding their babies do not seem to be important determinants of attachment. Rather, what seems to be important is whether mothers meet their babies' needs, and those needs are not limited to the traditional ones of being kept fed, dry, and warm. Babies also need to be stimulated, to have power over their environment by being able to get adults to respond to them, to be given autonomy of action, and to be accepted. Mothers who fulfill one of these needs also tend to fulfill the others.

On the basis of the existing research, it is impossible to tell whether some of these needs are more important than others. Research on rearing older children suggests that acceptance–rejection is most important. It generally finds that parental differences in child rearing, such as permissiveness versus restrictiveness and anxious involvement versus calm detachment, by themselves are not correlated with child behaviors. In contrast, acceptance and rejection are correlated with outcomes—acceptance with positive outcomes and rejection, sometimes in combination with other behaviors, with negative outcomes.

We can now reconsider whether feeding is an important determinant of attachment. It appears that merely feeding a baby (at least a monkey baby) does not produce attachment (as some interpretations of classic learning theory would expect). Nor does the handling of gratification of the sucking need alone seem crucial for attachment, as Freudians predicted. Both the surrogate studies with monkeys and Schaffer and Emerson's research support this conclusion. Nevertheless, it would be wrong to conclude, however, that what happens in feeding is irrelevant to the mother–infant attachment process. The same maternal characteristics of sensitivity and responsivity appear to operate in the feeding situation as they do in the general context of mother–infant interaction, and sensitivity in feeding (for example, allowing babies to decide when they have finished, or waiting until they open their mouths before feeding the next spoonful) is strongly related to quality of attachment (Ainsworth & Bell, 1969). This suggests that the feeding situation is not different in kind from other situations, although it may be particularly important in the early months because such a large amount of time is spent feeding.

---

[5]Imagine an analogue study in monkeys in which surrogate mothers would be equipped with robotic capabilities such that they would respond with appropriate gestures of padded arms, head movements, or body movements to appropriate auditory, tactual, motoric, and movement cues of infant monkeys. For example, an infant's approach might close a circuit (as happens in automatic doors) that would activate the surrogate's arm to reach out to hold the infant.

EARLY SOCIAL INTERACTIONS

For many infancy experts, social responses are by definition responses made differentially to one or a few individuals; that is, they are attachment responses. That is why attachment relationships have received our first and most extensive attention. Nevertheless, infants respond to humans long before they differentially respond to certain humans.

Nature of Early Social Interactions

Early responses are less clearly social in nature than later ones because young infants respond in the same ways (for example, by smiling) to both social and nonsocial stimuli. Whether they are indeed uniquely patterned social responses or simply part of the general set of processes by which infants come to respond to both the social and nonsocial world is unclear. The latter is what Papoušek and Papoušek (1974) call the fundamental cognitive response system. Those who believe there are unique social responses are generally ethologically or biologically oriented, while those who believe that social responses are not basically different from other responses are often interested in infants' abilities to learn or perceive. Two relevant instances of this controversy have appeared earlier in this book. One was in Chapter 6, where we discussed how a smile can be elicited in the first month of life first by auditory and then by visual stimulation. Both human and nonhuman sources of stimulation are effective. According to ethological theory, stimulation from the mother should be uniquely effective in eliciting smiling. In support of this, there is some evidence that the human voice, especially a high-pitched one, is the most effective stimulus (Eisenberg, 1969; Wolff, 1959), but these studies have not used a wide enough range of stimuli, social and nonsocial, to test the hypothesis adequately. Thus, the available evidence indicates that there is a general responsivity to auditory stimulation that is not specifically social, yet there may also be a particularly sensitive responsivity to human stimuli.

In Chapter 9 we described evidence that suggests that the ability to perceive faces develops in the same way as the ability to make perceptual discriminations of other nonhuman stimuli. This would support the beliefs of those who hypothesize that social responsivity develops from the general adaptation of the infant. Ethologists, in contrast, believe that infants have an innate ability to perceive that most human of stimuli, the face, and as we noted in Chapter 9, there is some, albeit as yet unconvincing, evidence in favor of this view.

While this controversy remains unresolved, some investigators have found a way of circumventing the whole problem by looking at the issue somewhat differently. They do not require that the infant understand the distinction between social and nonsocial stimuli or give unique "social" responses to "social stimuli." Rather, they regard any response made to a social stimulus as a social response. This allows them to go on to their major interest. How do the babies' responses interact with those of their mothers, and what effects do such interactions have on the subsequent social development of the infant? These questions coincide with those asked by parents, who are rarely concerned with the theoretical controversy. They sidestep the issue of whether infants understand the difference between social and nonsocial stimuli and whether they have unique social responses by regarding a social response as any response made to a social stimulus. A whole new area of research has evolved in this context of watching infants respond within a natural social situation, usually in face-to-face (or *en face*) situations.

We will first catalog those infant responses that seem to be important in these *en face* situations. We will mention the earliest ages at which such responses are found and will describe the role that they probably play in the developing social relationship.

Newborn babies seem remarkably asocial to many people. They do interact with adults by sucking, crying, and molding their bodies when held front-to-front, but these responses encourage caretaking rather than social responses in many caregivers. By the end of the first month, however, three very strong elicitors of social responses from others have begun to develop: sustained visual regard, smiling, and vocalizations. The first means exactly what it sounds like: They will focus on a stimulus (which is sometimes a person) for relatively long times (at least long enough to make it obvious). One of the stimuli they like to gaze at are eyes, although not eyes in unsmiling and unmoving faces (Brackbill, 1958; Stechler & Latz, 1966). The onset of eye-to-eye contact helps mothers feel less strange with their babies (Robson, 1967) and gives them a feeling that their babies are real social beings (Klaus & Kennell, 1970; Robson & Moss, 1970). The second infant behavior that elicits social responses from others is smiling. It occurs in response to the sight and sound of parents and others by the end of the first month. Babies' increased smiling at this point certainly helps parents perceive their infants as social beings. The third elicitor of social responses begins to appear by the fourth week when infants respond to vocalizations of others with gurgles. By the fifth week they vocalize in response to the vocalizations of others (although they don't necessarily make the same sounds) and will engage in exchanges of 10–15 vocalizations (Wolff, 1963, 1969).

Thus it is clear that very early in life babies do things that reward their mothers. And we have already shown that mothers do things that interest babies. Even newborn babies are attracted to contours such as the human hairline, to visual movement, to sounds, and to tactual stimulation (Chapter 9). The development of imitation was outlined in Chapters 7 and 10, where we noted that the infants' earliest imitations were of adult imitations of the infant's own vocalizations. Thus, mothers' imitations also reward babies. Mothers also frequently repeat a behavior over and over, particularly if their infants responded positively to it (Papoušek & Papoušek, 1977; Schoetzau & Papoušek, 1977; Stern, Beebe, Jaffe, & Bennett, 1977). This is highly rewarding to infants in two ways. First, infants respond positively to familiarization from repeated stimulation (McCall & Kagan, 1967; Lewis & Goldberg, 1969). Second, infants are rewarded by events that occur contingent on their own responses; in other words, when their own actions make things happen (Papoušek & Bernstein, 1969). Mothers and babies are thus well prepared to be mutually rewarding.

Robert R. Sears, in his presidential address to the American Psychological Association in 1951, noted that these mutually rewarding behaviors form the basis of mother–infant interactions. In the framework of learning theory

he described the way in which one person's actions are stimuli (or environmental events or rewards) for the other person. Mothers and their infants or children were the pairs he used as examples. He made a plea in this address for psychologists to combine individual and social behavior into a single theoretical system and be concerned with interacting pairs, or dyads. Unfortunately, only later did researchers use approaches that treated the mother and infant as a mutually interacting pair or dyad (Bell, 1968, 1971; Harper, 1971; Yarrow, Waxler, & Scott, 1971). One reason it has been hard for researchers to shift to this type of research is the lack of a statistical basis for analyzing the data of such sequences or for analyzing the dependencies of one actor's behavior upon the other actor. Nevertheless, the obvious importance of mother–infant interactions has resulted in recent attempts to develop ways of dealing with the complexities.

Different investigators describe the nature of these interactions differently, depending on their interests. Papoušek and Papoušek, like Sears, describe it in a learning context:

The most impressive feature of the interaction between infant and mother is the continuous sequence of short scenes in which the two members mutually stimulate and reinforce one another. Thus, the mother is not just a source of rich external stimulation or a selective reinforcing agent of behavioural expressions of her child. The child's spontaneous behaviour engages her too, and sets the occasion for her responding. The interaction of these two, therefore, tends to be reciprocal. Besides mutual stimulation and reinforcement, both members also learn how each can influence the other with his or her own behaviour. In sum, it is not simply the quantitative aspects of stimulation, but the structure, sequence and causal relations between individual components of behaviour which play the decisive roles. The discovery and mastery of the active and adaptive manipulation of a partner is a more decisive feature of mother–infant interaction than passive behavioural modification which is acquired through external reinforcement. (Papoušek & Papoušek, 1975, p. 254)

Trevarthen (1977) describes early mother–infant interactions as prespeech conversations.

He emphasizes their turn-taking nature—that first one partner is active and the other quiet, and then they reverse. He sees the beginning of language behavior in these interactions. Thoman (1981a) also views the early mother–infant interactions as communicative, but she sees their underlying nature as affective rather than cognitive. On the basis of neurological as well as other evidence she concludes that mother and infant behaviors are integrated by the affective behaviors of each member of the dyad as they are expressed, received, and reacted to. She cites a number of studies that have shown evidence of affect in facial expressions and in sucking patterns. Whether all of these sucking behaviors and facial expressions have meaning or not (a very real question), mothers react to them as if they had meaning.

Brazelton, Tronick, Adamson, Als, and Wise (1975), like Thoman, consider mother–infant interactions to be basically social–emotional phenomena. They describe the interactions as "a sequence of phases, each representing different states of the partner's mutual attentional and affective involvement" (p. 142). They are impressed with a different sort of rhythm than the turn taking described by Trevarthen. They describe alternation between social interactions (which often involve activity by both participants) and what they call disengagement, a sort of rest period between interactions. The following quotation describes an interaction between a 60-day-old infant and his mother that shows this sort of alternation:

Baby is looking off to side where mother will come in. He lies completely quiet, back in his baby seat, face serious, cheeks droopy, mouth half open, corners down, but there is an expectant look in his eyes as if he were waiting. His face and hands reach out in the same direction. As his mother comes in, saying, 'Hello' in a high-pitched but gentle voice, he follows her with his head and eyes as she approaches him. His body builds up with tension, his face and eyes open up with a real greeting which ends with a smile. His mouth opens wide and his whole body orients toward her. He subsides, mouths his tongue twice, his smile dies and he looks down briefly, while she continues to talk in

an increasingly eliciting voice. During this, his voice and face are still but all parts of his body point toward her. After he looks down, she reaches for and begins to move his hips and legs in a gentle containing movement. He looks up again, smiles widely, narrows his eyes, brings one hand up to his mouth, grunting, vocalizing, and begins to cycle his arms and legs out toward her. With this increasing activity, she begins to grin more widely, to talk more loudly and with higher-pitched accents, accentuating his vocalizations with hers and his activity with her movements of his legs. The grunting vocalizations and smiles, as well as the cycling activity of his arms and legs come and go in two-second bursts—making up small cycles of movement and attention toward her. She contains his hips with her hands as if to contain the peaks of his excitement.

Meanwhile, with her voice and her face, as well as with her hands, she both subsides with and accentuates his behaviour with her own. He looks down again, gets sober at 40 seconds, makes a pouting face. She looks down at his feet at this point, then comes back to look into his face as he returns to look up at her. She lets go of his legs, and they draw up into his body. He bursts out with a broad smile and a staccato-like vocalization for three repetitions. Each time, his face broadens and opens wide, his legs and arms thrust out toward her. She seems to get caught up in his bursts, and smiles broadly, her voice getting brighter, too. After each burst, he subsides to a serious face, limbs quiet, and her quieting response follows his.

At 70 seconds, he subsides completely, and looks down at his feet with a darkly serious face. She gets very still, her face becomes serious, her voice slows down and almost stops, the pitch becomes low. Her mouth is drawn down, reflecting his serious mouth. After three seconds, he begins to brighten again into a wide, tonguing smile. This time, he is more self-contained, holding back on the movement of his extremities and his excitement. She responds immediately, cocks her head coyly, smiles gently and her voice gently begins to build up again. He builds up to two more staccato vocalizations with smiles and jerky, cycling movements of his legs out toward her. She contains his hips, and this time her voice doesn't build up to a peak of excitement with him. She looks down after 6 seconds to pick up his arms with her hands as if to keep control over his build-up. He follows her downward look about ten seconds later, by looking down, too. His movements subside and his face becomes serious. She is quite serious also, at 90 seconds. (Brazelton et al., 1975, pp. 141–42)

These interactions occur very rapidly. The entire sequence quoted above lasted only 90 seconds. Also, the particular behaviors that occur are not constant. For example, turn taking might occur with smiles, nods, grunts, coos, or a variety of other responses. The particular responses might even change within an interaction. This is similar to the problem encountered in our discussion about attachment responses. In both cases the particular discrete responses, although easier to measure, turned out not to be psychologically meaningful, but an overall qualitative pattern can be discerned.

Thoman has chosen a somewhat different approach. Rather than categorize the very brief behaviors within these interactions, she has focused on patterns of behaviors between mothers and infants that occur over days, weeks, or months. She believes that labeling any one sequence of interactions as causal for behavior of either mother or infant may be trivial. Rather, she believes the behavior of both mother and infant are determined by all of their interactive experiences prior to the behavior in question. Thus, she records large numbers of behaviors in order to identify meaningful interactions that differ for different mother–infant pairs. She uses a coding system of about 75 categories that has a language structure with "nouns," "verbs," and "modifiers," which can be combined in descriptions of any one behavior. For example, this system can describe the proportion of time infants fuss when their mothers are looking at them or during social interactions. Her goal is to characterize stable individual patterns among dyads. This is a new element in the study of individual differences; that is, to study individual differences not only as they occur in infants or mothers but also in the dyads. Thoman (1981b) has described individual pairs who

exhibit synchrony or asynchrony in their interactions in the first 5 weeks of life.

In Thoman's view, the potential for these early communications between mothers and infants is biologically determined; that is, the interactive capabilities of infants have developed through the evolutionary process and provide a critical form of early adaptation that assures their survival. Even Papoušek and Papoušek (1975), who describe the interactions in learning terms, do not perceive mothers as systematically providing stimulation or reward to their infants. Rather, they see the mothers' behaviors to be social responses.

Importance of Early Social Interactions

The task of characterizing early social interactions is so immense that most researchers' efforts have centered on this important first step. Nevertheless, it appears that researchers in this area are making progress toward exploring the meaning of the early interaction patterns between mothers and young infants.

THE RELATION BETWEEN MOTHER AND INFANT BEHAVIORS WITHIN INTERACTIVE SESSIONS

Osofsky and Danzger (1974) have correlated the behaviors of mothers and newborn infants during their feeding interactions. They found that the babies' auditory responses were related to both the frequency and quality of maternal auditory stimulation during the feeding interaction (the correlations were substantial, accounting for about 25–50% of the variance). The infants' visual responsivity and motor responsivity during functional and nonfunctional handling by the mothers were also moderately correlated (accounting for over 20% of the variance) with the mothers' attentiveness and sensitivity to their babies and with mothers' facial movements and tactile or handling stimulation of their babies. A second, larger study by Osofsky (1976) found similar patterns of correlations between maternal sensitivity and infant responsiveness, although the correlations were of smaller magnitude.

Studies using the correlational approach can only show that two behaviors (or classes of behaviors) go together or are associated with each other. As usual, we note that correlational studies can tell nothing about whether one causes or leads to the other. The correlations Osofsky found may mean that attentive, sensitive mothers can more easily get their babies to be responsive than less attentive, less sensitive mothers, or that responsive babies tend to elicit attentive, sensitive behaviors from their mothers or that mothers and babies both influence each other in a reciprocal fashion. This research does demonstrate, however, that maternal behaviors generally perceived to be positive are related to infant behaviors that are also generally conceived to be positive.

Osofsky (1976) also presented evidence that not all infant behaviors are produced by the mother. The infant variable of interest was cuddling, which she assessed as part of the Brazelton exam (see Chapter 8, Table 8–7). She found that mothers' attempts to aid cuddling and to use eye contact in cuddling were negatively related to cuddling in their infants, that is, they resulted in less rather than more cuddling. Also the greater the arousal of the infant, the more effort was required from the mother to achieve cuddling. She pointed out that it is possible that babies requiring greater effort to cuddle were behaviorally, and possibly constitutionally, less cuddly. Several aspects of her data support such an interpretation, especially the negative relation between cuddliness and both state and overall reactivity. Indeed, there is some danger that cuddliness as measured by the Brazelton scale is confounded with a low arousal state and poor muscle tone.

Other research has focused on specifying behaviors in mothers that interfere with positive mother–infant interactions. Richards (1971) found that mothers differ in the type of responses they make to their babies when the babies are quiet. Some mothers continue to try to stimulate their infants, while others wait for the infants to "reply." The former overwhelm their babies and the babies "turn off" (either by crying or turning away or by lying motionless with nonconverging, staring eyes and sleeplike respiration), whereas babies of mothers who wait for their infants to reply are able to continue the interaction for longer periods of time. This can be conceptualized as one kind of maternal sensitivity.

Cohn and Tronick (1983) explored the effects of maternal behaviors experimentally by means of a simulation model. They had mothers of 3-month-old babies simulate depression by imagining how they felt on days when they were tired or depressed. The mothers were specifically instructed to look at their infants, speak in a flat uninteresting monotone, keep their faces relatively expressionless, and minimize body movement and touch contact with their infants. Cohn and Tronick demonstrated the effectiveness of this manipulation by rating the mothers' behaviors and found that mothers simulating depression were less likely to respond appropriately to infants' bids for attention (measured by a scale called elaboration) and were more hesitant and withdrawn (measured by a scale named undercontrol) than the same mothers were when they interacted normally with their babies. The 3-month-old babies responded differently to their mothers in the depressed and normal expression conditions. In the depressed condition they were more wary and exhibited more protest. They also engaged in more brief positive encounters, which were rare in normal interactions. Although simulated maternal depression may differ from an expression of genuine depression, it is at least clear that when mothers exhibit less elaboration and more undercontrol, it affects their babies' behaviors in a negative direction.

Taken together, these studies demonstrate that during the rapid fire interactions between young infants and their mothers, differences in behaviors of one member of the pair influence the behaviors of the other. They also confirm the findings of attachment research that maternal responsivity and sensitivity are important variables in mother–child interactions.

LONG-TERM OUTCOMES

Once differences in mother–infant interactions are established, the next step is to explore whether long-term consequences follow. For example, if some babies are constitutionally noncuddlers, and if attempts to cuddle them result in the babies' cuddling less (turning off), then perhaps mothers who insist on cuddling are creating difficulties in their interactions with their infants. Mothers who allow noncuddly infants to quiet themselves may be promoting a synchronous mother–infant relationship. Nevertheless, there may be a danger if mothers always allow their babies to exert autonomy with respect to their personality characteristics. Perhaps mothers should encourage their babies to develop just those aspects of temperament that the babies initially lack. This position argues that noncuddling babies should be encouraged to cuddle more frequently. We do not have directly relevant research that would enable us to make recommendations to mothers concerning this point. The attachment research is not directly relevant to the issues of whether mothers should encourage infants to develop characteristics they lack, but it clearly supports the notion that mothers should focus on establishing a synchronous relationship by permitting their babies to express their own needs and control themselves and their environment as much as possible.

Thoman (1981b) has examined synchrony in two mother–infant interactions in the first five months of life. In one pair, labeled N, the young baby was calm, alert, and very well organized, but both mother and infant exhibited a lack of synchrony in a sizeable proportion of their interactions. In the other pair, labelled M, the mother and infant exhibited superior synchrony, although the infant in the first month of its life was not so optimal as the infant in dyad N. At 1 year of age the infant in the M pair was developing in a very favorable fashion, while the N infant at 1 year cried more than any of the other 10 infants in the study. This is particularly striking because that baby had cried very little early in life. Similar kinds of asynchrony were exhibited in their 1 year interactions. The N baby also exhibited poor overall development (74 on Bayley Mental scale at 1 year and 84 on McCarthy scales at 2 years). Although it is difficult to draw any conclusions based on two mother–infant dyads, we want to point out that the sampling bias in this study is not as severe as in traditional case studies. Thoman initially selected her 10 dyads randomly from a normal population and then selected clear cases of her variables of interest. Furthermore, her conclusions match those of research done in another context. Thomas and Chess (1977) found that mutual adaptations (whether babies and parents fit each others' needs) rather than parent style or infant characteristics often determined the outcome, especially for babies somewhat outside the usual pattern of behavior. That finding also supports

the synchrony position, and adds a new ingredient, that synchrony may be more important for some babies than others.

The Role of Maternal Perceptions

The research described above was all based on observations of mothers actually interacting with their babies. Adults are also affected by their perceptions of situations independent of reality. It is likely that mothers' perceptions of their infants and of the patterns of mother–infant interaction also influence the developing relationship. Perhaps the first question to ask is how clearly mothers' perceptions match infants' behaviors. If mothers are always accurate in their perceptions of their babies, then there would be no need to be concerned with the issue of maternal perceptions at all; they would have no effect independent of the infants' behaviors. The research, however, suggests that mothers' perceptions reflect both their idea of what babies in general are like and their knowledge of their own babies in particular. For example, Ploof (1976) found that mothers' perceptions of their second-born babies became more similar to the babies' behaviors as they got to know the babies (during the first 4 months of the babies' lives) and less like their perceptions of average babies or of their first-borns. In addition, Ploof provided evidence that the mothers' perceptions of their infants were related to the infants' behaviors at the time of rating and also to their earlier behaviors. Ploof interprets her results to mean that the mothers' perceptions of their infants at 4 months are based on infants' particular characteristics as experienced over the first 4 months of interaction. This view is strengthened by Broussard and Hartner's (1971) finding that mothers' perceptions of their infants at birth were not related to their adjustment at 4 years of age, although their perceptions of the infants at 1 month were.

Ploof's research also suggests that mothers' perceptions of a baby are influenced by their knowledge of other babies, including their own. Ploof found direct evidence that mothers' perceptions of their first-borns were related to actual behaviors of their second-borns at 4 months. Those who had given high evaluations to their first children had second

504 SOCIAL DEVELOPMENT

children who were more alert, more rhythmic, and had good temperaments at 4 months. Babies whose mothers had low evaluations of their first-borns were unalert, arhythmic, and difficult at 4 months. Ploof's explanation that the mothers' perceptions that arose from their experiences with their first-borns were the cause of the second infants' behaviors is hardly the only possible one. The most obvious alternatives are that a mother who produces one genetically or constitutionally easy (or difficult) baby is likely to produce another of the same kind. Alternatively, a mother who has been effective (or ineffective) with her first child may be the same with her second. Obviously, these conditions could also occur in combination with each other.

Thus the research on maternal perceptions demonstrates that they are a factor that needs to be dealt with. Whether mothers' perceptions of their infants actually cause mothers to behave in ways that cause different infant behaviors is still an open question, which we think will become a lively research topic in the next decade. To answer this question in such a way that it will be possible to differentiate among the alternative explanations described in the last paragraph, a way must be found to separate the influence of the mothers' perceptions from the reality of the infants' behaviors. So far, the evidence shows only that maternal perceptions are related to infant outcomes and not that the maternal perceptions themselves are the real causal factor.

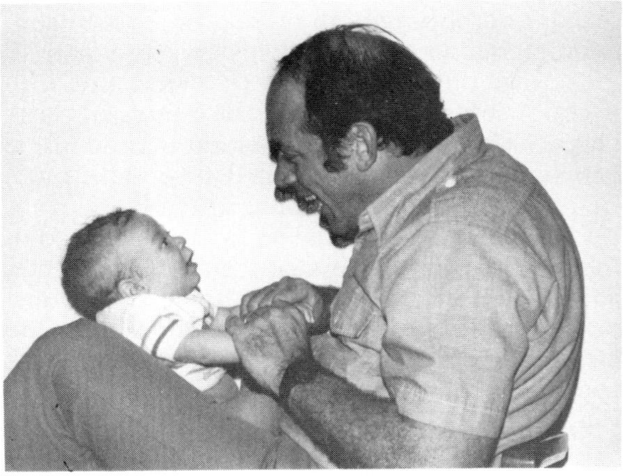

THE FATHER'S ROLE IN INFANTS' SOCIAL DEVELOPMENT

Most of our discussion so far in this chapter has concerned mother–infant social relationships. Fathers traditionally have been considered to have little interest or involvement in the care and nurture of infants. Father–infant interactions were rarely studied because in western culture, and in the psychoanalytic, behavioristic, and ethological theories that have developed in western cultures, mothers have been considered the primary (or only important) influence on infants. Indeed, Nash in a 1965 review of fathers in contemporary literature and in the current psychological literature

FIGURE 12–5. Parent-infant love is not limited to mothers and babies. Here an American father plays with his young infant (top) and a Balinese father serves as a secure base for exploration (bottom).

concluded that there was virtually no research concerning the role of fathers in infant development. Since Nash's review there has been considerably more study of the relations between fathers and their infants and of the roles fathers play in the social and cognitive development of their infants (Figure 12–5.) Although we are greatly encouraged by this increased attention, we find that the results are difficult to present with confidence because so many of the studies are done with rather small samples and it is difficult to assess how typical the babies and the fathers of these small samples are. Today this topic is very popular, because of the general climate of the times (feminism, more working mothers of young infants, more single parent homes). As Yogman (1982) pointed out in his recent review, this popularity has perhaps led to even more writing than research.

Fathers and Childbirth

As we noted in Chapter 5, fathers are increasingly involved in the birth process in western society and generally feel very positive about it. Entwisle and Doering (1981) found that 95% of men who were in the delivery room at the birth of their babies felt positive about the experience and about 25% of them reported it as a "peak experience." In comparison, fathers who spent time in the waiting room were generally neutral in their reactions. More fathers (51%) than mothers (25%) held their babies while in the delivery room. Although it is tempting to use these data to suggest that such experiences strengthen the involvement of fathers with their babies, this conclusion may not be warrented for two reasons. First, it may be the fathers' attitudes rather than the childbirth experiences that are crucial. In a recent exploratory study Grossman and Volkmer (1984) found that fathers who wished to participate in childbirth were more interested in infancy and in spending time with their babies than those who were not, regardless of whether they actually participated. Second, it appears that early postbirth contacts are more important than the childbirth experience. This has been found in a study (Greenberg & Morris, 1974) of 30 fathers of first sons, half of whom were present at delivery. Lind (1974) found that fathers who were permitted to feed and diaper their babies in the hospital continued to do more caretaking at home 3 months later. Similarly, fathers of babies delivered by Caesarean section, who presumably spent more time caring for their babies while the mothers were in the hospital, spent more time in caretaking when their babies were 5 months old (Pedersen, Zaslow, Cain, & Anderson, 1980). These studies are extremely suggestive, but far too limited to permit confident conclusions. The problems of doing and interpreting research in this area directly parallel those for research on maternal bonding, discussed in

Chapter 5. Primary among these is that fathers who choose to be involved with their babies during and immediately after delivery may differ in important ways from fathers who do not. Only experimental research can determine whether and which of fathers' experiences during their babies' birth and early experience affect their later relationships.

How Fathers Interact with Their Babies

In the United States, the cultural stereotype of fathers, reflected in Parsons and Bales' (1955) social role theory, is that they are disciplinarians, socializers, and teachers of instrumental activity for their children. It is considered inappropriate for them to be nurturant toward their infants (Josselyn, 1956), and their influence on their children is expected to begin only after infancy.

Whether fathers share this cultural stereotype seems to depend on what fathers are sampled. In a recent Australian study only 34% of the fathers felt they had the ability to care for children, although 60% of the mothers felt their husbands had such ability (Russell, 1980). In addition, most fathers felt that their parental role began after infancy. Other samples fit the stereotype less well. Cordell (1978) interviewed a subset of Parke and Sawin's (1977) sample. Although the majority of these men (14 of the sample of 25) accepted the stereotypical roles of provider, disciplinarian, and socializer, they did not accept the other stereotypic characteristics. Most of these fathers (16 of the 25) felt their functions as parents included emotional support both in the sense of being responsive to their infants' needs and sharing their infants' activities and joys. They all included routine care as part of their function. Furthermore, they did not perceive their role to be teacher or male role model.

Studies of fathers' behaviors toward their infants also indicate that these cultural stereotypes are oversimplified. Consistent with the stereotype, several studies have found that fathers tend to be little involved in caretaking (Kotelchuck, 1976; Richards, Dunn, & Antonis, 1977). For example, Kotelchuck found that only 7.5% of the fathers in his sample shared caretaking equally with their wives and only 25% had regular caretaking responsibilities. As would be expected from this large difference in caretaking responsibilities, fathers tend to spend much less time with their babies than do mothers (Kotelchuck, 1976; Pedersen & Robson, 1969). For example, Kotelchuck found that fathers spent an average of 3.2 hours per day with their infants versus mothers' 9.0 hours. Other studies have shown far shorter times for fathers' interactions with their infants.

Nevertheless, although fathers are less involved quantitatively with their infants, many do interact with them throughout infancy in ways that are more similar to mothers than different. Parke and his collaborators (Parke & O'Leary, 1976; Parke & Sawin, 1975, 1977), in extensive behavioral observations of a sample, some of whom had been found by Cordell (1978) not to conform well to the conventional fathering stereotype, found that indeed these fathers were as affectionate, sensitive, and responsive as mothers, although in somewhat different ways. Mothers engaged in more routine caregiving (wiping faces, grooming) and more frequent kissing, whereas fathers provided more visual and auditory stimulation through toys and through imitating their infants' facial expressions and mouth movements. Interestingly, the fathers perceived their newborns as needing more affection than did the mothers, but there were no related behavioral differences. Thus, in terms of meeting the emotional needs of their babies, which appears to be the crucial ingredient in the development of attachment, these middle-class, white fathers appear to be as motivated and adequate as mothers.

Parke and his collaborators' findings that fathers do stimulate their infants, although in ways different from those of mothers, has been corroborated both early in infancy (Yogman et al., 1977) and later. Fathers engage in proportionately more play and less caregiving than mothers, although in overall quantity mothers play more with their infants than do fathers simply because they are usually available for more hours per day. Furthermore, in the United States fathers play more physical games and mothers more quiet, nonphysical games (Belsky, 1979b; Clark-Stewart, 1978, 1980; Field, 1978; Lamb, 1977a, 1977b; Power & Parke, 1979), although this difference is not found in Sweden (Lamb, Frodi, Frodi, & Hwang, 1982; Lamb, Frodi, Hwang, & Frodi, 1983; Lamb, Frodi, Hwang, Frodi, & Steinberg, 1982).

Babies' Attachments to Their Fathers

Most of the traditional theories of infant development assumed that infants first form a single exclusive attachment to mothers and only later and secondarily (if at all) would they form attachments to fathers. It is now known that this is not true. Research in the 1960s demonstrated that infants cry when their fathers leave them (Schaffer & Emerson, 1964) and exhibit positive greeting behaviors to their fathers (Pedersen & Robson, 1969). These findings were both based on reports of naturalistic situations. What about responses in the laboratory or home to the Ainsworth-Wittig strange situation of similar tasks? Kotelchuck (1976) showed that infants at 12 months or older tended to cry when either the mother or the father left the room, but not when a stranger did. They also stayed near the door regardless of which parent left and touched the parent who returned to the room, but did neither for the stranger. Other studies that have shown attachment to both parents at different ages between 8 and 30 months in home or laboratory are too numerous to mention. Furthermore, Yogman and his collaborators (Yogman et al., 1976a, 1976b; Yogman, 1982) have found that by 2 months of age babies respond more positively to their fathers than to strangers, which shows the early beginnings of this responsiveness.

These findings should not be overgeneralized, however. Just because babies attach to both parents does not mean that there are no differences. At this point there is only a hint of the nature of such differences. Some studies find that infants respond similarly to their mothers and fathers, others find differential reactions. The degree of stress in the situation may be one determining factor in whether or not differences are found. Under high stress it appears there may be more preference for (or effectiveness of) the mother (Lamb, 1976a, 1976b, but not replicated in Lamb, 1977a). In contrast, in some contexts toddlers have been found to prefer their fathers as playmates

(Clarke-Stewart, 1978; Lamb, 1977a, 1977b), although these preferences are not universal (Lamb, Frodi, Hwang, & Frodi, 1983) and they may only represent responses to the father's own behaviors (Belsky, 1979b; Clarke-Stewart, 1978; Lamb, 1977b).

Sources of Differences Between Fathers and Mothers

A large part of the cultural stereotypes about fathers' roles stems from a belief in the existence of a "maternal instinct," that is, that mothers are biologically equipped to care effectively for infants and fathers are not. In a study of attitudes of Australian parents, Russell (1980) found that 51% of the mothers and 71% of the fathers believed this maternal instinct existed.

To demonstrate convincingly the truth or falseness of a biologically-based sex difference is a difficult endeavor, and evidence that convinces a doubter on either side is not likely to appear in the near future. Nevertheless, it is safe to say that no strong evidence exists to support a conviction that biological factors are of overriding importance in explaining parenting. Examinations of fathering in other species and other human cultures reveal that paternal roles vary widely. Within most categories of animals (primate, mammals, fishes, invertebrates), species exist in which fathers play an active or even predominant role in parenting (see, for example, Bailey, 1982; Earls & Yogman, 1978). Thus, it is difficult to argue that females are evolutionarily adapted to be exclusive parents. Also, although it is possible that maternal hormones produced during pregnancy and childbirth may influence maternal behaviors, no strong evidence exists for their role in human mothering other than for lactation (see the section on bonding in Chapter 5). It is even possible that interaction with his infant might stimulate hormone production related to caregiving in the male, too. This occurs for such species as stickleback fish, after all. Moreover, there is evidence that certain personality traits are more important than biological sex in determining responsivity to infants (Bem, Martyna, & Watson, 1976). College students who were classified as more expressive (a stereotypically female trait) exhibited more affectionate behaviors to an infant than did other students, regardless of whether they were male or female. Their sex did not influence their behaviors nor did their score on a typically masculine trait, instrumental orientation. Consistent with these findings was a study by Russell (1978) that found that men who scored high on both feminine (expressive) and masculine (instrumental) behaviors took more caretaking responsibility than "masculine" males. Thus the personality of the parent, rather than biological sex, may turn out to be the most important determinant of parenting.

Related to this are the results of a study by Easterbrooks (1982), who correlated an array of father variables with toddlers' behaviors (including responses to Ainsworth and Wittig's strange situation). She found that individual differences in fathers' attitudes and perceptions were more related to toddlers' attachment and task-oriented behaviors than was the time fathers spent alone with their toddlers. These results suggest that, as with mothers, it is not just the presence or absence of the father that determines his relationship with his infants, although that is clearly important (see review by Belsky, 1981), but his personal characteristics and reactions to the infant.

Another line of evidence concerning the hypothesis that there is a maternal instinct is the research on whether fathers and mothers respond differentially to infants' cries (discussed in Chapter 6). The evidence overall does not lend strong support to the hypothesis that females are genetically predisposed to respond to babies' cries and males are not, although there is some evidence that women are more accurate in their perceptions of infants' cries. This superior sensitivity is probably a joint result of women's greater expressiveness (the culturally approved norm) and their greater experience with caretaking.

The power of cultural context is obviously strong in parenting. Parke and Sawin's fathers responded to their subcultural norm as surely as more traditional males respond to traditional norms. It is important not to see these as two monolithic norms—traditional, masculine (instrumental) noncaretakers versus nontraditional, egalitarian, expressive (feminine or androgenous) males who are indistinguishable from mothers. The situation is much more complex. Indeed, a recent German study (Steingüber, Nolten, & Bisping, 1984) with excellent methodology has shown that mothers during their hospital stay are extremely good at picking out their babies' cries when their cries are paired with those of 9 other babies. They do show improved performance from day 3 to day 5, at which time they are essentially perfect. But, nonmothers trained to recognize an anger cry, and given the same test as the mothers but with an arbitrarily assigned baby's cry to recognize, do extremely well also.

Different aspects of fathering—amount of caretaking, degree to which responsibility for care is assigned to father, amount and kind of emotional support father provides, differences in behaviors to sons versus daughters, and many more—may all operate in different ways both in different cultures and in different families within a culture (see, for example, the review in Parke, 1979). Until the research reflects this complexity, there is likely to be slow progress in isolating differences between mothers and fathers.

The Family Context

Fathers and infants do not interact in a vacuum. The parents' marital relationship, their individual parenting styles, and the individual characteristics of their babies all influence each other in a complex family system. Little research has addressed the variables involved in this system, but a few scattered studies and one integrative review (Belsky, 1981) have appeared. The bulk of the available research has examined the influence one parent has on the way the other interacts with the infant. Primary in this category has been Pedersen and his collaborators (Pedersen, Anderson, & Cain, 1977, 1979; Pedersen, Rubenstein, & Yarrow, 1979). These studies have found that when fathers were negative concerning their wives, the wives scored lower in competence at feeding their newborns and were more negative toward their 5-month-olds. In contrast, when fathers were impressed with their wives as mothers, mothers exhibited more feeding skill.

Mothers' interactions with their husbands also are related to his fathering. Belsky (1979a) found that when mothers and fathers talked to each other about the baby, fathers were more involved with their babies, even when the father and baby were alone together.

Summary and Conclusions

The research on fathering, although limited, has accomplished a major task of dispelling some of the untested assumptions about fathers in western cultures. It is clear that many fathers are actively involved in the development of their infants even when not involved in a major way in their caretaking. In response to such involvement infants generally become attached to their fathers who then serve as secure bases for exploration in much the same way as mothers do.

Infant–mother and infant–father interactions differ in a variety of ways, and presumably for a variety of reasons. Research has only begun to reveal some of the many factors that influence these two kinds of interactions. It is clear that the cultural roles of father and mother are a major influence, but so are the parents' personalities, which do not always match their biological sex. Furthermore, father, mother, and infant all operate within a complex family system so that interactions between any two members can change the functioning of that system. Finally, the sex of the infant adds another layer of complexity. Both mothers and fathers treat boy and girl babies in different ways. Because all of these factors operate together, wide variability in the research results is to be expected. Single studies of a small sample of upper middle-class families are likely to yield results that are very restricted in their generality. It seems likely that research in this field in the next 10 years will focus on these various components and will provide a more complete picture of the role of the father.

DISCUSSION ISSUES
Role of Early Experience

Freud popularized the notion that what happens to babies during their infancy has greater influence on their social and emotional development than events during any other time of development. In this and the next chapter we examine the extensive research designed to find out what kinds of experiences are crucial. Our focus in this chapter has been on the kinds of experiences in infancy that promote good social development during the early years. In the next chapter we will discuss the implications for long-term development embodied in the critical periods hypothesis.

The research, both experimental studies with laboratory animals and correlational research with humans, strongly indicates that the essence of mother–infant relationships does not lie in the feeding situation. Whether the attachment figure feeds or diapers the baby does not by itself determine the babies' attachment. Rather, the person who accepts the baby, is socially responsive, and is sensitive to the baby's needs is the one to whom babies attach most securely and intensely. Moreover, the extent to which infants and their significant adults are mutually rewarding exerts an influence independent of the individual characteristics of child and adult. This relationship develops from the time of birth and is reflected in both early and later interactions between parents and infants.

Most people assume that whether and how infants attach to their caregivers is important to both their immediate and their long-term development. Most of the research that addresses this question has examined the long-term consequences to the infant of not having a single intense attachment to their mothers. We will discuss that research in the next chapter. There are a few studies that explore variations in the quality of attachment among infants who all have intact families. These studies find that babies who are securely attached tend to be advantaged with respect to both cognitive and social development.

One important implication of these findings is that attachment is not the exclusive domain of the biological mother, which it would be if sucking (through breast feeding) were the primary mechanism by which attachment developed. Babies form strong, secure attachments to fathers and, as we will see in the next chapter, to alternative caregivers as well. There is no consistent evidence that such multiple attachments produce diffusion in emotional relationships or any other negative outcome.

Research Issues

The study of attachment provides several good examples of research issues. Measuring complex phenomena such as attachment poses many problems of measurement and research strategy.

MULTIPLE MEASURES

A number of quite different measures of attachment have been used, including stranger anxiety, amount of protest at separation, and reunion behaviors after separation. As is often the case with different operational definitions of a concept, two measures do not always yield comparable results. Stranger anxiety seems to measure something different from protest at separation and reunion behaviors, whereas the latter two measures apparently tap the same dimensions. Currently most of the research is focused on measures surrounding maternal separations.

Although such a narrow focus assures comparability across studies, it limits the degree to which the results can be generalized. Measures involving separation tap the mother's role as a provider of security. Mothers fulfill other needs as well, which can be measured. Consider as examples measures such as sharing toys with mother or asking for help in solving a problem. Mothers' role as playmate and stimulator are not usually measured in separation measures.

LIMITATIONS OF LABORATORY RESEARCH

A second limitation of separation measures is that they are usually generated in a laboratory environment rather than in a natural setting. A laboratory setting allows researchers maximum control over the standardization of their procedures and they can thereby eliminate many extraneous variables. The laboratory situation is quite different from natural surroundings, however, and the findings produced in such an environment may be true only in laboratory settings and not in the real world. In the Ainsworth strange situation, for example, infants are put into a strange room with unusual walls (one-way mirrors), and a melange of toys, many of which are very strange to the child, and exposed to brief encounters with strangers. They are likely to explore less, to stay closer to the mother, and to cling to the mother much more than they would at home. Even worse, babies who are more fearful may cling to their mothers more and protest their departure more vehemently and may thereby appear to be more attached rather than more fearful. Thus, a different phenomenon is being studied in the laboratory (attachment behaviors under stress) and the results may not generalize to situations in which attachment behaviors occur in a context of security or familiarity.

The limitations of laboratory research are made much more severe when the laboratory study is an analogue study. In the Roedell and Slaby study, experimenters took the role of mothers and the experimental treatments were a homogeneous subset of the behaviors that the experimenters hypothesized were the crucial ones in real life mother–child relationships. Thus, an analogue study is one giant step further removed from the natural world than are other laboratory studies.

Even further removed from the reality of human infants growing up in their natural world are animal studies. Studying lower animals is a traditional way of overcoming the limitations of correlational studies and of controlling the pre-experimental experiences of the subjects. Nevertheless the cost of this control is that generalizing to humans in their natural environment is even more risky.

In all these different forms of laboratory research, there is a really problematic trade-off between the increased control possible in a laboratory study and the decreased generalizability. There is really no direct way around the problem in an individual study. Considering a mix of naturalistic, less well-controlled studies and the better controlled laboratory studies is much more convincing than considering either alone. We discussed some examples in which laboratory studies were corroborated by more naturalistic studies: One was the conclusion that feeding–sucking was not a primary determinant of attachment, as was found both in laboratory studies with monkeys and in correlational studies with monkeys.

INDIVIDUAL DIFFERENCES

This chapter also provided two good examples of the advances made when individual differences underlying general phenomena are studied. Most of the research we discussed in this chapter deals with what is true for most babies most of the time. Most babies in western cultures experience stranger anxiety and

protest when their mothers leave them at some times in their infancy. Nevertheless, these phenomena are not universal—not all babies usually protest when their mothers leave them and most babies protest under some circumstances and not others. In most research studies individual differences are a hidden phenomenon until someone decides to look explicitly at them. Ainsworth noted that during reunion after separation, although most babies exhibited happiness and relief at seeing their mothers, others exhibited negative emotions as well. Because this subset was a fairly substantial minority, Ainsworth thought it worthwhile to explore them as separate groups.

Individual differences often serve as a springboard for future research that clarifies causal relations. For example, Weinraub and Lewis (1977) explored the basis of individual differences in protest at separation and found that babies of mothers who sneaked out of the room were more likely to protest than babies whose mothers told them that they were going to leave for a few minutes. Weinraub (1977) then studied this phenomenon experimentally by randomly assigning mothers to one of two groups. One group of mothers informed their babies of their departure and the other group sneaked out. The results confirmed the results of the correlational study.

Unfortunately, most researchers ignore individual differences. It is important to remember that individual differences underlie virtually every general finding, at least to the extent to which the phenomenon holds for every baby and often whether it holds at all for every baby.

Parenting

Clearly this chapter deals with issues that are at the very heart of parenting. The parental question that arises is: How can parents interact with their babies to optimize their attachment and future social development? Bear in mind that these same interactions influence the baby's exploration of the world and cognitive development. Some of the implications for later development of various special circumstances in infants' life histories (to be dealt with in the next chapter) will also be involved with issues of attachment.

Both psychoanalytic and ethological theories have focused on mother–infant attachment to the neglect of attachment to other persons, a focus that indicates both historical and cultural bias. Infants have been cared for and attached to persons other than mothers in many times and places. In contemporary western culture, fathers and other caretakers are becoming common alternative caretakers, particularly for working mothers. Fathers play an important role both directly, in terms of their relationships with their infants, and indirectly, in terms of their relationships to their wives. Whether their relationships to their infants are similar to or complementary to that of their wives is still a matter of conjecture. For a lay survey of this topic, see Parke (1981).

Both Freudian and learning psychologists theorized that the development and quality of attachment depends on the sucking–feeding relationship between mother and infant. Research has frequently failed to confirm this view. This should be comforting to mothers and fathers who, for one reason or another, do not serve as primary feeders of their infants.

The maternal characteristics that do seem to be associated consistently with secure attachment are acceptance, sensitivity, and responsiveness to babies' needs and signals (including those for noninterference). It would be nice to be able to tell parents how to attain these characteristics, but that is not easy. Even acceptance, which appears to be straightforward and accessible to most parents, is a complex variable.

Mothers who want children and feel a strong attachment to them may not always act in accepting, sensitive ways. If such behaviors are fairly common the baby may perceive rejection where none is intended. Increased knowledge about infants can help such parents in several ways. First, factual knowledge about infants' signals and needs can obviously help. One example is the nature of infants' cries, discussed in Chapter 6. Another example is infants' need for their parent as a secure base from which to explore the world. Awareness of this need allows parents to structure the situation such that the infant can check in—by a glance, a call, a touch, or an interaction. This can be done by opening doors between rooms if parents and infant are in different rooms, or taking the child along as the parent moves from room to room. Notice that in this circumstance knowing what the infant needs may free the parents if they realize that the infant is not demanding constant attention, but rather intermittent reassurance and attention.

Second, knowledge about normal developmental change can help parents put their own infants' behaviors into context. We have discussed two examples of such natural developmental phenomena, stranger anxiety and protest at separation. Knowing that most babies develop stranger anxiety in the middle of their first year of life will prevent parents from worrying that their baby has suddenly changed from a friendly baby to a "scaredy cat." Likewise, knowing that toddlers typically exhibit strong emotional reactions to separation can prevent parents from worrying about their children becoming dependent adults because of something the parents did. Knowing that it is just a phase may permit parents to respond more sensitively, rather than feel that they cannot give in for fear of the long-term consequences for their babies' development.

Third, putting the behaviors of their own children in the context of the large range of common behaviors may also help parents keep perspective. For example, many children are strong finger suckers for years. This is as normal as giving up sucking in the first year of life is. Likewise, there are great individual differences among babies in when they show stranger anxiety and protest at separation and the degree to which they show these phenomena. Most such individual variations are within the normal range of infant behaviors and often reflect the specific context of the incident, the general life experiences of the infant, and constitutional characteristics of the infant rather than influences of parents. If parents understand that these mammoth individual differences are the rule, they can accept their child's idiosyncracies rather than worry about them.

If it is difficult to be an optimal parent in the best of circumstances—loving and well-meaning parents in economically and environmentally good situations—it is of course more difficult when these optimal conditions are not met. Mothers who feel strongly ambivalent, because they didn't want a child or because their life has become intolerably hard because of the baby, or because they find mothering unexpectedly unrewarding, will find it difficult to exhibit acceptance to their babies. Such parents need support systems that help deal with life circumstances, such as part-time child care, counseling or therapy, or help in finding a job. Since the rise of the nuclear family and the decrease in family size, these supports are not always available through the family network nor are they always available from social institutions. Sometimes even when they are available they are not easy to find. Parents need to understand that their relationship with their infants can go awry through no fault of either, and this realization should encourage them to search for help and not feel guilty about asking for it.

In other circumstances a baby may be wanted and circumstances may be adequate or even superior, but the parents' images of what their baby must be like is sufficiently rigid or unrealistic to allow for no modification by educaton. Such parents may not want to change their expectations to be more realistic, or to accept the child as is, and they may not accept educational messages or seek help, although they may need it the most. The ray of hope for children in these circumstances is that there is considerable evidence that corrective measures after infancy can reverse bad effects. Children who are not accepted at one age for being too immature in some way may be accepted when they do become more mature in the course of time. In addition, some infants are more resilient than others and seem able to develop in appropriate ways despite experiences that seem far from optimal. The topic of individual differences in resilience (or psychological and physical toughness) is one which is very little understood. This is true for the questions of why some babies exposed to noxious agents during embryonic or fetal life are only mildly affected and others seriously, or why some babies with less than optimal attachment to their mothers develop in an appropriate fashion and others don't.

SUMMARY

Attachment to Mother

Belief in the importance of infants' early attachment to their mothers was first popularized by Freud's theory and has been maintained in most later theories. Freud and Erikson both believed that the mother–infant relationship was the prototype for all subsequent relationships. Freud believed that this relationship was established through sucking experiences, whereas Erikson included other aspects of the mother–infant relationship in addition to sucking.

Bowlby integrated Freudian and ethological views in his theory of attachment. He determined that five behavioral systems within the infant (following, clinging, crying, smiling, sucking) are focused on the mother and form the basis of the infant's attachment. Development of each of these response systems depends on both experience and maturation. Bowlby described four stages of attachment, three of which occur in infancy and have been documented by Ainsworth's work. As is true for Piagetian stages, all children apparently go through each stage in the same sequence although not at the same ages. Stage one is undiscriminating social responsiveness, in which infants orient to salient features of the environment, including human faces and voices, gain and maintain contact with humans, and use special signaling behaviors. They do not, however, show consistent preference for one or a few individuals. Stage two is discriminating social responsiveness, in which infants respond differently to familiar figures compared to relative strangers. Transition to this stage requires development of perceptual and learning abilities. Stage three is active initiative in seeking proximity and contact with the attachment figure. Locomotion and control of body movements facilitate this stage. Because transitions between stages are both gradual and uneven, an infant's attachment behaviors at any particular time may include behaviors characteristic of an earlier and of a still developing stage. They are also, of course, influenced by the specific situation.

Most current studies of attachment are concerned with the third stage, active initative in seeking proximity contact, which develops around 7 months of age. Early work primarily used as a measure of attachment the child's protests when separated from the mother and indications of fear of strangers. Later work has de-emphasized stranger anxiety as a measure because stranger anxiety waxes and wanes according to a different developmental timetable than does protest at separation. Ainsworth's tripartite classification of quality of attachment, based on reunion behaviors, has been selected by many researchers as a more viable measure of attachment. Researchers find evidence that these global patterns of attachment are stable over time when the infants are in stable environments.

FUNCTIONS OF ATTACHMENT

Attachment is seen as a biological mechanism for survival whereby infants stay close to their mothers, with the result that the mothers can protect their babies from dangers in the environment. The security mothers provide makes a secure base which allows infants to explore the world around them. Between 6 months and 2 years, toddlers typically explore strange situations more readily when mother is present. Mothers also serve as an emotional support, a source of stimulation, and a playmate.

The degree to which maternal–infant attachments form the basis for later personal relationships is of particular interest to those concerned with mental health. Both Freud and Erikson believed that poor attachment in infancy would prevent children from ever forming healthy personal relationships. Erikson further believed that trust in institutions would be negatively affected. Nevertheless, Erikson argued that the negative effects of poor early attachment experiences can be ameliorated later through therapy or an improved environment. Thus, these two theories hypothesize that infancy is a sensitive period rather than a critical period. In this chapter we reviewed short-term longitudinal studies that found that babies who were securely attached were more likely than insecurely attached infants to exhibit desirable cognitive and social characteristics later in the preschool years. These studies, however, are quite sporadic and, because of their correlational nature, are open to other interpretations than that the mother–infant relationship in infancy caused the results. It may be that the same maternal behaviors that foster security may also support the development of social competence in young children, or it may be that babies who are easy and rewarding to mothers stimulate responsiveness and acceptance (maternal characteristics that promote attachment) in mothers, teachers, and peers.

THE MOTHER'S ROLE

Of central concern to researchers studying attachment is what maternal behaviors influence the development of attachment. The Harlow experiments with monkeys showed that contact comfort was more important than nursing in developing a secure base. Studies with humans suggest that variables involving sucking or feeding are also unimportant for humans. In contrast, contact comfort may be important for human babies only when it occurs as part of a larger context of social interaction, that is, when it is an appropriate response to the infant's responses. Indeed it is the mother's sensitivity and responsiveness to her infant's needs (for example, for handling or for being left alone) and her stimulation that seem to be related to the quality of her infant's attachment.

Early Social Interactions

Some researchers believe that newborns exhibit biologically based, specifically social, responses. Others believe that newborns are incapable of differentiating between social and nonsocial stimuli and so their responses to people are no different (from the babies' points of view) than their responses to nonsocial stimuli. A third group feels it doesn't matter because in either case newborn infants do respond to other people and these interactions can thus be studied.

During the first few months, babies' behaviors become increasingly effective in eliciting social responses from caretakers. Beginning at birth with sucking, crying, and molding their bodies when held front-to-front, they move on to sustained visual regard, smiling, wriggling, cooing, gurgling, and responsive vocalization—all behaviors that are rewarding to their mothers.

In addition to motion, sounds, and tactual stimulation, babies respond positively to adult imitations of their own vocalizations and to other enjoyable behaviors that are repeated over and over again. Familiarization through repetition and making things happen through their own actions are both rewarding to infants.

Researchers today view mothers and infants as a dyad in which both can synchronize their activities to stimulate and reinforce each other. Early mother–infant interactions have been described by some investigators as pre-speech conversations between active turn-taking partners. Other investigators have described social interactions between mother and infant as pulsing engagement and disengagement; that is, active interchanges of motions, sounds, and expressions, and then momentary periods of rest. Some researchers think of mothers and infants as a single system with feedback response loops. One reason it has been hard for researchers to become involved in this kind of research is the lack of statistical tools for analyzing the data of such rapid sequential behaviors. By recording large numbers of varied behaviors, they hope to identify meaningful clusters that will be different for different mother–child dyads. One promising hypothesis that needs further research is that dyads whose interactions result in babies "turning off" may be at risk for future difficulties, but pairs who consistently have synchronized interactions may become securely attached and develop in a normal fashion.

The Father's Role in Infants' Social Development

Because of the strong traditional belief that only mothers are important to infants' development, the nature of father–infant interactions and the role fathers play in infants' development was little studied before the 1970s. Changing beliefs about male and female roles have made this a lively research topic. Undoubtedly in part because of these changing beliefs, fathers vary greatly in the extent to which they conform to traditional norms, and those who reject the traditional role of paternal involvement spend more time with their babies. Thus, it should come as no surprise that studies exploring differences between fathers and mothers produce widely varying results. Some find fathers very similar to mothers in their interactions with infants, but others find that fathers do less caretaking and engage in more games and rough-and-tumble play. Research typically shows that toddlers exhibit specific attachments to both mother and father, although some studies find that infants under

stress may prefer the mother. As these results indicate, there is little evidence that fathers have a single, clearly defined role to play, as would be expected if paternal behavior were biologically determined. In fact, it appears that personality is a greater determinant of parenting behavior than is biological sex. Lastly, it is clear that fathers, mothers, and infants constitute a dynamic interactive system in which each influences both others, and the relationship between each pair affects the third.

REFERENCES

Ainsworth, M.D.S. (1963). The development of infant–mother interaction among the Ganda. In B.M. Foss (Ed.), *Determinants of infant behaviour* (Vol. 2, pp. 67–112). London: Methuen.

Ainsworth, M.D.S. (1967). *Infancy in Uganda: Infant care and the growth of love.* Baltimore: Johns Hopkins University Press.

Ainsworth, M.D.S. (1972). Attachment and dependency: A comparison. In J.L. Gewirtz (Ed.), *Attachment and dependency* (pp. 97–137). Washington, DC: Winston.

Ainsworth, M.D.S. (1973). The development of infant–mother attachment. In B.M. Caldwell & H.N. Ricciuti (Eds.), *Review of child development research* (Vol. 3, pp. 1–94). Chicago: University of Chicago Press.

Ainsworth, M.D.S. (1974). Infant–mother attachment and social development: Socialization as a product of reciprocal responsiveness to signals. In M. Edwards (Ed.), *The integration of the child into the social world.* Cambridge, England: Cambridge University Press.

Ainsworth, M.D.S., & Bell, S.M.V. (1969). Some contemporary patterns of mother–infant interaction in the feeding situation. In J.A. Ambrose (Ed.), *Stimulation in early infancy* (pp. 133–170). London: Academic.

Ainsworth, M.D.S., & Bell. S.M. (1970). Attachment, exploration, and separation: Illustrated by the behavior of one-year-olds in a strange situation. *Child Development, 41,* 49–67.

Ainsworth, M.S., Bell, S.M.V., & Stayton, D.J. (1971). Individual differences in strange-situation behavior of one-year-olds. In H.R. Schaffer (Ed.), *The origins of human social relations* (pp. 17–52). New York: Academic.

Ainsworth, M.D.S., & Wittig, B.A. (1969). Attachment and exploratory behavior of one-year-olds in a strange situation. In B.M. Foss (Ed.), *Deter-*

minants of infant behaviour (Vol. 4, pp. 111–136). London: Methuen.

Arsenian, J.M. (1943). Young children in an insecure situation. *Journal of Abnormal and Social Psychology, 38*, 225–249.

Bailey, W.T. (1982, March). *Affinity: An ethological theory of the infant–father relationship.* Paper presented at the Third International Conference on Infant Studies, Austin, TX.

Bell, R.Q. (1968). A re-interpretation of the direction of effects in studies of socialization. *Psychological Review, 75*, 81–95.

Bell, R.Q. (1971). Stimulus control of parent or caretaker behavior by offspring. *Developmental Psychology, 4*, 63–72.

Bell, S. (1970). The development of the concept of object as related to infant–mother attachment. *Child Development, 41*, 291–311.

Belsky, J. (1979a). The interrelation of parental and spousal behavior during infancy in traditional nuclear families: An exploratory analysis. *Journal of Marriage and the Family, 41*. 62–68.

Belsky, J. (1979b). Mother–father–infant interaction: A naturalistic observational study. *Developmental Psychology, 15*, 601–607.

Belsky, J. (1981). Early human experience: A family perspective. *Developmental Psychology, 17*, 3–23.

Bem, S.L., Martyna, W., & Watson, C. (1976). Sex typing and androgyny: Further explorations of the expressive domain. *Journal of Personality and Social Psychology, 34*, 1016–1023.

Bowlby, J. (1958). The nature of the child's tie to his mother. *International Journal of Psychoanalysis, 39*, 350–373.

Bowlby, J. (1969). *Attachment and loss: Vol. 1. Attachment.* New York: Basic Books.

Brackbill, Y. (1958). Extinction of the smiling response in infants as a function of reinforcement schedule. *Child Development, 29*, 115–124.

Brazelton, T.B., Tronick, E., Adamson, L., Als, H., & Wise, S. (1975). Early mother–infant reciprocity. In M.A. Hofer (Ed.), *Parent–infant interaction.* London: Ciba.

Bretherton, I., & Ainsworth, M.D.S. (1974). Responses of one-year-olds to a stranger in a strange situation. In M. Lewis & L. Rosenblum (Eds.), *The origins of fear* (pp. 131–164). New York: Wiley.

Bronson, G.W. (1968). The year of novelty. *Psychological Bulletin, 69*, 350–358.

Bronson, G.W. (1972). Infants' reactions to unfamiliar persons and novel objects. *Monographs of the Society for Research in Child Development, 37*(3, Serial No. 148).

Broussard, E.R., & Hartner, M.S.S. (1971). Further considerations regarding maternal perception of the first born. In J. Hellmuth (Ed.), *Exceptional infant: Studies in abnormalities* (Vol. 2, pp. 432–449). New York: Brunner/Mazel.

Cairns, R.B. (1966). Development, maintenance, and extinction of social attachment behavior in sheep. *Journal of Comparative and Physiological Psychology, 62*, 298–306.

Cairns, R.B. (1972). Attachment and dependency: A psychobiological and social learning synthesis. In J.L. Gewirtz (Ed.), *Attachment and dependency* (pp. 29–80). New York: Winston.

Cairns, R.B., & Johnson, D.L. (1965). The development of interspecies social attachment. *Psychonomic Science, 2*, 337–338.

Campos, J., Emde, R., & Gaensbauer, T. (1975). Cardiac and behavioral interrelationships in the reactions of infants to strangers. *Developmental Psychology, 11*, 589–601.

Carr, S., Dabbs, J., & Carr, T. (1975). Mother–infant attachment: The importance of the mother's visual field. *Child Development, 46*, 331–338.

Clarke-Stewart, K.A. (1973). Interactions between mothers and their young children: Characteristics and consequences. *Monographs of the Society for Research in Child Development, 38*(6, Serial No. 153).

Clarke-Stewart, K.A. (1978). And daddy makes three: The father's impact on mother and child. *Child Development, 49*, 466–478.

Clarke-Stewart, K.A. (1980). The father's contribution to children's cognitive and social development in early childhood. In F.A. Pedersen (Ed.), *The father–infant relationship: Observational studies in a family setting.* New York: Holt, Rinehart, & Winston.

Cohn, J.F., & Tronick, E.Z. (1983). Three-month-old infants' reaction to simulated maternal depression. *Child Development, 54*, 185–193.

Cordell, A.S. (1978). *The father–infant relationship.* Unpublished doctoral dissertation, University of Chicago.

Corter, C.M., Rheingold, H.L., & Eckerman, C.O. (1972). Toys delay the infant's following of his mother. *Developmental Psychology, 6*, 138–145.

Cox, F.N., & Campbell, D. (1968). Young children in a new situation with and without their mothers. *Child Development, 39*, 123–131.

Earls, F., & Yogman, M. (1978). The father–infant relationship. In J. Howells (Ed.), *Modern per-*

spectives in the psychiatry of infancy. New York: Brunner/Mazel.

Easterbrooks, M.A. (1982, March), *Father involvement, parenting characteristics and toddler development.* Paper presented at the Third International Conference on Infant Studies, Austin, TX.

Eckerman, C.O., & Rheingold, H.L. (1974). Infants' exploratory responses to toys and people. *Developmental Psychology, 10,* 255–259.

Eisenberg, R.B. (1969). Auditory behavior in the human neonate: Functional properties of sound and their ontogenetic significance. *International Audiology, 8,* 34–44.

Entwisle, D.R., & Doering, S.G. (1981). *The first birth.* Baltimore: Johns Hopkins University Press.

Erikson, E.H. (1963). *Childhood and society.* New York: Norton.

Feldman, S., & Ingham, M. (1975). Attachment behavior: A validation study in two age groups. *Child Development, 46,* 319–330.

Field, T. (1978). Interaction patterns of primary versus secondary caretaker fathers. *Developmental Psychology, 14,* 183–185.

Fox, N. (1977). Attachment of kibbutz infants to mother and metapelet. *Child Development, 48,* 1228–1239.

Freud, S. (1938). Three contributions to the theory of sex. In A.A. Brill (Trans. and Ed.), *The basic writings of Sigmund Freud* (pp. 553–629). New York: Modern Library. (Original work published in 1905.)

Gershaw, N.J., & Schwartz, T.C. (1971). The effects of a familiar toy and mother's presence on exploratory and attachment behaviors in young children. *Child Development, 42,* 1662–1666.

Gewirtz, J.L. (1972a). Attachment, dependence, and a distinction in terms of stimulus controls. In J.L. Gewirtz (Ed.), *Attachment and dependency* (pp. 139–177). Washington, DC: Winston.

Gewirtz, J.L. (1972b). On the selection and use of attachment and dependence indices. In J.L. Gewirtz (Ed.), *Attachment and dependency* (pp. 179–215). Washington, DC: Winston.

Greenberg, M., & Morris, N. (1974). Engrossment: The newborn's impact upon the father. *American Journal of Orthopsychiatry, 44,* 520–531.

Grossmann, K.E., & Wolkmer, H.-J. (1984). Fathers' presence during birth of their infants and paternal involvement. *International Journal of Behavioral Development, 7,* 157–165.

Harlow, H.F. (1958). The nature of love. *American Psychologist, 13,* 673–685.

Harlow, H.F., & Harlow, M.K. (1966). Learning to love. *American Scientist, 54,* 1–29.

Harlow, H.F., & Zimmerman, R.R. (1959). Affectional responses in the infant monkey. *Science, 130,* 421–432.

Harper, L.V. (1971). The young as a source of stimuli controlling caretaker behavior. *Developmental Psychology, 4,* 73–88.

Hebb, D.O., & Riesen, A.H. (1943). The genesis of irrational fears. *Bulletin of the Canadian Psychological Association, 3,* 49–50.

Josselyn, I.M. (1956). Cultural forces, motherliness, and fatherliness. *American Journal of Orthopsychiatry, 26,* 264–271.

Klaus, M.H., & Kennell, J.H. (1970). Mothers separated from their newborn infants. *Pediatric Clinics of North America, 17,* 460–463.

Kotelchuck, M. (1976). The infant's relationship to the father: Experimental evidence. In M.E. Lamb (Ed.), *The role of the father in child development* (pp. 329–344). New York: Wiley.

Lamb, M.E. (1976a). Effects of stress and cohort on mother– and father–infant interaction. *Developmental Psychology, 12,* 435–443.

Lamb, M.E. (1976b). Twelve month olds and their parents: Interaction in a laboratory playroom. *Developmental Psychology, 12,* 237–244.

Lamb, M.E. (1977a). The development of mother–infant and father–infant attachments in the second year of life. *Developmental Psychology, 13,* 637–648.

Lamb, M.E. (1977b). Father–infant and mother–infant interaction in the first year of life. *Child Development, 48,* 167–181.

Lamb, M.E. (Ed.) (1981). *The role of the father in child development.* New York: Wiley.

Lamb, M.E., Frodi, A.M., Frodi, M., & Hwang, C.-P. (1982). Characteristics of maternal and paternal behavior in traditional and nontraditional Swedish families. *International Journal of Behavioral Development, 5,* 131–141.

Lamb, M.E., Frodi, M., Hwang, C.P., & Frodi, A.M. (1983). Effects of paternal involvement on infant preferences for mothers and fathers. *Child Development, 54,* 450–458.

Lamb, M.E., Frodi, A.M., Hwang, C.-P., Frodi, M., & Steinberg, J. (1982). Mother– and father–infant interactions involving play and holding in traditional and nontraditional Swedish families. *Developmental Psychology, 18,* 215–221.

Lester, B.M., Kotelchuck, M., Spelke, E., Sellers, M.J., & Klein, R.E. (1974). Separation protest in Guatemalan infants: Cross cultural and cognitive findings. *Developmental Psychology, 10,* 79–85.

Lewis, M., & Goldberg, S. (1969). Perceptual–cognitive development in infancy: A generalized expectancy model as a function of mother–infant interaction. *Merrill-Palmer Quarterly, 15,* 81–100.

Lind, J. (1974, October). *Observations after delivery of communications between mother–infant–father.* Paper presented at the International Congress of Pediatrics, Buenos Aires.

Maccoby, E., & Feldman, S. (1972). Mother-attachment and stranger-reactions in the third year of life. *Monographs of the Society for Research in Child Development, 37*(1, Serial No. 146).

Main, M. (1973). *Exploration, play, and cognitive functioning as related to child–mother attachment.* Unpublished doctoral dissertation, Johns Hopkins University, Baltimore, MD.

Matas, L., Arend, R., & Sroufe, L. (1978). Continuity in adaptation in the second year: Quality of attachment and later competence. *Child Development, 49,* 547–556.

McCall, R.B., & Kagan, J. (1967). Stimulus–schema discrepancy and attention in the infant. *Journal of Experimental Child Psychology, 5,* 381–390.

Morgan, G.A., & Ricciuti, H.N. (1969). Infant's responses to strangers during the first year. In B.M. Foss (Ed.), *Determinants of infant behaviour* (Vol. 4, pp. 253–272). London: Methuen.

Nash, J. (1965). The father in contemporary culture and current psychological literature. *Child Development, 36,* 261–297.

Osofsky, J.D. (1976). Neonatal characteristics and mother–infant interaction in two observational situations. *Child Development, 47,* 1138–1147.

Osofsky, J.D., & Danzger, B. (1974). Relationships between neonatal characteristics and mother-infant interaction. *Developmental Psychology, 10,* 124–130.

Papoušek, H., & Bernstein, P. (1969). The functions of conditioning stimulation in human neonates and infants. In A. Ambrose (Ed.), *Stimulation in early infancy* (pp. 229–252). London: Academic.

Papoušek, H., & Papoušek, M. (1974). Mirror image and self recognition in young human infants. A new method of experimental analysis. *Developmental Psychology, 7,* 149–157.

Papoušek, H., & Papoušek, M. (1975). Cognitive aspects of preverbal social interaction between human infants and adults. In M. O'Connor (Ed.), *Parent-infant interaction.* Amsterdam: Elsevier.

Papoušek, H., & Papoušek, M. (1977). Mothering and the cognitive head-start: Psychobiological con-

siderations. In H.R. Schaffer (Ed.), *Studies in mother–infant interaction.* London: Academic.

Parke, R.D. (1981). *Fathers.* Cambridge, MA: Harvard University Press.

Parke, R.D., & O'Leary, S.E. (1976). Family interaction in the newborn period: Some findings, some observations and some unresolved issues. In K.F. Riegel & J.A. Meacham (Eds.), *The developing individual in a changing world: Vol. 2. Social and Environmental Issues* (pp. 653–663). Chicago: Aldine.

Parke, R.D., & Sawin, D.B. (1975, April). *Infant characteristics and behavior as elicitors of maternal and paternal responsibility in the newborn period.* Paper presented at the biennial meeting of the Society for Research in Child Development, Denver.

Parke, R.D., & Sawin, D.B. (1977, March). *The family in early infancy: Social interactional and attitudinal analyses.* Paper presented at the biennial meeting of the Society for Research in Child Development, New Orleans.

Parsons, T., & Bales, R.F. (1955). *Family, socialization and interaction process.* New York: Free Press.

Pastor, D.L. (1980). *The quality of mother–infant attachment and its relationship to toddler's initial sociability with peers.* Paper presented at the Second International Conference on Infant Studies, New Haven, CT.

Pedersen, F.A., Anderson, B.J., & Cain, R.L. (1977, March). *An approach to understanding linkages between the parent–infant and spouse relationships.* Paper presented at the biennial meeting of the Society for Research in Child Development, New Orleans.

Pedersen, F.A., Anderson, B.J., & Cain, R.L. (1979, March). *Parent–infant interaction observed in a family setting at age 5 months.* Paper presented at the biennial meeting of the Society for Research in Child Development, San Francisco.

Pedersen, F.A., & Robson, K.S. (1969). Father participation in infancy. *American Journal of Orthopsychiatry, 39,* 466–472.

Pedersen, F.A., Rubenstein, J., & Yarrow, L.J. (1979). Infant development in father-absent families. *Journal of Genetic Psychology, 135,* 151–161.

Pedersen, F.A., Zaslow, M.T., Cain, R.L., & Anderson, B.J. (1980, April). *Caesarean birth: The importance of a family perspective.* Paper presented at the Second International Conference on Infant Studies, New Haven, CT.

Ploof, D. (1976, April). *The reciprocal effects of maternal perceptions and infant characteristics in the early mother–infant interaction.* Paper presented at the meeting of the Eastern Psychological Association, Washington, DC.

Power, T.G., & Parke, R.D. (1979, March). *Toward a taxonomy of father–infant and mother–infant play patterns.* Paper presented at the biennial meeting of the Society for Research in Child Development, San Francisco.

Rheingold, H.L. (1969). The effect of a strange environment on the behavior of infants. In B.M. Foss (Ed.), *Determinants of infant behaviour* (Vol. 4, pp. 137–168). London: Methuen.

Rheingold, H.L., & Eckerman, C.O. (1969). The infant's free entry into a new environment. *Journal of Experimental Child Psychology, 8,* 217–283.

Rheingold, H.L., & Eckerman, C.O. (1970). The infant separates himself from his mother. *Science, 168,* 78–83.

Rheingold, H.L., Hay, D.F., & West, M.J. (1976). Sharing in the second year of life. *Child Development, 47,* 1148–1158.

Richards, M.P.M. (1971). A comment on the social context of mother–infant interaction. In H.R. Schaffer (Ed.), *The origins of human social relations* (pp. 187–193). New York: Academic.

Richards, M.P.M., Dunn, J.F., & Antonis, B. (1977). Caretaking in the first year of life: The role of fathers, and mothers' social isolation. *Child: Care, Health, and Development, 3,* 23–26.

Robson, K.S. (1967). The role of eye-to-eye contact in maternal infant attachment. *Journal of Child Psychology, 8,* 13–25.

Robson, K.S., & Moss, N.A. (1970). Patterns and determinants of maternal attachment. *Journal of Pediatrics, 77,* 976.

Roedell, W.C., & Slaby, R.G. (1977). The role of distal and proximal interaction in infant social preference formation. *Developmental Psychology, 13,* 266–273.

Rosenthal, M. (1973). Attachment and mother–infant interaction: Some research impasses and a suggested change in orientation. *Journal of Child Psychology and Psychiatry and Allied Disciplines, 14,* 201–207.

Ross, H.S., Rheingold, H.L., & Eckerman, C.O. (1972). Approach and exploration of a novel alternative by 12-month-old infants. *Journal of Experimental Child Psychology, 13,* 85–93.

Russell, G. (1978). The father role and its relation to masculinity, femininity and androgyny. *Child Development, 49,* 1174–1181.

Russell, G. (1980, July). *Fathers as caregivers: Possible antecedents and consequences.* Paper presented to a study group on Fathers and Social Policy, University of Haifa, Israel.

Schaffer, H.R., & Emerson, P.E. (1964). The development of social attachments in infancy. *Monographs of the Society for Research in Child Development, 29*(3, Serial No. 94).

Schoetzau, A., & Papoušek, H. (1977). Mothers' behavior in making eye contact with newborn infants. *Zeitschrift für Entwicklungpsychologie und Pädagogische Psychologie, 9,* 231–239.

Sears, R.R. (1943). *Survey of objective studies of psychoanalytic concepts.* New York: Social Science Research Council.

Sears, R.R. (1951). A theoretical framework for personality and social behavior. *The American Psychologist, 6,* 476–483.

Sluckin, W. (1965). *Imprinting and early learning.* Chicago: Aldine.

Solomon, R. & Décarie, T. (1976). Fear of strangers: A developmental milestone or an overstudied phenomenon? *Canadian Journal of Behavioral Science, 8,* 351–362.

Spitz, R.A. (1950). Anxiety in infancy: A study of its manifestations in the first year of life. *Journal of Psychoanalysis, 31,* 132–143.

Sroufe, L.A. (1977). Wariness of strangers and the study of child infant development. *Child Development, 48,* 731–746.

Sroufe, L.A. (1979). Socioemotional development. In J.D. Osofsky (Ed.), *Handbook of infant development* (pp. 462–516). New York: Wiley.

Sroufe, L.A., & Waters, E. (1977). Attachment as an organizational construct. *Child Development, 48,* 1184–1199.

Stechler, G. & Latz, E. (1966). Some observations on attention and arousal in the human infant. *Journal of the American Academy of Child Psychiatry, 5,* 517–525.

Steingüber, H.J., Nolten, G., & Bisping, R. (1984, September). *Mothers' capability to discriminate the cries of their newborn infants.* Paper presented at the XXIIIrd International Congress of Psychology, Acapulco, Mexico.

Stern, D.N., Beebe, B., Jaffe, J., & Bennett, S.L. (1977). The infants' stimulus world during social interaction: A study of caregiver behaviors with particular reference to repetition and timing. In H.R. Schaffer (Ed.), *Studies in mother–infant interaction.* New York: Academic.

Thoman, E.B. (1981a). Affective communication as the prelude and context for language learning. In R.L. Schiefelbusch & D. Bricker (Eds.), *Early language: Acquisition and inervention.* Baltimore: University Park Press.

Thoman, E.B. (1981b). Early communication as the prelude to later adaptive behaviors. In M.J. Begab, H.C. Haywood, & H.L. Garber (Eds.), *Psychosocial influences in retarded performance. Vol. 2. Strategies for improving competence.* Baltimore: University Park Press.

Thomas, A., & Chess, S. (1977). *Temperament and development.* New York: Brunner/Mazel.

Thompson, R.A., Lamb, M.E., & Estes, D. (1982). Stability of infant–mother attachment and its relationship to changing life circumstances in an unselected middle-class sample. *Child Development, 53,* 144–148.

Tiedemann, D. (1927). Tiedemann's observations on the development of the mental faculties of children (S. Langer, Trans.). *Pedagogical Seminary and Journal of Genetic Psychology, 34,* 205–230. (Original work published in 1897.)

Trevarthen, C. (1977). Descriptive analyses of infant communicative behaviour. In H.R. Schaffer (Ed.), *Studies in mother–infant interaction.* New York: Academic.

Vaughn, B., Egeland, B., Sroufe, L.A., & Waters, E. (1979). Individual differences in infant–mother attachment at twelve and eighteen months: Stability and change in families under stress. *Child Development, 50,* 971–975.

Waters, E. (1978). The reliability and stability of individual differences in infant–mother attachment. *Child Development, 49,* 483–494.

Waters, E., Wippman, J., & Sroufe, L.A. (1979). Attachment, positive affect, and competence in the peer group: Two studies in construct validation. *Child Development, 50,* 821–829.

Weinraub, M. (1977, March). *Children's responses to maternal absence: An experimental study.* Paper presented at the biennial meeting of the Society for Research in Child Development, New Orleans.

Weinraub, M., & Lewis, M. (1977). The determinants of children's responses to separation. *Monographs of the Society for Research in Child Development, 42*(4, Serial No. 172).

Wolff, P.H. (1959). Observations on newborn infants. *Psychosomatic Medicine, 21,* 110–118.

Wolff, P.H. (1963). Observations on the early development of smiling. In B.M. Foss (Ed.), *Determinants of infant behaviour* (Vol. 2, pp. 113–138). London: Methuen.

Wolff, P.H. (1969). The natural history of crying and other vocalizations in early infancy. In B.M. Foss (Ed.), *Determinants of infant behaviour* (Vol. 4, pp. 221–280). London: Methuen.

Yarrow, M.R., Waxler, C.Z., & Scott, P.M. (1971).

Child effects on adult behavior. *Developmental Psychology, 5,* 300–311.

Yogman, M.W. (1982). Development of the father–infant relationship. In H.E. Fitzgerald, B.M. Lester, & M.W. Yogman (Eds.), *Theory and research in behavioral pediatrics* (Vol. 1, pp. 221–279). New York & London: Plenum.

Yogman, M.W., Dixon, S., Tronick, E., Adamson, L., Als, H., & Brazelton, T.B. (1976a, April). *Development of social interaction.* Paper presented at the meeting of the Eastern Psychological Association, New York.

Yogman, M.W., Dixon, S., Tronick, E., Adamson, L., Als, H., & Brazelton, T.B. (1976b, May). *Parent–infant interaction.* Paper presented at the meeting of the American Pediatric Society—Society for Pediatric Research.

Yogman, M.W., Tronick, E., Dixon, S., Keefer, C., Als, H., & Brazelton, T.B. (1977, March). *The goals and structure of face-to-face interaction between infants and fathers.* Paper presented at the biennial meeting of the Society for Research in Child Development, New Orleans.

INFLUENCE OF ENVIRONMENT: DEPRIVATION AND ENRICHMENT

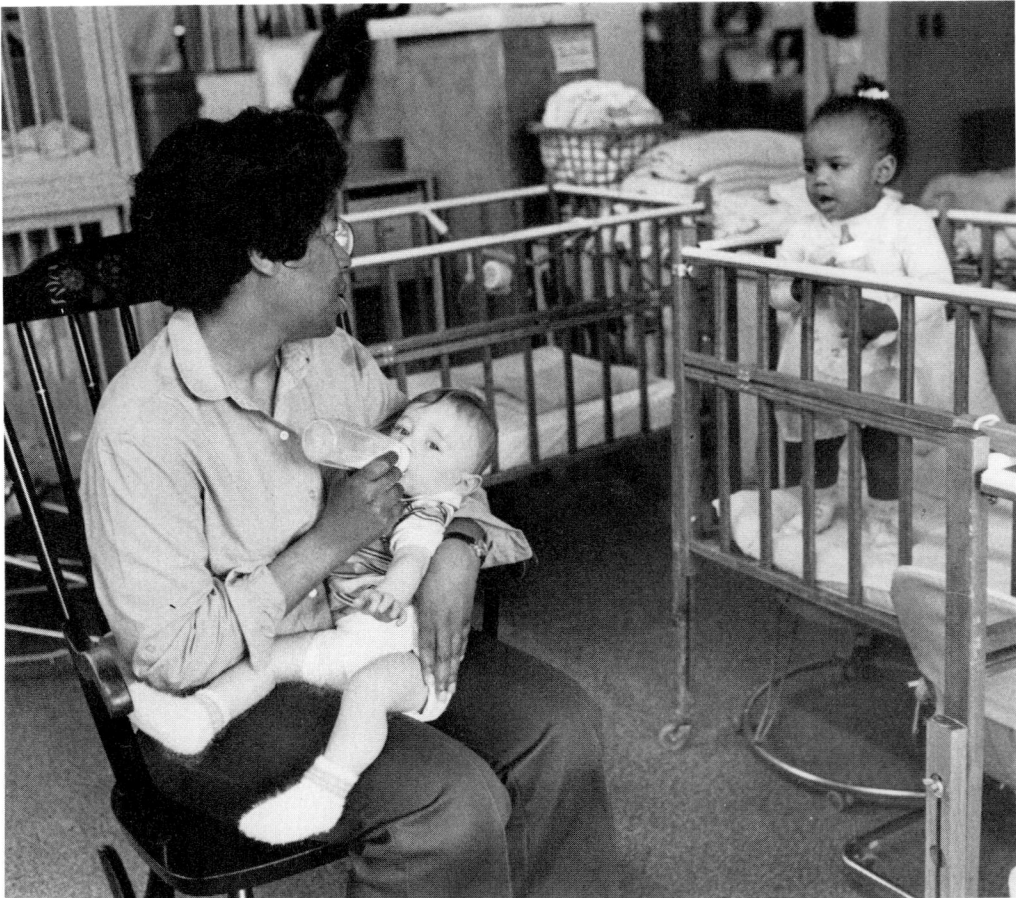

CHAPTER 13

In the last chapter we described the common critical periods hypothesis that babies must develop their affectional relationship with their mothers during infancy or they will be unable to develop normally. Our primary focus in this chapter will be research that examines this hypothesis by looking at the effects of various types of deprivation and its timing. One way of testing such a hypothesis is to examine the lives of children who were deprived of that maternal bond. Because researchers would not want to deprive babies of their mothers for the sake of science, they must look at so-called "experiments of nature," unavoidable occurrences in the natural world that provide the deprivation conditions whose effects they are interested in. The most severe case of maternal deprivation probably occurs in orphanages. Because care in orphanages is provided by paid caretakers who often have a large number of babies to care for and who work in shifts, the substitute care seems to be quite different from that a mother would provide. Thus researchers have been interested in studying the effects of deprivation during the presumed critical period of infancy by studying institutionalized infants. A related set of experiments of nature occurs when institutionalized children leave the institution for adoptive homes or other settings. By studying these children at different ages researchers can examine the long-term effects of deprivation. If indeed there is a critical period for the formation of attachment, infants adopted after that critical period should show long-term effects of their early deprivation.

By studying or manipulating the environment of orphanages and the subsequent different placements of orphanage children, researchers can get some idea of whether maternal deprivation itself produces ill effects. Orphanage children are indeed deprived of their mothers, but they are also often deprived of other sorts of environmental stimulation that home-reared infants enjoy. In some institutions, the children are not played with, taken places, or provided with toys to anywhere near the extent that home-reared infants are. Changes in the physical environment and in caretaking arrangements that lead to improved behaviors in orphanage children suggest that deprivation of the mother is not the only important variable in early deprivation. In general the research finds few permanent deficits from even severe early deprivation so long as an adequate environment is provided by 2 years of age.

Other natural experiments that permit examination of the effects of early maternal deprivation are studies of communal child rearing in other cultures and of day care in the United States. The argument goes like this. If mother is the crucial source of early psychological growth in the child, then partial deprivation of mother as a result of the multiple mothering that is part of communal care and day care should have deleterious effects. Studies of multiple mothering in situations in which infants experience adequate stimulation—things to look at, touch, play with, and so forth—provide a good test of the effect of the mother herself. This research is quite consistent in showing that multiple mothering is not harmful even when the biological mother spends much less time with her baby than the other caretaker or caretakers do.

The opposite of deprivation—enrichment—can also add to our understanding of the role of early experience. Research on enrichment has focused on the societally important goal of preventing or ameliorating the negative effects of deprivation by providing enriching experiences. Unlike human deprivation research, that on enrichment can be done in a truly experimental fashion. The limited research available has found intervention moderately successful, which suggests that deprivation effects are both preventable and correctable.

Finally we will examine a small part of the vast animal literature on the effects of early experience. The research we will review suggests that deprivation and enrichment affect various aspects of brain functioning and of behavior and that various kinds of early experience affect animals of varying genetic constitutions differently.

INSTITUTIONALIZATION

Early Studies

The great interest in studying institutionalized infants stems from the early to mid-1940s when several studies pointed to the dire consequences that being institutionalized had for infants. Spitz (1945, 1946) coined the term "hospitalism" for the syndrome shown by these infants. They failed to gain weight, many died in a measles epidemic, and they had great trouble in relationships with people. They also reached the normal developmental milestones (sitting, walking, talking) very late. Goldfarb (1945a, 1945b) presented similar data and later presented a re-analysis (1955).

At about the same time, Skodak and Skeels (1945, 1949) published the initial follow-up of their series of studies of an experiment of nature that suggested that these dire consequences were not an inevitable result of institutionalization. This experiment of nature began at overcrowded, unstaffed, poorly equipped orphanages in Iowa (Skeels, 1936; Skodak, 1939). Skeels served as staff psychologist for these orphanages and for several institutions for the retarded. His experiment began by accident. Two little girls, 13 and 16 months of age, had been committed to the orphanage because of neglect by their relatives. They were malnourished and had developmental levels of 6 and 7 months, respectively (DQs = 46 and 35), but had no physical defects. Because they clearly seemed to be retarded, they were transferred to a home for the retarded where they were placed in a ward of mentally deficient women. On Skeel's visit to that institution 6 months later he found that the two little girls were alert and responsive and not recognizable as the two children with the hopeless prognosis he had seen earlier. When he retested them he found them close to normal, but didn't believe the tests could be valid so they were left in the institution. New tests 12 months later and again when they were 40 and 35 months old showed development well within the normal range. The girls were transferred back to the orphanage and shortly afterward were adopted.

To find out why their development had changed so radically, Skeels examined their daily living situation and found that they had been made pets of the ward:

> . . . the older and brighter girls became very attached to the children and would play with them during most of their waking hours. Moreover, the attendants on the ward took a great fancy to the babies, and took them with them on their days off, took them to the store, bought them toys, picture books, and play materials. (Skeels & Dye, 1939, p. 5)

In the total program of the orphanage at that time, children whose development was so delayed that adoptive placement was out of the question remained there awaiting eventual transfer to an institution for the retarded. In the light of the experience with the two little girls, Skeels was able to get such children accepted as "house guests" in the state school for the retarded. For the most part only one guest child was assigned to each elite ward, but sometimes there were more children than elite wards. Periodic re-evaluations were to be made and the children committed to the institution only if they did not improve. Thirteen children became house guests during the course of the program. The average age at transfer was 19 months (range, 7 to 36) and the IQs averaged 64 (range, 35 to 89). A number showed severe motor retardation or other abnormal behaviors. Most spent 1 to 2 years as house guests (range, 6 months to 52 months). The development of these 13 children was varied but positive. All showed a gain in IQ, ranging from 7 to 58 points. Eleven of the children showed gains of over 17 points (which is greater than 1 standard deviation).

Skeels was able to select a contrast group from among the children who had remained at the orphanage until placement or institutionalization. Their initial IQs were higher (range 50 to 103), but their ages at first assessment were similar and their home backgrounds were as poor as those of the experimental group (those transferred to the institution for the retarded). For example, the mothers of both groups had averaged only an eighth grade education and the mothers' IQs when known were, with one exception, below normal (mean of 70 for the experimental group and 63 for the contrast group).

Although the contrast group started off somewhat more advantaged, their subsequent development was markedly inferior to that of the experimental group. Only one child maintained his IQ (2 points gained); the rest lost an average of 26 IQ points (range 9 to 45 points). Of the 12, 10 lost more than 15 points (or changed 1 standard deviation in the opposite direction from that of the experimental group).

What happened to the experimental children after their "visit" in the institution for the retarded? Of the 13 guests, one remained in the institution until adulthood, 11 were adopted, and 1 was returned to the orphanage for some years and later committed to the institution for the retarded. The adoptive homes were lower middle class but somewhat better than the children's natural homes.

About 2½ years after the adopted children were placed in their new homes, all 25 children were followed up. The average IQ for the experimental group was 96 and for the adopted members of that group it was 101. Only 1 of the adoptees, who was in the poorest of the adoptive homes, had a loss (−5 points). The two children who weren't adopted lost IQ points (17 points for the child returned to the orphanage and 9 for the child kept in the home for the retarded). The average IQ of the contrast group was 66, and 8 of the 12 had dropped markedly. Two were transferred at 41 months to the state school for the retarded and treated like the original experimental group. The IQ of one of these two children improved from 54 to 80. The other child failed to improve.

IQ is not the most important measure of people's adaptation in this world. In a rare show of persistence, and perhaps prodded by the current fashion in psychology of considering lack of early attachment to have dire consequences, Skeels (1966) again followed up these children when they reached adulthood. Of the 13 experimental children, not one was in an institution. All were self-supporting in skilled or semiskilled jobs. Of the 12 contrast children, 5 had ended up in institutions, and 5 of the 6 who worked were in unskilled jobs (the 12th had died). The median grade completed by the experimental group was the twelfth, by the contrast group the third. Four of the experimental group had attended college and one had graduated and then earned a Ph.D. at a major university. None of the contrast group attended college. Eleven of the 13 former guests had married and 9 were parents. Their children had an average IQ of 105 and were progressing satisfactorily in school. Of the contrast group only two had married and only one of these marriages had lasted.

Although there are many methodological problems with this study (small number of subjects, lack of random assignments of subjects to groups, extreme diversity of the sample), the results are so striking that its conclusions are difficult to ignore. They suggest that early deprivation effects can be overcome by providing a more stimulating environment. They also suggest that such enrichment needs to be continued; the children who returned to the earlier, less stimulating environment again declined in IQ.

The Skeels and Skodak studies did not systematically examine the relevant differences between the orphanages and the institution for the retarded. Skeels attributed the effect to an abundance of attention and experiential stimulation from many sources and a one-on-one relationship with a loving adult (because the older retarded girls tended to "adopt" one baby). An equally good claim could be made that these babies were being raised by multiple mothers, because there was a whole ward for them to play with.

What Produces the Retardation Effects of Institutions?

Skeel's study was greatly criticized for methodological defects, and so it had little impact on social policies.[1] Nevertheless, subsequent research has confirmed his findings that deprived children's development improves dramatically when their environment becomes more stimulating. The later studies have also helped to clarify conditions under which children institutionalized during infancy can later develop within the normal range. One nice demonstration of that is a comparison by Dennis (1960) of the development of infants in two institutions in Tehran. (Neither is necessarily representative of institutions in Tehran, which has many institutions for foundlings, orphans, half orphans, and others needing care). Children in the poorer institution showed profoundly retarded motoric development. For example, 85% of them were not yet walking in their fourth year. He even found that the unusual pattern of scooting rather than creeping was the modal pattern of prewalking locomotion. Nevertheless, they did not show the profound marasmus (or wasting away) from psy-

---

[1]In fact, such criticisms are still being made (see Longstreth, 1981).

chological causes that Spitz had described. Children from the second institution did not even show marked retardation in motor skills. A comparison of the two institutions suggests some possibly crucial differences in the environments of the children. The better institution was a new demonstration institute and was set up to provide more adequate stimulation. In the first institution there was 1 attendant for every 8 infants and the caretakers were untrained; in the demonstration orphanage there was 1 trained attendant for every 3–4 infants. Infants in the first orphanage were fed lying in bed, were never placed in a prone position (lying face down), and were never propped up, although they were placed on the floor once they could sit up. Infants in the demonstration project, in contrast, were held while being fed, were placed in the prone position (which leads to better motoric organization in newborns), were propped in their cribs, and were placed in playpens after 4 months of age. The motoric retardation at the first institution, then, very likely resulted from the lack of practice and use of appropriate muscles.

Further evidence of the causes of institutional retardation has been provided by Hunt and his collaborators (Hunt, Mohandessi, Ghodessi, & Akiyama, 1976; Hunt, Paraskevopoulos, Schickedanz & Uzgiris, 1975; Paraskevopoulus & Hunt, 1971). They explored the importance of the number of children per caregiver (child:caregiver ratio), what caregivers might do to foster cognitive development, and the role of visual and auditory stimulation independent of caregivers. Two studies explored the child:caregiver ratio. One used the same technique as Dennis had used. Paraskevopoulos and Hunt found two institutions in Athens, Greece, that appeared to differ mainly in the child:caregiver ratio. The babies at an orphanage with a 10:1 ratio were much slower to develop cognitively (as measured by the Hunt and Uzgiris ordinal scales of Piagetian-based cognitive development) than babies at an institution with a 3:1 ratio (the latter was a demonstration institute, as was Dennis's better orphanage). In the second study, Hunt and his collaborators (1976) studied the same institution in Teheran which Dennis had found to foster retardation, but introduced various experimental changes and assessed their effects. One intervention was to change the ratio

from 10:1 to 10:3 (they called it 10:3 rather than 3:1 to note that each infant received care from about 3 caregivers, not one). The caregivers were not specially tutored in any way. The increase in the infants' motoric development was quite spectacular. The age at which they stood and "cruised" around their cribs holding on to the edge was about 30 weeks earlier than infants in the same institution who had experienced the 10:1 ratio. Time-sampling observations suggested that the caregivers in the low child:caregiver ratio carried the babies in their arms and put them in strollers (where their feet could touch the floor) much more frequently than was possible in the 10:1 situation. Hunt surmised that this increase in muscular practice was what fostered their development. The effects of the lower caregiver ratio on cognitive development were less clear. When the infants of the 10:3 condition were 11–13 months old, they were still quite retarded cognitively, but during the second year they made spectacular gains. They reached top-level performance in all the Uzgiris–Hunt scales much earlier than did infants who had the standard 10:1 ratio. On some of the scales, they were even within the range of home-reared infants. Nevertheless, there was one hitch in the procedure that may have affected the results. Hunt visited the babies at the end of their first year. Because they were still so cognitively retarded, he introduced an informal experiment in eliciting vocal imitation and managed to get 2 of the infants to advance on that scale. The caregivers, who watched this procedure, instituted it with the other infants, who also showed sudden development in vocal contagion. The sudden improvement in cognitive development in the second year may have stemmed from this intervention and its consequences. The caregivers were surprised that imitating the infants had such good effects and may subsequently have watched the testing procedures to get more ideas of ways to stimulate their charges.[2]

In their second manipulation, Hunt and his collaborators introduced visual and auditory experiences in a progression designed to

---

[2] In an earlier intervention study, Dennis (1960) had failed to find significant effects and then had found that the caregivers of the control group were copying the experimental procedures.

increase both in complexity and in the extent to which the infants controlled them. These conditions fostered earlier development in the intermediate steps of the Hunt–Uzgiris scales (the first year of life) relative to the 10:3 ratio condition, but approximately the same developmental progress for the final steps of sensorimotor development.

Their last manipulation (Hunt, 1981, 1982) involved trained caregivers in a 3:1 ratio. The training included Badger's (1973, 1977) program for training mothers of infants and toddlers used in the United States. It involves teaching mothers to (1) recognize and respond to early signs of distress in their infants; (2) recognize their infants' reactions of interest, boredom, and distress to environmental stimuli; and (3) provide playthings and actions that bring forth interest rather than boredom or distress. In addition, the caregivers were taught how to foster vocal imitation and to talk to the infant about what the caregiver was doing when caring for the infant. This condition was the most successful of all. These babies achieved both the intermediate and final steps on the Uzgiris–Hunt scales earlier than those in any of the other conditions. They even achieved the final steps on 5 of the 7 scales earlier than the offspring of professional parents in the United States.

Hunt's research shows clearly that motoric and cognitive retardation need not be an inevitable consequence of institutionalization. The interventions Hunt instituted were relatively simple changes and yet they had profound effects. This research also reveals something about the kinds of early experience that foster development. Simply providing enough caretakers that they can engage in something other than pure caretaking activities has strong effects, but it is not enough. What is enough for the first year is perceptual stimulation that increases in complexity as the infant develops and that is responsive to the infants' behaviors. For the second year of life, however, something more is necessary for normal development. What that something is is not entirely clear from Hunt's research. His best condition involved both systematic and extensive cognitive stimulation and a deep affectional relationship with a caregiver (when these babies were adopted their caregivers were demonstrably sad at losing "their" infants). Thus, the in-

TABLE 13–1
DQs of Babies in Brossard and Décarie's Experimental Situation

Stimulation group	Prior to intervention	5 weeks later	10 weeks later
Perceptual	104	86	103
Social	102	89	102
Mixed	110	91	94
Control	102	86	83

fants' advancement may have been due to either of these manipulations or to the combined effects of both.

Brossard and Décarie (1971) carried out an experiment similar to but much more limited than Hunt's experimental intervention in the Teheran orphanage. They studied 4 groups of 12 infants matched on sex, age (at 2 to 2½ months), and developmental quotients. One group was the control and received normal institutional treatment. The three experimental groups received 15 minutes per day, 5 days per week, of systematic stimulation. The extra stimulation of one group was perceptual: a mobile that could be seen, touched, and made to make noise and a series of nonhuman everyday sounds from a tape recording. Another treatment group was socially stimulated: One of two adults (each adult assigned to half the babies) sang, talked to, smiled, caressed, carried, and rocked the babies in a strict sequence. The third experimental group received half of both the perceptual stimulation and the social stimulation programs.

The babies were evaluated by a series of measures (the Griffiths Mental Development Scale, a Piagetian object concept scale, observational records of spontaneous behavior and interaction patterns, and gross motor activity.) Table 13–1 presents the DQs for the babies at the onset of the experiment, after 5 weeks, and after 10 weeks (when the babies were 4–5 months old). The DQs of the control groups decreased, which shows that this institution did not provide an adequate environment for normal psychological development. Both the perceptual stimulation and social stimulation groups were higher than the controls after 10 weeks of stimulation (when the babies were 4–5 months of age), but had not differed after 5 weeks. Contrary to Brossard and Décarie's expectations, the mixed stimulation group was not only not superior to either single type of stimulation alone; it was, in fact, inferior to them. This study provides general support for the findings of Hunt and his collaborators. In the first year of life both pure perceptual stimulation and social stimulation, even in relatively small doses, prevent the development of retardation that would otherwise be the lot of these institutionalized babies. Because Brossard and Décarie's study did not extend into the second year, it did not speak to Hunt's conclusion that purely perceptual stimulation is not as facilitative in the second year as intervention that includes social stimulation. We believe that the inferior results of the mixed stimulation condition may be an artifact of Brossard and Décarie's method. The social and perceptual stimulations were isolated from each other and the babies received less than 10 minutes per day of each. Hunt's trained caregiver condition was also a mixed condition: The caregivers were trained to be responsive socially and to provide playthings appropriate to the babies' immediate needs. Either the more extensive nature of this intervention or the embedding of the perceptual stimulation within the context of a responsive relationship, or the combination, may have been the key to its success.

Hunt and colleagues and Brossard and Décarie found that specific interventions had specific effects. The trained caregiver condition of Hunt and colleagues was designed to overcome specific defects of the Badger training program. In the original research on that training program, Badger had found that poverty level infants with training were much more advanced (on the Object Permanence scale) than babies from professional homes with no special training. This seemed to result from the kind and timing of playthings the trained poverty-level mothers had introduced. However, these same infants were just as retarded in the development of vocal imitation, which had not been included in the training program, as they were advanced on the Object Permanence scale. Because of this, and as a result of their experience in Teheran, Hunt and colleagues included vocal imitation in their final training program. Their intervention also produced specific effects, usually in the pre-

dicted direction. For example, the infants exposed to perceptual stimulation were somewhat retarded motorically compared to the infants who had merely had additional untrained caregivers, but they were advanced in the first year on cognitive scales and on the final levels for scales involving language. The babies that were carried around would be expected to have had more motoric exercise, and those experiencing auditory stimulation matched to their progress (the caregivers generally tended not to talk to their charges) would be expected to have developed more rapidly on relevant cognitive scales. Likewise, the babies exposed to tutored caregivers were advanced in those domains relevant to the training (such as object permanence). They were retarded, however, in demonstrating knowledge of the whereabouts of familiar others and in the spontaneous naming of familiar objects.

The meaning of the specificity of these effects is a complex issue. Many of them obviously reflect a pure specificity effect; that is, babies advance in a particular domain when they are exposed to the specific relevant experiences. Other effects do not seem to conform to predictions, perhaps because the necessary specific experiences for these achievements are not known. (If this is so, a wonderful goal for future intervention research could be to figure out what experiences are relevant for different achievements.) It may be, however, that the results that do not conform to specificity expectations may represent part of a nonspecific pattern that is still unknown.

High-quality Institutions

The research in inadequate orphanages clearly shows the importance of stimulation in infancy and demonstrates that rather simple environmental interventions can make great inroads against developing retardation. These data suggest that so-called "institutionalization effects" are not due to institutionalization as such, but depend on the quality of the institution. In high-quality institutions infants apparently are not at intellectual or social risk. One well-documented study demonstrates this quite well. Tizard (1977) studied children who spent their first 2 years in a group of British orphanages that were designed to provide optimal physical environments and stimulation in the provision both of toys and of social interactions with staff and with other infants. For example, the children were read to and taken on outings regularly. There was at least one caregiver for every three children for most of the time (and for many of the children, all of the time). Generally these orphanages attempted to provide a home-like environment with its level and quality of stimulation, but there was one major exception. Close personal relationships between caregivers and children were discouraged. Care for each child was divided among the staff and the staff were discouraged from spending too much time with any one child. By the age of 24 months the average child had been looked after for at least a week by 24 different people and by $4\frac{1}{2}$ years, by 50.

Tizard first studied these children at 2 years of age. Their IQs were measured and their general development was compared to that of a control group of working class children in two-parent families. The intellectual development of the nursery children as measured by the IQ test was slightly retarded (mean mental age of 22 months) compared to that of home-reared controls (slightly above the average, a mean of 25 months). Most of this retardation seemed to be in language development, which was independently observed during play. The institutionalized children spoke less frequently and used a more limited vocabulary than their working class counterparts.

Generally, social development of the institutionalized group was normal. None of the children seemed grossly disturbed or unhappy, and so-called "institutional" behaviors, such as rocking and headbanging, were rare. The difference most striking to Tizard was the infantile attachment behaviors. When their nurse entered the room, 60% of the institutionalized children ran to be picked up, but none of the home-reared children did so when their mothers entered the room. The institutionalized children were more likely to protest at separation and to exhibit stranger anxiety. Other possible signs of immaturity or anxiety were that the institutionalized children were more likely to suck their thumbs, to wet their pants, to cry over minor mishaps. They were also very reluctant to share toys. This was characteristic of 90% of institutionalized chil-

dren versus only 53% of home-reared. On a few dimensions, however, the institutionalized children seemed more mature. Most of them occupied themselves well on their own, but only about half the home-reared group did; and only 3% of the nursery children woke during the night but about one third of the home-reared sample did.

Thus, children being reared in a high-quality institution seem developmentally and emotionally quite similar to home-reared children. The few differences might reflect a general, slight retardation or they might reflect specifics of the institutional setting. For example, the orphanage children might be more insecure in attachments because they were discouraged from putting their trust in any one caregiver. They might have more difficulty in getting along with peers because the staff did not teach them to cooperate. Indeed, the way the staff dealt with competition for adult attention among the children was to avoid the situation by not spending a concentrated period of time with any child.

These studies make it crystal clear that being raised in an institution does not necessarily condemn a child to a life of motoric, intellectual, and linguistic retardation or to profound inability to relate to people. They also provide guidelines for the design of institutions and care of children in an institutional setting. The good orphanages always seem to have a low child:caregiver ratio and always seem to provide sensory and intellectual stimulation. They do not, however, necessarily provide a single continuing relationship with a single other person, let alone with the child's mother.

Long-term Effects of Institutionalization During Infancy

Naturally, interest in the effects of institutionalization is not limited to the period during infancy. People are also interested in what happens to these children as they grow up, particularly when they leave the institution. They want to know whether initial deficits can be overcome by later development and whether infants reared in quality institutions nonetheless are at risk for later development.

Experiments of nature allow investigation of these questions. Researchers can study children who moved from one institutional setting to another or who were adopted, as Skeels and Skodak did. Studies of children who have left a deprived environment provide a good test of whether or not infancy is a critical period for later development. According to the strictest version of the critical periods hypothesis, normal post-infancy environments would not be sufficient to overcome the permanent deficiencies produced by early deprivation. Studies of children who have been adopted from good institutional environments can help to pinpoint aspects of institutionalization that might produce the effects found.

Most of the studies relevant to long-term effects have used intellectual development as the major dependent variable. Freud, the most well-known critical periods proponent in psychology, was primarily interested in emotional development, yet that is rarely measured. The reason for this is simple. Psychologists understand, and most important, can measure intellectual development far better than they can measure emotional development. To invest the amount of time, energy, and money required by longitudinal studies of effects of early experiences argues against using only poor measures of the effects. Failure to get the expected results can then as easily be due to the low reliability or validity of the measures used as to a false hypothesis. If consistent effects on intellectual development can be shown, at least the argument can be made that some psychological (rather than physical or medical) function is affected in a certain way.

LONG-TERM EFFECTS ON INTELLECTUAL DEVELOPMENT

One of the best research projects on the topic of permanence of early deprivation is the series of studies on the Crèche, a Lebanese orphanage run by French nuns (Dennis, 1973). Children stayed in the Crèche from infancy to the age of 6 years. The Crèche provided good physical care—the children were adequately fed, clothed, and kept warm and dry. There was, however, only 1 caregiver for every 10 infants and many of the caregivers were of below average intelligence (and many had themselves been raised in the Crèche). Thus, the infants received little stimulation. They were laid on their backs in cribs with white crib bumpers. The ceilings were white. They stayed in these

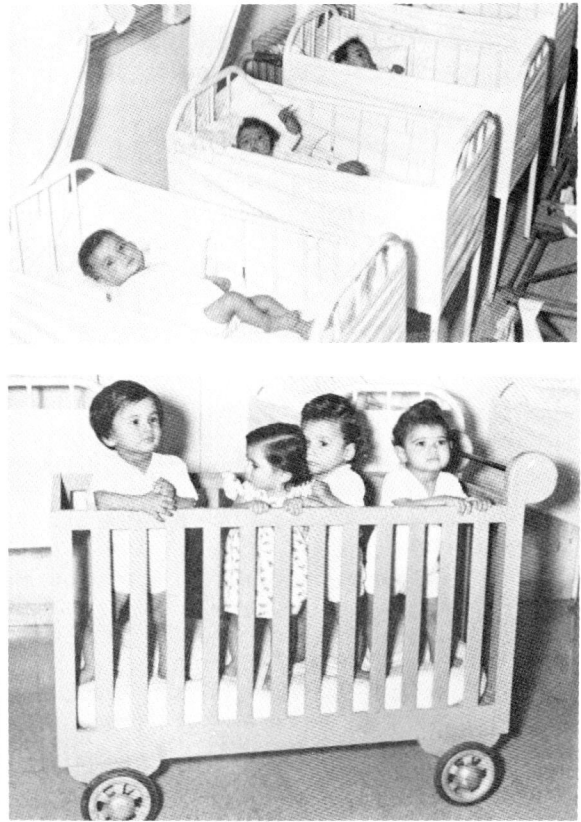

FIGURE 13–1. Typical scenes at the Crèche, the orphanage extensively studied by Dennis. (a) These are 2-year-olds in their cribs. Notice that their visual experience is severely restricted by the white crib bumpers, the homogeneity of the surrounding visual environment, and the lack of playthings. The children's physical and motoric retardation is evident. (b) Crèche children in a "play" pen. There are very few playthings and no structured activities. The children are crowded together and yet are remarkably noninteractive and passive. (From Children of the Crèche by Wayne Dennis. Appleton-Century-Crofts, 1973.)

cribs all the time except for changing and their daily baths. Thus, there was little perceptual variation in their environment (see Figure 13–1). They were fed and changed on a schedule and so their crying was not responded to. The attendants talked to them very infrequently. This means that the infants had little control over their environment. It should be no surprise that these circumstances led to extreme retardation of motoric, linguistic, and intellectual development. The children often did not sit up until 1 year of age or walk until 4 or 5 years. At 6 years, when these children left the Crêche, they had IQs of approximately 50, which is half the normal IQ and is well into the retarded range.

What happened to the children after they left the Crêche provides a relatively neat experiment of nature. The girls and boys were transferred to separate institutions. The girls were transferred to a home staffed by low-level workers and trained to do low-level work themselves. This institution was as unstimulating as the original one. At age 16 these girls had an average IQ of 50 with most being between 30 and 60. In contrast, the boys were sent to an institution with many more opportunities for stimulation. They received training to become regular workers and were regularly taken on outings. At 15 their average IQ was 80.

In 1956 a new experiment of nature began at the Crêche. Adoption became legal in Lebanon in that year and children of all ages were swooped out of the Crêche and into homes. Dennis followed up children who had been adopted from the Crêche at various ages from shortly after birth to 8 years. He then compared those who had been adopted early (before 2 years) to those adopted later (2–4 years and 4–8 years).

Children who were adopted by two years of age regained normal IQs. Their IQs at the time of adoption were 50, but within several years their average IQ increased to almost 100 (average for home-reared infants). Similar recovery has been found in other studies of deprived children adopted within the first several years of life (Clark & Hanisee, 1982; Scarr & Weinberg, 1976).

In contrast, the children in Dennis's study who were adopted later showed permanent deficits. Furthermore, of these, those who were adopted closer to 2 years suffered less severe permanent retardation than those who were adopted at still later ages. This permanent retardation was a residue from their earlier institutionalization and was not caused by later inability to learn or progress intellectually. Their rate of development once they left the Crêche was normal, exactly like that of home-reared children (that is, they gained one year of mental age for each year of chronological age). This was true for all the children adopted after

2 years of age regardless of their age at adoption. Because the children adopted at later ages developed at a normal rate once they left the Crêche, their permanent deficit was caused by their failure to make up for the deprivation suffered in the Crêche; that is, they did not show the catch-up in intellectual growth that the children adopted as infants did. This also explains why those adopted at older ages were more retarded than those adopted between 2 and 4 years. The older children had suffered more initial deficit in terms of mental age. A 4-year-old with an IQ of 50 has a mental age of 2 years, but an 8-year-old with an IQ of 50 has a mental age of 4. By 12 years of age, the child adopted at 4 had 8 years of normal growth, hence 8 additional years of mental age. Thus he had a mental age of 10 (2 + 8 = 10 years MA) and hence an IQ of 83 (10/12 × 100 = 83). The child adopted at 8, in contrast, had had only 4 additional years of normal mental growth by 12 years of age. That child had a mental age of 8 (4 + 4 = 8 years MA) and hence an IQ of 67 (8/12 × 100 = 67). Thus neither of these late adopted children reached a normal IQ, and the one adopted later had a lower IQ.

These data demonstrate rather conclusively that deprivation during the first 2 years can be overcome. In other words, so long as the later environment is normal (not supernormal) there are no permanent deficits. Therefore, if there is a critical period for intellectual development, then it is not the first 2 years. That leaves the possibility that there is a critical period sometime between 2 and 8 years.

The environment necessary to promote sensorimotor development is relatively simple to obtain. Babies need objects to see, to hear, and to manipulate. The emotional needs of infants, particularly in the first year of life, may be equally easy to meet. Responding to babies' distress and providing appropriate stimulation seem to be the keys. Only the most deprived environments, such as some orphanages, fail to fulfill these basic needs, and it is relatively easy to overcome these deficits by providing toys and other environmental supports and enough staffing so that the staff can be responsive and provide some noncaretaking stimulation. By 18 months to 2 years of age, children are developing language and other forms of mental representation. At this time then, the amount and quality of language and communication through language becomes important in their development (Atkin et al., 1977). Furthermore, the increased cognitive power brought about by mental representation makes children more responsive to many other aspects of their environment, such as picture books and make-believe toys. The ensuing cognitive development may well have a snowball effect in that as children assimilate these more complex aspects of their environment, their understanding develops and they need ever more complex environments. It is right at the 18–24 month period that day care (which we will discuss shortly) and other forms of early intellectual intervention (Levenstein, 1977; Levenstein, Kochman, & Roth, 1973; Levenstein, Kochman, Roth, & Sunley, 1968; White & Watts, 1973) begin to have an effect on intellectual development.[3] These developing abilities of symbol formation and their cognitive consequences may actually operate in a critical periods fashion, an hypothesis that is made plausible by Epstein's (1974a, 1974b) evidence that spurts in head size independent of physical growth occur between 2 and 4 years, during the onset of mental representation, and between 6 and 8 years, during the onset of Piaget's concrete operational period.[4] He infers that these spurts reflect brain growth spurts and he has found that they occur at the same ages as spurts in IQ. These two spurts both lie within the ages for which Dennis found permanent effects and thus strengthen the argument for a post-infancy critical period, because the clearest demonstrations of critical periods have involved physiological mechanisms (recall the prenatal critical periods described in Chapter 4 and the critical periods of perception described in Chapter 9). Although finding such physiological growth spurts makes the critical periods hypothesis more plausible, it is not compelling evidence. Not all biological growth operates according to the principles of critical periods. The phenomenon of catch-up growth after deprivation-produced retardation has been documented for physical growth and is

closer to Piaget's model for intellectual growth than is a critical periods notion.

Dennis's data are consistent with the notion of a post-infancy critical period, but they are also consistent with an interpretation that stresses the importance of the duration of deprivation. This alternative interpretation is that the length of deprivation, not the timing of deprivation, determines the possibility of catch-up growth. Dennis's data suggest that deprivation must last longer than 2 years to have a permanent effect and that after 2 years, the degree of retardation increases regularly (in a linear fashion) as the duration of deprivation increases.

Regardless of whether the later critical period or the duration interpretation is correct, this experiment of nature does not necessarily mean that those who were institutionalized for longer than 2 years could under no circumstances overcome their deficits. The post-infancy experiences of the boys transferred to a more enriching institution and of the children adopted into normal homes cannot be considered optimal. It might be that with optimal experiences (perhaps trained or especially understanding parents, or special school experiences), these seemingly permanent deficits might be overcome. We will discuss the available research on the effects of enrichment on noninstitutionalized children later in this chapter.

Luckily there is corroborative evidence for Dennis's findings that retardation in infancy is not necessarily permanent from another experiment of nature. Kagan (1976a) studied children in an isolated, subsistence level farming village in northern Guatemala. These children spent the first year of their lives (until they become mobile at 13–16 months), inside windowless bamboo huts. At noon the huts let in as much light as dusk outside. They contain a few objects, such as an open fire, wood, and pots, but no conventional toys. The infant spends about one third of his time in a sling on his mother, a third on a straw mat, and a third asleep in his hammock. Parents, relatives, and older children play or talk to him only 10% of the time. This is compared to 25–40% in homes in the United States (Clarke-Stewart, 1973). Kagan and his collaborators tested these babies at 1 year of age and found them 3–4 months behind United States children on vari-

---

[3] We should point out that White and Watts (1973) conclude from their data that the critical period is between 10 and 18 months, because differences between treatment groups are evident by 18–24 months.

[4] There are also later spurts, but they are not relevant to either Dennis's data or this book.

ous measures of development, including Piagetian object permanence and stranger anxiety. The overall appearance of the babies was also quite different from that of United States toddlers. The Guatemalan babies were quiet, nonsmiling, minimally alert, motorically flaccid, and temperamentally passive. The comparable profile for middle class Unites States toddlers is that they are highly vocal, smiling, alert, and active. Despite this rather severe retardation, by preadolescence these children were essentially normal on a variety of cognitive tasks, including tests of memory and inferential abilities. Here, then, is a second case in which early environmentally-produced retardation is not permanent. In both cases, the subsequent environment was not particularly optimal. Kagan's study, however, does more than replicate Dennis's findings with Crèche children. The Guatemalan children were not deprived of their mother although they were deprived of sensory and intellectual stimulation, and, to a large part, of a responsive social environment. They were initially quite retarded in spite of their opportunity to form a one-to-one relationship with their mother.

Another important study that explored the effects of early institutionalization and involved late adoption is that of Tizard (1977), which we described in part earlier. The children in this study had spent the first 2 to 7 years of life in good orphanages. Most of the children were adopted or returned to their own homes (restored) between 2 and 4 years, but a small group left their institutions for private homes only when they were between 4 and 7 years of age. These restored and adopted children experienced markedly different environments, and the differential effects on the children reveal something about the role of the later environment on their development. To assess the effects of early institutionalization, Tizard needed a control group of home-reared children. Because the children in the orphanages came primarily from working class homes, Tizard used a working class home-reared group for most of her dependent measures. It soon became clear that this control group was sometimes inappropriate because the adoptive parents were mostly middle class. Thus on occasion Tizard tested a middle class home-related group for comparison.

This study differs from those of Dennis and Kagan in that the early institutional experiences of these children did not result in gross retardation. Thus, it is not a good test of the long-term effects of early intellectual deprivation. It is, however, an excellent test of the effects of early deprivation of a one-to-one relationship with either a mother or a caretaker, because the staff were discouraged from showing interest in any one child and the children were cared for by large numbers of people. Indeed, of the research we have discussed this study is the purest test of the deprivation of a mother figure, exactly because the babies were not deprived in other respects. In addition, this study is somewhat unique in that it assessed the impact of institutionalization and later adoption on emotional as well as intellectual development.

We will first discuss Tizard's findings with respect to intellectual development, which can be compared to the studies of Dennis and Kagan. We will begin with the findings for the children who left the institution between 2 and 4 years. At 2 years of age (when they were still in the orphanages) these children were slightly below average in IQ, but by $4\frac{1}{2}$ years the adopted children (who had been adopted for 6–18 months) were above average in IQ (average was 115), and the restored children were average. Both groups of children were tested again at 8 years of age. The results of the IQ testing were virtually identical to the earlier tests and tests of school achievement were comparable. Thus, it is clear that there need be no long-term deleterious effects on intellectual development of not having a mother during infancy so long as an otherwise sufficiently stimulating environment is provided.

There were, however, obvious differences between the restored and adopted children. Both groups of children had had similar experiences during their first 2 years of life, but those who were adopted had better intellectual development subsequently. Not only did the adopted children perform better intellectually, they also were more cooperative in the testing situation. For example, two thirds of them concentrated well but over 73% of the restored children had very poor concentration. These differences in test taking behaviors undoubtedly account for at least part of the difference in intellectual performance, because it takes concentration and cooperativeness to do one's best in a test.

The general implication of these differences is that later environment also affects IQ. The parents of these two groups differed in many ways. The adoptive parents were very anxious to have a child and many had been waiting a long time to adopt. They were generally very accepting of their children, even in cases in which the children's teachers saw the children as problems. The natural parents generally were conflicted about their children, as was evidenced by their having left the babies in the orphanage. The mothers often had had other children since the institutionalized child and were often living with a man who was not the subject child's father. Thus, the restored children often entered new, intact families with younger children. Furthermore, the adoptive parents were better off financially than the natural parents and were more likely to read to and play with their children and to provide many toys.

In general, then, it appears that the adopted children entered a more emotionally accepting and intellectually stimulating environment than the restored children did. After several years in these environments the adopted children both approached intellectual tasks in a more positive fashion and performed better on them. Because the two groups were similar in intellectual performance when they left the institution, these differences can be attributed to their later environments.

Tizard also followed up a few children who were adopted or restored to their natural parents between the ages of $4\frac{1}{2}$ and 7 years. She was able to gather data on only 5 adopted children and 4 restored children in this age range, so conclusions from these data are speculative, but they are intriguing nevertheless. Unlike the earlier adopted children, only one of these later adopted children increased in IQ from 4 years (before leaving the institution) to 8 years, and the others, if anything, declined. Of the restored children, two stayed the same and two declined. Thus the children adopted later did not show the clear intellectual improvement that children adopted earlier did. These data show a similar pattern to those of Dennis, in that the earlier adopted children did better in-

tellectually than the later adopted. (Dennis's subjects all showed IQ improvements and Tizard's did not, but that is likely to be because Dennis's children started their home lives with much lower IQs.) The major differences between the results of the two studies is that the age at which the shift from greater than average mental (MA) growth to average mental (MA) growth was 2 years earlier for the children in Dennis's study. The most likely interpretation of this difference is that the more severe the deprivation, the earlier the age after which a normal family life will not suffice to overcome the effects.

As we pointed out in connection with the Dennis study, improvement for later adoptees might have been greater if their environments had been more optimal. Tizard noted some ways in which the environment of the later adopted children might have been less optimal than those of the earlier adopted. First, later adoptees were in school and so had less time to experience one-to-one stimulation from their parents. Second, their parents did not expect their children to excel in school and were prepared to accept that. Thus, they may not have pushed them to do their best or they may have created conditions for a self-fulfilling prophecy of low average performance. Tizard did not argue that the children were beyond a stage at which the mother's influence could make a difference. She argued that, assuming the child to be equally vulnerable, the environment of the later adopted children was not as facilitative as it would have been had they been adopted earlier.

Before we describe Tizard's findings on social and emotional development, let us summarize the findings on the effects of early deprivation on intellectual development. Early deprivation of sensory–perceptual–intellectual stimulation alone (Kagan's Guatemalan babies), and combined with maternal deprivation (Dennis's Crèche babies), caused severe intellectual retardation. In either case, if the subsequent environments were more stimulating, the babies' mental development became normal. Early deprivation of mother when sensory–perceptual–intellectual stimulation was adequate resulted in essentially normal intellectual performance. Whether the early deprivation effects were completely overcome depended in part on the age at which the environment was changed and in part on the quality of the subsequent environment. What has been most surprising to many people is that the effects of even 2 years of severe deprivation could be overcome. Thus, it is clear that the version of the critical periods hypothesis that says that infancy is a critical period with permanent effects on intellectual development is wrong. There may be a critical period that starts somewhere between 1 and 2 or after 2 years, but the data are also consistent with the hypothesis that it is the duration of the deprivation and not the timing that produces effects that seem irreversible.

LONG-TERM EFFECTS ON SOCIAL AND EMOTIONAL DEVELOPMENT

Tizard's is one of the few studies that measured systematically the effects of deprivation on the social and emotional development of humans. She gathered four kinds of data at $4\frac{1}{2}$ years and 8 years: children's initial responses to the psychologist (prior to being tested), children's behaviors during testing (assessed by the tester), parents' reports of children's behavior problems and attachment, and teachers' reports of children's behavior problems. For each of these categories, the data were gathered in a systematic fashion. For example, parents were asked a series of questions about specific behaviors, such as "Will he sit still through a meal?" and "Has he woken in the night for the past four weeks?" Asking specific questions rather than general questions such as "Is he restless?" is a good method to minimize bias in the mothers' reports. The responses of the parents were then categorized as reflecting severe, moderate, or negligible problems in each area. For example, a child who awoke and called out at least three times a week was rated as having severe sleep problems.

We shall concentrate on the results for the 24 adopted children, because they experienced the more optimal post-infancy environment and therefore are more relevant to the question of recovery. In general the adopted children did not show evidence of emotional disturbance. In fact, at age $4\frac{1}{2}$ they showed fewer problems than the home-reared working class controls, although that might be attributable to social class differences (remember that the adoptive homes were generally more middle class). At 8

years of age the adoptive children seemed very similar to a middle-class control group in terms of behavior problems. The only consistent problems the parents reported were that the adopted children tended to be overly friendly to strangers and overly seeking of attention at both $4\frac{1}{2}$ and 8 years. A few of the 20 children studied at 8 years appeared to have significant problems. Parents reported that 2 were "too good" (overinhibited), 3 were impulsive and had to be watched, and 1 had temper tantrums. Of the 6 who had been described as difficult while in the orphanage, 3 showed great improvement at $4\frac{1}{2}$ years, but all 6 still exhibited more problems than the others at 8 years.

Teachers had much more negative impressions of the adopted children at 8 years than the parents did. On a scale of behavior problems (the Rutter B scale, on which a score of 9 or greater is believed to indicate that the child may need special help) the average score for the adopted children was 10. The mean for classmates who served as controls was 3 and that for the original working class control sample was 5. Some of the specific problems noted by the teachers were that the children were restless, fidgety, quarrelsome, disobedient, lying, resentful or aggressive when corrected, and attention seeking. Tizard noted that the parents and teachers generally agreed on the behaviors that the children exhibited even though they disagreed on whether the children had problems. This suggests that the excessive attention seeking may have created the school problems, because such needs would be more difficult to meet in the school situation. If so, the children's subsequent frustration could well result in fidgeting, quarreling with other children, and so forth. Indeed, several mothers noted that the schools were unable to cope with their children's attention seeking, while they, the mothers, found it little bother.

The most crucial of the social-emotional measures for the critical periods hypothesis, as seen by Freud, Erikson, Bowlby, and others, is attachment. These children had had very little opportunity to form a close attachment to an adult in their first several years of life and at 2 years responded indiscriminately to familiar adults. There is no standard measure of attachment in 4-year-olds, so Tizard used parental reports. The adoptive parents often spontaneously commented that their adopted children were exceptionally affectionate. Most of them, however, were affectionate to anyone they knew well and four were affectionate to strangers as well. This could have reflected shallow and indiscriminate affections, a stereotype often said to characterize institutionalized children. Alternatively, this general affectionate tendency could reflect their experience in an institution in which all adults were presumably friendly, helpful, and to be trusted, and they simply generalized this experience to the outside world. To try to find out whether these children also had a specific affectionate relationship to one or both parents, Tizard asked the parents whether the child preferred being put to bed or comforted when ill by one or both parents rather than by a less familiar person. Half preferred to be put to bed by a parent and over 70% preferred to be comforted by a parent. These numbers are comparable to those of the working class home-reared group. (Nevertheless, the adopted children were much more likely to allow a stranger to put them to bed.) Finally, 20 of the 24 mothers were absolutely convinced that their adopted children were deeply attached to them.

By 8 years of age, the adopted children were more discriminating in their affection. Only one was affectionate with strangers. There were still only 4 of the 20 children (4 children were not retested at 8 years) who did not seem deeply attached to their mothers, by their mothers' report. Of these 4, 3 were the same children whose mothers had expressed the same doubts when the children were $4\frac{1}{2}$. The emotional responses of 3 of these 4 children did not fit the stereotype that adopted children are shallow and flat emotionally; these children seemed actually hostile to their parents. Tizard also noted that such reservations about their children's attachment occurred in 3 of the 30 mothers of the home-reared children as well.

The teachers of the adopted children reported that these children were not liked by their peers and that they frequently were quarrelsome. Nevertheless, they often formed good relations with their younger and older siblings. Their problems seemed limited to those with their agemates. This is the reverse of the pattern of the home-reared children, who more frequently had problems relating to their siblings and got along well with their agemates at school.

Thus, most of the adopted children appeared to have been able to establish strong, personal ties to their new parents and to siblings. They had more difficulty with relationships in school, both with their teachers, who found them more difficult to handle than other children, and with their peers. These school difficulties, however, did not prevent them from performing well academically.

The description of the children restored to their mothers is in general similar to that of the adopted children. When the two groups did differ, however, it was the restored group that was always worse. For example, 44% of restored children were described as very restless but only 28% of adopted children and no control children were so described. For the most persistent problem, attention seeking from both strangers and teacher, 78% of the restored children, 61% of the adopted, and 7% of the controls were so described.

Another study of infants adopted from a quality institution concentrated on the long-range effects on social and emotional development as measured by personality tests (Gardner, Hawkes, & Burchinal, 1961). These children had generally been adopted at an earlier age (about 1 year). This group was made up of those who had lived in a home management house run by home economics students as part of their university training. These infants were exposed to a new group of "mothers" every few days. Hence, like Tizard's subjects, they had no opportunity to form an intense attachment to any specific person, although presumably they received optimal care in other ways. To determine whether they had suffered any lasting emotional harm, they were followed up when they were from 8 to 17 years old. Due to the wide age span, the controls were selected from the same schools and matched for sex, age, and intelligence. Batteries of personality tests were administered. They indicated that the institutionalized and then adopted children did not differ from the controls in terms of personality processes, frustration tolerance, anxiety levels, personal or social adjustments, or school achievement. These results corroborate Tizard's findings of minimal emotional differences between home-reared babies and babies reared for their first one or two years in quality institutions in which one-to-one relationships were discouraged.

What can be concluded from these studies about the critical role of experiences during infancy in social and emotional development? It is clear from Tizard's study that when they were given parents who cared a lot and who worked very hard to give love and affection and a good environment to their children, most children deprived of a mother figure in infancy became attached. Therefore, it seems that the dire predictions made by Freud and others of later inability to love as a result of early deprivation of a primary love object are wrong. Furthermore, there is no clear evidence for major personality problems. Gardner and colleagues' adopted subjects did not differ from controls on personality tests. Tizard's adopted children were not so difficult that their adopted parents found them problems to raise. In the eyes of the adopted parents, the children were turning out quite nicely. Nevertheless, it is impossible to conclude that these children suffered no long-term effects, primarily because of the teachers' ratings when the children were 8 years of age. At this point, around half of the adopted children were considered to be greater problems than their classmates and were judged to have difficulties with their peers. It is possible that adopting by 2 years of age is more deleterious than adopting by 1 year of age, because Tizard's study found some negative findings and Gardner's did not. It is impossible to be sure, however, because the dependent measures used in the two studies were wholly different.

Tizard's study also showed clearly the importance of later child rearing. Whether or not infancy is critical in the sense of experiences having permanent effects, what happened to the children in their later years strongly influenced their adaptations. Whenever the two groups of previously institutionalized children differed, the children restored to their natural parents were consistently worse off than the adopted children. What the important differences were between the environments of the restored and adopted children can only be guessed. These environments differed on both emotional and intellectual dimensions. The adoptive parents (including the fathers) tended to be more accepting and less ambivalent toward their children and they provided more enriching experiences for them. Both of these kinds of differences are likely to be important.

MULTIPLE MOTHERING

The question of the possibly harmful effects of multiple mothering has been extremely controversial because of the strong theoretical support given by Freud and his followers to the wide-spread belief that all infants ought to be cared for by their own biological mothers. The effects found in the early studies of institutionalization were interpreted as being due to the absence of a mother, even though children in those institutions also suffered many other deprivations—of fathers, toys, sensory and perceptual stimulation, attention, and even exercise. So powerful has this belief system been that babies were removed from home economics "homes" (such as that studied by Gardner et al.). Even the Harlow studies on the effects of various rearing conditions in monkeys have been (wrongly) interpreted as demonstrating the need for a full-time mother. Thus, authors of popular and professional articles and books have assumed that all children have the inalienable right to the total attention of their mothers for at least 3 years, after which that attention may have to be shared with a new baby, a process that may be repeated in another few years.

The strength of this belief system is somewhat surprising, considering how really rare the nuclear family with mother as full-time caregiver is. The nuclear family with a nonworking mother became the norm in western societies only after urbanization and the increased mobility of modern times, and it is the norm only for part of that culture. The poor have never had the option and the rich in many times and places have placed their children in the primary care of a nursemaid or governess.[5] In many other cultures, children are routinely left in the care of relatives (adults or children) or other members of the community while the mother works.

The traditional Freudian view that all children must establish an exclusive love relationship with their mothers actually includes several hypotheses. In this chapter we discuss two

---

[5] An excellent description of the effects of child nurses on the roles of both women and children and the abuse of children, in earlier times, including during the Industrial Revolution, is included in Piers (1978) *Infanticide: Past and present.*

aspects: (1) Do babies deprived of any deep attachment suffer irreversible effects from such deprivation, and (2) should babies experience one deep relationship rather than several attachments? The research on institutionalization is relevant to the first question. We can summarize three tentative conclusions based on that research: (1) Infants who had formed no single intense relationship during infancy but were not otherwise deprived were neither permanently retarded nor grossly abnormal, although some may have suffered some emotional consequences even if subsequently placed in good homes (Dennis, 1973; Gardner et al., 1961; Jaffee & Fanshel, 1970; Tizard, 1977). (2) Deep, meaningful relationships with significant others are possible even if the early prototypical mother–infant relationship had not been formed during the hypothetically critical period of infancy (Gardner et al., 1961; Jaffee & Fanshel, 1970; Tizard, 1977). (3) The presence of a biological mother is not sufficient to overcome intellectual deficit if the environment is restrictive (Kagan, 1976a). Although arguments can be found against each of these conclusions that would soften or eliminate their negative impact on Freudian theory, the research clearly provides no positive support for the Freudian notion of the crucial role of an exclusive strong attachment to mother.

In this section we will address the second question, whether attachment to several figures does any harm. According to Freudian theory, the mother–infant relationship must be primary. Secondary attachments to other people are fine so long as they do not diffuse the all-important primary relationship. In this view, mothers who share the caregiving role put their babies at risk. Research is available on two natural situations relevant to this issue: studies of other cultures in which multiple mothering is the norm and studies of infant day care in the United States, in which infants spend full days in a day care center.

Studies of multiple mothering in which the biological mother is one of the "mothers" also allow us to address other questions of concern to mothers of all sorts. Can both mothers and substitute caregivers provide a secure base for exploration? Do infants come to prefer the mother or the caregiver? Is it important that the caregivers be stable or will changing caregivers do just as well? What sorts of multiple rearing environments are best? All of these questions are of crucial importance in the United States today, because, like it or not, many infants are being reared by multiple caretakers. Today 46% of children in the United States have working mothers, including 37% of children under 5 years of age (1976 Department of Labor statistics). Many mothers work because of economic necessity and many work because they feel that they can be happier (and more successful parents) if they pursue a career. The extent of the practice makes it crucial to find out whether children are adversely affected and, if so, what forms of care can avoid the adverse effects.

Communal Rearing

The Israeli kibbutz is a largely agricultural collective settlement. The first ones were begun by Zionists long before the state of Israel itself was established. Thus, some kibbutzim (plural of kibbutz) have existed over several generations. Although kibbutzim vary, a general characterization for the care of children can be made. Communal care begins at 4 days of age, when babies are transferred from the hospital to an infant house under the care of a professional caretaker called a metapelet (plural, metaplot). The mother, who has a 6-week maternity leave, may care for her baby as much as she wants, although the baby sleeps in the infant house. After 6 weeks the mother gradually resumes her normal kibbutz duties and the metapelet takes over the child care (Figure 13–2). At around 3–4 months of age a group of infants are put under the care of a second metapelet, who remains their primary caregiver until the children enter preschool. The mother assumes a regular work load (7–8 hours a day) and the metapelet assumes responsibility for the children. Even though the metapelet has responsibility during this first year of life, the mother spends twice as much time with the baby as the metapelet does (Gewirtz & Gewirtz, 1968). The mother's time with her infant gradually diminishes until, by the age of 1½ years, the children spend only a few hours a day with their parents.

The relative roles of the parents and of the metaplot are clearly defined. The parents are to be "friends" and the metaplot are to care for

FIGURE 13–2. Toddlers and their metapelet on the playpen porch of a kibbutz. Note the child from the neighboring group trying to interact. (Photograph courtesy of Jeannette Stone.)

and socialize the children. The metapelet is to train the children to eat by themselves, to wash and dress themselves, to eliminate in the toilet; she is to answer their questions about sex, to define the limits for their aggressive behaviors, and to place demands on them in all spheres of activity. Physical punishment is taboo; the primary forms of discipline are explanation or isolation from the group or both. The other children also contribute directly to their peers' socialization. They directly imitate the metapelet's admonishments and also sometimes invent their own wordings for sanctions. They also sometimes use the physical punishment that the metapelet avoids (Faigin, 1958).

Communal rearing in kibbutzim apparently has no negative influence on motoric and mental development of infants. Kohen-Raz (1968) conducted an extensive and well-controlled study of 130 communally-raised kibbutz infants, 152 infants reared in regular private homes, and 79 infants raised in institutions. Infants ranged from 1 to 27 months of age. Although the educational level of the parents of home-reared infants was higher than that of the kibbutz parents, the difference probably reflected the social structure of the kibbutz rather than the abilities of the parents.

There were also no differences in ethnic origins between these groups. In contrast, the institutionalized children presumably came from the lower socioeconomic strata, although records on them were not available.

The kibbutz babies came from 21 kibbutzim selected as a representative sample of all those in Israel in which infants lived in separate infant houses. (Size and age of kibbutz, geographic area, and the four major political movements were all proportionally represented so that the results can be generalized to all kibbutz-reared infants who live in separate infant houses.)

Home-reared babies were chosen at random from about 670 infants living in Jerusalem and Rehovoth. The institutionalized babies were selected from the total infant population in 5 baby homes located in Jerusalem, Tel Aviv, and Haifa. A shortage of such babies plus epidemics current at the time of the study made a truly representative group of institutionalized babies unachievable. Sick babies, prematures, forceps or vacuum extraction deliveries, and those with known physical or neurological defects were excluded.

All babies were evaluated by the Bayley scales in their natural surroundings by a highly trained group of examiners with the participation of mothers or caretakers. Both kibbutz and home-reared infants tended to score above the United States norms on the mental scales. This was to be expected because of the parents' educational and social level. Kibbutz infants excelled over home-reared babies in the earlier months but this difference tended to disappear with age. The institutionalized babies were inferior to the other Israeli groups and to the United States norms.

The motor scores did not differ as much among the various groups as the mental scales did. Nevertheless, the institutionalized babies were motorically retarded at all ages prior to 15 months (except for the 10-month sample), but at 18, 24, and 27 months they appeared to have caught up with the noninstitutionalized groups.

The relation of mental development to a number of environmental and family-background variables was assessed where these were known. We will describe a few findings of special relevance to our concerns. There was no relation between the frequency of caretaker changes and the DQ. There was some tendency for first-born infants to score higher than later borns (see also Gewirtz & Gewirtz, 1965), which Bayley (1965) reported for United States home-reared subjects. However, this difference was found only in the kibbutz group, not in the Israeli home-reared group. There was also a tendency for male infants from private homes where the mothers worked (most in full-time jobs) to have higher DQs than those whose mothers stayed home. Other evidence in our discussion of day care also suggests that multiple mothering can in some circumstances help intellectual development.

Certainly these data show that the separation of infants from mothers for large parts of the day and night and their collective education by other female adults and with other infants do not have an adverse effect on their motor or mental development. Hence these findings with kibbutz children confirm the conclusions of the studies of institutionalization that a single female caretaker is not a prerequisite for normal intellectual development in the first two years of life, the exact time that has often been supposed to be most important.

Social development is, as we said before, difficult to measure. In infants the major measure used is attachment. By that measure kibbutz infants are clearly attached to their mothers. They show very few differences in any of the attachment behaviors (protest, proximity behaviors, distance–attention behaviors) from those of home-reared United States infants (Levy-Shiff, 1983; Maccoby & Feldman, 1972). When differences have been found, as Fox (1977) found with reunion behaviors, the kibbutz babies showed greater attachments to their mothers than to their metaplot.

These studies clearly show that multiple mothering does not disrupt attachment to mother, even when someone else has the major responsibility of child rearing and socialization. Although the kibbutz mothers spend a good deal of time with their babies during the children's first year of life, by the time the babies are 1½ years of age, the mother's time is limited to 3 hours a day. The studies cited above all included babies older than that age. Why might mothers be so effective in eliciting attachment in their babies even when they see their infants for only a few hours a day? One reason is that there is growing evidence that the quality of time parents and infants spend together is more important than the quantity. Schaffer and Emerson (1964), in their study of family-reared Scottish infants, found that intensity of attachment was not related to the total amount of time infants and mothers spend together; that is, those babies who spent the most time with their mothers were not necessarily the most attached. Rather, how the mother acted—how much time she spent playing with her infant and how responsive she was—was related to the intensity of attachment. In the kibbutz, parent–child time is considered very important and parents are freed of all other responsibilities for that period. Their job is to be friends with the child. Thus, the amount of play and emotional support is likely to be very high. There is some independent evidence of this, although with much older children. Avgar, Bronfenbrenner, and Henderson (1977) asked 10–14-year-old children a series of questions about their impressions of parents. They found that kibbutz children reported more support (nurturance, help with homework, consistency of expectations, encouragement of autonomy) and less discipline (particularly physical punishment and strictness) than home-reared children.

A second factor that may be important is that the mother and father are the stable adults in the infants' life. The kibbutz system is set up so that in theory the infant has only one metapelet from the age of 3–4 months until preschool years, but in actuality they have many more because of high turnover. In Fox's (1977) study, he tried to limit his sample to children whose metapelet had been with them for over 4 months, and had to relax even that criterion on occasion.

Both of these factors may well be important. At this time it is possible only to guess why babies attach to their mothers as well or better than they do to their metaplot, but that they do so is a strong and replicated finding. Furthermore, there are analogous findings with day care babies in the United States.

Relatively little evidence on other aspects of social and emotional development is available. Faigin (1958) conducted 6 months of extensive observations of 2- and 3-year-olds at two kibbutzim with different philosophies. She described the everyday events and activities that occurred with some frequency and made systematic observations of several categories of aggression and dependency, two categories of behaviors that were popular when learning theory dominated child psychology. In aggression she included physical aggression with intent to hurt, instrumental physical aggression (that designed to achieve a goal such as getting a toy or attention), defense, and verbal aggression. Dependency included crying, affection to adults and to peers, instrumental dependency (asking help to achieve a goal), displaying achievements, and thumbsucking. Recall that crying and affection are also behaviors included in attachment measures. They may, however, have different meaning because the children here were older (and in most cultures separation fears are waning by 2 years) and because they were observed in everyday, uncontrolled situations rather than in a specific stress situation such as Ainsworth's.

Faigin unfortunately did not include a control group of nonkibbutz children so it is impossible to ascribe any of her findings to communal child rearing. Nevertheless, as a description of the behaviors of preschoolers in a kibbutz, certain of her findings are enlightening.

The amount of aggression was well within normal limits. Half of the 31 children in the two kibbutzim showed no or one instance of physical aggression in an average 15-minute period. Furthermore, the only forms of aggression that occurred with any frequency were physical aggression. Verbal aggression was nonexistent, which is surprising because verbal aggression is often more frequent than physical aggression in studies of nursery schools in the United States. The difference, however, may be due to age differences or to general differences between Israel and the United States in their socialization practices rather than to communal rearing. The kibbutz children in this study were younger than most children in United States nursery school samples and may be less verbally adept. They may also have experienced more tolerance for physical aggression and less tolerance for verbal aggression.

Although overall these kibbutz children were not very aggressive, there were large individual differences in the amount of physical aggression they exhibited. Several children were very aggressive. The worst (a 2-year-old) had 20 instances of physical aggression in an average 15 minutes. The small size of the sample and the lack of adequate controls mean that it is impossible to guess whether these very aggressive children were unusual. Nonetheless, it is clear that individuality was not eliminated by regimentation of the kibbutz, as was predicted by many detractors.

Overall, dependency responses were much more frequent than aggressive responses (about three times as frequent—an average of over 30 responses per child in an hour). This was not true, however, when responses to other children were considered separately. For the youngest children aggressive responses were more frequent than affectionate responses (the only dependency behavior measured toward children). For older children they were approximately equal. This frequency of dependency responses does not appear to be unusually high, particularly because it included both crying and affectionate responses. In sum, Faigin's exploratory study failed to show any major disturbance in the development of aggression or dependency, although its methodological limitations make it impossible to draw any firm conclusions.

The studies of kibbutz infants suggest that they behave very much like home-reared babies. That does not answer the equally important question of whether there are long-term negative consequences of kibbutz rearing. The evidence indicates that kibbutz children do not seem to have overall higher incidences of psychiatric problems. Some problems appear to be more frequent among kibbutz children than in the Israeli population at large (thumb-sucking for example), but others (such as eating problems, male homosexuality, and juvenile delinquency) are less frequent in kibbutzniks (Kaffman, 1965; Nagler, 1963). It is still possible that there could be subclinical differences in emotionality (that is, differences that are not necessarily maladaptive or not maladaptive enough to be considered pathological), but such more subtle effects are difficult to measure. Unfortunately many of the studies designed to get at them have used clinical interviews or projective tests that may be vulnerable to investigator bias. Indeed, the conclusions from these studies have been as varied as the theoretical biases of the researchers (Bettelheim, 1969; Handel, 1961; Kardiner, 1954; Pelled, 1964; Rabin, 1957, 1958, 1961; Spiro, 1958). Considered as a whole, these studies have failed to show consistent findings of inferior or even changed emotional structure with respect to the Freudian hypotheses of diluted or flat affective relationships, disturbed Oedipal resolution, and so forth. Even those who have reached negative conclusions about communal child rearing grudgingly admit that the kibbutz members do all right in life. For example, Kardiner (1954) concluded that "the social emotions are learned, but not integrated" by kibbutz children and that kibbutz members are well controlled and do not allow "a breakdown of the learned social behavior to the extent that society is abandoned to uncontrolled anxiety and rage." He believes that this is achieved by their repressing[6] envy and greed and by exhibiting high self-criticism and social vigilance. Reading between the lines, we see that the kibbutzniks Kardiner observed did not show the gross distortions in positive affect, high anxiety, rage, and insecure relationships with others that he expected. He therefore had

to conclude either that the feelings were present but repressed (not apparent) or that his hypotheses were wrong, and he preferred the former. Other studies have failed to find any substantial differences between kibbutzniks and family-reared Israelis. One of the most extensive was that of Rabin (1961). He used three projective techniques (Rorschach, Sentence Completion, and Thematic Apperception Test) with 17-year-olds. He found that kibbutz adolescents were at least as well adjusted as family-reared Israelis, and perhaps more spontaneous. Kibbutzniks were equally positive toward their parents, had less conflict with them, and involved them less in their fantasies.

Our summary of studies of children raised in kibbutzim is easy. Although there are some differences from family-reared children, kibbutzniks do not seem to be at a major disadvantage from having been partially deprived of their mothers (or from having had too many mothers, whichever way one looks at it). They show strong and normal attachment to their mothers and to their metaplot and they appear to end up as emotionally normal children, adolescents, and adults. Indeed, as adults they have contributed a greater proportion of leaders of Israeli society (both military and civilian) than any other group.

The kibbutzim are unusual environments in several ways other than their communal child rearing system. They are socialistic and communal in all aspects of living. Further, each exists as an isolated settlement in a much larger cultural context; only 2% of Israelis live on kibbutzim. Finally, they grew from ideological fervor rather than from societal evolution. There is no way of knowing whether the outcomes for their children are really due to the communal child rearing or to some other difference between the kibbutz environment and other Israeli environments. For example, Avgar and colleagues (1977), in their study of children's emotional attitudes toward their parents and others, compared kibbutz children with children of moshavim, which are cooperative agricultural settlements based on family structures rather than communal child rearing. They found that moshav children were more like children of kibbutzim than they were like family-reared urban Israeli children. This suggests that the cooperative, rural, agricultural setting of kibbutzim and moshavim are respon-

---

[6]Repression is a Freudian term that means that unacceptable feelings are not acknowledged consciously or directly in behavior, but that these feelings come out in hidden, distorted ways.

sible for some differences from the family-reared sample.[7]

It is therefore reassuring to find comparative research on another multiple mothering situation. Leiderman and Leiderman (1974) studied the Kikuyu of Kenya. In this culture some babies are raised primarily by their mothers whereas other babies are shared between mothers and one or more other caretakers, most often older sisters. Thus, this culture provides a contrast between single and multiple mothering within the same general cultural context (the same village). The Leidermans measured both the development of attachment and cognitive development in the third and fourth quarters of the first year of life.

The infants in both groups were clearly attached to their mothers as measured both by positive affective responses and by protest at separation. They were also attached to their caretakers. Attachment to mothers and caretakers was equally strong, as measured by the babies' positive affective behaviors. As judged by protest at separation, the caretakers became secure bases later than the mothers did, but the caretakers nevertheless became secure bases by the end of the first year. This difference seems reasonable because the mothers generally spent much more time with the baby for the first 6 months of life.

The only evidence for any differences between single and multiple mothering groups was that the multiply-mothered babies were more apprehensive of strangers than were the singly-mothered babies. Similar apprehension towards or lack of cooperation with strangers also has been found in kibbutz babies (Levy-Shiff, 1983; Maccoby & Feldman, 1972) and in Guatemalan infants from a village (San Marcos) with little variety of experience (Kagan, 1976b; Kagan, Kearsley, & Zelazo, 1978). The Leidermans raised the possibility that such apprehension may be a more sensitive measure of insecurity than babies' behaviors in the more familiar situation of presence of and departure from the mother or caretaker. Maccoby and Feldman did not attribute the apprehension to general insecurity (remember the arguments for this position in Chapter 12) but rather sug-

gested that the kibbutz babies were afraid of strangers simply because they saw fewer strangers in their world than did family-reared children. This may also be true of the Kikuyu children and of the Guatemalans from San Marcos. Kikuyu mothers who were primary caretakers took care of their babies over 75% of the time. It is likely that when these mothers left their babies, they left them with various strangers. Those with a secondary caretaker were probably left with that familiar caretaker and not with strangers. Institutionalized children also have little opportunity for meeting strangers outside the context of caretaker adults.

The strongest difference between singly-mothered and multiply-mothered babies in the Kikuyu was in cognitive development. Multiply-mothered babies were *advanced* relative to singly-mothered babies, but the effect was significant only for the economically poorest in the group. It appears that the caregiver provides some perceptual and cognitive stimulation to poor babies that their mothers are too busy or too preoccupied to provide. This finding supports research findings on babies in the United States that show the infants from economically disadvantaged homes are particularly vulnerable to environmental effects (for example, Hess, 1970) and that good infant day care provides enhanced cognitive development for babies from lower class homes (see, for example, Caldwell, 1964, 1974) as we will discuss next.

Day Care

Day care is the United States version of polymatric rearing (by more than one mother) and is more similar to the Kikuyu system than to the kibbutz. Typically, American children who are cared for by two or more caretakers live with their mothers and are either taken to an alternative caretaker or are cared for in their homes by an alternative caretaker. The research on American polymatric situations is almost exclusively on day care centers, and little is known about the effects of being cared for by relatives, paid caregivers in the home, or by family day care, in which a small number of children are cared for in the home of the alternative caregiver. Even though we will restrict

---

[7]For a more comprehensive review of issues of socialization and development from the cross-cultural perspectives provided in Israel, see Greenbaum and Kugelmass (1980).

our attention to day care centers, we are still faced with a wide range of settings. Comparing different day care centers is sometimes like comparing apples and oranges. The child-to-caregiver ratios vary, the training of the caregivers varies, the stability of the group providing care varies, the policy with respect to encouraging specific attachments varies, and the aims and curriculum (nature and variety of activities) vary. Furthermore, the relation of family to center, which includes such factors as the reasons parents choose day care (and the family's fit to the aims of the center), the consistency between day care and family practices, and the nature and extent of family support provided by the center, varies.

Most of the systematic research has been done in centers set up to provide models of good infant day care. They typically have low child:caregiver ratios (1:1, 2:1, or 3:1 ratios for babies under 1 year of age) and have programs designed to foster development. Studies of this type of center have consistently shown no negative effects on intellectual development, even for infants in day care from early infancy (Ricciuti's excellent 1976 review cites 11 studies supportive of this conclusion covering model day care centers that differ from each other in many ways). In fact, far from producing retardation, model day care centers designed to optimize intellectual development have sometimes had positive effects on intellectual development. In general, such effects have been modest, but the improvement has been dramatic in some instances when day care provided experiences comparable children did not have at home. We will give two examples. Robinson and Robinson (1971) found that the facilitation of intellectual development of children in the model day care program they studied was much more dramatic for the more disadvantaged Black children than for the more advantaged white children. Part of the reason for the large effects in the disadvantaged group was that the intellectual performance of the controls who had no day care decreased during their second year of life. This strongly suggests that day care was providing experiences that non-day-care disadvantaged children may fail to get. Our second example comes from a study of Chinese-American and American infants, also in a model day care center (Kagan, Kearsley, & Zelazo, 1978). At 29 months of age the Chinese-American children in day care (many of whose families were not English speaking) scored higher on a test of basic language concepts than their home-reared controls. In contrast, the Caucasian children in the same day care setting scored lower than their home-reared controls. Similar results have been found in several other studies as well (Garber & Herber, 1981; Golden et al., 1978; Heber, Garber, Harrington, Hoffman, & Falender, 1972; Lally, 1973, 1974; Ramey & Smith, 1976).

The facilitation of intellectual development for day care infants typically does not appear until the infants are 18 to 24 months of age (see, for example, Beller, Laewen, & Stahnke, 1981; Fowler & Kahn, 1974, 1975; Heber et al., 1972; Ramey & Smith, 1976; Robinson & Robinson, 1971). This consistent finding parallels those from the studies of institutionalization that found that intellectual deprivation during the first 2 years is reversible. It is not clear whether the effects are cumulative, that is, whether it takes 2 years of day care to produce the positive effects. It may be that if day care is to supplement children's home environments, it may not be necessary or even helpful to place children in day care while they are infants. Starting day care between 1 and 2 years of age may be equally effective. Of course, the research also shows that starting day care in infancy is not harmful to children's intellectual development.

If infant day care promotes intellectual development, then it is important to ask whether such positive effects last over long time periods. Most follow-up studies of day care programs have found that the superiority of day care children compared to home-reared children on measures such as IQ disappears by 5 years of age (Clarke-Stewart & Fein, 1983). Long-term effects on other measures have been found in an analysis of 14 experimental preschool programs. Although IQ improvements were maintained for only 2 years after intervention, adolescents who had been in these model preschool programs were less likely to have repeated a grade or to have been placed in special education or to have exhibited behavior problems than those not in the program (Darlington, Royce, Snipper, Murray, & Lazar, 1980; Lazar & Darlington, 1982; Schweinhart & Weikart, 1980).

In terms of multiple mothering, these studies of model day care facilities lead to exactly the same conclusion as those reached in the studies of orphanage children, kibbutz, and Kikuyu children: Multiple mothering can be at least as adequate a situation for intellectual development as exclusive care by mothers alone. Because the findings from research using several different operational definitions of multiple mothering are consistent, confidence in the validity of the outcomes is much higher.

Although the research using model day care centers is very informative, it is important not to take for granted that the conclusions of these studies can be generalized to more typical day care settings, which often have much higher child:caregiver ratios and often do not have programs carefully designed to promote intellectual development. Comparable research on such typical day care settings is rare. Three such studies yielded conflicting conclusions. Golden and colleagues (1978) did an extensive study of high-risk children, some of whom were reared at home by their mothers and others who were in 31 licensed day care centers or family day care. They found no retardation from day care.

In contrast, somewhat lowered intellectual functioning in day care centers with child:caregiver ratios from 16:1 to 24:1 was found by Peaslee in a dissertation cited by Ricciuti (1976). Unfortunately, the day care infants in this study may have differed in important ways from the home-reared infants because they were only roughly equated in social class and whether families were intact. The third study, which examined all the children in a parish (county) in Bermuda, found lower IQ at 2 years of age for Black children in day care centers with large groups, but did not find intellectual deficits for white children (Schwarz et al., 1981). The inconsistencies found in these three studies indicate that there are extraneous variables that are not being controlled. Group size and amount of time spent in care are two factors that were found to be correlated with IQ by Schwarz and colleagues.

Let us now turn to the effects of day care on emotional development. This is, of course, the area of greatest concern to psychoanalytically-oriented pediatricians, psychiatrists, and psychologists, who expect emotional disturbances to show up first in mother–infant relationships. The most frequent ways this has been tested have been by Ainsworth's test of attachment, the strange situation, or by other sorts of direct observations of mother–infant interactions. The majority of these studies have found no difference between day care and home-reared infants. The few that have found differences are about equally divided between those favoring day care and those favoring exclusive home rearing (see Belsky & Steinberg's extensive review of these studies, 1978). Although these studies are somewhat less consistent than those on intellectual development, they offer quite impressive confirmation of the hypothesis that day care is not harmful to the development of infants' attachment, for two reasons. First, in those studies that find differences between day care and home-reared infants, most of the differences are minor (see, for example, Schwartz, 1983). Only one (Blehar, 1974) found extensive differences: less secure attachment in day care children. Her findings, furthermore, are suspect because several subsequent studies have failed to find deleterious effects (Kagan et al., 1978; Moskowitz, Schwarz, & Corsini, 1977; Portnoy & Simmons, 1978). Moskowitz and colleagues attribute the discrepancy between Blehar's findings of differences in attachment and their own finding of no differences to Blehar's failure to control for experimenter bias. The second reason we find these studies impressive is that the day care centers in the studies of attachment are much more varied than those in the studies of intellectual development. Many were existing for-profit day care centers rather than university-related model centers, and the child:caregiver ratio was as high as 9:1. Even for high-risk children in rather minimal day care centers, there is evidence that attachment is not disturbed (e.g., Moskowitz et al., 1977).

Measures of emotional development other than attachment to the mother have not been included in most studies. Two studies that have used other measures—one a study of a model day care setting and one of a less advantaged setting—differed in their findings. A study by Kagan and colleagues (1978) using a model center measured emotional development by observations of the children interacting with other children at 13, 20, and 29 months of age, by mothers' judgments, and by frequent measures of separation anxiety. They found no strong differences between day care and home-reared babies (although they did find differences between Chinese and Caucasian children). There were no differences between day care and home-reared infants in disobedience or aggression, and generally they were similar in emotional development except in their relations to strange adults, where day care infants were less shy and more patient.

In contrast, Schwarz and colleagues (1981) did find differences between home-reared and day care Black infants cared for in a number of day care centers that were not models. Using several measures of social responsiveness they found that infants in day care were consistently less responsive and less communicative, although the size of these effects were small. The characteristics of the different day care situations that were related to these measures were: the amount of time spent at the center (a variable Schwartz, 1983, also found related to negative behaviors at 18 months in the strange situation), the size of the group, and the child : caregiver ratio. Thus their data suggest that emotional development is likely to be affected by day care settings when the centers are inadequate.

Considering the research on the relation between day care and infants' emotional development, there is little evidence for the dire predictions of emotional difficulties made by the Freudians. Most important, there is little replicated evidence that attachment, which is the basis for emotional development according to Freud, is at all impaired by infant day care even when the setting is not optimal. Nonetheless there is some indication that under certain circumstances, day care infants might be negatively affected. Furthermore, some infants are likely to be more vulnerable. Relatively little research has focused on circumstances that might negatively influence the day care experience, such as the age at which day care is entered; the home environment, including the quality of the relationship between mother and infant; the quality of attachment of infants to day care workers; the stability of the caregivers; and the congruence of the child rearing practices of the caregivers and the parents. We shall consider the evidence that does exist.

One factor that has often provoked concern is the age at which day care is started. Existing research has focused on two separate questions. Ricciuti and his collegues (Ricciuti, 1974, 1976; Ricciuti & Poresky, 1973; Willis & Ricciuti, 1974) were interested in when, within the period of infancy, it is better to start infants in day care. Not surprisingly they found that infants who enter day care at the height of stranger anxiety (7–12 months) may have more difficulty adjusting than those who enter either earlier or later. Whether such infants suffer a disruption in attachment or any long-term effects of this initial disturbance is not known. Portnoy and Simmons (1978) found that 3–4-year-olds who had experienced day care in infancy did not differ in attachment to their mothers from children who had stayed at home during infancy.

Another variable that might influence whether day care disrupts attachment is, of course, the home environment, including the characteristics of the mother. Farran and Ramey (1977) found that day care children whose mothers were more involved with them explored a strange situation more freely (that is, presumably they were more securely attached). Other studies have comparable findings (Hock, 1976; Ross, Kagan, Zelazo, & Kotelchuk, 1975).

A related set of issues on the effects of day care concern the caregiver. If day care children become attached to their caregivers, does this attachment compete with or dilute their attachment to their mothers? Does the stability of the caregiver influence the outcome? Does inconsistency between the kind of care given by the caregiver and by the parents disrupt the emotional development of the child?

The answers to the first two questions seem clear. Day care babies do form attachments to caregivers and generally prefer them to strangers, but they prefer their mothers to their caretakers (Cummings, 1980; Farran & Ramey, 1977; Kagan et al., 1978; Ricciuti, 1974; Ricciuti & Poresky, 1973). This was found even in a sample in which most of the infants lived in extended families and usually went from the day care center to relatives or neighbors because their mothers were not at home at night (Farran & Ramey, 1977). These findings seem similar to those found in comparisons of kibbutz' infants' attachments for mothers versus metaplot.

INFLUENCE OF ENVIRONMENT: DEPRIVATION AND ENRICHMENT

The other questions with respect to caregivers have received little study. The importance of stability of caregivers has rarely been experimentally studied, but two studies have correlated variations in stability of caregivers with infant behavior. Cummings (1980) examined differences between infants with stable and nonstable caregivers. Nonstable caregivers were defined as those a child had experienced at the day care center for at least 1 month (that is, they were not strangers). Stable caregivers had worked in the center with the experimental children at least 100 hours more than the unstable caregivers. In a laboratory strange situation test both kinds of caregivers were preferred to a stranger, and no preference was shown the stable caregiver relative to the unstable caregiver. The children did, however, prefer to be left with the stable caregiver when the mother left them at the day care center. In Kagan and colleagues' setting (1978), all caregivers were stable by Cummings' criteria but there were differences in the extent of relationship with caregivers because infants were given a primary caregiver. Over the course of their experience (the first 29 months of life) the children would run to their primary caregiver for comfort and help first, and to secondary personnel if their primary person was unavailable.

These studies unfortunately do not address the most crucial question of whether there are any long-term deleterious effects of instability of caregivers. Such studies are sorely needed, because many day care centers are set up to minimize the development of child–caregiver attachments by rotating caregivers, and many others do so out of staffing necessities. More and more experts today recommend stable caregivers so that the children have a base of security and consistency of caregiving. The Cummings study provides limited support for this opinion, because the children were less stressed when they were left at the day care center in the hands of a stable caregiver. The evidence from other settings is also tenuous. It appears that kibbutzim often have high metaplot turnover (although stability is supposedly built in), yet kibbutzniks apparently grow up to be normal. Tizard's institutionalized children experienced systematic attempts to prevent attachment. They were able to form attachments later, although they apparently suffered some emotional sequelae. The infants in Gardner and colleagues' sample, reared in home management houses which had perhaps the least stable set of caretakers, appeared to have no long-range personality defects. Our best guess, then, on the basis of woefully inadequate evidence, is that high turnover in caregivers is not a major detriment to the development of children, but that some stability is desirable, at least in the short run.

The question of consistency between child rearing techniques of parents and caretakers is even less studied. One of the most popular beliefs in child rearing is that children need a consistent, stable environment. Consistent feedback from the environment is necessary for learning, and inconsistency has been suggested as the cause of various sorts of psychopathology and as one of the major factors accounting for the deleterious effects of disadvantaged homes. Furthermore, parents frequently complain that the inconsistency between the care provided by grandparents on visits and parental care creates "re-entry" problems when children return to their parents. There is little direct evidence on even the degree of inconsistency that exists between parents and day care personnel, parents and family day care providers, or kibbutz parents and metaplot. It is likely, however, that unless parents make an effort to find a caretaker who shares their child rearing philosophy, child rearing techniques are bound to vary quite substantially between parents and caretakers. Kagan and colleagues' study (1978) included a clear case of such inconsistency in that the Chinese babies were being raised in traditional Chinese families but attended a Western style day care center. The researchers gathered impressionistic evidence with respect to the infants' behaviors in these two diverse settings during their frequent parent–teacher interchange sessions. They found that the children evidently conformed to each of the two disparate rearing conditions. The Chinese children were evidently as quiet and nonassertive as their siblings in their homes, but more outgoing and "American" in day care. The American children, particularly those of the middle class, experienced some inconsistency in the opposite direction. Parents often commented on how much better behaved and more compliant their children were at day care than at home. Thus, it appears that even very young children can respond appropriately to two different rearing environments and thrive in both. We hope that this study marks the beginning of an area of active research, in which differences and inconsistencies in rearing are more precisely analyzed and infants' responses are more closely and systematically measured.

Epilogue

This analysis of the effects of multiple mothering has consistently led to the conclusion that there are very few negative outcomes if a baby has more than one caregiver, so long as the alternative care is good. This review also suggests that a caregiver who is a stable, though not always present, individual in the baby's life is important. Babies seem always to prefer those most stable caregivers, their mothers, and the most negative outcomes from multiple mothering were found in one of the studies in which the children were denied any stable caregiver.

It is interesting, in the light of the evidence presented above, to consider the state of expert advice in this area. Etaugh (1980) reviewed the child care books and articles that appeared in leading women's magazines from 1956 to 1976 for what they had to say on the effects of day care.[8] It was possible to divide the evaluations into three categories: harmful, not harmful or beneficial, and mixed. The last category included articles that endorsed part-time employment for mothers who wished to work or advocated that good day care programs should be established for mothers who must work.

What is the tally of these views over the years? From 1956 to 1959 little appeared on the topic. There was one article in each category, and the principal parenting book (Dr. Spock's 1946 edition of *Baby and Child Care*) was negative. The distribution for the decade of the sixties and for 1970–1976 is shown in Table

TABLE 13–2
Attitudes Toward Day Care Expressed in Books and Articles, 1960–1976

	Positive	Negative	Mixed
1960–1969			
Books	1	10	2
Articles	9	6	3
1970–1976			
Books	8	10	8
Articles	11	4	0

NOTE. Based on data reported by Etaugh (1980).

13–2. It documents a marked shift toward a more positive view of day care. Nevertheless, there were still plenty of negative opinions, particularly in books. Spock's 1970 articles in *Redbook* were still highly negative, though his 1974 book is much milder. The third edition of his *Baby and Child Care* (1976) does a major turnaround and stresses the responsibilities of both parents for both child care and careers. Another pediatrician (Salk, 1974) takes a dim view of working mothers or day care for infants. So do a number of psychologists, some based on psychoanalytic precepts and some on arguments for the necessity of maternal stimulation and provision of attachment. Still another pediatrician (Brazelton, 1974, portions of which have been excerpted in *Redbook* articles as well) goes so far as to argue that separation from parents affects children adversely in unobservable ways that cannot be measured. His position at that time appeared to rule out the relevance of scientific data altogether. He did console parents or reduce their guilt by allowing for the possibility that a good nurturant day care center might compensate for some of the damage. Recently he seems to be softening his stand still further.

Parents who consulted child-rearing books (and, to a lesser extent, articles) as recently as 1976 were likely to be advised that putting infants into day care is likely to be harmful to them. Such advice contrasts sharply with the evidence, even that available at the time. This contrast between expert advice and evidence is, unfortunately, not uncommon. We hope that knowing this will help parents to be cautious or appropriately skeptical about expert advice and will motivate them to investigate available

---

[8]Only three magazines have shown a sustained interest in this topic (*Ladies Home Journal, Redbook,* and *Parents*) and they accounted for 28 of the 31 articles found in the seven magazines.

evidence themselves rather than rely on advice of supposed experts.

PREVENTING OR OVERCOMING DEPRIVATION EFFECTS THROUGH INTERVENTION PROGRAMS

Although our discussion so far in this chapter has focused on deprivation, actual or potential, the twin topic of enrichment has never been far away. Indeed we have discussed intervention in both institutionalized and in day care infants. These are examples of preventive intervention studies that introduced an enrichment program to a population of infants who would be expected to suffer deprivation effects if no one intervened and then measured whether such deprivation effects were thereby prevented. In the section on preventive interventions we will briefly summarize the outcomes of the two types of preventive interventions already discussed. Then we will discuss a new type of preventive intervention program in which the primary target of the intervention is the mother (or day care provider) or the caregiver–infant pair, or both. Researchers hope that this type of program will have more long-lasting effects, because if caregivers can be taught how to interact with babies successfully, then the improved environment should continue to have effects on the target children and their siblings when the intervention is over.

The last section of our discussion of intervention programs will be devoted to programs that provide experiences to children who have already developed deprivation effects. The adoption studies we discussed earlier are in a sense of this type, because these children were removed from a deprived environment and put into a more advantageous one. When there are still some remaining effects after adoption, as Dennis found, for example, in the intellectual achievement of children adopted after 2 years of age, adoption studies cannot answer the question of whether such effects could be eliminated. To do that, intervention studies are needed that provide experiences not necessarily provided by the normal environment. Such optimal experiences may overcome deprivation in situations where the normal environment does not. This kind of research is particularly germane to the question of whether the effects of critical periods are permanent. The available research has used animals as subjects.

Preventive Intervention Programs with Humans

We discussed several intervention programs in our analysis of the relative impact of the various kinds of deprivation experienced by institutionalized infants. These interventions were remarkably successful in preventing retardation in the specific domains of intervention. Furthermore, institutions that focused on providing enrichment experiences were successful in preventing retardation. Model day care programs designed to provide enrichment also prevented intellectual retardation. Because so many successful projects used such varied kinds of interventions, it is safe to conclude that the details of the kind of enrichment activities are not crucial, so long as enrichment is provided and so long as enough active and involved caregivers are provided to give such experiences.

The recent trend in intervention programs is to focus on training the caregivers. Some programs train mothers and others train day care providers. We will describe three of the first kind and one of the second, to give a flavor of the kinds of intervention provided and their effectiveness.

The first set of studies has been spurred by a program of the United States Government, the Parent–Child Development Project (PCDC; see Andrews, 1981; Andrews et al., 1982, for summaries). The PCDC sponsored multi-dimensional programs that intervene with low-income parents of infants between birth and 3 years. Three such programs, in Birmingham, Houston, and New Orleans, were started in 1970–1971 and continue today. In Birmingham and New Orleans, the families begin the program when the infants are 2 and 3 months old, respectively, and in Houston the families start when the infant is 1 year old. The Houston program also differs in that the participants are relatively less disadvantaged. All three programs focus on the parents, but vary in the extent to which the infants themselves are incorporated into the project, from Birmingham, in which the training focuses on the mother–child dyads, to New Orleans, in which the infants are not directly involved.

Positive maternal behaviors (for example, giving emotional support, asking questions, interfering less) increased for all three programs, but these effects were found only after 2 years in the Birmingham and New Orleans programs and after 3 years in the Houston program.

Only the New Orleans program evaluated effects on mothers' negative behaviors toward their children. Mothers' decline in negative behaviors was only of borderline significance ($p < .06$). Thus it appears easier to increase positive behaviors than to change negative ones.

The children also showed positive changes. In all three studies the Stanford-Binet IQ scores at 3 years were higher for the intervention children than for their controls. It appears that these differences were still there 1 year after completion of the program (at 4 years). Thus, it is clear that mothers can be taught skills while their babies are small that will influence their children's intellectual development.

Beller, Laewen, and Stahnke (1981) have begun a similar intervention study designed to help day care providers. The goal of the training was to change the orientation of the day care workers from that of custodial caretakers to that of active participants in the development of their charges. To accomplish this, the researchers taught the caregivers how to keep charts of behavioral development so that they would become more aware of development and more sensitive to the progression of their charges. On the basis of the developmental charts, caregivers learned to provide educational activities by using the children's strengths to help develop their weak points. The care providers were taught both through workshops and through interactive modeling sessions in the natural situation. For one group of children intervention began when they were from 4 to 7 months old and for a second group when they were 14–17 months old. It ended 6 months later.

The training procedures were effective for changing behaviors in the specific situations trained—feeding, diapering, and toilet situations. Whether training generalized beyond these situations must be determined by future analysis. Within the specific situations caregivers became more communicative and attentive and provided more opportunities for the children to learn. They intruded less into the children's ongoing behavior and adapted more to the needs of the children. These changes in caregiver behaviors had positive effects on the children in: independence of body care, awareness of surroundings, socio-emotional development, play activities, speech and cognition, and motoric function. Changes were always greater in the older group, and only the older experimental children had higher DQs than the control infants at the end of the study. The finding of larger effects with toddlers is consistent with the research on model day care centers.

As was true in the maternal intervention program, negative caretaker behaviors were not changed. The trained caregivers did not change in their communication of negative feelings or in exerting pressure or criticism, and this was paralleled by the data showing that the experimental children exhibited as much stress as control children.

These studies corroborate one of the most widely believed hypotheses about infant development, that how infants' caregivers act makes a large difference in how infants behave and develop. Perhaps more important, they help to specify that hypothesis. A major component of all the programs was provision of more information about the nature of infants and the training of specific skills. As we have seen, in all programs the caregivers became more positive, attentive, and cognitively enriching. The effects, however, were limited to the caregivers' positive behaviors. In the studies that measured caregivers' negative behaviors, no improvement was found. It is tempting to speculate on this difference. It may be that intervention programs provide mothers with skills whereby they can promote successful positive behaviors in their charges and can enjoy more fully the company of the infants. These skills may not change the ways in which adults experience negative emotions or communicate negative messages to their babies. These negative behaviors may require their own specific interventions.

Therapeutic Interventions with Animals

Intervention studies with infrahuman animals are possible because rearing intelligent mammals under conditions of severe deprivation produces profound effects on social and emotional development. First we will describe the effects of such deprivation and then we will describe interventions designed to overcome them.

Experimental animals who are isolated are typically raised in solitary cages with no direct contact with either humans or other animals. They have no toys or other objects of amusement. Their sensory environment is limited to the sights of their four walls and the muted sounds of the laboratory (such as other animals, human keepers, scraping of food and water dishes). Animals kept in these isolation conditions for a long enough period, become very peculiar. For example, dogs demonstrate greatly heightened diffuse activity, diminished social capacity, and a tendency to epileptic-like seizures. They also exhibit a curious apparent insensitivity to pain (Melzack & Scott, 1957). For example, they might repeatedly approach and touch a lighted match without obvious signs of distress, but rather only with generalized excitement. Thompson (1955) summarized the dogs' behaviors as appearing to reflect retarded development. As full-grown dogs, they showed the excitability and diffuseness typical of puppies.

Similar effects are found in rhesus monkeys (but not in all species of monkeys). Isolated monkeys sit immobile in their cages or pace in circles with stereotyped gestures or clasp their heads in their arms and rock for long periods of time. They aggress against themselves, especially when approached by humans, and don't exhibit appropriate social aggression when they encounter agemates. They exhibit avoidance and fear of both normal and unusual environmental stimuli (including others of their own species, humans, masks, and toys). When they reach sexual maturity, they are unable to mate. They seem interested, approach the opposite sex, show parts of the sexual pattern, but only rarely succeed in mating and then only after extensive support from experienced animals and with the help of humans. Interestingly, isolation has little effect of rhesus' intellectual abilities although they are not always able to exhibit their potential.

The strength of the isolation effects on rhesus monkeys depends on both the duration and timing of the isolation, which supports a critical period hypothesis. Twelve months of isolation produces more severe effects than 6 months (Rowland, 1964). These isolation effects occur only if the monkeys are isolated from birth. If they are first allowed to develop social affections and then are isolated, the effects are far less marked (Clark, 1968; Harlow & Novak, 1973; Harlow & Suomi, 1971).

Similarly, let us note that isolation of puppies from other dogs and humans has been shown to produce abnormal social behaviors and even learning deficits, and that these seem to develop in ways that support a critical period hypothesis (Scott, 1958; Scott & Marston, 1950; Scott, Stewart, & DeGhett, 1973; and see Scott, 1967, for a review). Even learning to avoid a painful stimulus was seriously affected (Melzak & Scott, 1957). Furthermore, it had been shown that in dogs the effects of isolation and of treatments depend on genetic factors, that is, on the breed of dog (Fuller & Clark, 1966).

Attempts to overcome isolation effects have been instituted with both dogs and rhesus monkeys. Such research has the potential to test the critical periods hypothesis because that hypothesis predicts that recovery from early isolation should be impossible. Furthermore, discovering what works and what doesn't work to overcome isolation effects reveals something about the nature of the deprivation.

The research with dogs has demonstrated that fear plays an important role in producing isolation effects or keeping them operative. Fuller & Scott (1967) discovered that if tranquilized, the puppies reared in isolation would approach harmless objects, such as the human experimenters they earlier had avoided, and could learn mazes which they had not been able to do previous to the use of tranquilizers. Later, after the effects of the tranquilizers wore off, the puppies were still willing to approach harmless objects. These studies are impressive in two ways. First, they showed that a relatively brief experience after the so-called critical period for socialization could eliminate deleterious effects of isolation. Second, the intervention merely allowed the animals to deal with the environmental stimuli when in a calm state. This suggests that fear or excitement prevented the isolates from being able to process stimuli accurately. Reasoning backward then, it is possible to infer that what happens during isolation is that the animals develop abnormal fear responses to almost all stimuli. This highlights one of the purported roles of attachment figures, discussed in Chapter 12. They provide a secure base from which the young can explore without interference from fear.

The second area of research on overcoming deprivation effects involves rhesus monkeys. Although several therapeutic attempts failed, Harlow and his collaborators found a therapy that works. They exposed isolate monkeys to younger (3-month-old) monkeys for 1–2 hours several days a week for 6 months. Monkeys who had been isolated for 6 months showed virtually complete recovery (Suomi & Harlow, 1972). Twelve-month isolates showed remarkable recovery in social situations and improved in the appropriateness of their behaviors while alone, although not all their peculiar behaviors disappeared (Novak & Harlow, 1975). These researchers suggest that younger peers are effective therapy agents for two major reasons. First, the peers repeatedly initiated social contact and did so without aggression. They were successful at such attempts because the isolates were immobile and withdrawn. The persistence of the therapists eventually paid off, a reciprocal relationship was established, and the isolates' self-directed activities (such as huddling and rocking) decreased. This set the stage for the development of more complex social interactions, which is the second advantage of the immature peers. Their social patterns were simple at the beginning of therapy and their play became more complex as the therapy progressed.

Thus, as with the research with puppies, this research provides little evidence for a strict critical period because the isolation effects were largely reversible. A sensitive period hypothesis is still viable, however, because timing is important. Isolation effects do not develop if monkeys are raised with same-age peers for the first six months. After six months of total isolation, exposing isolates to socially competent agemates (rather than younger monkeys) does not overcome the negative effects (Harlow, Dodsworth, & Harlow, 1965).

Although it is exceedingly dangerous to generalize from dogs and rhesus monkeys to humans, the information gathered from this research can be used to suggest possible interventions to try with humans. Such interventions could take the following forms: (1) Taking great care to ameliorate children's fear responses, (2) providing a persistent, actively initiating, and reliable love object, and (3) matching the emotional and intellectual capabilities of the child with the demands the environment produces (a notion that Hunt has repeatedly suggested). In fact, younger peers often provide just such an environment for older children and might, under carefully supervised circumstances, be helpful.

BIOLOGY AND THE EFFECTS OF EXPERIENCE

Unlike many topics in infant research, those discussed in this chapter have been studied extensively and ingeniously with humans. The two strategies of "natural experiments" and intervention experiments have provided a rather clear picture of the effects of deprivation and intervention. We have focused on research with humans whenever doing so provides a consistent pattern of results. Nevertheless, as we have frequently noted in this book, research with humans has different practical and ethical limitations than does animal research. We would therefore like to report on a few classic studies with laboratory animals that either corroborate the conclusions reached from studying humans or make points the research with humans is as yet unable to make.

Physiological Effects of Early Experience

Rosenzweig and his collaborators have produced a body of research that examined the effects of enrichment and deprivation on brain growth. Their impoverished rat pups were even worse off than the worst orphanage groups, except that they could eat and drink whenever they wanted and as much as they wanted. They were in individual cages, could not see or touch other rats, and were in quiet, dimly lit rooms. Each impoverished rat pup had a littermate

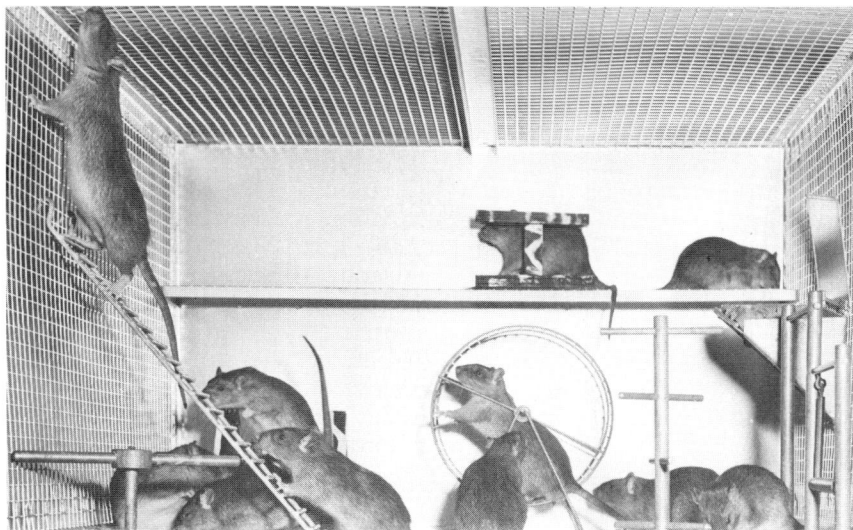

FIGURE 13–3. The enriched environment of the rats raised by Rosenzweig. (Photo courtesy of Mark R. Rosenzweig.)

who lived in an enriched environment with 10 or 12 other pups. They lived in a large cage with a different selection of toys such as ladders, wheels, boxes, and platforms each day (Figure 13–3). Each day they were taken in groups of 5 or 6 for half-hour exploratory sessions into a larger field with barriers that changed daily. After 30 days some formal training in mazes (what might be called "cognitively enriched day care") was given. For 101 out of 130 such pairs, the weights of the cortex of the brain was higher for the enriched pup than for the impoverished littermate (in contrast to their body weights which were lower). In addition, the ratio of the weight of the cortex to that of the rest of the brain was also higher in the enriched littermate for 115 of the 130 pairs. Actually, Bennett and colleagues (Bennett, Diamond, Krech, and Rosenzweig in a series of studies and publications cited in Rosenzweig, 1966) were able to affect the size of different portions of the brain according to the particular types of enrichment provided. In addition to the brain weight differences, this group has been able to demonstrate biochemical differences in the brain (Bennett, Diamond, Krech, & Rosenzweig, 1964; Bennett & Rosenzweig, 1971).

Some of this same group of workers and others have gone on to show that brain struc-

ture is altered by environmental differences. Both the numbers and branching of dendritic spines (Globus, Rosenzweig, Bennett, & Diamond, 1973; Greenough & Volkmar, 1973) and the synapses in the cerebral cortex of rats are affected by the environments (enriched, impoverished or standard rat colony) in which they have lived (Diamond, Linder, Johnson, Bennett, & Rosenzweig, 1975). Such effects have been demonstrated in other rodents (Rosenzweig & Bennett, 1978). In addition, environmental enrichment has been shown to affect the results of brain lesions. It both aids the recovery of learning capacity and affects the actual brain measures (Will, Rosenzweig, & Bennett, 1976; Will, Rosenzweig, Bennett, Hebert, & Morimoto, 1977). Their original studies exposed the rat pups to the different environments starting at weaning when it was assumed their brains would be more plastic. This timing would also capture a supposed initial critical or sensitive period for stimulation. Later studies showed that adult rats exposed for the same length of time (80 days) to the same enriched conditions showed the same sort of increased brain growth (Rosenzweig, 1983).

All of these animal studies suggest considerable plasticity both of brain development and of behavior. They also suggest that the growth, structure, and biochemistry of the brain are affected by environmental manipulations, and that these effects are not limited to early critical periods of development or to intact organisms. The results are in fact congruent with the human adoption studies, and, together, they argue against the hypothesis that the effects of early damage or environmental deprivation are irreversible. Both human and animal studies argue that even late intervention can sometimes be successful.

Interaction of Effects of Experience with Characteristics of the Organism

Most of the research discussed in this chapter has ignored the problem of individual differences. The issues have been stated in terms of the general case; for example, does institutionalization affect infants? Even when individual differences were obtained, as in the 4 of Tizard's 24 adopted babies who did not attach to their adopted parents, the reasons for the different outcomes of the minority were not explored. The avoidance of individual differences clearly masks a very large source of influence on outcomes. The same environmental event or situation is not likely to affect each and every infant to the same degree or even in the same way. A few studies with laboratory animals have explored individual differences operationalized as demonstrable genetic differences (that is, strain or breed differences). These studies all found an interaction between the environmental manipulation and the genetic constitution of the individual (or group) exposed. Thus they established that at least in some restricted circumstances (genetically based individual differences in infrahuman animals) a particular environmental event affects one individual in one way and another individual in another way.

Cooper and Zubek (1958) explored the influence of enrichment and deprivation on rats of varying genetic potential for learning. They produced rats of varying learning ability by breeding rats to be good or poor at running mazes (considered a standard test of rat intelligence; see Figure 13–4). These rats had been bred repeatedly over many generations until they formed two distinct groups with nonoverlapping distributions (that is, the brightest rat

FIGURE 13–4. A rat running a maze.

in the maze-dull group was poorer at running mazes than the dullest rat in the maze-bright group). Rat pups from each of these groups were subjected to one of three rearing conditions: normal laboratory environment, deprived environment, or enriched environment. They were then tested for the number of trials it took them to learn a maze. The results are reproduced in Table 13–3. Notice that any general statement about the effects of enriched or deprived environments is misleading. An enriched environment improved performance compared to a normal environment, but only for rats who were maze-dull (average of 119 versus 164 errors on the test maze). An enriched environment had no effect on maze-bright rats (111 versus 117 mean errors). Likewise, a restricted environment affected the two groups of rats differently. It was no worse than a normal laboratory environment for maze-dull rats (169 versus 164 mean errors), but did affect the learning ability of maze-bright rats (169 versus 117 mean errors). From the point of view of the prognosis for rats of varying genetic ability, the data show that differences in genetic potential are maximized in the normal laboratory environment and minimized in both enriched and deprived environments. A normal environment permitted maze-bright

TABLE 13–3
Mean Errors on Running a Maze for Rats of Varying Genetic Potential and Subjected to Different Rearing Environments

Genetic potential	Rearing environment		
	Restricted	Normal	Enriched
Maze-bright	169	117	111
Maze-dull	169	164	119

rats to reach their genetic potential, whereas maze-dull rats reached their potential only in an enriched environment.

It is dangerous to draw any precise conclusions about the effects of the interaction between environment and genetics on learning ability in human babies on the basis of this study. Nevertheless, the study is important in that it suggests that the abilities children bring to their environments will influence what they get out of them.[9] Furthermore, the research on genetic influences on IQ later in childhood demonstrates consistently that there are genetic differences in intellectual potential and that they interact with environment. Thus, Cooper and Zubek's study at the least suggests a potential for the influence of individual differences on environmental effects.

The other studies we are going to describe examined the interaction of environmental and genetic differences on social and emotional development. In this case groups with different genetic constitutions were formed by comparing different genetic strains (rats) or breeds (dogs). Although we do not know the nature of the genetic differences, we can be certain that there were some because strains and breeds are highly inbred.

First let us consider the work in rats on the effects of maternal stress during pregnancy on the behavior of the offspring. Thompson (1955) showed that pregnant rats exposed to a tone that had signalled electric shocks before they were pregnant had offspring that were more "emotional." These rat pups defecated more and explored less in the situation of being

placed in an open field, a situation that is stressful to a rat. A number of efforts to replicate Thompson's findings failed and some succeeded. It turned out that the crucial determinant of positive findings was the particular strain of rats used (Joffe, 1969). In short, in this study the effect of a prenatal environmental event on rats depended on the genotype of rat that is exposed to it.

Second, let us look at the effects of particular disciplinary techniques on the behavior of the dogs. Freedman (1958) studied this problem using four breeds of dogs—Shetland sheep dogs, wire-haired fox terriers, beagles, and basenjis. Each litter of 4 pups (2 litters per breed) was divided into 2 pairs based on similarity (both physical and behavioral) and one member of each pair was assigned to one of two rearing conditions, indulgent or disciplined. These were applied daily in two 15-minute periods of interaction with a single human caretaker from their third to eighth week. Indulged puppies were encouraged in any activity they initiated and were never punished. The disciplined pups were at first restrained in the experimenter's lap and later trained to sit, stay, come on command, and finally to follow on a leash. All were then tested for the next 8 days for obedience to the command not to eat the meat in a dish in the room with them. The adult rearer spent 3 minutes swatting them and shouting No! each time they attemped to eat. The dogs were then left alone and watched through a one-way mirror to see whether they started to eat in the next 10 minutes, and how soon they started.

To all intents and purposes the rearing made no long-term difference to either the Shetland sheep dogs or basenjis. After the first few days, basenjis all ate within 3 minutes of being left and no Shetland sheep dog ate even after being left for 10 minutes. Thus, these two breeds behaved very differently and their behavior was dependent more on their breed than on the rearing variable.

For the wire-haired fox terriers and beagles there was also a breed difference: Wiredhaireds waited longer than beagles to eat. Unlike the Shetland sheep dogs and basenjis, however, the other two species also showed differences based on rearing. Indulged dogs waited longer to eat than disciplined dogs. Thus, we see that the breed affected both

---

[9]This line of reasoning has been carried even further by some workers in the field of behavior genetics. They discuss the ways in which the genotype causes the child to seek certain environments, thus leading to a certain phenotype (see, for example, Scarr and McCartney, 1983).

obedience and the effectiveness of rearing conditions. One breed (Shetlands) was obedient regardless of rearing, one (basenjis) was disobedient regardless of rearing, and the other two were obedient only when indulgently reared.

Our third example is of breed differences in the effects of social isolation. Sackett, Holm, & Ruppenthal (1976) showed that pigtailed macaque monkeys did not develop the isolate syndrome (withdrawn, personally bizarre, abnormal in social, sexual, and exploratory behavior) described by Harlow and Harlow (1965) to the same extent as the Harlows' rhesus monkeys had. They were not deficient in exploratory behavior and they showed some positive social behaviors when placed with socially normal agemates after rearing in isolation. Nevertheless, compared to normally reared controls, they did have deficits that were similar to, but less serious than, those of the rhesus. Sackett, Ruppenthal, Holm, and Greenough (1981) decided to investigate these species differences further in a study of crab-eating, pigtailed, and rhesus macaques. They all showed different behaviors during isolation and were differently affected in their post-rearing social interactions. Not only did rearing in isolation produce markedly varied amounts of isolate syndrome behaviors among the different species, but the amount of isolate syndrome behavior did not predict the degree of exploratory behavior or even the degree of positive social behavior.

These examples make it very clear that in both intellectual and social-emotional development the influence of the environment depends on the strain studied. Although there is no comparable evidence with humans, it seems likely that individual differences exert at least as great an influence on human babies.

DISCUSSION ISSUES

The Critical Periods Hypothesis

The deprivation literature provides some evidence about the existence of long-term effects of deprivation. According to the critical periods notion, the environmental events that happen during a particular period are crucial for the development of a particular system. The original critical periods hypothesis—that

each period has a beginning and an end, that there must be a maturational underpinning that governs the existence of the period, and that there must be permanent, unchanging effects—was derived from embryology and has had to be modified to be applied to psychological development. This was seen in Chapter 9 on perception, where we showed that visual deprivation during the critical period caused permanent physiological effects, but that substantial behavioral recovery occurred.

The evidence for a critical period in intellectual and social and emotional development is even less supportive of a strict critical periods hypothesis. This is particularly clear for intellectual development. The evidence from behavioral studies both humans and animal and from studies of brain development in animals indicates that at least infancy is not a critical period. Although the evidence with humans is not incompatible with the hypothesis that the preschool period may be critical for intellectual development, there is no evidence that supports a critical period notion in preference to a noncritical periods interpretation.

The evidence for a critical period for social and emotional development is weaker. The data with animals suggest that it may never be too late to provide enrichment. As we discussed in Chapter 12, the particular environmental events that Freud believed to be crucial are not. That does not imply, however, that he was incorrect in hypothesizing that infancy is a critical period for the development of personality. Nevertheless, it is difficult to evaluate even this general tenet of his theory, because researchers must always refer to specific dependent variables. We showed in Chapter 6 that individual differences in orality at age 8 could be predicted from infant experiences, although not from the particular experiences hypothesized by Freud. In this chapter we showed that early deprivation of mother did not lead to difficulties in later attachment (at least from the adoptive mother's point of view) or to serious emotional disturbances, but that it was related to school problems and to unpopularity with peers. Research with animals also showed that even severe emotional disturbances of the sort predicted by Freud could be overcome by rather simple therapeutic interventions.

Those who are reluctant to give up a critical periods hypothesis altogether have reformulated it as a sensitive period. A sensitive period is conceived to be a time that is optimal for a particular kind of development. It is possible for the same development to occur earlier or later than this sensitive period, but it is easier for that development to occur at this time. The question of the role of maturation in sensitive periods is usually left unresolved because the answer is so difficult to determine. Many researchers assume that there is such a maturational underpinning, but it is possible to conceive of a sensitive period that is entirely environmentally determined. The boundaries of a sensitive period are also much less well defined than those of a critical period (although the boundaries in a critical period are usually less clear than originally thought). Finally, the effects of a sensitive period are not thought to be permanent, even though they may last a long time or require therapy. A child may compensate for early inadequate development, although that will be harder to do at older ages. The evidence (animal and human) does not clearly support a sensitive period hypothesis, although some of it may be seen as compatible with such an interpretation.

Research Issues

Deprivation and enrichment have been explored with three major research strategies that complement each other: experiments of nature, intervention studies in naturalistic situations, and laboratory experiments with animals. Research on the effects of early experience has probably used the experiment of nature to better advantage than any other research discussed in this book. It is impossible to conduct true experiments on the effects of severe deprivation, but researchers can examine what happens when infants do grow up in depriving environments. Situations in which the early environments change, as in the adoption studies, are particularly valuable because they allow assessment of long-lasting effects of deprivation during infancy without the confounding influence of later deprivation. Furthermore, comparison of the wide variety of circumstances infants are exposed to helps to separate different aspects of deprivation. For example, we compared situations involving de-

privation of stimulation only to situations involving maternal deprivation with adequate stimulation.

Nevertheless, experiments of nature are quasi-experiments, not true experiments. Subjects are not randomly assigned to deprived and nondeprived circumstances and thus such studies all are subject to all the same dangers of extraneous variables as correlation studies are. It is likely, for example, that orphanage babies experienced a substantially different prenatal environment than home-reared controls. They may have differing genetic characteristics as well. Consider the following example of how such differences might confound research outcomes. If Tizard's adopted babies experienced more prenatal maternal stress than their home-reared controls, they may have become constitutionally more emotional, which in turn may have been responsible for some of their difficulties in school.

Intervention studies provide a good adjunct to experiments of nature. Against a background of environmental deprivation, various kinds of environmental enrichment can be added and thus the influences of that particular component can be assessed independent of other variables. This strategy has been used successfully in orphanage, day care, and maternal intervention studies. Intervention studies can be experiments in that subjects can theoretically be randomly assigned to groups. In so doing, researchers can control for the potentially confounding subject variables that plague experiments of nature.

Unfortunately, not all intervention studies have used experimental procedures for practical reasons. A popular compromise is to assign a center to conditions at random. For example, Center A gets the experimental treatment and Center B serves as control. This does not solve the problem, however, because the centers may be different in ways that confound the results. For example, Center A may have a director who successfully motivates the caregivers to provide more attention than the caregivers provide in Center B. When an intervention program is then introduced, the caregivers in Center A may be more effective in using the procedures than those in Center B would have been. Conversely, if Center B was chosen for the intervention, the performance of its infants might improve, yet they would not improve more than the infants in Center A who were improving due to the director's influence.

Even when subjects are randomly assigned within a center, interventions executed in the center may not work as well. Recall that one of Dennis's intervention experiments in an orphanage failed because the control group caregivers imitated the actions of the experimental group caregivers.

Finally, researchers are limited in the kinds of interventions they can introduce. They usually choose multiple interventions rather than single interventions to maximize their chances of success. This design does not permit them to determine which aspects of their intervention are the effective ones. This use of multiple interventions is preferable on ethical grounds, however, because both the participants and the funding agencies(usually supported by tax dollars) deserve the best possible shot.

The limitations we have just described are intrinsic to research in naturalistic settings. They are the price researchers pay for the advantages of avoiding the problems of generalization (from another species to humans; from laboratory to life). Such intrinsic limitations can be overcome only by supplementing such studies with others that use methodology without these limitations. Laboratory studies with other species are the alternative of choice. They have exactly the reverse characteristics: They can effectively use random assignment of subjects to groups and they can independently vary a number of component variables to test their relative impact, but they do not solve the problem of whether generalization to real-life situations with real humans is appropriate. As we discussed in Chapter 12, it is possible to have increased confidence in research conclusions when findings from two research strategies corroborate each other.

The research described in this chapter also provides clear examples of the problems of operational definitions of dependent measures. To study the effects of deprivation and enrichment on intellectual development, researchers have available the IQ test, Piagetian-based cognitive tests, and other standard cognitive tests, all of which have demonstrated reliability and validity as indicators of group differences (de-

spite their errors in predictions for an individual). Thus findings can be compared and contrasted across studies that vary in many other ways. There are no equivalent standard measures for assessing social or emotional development. Attachment as measured by Ainsworth's strange situation is by far the most common dependent measure used, but it is most appropriately used with toddlers. Seeking proximity, protest at separation, and even strong reunion behaviors are often interpreted to reflect overdependency in older children rather than attachment. There is no outstanding alternative measure of children's attachment to their mothers or of the quality of their interpersonal relationships in general. Tizard relied on the judgments of the children's mothers. Although she used the most methodologically sound interview technique—a highly structured interview that asked mothers about specific behaviors—ultimately the validity of the measure rests on the objectivity of the mothers. Because mothers are—and should be—biased, maternal judgments are suspect. For example, recall that Tizard asked the mothers whether the child preferred being comforted by a parent. It is well known from research on human cognition that when asked such a question mothers are unlikely to count instances and then determine in what proportion of such instances the child exhibited a preference. Unless specifically asked to record instances, mothers do not compute the proportion of instances in which their child exhibited a preference for one person. Rather, a mother is likely to remember certain instances that stood out and, given a mother's strong need to be loved, the instances that are likely to stand out are those in which the child exhibited a strong preference. This is indeed why psychologists generally prefer behavioral measures.

Gardner and colleagues (1961) and Kagan and colleagues (1978) measured other aspects of emotional development. Gardner and colleagues used standard personality tests and Kagan and colleagues focused on objective observations of children in social interactions. Using varied dependent variables is not necessarily bad. They may all be valid and simply measure different aspects of social-emotional development. Unfortunately, unless most studies use all (or most) of the available dependent measures, assessment of the validity of any one dependent variable must wait until a large enough body of literature exists for each dependent variable. In the meantime it is extremely difficult to compare studies that use different dependent variables, because each may measure something different from the others.

Parenting

The portion of this chapter that deals with institutionalization has very few implications for parenting. One remote one is that if family circumstances are such that an infant (normal or otherwise) has to be institutionalized, every possible effort should be made to see to it that the institution is as good as possible; in other words, that the infant-to-caretaker ratio is as low as possible and that the philosophy of the caretakers is concerned with enrichment. The other, somewhat remote, implication for parenting is for adoptive parents. Those who adopt infants need not expect lasting developmental delays. Even for infants adopted from nonoptimal institutions there is a strong likelihood that adequate social and intellectual development can be achieved. Parents who adopt children, particularly older children, should be prepared to devote adequate time and effort to promoting their development. Tizard's data suggest adoptive parents need a high tolerance for attention-seeking behaviors and a willingness to provide an extra measure of security in response to such attention-seeking and attachment behaviors. The research on therapy of isolate monkeys suggests that treating children as if they were considerably younger and leading them through the stages of cognitive and social development may be a valuable approach.

Our review of multiple mothering research indicated that babies in such situations are not at risk. Various forms of multiple mothering are quite common in the United States. Many people are interested in alternative family patterns, such as extended families and communes. Anyone especially interested in this type will want to refer to Eiduson and Alexander (1978).

Multiple mothering also occurs when both parents work. In the United States about 40%

of all mothers with children under 5 years of age work. The kind of multiple mothering these children experience varies. In some families the mother or father (or sometimes both) takes a leave of absence from work to be home with the infant. Other parents arrange their work schedules to permit them to do most of the parenting between them. All others, including single parents, must find some alternative care for their babies. Some have relatives who can help. The rest must find some kind of day care. The data in this chapter should reassure parents. There is no convincing evidence that quality day care (day care by appropriate persons who do not have too many infants to look after) harms infants. Neither their social nor intellectual development seems at risk. In fact, quality day dare is advantageous for the intellectual development of disadvantaged children. Unfortunately, in many places it is very difficult to find quality day care. There is little research evidence on the effects of average sorts of day care, and that which exists yields inconsistent results.

Average to high-quality day care has been much more available in many countries than it has been in the United States, except for the period of World War II when women were needed in the work force (Robinson et al., 1979). Currently, more businesses and industries are again providing day care and finding that it is cost effective.

This chapter and Chapter 12 also addressed more general questions with respect to parenting, particularly with respect to so-called critical experiences in infancy. First, it is clear that several of the experiences believed by some to be crucial to psychologically healthy development are not. Babies do not need to experience a single exclusive relationship with their mothers—they do not need to be nursed, fed, changed, weaned, or toilet trained by their mothers. Babies will not even be harmed by unstimulating environments in the first year or two of life. If they are so invulnerable to relatively great deprivations, they will probably also thrive through the less serious mistakes all well-intentioned parents make. This does not mean that parents would not profit from learning more about children and about parenting. The maternal intervention studies demonstrated that such experience facilitates infant development (although only after a while and not necessarily in all mother–infant dyads), but note that the mothers in these studies were all disadvantaged. Furthermore, the child-rearing literature concerning post-infancy suggests that parents can behave in particular ways that facilitate their children's development. For example, parents who are concerned that their children develop positive behaviors and interests (such as sharing and good school progress), and who provide and enforce rules for appropriate and inappropriate behaviors, are likely to have children who turn out well in all sorts of ways (Baumrind, 1966, 1967, 1972). Thus, it seems clear both that parents are important to their children's development and that infants are not psychological china dolls who will be ruined unless the parents are perfect.

SUMMARY

In the 1940s Spitz documented that children in orphanages failed to thrive and were retarded. Both then and for a considerable period of time thereafter it was thought that these conditions were due to a lack of mothering, but this view has subsequently been shown to be wrong by several lines of research. First, in institutions that typically produced retardation, providing additional perceptual and intellectual stimulation or additional opportunities for exercise of motor capacities, or both, did a great deal to lessen the retardation of development normally found in old-fashioned orphanages. It is clear that providing stimulation in a particular mode fosters development in that mode (for example, vocal stimulation facilitates vocal behaviors) but it is not known whether certain kinds of stimulation facilitate in nonspecific ways. Further, the amount of time devoted to extra stimulation does not have to be large. Second, children in orphanages with low child : caregiver ratios and enrichment programs exhibited normal intelligence and generally good emotional development. Third, Guatemalan infants who spend their first year of life in a cognitively impoverished environment suffered retardation despite an unimpaired relationship with their mothers. Thus, it seems quite clear that institutionalization effects are produced by inadequate stimulation of infants'

developing cognitive abilities and not by lack of a mother or by institutionalization as such.

Because for many years infancy was thought to be a critical period for development of both intellectual and social-emotional functioning, institutionalization effects were thought to be permanent. Nevertheless, studies that followed the development of children after they left the deprived environments of institutions and moved into more normal, stimulating environments have demonstrated that such effects are not irreversible. Dennis's study of the Crèche children adopted at different ages showed that those adopted by 2 years of age had no lasting deficit. Children who were severely deprived for longer than the first 2 years did not entirely make up for their earlier deficit, although they developed at a normal rate after being adopted. It is impossible to determine from these data whether the permanent deficits occurred because the children were deprived for such a long time, or whether the post-infancy period is a crucial time for intellectual development. Also unanswered is the question of whether special enrichment for them or training for their adoptive parents could erase the deficits found among those adopted after 2 years of age. These conclusions from Dennis's research were confirmed by the later research of Kagan and of Tizard. Evidence concerning subsequent social-emotional development after early deprivation is more difficult to obtain because of the paucity of adequate measures. Nonetheless, the available research indicates that there are no startling negative effects. Tizard's findings suggested that adopted children had good relationships with their parents and with their siblings, but were more likely to have difficulties with school peers and with teachers. Gardner and colleagues found no personality deficits as measured by standard personality tests.

We next explored whether having multiple mothers is harmful in situations in which infants are able to form a specific attachment to their own mother. Such situations occur in cultures that practice communal child rearing and in day care in the United States. Studies have shown that infants develop strong, specific attachments to both their mothers and their alternative caretakers and that, in general, children's attachments are stronger to their mothers. There is little reliable evidence for any resultant important difficulties in social-emotional development.

Many of the studies of day care are of centers designed to maximize development. In such centers, intellectual development may be superior to that of home-reared infants for children from disadvantaged backgrounds. It is fairly easy to design or to select day care centers that promote intellectual development. The specifics of the program do not seem to be crucial. So long as the centers focus on fostering such development and provide stimulating experiences—such as activities, reading, conversations, field trips—children develop well. It is more difficult to specify what promotes social-emotional development. Although there is little evidence, it may be less disruptive to provide children with stability in their caregivers. With respect to consistency of caregiving between home and center, the limited research suggests that children can easily deal with inconsistencies.

The research that provided enrichment programs in orphanages and in model day care programs demonstrated that it is both possible and feasible to provide programs that prevent intellectual retardation in children who might otherwise suffer such effects. Recent programs that have focused on intervening with caregivers have been successful in teaching caregivers about children, in training specific skills, and in increasing caregivers' positive behaviors, although not in decreasing their negative behaviors. Such changes have demonstrable effects on children's development. In both the day care and the home intervention studies, the interventions were apparently more effective in the second year of life. This may be because effects are cumulative (it takes 2 years to work) or because a shorter intervention at a later age is more effective.

The research on therapeutic intervention with infrahuman animals indicates that deprivation effects on social-emotional development can be overcome with appropriate experiences. This makes it clear that a critical periods hypothesis is not viable and that even a sensitive periods hypothesis may not be sufficient to explain subsequent plasticity. This research also suggests the need in such interventions to (1) overcome fear so that the animals can learn to cope, (2) provide social interaction in a context that is safe for the deprived

animal, and (3) match the environmental demands with the animals' capabilities, moving gradually from simpler to more complex situations.

In the last section of the chapter we reviewed research with animals that further elucidated the mechanisms of deprivation and intervention. First, studies of the effects of enrichment and deprivation on brain development in rats demonstrate that enriched experiences stimulate the brain's growth and its structural development, but that such growth, as measured by current biochemical means, is no greater during infancy than in adulthood. This suggests that these effects do not operate by a critical periods mechanism. Second, the animal research makes it quite clear that genetic differences produce large individual differences in susceptibility to particular environmental experiences.

REFERENCES

Andrews, S.R. (1981). Mother–infant interaction and child development: Findings from an experimental study of parent-child programs. In M.J. Begab, H.C. Haywood, & H.L. Garber (Eds.), *Psychosocial influences in retarded performance: Strategies for improving competence* (Vol. 2, pp. 245–256). Baltimore: University Park Press.

Andrews, S.R., Blumenthal, J.B., Johnson, D.L., Kahn, A.J., Ferguson, C.J., Laseter, T.M., Malone, P.E., & Wallace, D.B. (1982). The skills of mothering: A study of parent child development centers. *Monographs of the Society for Research in Child Development*, 47(6, Serial No. 198).

Atkin, R., Bray, R., Davison, M., Herberger, S., Humphreys, L., & Selzer, V. (1977). Cross-lagged panel analysis of sixteen cognitive measures at four grade levels. *Child Development*, 48, 944–952.

Avgar, A., Bronfenbrenner, U., & Henderson, C.R., Jr. (1977). Socialization practices of parents, teachers, and peers in Israel: Kibbutz, moshav, and city. *Child Development*, 48, 1219–1227.

Badger, E. (1973). *Mother's guide to early learning.* Paoli, PA: McGraw-Hill.

Badger, E. (1977). The infant stimulation/mother training project. In B. Caldwell & D. Stedman (Eds.), *Infant education: A guide for helping handicapped children in the first three years.* New York: Walker.

Baumrind, D. (1966). Effects of authoritative parental control on child behavior. *Child Development, 37,* 887–907.

Baumrind, D. (1967). Child care practices anteceding three patterns of preschool behavior. *Genetic Psychology Monographs, 75,* 43–88.

Baumrind, D. (1972). Socialization and instrumental competence in young children. In W.W. Hartup (Ed.), *The young child: Reviews of research* (Vol. 2, pp. 202–224). Washington, DC: National Association for the Education of Young Children.

Bayley, N. (1965). Comparisons of mental and motor test scores for ages 1–15 months by sex, birth order, race, geographical location, and education of parents. *Child Development, 36,* 379–412.

Beller, E.K., Laewen, H., & Stahnke, M. (1981). A model of infant education in day care. In M.J. Begab, H.C. Haywood, & H.L. Garber (Eds.), *Psychosocial influences in retarded performance: Strategies for improving competence* (Vol. 2). Baltimore: University Park Press.

Belsky, J., & Steinberg, L.D. (1978). The effects of day care: A critical review. *Child Development, 49,* 929–949.

Bennett, E.L., Diamond, M.C., Krech, D., & Rosenzweig, M.R. (1964). Chemical and anatomical plasticity of the brain. *Science, 146,* 610–619.

Bennett, E.L., & Rosenzweig, M.R. (1971). Chemical alterations produced in brain by environment and training. In A. Lajtha (Ed.), *Handbook of neurochemistry* (Vol. 6). New York: Plenum.

Bettelheim, B. (1969). *The children of the dream.* New York: Macmillan.

Blehar, M.C. (1974). Anxious attachment and defensive reactions associated with day care. *Child Development, 45,* 683–692.

Brazelton, T.B. (1974). *Toddlers and parents.* New York: Delacorte Press.

Brossard, M., & Décarie, T.G. (1971). The effects of three kinds of perceptual–social stimulation on the development of institutionalized infants: Preliminary report of a longitudinal study. *Early Child Development and Care, 1,* 111–130.

Caldwell, B.M. (1964). The effects of infant care. In M.L. Hoffman (Ed.), *Review of child development research* (Vol. 1). New York: Russell Sage Foundation.

Caldwell, B.M. (1974). A decade of early intervention programs: What we have learned. *American Journal of Orthopsychiatry, 44,* 491–496.

Clark, D.L. (1968). *Immediate and delayed effects of*

early, intermediate, and late social isolation in the rhesus monkey. Unpublished doctoral dissertation, University of Wisconsin, Madison.

Clark, E.A., & Hanisee, J. (1982). Intellectual and adaptive performance of Asian children in adoptive American settings. *Developmental Psychology, 18,* 595–599.

Clarke-Stewart, K.A. (1973). Interactions between mothers and their young children: Characteristics and consequences. *Monographs of the Society for Research in Child Development, 38(6–7,* Serial No. 153).

Clarke-Stewart, K.A., & Fein, G.G. (1983). Early childhood programs. In P.H. Mussen (Ed.), *Handbook of child psychology* (4th ed., Vol. 2, pp. 917–999). New York: Wiley.

Cooper, R.M., & Zubek, J.P., (1958). Effects of enriched and restricted early environments on the learning ability of bright and dull rats. *Canadian Journal of Psychology, 12,* 159–164.

Cummings, E.M. (1980). Caregiver stability and day care. *Developmental Psychology, 16,* 31–37.

Darlington, R.B., Royce, J.M., Snipper, A.S., Murray, H.W., & Lazar, I. (1980). Preschool programs and the later school competence of children from low-income families. *Science, 208,* 202–204.

Dennis, W. (1960). Causes of retardation among institutional children: Iran. *The Journal of Genetic Psychology, 96,* 47–59.

Dennis, W. (1973). *Children of the Crèche.* New York: Appleton-Century-Crofts.

Diamond, M.C., Lindner, B., Johnson, R., Bennett, E.L., & Rosenzweig, M.R., (1975). Differences in occipital cortical synapses from environmentally enriched, impoverished, and standard colony rats. *Journal of Neuroscience Research, 1,* 109–119.

Eiduson, B.T., & Alexander, J.W. (1978). The role of children in alternative lifestyles. *Journal of Social Issues, 34,* 149–167.

Epstein, H.T. (1974a). Phrenoblysis: Special brain and mind growth periods. I: Human brain and skull development. *Developmental Psychobiology, 7,* 207–216.

Epstein, H.T. (1974b). Phrenoblysis: Special brain and mind growth periods. II: Human mental development. *Developmental Psychobiology, 7,* 217–224.

Etaugh, C. (1980). Effects of nonmaternal care on children: Research evidence and popular views. *American Psychologist, 35,* 309–319.

Faigin, H. (1958). Social behavior of young children in the Kibbutz. *Journal of Abnormal and Social Psychology, 56,* 117–129.

Farran, D., & Ramey, C. (1977). Infant day care and attachment behaviors toward mothers and teachers. *Child Development, 48,* 1112–1116.

Fowler, W., & Khan, N. (December, 1974). *The development of a prototype infant and child day care center in metropolitan Toronto.* Year III Progress Report.

Fowler, W., & Khan, N. (1975, December). *The development & prototype infant and child day care center in metropolitan Toronto.* Year IV Progress Report.

Fox, N. (1977). Attachment of Kibbutz infants to mother and metapelet. *Child Development, 48,* 1228–1239.

Freedman, D.G., (1958). Constitutional and environmental interactions in rearing of four breeds of dogs. *Science, 127,* 585–586.

Fuller, J.L., & Clark, L.D. (1966). Genetic and treatment factors modifying the postisolation syndrome in dogs. *Journal of Comparative and Physiological Psychology, 61,* 251–257.

Fuller, J.L., & Scott, J.P. (1967). Experiential deprivation and later behavior. *Science, 158,* 1648–1652.

Garber, H.L., & Heber, R. (1981). The efficacy of early intervention with family rehabilitation. In M.J. Begab, H.C. Haywood, & H.L. Garber (Eds.), *Psychosocial influences in retarded performance* (Vol. II, pp. 71–88). Baltimore: University Park Press.

Gardner, D.B., Hawkes, G.R., & Burchinal, L.G. (1961). Noncontinuous mothering in infancy and development in later childhood. *Child Development, 32,* 225–234.

Gewirtz, H.B., & Gewirtz, J.L. (1968). Visiting and caretaking patterns for kibbutz infants: Age and sex trends. *American Journal of Orthopsychiatry, 38,* 427–443.

Gewirtz, J.L., & Gewirtz, H.B. (1965). Stimulus conditions, infant behaviors, and social learning in four Israeli child-rearing environments: A preliminary report illustrating differences in environment and behavior between the 'only' and the 'youngest' child. In B.M. Foss (Ed.), *Determinants of infant behavior* (Vol. 3). New York: Wiley.

Globus, A., Rosenzweig, M.R., Bennett, E.L., & Diamond, M.C. (1973). Effects of differential experience on dendritic spine counts. *Journal of Physiological and Comparative Psychology, 82,* 175–181.

Golden, M., Rosenbluth, L., Grossi, M., Policare, H., Freeman, H., & Brownlee, E. (1978). *The New York city infant day care study.* New York: Medical and Health Research Association of New York City.

Goldfarb, W. (1945a) Psychological privation in infancy and subsequent adjustment. *American Journal of Orthopsychiatry, 15,* 247–255.

Goldfarb, W. (1945b). Effects of psychological deprivation in infancy and subsequent stimulation. *American Journal of Psychiatry, 102,* 18–33.

Goldfarb, W. (1955). Emotional and intellectual consequences of psychological deprivation in infancy: A re-evaluation. In E.H. Koch & J. Zubin (Eds.), *Psychopathology of childhood.* New York: Grune & Stratton.

Greenbaum, C.W., & Kugelmass, S. (1980). Human development and socialization in cross-cultural perspective: Issues arising from research in Israel. In N. Warren (Ed.), *Studies in cross-cultural psychology* (Vol. 2). London: Academic.

Greenough, W.T., & Volkmar, F.R. (1973). Pattern of dendritic branching in occipital cortex of rats reared in complex environments. *Experimental Neurology, 40,* 491–504.

Handel, A. (1961). Self-concept of the kibbutz adolescent (Hebrew). *Megamot, 11,* 142–159. (Abstract in Rabin, A.I. (1971). *Kibbutz studies.* E. Lansing: Michigan State University Press.

Harlow, H.F., Dodsworth, R.O., & Harlow, M.K. (1965). Total social isolation in monkeys. *Proceedings of the National Academy of Sciences, 54,* 90–96.

Harlow, H.F., & Harlow, M.K. (1965). The affectional systems. In A.M. Schrier, H.F. Harlow, & F. Stollnitz (Eds.), *Behavior of nonhuman primates* (Vol. 2). New York: Academic.

Harlow, H.F., & Novak, M.A. (1973). Psychopathological perspectives. *Perspectives in Biology and Medicine, 16,* 461–478.

Harlow, H.F., & Suomi, S.J. (1970). The nature of love—Simplified. *American Psychologist, 25,* 161–168.

Harlow, H.F., & Suomi, S.J. (1971). Production of depressive behaviors in young monkeys. *Journal of Autism and Childhood Schizophrenia, 1,* 246–255.

Heber, R., Garber, H.L., Harrington, S., Hoffman, C., & Falender, C. (1972). *Rehabilitation of families at risk for mental retardation.* Progress Report. Madison: University of Wisconsin, Rehabilitation & Training Center.

Hess, R.D. (1970). Social class and ethnic influences on socialization. In P. Mussen (Ed.), *Carmichael's manual of child psychology* (3rd ed., Vol. 2, pp. 457–557). New York: Wiley.

Hock, E. (1976). *Alternative approaches to child rearing and their effects on the mother–infant relationship* (Final report, grant No. OCD-490). Washington, DC: Office of Child Development, Department of Health, Education, and Welfare.

Hunt, J.McV. (1981). Language acquisition and experience: Tehran. Unpublished manuscript, University of Illinois, Urbana.

Hunt, J.McV. (1982). Facilitating the development of social competence and language skill. In L.A. Bond & J.M. Jaffe (Eds.), *Facilitating infant and early childhood development.* Hanover, NH & London: University Press of New England.)

Hunt, J.McV., Mohandessi, K., Ghodessi, M., & Akiyama, M. (1976). The psychological development of orphanage-reared infants: Interventions with outcomes (Tehran). *Genetic Psychology Monographs, 94*, 177–226.

Hunt, J.McV. Paraskevopoulos, J., Schickedanz, D., & Uzgiris, I.C. (1975). Variations in the mean ages of achieving object permanence under diverse conditions of rearing. In B.L. Friedlander, G.M. Sterritt, & G.E. Kirk (Eds.), *The exceptional infant: Vol. 3. Assessment and intervention.* New York: Brunner/Mazel.

Jaffee, B., & Fanshel, D. (1970). *How they fared in adoption: A follow-up study.* New York: Columbia University Press.

Joffee, J.M. (1969). Prenatal determinants of behavior. *International Series of Monographs in Experimental psychology* (Vol. 7). Oxford: Pergamon Press.

Kaffman, M. (1965). A comparison of psychopathology: Israeli children from Kibbutz and from urban surroundings. *American Journal of Orthopsychiatry, 35*, 509–520.

Kagan, J. (1976a). Resilience and continuity in psychological development. In A.M. Clarke & A.D.B. Clarke (Eds.), *Early experience: Myth and evidence* (pp. 97–121). New York: Free Press.

Kagan, J. (1976b). Emergent themes in human development. *American Scientist, 64*, 186–196.

Kagan, J., Kearsley, R.B., & Zelazo, P.R. (1978). *Infancy: Its place in human development.* Cambridge, MA: Harvard University Press.

Kardiner, A. (1954). The roads to suspicion, rage, apathy, and societal disintegration. In I. Galdston (Ed.), *Beyond the germ theory.* New York: Health Education Council.

Kohen-Raz, R. (1968). Mental and motor development of Kibbutz, institutionalized, and home reared infants in Israel. *Child Development, 39*, 488–504.

Lally, R. (1973). *The Family Development Research Program.* Progress Report. Syracuse, NY: Syracuse University.

Lally, R. (1974). *The Family Development Research Program.* Progress Report. Syracuse, NY: Syracuse University.

Lazar, I., & Darlington, R.B. (1982). Lasting effects of an early education. *Monographs of the Society for Research in Child Development, 47,* (2–3, Serial No. 195).

Leiderman, P.H., & Leiderman, G.F. (1974). Affective and cognitive consequences of polymatric infant care in the East African Highlands. In A.D. Pick (Ed.), *Minnesota Symposia on Child Psychology* (Vol. 8, pp. 81–110). Minneapolis: University of Minnesota Press.

Levenstein, P. (1977). The mother–child home program. In M.C. Day & R.K. Parker (Eds.), *The preschool in action: Exploring early childhood programs* (2nd ed.). Boston: Allyn & Bacon.

Levenstein, P., Kochman, A., & Roth, B. (1973). From laboratory to real world: Service and delivery of the mother–child home program. *American Journal of Orthopsychiatry, 43*, 72–78.

Levenstein, P., Kochman, A., Roth, B., & Sunley, R. (1968). Stimulation of verbal interaction between disadvantaged mothers and children. *American Journal of Orthopsychiatry, 38*, 116–121.

Levy-Shiff, R. (1983). Adaptation and competence in early childhood: Communally raised Kibbutz children versus family raised children in the city. *Child Development, 54*, 1606–1614.

Longstreth, L.E. (1981). Revisiting Skeels' final study: A critique. *Developmental Psychology, 17*, 620–625.

Maccoby, E., & Feldman, S.S. (1972). Mother-attachment and stranger-reactions in the third year of life. *Monographs of the Society for Research in Child Development, 37*(1, Serial No. 146).

Melzak, R., & Scott, J.P. (1957). The effects of early experience on the response to pain. *Journal of Comparative and Physiological Psychology, 50*, 155–161.

Moskowitz, D., Schwarz, J., & Corsini, D. (1977). Initiating day care at three years of age: Effects on attachment. *Child Development, 48*, 1271–1276.

Nagler, S. (1963). Clinical observation on Kibbutz children. *The Israeli Annals of Psychiatry and Related Disciplines, 1*, 201–216.

Novak, M.A., & Harlow, H.F. (1975). Social recovery of monkeys isolated for the first year of life: 1.

Rehabilitation and therapy. *Developmental Psychology, 11,* 453–465.

Paraskevopoulos, J., & Hunt, J.McV. (1971). Object construction and imitation under differing conditions of rearing. *Journal of Genetic Psychology, 119,* 301–321.

Pelled, N. (1964). On the formation of object-relations and identifications of the kibbutz child. *The Israel Annals of Psychiatry and Allied Disciplines, 2,* 144–161.

Piers, M. (1978). *Infanticide: Past and present.* New York: Norton.

Portnoy, F., & Simmons, C. (1978). Day care and attachment. *Child Development, 49,* 239–242.

Rabin, A.I. (1957). Personality maturity of kibbutz (Israeli collective settlement) and non-kibbutz children as reflected in Rorschach findings. *Journal of Projective Techniques, 21,* 148–153.

Rabin, A.I. (1958). Some psychosexual differences between kibbutz and non-kibbutz Israeli boys. *Journal of Projective Techniques, 22,* 328–332.

Rabin, A.I. (1961). Kibbutz adolescents. *The American Journal of Orthopsychiatry, 31,* 493–504.

Ramey, C., & Smith, B. (1976). Assessing the intellectual consequences of early intervention with high-risk infants. *American Journal of Mental Deficiency, 81,* 318–324.

Ricciuti, H.N. (1974). Fear and the development of social attachments in the first year of life. In M. Lewis & L.A. Rosenblum (Eds.), *The origins of fear* (pp. 73–106). New York: Wiley.

Ricciuti, H.N. (1976, October). *Effects of infant day care experience on behavior and development: Research and implications for social policy.* Review prepared for the Office of the Assistant Secretary for Planning and Evaluation, Dept. of Health, Education and Welfare, Washington, DC.

Ricciuti, H.N., & Poresky, R. (1973, March). *Development of attachment to caregivers in an infant nursery during the first year of life.* Paper presented at the biennial meeting of the Society for Research in Child Development, Philadelphia.

Robinson, H., & Robinson, N. (1971). Longitudinal development of very young children in a comprehensive day care program: The first two years. *Child Development, 42,* 1673–1683.

Robinson, N.M., Robinson, H.B., Darling, M.A., & Holm, G. (1979). *A world of children: Daycare and preschool institutions.* Belmont, CA: Brooks/Cole.

Rosenzweig, M.R. (1966). Environmental complexity, cerebral change, and behavior. *American Psychologist, 21,* 321–332.

Rosenzweig, M.R. (1983, August). *Experience, memory and the brain.* Paper presented to the annual meeting of the American Psychological Association, Anaheim, CA.

Rosenzweig, M.R., & Bennett, E.L. (1978). Experiential influences on brain anatomy and brain chemistry in rodents. In G. Gottlieb (Ed.), *Studies on the development of behavior and the nervous system: Vol. 4, Early influences.* New York: Academic.

Ross, G., Kagan, J., Zelazo, P., & Kotelchuk, M. (1975). Separation protest in infants in home and laboratory. *Developmental Psychology, 11,* 256–257.

Rowland, G.L. (1964). *The effects of total isolation upon the learning and social behavior of rhesus monkeys.* Unpublished doctoral dissertation, University of Wisconsin, Madison.

Rutter, M. (1979). Maternal deprivation 1972–1978: New findings, new concepts, new approaches. *Child Development, 50,* 283–305.

Sackett, G.P., Holm, R.A., & Ruppenthal, G.C. (1976). Social isolation rearing: Species differences in behavior of Macaque monkeys. *Developmental Psychology, 12,* 283–288.

Sackett, G.P., Ruppenthal, G.C., Holm, R.A., & Greenough, W.T. (1981). Social isolation rearing effects in monkeys vary with genotype. *Developmental Psychology, 17,* 313–318.

Salk, L. (1974). *Preparing for parenthood.* New York: McKay.

Scarr, S., & McCartney, K. (1983). How people make their own environments: A theory of genotype → environment effects. *Child Development, 54,* 424–435.

Scarr, S., & Weinberg, R.A. (1976). IQ test performance of black children adopted by white families. *American Psychologist, 10,* 726–739.

Schaffer, H.R., & Emerson, P.E. (1964). The development of social attachments in infancy. *Monographs of the Society for Research in Child Development, 29*(3, Serial No. 94).

Schwarz, J.C., Scarr, S.W., Caparulo, B., Furrow, D., McCartney, K., Billington, R., Phillips, D., & Hindy, C. (August, 1981). *Center, sitter, and home day care before age two: A report on the first Bermuda infant care study.* Paper presented at the annual meeting of the American Psychological Association, Los Angeles.

Schwartz, P. (1983). Length of day-care attendance and attachment behavior in eighteen-month-old infants. *Child Development, 54,* 1073–1078.

Schweinhart, L.J., & Weikart, D.P. (1980). Young children grow up: The effects of the Perry Preschool Program on youths through age 15. *Monographs of the High Scope Educational Research Foundation*, No. 3.

Scott, J.P. (1958). Critical periods in the development of social behavior in puppies. *Psychomatic Medicine, 20*, 42–54.

Scott, J.P. (1967). The development of social motivation. In D. Levine (Ed.), *Nebraska symposium on motivation* (Vol. 15, pp. 111–132). Lincoln: University of Nebraska Press.

Scott, J.P., & Marston, M. (1950). Critical periods affecting the development of normal and maladjustive social behavior of puppies. *Journal of Genetic Psychology, 77*, 25–60.

Scott, J.P., Stewart, J.M., & DeGhett, V.J. (1973). Separation in infant dogs: Emotional response and motivational consequences. In J.P. Scott & E.C. Senay (Eds.), *Separation and depression: Clinical and research aspects* (pp. 3–32). Washington, DC: American Association for the Advancement of Science.

Skeels, H.M. (1936). The mental development of children in foster homes. *Pedagogical Seminary & Journal of Genetic Psychology, 49*, 91–106.

Skeels, H.M. (1966). Adult status of children with contrasting early life experiences. *Monographs of the Society for Research in Child Development, 31*(3).

Skeels, H.M., & Dye, H.B. (1939). A study of the effects of differential stimulation of mentally retarded children. *Proceedings of American Association on Mental Deficiency, 44*, 114–136.

Skodak, M. (1939). Children in foster homes: A study of mental development. *University of Iowa Studies in Child Welfare, 16*(1).

Skodak, M., & Skeels, H.M. (1945). A follow-up study of children in adoptive homes. *Journal of Genetic Psychology, 66*, 21–58.

Skodak, M., & Skeels, H.M. (1949). A follow-up study of one hundred adopted children. *Journal of Genetic Psychology, 75*, 85–125.

Spiro, M.E. (1958). *Children of the kibbutz.* Cambridge, MA: Harvard University Press.

Spitz, R.A. (1945). Hospitalism: An inquiry into the genesis of psychiatric conditions in early childhood. In R.S. Eissler (Ed.), *Psychoanalytic study of the child.* New Haven: Yale University Press.

Spitz, R.A. (1946). Hospitalism: A follow-up report. *Psychoanalytic Study of the Child, 2*, 113–118.

Spock, B.J. (1946). *Baby and child care* (1st ed.). New York: Simon & Schuster.

Spock, B.J. (1974). *Raising children in a difficult time.* New York: Norton.

Spock, B.J. (1976). *Baby and child care* (3rd ed.). New York: Pocket Books.

Suomi, S.J. (1976). Mechanisms underlying social development: A reexamination of mother–infant interactions in monkeys. In A.D. Pick (Ed.), *Minnesota Symposia on Child Psychology* (Vol. 10, pp. 201–228). Minneapolis: University of Minnesota Press.

Suomi, S.J., & Harlow, H.F. (1972). Rehabilitation of isolate-reared monkeys. *Developmental Psychology, 6*, 487–496.

Thompson, W.R. (1955). Early environment—Its importance for later behavior. In P.H. Hoch & J. Zubin (Eds.), *Psychopathology of childhood.* New York: Grune and Stratton.

Tizard, B. (1977). *Adoption: A second chance.* New York: Free Press.

White, B.L., & Watts, J. (1973). *Experience & environment: Major influences on the development of the young child* (Vol. 1). New York: Prentice-Hall.

Will, B.E., Rosenzweig, M.R., & Bennett, E.L. (1976). Effects of differential environments on recovery from neonatal brain lesions, measured by problem solving scores and brain dimensions. *Physiology and Behavior, 16*, 603–611.

Will, B.E., Rosenzweig, M.R., Bennett, E.L., Hebert, M., & Morimoto, H. (1977). Relatively brief environmental enrichment aids recovery of learning capacity and alters brain measures after postweaning brain lesions in rats. *Journal of Comparative and Physiological Psychology, 91*, 33–50.

Willis, A., & Ricciuti, H.N. (January, 1974). *Longitudinal observations of infants' daily arrivals at a day care center* (Technical Report). Ithaca, NY: Cornell University.

Willis, A., & Ricciuti, H.N. (1975). *A good beginning for babies: Guidelines for group care.* Washington, DC: National Association for the Education of Young Children.

Delivery (Continued)
160–163; forceps, 160, 197; Caesarean section, 160–163; drugs during, 163–170, 197–198; childbirth practices, 172–182; criticisms of practices, 172–175; as surgical, 175, 198; at home, 181–182, 198. See also Childbirth
DeLoache, J.S., 214, 233, 279, 363
DeLucia, C., 210, 347
Dempsey, J.R., 273, 315n12
Denhoff, E., 321
Dennis, M.G., 298
Dennis, W., 209, 298, 299, 524, 525n2, 531, 548, 557. See also Crèche
Denver Developmental Screening Test, 324, 328
Deoxyribonucleic acid (DNA), 22, 29
Dependency, 481n1; in kibbutz children, 540
Dependent variable, 11, 16; in research design, 14; and operational definition, 57; neurological tests as, 320, 328, 333
Deprivation: institutionalization, 522–536; multiple mothering, 536–547; overcoming effects of, 547–551; research issues on, 556–558
Depth perception, 376–383; looming, 379–399; binocular perception, 379–380; and the visual cliff, 380–382; pictorial cues, 382
Dereux, J.F., 130
Derryberry, D., 244
Design, research, 14–15, 16
Desmonts, G., 109
Desor, J.A., 349
Detterman, D.K., 359
DeVault, S., 137, 138
Development: continuity of, 244–245; role of imitation in, 270–273; physical, 290–296, 332; motor, 296–310, 332–333; testing of, 310–328; perceptual, 343–386; cognitive, 401–471. See also Cognitive development; Motor development; Perceptual development; Physical development; prenatal development
Development quotient (DQ), 316, 324, 333
Devieux, J., 469
Dews, P.B., 384
DiFranco, D., 305, 376
Diabetes, 110, 111, 145
Diamond, M.C., 552
Diamond, R.M., 309
Diano, A., 119
Dick-Read, G., 172; childbirth without fear, 176, 198
Diethylstilbestrol (DES), 117
"Difficult" child, the, 243, 245, 250
Dijkstra, J., 310
Dirks, J., 371, 372
Disbrow, M.A., 207
Discriminating social responsiveness, 482
Discrimination learning, 345
Dishabituation of orienting response, 272
Dishotsky, N.I., 119
Disorders of genes and chromo-

somes, 69–88, 133; incidence and mortality, 70–71; in special populations, 71; specific, 71; chromosomal abnormalities, 72–81; abnormalities of sex chromosomes, 77–81; abnormalities from gene defects, 81–86; screening for, 83–85; and Rh factor, 86–88; counseling for, 88–94
Divorce, 186
Dixon, E., 464
Dmitriev, V., 76
Dobbing, J., 142
Dobson, V., 366
Dockeray, F.C., 346
Dodds, C., 279
Dodds, J.B., 324
Dodsworth, R.O., 551
Dodwell, P.C., 305, 354, 376
Doering, S.G., 191, 505
Dogs: deprivation in, 550–551; effect of discipline on, 554
Dolby, R.M., 160, 166, 167, 170
Dollinger, S.J., 272
Donahue, M., 454
Donovan, C.M., 233, 234, 235, 241
Dooling, E., 126, 127
Dougherty, L.M., 229
Douglas, J.W.B., 50
Dowd, J.M., 355
Dowler, J.K., 121, 166, 167
Dowling, K., 361
Down's syndrome, 72–77, 98; characteristics, 72–73; frequency, 73; forms and mechanisms, 73–74; social issues, 74–77, 97; preschool programs for, 76; and radiation, 133
Doxsey, P.A., 430
Drake, D., 469
Dressler, M., 45
Dreyfus-Brissac, C., 207, 208
Drillien, C.M., 48, 50, 51, 139, 327
Driscoll, J.W., 234
Drugs, effect on fetus, 105, 115–132, 146; thalidomide, 115–116; steroid hormones, 116–118; psychotropic, 118–120; cigarette smoking, 120–125; alcohol, 125–131; other, 131–132
Drugs used during delivery, 163–170, 193; types, 163–164; difficulties of establishing effects, 164–166; effects, 166–170; pre-anesthetics, 166–167; regional anesthetics, 167–169; general anesthetics, 169; overall level of medication, 169–170; oxytocin, 170–171; conclusions, 171–172; as statistical problem, 195
Dubowitz, L.M.S., 45
Dubowitz, V., 45
Ducasse, G., 70
Dumais, S.T., 365, 379, 380
Dunkeld, J., 307
Dunn, J.F., 237, 505
Dunst, C.J., 430
Dyad, 453; mother-infant, 499, 513–514
Dye, H.B., 523

E
Ear, development of, 28
Earls, F., 407

Easterbrooks, M.A., 307
Eckerman, C.O., 488, 489
Eckhoff, E., 139
Ecological validity, 351; in audition, 356
Ectodermal cells, 28
Ectopic pregnancies, 26
Education: effect of mother's, 50; as preparation for childbirth, 197
Effects: short-term vs. long-term, 194–195; role of chance in, 195
Egeland, B., 319, 486
Ehrhardt, A.A., 117
Eichorn, D.H., 75, 346n2, 354
Eiduson, B.T., 558
Eilers, R., 457, 471
Eimas, P., 455, 457
Eisdorfer, C., 218
Eisenberg, P., 378
Eisenberg, R.B., 356, 358, 498
Eisenberg-Berg, N., 271
Elder, J., 191
Electroencephalogram (EEG), 208
Elias, P.K., 244
Elicitation, of response by stimulus, 260, 263–265
Ellis, F.W., 128
Ellis, M.K., 223
Emanuel, I., 113
Embedded sentences, 461
Embryo, 28
Embryology, 4
Embryonic stages of development, 28–31; initial differentiation, 28–29; three to four weeks after conception, 29–31; five to eight weeks, 31; critical periods in, 55
Emde, R.N., 73, 190, 191, 230, 238, 239, 318, 488
Emerson, P.E., 488, 493, 495, 497, 506, 537
Emitted response, 263
Emotional development: in child care centers, 544–547; and critical period hypothesis, 555; lack of measures for, 557. See also Attachment; Social development
Emotions. See Affective behaviors
Empirically based tests, 326
Empiricism, 343; in associationism, 402
Endman, M., 354, 358
Endodermal cells, 28
Endometrium, 26n1
Engelmann, T.G., 207
Engen, T., 351
Engle, P.L., 290, 322
Enkin, M.W., 178
Enright, M., 276, 277
Entrainment, in sleep patterns, 208
Entwisle, D.R., 191, 505
Environment: role of in development, 2, 16, 141; and study of genetics, 3; and critical periods, 4, 55; postnatal, of prematures, 49–51; and the phenotype, 67, 69; and constitutional abnormalities, 94; influence of prenatal, on con-

stitution, 105–106; direct effects of on embryo and fetus, 132–135; radiation, 133–134; differing impacts of, 245; and learning, 280; and secular trends, 291; and development of motor skills, 298–301, 332; in perceptual development, 343–344; Piaget on role of, 405, 442; and information processing theories, 431; in skills theory, 431–432; providing a favorable, 444; and language development, 466, 468, 474; deprivation and enrichment in, 528–536; and genetic potential, 553–554
Enzymes, 68; hexosamidase A, 82
Episiotomies, 175
Epistemology, 3; Piaget's interest in, 401
Epstein, H.T., 531
Epstein-Barr virus, 109
Erhard, P., 124
Erikson, Erik, 480, 490, 512, 513
Ernhart, C.B., 159, 160, 320
Escalante, J.M., 161
Escalona, S.K., 215, 245, 422
Esposito, A., 265
Estes, D., 487
Etaugh, C., 547
Ethical problems, in genetic abnormalities, 91, 96
Ethnic groups and genetic syndromes: Ashkenazic Jews, and Tay-Sachs disease, 83, 97; sickle cell anemia in blacks, 92, 97
Ethology: impact of, 183; concept of attachment in, 481; on social response, 498
Etzel, B.C., 238
Evans, W.F., 429
Evolution, function of attachment in, 487, 490
Evrard, J.R., 161
Expectations: influence of on observation, 6, 196; control of, 7–9; and replicability, 15
Experience: empiricists and nativists on, 343; vs. maturation in vision, 381–382, 383; physiological effects of early, 551–553; interaction of with characteristics of organism, 553–555
Experiments: as research technique, 11–12, 16; and research design, 14; effect of experimenter's beliefs on, 281
Exploration by infants, and attachment, 488, 490
Extinction, 260
Extraneous variables, 11; in teratology research, 143–144
Eyeblink (auropalpebral reflex), and audition, 353, 354
Eyes: development of, 41–42; formation of lens as critical period, 55. See also Vision

F
Fabro, S., 127
Faces: perception of, 369–372, 435; recognition of, and attachment, 482
Facial expressions: in taste, 349; in communication, 473. See also Affective behaviors

Hall, G. Stanley, 322
Halle, M., 457
Haller, M., 358
Hallock, N.H., 315n12
Halton, A., 305, 376
Halton, M., 355
Halverson, H.M., 304
Hamerton, J., 70
Hamil, B.M., 228
Hamm, M., 267
Handel, A., 541
Hanisee, J., 530
Hans, S.L., 119
Hansman, C., 45
Hanson, S.W., 129
Hardy, J.B., 121
Harlap, S., 126, 128
Harlow, H.F., 270, 482, 488, 492, 513, 536, 550, 551
Harlow, M.K., 482, 492, 513, 536, 551
Harmon, R.J., 238, 239
Haronsseau, H., 126
Harper, L.V., 499
Harper, P.A., 44n8, 47, 50, 51
Harrington, S., 543
Harris, L., 354
Harris, P.L., 427
Harris, W.T., 3
Hartman, A.F., 160
Hartner, M.S.S., 168, 503
Harvey, L.O., Jr., 368
Hatch, J., 273
Hatshepshut, 179
Hattori, H., 134
Hawkes, G.R., 535
Hawkins, M.M., 123
Hay, D.F., 490
Hayden, A.H., 76
Hayes, L.A., 267
Haynes, H., 366
Head: operant conditioning of turning, 263; growth of circumference of, 294, 332, 531; control of, 302
Heald, F.P., 84
Healy, M.J.R., 294
Hearing. See Audition
Heart (circulatory system), development of, 22
Heartbeat, sound of mother's, 359
Heart rate: and habituation, 272–273; and taste, 349–350
Hebb, D.O., 485
Heber, R., 543
Hebert, M., 552
Height, 292–294; and physiological development, 290, 291, 332; secular trends in, 291
Heimer, B., 46
Hein, A., 309
Held, R., 307, 309, 365, 366, 380, 385
Hembree, E.A., 229
Hemisyndrome, 312, 333
Hemmink, F., 58
Hemophilia, 68, 89
Hen-Tov, A., 370
Henderson, C., 381
Henderson, C.R., 539
Henker, B.A., 370
Hepatitis B., 109
Herberger, S., 531
Herbst, A., 117
Heredity: in development, 2, 16; and environment, 2–4; and genetics, 3, 94; and genotype, 67–69; and learning, 280; and development of motor skills, 298–301

Herman, C.S., 127, 128
Hernandez-Garcia, J.M., 161
Heroin, 118–119
Heroux, L., 371
Hershenson, M., 363, 379, 440
Hertig, A., 70
Hertzig, M.E., 213, 243
Hess, P., 365
Hess, R.D., 542
Heterozygous carriers, **81**
Hetzer, H., 240, 266, 324
Heuyer, C., 126, 130
Hewitt, D., 136, 139
Hiatt, S., 229, 381
Hicks, L., 430
Hill, K.T., 422
Hirsch, H.V.B., 384, 385
Hirschhorn, K., 78
Hitler, A., 245
Hobbes, Thomas, 402
Hobbins, J., 89
Hock, E., 545
Hockman, C.H., 137
Hodges, G., 126, 130
Hoffman, C., 543
Hoffman, M.L., 266
Hofsten, C. von, 305, 307, 376
Hohmann, A., 385
Holden, R.H., 44, 45, 110, 138
Holland, W.W., 122
Holliday, M.A., 84
Holm, G., 558
Holm, R.A., 555
Holmberg, H., 190
Holmes, D.L., 50, 322
Holophrases: use of by young children, 460–461, 474; two-part relations in, 461
Holtzman, N.A., 84
Home environment, effect on prematures, 50–51, 52
Home deliveries, 181–182, 198
HOME scales, 50; and prematures, 51
Honzik, M.P., 225, 228, 327, 328
Horgan, D., 461
Hormonal disorders, maternal, 110–111, 145; hypothyroidism, 110; hyperthyroidism, 110; diabetes, 110, 111
Hormones: and the placenta, 27; and maternal stress, 139–140
Horn, H., 279
Horneman, G., 190
Horner, F.A., 48
Horowitz, F.D., 169, 212, 213, 246, 274, 316, 317, 318, 351, 370, 373
Hospital: intervention and prematurity, 52; childbirth in, 172–173; criticisms of delivery practices in, 173–175, 181; exclusion of significant persons by, 173; separation of mother and infant by, 174, 182, 184; length of stay in, 175; vs. home delivery, 181–183; and prematures, 184; present options in, 197
Hospitalization, effect on attachment, 482
Hotchner, T., 145, 197
Houghton, S.A., 83, 84, 86
Hoversten, G.H., 354
Howland, H.C., 366
Hoyer, L., 89
Hsia, D.Y-Y., 78, 84
Hubby, M., 117
Hubel, D.H., 368, 384
Hubert, N.C., 244

Hubley, P., 376
Hudson, F.P., 84
Huebner, R.R., 229
Huitt, W.G., 244
Hume, David, 402
Humphreys, L., 531
Hunt, J.McV., 270, 324, 325, 326, 327, 334; replications of Piaget's work by, 422, 424; scales of Uzgiris and, 444; on deprivation, 524–526, 527, 551
Huntington, L., 233
Husaim, J.S., 436
Hutchings, D.E., 116, 140
Hutt, C., 356, 358
Hutt, S.J., 215, 216, 356, 358
Hwang, C.P., 506, 507
Hwang, P., 190
Hydrocephalus, **131,** 133
Hydrocephaly, 294
Hyperexcitability syndrome, 312, 333
Hypothesis, testing of, 386–387

I

Identical (monozygotic) twins, **43**
Ignatoff, E., 54, 224
Illegitimacy, and stress, 139
Illingworth, R.S., 327, 328
Imipramine, 132
Imitation, 265–272; Piaget on, 8–9; development of, 265–269; inexact and same-class, **265,** 424; later development, 269–270; immediate, **270;** delayed, **270;** mechanisms of, 270; in infant development, 270–272; use of alternative interpretations in, 280; and learning, 281–282; in Piaget's Stage II, 405; in Stage III, 410; in Stage V, 418; in Stage VI, 421; research to test Piaget's theory, 424–426; neonatal, 424; early forms vs. later, 425; in cognitive development, 425; controversy over, 441; in language development, 469–470, 474; in social situations, 499
Implantation, 25, 26
Imprinting, **481**
Independent variable, **11,** 16; in research design, 14; and operational definition, 57
Indirect effects, **78**
Individual differences: in correlational studies, 510, 512; in kibbutz children, 540; in effects of deprivation, 553
Inexact or same-class imitation, **265;** use in learning, 271
Infant Behavior Record (IBR), 326
Infants: neurological testing of, 322–328, 333–334; responses to sound, 352, 358; to vision, 361; visual acuity of, 365; securely attached, 480; resistant, 486; avoidant, 486; function of attachment in, 487–490. See also Newborns; Prematures
Infectious diseases, maternal, 106–110; rubella, 106–107; syphilis, 107–108; organisms that infect the baby at birth, 108–109; other, 109; implications of knowledge of, 109–110
Influenza, 109

Information processing, 431
Ingemarsson, I., 158
Ingham, R.R., 489
Ingram, D., 465
Ingram, T.T.S., 221, 222
Inhalant anesthetics, 131
Innate characteristics, **3**
Input factors: in language development, 468–469; in imitation, 469–470
Institutionalization, 522–536, 559; early studies of, 522–524, 559; retardation effects of, 524–527; high-quality institutions, 527–528; long-term intellectual effects of, 528–534; long-term social and emotional effects of, 534–536; and attachment, 537; intervention programs, 548, 559
Insulin, 132
Intellectual effects: of deprivation, 528–534; Tizzard's data on, 532–533; of day care, 543–544; and critical period theory, 555
Intelligence: effect of prematurity on, 48–49, 50; lowered, and alcohol, 127–128; theories of, 245. See also Cognitive development
Intelligence quotient (IQ): and SES of mother, 50; and fine motor development, 310; and NBAS, 322; origin of, 322–323, 333; scoring, 323; and institutionalization, 530; effect of environment on, 533
Intentionality, and attachment, 483
Interaction effect, **50**
Interpretation of behavior, 6–7; alternative, 8–9, 16, 95–96; effect of experimenter's beliefs on, 281
Intervention: to reduce risks of prematurity, 52; hospital, 52–53; social interaction, 53–54; to reduce effects of deprivation, 548–551, 556, 559. See also Enrichment
Intonation contours, 452; use in holophrastic utterances, 460, 474
Invariance, **372;** abstraction of perceptual, 372; and movement, 373
Irritability on G/R, as prediction for prematures, 321
Irwin, O.C., 209, 347n2, 458
Israel, study of kibbutzim in, 537–541
Izard, C.E., 229, 230

J

Jackson, E., 325, 433
Jacobs, B.S., 48
Jacobs, H.L., 359
Jacobs, P.A., 70
Jacobson, J.L., 140
Jacobson, S.W., 121, 269, 424, 425
Jacobson, W.S., 140
Jaffe, J., 499
Jaffee, B., 537
Jäger, R., 375
Jakobsen, K., 190
Jakobson, R., 451, 457
James, L.S., 168
Jameson, S., 139

Stages of development, 531; Piaget on, 404–421; sequence of, 422
Stage I (Piaget), 405–406
Stage II (Piaget), 440; primary circular reactions, 406–408
Stage III (Piaget), 440; secondary circular reactions, 408–411; attention to object, 408–409; making interesting spectacles last, 409; classifying and relating, 409; relating means and ends, 409; discovering quantitative relations, 409–410; discovering object permanence, 410; discovering motor recognition, 410; advances in imitation, 410; ignoring novel features, 410
Stage IV (Piaget), 441, 483; coordination of secondary schemes, 411–415; means-end behavior, 411; ability to anticipate, 413; signs vs. signals, 413; advance in object permanence, 413; advance in imitation, 413–415; limitations of, 415
Stage V (Piaget), 441; tertiary circular reactions, 415–419; "experiments in order to see," 417; active experimentation, 417; means-end behavior, 417; problem-solving, 417–418; notions of causality, 418; elaboration of object, 418
Stage VI (Piaget), 441; invention of means through mental combinations, 419–421
Stagno, S., 106n1, 108
Stahnke, M., 543, 549
Stamps, L.E., 262
Standley, K., 168–169
Stanford-Binet Test, 186, 188, 322; and performance on fine motor skills, 327
Starkey, D., 355, 436, 438
Starr, R.H., Jr., 119
Startles, 239
State, 207, 249; activities of, 207; classification of, 214–216; and the baby's day, 216–217; responsiveness, 217–219; in study of newborns, 219–220; in preterm babies, 220–221; and conditioning, 261, 282; in neurological testing, 310; in MBAS, 315; and research in addition, 353
Statistical controls, 143
Statistics, role of in research, 195
Stayton, D.J., 486, 496
Stechler, G., 499
Stedman, D.J., 75
Steele, W.G., 136
Steffa, M., 185, 189
Stein, Z.A., 112, 126, 129
Steinberg, B., 276, 278
Steinberg, J., 506
Steinberg, L.D., 544
Steiner, J.E., 262, 349, 351
Steingüber, H.J., 507–508
Steinhausen, H.C., 84
Steinschneider, A., 166, 168, 272, 273, 274, 354
Stenberg, C.R., 230
Stereopsis, 379
Stern, D.N., 272, 362, 499
Stern, E., 50, 208
Stern, G.S., 234

Stern, J.A., 159
Stern, J.D., 376
Stern, W., 323
Steroid hormones, 116–118, 146; sexual hormones, 117–118; adrenal hormones, 118
Stevenson, M.B., 270, 424
Steward, S.L., 70
Stewart, A., 48n10
Stewart, A.M., 136, 139
Stewart, J.M., 550
Stickle, G., 71
Stimulation: function of attachment, 489–490; in intervention programs, 559
Stimulus: conditional, 260; unconditional, 260; tracking a moving, 361–362; scanning a stationary, 362–363; visual, 363–383. See also Conditioning
Stingle, K.G., 270
Stockard, C.R., 129
Stocking, M., 78
Stoller, A., 109
Stott, D.H., 122, 123, 135, 136, 138, 139
Stout, M.S., 70
Stoutsenberger, K., 229
Strabismus, 385, 387
Strangers: fear of, 484, 488, 512–513; anxiety not measure of attachment, 485, 509; fear of, in kibbutzim, 542
Strauss, M.E., 119, 316
Strauss, M.S., 277, 363, 372, 374, 435, 436
Strauss, S., 365
Streeter, L., 457
Streissguth, A.P., 126, 127, 128, 129, 316
Stress: prenatal, 105, 132, 135–140, 147; physical, 135–136; psychological, 136–140; effects of in early experience, 141–142
Stringer, S., 54
Stuart, H.C., 294
Study of infants: reasons for, 204; approaches to, 2; history of, 2; by baby biographers, 5–10; by normative/descriptive studies, 10; modern research techniques, 11–13; research issues, 13–16
Stutsman, R., 325
Sucking, 207, 221–229, 249; rooting and sucking reflexes, 221–222; and eating, 222–223; changes in prenatal, 223; and experience, 223–224; socialization of, 224–229; practical issues, 229, 248; operant conditioning of, 263; measure of taste, 349, 350; in Freudian theory, 480, 497, 511; and attachment, 509, 511
Sudden Infant Death Syndrome (SIDS), 121, 170; and cigarette smoking, 121; and LTA, 320
Sugarman, S., 434, 438, 439, 441
Sulik, K.K., 127, 129
Sullivan, J.W., 212, 213, 317
Sullivan, M.W., 241, 263, 276, 277, 278
Sullivan, W.C., 126
Sun, K.H., 349
Sunley, R., 531
Suomi, S.J., 550, 551
Super, C.M., 300–301

Suprasegmental cues, 452; in babbling, 453, 473
Susman, E.J., 245
Susser, M.W., 47, 112, 123, ,126, 129
Sutherland, G.R., 70, 77
Sutherland, J.M., 223
Svedja, M.J., 190, 191, 196, 381
Svenningsen, N.W., 158
Swaddling: and state, 219–220; as soothing, 237
Swallowing, 223
Sweat gland functioning, 347
Symbol, 438; and language, 442
Symbolization and concepts, 438–439, 441
Synapse, 217
Synchrony: vs. asynchrony in Fischer's theory, 433; mother-infant, 502–503
Syndrome, 106
Syntax, child's knowledge of, 474

T

Tactile-Adaptive score (TA), 313, 320
Tactile sensitivity, 346–348; sex differences in, 346, 347; responsivity to aversive stimuli, 346–347; to nonaversive stimuli, 347–348; and crawling, 381
Taeusch, H.W., 54, 111, 117
Taguchi, K., 354, 356
Taine, M.H., baby biography by, 7
Talbot, E., 2, 5–6
Talmadge, M., 137
Tanner, J.M., 290, 292, 294, 295
Taraldson, B., 319
Taste, 249–350
Taub, H.B., 46
Tauscher, J., 134
Tay-Sachs disease, 70, 82, 82–83, 98
Taylor Manifest Anxiety Scale, 138
Teachers, assessment of temperament by, 244
Teichmann, H., 52
Teller, D.Y., 363, 364
Temperament, 243–244, 248; research on, 243–244; assessment of, 244; and NBAS, 333
Teratogens, 105, 145; measures of effects of, 105–106
Teratology, 140; issues in, 140–141; complexities in, 141; development affected by, 141
Terman, L.M., 322
Terrace, H.S., 423
Test-retest reliability, 317, 329, 333
Tests, neonatal neurological, 313–318, 333; Graham Behavioral Test, 313; Graham/Rosenblith Behavioral Test, 313–315; Brazelton or Newborn Behavior Assessment Scales, 315–316; reliability of, 316–318, 329; validity of, 318, 329–330; as dependent variables, 319; long-term predictive value of, 320–322; fairness of, 331. See also Neurological testing
Thach, B.T., 348
Thacker, S.B., 159, 175
Thalassemia, 91

Thaler, I., 120
Thalidomide, 115–116, 142, 146
Thane, K., 191, 192
Thelen, E., 221, 272
Theorell, K., 232
Thoman, E.B., 50, 208, 210, 212, 223, 282; on communication of mother-infant dyad, 500, 501, 503
Thomas, A., 213, 243, 503
Thomas, D., 459
Thomas, D.B., 160, 167, 170
Thomas, H., 326, 372
Thompson, H., 210, 297, 301
Thompson, J., 222
Thompson, R.A., 487
Thompson, W.R., 136, 137, 550, 554
Thomson, A.M., 48, 50, 51, 113, 294
Thorndike, B., 166, 169
Thorndike, E.L., 246
Thorpe, J., 73
Thumb-sucking, 225, 229, 248, 511, 541
Thurston, D., 159, 320
Thurstone, L.L., 245
Thyroid: and Cretinism, 86; maternal disorders of, 110
Tiedemann, Dietrich, 4, 11, 493; baby biography by, 5, 6, 7, 16; on audition, 353
Tiers: in skills theory, 433; levels in Tier I, 433
Timney, B., 380
Ting, G., 221, 273
Tizard, J.P.M., 46, 527–528, 537, 556, 559; on intellectual deprivation, 532–534; on social and emotional deprivation, 534–536, 546, 553; measures of attachment used by, 557; suggestions for adoptive parents, 558
Toilet training, and attachment, 493–494
Tonascia, J.A., 124
Tongue, stimuli to, 348
Tonkova-Yampolskaya, R., 453
Topinka, C.V., 276, 278
Touch, 41, 346–348. See also Tactile sensitivity
Touching, 237; and laughing, 241
Toxoplasmosis, 109
Trait, 212; activity level as, 212; or temperament, 243–244
Tranquilizers: during delivery, 163, 166–167, 197–198; meperidine, 166, 167; Largon, 166; secobarbital (Seconal), 167; scopolamine, 167
Translocation, 74, 133
Trause, M.A., 189, 234
Trehub, S.E., 278, 354, 356, 358
Trevarthen, C., 305, 307, 376, 425, 499–500
Trisomy 18, 21, 77
Trisomy 21, 21
Trisomy X, 78, 95
Tronick, E.Z., 168, 315, 316, 321, 322, 361, 377, 500, 502
Truby, H.M., 231, 453
Truswell, L., 461
Tryphonopoulou, Y.A., 316
Tuberculosis, tests for, 134
Tucker, B.E., 158, 161, 234
Tudor-Hart, B.H., 240
Tulkin, S., 469
Tulloch, J.D., 359
Turkewitz, G., 354, 356